Fodor's 2008

SPAIN

Where to Stay and Eat for All Budgets

Must-See Sights and Local Secrets

Ratings You Can Trust

Fodor's Travel Publications New York, Toronto, London, Sydney, Auckland
www.fodors.com

FODOR'S SPAIN 2008
Editor: Debbie Harmsen; Maria Teresa Burwell

Editorial Production: Evangelos Vasilakis
Editorial Contributors: Christopher Culwell, Ben Curtis, Erica Duecy, Ignacio Gómez, Michael Kessler, Jared Lubarsky, Mary McLean, Norman Renouf, Helio San Miguel, George Semler, Will Shank, Stephen "Kip" Tobin
Maps & Illustrations: David Lindroth, *cartographer*; William Wu; with additional cartography provided by Henry Colomb, Mark Stroud, and Ali Baird, Moon Street Cartography; Bob Blake and Rebecca Baer, *map editors*
Design: Fabrizio LaRocca, *creative director*; Guido Caroti, Siobhan O'Hare, *art directors*; Tina Malaney, Chie Ushio, Ann McBride, *designers*; Melanie Marin, *senior picture editor;* Moon Sun Kim, *cover designer*
Cover Photo (The Corrida, San Fermin Festival, Pamplona): Alan Copson/age fotostock
Production/Manufacturing: Angela McLean

COPYRIGHT
Copyright © 2008 by Fodor's Travel, a division of Random House, Inc.

Fodor's is a registered trademark of Random House, Inc.

All rights reserved. Published in the United States by Fodor's Travel, a division of Random House, Inc., and simultaneously in Canada by Random House of Canada, Limited, Toronto. Distributed by Random House, Inc., New York.

No maps, illustrations, or other portions of this book may be reproduced in any form without written permission from the publisher.

ISBN 978–1–4000–1816–1

ISSN 0071–6545

SPECIAL SALES
This book is available at special discounts for bulk purchases for sales promotions or premiums. Special editions, including personalized covers, excerpts of existing books, and corporate imprints, can be created in large quantities for special needs. For more information, write to Special Markets/Premium Sales, 1745 Broadway, MD 6-2, New York, New York 10019, or e-mail specialmarkets@randomhouse.com.

AN IMPORTANT TIP & AN INVITATION
Although all prices, opening times, and other details in this book are based on information supplied to us at press time, changes occur all the time in the travel world, and Fodor's cannot accept responsibility for facts that become outdated or for inadvertent errors or omissions. So **always confirm information when it matters,** especially if you're making a detour to visit a specific place. Your experiences—positive and negative—matter to us. If we have missed or misstated something, **please write to us.** We follow up on all suggestions. Contact the Spain editor at editors@fodors.com or c/o Fodor's at 1745 Broadway, New York, NY 10019.

PRINTED IN THE UNITED STATES OF AMERICA
10 9 8 7 6 5 4 3 2 1

Be a Fodor's Correspondent

Your opinion matters. It matters to us. It matters to your fellow Fodor's travelers, too. And we'd like to hear it. In fact, we need to hear it.

When you share your experiences and opinions, you become an active member of the Fodor's community. That means we'll not only use your feedback to make our books better, but we'll publish your names and comments whenever possible. Throughout our guides, look for "Word of Mouth," excerpts of your unvarnished feedback.

Here's how you can help improve Fodor's for all of us.

Tell us when we're right. We rely on local writers to give you an insider's perspective. But our writers and staff editors—who are the best in the business—depend on you. Your positive feedback is a vote to renew our recommendations for the next edition.

Tell us when we're wrong. We're proud that we update most of our guides every year. But we're not perfect. Things change. Hotels cut services. Museums change hours. Charming cafés lose charm. If our writer didn't quite capture the essence of a place, tell us how you'd do it differently. If any of our descriptions are inaccurate or inadequate, we'll incorporate your changes in the next edition and will correct factual errors at fodors.com immediately.

Tell us what to include. You probably have had fantastic travel experiences that aren't yet in Fodor's. Why not share them with a community of like-minded travelers? Maybe you chanced upon a beach or bistro or B&B that you don't want to keep to yourself. Tell us why we should include it. And share your discoveries and experiences with everyone directly at fodors.com. Your input may lead us to add a new listing or highlight a place we cover with a "Highly Recommended" star or with our highest rating, "Fodor's Choice."

Give us your opinion instantly at our feedback center at www.fodors.com/feedback. You may also e-mail editors@fodors.com with the subject line "Spain Editor." Or send your nominations, comments, and complaints by mail to Spain Editor, Fodor's, 1745 Broadway, New York, NY 10019.

You and travelers like you are the heart of the Fodor's community. Make our community richer by sharing your experiences. Be a Fodor's correspondent.

¡Buen Viaje!

Tim Jarrell, Publisher

CONTENTS

SPAIN IN FOCUS

CONTENTS

CLOSE UPS

MAPS

ABOUT THIS BOOK

Our Ratings

Sometimes you find terrific travel experiences and sometimes they just find you. But usually the burden is on you to select the right combination of experiences. That's where our ratings come in.

As travelers we've all discovered a place so wonderful that its worthiness is obvious. And sometimes that place is so experiential that superlatives don't do it justice: you just have to be there to know. These sights, properties, and experiences get our highest rating, **Fodor's Choice,** indicated by orange stars throughout this book.

Black stars highlight sights and properties we deem **Highly Recommended,** places that our writers, editors, and readers praise again and again for consistency and excellence.

By default, there's another category: any place we include in this book is by definition worth your time, unless we say otherwise. And we will.

Disagree with any of our choices? Care to nominate a place or suggest that we rate one more highly? Visit our feedback center at www.fodors.com/feedback.

Budget Well

Hotel and restaurant price categories from ¢ to $$$$ are defined in the opening pages of each chapter. For attractions, we always give standard adult admission fees; reductions are usually available for children, students, and senior citizens. Want to pay with plastic? **AE, D, DC, MC, V** after restaurant and hotel listings indicate if American Express, Discover, Diners Club, MasterCard, and Visa are accepted.

Restaurants

Unless we state otherwise, restaurants are open for lunch and dinner daily. We mention dress only when there's a specific requirement and reservations only when they're essential or not accepted—it's always best to book ahead.

Hotels

Hotels have private bath, phone, TV, and air-conditioning and operate on the European Plan (aka EP, meaning without meals), unless we specify that they use the Continental Plan (CP, with a continental breakfast), Breakfast Plan (BP, with a full breakfast), or Modified American Plan (MAP, with breakfast and dinner) or are all-inclusive (including all meals and most activities). We always list facilities but not whether you'll be charged an extra fee to use them, so when pricing accommodations, find out what's included.

Many Listings

- ★ Fodor's Choice
- ★ Highly recommended
- ⊠ Physical address
- ✥ Directions
- Mailing address
- ☎ Telephone
- Fax
- On the Web
- E-mail
- Admission fee
- ⊙ Open/closed times
- Ⓜ Metro stations
- Credit cards

Hotels & Restaurants

- Hotel
- Number of rooms
- Facilities
- Meal plans
- ✕ Restaurant
- Reservations
- Smoking
- BYOB
- ✕ Hotel with restaurant that warrants a visit

Outdoors

- Golf
- Camping

Other

- Family-friendly
- ⇨ See also
- Branch address
- ☞ Take note

Experience Spain

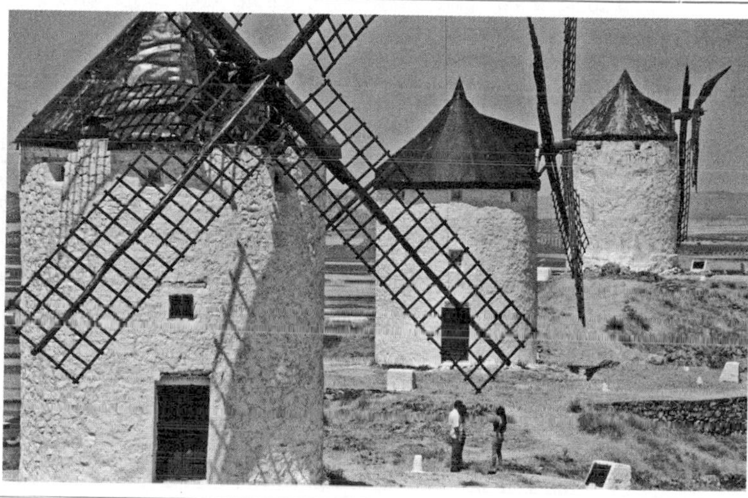

Consuegra, Toledo province

WORD OF MOUTH

"The most unusual thing about Spain is how gregarious the Spaniards are. Just sitting at a café, eating tapas, and enjoying sangria while watching the locals enjoy life is a joy. In the summer, people of all ages (from babies to the very old) congregate in the squares until very late at night walking, talking, drinking . . . Just thinking about it, I long to be there experiencing that!"

—cruiseluv

www.fodors.com/forums

WHAT'S NEW IN SPAIN

Once a well-kept secret, sequestered within a military-dominated dictatorship, Spain emerged late in the 20th century with a new sense of freedom and revived passion for life. It grew stronger politically and economically as it joined forces with other nations in the European Union and adopted the euro for its currency. Culturally, too, Spain has spread its wings. Spain's culinary scene, for example, is soaring to new heights, with innovative chefs like Catalonian Ferran Adrìa leading the world's molecular gastronomy movement (⇨ "Spain's Food Revolution" in Chapter 8).

Here's a look at what's new this year …

Valencia Continues Sporting Success

Hot on the heels of Valencia's 2007 America's Cup, the city will be busy preparing for its next big sporting challenge—becoming the latest addition to the Formula 1 circuit. Set to use much of the infrastructure put in place for the past summer's sailing challenge, this will be an urban circuit similar to Monte Carlo, and is likely to be dubbed the Mediterranean Gran Prix. The city is also due to hold the world indoor athletics championships in March 2008.

Election Year!

2008 will be the most important year in the history of the PSOE, the Spanish socialist party, as President Jose Luis Rodriguez Zapatero attempts to hold onto the leadership of the government. He came to power in 2004, shortly after the March 11 Madrid train bombings, when the furious nation voted out the Partido Popular, whose support of the war in Iraq was popularly blamed for the Madrid attacks. Since then, Mariano Rajoy, the leader the Partido Popular, now Spain's leading opposition party, has done little to endear himself to the Spanish population. Despite the fact that the PSOE could have done better with their failed peace negotiations with Basque Separatists ETA, and have angered many Spaniards by handing over too much power to regions such as Catalonia, they have every chance of being re-elected.

Penelope

After her 2007 "Best Actress" Oscar nomination for Pedro Almodovar's *Volver,* Penelope Cruz stars in two major productions set to hit the big screen in 2008—*Elegy,* where she stars alongside Ben Kingsley, and Woody Allen's Spanish project, which goes by the preproduction title of *Midnight in Barcelona.* Allen's latest muse, Scarlett Johansson, will be starring alongside Cruz and Spanish heartthrob Javier Bardem.

La Leti

The future queen of Spain, Letizia Ortiz, who shot to fame with her marriage to Prince Felipe in 2004, will continue to dominate the gossip magazines in 2008. Media interest in the princess rocketed with the tragic alleged suicide of her younger sister, Erika Ortiz, in February 2007. With her second child now entering her first year, and speculation over her happiness in the Royal Family, La Leti will continue to be constantly under the media microscope.

Art in Madrid

While Madrid's contemporary artists might not be making much of an impact of the international scene, the galleries themselves have the usual impressive range of exhibitions on offer in 2008. The Prado is bolstering its impressive Velazquez collection with paintings on

loan from London's National Gallery, including *La Venus del Espejo,* to offer the greatest retrospective of the painter's work seen to date, on show until the end of January. The gallery is also offering a touring exhibition of works by Goya and Sorolla that will be visiting major Spanish cities such as Valencia, Salamanca, Toledo, and Santiago de Compostela throughout 2008.

USARrt at the Guggenheim

Bilbao's Guggenheim is celebrating 300 years of artistic experimentation in the United States of America, with USARrt, running from October 2007 through to the beginning of February 2008. A joint effort by the Guggenheim Foundation and the Terra Foundation for American Art, the exhibition aims to bring together more than 200 works from public and private collections in the States.

Spain Spreads Online

Although Spain already has one of the highest adoption rates of broadband Internet in Europe, the government is set to pass a law that aims to insure that every home in the country has access to an affordable high-speed Internet connection by the end of 2008. At the same time, Málaga has its hopes set on becoming the first Spanish city to offer free Wi-Fi to all its citizens, closely followed by Madrid, although this will depend on the PSOE (socialists) winning local elections and fulfilling electoral promises in 2007, which seems unlikely in the right-wing capital.

Rock in Rio and at Rocket

Rock in Rio, the world's biggest music festival, that in its six-year history has entertained an audience of more 4 million with the performances of 400 artists, is landing in Madrid in 2008 at the end of June. Concerts will be held just outside the city center at Arganda del Rey, in an area the size of 20 football stadiums, with 70 internationally renowned artists playing to 100,000 spectators a day throughout the five-day festival. If you fancy something a little more down-to-earth, Granada is again hosting the **Rocket Festival.** Like a miniversion of the world-famous Burning Man festival, this May event mixes art exhibits with contemporary and traditional music—expect everything from flamenco to blues, jazz, rock and reggae.

Expo 2008

2008 is a big year for Zaragoza, as it hosts the International Exhibition from June 14 to September 14, a gathering of more than 80 nations in the style of great events from the past such as the 1889 Paris Exhibition, for which the Eiffel Tower was built. Although nothing so ambitious is planned for Zaragoza, the Bridge Pavilion is an architecturally impressive exhibition space designed by Zaha Hadid—the twisting bridge of steel and light crosses the Ebro River and leads into the main exhibition site. The theme is water and sustainable development, with the organizers hoping to establish clean water as a universal human right.

Barcelona: Euroscience 2008

From July 18 until July 22, Barcelona's average IQ is set to soar as 5,000 scientists and 30,000 science fans flood the city for the EuroScience Open Forum. The aim of the convention is to promote debate, communication, and development within the sciences, with themes covering everything from global warming, science, and art to demography in an aging Europe, and the human mind.

WHAT'S WHERE

The following numbers refer to chapters.

2 Madrid. Its boundless energy makes sights and sounds larger than life. The Prado, Reina Sofía, and Thyssen-Bornemisza pack thousands of Spanish and other European masterworks into an art-saturated half-mile. Sunday's crowded flea market in El Rastro is thick with overpriced oddities. The cafés in the Plaza Mayor and the wine bars in the nearby Cava Baja are abuzz, and nightlife stretches into the wee hours around Plaza Santa Ana.

3 Castile-La Mancha & Castile-León. The Spanish heartland—*meseta*—is an arid reach of windy skies and wide vistas. Castille-León is cut with rocky gorges and fringed with gaunt mountains. Salamanca, Segovia, León, and Burgos exude a seriousness marked with religiosity and a hardworking simple life. Castille-La Mancha is punctuated by Toledo's austerity, Cuenca's quirky natural architecture, and Soria's and Sigüenza's medieval preservation.

4 Galicia & Asturias. On the way to Santiago de Compostela to pay homage to St. James, Christian pilgrims once crossed Europe to a corner of Spain so remote it was called *finis terrae* (end of the earth). Santiago still resonates with mystic importance. In the more mountainous Asturias, towns are among green hills in the highlands, and sandy beaches stretch out along the Atlantic. The jagged Picos de Europa mountain range towers massively to the south.

5 Bilbao & the Basque Country. Greener, cloudier, and stubbornly independent in spirit, the Basque region that takes up part of the north is a country within a country, with its own language and culture as well as its own coastline on the Bay of Biscay, one of the peninsula's wildest and toughest shores.

6 The Pyrenees. Cut by some 23 steep north–south valleys on the Spanish side alone, with four independent geographical entities—the valleys of Camprodón, Cerdanya, Aran, and Baztán—the Pyrenees has a wealth of areas to explore, with a dozen highland cultures and languages to match.

7 Barcelona. The city's main street La Rambla, is a mass of strollers, artists, street entertainers, vendors, and vamps, all preparing you for Barcelona's energy and creativity best captured in startling architectural landmarks. Antoni Gaudí's sinuous Casa Milà and unique Sagrada Família church remain Moderniste masterpieces.

Bay of Biscay
BASQUE COUNTRY (EUSKADI)
Santander
San Sebastián
CANTABRIA
Bilbao
5
FRANCE
Vitoria
Pamplona
Treviño
NAVARRE
ANDORRA
Burgos
Logroño
LA RIOJA
PYRENEES
Palencia
Huesca
6
Girona
CATALONIA
Soria
3
Valladolid
Duero
Zaragoza
Lleida
COSTA BRAVA
CASTILE–LEÓN
ARAGON
7
Tarragona
BARCELONA
Segovia
Tortosa
COSTA DORADA
Ávila
MADRID
2
Teruel
Balearic Sea
Toledo
Aranjuez
Cuenca
Castellón de la Plana
Minorca
COSTA DEL AZAHAR
Mallorca
CASTILE–LA MANCHA
Requena
Valencia
Alcazár
Guadiana
Júcar
BALEARIC ISLANDS
Ibiza
Ciudad Real
Albacete
Segura
VALENCIA
Formentera
Valdepeñas
COSTA BLANCA
Alicante
MURCIA
Murcia
Jaén
Córdoba
Cartagena
0
100 miles
ANDALUSIA
Lorca
0
150 km
Antequera
Granada
Almería
Mediterranean Sea
Málaga
COSTA DEL SOL
COSTA DE ALMERIA
ALGERIA
Melilla
MOROCCO

WHAT'S WHERE

8 Catalonia & the Levante. A cultural connection with France and Europe at large is what defines Catalonia. The citrus-scented, mountain-backed plain of the Levante is dotted with Christian and Moorish landmarks. And Valencia's signature dish, *paella*, fortifies visitors off touring the area's Roman ruins.

9 The Balearic Islands. These islands remain infamous as Europe's playground. Ibiza blasts to life nightly, but even this isle has its quiet coves. Majorca combines tourist-clogged pockets with undiscovered rugged mountains. Minorca includes the historic cities of Ciutadella and Mahón. Formentera, pastoral in comparison, retains a wild beauty.

10 The Southeast. Here you have party-till-dawn resort towns like Beidorm as well as little villages where time seems suspended in the last century. The Costa Blanca area with rice paddies and fragrant orange groves leads to the palm-fringed port city of Alicante. In La Manga del Mar Menor, tired travelers treat themselves to a saltwater soak.

11 Andalusia. Eight provinces, five of which are coastal (Huelva, Cádiz, Málaga, Granada, and Almería) and three that are landlocked (Seville, Córdoba, and Jaén), compose this southern Spain autonomous community known for its Moorish influences. Highlights are the romantic Alhambra and seductive Seville.

12 The Costa del Sol. With more than 320 days of sunshine a year, the northern Europeans can't stay away. The main holiday resorts are built up with high-rise hotels, shopping centers, and sprawling housing developments near the beach. Marbella, a longtime glitterati favorite, has a pristine Andalusian old quarter. Villages such as Casares seem immune to the goings-on along the coast, and the ancient town of Ronda straddles a giant river gorge.

13 Extremadura. Remote and rustic defines Spain's far west borderland with Portugal. Highlights include prosperous Cáceres, packed with medieval and Renaissance churches and palaces; Trujillo, lined with mansions of Spain's imperial age; ancient Mérida, Spain's richest trove of Roman remains; and the Jerte Valley, which turns white in late March with the blossoming of its 1 million cherry trees.

Bay of Biscay
BASQUE COUNTRY (EUSKADI)
Santander
San Sebastián
CANTABRIA
Bilbao
FRANCE
Trevino
NAVARRE
ANDORRA
PYRENEES
Burgos
Logroño
LA RIOJA
Huesca
Girona
Palencia
CATALONIA
Soria
Ebro
Zaragoza
Lleida
Valladolid
Duero
COSTA BRAVA
CASTILE-LEÓN
ARAGON
8
Barcelona
Tarragona
Segovia
Tortosa
COSTA DORADA
Tajo
Ávila
MADRID
Teruel
Balearic Sea
Castellón de la Plana
Minorca
Toledo
Aranjuez
Cuenca
COSTA DEL AZAHAR
Majorca
CASTILE-LA MANCHA
Requena
Jucar
Valencia
BALEARIC ISLANDS
Alcazár
Guadiana
VALENCIA
Ciudad Real
Ibiza
9
Albacete
10
Valdepeñas
Formentera
Segura
Alicante
COSTA BLANCA
0
100 mile
Córdoba
11
MURCIA
0
150 km
Jaén
Murcia
Cartagena
ANDALUSIA
Lorca
Mediterranean Sea
Antequera
Granada
Almería
12
Málaga
COSTA DE ALMERIA
COSTA DEL SOL
Ceuta
Melilla
MOROCCO

SPAIN PLANNER

Peak Times to . . .

. . . go skiing in the Pyrenees: December–April

. . . see wildflowers in bloom in the Southeast: April–June

. . . sunbathe in the Balearic Islands: May–October

. . . play golf in Costa del Sol: October–June

. . . do sightseeing in Madrid: April–June

. . . bird-watch in Extremadura: late February

. . . hike the rolling hills of the Basque Country: April–June or September and October

. . . participate in Barcelona's cultural celebrations: April and May

. . . shout *Olé!* at the bullfighters in Seville: April–October

. . . walk along the coast in Catalonia: May–September

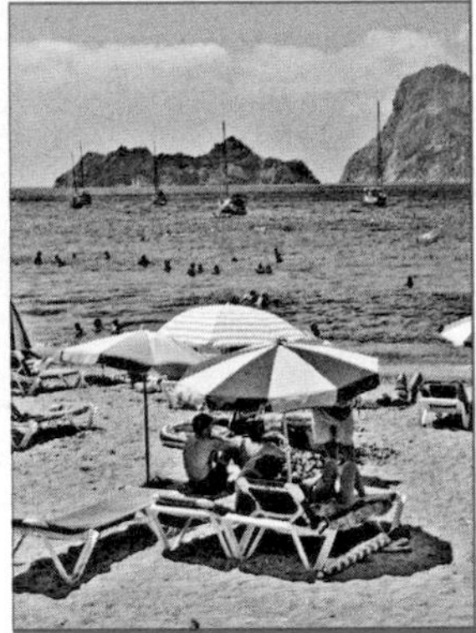

Getting There & Around

Most flights into Spain go to Madrid or Barcelona, though certain destinations in Andalusia are popular with carriers traveling from England and other European countries. You can also reach Spain via a ferry from the United Kingdom into northern Spain, a ferry or catamaran from Morocco into southern Spain, or on a cruise—Barcelona is Spain's main port-of-call, but other ports-of-call include Málaga, Cádiz, Gibraltar, Valencia, A Coruna, and stops on the Balearic Islands. From France or Portugal you can drive in or take a bus.

Once in Spain, you can travel by bus, car, or train. The bus is usually much faster than the train, and bus fares tend to be lower as well. Service is extensive, though less frequent on weekends. Various bus companies service the country, but Spain's major national bus line is Alsa-Enatcar (☎902/422242).

If you choose to travel by train, you can take RENFE trains, which are economical if they're short routes with convenient schedules (such as the commuter trains around Madrid and Barcelona); or take the AVE, Spain's high-speed train, which is wonderfully fast—it can go from Madrid to Seville in under three hours. ■TIP→ **If you want a rail pass, including a Eurailpass, you must purchase it before you leave for Europe.**

The big-chain car rental companies all have branches in Spain, though the online outfit Pepe Car (⊕www.pepecar.com), may have better deals. Its modus operandi is the earlier you book, the less you pay. Note that in Spain, most vehicles have a manual transmission. ■TIP→ **If you don't want a stick shift, reserve well in advance and specify automatic transmission.**

A few rules of the road: Children under 10 may not ride in the front seat, and seat belts are mandatory for all passengers. ■TIP→ **Follow speed limits. Rental cars are frequently targeted by police monitoring speeding vehicles.**

For more on bus, train, and car trave, see Spain Essentials in the back of the book.

Spain Etiquette 101

SOCIAL MORES

If you're in town for business or meeting new people, use the formal *usted* in conversation spoken in Spanish.

Don't smoke in shopping malls and cinemas. Look for signs that say *Se permite fumar* if you want to smoke at a restaurant.

DRESS

In southern Spain you will find that many of the women at beaches wear bikini bottoms and nothing else; however, no matter how modest your swimsuit is, be sure to bring a coverup for eating or shopping at nearby establishments.

When visiting churches, dress conservatively—no shorts or anything gaudy or unkempt

TIPPING

Do not tip more than 10% of the restaurant bill.

Tip tour guides €2.

Tip taxi drivers 10% plus a little for each bag.

Hotel staff (doorman who gets you a cab, room service attendant, maids, and porters) should get €0.50—the porter gets this amount per bag and the maid per night.

What Things Cost in Spain (in euros)

Cup of coffee	1.20
Glass of Wine	2.50
Glass of Beer	2
Sandwich	4
One-Mile Taxi Ride in the City	4
Museum Admission	6

If You Like

Mountains: The Pyrenees, Picos de Europa (Asturias)

Beaches: Costa del Sol, the Southeast, Balaeric Islands, Andalusia, Catalonia & the Levante, Galicia

Cosmopolitan Culture: Barcelona, Bilbao, Valencia

Old-World charm: Madrid, Andalusia, Galicia, the Basque Country

Border Excursions: the Pyrenees (France), Santander (England), Extremadura (Portugal), Gibraltar (Morocco)

National Parks & Reserves: Picos de Europa (Asturias), Monfragüe (Extremadura), Doñana (Andalusia), Cabo de Gata (the Southeast)

TOP FESTIVALS & EVENTS

Carnaval dances through Spain in February just before Lent, most flamboyantly in Cádiz, Sitges, Santa Cruz de Tenerife, and Las Palmas de Gran Canaria.

Semana Santa (Holy Week) is the week before Easter and is Spain's most spectacular feast of all, celebrated most elaborately in Seville.

Feria de Abril brings horseback parades and a carnival atmosphere to Seville in April.

The **Fiesta de San Fermín** and the accompanying running of the bulls through Pamplona's streets unleash wine, bravado, and merriment.

SPAIN TODAY

Politics

Spain's socialist party, led by José Luis Rodriguez Zapatero, continues to hold power after the terrible events of March 11, 2004, dropped them into power against all the odds. With elections looming three days after the tragic train bombings that killed 198, the ruling Partido Popular did their best to persuade the country that the atrocity had been carried out by the Basque separatists, ETA. When the country quickly discovered that Al Qaeda was in fact responsible, they blamed the Partido Popular and the country's involvement in Iraq, and voted them out despite the fact that they had been clear favorites to win the elections only days before.

Once in power, the socialists were forced to keep certain preelectoral promises they never expected to be able to put into place. Gay marriage became legal, and the Plan Hidrologico Nacional, a much-debated plan to divert water from the water-logged north to the parched south of the country, was scrapped almost overnight. The historic ceasefire declared by ETA on March 22, 2006, looked set to place Zapatero's government firmly in the annuls of Spain's history, until the terrorist organization dashed everyone's hopes of lasting peace by bombing a car park in Madrid's Barajas airport on December 30, 2006, killing two civilians caught in the blast, and finally officially ending the ceasefire and promising a return to violence on June 6, 2007.

With elections due in 2008, the Partido Popular is doing itself few favors by presenting fierce, yet decidedly petty, parliamentary opposition. Railing against the government's every move, and refusing to participate in any demonstration organized by the socialists, no matter how worthy the cause, they are creating a damaging image for a party that once seemed set to rule the country for decades.

The Economy

The introduction of the euro in January 2002 saw a major change in Spain's economy, as shopkeepers, hoteliers, restaurateurs, and real estate agents all rounded up prices in an attempt to make the most of the change over from the old currency, and the country became markedly more expensive. A lunchtime set menu that in peseta terms was worth 5.50 euros in 2001, for example, was rounded straight up to 6 euros with the introduction of the new currency. Nevertheless, this did nothing to harm Spain's immense tourism machine: Spain is the second biggest tourist destination in the world, after France, receiving 60 million visitors a year, who contribute around 12% to the country's GDP.

Coupled with the euro price hike was an unprecedented rise in real estate values, with house prices skyrocketing by an average of 10% per annum since 1998, reaching the 18% mark in 2003 and 2004. This did nothing to hold back the country's booming construction industry. As economic immigrants continue to flood into major cities, and as Spaniards and expats alike continue to demand holiday homes on the coast, building sites and tower cranes are a familiar part of the Spanish landscape.

Immigration is a major factor in Spain's changing economy and demography. With an average influx of half a million immigrants a year, foreigners now constitute 10% of the country's population. Moroccans (14%), Ecuadorians (11%),

and Romanians (10%) make up the bulk of these new arrivals. One of the most important benefits of this immigration has been an increase in Spain's birthrate, which at the beginning of the millennium had been among the lowest in the world. The country's aging population had previously been seen as a major problem for the stability of the country's economic future.

Religion

The state-funded Catholic church, closely tied to the right wing Partido Popular, and with the national Cadena Cope radio station as its voice, continues to hold considerable social and political influence in Spain, with members of secretive groups such as *Opus Dei* and the *Legionarios de Cristo* holding key government and industry positions.

Despite the church's remaining influence, at street level Spain has become a distinctly secular country, as shown by the fact that 70% of Spaniards supported the decidedly un-Catholic 2005 law allowing gay marriage. And although more than 75% of the population claim to be Catholic, less than 20% go to church on a regular basis.

The most striking changes to the religious landscape in Spain in recent years have come as a result of Spain's rocketing immigration. There are more than 1 million Muslims in Spain, making Islam the country's second biggest religion. Meanwhile, Catholic masses have been greatly bolstered over the last decade by strongly Catholic South American and Polish immigrants.

Cultural Mores

Many of the cultural misunderstandings for visitors to Spain center around the dinner table. For starters, you have to get used to sitting down to eat when the Spanish do. No earlier than 1:30 PM for lunch, preferably after 2, and definitely not before 9 PM for dinner. Any earlier and you may well find the kitchen is closed and the waiter is not too happy that you have disturbed his late morning or early evening rest.

Speaking of waiters, it's safest to expect surly—if not downright grumpy—behavior as the norm. Waiters are paid a reasonable flat rate in Spain, and do not expect to make their living from tips, a good thing considering that tipping is often ignored completely by the Spanish, perhaps rising to a meager 5% on big meals, and only if the waiter is particularly nice. The lack of an end-of-the-meal payoff incentive has led to a culture of terrible customer service in many establishments.

Dining is not the only part of Spanish life with a bizarre timetable. Outside of major cities such as Madrid and Barcelona you can expect to find most shops shut from 2 until 5. During this time, shopkeepers go home to eat the main meal of the day, and perhaps snooze for a while. It's best to work this into your plans on an "if you can't beat them, join them" basis, taking a quick siesta at the hotel after lunch in preparation for a long night out on the town.

Science

In recent decades, Spanish science has been plagued by a brain-drain of its best minds to other European countries and the USA, as chronic under-funding leads intellects to seek research grants abroad. Juan Ignacio Cirac, a world-renowned theoretical physicist, is a perfect example—he left for the University of Colo-

SPAIN TODAY

rado in 1991, and is now director of the Max Planck Institute of Quantum Optics in Germany.

Despite funding problems, Spain still remains a world leader in various fields, noticeably medical and organ transplants. In 2006, doctors at Hospital La Fe, in Valencia, successfully carried out a double hand transplant on a 47-year-old woman who had lost her hands in an accident 28 years before. Spain has also been chosen to manage a worldwide organ transplant database, aimed at preventing illegal international organ trafficking.

Another area in which Spain excels is in the promotion of renewable energies. Wind farms are an increasingly common site on the country's high plains, and 2007 saw the launch of the world's biggest solar power farm, in Beneixama, in the province of Alicante. Costing 150 million euros, the 100,000 solar panels produce 30 million kilowatts an hour, providing energy for more than 12,000 homes.

The Arts

Spain's devotion to the arts is clearly shown by the attention, both national and international, paid to its annual Principe de Asturias prize, where Prince Filipe hands out accolades to international high achievers such as Woody Allen and Paul Auster, and home-grown talent such as Santiago Calatrava and Pedro Almodovar. While Calatrava takes the world of architecture by storm (think Athens Olympic Sports Complex and New York's upcoming 80 South Street project), Almodovar and his eternal muse Penelope Cruz continue to flourish at home and abroad with movies such as *Volver.* With Spanish household names such as Paz Vega and Javier Bardem also making a splash in Hollywood, film is without doubt at the forefront of the Spanish arts scene.

Spanish music, however, continues to be a very local affair. A host of *Pop Idol*–style shows (*Pop Idol* was the British precursor to *American Idol*), noticeably *Operacion Triunfo,* have churned out youthful stars such as David Bisbal and Chenoa, that despite gathering huge followings in Spain and in parts of South America, will never really make it on the international scene. Conversely, big international bands, such as The Rolling Stones, Elton John, and U2 can often be found touring in Spain, while the summer festival scene, including the Festival Internacional de Benicássim, Womad, and Summercase, serve up top names to revelers who come from all over Europe to soak up the music in the sun.

While authors such as Miguel Delibes, Rosa Montero, and Maruja Torres flourish in Spain, very few break onto the international scene, with the exception of Arturo Perez Reverte, whose books include *Captain Alatriste* and *The Fencing Master,* and Carlos Ruiz Zafón, author of the internationally acclaimed *Shadow of the Wind.* Spain's contribution to the fine arts is still dominated by two names: the Mallorcan-born artist Miguel Barceló, and the Basque sculptor Eduardo Chillida, who died in 2002, and whose work can be seen in his Chillida-Leku museum close to San Sebastian.

Sports

Sports play such an important part in Spanish life that until *20Minutos,* an all-news tabloid distributed free in big cities, took over the top spot in 2006, Spain's biggest selling daily paper was *Marca,* which is dedicated 100% to sports, and

mostly soccer at that. With Real Madrid and Barcelona now firmly established as International brands, and La Liga recognized as the world's most exciting league, soccer still remains the nation's firm favorite, second only to motor racing.

When Fernando Alonso won the Formula One championship in 2005 and 2006, national pride reached levels of near frenzy. The Asturian was paraded around his native Oviedo in an open-topped bus like a returning hero of days gone by. Second only to Alonso in terms of national pride is Dani Pedrosa, the prodigious motorcycling star who, having triumphed in the 125 and 250cc Moto GP events, now threatens to topple the legendary Valentino Rossi from his place in the GP class. So fanatical in fact are the Spanish about motorcycle racing, that the Grand Prix circuit passes through Spain three times every year, visiting Jerez, Valencia, and Montmeló (near Barcelona), while no other country is visited more than once.

Cycling is also big in Spain, with the Vuelta, Spain's version of the Tour de France, crisscrossing the country every year in September. Barely out of his teens, Mallorcan-born Rafa Nadal is making a striking impact on the international tennis scene, enlivening grand slam finals worldwide with his epic battles against the all-powerful Roger Federer. Finally, Spain looks set to relaunch its unsuccessful 2012 Madrid Olympic bid for 2016, where, if all else fails, we can expect great things from another source of national pride: the female synchronized swimming team.

Media

The Spanish press has long been dominated by three major national newspapers, *El País* (left wing), *El Mundo* (right wing), and *ABC* (right wing). Although the introduction of a number of free newspapers, including *20Minutos, Metro,* and *¡Qué!,* has undermined their sales, *kioskos* (the press stands on every street corner) still do a brisk daily trade in these traditional newspapers and a host of gossip magazines such as *¡Qué Me Dices!* and *10 Minutos.*

Gossip unfortunately dominates a lot of Spanish television as well, which is not renowned for the quality of its programming. C-grade celebrity chasing, scandal-raking panels, and South American soaps dominate most daytime schedules, even on state-run Television Española's main channels, TV1 and La 2. On these and independent channels such as Tele 5 and Antenna 3, advertising stretches well beyond official guidelines, with regular 15- to 20-minute commercial breaks stretching movies out for hours.

It's not surprising then that many Spaniards hold such a high regard for the radio, with state-run Radio Nacional de España, church funded Cadena Cope, and independent Cadena Ser producing high-quality current affairs and news programs.

SPAIN TOP ATTRACTIONS

La Alhambra, Granada

(A) Nothing can quite prepare you for the Moorish grandeur of Andalusia's greatest monument. The ornamental palace is set around sumptuous courtyards and gardens complete with bubbling fountains, magnificent statues, and brilliantly colored flower beds. From the Generalife gardens, there are evocative, camera-clicking views of the Albayzín, the ancient wealthy neighborhood of Moorish Granada. (⇨ Chapter 11.)

Toledo

(B) This sumptuous, historically rich city is Castile's crowning glory. Toledo is often cited as being Spain's spiritual capital, and past inhabitants—including Jews, Romans, and Muslims—have all felt its spiritual pull. This open-air museum of a city is an architectural tapestry of medieval buildings, churches, mosques, and synagogues threaded by narrow cobbled streets and squares. The location is similarly awesome: Toledo is on a ridge high above the Río Tajo. The only downside is the fleets of bus tours that clog the streets; visit at dusk. (⇨ Chapter 3.)

La Sagrada Família, Barcelona

(C) *The* symbol of Barcelona, Gaudí's extraordinary unfinished cathedral should be included on everyone's must-see list. The pointed spires, with organic shapes that resemble a honeycombed stalagmite, give the whole place a sort of fairytale quality. (⇨ Chapter 7.)

Guggenheim, Bilbao

(D) All swooping curves and rippling forms, the architecturally innovative museum—one of architect Frank Gehry's most breathtaking projects—was built on the site of the city's former shipyards. It was appropriately inspired by the shape of a ship's hull. The museum collection is pretty good as well, including such

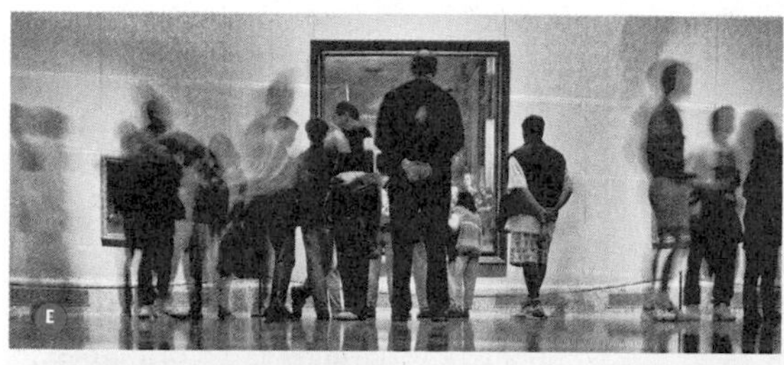

smock-and-beret masters as Picasso and Miró, as well temporary avant-garde exhibits. (⇨ Chapter 5.)

Museo del Prado, Madrid

(E) Set in a magnificent Neoclassical building on one of the capital's most elegant boulevards, the Prado is Spain's answer to the Louvre and a regal home to renowned Spanish masterpieces. Much of the collection dates back to the museum's inauguration in 1819. (⇨ Chapter 2.)

Mérida's Roman Ruins

(F) Your instinct may be to rub your eyes in disbelief. Here, plopped in the center of a somewhat drab modern town is the largest Roman city on the Iberian Peninsula. Ogle at the fabulously preserved Roman amphitheater with its columns, statues, and tiered seating, or the humbler, yet equally beguiling, 2nd-century house with tiled mosaics and frescoes. (⇨ Chapter 13.)

Cuenca's Hanging Houses

(G) The old town of Cuenca is all honey-color buildings, handsome mansions, ancient churches, and earthy local bars. Seek out the famous Casas Colgadas or "Hanging Houses" with their facades precipitously dipping over a steep ravine. Dating from the 15th century, the balconies appear as an extension of the rock face. (⇨ Chapter 3.)

San Lorenzo de El Escorial

(H) Seriously over-the-top, this giant palace-monastery (with no less than 2,673 windows) built by the megalomaniac Felipe II, causes visitors to stop in their tracks with wonder. The exterior is undeniably austere, but inside, *salas* (rooms) like the Bourbon apartments and library are positively lush with their rich colorful tapestries, ornate frescoes, and paintings by such masters as El Greco, Titian, and José de Ribera. (⇨ Chapter 2.)

SPAIN'S TOP EXPERIENCES

Stroll with Your Sweetheart on Festa de Sant Jordi

Barcelona's Festa de Sant Jordi is like Valentine's Day with a Catalan twist. Celebrating St. George, the patron saint of Barcelona, for his heroism in allegedly saving a princess from a dragon, this day has come to be associated with chivalry and romance. All over the city you'll find couples strolling, smooching, and buying each other tokens of affection—tradition dictates that the men buy their true love a rose, and since the Festa de Sant Jordi shares a date with International Book Day, women reciprocate by buying their beau a book. The result is fragrant, rose-scented streets lined with bookstalls. For locals, the urge to play hooky from work runs high, and a giddy, playful, flirtatious vibe lasts until the wee hours.

Have the Ultimate Food Fight in Buñol

Buñol, a tiny town outside Valencia, may hold the key to the best stress relief without a prescription. Every year on the last Wednesday of August townsfolk hold La Tomatina, a giant tomato-throwing extravaganza. The modest town of 9,000 swells to three times its size, as visiting tomato-chuckers ride the RENFE in to participate. The affair, with unknown origins (some say it mushroomed from a tomato thrown at a pedestrian), now literally paints the town red as hundreds of thousands of tomatoes are thrown. It's the tomato version of a snowball fight, in all its bloody glory.

Dance Till Dawn in Ibiza

If Spain is a country for night owls and 3 AM dance marathons, then Ibiza is its party capital. Unapologetically hedonistic, this little island knows how to throw it down. Where else would you find a club with a pool? Or a "Discobus" to shuttle tipsy clubbers to the next multi-floor nightclub? Models, film stars, and beautiful people working on their tans all flock to the beaches and the throbbing music.

Surf the Seas

Tarifa, located on the Atlantic Coast in Cadíz Province, has fast become the wind- and kite-surfing capital of Europe, and every year seems to attract more devotees from all over the world. Silhouetted against a bold blue backdrop, the vivid sails flutter in the breeze like tropical butterflies. The most popular beaches for the sport are just northwest of the town along what is known as the Costa de la Luz (Coast of Light)—wide stretches of silvery white sand, washed by magical rollers and flanked by rolling dunes. The winds here are the eastern Levante and the western Poniente, which can be a gusty problem if you are trying to read the paper under a beach umbrella, but ideal for surfing the waves. There are plenty of places here where you can enroll in courses and rent gear.

Play Top Chef at the Spanish Market

Markets (*mercados*) are the key to delicious local cuisine and represent an essential part of Spanish life, largely unaffected by competition from supermarkets and hypermarkets. You'll find fabulous produce sold according to whatever is in season: counters neatly piled with shiny purple eggplants, blood-red peppers, brilliant orange cantaloupes and all variety of fruit, including fresh figs, a couple sliced open to show their succulent pink flesh. Some towns have markets on one or two days a week only, while others have daily fruit and vegetable markets from Monday through Saturday. Take the opportunity to get a culinary education. Vendors

are authorities and connoisseurs on their offerings and are only too happy to share their secrets.

Hit the Slopes in the Pyrenees

Simply drinking in the view around the Vall d'Aran with a pair of skis clapped to your feet is worth the trip, but then the skiing itself is world famous. Just note all the accents from neighboring countries that come to Spain for peak snow conditions (with a boost from the artificial snow machines). Trust us, uttering the phrase "I went skiing in the Pyrenees" to your friends never gets old.

Dance in the Streets during the Ferias

Throughout Spain and particularly Andalusia, the year revolves around *ferias* (fairs), which are far more than a holiday from work. While city-based *ferias* are rich and glittering affairs attracting millions of visitors, others, such as the *feria* of Casares village near the Costa del Sol, is more an exuberant street party. The most famous fair of all is Seville's Feria de Abril (April Fair), when sultry foot-stomping señoritas wear traditional, brilliantly colored flamenco dresses. From 1 to 5 every afternoon, Sevillana society parades around in carriages drawn by glossy high-stepping horses. The atmosphere is electric and infectious and, like all *ferias,* the charm lies in the universal spontaneity of enjoyment.

Catch the Carnaval

Second only to Rio in terms of revelry and costumes, the annual *Carnaval* in Spain can reach serious partying proportions. Aside from the Canary Islands (legendary for its full-on fiestas), Cadíz in southern Spain is famous for its annual extravaganza of drinking, dancing, and dressing up—the more outrageous the better. The celebrations typically carry on for 10 days. There are processions of costumed groups and everyone is dressed up, including a healthy number of drag queens. Book your hotel months in advance, because you're not likely to find a single vacancy in town during the celebration.

Drink Like a Madrileño

To experience Madrid like a local, you have to eat and drink like a local, and in the capital an aperitif is a crucial part of daily life. In fact, there are more bars per square meter than any other capital in Europe, so finding a venue poses no great challenge. Go the traditional route and try a *vermut* (vermouth) on tap, typically served with a squirt of soda. Or go for a glass of ice-cold fino (dry sherry) with its common tapas accompaniment of a couple of *gambas* (prawns). *Cervecerías* are also rife in the capital. These beer houses typically serve several local varieties on tap. In Madrid's Plaza Santa Ana some of the best-loved *cervecerías* line the pretty central square. Turn to your neighbor and give your best "¡Salud!"

Spot Celebrities on the Costa

The Monte Carlo of Costa del Sol, Puerto Banús is *the* place to pick up your made-to-measure gold chain or meet up with members of the local Ferrari Club. The buildings reflect a tantalizing combination of traditional Andaluz and Moorish design, while the position, cradled by lofty mountains overlooking the Mediterranean, is suitably stunning. The harbor is the port of call to some of the most lavish yachts in the world, so don't be surprised if you have to shift your credit card into overdrive to eat here. It is well worth stopping for a drink or just to ogle at the rich, famous, and wannabe celebs.

QUINTESSENTIAL SPAIN

La Siesta

The unabashed Spanish pursuit of pleasure and the unswerving devotion to establishing a healthy balance between work and play is nowhere more apparent than in this midday shutdown. However, as air-conditioning, fitness clubs, and other distractions gain ascendancy in modern Spain, and Mom-cooked lunches, once a universal ritual, become all but extinct in the two-salary, 21st-century Spanish family, the siesta question is increasingly debated. The classic midday snooze described by novelist Camilo José Cela as "de padrenuestro y pyjama" (with a prayer and pajamas) is rarely practiced these days, but the fact remains that most stores and businesses close from 1:30 to 4:30 or later; whether they're sleeping, feasting, exercising, or canoodling, one thing is certain: they're not working.

El Fútbol

The Spanish National Fútbol (soccer) League and the *tortilla de patata* (potato omelet) have been described as the only widely shared phenomena that bind the nation together. In the case of the league, the tie that binds often resembles tribal warfare, as bitter rivalries centuries old are played out on the field. Some of these, such as the Real Sociedad (San Sebastián)—Athletic de Bilbao feud, are fraternal in nature, brother Basques battling for boasting rights, but others, such as the Madrid-Barcelona stand-offs, are as basic to Spanish history as Moros y Cristianos (a reenactment of the battle between the Moors and the Christians). The beauty of the game is best appreciated in the stadiums, but local sports bars, many of them official fan clubs of local teams, is where you see *fútbol* passions at their wildest.

If you want to get a sense of Spanish culture and indulge in some of its pleasures, start by familiarizing yourself with the rituals of daily life. These are a few things you can take part in with relative ease.

El Paseo

One of the most delightful Spanish customs is *el paseo* (the stroll), which traditionally takes place during the early evening, and is common throughout the country, but particularly in *pueblos* and towns. Given the modern hamster-wheel pace of life, there is something appealingly old-fashioned about families and friends walking around at a leisurely pace with no real destination or purpose. In fact, if you were to set off for a jog at dusk in a small village here, you would likely be viewed with amusement or even suspicion. Dress is usually formal or fashionable: elderly señoras with their boxy tweed suits, men with jackets slung, capelike, round the shoulders, teenagers in their latest Zara gear, and younger children in their Sunday best. El paseo provides everyone with an opportunity to participate in a lively slice of street theater.

Sunday Lunch

The Spanish love to eat out, especially on Sunday, the traditional day when families will drive to restaurants for long leisurely lunches. Depending on the time of year, this is most likely to be a seaside *chiringuito* or rural *venta*. The latter thrive, particularly in southern Spain, born from bygone days when much of the region's seasonal work was done by itinerant labor. Cheap, hearty meals were much in demand and some enterprising country housewife saw the opportunity and decided to provide *ventas* (meals for sale); an idea that quickly mushroomed. Ventas are still a wonderfully good value today, not just for the food, but also for the atmosphere: long scrubbed wooden tables, large noisy Spanish families, and a convivial informality. Sunday can be slow. So relax, and remember that all good things are worth waiting for ...

IF YOU LIKE

Art

During the Spanish Golden Age (1580–1680), the empire's wealth flowed to the imperial capital of Madrid, and Spanish monarchs used it not only for defense and civil projects but to finance the arts. Painters from El Greco to Rubens, and writers from Lope de Vega to Cervantes, were drawn to the luminous (and solvent) royal court. For the first time in Europe, the collecting of art became an important symbol of national wealth and power.

- **Centro de Arte Reina Sofia, Madrid.** The modern collection focuses on Spain's three great modern masters: Pablo Picasso, Salvador Dalí, and Joan Miró. It houses Picasso's *Guernica*.
- **Museo de Bellas Artes, Seville.** Among the fabulous works are those of Murillo, Zurbarán, Valdés Leal, and El Greco, and there are examples of Seville Gothic art, baroque religious sculptures, and Sevillian art of the 19th and 20th centuries.
- **Museo del Prado, Madrid.** One of the world's greatest museums, it holds masterpieces by Italian and Flemish painters. But its jewels are the works of Spaniards: Goya, Velázquez and El Greco.
- **Museo Thyssen-Bornemisza, Madrid.** An ambitious collection of 800 paintings traces the development of Western humanism as no other in the world.
- **Museo Guggenheim, Bilbao.** The world-famous mesmerizing building houses works from the Venetian and the New York Guggenheim collections, but also from big-name Spanish modern artists.

Beaches

Virtually surrounded by bays, oceans, gulfs, straits, and seas, Spain is a beach-lover's dream as well as an increasingly popular destination for water-sports enthusiasts. August beaches are overcrowded and to be avoided, whereas winter beaches offer solitude and sunshine without the stifling heat.

Known for its warm-water temperatures and the healing properties of its brine and iodine content, the Mar Menor in Costa Blanca offers year-round beach fun.

Beaches on the Costa del Sol from Málaga to Estepona are warm enough for swimming year-round, though the overdeveloped high-rise apartments that have replaced fishing villages along this strip are ugly and depressing. The Costa de La Luz, just beyond Algeciras, presents a very different picture with its white sandy beaches and a refreshing lack of concrete, particularly around Tarifa, which is famous for its water sports.

Matalascañas, at the western end of the Andalusian coast, and La Antilla, west of Huelva, are fine beaches except in late July and August when there's no towel space on the sand. South of Huelva are Cadíz's Atlantic wild and very windy beaches, appreciated by water-sports fans and by locals fleeing from the Mediterranean clamor and crowds.

Spain's northern coast, from the French border at Hondarribia to the border with Portugal at the Río Miño offers a variety of urban beaches and remote strands, while the Balearic archipelagoes have year-round beaches—though they can be too cold for swimming from November to May.

Food

Spanish cooking has come into its own over the last 20 years. The Mediterranean diet, with its emphasis on olive oil, fish, vegetables, garlic, onions, and red wine, is now understood to be not only delicious but a healthy way to eat. Innovative chefs, including Ferran Adrià and Pedro Subijana, and such masters as Juan Mari Arzak and Santi Santamaría, are making Spain's regional cuisines famous throughout the world, and newer stars—Martin Berasategui, Sergi Arola, Fermí Puig, and Carme Ruscalleda Puig—are filling the firmament with new aromas and textures.

- **Arzak, San Sebastián.** The traditional Basque food at this extremely popular, internationally renowned restaurant is jazzed up by the owner's imaginative culinary flair.
- **Tragabuches, Ronda.** This stylish restaurant dishes ups innovative cuisine and has a superb taster's menu of five courses and two desserts.
- **El Celler de Can Roca, Girona, Costa Brava.** Perhaps for its oddball combinations, the best restaurant in town is also one of Catalonia's top six.
- **El Chaflán, Madrid.** Come for white-truffle sampler week but find new and sophisticated dishes anytime.
- **La Broche, Madrid.** El Bulli's Ferran Adrià's best disciple plays with texture and temperatura, drawing on his Catalonian roots but also turning his back on them when inspiration calls.
- **El Racó de Can Fabes, Sant Celoni.** One of Spain's top four restaurants, it's well worth the train ride from Barcelona.

Exploring the Outdoors

Crisscrossed with mountain ranges, Spain has areas that are ideal for walking, mountain biking, and backpacking. The Pyrenees offer superior hiking and trekking on well-marked trails from the Atlantic Bay of Biscay to the Mediterranean, among them the 40- to 45-day GR-11 trail that runs from the Atlantic Ocean to the Mediterranean Sea. The Sierra de Gredos, west of Ávila, and the Sierra de Guadarrama, north of Madrid, are also popular for climbing and trekking. Hiking is also excellent in the interior of Spain, in the Alpujarra Mountains southeast of Granada, and in the numerous national parks, such as mountainous Picos de Europa. Still in vogue after hundreds of years is the Pilgrimage Road to Santiago de Compostela; it traverses the north of Spain from either Roncesvalles in Navarra or the Aragonian Pyrennees to Galicia. Mountain streams in the Pyrenees and other ranges throughout Spain offer trout- and salmon-fishing opportunities that can combine nicely with hiking and camping expeditions. Perhaps the best part of Spain's outdoor space and activities is that they often bring you nearer to some of the finest architecture and cuisine in Iberia.

- **Doñana National Park, Andalusia.** One of Europe's last tracts of true wilderness includes wetlands, beaches, shifting sand dunes, marshes, 150 species of rare birds, and countless kinds of wildlife, including the endangered imperial eagle and lynx.
- **Ordesa and Monte Perdido National Park, the Pyrenees.** Hike in Spain's version of the Grand Canyon. The 57,000-acre park features waterfalls, caves, forests, meadows, and more.

GREAT ITINERARIES

MADRID & THE SOUTH

Days 1–3: Welcome to Madrid

The elegant Plaza Mayor is the perfect jumping-off point for a tour of the Spanish capital. To the west, see the Plaza de la Villa, Royal Palace, the opera house and the royal convents; to the south wander around the maze of streets of La Latina and the Rastro and indulge yourself in local tapas. Start or end the day with a visit to the Prado, the Museo Thyssen-Bornemisza, or the Centro de Arte Reina Sofía.

On Day 2, visit the sprawling Barrio de las Letras. Around Plaza de Santa Ana, it was the favorite neighborhood of writers during the Spanish golden literary age in the 17th century, and it is still cramped with theaters, cafés, and good tapas bars. It borders the Paseo del Prado on the east, allowing you to comfortably walk to any of the art museums in the area. If the weather is pleasant, take an afternoon stroll in the Parque del Buen Retiro.

For your third day in the capital, wander along Chueca and Malasaña, the two neighborhoods most favored by young Madrileños. Fuencarral, a landmark street that serves as the border between the two is one of the city's trendiest shopping enclaves. From there you can walk to the Parque del Oeste and the Templo de Debod—the best spot from which to see the city's sunset. Among the lesser-known museums, consider visiting the captivating Museo Sorolla, Goya's frescoes and tomb at the Ermita de San Antonio de la Florida, or the Real Academia de Bellas Artes de San Fernando for classic painting. People-watch at any of the terrace bars in either Plaza de Chueca or Plaza 2 de Mayo in Malasaña. *See Chapter 2 for details on Madrid.*

Logistics: If you are traveling light, the subway (Metro) or the bus will take you from the airport to the city for €1 to €1.25. A taxi will do the same for around €25 to €30. Once in the center consider either walking or taking the subway rather than driving in gridlock traffic.

Days 4 & 5: Castilian Charmers

Making excellent half- or one-day side trips from the capital are Toledo and Segovia, two of the oldest Castilian cities—both with delightful old quarters dating back to the Romansand El Escorial, which houses the massive monastery built by Felipe II. Two other nearby towns also worth visiting are Aranjuez and Alcalá de Henares. See Chapter 3 for details on these Castilian cities.

Logistics: In 2007, Toledo and Segovia became part of the high-speed train line (AVE), so you can get to both of them in a half-hour from Madrid. To reach the old quarters of both cities take a bus or cab from the train station. Or take the bus from Madrid; by bus is also the best way to get to El Escorial. Reach Aranjuez and Alcalá de Henares via the intercity train system.

Day 6: Córdoba & Its Mosque or Extremadura

This capital of both Roman and Moorish Spain was also the center of Western art and culture between the 8th and 11th centuries. Córdoba's sprawling mosque (now a cathedral) and the medieval Jewish Quarter bear witness to the city's brilliant past. From Madrid you can rent a car and visit the lesser-known cities north of Extremadura (Guadalupe, Trujillo, and Cáceres). You can sleep over in Cáceres,

a UNESCO World Cultural Heritage city, and return to Madrid the next day. *See Chapter 11 for Córdoba and Chapter 13 for Extremadura.*

Logistics: The AVE train will take you to Córdoba from Madrid in under two hours. A good alternative is to sleep over in Toledo, also on the route heading south, and then head to Córdoba the next day. Once in Córdoba, take a taxi for a visit out to the summer palace at Medina Azahara.

Days 7 & 8: Seville

Seville's Giralda tower, cathedral, bullring, and Barrio de Santa Cruz are visual feasts. Forty minutes south you can sip the world-famous sherries of Jerez de la Frontera, then munch jumbo shrimp on the beach at Sanlúcar de Barrameda. For more on Seville, *see Chapter 11.*

Logistics: From Seville's AVE station, take a taxi to your hotel. After that, walking and hailing the occasional taxi are the best ways to explore the city.

Days 9 & 10: Granada

The hilltop Alhambra palace, Spain's most visited attraction, was conceived by the Moorish caliphs as heaven on earth. Try any of its famous tapas bars and tea-shops, and also roam the magicical steep streets of the Albayzín, the ancient Moorish quarter. For more on Andalusia, see Chapter 11.

Logistics: The Seville-to-Granada leg of this trip is best accomplished by renting a car. However, the Sevilla-to-Granada trains (four daily, just over three hours, costing less than €21) are an alternative. An alternative route is to head first from Madrid to Granada, skipping Córdoba, and then from Granada to Seville.

> **TIP**
>
> Spain's modern freeways are as good as any in the world—with the exception of the signs, which have writing that's often too small to decipher while comfortably travelling at the routine speed of 120 km/h (74 mph).

GREAT ITINERARIES

BARCELONA & THE NORTH

Days 1–3: Welcome to Barcelona

To get a feel of Barcelona, begin with the Rambla neighborhood and Boqueria market. Then set off for the Gothic Quarter to see the Catedral de la Seu, Plaça del Rei, and the Catalan and Barcelona government palaces in Plaça Sant Jaume. Next, cross Via Laietana to the Barri de la Ribera (waterfront neighborhood), which contains the paradigmatic Catalan Gothic Santa Maria del Mar and Museu Picasso.

Make Day 2 a Gaudí day. Visit the Temple Expiatori de la Sagrada Família first thing, followed by Parc Güell. In the afternoon tour Casa Vicens, then Casa Milà and Casa Batlló, part of the Manzana de la Discòrdia on Passeig de Gràcia. Palau Güell, off the lower Rambla, is probably too much Gaudí for one day, but don't miss it. (In our in-focus feature "Gaudí: Architecture Through the Looking Glass" in Chapter 7, learn all about this prolific artist and the ornamental style of Barcelona's Moderniste architecture.)

On Day 3, climb Montjuïc for the Museu Nacional d'Art de Catalunya, in the hulking Palau Nacional. Investigate the Fundació Miró, Estadi Olímpic, the Mies van de Rohe Pavilion and Casaramona (aka Caixaforum). At lunchtime, take the cable car across the port for seafood in Barceloneta. See Chapter 7 for more on Barcelona.

Logistics: The bus will take you from the airport to the city for €4.75. A taxi will do the same for around €23. In Barcelona's city center, walking or taking the subway is better than cabbing it.

Days 3 & 4: San Sebastián

San Sebastián is one of Spain's most beautiful—and delicious—cities. Belle epoque buildings nearly encircle the tiny bay, and tapas bars flourish in the old quarter. Visiting San Sebastián without a look at Pasajes de San Juan is a mistake. Likewise, an excursion to Hondarribia is a must. The cider mills in Astigarraga are another important off–San Sebastián visit. For more on San Sebastián, see Chapter 5.

Logistics: Whether you arrive by plane, train, or car, you'll need a car to explore the Basque Country properly. Although there is no need for a car in San Sebastián proper, visits to cider houses in Astigarraga, Chillida Leku on the outskirts of town, and many of the finest restaurants around San Sebastián, are possible only by car. (Of course, if you go by taxi, you won't have to worry about getting lost.) The freeway west to Bilbao is beautiful and fast, but the coastal road through Orio, Zarautz, Guetaria, and Zumaia is recommended at least as far as Zumaia.

Days 5 & 6: The Basque Coast

The Basque coast between San Sebastián and Bilbao is lined with beaches, rocky cliffs, and picture-perfect fishing ports. The wide beach at Zarautz, the fishermen's village of Guetaria, the Zuloaga Museum in Zumaia, Mundaka's famous left-breaking surfing wave, and Bermeo's port and fishing museum should all be near the top of your list. See Chapter 5 for information on Basque Country.

Logistics: To see the Basque coast, forget about time and wind along the coastal roads that twist through places such as Elantxobe, Bakio, Mundaka, and San Juan Gaztelugatxe. From Bilbao there is a train, the Euskotren, that runs from

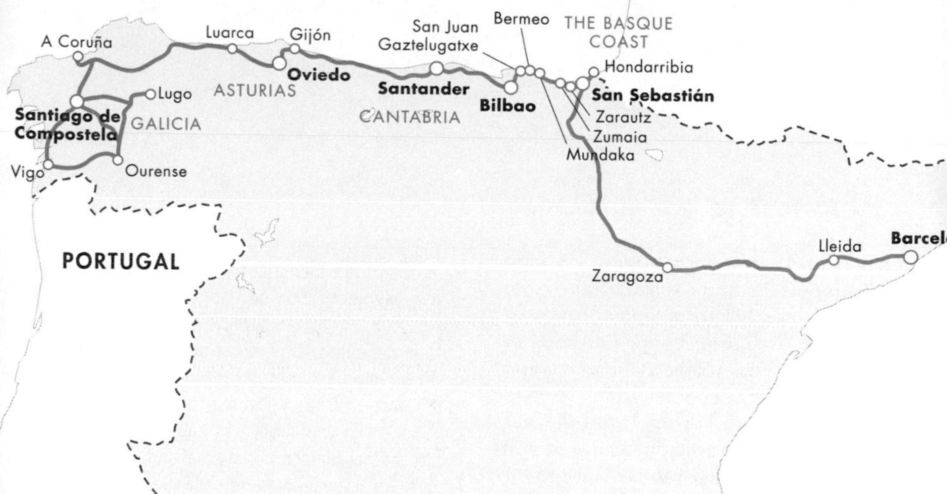

the Atxuri station through the Urdaibai wetlands and the Ría de Gernika to Mundaka.

Days 7 & 8: Bilbao

Bilbao's Guggenheim Museum is worth a trip for the building itself, and the Museum of Fine Arts has an impressive collection of Basque and Spanish paintings. Restaurants and tapas bars are famously good in Bilbao, and the city's cultural offerings, from opera to jazz to bullfights (in August), has always been first-rate. See Chapter 7 for more details on Bilbao.

Logistics: In Bilbao, use the subway or the Euskotram, which runs up and down the Nervión estuary.

Days 9 & 10: Santander & Cantabria

The elegant beach town Santander has an excellent summer music festival. Santillana del Mar is one of Spain's best Renaissance towns, and the museum at the Altamira Caves displays famous early-day cave paintings. Exploring the Picos de Europa will take you through some the peninsula's wildest reaches, and the port towns along the coast provide some of Spain's wildest and purest beaches. See Chapter 7 for more on Santander and other Cantabria destinations.

Logistics: Santander stretches for several miles along its Sardinero beachfront. There is little traffic, except in mid-August, but parking is expensive and scarce, so it's better to make use of the bus service. For explorations into the towns and hills of Cantabria, an automobile is indispensable.

Days 11–13: Oviedo & Asturias

The coast road through Ribadesella and cider capital Villaviciosa to Oviedo is a scenic tour punctuated with numerous tempting beaches. Oviedo, its cathedral, and its pre-Romanesque churches are worlds away from Córdoba's Mezquita and Granada's Alhambra. Gijón is a fishing and freight port, summer resort, and university town, and the villages along the coast such as Cudillero and Luarca remain quite unspoiled and serve wonderful fish and seafood. See Chapter 4 for details on Asturias.

Logistics: The A8 coastal freeway gets you quickly and comfortably from points east to Oviedo and just beyond. From there west into Galicia the two-lane N634 and the coastal N632 are the slow but scenic routes to Santiago de Compostela.

Days 14–16: Santiago de Compostela & Galicia

Spain's northwest corner, with Santiago de Compostela at its spiritual and geographic center, is a green land of bagpipes and apple orchards. Lugo, Ourense, A Coruña, and Vigo are the major cities, and the Albariño wine country, along the Río Miño border with Portugal, and the *rías* (estuaries), full of delicious seafood, will keep you steeped in *enxebre*—Gallego for "local specialties and atmosphere." See Chapter 4 for more on Galicia.

Logistics: Once in Galicia, the four-lane freeways AP9 and A6 whisk you from Lugo and Castro to Santiago de Compostela and down into the Rías Baixas. Cars are the only way to tour Galicia, and the slower the better. The AC552 route around the upper northwest corner and the Rías Altas turns into the AC550 coming back into Santiago.

TIP

Be prepared for bilingual traffic signs and local spellings that do not match your map, which probably adheres to the "traditional" Castilian spelling. (Languages across the north of Spain go from Basque or Euskera in the eastern Basque Country; to Castilian Spanish in Santander and Cantabria; to Bable, a local dialect, in Asturias; and Gallego, a Portuguese-like Romance language, in Galicia.)

FAQ

What are my lodging options in Spain? For a slice of Spanish culture, check out the paradores; to indulge your pastoral fantasies, a *casa rural* (country house), Spain's version of a bed-and-breakfast. On the other end of the spectrum are luxurious high-rise hotels along the coastline, and chain hotels in the major cities. Traveling with your family? Consider renting an apartment. If you only need a simple, clean place to tuck in for the night, hostels provide the ultimate savings.

Do I need to book hotels beforehand, or can I just improvise once I'm in Spain? In big cities or popular tourist areas it's best to book in advance. In smaller towns and rural areas you can usually find something on the spot, except when local fiestas are on—for those dates you may have to book months in advance.

How can I avoid looking like a tourist in Spain? Ditch the white tennis-shoes and shorts for a start. Also, try to avoid baseball caps, and carry your maps and guidebook discreetly. Some suggest buying an entire Spanish wardrobe at fashion chain Zara, but that may be a bit overboard.

Do shops really close for siesta? In general, shops will close from 2 PM to 5 PM, particularly in small towns and villages. The exceptions are supermarkets and large department stores, which tend to be open from 9 AM to 9 PM. Shops in the center of Madrid and Barcelona and at major resorts often stay open all day.

How much should I tip at a restaurant? You won't find a service charge on the bill, but the tip is included. For stellar service, leave a small sum in addition to the bill, but not more than 10%. If you're indulging in tapas, just round out the bill to the nearest euro. For cocktails, tip about €0.5 a drink.

If only have time for one city, should I choose Barcelona or Madrid? It depends on what you're looking for. Madrid will give you world-class art and much more of a sense of a workaday Spanish city, while cosmopolitan Barcelona has Gaudí, Catalan cuisine, and its special Mediterranean atmosphere.

Can I get dinner at 7, or do I really have to wait until the Spanish eat at 9? If you really can't wait, head for the most touristy part of town; there you should be able to find bars and cafés that will serve meals at any time of day. But it won't be nearly as good as the food the Spaniards are eating a couple of hours later.

How easily is it to cross the border from Spain into neighboring countries? Spain, Portugal, and France are members of the EU, so borders are open. Trains travel between Madrid and Lisbon (about €57), and between Madrid and Paris (about €75). U.S. citizens need only a valid passport to enter Morocco; ferries run regularly to Tangier for about €30 one-way.

Can I bring home the famous Iberico ham, Spanish olives, almonds, or baby eels? Products you can legally bring into the United States include olive oil, cheese, olives, almonds, wood-smoked paprika, and saffron. Ibérico ham, even vacuum-sealed, is not legal, so you may not get past customs agents and their canine associates. If caught, you risk confiscation and fines. And don't even think about trying to bring back the *angulas* (eels) ...

For help on trip planning, see Spain Essentials in the back of the book.

HISTORY YOU CAN SEE

Ancient Spain

The story of Spain, a romance-tinged tale of counts, caliphs, crusaders, and kings, begins long before written history. The Basques were among the first here, fiercely defending the green mountain valleys of the Pyrenees. The Iberians came next, apparently crossing the Mediterranean from North Africa around 3,000 BC. The Celts arrived from the north about a thousand years later. The seafaring Phoenicians founded Gadir (now Cádiz) and several coastal cities in the south three millenniums ago. The parade continued with the Greeks, who settled parts of the east coast, and then the Carthaginians, who founded Cartagena around 225 BC—and who dubbed the then-wild, forested and game-rich country Ispania, after their word for rabbit: *span*.

What to See: Near Barcelona, rocket yourself back almost 3,000 years at **Ullastret,** a settlement occupied by an Iberian people known as the Indiketas. On a tour, actors guide groups through the homes and fortifications of some of the Peninsula's earliest inhabitants, the defensive walls attesting to the constant threat of attack and the bits of pottery evidence of the settlement's early ceramic industry. Not far away in **Empúries,** are ruins of the Greek colony established in the 6th century BC. Meanwhile, at the **Museo de Cádiz,** view sarcophagi dating back to the 1,100 BC founding of the city.

The Roman Epoch

Modern civilization began with the Romans, who expelled the Carthaginians and turned the peninsula into three imperial provinces. It took the Romans 200 years to subdue the fiercely resisting Iberians, but their influence is seen today in the fortifications, amphitheaters, aqueducts, and other ruins in cities across Spain, as well as in the country's legal system, and in the Latin base of Spain's Romance languages and dialects.

What to See: Segovia's nearly 3,000-foot-long **Acueducto Romano** is a marvel of Roman engineering. Mérida's Roman ruins are some of Spain's finest, including its **bridge, theater,** and **outdoor amphitheater.** Tarragona was Rome's most important city in Catalonia, as the **walls, circus,** and **amphitheater** bear witness, while Zaragoza boasts a **Roman amphitheater** and a **Roman fluvial port** that dispatched flat-bottomed riverboats loaded with wine and olive oil down the Ebro.

SPAIN TIMELINE

1100 BC Earliest Phoenician colonies, including Cádiz, Villaricos, Almuñecar, and Málaga.

237 BC Carthaginians land in Spain. Natives include Basques in the Pyrenees, Iberians in the south, and Celts in the northwest.

206 BC Romans expel Carthaginians from Spain and gradually conquer peninsula.

AD 74 Roman citizenship extended to all Spaniards.

419 Visigothic kingdom established in northern Spain, with capital at Toledo.

711–12 Visigothic kingdom destroyed by invading Muslims (Moors), who create emirate, with capital at Córdoba.

The Visigoths & Moors

In the early 5th century, invading barbarians crossed the Pyrenees to attack the weakening Roman empire. The Visigoths became the dominant force in northern Spain by 419, establishing their kingdom at Toledo and eventually adopting Christianity. But the Visigoths, too, were to fall before a wave of invaders. The Moors, an Arab-led Berber force, crossed the Strait of Gibraltar in 711 and swept through Spain in an astonishingly short time, launching almost eight centuries of Muslim rule. The Moors brought with them citrus fruits, rice, cotton, sugar, palm trees, glassmaking, and the complex irrigation system still used around Valencia. The influence of Arabic in modern Spanish includes words beginning with "al," such as *albóndiga* (meatball), *alcalde* (mayor), *almohada* (pillow), and *alcázar* (fortress), as well as prominent phonetic characteristics ranging from the fricative "j" to, in all probability, the lisping "c" (before "e" and "i") and "z." The Moorish and Mudéjar (Moorish decorative details) architecture found throughout most of Spain tells much about the splendor of the Islamic culture that flourished here.

What to See: Moorish culture is most spectacularly evident in Andalusia, derived from the Arabic name for the Moorish reign on the Iberian Peninsula, al-Andalus, which meant "western lands." The fairy-tale **Alhambra** palace overlooking Granada captures the refinement of the Moorish aesthetic, while the earlier, **9th-century mosque** at Córdoba bears witness to the power of Islam in al-Andalus.

Spain's Golden Age

By 1085, Alfonso VI of Castile had captured Toledo, giving the Christians a firm grip on the north. In the 13th century, Valencia, Seville, and finally Córdoba—the capital of the Muslim caliphate in Spain—fell to Christian forces, leaving only Granada in Moorish hands. Nearly 200 years later, the so-called Catholic Monarchs—Ferdinand of Aragón and Isabella of Castile—were joined in a marriage that would change the world. Finally, on January 2, 1492, 244 years after the fall of Córdoba, Granada surrendered and the Moorish reign was over.

The year 1492 was the beginning of the nation's political golden age: Christian forces conquered Granada and unified all of current-day Spain as a single king-

813 Discovery of remains of St. James; the cathedral of Santiago de Compostela is built and becomes a major pilgrimage site.

1085–1270 Main years of the Reconquest.

1478 Spanish Inquisition begins.

1479–1504 Isabella and Ferdinand rule jointly.

1492 Granada, the last Moorish outpost, falls. Christopher Columbus, under Isabella's sponsorship discovers America, setting off a wave of Spanish exploration. Ferdinand and Isabella expel Jews and Muslims from Spain.

1516 Ferdinand dies. His grandson Charles I inaugurates the Habsburg dynasty.

1519–22 First circumnavigation of the world by Ferdinand Magellan's ships.

ca. 1520–1700 Spain's Golden Age.

dom; in what was, at the time, viewed as a peace-keeping measure promoting national unity, Jews and Muslims who did not convert to Christianity were expelled from the country. The departure of educated Muslims and Jews was a blow to the nation's agriculture, science, and economy that would take nearly 500 years to expiate. The Catholic monarchs and their centralizing successors maintained Spain's unity, but they sacrificed the spirit of international free trade that was bringing prosperity to other parts of Europe. Carlos V weakened Spain with his penchant for waging war, and his son, Felipe II (Phillip II), followed in the same expensive path, defeating the Turks in 1571 but losing the "Invincible Spanish Armada" in the English Channel in 1588.

What to See: Celebrate Columbus's voyage to America with **festivities in Seville, Huelva, Granada, Cádiz, and Barcelona,** all of which display venues where "The Discoverer" was either commissioned, confirmed, set out, returned, or buried. Wander through the somber **El Escorial,** a monastery northwest of Madrid whose construction Felipe II oversaw and which is the resting place of Carlos V.

War of the Spanish Succession

The 1700–14 War of the Spanish Succession ended with the fall of Barcelona, which had sided with the Hapsburg Archduke Carlos against the Bourbon Prince Felipe V. El Born market, completed in 1876, covered the buried remains of the Ribera neighborhood where the decisive battle took place. Ribera citizens were required to tear down a thousand houses to clear space for the Ciutadella fortress, whose fields of fire were directed, quite naturally, toward the city the Spanish and French forces had taken a year to subdue. The leveled neighborhood, then about a third of Barcelona, was plowed under and forgotten by the victors, though never by Barcelonians.

What to See: In Barcelona, walk among the preserved 17th-century **Ribera neighborhood,** including several houses shattered by cannon balls. Check out the nearby **Fossar de les Moreres cemetery** next to the Santa Maria del Mar basilica; it is still a powerful symbol for Catalan nationalists who gather there every September 11, Catalonia's National Day, commemorating the fall of the city in 1714.

1605 Miguel de Cervantes publishes the first part of Don Quijote de la Mancha.

1618–1648 Thirty Years' War: a dynastic struggle between Habsburgs and Bourbons.

1701–14 War of the Spanish Succession. Claimants to the throne are Louis XIV of France, Holy Roman Emperor Leopold I, and electoral prince Joseph Ferdinand of Bavaria.

1756–63 Seven Years' War: Spain and France versus Great Britain.

1808 Napoleon takes Madrid.

1809–14 The Spanish War of Independence: Napoleonic armies thrown out of Spain.

1834–39 First Carlist War: Don Carlos contests the crown and begins an era of upheaval.

1873 First Spanish Republic declared. Three-year Second Carlist War begins.

Spanish Civil War

Spain's early 19th-century War of Independence required five years of bitter guerrilla fighting to rid the peninsula of Napoleonic troops. Later, the Carlist Wars set the stage for the Spanish civil war (1936–39), in which more than half a million people died. Intellectuals and leftists sympathized with the elected government, and the International Brigades, with many American, British, and Canadian volunteers, took part in some of the worst fighting, including the storied defense of Madrid. But General Francisco Franco, backed by the Catholic Church, got far more help from Nazi Germany, whose Condor legions destroyed the Basque town of Gernika (in a horror made infamous by Picasso's monumental painting, *Guernica*), and from Fascist Italy. For three years, European governments stood quietly by as Franco's armies ground their way to victory. After the fall of Barcelona in January 1939, the Republican cause became hopeless and Franco's Nationalist forces entered Madrid on March 27, 1939.

What to See: Snap a shot of **Madrid's Plaza Dos de Mayo,** in the Malasaña neighborhood; it is the site of the heroic stand of officers Daoiz and Velarde against vastly superior French forces at the start of the popular uprising against the French. The archway in the square is all that remains of the armory Daoiz and Velarde defended to the death. Trace the shrapnel marks on the wall of the **Sant Felip Neri church** in Barcelona, material evidence of the 1938 bombing of the city by Italian warplanes under Franco's orders. East of Zaragoza, the town of **Belchite** was the scene of bloody fighting during the decisive Battle of the Ebro. The town has been left exactly as it appeared on September 7, 1937, the day the battle ended.

HIDDEN MEANINGS

It's interesting to note that what is *not* present in Spain is just as revealing. For example, there are no Roman ruins in Madrid, since it was founded as a Moorish outpost in the late 10th century and was not the capital of Spain until 1560, a recent date in Spanish history. Likewise, Barcelona has no Moorish architecture—the Moors sacked Barcelona but never established themselves there, testifying to Catalonia's medieval past as part of Charlemagne's Frankish empire, while then-Spain was part of Al-Andalus, the 781-year Moorish sojourn on the peninsula.

1898 Spanish-American War: Spain loses Cuba, Puerto Rico, and the Phillipines.

1936–39 Spanish civil war; more than 600,000 die. Gen. Francisco Franco wins and rules Spain for the next 36 years.

1977–78 First democratic election in 40 years; new constitution restores civil liberties and freedom of the press.

1992 Olympic Games held in Barcelona.

2000 Juan Carlos celebrates 25 years as Spain's king.

2004 Terrorist bombs on Madrid trains claim more than 200 lives.

LANGUAGES OF SPAIN

Spanish

Often identified as *castellano* or Castilian Spanish, **Spanish** is the main language spoken throughout Spain. A Romance language derived from Latin, Spanish contains considerable Arabic influence as a result of the nearly eight centuries of Moorish presence on the Iberian Pensinsula. The first recorded use of Spanish was the *Roman paladino,* recited by the poet Gonzalo de Berceo in the 13th century at the Monasterio de Suso in La Rioja. Two centuries later, Antonio de Nebrija's famous Spanish grammar book helped spread Spanish throughout Spain's sprawling global empire. Felipe V, in 1714, decreed Spanish the official language of Spain. Spanish is presently spoken by more than 400 million people around the world.

Spain's Other Languages

Spain's other main languages, most of which predate Castilian Spanish, include the Romance languages Catalan and Gallego (or Galician-Portuguese), and the non-Indo-European Basque language, Euskera. A third tier of local dialects include Asturiano (or Bable), Aranés, and the variations of Fabla aragonesa, the languages of the north-central community of Aragón. In Extremadura the provincial dialect is Extremaduran.

Catalan is spoken in Barcelona and in Spain's northeastern autonomous community of Catalonia, in southern France's Roussillon region, in the city of L'Alguer on the Italian island of Sardinia, and in Andorra (where it is the national language). It is derived from Provençal French and is closer to Langue d'Oc and Occitan than to Spanish, as is clarified by eminent Spanish philologist Ramón Menéndez Pidal (1869–1968) in his *Orígenes del Español.* Both **Valenciano** and **Mallorquin**, spoken respectively in the Valencia region and in the Balearic Islands in the Mediterranean east of Barcelona, are considered dialects of Catalan.

Gallego is spoken in Galicia in Spain's northwestern corner and more closely resembles Portuguese than Spanish.

Euskera, the Basque language, is Spain's greatest linguistic mystery. Links to Japanese, Sanskrit, Finnish, Gaelic, or the language of the lost city of Atlantis have proven to be false leads or pure mythology. The best theory on Euskera, developed by Menéndez Pidal in his *En Torno a la Lengua Vasca* (*On the Basque Language*) suggests that a language similar to Euskera was spoken by the aboriginal inhabitants of the Iberian Peninsula and was best defended in the remote hills of the Basque Country. Euskera is presently spoken by about a million inhabitants of the Spanish and French Basque provinces.

Asturiano (or Bable) is a Romance language (sometimes called a dialect) spoken in Asturias and in parts of León, Zamora, Salamanca, Cantabria, and Extremadura by some 700,000 people.

Aranés (or Occitan), derived from Gascon French, is spoken in Catalonia's westernmost valley, the Vall d'Arán.

Fabla aragonesa is the collective term for all of Aragón's mountain dialects. Aragón has some 15 active dialects, including Patués, Chistabino, Pandicuto, Tensino, and Ribagorzano. All are more closely related to Gascon French and Occitan than to Spanish.

Extremaduran, a Spanish dialect, is spoken in Extremadura.

Gain access to the inner chambers of paradores in Santiago de Compostela (left) and Sigüenza (above).

A NIGHT WITH HISTORY

Spain's nearly 100 paradores all have one thing in common: heritage status. More often than not they also have a killer view. If a visitor plans a trip with stays at a number of paradores, he has the chance to experience an authentic slice of Spanish culture around the country. Spaniards themselves love the paradores and make up about 70 percent of visitors.

Accommodations come in all manner of distinguished settings, including former castles, convents, and Arab fortresses—soon, in Madrid, you'll even be able to check into a former women's prison. Talk about ex-cell-ent sleeping....

Even if you find yourself in a parador that's a (ho-hum) stately historic home, you'll most likely be perched above, or nestled in, some lovely surroundings—from the *pueblos blancos* (whitewashed villages) and verdant golf courses of Andalusia to the rolling fields, mountains, and beaches of northern Spain.

THE PARADOR'S TRUE CHARM: PAY LESS, GET MORE

Why pay top-euro prices when you can get top-notch quality for considerably less? In most cases, the accommodations, interior decoration, and cuisine at paradores are just as good and, in many cases, vastly superior to that of four- and five-star hotels. Just as strong a selling point is that paradores have the luxury of beautiful and peaceful settings. The variety of settings is perhaps what attracts most visitors, from a balcony overlooking the Alhambra or views of snow-peaked mountains to sweeping views of plains in countryside venues.

FROM ROYAL HUNTING LODGE TO FIRST PARADOR

An advocate for Spain tourism in the early 20th century, King Alfonso XIII was eager to develop a countrywide hotel infrastructure that would cater to local and overseas travelers. He directed the Spanish government to set up the Royal Tourist Commission to mull it over, and in 1926, commissioner Marquis de la Vega Inclán came up with the parador ("stopping place") idea and searched for where to build the first such inn. His goal was to find a setting that would reflect both the beauty of Spain and its cultural heritage. He nominated the wild Gredos Mountains, where royalty came to hunt and relax, a few hours west of Madrid.

King Alfonso XIII

By October of 1928, the Parador de Gredos opened at a spot chosen by King Alfonso himself, amid pine groves, rocks, and the clear waters of Avilá. In 1937, this parador is where the fascist Falange party was established, and a few decades later, in 1978, it's where national leaders drafted the Spanish Constitution.

SPAIN'S PARADOR CHAIN

When Alfonso gave his blessing to the establishment of Spain's first parador, he probably didn't realize that he was sitting on a financial, cultural, and historical gold mine. But after it opened, the Board of Paradores and Inns of Spain was formed and focused its energies on harnessing historical, artistic, and cultural monuments with lovely landscapes into a chain—an effort that has continued to this day.

The number of state-run paradores today approaches nearly 100, with the latest two being the Parador La Granja on the grounds of the royal summer home of Carlos III and Isabel de Farnesio in Segovia, and the Parador de Gran Canaria in Cruz in Tejeda in Las Canarias. Three others are scheduled to open in 2008.

Pillow Talk

Grace Kelly

Given that many paradores were once homes and residences to noble families and royalty, it's no surprise that they've continued to attract the rich and famous. Italian actress Sophia Loren stayed at the Parador de Hondarribia, as did distinguished Spanish writer José Cela. Meanwhile, the Cardona's castle and fortress was the backdrop for Orson Welles's movie *Falstaff.* Topping the list, though, is the Parador de Granada. President Johnson, Queen Elizabeth, actress Rita Hayworth, and even Franco himself have all stayed here. Additionally, Grace Kelly celebrated some of her honeymoon trip with Prince Rainier of Monaco in these hallowed walls, and many a Spanish intellectual and artist also have gotten cozy in this charming, sophisticated abode.

WHAT TO EXPECT

Walk where famous people have walked in the Parador de Granada's courtyard.

Paradores have been restored to provide modern amenities. Depending on the location, some have swimming pools, while others have fitness rooms and/or saunas. Most paradores have access to cable TV, but if they veer more toward four-star status, English channels may be limited to news services such as CNN and BBC World, though films may be available via a pay-for-view service. Some rooms have DVDs and a rental service. Laundry facilities are available at almost all of the paradores. Internet access is limited.

Lodging at the paradores is generally equivalent to a four-star hotel and occasionally a five-star. The dining is what sets the paradores apart—you'd pay considerably more to eat the quality of food they serve at the same caliber restaurant in town. Another advantage of the paradores is that unlike hotels, the room rates do not vary much in the peak months of June, July, and August.

Cost: Prices at the paradores vary, depending on location and time of year. In general, one-night stays range from €95 to €200, though the Parador de Granada will hit your wallet for at least 60 euros more per night. July through September and Easter Week tend to be the most expensive times.

GREAT FOR DAY VISITS, TOO

While paradores are a great means of accommodation, they also attract huge numbers of day visitors. The reasons for this are two-fold. First, the buildings are often spectacular and historically significant and many contain great views. Secondly, the restaurants are consistently excellent but reasonable priced. Each parador strives to use local produce and reproduce the traditional gastronomy found in its region.

FODOR'S CHOICE PARADORES

PARADOR DE GRANADA

Location: Granada, Andalusia

Why Visit: Situated within the walls of the Alhambra, this former 15th-century monastery is Spain's most popular (and most expensive) parador. Originally a Moorish nobleman's house, it later became the first holy place for Christians in Granada. The building has survived abandonment by the monks and French occupation, and at different times has housed the poor and the military. It opened as a parador in 1949.

Lodging & Dining Highlights: Spacious rooms are tastefully decorated in a classic Moorish style, many with patios. An excellent restaurant serves great local cuisine—try the Tortilla de Sacromonte (omelet of eggs, brains, and sweetbreads) and Moraga de Sardinas (oven-baked sardines).

PARADOR DE SIGÜENZA

Location: Sigüenza, Castilla-La Mancha

Why Visit: This sprawling 12th-century Moorish citadel is arguably the finest architectural example of all the parador castles. Its appointments include a splendid courtyard, stately corridors, and elegantly rustic furniture, all of which give the parador a strong medieval ambience. The best thing about the parador is its access to Siguenza, in Don Quixote territory.

Lodging & Dining Highlights: The rooms, many with a terrace, are decked out with traditional furniture from the region. All the local delicacies are here: fried bread crumbs with bacon and fried eggs, roast suckling kid, and cod prepared with manchego cheese. If you like game, there's also deer and partridge.

PARADOR DE CARDONA

Location: Cardona, Catalonia

Why Visit: As you approach Cardona along the highway from Manresa you can see the gigantic, 9th-century castle, church, and tower looming 10 km (6.2 mi) away. Perhaps there are more ornate and architecturally refined castles in Spain, but there is surely not one as towering and omnipresent as Cardona's. What draws crowds to the area are the famous salt mines, where visitors can take underground tours.

Lodging & Dining Highlights: Rooms tend to vary; some are spacious, while others are simple yet still remarkable, due to the lovely views of the valley. The food is nothing short of superb. Shoulder of lamb, salted octopus, seafood bisque, and leg of duck are all equally good, and there's a great selection of wines.

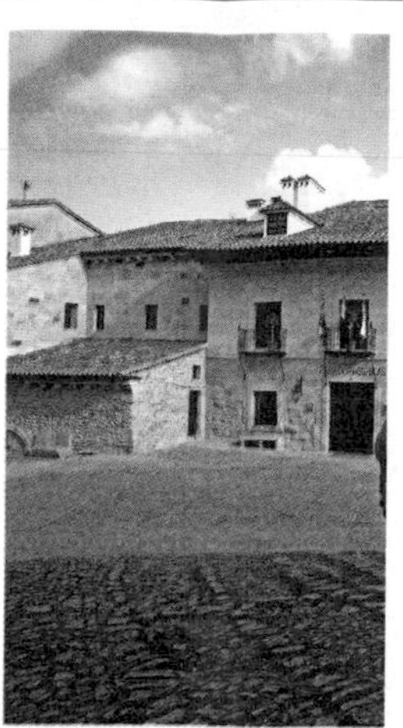

PARADOR DE SANTILLANA GIL BLAS

Location: Santillana del Mar, Cantabria

Why Visit: French philosopher and writer Jean-Paul Sarte once described the village of Santillana de Mar as the most beautiful village in Spain. Few would disagree. If you're after peace and quiet, this is the parador for you. Set in a former noble family's residence in the mountains, the Parador Santillana del Mar has a history as a haven for writers in the 1940s, and later, as a theater, attended by the likes of King Alfonso XIII.

Lodging & Dining Highlights: The rooms are comfortable without being spectacular. Rather, it's the peaceful ambience that's the attraction here—and the mountain food: try the *cocido montañ*, a dish of boiled white beans, vegetables, bacon and sausages; also worth sampling is *sorropotún*, Cantabrian hakefish with green asparagus and the *quesada* cheese pudding.

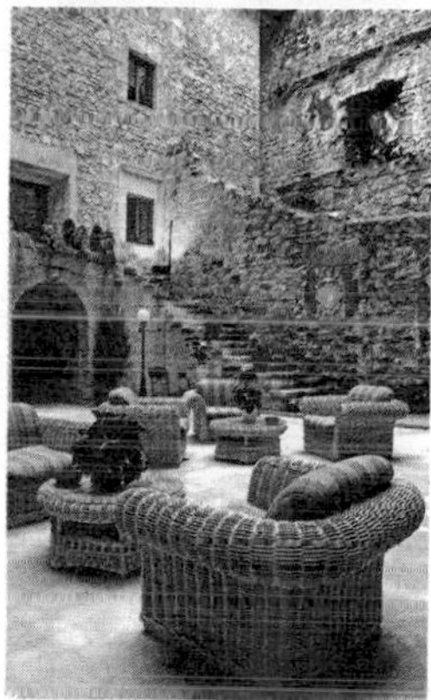

PARADOR DE HONDARRIBIA

Location: Hondarribia, Pais Vasco

Why Visit: This 10th century castle-cum-fortress may look severe on the outside, but indoors, plentiful nooks and crannies, spaces adorned with arches, wrought-iron appointments, and coffered ceilings envelop the traveler in an atmosphere of indescribable beauty. Lances, cannons, and armour make up the interior decor, and two terraces, with their sweeping views of the French coastline, top off a stay here. The parador is in the heart of Hondirribia, an elegant and stunning border town renowned for its food.

Lodging Highlights: Rooms are comfortable and elegant, some with stunning views of the sea. There's no dining facilities on the premises.

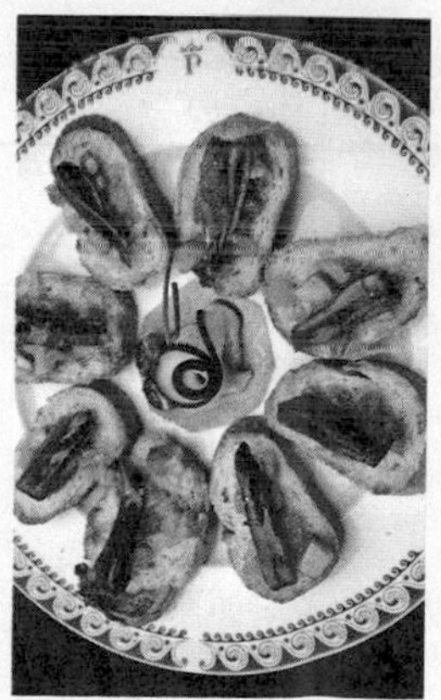

In the Works: New Paradores to Open Soon

Three new paradores are scheduled to open in 2008 in Madrid, Murcia, and Castellón. Here is a brief description of each:

- **Pardor de Alcalá de Henares** is set in a former women's prison on Madrid's Calle Colegios, just across the street from the Hostería del Estudiante parador.
- The 83-room **Parador de Lorca**, in Murcia, has a distinguishing tower and a view of the nearby one-time Arab fortress.
- Offering a prayerful night's sleep, the 15th-century San Francisco convent is set to open as the **Parador de Morella** in Castellón.

MORE PARADORES WORTH VISITING

With its Spanish plateresque façade, the Parador de León adorns the Plaza de San Marcos.

PARADOR DE CANGAS DE ONIS, *Asturias.* This is a beautiful former monastery set in the lush mountains of Picos de Europa.

PARADOR DE GOMERA, *Canarias.* Great ocean views of Tenerife Island, a pool, and gardens make a visit here a tropical stay.

PARADOR DE LEON, *Castilla y León.* Pure luxury sums up this five-star monastery, with arguably the best restaurant in the parador network.

PLASENCIA, *Extremadura.* Built in Gothic style through and through, this pretty convent lies in the heart of Plasencia's beautiful old quarters.

SANTIAGO DE COMPOSTELA, *Galicia.* Considered to be the world's oldest hotel, this is the meeting point for the many pilgrims who've traveled the long road to Santiago. Set in one of the city's famous squares, Plaza do Obradoiro, the parador boasts beautiful rooms, lots of space, and tantalizing Galician cuisine, including pulpo gallego (octupus) and percebes (gooseneck barnacles).

SANTO DOMINGO DE LA CALZADA, *La Rioja.* This 12th-century hospital, also known for sheltering pilgrims en route to Santiago, is popular for its restaurant (stuffed peppers are a staple) and its wines—it is, after all, situated in La Rioja, Spain's wine capital, and offers good value wines such as Marqués de Vargas and Allende.

■TIP→ Popular paradores such as the two in Granada and Santiago de Compestela are in huge demand and need to be booked up to six months in advance. Booking can be done by telephone or via the Internet.

PARADOR INFORMATION

For more information about paradores, consult the official parador Web site, 🌐 www.paradores.es/english, e-mail ✉ reservas@parador.es, or call ☎ 34 902/547979.

Madrid

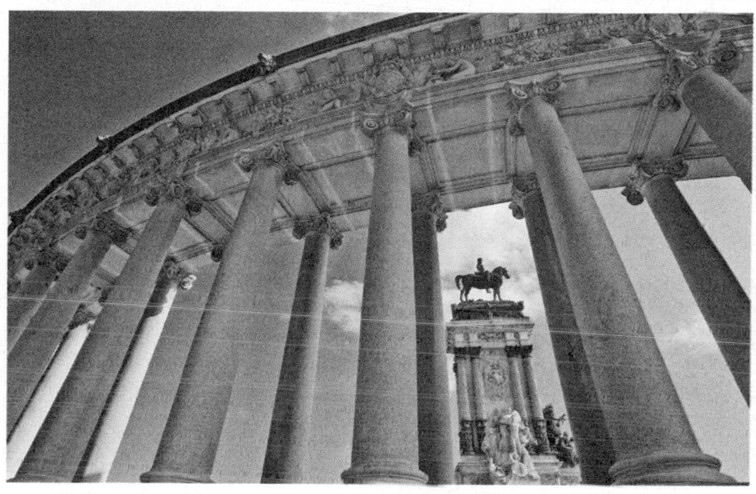

Parque del Retiro

WORD OF MOUTH

"Strolling through Madrid at night is, if possible, even more breathtaking than during the day. The architecture defies my vocabulary, and a new amazing sight seems to appear around every corner. I could've kept walking all night but had to stop for the *churros* and chocolate that everyone writes and talks about so often. . . ."

—Chicago Heather

www.fodors.com/forums

WELCOME TO MADRID

TOP REASONS TO GO

★ **Strolling the Centro Histórico:** The Plaza Mayor on any late night when it's almost empty is the place that best evokes the glory of Spain's Golden Age.

★ **Painting the Past:** Find a pleasant mix of art and architecture in the Prado, the Reina Sofía, and the Thyssen, all of which display extensive and impressive collections.

★ **Relaxing on the Green:** Visit the Retiro Gardens on a Sunday morning, when it's at its most boisterous, to unwind and take in the sun and merrymaking.

★ **Bar Hopping:** Indulge in a *madrileño* way of socializing. Learn about the art of tapas and sample local wines while wandering among the bars of Cava Baja.

★ **Famous Nightlife:** When other cities turn off their lights, *madrileños* swarm to the bars of the liveliest neighborhoods—Malasaña, Chueca, and more—and stretch the party out until dawn.

1 La Latina. La Latina is known to *madrileños* for its great daytime atmosphere, especially on the weekends. It has the city's highest concentration of aristocratic buildings and great yet affordable bars and restaurants.

2 Barrio de las Letras. This area, home to the city's first open-air theaters in the late 16th century, is where all the major Spanish writers eventually settled. A bohemian spirit is preserved; there's a good nightlife and some of the city's trendiest hotels.

GETTING ORIENTED

Sitting on a plateau 2,165 feet above sea level, and bordered in the north by a mountain range, Madrid is Europe's highest capital. Dating from the 9th century, the almond-shaped historic center is concentrated in a small area that can easily and pleasantly be covered on foot. The newer neighborhoods (Chamberí, Salamanca, Argüelles, Embajadores) are easily pinpointed on a map by their clean-cut layout, which contrasts with the chaotic maze of streets left behind by the Hapsburg monarchs.

3 Chueca & Malasaña. These neighborhoods offer eclectic, hip restaurants, shops run by young proprietors selling a unique variety of goods, and landmark cafés where young people sip cappuccinos, read books, and surf the Web.

4 Palacio. Here, in the oldest part of the city, you'll find old taverns, traditional pastry shops, and old businesses. The narrow streets have such names as Bordadores (Embroiders), Coloreros (Dyers), and Cuchilleros (Knife-makers)—reminders of those who used to work here.

5 Salamanca. Born out of the late-19th-century expansion, Salamanca has long been the upper middle class's favorite enclave. Here are the largest numbers of designer shops and a good share of the most sophisticated and expensive restaurants.

MADRID PLANNER

When to Go

Madrid is quite hot and dry in summer—with temperatures reaching 95°F to 105°F in July and August—and chilly in winter—with minimum temperatures in the low 30s or slightly below in January and February, even though snow in the city is rare. **The most pleasant time to visit the city is spring, especially in May,** when the city honors its patron saint and bullfighting season begins. June is also a good month, as are the last four months of the year. In fact, in September and October it's likely you can still wear a T-shirt.

Avoid traveling to Madrid in July and August—especially August; even though fares are better and there are plenty of concerts and open-air activities, many locals flee to the coast or to the mountains, and so many restaurants, bars, and shops are closed for vacation.

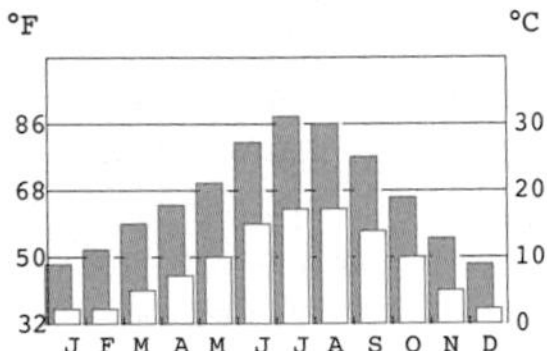

Getting There & Around

There are regular flights from the United States and all major European cities to Madrid. The massive Terminal 4 (T-4), inaugurated in 2006, handles flights from 32 companies, including Aer Lingus, American Airlines, British Airways, Iberia, and Virgin Express. All other American and British airlines depart from and arrive at Terminal 1. The terminals are connected by a bus service and also to a subway line that takes you to the city center in 30 to 45 minutes for €2.

With the exception of those connecting to Madrid and Barcelona, local flights tend to be expensive. Iberia, Air Europa, Spanair, and Vueling cover the Madrid-Barcelona route. The late 2007 opening of a high-speed train line (AVE) that reaches the center of Barcelona in less than four hours will push prices lower. Spanair usually has the best discounts. The airline Web sites and local flight consolidators, such as *www.edreams.com* and *www.terminala.com*, can help you get the best price for local flights.

Because Madrid is in the geographical center of Spain, all of the major train lines depart from one of its two main train stations (Chamartín and Atocha) or at least pass through Madrid. Although traveling by train is comfortable, for some destinations it's better to take the bus. This holds true for Segovia and Toledo, unless you choose to take the more expensive high-speed train. *See the By Train section in Spain Essentials at the end of the chapter for information on routes and on how to buy tickets.*

Once in the city you'll find that all the historic neighborhoods are in close proximity and can best be enjoyed when explored on foot. However, the metro, which runs frequently (open 6 AM–1:30 AM), is a fast and—at €1 no matter how far you travel—cheap alternative. Taxis are another good deal and are easily hailed in the street—except when it rains or on weekend nights, at which point they're exceedingly hard to come by.

See Madrid Essentials at the end of this chapter for transportation contact information.

Planning Your Time

Madrid's most valuable art treasures are all on display in a few blocks of Paseo del Prado. This area is home to the Prado, with its astounding selection of masterworks from Velázquez, Goya, El Greco, and others; the Centro de Arte Reina Sofía, with an excellent collection of contemporary art, and the Thyssen Museum, with a singular collection that stretches from the Renaissance to the 21st century. Each can take a number of hours to explore, so it's best to alternate museum visits with less overwhelming attractions. If you're running short on time and want to pack everything in, replenish your energy at any of the tapas bars or restaurants in the Barrio de las Letras (behind the Paseo del Prado, across from the Prado Museum).

Any visit to Madrid should include a walk in the old area between Puerta del Sol and the Royal Palace. Leave the map in your back pocket as you come across the Plaza Mayor, the Plaza de la Villa, and the Plaza de Oriente, and let the streets guide you to some of the oldest churches and convents standing. End or begin the day visiting the Royal Palace, built some centuries later than many of the churches but nonetheless quite staggering.

What It Costs In Euros

	¢	$	$$	$$$	$$$$
RESTAURANTS	under €8	€8–€12	€12–€18	€18–€25	over €25
HOTELS	under €50	€50–€80	€80–€150	€150–€225	over €225

Restaurant prices are per person for a main course at dinner. Hotel prices are for two people in a standard double room in high season, excluding tax.

Discounts & Deals

For €39, €49, or €59 for one, two, or three days, respectively, you can get the **Madrid Card,** which gives you entry to 40 museums and monuments, a tourist bus called Madrid Visión, all the guided visits in the Discover Madrid program, and admission to Faunia zoo. Purchase it at tourist offices, on Madrid Visión buses, and at its kiosk next to the Prado Museum on Felipe IV, at Viajes Brújula at Atocha and Chamartín train stations, and at Sol Pentour on Puerta del Sol 6. It's also available at *www.madridcard.com.*

Madrid Card Cultura covers entry to dozens of museums and Discover Madrid visits; it sells for €25, €29, or €35 for one, two, or three days, respectively.

The **Abono Turístico** (Tourist Pass) allows unlimited use of public buses and the subway for a period of one (€3.50) to seven (€18.40) days. Purchase it at tourist offices, subway stations, or select newsstands.

Safety

Madrid is quite safe a city, and it is hard to find yourself on an empty street. Theft of personal property—a wallet, a purse that's left hanging off a chair, a camera, etc.—is nonetheless common. Keep this in mind when you're in a crowded place such as the subway.

By Ignacio Gómez

SWASHBUCKLING MADRID CELEBRATES ITSELF AND life in general around the clock. A vibrant crossroads, Madrid—the Spanish capital since 1561—has an infectious appetite for art, music, and epicurean pleasure, and it has turned into a cosmopolitan modern urban center while fiercely preserving its traditions. The rapid political and economic development of Spain following the arrival of democracy in 1977, the integration of the country in the European Union a decade later, and the social upheaval brought in by the many immigrants settling here after the new millennium have put Madrid back onto the world stage with an energy redolent of its 17th-century golden age, when painters and playwrights swarmed to the flame of Spain's brilliant royal court.

The modern-day city spreads eastward into the 19th-century grid of the Barrio de Salamanca and sprawls northward through the neighborhoods of Chamberí and Chamartín. But the Madrid to explore thoroughly on foot is right in the center, in Madrid's oldest quarters, between the Royal Palace and Madrid's midtown forest, the Parque del Buen Retiro. Wandering around the sprawling conglomeration of buildings with ancient red-tile rooftops punctuated by redbrick Mudejar churches and buildings with gray-slate roofs and spires left by the Habsburg monarchs, you are more likely to grasp what's probably the city's major highlight: the hustle and bustle of a truly optimistic people who are elated when they're outdoors.

Then there are the paintings, the artistic legacy of one of the greatest global empires ever assembled. King Carlos I (1500–58), who later became emperor Carlos V, made sure the early masters of all European schools found their way to Spain's palaces. The collection was eventually placed in the Prado Museum, part of the grand Madrid built in the 18th century by Carlos III. Among the Prado, the contemporary Reina Sofía museum, the eclectic Thyssen-Bornemisza collection, and Madrid's smaller artistic repositories—the Real Academia de Bellas Artes de San Fernando, the Convento de las Descalzas Reales, the Sorolla Museum, and the Lázaro Galdiano Museum—there are more paintings than anyone can hope to contemplate in a lifetime.

But the attractions go beyond the well-known baroque landmarks. Now embarked in an expansion plan, Madrid has made sure some of the world's best architects leave their imprint on the city. This is the case with Jacques Herzog and Pierre de Meuron, who are building a new arts center, Caixa Forum, scheduled to open late in 2007 across from the Botanical Garden, and with the major renovations by Rafael Moneo and Jean Nouvel of the Museo del Prado and the Centro Reina Sofía. Other projects include the massive but stylish new airport terminal, which began operating in early 2006, and the daring renovation project of the whole area of Paseo del Prado that's been entrusted to Portuguese architect Alvaro Siza.

Madrid is also ideally placed for getaways to dozens of Castilian destinations—Toledo, Segovia, Alcalá de Henares, and El Escorial.

EXPLORING MADRID

The real Madrid is not to be found along its major arteries, such as Gran Vía and the Paseo de la Castellana. To find the quiet, intimate streets and squares that give the city its true character, duck into the warren of villagelike byways in the downtown area that extends 2½ km (1½ mi) from the Royal Palace to the Parque del Buen Retiro and from Plaza de Lavapiés to the Glorieta de Bilbao. Broad *avenidas,* twisting medieval alleys, grand museums, stately gardens, and tiny, tile taverns are all jumbled together, creating an urban texture so rich that walking is really the only way to soak it in. **■TIP→ Petty street crime is a serious problem in Madrid, and tourists are frequent targets. Be on your guard, and try to blend in by keeping cameras concealed, avoiding obvious map reading, and securing bags and purses, especially on buses and subway and outside restaurants.**

Madrid is composed of 21 districts, each broken down into several neighborhoods. The most central district is called just that, Centro. It stretches from Recoletos and Paseo del Prado in the east to behind the Royal Palace in the west, and from Sagasta and Alberto Aguilera in the north to Ronda de Valencia and Ronda de Segovia in the south. Within this district you'll find all of Madrid's oldest neighborhoods: Palacio, Sol, La Latina, Lavapiés, Barrio de las Letras, Malasaña, and Chueca. Other well-known districts, which we'll call neighborhoods in this chapter for the sake of convenience, are Salamanca, Retiro, Chamberí (north of Centro), Moncloa (east of Chamberí), and Chamartín.

Numbers in the text correspond to numbers in the margin and on chapter maps.

MEDIEVAL & HAPSBURG MADRID

The narrow streets of this old section, which includes the Palacio, La Latina, and Sol neighborhoods—part of Madrid's greater Centro region—wind back through the city's history to its beginnings as an Arab fortress. These historic quarters are not so readily apparent as the ancient neighborhoods in the nearby cities of Toledo and Segovia, nor are they so grand, but make time to explore their quiet alleys.

WHAT TO SEE: MAIN ATTRACTIONS

18 **Basílica de San Francisco el Grande.** In 1760 Carlos III built this impressive basilica on the site of a Franciscan convent, allegedly founded by St. Francis of Assisi in 1217. The dome, 108 feet in diameter, is the largest in Spain, even larger than that of St. Paul's in London. The seven main doors were carved of American walnut by Casa Juan Guas. Three chapels adjoin the circular church, the most famous being that of **San Bernardino de Siena,** which contains a Goya masterpiece depicting a preaching San Bernardino. The figure standing on the right, not looking up, is a self-portrait of Goya. The 16th-century Gothic choir stalls came from La Cartuja del Paular, in rural Segovia Province. ✉ *Pl. de San Francisco, La Latina* ☎ *91/365–3800* 🎫 *€3 guided tour* ⏲ *Oct.–May,*

Tues.–Fri. 11–12:30 and 4–6:30, Sat. 11–noon; June–Sept., Tues.–Fri. 11–12:30 and 5–7:30, Sat. 11–noon.

2 **Convento de las Descalzas Reales** *(Convent of the Royal Discalced, or Barefoot, Nuns).* This 16th-century building was restricted for 200 years to women of royal blood. Its plain, brick-and-stone facade hides paintings by Zurbarán, Titian, and Brueghel the Elder—all part of the dowry the novices had to provide when they joined the monastery—as well as a hall of sumptuous tapestries crafted from drawings by Peter Paul Rubens. The convent was founded in 1559 by Juana of Austria, one of Felipe II's sisters, who ruled Spain while he was in England and the Netherlands. It houses 33 different chapels—the age of Christ when he died and the maximum number of nuns allowed to live at the monastery at the same time—and more than 100 sculptures of Jesus as a baby. About 30 nuns (not necessarily of royal blood) still live here, cultivating their own vegetables in the convent's garden. **■ TIP→ You must take a tour in order to visit the convent; it is conducted in Spanish only.** ✉ *Plaza de las Descalzas Reales 3, Palacio* ☎ *91/454–8800* 🎫 *€5, €6 combined ticket with Convento de la Encarnación* ⏱ *Tues.–Thurs. and Sat. 10:30–12:30 and 4–5:30, Fri. 10:30–12:30, Sun. 11–1:30.*

RAINY DAY TREAT

Despite what ads say, Madrid is not always sunny. If you hit a rainy or a chilly day, walk along the western side of the Convento de las Descalzas Reales until you see on your left the Chocolatería Valor (✉ *Calle Postigo de San Martín 7, Centro*); there you'll find the thick Spanish version of hot chocolate, perfect for dipping cripsy churros.

5 Fodor'sChoice ★ **Palacio Real.** The Royal Palace was commissioned in the early 18th century by the first of Spain's Bourbon rulers, Felipe V, on the same strategic site where Madrid's first Alcázar (Moorish fortress) was built in the 9th century. Before you enter, admire the classical French architecture on the graceful **Patio de Armas.** King Felipe was obviously inspired by his childhood days at Versailles with his grandfather Louis XIV. Look for the stone statues of Inca prince Atahualpa and Aztec king Montezuma, perhaps the only tributes in Spain to these pre-Columbian American rulers. Notice how the steep bluff drops westward to the Manzanares River—on a clear day, this vantage point commands a view of the mountain passes leading into Madrid from Old Castile; thus it's easy to see why the Moors picked this spot for a fortress.

Inside, 2,800 rooms compete with each other for over-the-top opulence. A nearly two-hour guided tour in English winds a mile-long path through the palace. Highlights include the **Salón de Gasparini,** King Carlos III's private apartments, with swirling, inlaid floors and curlicued, stucco wall and ceiling decoration, all glistening in the light of a 2-ton crystal chandelier; the **Salón del Trono,** a grand throne room with the royal seats of King Juan Carlos and Queen Sofía; and the **banquet hall,** the palace's largest room, which seats up to 140 people for state dinners. No monarch has lived here since 1931, when Alfonso XIII was deposed after a republican electoral victory. The current king and queen live in the far simpler Zarzuela Palace on the outskirts of Madrid, using this palace only for official occasions.

Also visit the **Museo de Música** (Music Museum), where five stringed instruments by Stradivarius form the world's largest such collection; the **Painting Gallery,** which displays works by Spanish, Flemish, and Italian artists from the 15th century onward; the **Armería Real** (Royal Armory), with historic suits of armor and frightening medieval torture implements; and the **Real Oficina de Farmacía** (Royal Pharmacy), with vials and flasks used to mix the king's medicines. The Royal Palace is closed during official receptions. ✉ *Calle Bailén s/n, Palacio* ☎ *91/454–8800* ✉ *€8, guided tour €9; Royal Armory only €3.40* ⊙ *Apr.–Sept., Mon.–Sat. 9–6, Sun. 9–3; Oct.–Mar., Mon.–Sat. 9:30–5, Sun. 9–2.*

17 **Plaza de la Paja.** At the top of the hill, on Costanilla San Andrés, the Plaza de la Paja was the most important square in medieval Madrid. The plaza's jewel is the **Capilla del Obispo** (Bishop's Chapel), built between 1520 and 1530; this was where peasants deposited their tithes, called *diezmas*—literally, one-tenth of their crop. The stacks of wheat on the chapel's ceramic tiles refer to this tradition. Architecturally, the chapel marks a transition from the blockish Gothic period, which gave the structure its basic shape, to the Renaissance, the source of the decorations. Go inside to see the intricately carved polychrome altarpiece by Francisco Giralta, with scenes from the life of Christ. Opening hours are erratic; try to visit during Mass or on feast days. The chapel is part of the complex of the domed church of **San Andrés,** one of Madrid's oldest, which for centuries held the remains of Madrid's male patron saint, San Isidro Labrador (they are now with his wife's, at the Real Colegiata de San Isidro, on nearby Calle Toledo). The church was severely damaged during the civil war. St. Isidore the Laborer was a peasant who worked fields belonging to the Vargas family. The 16th century **Vargas Palace** forms the eastern side of the Plaza de la Paja. According to legend, St. Isidro worked little but had the best-tended fields thanks to many hours of prayer. When Señor Vargas came out to investigate the phenomenon, Isidro made a spring of sweet water spurt from the ground to quench his master's thirst. A hermitage (Ermita de San Isidro), now on Paseo de la Ermita del Santo, west of the Manzanares River, was built next to the spring in 1528. Every May 15 there's a procession followed by festivities in the meadow next to the hermitage. (In olden days, his remains were traditionally paraded through the city in times of drought.) ✉ *Plaza de la Paja, La Latina.*

4 **Plaza de Oriente.** The stately plaza in front of the Royal Palace is surrounded by massive stone statues of Spanish monarchs. These sculptures were meant to be mounted on the railing on top of the palace, but Queen Isabel of Farnesio, one of the first royals to live in the palace, had them removed because she was afraid their enormous weight would bring the roof down. (Well, that's what she *said.* According to palace insiders, the queen wanted the statues removed because her own likeness had not been placed front and center.) A Velázquez painting of King Felipe IV is the inspiration for the statue in the plaza's center. It is the first equestrian bronze ever cast with a rearing horse. The sculptor,

THE ART WALK

With a visit to the Prado—at least two or three hours—and a short stroll in Parque del Buen Retiro, you can do this walk in about five hours. Set aside a morning or an afternoon each to return to the Reina Sofía and Thyssen-Bornemisza.

■ **TIP→The** *Paseo del Arte* **(Art Walk) pass allows you to visit the three museums for €14.40. You can buy it at any of the three museums, and you don't have to visit all of them on the same day.**

Madrid's three major art museums are all within walking distance of one another via the Paseo del Prado. The Paseo was designed by Carlos III as a leafy nature walk with glorious fountains and a botanical garden for respite in scorching summers.

Start on **Plaza de las Cortés,** down Calle San Jerónimo, right next to the **Plaza Santa Ana** ㉛ tapas area. The granite building on the left, its stairs guarded by bronze lions, is the Congreso, lower house of Las Cortes, Spain's parliament. Walk past the landmark Westin Palace on the right to the **Fuente de Neptuno** ㉗, in the Plaza Cánovas del Castillo, on the wide Paseo del Prado. The **Museo del Prado** ㊽ is across the boulevard to the right. On your left is the **Museo Thyssen-Bornemisza** ㉘, and across the plaza on the left is the elegant Ritz hotel, alongside the obelisk dedicated to all those who have died for Spain. Tackle one or both of these museums now, or continue strolling.

Turning right and walking south on Paseo del Prado, you can see the **Jardín Botánico** ㊾ on the left and **Estación de Atocha** ㊿, a railway station on the southern edge of the Glorieta (roundabout) del Emperador Carlos V resembling the overturned hull of a ship. The **Centro de Arte Reina Sofía** 51, site of Picasso's *Guernica,* is across the street in the building with the exterior glass elevators, best accessed by walking up Calle Atocha from the station and taking the first left.

A block after the Ministry of Agriculture (noted by the immense pile of painted tiles and winged statues), make a left on Calle Alfonso XII, which puts the Anthropology Museum on your left. Calle Alfonso XII runs along the west side of the vast **Parque del Buen Retiro** 53 (most just call it Parque del Retiro). If you walk down Felipe IV, which ends at the back of the Casón del Buen Retiro, you can get back to the Plaza Cánovas del Castillo and the Fuente de Neptuno.

Back at the fountain, turn right and walk up the right side of Paseo del Prado (or, even better, the central promenade). After passing the **Museo Naval** ㉖, cross Calle Montalbán, down which the **Museo Nacional de Artes Decorativas** 55 is located. Finally, you'll reach the **Plaza de la Cibeles** ㉒. Turn right at Cibeles, walk up Calle Alcalá, and you can see Madrid's unofficial symbol, the Puerta de Alcalá, and, again, the Parque del Buen Retiro. Continue north for the **Museo Arqueológico** ㊹, which adjoins the National Library, and the **Plaza Colón** ㊺.

Consider also visiting the **Museo Sorolla,** ㊻ on Calle Martínez Campos, in Chamberí, or **Museo Láw Galdiano,** ㊼ on Calle Serrano, in Salamanca.

Italian artist Pietro de Tacca, enlisted Galileo's help in configuring the statue's weight so it wouldn't tip over. For most madrileños, the Plaza de Oriente is forever linked with Francisco Franco. The *generalísimo* liked to speak from the roof of the Royal Palace to his followers as they crammed into the plaza below. Each year, on the November anniversary of Franco's death, the plaza fills with supporters, most of whom are old-timers, though occasionally skinheads from other countries come waving swastikas in a fascist tribute. ✉*Plaza de Oriente, Palacio.*

16 **Plaza Mayor.** Austere, grand, and often surprisingly quiet compared with the rest of Madrid, this 360-foot by 300-foot public square—finished in 1620 under Felipe III, whose equestrian statue stands in the center—is one of the largest in Europe. It has seen it all: autos-de-fé (trials of faith, i.e., public burnings of heretics); the canonization of saints; criminal executions; royal marriages, such as that of Princess María and the King of Hungary in 1629; bullfights (until 1847); masked balls; and all manner of other events. It is still the site of special events.

This space was once occupied by a city market, and many of the surrounding streets retain the names of the trades and foods once headquartered there. Nearby are Calle de Cuchilleros (Knifemakers' Street), Calle de Lechuga (Lettuce Street), Calle de Fresa (Strawberry Street), and Calle de Botoneros (Buttonmakers' Street). The plaza's oldest building is the one with the brightly painted murals and the gray spires, called Casa de la Panadería (Bakery House) in honor of the bread shop over which it was built; it is now the tourist office. Opposite is the Casa de la Carnicería (Butcher Shop), now a police station.

The plaza is closed to motorized traffic, making it a pleasant place to sit at one of the sidewalk cafés, watching alfresco artists, street musicians, and madrileños from all walks of life. Sunday morning brings a stamp and coin market. Around Christmas the plaza fills with stalls selling trees, ornaments, and nativity scenes. ✉*Plaza Mayor, Sol.*

14 **San Nicolás de los Servitas** *(Church of St. Nicholas of the Servitas).* This church tower is one of the oldest buildings in Madrid. There's some debate over whether it once formed part of an Arab mosque. It was more likely built after the Christian Reconquest of Madrid in 1085, but the brickwork and the horseshoe arches are evidence that it was crafted by either Mudejars (Moorish workers) or Spaniards well versed in the style. Inside, exhibits detail the Islamic history of early Madrid. ✉*Near Plaza de San Nicolás, La Latina* ☎*91/559–4064* *Donation suggested* ⏲*Tues.–Sat. 8:30* AM*–9:30* AM *and 6:30–9* PM*, Sun. and Mon. 8:30–2 and 6–9; groups by appointment.*

ALSO WORTH SEEING

13 **Arab Wall.** The remains of the Moorish military outpost that became the city of Madrid are visible on Calle Cuesta de la Vega. The sections of wall here protected a fortress built in the 9th century by Emir Mohammed I. In addition to being an excellent defensive position, the site had plentiful water and was called *Mayrit,* Arabic for "source of life" (this is the likely origin of the city's name). All that remains of the *medina*—the old Arab city that formed within the walls of the fortress—is the

neighborhood's crazy quilt of streets and plazas, which probably follow the same layout they followed more than 1,100 years ago. The park **Emir Mohammed I,** alongside the wall, is the site of concerts and plays in summer. ✉*C. Cuesta de la Vega, Centro.*

19 ★ **Cava Baja.** The epicenter of the fashionable and historic La Latina neighborhood, the narrow streets south of Plaza Mayor and across Calle Segovia are crowded with excellent tapas bars and traditional restaurants. Its lively atmosphere spills over into nearby streets and squares, including Almendro, Cava Alta, Plaza del Humilladero, and Plaza de la Paja. ✉*Across Calle Segovia, La Latina.*

7 **Campo del Moro** *(Moors' Field).* Below the Sabatini Gardens, but accessible only by an entrance on the far side, is the Campo del Moro. Enjoy the clusters of shady trees, winding paths, and lawn leading up to the Royal Palace. Inside the gardens is a **Museo de Carruajes,** displaying royal carriages and equestrian paraphernalia from the 16th through 20th century. ✉*Paseo Virgen del Puerto s/n, Palacio.*

3 **Convento de la Encarnación** *(Convent of the Incarnation).* Once connected to the Royal Palace by an underground passageway, this Augustinian convent now houses less than a dozen nuns. Founded in 1611 by the wife of Felipe III, it has several artistic treasures, including a reliquary where a vial with the dried blood of St. Pantaleón is said to liquefy every July 27. The ornate church has superb acoustics for medieval and Renaissance choral concerts. ✉*Plaza de la Encarnación 1, Palacio* ☎*91/454–8800 tourist information office* 🎟*€3.60, €6 combined ticket with Convento de las Descalzas Reales* ⏲*Tues.–Thurs. and Sat. 10:30–12:45 and 4–5:45, Fri. 10:30–12:45, Sun. 11–1:45.*

12 **Catedral de la Almudena.** The first stone of the cathedral (which adjoins the Royal Palace) was laid in 1883 by King Alfonso XII, and the result was consecrated by Pope John Paul II in 1993. Built on the site where the old church of Santa María de la Almudena stood (thought to be the city's main mosque during Arab rule), the new cathedral was intended to be Gothic in style, with needles and spires; funds ran low, so the design was simplified into the existing, more austere classical form. The cathedral has a wooden statue of Madrid's female patron saint, the Virgin of Almudena, reportedly discovered after the 1085 Christian Reconquest of Madrid. Legend has it that when the Arabs invaded Spain, the local Christian population hid the statue of the Virgin in a vault carved in the old Roman wall that encircled the city. When Christians reconquered Madrid in 1085, they looked for it, and after nine days of intensive praying—others say it was after a procession honoring the Virgin—the wall opened up to show the statue framed by two lighted candles. Its name is derived from the place where it was found: the wall of the old citadel (in Arabic, *almudeyna*). ✉*C. Bailén 10, Palacio* ☎*91/542–2200* 🎟*Free* ⏲*Daily 9–9.*

30 **Museo del Traje** *(Costume Museum).* This museum traces the evolution of dress in Spain, from the old burial garments worn by kings and nobles (very few pieces of which have withstood the erosion of time) and the introduction of French fashion by Phillip V, to the 20th-cen-

tury creations of couturiers such as Balenciaga and Pertegaz. The 18th century claims the largest number of pieces. The explanatory notes are in English. The museum has a superb restaurant. To get here, from Moncloa take Bus 46 or walk along the northeastern edge of Parque del Oeste. ✉ *Av. Juan de Herrera 2, Ciudad Universitaria* ☎ *91/549–7150* 🌐 *http://museodeltraje.mcu.es* *€3, free Tues. after 2:30 and Sun.* ⊙ *Tues.–Sat. 9:30–7, Sun. 10–3.*

2

1 **Puerta del Sol.** Crowded with people and exhaust and now the construction of a massive underground station that has been delayed several times due to the discovery of archaeological remains, Sol is the nerve center of Madrid's traffic. The city's main subway interchange is below, and buses fan out from here. A brass plaque in the sidewalk on the south side of the plaza marks Kilometer 0, the spot from which all distances in Spain are measured. The restored 1756 French-neoclassical building near the marker now houses the offices of the regional government, but during Franco's reign it was the headquarters of his secret police, and it's still known folklorically as the Casa de los Gritos (House of Screams). Across the square is a bronze statue of Madrid's official symbol, a bear with a *madroño* (strawberry tree), and a statue of King-Mayor Carlos III on horseback. ✉ *Puerta del Sol, Sol.*

11 **Teatro Real** *(Royal Theater).* Built in 1850, this neoclassical theater was long a cultural center for madrileño society. A major restoration project has left it filled with golden balconies, plush seats, and state-of-the-art stage equipment for operas and ballets. ✉ *Plaza de Isabel II, Palacio* ☎ *91/516–0660* 🌐 *www.teatro-real.com.*

CENTRAL MADRID (CENTRO)

The following section includes attractions in the Centro district outside the Palacio, La Latina, and Sol neighborhoods (Medieval and Hapsburg Madrid); it also includes the Moncloa neighborhood.

WHAT TO SEE: MAIN ATTRACTIONS

28 **Museo Thyssen-Bornemisza.** The newest of Madrid's three major art centers, the Thyssen occupies spacious galleries washed in salmon pink and filled with natural light in the late-18th-century Villahermosa Palace, finished in 1771. This ambitious collection of 800 paintings traces the history of Western art with examples from every important movement, from the 13th-century Italian Gothic through 20th-century American pop art. The works were gathered from the 1920s to the 1980s by Swiss industrialist Baron Hans Heinrich Thyssen-Bornemisza and his father. At the urging of his wife, Carmen Cervera (a former Miss Spain), the baron donated the entire collection to Spain in 1993. A renovation in 2004 increased the number of paintings on display to include the baron's wife's personal collection. Critics have described the museum's paintings as the minor works of major artists and the major works of minor artists, but, be that as it may, the collection traces the development of Western humanism as no other in the world.

Fodor's Choice ★

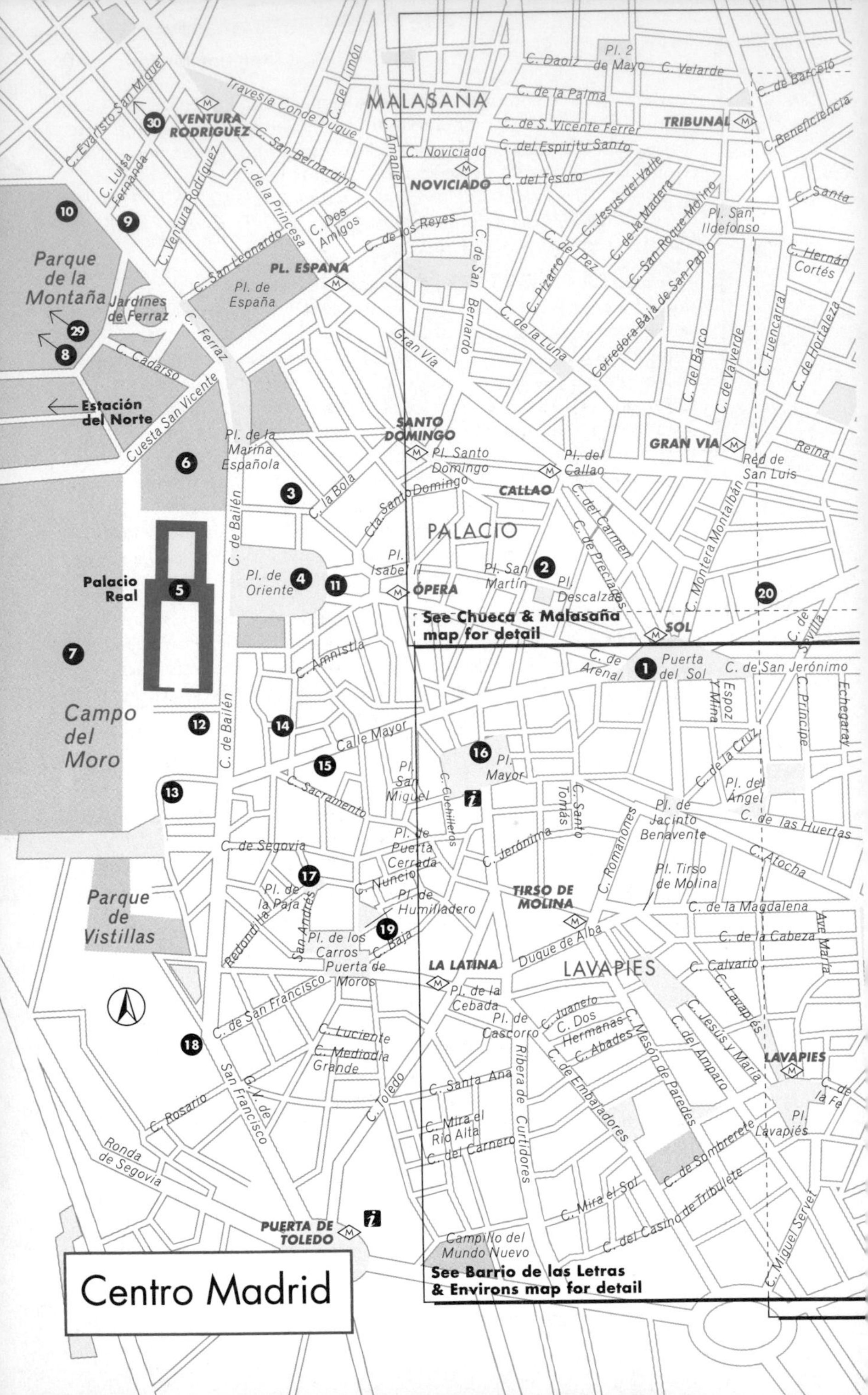
Centro Madrid
MALASAÑA
PALACIO
LAVAPIES
VENTURA RODRIGUEZ
NOVICIADO
TRIBUNAL
PL. ESPANA
SANTO DOMINGO
CALLAO
GRAN VIA
ÓPERA
SOL
TIRSO DE MOLINA
LA LATINA
LAVAPIES
PUERTA DE TOLEDO
Parque de la Montaña
Jardines de Ferraz
Estación del Norte
Palacio Real
Campo del Moro
Parque de Vistillas
See Chueca & Malasaña map for detail
See Barrio de las Letras & Environs map for detail
Pl. de España
Pl. de la Marina Española
Pl. de Oriente
Pl. Isabel II
Pl. Santo Domingo
Pl. del Callao
Pl. San Martín
Pl. Descalzas
Puerta del Sol
Pl. Mayor
Pl. San Miguel
Pl. de Puerta Cerrada
Pl. de la Paja
Pl. de Humilladero
Pl. de los Carros
Puerta de Moros
Pl. de la Cebada
Pl. de Cascorro
Pl. Tirso de Molina
Pl. de Jacinto Benavente
Pl. del Ángel
Pl. Lavapiés
Pl. 2 de Mayo
Pl. San Ildefonso
Red de San Luis
Campillo del Mundo Nuevo
Gran Vía
Calle Mayor
Cuesta San Vicente
Travesia Conde Duque
Ronda de Segovia
G.V. de San Francisco
Duque de Alba
Ribera de Curtidores
Cta Santo Domingo
C. Evaristo San Miguel
C. Luisa Fernanda
C. Ventura Rodriguez
C. de la Princesa
C. San Bernardino
C. del Limón
C. Amaniel
C. Daoiz
C. Velarde
C. de Barceló
C. de la Palma
C. de S. Vicente Ferrer
C. del Espiritu Santo
C. de Beneficiencia
C. Noviciado
C. del Tesoro
C. Santa
C. Dos Amigos
C. de los Reyes
C. de San Bernardo
C. Jesús del Valle
C. de la Madera
C. San Roque Molino
C. Pizarro
C. de Pez
C. Corredera Baja de San Pablo
C. Hernán Cortés
C. San Leonardo
C. Ferraz
C. Cadarso
C. de la Luna
C. del Barco
C. de Valverde
C. Fuencarral
C. de Hortaleza
Reina
C. de Bailén
C. la Bola
C. del Carmen
C. de Preciados
C. Montera Montalbán
C. de Sevilla
C. Amnistía
C. de Arenal
C. de San Jerónimo
C. Espoz y Mina
C. Príncipe
Echegaray
C. Sacramento
C. Cuchilleros
C. Santo Tomás
C. Romanones
C. de la Cruz
C. de las Huertas
C. Atocha
C. de Segovia
C. Jerónima
C. Nuncio
C. Baja
C. Redondilla
San Andrés
C. de San Francisco
C. de la Magdalena
C. de la Cabeza
Ave María
C. Calvario
C. Lavapiés
C. Juanelo
C. Dos Hermanas
C. Abades
C. Mesón de Paredes
C. del Amparo
C. Jesús y María
C. de Embajadores
C. de la Fe
C. Luciente
C. Mediodía Grande
C. Toledo
C. Santa Ana
C. Rosario
C. Mira el Río Alta
C. del Carnero
C. Mira el Sol
C. de Sombrerete
C. del Casino de Tribulete
C. Miguel Servet
1 2 3 4 5 6 7 8 9 10 11 12 13 14 15 16 17 18 19 20 29 30

Arab Wall **13**
Banco de España **21**
Basílica de San Francisco el Grande **18**
Campo del Moro **7**
Casa de América **24**
Catedral de la Almudena **12**
Cava Baja **19**
Convento de la Encarnación **3**
Convento de las Descalzas Reales **2**
Ermita de San Antonio de la Florida **8**
Fuente de Neptuno **27**
Jardines Sabatini **6**
Museo del Traje **30**
Museo Naval **26**
Museo Thyssen-Bornemisza **28**
Palacio de Comunicaciones **23**
Palacio Real **5**
Plaza de la Cibeles **22**
Plaza de Oriente **4**
Plaza de la Paja **17**
Plaza de la Villa **15**
Plaza Mayor **16**
Puerta de Alcalá **25**
Puerta del Sol **1**
Real Academia de Bellas Artes de San Fernando **20**
San Nicolás de los Servitas **14**
Teatro Real **11**
Teleférico **9**
Templo de Debod **10**
Zoo-Aquarium **29**

One of the high points here is Hans Holbein's *Portrait of Henry VIII* (purchased from the late Princess Diana's grandfather, who used the money to buy a Bugatti sports car). American artists are also well represented; look for the Gilbert Stuart portrait of George Washington's cook, and note how closely the composition and rendering resemble the artist's famous painting of the Founding Father. Two halls are devoted to the impressionists and postimpressionists, including many works by Pissarro and a few each by Renoir, Monet, Degas, Van Gogh, and Cézanne. Find Pissarro's *Saint-Honoré Street in the Afternoon, Effect of Rain* for a jolt of mortality, or Renoir's *Woman with a Parasol in a Garden* for a sense of bucolic beauty lost.

Within 20th-century art, the collection is strong on dynamic German expressionism, with some works by Georgia O'Keeffe and Andrew Wyeth along with Hoppers, Bacons, Rauschenbergs, and Lichtensteins. The temporary exhibits can be fascinating, and in summer, are sometimes open until 11 PM. A rooftop restaurant serving tapas and drinks, is open in the summer until past midnight. ✉ *Paseo del Prado 8, Centro* ☎ *91/369–0151* 🌐 *www.museothyssen.org* 🎫 *Permanent collection €6, temporary exhibition €5, combined €9* ⏲ *Tues.–Sun. 10–7.*

■ **TIP→** *See* **"The Art Walk" box for how to include the Museo Thyssen-Bornemisza as part of an art-theme excursion.**

22 **Plaza de la Cibeles.** A tree-lined walkway runs down the center of Paseo del Prado to the grand Plaza de la Cibeles, where the famous Fuente de la Cibeles (Fountain of Cybele) depicts the nature goddess driving a chariot drawn by lions. Even more than the officially designated bear and arbutus tree, this monument, beautifully lighted at night, has come to symbolize Madrid—so much so that during the civil war, patriotic madrileños risked life and limb to sandbag it as Nationalist aircraft bombed the city. ✉ *Plaza de la Cibeles, Centro.*

20 **Real Academia de Bellas Artes de San Fernando** *(St. Ferdinand Royal Academy of Fine Arts).* Designed by Churriguera in the waning baroque years of the early 18th century, this museum showcases 500 years of Spanish painting, from Ribera and Murillo to Sorolla and Zuloaga. The tapestries along the stairways are stunning. Because of a lack of personnel, now they show only the first floor, which displays paintings up to the 18th century, including Goya. The same building houses the **Instituto de Calcografía** (Prints Institute), which sells limited-edition prints from original plates engraved by Spanish artists, including Goya. Check listings for classical and contemporary concerts in the small upstairs hall. ✉ *Alcalá 13, Sol* ☎ *91/524–0864* 🎫 *€3, free Wed.* ⏲ *Tues.–Fri. 9–7, Sat.–Mon. 9–2:30; free guided tour Wed. 5–7.*

ALSO WORTH SEEING

21 **Banco de España.** This massive 1884 building, Spain's central bank, takes up an entire block. It's said that part of the nation's gold reserves are held in vaults that stretch under the Plaza de la Cibeles traffic circle all the way to the fountain. (Some reserves are also stored in Fort Knox, in the United States.) The bank is not open to visitors, but its style of architecture is worth viewing. If you can dodge traffic well enough to

reach the median strip in front of it, you can take a fine photo of the fountain and palaces with the Puerta de Alcalá arch in the background. ✉*Paseo del Prado s/n, at Plaza de la Cibeles, Centro.*

24 **Casa de América.** A cultural center and art gallery focusing on Latin America, the Casa is in the allegedly haunted Palacio de Linares, built by a man who made his fortune in the Americas and returned to a life of incestuous love and strange deaths. ✉*Paseo de Recoletos 2, Centro* ☎*91/595–4800* 🌐*www.casamerica.es* *Free* *Sept.–July, Tues.–Sat. 11–2 and 5–8, Sun. 11–2.*

2

8 **Ermita de San Antonio de la Florida (Goya's tomb).** Built from 1792 to 1798 by the Italian architect Francisco Fontana, this neoclassical church was financed by King Carlos IV, who also commissioned Goya to paint the vaults and the main dome. The painter, who by that time was already deaf, took 120 days to complete his assignment. He painted them alone with the help of a little boy who would stir the pigments for him. This gave him absolute freedom to depict events of the 13th century (Saint Anthony of Padua resurrecting a dead man) as if they had happened five centuries later, and using naturalistic images never used before to paint religious scenes. Opposite the image of the frightening dead man on the main dome Goya painted himself as a man covered with a blackish cloak. The frescoes' third-restoration phase ended in 2005, and now visitors can admire them in their full splendor. The painter, who died in Bordeaux in 1828, is buried here (without his head, since it was stolen in France), under an unadorned gravestone. ✉*Glorieta de San Antonio de la Florida 5, Príncipe Pío* ☎*91/542–0722* *Free* *Tues.–Fri. 9:30–8, Sun. 10–2.*

27 **Fuente de Neptuno** *(Neptune's Fountain).* At Plaza Canovas del Castillo, midway between the Palace and Ritz hotels and the Prado and Thyssen-Bornemisza museums, this fountain is at the hub of Madrid's Paseo del Arte. It was a rallying point for Atlético de Madrid soccer triumphs (counterpoint to Real Madrid's celebrations at the Fuente de la Cibeles up the street). It's been quiet here for the past few years, with Atlético mired in second division (a concept comparable to the New York Yankees slipping down to the minors). With Atlético's return to first division in spring of 2002, the Fuente de Neptuno is waiting to revive its pivotal role in Madrid life. ✉*Plaza Canovas del Castillo, Centro.*

6 **Jardines Sabatini** *(Sabatini Gardens).* The formal gardens to the north of the Royal Palace are crawling with stray cats—but are nonetheless a pleasant place to rest or watch the sun set. ✉*C. Bailén s/n, Centro.*

26 **Museo Naval.** Anyone interested in Patrick O'Brian's painstakingly detailed naval novels or in old vessels and war ships will be bouncing off the walls experiencing the 500 years of Spanish naval history displayed in this museum. The collection, which includes documents, maps, weaponry, paintings, and hundreds of ship models of different sizes, is best enjoyed by those who speak some Spanish. Beginning with Queen Isabella and King Ferdinand's reign and the expeditions led by Christopher Columbus and the conquistadors, exhibits also reveal how Spain built a naval empire that battled Turkish, Algerian, French,

Portuguese, and English armies and commanded the oceans and the shipping routes for a century and a half. Moving to the present day, the museum covers Spain's more recent shipyard and naval construction accomplishments. *Paseo del Prado 5, Cibeles 91/3523–8789 www.museonavalmadrid.com Free Tues.–Sun. 10–2. Guided tour, in Spanish only, weekends at 11:30.*

23 **Palacio de Comunicaciones.** This ornate building on the southeast side of Plaza de la Cibeles, built at the start of the 20th century, is Madrid's main post office, a massive stone compound of French, Viennese, and traditional Spanish influences. Even if you aren't planning on mailing any postcards, it's worth visiting its main hall. *Plaza de Cibeles, Centro 902/197197 Weekdays 8:30 AM–9:30 PM, Sat. 8:30–2.*

15 **Plaza de la Villa.** Madrid's town council has met in this medieval-looking complex since the Middle Ages, though plans are afoot to move city hall headquarters to the post office building at Plaza Cibeles. The oldest building is the **Casa de los Lujanes,** on the east side—it's the one with the Mudejar tower. Built as a private home in the late 15th century, the house carries the Lujanes crest over the main doorway. Also on the plaza's east end is the brick-and-stone **Casa de la Villa,** built in 1629, a classic example of Madrid design with clean lines and spire-topped corner towers. Connected by an overhead walkway, the **Casa de Cisneros** was commissioned in 1537 by the nephew of Cardinal Cisneros. It's one of Madrid's rare examples of the flamboyant plateresque style, which has been likened to splashed water. *C. Mayor, Centro Closed to public except for free guided tour in Spanish Mon. at 5.*

25 **Puerta de Alcalá.** The triumphal arch was built by Carlos III in 1778 to mark the site of one of the ancient city gates. You can still see the bomb damage inflicted on it during the civil war. *C. de Alcalá s/n, Retiro.*

9 **Teleférico.** Kids love this cable car, which takes you from the Rosaleda gardens in the Parque del Oeste to the center of Casa de Campo. The walk from where the cable car drops you off to the zoo and theme park is at least 2 km (1 mi), and you'll probably have to ask for directions; it's easier to ride out, turn around, and come back. *Estación Terminal Teleférico, Paseo de Pintor Rosales, at C. Marques de Urquijo, Moncloa 91/541–7450 €3.50 one-way, €4.80 round-trip Apr.–Sept., daily noon–dusk; Oct.–Mar., weekends noon–dusk.*

10 **Templo de Debod.** This authentic 4th-century BC Egyptian temple was donated to Spain in gratitude for its technical assistance with the construction of the Aswan Dam. It's near the site of the former Montaña barracks, where madrileños bloodily crushed the beginnings of a military uprising in 1936. The western side of the small park around the temple is the best place to watch Madrid's outstanding sunset. *Pintor Rosales, Centro 91/765–1008 Free Oct.–Mar., Tues.–Fri. 9:45–1:45 and 4:15–6:15, weekends 10–2; Apr.–Sept., Tues.–Fri. 10–2 and 6–8, weekends 10–2; free guided tour Sat. at 11:30 and 12:30.*

29 **Zoo-Aquarium.** One of the most comprehensive zoological parks in Europe, Madrid's zoo houses a large variety of animals (including rari-

ties such as an albino tiger) that are grouped according to their geographical origin. It also has a dolphinarium and a wild bird reservoir that hold entertaining exhibitions twice a day on weekdays, and several more on weekends. To get a good seat, arrive a few minutes before the show begins, especially on the weekend. Give yourself at least three to four hours to stroll through the entire park. To enjoy the outdoors, bring your own food and eat at one of the picnic zones. The zoo is in the Casa de Campo, a large park right outside the western part of the city. It is best reached via subway to Príncipe Pío and then Bus 33. ✉*Moncloa* ☎*91/512–3770* 🌐*www.zoomadrid.com* 🎫*€15.90* ⏲*Winter, daily 11–6; summer, daily 10:30–7:30 (sometimes until 8 or 9* PM*).*

THE BARRIO DE LAS LETRAS & ENVIRONS

The Spanish word *castizo* means "authentic," and *los madrileños castizos* are Madrid's equivalent of London's cockneys. The castizos have traditionally lived in the Barrio de las Letras and a handful of other up-and-coming neighborhoods, such as Chueca, Malasaña, Lavapies, and the Rastro. However, the madrileños castizos are now in retreat, their place increasingly taken up by a growing number of immigrants and young Spanish professionals willing to withstand the chaos of living within these lively and creative enclaves.

The Barrio de las Letras, long favored by tourists for its clean-cut looks and its many fun places, was named for the many writers and playwrights who historically set up house within a few blocks of Plaza de Santa Ana. The City Hall's decisions to restrict traffic to residents only and to close Calle Huertas (full of bars and clubs) to vehicle traffic have added to the charm of walking and socializing in this neighborhood.

Malasaña and Chueca, once known primarily for their nightlife and mostly unsafe streets, are the two neighborhoods that have changed the most in the past decade. Money from City Hall and from private investors has helped renovate buildings and public zones, which has drawn prosperous businesses and many professional and young inhabitants to these areas. Chueca especially has been totally transformed by the gay community. Both neighborhoods now make for pleasant walks and have many good nightclubs and inexpensive restaurants.

The Lavapiés neighborhood has the highest concentration of immigrants—mostly Chinese, Indian, and North African—in Madrid. As a result, the area has plenty of ethnic markets and inexpensive restaurants as well as bustling crowds, especially at the Plaza de Lavapíes. The Plaza Tirso de Molina, near the Rastro, was rehabilitated and converted into a flower market, but Lavapiés still looks more rundown than the other parts of Castizo Madrid.

Within some of these neighborhoods, especially Lavapies and the Rastro, there is a growing number of immigrants as well as problems that come with unemployment. Purse snatching and petty crime are not uncommon, so be alert and keep your valuables within your sight.

Barrio de las Letras

KEY
Metro Stops
Tourist info

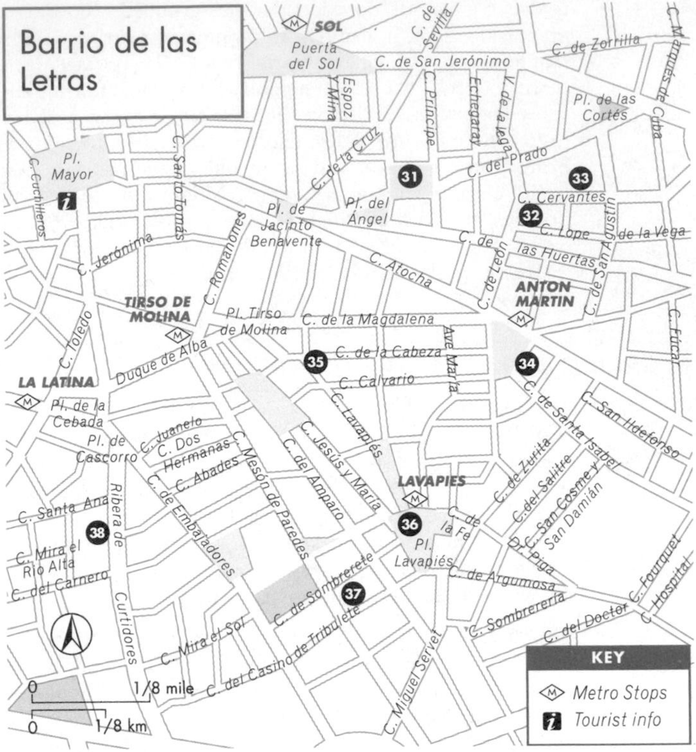

However, the streets surrounding the Plaza Santa Ana are more interesting after dark, as they pack some of Madrid's best tapas bars and nightspots.

WHAT TO SEE: MAIN ATTRACTIONS

42 **Centro de Conde Duque.** Built by Pedro de Ribera in 1717–30 to accommodate the Regiment of the Royal Guard, this building of gigantic proportions (its facade is 250 yards long) was used as a military academy and an astronomical observatory in the 19th century. A fire damaged the upper floors in 1869, and after some decay it was partially renovated and turned into a cultural and arts center. The center features temporary art exhibitions in some of its spaces, including the public and historical libraries. In summer, outdoor concerts are held in the main plaza. ✉*Conde Duque 9 and 11, Malasaña* ⏲*Tues.–Sat. 10–9, Sun. 11–2:30 exhibitions only.*

43 **Museo Municipal de Arte Contemporáneo.** To reach this museum inside the Centro de Conde Duque, take the door to your right after the entrance and walk up the stairs. Founded in 2001, the museum displays on two floors 200 modern artworks acquired by City Hall since 1980. The paintings, graphic artwork, sculpture, and photography are mostly by local artists. ✉*Conde Duque 9 and 11, Malasaña* ☎*91/588–5928* 🎟*Free* ⏲*Tues.–Sat. 10–9, Sun. 11–2:30.*

NEED A BREAK?

While on San Bernardo, before crossing over to the Convent of Monsterrat on Calle Quiñones, stop for an ice-cream break at what is probably Madrid's tastiest, most fashionable, and priciest ice-cream parlor, Giangrossi ✉ *Alberto Aguilera 1, Malasaña.* Although the name sounds Italian, it happens to be an Argentine chain. In addition to the one on Alberto Aguilera, there are branches on the corner of Hermosilla and Velazquez, and on Cava Baja. Creative flavors include *dulce de leche* (a very sweet caramel spread well known in South America), mascarpone, and *turrón* (a type of candy eaten at Christmas, usually with dried fruit in it), as well as pink grapefruit, pineapple, and melon sorbets. What's with the funny-looking, triangular scoops? That's the way they serve a cone in Argentina.

38 **El Rastro.** Named for the *arrastre* (dragging) of animals in and out of the slaughterhouse that once stood here and, specifically, the *rastro* (blood trail) left behind, this site explodes into a rollicking flea market every Sunday from 10 to 2. For serious browsing and bargaining, any *other* morning is a better time to turn up treasures such as old iron grillwork, a marble tabletop, or a gilt picture frame, but Sunday brings out truly bizarre bric-a-brac ranging from stolen earrings to sent postcards

A GOOD WALK: BARRIO DE LAS LETRAS

Allow between one and a half and two hours for this tour.

Begin in the Barrio de las Letras, at the **Plaza Santa Ana** ㉛, hub of the theater district in the 17th century and now a center of nocturnal activity. The plaza's notable buildings include, at the lower end, the Teatro Español. Walk up to the sunny Plaza del Ángel (next to the Reina Victoria hotel) and turn down Calle de Las Huertas, past the ancient olive tree and plant nursery behind the San Sebastián church—it was once the church cemetery. This was the final resting place of Lope de Vega, whose sepulchre is displayed inside the church. Walk down Huertas to No. 18, Casa Alberto, an ancient (though still excellent) bar and restaurant as well as the house where Miguel de Cervantes was living when he finished some of his most important works, including the second part of *Don Quijote*. Continue to Calle León, named for a lion kept here long ago by a resident Moor. A short walk to your left brings you to the corner of Calle Cervantes. As the plaque on the wall overhead attests, *Don Quijote's* author died on April 23, 1616, in what is now called the **Casa de Cervantes** ㉜. Down the street, at No. 11, is the **Casa de Lope de Vega** ㉝, where the "Spanish Shakespeare," Fray Lope Félix de la Vega Carpio, lived and worked.

A right from Calle Cervantes onto Calle Quevedo takes you past the Basque *sidrería* (cider house) Zerain—where you can catch cider in your glass as it spurts directly from the barrel—down to the corner across from the convent and church of the Trinitarias Descalzas (Discalced, or Barefoot, Trinitarians, a cloistered order of nuns). Just before the corner, on the wall to your left, is a plaque honoring Quevedo, the 17th-century poet who gives the street its name, and who lived in a building that was once on this site. (Credited with having the best command of the Spanish language ever, Quevedo acquired the building and ousted a tenant who couldn't pay his bills because of his gambling debts. This tenant just happened to be another famous poet, Góngora, with whom Quevedo sustained a poetry rivalry that had lasted for decades.)

to thrown-out love letters. Even so, people-watching is the best part. ✉ *Ribera de los Curtidores s/n, Lavapies/Centro.*

㊶ **Plaza del 2 de Mayo.** On this unassuming square stood the Monteleón Artillery barracks, where some brave Spanish soldiers and citizens fought Napoléon's invading troops on May 2, 1808. The arch that now stands in the middle of the plaza was once at the entrance of the old barracks, and the sculpture under the arch represents captains Daoiz and Velarde. All the surrounding streets carry the names of that day's heroes. The plaza, now filled with spring and summer terraces, makes a good place to stop for a drink. One of the most popular cafés, Pepe Botella, carries the demeaning nickname the people of Madrid gave to Joseph Bonaparte, Napoléon's brother, who ruled Spain from 1808 to 1813: Botella ("bottle" in English) is a reference to his alleged—but false—fondness for drink. ✉ *Plaza del 2 de Mayo, Malasaña.*

31 **Plaza Santa Ana.** This plaza was the heart of the theater district in the 17th century—the golden age of Spanish literature—and is now the center of Madrid's thumping nightlife. A statue of 17th-century playwright Pedro Calderón de la Barca faces the **Teatro Español, where** playwrights such as Lope de Vega, Tirso de Molina, Calderón de la Barca, and Valle Inclán have released some of their plays. (Opposite the theater and off to the side of a hotel is the diminutive **Plaza del Ángel,** with one of Madrid's best jazz clubs, the Café Central.) One of Madrid's most famous cafés, the former Ernest Hemingway hangout **Cervecería Alemana,** is on Plaza Santa Ana and is still catnip to writers and poets. ✉*Plaza de Santa Ana s/n, Barrio de las Letras.*

ALSO WORTH SEEING

35 **Cárcel de la Inquisición** *(Inquisition Jail).* Unmarked by any historical plaque, the former jail is now a large tapas bar, the **Taberna de Lavapiés,** named for the old Jewish Quarter. Here Jews, Moors, and others designated unrepentant heathens or sinners bent to the inquisitors' whims; the prison later became a Cárcel de la Corona (Crown Prison) for the incarceration of wayward soldiers, priests, and nuns. Ask a bartender if you can see the original, two-story medieval patio out back—it's tiny, but highly evocative. ✉*Southeast corner of C. Cabeza and C. Lavapiés, Lavapiés* ☎*91/369–3218* ⏲*Daily 9* AM*–2* AM.

32 **Casa de Cervantes.** A plaque marks the private home where Miguel de Cervantes Saavedra, author of *Don Quijote de la Mancha,* committed his final words to paper: "*Puesto ya el pie en el estribo, con ansias de la muerte …*" ("One foot already in the stirrup and yearning for death . . ."). The Western world's first runaway best seller, and still one of the most widely translated and read books in the world, Cervantes' spoof of a knightly novel playfully but profoundly satirized Spain's rise and decline while portraying man's dual nature in the pragmatic Sancho Panza and the idealistic Don Quijote, ever in search of wrongs to right. ✉*C. Cervantes and C. León, Santa Ana.*

33 **Casa de Lope de Vega.** Considered the Shakespeare of Spanish literature, Fray Lope Félix de la Vega Carpio (1562–1635) is best known as Lope de Vega. A contemporary and adversary of Cervantes, he wrote some 1,800 plays and enjoyed great success during his lifetime. His former home is now a museum with an intimate look into a bygone era: everything from the whale-oil lamps and candles to the well in the tiny garden and the pans used to warm the bedsheets brings you closer to the great dramatist. Don't miss the Latin inscription over the door: PARVA PROPIA MAGNA / MAGNA ALIENA PARVA (small but mine big / big but someone else's small). ✉*C. Cervantes 11, Santa Ana* ☎*91/429–9216* 🎟*€2, free Sat.* ⏲*Sept.–July, Tues.–Fri. 9:30–2, Sat. 10–2.*

39 **Casa Longoria.** A modernist palace commissioned in 1902 by the businessman and politician Javier González Longoria, the Casa Longoria was built by José Grases Riera, a Catalan architect who was also a disciple of Gaudí. The winding shapes, the plant motifs, and the wrought-iron balconies are reminiscent of Gaudí's works in Barcelona. The building's jewel is its main iron, bronze, and marble staircase;

unfortunately this is off-limits to tourists, because the building is now in private hands. ✉ *Fernando VI 4, Chueca.*

34 **Cine Doré.** A rare example of Art Nouveau architecture in Madrid, the hip Cine Doré shows movies from the Spanish National Film Archives and eclectic foreign films for €2.50 per session. Show times are listed in newspapers under "*Filmoteca.*" The pink neon-trimmed lobby has a sleek café–bar and a good bookshop. ✉ *C. Santa Isabel 3, Lavapiés* ☎ *91/369–1125* ⏲ *Tues.–Sun.; 4 shows daily, 1st starting at 5:30* PM.

37 **Corrala.** This structure is not unlike the rowdy outdoor areas (*corrales*) used as Madrid's early makeshift theaters; they were usually installed in a vacant lot between two apartment buildings, and families with balconies overlooking the action rented out seats to wealthy patrons of the arts. There's a plaque here to remind you that the setting for the famous 19th-century *zarzuela* (light opera) *La Revoltosa* was a corrala like this one. City-sponsored musical-theater events are occasionally held here in the summer. The ruins across the street were once the **Escolapíos de San Fernando,** one of several churches and parochial schools that fell victim to anti-Catholic sentiments during the civil war. ✉ *C. Mesón de Paredes and C. Sombrerete, Lavapiés.*

40 **Museo Municipal.** Founded in 1929 on what was formerly a hospice from the 17th century, the museum displays paintings, drawings, pictures, ceramics, furniture, and other objects explaining Madrid history. There is a good exhibition on Madrid that will be best enjoyed by those who speak Spanish and who already know a bit about the city's history. But the ornamented facade—a baroque jewel by Pedro de Ribera—and the painstakingly precise, nearly 18-foot model of Madrid, a project coordinated by León Gil de Palacio in 1830 are two exhibits almost everyone can enjoy. ✉ *Fuencarral 78, Malasaña* ☎ *91/532–6499* 🎫 *Free* ⏲ *Tues.–Fri. 9:30–8; weekends 10–2.*

NEED A BREAK?

If you get nostalgic, but are looking for something a little refined go for the creative French-Canadian gourmet versions of an American burger at Home Burger Bar (✉ *Calle Espíritu Santo 25, Malasaña* ☎ *915229728*) just a couple of blocks away from the Museo Municipal.

36 **Plaza Lavapiés.** The heart of the historic Jewish barrio, this plaza remains a neighborhood hub. To the left is the Calle de la Fe (Street of Faith), which was called Calle Sinagoga until the expulsion of the Jews in 1492. The church of **San Lorenzo** at the end was built on the site of the razed synagogue. Legend says Jews and Moors who chose baptism over exile had to walk up this street barefoot to the ceremony to demonstrate their new faith. ✉ *Top of Calle de la Fe, Lavapiés.*

SALAMANCA

The sophisticated set spends time in Salamanca, one of Madrid's 21 districts. Hugging Central Madrid's northeast quadrant, this section of town is where you find plenty of shops—the designer variety, as well as artsy and gourmet—and places to eat that will deplete your wallet's

CLOSE UP

The Events of May 2nd

In 1808 Spain was ruled by Carlos IV, a king more interested in hunting than in the duties attached to government. The king delegated power to his wife, María Luisa, and she to the chief minister, Godoy, one of the country's most despised statesmen of all time. He succeeded in tripling the country's debt in 20 years, and signed the secret Convention of Fontainebleau with Napoléon, which allowed the French troops to freely cross Spain on their way to Portugal. Napoléon's plans were different—he intended to use the convention as an excuse to annex Spain to his vast domains. While the French troops entered Spain, the Spanish people, tired of the inept king and the greedy Godoy, revolted against the French in Aranjuez on March 17, 1808, hoping Napoléon would hand the throne over to the king's elder son, Prince Ferdinand. In the following days Carlos IV abdicated, and his son was proclaimed the new king, Fernando VII. Napoléon had already chosen a person for that job, though—one of his brothers, José Bonaparte. The shrewd French emperor managed to attract the Spanish royal family to France and had Carlos IV, his wife, and Ferdinand VII imprisoned in Bayona, France, and his brother placed on the Spanish throne.

When French General Murat arrived in Madrid a few days later, on March 23, 1808, with 10,000 men (leaving 20,000 more camped outside the city) following Napoléon's orders, Madrid's Captain General Francisco Javier Negrete ordered the Spanish troops to remain in their military quarters, arguing that resistance was futile. On the morning of May 2, a raging group of civilians revolted in front of the Palacio Real, fearing the French troops intended to send Francisco de Paula, King Carlos IV's youngest son, to Bayona with his brother and father. Gunfire ensued, and word of the events spread all over the city. People rose up, fighting the mightier French troops with whatever they could use as weapons. Two captains, Daoiz and Velarde, and a lieutenant, Ruiz, disobeyed Negrete's orders and quartered at the Monteleón Artillery barracks, which stretched from what is now Plaza de 2 de mayo to Calle Carranza. Helped by a small group of soldiers and some brave citizens who had marched to the barracks from the Royal Palace, the group resisted the French for three hours, doing so with very little ammunition, since they couldn't access the armory.

Daoiz and Velarde died in the bloody fight. Ruiz managed to escape, only to die from his wounds later. Murat's forces executed soldiers and civilians throughout the city, including in the Casa de Campo, captured by Goya in one of his two famous paintings of the executions. The events marked the beginning of the five-year War of Independence against the French. The remains of the three military heroes, together with those who were executed at Paseo del Prado, are now held in an obelisk-mausoleum at Plaza de la Lealtad.

Paradoxically, José Bonaparte proved to be a good ruler, implementing some wise renovations in the then quite congested and unhygienic city. He built new squares, enlarged key streets, and moved some of the cemeteries outside the city.

contents. It borders on the west with Chamberí, a mainly residential neighborhood with good dining and nightlife options.

WHAT TO SEE: MAIN ATTRACTIONS

44 **Museo Arqueológico** *(Museum of Archaeology)*. The biggest attraction here is a replica of the early cave paintings in Altamira. (Access to the real thing, in Cantabria Province, is highly restricted.) Also here, look for *La Dama de Elche,* a bust of a wealthy, 5th-century BC Iberian woman, and notice that her headgear is a rough precursor to the mantillas and hair combs still associated with traditional Spanish dress. The ancient Visigothic votive crowns are another highlight; discovered in 1859 near Toledo, they are believed to date back to the 8th century. The museum shares its neoclassical building with the **Biblioteca Nacional** (National Library). ✉*Calle Serrano 13, Salamanca* ☎*91/577–7912, 91/580–7823 library* ⊕*http://man.mcu.es* 🎫*€3, free Sat. after 2:30 and all day Sun.* ⏲*Museum Tues.–Sat. 9:30–8:30, Sun. 9:30–2:30. Library weekdays 9–9, Sat. 9–2.*

46 **Museo Sorolla.** See the world through the exceptional eye of Spain's most famous impressionist painter, Joaquín Sorolla (1863–1923), who lived and worked most of his life at the home and garden he designed. Entering this diminutive but cozy domain is a little like stepping into a Sorolla painting, because it's filled with the artist's best-known works, most of which shimmer with the bright Mediterranean light and color of his native Valencia. ✉*General Martinez Campos 37, Chamberí* ⊕*http://museosorolla.mcu.es* ☎*91/310–1584* 🎫*€2.40, free Sun.* ⏲*Tues.–Sat. 9:30–3, Sun. 10–3.*

ALSO WORTH SEEING

47 **Museo Lázaro Galdiano.** This stately mansion of writer and editor José Lázaro Galdiano (1862–1947), located just a 10-minute walk across the Castellana from the Museo Sorolla, has decorative items and paintings by Bosch, El Greco, Murillo, and Goya, among others. The remarkable collection comprises five centuries of Spanish, Flemish, English, and Italian art. Bosch's *St. John the Baptist* and the many Goyas are the stars of the show, with El Greco's *San Francisco de Assisi* and Zurbarán's *San Diego de Alcalá* close behind. It was completely renovated in 2005. ✉*Calle Serrano 122, Salamanca* ⊕*www.flg.es* ☎*91/561–6084* 🎫*€4, free Sun.* ⏲*Wed.–Mon. 10–4:30.*

45 **Plaza Colón.** Named for Christopher Columbus, this plaza has a statue of the explorer (identical to the one in Barcelona's port) looking west from a high tower in the middle of the square. Beneath the plaza is the **Centro Cultural de la Villa** (☎*91/480–0300*), a performing-arts facility. Behind Plaza Colón is **Calle Serrano,** the city's premier shopping street (think Gucci, Prada, and Loewe). Stroll in either direction on Serrano for some window-shopping. ✉*Plaza Colón, Salamanca* .

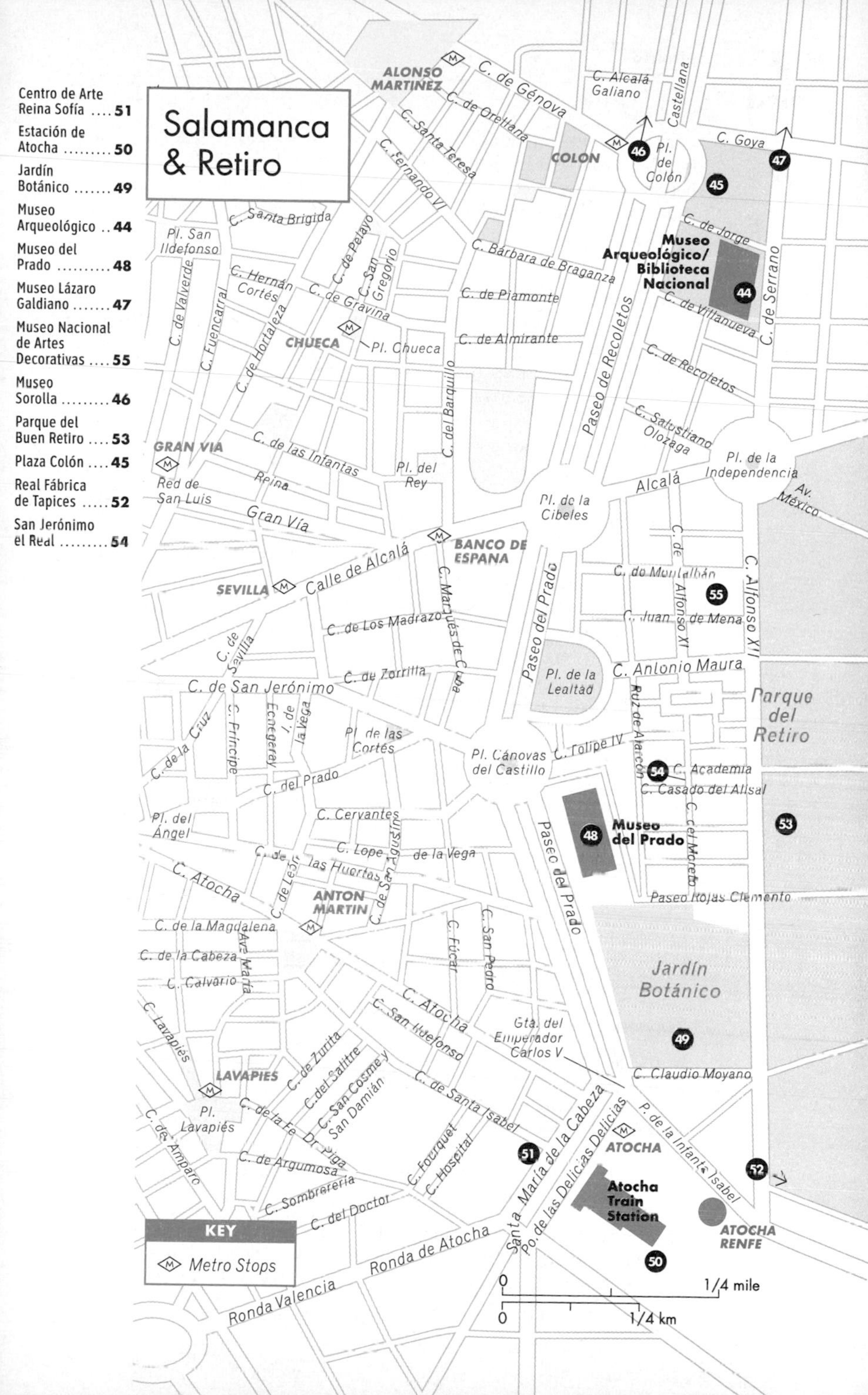

Salamanca & Retiro
Centro de Arte Reina Sofía 51
Estación de Atocha 50
Jardín Botánico 49
Museo Arqueológico .. 44
Museo del Prado 48
Museo Lázaro Galdiano 47
Museo Nacional de Artes Decorativas 55
Museo Sorolla 46
Parque del Buen Retiro 53
Plaza Colón 45
Real Fábrica de Tapices 52
San Jerónimo el Real 54
Museo Arqueológico/ Biblioteca Nacional
Museo del Prado
Atocha Train Station
Parque del Retiro
Jardín Botánico
ALONSO MARTINEZ
COLON
CHUECA
GRAN VIA
BANCO DE ESPANA
SEVILLA
ANTON MARTIN
LAVAPIES
ATOCHA
ATOCHA RENFE
C. de Génova
C. de Orellana
C. Santa Teresa
C. Fernando VI
C. Alcalá Galiano
Castellana
Pl. de Colón
C. Goya
C. de Jorge
C. de Serrano
C. Santa Brigida
Pl. San Ildefonso
C. de Pelayo
C. San Gregorio
C. Bárbara de Braganza
C. Hernán Cortés
C. de Gravina
C. de Piamonte
C. de Villanueva
C. de Valverde
C. Fuencarral
C. de Hortaleza
Pl. Chueca
C. de Almirante
Paseo de Recoletos
C. de Recoletos
C. del Barquillo
C. Salustiano Olózaga
C. de las Infantas
Pl. del Rey
Pl. de la Independencia
Red de San Luis
Reina
Gran Vía
Pl. de la Cibeles
Alcalá
Av. México
Calle de Alcalá
C. Marqués de Cuba
C. de Montalbán
C. de Alfonso XI
C. Alfonso XII
C. de Los Madrazo
C. Juan de Mena
C. de Sevilla
Paseo del Prado
Pl. de la Lealtad
C. Antonio Maura
C. de Zorrilla
C. de San Jerónimo
Ruiz de Alarcón
C. de la Cruz
C. Príncipe
Echegaray
V. de la Vega
Pl. de las Cortés
Pl. Cánovas del Castillo
C. Felipe IV
C. Academia
C. Casado del Alisal
C. del Prado
C. Cervantes
Pl. del Ángel
C. Lope de la Vega
C. del Moreto
C. de las Huertas
C. de León
C. de San Agustín
C. Atocha
Paseo Rojas Clemente
C. de la Magdalena
Ave María
C. de la Cabeza
C. Calvario
C. Fúcar
C. San Pedro
C. Lavapiés
C. San Ildefonso
Gta. del Emperador Carlos V
C. Claudio Moyano
C. de Zurita
C. del Salitre
C. San Cosme y San Damián
C. de Santa Isabel
Pl. Lavapiés
C. de la Fe
Dr. Piga
P. de la Infanta Isabel
C. de Amparo
C. de Argumosa
C. Fourquet
C. Hospital
Santa María de la Cabeza
Po. de las Delicias
Delicias
C. Sombrerería
C. del Doctor
Ronda de Atocha
Ronda Valencia
KEY
Metro Stops
0
1/4 mile
0
1/4 km

RETIRO

Lush with natural offerings, Madrid's Retiro district lies just east of the Paseo del Prado (Madrid's Art Walk boulevard). The small area between the western edge of the park and the Paseo del Prado hides some of the city's most expensive and sought-after houses.

WHAT TO SEE: MAIN ATTRACTIONS

51 **Centro de Arte Reina Sofía** *(Queen Sofía Art Center)*. Madrid's museum of modern art is in a converted hospital, the classical granite austerity of which is somewhat relieved (or ruined, depending on your point of view) by the playful pair of glass elevator shafts on its facade. Three separate buildings joined by a common vault were added to the original complex in a renovation that was completed at the end of 2005. The first contains an art bookshop and a public library, the second a center for contemporary exhibitions, and the third an auditorium and restaurant/cafeteria managed by Sergi Arola of La Broche. The latter, although expensive, makes an excellent stop for a refreshment, be it a cup of tea or coffee, a snack, or even a cocktail.

Fodor's Choice ★

The collection focuses on Spain's three great modern masters—Pablo Picasso, Salvador Dalí, and Joan Miró—and has contributions from Juan Gris, Jorge Oteiza, Pablo Gargallo, Julio Gonzalez, Eduardo Chillida, and Antoni Tàpies. Take the elevator to the second floor to see the heavy hitters, then to the fourth floor for the rest of the permanent collection. The other floors have traveling exhibits. Exhibition rooms are numbered 1 to 45, beginning chronologically with the turn-of-the-20th-century birth of Spain's modern movement on the second floor and continuing to contemporary artists such as Eduardo Chillida in Rooms 42 and 43 on the fourth floor. The free English-language guidebooklet is excellent, as are the plastic-covered notes at each display.

The museum's showpiece is Picasso's *Guernica,* in the center hall on the second floor. The huge black-and-white canvas depicts the horror of the Nazi Condor Legion's bombing of the ancient Basque town of Gernika in 1937, during the Spanish civil war. The work is something of a national shrine. *Guernica* did not reach Madrid until 1981, as Picasso had stipulated in his will that the painting return to Spain only after democracy was restored.

The room in front of *Guernica* has surrealist works, with six canvases by Miró. Room 10 belongs to Salvador Dalí, hung in three *ámbitos* (areas). The first has the young artist experimenting with styles, as in his classical landscape *Paisaje de Cadaqués* and his cubist self-portrait; the second shows the evolving painter of the Buñuel portrait and portraits of the artist's sister; and the third includes the full-blown surrealist work *The Great Masturbator* (1929), and *The Enigma of Hitler* (1939), with its ghostly umbrella and broken, dripping telephone.

The rest of the museum is devoted to more recent art, including works by Spanish sculptor Eduardo Chillida and paintings by Barcelona artist Antoni Tàpies. ✉*Santa Isabel 52, Atocha* ☎*91/467–5062* 🌐*http://*

museoreinasofia.mcu.es 🎫*€6, free Sat. after 2:30 and all day Sun.* ⏲*Mon. and Wed.–Sat. 10–9, Sun. 10–2:30.*

■ TIP→ *See* **"The Art Walk" box for how to include the Centro de Arte Reina Sofía as part of an art-theme excursion.**

48 Fodor'sChoice ★ **Museo del Prado** *(Prado Museum). See the in-focus feature "El Prado: Madrid's Brush with Greatness."* A five-minute walk from the museum, and free with a Prado ticket, is the **Casón del Buen Retiro.** This annex, once a ballroom, and the formal gardens in the Retiro are all that remain of Madrid's second royal complex—at one time it filled the entire neighborhood. On display are 19th-century Spanish paintings and sculpture, including works by Sorolla and Rusiñol. A regal restoration of the complex will yield new halls devoted to 17th- and 19th-century Spanish art. At this writing, the halls were scheduled to open by early 2008. ✉*C. Alfonso XII s/n, Retiro* ☎*91/330–2867* 🌐*http://museoprado.mcu.es* 🎫*€6, free Sun.* ⏲*Tues.–Sat. 9–7, Sun. 9–2.*

NEED A BREAK?

La Dolores (✉*Plaza de Jesús 4, Santa Ana* ☎*91/429–2243*) is an atmospheric ceramic-tile bar that's the perfect place for a beer or glass of wine and a plate of olives. It's a great alternative to the Prado's basement cafeteria and is just across the Paseo, then one block up on Calle Lope de Vega.

53 **Parque del Buen Retiro** *(The Retreat).* Once the private playground of royalty, Madrid's crowning park is a vast expanse of green encompassing formal gardens, fountains, lakes, exhibition halls, children's play areas, outdoor cafés, and a **Puppet Theater** featuring free slapstick routines that even non-Spanish speakers will enjoy. Shows take place on Saturday at 1 and on Sunday at 1, 6, and 7. The park is especially lively on weekends, when it fills with street musicians, jugglers, clowns, gypsy fortune-tellers, and sidewalk painters along with hundreds of Spanish families out for a walk. The park holds a book fair in May and occasional flamenco concerts in summer. From the entrance at the Puerta de Alcalá, head straight toward the center and you can find the **Estanque** (lake), presided over by a grandiose equestrian statue of King Alfonso XII, erected by his mother. Just behind the lake, north of the statue, is one of the best of the park's many cafés. If you're feeling nautical, you can rent a boat and work up an appetite rowing.

The 19th-century **Palacio de Cristal** (Crystal Palace), southeast of the Estanque, was built to house exotic plants from the Philippines, a Spanish possession at the time. This airy marvel of steel and glass sits on a base of decorative tile. Next door is a small lake with ducks and swans. Along the Paseo del Uruguay at the park's south end is the **Rosaleda** (Rose Garden), bursting with color and heavy with floral scents for most of the summer. West of the Rosaleda, look for a statue called the **Ángel Caído** (Fallen Angel), which madrileños claim is the only one in the world depicting the prince of darkness before (during, actually) his fall from grace. ✉*Puerta de Alcalá, Retiro* 🎫*Free.*

Continued on page 85

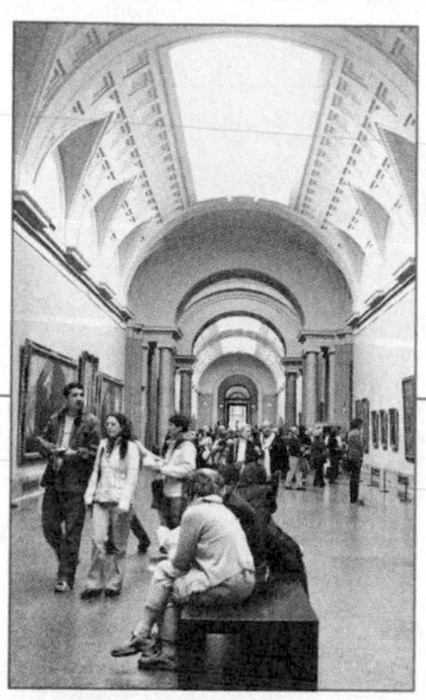

EL PRADO: MADRID'S BRUSH WITH GREATNESS

Don't let the Prado's immense size intimidate you. You can't see it all in a day. But if you zero in on some of the museum's undisputed masterpieces, then you can have a rich art experience without collapsing.

Let's face it: While the Prado has sculptures, drawings, and other treasures spanning centuries, it's "why-go"—it's "*must*-go"—is its paintings.

Most of the attention, all of it deserved, goes to the Prado's perennial headliners: Diego Velazquez, El Greco, and Francisco Goya. The museum's most famous canvas is Velázquez's *Las Meninas* (*The Maids of Honor*), which combines a self-portrait of the artist at work with a mirror reflection of the King Philip IV and Queen Doña Mariana of Austria in a revolutionary interplay of space and perspectives. Picasso was so taken with this work that he painted several copies of it in his own abstract style (most of these are on display in the Picasso Museum in Barcelona). If you find fellow visitors taken with the painting and need to wait a bit before studying it, you can while away some time with the 46 other Velázquez works in the collection; the Prado owns all but a handful of the paintings ever created by the artist.

Likewise, of the Prado's 42 El Grecos, the two that stir up the most interest are his passionately spiritual *The Resurrection* and *The Adoration of the Shepherds*. And Goya fans will have 119 oil-on-canvas paintings for their delectation, including one of his more scandalous works, *The Naked Maja*.

CONTACT INFORMATION

✉ Paseo del Prado s/n, 28014 Madrid
☎ (+34) 91 330 2800.

HOURS OF OPERATION

9AM to 8PM, Tuesday through Saturday and 9AM to 7PM on Sunday, except 9AM to 9PM on Christmas Eve, New Year's Eve, and Three Kings Day (January 6). The museum is closed every Monday of the year, as well as New Year's Day, Good Friday, Fiesta del Trabajo (May 1), and Christmas.

ADMISSION

€6. Reduced-price admission is available for students under 25. Admission is free for all on Sundays.

GETTING THERE

Ⓜ The nearest Metro/train stop to the museum is Atocha (line 1); to reach the Prado by bus, take line 9, 10, 14, 19, 27, 34, 37, or 45.

The Trinity by El Greco, 1577. Oil on canvas.

A MUCH-NEEDED FACE LIFT

A collective "it's about time" rang forth during the Prado's long-awaited facelift. Although the Prado is the most-visited tourist destination in Spain, its patrons were frequently stymied by erratic opening hours and especially frustrated by the lack of amenities that they take for granted in other museums of the Prado's stature. The Madrid museum, one of Europe's best, had languished comfortably, but maddeningly, in the status quo of the 19th century. A gleaming new addition by Spanish architect Rafael Moneo, which opened in June 2007, brought an end to all that.

(top) A Velázquez statue graces the museum's old entrance. (bottom) Visitors now enter via a new $202 million wing, designed by Rafael Moneo.

Like I. M. Pei's pyramid at Paris's Louvre, Moneo's new steel-and-glass wedge has thrust the Prado dynamically into the 21st century. With the expansion, the Prado has doubled its exhibition space to a total of 16,000 square meters (52,800 square feet). Visitors now enter into a reception hall in the new wing and walk through a corridor to the green space of the Retiro Park, where the building connects with the formerly sleepy cloister of the Jerónimos Church beyond. In between is a 400-seat auditorium, temporary exhibitions, a library, studios for art conservation, and expanded shops and eateries.

The best part of the expansion is that the museum now showcases thousands more of its collection. Previously, more than three-quarters of the 9,000 paintings of art in Prado's world-class collection remained in storage, with only 2,000 of the most intriguing pieces on display in the elegant 1819-vintage galleries. A re-hang is underway, as curators fit in some of these previously hidden works.

El Prado

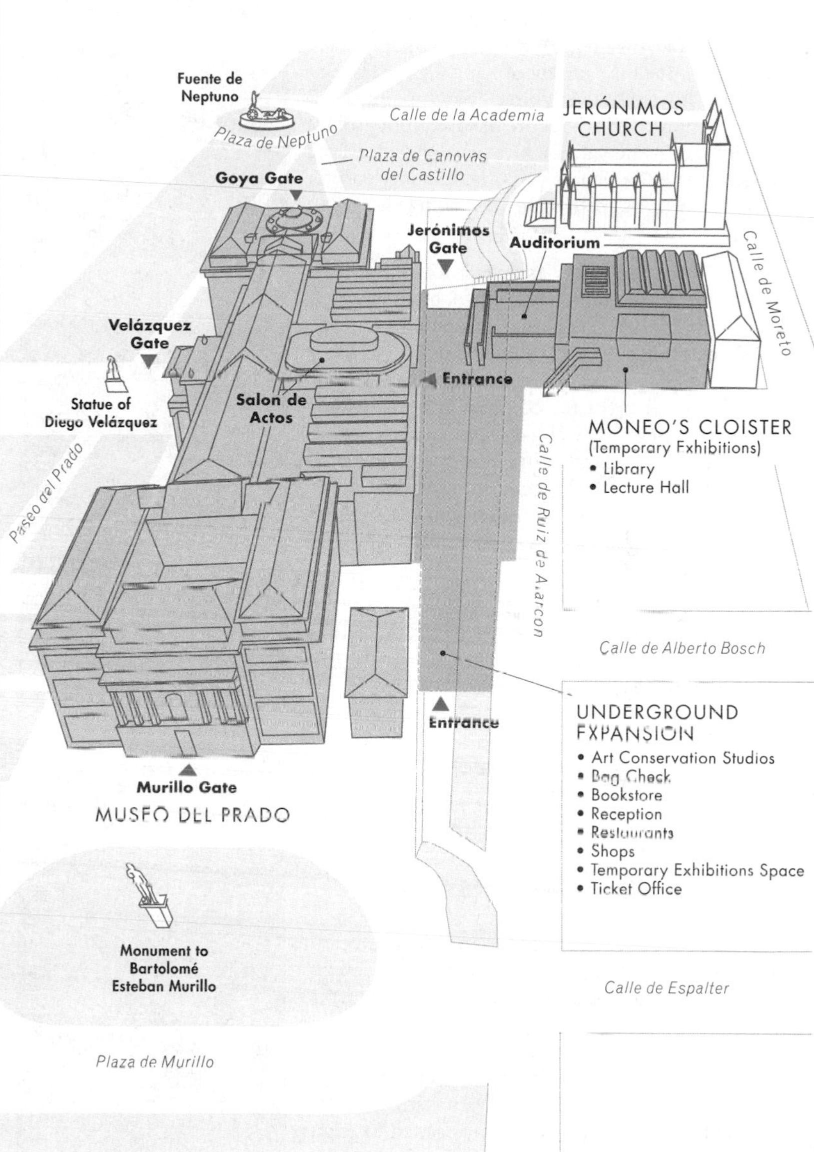
Fuente de Neptuno
Plaza de Neptuno
Calle de la Academia
JERÓNIMOS CHURCH
Plaza de Canovas del Castillo
Goya Gate
Jerónimos Gate
Auditorium
Calle de Moreto
Velázquez Gate
Statue of Diego Velázquez
Salon de Actos
Entrance
MONEO'S CLOISTER
(Temporary Exhibitions)
• Library
• Lecture Hall
Calle de Ruiz de Alarcon
Paseo del Prado
Calle de Alberto Bosch
UNDERGROUND EXPANSION
• Art Conservation Studios
• Bag Check
• Bookstore
• Reception
• Restaurants
• Shops
• Temporary Exhibitions Space
• Ticket Office
Entrance
Murillo Gate
MUSEO DEL PRADO
Monument to Bartolomé Esteban Murillo
Calle de Espalter
Plaza de Murillo

THREE GREAT MASTERS

Francisco de Goya

FRANCISCO DE GOYA 1746–1828
Goya's work spans a staggering range of tone, from bucolic to horrific, his idyllic paintings of Spaniards at play and portraits of the family of King Carlos IV contrasting with his dark, disturbing "black paintings." Goya's attraction to the macabre assured him a place in posterity, an ironic statement at the end of a long career in which he served as the official court painter to a succession of Spanish kings, bringing the art of royal portraiture to unknown heights.

Goya found fame in his day as a portraitist, but he is admired by modern audiences for his depictions of the bizarre and the morbid. Beginning as a painter of decorative Rococo figures, he evolved into an artist of great depth in the employ of King Charles IV. The push-pull between Goya's love for his country and his disdain for the enemies of Spain yielded such masterpieces as *Third of May 1808,* painted after the French occupation ended. In the early 19th century, Goya's scandalous *The Naked Maja* brought him before the Spanish Inquisition, whose judgment was to end his tenure as a court painter.

Diego Velázquez

DIEGO VELÁZQUEZ 1599–1660
A native of Seville, Velázquez gained fame at age 24 as court painter to King Philip IV. He developed a lifelike approach to religious art in which both saints and sinners were specific people rather than generic types. The supple brushwork of his ambitious history paintings and portraits was unsurpassed. Several visits to Rome, and his friendship with Rubens, made him the quintessential baroque painter with an international purview.

Domenikos Theotokopoulos

DOMENIKOS THEOTOKOPOULOS (AKA "EL GRECO") 1541–1614
El Greco's art was one of rapture and devotion, but beyond that his style is almost impossible to categorize. "The Greek" found his way from his native Crete to Spain through Venice; he spent most of his life in Toledo. His twisted, elongated figures imbue both his religious subjects and portraits with a sense of otherworldliness. While his palette and brushstrokes were inspired by Italian Mannerism, his approach to painting was uniquely his own. His inimitable style left few followers.

SIX PAINTINGS TO SEE

SATURN DEVOURING ONE OF HIS SONS (1819)
FRANCISCO DE GOYA Y LUCIENTES
In one of fourteen nightmarish "Black Paintings" executed by Goya to decorate the walls of his home in the later years of his life, the mythological God Kronos, or Saturn, cannibalizes one of his children in order to derail a prophecy that one of them would take over his throne. *Mural transferred to canvas.*

Saturn Devouring One of His Sons

THE GARDEN OF DELIGHTS OR LA PINTURA DEL MADROÑO (1500)
HIËRONYMUS BOSCH
Very little about the small-town environment of the Low Countries where the Roman Catholic Bosch lived in the late Middle Ages can explain his thought-provoking, and downright bizarre, paintings. His depictions of mankind's sins and virtues, and the heavenly rewards or demonic punishments that await us all, have fascinated many generations of viewers, who have called the devout painter a "heretic," and most recently compared him to Salvador Dalí for his disturbingly twisted renderings. In this three panel painting, Adam and Eve are created, mankind celebrates its humanity, and hell awaits the wicked, all within a journey of 152 inches! *Wooden Triptych.*

The Garden of Delights

LAS MENINAS (THE MAIDS OF HONOR) (1656-57)
DIEGO VELÁZQUEZ DE SILVA
Velázquez's masterpiece of spatial perspective occupies pride-of place in the center of the Spanish baroque galleries. In this complex visual game, *you* are the king and queen of Spain, reflected in a distant hazy mirror as the court painter (Velázquez) pauses in front of his easel to observe your features. The actual subject is the Princess Margarita, heir to the throne in 1656. *Oil on canvas.*

Las Meninas

STILL LIFE (17th Century; no date)
FRANCISCO DE ZURBARÁN
Best known as a painter of contemplative saints, Zurbarán, a native of Extremadura who found success working with Velázquez in Seville, was a peerless observer of beauty in the everyday. His rendering of the surfaces of these homely objects elevates them to the stature of holy relics, urging the viewer to touch them. But the overriding mood is one of serenity and order. *Oil on canvas.*

Still Life

DAVID VICTORIOUS OVER GOLIATH (1599)

MICHELANGELO MERISI (CARAVAGGIO)

Caravaggio used intense contrasts between his dark and light passages (called *chiaroscuro* in Italian) to create drama in his bold baroque paintings. Here, a surprisingly childlike David calmly ties up the severed head of the giant Philistine Goliath, gruesomely featured in the foreground plane of the picture. The astonishing realism of the Italian painter, who was as well known for his tempestuous personal life as for his deftness with a paint brush, had a profound influence on 17th century Spanish art. *Oil on canvas.*

David Victorious over Goliath

THE TRINITY (1577)

DOMENIKOS THEOTOKOPOULOS (EL GRECO)

Soon after arriving in Spain, Domenikos Theotokopoulos created this view of Christ ascending into heaven supported by angels, God the Father, and the Holy Spirit. It was commissioned for the altar of a convent in Toledo. The acid colors recall the Mannerist paintings of Venice, where El Greco was trained, and the distortions of the upward-floating bodies show more gracefulness than the anatomical contortions that characterize his later works. *Oil on canvas.*

The Trinity

PICASSO AND THE PRADO

The Prado contains no modern art, but one of the greatest artists of the 20th century had an important history with the museum. **Pablo Picasso** (1891–1973) served as the director of the Prado during the Spanish civil war, from 1936 to 1939. The Prado was a "phantom museum" in that period, Picasso once noted, since it was closed for most of the war and its collections hidden elsewhere for safety.

Later that century, the abstract artist's enormous *El Guernica* hung briefly on the Prado's walls, returning to Spain from the Museum of Modern Art in 1981. Picasso had stipulated that MoMA give up his anti-war masterpiece after the death of fascist dictator Francisco Franco, and it was displayed at the Prado and the Casón del Buen Retiro until the nearby Reina Sofia was built to house it in 1992.

Picasso with his wife Jacqueline Roque

Picasso in his atelier

ALSO WORTH SEEING

50 **Estación de Atocha.** A steel-and-glass hangar, Madrid's main railroad station was built in the late 19th century by Alberto Palacio Elissague, the architect who became famous for his work with Ricardo Velázquez in the creation of the Palacio de Cristal (Crystal Palace) in Madrid's Retiro Park. Closed for years, and nearly torn down, Atocha was restored and refurbished by Spain's internationally acclaimed architect Rafael Moneo. ✉*Paseo de Atocha s/n, Retiro* ☎*91/420–9875.*

49 **Jardín Botánico** *(Botanical Garden).* Just south of the Prado Museum, the gardens provide a pleasant place to stroll or sit under the trees. True to the wishes of King Carlos III, they hold many plants, flowers, and cacti from around the world. ✉*Plaza de Murillo 2, Retiro* ☎*91/420–3017* 🌐*www.rjb.csic.es* 🎫*€2* ⏲*Nov.–Feb., daily 10–6; Mar. and Oct., daily 10–7; Apr. and Sept., daily 10–8; May–Aug., daily 10–9.*

55 **Museo Nacional de Artes Decorativas.** This palatial building showcases 60,000 textiles, pieces of furniture—including some installed in reconstructed period rooms—jewelry, ceramics, glass, crystal, and metalwork items. The collection, displayed in chronological order, starts with medieval and Renaissance items on the first floor and ends with the 18th- and 19th-century pieces on the top floor. The ground floor is taken up by temporary exhibitions and some avant-garde works. ✉*Montalbán 12, Cibeles* ☎*91/532–6499* 🌐*http://mnartesdecorativas.mcu.es* 🎫*€2.40, free Sun.* ⏲*Tues.–Sat. 9:30–3, Sun. 10–3. Guided tour, in Spanish only, Sun. at 11:30.*

52 **Real Fábrica de Tapices.** Tired of the previous monarchs' dependency on the Belgium and Flemish thread mills and craftsmen, King Philip V decided to establish the Royal Tapestry factory in Madrid in 1721. It was originally housed near Alonso Martínez, and moved to its current location in 1889. From early on some of Europe's best artists collaborated in the factory's tapestry designs. The most famous was Goya, who produced 63 cartoons (rough plans), some of which can be seen at the Prado Museum. It's said that he put so much detail into them that the craftsmen complained he'd made their work miserable. The factory, still in operation, applies traditional weaving techniques from the 18th and 19th centuries to modern and classic designs—including Goya's. Carpets are available for sale (you can suggest your own design), at skyrocketing prices (€840 a square meter [10-¾ square feet] for carpets, €9,000–€12,000 a square meter for tapestries). The factory also runs a training center that teaches traditional weaving techniques to unemployed teenagers, who later become craftspeople. ✉*Fuenterrabía 2, Atocha* ☎*91/434–0550* ⏲*Weekdays 9–2; guided tour every 45 min starting at 9.*

54 **San Jerónimo el Real.** Ferdinand and Isabella used this church and cloister as a *retiro,* or place of meditation—hence the name of the nearby park. The building was devastated in the Napoleonic Wars, then rebuilt in the late 19th century. ✉*Moreto 4, behind Prado Museum, Retiro* ☎*91/420–3578* ⏲*Daily 10–1 and 5–8:30.*

TAPAS BARS & CAFÉS

The best tapas areas are in the neighborhoods of La Latina, Chueca, Sol, Santa Ana, Salamanca, and Lavapiés. Trendy La Latina's best concentration of good tapas bars are in Plaza de la Paja and on Cava Baja, Cava Alta, and Almendro streets. Chueca is colorful and lively, and the tapas bars there reflect this casual and cheerful spirit in their food and decor. The bars around Sol are quite traditional (many haven't changed in decades), but the larger concentration of tourists and passersby there mean they don't always have to strive for the better food and service. In touristy Santa Ana, avoid the crowded and usually pricey tapas bars in the main plaza and instead get into the ones on the side streets. The tapas bars in the Salamanca neighborhood are more sober and traditional, but the food is often excellent. In Lavapiés, the neighborhood with the highest concentration of immigrants, there are plenty of tapas bars serving Moroccan, African, and Asian-inspired food.

Most of the commendable cafés you'll find in Madrid can be classified into two main groups. The ones that've been around for many years (Café Gijóon, Café del Círculo, Café de Oriente, Libertad 8), where writers, singers, poets, and discussion groups still meet and where conversations are usually more important than the coffee itself; and the new ones (Faborit, Diurno, Laan Café, Delic, Anglona), which are more tailored to the hip and hurried urbanite and tend to have a more varied product selection, modern decor and Wi-Fi access.

TAPAS BARS

CHUECA

★ **El Bocaíto.** This place has three dining areas and more than 130 tapas on the menu, including 15 to 20 types of *tostas* (toast topped with prawns, egg and garlic, pâté with caviar, cockles, and so on), and surely the best *pescaito frito* (deep-fried whitebait) in the city. ✉*Libertad 6, Chueca* ☎*91/532–1219* ⏲*Closed Sun. and Aug.*

★ **Gastromaquia.** Ordinary looking from the outside, this place hides a secret in the kitchen: chef Iván García, who used to run a fashionable restaurant but has traded the stressful demands of high cuisine for the pleasures of miniature creation. The menu isn't very long, and it certainly doesn't dig deep into your pocket. Try the blood-pudding risotto, stuffed tomatoes, bean salad, or grilled perch. ✉*Pelayo 8, Chueca* ☎*91/522–6413* ⏲*No dinner Sun. and Mon.; no lunch Tues.*

La Bardemcilla. This homey bar belongs to Javier Bardem's family—note the actor's family pictures on the walls. There are plenty of tables, and there's a good selection of wines and tapas. Highlights include the grilled vegetables, *huevos estrellados,* (fried eggs with potatoes and sausage), and the *croquetas* (béchamel and meat—usually chicken or ham—with a fried bread-crumb crust). There's a fixed-price lunch for less than €10. ✉*Augusto Figueroa 47, Chueca* ☎*91/521–4256* ⏲*Closed Sun. No lunch Sat.*

2

LA LATINA

Casa Lucas. Some of the favorites at this small, cozy bar with a short but creative selection of homemade tapas include the *Carinena* (grilled pork sirloin with caramelized onion), *Madrid* (scrambled eggs with onion, *morcilla,* or blood pudding, and pine nuts in a tomato base), and *huevos a la Macarena* (puff pastry with mushrooms, fried artichokes, fried ham, béchamel, and pine nuts). ✉*Cava Baja 30, La Latina* ☎*91/365–0804* ⏲*No lunch Wed.*

El Almendro. Getting a weekend seat in this rustic-looking old favorite is quite a feat. Drop by any other time and you'll be served great *roscas* (round hot bread filled with various types of cured meats), *huevos rotos* (fried eggs with potatoes), *pistos* (sautéed vegetables with a tomato base), or *revueltos* (a favorite is the *habanero,* scrambled eggs with fava beans and blood pudding). Note that drinks and food need to be ordered separately (a bell rings when your food is ready). ✉*Almendro 13, La Latina* ☎*91/365–4252.*

★ **Juana la Loca.** This tempting spot serves sophisticated and unusual tapas that can be as pricey as they are delightful (don't miss the *tortilla de patatas*—Spanish omelet). If you drop by the bar during the weekend, go early: the tapas will be at their freshest. On weekdays, order by the menu. ✉*Plaza Puerta de Moros 4, La Latina* ☎*91/364–0525* ⏲*Closed Mon.*

Matritum. This is one of those places where the wine list is three times the size of the food menu. Matritum is also quieter and cozier than most of the other places in this bar-filled neighborhood. Some of the star tapas include *patatas a los cinco quesos* (five-cheese potatoes), *vieiras gratinadas* (grilled grated scallops), and *delicias de berenjena* (eggplant in three textures with sun-dried tomatoes and goat cheese). ✉*Cava Alta 17, La Latina* ☎*91/365–8237* ⏲*No lunch weekdays.*

Taberna de Cien Vinos. If you're a wine buff, don't leave La Latina without stopping here. Have one of the many Spanish wines available by the glass with the dish of the day. ✉*Nuncio 17, La Latina* ☎*91/365–4704* ⏲*Closed Mon. No dinner Sun.*

LAVAPIÉS

La Bodega de Lete. This place shares the laid-back spirit of the neighborhood in its bold colors and unassuming decor, but it's for the simple yet superb *raciones* (large portions for several to share) that people choose to wait for one of its six tables. Share an *entraña* (a cut of grilled beef), the *patatas chimichurri* (potatos with a sauce of garlic, oregano, and parsley), or the Atlantic salad—all with the young house Rioja—yet still smile with satisfaction when the tab comes. ✉*Buenavista 42, Lavapiés* ☎*91/530–0259* ⏲*Closed Mon. No dinner Sun. No lunch Tues.–Fri.*

MALASAÑA

Bodega de la Ardosa. Big wooden barrels serve as tables at this charming tavern with more than 100 years of history. There's great vermouth and draft beer, along with specialties such as *salmorejo* (thick, cold tomato soup that's similar to gazpacho), a very juicy *tortilla de patatas* (Spanish omelet) made by the owner's mother, and *croquetas,* including varieties with béchamel and prawns (*carabineros*) as well as aromatic cheese (*Cabrales*). You'll always hear a good selection of jazz here. ✉*Colon 13, Malasaña* ☎*91/521–4979.*

PALACIO

★ **Taberneros.** This museumlike wine bar has wine racks and decanters exhibited all over the tavern, and a menu that includes both local specialties (*croquetas,* grilled mussels, duck sirloin, fresh liver) and Asian-inspired ones (tuna burger, sirloin in soy sauce). A tapas sampler and a weekly lunch menu are also available. Show up early or prepare to wait awhile. ✉*Santiago 9, Palacio* ☎*91/542–2460* ⊗*Closed Mon.*

RETIRO

★ **Laredo.** The nine tables here are some of the most sought after in the city—you need to reserve two or three days in advance—but you can also walk in and order at the bar. Variety and quality walk hand in hand here: Laredo serves fresh and simple food (asparagus, prawns, and clams), as well as more scrumptous and elaborate dishes, such as the superb mushroom risotto with duck liver, rice with chicken, small rabbit chops, and mushroom *croquetas.* The exhaustive menu will tire out your eyes (it's better to follow the waiters' advice). ✉*Menorca 14, Retiro* ☎*91/573–3061* ⊗*Closed Sun and Aug.*

SALAMANCA

★ **Estay.** A two-story bar and restaurant with functional furnishings, this place has quickly become a landmark among the city's posh crowd. The tapas menu is plentiful and diverse. Specialties include the *tortilla española con atún y lechuga* (Spanish omelet with tuna fish and lettuce), and the *rabas* (fried calamari). There is a dish of the day for €12, and a few tapas samplers. ✉*Hermosilla 46, Salamanca* ☎*91/578–0470* ⊗*Closed Sun.*

Jurucha. If you're shopping in the Serrano area, this is the place to go for a quick bite. There's a long bar with all the food on display; tapas highlights include the *gambas con allioli* (prawns with a garlic-mayo sauce), fried *empanadillas* (small empanadas), and Spanish omelets. A small seating space has wooden stools, and there are tables at the back. ✉*Ayala 19, Salamanca* ☎*91/575–0098* ⊗*Closed Sun and Aug.*

BARRIO DE LAS LETRAS

Casienhuertas. The tapas menu here is overseen by chef Roberto Limas and includes juicy meat skewers and toasts as well as such outstanding creations as fresh poached egg with fried bread, leek, and butter sauce (a customer favorite) and tempura-fried zucchini flower stuffed with rapsberry and mango. This place has quickly gained a reputation of its own in the Barrio de las Letras. It has an extensive wine menu with many hard-to-find French names. ✉*Lope de Vega 20, Barrio de las Letras* ☎*91/389–6188* ⊗*Sun. and Mon.*

El Cervantes. Clean, comfortable and very popular among locals, this place serves plenty of hot and cold tapas. A good choice here is the *pulpo a la gallega* (octopus with potatoes, olive oil, and paprika). You may also want to go for the tapas sampler. ✉*Plaza de Jesús 7, Barrio de las Letrasa* ☎*91/429–6093.*

La Dolores. Usually crowded and noisy, this bar serves one of the best draft beers in Madrid. It also has a decent selection of pricey tapas, which you can enjoy at one of the few tables in the back. ✉*Plaza de Jesús 4, Barrio de las Letras* ☎*91/429–2243.*

CAFÉS

CHAMBERÍ

Cacao Sampaka. Heaven on earth for any chocolate lover, the café–shop sells cute little paninis, tantalizing blends of fresh juices, a great selection of pastries, and, of course, chocolate in just about every form and flavor imaginable. ✉*Orellana 4, Chamberí* ☎*91/319–5840* ⏲*Closed Sun. except 1st Sun. of month.*

SOL

Café del Círculo *(La Pecera).* Spacious and elegant, with large velvet curtains, marble columns, hardwood floors, painted ceilings, and sculptures scattered throughout, this eatery inside the famous art center Círculo de Bellas Artes feels more like a private club than a café. Expect a bustling, intellectual crowd. ✉*Marqués de Casa Riera 2, Sol* ☎*91/522–5092.*

Chocolatería San Ginés. Gastronomical historians suggest that the practice of dipping explains the reason for Spaniards' lasting fondness for hot, thick chocolate. Only a few of the old places where this hot drink was served exclusively (with crisp churros), such as this *chocolateri,* remain standing. Open from 6 PM to 7 AM, it also has the privilege of being the last stop of the bleary-eyed after a night out. ✉*Pasadizo de San Ginés, enter by Arenal 11, Sol* ☎*91/365–6546* ⏲*Closed Mon.*

Faborit. A chain store bold enough to open next door to Starbucks had better serve some great coffee and for less money. Faborit does, and offers a warm, high-tech environment (a hanging screen displays the variety of coffees and teas and their prices) to boot. Whether your feet hurt and the sun is blazing, or it's chilly out and you're tired of shivering, indulge in the mug cappuccino with cream or the chai cappuccino—you'll still be able to splurge later. The café is two blocks away from the neighborhood Sol. ✉*Alcalá 21, Sol* ☎*91/521–8616.*

PALACIO

Café de Oriente. This landmark has a magnificent view of the Royal Palace and its front yard. Divided into two sections—the left one serves tapas and raciones and the right one serves more elaborate food—the café also has a splendid terrace that's open when the sun is out. ✉*Plaza de Oriente 2, Palacio* ☎*91/547–1564.*

MALASAÑA

El Jardin Secreto. This place has a romantic and exotic setting, with eclectic furniture and lamps (both for sale), savory chocolates, and a generous selection of tasty pastries. It's the perfect place to sip infusions and unwind. ✉*Conde Duque 2, Malasaña* ☎*91/364–5450.*

CHUECA

Areia. An old pub converted into a lounge, Areia is furnished with North African and Asian knickknacks and furniture. Cushioned seating in many forms (there's even an Asian-looking wood canopy bed in the back), very low lighting, and lots of nooks make this a cozy place to share a drink. Best to go in the afternoon or early at night to be sure you get a cushion of your own. ✉*Hortaleza 92, Chueca* ☎*91/310–0307.*

Café Gijón. Madrid's most famous literary café has hosted highbrow *tertulias* (discussion groups that meet regularly to hash out the political and artistic issues of the day) since the 19th century. ✉*Paseo de Recoletos 21, Chueca* ☎*91/521–5425.*

Café Libertad. More than just a café, this Madrid staple is a music and poetry venue—almost every famous songwriter, musician, and poet has passed through this decadent and charming, evenings-only hangout (it opens at 4 PM and entertainment starts at 9 PM). ✉*C. de la Libertad 8, Chueca* ☎*91/532–1150* 🌐*www.libertad8cafe.com.*

Diurno. A Chueca landmark, this café, DVD rental stop, and takeout is the type of place where you'd expect to run into your yoga teacher. Spacious, with large windows facing the street, sleek white chairs and couches, and lots of plants, Diurno serves healthful snacks and sandwiches as well as indulgent coffee-shop desserts. ✉*San Marcos 37, Chueca* ☎*91/522–0009.*

La Sueca. Light plays an important role in the Scandinavian-esque decor of this inviting space, where there are stripped wood floors, leather stools in primary colors, and large, white-wood tables. Besides the savory Baileys Irish Cream and chocolate cakes, La Sueca also carries baked potatoes with different toppings. ✉*Hortaleza 67, Chueca* ☎*91/319–0487.*

Maison Blanche. In front is a gourmet shop selling bagels as well as other breads, rice, and pastas, and in back is a restaurant-café with white-marble floors and iron columns painted white. On offer are international dishes such as crepes, couscous, pastas, and salads. If you have a sweet tooth, don't miss the tiramisu or chocolate cake. ✉*C. Piamonte 10, Chueca* ☎*91/522–8217* ⏲*Closed Sun. nights after 5* PM.

LA LATINA

Anglona. A good option for those dining in La Latina neighborhood, this small café serves a variety of hot chocolates (with cognac, caramel, mint, and more) and imported teas, as well as some sweets, including chocolate cake, carrot cake, and custard crème millefeuille. At night, with jazz or bossanova in the background, customers go for the *mojitos* (a cocktail made of rum, fresh mint and lime juice) and the *caipirinhas* (a Brazilian drink made with lime and sugar cane liquor). ✉*Príncipe de Anglona 3, La Latina* ☎*91/365–0587* ⏲*Closed Mon.*

Delic. This warm and inviting café is a hangout for Madrid's trendy crowd. Besides the *patatitas con mousse de parmesano* (potatoes with a Parmesan-cheese mousse) and zucchini cake, homesick travelers will find carrot cake, brownies, and pumpkin pie among the selections. ✉*Costanilla de San Andrés 14, Plaza de la Paja, La Latina* ☎*91/364–5450* ⏲*Closed Mon. and Aug. 1–15.*

2

WHERE TO EAT

The current variety of food options and the riveting decor of some of the better restaurants in Madrid put the city on par with other European capitals when it comes to dining. Top Spanish chefs, who often team up with hotels, fearlessly borrow from other cuisines and reinvent traditional dishes. The younger crowd as well as movie celebrities and artists flock to the casual Malasaña, Chueca, and La Latina neighborhoods, for the affordable restaurants and tapas bars with truly scintillating small creations. When the modern gets tiresome, faithful *madrileños*—from ministers to students—crave the traditional and seek out such local enclaves as Casa Ciriaco, Casa Botín, and Casa Paco for some unpretentious and hearty home cooking.

THE CUISINE

Madrid's traditional cuisine is based on the roasts and thick soups and stews of Castile, Spain's high central *meseta* (plain). Roast suckling pig and lamb are standard Madrid feasts, as are baby goat and chunks of beef from Ávila and the Sierra de Guadarrama. *Cocido madrileño* and *callos a la madrileña* are local specialties. The white and green asparagus, formerly grown by the kings in Aranjuez and now coming from other regions, are also favorites. *Cocido* is a hearty winter meal of broth, garbanzo beans, vegetables, potatoes, sausages, pork, and hen. The best cocidos are simmered in earthenware crocks over coals and served in three courses: broth, beans, and meat. Cocido anchors the midday winter menu in the most elegant restaurants as well as the humblest holes-in-the-wall. *Callos* are simpler concoctions of veal tripe stewed with tomatoes, onions, hot paprika, and garlic. *Jamón serrano* (serrano ham)—a specialty from the livestock lands of Teruel, Extremadura, and Andalusia—has become a Madrid staple; wanderers are likely to come across bars and restaurants where legs of the dried delicacy dangle in store windows or in bars.

The house wine in basic Madrid restaurants is often a sturdy, uncomplicated Valdepeñas from La Mancha. Serious dining is normally accompanied by a Rioja or a more powerful, complex Ribera de Duero, the latter from northern Castile. Ask your waiter's advice; a smooth Rioja, for example, may not be up to the task of accompanying a cocido or a roast suckling pig. After dinner, try the anise-flavor liqueur (*anís*) produced outside the nearby village of Chinchón.

BEST BETS FOR MADRID DINING

Need a cheat sheet for Madrid's thousands of restaurants? Fodor's writers have selected some of their favorites by price, cuisine, and experience in the lists shown here. You can also search by neighborhood or find specific details about a restaurant in our full reviews—just peruse the following pages. Happy dining in Spain's capital. ¡Buen provecho!

Fodor'sChoice ★

Asiana, $, Chueca

Casa Paco, $$$, La Latina

El Chaflán, $$$$, Chamartín

Goizeko Wellington, $$$$, Salamanca

La Broche, $$$$, Chamberí

La Trucha, $-$$, Barrio de las Letras

Zalacaín, $$$$, Salamanca

HIGHLY RECOMMENDED

Arabia, $, Chueca

Boccondivino, $$$, Salamanca

Casa Benigno, $$$, Chamartín

Casa Botín, $$-$$$, La Latina

Casa Ciriaco, $$, La Latina

Dassa Bassa, $$$, Salamanca

El Landó, $$$, La Latina

Espacio Alboroque, $$$$, Antón Martín

La Biblioteca del Santo Mauro, $$$$, Chamberí

La Gamella, $$$, Retiro

La Gastroteca de Santiago, $$$, Ópera

La Terraza—Casino de Madrid, $$$$, Sol

Le Petit Bistro, $$-$$$, Barrio de las Letras

Santceloni, $$$$, Chamberí

Taberna Bilbao, $-$$, La Latina

Viridiana, $$$$, Retiro

By Price

¢

Bazaar, Chueca

Casa Mingo, Moncloa

La Finca de Susana, Centro

Nueva Galicia, Sol

$

Arabia, Chueca

La Musa, Malasaña

Mercado de la Reina, Chueca

Pulcinella, Chueca

Taberna Bilbao, La Latina

$$

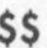

Casa Ciriaco, La Latina

Champagnería Gala, Antón Martín

Le Petit Bistro, Barrio de las Letras

Paulino de Quevedo, Chamberí

$$$

Boccondivino, Salamanca

Citra, Salamanca

Dassa Bassa, Salamanca

La Gamella, Retiro

La Gastroteca de Santiago, Ópera

Sacha, Chamartín

$$$$

El Chaflán, Chamartín

Espacio Alboroque, Anton Martín

Goizeko Wellington, Salamanca

La Terraza—Casino de Madrid, Sol

Viridiana, Retiro

By Cuisine

TRADITIONAL SPANISH

Casa Botín, $$–$$$, La Latina

Casa Ciriaco, $$, Palacio

El Landó, $$$, La Latina

La Bola, $$, Ópera

CONTEMPORARY SPANISH

Citra, $$$, Salamanca

Dassa Bassa, $$$, Salamanca

Espacio Alboroque, $$$$, Anton Martín

Goizeko Wellington, $$$$, Salamanca

La Gastroteca de Santiago, $$$, Ópera

Sacha, $$$, Chamartín

Zalacaín, $$$$, Salamanca

EXPERIMENTAL CUISINE

Asiana, $$$$, Chueca

La Broche, $$$$, Chamberí

La Terraza—Casino de Madrid, $$$$, Sol

Santceloni, $$$$, Chamberí

Viridiana, $$$$, Retiro

TAPAS

Citra, $$$, Salamanca.

El Bocaíto (tapas bar), Chueca

Estay (tapas bar), Salamanca

Gastromaquia (tapas bar), Chueca

Juana la Loca (tapas bar), La Latina

Laredo (tapas bar), Retiro

La Trucha, $–$$, Barrio de las Letras

Mercado de la Reina, $–$$, Chueca

Paulino de Quevedo, ¢¢, Chamberí

Taberna Bilbao, $–$$, La Latina

Taberneros (tapas bar), Palacio

For tapas-bar listings, see previous section of chapter.

STEAK HOUSE

Asador Casa Matias, $$$ Plaza España

Asador Frontón I, $$$, Lavapiés

Casa Paco, $$$, La Latina

Julián de Tolosa, $$$–$$$$, La Latina

PAELLA

Casa Benigno, $$$, Chamartín

Champagnería Gala, $$, Antón Martín

SEAFOOD

El Pescador, $$$–$$$$, Salamanca

La Trainera, $$$$, Salamanca

By Experience

BEST BANG FOR YOUR BUCK

Arabia, $, Chueca

Bazaar, ¢–$, Chueca

Le Petit Bistro, $$–$$$, Barrio de las Letras

Pulcinella, $–$$, Chueca

Taberna Bilbao, $–$$, La Latina

QUAINT & COZY

Arabia, $, Chueca

Casa Benigno, $$$, Chamartín

Come Prima, $$$, Barrio de las Letras

Genoveva de Barri, $$, Ópera

La Galette, $$, Salamanca

Le Petit Bistro, $$–$$$, Barrio de las Letras

Sacha, $$$, Chamartín

YOUNG & HAPPENING

Al Norte, $$$, Palacio Real

La Musa, ¢–$, Malasaña

Le Dragon, $$, Salamanca

Mercado de la Reina, $–$$, Chueca

Nina, $–$$, Malasaña

SUMMER DINING

Bokado, $$$–$$$$, Moncloa

La Biblioteca del Santo Mauro, $$$$, Chamberí

La Terraza—Casino de Madrid, $$$$, Sol

Pedro Larumbe, $$$–$$$$, Salamanca

Sacha, $$$, Chamartín

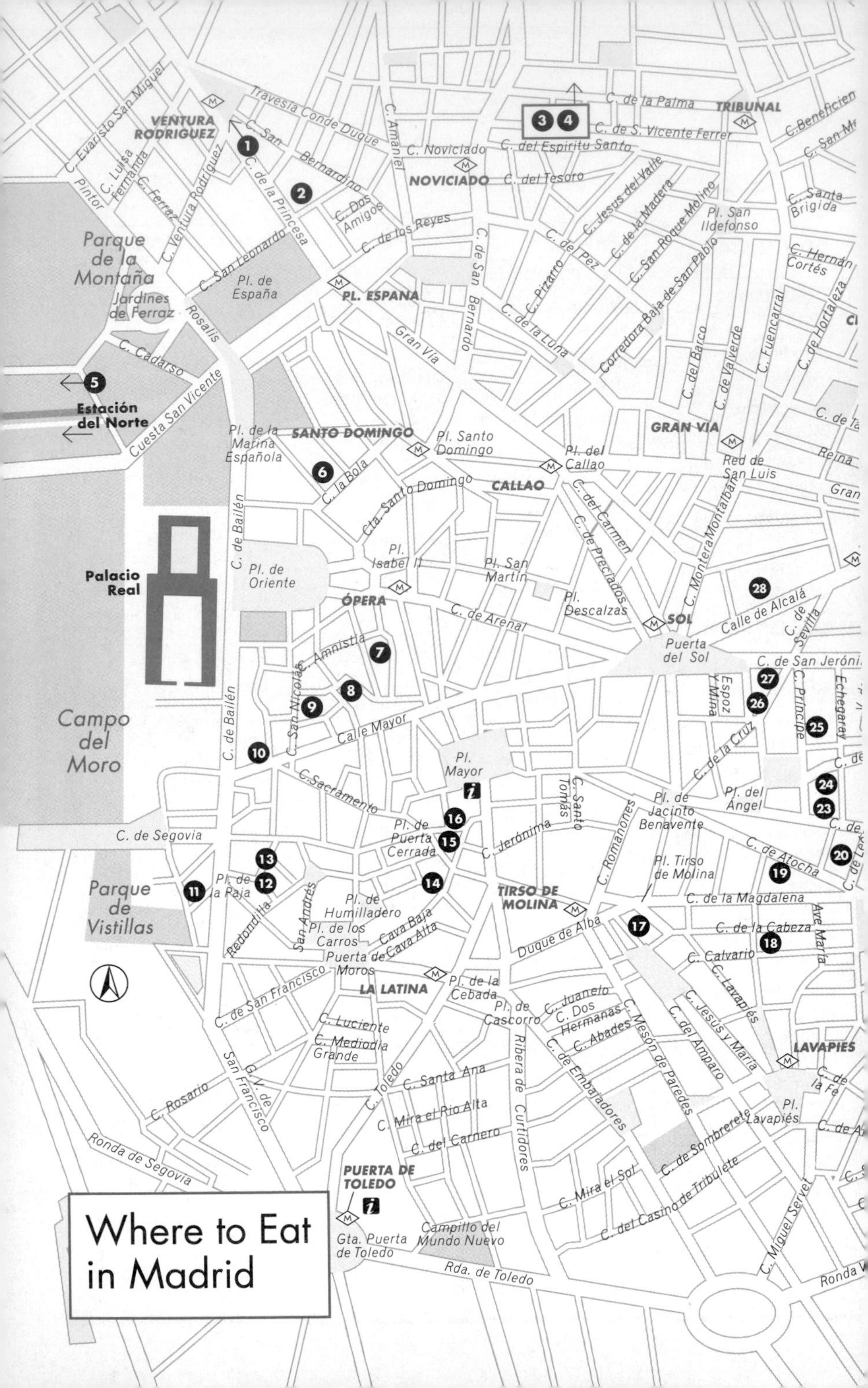

Where to Eat in Madrid
Parque de la Montaña
Jardines de Ferraz
Estación del Norte
Palacio Real
Campo del Moro
Parque de Vistillas
Pl. de España
PL. ESPAÑA
VENTURA RODRIGUEZ
NOVICIADO
TRIBUNAL
SANTO DOMINGO
CALLAO
GRAN VIA
ÓPERA
SOL
TIRSO DE MOLINA
LA LATINA
LAVAPIES
PUERTA DE TOLEDO
Pl. de Oriente
Pl. Isabel II
Pl. San Martín
Pl. Descalzas
Pl. Santo Domingo
Pl. del Callao
Pl. de la Marina Española
Puerta del Sol
Pl. Mayor
Pl. de Puerta Cerrada
Pl. de la Paja
Pl. de Humilladero
Pl. de los Carros
Puerta de Moros
Pl. de la Cebada
Pl. de Cascorro
Pl. de Jacinto Benavente
Pl. Tirso de Molina
Pl. del Ángel
Pl. Lavapiés
Pl. San Ildefonso
Red de San Luis
Gta. Puerta de Toledo
Campillo del Mundo Nuevo
Gran Vía
Calle Mayor
Calle de Alcalá
C. de Arenal
C. de Bailén
C. de Segovia
C. de la Princesa
C. San Bernardino
Travesía Conde Duque
C. de la Palma
C. de S. Vicente Ferrer
C. del Espiritu Santo
C. del Tesoro
C. Noviciado
C. Amaniel
C. de San Bernardo
C. de los Reyes
C. Dos Amigos
C. San Leonardo
C. Ventura Rodriguez
C. Evaristo San Miguel
C. Luisa Fernanda
C. Ferraz
Pintor Rosales
C. Cadarso
Cuesta San Vicente
C. la Bola
Cta. Santo Domingo
C. del Carmen
C. de Preciados
C. Montera
C. de la Luna
C. de Pez
C. Pizarro
C. Jesus del Valle
C. de la Madera
C. San Roque
Corredera Baja de San Pablo
C. del Barco
C. de Valverde
C. Fuencarral
C. de Hortaleza
C. Santa Brigida
C. Hernán Cortés
C. Beneficiencia
Reina
C. de San Jerónimo
C. de Sevilla
C. Príncipe
Echegaray
Espoz y Mina
C. de la Cruz
C. Santo Tomás
C. Romanones
C. Jerónima
C. de Atocha
C. de la Magdalena
C. de la Cabeza
Ave María
C. Calvario
C. Lavapiés
C. Jesús y María
C. del Amparo
C. Mesón de Paredes
C. de Embajadores
Duque de Alba
C. Juanelo
C. Dos Hermanas
C. Abades
Ribera de Curtidores
C. de la Fe
C. de Sombrerete
C. del Casino de Tribulete
C. Mira el Sol
C. Miguel Servet
Rda. de Toledo
Ronda de Segovia
C. de San Francisco
G.V. de San Francisco
C. Rosario
C. Toledo
C. Santa Ana
C. Mira el Rio Alta
C. del Carnero
C. Luciente
C. Mediodia Grande
Cava Baja
Cava Alta
San Andrés
Redondilla
C. Sacramento
C. San Nicolás
C. Amnistía

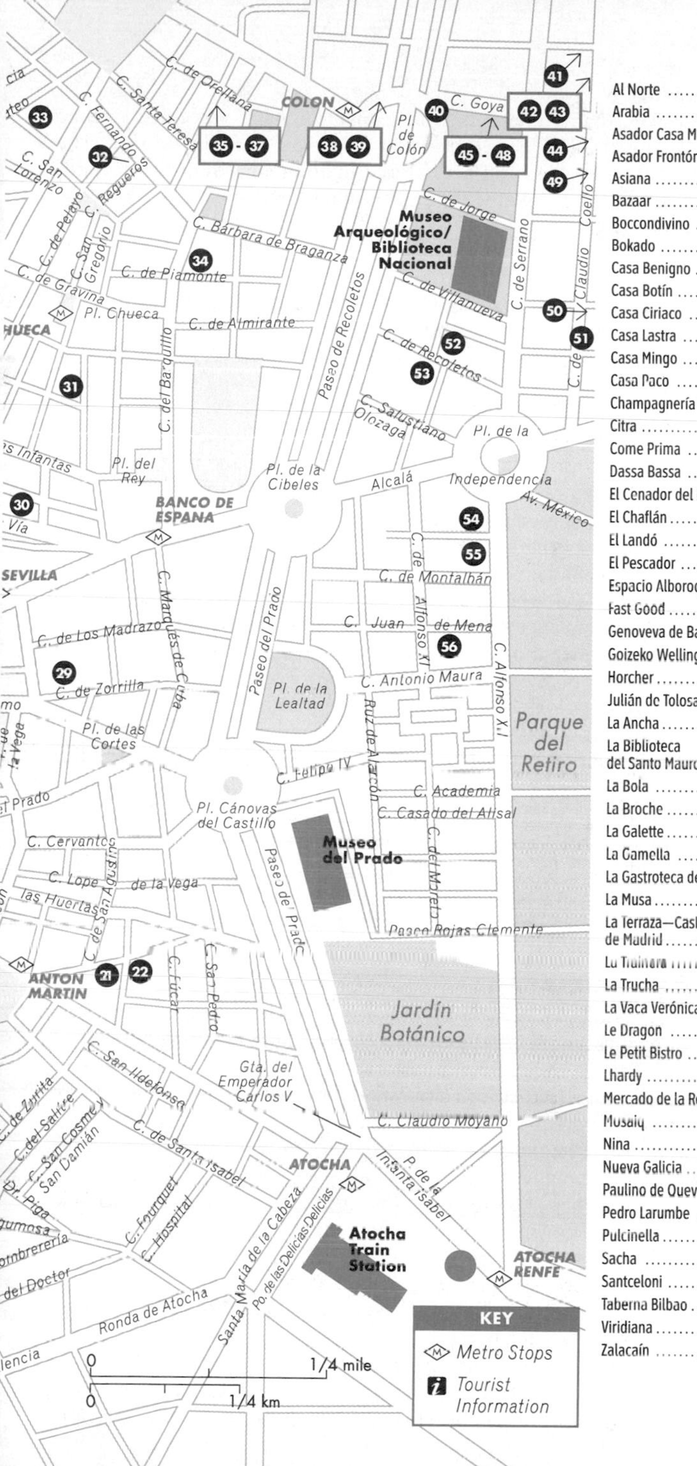

- Al Norte 9
- Arabia 34
- Asador Casa Matias 2
- Asador Frontón I. 17
- Asiana 33
- Bazaar 31
- Boccondivino 41
- Bokado 1
- Casa Benigno 46
- Casa Botín 16
- Casa Ciriaco 10
- Casa Lastra 18
- Casa Mingo 5
- Casa Paco 15
- Champagnería Gala 21
- Citra 49
- Come Prima 23
- Dassa Bassa 53
- El Cenador del Prado 24
- El Chaflán 40
- El Landó 11
- El Pescador 43
- Espacio Alboroque 19
- Fast Good 42
- Genoveva de Barri 7
- Goizeko Wellington 50
- Horcher 54
- Julián de Tolosa 14
- La Ancha 29
- La Biblioteca del Santo Mauro 37
- La Bola 6
- La Broche 39
- La Galette 51
- La Gamella 55
- La Gastroteca de Santiago 8
- La Musa 3, 12
- La Terraza—Casino de Madrid 28
- La Trainera 44
- La Trucha 25
- La Vaca Verónica 22
- Le Dragon 52
- Le Petit Bistro 20
- Lhardy 27
- Mercado de la Reina 30
- Mosaiq 35
- Nina 4
- Nueva Galicia 26
- Paulino de Quevedo 36
- Pedro Larumbe 45
- Pulcinella 32
- Sacha 38
- Santceloni 47
- Taberna Bilbao 13
- Viridiana 56
- Zalacaín 48

CHAMARTÍN

$$$$ Fodor's Choice ★ **El Chaflán.** Juan Pablo Felipe has converted what was once a venue for traditional Cantabrian cuisine into a temple of sophistication. The soothing pastel tones, indirect colored lighting, and minimalist atmosphere evoke comfort and style. The open kitchen gives you a view of the master chef at work. The dishes and the sampler menu change constantly to reflect the chef's innovative style. The seasonal highlights include a unique gazpacho (a transparent golden gelatin obtained from a mix of tomato water, olive oil, and vinegar, with cumin bread, pepper, and ham on top), an exceptionally creamy mushroom risotto, and savory red-tuna dishes. *Av. de Pio XII 34, Chamartín 91/345–0450 AE, DC, MC, V Closed Sun., Easter, and 2 wks in Aug. No lunch Sat.*

$$$ ★ **Casa Benigno.** Owner-creator Don Norberto takes gracious care in what he does by providing a carefully edited menu and some painstakingly selected wines and olive oils to enthusiastic customers. Inside a casual and understated hideaway, the few tables breathe craftsmanship in every corner. Enriching the experience are ceramic plates from Talavera, great Danish herring, the best rice in the city (cooked with extra-flat paella pans made especially for the restaurant), and a chef with an astounding knowledge of food, who markets his own brand of tuna, olive oil, and vinegar and generously talks with all his guests without ever looking at his watch. *Benigno Soto 9, Chamartín 91/416–9357 Reservations essential AE, DC, MC, V No dinner Sun. Closed Christmas and Easter wks.*

$$$ **Sacha.** Playful sketches decorate the walls of this French bistro–like restaurant filled with oversize antique furniture. The cuisine is provincial Spanish—with a touch of imagination. The *lasaña de erizo de mar* (sea urchin lasagna), *arroz con setas y perdiz* (rice with mushrooms and partridge), and the *Villagodio* (a thick grilled cut of beef) are some of the house specialties. *Juan Hurtado de Mendosa 11, Chamartín 91/345–5952 Reservations essential AE, DC, MC, V Closed Sun. and Aug.*

CHUECA & MALASAÑA

$$$$ Fodor's Choice ★ **Asiana.** Young chef Renedo and his Swedish colleague Andy Borman surprise even the most jaded palates in a unique setting—Renedo's mother's Asian antiques furniture store, which used to be a ham-drying shed. They bring to their job a bursting and contagious enthusiasm for cooking and experimentation as well as painstaking attention to detail. Sit among a Vietnamese bed, a life-size Buddha, and other merchandise for sale while enjoying the perfectly balanced and eclectic 10-dish fixed menu. Borman has departed from the former traditional Spanish cooking base drawing inspiration from his years in Thailand and Vietnam, and from his Scandinavian origins. The menu can be altered to meet special dietary needs. *Travesía de San Mateo 4, Chueca 91/310–4020 or 91/310–0965 Reservations essential MC, V Closed Sun. and Mon. No lunch.*

$–$$ **Mercado de la Reina.** Plentiful and inexpensive tapas and succulent larger portions—scrambled eggs with a variety of meats and vegetables, tasty local cheeses, and salads—make this large and tastefully decorated

(top left) Wine makers roll barrels of sherry in Cádiz, (top right) an Asturian house is tucked away in the region's verdant countryside, and (bottom) whimsical, scaly creatures adorn Gaudí's Casa Battlló.

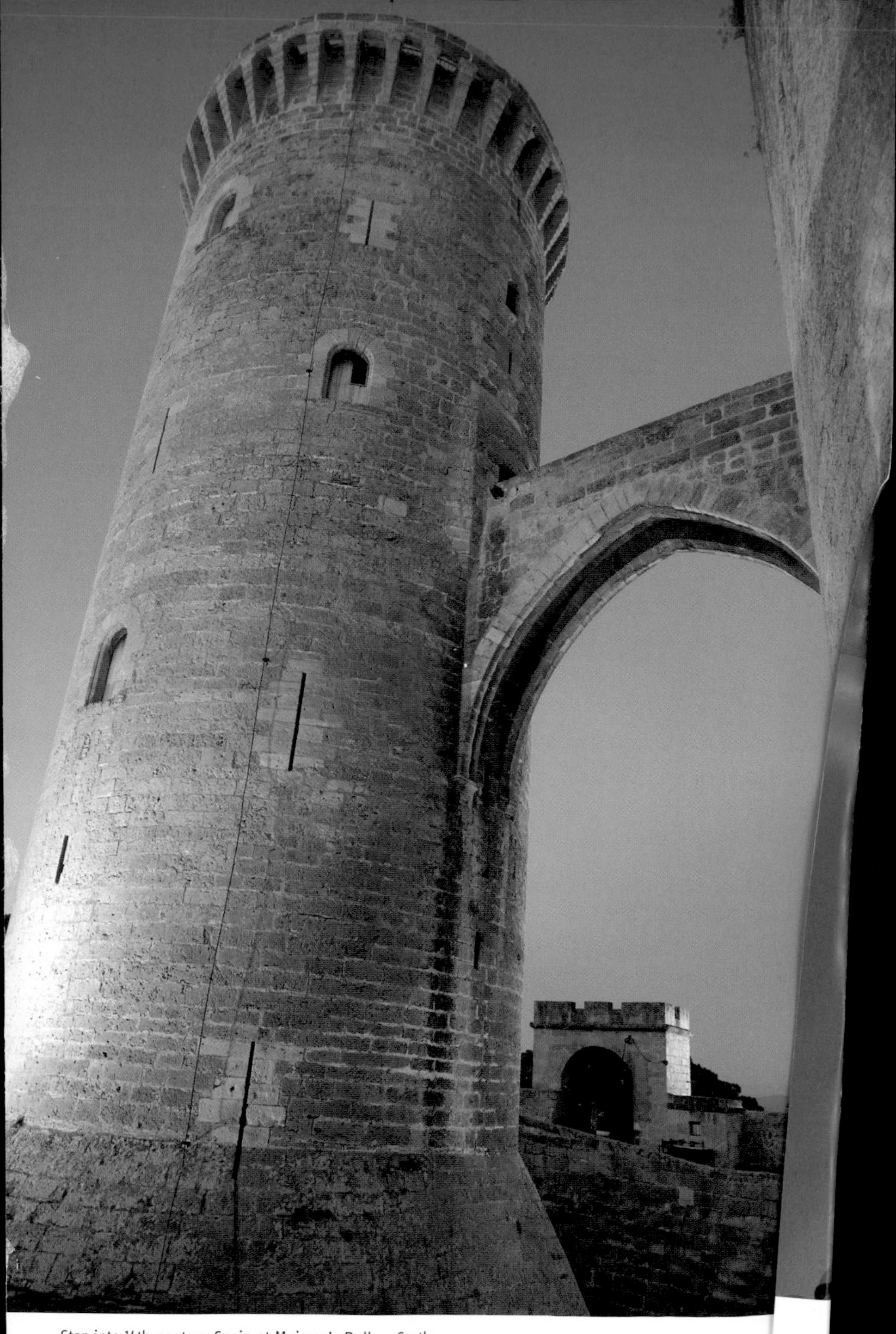

Step into 14th-century Spain at Majorca's Bellver Castle.

(top) Valencia's City of Arts & Sciences complex abuts the Turia River. (bottom) Alcazaba is the original fortress of Granada's Moorish marvel, Alhambra.

(top left) Viura grapes are harvested for white wine in the Rueda region, (top right) candles reflect pilgrims' devotion at Montserrat's monastery, (bottom) and a Moroccan Barbary Ape sits atop a cannon in Gilbraltar.

An architectural triumph of titanium, the Guggenheim Museum is Bilbao's top attraction.

(top left) Galicia's Celtic roots pop up near Torre de Hercules in its modern port city of A Coruña, (top right) Tapas entice in Jerez de la Frontera. (bottom) In Olite, the parador originated as a French-style castle.

(top) Guernica at the Queen Sofía Art Center is one of Picasso's works not to be missed in Madrid. (bottom) Men dressed with cow bells try to scare off evil spirits during La Endiablada in Cuenca.

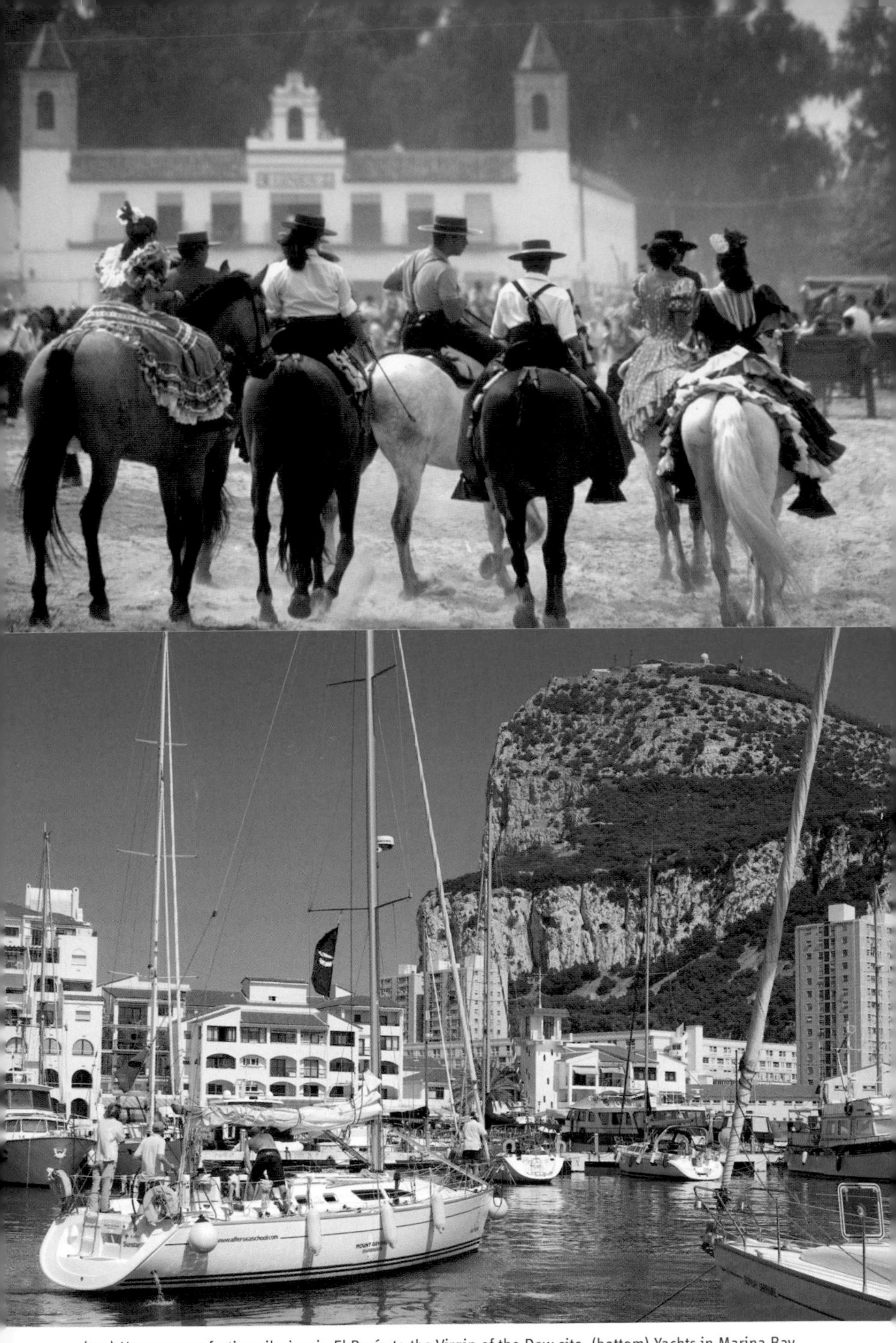

(top) Horses carry festive pilgrims in El Rocío to the Virgin of the Dew site. (bottom) Yachts in Marina Bay transport vacationers around the Rock.

bar–restaurant a very handy stop for people who want to replenish themselves without having to sit through a long meal. Where else can you sip a beer standing next to an olive tree? There's also a more formal dining area with long tables where groups and families can share some of the more elaborate meat and fish options; a bar and lounge downstairs accommodates those who want to keep the night rolling. ✉*Gran Vía 12, Centro* ☎*91/521–3198* ▭*AE, MC, V.*

MEALTIMES

Madrileños tend to eat their meals even later than people in other parts of Spain, and that's saying something. Restaurants open for lunch at 1:30 and fill up by 3. Dinnertime begins at 9, but reservations for 11 are common, and a meal can be a lengthy (up to three hours) affair. If you face hunger meltdown several hours before dinner, make the most of the early-evening tapas hour.

2

$–$$ ✕**Nina.** One of the first local restaurants to bring sophistication and refinement to a neighborhood best known for its wild and unrestricted spirit, Nina is in an airy loft-like interior with high ceilings, iron columns, exposed brick-and-alabaster walls, and dark hardwood floors. Waiters dressed in black serve the creative Mediterranean cuisine with an Eastern touch to a mostly young and hip crowd. Highlights include the goat cheese *milhojas* (pastry puffs), glazed codfish, *bacalao* (salt cod) with honey sauce and the venison and mango in a mushroom sauce. It has a good weekday fixed-price lunch menu and serves brunch on the weekends. ✉*Manuela Malasaña 10, Malasaña* ☎*91/591–0046* ⏲*AE, DC, MC, V.*

$–$$ ✕**Pulcinella.** Tired of not being able to find a true Italian restaurant in the city, owner Enrico opened up this homey trattoria, filled with memorabilia of Italian artists. It seems like a direct transplant from Naples. Superb pastas and the best pizzas in the city cooked in a brick oven are the stars here. ✉*Regueros 7, Chueca* ☎*91/319–7363* ✍*Reservations essential* ▭*AE, DC, MC, V.*

$ ★ ✕**Arabia.** After you cross the heavy wool rug hanging at this restaurant's entrance, you may feel as if you've entered a warm Aladdin's cave, decorated with adobe, wood, brass work, whitewashed walls, and lavish palms. Full of young boisterous madrileños, it's a great place to get such elaborate Moroccan dishes as stewed lamb with honey and dry fruits or a vegetarian favorite such as couscous with milk and pumpkin. To start, try the best falafel anywhere outside of Morocco or the yogurt cucumber salad. Be sure to make a reservation if you want to eat here on the weekend. ✉*Piamonte 12, Chueca* ☎*91/532–5321* ⏲*Closed Mon. No lunch Tues.–Fri.*

¢–$ ✕**Bazaar.** Owners of La Finca de Susana opened up this Chueca restaurant, which resembles an old-fashioned convenience store. Done in tones of white, Bazaar serves low-price and creative Mediterranean food of reasonable quality in a trendy environment. The square-shape upper floor has big windows facing the street, high ceilings, columns, and hardwood floors; the downstairs is bigger although less interesting. While watching the young passersby through the large windows upstairs, order the tuna *rosbif* (roasted and sliced thinly like beef) with mango chutney, or the tender ox with Parmesan and arugula. For dessert, a popular choice is the *chocolatísimo* (chocolate soufflé). To get a table, arrive by 1 for lunch and by 8:30 for dinner. ✉*C. Libertad 21, Chueca* ☎*91/523–3905* ✍*Reservations not accepted* ▭*MC, V.*

¢–$ ✕**La Musa.** The trendy, elegant vibe and the creative and inexpensive menu of unique salads and tapas (try the *bomba,* a potato filled with meat or vegetables in a spinach sauce, or the huge meat and vegetable brochettes) draw a stylish young crowd. There's a breakfast menu during the week as well as a good fixed-price lunch menu. Just a few blocks away the same owners have another restaurant, Ojalá (Calle San Andrés 1). The menu is more or less the same, but Ojalá also has a chill-out room downstairs with white cushions and sand on the floor. There's a second, bigger La Musa in La Latina neighborhood; it also has a cocktail lounge. Show up early or expect to wait. ✉*Manuela Malasaña 18, Malasaña* ✍*Reservations not accepted* ☎*91/448–7558* ▭*AE, DC, MC, V.*

LA LATINA

$$$–$$$$ ✕**Julián de Tolosa.** This rustic, designer-decorated spot is famous for *alubias rojas* (red kidney beans) from the Basque town of Tolosa. The *ibérico* (acorn-fed) ham here is fine sliced and juicy, and the two-person *chuletón* (T-bone steak) is excellent. The *pimientos de piquillo* (roasted sweet red peppers) come to the table sizzling and may just be the best in the world. Try a Basque *txakolí*(tart, young white wine) with your first course and a Ribera de Duero later. Let maître d' and owner Angela talk you into a small flask of *pacharán,* the famous Basque sloe-berry liqueur, served over coffee. ✉*Cava Baja 18, La Latina* ☎*91/365–8210* ✍*Reservations essential* ▭*DC, MC, V* ⊙*No dinner Sun.*

$$$ Fodor'sChoice ★ ✕**Casa Paco.** This Castilian tavern wouldn't have looked out of place two or three centuries ago. Squeeze past the old, zinc-top bar, crowded with madrileños downing shots of Valdepeñas red wine, and into the tile dining rooms. Feast on thick slabs of red meat, sizzling on plates so hot that the meat continues to cook at your table. The Spanish consider overcooking a sin, so expect looks of dismay if you ask for your meat well done (*bien hecho*). You order by weight, so remember that a *medio kilo* is more than a pound. To start, try the *pisto manchego* (La Mancha version of ratatouille) or the Castilian *sopa de ajo* (garlic soup). ✉*Puerta Cerrada 11, La Latina* ☎*91/366–3166* ✍*Reservations essential* ▭*DC, MC, V* ⊙*Closed Sun. and Aug.*

$$$ ★ ✕**El Landó.** This *castizo* (authentic or highly traditional) restaurant with dark-wood-panel walls and lined with bottles of wine serves classic Spanish food. On the staircase that leads to the main dining area are pictures of famous celebrities who have eaten at this typically noisy landmark. Specialties of the house are *huevos estrellados* (fried eggs with potatoes and sausage), grilled meats, a good selection of fish (sea bass, haddock, grouper) with many different sauces, and steak tartare. As you sit down for your meal, you'll immediately be served a plate of bread with tomato, a salad, and Spanish ham. ✉*Plaza Gabriel Miró 8, La Latina* ☎*91/366–7681* ✍*Reservations essential* ▭*AE, DC, MC, V* ⊙*Closed Sun. and Aug.*

$$–$$$ ★ **Casa Botín.** The *Guinness Book of Records* calls this the world's oldest restaurant (1725), and Hemingway called it the best. The latter claim may be a bit over the top, but the restaurant *is* excellent and extremely charming (and so successful that the owners opened a "branch" in Miami, Florida). There are four floors of tile and wood-beam dining rooms, and, if you're seated upstairs, you'll pass ovens dating back centuries. Musical groups called *tunas* (mostly made up of students dressed in old costumes) often drop in to meander among the hordes. Specialties are *cochinillo* (roast pig) and *cordero* (roast lamb). It's rumored Goya washed dishes here before he made it as a painter. *Cuchilleros 17, off Plaza Mayor, La Latina 91/366–4217 AE, DC, MC, V.*

$$ ★ **Casa Ciriaco.** At Madrid's most traditional restaurant—host to a long list of Spain's illustrious, from royalty to philosophers and painters to bullfighters—expect simple home cooking in an unpretentious environment. You can get a flask of Valdepeñas or a split of a Rioja reserve to accompany the *perdiz con judiones* (partridge with broad beans). The *pepitoria de gallina* (hen in an almond sauce) is another favorite. *C. Mayor 84, La Latina 91/559–5066 AE, MC, V Closed Wed. and Aug.*

$–$$ ★ **Taberna Bilbao.** Run by a couple, this popular tavern—highly praised by local restaurant owners and restaurant goers—is somewhere between a tapas bar and a restaurant. It has three small dining areas, floor and walls of red Italian marble, plain wooden furniture, and a menu that is representative of Basque cuisine. Try any of the fish or mushroom *revueltos* (scrambled eggs), the *habas* (fava beans), or the *bacalao* (cod). And order a glass of *txakolí* (tart, young Basque white wine). *Costanilla de San Andrés 8, Plaza de la Paja, La Latina 91/365–6125 Reservations essential DC, MC, V Closed 1st 2 wks of Sept. and Feb. No lunch Mon.*

LAVAPIÈS & ANTÓN MARTÍN

$$$$ ★ **Espacio Alboroque.** Chef Andrés Madrigal unleashes his creativity in a completely rehabilitated 19th-century mansion with two dining floors filled with contemporary artwork. The young chef delivers to privileged customers a €75 eight-course joyful fixed menu that changes every two to three weeks. He and his team subtly reinvent such traditional dishes as sole meunière, royal hare (a traditional French dish made with stuffed, marinated hare and simmered for many hours; what's particular here is that they simmer it for many more hours than the average), and Andalusian shrimp omelet—a good choice here because the restaurant cooks all the ingredients separately before combining them. The restaurant has a mind-blowing wine cellar, and there's a courtyard for summer dining. *Calle Atocha, 34, Antón Martín 91/389–6570 AE, DC, MC, V No lunch weekends, no dinner Mon.*

$$$ **Asador Frontón I.** Fine meat and fish are the headliners here. Uptown's Asador Frontón II is swankier, but this downtown original is more charming. Appetizers include *anchoas frescas* (fresh grilled anchovies) and *pimientos rellenos con bacalao* (peppers stuffed with cod). The huge *chuletón* (T-bone steak), seared over charcoal and sprinkled with

sea salt, is for two or more; order *cogollo de lechuga* (lettuce hearts) to accompany. The *cogotes de merluza* (hake jowls) are supremely light and aromatic. ✉*Tirso de Molina 7, entrance on Jesus y Maria, 1, Lavapiés* ☎*91/369–1617* ✍*Reservations essential* ▭*AE, DC, MC, V* ⊙*Closed 1 wk in Aug. No dinner Sun.*

$$–$$$ ★ ✕**Le Petit Bistro.** Carlos and his wife, Frederique, took on a great challenge to convert what was once a bullfighting-theme tavern into a Parisian bistro. Although some elements, such as the long brass copper bar, hint at its *castizo* (authentic as in old and traditional) origins, there's much that's truly French here, including the service, a superb Sunday brunch, and the wine and cocktails. Specialties include brie *croquetas* (in a bread-crumb crust and deep fried), the assortment of oysters, and the chateaubriand steak with butter, tarragon, and white vinegar. ✉*Plaza de Matute 5, Barrio de las Letras* ☎*91/429–6265* ▭*AE, MC, V* ⊙*Closed Mon. No dinner Sun.*

$$ ✕**Casa Lastra.** Established in 1926, this Asturian tavern is popular with Lavapiés locals. The rustic, half-tile walls are strung with relics from the Asturian countryside, including wooden clogs, cow bells, sausages, and garlic. Specialties include *fabada* (Asturian white beans stewed with sausage), *fabes con almejas* (white beans with clams), and *queso de cabrales,* aromatic cheese made in the Picos de Europa. Great hunks of crisp bread and hard Asturian cider complement a hearty meal; desserts include tangy baked apples. There's an inexpensive fixed-price lunch menu on weekdays. ✉*Olivar 3, Lavapiés* ☎*91/369–0837* ▭*MC, V* ⊙*Closed Wed. and July. No dinner Sun.*

$$ ✕**Champagnería Gala.** Hidden on a back street not far from Calle Atocha and the Reina Sofía museum, this cheerful Mediterranean restaurant is usually packed, thanks to the choice of paellas, *fideuás* (paellas with noodles instead of rice), risottos, and hearty bean and chickpea stews—all served with salad, dessert, and a wine jar. The same type of rice must be ordered for tables of four and fewer. The front dining area is modern and festive; the back room incorporates trees and plants in a glassed-in patio. ✉*Moratín 22, Antón Martín* ☎*91/429–2562* ✍*Reservations essential* ▭*No credit cards* ⊙*Closed Mon.*

$$ ✕**La Vaca Verónica.** In the golden-age literary quarter, this romantic little hideaway gathers a following for its *carne a la plancha* (grilled meat with potatoes and peppers), *pescado a la sal* (fish cooked in a shell of salt), homemade pastas with various seafood dressings, and terrific salads. The pasta *a los carabineros* (with scarlet shrimp) is seductive. ✉*Moratín 38, Antón Martín* ☎*91/429–7827* ▭*AE, DC, MC, V* ⊙*No lunch Sat.*

MONCLOA

$$$–$$$$ ✕**Bokado.** Chefs Mikel and Jesús Santamaría, best known for breaking ground in the world of tapas in both Navarra and the Basque Country, have brought their talent to Madrid. Away from the bustling city center and five minutes from Moncloa, the restaurant, a spacious, elegant, and design-rich setting, is part of the Museo del Traje's building. There's even a terrace and garden that's ideal for summer dining. The menu is a modern example of the fancy combinations that make Basque cuisine renowned, such as oysters, monkfish, haddock, stews, mushroom

delicacies, and savory game dishes. ✉*Av. Juan de Herrera 2, Moncloa* ☎*91/549–0041* ▭*AE, MC, V* ⊙*Closed Sun. and Mon.*

¢ ✕**Casa Mingo.** This bustling place, built into a stone wall beneath the Estación del Norte (across the street from the hermitage of San Antonio de la Florida), resembles an Asturian cider tavern. Expect to share long tables with other diners; the only items on the menu are succulent roast chicken, cheese, salad, and sausages, all to be taken with *sidra* (hard cider). Small tables are set up on the sidewalk in summer. If you don't come early (1 for lunch, 8:30 for dinner), you may have to wait for a table. ✉*Paseo de la Florida 34, Moncloa* ☎*91/547–7918* ✍*Reservations not accepted* ▭*No credit cards.*

PALACIO

$$$ ✕**Al Norte.** In the colonnaded bland brick building that looks completely out of place in the neighborhood, and near one of the oldest churches in Madrid, this sophisticated restaurant specializes in Atlantic, especially Asturian and Galician, dishes. This allows for a great variety of soups, stews, and meats (such as roasted piglet, wild boar, or venison) in winter; a good selection of salads and fish in summer; and regional staples such as *tortos,* the Austurian corn-and-wheat fried cakes, year-round. Other features include an elaborate and unusual ice-cream menu and a terrace for summer dining. ✉*San Nicolas 8, Palacio Real* ☎*91/547–2222 or 91/559–3604* ✍*Reservations essential* ▭*AE, DC, MC, V* ⊙*No dinner Sun.*

$$$ ✕**Asador Casa Matias.** Like Julián de Tolosa, its kin (with the same owner), this restaurant a block off Plaza de España draws crowds for its juicy meats (you can see the hearty portions of meat being grilled in the exposed kitchen) and its tender red peppers. The menu includes other good options, too, such as the thick stews or the whitefish dishes. The interior makes extensive use of wood and slate, and huge barrels full of cider are scattered around the two floors. The apple-green and deep-yellow walls and ceilings subdue the rustic look a bit. ✉*C. San Leonardo 12, Plaza España* ☎*91/541–7683 or 91/541–1046* ✍*Reservations essential* ▭*AE, DC, MC, V* ⊙*No dinner Sun.*

$$$ ★ ✕**La Gastroteca de Santiago.** Among the trendy new restaurants that force you to rest comfortably in the hands of a talented chef, this one offers the best value, with fixed-price menus that change every few weeks and expert wine advice. Here you'll see where contemporary creative Spanish cuisine is heading without having to guess what's on your plate. The restaurant sits only 16 people—the open kitchen is as big as the dining area—and offers a short (€42) and a long (€65) fixed-price menu. The long menu comprises five small appetizers, two main courses, a cheese sampler, and two desserts. There are some à la carte options for those without such a voracious appetite. ✉*Plaza de Santiago 1, Ópera* ☎*91/548–0707* ✍*Reservations essential* ▭*AE, MC, V* ⊙*Closed Sun.*

$$ ✕**Genoveva de Barri.** A few blocks from Palacio Real, this charming restaurant is on a *callejuela* (small street) that's easy to miss. Young chef and sommelier Gonzalo Lara broke away from his father (owner and chef of the acclaimed Laray) to experiment on his own. The result is a bare space with a handful of tables and a few baroque touches:

white-and-gold wallpaper, fringed mirrors, and a hanging crystal lamp. The short menu is full of surprises: duck tartare; scrambled eggs with lobster, asparagus, and mushrooms; and an unconventional, although expert, selection of wines. ✉*Espejo 10, Ópera* ☎*91/547–8014* *Reservations essential* ▭*AE, V* ⊙*Closed on Sun.*

$$ ✕**La Bola.** First opened as a *botellería* (wine shop) in 1802, La Bola developed slowly into a tapas bar and then a full-fledged restaurant. The traditional setting is the draw: the bar is original, and the dining nooks, decorated with polished wood, Spanish tile, and lace curtains, are charming. The restaurant belongs to the founding family, with the seventh generation currently in training. The house specialty is *cocido a la madrileña* (a hearty meal of broth, garbanzo beans, vegetables, potatoes, and pork). ✉*Bola 5, Ópera* ☎*91/547–6930* ▭*No credit cards* ⊙*No dinner Sun. Closed Sun. in Aug. No dinner Sat. in Aug.*

RETIRO

$$$$ ✕**Horcher.** The faithful continue to fill this very traditional shrine to fine dining, once Madrid's best restaurant. Wild boar, venison, hare, partridge, wild duck, as well as some very unique hamburgers (ostrich and turkey, monkfish, and swordfish) are standard fare. Fish and meat Stroganoff, pork chops with sauerkraut, and *baumkuchen* (a chocolate-covered fruit-and-cake dessert) reflect the restaurant's Germanic roots. The dining room is decorated with rust-color brocade and antique Austrian porcelain; an ample selection of French and German wines rounds out the menu. ✉*Alfonso XII 6, Retiro* ☎*91/522–0731* *Reservations essential* Jacket and tie ▭*AE, DC, MC, V* ⊙*Closed Sun. and Aug. No lunch Sat.*

$$$$ ★ ✕**Viridiana.** This place has a relaxed, somewhat cramped bistro feel, its black-and-white scheme punctuated by prints from Luis Buñuel's classic anticlerical film, the restaurant's namesake. Iconoclast chef Abraham Garcia says "market-based" is too narrow a description for his creative menu, which changes every two weeks. Some standard dishes include *foie de pato con chutney de rosas* (duck foie with rose chutney) and *huevos sobre mousse de hongos* (eggs on a mushroom mousse). Or try the superb duck pâté drizzled with sherry and served with Sauternes or Tokay wine. ✉*Juan de Mena 14, Retiro* ☎*91/531–1039* *Reservations essential* ▭*AE, MC, V* ⊙*Closed Sun. and wk before Easter.*

$$$ ★ ✕**La Gamella.** Some of the American-born former chef Dick Stephens's dishes—Caesar salad, hamburger, steak tartare—are still on the reasonably priced menu at this perennially popular dinner spot. The new selections are a fusion of Mediterranean and American dishes. The sophisticated rust-red dining room, batik tablecloths, oversize plates, and attentive service remain the same. The lunchtime *menú del día* (fixed menu) is a great value. ✉*Alfonso XII 4, Retiro* ☎*91/532–4509* ▭*AE, DC, MC, V* ⊙*Closed Sun. No lunch Sat.*

SALAMANCA & CHAMBERÍ

$$$$ Fodor'sChoice ★ ✕**Goizeko Wellington.** Aware of the more sophisticated palate of Spain's new generation of diners, the owners of the Madrilenean traditional dreamland that is Goizeko Kabi have opened a new restaurant that shares the virtues of its kin but none of its stuffiness. The menu deliv-

ers the same quality of *bacalaos* (codfish), *kokotxas de merluza* (hake jowls), and *chipirones encebollados* (baby squid sauteed in onions), and also includes pastas, risottos, and carpaccios. The decor blends citrus-yellow walls and indirect, intimate lighting with elements such as lattices and screens to help make things look warm and modern. ✉ *Villanueva 34, Salamanca* ☎ *91/577–6026* ⚠ *Reservations essential* ▭ *AE, DC, MC, V* ⊙ *Closed Sun. No lunch Sat. in July and Aug.*

$$$$ ★ ✕ **La Biblioteca del Santo Mauro.** After restoring the El Amparo restaurant to its former self, Vasque chef Carlos Posadas has brought his talent to this simply decorated restaurant in the former library of the Duke of Santo Mauro, inside the hotel of the same name. Here he delves into the realms of Mediterranean and classic Spanish cuisine to produce light and reinterpreted seasonal dishes using meat (pigeon, venison, veal) and fish (sea bass, hake, turbot). Diners are surrounded by tall antique wood bookshelves that contain some of the original volumes and still distill a noble aroma; on the weekends extra tables are set in the old dance room, and in summer clients can dine in the garden, which has some of the city's oldest chestnut trees. ✉ *C. Zurbano 36, Chamberí* ☎ *91/319–6900* ⚠ *Reservations essential* ▭ *AE, DC, MC, V.*

$$$$ Fodor's Choice ★ ✕ **La Broche.** Sergi Arola, a Ferran Adrià disciple, has vaulted directly to the top of Madrid dining. The minimalist dining room here allows you to concentrate on the hot-cold, surf-and-turf counterpoints of the seasonal menu. (Surf and turf has become a hallmark of the chef's style; playing with food temperature is also a distinctive trait.) The *menú de degustación* (sampler menu) permits Sergi and his staff to run you through contrasts, generally progressing from light to dark, fish to foie, seafood to tenderloin. ✉ *Miguel Angel 29, Chamberí* ☎ *91/399–3437* ⚠ *Reservations essential* ▭ *AE, DC, MC, V* ⊙ *Closed weekends, Easter wk, and Aug.*

$$$$ ✕ **La Trainera.** With its nautical theme and maze of little dining rooms, this informal restaurant is all about fresh seafood—the best that money can buy. Crab, lobster, shrimp, mussels, and a dozen other types of shellfish are served by weight in *raciones* (large portions). Although many Spanish diners share several plates of these shellfish as their entire meal, either the grilled hake, sole, or turbot makes an unbeatable second course. To accompany the legendary *carabineros* (giant scarlet shrimp), skip the listless house wine and go for a bottle of Albariño, from the southern Galician coast. ✉ *Lagasca 60, Salamanca* ☎ *91/576–8035* ▭ *AE, DC, MC, V* ⊙ *Closed Sun. and Aug.*

$$$$ ★ ✕ **Santceloni.** Santi Santamaría's Madrid branch of his Racó de Can Fabes (near Barcelona) has proved an immediate and major success in the Spanish capital. With one of the reigning troika of chief Spanish chefs, Santamaría serves in an elegant and sophisticated environment, where the service is equally impeccable as the food, exquisite combinations of Mediterranean ingredients accompanied by a comprehensive and daring wine list. Go with an appetite and lots of time (a minimum of three hours) because a meal here is ceremonious. If you're a meat lover, don't leave without trying the *jarrete* (veal shank). And if you love cheese you'll ga-ga over the splendid cheese sampler offered right before dessert. ✉ *Paseo de la Castellana 57, Chamberí* ☎ *91/210–8840*

Reservations essential *AE, DC, MC, V* *Closed Sun. and Aug. No lunch Sat.*

$$$$ Fodor's Choice ★ **Zalacaín.** This place introduced nouvelle Basque cuisine to Spain in the 1970s and has since become a Madrid classic. It's particularly known for using the best and freshest seasonal products available, as well as for having the best service in town. From the variety of fungi and game meat to the hard-to-find seafood served, the food here tends to be unusual—you won't find many of these sorts of ingredients, or dishes, elsewhere. The restaurant has a deep-apricot color scheme that is made more dramatic by dark wood and gleaming silver. Inside, you'll feel like you're in an exclusive villa. *Alvarez de Baena 4, Salamanca* *91/561–4840* *Reservations essential* Jacket and tie *AE, DC, V* *Closed Sun., Aug., and Holy Week. No lunch Sat.*

$$$–$$$$ **El Pescador.** Cross the rustic front door, and you'll forget you're in a city without a sea. Fishnets, anchors, and other fishing paraphernalia line the walls, but it's the smell that hints that this restaurant belongs to the best fish market in town. The owner is so proud of the freshness of his superb sole, turbot, grouper, and sea bass that the fish (oven-cooked, grilled, or with salsa) all come plain. The starters, an encyclopedia of seafood, include barnacles, crayfish, oysters, shrimp, and more. Quench your thirst with the Albariño white wine specially made for the house. *C. J. Ortega y Gasset 75, Salamanca* *91/402–1290 or 91/402–2304* *Reservations essential* *MC, V* *Closed Sun., Easter, and Aug.*

$$$–$$$$ **Pedro Larumbe.** This restaurant is literally the pinnacle of the ABC shopping center between Paseo de la Castellana and Calle Serrano. Dining quarters include a summer roof terrace (that turns into a lively bar after dinner) and an Andalusian patio. For over a decade chef-owner Pedro Larumbe has built himself a reputation for a market food that respectfully breaks away from tradition and which features such contemporary dishes as semi-wild duck with chickpea humus and red Swiss-chard, or codfish with a spider-crab stew and a roasted-pepper soup. The dessert buffet is an art exhibit. A good wine list complements the fare. *Paseo de la Castellana 34, at Calle Serrano 61, Salamanca* *91/575–1112* *AE, DC, MC, V* *Closed Sun. and Holy Week. No lunch Sat.*

$$$ ★ **Boccondivino.** After years of low-quality Italian restaurants, madrileños are witnessing the resurrection of Transalpine gastronomy, thanks to a handful of star-studded newcomers. Surely at the top of everybody's list is this Sardinian restaurant, decorated in gray and blue tones, whose menu is a feast for both the eye and the stomach. Dinners include *malloreddus* (a small shell-shape wheat pasta) either with sheep's-milk cheese and black truffle or eggplant and curd cheese; Carneroli rice risottos; and dishes made with spicy Italian pork sausages. Along with the painstakingly selected homemade cheeses, everything here feels more authentic than what Madrid is used to. There's also a good selection of savory and fruity wines from Sardinia and sweet delicacies such as *seada*, a pastry filled with milk-based curd and a special honey made with truffles. *C. Castelló 81, Salamanca* *91/575–7947* *AE, DC, MC, V* *Closed Sun.*

$$$ ✕ **Citra.** Young cooking wizard Elías Murciano understands that today's youngsters can be tomorrow's customers. That's why his sober yet elegant restaurant is separated into two well-defined areas. The bar and the tables next to the entrance allow for casual dining: customers are offered a selection of sophisticated tapas (smaller portions of the regular courses), and a five-tapas sampler for €25. The upper floor is where the daring but balanced creations of the young Venezuelan chef, trained in top-notch Spanish and French restaurants, achieve their greatest splendor: highlights include marinated salmon with an algae foam, mushroom risotto, superb venison steak, and delicious scallops over caramelized mushroom. For dessert, don't miss the chocolate soufflé. ✉ *C. Castelló, 18, Salamanca* ☎ *91/575–2866* ✍ *Reservations essential* ▭ *AE, MC, V* ⏲ *Closed Sun.*

$$$ ★ ✕ **Dassa Bassa.** What look like stairs leading you into a disco actually open up into an old underground coal bunker, now a trendy restaurant. The young chef Darrio Barrio combines conventional recipes with more adventuresome creations inspired by his stints with Adriá, Larumbe, and Subijana. The menu changes according to what's available in the market. Some recent highlights were sardines marinated in Moroccan tea, *verdinas* (small green beans) with pheasant, and caramelized suckling pig. ✉ *C. Villalar 7, Salamanca* ☎ *91/576–7397* ✍ *Reservations essential* ▭ *AE, DC, MC, V* ⏲ *Closed Sun. and Mon.*

$$ ✕ **La Galette.** This quaint place will satisfy both vegetarians and nonvegetarians. In the evening it's candlelighted, and baroque music plays in the background. Specialties include apple *croquetas* (béchamel and apple mixed in a bread-crumb crust and then deep-fried), spinach with tofu, onion soup, and zucchini soup. ✉ *C. Conde de Aranda 11, Salamanca* ☎ *91/576–0641* ▭ *AE, DC, MC, V.*

$$ ✕ **Le Dragon.** A more humble competitor to other big-shot Chinese restaurants such as Asia Gallery and Tse-Yang, Le Dragon attracts a younger, less stuffy crowd because of its tasteful combination of food (Chinese with a Japanese influence) and decor. Creatively using screens, panels, and lighting, the restaurant sets up an intimate and distinctive atmosphere between its many tables. The regulars go for the crispy duck, crispy noodles with shrimp, and dim sum. Another option is the extensive sampler menu for two or more people (€24 each). ✉ *C. Gil de Santivañes 2, Salamanca* ☎ *91/435–6668 or 91/435–6669* ✍ *Reservations essential* ▭ *AE, DC, MC, V.*

$$ ✕ **Paulino de Quevedo.** What appears to be a completely refurbished barn serves as the dining room for a big-name chef in traditional Spanish cooking who opened this second restaurant (the first is called Paulino) aimed at a more sophisticated crowd. The menu takes traditional dishes on a detour to create stars such as the grilled haddock with *calcots* (a type of tender scallion from Cataluña), or the fresh foie with sautéed corn and mango ice cream. Some of the best tapas in Madrid (main courses in miniature plus original creations) are served in the front casual dining area. The tablecloths and cutlery are both reminders of the owner's own *castizo* origins. ✉ *C. Jordán 7, Chamberí* ☎ *91/591–3929* ✍ *Reservations essential* ▭ *AE, DC, MC, V* ⏲ *Closed Sun. and Aug.*

$$ ✕**Mosaiq.** At this sumptuous restaurant, made fashionable by its trendy young crowd, the enclosed patio and its ceramic-tile and wrought-iron furniture are perfect for lunch or summer dining. Below it is an intimate dining area with transparent fabric used as partitions, cushioned seating, small leather stools, and large brass plates as tables. The top floor has a curtained area with colorful rolls of fabric that make you feel like you're having lunch in a textile market, plus another, more conventional dining area. The menu is traditional Moroccan with some not-so-risqué options to accommodate the Spanish taste; go for the sampler starter and any of the tagine or shawarma dishes. ✉*C. Caracas 21, Salamanca* ☎*91/308–4446* *Reservations essential* ▭*AE, MC, V.*

¢ ✕**Fast Good.** At the first location, the food was neither fast nor exceptionally good. With the opening of the second restaurant, the Ferran Adrià–sponsored project for healthful, creative, fresh fast food has improved, making this a great alternative dining and take-out option. The menu, divided into cold and hot choices, includes an interesting combination of gourmet salads with their own particular dressings, *bocatines* (finger sandwiches), hamburgers, paninis, fries fried in olive oil that is changed on a daily basis, fresh juice combinations, and three rich flavors of flan: chocolate, coffee, and fresh cheese. The decor is lively and meant to accommodate groups or those dining alone. ✉*C. Juan Bravo 3, Salamanca* ☎*91/577–4151.*

SOL, SANTA ANA & BARRIO DE LAS LETRAS

$$$$ ★ ✕**La Terraza—Casino de Madrid.** This rooftop terrace just off Puerta del Sol is in one of Madrid's oldest, most exclusive clubs (the *casino* is a club for gentlemen, not gamblers). The food is inspired and overseen by Ferran Adrià, who runs his own famous restaurant, El Bullí, near Roses in Catalonia. Francisco Roncero's creations closely follow Adrià's trademarks: try any of the light and tasty mousses, foams, and jellies, or indulge in the unique tapas—experiments of flavor, texture, and temperature. There's also a sampler menu. ✉*Alcalá 15, Sol* ☎*91/521–8700* *Reservations essential* ▭*AE, DC, MC, V* ⏲*Closed Sun. and Aug. No lunch Sat.*

$$$$ ✕**Lhardy.** Serving Madrid specialties for more than 150 years, Lhardy looks about the same as it must have on day one, with dark-wood paneling, brass chandeliers, and red-velvet chairs. Most people come for the traditional *cocido a la madrileña* (a hearty meal of broth, meat, and garbanzo beans) and *callos a la madrileña* (veal tripe stewed with onions and tomatoes). Game, sea bass, and soufflés are also available. Dining rooms are upstairs; the ground-floor entry doubles as a delicatessen and stand-up coffee bar that fills on chilly winter mornings with shivering souls sipping steaming-hot *caldo* (broth) from silver urns. ✉*Carrera de San Jerónimo 8, Sol* ☎*91/522–2207* ▭*AE, DC, MC, V* ⏲*Closed Aug. No dinner Sun.*

$$$ ✕**Come Prima.** There are fancier and surely more expensive Italian restaurants in the city, but none as warm or authentic. Decorated with black-and-white photos of Italian actors and movie scenes, the restaurant is divided into three nooks. The bistrolike front with the green-and-white checkered tablecloths is the most charming. The portions are large, eye-catching, and tastefully presented; diners love risottos such

as the Milanesa with lobster and the risotto porcini. The menu also offers fresh pasta dishes and surprises such as liver- or pumpkin-filled ravioli, and the timbale *Come Prima* (a molded pasta cake filled with vegetables). ✉ *C. Echegaray 27, Barrio de las Letras* ☎ *91/420–3042* ✍ *Reservations essential* ▭ *MC, V* ⊙ *No lunch Sun. and Mon.*

$$–$$$ ✕ **La Ancha.** The traditional Spanish menu includes some of the best lentils, meat cutlets, and croquettes in Madrid, as well as more elaborate dishes, such as the juicy *tortilla con almejas* (Spanish omelet with clams). Both locations of the restaurant belong to the same family and are unpretentious inside but are outstanding in terms of quality. The original Prícipe de Vergara location has a tented patio for the summer; the newer one behind the Congress is often filled with politicians. ✉ *Príncipe de Vergara 204, Chamartín* ☎ *91/563–8977* ✉ *Zorrilla 7, Centro* ☎ *91/429–8186* ▭ *AE, DC, MC, V* ⊙ *Closed Sun. and 1 wk in Aug.; Zorrilla branch closed 3 wks in Aug.*

$$ ✕ **El Cenador del Prado.** The name means "The Prado Dining Room," and the settings include a boldly painted dining area and plant-filled conservatory, as well as a separate baroque salon (a sitting area, mainly occupied by large groups). The innovative menu has French and Asian touches, as well as exotic Spanish dishes. The house specialty is *patatas a la importancia* (sliced potatoes fried in a sauce of garlic, parsley, and clams); other options include black rice with baby squid and prawns, and sirloin on a pear pastry puff. For dessert try the *bartolillos* (custard-filled pastries). ✉ *C. del Prado 4, Retiro* ☎ *91/429–1561* ▭ *AE, DC, MC, V* ⊙ *Closed 1 wk in Aug. No dinner Sun.*

$–$$ ✕ **La Trucha.** This Andalusian deep-fry specialist, decorated with hanging hams, ceramic plates, and garlic, is one of the happiest places in Madrid. The staff is jovial, and the house specialty, *trucha a la truchana* (trout stuffed with ham and ample garlic), is a work of art. Other star entrées are *chopitos* (baby squid), *pollo al ajillo* (chunks of chicken in crisped garlic), and *espárragos trigueros* (wild asparagus). *Jarras* (pitchers) of chilled Valdepeñas seem to function like laughing gas in this magical little bistro. The Nuñez de Arce branch, near the Hotel Reina Victoria, is usually less crowded. ✉ *Manuel Fernandez y Gonzalez 3, Barrio de las Letras* ☎ *91/429–5833* ✉ *Nuñez de Arce 6, Santa Ana* ☎ *91/532–0890* ▭ *AE, MC, V* ⊙ *Nuñez de Arce branch closed Sun., Mon., and Aug.*

Fodor's Choice ★

¢ ✕ **Nueva Galicia.** This small family-run bar and restaurant has long been one of the best values in the center of Madrid—it's two blocks from the Puerta del Sol. You can eat inside or at tables on the pedestrian-only side street. A starter, main course, dessert, and a full bottle of wine can be had for a ridiculously low €7.50; or you can choose to share some of the larger portions (*raciones*). ✉ *Cruz 6, Sol* ☎ *91/522–5289* ▭ *No credit cards* ⊙ *Closed Sun. and Aug.*

WHERE TO STAY

From the beginning of the new millennium, Madrid has added more than 15,000 new hotel rooms, and 10,000 more will be available in the next few years.

Plenty of the new arrivals are medium-price chain hotels that try to combine striking design with affordable prices. One step higher is the handful of new hotels that lure a good portion of the city's hippest crowd with top-notch design and superb food and nightlife. These have caused quite a stir in the five-star range and forced some of the more traditional hotels long favored by dignitaries, star athletes, and artists to enhance their food and service. Meanwhile, *hostals* and small hotels have shown that low prices can walk hand in hand with good taste and friendly service.

DEALS & DISCOUNTS

Most hotels offer special weekend plans and special prices of up to 30% or more off during the month of August. Prices fluctuate, even with hotels of the same category belonging to the same chain, so it's best to shop around. *Hostal* rooms found on the upper floors of apartment buildings often go for €50 or less. These cheap lodgings are frequently full, especially on the weekends, and sometimes don't take reservations, so you simply have to try your luck door-to-door. Many are in the old city, in the trapezoid between the Puerta del Sol, the Atocha Station, the Basílica de San Francisco on calle Bailén, and the Royal Palace; start your quest around Plaza Santa Ana or on the streets that are behind Puerta de Sol, near Plaza Mayor and calle Atocha.

CENTRO & CHUECA

$$$–$$$$ **De Las Letras.** This hotel inspired by literature (it even has a book catalog in every room) is a seamless mix of modern pop interior design that respects and accents the original details of the 1917 structure (glazed tiles, canopies, original wood-and-iron elevator, wooden staircase, and stone carvings). Rooms are painted in tones of ocher, orange, or burgundy, with high ceilings, wooden floors, indirect lighting, and over-the-top modern bathrooms, and the junior suites have a terrace with a whirlpool bath. The hotel has a charming rooftop terrace bar open

2

WHERE SHOULD I STAY?

	Neighborhood Vibe	Pros	Cons
Barrio de las Letras (including Carrera de San Jerónimo and Paseo del Prado)	A magnet for tourists, this classic literary nest has gone up a few notches with the pedestrianization of some streets and the traffic restrictions. It features the most exciting recent hotel openings.	Completely revamped—new street lights, paved roads, and a renovated Plaza de Santa Ana and Plaza del Ángel (still under construction)—plus the emergence of posh hotels and restaurants;	Noisy, especially around Plaza de Santa Ana; some bars and restaurants overprice due to the tourists.
Chueca & Malasaña	Vibrant and bustling, this is the area where you want to be if you're past your twenties but still don't want to be in bed before midnight.	These barrios burst with a bit of everything: a busy nightlife, alternative shops, charming cafés, and fancy and inexpensive local and international restaurants.	Extremely loud, especially on the weekends; dirtier than most other neighborhoods.
Sol & the Royal Palace	Anchored by the locally flavored Plaza Mayor, this historic quarter is full of narrow streets and taverns.	Has the most traditional feel of any neighborhood in Madrid; lodging and dining of all sorts, including many inexpensive yet usually indistinctive hostals and old flavor taverns.	Can be tough to navigate; a lot of history; many tourist traps.
Salamanca	Swanky, posh, and quite safe, this is a neighborhood many high-end hotels and restaurants call home.	Quiet at day's end; plenty of good restaurants; the city's major upscale shopping district.	It's blander and has less character than other districts, which is reflected in the hotels; expensive.
Callao & Gran Vía	This big commercial area has some of the city's most crowded streets—especially on the weekends.	Easy access to museums and sightseeing points; a few fancy restaurants and hotels; on the edge of Gran Ví but close to the junction with Alcalá.	When the shops close it gets quite deserted and lugubrious; plenty of ramshackle buildings and grime.

to everyone. Enjoying a meal or a cocktail in the restaurant–lounge on the street level, you would never think you're around the corner from the bustling Gran Vía. ✉ *Gran Vía 11, Centro, 28013* ☎ *91/523–7980* 📠 *91/523–7981* 🌐 *www.hoteldelasletras.com* ⇨ *103 rooms, 1 suite, 6 junior suites* ♿ *In-room: DVD, Wi-Fi. In-hotel: restaurant, bar, gym, public Wi-Fi, parking (fee)* 💳 *AE, DC, MC, V.*

$$$ Fodor's Choice ★ **Hotel Intur Palacio San Martín.** In an unbeatable location across from one of Madrid's most celebrated monuments (the Convent of Descalzas), this hotel, once the old U.S. embassy and later a luxurious residential building crowded with noblemen, still exudes a kind of glory. The entrance leads to a glass-dome atrium that serves as a tranquil sitting area. The hotel has preserved an antique elevator, and many of the ceilings are carved and ornate. The rooms are spacious and carpeted; request one facing the big plaza. ✉ *Plaza de San Martín 5, Cen-*

tro, 28013 ☎91/701–5000 📠91/701–5010 🌐www.intur.com ⇨93 rooms, 8 suites ♿In-room: safe, Wi-Fi. In-hotel: restaurant, gym, public Wi-Fi, parking (fee) 💳AE, DC, MC, V.

$$$ **Hotel Preciados.** In a 19th-century building on the quieter edge of one of Madrid's main shopping areas, this hotel is both charming and convenient. The rooms are modern and sophisticated, with hardwood floors and opaque glass closets. Some of the "double superiors" (slightly more expensive) have slanted ceilings and skylights in the bathrooms. ✉*C. Preciados 37, Centro, 28013 ☎91/454–4400 📠91/454–4401 🌐www.preciadoshotel.com ⇨74 rooms, 6 suites ♿In-room: Wi-Fi. In-hotel: restaurant, bar, gym, public Wi-Fi, parking (fee) 💳AE, DC, MC, V.*

$$$ **Petit Palace Ducal.** At the core of Madrid's most youthful shopping district, this former hostel is now a modern high-tech hotel that preserves some of the original elements (such as the wrought-iron elevator and staircase). The rooms have dark-wood floors and headboards and track lighting; some have bunk beds and can house up to five people. The café, open to the public, has large windows that face the street. ✉*Hortaleza 3, Chueca, 28004 ☎91/521–1043 📠91/521–5064 🌐www.hthoteles.com ⇨58 rooms ♿In-room: safe, Wi-Fi. In-hotel: restaurant, public Wi-Fi, public Internet 💳AE, DC, MC, V.*

$$$ **Quo Puerta del Sol.** Between Santa Ana and Sol, this modern and design-oriented boutique hotel has rooms with views of the city center that are equipped with cutting-edge technology, dark hardwood floors, and modern touches such as the stainless-steel-and-glass sinks in the bathrooms. Common areas may not be ample in size but are nonetheless charming, trendy, and full of character. ✉*C. Sevilla 4, Centro, 28014 ☎91/532–9049 📠91/531–2834 🌐www.hotelesquo.com ⇨61 rooms, 1 junior suite ♿In-room: Ethernet, Wi-Fi. In-hotel: restaurant, public Wi-Fi, parking (fee) 💳AE, DC, MC, V.*

$$$ **Tryp Ambassador.** On an old street between Gran Vía and the Royal Palace, the Ambassador occupies the renovated 19th-century palace of the Dukes of Granada. The facade—restored in 2007—a magnificent front door, and a graceful three-story staircase recall the building's aristocratic past. The rest has been transformed into elegant, somewhat soulless lodgings favored by executives. Large guest rooms have sitting areas, wooden floors, and mahogany furnishings. The greenhouse restaurant, filled with plants and songbirds, is especially pleasant on cold days. ✉*Cuesta Santo Domingo 5 and 7, Ópera, 28013 ☎91/541–6700 📠91/559–1040 🌐www.solmelia.com ⇨183 rooms, 25 suites ♿In-room: Wi-fi. In-hotel: restaurant, bar, airport shuttle, public Wi-Fi, parking (fee) 💳AE, DC, MC, V.*

$$ **Abalú.** Each of the 10 rooms of this hotel at the core of one of the city's youngest and liveliest neighborhoods is a small oasis of unusual and pleasant taste. Designer Javier Delgado's mission is to make each room special, with a hodgepodge of unique accessories, such as the black stenciled butterflies scattered along the walls of the White Room. If you're interested in feeling Malasaña's vibe and are not easily daunted by noise, ask for one of the three rooms facing the street. At the time of this writing, another five rooms and a cafeteria were to be added

in 2007. ✉ *Pez 19, Centro, 28004* ☎ *91/531–4744* 📠 *91/521–4492* 🌐 *www.hotelabalu.com* ⟲ *10 rooms,* *In-room: safe, Wi-Fi, DVD (some)* ▭ *AE, MC, V* 🍴 *CP.*

$$ **Liabeny.** Although unassuming in style and a bit outdated, this 1960s hotel near a plaza (and several department stores) between Gran Vía and Puerta del Sol has large and comfortable rooms with floral fabrics and big windows. Interior and top-floor rooms are the quietest. ✉ *Salud 3, Centro, 28013* ☎ *91/531–9000* 📠 *91/532–7421* 🌐 *www.liabeny.es* ⟲ *220 rooms* *In-room: dial-up, Wi-Fi. In-hotel: restaurant, bar, gym, public Wi-Fi, parking (fee)* ▭ *AE, DC, MC, V.*

$$ **Room Mate Mario.** More than just a good deal, this modern and stylish hotel is in the city center, steps away from the major sites and nightlife. Although small and limited in services, its bold modern style—reflected in original silk printed headboards and combinations of white, gray, and black tones—and friendly service are a breath of fresh air among the traditional and neoclassic hotel options in Madrid. ✉ *Campomanes 4, Centro, 28013* ☎ *91/548–8548* 📠 *91/559–1288* 🌐 *www.room-matehoteles.com* ⟲ *54 rooms, 3 suites* *In-room: dial-up, Wi-Fi. In-hotel: laundry facilities* ▭ *AE, DC, MC, V* 🍴 *CP.*

$ **Mora.** This cheery hotel with a sparkling, faux-marble lobby and bright, carpeted hallways is across the Paseo del Prado from the Botanical Garden. Guest rooms are modestly decorated (those on the fourth floor are newer) but are large and comfortable; those on the street side have great views of the gardens and the Prado, and double-pane windows keep them fairly quiet. For breakfast and lunch, the café is excellent, affordable, and popular with locals. ✉ *Paseo del Prado 32, Centro, 28014* ☎ *91/420–1569* 📠 *91/420–0564* 🌐 *www.hotelmora.com* ⟲ *62 rooms* *In-hotel: restaurant* ▭ *AE, DC, MC, V.*

CHAMBERÍ, RETIRO & SALAMANCA

$$$$ Fodor'sChoice ★ **AC Palacio del Retiro.** An early-20th-century restored palatial building owned by a noble family with extravagant habits (the elevator carried the horses up and down from the exercise ring on the roof), this spectacular hotel closely follows the path of the first opened AC Santo Mauro: tasteful, modern decor in a historical building. Palacio preserves even more of its grandiose past: baseboards and fountains covered with ceramics from Talavera, original Parisian stained-glass windows, marble floors and columns, and original moldings. All rooms have superb views of the nearby Retiro Park. The double superior rooms' bathroom doors are full-size Lichtenstein silk-screen prints. ✉ *Alfonso XII 14, Retiro, 28014* ☎ *91/523–7460* 📠 *91/523–7461* 🌐 *www.ac-hotels.com* ⟲ *51 rooms* *In-room: safe, Wi-Fi. In-hotel: restaurant, bar, public Wi-Fi, parking (fee)* ▭ *AE, DC, MC, V.*

$$$$ Fodor'sChoice ★ **AC Santo Mauro.** Once the Canadian embassy, this turn-of-the-20th-century mansion is now an intimate luxury hotel, an oasis of calm a short walk from the city center. The neoclassical architecture is accented by contemporary furniture in white, gray, eggplant, and black hues. Some of the rooms in the main building still maintain the original details and fixtures. The top-notch restaurant is in what used to be the mansion's library. Views vary; request a room with a terrace overlooking the gardens. ✉ *Zurbano 36, Chamberí, 28010* ☎ *91/319–6900*

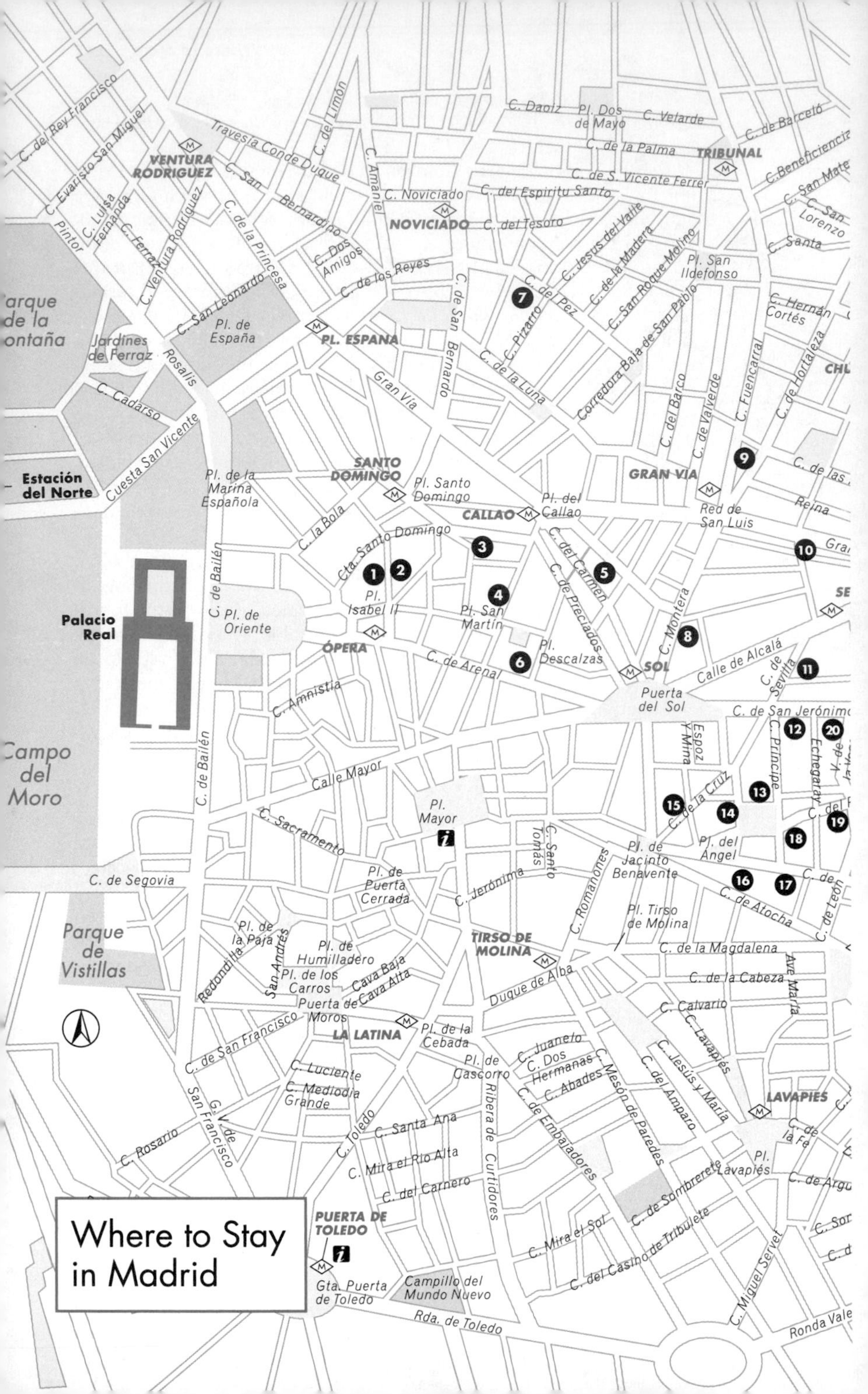

Where to Stay in Madrid
VENTURA RODRIGUEZ
NOVICIADO
TRIBUNAL
PL. ESPAÑA
SANTO DOMINGO
CALLAO
GRAN VÍA
ÓPERA
SOL
TIRSO DE MOLINA
LA LATINA
LAVAPIES
PUERTA DE TOLEDO
Palacio Real
Estación del Norte
Campo del Moro
Parque de Vistillas
Pl. de España
Pl. Mayor
Puerta del Sol
Calle Mayor
Calle de Alcalá
Gran Vía
C. de Arenal
C. de Atocha
C. de Bailén
C. de Toledo
Rda. de Toledo
Gta. Puerta de Toledo
Campillo del Mundo Nuevo
Pl. Lavapiés

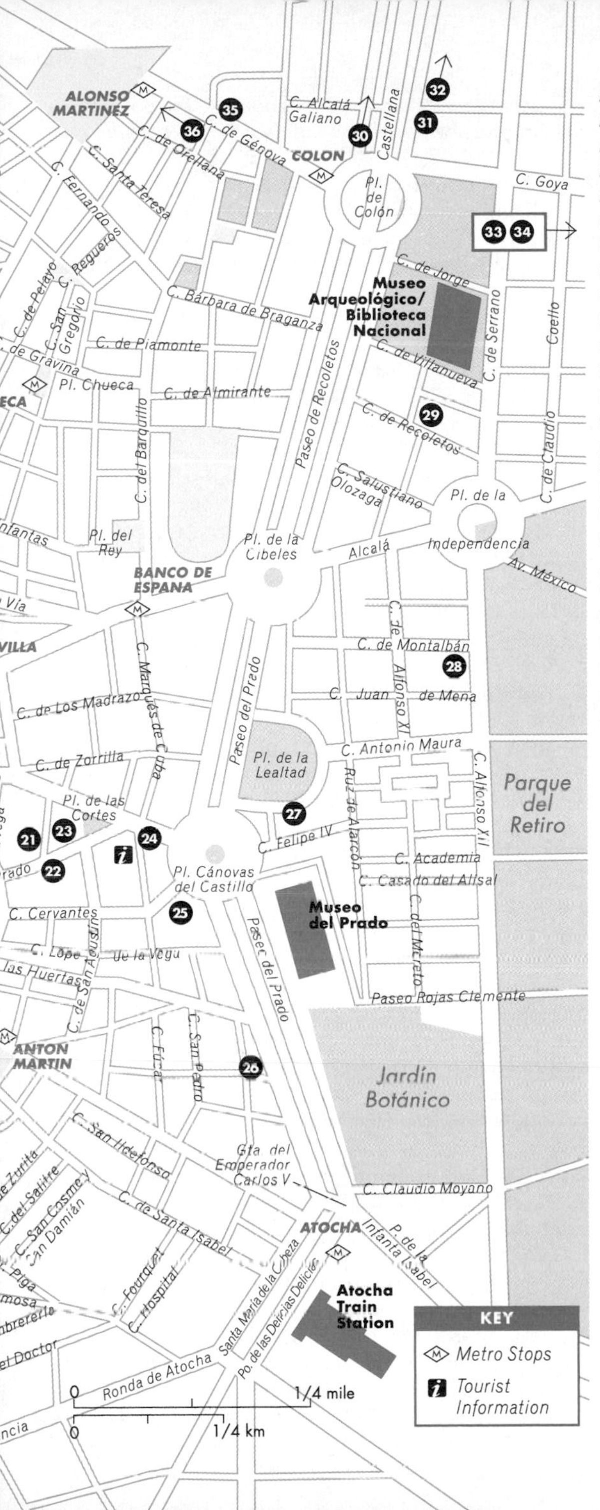

Abalú **7**
AC Palacio del Retiro **28**
AC Santo Mauro **36**
Alicia Room Mate **18**
Ateneo Hotel..........................**8**
Catalonia Moratín **16**
De Las Letras **10**
Gran Hotel Canarias **25**
Gran Meliá Fénix **31**
Hesperia Madrid **30**
Hostal Adriano **15**
Hostal Villar **13**
Hotel Bauzá **33**
Hotel Catalonia Las Cortes **19**
Hotel Intur Palacio San Martín **4**
Hotel Preciados **3**
Hotel Urban **20**
Inglés **12**
Jardín de Recoletos **29**
Liabeny **5**
ME Reina Victoria **14**
Mora **26**
NH Lagasca **34**
Orfila **35**
Petit Palace Arenal **6**
Petit Palace Ducal **9**
Puerta de América **32**
Quo Puerta del Sol **11**
Ritz **27**
Room Mate Mario **2**
7 Colors **17**
Suite Prado **21**
Tryp Ambassador **1**
Villa Real **23**
Vincci Soho **22**
Westin Palace **24**

91/308–5477 www.ac-hotels.com 51 rooms In-room: VCR, Wi-Fi. In-hotel: restaurant, bar, pool, gym, public Wi-Fi, parking (fee) AE, DC, MC, V.

$$$$ **Gran Meliá Fénix.** An impressive lobby with marble floors and columns decorated with antique furniture, and a blue stained-glass dome ceiling define the style of this completely refurbished Madrid institution. The hotel overlooks Plaza de Colón on the Castellana and is a mere hop from the posh shops of Calle Serrano. Its spacious rooms are decorated in reds and golds and are amply furnished; flowers abound. Ask for a room facing the Plaza de Colón; otherwise, the view is rather dreary. *Hermosilla 2, Salamanca, 28001 91/431–6700 91/576–0661 www.solmelia.com 216 rooms, 9 suites In-room: dial-up, Wi-Fi. In-hotel: 3 restaurants, bar, gym, spa, parking (fee) AE, DC, MC, V.*

$$$$ **Hesperia Madrid.** A bit far from the historic area but still in the commercial center, Hesperia welcomes visitors with a long, remarkably sophisticated lobby decorated by renowned designer Pasqua Ortega. Designed using materials such as limestone and light woods, it provides a soothing contrast to the bustling Castellana street outside and ends in a *patio de luces* (atrium) surrounded by the open restaurant La Manzana and common spaces, which have live harp and piano music in the afternoons. Carpeted rooms, though less impressive in terms of size and decor, have all sorts of facilities, including a pillow menu to make sure you feel at home. *Paseo de la Castellana 57, Salamanca, 28046 91/210–8888 91/210–8899 www.hesperia-madrid.com 139 rooms, 32 suites In-room: Ethernet, dial-up, Wi-Fi. In-hotel: 2 restaurants, bar, gym, concierge, public Wi-Fi, parking (fee) AE, DC, MC, V.*

$$$$ ★ **Orfila.** This elegant 1886 town house, hidden away on a leafy little residential street not far from Plaza Colón, has every comfort of a larger hotel, but more intimate, personalized surroundings. Originally the in-town residence of the literary and aristocratic Gomez-Acebo family, Orfila 6 was an address famous for theater performances in the late 19th and early 20th centuries. The restaurant, garden (superb for summer dining), and tearoom have period furniture; guest rooms are draped with striped and floral silks. *Orfila 6, Chamberí, 28010 91/702–7770 91/702–7772 www.hotelorfila.com 20 rooms, 12 suites In-room: dial-up, Wi-Fi. In-hotel: restaurant, bar, gym, public Wi-Fi, parking (fee) AE, DC, MC, V.*

$$$$ ★ **Puerta de América.** Inspired by Paul Eluard's *La Liberté* (whose verses are written across the facade), the owners of this hotel granted an unlimited budget to 19 of the world's top architects and designers. The result: 12 hotels in one, with floors by Zaha Hadid, Norman Foster, Jean Nouvel, David Chipperfield, and more. Pick online the floor of your choice; most popular are the futuristic all-white layout by Hadid, an elegant black wood and white leather proposal by Foster, and the imaginative re-creation of space by Ron Arat. There's also a reputed restaurant and two bars (one on the rooftop) just as impressive in design. The only snag: the location, away from the city center. *Avenida de América 41, Prosperidad, 28002 91/744–5400 91/744–*

5401 ⊕www.hotelpuertamerica.com ☞308 rooms, 22 junior suites, 12 suites ♨In-room: safe, Wi-Fi. In-hotel: restaurant, bars, public Wi-Fi, gym, pool, parking (fee) ▭AE, DC, MC, V.

$$$$ **Ritz.** Alfonso XIII, about to marry Queen Victoria's granddaughter, encouraged the construction of this hotel, the most exclusive in Spain, for his royal guests. Opened in 1910 by the king himself (who personally supervised construction), the Ritz is a monument to the belle epoque, its salons furnished with rare antiques, hand-embroidered linens, and handwoven carpets. All of the rooms (that are slowly being revamped for its centennial) have canopy beds, and some have views of the Prado. The famous and pricey restaurant, Goya, serves a Sunday brunch feast that is accompanied by the soothing strains of harp music; from February to May, you'll enjoy chamber music during weekend tea and supper. *⊠Plaza de la Lealtad 5, Retiro, 28014 ☎91/701–6767 ℻91/701–6776 ⊕www.ritzmadrid.com ☞167 rooms ♨In-room: dial-up, Wi-fi. In-hotel: restaurant, bar, gym, public Wi-fi, parking (fee) ▭AE, DC, MC, V.*

$$$$ ★ **Villa Real.** For a medium-size hotel that combines elegance, modern amenities, friendly service, and a great location, look no further: the Villa Real faces Spain's parliament and is convenient to almost everything, particularly the Prado and Thyssen-Bornemisza museums. The simulated 19th-century facade gives way to an intimate lobby with modern furnishings. Many rooms are split level, with a small sitting area. Some suites have whirlpool baths. *⊠Plaza de las Cortés 10, Retiro, 28014 ☎91/420–3767 ℻91/420–2547 ⊕www.derbyhotels.es ☞94 rooms, 20 suites ♨In-room: Wi-Fi. In-hotel: restaurant, bar, public Wi-Fi, parking (fee) ▭AE, DC, MC, V.*

$$$$ ★ **Westin Palace.** Built in 1912, Madrid's most famous grand hotel is a belle epoque creation of Alfonso XIII and has hosted the likes of Salvador Dalí, Marlon Brando, Rita Hayworth, and Madonna. Guest rooms are high-tech and generally impeccable; banquet halls and lobbies have been beautified, and the facade has been restored. The Art Nouveau stained-glass dome over the lounge remains exquisitely original, and guest room windows are double-glazed against street noise. The suites are no less luxurious than the opulent public spaces with Bang & Olufsen CD players, spacious bathrooms, double sinks, hot tubs, and separate shower stalls. It now hosts the very popular Asia Gallery restaurant. *⊠Plaza de las Cortés 7, Retiro, 28014 ☎91/360–8000 ℻91/360–8100 ⊕www.palacemadrid.com ☞465 rooms, 45 suites ♨In-room: dial-up, Wi-Fi. In-hotel: 2 restaurants, bar, gym, public Wi-Fi, parking (fee) ▭AE, DC, MC, V.*

$$$–$$$$ ★ **Gran Hotel Canarias.** Once the residence of a count, this fully restored hotel, a block away from the Prado, is a reasonable yet luxurious alternative to the five-star hotels that populate the area. In the common areas you find odd combinations such as a brown-leather couch and period chairs, but guest rooms are spacious, with hand-painted Canarian motifs, bold-color carpets from the Royal Factory of Tapestries, and wooden furniture. Bathrooms are tiled in green marble with huge mirrors and showers. The cafeteria, open to the public, is a magnet for the passersby. *⊠Plaza Cánovas del Castillo 4, Retiro, 28014 ☎91/330–*

2400 ☎91/360–0798 @www.granhotelcanarias.com 114 rooms, 5 suites In-room: safe, Ethernet, Wi-Fi. In-hotel: restaurant, gym, public Wi-FI, parking (fee) AE, DC, MC, V.

$$$–$$$$ **Hotel Bauzá.** With a balanced combination of modern style and elegance, this hotel has dark-wood floors, stereos in every room, and other details, such as the environmentally friendly bikes with motorized bicycles for guests, that make it a good alternative to the higher-end hotels. The rooms have functional yet distinctive furniture (each room is decorated with an original photograph signed by the artist), and the bathrooms are beautifully tiled. The restaurant serves Mediterranean-fusion food and has great views of one of Madrid's great shopping streets, Calle Goya. *✉Calle Goya 79, Salamanca, 28001 ☎91/435–7545 91/431–0943 @www.hotelbauza.com 167 rooms, 3 suites, 7 apartments In-room: Ethernet, Wi-Fi. In-hotel: restaurant, bar, public Wi-Fi, gym, parking (fee) AE, DC, MC, V.*

$$$ **Jardín de Recoletos.** This sleek apartment hotel offers great value on a quiet street close to Plaza Colón and upmarket Calle Serrano. The large lobby has marble floors and a stained-glass ceiling, and adjoins a café, restaurant, and the hotel's restful private garden. The large rooms, with light-wood trim and beige-and-yellow furnishings, include sitting and dining areas. "Superior" rooms and suites have hydromassage baths and large terraces. Book well in advance. *✉Gil de Santivañes 6, Salamanca, 28001 ☎91/781–1640 91/781–1641 36 rooms, 7 suites In-room: kitchen, VCR, dial-up, Wi-Fi. In-hotel: restaurant, room service, public Wi-Fi, parking (fee) AE, DC, MC, V BP.*

$$$ **NH Lagasca.** In the heart of the elegant Salamanca neighborhood, this hotel combines large, brightly decorated rooms with an unbeatable location two blocks from Madrid's main shopping street, Calle Serrano. Half of the rooms were renovated in early 2007 and have a more modern look than the rest. The remaining rooms and the lobby, which although a bit unappealing serves its purpose as a meeting place, will be revamped in 2008. Note that just a few more euros will get you a larger room. *✉Lagasca 64, Salamanca, 28001 ☎91/575–4606 91/575–1694 @www.nh-hotels.com 100 rooms In-room: safe, Wi-Fi. In-hotel: restaurant, bar, public Wi-Fi, parking (fee) AE, DC, MC, V.*

SOL, SANTA ANA & BARRIO DE LAS LETRAS

$$$$ ★ **Hotel Urban.** With a stylish mix of the ancient (New Guinean carvings in the lobby, a small Egyptian museum, and antique Chinese or Burmese statues in every room, all belonging to the owner, a renowned art collector) and daring sophistication (the tall alabaster column that majestically stands in the lobby's atrium, the tiled and gold inlaid wall on the main staircase, and the sleek cocktail bar), this is the hotel that best conveys Madrid's new cosmopolitan spirit. Rooms, done in dark hues, are less flamboyant, and some are small. There's a great restaurant here and an ultrachic bar on the roof, where the glamorous gather on summer nights to enjoy the views and sip a champagne cocktail. *✉Carrera de San Jerónimo 34, Barrio de las Letras, 28014 ☎91/787–7770 91/787–7799 @www.derbyhotels.com 96 rooms, 3 junior suites, 4 suites In-room: safe, Wi-Fi. In-hotel: 2 restaurants, bar, pool, gym, parking (fee) AE, DC, MC, V.*

$$$$ ★ **ME Reina Victoria.** A few bulls' heads hanging in the lounge and some abstract pictures of bull fighting scattered around this ultramodern hotel are all that remain to remind visitors that this was once the place where bullfighters convened before heading off toward Las Ventas. The old flair has been superseded by cutting-edge services in the rooms: a USB port (for recharging iPods, MP3 players and the like), a flat large-screen TV with surround sound, an advanced latex memory foam mattress, and a minibar twice the size you'd find elsewhere. Common areas have round-the-clock entertainment, the great restaurant is supervised by Asiana's talented chef, and two of the city's fanciest and busiest bars are here, including one rooftop establishment with a 360-degree panoramic view of the city. ✉ *Plaza Santa Ana 14, Santa Ana, 28014* ☎ *91/531–4500* 📠 *91/522–0307* 🌐 *www.solmelia.com* *182 rooms, 9 suites* *In-room: safe, DVD, Wi-Fi. In-hotel: restaurant, bars, laundry facilities, public Wi-Fi, some pets allowed, parking (fee)* 💳 *AE, DC, MC, V.*

$$$–$$$$ **Vincci Soho.** Faithful to its surname, this hotel seems as if it had been transplanted from London or New York into one of Madrid's busiest neighborhoods. Everything on its ground floor—the lamps, the mustard color circular divan that sits in front of the reception desk, the meeting lounges with velvet armchairs and silk screens, the steel butterfly cutouts on the restaurant walls—highlights elegance and imagination. There are no two rooms alike in shape—the hotel is made of five old private houses—but they're all comfortable and bright—even the interior ones, thanks to a large open courtyard that keeps the street noise out and lets the sun in. ✉ *Prado 18, Santa Ana, 28014* ☎ *91/141–4100* 📠 *91/141–4100* 🌐 *www.vinccihoteles.com* *167 rooms* *In-room: safe, Wi-Fi. In-hotel: restaurant, bar, public Wi-Fi, parking (fee)* 💳 *AE, DC, MC, V.*

$$$ **Catalonia Moratín.** The aristocratic corridor leading to the registration desk, the atrium (where the walls are partly made of original granite blocks), and the magnificent main wooden staircase, presided over by a lion statue—these are the elements that best reveal this building's 18th-century origins. The other common areas, including the restaurant and a reading room with a small library, have less character. Guest rooms are comfortable, with functional wooden furniture and striped curtains and bedspreads. Bathrooms have cream-color tiles and green marble sinks. ✉ *Calle Atocha 23, Sol, 28012* ☎ *91/369–7171* 📠 *91/360–1231* 🌐 *www.hoteles-catalonia.es* *63 rooms* *In-room: safe, Wi-Fi. In-hotel: restaurant, public Wi-Fi, bar* 💳 *AE, DC, MC, V.*

$$$ **Hotel Catalonia Las Cortes.** A late 18th-century palace formerly owned by the Duke of Noblejas, this hotel retains a good shred of its noble past: a gorgeous wooden staircase, some of the old moldings, and stained windows. It has a classic feel without being ostentatious or overwhelming. Rooms are elegant and wallpapered in grayish tones, whereas bathrooms—with more bland decor—are quite decent in size for the city's standards. Better still, it's just a few yards away from Plaza Santa Ana. ✉ *Prado 6, Santa Ana, 28014* ☎ *91/389–6051* 📠 *91/389–6052* 🌐 *www.hoteles-catalonia.com* *55 rooms, 8 junior suites, 2*

suites ♨In-room: safe, Wi-Fi. In-hotel: restaurant, bar, laundry facilities, public Wi-Fi, parking (fee) ▭AE, DC, MC, V.

$$$ **Petit Palace Arenal.** Near the bustling tourist area Sol, this fairly new and popular hotel maintains some of its location's original characteristics, including a wood staircase, some wooden beams, and the vaulted exposed-brick walls in the meeting and breakfast rooms downstairs. The rooms, tastefully done with deep-purple ceilings and outfitted with modern light fixtures and tempered-glass sinks, already show some wear and tear. This chain boutique hotel has two nearby locations with similar features: the Petit Palace Puerta del Sol on the same street but closer to Sol, and the Posada del Peine at C. Postas 17. *✉Arenal 16, Sol, 28013 ☎91/564–4355 🖷91/564–0854 ⊕www.hthoteles.com ⇐64 rooms ♨In-room: safe, Ethernet. In-hotel: restaurant, public Internet ▭AE, DC, MC, V.*

$$–$$$ **Suite Prado.** Popular with Americans on short stays, this stylish apartment hotel is near the Prado, the Thyssen-Bornemisza, and the Plaza Santa Ana tapas area. The attractive attic studios on the fourth floor have sloped ceilings with wood beams; there are larger suites (including some completely renovated rooms on the first floor) downstairs. All apartments are brightly decorated and have marble baths and basic kitchens. Breakfast is served daily, on request, by a friendly staff. Triple rooms are a great deal. *✉Manuel Fernández y González 10, Santa Ana, 28014 ☎91/420–2318 🖷91/420–0559 ⊕www.suiteprado.com ⇐18 suites ♨In-room: kitchen, dial-up, Wi-Fi. In-hotel: parking (fee) ▭AE, DC, MC, V.*

$$ **Alicia Room Mate.** The all-white lobby with curvaceous walls, ceiling, and lamps sets the mood for the mostly young urbanite visitors of this former trench coat factory that now, as a hotel, sells style at affordable prices. Carpeted rooms, although not spectacular in size, are very modern; the black slate bathrooms, all with showers, are in the bedroom separated only by a glass door. For just a few more euros you can upgrade to an executive room with a terrace or a minisuite with large windows overlooking Plaza Santa Ana. *✉Prado 2, Santa Ana, 28014 ☎91/389–6095 🖷91/369–4795 ⊕www.room-matehoteles.com ⇐34 rooms, 3 suites ♨In-room: Wi-Fi. In-hotel: bar, public Wi-Fi, parking (fee) ▭AE, DC, MC, V.*

$$ **Ateneo Hotel.** This hotel is in the restored 18th-century building that once housed the Ateneo, a club founded in 1835 to promote freedom of thought. The spacious rooms are done in cream-and-light-wood tones with parquet flooring and red-and-gold-striped spreads on the bed. Exterior rooms have balconies overlooking the crowded street, except those on the fourth floor, which have sloped ceilings and skylights above the beds. *✉Montera 22, Sol, 28013 ☎91/521–2012 🖷91/523–3136 ⊕www.hotel-ateneo.com ⇐38 rooms, 6 junior suites ♨In-room: dial-up ▭AE, DC, MC, V ¶○¶BP.*

$$ **Inglés.** Virginia Woolf was among the first luminaries to discover this place, in the middle of the old city's bar-and-restaurant district. Since Woolf's time, the Inglés has attracted more than its share of less-celebrated artists and writers. Half of the rooms were tiled and painted in 2005, and new bathrooms were installed, but the decor still resembles

the ornate and outdated lobby. The suites, which are double rooms with a salon, are nonetheless a bargain. You get twice the space for what you'd pay for a standard double elsewhere. Also, if your room faces Calle Echegaray, you can get an unusual aerial view of the medieval quarter, which is all red tiles and ramshackle gables. ✉ *Echegaray 8, Santa Ana, 28014* ☎ *91/429–6551* 📠 *91/420–2423* *58 rooms* *In-room: no a/c (some). In-hotel: restaurant, bar, gym, parking (fee)* 💳 *AE, DC, MC, V.*

$–$$ **7 Colors.** Primarily but not exclusively gay, this is the perfect place for those who love design but don't plan on spending too much time in their rooms. Based on the concept of color therapy, each room is decorated in a specific color with integrated bathrooms; you can play with the intensity of light to suit your mood. The yellow, red, and orange rooms have balconies and face the street. Get more space with the double superior room for a little extra. The rectangular white table at the entrance serves as a meeting and breakfast room. Reserve rooms in advance. ✉ *Huertas 14, 2nd exterior left, Santa Ana, 28012* ☎ *91/429–6935* 📠 *91/429–6935* 🌐 *www.7colorsrooms.com* *10 rooms* *In-hotel: public Internet* 💳 *AE, DC, MC, V* *CP.*

$ ★ **Hostal Adriano.** Tucked away on a street with dozens of bland competitors and a couple of blocks away from Sol, this option stands out for its price and quality. The rooms, although not especially big, are charming and far from the standard hostal fare. They are made unique by the brightly colored walls and comforter covers and by the furniture and accessories collected over the years by the two friendly Argentine owners. The best of the lot has been wallpapered with some old María Callas pictures and the musical score from *Tosca.* ✉ *De la Cruz 26, 4th fl., Santa Ana, 28012* ☎📠 *91/521–1339* 🌐 *www.hostaladriano.com* *22 rooms* *In-room: safe. In-hotel: public Internet* 💳 *MC, V.*

¢ **Hostal Villar.** Rooms here go from single to quadruple, with or without bathrooms (those facing the busy Calle Príncipe are among the ones without baths), and are reasonably large, clean, and comfortably decorated with matching bedspreads and curtains. The bathrooms, however, are rather small. The service is friendly and attentive. ✉ *Príncipe 18, Santa Ana, 28012* ☎ *91/531–6600* 📠 *91/521–5073* 🌐 *www.villar.es* *40 rooms, 27 with bath* *In-room: no TV (some)* 💳 *MC, V.*

NIGHTLIFE & THE ARTS

THE ARTS

As Madrid's reputation as a vibrant, contemporary arts center has grown, artists and performers have arrived in droves. Consult the weekly *Guía del Ocio* (published Friday) or the daily listings and the Friday supplements in any of the leading newspapers—*El País, El Mundo,* or *ABC,* all of which are understandable even if you don't read much Spanish. The Festival de Otoño (Autumn Festival), from late September to late November, blankets the city with pop concerts, poetry readings, flamenco, and ballet and theater from world-renowned companies. Other annual events include outstanding bonanzas of film, contemporary art, and jazz, salsa, rock, and African music, all at reasonable prices. Seats for the classical performing arts are best purchased through your hotel concierge, on the Internet, or at the hall itself. **El Corte Inglés** (☎*902/400222* 🌐*www.elcorteingles.es/entradas*) sells tickets for major concerts. **FNAC** (✉*Preciados 28, Sol* ☎*91/595–6100* 🌐*www.fnac.es*), a large retail media store, sells tickets to musical events. **Ticket Brokers** to try are **Tel-Entrada** (☎*902/101212* 🌐*www.telentrada.com*) and **Entradas.com** (☎*902/221622*).

CONCERTS & DANCE

In addition to concert halls listed below, the Convento de la Encarnación and the Real Academia de Bellas Artes de San Fernando museum (⇨Exploring Madrid) hold concerts. The modern **Auditorio Nacional de Música** (✉*Príncipe de Vergara 146, Salamanca* ☎*91/337–0100* 🌐*www.auditorionacional.mcu.es*) is Madrid's main concert hall, with spaces for both symphonic and chamber music. The resplendent **Teatro Real** (✉*Plaza de Isabel II, Ópera* ☎*91/516–0660* 🌐*www.teatro-real.com*) is the site of opera and dance performances.

The subterranean **Centro Cultural de la Villa** (✉*Plaza de Colón, Salamanca* ☎*91/480–0300 information, 902/101212 tickets*) has an eclectic program ranging from gospel and blues to flamenco and Celtic dance. The **Fundación Juan March** (✉*Castello 77, Salamanca* ☎*91/435–4240*) offers chamber music Monday and Saturday at noon, and Wednesday at 7:30 PM.

The **Círculo de Bellas Artes** (✉*Marqués de Casa Riera 2, Centro* ☎*902/422442* 🌐*www.circulobellasartes.com*), at the junction between Gran Vía and Alcalá, has concerts, theater, dance performances, art exhibitions, and other arts events. The **Centro de Conde Duque** (✉*Conde Duque 11, Centro* ☎*91/588–5834*) is best known for its summer live music concerts (flamenco, jazz, pop), but it also has free and often interesting exhibitions.

FILM

Of Madrid's 60 movie theaters, only 12 show foreign films, generally in English, with original sound tracks and Spanish subtitles. These are listed in newspapers and in the *Guía de Ocio* under "v.o."—*versión original,* that is, undubbed. Your best bet for catching a new release is the **Ideal Yelmo Cineplex** (✉*Doctor Cortezo 6, Centro* ☎*902/220922*). The excellent, classic v.o. films at the **Filmoteca Cine Doré** (✉*Santa Isabel 3, Lavapiés* ☎*91/369–1125*) change daily. However, there are also good theaters around the Plaza de España. **Alphaville** (✉*Martín de los Heros 14, Plaza de España* ☎*91/559–3836*) is a leading v.o. theater a block off Plaza de España. **Renoir Plaza de España** (✉*Martín de los Heros 12, Plaza de España* ☎*91/541–4100*) offers v.o. films. **Princesa** (✉*Princesa 3, Plaza de España* ☎*91/541–4100*) is a good option for original-version films. **Renoir Princesa** (✉*Princesa 5, Plaza de España* ☎*91/541–4100*) has two theaters in the underpass below what's popularly known as Plaza de los Cubos. The latest multiplex that opened in the city (in terms of v.o. movie theaters) is **Verdi** (✉*Bravo Murillo 28, Quevedo* ☎*91/447–3930*).

FLAMENCO

Spain's best flamenco habitat is Andalusia, there are a few possibilities in Madrid. Note that *tablaos* (flamenco venues) charge around €25 to €32 for the show only (with a complimentary drink included). You can save money by dining elsewhere and arriving in time for the show. But if you want to dine at the *tablaos* anyway, note that three of them, Carboneras, Corral de la Moreriá, and Café de Chinitas, also offer a show and fixed-menu option that's worth considering.

Café de Chinitas. It's expensive, but the flamenco is the best in Madrid. Reserve in advance; shows often sell out. The restaurant opens around 8:30 PM and the performance starts at 10:15 PM Monday through Saturday. ✉*Torrija 7, Ópera* ☎*91/559–5135* ⏲*Closed Sun.*

Casa Patas. Along with tapas, this well-known space offers good, relatively authentic (according to the performers) flamenco. Prices are more reasonable than elsewhere. Shows are at 10:30 PM Monday through Thursday, and at 9 PM and midnight on Friday and Saturday. ✉*Canizares 10, Lavapiés* ☎*91/369–0496* ⏲*Closed Sun.*

Corral de la Morería. Dinner à la carte and well-known visiting flamenco stars accompany the resident dance troupe here. Since Morería opened its doors in 1956, celebrities such as Frank Sinatra and Ava Gardner have left their autographed photos for the walls. Shows are nightly at 10 PM and midnight. ✉*Morería 17, on C. Bailén; cross bridge over C. Segovia and turn right, Centro* ☎*91/365–8446.*

Las Carboneras. A prime flamenco showcase, this place rivals Casa Patas as the best option in terms of quality and price. Performing here are young and less commercial artists as well as more established stars on tour. Nightly shows are staged at 9 and 10:30 Monday–Thursday and at 8:30 and 11 Friday and Saturday. ✉*Plaza del Conde de Miranda 1, Centro* ☎*91/542–8677* ⏲*Closed Sun.*

■ TIP→The best flamenco in Madrid is found at Café de Chinitas, whereas Café Central is the city's best-known jazz venue. For salsa, it's Azúcar."

THEATER

English-language plays are rare. When they do come to town, they're staged at any of a dozen venues. One theater you won't need Spanish for is the **Teatro de la Zarzuela** (✉*Jovellanos 4, Centro* ☎*91/524–5400*), which specializes in the traditional Spanish operetta known as *zarzuela*, a kind of bawdy comedy. **Calle Gran Vía** has become a small reproduction of the West End and Broadway, and here you'll find popular musicals adapted for the Spanish audience, as well as some local productions. The **Teatro Español** (✉*Príncipe 25, Santa Ana* ☎*91/360–1480*) brings big leading companies from all over the world and often performs Spanish classics. The **Compañía Nacional de Teatro Clásico** (✉*Teatro Pavón, Embajadores 9, Tirso de Molina* ☎*91/528–2819*) keeps 17th-century Spanish classics alive.

Continued on page 128

THE ART OF BULLFIGHTING

Whether you attend is your choice, but love it or hate it, you can't ignore it. Bullfighting in Spain is big. For all the animal-rights protests, attempted local bans, failed European parliamentary censures, and general world-wide antipathy, you'd be hard pressed to find a higher volume of fans than you would around Spain's bullrings between March and October.

Its opponents call it a blood sport, its admirers—Hemingway, Picasso, and Goya among them—an art form. The latter win when it comes to media placement: you won't find tales of a star matador's latest conquest on a newspaper's jump page with car racing stories; you'll spy bullfighting news alongside theater and film reviews. This is perhaps the secret to understanding bullfighting's powerful cultural significance and why its popularity has risen over the past decade.

Bullfighting is making certain people very, very rich, via million-dollar TV rights, fight broadcasts, and the 300-plus bull-breeding farms. The owners of these farms comprise a powerful lobby that receives subsidies from the EU and exemption from a 1998 amendment to the Treaty of Rome that covers animal welfare. The Spanish Ministry of Culture also provides considerable money to support bullfighting, as do local and regional governments.

The Spanish media thrive on it, too. The matador is perhaps Spain's last remaining stereotypical *macho hombre*, whose popularity outside the ring in the celebrity press is often dramatically disproportionate to what he achieves inside it.

How bullfighting came to Spain is an unsettled issue. It may have been introduced by the Moors in the 11th century or via ancient Rome, where human vs. animal events were held as a warm-up for the gladiators.

Historically speaking, the bull was fought from horseback with a javelin and was used by the noble classes as a substitute and preparation for war, like hunting and jousting. Religious festivities and royal weddings were celebrated by fights in the local plaza, where noblemen would ride competing for royal favor, with the populace enjoying the excitement. In the 18th century, the Spanish introduced the practice of fighting on foot. As bullfighting developed, men on foot started using capes to aid the horsemen in positioning the bulls. This type of fighting drew more attention from the crowds, thus the modern *corrida*, or fight, started to take form.

THE CASE AGAINST BULLFIGHTING

Animal welfare activists aggressively protest bullfighting for the cruelity it afflicts on both bulls and horses. The argue that the bulls die a cruel (usually slow and painful) death; in fact, activists argue, the bull is essentially butchered alive and bleeds to death. The horses involved are knocked around and sometimes die or are injured as they're used as shields for the picadors riding atop them.

Activists have had little success in banning the bullfight on a national level. However, while the sport is as popular as ever in the south of Spain and Madrid, it has been halted in several Catalonian towns, and in 2003, the Catalan regional parliament became the first in Spain to ban children under 14 from attending bullfights. Then, in 2004, the Barcelona City Council banned bullfighting altogether, a historic first in Spain. The decision still needs to be ratified by the regional government.

SUITING UP

Matadors are easily distinguished by their spectacular and quite costly *traje de luces* (suit of lights), inspired by 18th-century Andalusian clothing. This ensemble can run several thousand dollars, and a good matador uses at least six of them each season. The Matador's team covers the cost.

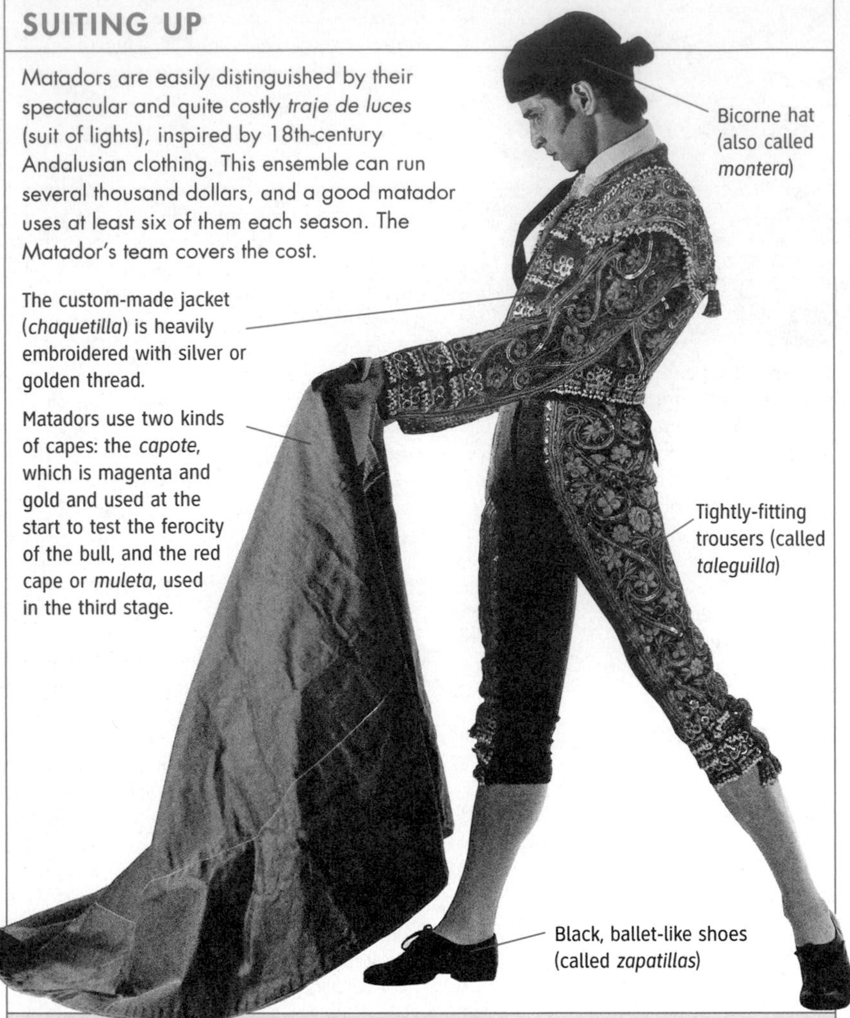

OTHER BULLFIGHTING TERMS

Alguacililllo—the title given to the two men in the arena who represent the presiding dignitary and apply his orders.

Banderilleros—the torero's team members who place a set of banderillas (barbed sticks mounted on colored shafts) into the bull's neck.

Corrida de toros—bullfight (literally, running of the bulls); sometimes just referred to as *corrida.*

Cuadrilla—the matador's team of three *banderilleros* and two *picadors.*

Matador or Torero—matador literally means "killer."

Paseíllo—the parade that the participants make when they enter the bullring.

Picador—lancers mounted on horseback.

Presidente—the presiding dignitary.

Varas—lances.

MATADOR LEGENDS, PAST AND PRESENT

YESTERDAY'S HEROES

Modern-day Spanish bullfighting's most famous son is **Juan Belmonte.** He's credited for the daring and revolutionary style that kept him and the bull always within inches of one another. **Manuel Rodríguez Sánchez** (Manolete), comes a close second. After hundreds of performances, and in Manolete's final year before retirement, he was mortally wounded in a *corrida* in Linares, Spain, resulting in a national mourning.

Manuel Rodríguez Sánchez

TODAY'S HOT MATADORS

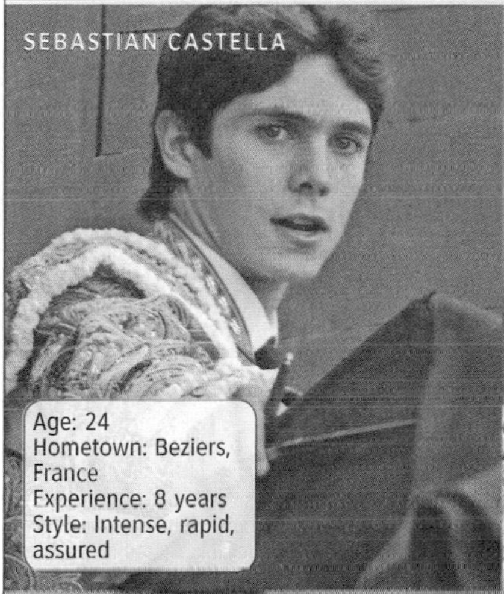

SEBASTIAN CASTELLA

Age: 24
Hometown: Beziers, France
Experience: 8 years
Style: Intense, rapid, assured

"EL JULI" (JULIÁN LÓPEZ ESCOBAR)

Age: 25
Hometown: Madrid
Experience: 10 years
Style: Nothing short of Spain's best—a master of his craft

EL FANDI (DAVÍD FANDILA MARÍN)

Age: 26
Hometown: Granada
Experience: 9 years
Style: Powerful, sharp, decisive

CÉSAR JIMÉNEZ

Age: 23
Hometown: Madrid
Experience: 6 years
Style: Creative, effortless, courageous

WHAT YOU'LL SEE

Modern-day bullfights in Spain follow a very strict ritual that's played out in 3 stages ("*tercios*" or "thirds").

1ST STAGE: TERCIO DE VARAS

After the procession of the matador and his *cuadrilla* (entourage), the bull is released into the arena. A trumpet sounds and the *picadors* (lancers on horseback) encourage the bull to attack the heavily padded horse. They use the lances to pierce the bull's back and neck muscles.

2ND STAGE: TERCIO DE BANDERILLAS

Three *banderilleros* (hit squad) on foot each attempt to plant barbed sticks mounted on colored shafts into the bull's neck and back. These further weaken the enormous ridges of the bull's neck and shoulder in order to make it lower its head. Rather than use capes, the banderilleros use their bodies to attract the bull.

3RD STAGE: TERCIO DE MUERTE (DEATH)

The torero reenters with his red cape and, if he so chooses, dedicates the bull to an individual, or to the audience. The *faena* (work), which is the entire performance with the *muleta* (cape), ends with a series of passes in which the matador attempts to maneuver the bull into a position so he can drive his sword between the shoulder blades and through the heart.

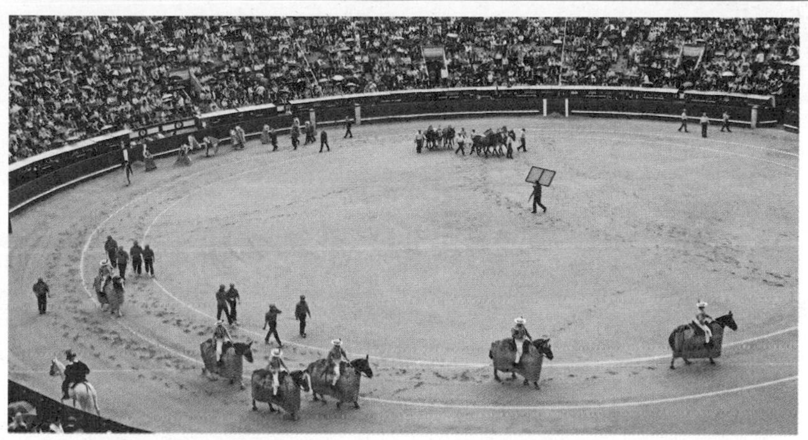

Lancers astride heavily padded horses parade around the bullring near the beginning of a fight.

HOW TO BEHAVE

The consummate bullfighting fan is both passionate and knowledgeable. The more learned respond according to the minutest details that occur inside the ring. Audiences are in fact part of the spectacle and their intervention during the event is often an indicator of the quality of the *corrida*.

For instance, during the *tercio de varas* or first third of the fight, when the matador confronts his adversary and performs with art and courage, he will be rewarded with an ovation. If a picador is over-zealous in the stabbing of the bull and leaves it too weak to fight, the crowd will boo him.

Similarly, the *estocada*, the act of thrusting the sword by the matador, can generate boos from the crowd if it's done clumsily and doesn't achieve a quick and clean death. A *trofeo* (trophy) is the usual indicator of a job well done. When the records of bullfights are kept, *trofeos* earned by the matador are always mentioned. If the crowd demands, the matador is allowed to take a lap of victory around the ring. If more than or about half the spectators petition the *presidente* by waving handkerchiefs, the presidente is obliged to award the matador with one ear of the bull.

If a matador performs particularly poorly, the audience may shift its support to the bull instead. A hapless matador may find himself being pelted with seat cushions as he makes his exit.

■TIP→ Many bullrings have eight or more entrances. It is always advisable to specify whether you want a seat in the sun *(sol)* or shade *(sombra)* or a mix of sun and shade as time passes *(sol y sombra)* as the bullfighting season coincides with the hot summer months. It's also recommended to take a cushion or rent one for €1 so you're not sitting on the hard concrete. Seats at the top rows in the sun can be as little as €5, whereas shaded bottom row seats can cost as much as €120. If you want tickets for a major bullfight, buy tickets well in advance—call 902/150025 or go online to www.taquillatoros.com.

STAR GAZING

It's not uncommon for local Spanish celebrities to attend bullfights, and during the most prestigious summer carnival, the San Isidro in Madrid, King Juan Carlos often makes an appearance.

NIGHTLIFE

Nightlife—or *la marcha*—reaches legendary heights in Madrid. It has been said that madrileños rarely sleep, largely because they spend so much time in bars—not drunk, but socializing in the easy, sophisticated way that's unique to this city. This is true of old as well as young, and it's not uncommon for children to play on the sidewalks past midnight while multigenerational families and friends convene over coffee or cocktails at an outdoor café. For those in their thirties, forties, and up who don't plan on staying out until sunrise, the best options are the bars along the Cava Alta and Cava Baja, Calle Huertas near Plaza Santa Ana, and Moratín near Antón Martín. Younger people have more options: Calle Príncipe and Calle De la Cruz—also in Santa Ana—and the Plaza de Anton Martín, especially the scruffier streets that lead onto Plaza Lavapiés. The biggest night scene—with a very mixed crowd—happens in Malasaña, which has plenty of trendy, smoke-filled hangouts on both sides of Calle San Vicente Ferrer, on Calle La Palma, and on the streets that come out onto Plaza 2 de Mayo. Also big is nearby Chueca, where tattoo parlors and street-chic boutiques break up the endless alleys of gay and lesbian bars, techno discos, and after-hours clubs.

BARS & NIGHTCLUBS

Jazz, rock, flamenco, and classical music are all popular in Madrid's many small clubs.

Bar Cock. Resembling a room at some very exclusive club (with all the waiters in suits), this bar with a dark-wood interior, cathedral-like ceilings, a big chimney, two engraved columns, and large leather chairs at every table serves about 20 different cocktails (hence the name). It caters to an older, more classic crowd. ✉*C. Reina 16, Chueca* ☎*91/532–2826.*

Café Belén. The handful of tables here are rarely empty on the weekends, thanks to the candlelight and cozy atmosphere—it attracts a young, mixed, postdinner crowd in the area and in search of the first drink of the night. Weekdays are mellower. ✉*C. Belen 5, Chueca* ☎*91/308–2747.*

Café Central. Madrid's best-known jazz venue is chic, and the musicians are often internationally known. Performances are usually from 10 PM to midnight. ✉*Plaza de Ángel 10, Santa Ana* ☎*91/369–4143.*

Café la Palma. With a bar in the front, a music venue for intimate concerts, and a chill-out room in the back, and a café in the center room, this is a must if you're in the Malasaña neighborhood. ✉*La Palma 62, Malasaña* ☎*91/522–5031.*

Castellana 8. Spacious and often with a DJ, this bar and restaurant is a perfect place for the professional and generally affluent crowd to go for the first cocktail of the night. It has a lively summer terrace, and you won't have to put up with a noisy crowd or elbow your way to the bar. ✉*Paseo de la Castellana 8, Colon* ☎*91/578–3487* ⊗*No dinner Sun.*

Costello. A multispace locale that combines a café and a lounge, Costello caters to a more relaxed and conversational crowd, with a bottom floor suited to partygoers with the latest in live and club music. On weekdays, it also features theater and stand-up comedy. ✉*Caballero de Gracia 10, Sol* ☎*91/522–1815.*

Del Diego. Arguably Madrid's trendiest cocktail bar, this place is frequented by a variety of crowds from movie directors to moviegoers. ✉*Calle de la Reina 12, Centro* ☎*91/523–3106* ⏲*Closed Sun.*

El Clandestino. This bar-café is a hidden hot spot with a local following. Jam sessions on the bottom floor (open only from Thursday to Saturday night) alternate mellow jazz with house and ambient music. ✉*Barquillo 34, Centro* ☎*91/521–5563* ⏲*Closed Sun.*

El Junco. Owners turned what was just another bar into a very happening jazz venue. The live music is a plus, but what really gets the crowd going and coming back for more are the DJs that mix late into the night. ✉*Plaza Santa Bárbara 10, Alonso Martínez* 🌐*www.eljunco.com* ☎*91/319–2081* ⏲*Closed Sun. and Mon.*

El Viajero. This establishment serves food but is best known by the madrileños who swarm around La Latina on the weekends for its middle floor bar, which is usually filled by those who jump from lunch to dinner and need a drink in between. Its irresistible terrace is usually packed. ✉*Plaza de la Cebada 11, La Latina* ☎*91/366–9064* ⏲*Closed Sun. night and Mon.*

Krypton Bar. Decorated with art toys, comic illustrations, and works by artists such as Frank Kozik and Marcus Evans, this place serves cocktails (including the sweet white Russian), plays soft and classic rock music, and offers an alternative to the louder clubs. ✉*Gonzalo de Córdoba 20, Bilbao* ☎*91/214–1412* ⏲*Closed Sun.–Wed.*

Larios Café. Cuban restaurant, bar, and disco, this art deco scene is a great place to sip a *mojito* (a refreshing Cuban cokctail made with mint, rum, lime, and sugar) any day of the week. The dance floor is open Thursday–Saturday night. ✉*Silva 4, Centro* ☎*91/547–9394.*

Los Gabrieles. This building has remarkable tile walls—advertisements from the turn of the 20th century, when this was a high-class brothel. On the same street are other night hangouts worth a look. ✉*Echegaray 17, Santa Ana* ☎*91/429–6261.*

Midnight Rose and The Penthouse. Two different spaces connected by an elevator that could easily be confused for a dance floor: the bottom lounge takes up most of the ground floor of the chic ME Reina Victoria, including the reception area; the rooftop terrace in the same hotel offers an unbeatable view of the city. ✉*Covarrubias 24, Chamberí* ☎*91/445–6886.*

Museo Chicote. Recently refurbished and regaining popularity, this landmark cocktail bar–lounge is said to have been one of Hemingway's haunts. ✉*Gran Vía 12, Centro* ☎*91/532–6737* ⏲*Closed Sun.*

Sol y Sombra. On a street filled with flamenco hangouts, this bar is designed around another very Spanish pasttime: bullfighting. However, Tomás Alía's work is so sleek and subtle that the theme might easily go unnoticed. There are jazz, R&B, and bossanova live performances early Thursday through Saturday. ✉*Echegaray 18, Santa Ana* ☎*91/542–5698* ⏲*Closed Sun. and Mon.*

Why not? Long and narrow and always packed with a very local (mostly gay) crowd from the neighborhood, this is a great place to hear '70s and '80s Spanish and American pop music. When it closes, the throng of people moves over to the even wilder Polana on C. Barbieri, which has the same owner. ✉ *C. San Bartolomé 6, Chueca* ☎ *91/523–0581.*

CABARET

Berlin Cabaret (✉ *Costanilla de San Pedro 11, Centro* ☎ *91/366–2034* ⏲ *Closed Sun.*) professes to provide cabaret as it was performed in Berlin in the '30s. Combining magic, chorus girls, and ribaldry, it draws an eccentric crowd for vintage café theater. On Friday and Saturday the fun lasts until daybreak.

DISCOS

Madrid's oldest and one of the hippest discos for all-night dancing to an international music mix is **El Sol** (✉ *C. Jardines 3, Centro* ☎ *91/532–6490*), open until 5:30 AM. There's live music beginning around midnight Thursday–Saturday. **Joy Eslava** (✉ *C. Arenal 11, Sol* ☎ *91/366–3733*), a downtown disco in a converted theater, is an old standby. **Palacio de Gaviria** (✉ *Arenal 9, Sol* ☎ *91/526–6069*), a maze of rooms turned into a disco, is mainly for foreigners. **Pachá** (✉ *Barceló 11, Centro* ☎ *91/447–0128* ⏲ *Closed Mon.–Wed.*) is always energetic. **Fortuny** (✉ *Fortuny 34, Chamberí* ☎ *91/319–0588*) attracts a celebrity crowd, especially in summer, when the lush outdoor patio opens. Put on your best dancing shoes: the door is ultraselective. Salsa has become a fixture in Madrid; check out the most spectacular moves at **Azúcar** (✉ *Paseo Reina Cristina 7, Atocha* ☎ *91/501–6107*). **Clamores** (✉ *Albuquerque 14, Chamberí* ☎ *91/445–7938* ⏲ *Closed after 11 PM Sun.*) plays live music until 2:30 AM. Attracting a sophisticated crowd, **Moma** (✉ *José Abascal 56, Chamberí* ☎ *91/399–4830* ⏲ *Closed Sun.–Tues.*) is a modern, chic disco decorated in lots of red and white. Dress policy is strict, so don't show up in sneakers and a T-shirt. **Golden Boite** (✉ *Duque de Sesto 54, Retiro* ☎ *91/573–8775*) is always hot from midnight on. For funky rhythms, try **Stella** (✉ *C. Arlabán 7, Centro* ☎ *91/531–6378* ⏲ *Closed Sun.–Wed.*). On Thursday it's called Mondo (electronic and house music); on Friday and Saturday it's the Room—a more mainstream scene. Show up late. **Shabay** (✉ *C. Miguel Ángel, 3, Chamberí* ☎ *91/319—7692*) rides on the ethnic wave that pervades the city, with lots of fusion music and Indian and South Asian remixes. The elegant, spacious setting is furnished with wicker seats, low tables, and plenty of candles. Flamboyant crowds show up late. Popular for its quiet summer terrace under the Puente de Segovia arches and its unbeatable electro-funk mixes, **Marula Café** (✉ *C. Caños Viejos, 3, Palacio Real* 🌐 *www.marulacafe.com* ☎ *91/366–1596*) is a cleverly designed narrow space with lots of illuminated wall art. Five minutes away from Plaza de Castilla **69 Pétalos** (✉ *C. Alberto Alcocer, 32, Chamartín* ☎ *No phone* ⏲ *Closed Sun.–Wed.*) is a popular disco among people in their thirties; here you'll find an eclectic music vibe—pop, hip-hop, swing, electronic—and on-stage performances by actors, go-go dancers, and musicians.

CLOSE UP

Summer Terraces

Madrid is blazing hot in the late spring and summer, and madrileños seem to have a nearly relentless yearning for nightlife. As a result, the city allows nearly 2,000 bars and restaurants to create outdoor spaces for enjoying the cool, dry summer nighttime air while sipping a beer.

For formal summer dining, we recommend some of the good hotel restaurants, most of which have private and peaceful gardens or roof terraces that avoid the street noise. Possibilities include the Ritz hotel, La Biblioteca del Santo Mauro, El Jardín de Orfila (the restaurant at the Hotel Orfila), and La Terraza del Casino. Three midrange restaurants with good terraces are Sacha, Bokado, and Pedro Larumbe—the latter's rooftop restaurant turns into one of Madrid's most fashionable terraces at night.

If you just want to grab a bite or an early-evening drink, drop by La Latina neighborhood, especially Plaza de la Paja or Plaza de San Andrés, across from the Church of San Andrés, or sit on any of the terraces at Plaza de Olavide, an enclave favored mostly by locals, near Malasaña and the Bilbao subway stop. Plaza Santa Ana is a pricier, more touristy alternative. Plaza Chueca, in the neighborhood of the same name, and the Mercado de Fuencarral (halfway between Gran Vía and Tribunal), the Plaza de 2 de Mayo, and the Plaza de las Comendadoras in the Malasaña neighborhood are always bustling and crowded with younger people.

The best nightlife is along the terraces on Castellana—especially at Ananda in the Atocha Train Station—at Terraza Atenas on Calle Segovia, and at the hotel rooftop bars that have spread out in the last few years: Urban Hotel, ME Reina Victoria, Puerta América, and De las Letras.

2

SPORTS & THE OUTDOORS

BICYCLING

Though bicycling in the city can be a risky option because of the heavy traffic and madrileños' disregard for regulations, the city parks and the surroundings towns are good for enjoyable rides. **Bravo Bike** (✉*Juan Álvarez Mendizábal 29, Sol* ☎*91/559–5523, 607/448440 ask for Kaspar* 🌐*www.bravobike.com*) is a trustworthy company that's been organizing one-day or multiday biking tours around Madrid (Toledo, Aranjuez, Chinchón, Segovia) and Spain (the pilgrimage to Santiago, the Andalucía route, and others) since 1999. They also have a guided city tour (€25) and rent bikes (€12 a day or less if you rent for a few days) if you're brave enough to head out on your own. The best way to contact them is by e-mail (info@bravobike.com). Another company that rents bicycles and organizes guided tours (in Madrid and all over Spain) is **Bike Spain** (✉*Plaza de Villa 1, entrance on calle Codo, Centro* ☎*91/559–0653, 677/356586 ask for Pablo* 🌐*www.bikespain.info*). The company charges between €10 to €15 for a half-day and one-day bike rental and €75 for a one-day guided trip to El Escorial including meals. Bike Spain also organizes the **Discover Madrid** (☎*91/588–2906 Patronato de Turismo*) bike tours for city hall. These take place every

Saturday (in English) and Sunday (in Spanish) at 10 AM and are a real bargain at €9.20 (includes rental fee).

To go out on your own, two good alternatives are the Retiro Park and the Casa de Campo. To get to the latter, you can take your bike on the subway, but only on weekends and holidays. You must ride in the first car, and you must enter at a station where attendants are present. Get off at the Casa de Campo subway stop. There you will find a map to the *anillo verde* (green ring), a special circuit for bicycles that runs along Casa de Campo and some other nearby parks.

GOLF

Eleven golf courses surround Madrid, and more are on the way. The successes of Seve Ballesteros, José María Olazabal, and Sergio García have created a new surge of interest in golf in Spain. Most golf clubs require proof of club membership. **Golf Olivar de la Hinojosa** (✉*Av. Dublín s/n, Barajas* ☎*91/721–1889* 🌐*www.golfolivar.com*), in Campo de las Naciones outside town, is open to the public, with two courses (one 18 holes, one 9) and golf lessons. They have a fixed all-week greens fee of €44. Reservations, essential on weekends, can be made up to one week in advance. **La Herrería Club** (✉*Ctra. Robledo de Chavela s/n, Escorial* ☎*91/890–5111* 🌐*www.golflaherreria.com*), in San Lorenzo de Escorial, is open to the public. Their greens fee is €65 during the week and €112 on weekends. However, weekend spots are usually reserved for members. Playing golf at La Herrería Club's 18-hole course, in the shadow of the monolithic Monastery of San Lorenzo del Escorial, is one of Spain's great golfing experiences.

HIKING

The northern section of the region around Madrid is lined by a mountain range, the Sierra de Guadarrama. Also running into some parts of Ávila and Segovia, the range is on its way to becoming Spain's 14th national park. Long favored by naturalists, writers (including John Dos Passos), painters, poets, and historians, it also attracts sporty madrileños looking to distance themselves from the chaos of the capital. The Sierra's eastern border lies at Puerto de Somosierra, west of the A1 highway heading to Burgos; the little town of Robledo de Chavela, southwest of El Escorial, marks the park's western edge. Near the middle of this long stretch sprouts another branch to the northeast, giving the Sierra de Guadarrama the shape of a fork, with the Valle de Lozoya in between the fork's tines. Hiking options are nearly limitless, but two destinations stand out because of their geological importance: the Parque de la Pedriza, a massive, orangish, fancifully shaped granite landscape in the Cuenca Alta del Manzanares, and the Peñalara's alpine cirques (basins) and lakes. The Peñalara is the park's highest peak—a holdover from the ice age that created the entire range.

The **Arawak Viajes Madrid** (✉*Peñuelas 12, Atocha* ☎*91/474–2524* 🌐*www.arawakviajes.com*) travel agency offers three or four different one-day trips every weekend to different spots in the Madrid Sierra (and to Guadalajara or Sierra de Gredos), plus a weekend trek every month. Prices to the Sierra de Guadarrama are usually around €20 to €25. You must reserve in advance and pay within one day of making the reservation. Buses depart from Estación de Autobuses Ruiz on Ronda de Atocha 12.

RUNNING

Your best running spots are the Parque del Buen Retiro, where a path circles the park and others weave under trees and through gardens, and the Parque del Oeste, with more uneven terrain but fewer people. The Casa de Campo is crisscrossed by numerous, sunnier trails.

2

SOCCER

Fútbol is Spain's number-one sport. Madrid has four teams, Real Madrid, Atlético Madrid, Rayo Vallecano, and Getafe. The two major teams are Real Madrid and Atlético Madrid. For tickets, either call a week in advance to reserve and pick them up at the stadium or stand in line at the stadium of your choice. The **Estadio Santiago Bernabeu** (✉ *Paseo de la Castellana 140, Chamartín* ☎ *91/398–4300* 🌐 *www.realmadrid.es*), which seats 75,000, is home to Real Madrid, winner of a staggering nine European Champion's Cups, the first in 1956. Atlético Madrid plays at the **Estadio Vicente Calderón** (✉ *Virgen del Puerto 67, Arganzuela* ☎ *91/366–4707 or 91/364–0888* 🌐 *www.clubatleticodemadrid.com*), on the edge of the Manzanares River south of town.

SWIMMING

Madrid has an antidote to the dry, sometimes intense heat of summer—a superb system of clean, well-run municipal swimming pools. A good option is **Piscina Canal Isabel II** (✉ *Plaza Juan Zorrilla, entrance off Av. de Filipinas, Chamberí* ☎ *91/533–1791*). It has grass, diving boards, and a wading pool for kids. Admission is about €4.

SHOPPING

Spain has become one of the world's centers for design of every kind. You'll have no trouble finding traditional crafts, such as ceramics, guitars, and leather goods (albeit not at countryside prices), but, at this point, the city is more like Rodeo Drive than the bargain bin. Known for contemporary furniture and decorative items as well as chic clothing, shoes, and jewelry, Spain's capital has become stiff competition for Barcelona. Keep in mind that many shops, especially those that are small and family run, close during lunch hours, on Sunday, and on Saturday afternoon. Shops generally accept most major credit cards.

DEPARTMENT STORES

El Corte Inglés. Spain's largest department store carries the best selection of everything, from auto parts to groceries, electronics, lingerie, and designer fashions. They also sell tickets for major sports and arts events, have their own travel agency, a restaurant (usually the building's top floor), and a great gourmet store. Madrid's biggest branch is the one on the corner of Calle Raimundo Fernández Villaverde and Castellana, which is not a central location. Try instead the one at Sol-

Callao (split into three separate buildings), or the ones at Serrano or Goya (these are also in two independent buildings). ✉*Preciados 1, 2, and 3, Sol* ☎*91/379–8000, 901/122122 general information, 902/400222 ticket sales* 🌐*www.elcorteingles.es* ✉*Callao 2, Centro* ☎*91/379–8000* ✉*Calle Goya 76 and 85, Salamanca* ☎*91/432–9300* ✉*Princesa 41, 47, and 56, Centro* ☎*91/454–6000* ✉*Calle Serrano 47 and 52, Salamanca* ☎*91/432–5490* ✉*Raimundo Fernández Villaverde 79, Chamartín* ☎*91/418–8800.*

Mango. The Turkish brothers Isaac and Nahman Andic opened their first store in Barcelona in 1984. Two decades later Mango has stores all over the world, and the brand rivals Zara as Spain's healthiest fashion venture. Mango's target customer is the young, modern, and urban woman. In comparison with Zara, Mango has fewer formal options. ✉*Fuencarral 70, Malasãa* ☎*91/523–0412* 🌐*www.mango.com* ✉*Fuencarral 140, Bilbao* ☎*91/445–7811* ✉*Calle Goya 83, Salamanca* ☎*91/435–3958* ✉*Hermosilla 22, Salamanca* ☎*91/576–8303.*

Zara. For those with young, functional, and designy tastes but slim wallets (picture hip clothes that won't last you more than one or two seasons), Zara—whose minimalist window displays are hard to miss—carries the latest looks for men, women, and children. Zara is self-made entrepreneur Amancio Ortega's textile empire flagship, which you will find all over the city. In 2003 it launched a new line, Zara Home, that sells design products for the house. Zara's clothes are considerably cheaper in Spain than in the United States or the United Kingdom. Zara has two outlet stores in Madrid—in the Gran Vía store and in Calle Carretas; both are called Lefties. If you choose to try your luck at the outlets, keep in mind that Monday and Thursday is when new deliveries arrive—and therefore the days when you have the best chance of finding good stuff. ✉*Centro Comercial ABC, Calle Serrano 61, Salamanca* ☎*91/575–6334* 🌐*www.zara.es* ✉*Gran Vía 34, Centro* ☎*91/521–1283* ✉*Velázquez 49, Salamanca* ☎*91/575–1476* ✉*Carretas 6, Sol* ☎*91/522–6945* ✉*Princesa 63, Centro* ☎*91/543–2415* ✉*Conde de Peñalver 4, Salamanca* ☎*91/435–4135.*

SHOPPING DISTRICTS

Madrid has three main shopping areas. The first, the area that stretches from Callao to Puerta del Sol (Calle Preciados, Gran Vía on both sides of Callao, and the streets around the Puerta del Sol), includes the major department stores (El Corte Inglés and the French music-and-book chain FNAC), and popular brands such as H&M and Zara.

The second area, far more elegant and expensive, is in the eastern Salamanca district, bounded roughly by Serrano, Juan Bravo, Jorge Juan (and its blind alleys), and Velázquez; the shops on Goya extend as far as Alcalá. The streets just off the Plaza de Colón, particularly Calle Serrano and Calle Ortega y Gasset, have the widest selection of designer fashions—think Prada, Loewe, Armani, or Louis Vuitton—as well as other mainstream and popular local designers (Purificación García, Pedro del Hierro, Adolfo Domínguez, or Roberto Verino). Hidden within Calle Jorge Juan, Calle Lagasca, and Calle Claudio Coello is the widest selection of smart boutiques from renowned young Spanish designers, such as Sybilla, Josep Font, Amaya Arzuaga, and Victorio & Lucchino.

Finally, for hipper clothes, Chueca is your best stop. Calle Fuencarral, from Gran Vía to Tribunal, is the street with the most shops in this area. On Fuencarral you can find name brands such as Diesel, Gas, and Billabong, but also local brands such as Homeless, Adolfo Domínguez U (selling the Galician designer's younger collection), and Custo, as well as some makeup stores (Madame B and Mac). Less mainstream and sometimes more exciting is the selection you can find on nearby Calles Hortaleza, Almirante, and Piamonte.

FLEA MARKET

On Sunday morning, Calle de Ribera de Curtidores is closed to traffic and jammed with outdoor booths selling everything under the sun—the weekly transformation into **El Rastro.** The crowds grow so thick that it takes awhile just to advance a few feet amid the hawkers and gawkers. Pickpockets abound here. Hang on to your purse and wallet, and be especially careful if you choose to bring a camera. The flea market sprawls into most of the surrounding streets, with certain areas specializing in particular products. Many of the goods are wildly overpriced. But what goods! The Rastro has everything from antique furniture to exotic parrots and cuddly puppies; from pirated cassette tapes of flamenco music to key chains emblazoned with symbols of the CNT, Spain's old anarchist trade union. Practice your Spanish by bargaining with the vendors over paintings, colorful Gypsy oxen yokes, heraldic iron gates, new and used clothes, and even hashish pipes. They may not lower their prices, but sometimes they'll throw in a handmade bracelet or a stack of postcards to sweeten the deal. Plaza General Vara del Rey has some of the Rastro's best antiques, and the streets beyond—Calles Mira el Río Alta and Mira el Río Baja—have some truly magnificent junk and bric-a-brac. The market shuts down shortly after 2 PM, in time for a street party to start in the area known as La Latina, centered on the bar El Viajero in Plaza Humilladero. Off the Ribera are two *galerías*, courtyards with higher-quality, higher-price antiques shops. All the shops (except for the street vendors) are open during the week.

SPECIALTY STORES

BOOKS

Casa del Libro (✉*Maestro Victoria 3, Centro* ☎*91/521–4898*), not far from the Puerta del Sol, has an impressive collection of English-language books, including city guides and translated Spanish classics. It's also a good source for maps, cookbooks, and gifts. Its discount store around the corner, on Calle Salud 17, sells English classics. **Booksellers** (✉*José Abascal 48, Chamberí* ☎*91/442–8104*), just off the upper Castellana near the Hotel Miguel Angel, has a large selection of books in English. **J&J** (✉*Espíritu Santo 47, Centro* ☎*91/521–8576*), a block off San Bernardo, is a charming café and bookstore run by a woman from Alabama and her Spanish husband. The store stocks a good selection of used books in English. Established in 1950, **La Tienda Verde** (✉*Maudes 23 and 38, Chamberí* ☎*91/535–3810* 🌐*www.tiendaverde.es*) is perfect for outdoor enthusiasts planning hikes, mountain-climbing expeditions, spelunking trips, and so forth; they have detailed maps and Spanish-language guidebooks.

BOUTIQUES & FASHION

The free magazine *InfoShopping* (in English and Spanish), distributed at tourist offices and upscale hotels, is a good resource, and provides detailed lists of both young and established Spanish fashion designers, as well as major international stores.

SALAMANCA The area with the most concentrated local fashion offering, especially on Calles Claudio Coello, Lagasca, and the first few blocks of Serrano. There you can find a good mix of mainstream designers, small-scale exclusive boutiques, and multibrand stores. Most mainstream designer stores are located on Calle Serrano. **Adolfo Domínguez** (✉*Calle Serrano 18 and 96, Salamanca* ☎*91/576–7053* 🌐*www.adolfo-dominguez.com*) is a Galician designer with simple, sober, and elegant lines for both men and women. Of his eight other locations in the city, the one at Calle Fuencarral 5, a block away from Gran Vía, is geared toward a younger crowd, with more affordable and colorful clothes. Also popular is the Madrileño designer **Pedro del Hierro** (✉*Calle Serrano 24 and 63, Salamanca* ☎*91/575–6906* 🌐*www.pedrodelhierro.com*), who has built himself a good reputation for his sophisticated but uncomplicated clothes for both sexes. **Purificación García** (✉*Calle Serrano 28 and 92, Salamanca* ☎*91/435–8013* 🌐*www.purificaciongarcia.es*) is also a good choice for women searching for contemporary all-day wear.

The top stores for non-Spanish fashions are mostly scattered along Ortega y Gasset, between Nuñez de Balboa and Serrano, but if you want the more exclusive of the local brands, head to the smaller designer shops unfolding along Calles Claudio Coello, Jorge Juan, and Lagasca. Start the tour on Calle Jorge Juan and its alleys, and then move northward along Claudio Coello and Lagasca toward the core of the Salamanca district. **Sybilla** (✉*Jorge Juan 12, at end of one of two cul-de-sacs, Salamanca* ☎*91/578–1322*) is the studio of Spain's best-known female designer. Her fluid dresses and hand-knit sweaters have made her a favorite with Danish former supermodel and now editor and designer Helena Christensen. Next to Sybilla is **Jocomomola** (✉*Jorge Juan 12, Salamanca* ☎*91/575–0005* 🌐*www.jocomomola.com*), which is Sybilla's younger and more affordable second brand. There you will find plenty of informal and provocative colorful pieces as well as some accessories. Across from Sybilla is **Roberto Torretta** (✉*Jorge Juan 12, at end of one of two cul-de-sacs, Salamanca* ☎*91/435–7989*), another designer with a celebrity following.

Alma Aguilar (✉*Jorge Juan 12, Salamanca* ☎*91/577–6698*) is known for using natural and prime fabrics (silks, cashmere, wool, crepe), and for her sundresses and romantic and feminine coats. For shoes to excite even the most jaded, drop by the small **Columela** (✉*Columela 6, Salamanca* ☎*91/435–1925*). You won't find Jimmy Choos or Manolo Blahniks here, but rather a more personal selection: Italy's Trans-parents and Costume National, France's L'Autre Chose, America's Marc Jacobs, local brands such as Juan Antonio López, and shoes made in Italy expressly for the store.

Young and highly praised Catalonian designer **Josep Font** (✉*Don Ramón de la Cruz 51, Salamanca* ☎*91/575–9716*) sells his seductive clothes a few blocks from the customary shopping route in the Salamanca neighborhood. Worth the detour, his clothes are distinctive and colorful, with original shapes and small, subtle touches such as ribbons or flounces that act as the designer's signature. The Gallician designer **Kina Fernández** (✉*Claudio Coello 75, Salamanca* ☎*91/426–2420*) has built a name for herself during the last three decades for clothes that are multipurpose, feminine, and very figure conscious. At **Victorio & Lucchino** (✉*Lagasca 75, Salamanca* ☎*91/431–8786* 🌐*www.victorioylucchino.com*) you can find sophisticated party dresses (many with characteristic Spanish features) in materials such as gauze, silk, or velvet, as well as more casual wear and a popular line of jewelry and accessories.

Brothers Custodio and David Dalmau are the creative force behind the success of **Custo** (✉*Claudio Coello 91, Salamanca* ☎*91/578–1322* ✉*Fuencarral 29, Chueca* 🌐*www.custo-barcelona.com* ☎*91/360–4636*), whose eye-catching T shirts can be found in the closets of such showbiz stars as Madonna and Julia Roberts. They have expanded their collection to incorporate pants, dresses, and accessories, never relinquishing the traits that have made them famous: bold colors and striking graphic designs.

If you're on a tight schedule, dropping by some of the multibrand fashion shops in the neighborhood may save you from a headache. **Nac** (✉*Génova 17, Chamberí* ☎*91/310–6050* ✉*Conde de Aranda 6, Salamanca* ☎*91/431–2515*) has a good selection of Spanish designer brands (Antonio Miró, Hoss, Josep Font, Jocomomola, and Ailanto). The store on Calle Génova is the biggest among the four they have in Madrid. **A quemarropa** (✉*Lagasca 58, Salamanca* ☎*91/435–7264*) sells very informal clothes for young and modern women from French and Italian designers such as Patrizia Pepe or Et-Vous, and from some Spanish ones such as Masscob.

A block west of Calle Fuencarral, on a narrow short street, is **the Deli Room** (✉*Santa Bárbara 4, Malasaña* ☎*91/521–1983*), a boutique with funky clothes from young Spanish designers (Josep Font, Ailanto, Miriam Orcaiz, and others). At **Ensánchez** (✉*Argensola 12, Chueca* ☎*91/319–5850*) sister-owners Nuria and Marta Sánchez sell highly original and unique accessories, especially handbags, scarves, and jewelry, from local and international designers. Chueca's trademark are its multibrand boutiques and the small multibrand fashion shops, often managed by eccentric and outspoken characters. A good example of this is **H.A.N.D** (✉*Hortaleza 26, Chueca* ☎*91/521–5152*), a cozy, tasteful store owned by two Frenchmen, Stephan and Thierry. They specialize in feminine, colorful, and young French prêt-à-porter designers (Stella Forest, La Petite, Tara Jarmon). Prominent designer **Jesús del Pozo** (✉*Almirante 9, Chueca* ☎*91/531–3646* 🌐*www.jesusdelpozo.com*) has clothes for both sexes. It's an excellent, if pricey, place to try on some classic Spanish style. **L'Habilleur** (✉*Plaza de Chueca 8, Chueca* ☎*91/531–3222*) is a fancy outlet selling samples and end-of-season designer clothes at a large discount. **Momo** (✉*Almirante 8, Chueca* ☎*91/521–5876* ✉*Jorge Juan 14, Salamanca* ☎*91/577–0704*) sells daily wear and fancier nighttime outfits from Spanish and other European designers. The highly energetic owner of **Próxima Parada** (✉*Piamonte 25, Chueca* ☎*91/310–3421*) enthusiastically digs into racks looking for daring garments from Spanish designers in her quest to quickly redefine and modernize her customers' look. The store also sells some original clothespins made by art-school students. **Uno de 50** (✉*Barquillo 41, Chueca,* ✉*Fuencarral 25, Malasaña* ☎*91/308–2953*) carries original, youngish, and inexpensive (all pieces less than €200) costume jewelry (mostly made in leather and a silver-plated tin alloy) and accessories by Spanish designer Concha Díaz del Río.

SOL The area around **Sol** is more mainstream, with big names such as Zara and H&M, and retail media and department stores (i.e., FNAC, El Corte Inglés). However, there are some interesting isolated stops such as **Seseña** (✉*De la Cruz 23, Sol* ☎*91/531–6840*), which since the turn of the 20th century has outfitted international celebrities in wool and velvet capes, some lined with red satin.

CERAMICS

Antigua Casa Talavera (✉*Isabel la Católica 2, Centro* ☎*91/547–3417*) is the best of Madrid's many ceramics shops. Despite the name, the finest wares sold here are from Manises, near Valencia, but the blue-and-yellow Talavera ceramics are also excellent. **Cántaro** (✉*Flor Baja 8, Centro* ☎*91/547–9514*) sells traditional handmade ceramics and pottery. **Cerámica El Alfar** (✉*Claudio Coello 112, Salamanca* ☎*91/411–3587*) has pottery from around Spain. **Sagardelos** (✉*Zurbano 46, Chamberí* ☎*91/310–4830*), specializing in modern Spanish ceramics from Galicia, has breakfast sets, coffeepots, and objets d'art.

FOOD & WINE

SALAMANCA **Lavinia** (✉*José Ortega y Gasset 16, Salamanca* ☎*91/426–0604* 🌐*www.lavinia.es*) claims to be the largest wine store in Europe. It has a large selection of bottles, books, and bar accessories, and even a restaurant where you can sample its products. In the middle of Salamanca's shopping area you can find **Mantequerías Bravo** (✉*C. Ayala 24, Salamanca* ☎*91/576–7641*), which has Spanish wines, olive oils, cheeses, and hams. You can find more than 120 different cheeses from all over Spain as well as almost 300 others from nearby countries such as France, Portugal, Italy, and Holland at **Poncelet** (✉*Argensola 27, Alonso Martínez* ☎*91/308–0221* 🌐*www.poncelet.es*). Marmalades, wines, and items to help you savor your cheese are also available.

SANTA ANA Just across from Los Gabrieles, behind Plaza Santa Ana, **Mariano Aguado** (✉*C. Echegaray 19, Santa Ana* ☎*91/429–6088*) is a charming 150-year-old wine store with a broad range of wines and fine spirits. The traditional food store **Gonzalez** (✉*León 12, Santa Ana* ☎*91/4295618*) holds a secret in back: a cozy and well-hidden bar where you can sample most of the fare they sell: canned asparagus; olive oil; honey; cold cuts; smoked anchovies, salmon, and other fish; and a good selection of Spanish cheeses and local wines. They also serve good, inexpensive breakfasts. Named after the current owner, the liquor store **David Cabello** (✉*Cervantes 6, Santa Ana* ☎*91/4295230*) has been in the family for more than 100 years. It's rustic and a bit dusty, and looks like a warehouse rather than a shop, but David knows what he's selling. Head here for a good selection of Rioja wines (some dating as far back as 1920) and local liqueurs, including anisettes and *pacharan,* a fruity liquor made with sloes (wild European plums).

LEATHER GOODS

On a street full of bargain shoe stores, or *muestrarios,* **Caligae** (✉*Augusto Figueroa 18 and 27, Chueca* ☎*91/531–5343*) is probably the best of the bunch. Posh **Loewe** (✉*Calle Serrano 26 and 34, Salamanca* ☎*91/577–6056* ✉*Gran Vía 8, Centro* ☎*91/532–7024* ✉*Westin Palace Hotel, Centro* ☎*91/429–8530* 🌐*www.loewe.es*) carries high-quality designer purses, accessories, and clothing made of butter-soft leather in dyed, jewel-like colors. The store on Serrano 26 displays the women's collection; items for men are a block away, on Serrano 34. Prices can hit the stratosphere. The owners of **Boxcalf** (✉*Jorge Juan 34, Salamanca* ☎*91/531–5343*), on the corner of one of Calle Jorge Juan's alleys, sell exclusive suede, nappa, and leather coats for women, as well as accessories, made in Majorca.

MUSIC

José Ramírez (✉*Calle de la Paz 8, Centro* ☎*91/531–4229*) has provided Spain and the rest of the world with guitars since 1882, and his store includes a museum of antique instruments. Prices for new ones range from €120 to €225 for children and €150 to €2,200 for adults, though some of the top concert models easily break the €10,000 mark. **Percusión Campos** (✉*Olivar 36, Lavapiés* ☎*91/539–2178*) is an easy-to-miss percussion shop-workshop where the young Canarian Pedro Navarro crafts his own *cajones flamencos* or flamenco box drums that are greatly appreciated among professionals. Prices range between €120 and €250 and vary according to the quality of woods used. **Real Música** (✉*Carlos III 1, Centro* ☎*91/540–1672*), around the corner from the Teatro Real, is a music lover's dream, with books, CDs, sheet music, memorabilia, guitars, and a knowledgeable staff.

SIDE TRIPS FROM MADRID

EL ESCORIAL

56 *50 km (31 mi) northwest of Madrid.*

Felipe II was one of history's most deeply religious and forbidding monarchs—not to mention one of its most powerful—and the great granite monastery that he had constructed in a remarkable 21 years (1563–84) is an enduring testament to his character. Outside Madrid in the foothills of the Sierra de Guadarrama, the **Real Monasterio de San Lorenzo de El Escorial** *(Royal Monastery of St. Lawrence of Escorial)* is severe, rectilinear, and unforgiving—one of the most gigantic yet simple architectural monuments on the Iberian Peninsula.

Felipe built the monastery in the village of San Lorenzo de El Escorial to commemorate Spain's crushing victory over the French at Saint-Quentin on August 10, 1557, and as a final resting place for his all-powerful father, the Holy Roman Emperor Carlos V. He filled the place with treasures as he ruled the largest empire the world has ever seen, knowing all the while that a marble coffin awaited him in the pantheon deep below. The building's vast rectangle, encompassing 16 courts, is modeled on the red-hot grille upon which St. Lawrence was martyred—appropriate enough, since August 10 was that saint's day. (It's also said that Felipe's troops accidentally destroyed a church dedicated to St. Lawrence during the battle and sought to make amends.)

El Escorial is easily reached by car, train, bus, or organized tour from Madrid. If you plan on taking public transportation, the bus is probably the best alternative. Herranz's Lines 661 (through Galapagar) and 664 (through Guadarrama) depart a few times every hour (they run less frequently on the weekends) from bay number 3 at the *Intercambiador* (station) at Moncloa. The 50-minute ride leaves you within a five-minute walk of the monastery. You can also take the *cercanías C-8a* (commuter train C-8a) from either Atocha or Chamartín. However, trains run less frequently than the buses and stop at the town of El Escorial, from where you must either take Bus L-4 (also run by Herranz) to San Lorenzo de El Escorial (where the monastery is) or take a strenuous, long walk uphill. To get to the **local tourist office** (✉ *Calle Grimaldi 2* ☎ *91/890–5313*), cross the arch that's across from the visitors' entrance to the monastery. The building and its adjuncts—a palace, museum, church, and more—can take hours or even days to tour. Easter Sunday's candlelight midnight Mass draws crowds, as does the summer tourist season.

The monastery was begun by Juan Bautista de Toledo but finished in 1584 by Juan de Herrera, who would eventually give his name to a major Spanish architectural school. It was completed just in time for Felipe to die here, gangrenous and tortured by the gout that had plagued him for years, in the tiny, sparsely furnished bedroom that resembled a monk's cell more than the resting place of a great monarch. It's in this bedroom—which looks out, through a private entrance, into

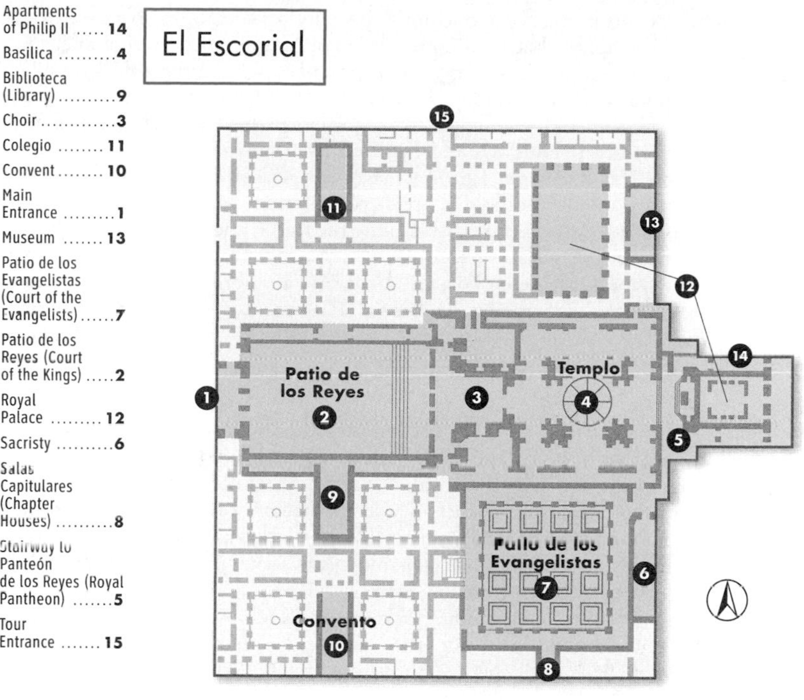

the royal chapel—that you most appreciate the man's spartan nature. Spain's later Bourbon kings, such as Carlos III and Carlos IV, had clearly different tastes, and their apartments, connected to Felipe's by the Hall of Battles, and which can be visited only with an appointment, are far more luxurious.

Perhaps the most interesting part of the entire Escorial is the **Panteón de los Reyes** (Royal Pantheon), a baroque construction room from the 17th century that contains the body of every king since Carlos I except three—Felipe V (buried at La Granja), Ferdinand VI (in Madrid), and Amadeus of Savoy (in Italy). The body of Alfonso XIII, who died in Rome in 1941, was brought to El Escorial in January 1980. The rulers' bodies lie in 26 sumptuous marble-and-bronze sarcophagi that line the walls (three of which are empty, awaiting future rulers). Only those queens who bore sons later crowned lie in the same crypt; the others, along with royal sons and daughters who never ruled, lie nearby, in the **Panteón de los Infantes** built during the reign of Elizabeth II in the third quarter of the 19th century. Many of the royal children are in a single circular tomb made of Carrara marble.

Another highlight is the monastery's surprisingly lavish and colorful **library,** with ceiling paintings by Michelangelo disciple Pellegrino Tibaldi (1527–96). The imposing austerity of El Escorial's facades makes this chromatic explosion especially powerful; try to save it for last. The library houses 50,000 rare manuscripts, codices, and ancient books, including the diary of St. Teresa of Ávila and the gold-lettered, illuminated Codex Aureus. Tapestries woven from cartoons by Goya, Rubens, and El Greco cover almost every inch of wall space in huge sections of the building, and extraordinary canvases by Velázquez, El Greco, David, Ribera, Tintoretto, Rubens, and other masters, collected from around the monastery, are displayed in the **Museos Nuevos** (New Museums). In the **basilica,** don't miss the fresco above the choir, depicting heaven, or Titian's fresco *The Martyrdom of St. Lawrence,* which shows the saint being roasted alive. ✉*San Lorenzo de El Escorial* ☎*91/890–5904 or 91/890–5905* *General admission €8; without Panteón, or after 4:30 €7; with guided tour €9* ⏲*Apr.–Sept., Tues.–Sun. 10–6; Oct.–Mar., Tues.–Sun. 10–5.*

WHERE TO EAT

$$$–$$$$ ✕**Charolés.** Some go to El Escorial for the monastery, and others go for Charolés. It's a landmark that attracts a crowd of its own for its noble bearing, with thick stone walls and vaulted ceilings, wooden beams and floors, and stuffy service; its summer terrace a block from the monastery; and its succulent dishes, such as the heavy beans with clams or mushrooms, and the game meats served grilled or in stews. It has an extensive wine menu generous in Riojas and Riberas del Duero. The four-course mammoth *cocido* (broth, chickpeas, meats, and in this case, also a salad) on Wednesday and Friday that tests the endurance of even those with the heartiest appetite. ✉*Calle Floridablanca 24* ☎*91/890–5975* ▭*AE, DC, MC, V.*

$$ ✕**La Cañada Real.** After visiting the massive monastery, this little restaurant with sketches of bullfighters on the walls is welcoming and cozy. It has fewer than 10 tables and a laid-back crowd. The menu includes a good selection of wines, grilled meats, salads, and hearty stews. The apple tart is a must for rounding off any meal. ✉*Calle Floridablanca 30* ☎*91/890–2703* ▭*MC, V* ⏲*No dinner Sun. and Mon.*

$$ ✕**La Horizontal.** Away from town and surrounded by trees in what used to be a mountain cabin, this family-oriented restaurant is coveted by madrileños who come here to enjoy the terrace in summer and the cozy bar area with a fireplace in winter. It has a good selection of fish and rice dishes, but the meats and seasonal plates are what draw the large following. Take Paseo Juan de Borbón, which surrounds the monastery, exit through the arches, and pass the *casita del infante* (Prince's Quarters) on your way up to the Monte Abantos, or get a cab at the taxi station on Calle Floridablanca. ✉*C. Horizontal s/n* ☎*91/890–3811* ▭*AE, MC, V* ⏲*No dinner Mon.–Wed. Nov.–Mar.*

VALLE DE LOS CAÍDOS

57 *13 km (8 mi) north of El Escorial on C600.*

Ranked as a not-to-be-missed visit until the death of Generalísimo Francisco Franco in 1975, this massive monument to fascism's victory over democracy (religion's victory over communism to some) in the 1936–39 Spanish civil war has become something of an anachronism

in modern democratic Spain. Now relegated to a rallying point for the extreme right on key dates, such as the July 18 commemoration of the military uprising of 1936 or the November 20 death of Franco, the Valley of the Fallen is just a few minutes north of El Escorial. A lovely pine forest leads up to a massive basilica carved out of a solid granite mountain. Topped with a cross nearly 500 feet high (accessible by elevator), the basilica holds the tombs of both General Franco and José Antonio Primo de Rivera, founder of the fascist Spanish Falange, but also the bodies of nearly 34,000 Spaniards (of both sides) who died during the civil war, and whose remains were removed from communal graves and buried here between 1959 and 1983.

The monument was built with the forced labor of postwar Republican prisoners and dedicated, rather disingenuously, to all who died in the three-year conflict. Tapestries of the Apocalypse add to the terrifying air inside as every footstep resounds off the polished marble floors and stone walls. An eerie midnight Mass is held here on Easter Sunday, the granite peak lighted by candlelight.

To get here by public transportation, take the 3:15 PM bus from the Herranz station at San Lorenzo de El Escorial. The bus makes a return drive at 5:30 (the bus plus the visit is €8.30). If you go by car, note that the adjacent Benedictine monastery has a *hospedería* (guesthouse) and a restaurant serving good, inexpensive food. ☎91/890–5611 *Basilica €5; combined with guided tour of El Escorial €10; combined with unguided tour of El Escorial €8.50 ⊙Apr.–Sept., Tues.–Sun. 10–6; Oct.–Mar., Tues.–Sun. 10–5.*

CHINCHÓN

58 *54 km (33 mi) southeast of Madrid, A3 to M832 to M311.*

A true Castilian town, the village of Chinchón seems a good four centuries removed. It makes an ideal day trip, especially if you save time for lunch at one of its many rustic restaurants; the only problem is that swarms of madrileños have the same idea, so it's often hard to get a table at lunchtime on weekends.

The high point of Chinchón is its charming **Plaza Mayor,** an uneven circle of ancient three- and four-story houses embellished with wooden balconies resting on granite columns. Restored in 2006–07 it's something like an open-air Elizabethan theater, but with a Spanish flavor—in fact, the entire plaza is converted to a bullring during the local fiestas, which take place by mid August, with temporary bleachers erected in the center and seats on the privately owned balconies rented out for splendid views.

East of the M311 runs the river Jarama. The stretch known as **Valle del Jarama** between the A3 and Ciempozuelos was the scene of one of the bloodiest battles of the Spanish Civil War. American volunteers in the Abraham Lincoln Battalion, part of the 15th International Brigade (comprised of volunteers from 26 nations), which fought with the democratically elected Spanish Republican government against Franco's military insurgency, were mauled here in a baptism of fire. Between 15,000 to 20,000 soldiers from both sides lost their lives on the river banks in a 20 day battle. Folk singer Pete Seeger immortalized the battle with "There's a valley in Spain called Jarama . . ." The trenches are still visible, and bits of rusty military hardware can still be found in the fields.

WHERE TO EAT

$$$ ✕**Parador de Chinchón (El Convento).** In the villa's best hotel, this restaurant compensates its less rustic decor with a more varied menu that includes many fish courses, vegetables such as the broad beans with sweet chives, pig's trotters, and the hearty *migas* (a traditional dish made with pieces of bread fried in olive oil, paprika, and garlic, and served with a variety of meats and a fried egg on top). It also has a fixed course €22 on the weekdays. ✉*Calle Los Huertos 1,* ☎*91/894–0836* ▭*MC, V.*

$$–$$$ ✕**Mesón de las Cuevas del Vino.** A rambling tavern with roaring fireplaces, a giant olive press in the main room, and immense antique wine and olive oil amphorae—signed by all the illustrious guests who have visited it—this is arguably the town's best-known restaurant. Madrileños swarm there for the suckling pig and the roasted lamb. For a starter, try the hearty beans, the roasted peppers (*asadillo*) or

the blood pudding. Wine tastings are held in the carved caves here, which only can be visited on weekends. ✉ *Calle Benito Hortelano 13* ☎ *91/894–0285* ♨ *Reservations essential* ▭ *MC, V* ⊙ *Closed Tues., dinner Sun., and Aug.*

$$ ✕ **Mesón el Duende.** A notch cheaper than its peers, this rustic restaurant is also smaller and hence a bit warmer. Besides the usual fare (charcoal-grilled lamb and suckling pig), this establishment also serves some comforting soups (Castilian and vegetarian) and succulent meats, such as the juicy veal steak (*churrasco*) and the tender lamb chops. It has two dining floors (one with a huge wine press in the middle), high ceilings, wooden beams, and walls lined up with posters of landmark bullfighting events. If you're short on time, stop to sip a beer or a red wine at the front bar. ✉ *Calle Grande 36* ☎ *91/894–0807* ▭ *MC, V* ⊙ *Closed Mon., and Aug.*

2

MONASTERIO DE EL PAULAR & LOZOYA VALLEY

59 *100 km (62 mi) north of Madrid.*

Rising from Spain's great central *meseta* (plain), the Sierra de Guadarrama looms northwest of Madrid like a dark, jagged shield separating Old and New Castile. Snowcapped for much of the year, the mountains are indeed rough hewn in many spots, particularly on their northern face, but there is a dramatic exception—the Lozoya Valley.

About 100 km (62 mi) north of the capital, this valley of pines, poplars, and babbling brooks is a cool, green retreat from the often searing heat of the plain. Madrileños come here for a picnic or a simple drive, rarely sharing the space with foreign travelers, to whom the area is virtually unknown.

You need a car to make this trip, and the drive is a pleasant one. Take the A6 northwest from Madrid and exit at signs for the Navacerrada Pass on the N601. As you climb toward the 6,100 foot mountain pass, you come to a road bearing to the left toward Cercedilla. (This little village, a popular base for hikes, is also accessible by train.) Just above Cercedilla, an old Roman road leads up to the ridge of the Guadarrama, where an ancient fountain, known as Fuenfría, for a long time produced the spring water that fed the Roman aqueduct of Segovia. The path traced by this cobble road is very close to the route Hemingway has his hero Robert Jordan take in *For Whom the Bell Tolls* and eventually takes you near the bridge that Jordan blows up in the novel. On the right is the exit for Navacerrada, a mountain village with a nice main plaza whose terraces get crowded during summer weekends with locals sipping beer and having tapas.

If you continue past the Cercedilla road, you come to a ski resort at the highest point of the Navacerrada Pass. Take a right here on M604 and follow the ridge of the mountains for a few miles before descending into the **Lozoya Valley.** The valley is filled with picnic spots along the Lozoya River, including several campgrounds. The monastery is on your left as you approach the floor of the Lozoya Valley.

Before visiting the monastery, stop across the road at the **Centro de Educación Ambiental Puente del Perdón** (☎*91/869–1757* ⏲*Daily 10–6*), which provides information on the area, including some lodging and eating options in Rascafría and nearby villages, and suggestions for interesting treks—one of the most beautiful is a route that takes you to La Cascada del Purgatorio, Purgatory Falls. Next to the center is El Arboreto Giner de los Ríos, an arboretum worth visiting.

The highlight of this excursion is the **Monasterio de El Paular** (☎*91/869–1425*), built by King Juan I in 1390 and the first Carthusian monastery in Castile. It was plundered five centuries later with the Disentailment of 1836, when the religious organizations' art treasures were taken by the state and its land and buildings auctioned. The state repurchased the monastery (at a much higher price) in two phases, one in 1874 and the other one in 1936, right before the beginning of the civil war. The winner of this last conflict, Francisco Franco, himself a devout Catholic, decided in 1948 to have a Benedictine monastery in Madrid, and nine years later (and 119 years after the last Carthusian left the building) the first monks arrived in El Paular. Nowadays fewer than a dozen Benedictine monks still live here, living and praying exactly as their predecessors did centuries ago. Tours (in Spanish only and conducted by one of the monks) are given Monday–Saturday at noon, 1, and 5 (on Thursday there's no 5 PM tour); Sunday tours are at 1, 4, and 5 October–April and at 1, 5, and 6 May–September. If you happen to get here on a Sunday, don't miss the noon Mass. You'll have the privilege of listening to the monks' Gregorian chants.

Attached to the monastery, the **Hotel Santa María de El Paular** (☎*91/869–1011* 🖷*91/869–1006* 🌐*www.hotelsantamariapaular.com*) is a cozy mountain hotel run by the same Westin chain that owns Madrid's Palace Hotel. The hotel has two good restaurants: Dom Lope, open daily and specializing in traditional Spanish food, and Trastámara, open weekends at lunch for great roasted lamb and suckling pig. Oteruelo del Valle, 1½ mi from Rascafría, also has some good eateries.

To end this excursion, from M604 in Rascafría turn right on a smaller and scenic road marked as Miraflores de la Sierra (M611). In that town turn right again, following signs for Colmenar Viejo, and then pick up a short expressway back to Madrid.

MADRID ESSENTIALS

To research prices, get advice from other travelers, and book travel arrangements, visit www.fodors.com.

TRANSPORTATION

For more on travel to and in Madrid, see the Madrid Planner at the beginning of the chapter.

BY AIR

Madrid is served by Madrid Barajas Airport (12 km [7 mi] east of the city), which with a capacity of up to 70 million passengers a year is Europe's fourth largest airport. It has four terminals and a bus service, *lanzadera,* which connects all of them and which departs every three minutes going from Terminal 1 to Terminal 4 in 10 minutes.

AIRPORT TRANSFERS The fastest way to get to all four terminals is the subway line number 8 (*Línea 8*). Terminal 2 (T-2) and the more remote Terminal 4 (T-4) each have a subway stop and from Terminal 2 you can walk or take the bus to the other two terminals. The metro runs every few minutes between Nuevos Ministerios (where you can check in your luggage) and Barajas Airport; it costs €1 plus a €1 airport supplement that you can pay at any subway stop or once you get on or leave from either of the two airport subway stops. The journey takes 20–30 minutes.

For a mere €1 there's also a convenient bus to Avenida de América, where you can catch the subway or a taxi to your hotel. From Avenida de América you can also take Bus 204, which takes you straight to T-4, and Bus 200, which takes you to the other three terminals. Buses leave every 15 minutes between 5:20 AM and 11:30 PM (slightly less often very early or late in the day).

In bad traffic, the 20-minute taxi ride to Madrid can take the better part of an hour, but it makes sense if you have a lot of luggage. Taxis normally wait outside the airport terminal near the clearly marked bus stop; expect to pay up to €25, more in heavy traffic (and more from Terminal 4, which is farther out), including a surcharge that goes up each year (it was €5 in 2007). Make sure the driver is on the meter—off-the-meter "deals" will surely cost you more. Some hotels offer shuttle service in vans; check with yours when you reserve.

Carriers **Air Europa** (☎ *902/401501* 🌐 *www.air-europa.com*). **Iberia** (☎ *902/400500* 🌐 *www.iberia.com*). **Spanair** (☎ *902/131415* 🌐 *www.spanair.es*). **Vueling** (☎ *902/333933* 🌐 *www.vueling.com*).

Contacts **Aeropuerto de Madrid Barajas** (✉ *Av. Hispanidad s/n* ☎ *902/353570* 🌐 *www.aena.es*).

BY BUS

Madrid has no central bus station; buses are generally less popular than trains (though they sometimes can be faster). Most of southern and eastern Spain (including Toledo) is served by the Estación del Sur. From the Estación de Avenida de América, two companies, Continental Auto and Alsa (which also has buses departing from the south station), serve mostly the north and the east, respectively. Alsa, for instance, runs two buses to Barcelona daily from Estación del Sur, and almost 20 from Avenida de América. Buses for much of the rest of the peninsula, including Cuenca, Extremadura, Salamanca, and Valencia, depart from the Auto Res station. There are also several smaller stations in Madrid, so inquire at travel agencies for the one serving your destination.

Estación de Avenida de América and Estación del Sur have subway stops (Avenida de América and Méndez Álvaro) that leave you right at the station. The Auto Res station is within a two-minute walk of the closer subway stop, Conde de Casal—however, the company will be moving all its fleet to Estación del Sur soon (date TBD). Call ahead or check its Web site to inquire about its current location. If you intend to go to Segovia, take the subway to the Príncipe Pío stop, get the Paseo de la Florida exit and walk on the left-hand side of the street until you get to La Sepulvedana bus station. La Sepulvedana bus company serves Segovia, Ávila, and La Granja. Herranz goes to El Escorial (it leaves from the Intercambiador de Moncloa; that is, the Moncloa bus station) and from there to the Valle de los Caídos. La Veloz has service to Chinchón, and Aisa goes to Aranjuez and from there to Chinchón.

Red city buses run from about 6 AM to 11:30 PM and cost €1 per ride. After midnight, buses called *búhos* ("night owls") run out to the suburbs from Plaza de Cibeles for the same price. Signs at every stop list all other stops by street name, but they're hard to comprehend if you don't know the city well. Pick up a free route map from the transportation authority's (EMT) kiosks on the Plaza de Cibeles or the Puerta del Sol, where you can also buy a 10-ride ticket called a Metrobus (€6.15) that's also valid for the subway. If you speak Spanish, call for information (☎902/507850). Drivers will generally make change for anything up to a €10 note. If you've bought a 10-ride ticket, step just behind the driver and insert it in the ticket-punching machine until the mechanism rings.

Bus Companies Aisa (✉*Estación Sur* ☎*902/198788* Ⓜ*Méndez Álvaro*). **Alsa** (✉*Av. de América 9, Salamanca* ☎*902/422242* 🌐*www.alsa.es* Ⓜ*Avenida de América*). **Continental Auto** (✉*Av. de América 9, Salamanca* ☎*91/745–6300* 🌐*www.continental-auto.es* Ⓜ*Avenida de América*). **Herranz** (✉*Intercambiador de Moncloa, Moncloa* ☎*91/896–9028* Ⓜ*Moncloa*). **La Sepulvedana** (✉*Paseo de la Florida 11, near Estación del Norte, Moncloa* ☎*91/559–8955* 🌐*www.lasepulvedana.es* Ⓜ*Príncipe Pío*). **La Veloz** (✉*Mediterrawneo 49, Atocha* ☎*91/409–7602* Ⓜ*Conde de Casal*).

Bus Stations Auto Res (✉*Fernández Shaw 1, Atocha* ☎*902/020999* 🌐*www.auto-res.net* Ⓜ*Conde de Casal*). **Estación del Avenida de América** (✉*Av. de América, 9, Salamanca* ☎*No phone* Ⓜ*Avenida de América*). **Estación del Sur**

(✉ *Méndez Álvaro s/n, Atocha* ☎ *91/468–4200* 🌐 *www.estaciondeautobuses.com* Ⓜ *Méndez Álvaro*).**Intercambiador de Moncloa** (✉ *Princesa 89, Moncloa* ☎ *No phone* Ⓜ *Moncloa*).

2

BY CAR

Felipe II made Madrid the capital of Spain because it was at the very center of his peninsular domains, and to this day many of the nation's highways radiate from Madrid like the spokes of a wheel. Originating at Kilometer 0—marked by a brass plaque on the sidewalk of the Puerta del Sol—these highways include the A6 (Segovia, Salamanca, Galicia); A1 (Burgos and the Basque Country); the A2 (Guadalajara, Barcelona, France); the A3 (Cuenca, Valencia, the Mediterranean coast); the A4 (Aranjuez, La Mancha, Granada, Seville); the A42 (Toledo); and the A5 (Talavera de la Reina, Portugal). The city is surrounded by the M30 (the inner ring road), and the M40 and M50 (the outer ring roads), from which most of these highways are easily picked up. To fight the heavy traffic leaving and getting into Madrid, the government set up an infrastructure plan that includes radial toll highways (marked R1, R2, R3, R4, and R5) that bypass the major highways by 50 to 60 km (31 to 37 mi), as well as the A41, a new toll highway connecting Madrid and Toledo. These options are worth considering, especially if you're driving on a summer weekend or a holiday.

Driving in Madrid is best avoided. Parking is nightmarish, traffic is heavy almost all the time, and the city's daredevil drivers can be frightening. August is an exception; the streets are then largely emptied by the mass exodus of madrileños on vacation.

BY SUBWAY

The subway grid covers all of the city and its surroundings. Depending on how often you're planning on using it, you can buy a €1 single ticket, the cheaper 10-ride Metrobus ticket, or a *billete de diez,* a daily ticket that costs €6.15 and can also be used on buses; the daily ticket is accepted by automatic turnstiles, so it helps you avoid long lines at ticket booths. You might consider buying the Abono Turístico (Tourist Pass) if you intend to be hopping on and off the metro for a few days; *see Discounts & Deals at the beginning of this chaper for a detailed explanation of this last ticket.* The metro system is open from 6 AM to 1:30 AM, though a few entrances close earlier. There are 12 metro lines, and system maps in stations detail their color-coded routes. Note the end station of the line you need, and follow signs to the correct corridor. Exits are marked SALIDA.

Contact **Metro Madrid** (☎ *902/444403* 🌐 *www.metromadrid.es*).

BY TAXI

Taxis work under three different tariff schemes. Tariff 1 is valid in the city center from 6 AM to 10 PM; meters start at €1.85. Supplemental charges include €5 to or from the airport, and €2.50 from bus and train stations. Tariff 2 is from 10 PM to 6 AM in the city center (and from 6 AM to 10 PM in the suburbs). During this period the meter runs faster and charges more per kilometer. Tariff 3 runs at night beyond the city limits. You'll find all tariffs listed on the taxi window.

Madrid Metro
Hospital del Norte
Pinar de Chamartín
Aeropuerto T4
Alameda de Osuna
Pueblo Nuevo
Henares
Arganda del Rey
Congosto
Villaverde Alto
La Peseta
Pitis
Herrera Oria
Las Tablas
Chamartín
Plaza Castilla
Mar de Cristal
Colombia
Nuevos Ministerios
Cuatro Caminos
Guzmán el Bueno
Canal
Moncloa
Argüelles
San Bernardo
Bilbao
Alonso Martínez
Gregorio Marañón
Avda. de América
Diego de León
La Elipa
Ventas
N. de Balboa
Manuel Becerra
Goya
Pl. de España
Noviciado
Tribunal
Callao
Gran Vía
Sol
Opera
Príncipe Pío
Príncipe de Vergara
Sainz de Baranda
Pacífico
Colonia Jardín
Casa de Campo
Acacias
Embajadores
Oporto
Plaza Elíptica
Legazpi
Puerta del Sur
Aluche
R. Manzanares
KEY
Metro Terminals
Metro Stations
Transfer Stations
Railway Lines
Train Stations

Available cabs display a LIBRE sign during the day, a green light at night. Spaniards do not usually tip cabbies, but if you're inspired, €0.50 is about right for shorter rides; you can go as high as 10% for a trip to the airport. You can call a cab through Tele-Taxi, Radioteléfono Taxi, or Radio Taxi Gremial.

Taxi Services Radio Taxi Gremial (☎ *91/447–5180*). **Radioteléfono Taxi** (☎ *91/547–8200*). **Tele-Taxi** (☎ *91/371–2131*).

BY TRAIN

Traveling by train is comfortable and safe, but for some destinations, especially regional ones, it's sometimes better to take the bus because the buses run more often.

For train schedules and reservations, go to any of Madrid's major train stations, visit a travel agent, go to the RENFE office on Alcalá 44 across from the Círculo de Bellas Artes, or call the RENFE number—they will transfer you to an English-speaking representative who can guide you through the procedure. If you use the phone to reserve a ticket, RENFE will hold your ticket for the next 72 hours, providing you go buy your ticket at least one day before departure—otherwise your reservation will be canceled. You can get the ticket from an automated machine at the station, if you pay with credit card, or at the service counter—you will have to take a number and stand in line. The best option however, is the RENFE Web site (www.renfe.es), which has an English-language section. Click on TIKNET, RENFE's online ticket sales service. You can buy regional destination tickets up to 15 days before departure, while long-distance and the fast-speed train tickets can be bought up to two months in advance.

Unfortunately, at this writing, not all train tickets are available online. This restriction applies to the *cercanías* (commuter trains), international trains, and some of the night and regional trains—for instance, you can buy a ticket online to go from Madrid to Granada or Salamanca, but not one for Madrid to Toledo or Segovia (unless you take the high-speed train, as you'll read below). The system is quite complex, even for locals, because RENFE works by type of train and not by destination. For example, you can buy tickets online for the Alaris, Altaria, Talgo, and AVE trains, but not for the Surexpress, the Lusitania, or the Elipsos. Since there are different trains covering the same route, it's not easy to figure out what you can buy online and what you cannot. To buy a ticket online, you must register and provide credit-card information. Also, note that you cannot buy a ticket online within two hours of departure. There's a 15% cancellation fee if you cancel more than two hours after making the purchase—if you wish to reschedule your ticket after buying it, you must do so at the counters at the train station. After you buy the ticket, you will be given a car and seat assignment and a *localizador* (localizer) number. You can then choose to print the ticket and reservations page up to one hour before departure or write down the car number, seat number, and localizer, and bring this information with you.

If it's the first time you've bought a ticket online through this service, you won't be able to print out the ticket. Instead you'll have to retrieve the tickets at the *venta anticipada* (advance sale) counter. Take a number and stand in line. **Be sure to bring the credit card you used when buying the ticket,** a form of ID, and the localizer. If you've bought tickets online before, you may bypass the counter and instead go directly to your assigned seat on the train. When the conductor comes around, show him the printed ticket or give him the localizer and he will issue the ticket on the spot. You will need your passport and, in most cases, the credit card with which you made the reservation.

The AVE trains work a little differently. If it's the first time you're buying, whether by phone or on the Internet, you'll have to retrieve the tickets at the sale counters; otherwise, you'll find a check-in gate before you get to the platform. There you can show the localizer and be issued a ticket, or you can proceed to the train if you have a printed ticket.

Commuter trains, which travel to El Escorial, Aranjuez, and Alcalá de Henares, run frequently throughout the day. The best way to get a ticket for such trains is to use one of the automated reservation terminals at the station (they're in the *cercanías* area). To purchase tickets for the regional lines that run less frequently but go to popular destinations such as Segovia or Toledo, you need to use the phone reservation system, the ticket counters at the station or in RENFE offices, or the automated reservations terminals at the main train stations. The high-speed AVE regional lines are an exception, and allow you to buy the ticket online. From mid-2007 you can reach Segovia from the Atocha station in a half and hour, the same time it takes you to get to Toledo. If you return within the same day, the ticket will cost you less than €15. Even if there are plenty of high-speed trains covering both routes daily, try to buy the tickets ahead of time, especially during high season. Also, keep in mind that the AVE stations in both Toledo and Segovia are located outside the city, meaning once there you'll have to either take a bus or a taxi to get to their old quarters.

TRAIN STATIONS Madrid has three main train stations: Chamartín, Atocha, and Norte, the last primarily for commuter trains. Remember to confirm which station you need when arranging a trip. Generally speaking, Chamartín, near the northern tip of Paseo de la Castellana, serves destinations north and west, including San Sebastián, Burgos, León, Oviedo, La Coruña, and Salamanca, as well as France and Portugal and the night train to Barcelona. Atocha, at the southern end of Paseo del Prado, serves towns near Madrid, including El Escorial, Segovia, and Toledo, and southern and eastern cities such as Seville, Málaga, Córdoba, Valencia, and Castellón, and the daily trains to Barcelona. Atocha also sends AVE (high-speed) trains to Córdoba, Seville, Zaragosa, Toledo, Segovia, Huesca, Lleida, and by late 2007, Barcelona. For some destinations, however, you can depart from either Atocha or Chamartín (this is the case for Toledo, Segovia, El Escorial, and Alcalá de Henares).

Train Information **Estación de Atocha** (✉ *Glorieta del Emperador Carlos V, Atocha* Ⓜ *Atocha* ☎ *91/528–4630*). **Estación Chamartín** (✉ *Agustín de Foxá* *s/n, Chamartín* Ⓜ *Chamartín* ☎ *91/315–9976).* **Estación de Príncipe Pío (Norte)** (✉ *P° de la Florida s/n, Moncloa* Ⓜ *Príncipe Pío* ☎ *902/240202 Renfe).* **RENFE** (☎ *902/240202* 🌐 *www.renfe.es).*

CONTACTS & RESOURCES

BANKS & EXCHANGING SERVICES

Banks usually are open 8:30 AM–2:30 PM during the week and 8:30 AM–1 PM on Saturday. However, May–September they're open only on the weekdays. Savings-and-loans banks have a different schedule—for instance, Caja Madrid is open weekdays 8:15 AM–2 PM and Saturday 11 AM–1:30 PM, although the latter may vary slightly depending on the office size and location. Caja Madrid also has special offices that are open continuously every day until 7 PM or 7:45 PM, in some of the city's key locations: train stations, airport terminals, and the city center (they've got one on Gran Vía 44). You'll find no trouble exchanging foreign currency into euros, especially in tourist areas (Puerta del Sol, Callao, Gran Vi), and always providing you intend to exchange reasonable amounts.

EMERGENCIES

In any emergency, call 112; an operator will redirect you to the appropriate number. Emergency pharmacies are required to be open 24 hours a day on a rotating basis; pharmacy windows and the major daily newspapers list pharmacies open round-the-clock that day. For English-speaking doctor referrals, try **Unidad Médica Angloamericana** (✉ *Conde de Aranda 1, Salamanca* ☎ *91/435–1823*), a private medical center.

The Madrid police run a phone service in several languages for tourists who are the victims of crimes; call 902/102112. Your complaint will be sent to the police station nearest to where the crime took place, and you will have two days to drop by the station and sign the report.

Emergency Services Ambulancias Cruz Roja (*Red Cross Ambulances* ☎ *91/522–2222*) are on call 24 hours a day. **Ambulancias SAMUR** (Red Cross Ambulances ☎ *112*) are always available.

Public Hospitals Hospital La Paz (✉ *Paseo de la Castellana 261, Chamartín* ☎ *91/358–2600).* **Hospital Universitario de la Princesa** (✉ *Diego de León 62, Salamanca* ☎ *91/520–2200).* **Hospital Universitario Gregorio Marañon** (✉ *C. Doctor Esquerdo 46, Moncloa* ☎ *91/586–8000).* **Hospital Universitario San Carlos** (✉ *Profesor Martín Lagos s/n, Moncloa* ☎ *91/330–3000).*

INTERNET & MAIL

A variety of Internet cafés and services exists throughout the city, especially in the Puerta del Sol neighborhood. Cyber Acceso, BBIGG, Cyberfutura, La Casa de Internet, and EasyInternetCafé are five of the largest ones. Shopkeepers and bartenders are good sources for finding a place to get online; station open daily 9–9. There is also a city tourist office with Wi-Fi access on the Plaza Mayor; it's open daily 9:30–8:30 and has six computer stations. Madrid's main post office, the Palacio de Comunicaciones, is at the intersection of Paseo de Recoletos and Calle de Alcalá, one long block north of the Prado Museum.

Internet Cafés **BBIGG** (✉ *Mayor 1, Sol* ⏲ *Weekdays 10 AM–midnight, weekends 10 AM–2 AM*). Cyber Acceso (✉ *Espoz y Mina 17, Sol* ☎ *91/532–2622* ⏲ *Mon.–Sat. 9 AM–11 PM, Sun. 11–11*). **Cyberfutura** (✉ *Montera 43, Sol* ☎ *91/521–7119* ⏲ *Mon.–Sat. 9 AM–1 AM, Sun. 10 AM–1 AM*). **EasyInternetCafé** (✉ *Alberto Aguilera 27, Moncloa* ⏲ *Mon.–Sat. 9 AM–10 PM, Sun. 9 AM–9 PM*).**La Casa de Internet** (✉ *Luchana 20, Bilbao* ☎ *91/594–4200* ⏲ *Daily 9 AM–12:30 AM*).

Post Office **Palacio de Comunicaciones** (✉ *Plaza de Cibeles s/n, Centro* ☎ *902/197197* ⏲ *Weekdays 8:30 AM–10 PM, Sat. 8:30–8 [after 2 PM, enter by C. Monteleón], Sun. 10–1*).

VISITOR INFORMATION

City Tourist Office **Madrid Municipal Tourist Office** (✉ *Plaza Mayor 27* ☎ *91/588–1636* 🌐 *www.esmadrid.com*).

Castile–León & Castile–La Mancha

Magaña, Soria province

WORD OF MOUTH

"I loved visiting the castle at Peñaranda del Duero, but the most impressive sight there for me was the Renaissance Palacio de Avellaneda. The rooms have the most impressive coffered ceilings, the artesonado (coffered ceiling) is striking—don't miss this!—and the pharmacy, Antigua Botica Ximeno, is the second oldest in Spain."

—Maribel

www.fodors.com/forums

WELCOME TO CASTILE–LEÓN & CASTILE–LA MANCHA

TOP REASONS TO GO

★ **Defying Gravity:** Overcome your vertigo with a walk across Cuenca's San Pablo Bridge.

★ **Searching for Pancho:** Ruminate along the windmilled route in Consuegra's wide-open horizon, absorbing Don Quijote's inspirational views.

★ **Toledo's Maze:** Enjoy getting lost in Toledo's labyrinthine streets.

★ **Soria's Serenity:** Stroll along the Duero River, where Antonio Machado used to write poetry.

★ **Timeless Trekking:** Mountaineer or ski in the Sierra de Gredos.

★ **Opulent Gardens:** Spend the afternoon picnicking in Aranjuez's royal gardens and desserting on the regional strawberries and cream, or wander through the Royal Palace of La Granja's San Ildefonso gardens, which rival those at Versailles.

★ **Medieval Musing:** Explore León's Gothic cathedral, with its mesmerizing, kaleidoscopic windows.

1 Segovia. The area north of Madrid prides itself with its rich and varied history, from the Roman aqueduct in Segovia to the 16th-century village of Pedraza de la Sierra.

2 Sierra de Gredos. The Gredos mountains provide a backdrop for Ávila, as well as quiet villages near Arenas de San Pedro.

3 León. The ancient area and current provincial capital, León is a fun university town with some of its Roman walls still in place.

4 Burgos. An early outpost of Christianity, this small city brims with medieval architecture and a multitude of nuns roam its streets.

5 Cuenca. The natural architecture of this hill-perched city merits at least two days of staring at it from the convent-turned-parador across the gorge. Spaniards from Madrid to Valencia flock to this peaceful village for weekend getaways.

6 Alcalá de Henares. Cervantes was born in this bustling university town near Madrid and is revered like a god. The town is renowned for its tapas.

Remains of the Convent of the Rosal in Cuenca.

7 Consuegra. Drive up to the same windmills that so characterize Don Quixote's masterpiece and inspired him to write the first modern novel.

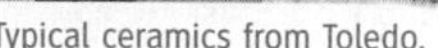
Typical ceramics from Toledo.

8 Toledo. A seriousness exudes from each corner and can be seen in its castle, massive cathedral, and all of El Greco's paintings.

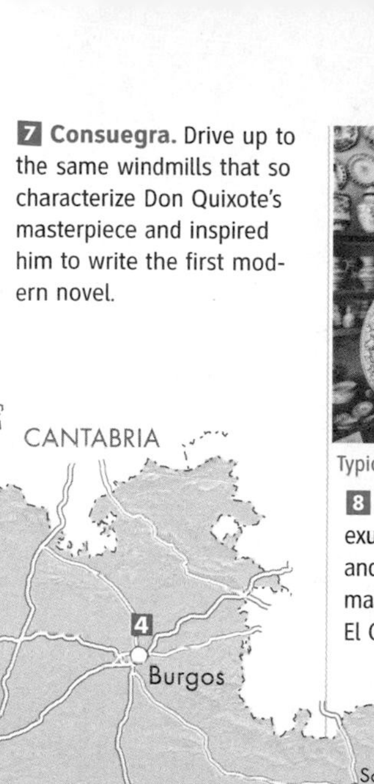

GETTING ORIENTED

Castile–León and Castile–La Mancha are like parentheses around Madrid, tilted about 45 degrees to the right. La Mancha's tourist hub is Toledo, once home to Spain's famous artist El Greco. In the larger region of Castile–León are the spectacular peaks of the Sierra de Gredos, the walled city of Ávila, and medieval Segovia, with its famed Roman aqueduct and Alcázar palace. Farther north is Salamanca, dominated by luminescent sandstone buildings, and the ancient capitals of Burgos and León.

Segovia province's Castle of Cuéllar.

CASTILE–LEÓN & CASTILE–LA MANCHA

When to Go

July and August can be brutally hot, while November through February can get bitterly cold, especially in the Sierra de Guadarrama. **May and October, when the weather is sunny but relatively cool, are the two best months to visit central Spain.**

Every town has its own festival, be it religious or a leftover pagan festival that isn't even sure of its origins. Semana Santa is the most important week of the year for many, some even spend the entire year preparing for the processions, costumes, and floats. **Cuenca's Easter celebration** and **Toledo's Corpus Christi** draw people from all over Spain. During the pre-Lenten carnival, León and nearby La Bañeza are popular party centers. Expect crowds and book accommodations months in advance if going during these times.

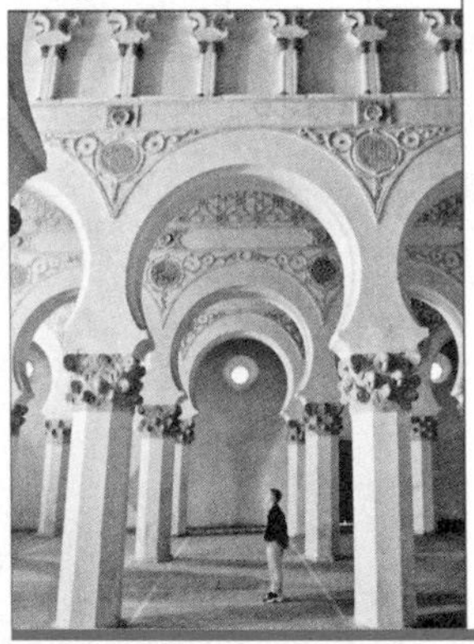

Getting There & Around

The major airport, and only international one, in Castile is Madrid's Barajas. From León and Valladolid, however, Iberia runs flights to all of Spain's major cities.

The two best ways to discover Castile are traveling by car or bus. Major divided highways—the A1 through A6—radiate out from Madrid, making all of Castile's major cities easily accessible by car. You can find the major rental outlets in Segovia, Ávila, Salamanca, Valladolid, Burgos, León, Ciudad Real, and, of course, Madrid. In recent years, the online outfit Pepe Car has been a big hit with travelers. With Pepe, in general, the earlier you book, the less you pay.

Bus connections between Madrid and Castilian destinations are excellent. Madrid's three main bus stations are Estación Sur de Autobuses (Méndez Alvaro), the bus station at the Conde de Casal Metro station, and the bus station one level above the Avenida de America Metro stop. Buses to **Segovia** (1½ hours) leave every hour from La Sepulvedana's headquarters, which are near Príncipe Pío. Larrea sends buses to **Ávila** from the Méndez Alvaro Metro stop. From the Conde de Casal Metro station, Alsa travels to **León** (4½ hours) and **Valladolid** (2¼ hours), and Auto Res serves **Cuenca** (2¾ hours) and **Salamanca** (3 hours). ⚠ **Avoid taking the bus at rush hours, as journeys can be delayed by more than an hour. Also note that because bus company operators sometimes do not speak English fluently, it's best to go online to find schedules and times.**

All the main towns in Castile-León and most in Castile-La Mancha are accessible by train from Madrid. However, trains tend to take longer than buses, have fewer daily departures, can be a rockier ride, and sometimes don't pass through certain cities. There are commuter trains from Madrid to Segovia (2 hours) and to Guadalajara (1 hour). Trains to Salamanca, Burgos, and León depart from Atocha and Chamartín; both stations also serve Ávila and Segovia, though Chamartín may have more frequent service.

See Castile Essentials at the end of this chapter for transportation contact information.

Planning Your Time

Madrid is the natural starting point for trips to Castillian destinations, most of which can be visited as either day or weekend trips. If you're traveling by car, it's quite possible to visit two nearby places in one day (e.g., Sigüenza/Mendinaceli). If you're traveling by train, we've included a few "Getting There" tips at key destinations with train information. (*See also By Train in the Castile Essentials section at the end of the chapter.*)

If you have three for four days for La Mancha, try this possible itinerary: visit site-brimming Toledo for a day and night before stopping off to see Quixote's windmills in Consuegra; afterward, swing northeast to Cuenca to enjoy its architecturally challenged old town. Complete your journey with a day and night in serene Sigüenza or Soria.

For Castile-León, an ideal three- or four-day trip would include Segovia, famous for its aqueduct and the gardens of the Palacio Real de la Granja, and Ávila—en route between Segovia and Ávila, stop by the medieval Castillo de Coca. You'll also want to visit Salamanca, both for its architecture and for its lively student-led night life. Farther north, Burgos's monasteries at Santo Domingo de Silos and San Pedro de Cardeñá are both well worth visiting—spending a night at one of the two is highly recommended.

WHAT IT COSTS In Euros

	$$$$	$$$	$$	$	¢
Restaurants	over €20	€15–€20	€10–€15	€6–€10	under €6
	$$$$	$$$	$$	$	¢
Hotels	over €180	€100–€180	€60–€100	€40–€60	under €40

Prices are per person for a main course at dinner. Prices are for two people in a standard double room in high season, excluding tax.

If You Like

Architecture

Alcalá de Henares. Birthplace of Cervantes, this town is rich in Renaissance-style structures.

Cuenca. The Hanging Houses hug the cliffs.

Salamanca. Wind through narrow streets with buildings done in plateresque style.

Toledo. It has a cathedral that resembles the great Gothic cathedral of Chartres in France.

Literary Heroes

Burgos. Visit the home of El Cid, Spain's legendary hero of the Christian Reconquest.

Consuegra. Watch the whirling of windmills in honor of Cervantes's Don Quijote.

Natural Wonders

Ciudad Encantada. Resembling a set from the *Flintstones*, or perhaps a Mars landscape, this series of limestone rock formations is about 30 minutes from Cuenca.

Sierra de Gredos. Head to Castile's premier hiking area.

Nightlife

Burgos. Get a free tapa with a drink at any bar in town.

León. Go for a tapas crawl in student-filled Plaza Mayor.

Roman Monuments

Segovia. It's engineering marvel is its Roman aqueduct.

3

Michael
ssler & Kip
bin

FOR ALL THE VARIETY IN the towns and countryside around Madrid, there's an underlying unity in Castile—the high, wide *meseta* (plain) of gray, bronze, and (briefly) green, split by the Guadarrama mountains just north of the capital. This central Spanish steppe is divided into what was historically known as Old and New Castile, the former north of Madrid, the latter south (known as "New" because it was captured from the Moors a bit later). No Spaniard refers to either as "Old" or "New" anymore, preferring instead Castilla y León or Castile-León for the area north of Madrid, and Castilla–La Mancha or Castile-La Mancha for the area to the south. The name Castilla refers to the great east–west line of castles and fortified towns built in the 12th century between Salamanca and Soria. Segovia's Alcázar, Ávila's fully intact city walls, and other bastions are among Castile's greatest monuments. Many have been converted into splendid hotels.

Stone, a dominant element in the Castilian countryside, gives the region much of its character. Gaunt mountain ranges frame the horizons; gorges and rocky outcrops break up flat expanses; and the fields around Ávila and Segovia are littered with giant boulders. Castilian villages are built predominantly of granite, and their solid, formidable look contrasts markedly with the whitewashed walls of most of southern Spain. Over the centuries, poets—most notably Antonio Machado, whose experiences at Soria in the early 20th century inspired his haunting *Campos de Castilla* (Fields of Castile)—and others have characterized Castile as austere and melancholy. There is a distinct, chilly beauty in the stark lines and soothing colors of these breezy expanses.

EXPLORING CASTILE

ABOUT THE RESTAURANTS

Castilian food is hearty stuff. Classic dishes are *cordero* (lamb) and *cochinillo* (suckling pig) roasted in a wood oven, while prized entrées include *perdiz en escabeche,* the marinated partridge of Soria, and *perdiz estofada a la Toledana,* the stewed partridge of Toledo. The mountainous districts of Salamanca, particularly the villages of Guijuelo and Candelario, are renowned for their hams and sausages—as the Spanish saying goes, "*Del cerdo se aprovecha todo*" ("All parts of the pig are there to be enjoyed"). A typical dish in the El Bierzo area, near León, is *botillo*—pig's tail, ribs, and cheeks stuffed into pig's stomach. Bean dishes are specialties of the villages El Barco (Ávila) and La Granja (Segovia), and *trucha* (trout) and *cangrejos de río* (river crab) are common in Guadalajara. Castile's most complex and exotic cuisine is perhaps that of Cuenca; here a Moorish influence appears in such dishes as *gazpacho pastor,* a hot terrine made with a mix of game, topped with grapes.

Among the region's sweets are the *yemas* (sugared egg yolks) of Ávila, *almendras garrapiñadas* (candied almonds) of Alcalá de Henares, *mazapán* (marzipan) of Toledo, and *ponche Segovia* (Segovian egg toddy). *Manchego* cheeses (from La Mancha) are staples throughout Spain, and Aranjuez is known for both its strawberries and asparagus.

Traditionally most of Spain's everyday wine has come from Castile—La Mancha's Valdepeñas region, the largest vineyard in the world. Winemakers such as Adolfo Muñoz and Carlos Falcó (Marqués de Griñón) have been cultivating new grape varietals such as Syrah and Petit Verdot with the traditional Cencibel (Tempranillo) and cabernet sauvignon vines. In Castile–León in the Duero Valley around Valladolid and Peñafiel, look for Vega Sicilia, Mauro, Pingus, Protos, Pesquera, Abadía Retuerta, and Pago de Carraovejas. The Rueda wine-growing region centered around Medina del Campo southwest of Valladolid produces fine white wines with the Verdejo varietal. Cuenca's very sweet Castilian liqueur *resolí,* made from aquavit, coffee, vanilla, orange peel, and sugar, is often sold in bottles in the shape of Cuenca's *Casas Colgadas* (Hanging Houses). It competes with neighboring Chinchon's age-old, extremely sweet Anis del Mono liqueur, brewed from herbs and anise.

ABOUT THE HOTELS

The majority of the oldest and most attractive paradors in Castile are in quieter towns such as Almagro, Ávila, Chinchón, Cuenca, León, and Sigüenza. Those in Toledo, Segovia, Salamanca, and Soria are modern buildings with magnificent views and, in the case of Segovia, have wonderful indoor and outdoor swimming pools. Of course, there are pleasant alternatives to paradors, such as Ávila's Palacio de Valderrábanos (a 15th-century palace next to the cathedral), Segovia's Infanta Isabel, Salamanca's Rector, and Cuenca's Posada San José, a 16th-century convent. Hostels in Castile range from quaint converted apartments that are reasonably priced to dingy and dilapidated and cost next to nothing. Avoid anything with two stars; they tend to have non- or poor-English speaking owners who cater to Spaniards traveling cheaply.

Numbers in the text correspond to numbers in the margin and on the chapter maps.

CASTILE–LA MANCHA

TOLEDO

Fodor'sChoice ★ *71 km (44 mi) southwest of Madrid.*

Long the spiritual capital of Spain, Toledo perches atop a rocky mount with steep ocher hills rising on either side, bound on three sides by the Río Tajo (Tagus River). When the Romans came in 192 BC, they fortified the highest point of the rock, where you now see the Alcázar. This stronghold was later remodeled by the Visigoths. In the 8th century, the Moors arrived.

The Moors strengthened Toledo's reputation as a center of religion and learning. Unusual tolerance was extended to those who practiced Christianity (the Mozarabs), as well as to the town's exceptionally large Jewish population. Today, the Moorish legacy is evident in Toledo's strong crafts tradition, the mazelike arrangement of the streets, and the predominance of brick rather than stone. For the Moors, beauty was a quality to be savored within rather than displayed on the surface, and it's significant that even Toledo's cathedral—one of the most richly endowed in Spain—is hard to see from the outside, largely obscured by the warren of houses around it.

Alfonso VI, aided by El Cid ("Lord Conqueror"), captured the city in 1085 and styled himself emperor of Toledo. Under the Christians, the town's strong intellectual life was maintained, and Toledo became famous for its school of translators, who spread to the West a knowledge of Arab medicine, law, culture, and philosophy. Religious tolerance continued, and during the rule of Peter the Cruel (so named because he allegedly had members of his own family murdered to advance himself), a Jewish banker, Samuel Levi, became the royal treasurer and one of the wealthiest men in town. By the early 1600s, however, hostility toward Jews and Arabs had grown as Toledo developed into a bastion of the Catholic Church.

As Florence had the Medici and Rome the papacy, so Toledo had its long line of cardinals, most notably Mendoza, Tavera, and Cisneros. Under these patrons of the arts, Renaissance Toledo emerged as a center of humanism. Economically and politically, however, Toledo began to decline in the 16th century. The expulsion of the Jews from Spain in 1492, as part of the Spanish Inquisition, had serious economic consequences for Toledo. When Madrid became the permanent center of the Spanish court in 1561, Toledo's political importance eroded, and the expulsion from Spain of the converted Arabs (Moriscos) in 1601 led to the departure of most of Toledo's artisan community. The years the painter El Greco spent in Toledo—from 1572 to his death in 1614—were those of the town's decline. Its transformation into a major tourist center began in the late 19th century, when the works of El Greco came to be widely appreciated after years of neglect. Today, Toledo is conservative, prosperous, and expensive.

Toledo's winding streets and steep hills can be exasperating, especially when you're looking for a specific sight. Take the entire day to absorb the town's medieval trappings, and expect to get a little lost.

■ TIP→ If you're traveling with children, look to Toledo's Tren Imperial (☎ 925/142274 🎟 €3.80, €2 kids ⏲ Daily 11–11), a fun little tourist train that chugs past many of the sights. It departs from the Plaza de Zocodover.

GETTING THERE The best way to get to Toledo from Madrid is the high-speed AVE train. The AVE leaves from Madrid eight times daily and gets you there in 35 minutes (the normal train takes 1½ hours). Buses leave every half hour from Méndez Alvaro/Estación del Sur and take 1¼ hours.

WHAT TO SEE

5 **Alcázar.** Closed for renovations until June 2008, the Alcázar ("fortress" in Arabic) was originally a Moorish citadel that stood here from the 10th century to the Reconquest. A tour around the exterior reveals the south facade, the building's most severe—the work of Juan de Her-

rera, of El Escorial fame. The east facade incorporates a large section of battlements. The finest facade is the northern, one of many Toledan works by Alonso de Covarrubias, who did more than any other architect to introduce the Renaissance style here. When the renovations are finished, the Alcázar will be the new site for the Museo del Ejercito (Military Museum), formerly in Madrid. The Alcázar's architectural highlight is Covarrubias's Italianate courtyard, which, like most other parts of the building, was largely rebuilt after the civil war, when the Alcázar was besieged by the Republicans. Though the Nationalists' ranks were depleted, they managed to hold on to the building. Franco later turned the Alcázar into a monument to Nationalist bravery; the office of the Nationalist general who defended the building, General Moscardó, has been left exactly as it was after the war, complete with peeling ceiling paper and mortar holes. Also visit the dark cellars, which evoke living conditions at the time of the siege. More cheerful is a ground-floor room full of beautifully crafted swords, a Toledo specialty introduced by Moorish silversmiths. At the top of the grand staircase are rooms displaying a vast collection of toy soldiers. ✉ *Calle Cuesta Carlos V 2* ☎ *925/221673* 💲 *€5* ⊙ *Tues.–Sun. 9:30–2:30.*

> **TOLEDO TO CIUDAD REAL HIGHLIGHTS**
>
> ■ In Toledo you can explore the mighty Gothic cathedral and the Sinagoga del Tránsito; contemplate El Greco's most famous painting, *El Entierro del Conde de Orgaz (The Burial of Count Orgaz)*; or just roam the winding lanes.
>
> ■ Aranjuez has the sumptuous Palacio Real.
>
> ■ Consuegra is the saffron capital of La Mancha.
>
> ■ Almagro, a hub during La Mancha's Age of Chivalry, has a preserved medieval theater.

⓫ **Casa de El Greco** *(El Greco's House)*. This house is on the property that belonged to Peter the Cruel's treasurer, Samuel Levi. El Greco once lived in a house owned by Levi, but it's pure conjecture that the artist lived here. The interior, decorated in the late 19th century to resemble a "typical" house of El Greco's time, is a fake, albeit a pleasant one. The museum next door has a few of El Greco's paintings, including a panorama of Toledo with the Hospital of Tavera in the foreground. ✉ *Calle Samuel Levi s/n* ☎ *925/224046* 💲 *€2.50, free Sat. afternoon and Sun. morning* ⊙ *Tues.–Sat. 10–2 and 4–9, Sun. 10–2.*

❼ **Cathedral.** Jorge Manuel Theotokópoulos was responsible for the cathedral's Mozarabic chapel, the elongated dome of which crowns the right hand side of the west facade. The rest of this facade is mainly early 15th century and has a depiction of Mary presenting her robe to Toledo's patron saint, the Visigothic Ildefonsus. Enter the cathedral from the 14th-century cloisters to the left of the west facade. The primarily 13th-century architecture was inspired by Chartres and other Gothic cathedrals in France, but the squat proportions give it a Spanish feel, as do the wealth and weight of the furnishings and the location of the elaborate choir in the center of the nave. Immediately to your right

A GOOD WALK: TOLEDO

The eastern end of the Tagus gorge, along Calle de Circunvalación, is a good place to park your car (except midday, when buses line up) and look down over most of historic Toledo. For quicker access to your car after a long day's walk, park by the Alcázar.

A complete tour starts at the **Puente de Alcántara** ❶. If you skirt the city walls traveling northwest, a long walk past the Puerta de Bisagra on Calle Cardenal Tavera brings you to the **Hospital de Tavera** ❷. If you enter the city wall, walk west and pass the **Museo de la Santa Cruz** ❸ to emerge in the **Plaza de Zocodover** ❹. Due south of here, on Calle Cuesta de Carlos V, is the **Alcázar** ❺; a short walk northwest on Calle Nueva brings you to the **Mezquita del Cristo de la Luz** ❻. From the southwestern corner of the Alcázar, a series of alleys descends to the east end of the **cathedral** ❼. Make your way around the southern side of the building, passing the mid-15th-century Puerta de los Leones. Emerging into the small square in front of the cathedral's west facade, you'll see the stately *ayuntamiento* (town hall) to your right.

Near the Museo de los Concilios, on Calle de San Clemente, take in the richly sculpted portal by Covarrubias on the Convento de San Clemente; across the street is the church of **San Román** ❽. Almost every wall in this part of town belongs to a convent, and the empty streets make for contemplative walks. This was a district loved by the Romantic poet Gustavo Adolfo Bécquer, author of *Rimas* (*Rhymes*), the most popular collection of Spanish verse before García Lorca's *Romancero Gitano*. Bécquer's favorite corner was the tiny square in front of the 16th-century convent church of **Santo Domingo** ❾, a few minutes' walk north of San Román, below the Plazuela de Padilla.

Backtrack, following Calle de San Clemente through the Plaza de Valdecaleros to Calle de Santo Tomé, to get to the church of **Santo Tomé** ❿. Downhill from Santo Tomé, off Calle de San Juan de Díos, is the **Casa de El Greco** ⓫. (Follow the signs, because this is a tricky labyrinth to navigate.) Next door to the Casa de El Greco is the 14th-century **Sinagoga del Tránsito** ⓬, financed by Samuel Levi, and the accompanying Museo Sefardí. From the synagogue, turn right up Calle de Reyes Católicos. A few steps past the town's other synagogue, **Santa María la Blanca** ⓭, is the late-15th-century church of **San Juan de los Reyes** ⓮. The town's western extremity is the **Puente de San Martín** ⓯.

as you enter the building is a beautifully carved plateresque doorway by Covarrubias, marking the entrance to the Treasury. The latter houses a small Crucifixion by the Italian painter Cimabue and an extraordinarily intricate late-15th-century monstrance by Juan del Arfe, a silversmith of German descent; the ceiling is an excellent example of Mudejar (11th- to 16th-century Moorish-influenced) workmanship.

From here, walk around to the ambulatory; off to the right side is a chapter house with a strange and quintessentially Spanish mixture of

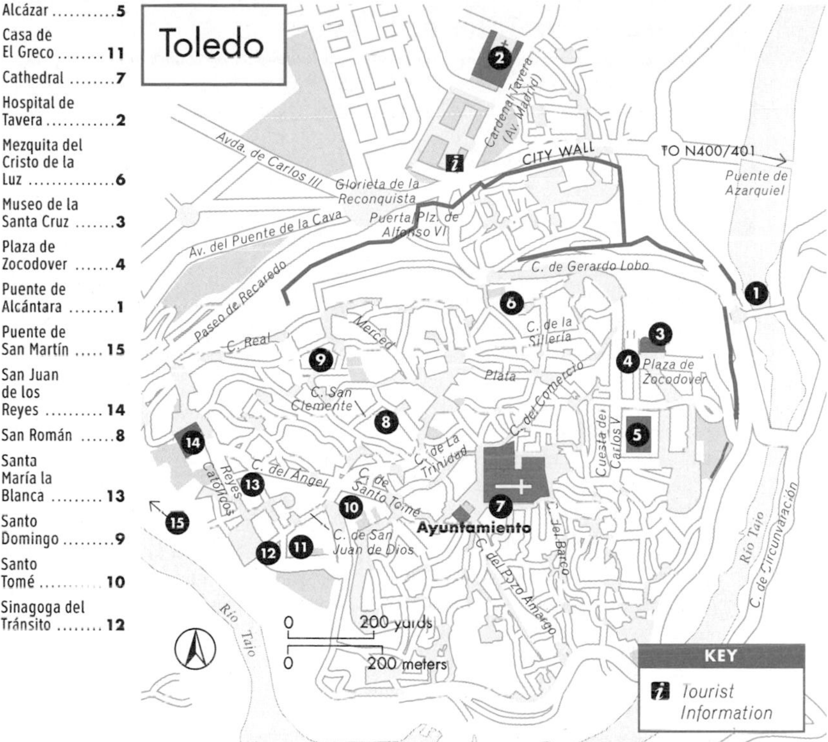

Italianate frescoes by Juan de Borgoña. In the middle of the ambulatory is an example of baroque illusionism by Narciso Tomé known as the *Transparente*, a blend of painting, stucco, and sculpture. Finally, off the northern end of the ambulatory, you'll come to the sacristy and several El Grecos, including one version of *El Espolio* (Christ Being Stripped of His Raiment). This painting is considered to be the first recorded instance of the painter in Spain. Before leaving the sacristy, look up at the colorful and spirited late-baroque ceiling painting by the Italian Luca Giordano. ✉ *Arco de Palacio 2* ☎ *925/222241* 💵 *€6* ⏲ *Mon.–Sat. 10–6:30, Sun. 2–6:30.*

10 **Santo Tomé.** Topped with a Mudéjar tower, this chapel was specially built to house El Greco's most famous painting, *The Burial of Count Orgaz*, and remains devoted to that purpose. The painting portrays the benefactor of the church being buried with the posthumous assistance of St. Augustine and St. Stephen, who have miraculously appeared at the funeral to thank him for all the money he gave to religious institutions named after them. Though the count's burial took place in the 14th century, El Greco painted the onlookers in contemporary costumes and included people he knew; the boy in the foreground is one of El Greco's sons, and the sixth figure on the left is said to be the artist himself. To avoid crowds in summer, come as soon as the building opens. ✉ *Pl. del*

CLOSE UP

El Greco: the Titan of Toledo

"Crete gave him his life, and brushes; Toledo, a better land, where he begins with Death to attain Eternity." With these words, the Toledan poet Fray Hortensio Paravicino paid homage to his friend El Greco—and to the symbiotic connection between El Greco and his adopted city of Toledo. El Greco's intensely individual and expressionist style—elongated and sometimes distorted figures, charged colors, and a haunting mysticism—was seen as strange and disturbing, and his work remained largely neglected until the late 19th century, when he found wide acclaim and joined the ranks of Velazquez and Goya as one of the old masters of Spanish painting.

Born Domenikos Theotokópoulos on the island of Crete, El Greco ("The Greek") received his artistic education and training in Italy, then moved to Spain around 1577, lured in part by the prospect of painting frescoes for the royal monastery of El Escorial. King Felipe II, however, rejected El Greco's work for being too unusual. It was in Toledo that El Greco came into his own, creating many of his greatest works and honing his singular style and unique vision. He remained here until his death in 1614.

The master painter immortalized the city and its citizens. In his masterpiece *The Burial of Count Orgaz,* which hangs in Toledo's Chapel of Santo Tomé, El Greco pays tribute to Toledan society. The burial onlookers, beneath a vibrant heaven full of angels, include many of El Greco's distinguished contemporaries, their white 16th-century ruff collars framing their angular, ascetic faces. Perhaps the most famous rendering of Toledo is El Greco's dramatic *View of Toledo,* in which Toledo's cityscape crackles with a sinister energy underneath a stormy sky.

Conde 4 ☎925/256098 🌐www.santotome.org 🎫€1.90 ⏲Mar.–mid-Oct., daily 10–6:45; mid-Oct.–Feb., daily 10–5:45.

❷ **Hospital de Tavera.** You can find this hospital, Covarrubias's last work, outside the walls beyond Toledo's main northern gate, Covarrubias's imposing Puerta de Bisagra. Unlike the former Hospital of Santa Cruz, this complex is unfinished and slightly dilapidated, but it is nonetheless full of character and has the evocatively ramshackle **Museo de Duque de Lema** in its southern wing. The most important work in the museum's miscellaneous collection is a painting by the 17th-century artist José Ribera. The hospital's monumental chapel holds El Greco's *Baptism of Christ* and the exquisitely carved marble tomb of Cardinal Tavera, the last work of Alonso de Berruguete. Descend into the crypt to experience some bizarre acoustical effects. *✉Calle Cardenal Tavera 2 ☎925/220451 🎫€4 ⏲Daily 10–1:30 and 3:30–5:30.*

❻ **Mezquita del Cristo de la Luz** *(Mosque of Christ of the Light).* A gardener will open the gate and show you around this mosque-chapel, in a park above the northern ramparts; if the gardener's not around, ask at the house opposite. Originally a tiny Visigothic church, the chapel was transformed into a mosque during the Moorish occupation; the Islamic arches and vaulting survived, making this the most important relic of Moorish Toledo. The chapel got its name when the horse of Alfonso VI, riding into Toledo in triumph in 1085, fell to its knees out front (a white stone marks the spot); it was then discovered that a candle had burned continuously behind the masonry throughout the time that the Muslims had been in power. Allegedly, the first Mass of the Reconquest was held here, and later a Mudejar apse was added (now shielded by glass). After you've seen the chapel, the gardener will take you across the ramparts to climb to the top of the Puerta del Sol, a 12th-century Mudéjar gatehouse. ✉ *Calle Cuesta de los Carmelitas Descalzas 10* ☎ *925/254191* 🎫 *€1.90* ⏲ *Oct. 1–Mar. 1, daily 10–5:45; Mar. 2–Sept. 30, daily 10–6:45. Closed 2–3:30 one unfixed day per week year-round.*

3 **Museo de la Santa Cruz.** This museum is in a beautiful Renaissance hospital with a stunning classical-plateresque facade; unlike Toledo's other sights, it's open all day without a break. The light and elegant interior has changed little since the 16th century, the main difference being that works of art have replaced the hospital beds; among the displays is El Greco's *Assumption* of 1613, the artist's last known work. A small **Museo de Arqueología** (Museum of Archaeology) is in and around the hospital's delightful cloister. ✉ *Calle de Miguel de Cervantes 3* ☎ *925/221402* 🎫 *Free* ⏲ *Mon.–Sat. 10–6:30, Sun. 10–2.*

4 **Plaza de Zocodover.** Toledo's main square was built in the early 17th century as part of an unsuccessful attempt to impose a rigid geometry on the chaotic Moorish ground plan. Nearby, you can find **Calle del Comercio,** the town's narrow and lively pedestrian thoroughfare, lined with bars and shops and shaded in summer by awnings.

1 **Puente de Alcántara.** Roman in origin, this is the town's oldest bridge. Next to it is a heavily restored castle built after the Christian capture of 1085 and, above this, a vast and depressingly severe military academy, a typical example of fascist architecture under Franco.

15 **Puente de San Martín.** This pedestrian bridge on the western edge of the town dates from 1203 and has splendid horseshoe arches.

14 **San Juan de los Reyes.** This convent church in western Toledo was erected by Ferdinand and Isabella to commemorate their victory at the Battle of Toro in 1476 and was intended to be their burial place. The building is largely the work of architect Juan Guas, who considered it his masterpiece and asked to be buried here himself. In true plateresque fashion, the white interior is covered with inscriptions and heraldic motifs. ✉ *Calle de Reyes Católicos 17* ☎ *925/223802* 🎫 *€1.90* ⏲ *Apr.–Oct., daily 10–6:45; Nov.–Mar., daily 10–6.*

8 **San Román.** A virtually unspoiled part of Toledo hides this early-13th-century Mudéjar church with extensive remains of frescoes inside. It has been deconsecrated and is now the **Museo de los Concilios y de la Cultura Visigótica,** and has statuary, manuscript illustrations, and jewelry. ✉ *Calle de San Clemente s/n* ☎ *925/227872* 🎫 *Free* ⏲ *Tues.–Sat. 10–2 and 3:30–6, Sun. 10–2.*

NEED A BREAK?

If the convolutions of Toledo's maze exhaust you, unwind at Palacio Sancara (✉ *Alfonso X El Sabio 6*). Around the corner from the church of San

Román, off Plaza Juan de Mariana, this Arabian café-bar has plush couches, low tables, soothing classical music, and colorful tapestries.

13 **Santa María la Blanca.** Founded in 1203, Toledo's second synagogue is nearly two centuries older than the more elaborate Tránsito. The white interior has a forest of columns supporting capitals of enchanting filigree workmanship. Stormed in the early 15th century by a Christian mob, the synagogue was later used as a carpenter's workshop, a store, a barracks, and a refuge for reformed prostitutes. ✉ *Calle de Reyes Católicos 4* ☎ *925/227257* 🎫 *€1.90* ⏲ *Apr.–Sept. daily 10–6:45; Oct.–Mar. daily 10–5:45.*

9 **Santo Domingo.** A few minutes' walk north of San Román is this 16th-century convent church, where you'll find the earliest of El Greco's Toledo paintings as well as the crypt where the artist is believed to be buried. The friendly nuns at the convent will show you around an odd little museum that includes documents bearing El Greco's signature. ✉ *Pl. Santo Domingo el Antiguo s/n* ☎ *925/222930* 🎫 *€1.80* ⏲ *Mon.–Sat. 11–1:30 and 4–7, Sun. 4–7.*

12 **Sinagoga del Tránsito.** Financed by Samuel Levi, this 14th-century rectangular synagogue is plain on the outside, but the inside walls are covered with intricate Mudéjar decoration, as well as Hebraic inscriptions glorifying God, Peter the Cruel, and Levi himself. It's said that Levi imported cedars from Lebanon for the building's construction, à la Solomon when he built the First Temple in Jerusalem. Adjoining the main hall is the **Museo Sefardí,** a small museum of Jewish culture in Spain. ✉ *Samuel Levi s/n* ☎ *925/223665* 🎫 *€2.50, free Sat. afternoon and Sun.* ⏲ *Mar.–Nov., Tues.–Sat. 10–9, Sun. 10–2; Dec.–Feb., Tues.–Sat. 10–2 and 4–9, Sun. 10–2.*

WHERE TO STAY & EAT

$$$–$$$$ ✕ **Asador Adolfo.** Steps from the cathedral but discreetly hidden away, this restaurant has an intimate interior with a coffered ceiling painted in the 14th century. Game, fresh produce, and traditional Toledan recipes are prepared in innovative ways. The *tempura de flor de calabacín* (fried zucchini blossoms in saffron sauce) makes for a tasty starter; King Juan Carlos I has declared Adolfo's partridge stew the best in Spain. Finish with a Toledan specialty, *delicias de mazapán* (marzipan delights). ✉ *Calle de La Granada 6* ☎ *925/227321* 🌐 *www.adolfo-toledo.com* ✍ *Reservations essential* 💳 *AE, DC, MC, V* ⏲ *Closed Mon. No dinner Sun.*

$$–$$$$ ✕ **Casón de los López de Toledo.** A vaulted foyer leads to a patio with marble statues, twittering caged birds, a fountain, and abstract religious paintings; in the dining room, carved wood abounds. The menu might include garlic-ravioli soup, braised rabbit with sesame sauce and mashed potatoes, or cod with manchego cheese, onions, and olive oil. Try the almond *mazapán* (marzipan) cake topped with cream cheese. Make reservations. ✉ *Calle Sillería 3* ☎ *902/198344* 📠 *925/257282* 🌐 *www.casontoledo.com* 💳 *AE, DC, MC, V* ⏲ *No dinner Sun.*

$–$$$ ✕ **Enebro Tapas Bar.** The motto here is, "Don't drink if you're not going to eat." Every drink ordered comes with an ample serving of *patatas* *bravas* (roast potatoes) and some combination of pizza, olives, and *croquetas* (croquettes). An enormous terrace offers gas lamps and umbrellas to provide heat in the winter and shade in the summer. Enebro, which is very popular with locals, is more of a place to take a break than have a full meal, though two people could share a *ración* (larger tapas plate) for a meal if need be. ✉ *Pl. Santiago de los Caballeros 1* ☎ *No phone* 🌐 *www.barenebro.com* ▭ *No credit cards.*

$–$$$ ✕ **Restaurante Maravilla.** Partridge, quail and seafood stand out at this homey, modestly priced spot, though the roast leg of lamb is hard to resist. ✉ *Pl. Barrio Rey 7* ☎ *925/228582* 🌐 *www.hotelmaravilla.com* ▭ *AE, DC, MC, V.*

3

$$$ ✕ **Parador de Toledo.** This modern building on Toledo's outskirts has an unbeatable panorama of the town. The architecture and furnishings nod to the traditional Toledan style, emphasizing brick and wood. The restaurant ($$$–$$$$) is stately and traditional, with top-quality regional wines and products. ■ **TIP→ Note that the hotel is under renovation until May 2008; it is open during renovation but at reduced capacity.** ✉ *Calle Cerro del Emperador s/n, 45002* ☎ *925/221850* 📠 *925/225166* 🌐 *www.parador.es* *76 rooms* *In-hotel: no pool or elevator (until renovation complete)* ▭ *AE, DC, MC, V.*

$$–$$$ ★ ✕ **Hostal del Cardenal.** Built in the 18th century as a summer palace for Cardinal Lorenzana, this quiet and beautiful hotel has rooms with antique furniture. Some rooms overlook the hotel's enchanting wooded garden, which lies at the foot of the town's walls. The restaurant, popular with tourists, has a long-standing reputation; the dishes are mainly local, and in season you can find delicious asparagus and strawberries from Aranjuez. ■ **TIP→ If you'll have a car with you, reserve a parking spot when you book your room, or you may not be guaranteed a spot.** ✉ *Paseo de Recaredo 24, 45004* ☎ *925/224900* 📠 *925/222991* 🌐 *www.hostaldelcardenal.com* *27 rooms* *In-hotel: restaurant, no elevator, laundry service, public Wi-Fi (some), parking (no fee), some pets allowed, no elevator* ▭ *AE, DC, MC, V.*

$$–$$$ **Hotel Alfonso VI.** Besides being smack in the middle of the historic district, this hotel has great views of the city from its summer terrace. The rooms are modern, clean, and inviting; the restaurant is done in the ubiquitous Mudéjar style and serves good food. ✉ *Calle General Moscardó 2, 45001* ☎ *925/222600* 📠 *925/214458* 🌐 *www.hotelalfonsovi.com* *83 rooms* *In-hotel: restaurant* ▭ *AE, DC, MC, V.*

$$–$$$ **Hotel Pintor El Greco.** Next door to the painter's house, this friendly hotel occupies what was once a 17th-century bakery. The modern interior is warm and clean, with tawny colors and antique touches, such as exposed-brick vaulting. The elevator goes to the second floor only. ✉ *Alamillos del Tránsito 13, 45002* ☎ *925/285191* 📠 *925/215819* 🌐 *www.hotel-pintorelgreco.com* *33 rooms* *In-hotel: laundry service, public Wi-Fi, parking (fee)* ▭ *AE, DC, MC, V.*

SHOPPING

The Moors established silver work, damascene (metalwork inlaid with gold or silver), pottery, embroidery, and marzipan traditions here, and next to San Juan de los Reyes a turn-of-the-20th-century art school keeps these crafts alive. For inexpensive pottery, stop at the large empo-

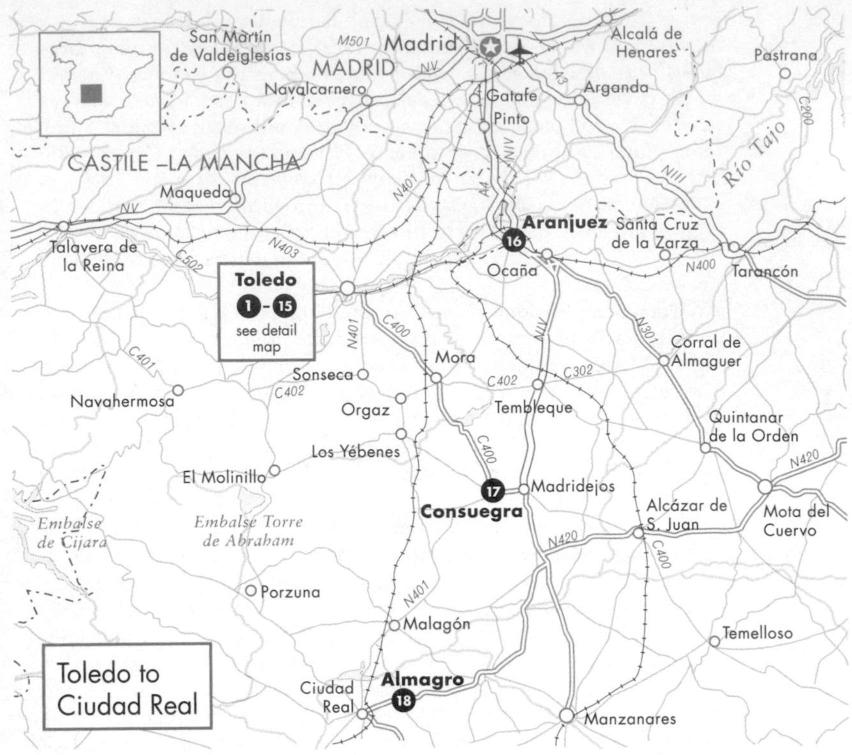

ria on the outskirts of town, on the main road to Madrid. Most of the region's pottery is made in Talavera la Reina, 76 km (47 mi) west of Toledo. At **Museo Ruiz de Luna** (✉*Pl. de San Augustín* ☎*925/800149* 🎟*Museum €0.60, weekends free* ⏲*Tues.–Sat. 10–2 and 4–6:30, Sun. 10–2*), watch artisans throw local clay, and to trace the development of Talavera's world-famous ceramics—chronicled through 1,500 tiles, bowls, vases, and plates dating back to the 15th century.

ARANJUEZ

16 *47 km (29 mi) south of Madrid, 35 km (22 mi) northwest of Toledo.*

Founded where the Tagus and Jarama rivers meet, Aranjuez was for centuries the spring quarters of the Hapsburg and Bourbon kings. Felipe V, the first of the Bourbon line, decided to transform the impressive Royal Palace, first built by Hapsburg's Felipe II in 1561, to meet the French aesthetic requirements of his time, and gave a boost to the construction of the impressive gardens and parks that surround the palace. Prohibiting people from settling near his lands (a prohibition perpetuated by other monarchs), Felipe II helped make Aranjuez a privileged green royal oasis praised by travelers visiting the court.

The Aranjuez of today is a medium-size town that still retains the splendor of its palace, gardens, and *sotos*—magnificent avenues in the northern part of the city with groves of trees—elms, ash trees, poplars, linden, and oaks. Try to visit Aranjuez in the spring or fall, when nature is showing off its brightest colors. And to see the quiet town liven up, plan to visit in May or June, when the first of two local festivals celebrates ancient music with an array of concerts in the royal gardens. All concerts are performed from their respective periods with the original instruments used to create each style of music. In spring and summer you can find street vendors selling strawberries with whipped cream by the riverbank near the palace—you can also get them at the city's food market, a restored building across from city hall.

3

GETTING THERE By commuter train (*tren de cercanías*), the ride from Madrid to Aranjuez is 50 minutes. Trains leave often from Madrid's Atocha Station. Another option is the *Tren de la Fresa (Strawberry Train)*. From April to mid-June, it departs on Saturday and Sunday from Atocha at 10:05 AM. After a 90-minute trip, you reach Aranjuez, where you get a guided tour of the city. On the way, train staff serve you strawberries, one of the region's best-known products. Round-trip fare is €24 for adults and €16 for children ages 2 to 12.

WHAT TO SEE

A 10-minute walk along the narrow avenue of Palacio Real will lead you onto the southeastern corner of the **Royal Palace.** The palace dates back to the year 1561, when Felipe II entrusted its design and construction to architect Juan Bautista de Toledo. The work was continued by Bautista's disciple, Juan de Herrera, but it was the Bourbon kings and architects (especially Giacomo Bonavia, who also built the facade) who decided to part with the austerity of the former dynasty, enlarging the palace to adapt it to the ostentatious baroque period and to the increasing number of members of the court. The inside of the palace reflects the taste of the last monarch who inhabited it (Elizabeth II, in the mid-1800s). East and north of the palace extend two gardens: the Parterre, designed during the Bourbon period, and the Island, originally designed by Herrera and mixing Spanish, Flemish, and Italian elements. A tourist train departs from the palace, making an hour tour of the city. *Av. del Palacio s/n 918/910740 Guided tour €5, special tour with access to royal family's rooms €6 Oct.–Mar., Tues.–Sun. 10–5:15; Apr.–Sept., Tues.–Sun. 10–6:15.*

The city's most impressive garden is the **Jardín del Príncipe** (*Calle de La Reina s/n 918/8924332 Free Oct.–Apr., 8 AM–6:30 PM, Mar.–Sept., 8 AM–8:30 PM*), which spreads between the Tagus course and Calle de la Reina. Designed at the end of the 18th century, it's divided into a dozen distinctive sections. In the northwestern corner of the garden is the old royal jetty and the **Museo de Falúas** (Felucca Museum) (*Calle de La Reina s/n 918/8924332 €3.40 Oct.–Mar., daily F10 AM–5:15 PM, Apr.–Sept., Tues.–Sun. 10 AM–6:15 PM*), home to seven impressive gondolas used by Spanish royalty for festive outings on the Tagus and other Spanish rivers. In the eighth garden to the east of Jardín del Príncipe is **La Casita del Labrador** (*Royal Laborer's*

House ☎*91/891–0304*) built by Carlos IV as a rustic escape from palace activity. During its construction, however, the king got carried away, creating an ostentatious small palace with all the sumptuous decorative arts of the period on display. The house can be visited only via a guided tour (*€5*), conducted in Spanish. Make a reservation in advance. When you've finished your tour, the best way to get back to town is to walk the path parallel to the Calle de la Reina, inside the park.

NEED A BREAK?

The city's most renowned restaurant is Casa Pablo (✉*Calle Almíbar 42* ☎*918/911451*), decorated with bullfighting paraphernalia. In the bar, you can get some tapas as well as something to quench your thirst.

CONSUEGRA

17 *78 km (48 mi) south of Aranjuez (Km 119 on A4).*

★ This small, historic town is dominated by a spectacular hilltop castle and 11 white **windmills.** You can drive straight up to the first windmill, **El Bolero** (restored to house the local tourist office), and walk upstairs to see the intricate 16th-century machinery. In October, the fields all around Consuegra are purple with **saffron crocuses.** These flowers appear overnight, and the three female stigmas must be handpicked from each one immediately. The stamens are then dried over braziers in private homes to become "red gold" worth €1,800 per kilogram. The process, which requires 4,000 crocuses to make 2 grams of saffron, has been used for 700 years. Consuegra's **Fiesta de la Rosa del Azafrán** (Saffron Festival), complete with competitions and saffron-based foods, is held here the last week of October.

Moors and Christians once did battle for the 10th-century **Castillo de Consuegra,** and during the second week in August the town reenacts their medieval conflict twice a day. In the 12th century the castle housed the Knights of St. John of Jerusalem, and here you can imagine that most notorious knight of all, Don Quijote, tilting at the windmills. The ramparts have classic views of the plains of La Mancha and saffron fields below. ✉*Calle del Aqueducto s/n* ☎*925/475731 tourist office and castle* *www.consuegra.es* €2 *Nov.–Mar., weekdays 9–2 and 3:30–6, weekends 10:30–2 and 3:30–6; Apr.–Oct., weekdays 9–2 and 4:30–7, Sat. 10–2 and 4:30–7, Sun. 10:30–2 and 4:30–7.*

ALMAGRO

18 *65 km (40 mi) south of Consuegra.*

The center of this noble town contains the only preserved medieval theater in Europe. The theater stands beside the ancient Plaza Mayor, where 85 Roman columns form two facing colonnades supporting green-frame 16th-century buildings. Near the plaza are granite mansions embellished with the heraldic shields of their former owners and a splendid parador in a restored 17th-century convent.

WHAT TO SEE

★ The **Corral de Comedias** theater stands almost as it did in the 16th century, when it was built, with wooden balconies on four sides and the stage at one end of the open central patio. During the golden age of Spanish theater—the time of playwrights Calderón de la Barca, Cervantes, and Lope de Vega—touring actors came to Almagro, which then prospered from mercury mines and lace making. The Corral is the site of an international theater festival each July. ✉*Pl. Mayor 18* ☎*926/861539* *€1.80* *www.corraldecomedias.com* ☞*Festival tickets: by credit card, Tele-Entrada, 926/882458; with cash, after mid-May, Palacio de los Medrano, San Agustín 7.*

The **Museo Nacional del Teatro** displays models of the Roman amphitheaters in Mérida (Extremadura) and Sagunto (near Valencia), both still in use, as well as costumes, pictures, and documents relating to the history of Spanish theater. ✉*Calle Gran Maestre 2* ☎*926/261014* *http://museoteatro.mcu.es* *Tues.–Fri. 10–2 and 4–7 (6–9 July), Sat. 11–2 and 4–6 (6–8 July), Sun. 11–2.*

WHERE TO STAY & EAT

$$–$$$ **El Corregidor.** Several old houses stuffed with antiques make up this fine restaurant and tapas bar. The menu centers on rich local fare, including game, fish, and spicy Almagro eggplant, a local delicacy. The €25 *menú de degustación* (house menu) yields seven savory tapas, and the €45 *menu Manchegomenu gastronómico,* a three-course meal that showcases regional specialties, including *pisto manchego,* a La Mancha–style vegetable ratatouille, and *ravioli de cordero* (lamb-stuffed ravioli). ✉*Pl. Fray Fernando de Córdoba 2* ☎*926/860648* *AE, DC, MC, V* *Closed Mon. Aug.–June.*

$$$ ★ **Parador de Almagro.** With cells, cloisters, and patios, this parador is a finely restored 17th-century Franciscan convent. Some rooms still resemble monks' cells, albeit with lots of modern conveniences. The restaurant ($$$–$$$$) serves fabulous *pisto manchego* (a La Mancha equivalent of ratatouille) and *migas,* fried spiced bread crumbs with chopped pork. There's also a bodega-style wine bar. ✉*Ronda San Francisco 3113270* ☎*926/860100* *926/860150* *www.parador.es* *54 rooms* *In-hotel: restaurant, bar, pool, laundry service* *AE, DC, MC, V.*

OFF THE BEATEN PATH

In 1255 Alfonso the Wise founded the university town of Ciudad Real, 22 km (14 mi) southwest of Almagro, as Villa Real. Only one of its original gate arches, the Puerta de Toledo—built in 1328—remains, and the extensive city wall has disappeared altogether. However, its cathedral, Santa María del Prado (✉*Paseo del Prado s/n*), has a magnificent baroque altarpiece by Giraldo de Merlo.

CUENCA

★ *167 km (104 mi) southeast of Madrid and 150 km (93 mi) northwest of Valencia.*

Though somewhat isolated, Cuenca makes a good overnight stop if you're traveling between Madrid and Valencia. The delightful old town is one of the strangest in Spain. It's built on a sloping, curling finger of rock whose precipitous sides plunge down to the gorges of the Huécar and Júcar rivers. Because the town ran out of room to expand, some medieval houses hang right over the abyss and are now a unique architectural attraction: the Casas Colgadas (Hanging Houses). The old town's dramatic setting grants spectacular gorge views, and its cobblestone streets, cathedral, churches, bars, and taverns contrast starkly with the modern town, which sprawls beyond the river gorges.

SOUTHEAST OF MADRID HIGHLIGHTS

Dramatic landscapes are the draw here: the rocky countryside and magnificent gorges of the Huécar and Júcar rivers make for spectacular views. Cuenca has an impressive museum devoted to abstract art, Ciudad Encantada its rock formations, and Alarcón, a medieval castle.

GETTING THERE From Madrid, buses leave for Cuenca about every 2 hours from Conde de Casal. From Valencia, four buses leave every 4–6 hours, starting at 8:30 am. Trains stop in Cuenca from either Madrid or Valencia twice a day, but this is not recommended as the train is bumpy, makes many stops, and is much slower than the bus.

WHAT TO SEE

Cuenca itself is loaded with monuments and has 14 churches and two cathedrals. Unfortunately, about half of the churches, convents, and monuments can only be viewed from the outside since visitors are not allowed inside. The best views are from the square in front of a small palace at the very top of Cuenca, where the town tapers out to the narrowest of ledges. Here, gorges are on either side of you, and old houses sweep down toward a distant plateau in front. The lower half of the old town is a maze of tiny streets, any of which will take you up to the Plaza del Carmen. From here the town narrows and a single street, Calle Alfonso VIII, continues the ascent to the Plaza Mayor, which you reach after passing under the arch of the town hall. Calle San Pedro shoots off from the northern side of Plaza Mayor; just off Calle San Pedro, clinging to the western edge of Cuenca, is the tiny Plaza San Nicolás, a pleasingly dilapidated square. Nearby, the unpaved Ronda del Júcar hovers over the Júcar gorge and commands remarkable views of the mountainous landscape.

Santa Maria de Gracia Cathedral, adjacent to the Plaza Mayor, looms large and casts an enormous shadow in the evening throughout the Plaza Mayor. Built during the Gothic era in the 12th century, many of its origins were covered by the Renaissance. Cuenca's cathedral bears a massive tryptic facade that has lost all its Gothic origins thanks to the

Renaissance. Inside are the tombs of the cathedral's founding bishops, an impressive portico of the Apostles and a Byzantine reliquary. ✉ *Pl. Mayor s/n* ☎ *969/224626* 🎫 *€2.80* ⏲ *Daily 9–1:30 and 4–6.*

The **Museo Diocesano de Arte Sacro** *(Diocesan Museum of Sacred Art)* is in what were once the cellars of the Bishop's Palace. The beautifully clear display includes a jewel-encrusted, Byzantine diptych of the 13th century; a Crucifixion by the 15th-century Flemish artist Gerard David; and two small El Grecos. From the Plaza Mayor, take Calle Obispo Valero and follow signs toward the Casas Colgadas. ✉ *Calle Obispo Valero 3* ☎ *969/224210* 🎫 *€2* ⏲ *Oct.–May, Tues.–Sat. 11–2 and 4–6, Sun. 11–2; June–Sept., Tues.–Sat. 11–2 and 5–8, Sun. 11–2.*

★ Cuenca's most famous buildings, the **Casas Colgadas** *(Hanging Houses)*, form one of Spain's finest and most curious museums, the **Museo de Arte Abstracto Español** (Museum of Spanish Abstract Art). Projecting over the town's eastern precipice, these houses originally formed a 15th-century palace, which later served as a town hall before falling into disrepair in the 19th century. In 1927 the cantilevered balconies that had once hung over the gorge were rebuilt, and finally, in 1966, the painter Fernando Zóbel decided to create (inside the houses) the world's first museum devoted exclusively to abstract art. The works he gathered are almost all by the remarkable generation of Spanish artists who grew up in the 1950s and were essentially forced to live abroad during the Franco regime: the major names include Carlos Saura, Eduardo Chillida, Lucio Muñoz, Manuel Millares, Antoni Tàpies, and Zóbel himself. ✉ *Calle Canónigos s/n* ☎ *969/212983* 🌐 *www.march.es/arte/cuenca/index.asp* 🎫 *€3* ⏲ *Tues.–Fri. 11–2 and 4–6, Sat. 11–2 and 4–8, Sun. 11–2:30.*

★ The **Puente de San Pablo,** an iron footbridge over the Huécar gorge, was built in 1903 for the convenience of the Dominican monks of San Pablo, who live on the other side. If you don't have a fear of heights, cross the narrow bridge to take in the vertiginous view of the river below and the equally thrilling panorama of the Casas Colgadas. A path from the bridge descends to the bottom of the gorge, landing you by the bridge that you crossed to enter the old town.

WHERE TO STAY & EAT

Much of Cuenca's cuisine is based around wild game: partridge, lamb, rabbit, and hen. Given the river's adjacency, trout is the fish of choice and is seen in many main courses and soups. Found in almost every town restaurant is Cuenca's paté, *morterualo,* a mixture of ham, rabbit, partridge, hen, liver, pork loin, and spices, as well as *galianos,* a thick stew served on wheat cake. For dessert, there are almond-based confections called *alajú,* which are enriched with honey, nuts, and lemon and *Semana Santa* (Holy Week) *torrijas,* made of bread dipped in milk, fried, and decorated with confectioner's sugar.

$$–$$$$ ✕**Mesón Casas Colgadas.** Run by the same management as El Figón de Pedro, this place offers much the same local fish and game but in a more pretentious manner. The white, very modern dining room is next to the Museum of Abstract Art in the gravity-defying Casas Colgadas. ✉ *Canónigos s/n* ☎ *969/223509* ✍ *Reservations essential* ▭ *AE, DC, MC, V* ⏲ *No dinner Mon.*

$$–$$$ Fodor'sChoice ★ ✕**El Figón de Pedro.** Owner Pedro Torres Pacheco, one of Spain's most famous restaurateurs, has done much to promote the excellence of Cuenca's cuisine. This pleasantly low-key spot in the lively heart of the modern town serves such local specialties as *ajoarriero,* a paste of pounded salt cod, garlic, and peppers served on toast, and *morteruelo,* a warm pâté made from the livers of wild game (such as rabbit and partridge) and served with garlic bread. For dessert, try the *alajú,* a Moorish sweet made with honey, bread crumbs, almonds, and orange water. To drink, try *resolí,* Cuenca's liqueur made from orange, coffee, and spices. ✉ *Calle Cervantes 13* ☎ *969/226821* ▭ *AE, DC, MC, V* ⏲ *Closed Mon. No dinner Sun.*

$–$$ ✕**La Ponderosa.** Famous around Spain for fine tapas and *raciones,* both to take home and consume on the premises, this place is always filled to the gills and booming. It is a completely no-smoking bar. ✉ *Calle de San Francisco 20* ☎ *969/213214* ▭ *DC, MC, V* ⏲ *Closed Sun. in June and July.*

$–$$ ✕**Las Brasas.** Meats cooked over wood coals and hearty bean concoctions excel here, with the kitchen and fire visible from the bar of this cozy, oak-floored enclave. The owners use vegetables from their garden to make a delicious *pucherete* (white-bean soup). ✉ *Alfonso VIII 105* ☎ *969/213821* ▭ *DC, MC, V* ⏲ *Closed Wed. and July.*

$$$ **Parador de Cuenca.** In the gorge beneath the Casas Colgadas is this exquisitely restored 16th-century convent of San Pablo. Rooms are furnished in a lighter and more luxurious style than the norm for Castilian houses of this vintage. ✉ *Subida a San Pablo s/n, 16001* ☎ *969/232320* 📠 *969/232534* 🌐 *www.parador.es* *63 rooms* *In-hotel: restaurant, bar, tennis court, pool, no-smoking rooms* ▭ *AE, DC, MC, V.*

$–$$$ ★ **Posada San José.** Installed in a 17th-century convent in Cuenca's old town, the *posada* (inn) clings to the top of the Huécar gorge. Furnishings are traditional, and the mood is informal and friendly. ✉ *Calle*

Julián Romero 4, 16001 ☎*969/211300* 🖷*969/230365* 🌐*www.posadasanjose.com* *29 rooms* *In-room: no a/c, no TV (some). In-hotel: restaurant, bar* 💳*AE, DC, MC, V.*

$ **Hostal Cánovas.** Near Plaza España, in the heart of the new town, this is one of Cuenca's best bargains. The lobby's not impressive, but the inviting rooms more than compensate with hardwood floors, gold-trim burgundy fabrics, and decorative white moldings. Brothers Edilio and Paulino, the owners, spent more than two years restoring the run-down 1878 building. ✉*Calle Fray Luis de León 38, 16001* ☎*969/213973* 🌐*www.hostalcanovas.com* *17 rooms* 💳*AE, MC, V.*

3

OFF THE BEATEN PATH

Ciudad Encantada *(Enchanted City)*. Not really a city at all, the Ciudad Encantada (35 km [22 mi] north of Cuenca) is a series of large and fantastic mushroomlike rock formations erupting in a landscape of pines. This commanding spectacle, deemed a "site of national interest," was formed over thousands of years by the forces of water and wind on limestone rocks. Of the ones with names, the most notable are *Cara* (Face), *Puente* (Bridge), *Amantes* (Lovers) and *Olas en el Mar* (Waves in the Sea). You can stroll through this enchanted city in under two hours.

ALARCÓN

20 *69 km (43 mi) south of Cuenca.*

This fortified village on the edge of the great plains of La Mancha stands on a high spur of land encircled almost entirely by a bend of the Júcar River. Alarcón's **castle** (✉*Av. Amigos de los Castillos 3)* dates from the 8th century, and in the 14th century it came into the hands of the *infante* (child prince) Don Juan Manuel, who wrote a collection of classic moral tales. Today the castle is one of Spain's finest paradors. If you're not driving, a bus to Motilla will leave you a short taxi ride away (call 969/331797 for a cab).

WHERE TO STAY & EAT

$$$–$$$$ **Parador de Alarcón.** This 8th- to 12th-century gorge-top castle ($$$$) is a fantasy come true, a fortress of Moorish origin decorated in a military motif. The turret room is the best and biggest; the rooms in the corner towers have arrow slit windows, and others have window niches where women did needlework. Dinner is served in an arched baronial hall complete with shields, armor, and a gigantic fireplace. ✉*Av. Amigos de los Castillos 3, 16213* ☎*969/330315* 🖷*969/330303* 🌐*www.parador.es* *14 rooms* *In-hotel: restaurant, bar, laundry service* 💳*AE, DC, MC, V.*

ALCALÁ DE HENARES

21 *30 km (19 mi) east of Madrid, off A2.*

A Roman town (Complutum) in the 1st century AD, and an Arab one (al-Qala ibn Salam, hence its current name) in the 8th century, Alcalá was the site of the first meeting between Christopher Columbus and

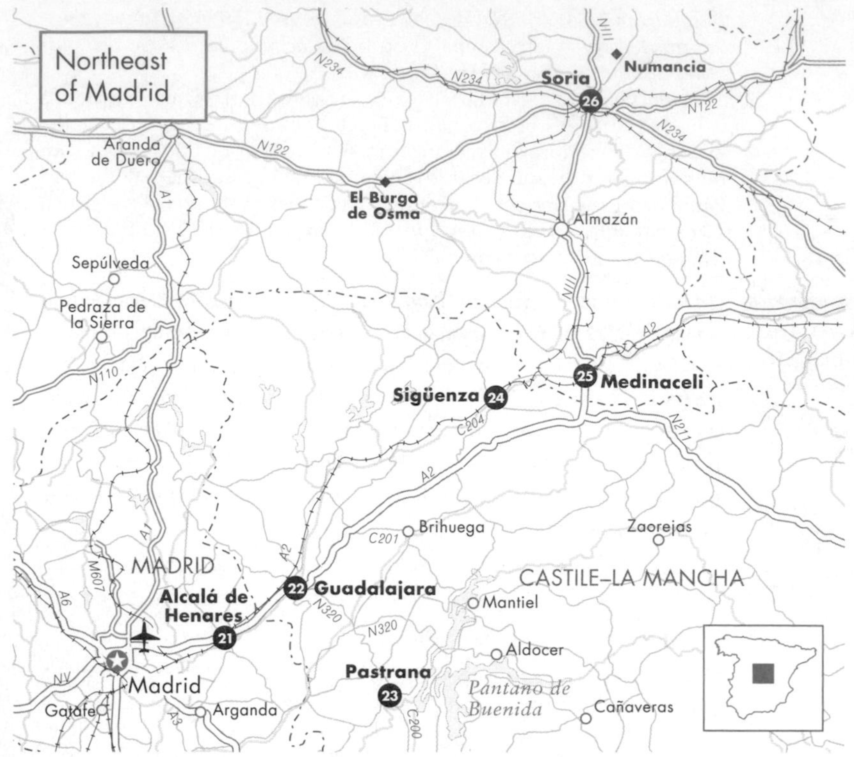

Isabella, and was also Cervantes' birthplace. By the early 1500s, it had become a major university town, attracting talented people from all over the country and beyond. A few centuries later, after some ups and downs, it remains a bustling gathering point for national and international students, a city that preserves many of its Renaissance architectural riches and is well worth a visit of half of or all of the day.

Alcalá has the largest concentration of storks in Spain and has gone to great lengths to ensure their successful cohabitation and has helped them from near-extinction to prosperity. You can see storks throughout Alcalá's rooftops, nesting on the tops of churches and the cathedral.

Every year from September 28 through November and April 20 until June 23 is the **Tren de Cervantes,** a train full of actors playing Cervantes' characters and sketches of Castillian comedy. The train leaves from Madrid's Atocha Station every Saturday and Sunday at 11 AM and returns from the Alcalá de Henares station, at Calle Pedro Lainez s/n, at 7 PM. The cost is €14 for adults and €9 for children.

GETTING THERE The best way to get to Alcalá is by a 40-minute commuter train ride from Madrid's Atocha Station. From the station to the northern corner of the university's law school, which marks the beginning of the old quarter, it is only a 10-minute walk along Paseo de la Estación.

WHAT TO SEE

The city's most significant building is **Colegio Mayor San Ildefonso** (✉ *Pl. San Diego s/n* ☎ *91/885–6487*), a part of Alcala de Henares' university and now the current university president's office. The university was founded by Cardinal Cisneros in 1499 to teach law, art, and theology; in 1514, medicine was added. Cisneros, Isabella's confessor, was a powerful and wise man who greatly influenced the politics and culture of his time. He coordinated the works that produced the first polyglot Bible (a translation of the holy scriptures in Latin, Greek, Hebrew, and Aramean). After a few centuries of glory, the university closed down in 1836 after the state began confiscating the Catholic Church's assets. Later the university was bought back by a group of citizens in 1850. The group's successors started renting the premises to the state in 1977 for the symbolic amount of 1 peseta a year, so that the university could reopen. The building has four patios and a magnificent chapel, done in a mix of Gothic, plateresque, and Mudejar styles, which houses Cisneros's highly ornamented sepulchre (his remains are safeguarded beneath Alcalá's cathedral's presbytery), carved in Carrara marble. The beautiful main lecture hall, the students' graduation exam room in the 16th and 17th centuries, is where Juan Carlos I, Spain's present-day king, awards the annual Premio Cervantes, the most distinguished literature award in the Spanish language. Students offer guided tours of the building several times a day—call in advance for one in English.

NORTHEAST OF MADRID HIGHLIGHTS

They're off the main tourist tracks, but the provinces of Guadalajara (in Castile–La Mancha) and Soria (in Castile–León) have a lot to offer and are easily accessible by train or bus. The rail from Madrid to Zaragoza passes through every town in this section, allowing a manageable excursion of two to three days. If you have a car, you can extend this trip with a countryside detour. Best two towns to linger at: Sigüenza, in Castile–La Mancha, for its architecture; and Medinaceli, in Castile–León, for its views.

The **Museo Arqueológico Regional** (*Regional Archaeological Museum*) traces the history of life in Madrid to the 18th century. ✉ *Pl. de las Bernardas* ☎ *91/879–6666* 💲 *Free* ⏲ *Tues.–Sat. 11* AM*–7* PM*, Sun. 11* AM*–3* PM.

On Plaza del Santos Niños is the **Catedral Magistral** (✉ *Pl. de los Santos Niños s/n* ☎ *No phone* 💲 *Free* ⏲ *9–1 and 5–8:30, Sat. 9–1 and 6–8:30, Sun. 10–1:30 and 6–8:30*), built in the late-Gothic style and still preserving some valuable elements despite a fire that severely damaged it in 1936. Across from the Catedral Magistral is one of the city's two **tourist offices** (✉ *Pl. de los Santos Niños s/n* ☎ *91/881–0634* ✉ *Callejón de Santa María 1* ☎ *91/889–2694*); the other is near the southeastern edge of the Colegio Mayor San Ildefonso's building, on Callejón Santa María. Don't miss the largest open-air sculpture museum in Europe, **Museo de Esculturas al Aire Libre** (✉ *Vía Complutense* ☎ *91/881–3934*). It houses more than 140 sculptures from famous contemporary Spanish artists, using many varieties of metals and minerals in an amazing boullibaise of styles. This free, sprawling attraction begins near Palacio Robispal.

■ **TIP→** If you're part of a group, you may want to buy guided tours in English (€115–€125) from **Promoción Turística de Alcalá** (✉ *Pl. de los Irlandeses 1* ☎ *91/882–1354* 🌐 *www.alcalaturismo.com*).

WHERE TO EAT

The best place to eat—for its location (on Colegio Mayor San Ildefonso) and for its food (great suckling pig, lamb, and venison, and other regional delicacies)—is the **Hostería del Estudiante** (✉ *Calle Colegios 3* ☎ *91/8880330*).

GUADALAJARA

22 *17 km (10 mi) northeast of Alcalá.*

This quiet, affluent provincial capital is popular with Madrid commuters, who own many of the villas with terra-cotta roofs that sprawl down its slopes.

Guadalajara was severely damaged in the civil war, but its **Palacio del Infantado** *(Palace of the Prince's Territory)* still stands and is one of the most important Spanish palaces of its period. Built between 1461 and 1492 by Juan Guas, the palace is a bizarre and potent mixture of Gothic, classical, and Mudéjar influences. The main facade is rich; the lower floors are studded with diamond shapes; and the whole is crowned by a complex Gothic gallery supported on a frieze pitted with intricate Moorish cellular work (the honeycomb motif). Inside is a fanciful and exciting courtyard. The ground floor holds the Museo de Bellas Artes, a modest provincial art gallery. ✉ *Pl. de los Caídos 1* ☎ *949/213301* 🎫 *Palace and museum free* ⏲ *Weekdays 9–9:30, Sat. 9–2:30 and 4–7:30, Sun. 10–2:30 and 5–7:30.*

EN ROUTE

East of Guadalajara extends the Alcarria, a high plateau crossed by rivers forming verdant valleys. It was made famous in the 1950s by one of the great classics of Spanish travel literature, Camilo José Cela's *Journey to the Alcarria*, in which Cela evoked the backwardness and remoteness of an area barely an hour from Madrid. Even today you can feel far removed from the modern world here.

PASTRANA

23 *46 km (28 mi) southeast of Guadalajara via N320 and the CM 2006 fork, 101 km (61 mi) east of Madrid.*

This pretty village of Roman origin was once the capital of a small duchy.

WHERE TO EAT

The tiny museum attached to Pastrana's **Colegiata** *(Collegiate Church)* displays a glorious series of Gothic tapestries. To see the museum, stop into the **tourist office** (✉ *Pl. de La Hora* ☎ *949/370672*) and they'll send someone to unlock the door for you. ✉ *Pl. del Ayuntamiento s/n, for Colegiata* ☎ *94/370027* 🎟 *€2.50* ⏲ *Daily 11:30–2 and 4:30–7.*

Even more of a gem is Pastrana's **Museo de Recuerdos de Santa Teresa de Avila y de San Juan de la Cruz** *(Museum of Santa Teresa de Avila and San Juan de la Cruz)* and **Museo de Ciencias Naturales** *(Museum of Natural Sciences)*, which share a building. A unique combination of mysticism, science, and art set in a stunning 16th- to 17th-century convent, the museums' treasures include medieval wood carvings, paintings by masters Luca Giordano and Sebastiano Ricci, memorabilia from the lives and works of Santa Teresa and St. John of the Cross, and a display of shells, woods, and birds from the Philippines brought back by missionary monks. *Convento del Carmen* ✉ *Crtra. de Almonacid de Zorita, Km 2* ☎ *949/370057* 🎟 *€2.40* ⏲ *Tues.–Sun. 11:30–2 and 3–6.*

CASTILE–LEÓN

SIGÜENZA

24 *86 km (53 mi) northeast of Guadalajara.*

Sigüenza has splendid architecture and one of the most beautifully preserved cathedrals in Castile.

WHAT TO SEE

An enchanting **castle,** overlooking wild, hilly countryside from above Sigüenza, is now a parador. Founded by the Romans but rebuilt at various later periods, most of the structure went up in the 14th century, when it became a residence for the queen of Castile, Doña Blanca de Borbón, who was banished here by her husband, Peter the Cruel.

Begun around 1150 and not completed until the early 16th century, Sigüenza's remarkable **cathedral** combines aspects of Spanish architecture from the Romanesque period to the Renaissance. The sturdy western front is forbidding, but hides a wealth of ornamental and artistic masterpieces. Go directly to the sacristan (the sacristy is at the north end of the ambulatory) for a guided tour, which is obligatory when visiting the cathedral. The late-Gothic cloister leads to a room lined with 17th-century Flemish tapestries. In the north transept is the late-15th-century plateresque sepulchre of Dom Fadrique of Portugal. The Chapel of the Doncel (to the right of the sanctuary) contains the tomb of Don Martín Vázquez de Arca, commissioned by Queen Isabella, to whom Don Martín served as *doncel* (page) before dying young (at 25) at the gates of Granada in 1486. ✉ *Pl. Mayor* 🎟 *€3* ⏲ *Tues.–Sun. 9:30–1:30 and 4:30–7. Guided tours Tues.–Sat. at 11, noon, 4:30, and 5:30, and Sun. at noon and 5:30.*

In a refurbished early-19th-century house next to the cathedral's west facade, the **Museo Diocesano de Arte Sacro** *(Diocesan Museum of Sacred Art)* contains a prehistoric section and much religious art from the 12th to 18th centuries. ✉ *Pl. Mayor* ☎ *949/391023* €3 ⏲ *Tues.–Sun. 11–2 and 4–7.*

The south side of the cathedral overlooks the arcaded **Plaza Mayor,** a harmonious Renaissance square commissioned by Cardinal Mendoza. The small palaces and cobbled alleys mark the virtually intact old quarter. Along Calle Mayor you'll find the palace that belonged to the doncel's family.

WHERE TO STAY & EAT

$$$ ★ ✕ **Parador de Sigüenza.** This mighty 12th-century fortress has hosted royalty for centuries, from Ferdinand and Isabella right up to the present king, Juan Carlos. Some rooms have four-poster beds and balconies overlooking the wild landscape. The excellent dining room ($$$–$$$$) makes a leisurely lunch essential; your choices might include roast kid, pheasant, or cod with truffles and cheese. ✉ *Pl. del Castillo s/n, 19250* ☎ *949/390100* *949/391364* *www.parador.es* *81 rooms* *In-hotel: restaurant, parking (fee)* *AE, DC, MC, V.*

MEDINACELI

25 *32 km (20 mi) northeast of Sigüenza.*

The preserved village of Medinaceli—literally "city in the sky"—commands exhilarating views from the top of a long, steep ridge. Dominating the skyline is a Roman triumphal arch from the 2nd or 3rd century AD, the only surviving triple archway of this period in Spain (the arch's silhouette is featured on road signs to national monuments throughout the country). The surrounding village, once the seat of one of Spain's most powerful dukes, was virtually abandoned by the end of the 19th century, and if you come here during the week, you can find yourself in a near ghost town. Madrileños have weekend houses here, as do several Americans. The town is archaic and beautiful, with houses overgrown by shrubs and trees, and unpaved lanes into wild countryside.

EN ROUTE

Approximately 56 km (35 mi) west of Soria, El Burgo de Osma is an enticing medieval and Renaissance town dominated by a Gothic cathedral and a baroque bell tower. There are also many historic buildings that have been elegantly restored.

$$–$$$ ★ ✕ **Virrey Palafox.** The white walls, wood-beam ceiling, and furnishings here are traditional Castilian, and the long dining room has a no-smoking section, a rarity in Spain. Produce is fresh and seasonal, vegetables are homegrown, and excellent local game is served year-round. The house specialty is fish, in particular *merluza Virrey* (hake stuffed with eels and salmon). Every Saturday and Sunday, starting on the last weekend in January and continuing through March, a pig is slaughtered and a feast ensues (€39, reservations required). ✉ *Calle Universidad 7* ☎ *975/340222* *AE, DC, MC, V* ⏲ *Closed Mon. No dinner Sun.*

A POETIC TALE

Soria has strong connections with Spain's finest 20th-century poet Antonio Machado (1875–1939). The Seville-born poet lived a bohemian life in Paris for many years before returning, at the age of 34, to teach French in Soria from 1909 to 1911. It was in Soria that Machado fell in love with and married his landlady's 16-year-old daughter, Leonor. When his young bride died only two years later, he felt he could no longer stay in a town so full of tragic memories. He moved on to Baeza, in his native Andalusia, and then to Segovia, where he spent his last years in Spain. Machado died in 1939 just after the end of the Spanish civil war in a refugee concentration camp in Collioure after escaping fascist forces as they entered Catalonia. His most successful work, *Campos de Castilla,* was greatly inspired by Soria and Leonor; both the town and the woman haunted him until his death. An oversize bronze head of Machado by sculptor Pablo Serrano is displayed outside the **school** where he taught, and his former classroom contains a tiny collection of memorabilia.

$$ **Il Virrey.** Under the same management as the Virrey Palafox, this pleasant hotel adjoins the 16th-century Convent of San Agustín. Constructed with traditional materials, rooms overlook the plaza and have marble floors, stone walls, and elegant decor. ✉*C. Mayor 2, 42300* ☎*975/341311* 📠*975/340855* 🌐*www.virreypalafox.com* *52 rooms* *In-room: safe. In-hotel: restaurant, concierge, laundry service, parking (fee).* 💳*AE, DC, MC, V.*

SORIA

26 *74 km (46 mi) north of Medinaceli via N111.*

Prosperous as a sheep farming center during the 15th-century European wool monopoly that laid the groundwork for Spain's Golden Age, this provincial capital has been marred to some degree by modern development. Still, the Duero River valley is splendid, as are the Romanesque monuments throughout the town and its hilly environs.

Soria is a comfortable base for exploring the surrounding countryside, which offers bountiful options for hiking and cycling through pine forests and along Roman roadways, plus rugged climbs with soaring vistas. Inquire at the Office of Tourism on Caballeros 17 for maps.

WHAT TO SEE

Nearly all roads to Soria converge onto the wide, modern promenade El Espolón, the location of the **Museo Numantino** *(Museum of Numancia).* Founded in 1919, the museum contains archaeological finds rich in prehistoric and Iberian items. One section on the top floor is dedicated to the important Iberian settlement at nearby Numancia that became famous in Spanish legend for its heroic resistance to invading Roman forces in 133 BC. As historical evidence has confirmed, Numancia resisted a lengthy siege, the few survivors choosing to take their own lives rather than fall into Roman hands. Even today, an ultra-defensive soccer or political strategy is invariably described as *una defensa numantina* (a Numancian defense). ⊠*Paseo del Espolón 8* ☎*975/221397* *€1.20, free weekends* ⊙*July–Sept., Tues.–Sat. 10–2 and 5–8, Sun. 10–2; Oct.–June, Tues.–Sat. 10–2 and 4–7, Sun. 10–2.*

The late-12th-century church of **Santo Domingo** (⊠*C. Aduana Vieja*) has a richly carved, Romanesque west facade. The imposing, 16th-century **Palacio de los Condes de Gomara** (*Palace of the Counts of Gomara* ⊠*C. Estudios*) is now a courthouse.

Dominating the hill just south of the Duero River is Soria's **Parador Antonio Machado** (⊠*Parque del Castillo s/n* ☎*975/240800*), which shares the Parque Municipal de El Castillo with the ruins of the town's castle. Calle de Santiago, which leads to the Parador, passes the church and cemetery of El Espino, where Machado's wife, Leonor, is buried.

Across the Duero River from Soria is the Monastery of **San Juan de Duero,** once the property of the Knights Hospitalers, a monastic military order of the Crusades. Outside the church are the curious ruins of a Romanesque cloister, with a stunning example of interlaced arching with Moorish echoes. The church itself, now maintained by the Museo Numantino, is a small museum of Romanesque art and architecture. ⊠*Piso de las Ánimas s/n* ☎*975/230218* *€0.60, free on weekends* ⊙*Oct.–June, Tues.–Sat. 10–2 and 4–7, Sun. 10–2; July–Sept., Tues.–Sat. 10–2 and 5–8, Sun. 10–2.*

The poet Machado wrote fondly of strolling along the Duero River from the Monastery of San Polo to the **Ermita de San Saturio,** a unique 18th-century chapel built into the step rocky hillside. You'll follow a polar-lined path from a parking and picnic area for about 1 km to a little chapel perched above the cave where the Anchorite St. Saturio fasted and prayed. You can climb up to San Saturio through the cave. ⊠*Paseo San Saturio s/n* ☎*975/180703* *Free* ⊙*Tues.–Sat. 10:30–2 and 4:30–6:30 (until 7:30 Jan.–Mar. and Nov.–Dec., until 8:30 July–Aug.), Sun. 10:30–2.*

WHERE TO STAY & EAT

$$$$ ✕**Mesón Castellano.** The most traditional restaurant in town, this cozy establishment has a large, open fire over which succulent *chuletón de ternera* (veal chops) are cooked. Another house specialty is *migas pastoriles* (soaked bread crumbs fried with peppers and bacon), a local dish. ⊠*Pl. Mayor 2* ☎*975/213045* *AE, DC, MC, V.*

$–$$$ ✕**Iruña Restaurant and Bar.** Offering an innovative menu of tapas and entrees, this is a fashionable choice for a drink or meal off the lively Plaza San Clemente. Try the *Torta del Casar* for an exquisite snack. ⊠*Pl. San Clemente 2* ☎*975/226831* *AE, DC, MC, V.*

$$$ **Parador de Soria Antonio Machado.** On a hilltop surrounded by trees and parkland and offering panoramic views of the Duero Valley, this modern parador resembles a luxurious alpine ski lodge. It's easy to see why Antonio Machado came often to this site for inspiration. ⊠*Parque del Castillo s/n, 42005* ☎*975/240800* *975/240803* *www.parador.*

es 67 *rooms* *In-hotel: restaurant, bar, parking, public Ethernet, laundry service* *AE, DC, MC, V.*

OFF THE BEATEN PATH

The bleak hilltop ruins of Numancia, an important Iberian settlement, are just a few minutes by car (4½ mi north) from Soria. Viciously besieged by the Romans in 135–134 BC, Numancia's inhabitants chose death rather than surrender. Their fearless courage inspired the adjective "*una defensa numantina*" (a Numancian defense) when referring to anything unrelentingly tenacious. Most of the foundations that have been unearthed date from the Roman occupation. ***Naciónal 111, Km 7 (1 Km away from pueblo Garray) 975/180712 €1 Oct.–May, Tues.–Sat. 10–2 and 4–6, Sun. 10–2; June–Sept., Tues.–Sat. 10–2 and 5–9, Sun. 10–2.***

SEGOVIA

Fodor's Choice ★

87 km (54 mi) north of Madrid.

Breathtaking Segovia—on a ridge in the middle of a gorgeously stark, undulating plain—is defined by its Roman and medieval monuments, its excellent cuisine, its embroideries and textiles, and its sense of well-being. An important military town in Roman times, Segovia was later established by the Moors as a major textile center. Captured by the Christians in 1085, it was enriched by a royal residence, and in 1474 the half-sister of Henry IV, Isabella the Catholic (married to Ferdinand of Aragón), was crowned queen of Castile here. By that time Segovia was a bustling city of about 60,000 (there are 53,000 today), but its importance soon diminished as a result of its taking the (losing) side of the Comuneros in the popular revolt against the emperor Carlos V. Though the construction of a royal palace in nearby La Granja in the 18th century revived the town's fortunes somewhat, it never recovered its former vitality. Early in the 20th century, Segovia's sleepy charm came to be appreciated by artists and writers, among them painter Ignacio Zuloaga and poet Antonio Machado. Today the streets swarm with tourists from Madrid—think twice about coming in summer.

If you approach Segovia on N603, the first building you see is the cathedral, which seems to rise directly from the fields. Between you and Segovia lies, in fact, a steep and narrow valley, which shields the old town from view. Only when you descend into the valley do you begin to see the old town's spectacular position, rising on top of a narrow rock ledge shaped like a ship. As soon as you reach the modern outskirts, turn left onto the Paseo E. González and follow the road marked **Ruta Panorámica**—you'll soon descend on the narrow and winding Cuesta de los Hoyos, which takes you to the bottom of the wooded valley that dips to the south of the old town. Above, you can see the Romanesque church of San Martín to the right; the cathedral in the middle; and on the far left, where the rock ledge tapers, the turrets, spires, and battlements of Segovia's castle, known as the Alcázar.

28 **Acueducto Romano.** Segovia's Roman aqueduct ranks with the Pont du Gard in France as one of the greatest surviving examples of Roman

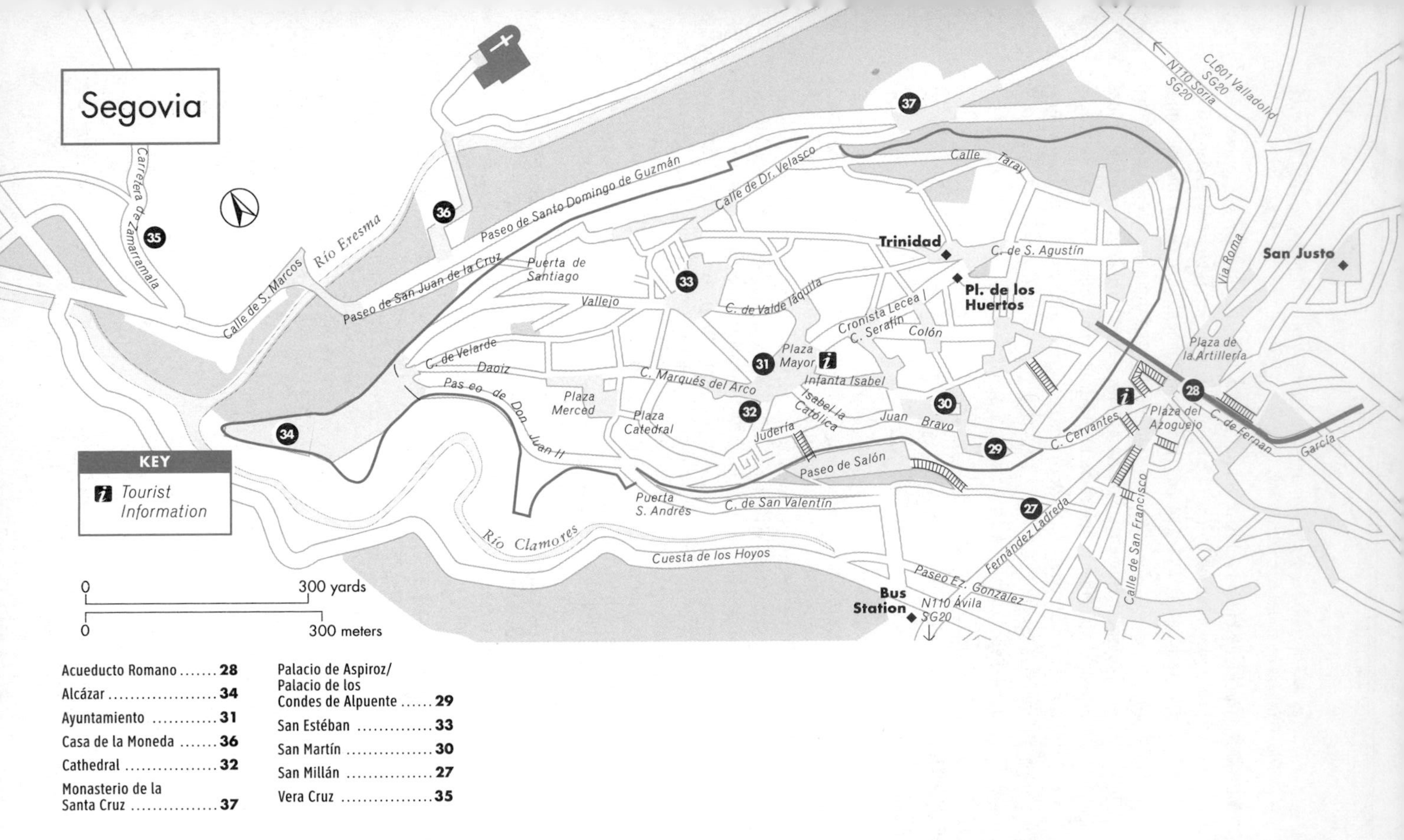
Segovia
KEY
Tourist Information
0
300 yards
0
300 meters
Acueducto Romano 28
Alcázar 34
Ayuntamiento 31
Casa de la Moneda 36
Cathedral 32
Monasterio de la Santa Cruz 37
Palacio de Aspiroz/ Palacio de los Condes de Alpuente 29
San Estéban 33
San Martín 30
San Millán 27
Vera Cruz 35
CL601 Valladolid SG20
N110 Soria SG20
N110 Ávila SG20
Carretera de Zamarramala
Calle de S. Marcos
Río Eresma
Paseo de San Juan de la Cruz
Paseo de Santo Domingo de Guzmán
Calle de Dr. Velasco
Calle Taray
Trinidad
C. de S. Agustín
Pl. de los Huertos
San Justo
Vía Roma
Plaza de la Artillería
Plaza del Azoguejo
C. de Fernan García
Calle de San Francisco
C. Cervantes
Puerta de Santiago
Vallejo
C. de Valde laquila
Cronista Lecea / C. Serafín
Colón
Plaza Mayor
Infanta Isabel
Isabel la Católica
Juan Bravo
C. Marqués del Arco
C. de Velarde
Daoiz
Pas eo de Don Juan II
Plaza Merced
Plaza Catedral
Judería
Paseo de Salón
Puerta S. Andrés
C. de San Valentín
Río Clamores
Cuesta de los Hoyos
Fernández Ladreda
Paseo Ez. Gonzalez
Bus Station

A GOOD WALK: SEGOVIA

Driving and parking are problematic on the narrow streets of old Segovia, so it's best to leave the car behind.

Beginning at the church of **San Millán** ㉗, go up Avenida de Fernández Ladreda until you come to the Plaza del Azoguejo, once the town center and marketplace. Directly in front of you are the arches of the grand **Acueducto Romano** ㉘. Turn away from the aqueduct, exit the plaza from the northwest corner, and head up the pedestrian shopping street Calle Cervantes. Continue up the same street, now called Calle de Juan Bravo, and veer off to the left onto Herrería for a look at the late-Gothic **Palacio de Aspiroz/Palacio de los Condes de Alpuente** ㉙. covered with Segovian *esgrafiado* plasterwork (incised with regular patterns). Back on Calle Juan Bravo and farther ahead, you'll come to the Plaza Martín, on which rises another Romanesque church, **San Martín** ㉚. Just to the west of the church is the Biblioteca y Archivo Historical (Library and Historical Archive), housed in a 17th-century stone structure that served as Segovia's jail until 1933. Off to the left of Juan Bravo, across from the Plaza Martín, is the refreshing Paseo de Salón, a small promenade at the foot of the town's southern walls. This walk was very popular with Spain's 19th-century queen, Isabel II.

At the Plaza del Corpus, where Juan Bravo splits into Calle de La Judería Vieja and Isabel la Católica, a right turn leads directly to the Plaza Mayor. A left turn leads up Calle de La Judería Vieja into the former Jewish quarter, where Segovia's Jews lived as early as the 13th century. Turn right on Calle de San Frutos, which runs along the east side of the cathedral; from here a short alley leads to the lively Plaza Mayor, an ideal place for lunch or an early evening drink. Facing the arcaded square are the 17th-century **ayuntamiento** ㉛ (town hall) and the eastern corner of the **cathedral** ㉜, its flying buttresses a favorite vantage point for storks. From the plaza, take Calle de Valdeláguila to the church of **San Estéban** ㉝. Touristy Calle de Los Leones slopes down from San Estéban toward the western extremity of the old town's ridge. At the western end of the square is the famous **Alcázar,** ㉞ from which you can see the church of **Vera Cruz** ㉟ and **Casa de la Moneda** (former Mint) ㊱. A walk along the city's peripheral road, Paseo de Santo Domingo de Guzmán, leads to the **Monasterio de la Santa Cruz** ㊲.

engineering. Spanning the dip that stretches from the walls of the old town to the lower slopes of the Sierra de Guadarrama, it's about 2,952 feet long and rises in two tiers—above what is now the Plaza del Azoguejo, whose name means "highest point"—to a height of 115 feet. The raised section of stonework in the center originally carried an inscription, of which only the holes for the bronze letters remain. The massive granite blocks are held together by neither mortar nor clamps, but the aqueduct has been standing since the end of the first century AD. The only damage it has suffered is the demolition of 35 of its arches by the Moors, and these were later replaced on the orders of Ferdinand and Isabella. Steps at the side of the aqueduct lead up to the walls of the old town. Because pollution from the freeway that passes through the aqueduct has weakened the structure, the road underneath has been closed to traffic. ⊠*Pl. del Azoguejo.*

34 **Alcázar.** Possibly dating from Roman times, this castle was considerably expanded in the 14th century, remodeled in the 15th, altered again toward the end of the 16th, and completely redone after being gutted by a fire in 1862, when it was used as an artillery school. The exterior, especially when seen from the Ruta Panorámica, is certainly imposing, but the castle is now little more than a pseudomedieval sham. The last remnant of the original structure is the guard tower through which you enter. Crowned by crenellated towers that seem to have been carved out of icing, the rampart can be climbed for superb views; the rest of the interior is a bit disappointing. ⊠*Pl. de la Reina Victoria Eugenia* ☎*921/460759* 🌐*www.alcazardesegovia.com* *€3.50, plus €1.50 extra to climb the tower* ⏲*Apr.–Sept., daily 10–7; Oct.–Mar., Mon.–Thurs. 10–6, Fri.–Sun. 10–7.*

32 **Cathedral.** Begun in 1525 and completed 65 years later, the cathedral was intended to replace an earlier one near the Alcázar, destroyed during the revolt of the Comuneros against Carlos V. It's one of the country's last great examples of the Gothic style. The designs were drawn up by the leading late-Gothicist Juan Gil de Hontañón but executed by his son Rodrigo, in whose work can be seen a transition from the Gothic to the Renaissance style. The interior, illuminated by 16th-century Flemish windows, is light and uncluttered, the one distracting detail being the wooden, neoclassical choir. You enter through the north transept, which is marked MUSEO; turn right, and the first chapel on your right has a lamentation group (carved figures who are lamenting) in wood by the baroque sculptor Gregorio Fernández. Across from the entrance, on the southern transept, is a door opening into the late-Gothic cloister—this and the elaborate door leading into it were transported from the old cathedral and are the work of architect Juan Guas. Under the pavement immediately inside the cloisters are the tombs of Juan and Rodrigo Gil de Hontañón; that these two lie in a space designed by Guas is appropriate, for the three men together dominated the last phase of the Gothic style in Spain. Off the cloister, a small museum of religious art, installed partly in the first-floor chapter house, has a white-and-gold 17th-century ceiling, a late example of Mudéjar *artesonado* work. ⊠*Pl. Mayor s/n* ☎*921/462205* *Cathedral free, cloister and museum €2* ⏲*Apr.–Oct., Mon.–Sat. 9–6:30, Sun. 9–2:30; Nov.–Mar., Mon.–Sat. 9–5:30, Sun. 9–2:30.*

31 **Ayuntamiento.** The 17th-century town hall stands on the active **Plaza Mayor.** It's closed to the public, but it's a great place to sit and watch the world go by. ⊠*Pl. Mayor.*

36 **Casa de la Moneda** *(Mint).* All Spanish coinage was struck here from 1455 to 1730. The mint, scheduled for reconstruction work, offers tours every first and third Saturday of the month, with English-language guides available by prior arrangement. Call or e-mail (info@

segoviamint.org) to reserve a tour. ✉ *C. de la Moneda, just south of Eresma River* ☎ *921/420921* ⊕ *www.segoviamint.org* 🎫 *Free.*

37 **Monasterio de la Santa Cruz.** Built in the 13th century, this church was established by St. Dominick of Guzmán, founder of the Dominican order, and rebuilt in the 15th century by Ferdinand and Isabella. Now it's a private university, La Universidad Sec, and during the academic year, you can see the Gothic interior with plateresque and Renaissance touches. ✉ *Calle Cardenal Zúñiga s/n* ☎ *921/471997.*

29 **Palacio de Aspiroz/Palacio de los Condes de Alpuente** *(Palace of the Counts of Alpuente).* This late-Gothic palace is covered with a type of plasterwork known as *esgrafiado,* (sgraffito) incised with regular patterns; the style was most likely introduced by the Moors and is characteristic of Segovian architecture. The building, now used for city administrative offices, is not open to the public. ✉ *Pl. del Platero Oquendo.*

33 **San Estéban.** Though the interior has a baroque facing, the exterior has kept some splendid capitals, as well as an exceptionally tall tower. Due east of the church square is the **Capilla de San Juan de Dios,** next to which is the former pension where the poet Antonio Machado spent his last years in Spain. The family who looked after Machado still owns the building and will show you the poet's room on request, with its kerosene stove, iron bed, and round table. The church is open for Mass only. ✉ *Pl. de San Estéban* ⏲ *Mass daily at 8* AM *and 7* PM.

30 **San Martín.** This unavoidable and elevated Romanesque church, on the main street between the aqueduct and cathedral, stands in a little plaza of the same name. It's open for Mass only. ✉ *Pl. San Martín* ☎ *921/443402* ⏲ *Mass daily at 8* AM *and 7* PM.

27 **San Millán.** A perfect example of the Segovian Romanesque, this 12th-century church is perhaps the finest in town apart from the cathedral. The exterior is notable for its arcaded porch, where church meetings were once held. The virtually untouched Romanesque interior is dominated by massive columns, whose capitals carry such carved scenes as the Flight into Egypt and the Adoration of the Magi. The vaulting on the crossing shows the Moorish influence on Spanish medieval architecture. It's open for Mass only. ✉ *Av. Fernández Ladreda 26, 5-min walk outside town walls* ⏲ *Mass daily at 8* AM *and 7* PM.

35 **Vera Cruz.** Made of the local warm-orange stone, this isolated Romanesque church was built in 1208 for the Knights Templar. Like other buildings associated with this order, it has 12 sides, inspired by the Church of the Holy Sepulchre in Jerusalem. Your trip pays off in full when you climb the bell tower and see all of Segovia profiled against the Sierra de Guadarrama. ✉ *Ctra. de Zamarramala s/n, on northern outskirts of town, off Cuestra de los Hoyos* ☎ *921/431475* 🎫 *€1.50* ⏲ *May–Sept., Tues.–Sun. 10:30–1:30 and 3:30–7; Oct. and Dec.–Apr., Tues.–Sun. 10:30–1:30 and 3:30–6:30.*

WHERE TO STAY & EAT

$$$$ ★ ✕ **Mesón de José María.** With a lively bar, this *mesón* (traditional tavern-restaurant) is hospitable, and its passionately dedicated owner is devoted to maintaining traditional Castilian specialties while concocting innovations of his own. The menu changes constantly according to what's in season. The large, old-style, brightly lighted dining room is often packed, and the waiters are uncommonly friendly. Although it's a bit touristy, it's equally popular with locals. ✉ *Calle Cronista Lecea 11* ☎ *921/461111* ▭ *AE, DC, MC, V.*

$$$–$$$$ ✕ **Casa Duque.** Founded in 1895 and still in the family, this restaurant, the oldest in Segovia, has an intimate interior, with homey wood beams and a plethora of fascinating *objetos*. Roasts are the specialty, but the *judiones de La Granja Duque*—enormous white beans from nearby La Granja served with sausages—are also excellent. ✉ *Calle Cervantes 12* ☎ *921/462487* 🌐 *www.restauranteduque.es* ✍ *Reservations essential* ▭ *AE, DC, MC, V.*

$$–$$$$ ★ ✕ **Mesón de Cándido.** Cándido began life as an inn near the end of the 18th century, and was declared a national monument in 1941. Tucked beside the aqueduct, it has a medley of small, irregular dining rooms decorated with memorabilia. Amid the dark-wood beams and Castilian knickknacks hang photos of the celebrities who have dined here, from Ernest Hemingway to Princess Grace of Monaco. Cándido's son now runs the place. If it's your first time here, the *cochinillo* (piglet), roasted in a wood-fire oven, is a great choice. The partridge stew or roast lamb are also memorable, especially on a freezing winter afternoon with sunlight lighting up the bright ocher aqueduct. ✉ *Pl. de Azoguejo 5* ☎ *921/425911* 🌐 *www.mesondecandido.es* ✍ *Reservations essential* ▭ *AE, DC, MC, V.*

$$$ ✕ **Parador de Segovia.** Architecturally one of the most interesting of Spain's modern paradors (if you like naked concrete), this low building is set on a hill overlooking the city; it's a very long walk to the city center. The rooms are cold in appearance, but from the large windows the panorama of Segovia and its aqueduct are spectacular. (The ground floors have views of hedges, so request a room with a view if you want one.) The restaurant ($$$$) serves Segovian and international dishes, such as *lomo de merluza al aroma de estragón* (hake fillet with tarragon and shrimp). ✉ *Ctra. de Valladolid s/n, 2 km (1 mi) from Segovia, 40003* ☎ *921/443737* 📠 *921/437362* 🌐 *www.parador.es* *113 rooms* *In-hotel: restaurant, pools, gym, parking (fee)* ▭ *AE, DC, MC, V.*

$$–$$$ **Infanta Isabel.** You'll get great views of the cathedral from this hotel perched on the Plaza Mayor—with an entrance on a charming, if congested, pedestrian shopping street. Rooms are light and feminine, with wrought-iron beds and little round tables; those on the plaza have floor-length shutters and small verandas. ✉ *Pl. Mayor 12, 40001* ☎ *921/461300* 📠 *921/462217* 🌐 *www.hotelinfantaisabel.com* *37 rooms* *In-hotel: restaurant* ▭ *AE, DC, MC, V.*

$$ **Las Sirenas.** If you stay here, not only will you be just steps from the Plaza Mayor, above Segovia's nicest shops, but you'll have the benefit of a prime downtown location, a pillared marble lobby, and, from the

best rooms, splendid balcony views of the church of San Millán. Sensuous and classical accents include statues of mermaids at the foot of a curving staircase and Greek vases on antique bedside tables. Drawbacks are the tiny showers and slightly faded furnishings, but it's a hard value to beat. ✉*C. Juan Bravo 30, 40001* ☎*921/462663* 🌐*www.hotelsirenas.com* 📠*921/462657* *39 rooms* *In-hotel: bar* 💳*AE, DC, MC, V.*

OFF THE BEATEN PATH

Fodor's Choice ★

While in the Segovia area, don't miss the Palacio Real de La Granja (Royal Palace of La Granja) stands in the town of La Granja de San Ildefonso, some 11 km (7 mi) southeast of Segovia (on N601) on the northern slopes of the Sierra de Guadarrama. The palace site was once occupied by a hunting lodge and a shrine to San Ildefonso, administered by Hieronymite monks from the Segovian monastery of El Parral. Commissioned by the Bourbon king Felipe V in 1719, the palace has been described as the first great building of the Spanish Bourbon dynasty. The Italian architects Juvarra and Sachetti, who finished it in 1739, were responsible for the imposing garden facade, a late-baroque masterpiece anchored throughout its length by a giant order of columns. The interior has been badly gutted by fire; the highlight is the collection of 15th- to 18th-century tapestries in a special museum. It's the gardens that are most notable—terraces, ornamental ponds, lakes, classical statuary, woods, and baroque fountains dot the mountainside. On Wednesday, Saturday, and Sunday evenings in the summer (May–September, 6–7 PM), the fountains are turned on, one by one, creating an effect to rival that of Versailles. The starting time has been known to change on a whim; call ahead. ☎***921/470020*** 🌐***www.patrimonionacional.es*** ***Palace €5, gardens free*** ***Palace Oct.–Mar., Tues.–Sat. 10–1:30 and 3–5, Sun. 10–2; Apr.–Sept., Tues.–Sun. 10–6. Gardens daily 10–sunset.***

SHOPPING

After Toledo, the province of Segovia is Castile's most important for crafts. Glass and crystal are specialties of La Granja, and ironwork, lace, and embroidery are famous in Segovia itself. You can buy good lace from the Gypsies in Segovia's Plaza del Alcázar, but be prepared for some strenuous bargaining, and never offer more than half the opening price. For genuine crafts, go to **San Martín 4** (✉*Pl. San Martín 4*), an excellent antiques shop. **Calle Daiza**, leading to the Alcázar, overflows with touristy ceramic, textile, and gift shops.

PEDRAZA DE LA SIERRA

38 *30 km (19 mi) northeast of Segovia.*

Though somewhat commercialized and overdone, Pedraza is still a striking 16th-century village. Crowning a rocky outcrop and completely encircled by its walls, it's perfectly preserved, with wonderful views of the Guadarrama Mountains. In the center of the village is the frail, irregularly shaped Plaza Mayor, lined with rustic wooden porti-

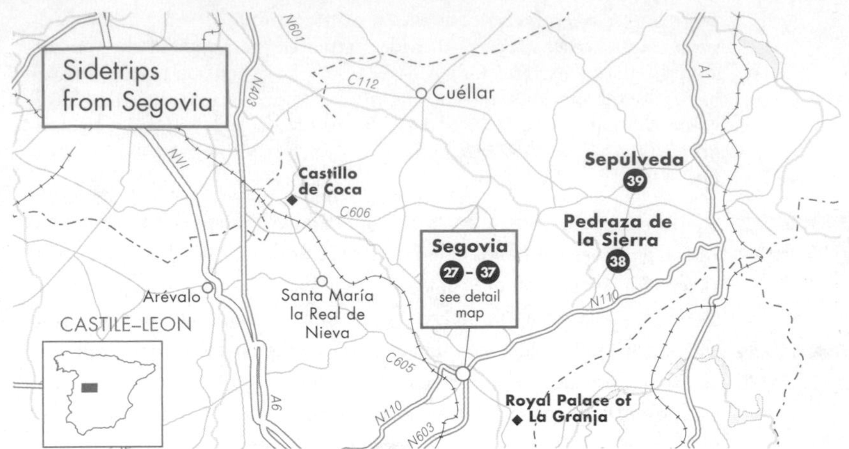

coes and dominated by a Romanesque bell tower. Pedraza's romance peaks on the first two Saturdays of July for the **Conciertos de las Velas** *(Candle Concerts)*, when the artificial lights in Pedraza are switched off and the entire town is bathed in the flickering glow of more than 35,000 candles, placed along the streets and in the Plaza Mayor. In the evening (at 10 PM) classical-music concerts take place in the Plaza Mayor and the castle. Concert tickets must be bought at least a month in advance. Contact the **Fundación Villa de Pedraza** or the Segovia tourist office (☎ *921/460334*) for tickets to the Candle Concerts in July. ✉ *C. Real 15, Pedraza, 40172* ☎ *921/509960* ⏲ *Tues. and Wed. 10–3:15.*

At the top of Pedraza de la Sierra is the Renaissance **Castillo Pedraza de la Sierra,** a 14th-century stone castle that the painter Ignacio Zuloaga bought as a private home in the early 20th century. Two sons of the French king Francis I were held hostage here after the Battle of Pavia, together with their majordomo, the father of the Renaissance, poet Pierre de Ronsard. Note that visiting times are valid except when Zuloaga's heirs are in residence. ☎ *921/509825* 🎫 *€4* ⏲ *Wed.–Sun. 11–2 and 4–6.*

WHERE TO STAY & EAT

$$$$ ✕ **El Yantar de Pedraza.** This traditional restaurant on the main square has wooden tables and beam ceilings. Famous for its roast meats, it's the place to come for that most celebrated Pedraza specialty, *corderito lechal en horno de leña* (baby lamb roasted in a wood oven). Dinner is served only for large groups and must be reserved in advance. ✉ *Pl. Mayor* ☎ *921/509842* 🌐 *www.elyantardepedraza.com* 💳 *AE, DC, MC, V* ⏲ *Closed Mon.*

$$–$$$ 🏨 **El Hotel de La Villa.** Heavy wooden beams everywhere, a roaring fire in the salon, and an elegant dining room make this Pedraza's chicest place to spend the night. A medieval Moorish oven for roasting lamb is in a corner of the restaurant. The bedrooms are an exquisite combination of heavy Castilian rustic and light postmodern design. ✉ *C. Calzada*

5, 40172 ☎921/508651 📠921/508653 🌐*www.elhoteldelavilla.com* ⇆*36 rooms, 2 suites* ♨*In-hotel: restaurant, bar* 💳*AE, DC, MC, V.*

$$ **La Posada de Don Mariano.** Originally a farmer's home, this antique and elegant building has intimate guest rooms filled with rustic furniture and antiques. The restaurant, Enebro, serves cochinillo and a good selection of red meat dishes. ✉*C. Mayor 14, 40172* ☎*921/509886* 📠*921/509887* 🌐*www.hoteldonmariano.com* ⇆*18 rooms* ♨*In-hotel: restaurant, bar* 💳*AE, DC, MC, V.*

3

SEPÚLVEDA

39 *24 km (15 mi) north of Pedraza de la Sierra, 60 km (37 mi) northeast of Segovia.*

A walled village with a commanding position, Sepúlveda has a charming main square, but its main attraction is the 11th-century **El Salvador,** the oldest Romanesque church in Segovia's province. It has a crude but amusing example of the porches found in later Segovian buildings: the carvings on its capitals, probably by a Moorish convert, are quite fantastical. ✉*Cerro de Somosierra.*

OFF THE BEATEN PATH

Perhaps the most famous medieval sight near Segovia—worth a detour between Segovia and Ávila or Valladolid—is the Castillo de Coca, 52 km (32 mi) northwest of the city. Built in the 15th century for Archbishop Alonso de Fonseca I, the castle is a turreted structure of plaster and red brick, surrounded by a deep moat. It looks like a stage set for a fairy tale, and indeed, it was intended not as a defense but as a place for the notoriously pleasure-loving Archbishop Fonseca to hold riotous parties. The interior, now occupied by a forestry school, has been modernized, with only fragments of the original decoration preserved. Note that opening hours are erratic; call ahead if possible. The restaurant is closed the first Tuesday of every month. 📠*921/586622* 🎫*€2.50* 🕐*May–Aug., weekdays 10:30–1 and 4:30–7, weekends 11–1 and 4–6; Sept.–Apr., weekdays 10:30–1 and 4:30–6, weekends 11–1 and 4–6. Closed 1st Tues. of every month..*

ÁVILA

40 *107 km (66 mi) northwest of Madrid.*

In the middle of a windy plateau littered with giant boulders, Ávila can look wild and sinister, especially with the Sierra de Gredos in the background. Modern development on its outskirts partially obscures Ávila's surrounding **walls,** which, restored in parts, look as they did in the Middle Ages. Begun in 1090, shortly after the town was reclaimed from the Moors, the walls were completed in only nine years—accomplished by the daily employment of an estimated 1,900 men. With 9 gates and 88 cylindrical towers bunched together, they are unique to Spain in form, unlike the Moorish defense architecture that the Christians adapted elsewhere. They're most striking when seen from outside town; for the best view on foot, cross the Adaja River, turn right on the

Carretera de Salamanca, and walk uphill about 250 yards to a monument of four pilasters surrounding a cross.

The walls reflect Ávila's importance during the Middle Ages. Populated by Alfonso VI mainly with Christians from Asturias, the town came to be known as Ávila of the Knights because of its many nobles. Decline set in at the beginning of the 15th century, with the gradual departure of the nobility to the court of Carlos V in Toledo. Ávila's fame later on was largely because of St. Teresa. Born here in 1515 to a noble family of Jewish origin, Teresa spent much of her life in Ávila, leaving a legacy of convents and the ubiquitous *yemas* (candied egg yolks), originally distributed free to the poor but now sold for high prices to tourists. Ávila is well preserved, but the mood is slightly sad, austere, and desolate. The quietude is dispelled during Fiestas de la Santa Teresa, beginning October 8. The weeklong celebration includes lighted decorations, parades, singing in the streets, and religious observances.

WHAT TO SEE

Cathedral. Its battlement apse forms the most impressive part of Ávila's walls. Entering the town gate to the right of the apse, you can reach the sculpted north portal (originally the west portal, until it was moved in 1455 by the architect Juan Guas) by turning left and walking a few steps. The present west portal, flanked by 18th-century towers, is notable for the crude carvings of hairy male figures on each side; known as "wild men," these figures appear in many Castilian palaces of this period. The Transitional Gothic interior, with its granite nave, is heavy and severe. The Lisbon earthquake of 1755 deprived the building of its Flemish stained glass, so the main note of color appears in the beautiful mottled stone in the apse, tinted yellow and red. Elaborate, plateresque choir stalls built in 1547 complement the powerful high altar of circa 1504 by painters Juan de Borgoña and Pedro Berruguete. On the wall of the ambulatory, look for the early-16th-century marble sepulchre of Bishop Alonso de Madrigal, a remarkably lifelike representation of the bishop seated at his writing table. Known as "El Tostado" (the Toasted One) for his swarthy complexion, the bishop was a tiny man of enormous intellect, the author of 54 books. When on one occasion Pope Eugenius IV ordered him to stand—mistakenly thinking him to still be on his knees—the bishop indicated the space between his eyebrows and hairline, retorting, "A man's stature is to be measured from here to here!" ✉ *Pl. de la Catedral s/n* ☎ *920/211641* 🎟 *€4* ⏲ *June–Aug., weekdays 10–7, Sat. 10–6:30, Sun. noon–6; Sept.–May, weekdays 10–5, Sat. 10–6, Sun. noon–6.*

The 15th-century **Mansión de los Deanes** *(Deans' Mansion)* houses the cheerful **Museo de Ávila,** a provincial museum full of local archaeology and folklore. It's a few minutes' walk east of the cathedral apse. ✉ *Pl. de Nalvillos 3* ☎ *920/211003* 🎟 *€1.20, weekends free* ⏲ *Tues.–Sat. 10–2 and 5–8, Sun. 10–2.*

In the **Convento de San José** *(de Las Madres)*, four blocks east of the cathedral on Calle Duque de Alba, is the **Museo Teresiano,** with musical instruments used by St. Teresa and her nuns. ✉ *Calle Las Madres 4*

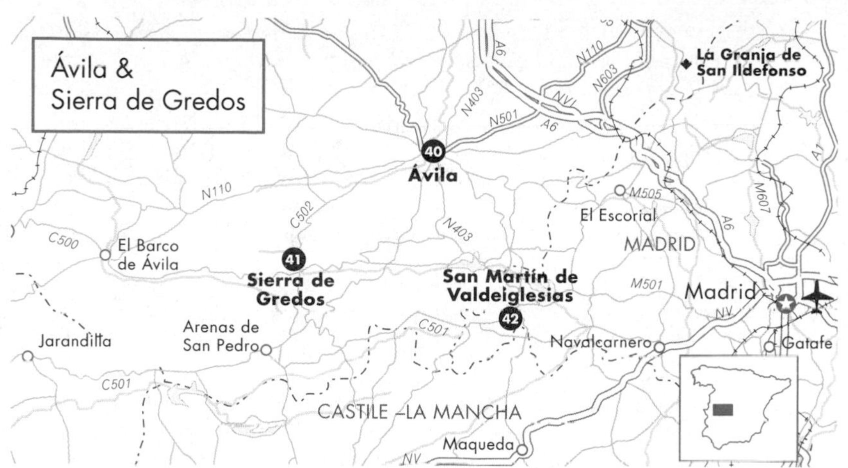

☎920/222127 🎫€1 ⏱Apr.–Oct., daily 10–1:30 and 4–7; Nov.–Mar., daily 10–1:30 and 3–6.

North of Ávila's cathedral, on Plaza de San Vincente, is the much-venerated Romanesque **Basílica de San Vicente** *(Basilica of St. Vincent)*, founded on the supposed site where St. Vincent was martyred in 303 with his sisters Sts. Sabina and Cristeta. The west front, shielded by a vestibule, has damaged but expressive Romanesque carvings depicting the death of Lazarus and the parable of the rich man's table. The sarcophagus of St. Vincent forms the centerpiece of the basilica's Romanesque interior; the extraordinary, Asian-looking canopy above the sarcophagus is a 15th-century addition. ✉*Pl. de San Vicente s/n* ☎*920/255230* 🎫*€1.40* ⏱*Daily 10–1:30 and 4–6:30.*

The elegant chapel of **Mosen Rubí** (circa 1516) is illuminated by Renaissance stained glass by Nicolás de Holanda. Try to persuade the nuns in the adjoining convent to let you inside. ✉*C. de Lopez Nuñez.*

At the west end of the town walls, next to the river in a farmyard nearly hidden by poplars, is the small Romanesque **Ermita de San Segundo** *(Hermitage of St. Secundus)*. Founded on the site where the remains of St. Secundus (a follower of St. Peter) were reputedly discovered, the hermitage has a realistic marble monument to the saint, carved by Juan de Juni. You may have to ask for the key in the adjoining house. ✉*Av. de Madrid s/n, toward Salamanca* 🎫*€0.60* ⏱*Summer, daily 10–1 and 3:30–6; fall–spring, daily 11–1 and 4–5.*

Inside the south wall on Calle Dama, the **Convento de Santa Teresa** was founded in the 17th century on the site of the saint's birthplace. Teresa's famous written account of an ecstatic vision in which an angel pierced her heart influenced many baroque artists, most famously the Italian sculptor Giovanni Bernini. The convent has a small museum with relics—including one of Teresa's fingers; you can also see the small and rather gloomy garden where she played as a child. The restaurant is closed Monday from October through Easter. ✉*Pl. de la Santa s/n*

☎920/211030 Museum €2 ⊙Museum, May–Sept., weekdays 10–1:30 and 3:30–5:30, Sat. 10–1 and 4–6; Apr.–Oct., weekdays 10–2 and 4–7, Sat. 10–1 and 4–6.

The **Museo del Convento de la Encarnación** is where St. Teresa first took orders and was then based for more than 30 years. Its museum has an interesting drawing of the Crucifixion by her disciple St. John of the Cross, as well as a reconstruction of the cell she used when she was a prioress here. The convent is outside the walls in the northern part of town. *⊠Paseo de la Encarnación s/n ☎920/211212 €1.05 ⊙May–Oct., weekdays 9:30–1 and 4–7, weekends 10–1 and 4–6; Nov.–Apr., weekdays 9:30–1:30 and 3:30–6, weekends 10–1 and 4–6.*

The most interesting architectural monument on Ávila's outskirts is the **Monasterio de Santo Tomás.** A good 10-minute walk from the walls among housing projects, it's not where you would expect to find one of the most important religious institutions in Castile. The monastery was founded by Ferdinand and Isabella with the financial assistance of the notorious Inquisitor-General Tomás de Torquemada, who is buried in the sacristy. Further funds were provided by the confiscated property of converted Jews who ran afoul of the Inquisition. Three decorated cloisters lead to the church; inside, a masterly high altar (circa 1506) by Pedro Berruguete overlooks a serene marble tomb by the Italian artist Domenico Fancelli. One of the earliest examples of the Italian Renaissance style in Spain, this influential work was built for Prince Juan, the only son of Ferdinand and Isabella, who died at 19 while a student at the University of Salamanca. After Juan's burial here, his heartbroken parents found themselves unable to return; in happier times they had often attended mass here, seated in the upper choir behind a balustrade exquisitely carved with their coats of arms. *⊠Pl. de Granada 1 ☎920/220400 €3 ⊙Tues.–Sun. 10–1 and 4–8.*

WHERE TO STAY & EAT

$$–$$$ ★ ✕**El Molino de la Losa.** Nearly straddling the serene Adaja River, with one of the best views of the town walls, El Molino is in a 15th-century mill, the working mechanism of which has been well preserved and provides much distraction for those seated in the animated bar. Lamb is roasted in a medieval wood oven, and the beans from nearby El Barco (*judías de El Barco*) are famous. The garden has a small playground for children. *⊠Bajada de la Losa 12 ☎920/211101 or 920/211102 ⊕www.elmolinodelalosa.com ▭AE, MC, V ⊙Closed Mon.*

$$ ✕**Mesón del Rastro.** In a wing of the medieval Palacio Abrantes, this restaurant has a bucolic Castilian interior with exposed stone walls and beams, low lighting, and dark-wood furniture. Try the lamb and El Barco beans; also worthwhile is the *caldereta de cabrito* (goat stew). The place suffers somewhat from its popularity with tour buses, and service is sometimes slow and impersonal. *⊠Pl. Rastro 1 ☎920/211218 ⊕www.mesondelrastro.com ▭AE, DC, MC, V.*

$–$$ ✕**Las Cancelas.** Locals flock to this little tavern ($$) for the €12 *menú del día* (fixed-price special). Push your way through the loud tapas bar to the dining room, where wooden tables are heaped with combination platters of roast chicken, french fries, sunny-side-up eggs, and chunks of home-baked bread. The local T-bone steak, *chuletón de Ávila,* is enormous. The succulent cochinillo bursts with flavor. A hotel has 14 rooms, which are simple, slightly ramshackle arrangements. ✉*Cruz Vieja 6* ☎*920/212249* 📠*920/212230* 💳*AE, DC, MC, V* ⊗*Closed Jan. 7–Feb. 3.*

$$$ **Parador de Ávila.** A largely rebuilt medieval castle attached to the town walls, Ávila's parador has the advantage of a garden, from which you can sometimes climb up onto the ramparts. The interior is unusually warm, done mostly in tawny tones, and the public rooms are convivial. Guest rooms have terra-cotta tile floors and leather chairs, and their bathrooms are spacious, gleamingly modern, and fashionably designed. ✉*Calle Marqués de Canales de Chozas 2, 05001* ☎*920/211340* 📠*920/226166* 🌐*www.parador.es* *61 rooms* *In-hotel: restaurant, bar* 💳*AE, DC, MC, V.*

$$–$$$ ★ **Palacio de los Velada.** Ávila's top hotel occupies a beautifully restored 16th-century palace in the heart of the city, right beside the cathedral. (It's ideal if you like to relax between sightseeing jaunts.) Upscale locals gather in the bar and the lovely Mediterranean courtyard. Rooms are modern and comfortable. ✉*Pl. de la Catedral 10, 05001* ☎*920/255100* 📠*920/254900* 🌐*www.veladahoteles.com* *145 rooms* *In-hotel: restaurant, bar* 💳*AE, DC, MC, V.*

SIERRA DE GREDOS

41 *79 km (49 mi) southwest of Ávila.*

The C502 from Ávila through the mountains follows a road dating from Roman times, when it was used to transport oil and flour from Ávila in exchange for potatoes and wood. In winter, the **Sierra de Gredos** (4,435 feet) gives the region a majestic, snowy backdrop. You can enjoy extensive views from the peak; soon after descending you'll see a perfectly preserved stretch of the Roman road, zigzagging down into the valley and crossing the modern road now and then. Today it's used by hikers, as well as by shepherds transporting their flocks to lower pastures in early December.

WHERE TO STAY

$$–$$$ **Parador de Gredos.** Built in 1926 on a site chosen by Alfonso XIII, this was the first parador in Spain. The stone architecture has a sturdy look and blends well with the magnificent surroundings. Rooms are standard parador, with heavy, dark furniture and light walls, and more than half have excellent views of the Sierra. An ideal base for hiking or climbing, the framers of Spain's Constitution met here in 1976 to draft the charter for today's constitutional monarchy. ✉*Ctra. Barraco–Béjar, Km 42, 05635, Navarredonda de Gredos* ☎*920/348048* 📠*920/348205* 🌐*www.parador.es* *74 rooms* *In-hotel: restaurant, bar, tennis court* 💳*AE, DC, MC, V.*

SPORTS & THE OUTDOORS

★ HIKING & MOUNTAIN CLIMBING The Sierra de Gredos is Castile's best area for hiking and mountaineering. You can base yourself at the parador or at one of six mountain huts with limited accommodations and facilities. For information contact **FEDME (Federación Española de Deportes de Montaña y Escalada)** (*Spanish Mountaineering and Climbing Federation* ✉*C. Floridablanca 84* ☎*93/426–4267* 🖷*93/426–2575* 🌐*www.fedme.es*) in Barcelona.

HORSEBACK RIDING Near the Gredos Parador, **Turactiv Gredos** (✉*Calle Barajas* ☎*608/920892*) offers gear and guides for horseback riding, canoeing, fishing, and archery. You can go riding at **Hípica de Bohoyo** (✉*Carretera Los Yardes, Bohoyo* ☎*920/341118* 🌐*www.turactiv.com*).

SAN MARTÍN DE VALDEIGLESIAS

42 *73 km (45 mi) west of Madrid.*

Just 6 km (4 mi) before San Martín, on the right side of the road, is a stone inscription in front of a hedge; this marks the site where, in 1468, Isabella the Catholic was acknowledged by the assembled Castilian nobility as rightful successor to Henry IV. The **Toros de Guisando,** or stone bulls, dating from the 6th century BC, are thought to have been used as territorial border markers for a Celtiberian tribe. Just three of many such bulls once scattered around the Castilian countryside (they take their name from the nearby Cerro Guisando, or Guisando Hill), they're now a symbol of the Spanish Tourist Board. To see these taurine effigies, head back east from Arenas on the C501; it's a pleasant drive through countryside bordered to the north by the Gredos range. ✉*Near Cerro Guisando, 6 km (4 mi) before San Martín, on right side of road, on other side of hedge with stone inscription* .

SALAMANCA

Fodor'sChoice ★ *205 km (127 mi) northwest of Madrid.*

Salamanca's radiant sandstone buildings, immense Plaza Mayor, and hilltop riverside perch make it one of the most attractive and beloved cities in Spain. Today, as it did centuries ago, the university predominates, providing an intellectual flavor, a stimulating arts scene, and nightlife to match, best experienced on the weekend.

If you approach from Madrid or Ávila, you'll first see Salamanca rising on the northern banks of the wide and winding River Tormes. In the foreground is its sturdy, 15-arch Roman bridge; above this soars the combined bulk of the old and new cathedrals. Piercing the skyline to the right is the Renaissance monastery and church of San Estéban. Behind San Estéban and the cathedrals, and largely out of sight from the river, extends a stunning series of palaces, convents, and university buildings that culminates in the Plaza Mayor. Despite considerable damage over the centuries, Salamanca remains one of Spain's greatest cities architecturally, a showpiece of the Spanish Renaissance. It is the

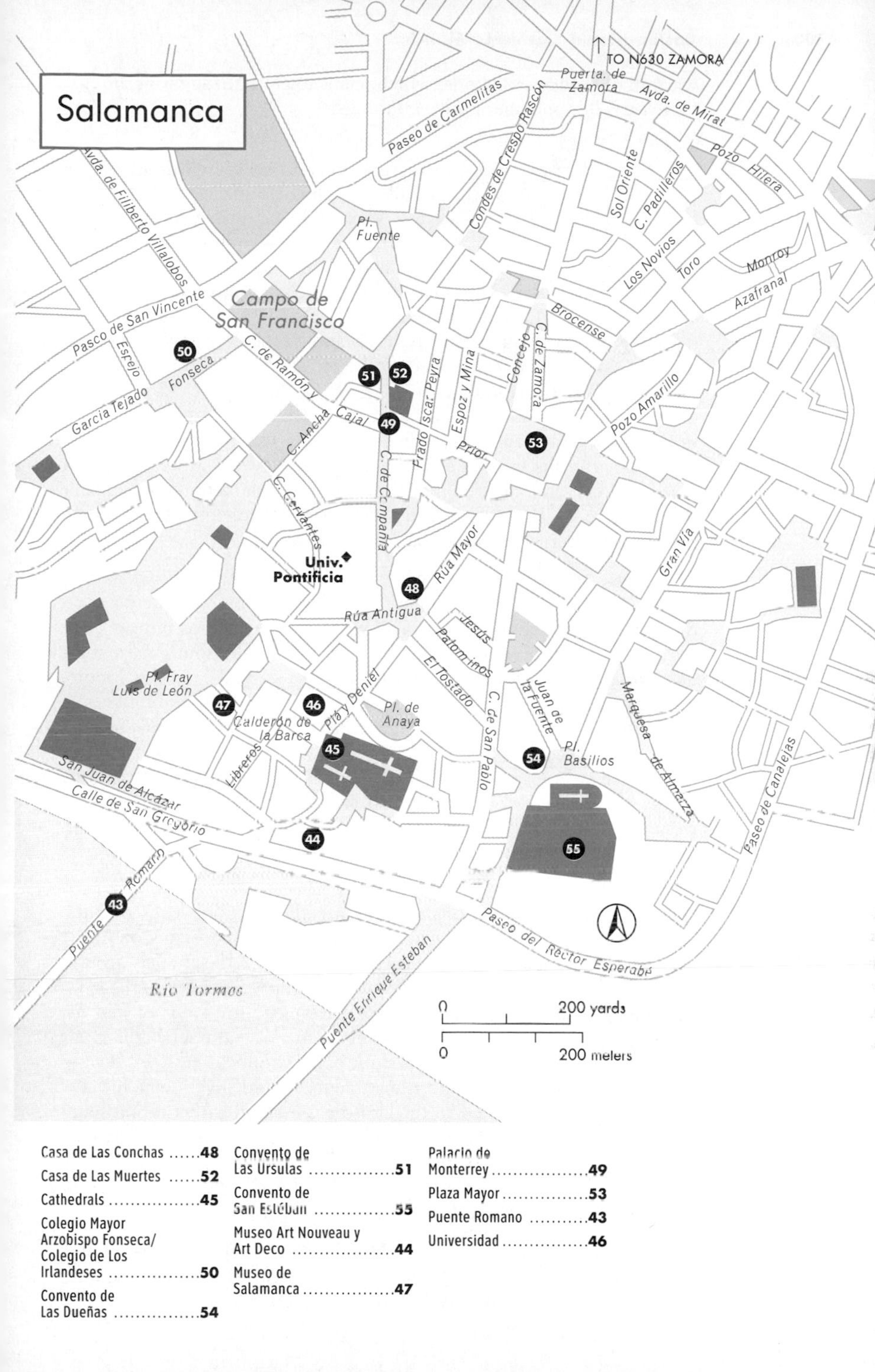
Salamanca
TO N630 ZAMORA
Puerta. de Zamora
Avda. de Mirat
Paseo de Carmelitas
Condes de Crespo Rascón
Sol Oriente
C. Padilleros
Pozo Hilera
Avda. de Filiberto Villalobos
Pl. Fuente
Los Novios
Toro
Monroy
Azafranal
Campo de San Francisco
Pasco de San Vincente
Brocense
Esrejo
Fonseca
C. de Ramón y Cajal
Prado
Iscar Peyra
Espoz y Mina
Concejo
C. de Zamora
Pozo Amarillo
García Tejado
C. Ancha
Prior
C. Cervantes
C. de Compañía
Univ. Pontificia
Rúa Mayor
Gran Vía
Rúa Antigua
Jesús
Palominos
Pl. Fray Luis de León
El Tostado
Pl. de Anaya
Pla y Deniel
Calderón de la Barca
Juan de la Fuente
Marquesa de Almarza
C. de San Pablo
Pl. Basilios
Libreros
San Juan de Alcázar
Calle de San Gregorio
Paseo de Canalejas
Puente Romano
Paseo del Rector Esperabé
Río Tormes
Puente Enrique Esteban
0 200 yards
0 200 meters
43
44
45
46
47
48
49
50
51
52
53
54
55

warmth of golden sandstone, which seems to glow throughout the city, that you will remember above all things.

WHAT TO SEE

45 For a complete exterior tour of the old and new **Cathedrals,** take a 10-minute walk around the complex, circling counterclockwise. Nearest the river stands the **Catedral Vieja** (Old Cathedral), built in the late 12th century, one of the most interesting examples of the Spanish Romanesque. Because the dome of the crossing tower has strange, plumelike ribbing, it's known as the Torre del Gallo (Rooster's Tower). The much larger **Catedral Nueva** (New Cathedral) dates mainly from the 16th century, though some parts, including the dome over the crossing and the bell tower attached to the west facade, had to be rebuilt after the Lisbon earthquake of 1755. Work began in 1513 under the direction of the distinguished late-Gothic architect Juan Gil de Hontañón, and as at Segovia's cathedral, Juan's son Rodrigo took over the work after his father's death in 1526. The New Cathedral's north facade (which contains the main entrance) is ornamental enough, but the west facade is dazzling in its sculptural complexity. Try to come here in late afternoon, when the sun shines on it.

The interior of the New Cathedral is as light and harmonious as that of Segovia's cathedral but larger. It's a triumphant baroque effusion designed by the Churrigueras. The wooden choir seems almost alive with active cherubim and saints. From a door in the south aisle, steps descend into the Old Cathedral, where boldly carved capitals supporting the vaulting are accented by foliage, strange animals, and touches of pure fantasy. Then comes the dome, which seems to owe much to Byzantine architecture; it's a remarkably light structure raised on two tiers of arcaded openings. Not the least of the Old Cathedral's attractions are its furnishings, including sepulchres from the 12th and 13th centuries and a curved high altar comprising 53 colorful and delicate scenes by the mid-15th-century artist Nicolás Florentino. In the apse above, Florentino painted an astonishingly fresh Last Judgment fresco.

From the south transept of the Old Cathedral, a door leads into the cloister, begun in 1177. From about 1230 until the construction of the main university building in the early 15th century, the chapels around the cloister served as classrooms for the university students. In the Chapel of St. Barbara, on the eastern side, theology students answered the grueling questions meted out by their doctoral examiners. The chair in which they sat is still there, in front of a recumbent effigy of Bishop Juan Lucero, on whose head the students would place their feet for inspiration. Also attached to the cloister is a small cathedral museum with a 15th-century triptych of St. Catherine by Salamanca's greatest native artist, Fernando Gallego. ✉ *Calle Cardenal Plá y Deniel s/n* ☎ *923/217476* 🎫 *New Cathedral free, Old Cathedral €3.50* ⏲ *Both cathedrals, Apr.–Sept., daily 10–7:30; Mar.–Oct., daily 10–1 and 4–6.*

54 **Convento de Las Dueñas** *(Convent of the Dames).* Founded in 1419, this convent hides a 16th-century cloister that is the most fantastically decorated in Salamanca, if not in the whole of Spain. The capitals of its two

superimposed Salamantine arcades are crowded with a baffling profusion of grotesques that can absorb you for hours. As you're wandering through, take a moment to look down. The interlocking diamond pattern on the ground floor of the cloister is decorated with the knobby vertebrae of goats and sheep. It's an eerie yet perfect accompaniment to all the grinning disfigured heads sprouting from the capitals looming above you. There's another reason to come here: the nuns make and sell excellent sweets. ✉ *Pl. Concilio de Trento* ☎ *923/215442* 🎫 *€1.50* ⏲ *Apr.–Oct., Mon.–Sat. 10:30–1 and 4:30–6, Sun. 11–12:45 and 4:30–6:45; Nov.–Mar., Mon.–Sat. 10:30–1 and 4:30–5:45, Sun. 11–12:45 and 4:30–5:45.*

53 **Plaza Mayor.** Built in the 1730s by Alberto and Nicolás Churriguera, Salamanca's Plaza Mayor is one of the largest squares in Spain, and many find it the most beautiful. Its northern side is dominated by the lavishly elegant, pinkish **ayuntamiento** (city hall). The square and its arcades are popular gathering spots for most of Salamancan society, and the many surrounding cafés make this the perfect spot for a coffee break. At night, the plaza swarms with students meeting "under the clock" on the plaza's north side. *Tunas* (strolling musicians in traditional garb) often meander among the cafés and crowds, playing for smiles and applause rather than tips.

46 **Universidad.** Parts of the university's walls, like those of the cathedral and other structures in Salamanca, are covered with large, ocher lettering recording the names of famous university graduates. The earliest names are said to have been written in the blood of the bulls killed to celebrate the successful completion of a doctorate. The **Escuelas Mayores** (Major Schools) dates to 1415, but it was not until more than 100 years later that an unknown architect provided the building with its gloriously elaborate facade. Immediately above the main door is the famous double portrait of Isabella and Ferdinand, surrounded by ornamentation that plays on the yoke-and-arrow heraldic motifs of the two monarchs. The double-eagle crest of Carlos V, flanked by portraits of the emperor and empress in classical guise, dominates the middle layer of the frontispiece. Perhaps the most famous rite of passage for new students is to find the carved frog that squats atop a skull at the very top left-hand corner. Legend has it that if you spot the frog on your first try, you'll pass all your exams and have a successful university career; for this reason, it's affectionately called *la rana de la suerte* (the lucky frog). It can be hard to pin down the elusive amphibian; if you're not having any luck, pop inside to the ticket booth, where they've kindly posted a detail of the frontispiece for precisely this purpose. You can then see the beloved frog all over town, on sweatshirts, magnets, pins, jewelry, and postcards.

The interior of the Escuelas Mayores, drastically restored in parts, comes as a slight disappointment after the splendor of the facade. But the *aula* (lecture hall) of Fray Luis de León, where Cervantes, Calderón de la Barca, and numerous other luminaries of Spain's golden age once sat, is of particular interest. Cervantes carved his name on one of the wooden pews up front. After five years' imprisonment for having translated the *Song of Songs* into Spanish, Fray Luis returned to this hall and began his lecture, "As I was saying yesterday ..."

Your ticket to the Escuelas Mayores also admits you to the nearby **Escuelas Menores** (Minor Schools), built in the early 16th century as a secondary school preparing candidates for the university proper. Passing through a gate crowned with the double-eagle crest of Charles V, you'll come to a green, on the other side of which is a modern building with a fascinating ceiling fresco of the zodiac, originally in the library of the Escuelas Mayores. A fragment of a much larger whole, this painting is generally attributed to Fernando Gallego. ✉ *Calle Fonseca, 4* ☎ *923/294550 or 923/294400* 🎫 *€4, free Mon. 9–2* ⏲ *Weekdays 9–2 and 4–7, Sat. 9–2 and 4–6:30, Sun. 10–1.*

NEED A BREAK?

Unwind at La Regenta (✉ *Calle Espoz y Mina 19–20* ☎ *923/123230*), a warm, plush, baroque-style café-bar that shines like a beacon of light (the flickering candle kind) in the thronged heart of town. Heavy green-and-gold curtains block most of the street noise, making the Plaza Mayor, a half a block off, a distant memory. Try a *café al caramelo* (coffee with caramel). In the evening you can order potent cocktails with names like "Kiss Me Boy" and "Sangre de Toro" (Bull's Blood).

48 **Casa de Las Conchas** *(House of Shells)*. This house was built around 1500 for Dr. Rodrigo Maldonado de Talavera, a professor of medicine at the university and a doctor at the court of Isabella. The scallop motif was a reference to Talavera's status as chancellor of the Order of St. James (Santiago), whose symbol is the shell. Among the playful plateresque details are the lions over the main entrance, engaged in a fearful tug-of-war with the Talavera crest. The interior has been converted into a public library. Duck into the charming courtyard, which has an upper balustrade carved with virtuoso intricacy in imitation of basketwork. ✉ *Calle de Compañía 2* ☎ *923/269317* 🎫 *Free* ⏲ *Weekdays 9–9, Sat. 9–2 and 4–7, Sun. 10–2 and 4–7.*

52 **Casa de Las Muertes** *(House of the Dead)*. Built in about 1513 for the majordomo of Alonso de Fonseca II, the house takes its name from the four tiny skulls that adorn its top two windows. Alonso de Fonseca II commissioned them to commemorate his deceased uncle, the licentious archbishop who lies in the Convento de Las Ursulas, across the street. For the same reason, the facade also bears the archbishop's portrait. The small square in front of the house was a favorite haunt of the poet, philosopher, and university rector Miguel de Unamuno, whose statue stands here. Unamuno supported the Nationalists under Franco at the outbreak of the civil war, but he later turned against them. Placed under virtual house arrest, Unamuno died in the house next door in 1938. During the Franco period, students often daubed his statue red to suggest that his heart still bled for Spain. ✉ *Rua Bordadores 6.*

50 **Colegio Mayor Arzobispo Fonseca/Colegio de Los Irlandeses** *(Irish College)*. This small college was founded by Alonso de Fonseca II in 1521 to train young Irish priests. It's now a residence hall for guest lecturers at the

university. This part of town was the most severely damaged during the Peninsular War of the early 19th century and still has a slightly derelict character. The interior, however, is a treat. To the right immediately inside is a late-Gothic chapel, and beyond it lies one of the most classical and genuinely Italianate of Salamanca's many courtyards. ✉ *Calle Fonseca 4* ☎ *923/294570* 🎫 *Free* ⏲ *Daily 10–2 and 4–7.*

51 **Convento de Las Ursulas** *(Convent of the Ursulines).* Archbishop Alonso de Fonseca I lies here, in a splendid marble tomb created by Diego de Siloe during the early 1500s. ✉ *Calle Las Ursulas 2* ☎ *923/219877* 🎫 *€2* ⏲ *Daily 11–1 and 4:30–6. Closed last Sun. of every month.*

55 **Convento de San Estéban** *(Convent of St. Stephen).* The convent's monks, among the most enlightened teachers at the university, were the first to take Columbus's ideas seriously and helped him gain his introduction to Isabella (hence his statue in the nearby Plaza de Colón, back toward Calle de San Pablo). The complex was designed by one of San Estéban's monks, Juan de Alava. The door to the right of the west facade leads you into a gloomy cloister with Gothic arcading, interrupted by tall, spindly columns adorned with classical motifs. From the cloister, you enter the church at its eastern end. The interior is unified and uncluttered but also dark and severe. The one note of color is provided by the ornate and gilded high altar of 1692, a baroque masterpiece by José Churriguera. The most exciting part of San Estéban, though, is the massive west facade, a thrilling plateresque work in which sculpted figures and ornamentation are piled up to a height of more than 98 feet. ✉ *Pl. Concilio de Trento* ☎ *923/215000* 🎫 *€2* ⏲ *Apr.–Sept., daily 10–2 and 4–8; Oct.–Mar., daily 10–2 and 4–7.*

44 **Museo Art Nouveau y Art Deco.** The museum is in the Casa Lis, a modernist building from the end of the 19th century. On display are 19th-century paintings and glass, as well as French and German china dolls, Viennese bronze statues, furniture, jewelry, enamels, and jars. ✉ *Calle Gibraltar 14* ☎ *923/121425* 🌐 *www.museocasalis.org* 🎫 *€2.50* ⏲ *Tues.–Fri. 11–2 and 4–7, weekends and holidays 11–8.*

47 **Museo de Salamanca** *(Museo de Bellas Artes).* Consisting mainly of minor 17th- and 18th-century paintings, this museum, also known as the Museo de Bellas Artes (Museum of Fine Arts), is interesting for its 15th century building, which belonged to Isabella's physician, Alvárez Abarca. ✉ *Patio de Escuelas Menores 2* ☎ *923/212235* 🎫 *€1.20, free weekends* ⏲ *Oct.–June, Tues.–Sat. 10–2 and 4–7, Sun. 10–2; July–Sept., Tues.–Sat. 10–2 and 5–8, Sun. 10–2.*

49 **Palacio de Monterrey.** Built after 1538 by Rodrigo Gil de Hontañón, the Monterrey Palace was meant for an illegitimate son of Alonso de Fonseca I. As in Rodrigo's other local palaces, the building is flanked by towers and has an open arcaded gallery running the length of the upper level. Such galleries—which in Italy you would expect to see on the ground floor—are common in Spanish Renaissance palaces and were intended to provide privacy for the women of the house and cool the floor below during the summer. Privately owned, the palace is not open to visitors, but you can stroll its grounds. ✉ *Calle de Compañía s/n.*

43 **Puente Romano** *(Roman Bridge)*. Next to the bridge is an Iberian stone bull, and opposite the bull is a statue commemorating Lazarillo de Tormes, the young hero of the eponymous (but anonymous) 16th-century work that is one of the masterpieces of Spanish literature.

WHERE TO STAY & EAT

$$$$ ✕**Chez Víctor.** Try this chic restaurant for a break from traditional Castilian food. Chef-owner Victoriano Salvador learned his trade in France and adapts French cuisine to Spanish taste, with whimsical touches all his own. Sample the traditional *carrillada de buey braseada con jengibre* (cheek of beef braised in ginger) or the more continental *hojaldre de verduras y foie con salsa de trufas* (puff pastry filled with leeks and julienned carrots in a truffle sauce). Desserts are outstanding, especially the chocolate ones. ✉*Espoz y Mina 26* ☎*923/213123* ▭*AE, DC, MC, V* ⊙*Closed Mon. and Aug. No dinner Sun.*

$$$$ ✕**Río de la Plata.** Off Calle de San Pablo, this tiny basement restaurant has been in business since 1958 and retains an old-fashioned character. The gilded yet quiet interior is a pleasant change of scenery, and the fireplace and local crowd provide warmth. The food is simple but carefully prepared, with good-quality fish and meat. ✉*Pl. Peso 1* ☎*923/219005* ▭*AE, MC, V* ⊙*Closed Mon. and July.*

$$$–$$$$ ✕**La Hoja Charra.** The restaurant off Plaza Mayor has a glass facade, high ceilings, butter-yellow walls, and minimalist art—all signs of a very different kind of Castilian dining experience. Young chef-owner Alberto López Oliva prepares an innovative menu of traditional fare with a twist. *Manitas, manzana, y langostinas al aroma de Módena* are pig trotters with prawns and apple slices, all in Módena vinegar; *perdiz al chocolate con berza* is partridge cooked in chocolate and served with cabbage. ✉*Pasaje Coliseum 19* ☎*923/264028* ▭*AE, MC, V* ⊙*Closed Mon. and last 2 wks of Feb. and Aug. No dinner Sun.*

$$–$$$$ ✕**El Candil Viejo.** Beloved by locals for its superb, no-nonsense Castilian fare, this tavern is an old favorite with professors in pinstripes and students on dates. Aside from a simple salad, the menu consists of meat, meat, and more meat, including pork, lamb, kid, sausage, and fantastic *marucha* (short ribs).The homemade sausages are especially good. For tapas, try the *farinato* sausage, made from pork, onion, eggs, and bread crumbs, or the *picadillo,* similar but spicier with pepper, garlic, and tomato. ✉*Calle Ventura Ruiz Aguilera 14–16* ☎*923/217239* ▭*AE, DC, MC, V* ⊙*Closed 3 wks in Jan.*

$–$$ ✕**El Grillo Azul.** A vegetarian restaurant is a rare sight in Spain, and this, the only one in Salamanca, has an adventurous menu of heaping dishes that easily trump any of the limp salads and veggie options you'll find elsewhere. Dig into the *arroz basmati con calabacín, zanahorias, y piñones* (basmati rice topped with zucchini, carrots, and pine nuts) or an omelet stuffed with almonds and mushrooms. ✉*C. El Grillo 1* ☎*923/219233* ▭*AE, DC, MC, V* ⊙*Closed Mon. No dinner Sun.*

¢–$$ ✕**Bambú.** At peak times, it's standing-room only at this jovial basement tapas bar catering to students. The floor may be littered with napkins, and you might have to shout to be heard, but it's the generous tapas and big sloppy *bocadillos* (sandwiches) that draw the crowds. Although paella is usually the exclusive domain of pricey paella restaurants, here (during lunch) you can enjoy a *ración* of paella, ladled out from a large *caldero* (shallow pan). Another bonus: even if you just order a drink, you'll be served a liberal helping of the "tapa of the day." ✉ *C. Prior 4* ☎ *923/260092* 🌐 *www.cafeteriabambu.com* 💳 *MC, V.*

$$$ **AC Palacio de San Estéban.** Near the cathedrals, this fancy hotel is in a former part of the 17th-century Convento de San Estéban. The rooms are modern, finished in cream and white with dark-wood trim. ✉ *Calle Arroyo de Santo Domingo 3, 37001* ☎ *923/262296* 📠 *917/268872* 🌐 *www.ac-hoteles.com* *51 rooms* *In-hotel: restaurant, bar, gym, laundry service, parking (fee), no-smoking rooms* 💳 *AE, DC, MC, V.*

$$$ ★ **Rector.** From the stately entrance to the high-ceiling guest rooms, this lovely hotel is a true European experience. The sitting areas, hallways, and breakfast room are all spotless, spacious, warm, and quiet, and the owners and staff are very helpful, and can tell you all about Salamanca. ✉ *Paseo Rector Esperabé 10* ☎ *923/218482* 📠 *923/214008* 🌐 *www.hotelrector.com* *14 rooms* *In-hotel: bar* 💳 *AE, DC, MC, V.*

$$ **San Polo.** Built on the foundations of the old Romanesque church by the same name—the ruins of which you can see through windows in the foyer and hall—the hotel is near the city center and has a friendly staff. The smallish rooms have light ocher tones, with white curtains. ✉ *Arroyo de Santo Domingo 2, 37008* ☎ *923/211177* 📠 *923/211154* 🌐 *www.hotelsanpolo.com* *37 rooms, 1 suite* *In-hotel: restaurant, bar, parking (fee)* 💳 *AE, DC, MC, V.*

$ **Hostal Plaza Mayor.** You can't beat the location of this great little *hostal,* just steps from the Plaza Mayor. Rooms are small but modern; the only drawback is the noise level on weekends (bring earplugs), when student *tunas* (musicians or bands) sing ballads at the plaza's crowded cafés until the wee hours. Reservations are advisable, as rooms fill up fast. ✉ *Pl. del Corrillo 20, 37008* ☎ *923/262020* 📠 *923/217548* *19 rooms* *In-hotel: restaurant* 💳 *MC, V.*

NIGHTLIFE

Particularly in summer, Salamanca sees perhaps the greatest influx of foreign students of any city in Spain—by day they study Spanish, and by night they fill Salamanca's bars and clubs to capacity. **Mesón Cervantes** (✉ *Entrance on southeast corner of Pl. Mayor* 🌐 *www.meson-cervantes.com*), an upstairs tapas bar, draws crowds to its balcony for a drink and an unparalleled view of the action. Bask in the romantic glow emanating from stained-glass lamps in the baroque-style **Posada de las Almas** (✉ *Pl. San Boal s/n*), the preferred cocktail-and-conversation nightspot for stylish students. Wrought-iron chandeliers hang from the high wood-beam ceilings, harp-strumming angels top elegant pillars, and one entire wall of shelves showcases colorful doll's houses. After 11, a well-dressed twenty- and thirtysomething crowd comes to dance at **Camelot** (✉ *Rua Bordadores 3* 🌐 *www.camelotsalamanca*), an ancient stone-wall warehouse in one corner of the 16th-century Convento de Las Ursulas. For good wine, heaping portions of tapas, and live music, try the **Café Principal** (✉ *Rua Mayor 9*). After-hours types end (if not spend) the night at **Café Moderno** (✉ *Gran Vía 75*), tucking into *chocolate con churros* at daybreak.

SHOPPING

On Sunday, the **Rastro** flea market is held on Avenida de Aldehuela. Buses leave from Plaza de España. The husband-and-wife team in tiny **Artesanía Duende** (✉*C. San Pablo 29* ☎*923/213622*) have been creating and selling unique wooden crafts for decades. Their music boxes, thimbles, photo frames, and other items are beautifully carved or stenciled with local themes, from the *bailes charros,* Salamanca's regional dance, to the floral designs embroidered on the hems of provincial dresses.

SPORTS & THE OUTDOORS

GOLF There are two golf courses near Salamanca. **Campo de Golf de Salamanca** (✉*Calle Monte de Zarapicos, Zarapicos* ☎*923/329102* 📠*923/329105* 🌐*www.golfysol.com*) is 18 km (12 mi) from Salamanca on the C517 and is more of a country club, with swimming pools, horseback riding, tennis, a gym, and a social club and bar. Three kilometers (2 mi) from Salamanca is **Golf Villa Mayor** (✉*Villamayor* ☎*923/337011* 📠*923/337007* 🌐*www.villamayorgolf.com*).

OFF THE BEATEN PATH

About an hour southwest (88 km/54 mi) from Salamanca are the preserved medieval walls of Ciudad Rodrigo, an interesting town with fewer tourists, surveying the fertile valley of the River Agueda. This small town has numerous well-preserved palaces and churches and makes an excellent overnight stop on the way from Spain to Portugal.

The cathedral (✉*Pl. de Herrasti* ☎*923/481424* 🎫*Cathedral free, museum €2.50* ⏲*Daily 10–1 and 4–6*) combines the Romanesque and transitional Gothic styles and has a great deal of fine sculpture. Look closely at the early-16th-century choir stalls, elaborately carved with entertaining grotesques by Rodrigo Alemán. The cloister has carved capitals, and the cypresses in its center lend tranquillity. The cathedral's outer walls are still scarred by cannonballs fired during the Peninsular War. A major Salamanca monument is its fortified medieval castle (✉*Pl. del Castillo*), part of which has been turned into a parador. From here you can climb onto the town's battlements.

ZAMORA

248 km (154 mi) northwest of Madrid.

Zamora, on a bluff above the Duero, is not conventionally beautiful, as its many attractive monuments are isolated from one another by ramshackle 19th- and 20th-century development. The town does have a lively, old-fashioned character, making it a pleasant place to pause.

WHAT TO SEE

Zamora is famous for its Holy Week celebrations. The **Museo de Semana Santa** *(Holy Week Museum)* houses the sculptures paraded around the streets in processions during that time. Of relatively recent vintage, these works have an appealing provincial quality—for instance, a Crucifixion group filled with what appears to be the contents of a hard-

Continued on page 214

Sherry wine at the *Feria del Caballo* of Jerez de la Frontera, Cádiz.

THE WINES OF SPAIN

Copitas (traditional sherry wine glasses) and casks at González Byass winery.

After years of being in the shadows of other European wines, Spanish wines are finally gunning for the spotlight—and what has taken place is nothing short of a revolution. The wines of Spain, like its cuisine, are currently experiencing a firecracker explosion of both quality and variety that has brought a new level of interest, awareness, and recognition throughout the world, propelling them into superstar status. A generation of young, hot-to-trot winemakers has jolted dormant areas awake, rediscovered long-forgotten local grapes, and introduced top international varieties. Even the most established regions submitted to makeovers to keep up with these dramatic changes and compete in the global market.

THE ROAD TO GREAT WINE

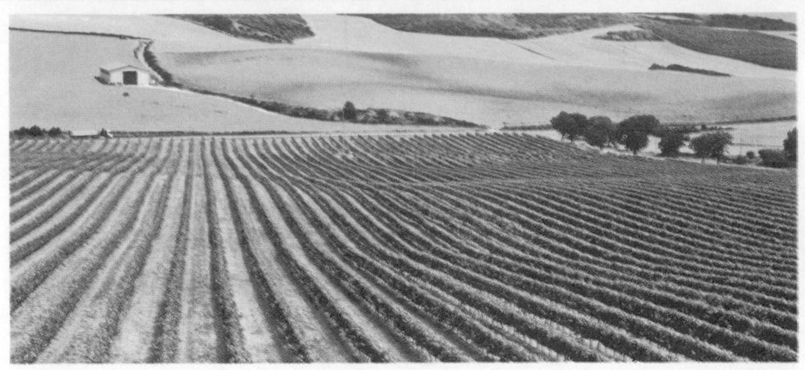

(top) Vineyard in Navarra. (below) Men with *cunachos* (grape baskets) near Málaga.

In the beginning, it wasn't so rosy. Spanish wine has a long and agitated history dating back to the time when the Phoenicians introduced viticulture over 3,000 years ago. Some wines achieved fame in Roman times, and the Visigoths enacted wine laws, but in the regions under Muslim rule, winemaking slowed down for centuries. Starting in the 16th century, wine trade expanded along with the Spanish Empire, and by the 18th and 19th centuries the Sherry region *bodegas* (wineries) were already established.

In the middle of the 19th century, seeds of change blossomed throughout the Spanish wine industry. In 1846 the estate that was to become Vega Sicilia, Spain's most revered winery, was set up in Castile. Three years later the famous Tío Pepe brand was established to produce the excellent dry *Fino* wines. Marqués de Murrieta and the Marqués de Riscal wineries opened in the 1860s creating the modern Rioja region and clearing the way for many centenary wineries. *Cava*—Spain's white or pink sparkling wine—was created the following decade in Catalonia.

After this flurry of activity, Spanish wines languished for almost a century. Vines were hit hard by phylloxera, and then a civil war and a long dictatorship left the country stagnant and isolated. Just 30 short years ago, Spain's wines were somehow split between the same dominant trio of Sherry, Rioja, and Cava, and loads of cheap, watered-down wines made by local cooperatives with little gumption to improve and even less expertise.

However, starting in the 1970s, a wave of innovation crashed through Rioja and emergent regions like Ribera del Duero and Penedés. In the 1990s, it turned into a revolution that spread all over the landscape—and it's still going strong. Today, Spain is the third largest wine producer in the world, makes enticing wines at all price ranges, in never before seen levels of quality and variety. As a result, in 2006 Spain became the second wine exporting country by volume, beating out France and trailing just behind Italy.

TYPE OF WINES BY AGING

A unique feature of Spanish wines is their indication of aging. DO wines (see "A *Vino* Primer" on following page) show this on mandatory back labels. They apply to white, rose, and sparkling wines, but are much more prevalent among reds, whose requirements are the following:

Joven or Cosecha

A young wine with less than the legal *crianza* barrel-aging period. This is the basic category. But quality-oriented winemakers have begun to shun the traditional aging regulations and have produced new, cutting-edge wines in this category. To distinguish the ambitious new reds from the charming easy drinking jovenés, check the price.

Crianza

A wine aged for at least 24 months, six of which are in barrels (12 in Rioja, Ribera del Duero, and Navarra). A great bargain in top vintages from the most reliable wineries and regions.

Reserva

A wine aged for a minimum of 36 months, at least 12 of which are in oak.

Gran Reserva

Traditionally the top of the Spanish wine hierarchy, and the pride of the centenary Rioja wineries. A red wine aged for at least 24 months in oak, followed by at least an additional 36 in the bottle before release.

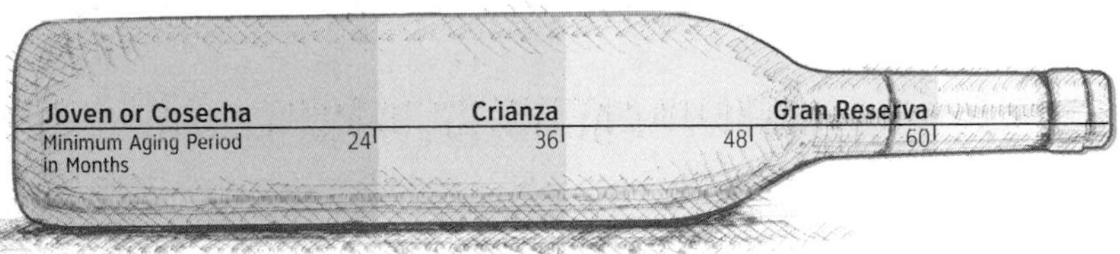

READING LABELS LIKE A PRO

A *VINO* PRIMER

Spain offers a daunting assortment of styles, regions, grapes, and terminology. But don't panic. A few guidelines can help you soldier through them. Save for a growing number of worthy exceptions, Spain's quality wines come from designated areas called *Denominaciones de Origen* (Appellations of Origin) or simply *DO* for short. Spain has more than 60, all of them with specific regulations designed to protect the personality of their wines. Four key elements account for the distinctive character in the best of them: diverse climates, varied soils, indigenous grape varieties, and winemaking practices.

1 The green and more humid areas of the Northwest deliver crisp, floral white albariños in Galicia's **Rias Biaxas.** In the **Bierzo** DO, the Mencía grape distills the essence of the schist slopes, where it grows into minerally infused red wines.

2 Moving east, in the iron-rich riverbanks of the Duero, Tempranillo grapes, here called "Tinto Fino," produces complex and age-worthy **Ribera del Duero** reds and hefty **Toro** wines. Close by, the **Rueda** DO adds aromatic and grassy whites from local Verdejo and adopted Sauvignon Blanc.

3 The **Rioja** region is a winemaker's paradise. Here a mild, nearly perfect vine-growing climate marries limestone and clay soils with Tempranillo, Spain's most noble grape, to deliver wines that possess the two main features of every great region: personality and quality. Tempranillo-based riojas evolve from a young cherry color and aromas of strawberries and red fruits, to a brick hue, infused with scents of tobacco and leather. Whether medium or full-bodied, tannic or velvety, these reds are some of the most versatile and food-friendly wines, and have set the standard for the country for over a century.

Nearby, **Navarra** and three small DO's in Aragón, deliver great wines made with the local Garnacha, Tempranillo, and international grape varieties.

4 South of Barcelona, a group of visionary winemakers, in less than a decade, revived the tiny and dormant medieval mountainous region of **Priorat.** Blending indigenous old Garnacha and Cariñena vines with mostly Cabernet and Syrah, they translated the brown

WINE + ARCHITECTURE

Calatrava's Ysios winery

Nothing symbolizes the current golden era of Spanish wines better than the winery projects completed by world-class architects. Just to name a few: **Rafael Moneo** built the new Chivite winery; **Zaha Hadid** is renovating the traditional López Heredia; **Frank Gehry** just opened the new Marqués de Riscal visitors center; **Santiago Calatrava** created Ysios with a curvy profile that mim-

slate soils into fascinating and powerful red wines, deeply different from the Rioja and Ribera del Duero wines. Their immense success has energized the areas along the Mediterranean coast—notably *Montsant, Empordà,* and *Jumilla*—and has provoked the emergence of new bold, rich, full-bodied, packed with fruit, and immediately appealing wines.

5 In the **central plateau south of Madrid,** rapid investment, modernization, and replanting is resulting in medium bodied, easy drinking, and fairly priced wines made with Tempranillo (here called "Cencíbel"), Cabernet, Syrah, and even Petit Verdot, that are opening the doors to more ambitious endeavors.

6 In sun-drenched Andalusia, where the white albariza limestone soils reflect the powerful sunlight while trapping the scant humidity, the fortified **Jerez** (Sherry) and **Montilla** emerge. In all their different incarnations, from dry *finos, manzanillas, amontillados, palo cortados,* and *olorosos,* to sweet creams and Pedro Ximénez, they are the most original wines of Spain.

ics the nearby mountains; **Philippe Mazières** made the new barrel-shaped CVNE winery; **Richard Rogers's** new Protos winery sits in stark contrast to the medieval castle above the hill. These flashy wineries, set in picturesque vine landscapes and quaint villages, are adding a new attraction to the growing enotourism industry (wine-related tourism).

Gehry's Marqués de Riscal winery

JUST OFF THE VINE

Beyond Tempranillo: The current wine revolution has recovered many native varieties. Albariño, Godello, and Verdejo among the white, and Callet, Cariñena, Garnacha, Graciano, Mandó, Manto Negro, Mencía, and Monastrell among the red are currently gaining momentum and will become more popular over the years.

Cult Wines: For most of the past century, Vega Sicilia Unico was the only true cult wine from Spain. The current explosion has greatly expanded the roster: L'Ermita, Pingus, Clos Erasmus, Artadi, Cirsion, Terreus, and Termanthia are the leading names in a list that grows every year.

Vinos de Pagos: *Pago,* a word meaning plot or vineyard, is the new legal term chosen to create Spain's equivalent of a *Grand Cru* hierarchy, by protecting quality oriented wine producers that make wine from their own estates.

V.O.S. and V.O.R.S: Sherry's most dramatic change in over a century is the creation of the "Very Old Sherry" designation for wines over 20 years of age, and the addition of "Rare" for those over 30, to easier distinguish their best, oldest, and most complex wines.

Petit Verdot: Winemakers in Spain are discovering that Petit Verdot, the "little green" grape of Bordeaux, ripens much easier in warmer climates than in its birthplace. This is leading to a dramatic increase in the presence of Petit Verdot in blends, and even to the production of varietals.

Innovative New Blends: A few wine regions have strict regulations concerning the varieties used in their wines, but most allow for experimentation. All over the country, *bodegas* are crafting wines with unsuspecting blends that involve local varieties, Tempranillo, and famous international grapes.

Andalusia's New Wines: For centuries, scorching southern Andalusia has offered world-class Sherry and Montilla wines. Now trailblazing winemakers are making serious inroads in the production of quality white, red, and new dessert wines, something deemed impossible a few years back.

Island Wines: In both the Balearic and Canary Islands the strong tourist industry helped to revive local winemaking. Although hard to find, the best Callet and Manto Negro based red wines of Majorca, and the sweet *malvasías* of Lanzarote will reward the adventurous drinker.

SUPERSTAR WINEMAKERS

Mariano García

Peter Sisseck

Alvaro Palacios

Josep Lluís Pérez

The current wine revolution has made superstars out of a group of dynamic, innovative, and visionary winemakers. Here are some of the top names:

Mariano García. His 30 years as winemaker of Vega Sicilia made him a legend. Now García displays his deft touch in the Duero and Bierzo through his four family projects: Mauro, Aalto, San Román, and Paixar.

Peter Sisseck. A Dane educated in Bordeaux, Sisseck found his calling in the old Ribera de Duero vineyards, where he crafted Pingus, Spain's quintessential new cult wine.

Alvaro Palacios. Palacios is the engine behind the current renaissance of Bierzo, and previously of Priorat, where he created L'Ermita, which is, along with Pingus, Spain's ultimate collector item.

Josep Lluís Pérez. From his base in Priorat and through his work as a winemaker, researcher, teacher, and consultant, Pérez (along with his daughter Sara Pérez) has become the main driving force in shaping the modern Mediterranean wines of Spain.

MATCHMAKING KNOW-HOW

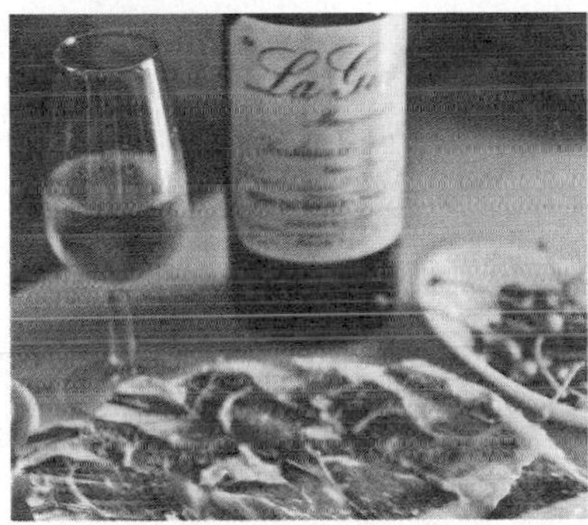
A pairing of wine with *jamon* and Spanish olives.

Spain has a great array of regional products and cuisines, and its avant-garde chefs are culinary world leaders. As a general rule, you should match local food with local wines—but Spanish wines can be matched very well with some of the most unexpected dishes.

Albariños and the white wines of Galicia are ideal partners of seafood and fish. Dry sherries complement Serrano and Iberico hams, *lomo, chorizo,* and *salchichón* (white dry saugage), as well as olives and nuts. Pale, light, and dry *finos* and *manzanillas* are the perfect aperitif wines, and the ideal companion of fried fish. Fuller bodied *amontillados, palo cortados*, and *olorosos* go well with hearty soups. Ribera del Duero reds are the perfect match for the outstanding local lamb. Try Priorat and other Mediterranean reds with strong chesses and barbecue meats. Traditional Rioja harmonizes well with fowl and game. But also take an adventure off the beaten path: *manzanilla* and *fino* are great with sushi and sashimi; Rioja *reserva* fit tuna steaks; and cream sherry will not be out of place with chocolate. ¡Salud!

ware store, including bales of rope, a saw, a spade, and numerous nails. The museum is in an unsightly modern building next to the church of Santa María. ✉*Pl. de Santa María la Nueva* ☎*980/532295* *€3* ⏲*Tues.–Sat. 10–2 and 5–8, Sun. 10–2.*

BREAD & WINE

Zamora, a densely fertile province, is divided by the Duero River into two distinct zones: the "land of bread" to the north, and the "land of wine" to the south. The area is most interesting for its Romanesque churches, the finest of which are in Zamora and Toro.

Zamora's **cathedral** is in a hauntingly beautiful square at the highest and westernmost point of the old town. Most of the building is Romanesque, but the exterior is most remarkable for its dome, which is flanked by turrets, articulated by spiny ribs, and covered in overlapping stones. The interior is notable for its early-16th-century carved choir stalls. The austere, late-16th-century cloister has a small museum, with an intricate *custodia* (monstrance, or receptacle for the Host) by Juan de Arce and some badly displayed but intriguing Flemish tapestries from the 15th and 16th centuries. ✉*Pl. Catedral* ☎*980/530644* *Cathedral free, museum €3* ⏲*Mar.–Sept., Tues.–Sun. 10–2 and 5–8; Oct.–Feb., Tues.–Sun. 10–2 and 4:30–6:30.*

Surrounding Zamora's cathedral to the north is a sizable park incorporating the heavily restored **castle,** begun in the 11th century. Now a municipal school, it's open to visitors only when classes are in session. Calle Trascastillo, descending south from the cathedral to the river, allows for views of the fertile countryside to the south and the town's old **Roman bridge.** ✉*Calle Trascastillo s/n.*

WHERE TO STAY & EAT

$$$–$$$$ ✕**El Rincón de Antonio.** Zamora's finest *cocina de autor* (original cuisine) comes off the burners from behind this stone facade, decorated in sleek contemporary lines. Local upland ingredients and seafood dishes from the Iberian coasts balance a constantly changing menu rich in creativity. ✉*Rúa de los Francos 6* ☎*980/535370* 🌐*www.elrincondeantonio.com* 💳*AE, DC, MC, V* ⏲*No dinner Sun.*

$$$ **Parador de Zamora.** This restored 15th-century palace is central yet quiet, with a distinctive patio courtyard adorned with coats of arms and classical medallions of historical and mythological figures. The views are excellent, and the staff is friendly and resourceful. ✉*Pl. de Viriato 5, 49001* ☎*980/514497* 📠*980/530063* 🌐*www.parador.es* *52 rooms* *In-hotel: restaurant, bar, pool* 💳*AE, DC, MC, V.*

TORO

57 *33 km (20 mi) east of Zamora.*

Above a loop of the Duero River and commanding extensive views over the vast plain to the south, Toro was once a provincial capital. In 1833 it was absorbed into the province of Zamora—a loss of status that worked in some ways to its advantage. Zamora developed into a thriving modern town, but Toro slumbered and preserved its old appear-

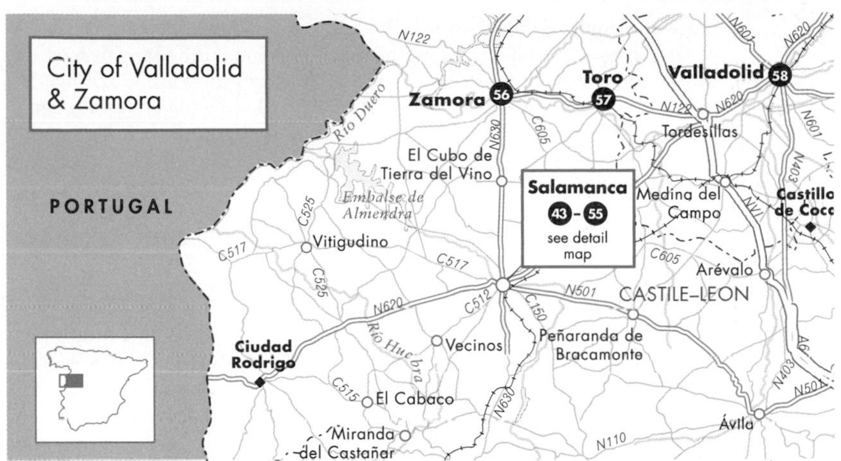

ance. The town is crowded with Romanesque churches, of which the most important is the **Colegiata**, begun in 1160. The protected west portal, or Portico de La Gloria, has colorfully painted, perfectly preserved statuary from the early 13th century. The Serbian-Byzantine dome is also prominent. In the sacristy is an anonymous 15th-century painting of the Virgin, a moving work in the so-called Hispano-Flemish style titled *La Virgen de la Mosca* (The Virgin of the Fly) for the fly painted on the Virgin's robe. ✉*Pl. de la Colegiata* ☎*980/694747 tourist office* 🌐*www.toroayto.es* 💷*€1* ⏲*Mar.–Nov., daily 10–2 and 4:30–6:30; Dec.–Feb. daily 10:30–2 and 5–7:30; Mon. open for Mass only (at 10* AM *and 11* AM*).*

VALLADOLID

58 *96 km (60 mi) east of Zamora, 193 km (120 mi) northwest of Madrid.*

Modern Valladolid, capital of Castile-León, is a sprawling industrial center in the middle of a flat stretch of Castilian terrain. The surrounding countryside has a desolate, wintry sort of beauty, its vast, brittle fields unfolding grandly toward the horizon, punctuated here and there with swaths of green. The city has an important place in Spain's history: Ferdinand and Isabella were married here, Felipe II was born and baptized here, and Felipe III made Valladolid the capital of Spain for six years. Though not as scenic as Zamora, Valladolid has the National Museum of Sculpture and plenty of interesting history.

WHAT TO SEE

Fodor's Choice ★ From the bus station, train station, or wherever you park your car, hop a taxi to the **Museo Nacional de Escultura** *(National Museum of Sculpture)*, at the northernmost point in the old town. The late-15th-century Colegio de San Gregorio, in which the main museum is housed, is a masterpiece with playful, naturalistic detail. The facade is especially fantastic, with ribs in the form of cut-back trees, sprouting branches, and—to complete the forest motif—a row of wild men bearing mighty clubs. Across the walkway from the main museum is a Renaissance palace that houses temporary exhibitions. The main museum is arranged in rooms off an elaborate, arcaded courtyard. Its collections do for Spanish sculpture what those in the Prado do for Spanish painting—the only difference is that most people have heard of Velázquez, El Greco, and Goya, but fewer are familiar with Alonso de Berruguete, Juan de Juni, and Gregorio Fernández, the three artists represented here.

Attendants and directional cues encourage you to tour the museum in chronological order. Begin on the ground floor, with Alonso de Berruguete's remarkable sculptures from the dismantled high altar in Valladolid's church of San Benito (1532). Berruguete, who trained in Italy under Michelangelo, is the most widely appreciated of Spain's post-medieval sculptors. He strove for pathos rather than realism, and his works have an extraordinarily expressive quality. The San Benito altar was the most important commission of his life, and the fragments here allow you to scrutinize his powerfully emotional art. In the museum's elegant chapel (which you normally see at the end of the tour) is a Berruguete retable from 1526, his first known work; on either side kneel gilded bronze figures by the Italian-born Pompeo Leoni.

Many critics of Spanish sculpture think that decline set in with the late-16th-century artist Juan de Juni, who used glass for eyes and pearls for tears. Juni's many admirers, however, find his works intensely exciting, and the works are, in any case, the highlights of the museum's upper floor. Dominating Castilian sculpture of the 17th century was Galician-born Gregorio Fernández, in whose works the dividing line between sculpture and theater becomes tenuous. Respect for Fernández has been diminished by the number of vulgar imitators his work has spawned, but at Valladolid you can see his art at its best. The enormous, dramatic, and moving sculptural groups assembled in the last series of rooms form a suitably spectacular climax to this fine collection. ✉ *Calle Cadenas de San Gregorio 1–3* ☎ *983/250375* 🌐 *http://museoescultura.mcu.es* 🎫 *€2.40, Sat. 4–6 and Sun. 10–2 free* ⏲ *Sept. 21–Mar. 20, Tues.–Sat. 10–2 and 4–6; Mar. 21–Sept. 20, Tues.–Sat. 10–2 and 4–9, Sun. 10–2.*

San Pablo (✉ *Pl. de San Pablo*), a late-15th-century church, has an overwhelmingly elaborate facade.

Though the foundations of Valladolid's **cathedral** were laid in late-Gothic times, the building owes much of its appearance to designs executed in the late 16th century by Juan de Herrera, the architect of the Escorial. Further work was carried out by Alberto de Churriguera in the early 18th century. The Juni altarpiece is the one bit of color in an otherwise visually chilly place. ✉ *Pl. de la Universidad 1* ☎ *983/304362* 🎫 *Cathedral free, museum €2.50* ⏲ *Tues.–Fri. 10–1:30 and 4:30–7, weekends 10–2.*

The main **university building** (✉ *Pl. de la Universidad*) sits opposite the garden just south of the cathedral. The exuberant and dynamic late-baroque frontispiece is by Narciso Tomé, creator of the remarkable

THEY WERE HERE

Valladolid is where three famous Spanish men were born, lived part of their lives, or died. Two of their homes are open to the public.

The **birthplace of Felipe II** (✉*Corner of Calle Angustias*) is a private brick home not open to the public.

An interesting remnant of Spain's golden age is the tiny house where the writer Miguel de Cervantes lived from 1603 to 1606. A haven of peace set back from a noisy thoroughfare, **Casa de Cervantes** *(Cervantes's House)* is best reached by taxi. It was furnished in the early 20th century in a pseudo-Renaissance style by the Marquis of Valle-Inclan—the creator of the El Greco Museum in Toledo. ✉*Pl. Rastro 7* ☎*983/308810* 🌐*http://museocasacervantes.mcu.es* 🎫*€2.40, free Sun.* ⏲*Tues.–Sat. 9:30–3, Sun. 10–3.*

The house where Christopher Columbus died is now the **Museo de Colón** *(Columbus Museum)* with a well-arranged collection of objects and explanatory panels illuminating the explorer's life. ✉*Plaza de Colón s/n* ☎*983/291353* 🎫*Free* ⏲*Tues.–Sat. 10–2 and 5–7, Sun. 10–2.*

Transparente in Toledo's cathedral. Valladolid's Calle Librería leads south from the main building to the magnificent **Colegio de Santa Cruz** (✉*Pl. Colegio de Santa Cruz*), a large university college begun in 1487 in the Gothic style and completed in 1491 by Lorenzo Vázquez in a tentative, pioneering Renaissance mode. Inside is a courtyard.

WHERE TO STAY & EAT

$$$–$$$$ ✕**La Dovela.** Valladolid's most famous and stylish restaurant counts members of the Spanish royal family among its guests. Specialties include meat roasted in a wood oven and *rape Castellano Gran Mesón* (breaded monkfish with clams and peppers). The daily five-course *menú de degustación* (tasting menu) at €25 is an excellent value, and the cozy downstairs bar serves a creditable *vino de la casa* (house wine) and a great selection of tapas. ✉*Paseo Zorrilla 10* ☎*983/338785* ▭*AE, DC, MC, V.*

$$–$$$ 🏨**Olid Meliá.** This hotel sits on a modern block amid one of Valladolid's oldest and most attractive districts. The building was erected in the early 1970s, and the rooms have blond-wood furniture. For a splurge, you can book a room with a sauna or hot tub. The first two floors have a pristine, marble elegance. ✉*Pl. de San Miguel 10, 47003* ☎*983/357200* 🖷*983/336828* 🌐*www.solmelia.com* *211 rooms* *In-hotel: restaurant, bar* ▭*AE, DC, MC, V.*

NIGHTLIFE

Valladolid is a university town with a dynamic nightlife. The cafés on the Plaza Mayor are the best places to people-watch as evening falls. Tapas are good in the Zona Santa María la Antigua and on the adjacent Calle Marqués and Calle Paraíso. The modern Zona Paco Suárez is popular with students. More fashionable and less rowdy are the Zona Cantarranas and hidden hot spots around the Plaza del Salvador. Make for the boisterous, standing-room-only **Bar El Corcho** (✉*Calle Correo*

2 ☎983/330861), just off the Plaza Mayor, for Castilian tapas—the house specialty is *tostada de gambas,* toasted French bread heaped with shrimp and drizzled with olive oil. A hopping dance spot is **Disco Bagur** (✉*C. de la Pasión 13*), off Plaza Mayor.

BURGOS

240 km (149 mi) north of Madrid.

On the banks of the Arlanzón River is this small city with some of Spain's most outstanding medieval architecture. The first signs of Burgos, if you approach on the A1 from Madrid, are the spiky twin spires of its cathedral, rising above the main bridge. Burgos's second glory is its heritage as the city of El Cid, the part-historical, part-mythical hero of the Christian Reconquest of Spain. The city has been known for centuries as a center of both militarism and religion, and even today you can see more nuns on its streets than almost anywhere else in Spain. Burgos was born as a military camp in 884—a fortress built on the orders of the Christian king Alfonso III, who was having a hard time defending the upper reaches of Old Castile from the constant forays of the Arabs. It quickly became vital in the defense of Christian Spain, and its identity as an early outpost of Christianity was sealed with the founding of the Royal Convent of Las Huelgas, in 1187. Burgos also became a place of rest and sustenance for Christian pilgrims on the Camino de Santiago.

WHAT TO SEE

59 ★ Start your tour of the city with the **cathedral,** the city's high point, which contains such a wealth of art and other treasures that the local burghers actually lynched their civil governor in 1869 for trying to take an inventory of it. The proud Burgalese apparently feared that the man was angling to remove the treasures. Most of the outside of the cathedral is sculpted in the Flamboyant Gothic style. The cornerstone was laid in 1221, and the two 275-foot towers were completed by the middle of the 14th century, though the final chapel was not finished until 1731. There are 13 chapels, the most elaborate of which is the hexagonal Condestable Chapel. You'll find the **tomb of El Cid** (1026–99) and his wife, Ximena, under the transept. El Cid (whose real name was Rodrigo Díaz de Vivar) was a feudal warlord revered for his victories over the Moors; the medieval *Song of My Cid* transformed him into a Spanish national hero.

At the other end of the cathedral, high above the West Door, is the **Reloj de Papamoscas** (Flycatcher Clock), so named for the sculptured bird that opens its mouth as the mechanism marks each hour. The grilles around the choir have some of the finest wrought-iron work in central Spain, and the choir itself has 103 delicately carved walnut stalls, no two alike. The 13th-century stained-glass windows that once shed a beautiful, filtered light were destroyed in 1813, one of many cultural casualties of Napoléon's retreating troops. ✉*Between Pl. del Rey San Fernando and Pl. de Santa María* ☎*947/204712* 🌐*www.catedraldeburgos.es* 🎫*Museum and cloister €4* ⏲*Mar. 19–June and Oct., daily*

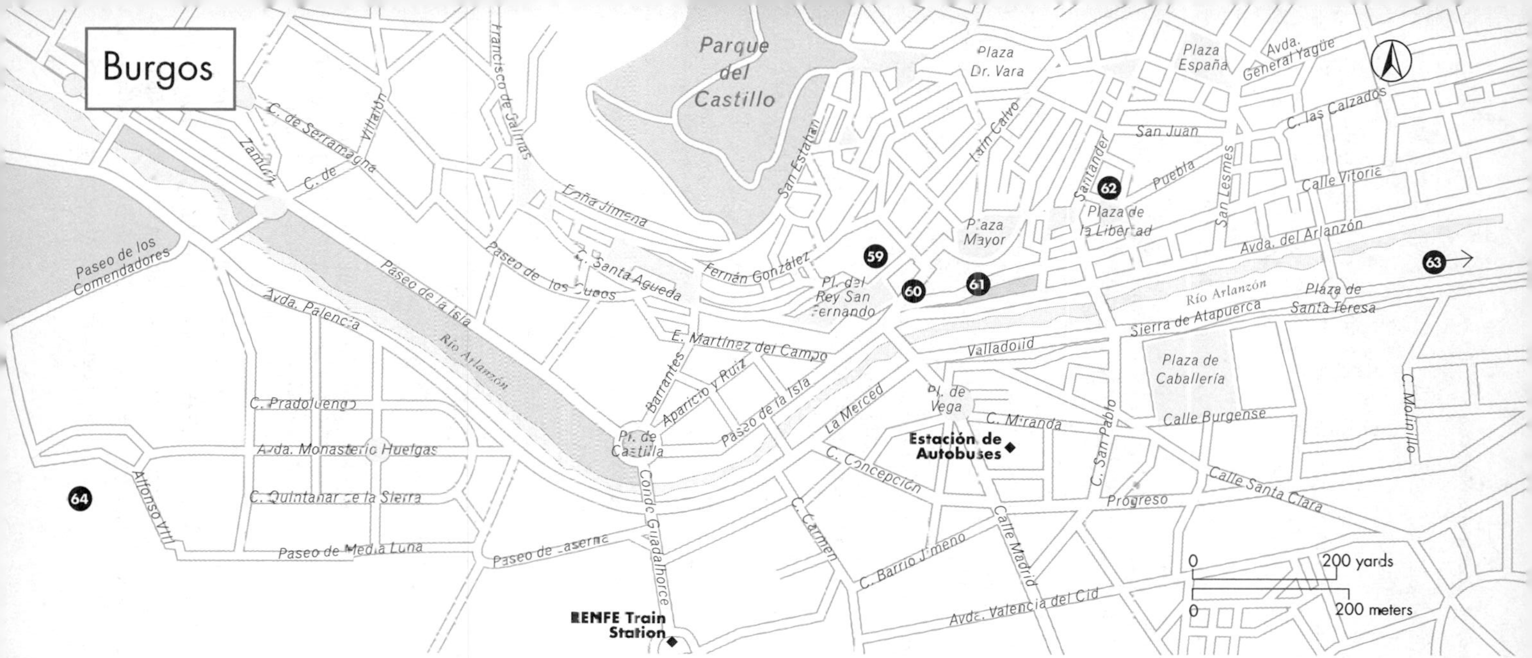

Burgos

Parque del Castillo
Plaza Dr. Vara
Plaza España
Avda. General Yagüe
C. las Calzadas
San Juan
Calle Vitoria
Puebla
San Lesmes
Santander
Plaza de la Libertad
Laín Calvo
San Esteban
Plaza Mayor
Avda. del Arlanzón
Río Arlanzón
Plaza de Santa Teresa
Sierra de Atapuerca
Valladolid
Fernán González
Pl. del Rey San Fernando
E. Martínez del Campo
Francisco de Salinas
Doña Jimena
C. Santa Agueda
Paseo de los Cubos
C. de Serramagna
Villalón
C. de Zamora
Paseo de los Comendadores
Paseo de la Isla
Avda. Palencia
Río Arlanzón
C. Pradoluengo
Avda. Monasterio Huelgas
C. Quintanar de la Sierra
Paseo de Media Luna
Alfonso VIII
Barrantes
Aparicio y Ruiz
Paseo de la Isla
Pl. de Castilla
La Merced
Pl. de Vega
C. Miranda
Estación de Autobuses
C. San Pablo
Plaza de Caballería
Calle Burgense
C. Molinillo
Calle Santa Clara
Progreso
C. Concepción
C. Carmen
Calle Madrid
C. Barrio Jimeno
Avda. Valencia del Cid
Conde Guadalhorce
Paseo de Laserna
RENFE Train Station

0 200 yards
0 200 meters

- Arco de Santa María 60
- Cartuja de Miraflores 63
- Casa del Cordón 62
- Cathedral 59
- Espolón 61
- Monasterio de Las Huelgas Reales 64

3

9:30–1:15 and 4–7; July–Sept., daily 9:30–7:15; Nov.–Mar. 18, daily 10–1:15 and 4–6:45.

60 Across the Plaza del Rey San Fernando from the cathedral is the city's main gate, the **Arco de Santa María**; walk through toward the river and look above the arch at the 16th-century statues of the first Castilian judges; El Cid; Spain's patron saint James; and King Carlos I.

61 The Arco de Santa María fronts the city's loveliest promenade, the **Espolón.** Shaded with black poplars, it follows the riverbank.

62 The **Casa del Cordón,** a 15th-century palace, is where the Catholic Monarchs received Columbus after his second voyage to the New World. It's now a bank. ✉*Pl. de Calvo Sotel.*

63 Founded in 1441, the **Cartuja de Miraflores** is a florid Gothic charter house; its Isabelline church has an altarpiece by Gil de Siloe that is said to be gilded with the first gold brought back from the Americas. To get there, follow signs from the city's main gate. ✉*3 km (2 mi) east of Burgos, at end of a poplar- and elm-lined road* 🌐*www.cartuja.org* *Free* ⏲*Church open for Mass Mon.–Sat.at 9 AM, Sun. at 7:30 and 10:15 AM; main building Mon.–Sat. 10:15–3 and 4–6, Sun. 11–3 and 4–6.*

64 On the western edge of town—a mile-long walk from the town center—is the **Monasterio de Las Huelgas Reales,** still run by nuns. Founded in 1187 by King Alfonso VIII, the convent has a royal mausoleum. All but one of the royal coffins were desecrated by Napoléon's soldiers; the one that survived contained clothes that form the basis of the convent's textile museum. ✉*1½ km (1 mi) southwest of town, along Paseo de la Isla and left across Malatos Bridge* ☎*947/201630* 🌐*www3.planalfa.es/lashuelgas* *€5, Wed. free for EU citizens* ⏲*Tues.–Sat. 10–1 and 3:45–5:30, Sun. 10:30–2.*

WHERE TO STAY & EAT

$$–$$$ ★ ✕ **Casa Ojeda.** Across from the Casa del Cordón, this popular restaurant is known for inspired renditions of Burgos classics, especially roast lamb. ✉*C. Vitoria 5* ☎*947/209052* 🌐*www.grupojeda.com* 💳*AE, DC, MC, V* ⏲*Closed Sun.*

$$$ ✕🏨 **Mesón del Cid.** Once a 15th-century printing press, this family-run hotel and restaurant ($$$$) has been hosting travelers and serving Burgalese food for four generations. Guest rooms face the cathedral and are done in traditional Castilian style. The dining rooms have hand-hewn beams and views of the cathedral. The *pimientos rellenos* (peppers stuffed with meat) are excellent, as is the *sopa de Doña Jimena* (garlic soup with bread and egg). ✉*Pl. Santa María 8, 09003* ☎*947/208715* 📠*947/269460* 🌐*www.mesondelcid.es* *56 rooms* *In-hotel: restaurant, bar, parking (no fee)* 💳*AE, DC, MC, V.*

EN ROUTE

For a sojourn with those masters of the Gregorian chant, the double-platinum monks of *Chant* fame, stop at the Monastery of Santo Domingo de Silos, 58 km (36 mi) southeast of Burgos. Single men can stay here for up to eight days. Guests are expected to be present for breakfast, lunch, and dinner but are otherwise left to their own devices. If the monastery is full, try

to drop in for a vespers service. Quite close to Burgos to the southeast (10 km [6 mi]) is the **Monastery of San Pedro de Cardeña**, a lodging that allows couples and even families—possibly thanks to the monastery's importance in the story of El Cid, the medieval Spanish hero who left his wife and children there when banished into exile.

> **EL CAMINO**
>
> West of Burgos, the N120 to León crosses the ancient Way of St. James, occasionally revealing lovely old churches, tiny hermitages, ruined monasteries, and medieval villages in rolling fields. West of León, you can actually follow the well-worn Camino as it approaches Galicia and the very last stops on a pilgrimage route that began all the way back in France or Portugal. Making its way toward the giant cathedral in Santiago de Compostela, this Castilian leg of the Camino passes through medieval towns and quiet valleys as the terrain gets greener, wetter, and hillier. *See Chapter 4 for more on El Camino.*

NIGHTLIFE

Due to its university students, Burgos has a lively *vida nocturna* (nightlife). House wines and *cañas* (small glasses of beer) flow freely at the crowded tapas bars along Calles Laín Calvo and San Juan, near the Plaza Mayor. Calle Puebla, a small, dark street off Calle San Juan, also gets constant revelers, who pop into Café Principal, La Rebotica, and Spils Cervecería for a quick drink and morsel before moving on. When you order a drink at any Burgos bar, the bartender plunks down a free *pinchito* (small tapa)—a long-standing tradition. The late-night bar scene centers on **Las Llanas**, near the cathedral.

SHOPPING

A good buy is a few bottles of local Ribera de Duero *tinto* wines, now strong rivals to those of Rioja-Alta. Burgos is also known for its cheeses. **Casa Quintanilla** (✉ *C. Paloma 17*) is a good spot to pick up some *queso de Burgos*, a fresh ricottalike cheese.

EN ROUTE

Off the Nacional-120 highway west of Burgos, about 25 km (16 mi) turn right, and soon you'll be in the village of **Sasamón**, where the 15th-century hilltop church of Santa María la Real, with a magnificent carved portico, stands beside a tree-lined plaza with a tinkling fountain. You can visit on weekdays 11–2 and 4–6. Pick up keys to the church in the nearby Bar Gloria. On the north side of the village is the tiny Ermita de San Isidro Hermitage. If the hermitage is closed, peer through the small window in the door to see, right in the middle of the aisle, its surreal, 20-foot-tall 16th-century Gothic cross. Carved of stone, it depicts the expulsion of Adam and Eve from paradise.

FRÓMISTA

65 *70 km (44 mi) northwest of Burgos.*

Take the small road south from Castrojeriz to Itero de la Vega and Boadillo del Camino to reach Frómista. Just before you arrive, the road

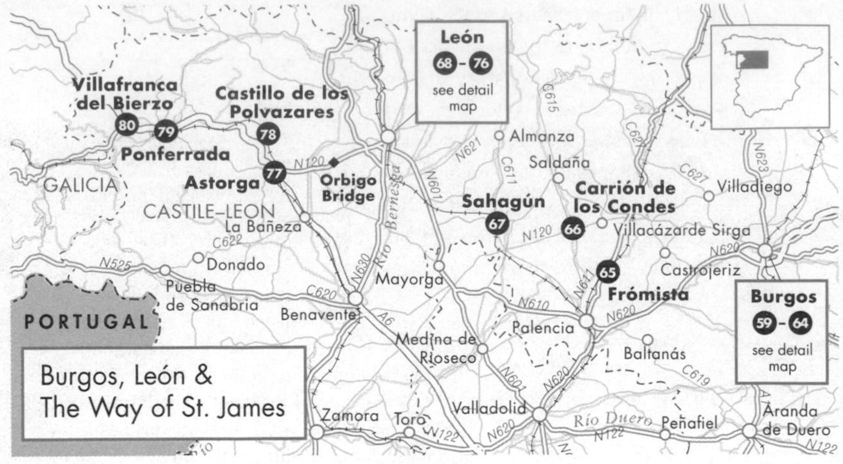

crosses the Canal de Castilla, begun in 1753 with the dubious idea of linking Salamanca with the port of Santander—and never completed. The town of Frómista has four hospices for present-day pilgrims, and its architectural gem is the 1066 church of **San Martín** (✉*Plaza San Martín, s/n* ⏲*Apr. 1 to June 30 and Oct. 1–15, daily 10–2 and 4:30–8; Oct. 16–Mar. 31, daily 10–2 and 3:30–6:30*). Richly sculpted inside, it was part of a monastery in the 11th century, which might explain the geographical breathing room it still enjoys.

WHERE TO EAT

$$$–$$$$ ✕ **Hostería de los Palmeros.** Here in a 17th-century pilgrims' hospital, the kitchen serves good fish, game in season, and baby lamb. Dine on an outdoor terrace or in the rather formal upstairs dining room, with a view of the storks' nests on the church of San Telmo, across the highway. ✉*Pl. San Telmo 4* ☎*979/810067* ▭*AE, DC, MC, V.*

EN ROUTE

As you drive toward Carrión de los Condes, turn right into the village of Villalcázar de Sirga, which is 13 km (8 mi) west of Frómista. The Templar church of Santa María la Blanca has a towering double-arch entrance and the polychrome 13th-century tombs of Felipe, brother of Alfonso X the Learned, and Leonor, his wife.

CARRIÓN DE LOS CONDES

66 *7 km (4½ mi) west of Villalcázar de Sirga.*

Drive through this busy town, heading west, and cross the River Carrión to reach the **Real Monasterio San Zoilo** on the left. Begun in the 10th century, this former Benedictine monastery has magnificent 16th-century Gothic-Renaissance cloisters and the elaborate tombs of the *condes* (counts) of Carrión. You can visit weekdays 10:30–2 (plus 4–8 June–August) and on weekends 10:30 to 2 and 4 to 8 year-round.

WHERE TO STAY

$$–$$$ ★ **Hotel Real Monasterio San Zoilo.** This former Benedictine monastery dates back to the 10th century, and its spectacular entrance leads to impressive public rooms with exposed bricks and timbers. The vast refectory can seat 330. One floor up is the restaurant Las Vigas ($$$$), which serves decent Castilian fare at tables set below a forest of medieval beams (*vigas*). The large rooms are well furnished, and the "Habitación del Conde" suite is especially grand. ✉*Carrión de los Condes, 34120* ☎*979/880050* 🖷*979/881090* 🌐*www.sanzoilo.com* *45 rooms, 5 suites* *In-hotel: restaurant, bar* 💳*AE, DC, MC, V.*

SAHAGÚN

67 *44 km (27 mi) west of Carrió de los Condes.*

Near rolling fields of wheat, Sahagún was allegedly founded by Charlemagne after he conquered the Moors by the nearby River Cea; in fact the town is a center of Mudéjar craftsmanship, as evidenced in the brick bell towers and trilobed apses of the 12th-century churches of San Tirso and San Lorenzo. Nuns in the Monasterio de Santa Cruz usually allow visitors to see the treasures, which include a beautifully carved medieval silver casket.

WHERE TO EAT

$$–$$$ ✕**Luis.** With a long bar overlooking the narrow Plaza Mayor, this popular, family-run restaurant cooks local produce with flair. At €10, the *puerros de Sahagún rellenos de mariscos* (Sahagún leeks stuffed with shellfish) are highly recommended, and there's a good selection of salads. Breakfast, lunch, and dinner are served daily. ✉*Pl. Mayor 9* ☎*987781085* 💳*AE, MC, V.*

LEÓN

333 km (207 mi) northwest of Madrid, 216 km (134 mi) west of Burgos.

The ancient capital of the group of Castile–León sits on the banks of the Bernesga River in the high plains of Old Castile. Historians say that the name of the city, which was founded as a permanent camp for the Roman legions in AD 70, has nothing to do with the proud lion that has been its emblem for centuries but is instead a corruption of the Roman word *legio* (legion). The capital of Christian Spain was moved to León from Oviedo in 914 as the Reconquest spread southward, launching the city's richest era. Walls went up around the old Roman town, and you can still see parts of the 6-foot-thick ramparts in the middle of the modern city. Today, León is a wealthy provincial capital and prestigious university town. The wide avenues of western León are lined with boutiques, and the twisting alleys of the half-timbered old town hide the bars, bookstores, and *chocolaterías* most popular with students. As you're wandering the old town, look down occasionally and you just might notice small brass scallop shells set into the street. The scallop is the symbol of St. James; the shells were installed by the town government to mark the path for modern-day pilgrims.

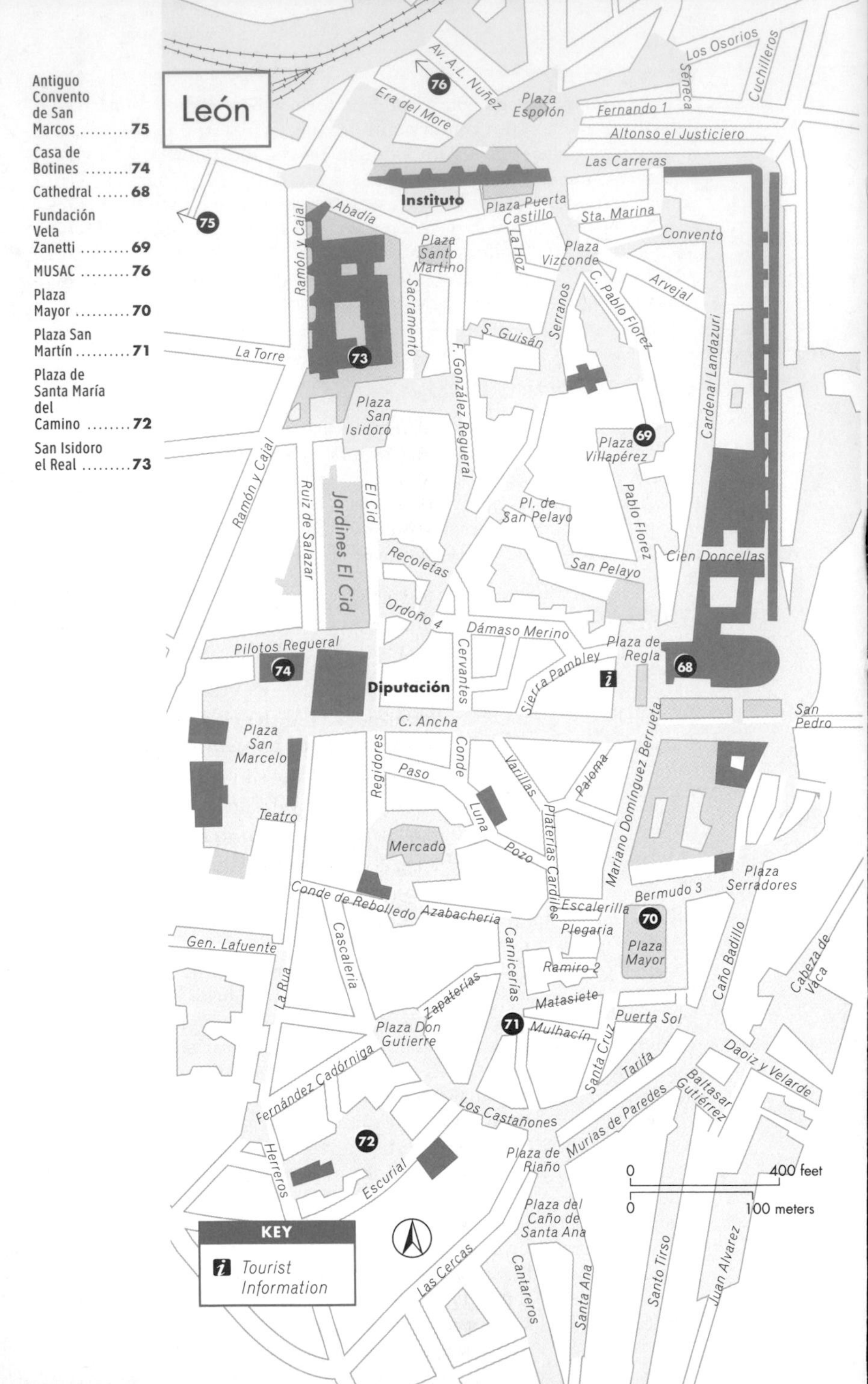
León
Antiguo Convento de San Marcos 75
Casa de Botines 74
Cathedral 68
Fundación Vela Zanetti 69
MUSAC 76
Plaza Mayor 70
Plaza San Martín 71
Plaza de Santa María del Camino 72
San Isidoro el Real 73
Av. A.L. Nuñez
Era del More
Plaza Espolón
Los Osorios
Séneca
Cuchilleros
Fernando 1
Alfonso el Justiciero
Las Carreras
Instituto
Plaza Puerta Castillo
Sta. Marina
Convento
Abadía
Ramón y Cajal
Plaza Santo Martino
La Hoz
Plaza Vizconde
C. Pablo Florez
Arvejal
Sacramento
S. Guisán
Serranos
La Torre
F. González Regueral
Cardenal Landazuri
Plaza San Isidoro
Plaza Villapérez
Ruiz de Salazar
Jardines El Cid
El Cid
Pl. de San Pelayo
Pablo Florez
Recoletas
San Pelayo
Cien Doncellas
Ordoño 4
Dámaso Merino
Pilotos Regueral
Cervantes
Plaza de Regla
Sierra Pambley
Diputación
C. Ancha
San Pedro
Plaza San Marcelo
Regidores
Conde
Paso
Varillas
Paloma
Mariano Domínguez Berrueta
Luna
Teatro
Mercado
Pozo
Platerías
Cardiles
Plaza Serradores
Conde de Rebolledo
Azabachería
Escalerilla
Bermudo 3
Gen. Lafuente
Cascalería
Carnicerías
Plegaria
Plaza Mayor
Caño Badillo
Cabeza de Vaca
Ramiro 2
La Rua
Zapaterías
Matasiete
Puerta Sol
Plaza Don Gutierre
Mulhacín
Santa Cruz
Tarifa
Daoiz y Velarde
Fernández Cadórniga
Baltasar Gutiérrez
Los Castañones
Murias de Paredes
Herreros
Escurial
Plaza de Riaño
0
400 feet
0
100 meters
Plaza del Caño de Santa Ana
KEY
Tourist Information
Las Cercas
Cantareros
Santa Ana
Santo Tirso
Juan Alvarez

WHAT TO SEE

68 ★ León is proudest of its soaring Gothic **cathedral,** on the Plaza de Regla. Its soaring upper reaches are built with more windows than stone. Flanked by two aggressively square towers, the facade has three arched, weatherworn doorways, the middle one adorned with slender statues of the apostles. Begun in 1205, the cathedral has 125 long, slender stained-glass windows; dozens of decorative small ones; and three giant, spectacular rose windows. On sunny days, the glass casts bejeweled shafts of light on the beautifully spare, pale-sandstone interior; the windows themselves depict abstract floral patterns as well as various biblical and medieval scenes. A glass door to the choir gives an unobstructed view of nave windows and the painted altarpiece, framed with gold leaf. The cathedral also contains the sculpted tomb of King Ordoño II, who moved the capital of Christian Spain to León. The **museum** has giant medieval hymnals, textiles, sculptures, wood carvings, and paintings. Look for the carved wood Mudéjar archive, with a letter of the alphabet above each door: it's one of the world's oldest file cabinets. ✉*Pl. de Regla* ☎*987/875770* 🌐*www.catedraldeleon.org* 🎟*Cathedral free (€1.70 with guide), museum €3.50, cloister €1* 🕒*Cathedral Oct.–June, Mon.–Sat. 8:30–1:30 and 4–7, Sun. 8:30–2:30 and 5–7; July–Sept., Mon.–Sat. 8:30–1:30 and 4–8, Sun. 8:30–2:30 and 5–8. Museum Oct.–May, weekdays 9:30–1:30 and 4–7, Sat. 9:30–1:30; June–Sept., weekdays 9:30–2 and 4–7:30, Sat. 9:30–2 and 4–7.*

69 Hidden away just north of the cathedral is the **Fundación Vela Zanetti,** a contemporary, wood-and-windows art museum inside a 15th-century mansion. Zanetti was a 20th-century Castilian artist with a fondness for warm tones and a special interest in human rights. Some of his portraits recall El Greco. Art-lovers will find this widely unknown museum a pleasant surprise. ✉*C. Pablo Flórez s/n* ☎*987/244121* 🎟*Free* 🕒*Tues.–Fri. 10–1:30 and 5–8, weekends 5–8.*

70 The **Plaza Mayor,** in the heart of the old town, is surrounded by simple half-timber houses. On Wednesday and Saturday, the arcaded plaza bustles with farmers selling produce and cheeses. Many farmers still wear wooden shoes called *madreñas,* which are raised on three heels, two in front and one in back. They were designed to walk on mud in this usually wet part of Spain.

71 Most of León's tapas bars are in the 12th-century **Plaza San Martín.** This area is called the Barrio Húmedo, or Wet Neighborhood, for the large amount of wine spilled here late at night.

72 Southwest of the Plaza San Martín is the **Plaza de Santa María del Camino,** which, as the plaque here points out, used to be called Plaza del Grano (Grain Square) and hosted the local corn and bread market. Also here is the church of **Santa María del Camino,** where pilgrims stop on their way west to Santiago de Compostela. The strange allegorical fountain in the middle depicts two chubby angels clutching a pillar, symbolizing León's two rivers and the capital.

73 ★ The sandstone basilica of **San Isidoro el Real,** on Calle Cid, was built into the side of the city wall in 1063 and rebuilt in the 12th century.

> **KID'S PLAY**
>
> León has a long **park** on the banks of the Bernesga River, with playground equipment every 100 feet or so.

The **Panteón de los Reyes** (Royal Pantheon), adjoining the basilica, has been called the Sistine Chapel of Romanesque art for the vibrant 12th-century frescoes on its pillars and ceiling. The pantheon was the first building in Spain to be decorated with scenes from the New Testament. Look for the agricultural calendar painted on one archway, showing which farming task should be performed each month. Twenty-three kings and queens were once buried here, but their tombs were destroyed by French troops during the Napoleonic Wars. Treasures in the adjacent **Museo de San Isidoro** include a jewel-encrusted agate chalice, a richly illustrated handwritten Bible, and many polychrome wood statues of the Virgin Mary. ✉*Pl. de San Isidoro 4* ☎*987/876161* *Basilica free, Royal Pantheon and museum €3.50* ⏲*July and Aug., Mon.–Sat. 9–8, Sun. 9–2; Sept.–June, Mon.–Sat. 9–1:30 and 4–7, Sun. 10–2.*

74 Just south of the old town is the **Casa de Botines,** a multigabled, turreted, granite behemoth designed in the late 1800s by that controversial Catalan Antoni Gaudí. It now houses a bank. ✉*Off Ruiz de Salazar.*

75 Fronted by a large, airy pedestrian plaza, the sumptuous **Antiguo Convento de San Marcos** is now a luxury hotel, the Parador Hostal San Marcos. Originally a home for knights of the Order of St. James, who patrolled the Camino de Santiago, and a pit stop for weary pilgrims, the monastery you see today was begun in 1513 by the head of the order, King Ferdinand, who thought that knights deserved something better. Finished at the height of the Renaissance, the plateresque facade is a majestic swath of small sculptures (many depicting knights and lords) and careful ornaments. Inside are an elegant staircase and a cloister full of medieval statues. Have a drink in the bar—its tiny windows are the original defensive slits. The building also houses León's **Museo Arqueológico,** famous for its 11th-century ivory Carrizo crucifix. ✉*Pl. de San Marcos s/n* ☎*987/245061* *Museum, €2.50* ⏲*Museum, Mon. 10–2, Tues.–Sat. 10–2 and 5–8:30.*

76 **MUSAC (Museo de Arte Contempar[ac]aneo de Castilla y Léon)** *(Museum of Modern Art of Castillo y León)* reflects the modern León while paying homage to its history with its own cluster of buildings whose exteriors are cascaded with rectangular stained glass, like its cathedral. This "Museum of the Present" brings art to the people by offering varied workshops and activities for children amid exhibiting modern creations from all over the globe. Films and concerts are also put on throughout the year. ✉*Av. de Los Reyes Leoneses 24* ☎*987/090000* 🌐*www.musac.org.es* *Free* ⏲*Tues.–Sun. 10–3 and 4–9.*

WHERE TO STAY & EAT

$$–$$$$ ✕**Nuevo Racimo de Oro.** Upstairs in a ramshackle 12th-century tavern in the heart of the old town, this rustic restaurant, once a hostel and hospital for weary pilgrims, now specializes in roast lamb cooked in

a wood-fire clay oven. The spicy *sopa de ajo leonese* (garlic soup) is a classic, and *solomillo Racimo al hojaldre* (veal in puff pastry) makes a tasty entrée. Worth trying is *Tarta de San Marcos,* a lemon cake served with whipped cream. ✉*Pl. San Martín 8* ☎*987/214767 or 987/260146* 🌐*www.racimodeoro.com* ▭*AE, DC, MC, V* ⏲*Closed Sun. June–Sept. No dinner Tues. Closed Wed. Oct.–May.*

$–$$$ ✕**Casa Pozo.** This longtime favorite is across from City Hall on the historic Plaza de San Marcelo. Past the small bar, the bright dining rooms are furnished with heavy Castilian furniture. Owner Gabriel del Pozo Alvarez—called Pin—supervises the busy kitchen while his son, also called Pin, is maître d'. Specialties include roast lamb, river crabs with clams, cod with pimiento and olive oil, and deep-fried hake. ✉*Pl. de San Marcelo 15* ☎*987/223039* ▭*AE, DC, MC, V* ⏲*No dinner Sun.*

3

$$$ ✕🏨 **Parador de León.** The magnificent Parador Hotel San Marcos occupies a restored 16th-century monastery built by King Ferdinand to shelter pilgrims walking the Camino de Santiago; the bridge beside it has helped pilgrims cross the Río Bernesga for centuries. The huge, ornamental, plateresque facade also fronts a church and museum of archaeology (which is in the Antiguo Monasterio de San Marcos). Hallways and guest rooms have antiques, high-quality reproductions, and some nice contemporary art. One wing is modern; if you want a more medieval look, ask for a room in the old section. The elegant dining room ($$–$$$$) offers 10 hot and cold regional appetizers for €13, and main dishes from €14 to €32. ✉*Pl. de San Marcos 7, 24001* ☎*987/237300* 📠*987/233458* 🌐*www.parador.es* 🛏*230 rooms* 👍*In-hotel: 2 restaurants, bar, pool, parking (fee)* ▭*AE, DC, MC, V.*

Fodor's Choice ★

$$ 🏨 **Hotel Paris.** Rooms here are comfortable, and the classic basement *mesón* (tavern) snuggles up to the stone of a Roman wall. The hotel is on the modern thoroughfare heading east from Plaza Santo Domingo, halfway between the cathedral and the new town. ✉*Calle Ancha 18, 24003* ☎*987/238600* 📠*987/271572* 🌐*www.hotelparisleon.com* 🛏*55 rooms* 👍*In-hotel: restaurant, bar* ▭*AE, DC, MC, V.*

NIGHTLIFE

Most of León's liveliest hangouts are clustered in Plaza Mayor and Plaza San Martín, with the former drawing couples and families and the latter a university crowd. The streets are packed with tapas bars. In the Plaza Mayor, you might want to start your crawl at **Universal, Mesón de Don Quijote, Casa Benito,** or **Bar La Plaza Mayor.** In the Plaza San Martín, the **Latino Bar at No. 10** serves a glass of house wine and your choice of one of four generous tapas. **Cozy Prada a Tope** serves the local Bierzo wine out of a big barrel.

SHOPPING

Tasty regional treats include roasted red peppers, potent brandy-soaked cherries, and candied chestnuts. You can buy these in food shops all over the city. The shop **Cuesta Castañón** (✉*Calle Castañones 2* ☎*987/260750*), near Plaza San Martín, has a great selection of wines, cured meats, cookies, preserves, and bottled delicacies, not to mention books on related topics. Friendly owner José María González lets you sample the stock. At **Hojaldres Alonso** (✉*Calle Ancha 7* ☎), near the cathedral, you can browse through the shelves of local goodies (candied nuts, preserves), all produced at their factory in nearby Astorga, and then head to the café in the back. The focus here is on the baked goods, particularly the *hojaldres* (puff pastries) and *torrijas*, a Castilian version of French toast. The café is a favorite among locals who come for their early evening *merienda* (usually between 6 and 8), Spain's answer to the afternoon tea. You can shop while having tapas at **Prada a Tope** (✉*Pl. San Martín 1* ☎*987/257 221*), where they're packaged by the house. For fine, funky gifts, visit **Tricosis** (✉*C. Mulhacín 3* ☎*987/202953*), a gallery opened by art students from the universities of León and Gijón. Colorful papier-mâché and experimental media form outstanding lamps, candleholders, vases, and frames.

ASTORGA

77 *46 km (29 mi) southwest of León.*

Astorga, where the pilgrimage roads from France and Portugal merge, once had 22 hospitals to lodge and care for ailing travelers. The only one left today is next to the cathedral. The **cathedral** itself is a huge 15th-century building with four statues of St. James.

WHAT TO SEE

The **Museo de la Catedral** displays 10th- and 12th-century chests, religious silverware, and paintings and sculptures by various Astorgans. ✉*Pl. de la Catedral* ☎*987/615429* €2.50 *Oct.–Dec. and Feb., daily 11–2 and 3:30–6:30; Mar.–Sept., daily 10–2 and 4–8.*

Fodor's Choice ★ Just opposite Astorga's cathedral is the fairy-tale, neo-Gothic **Palacio Episcopal** *(Archbishop's Palace)*, designed for a Catalan cleric by Antoni Gaudí in 1889. Visiting the palace the last week of August, during Astorga's Fiesta de Santa María, is a treat for the senses; fireworks explode in the sky, casting rainbows of light over Gaudí's ornate, mystical towers. No expense was spared in creating this building, site of the **Museo del Camino** (Museum of the Way). The collection has folk items, such as the standard pilgrim costume—heavy black cloak, staff hung with gourds, and wide-brimmed hat bedecked with scallop shells—as well as contemporary Spanish art. ✉*Adjacent to cathedral, on Pl. de la Catedral* ☎*987/616882* €2.50 *Mar. 20–Sept. 20, Tues.–Sat. 10–2 and 4–8, Sun. 10–2 (and 4–8 in Aug.); Sept. 21–Mar. 19, Tues.–Sat. 11–2 and 4–6, Sun. 11–2.*

WHERE TO STAY & EAT

$–$$$ ✕**Restaurante Serrano.** Popular with locals, and occasionally serving the likes of game, wild mushrooms, and pork during special gastronomic weeks, this mesón serves both contemporary cuisine and traditional roasts of baby lamb. ✉*Calle Portería 2* ☎*987/617866* *AE, MC, V* *Closed last 2 wks in June. No dinner Mon.*

$–$$ ✕**La Peseta.** Family-run since 1871, the restaurant ($$–$$$) here persists in good home cooking, especially the four-dish marathon *cocido maragato*, a kind of country stew. The 18-room inn upstairs offers decent and economical rooms. ✉*Pl. de San Bartolomé 3* ☎*987/617275*

☎987/615300 🛏18 rooms 💳AE, DC, MC, V ⏲Closed last 2 wks in Oct. and Jan. No dinner Sun. or Tues.

CASTILLO DE LOS POLVAZARES

78 *51 km (32 mi) west of León, 5 km (3 mi) northwest of Astorga.*

A 15-minute drive from Astorga is Castillo de los Polvazares, a 17th-century village built on the site of a fortified Roman settlement. The city's 30-odd residents live in stone houses emblazoned with crests above their green doorways. Walk down the stone streets and look for storks' nests on top of the village church. Castillo de los Polvazares is in León's Maragatería region, whose people are believed to be a mixture of the ancient Celts and Phoenicians. These traders resisted the Roman invasion of the Iberian Peninsula and reached the height of their prowess as muleteers in the 18th and 19th centuries (hence the wide doorways around town), transporting gold from the Americas to the royal court in Madrid.

PONFERRADA

79 *64 km (40 mi) west of Astorga on NVI.*

In a hilly region with fertile valleys, Ponferrada is a mining and industrial center that gets its name from an iron toll bridge built by a local bishop in the 1100s.

The tall, slim turrets of the 13th-century **Castillo de los Templarios** *(Templars' Castle)* on the western edge of town has sweeping views of the countryside and may once have been used by the Knights of the Order of St. James to police the route. *✉Calle Florez Osorio 4 ☎987/414141 🎫€2.50 ⏲Apr. and May, Tues.–Sat. 10–2 and 4:30–8, Sun. 10–2; June–mid-Sept., Tues.–Sun. 10:30–2 and 5–9; mid-Sept.–Mar., Tues.–Sat. 10:30–2 and 4–7, Sun. 11–2.*

OFF THE BEATEN PATH

Las Medulas. Leave Ponferrada heading west on the A6 (toward A Coruña), and take the Las Médulas–Puente de Domingo exit to the N536 toward Carucedo. Turning right here, you can either follow the signs to a viewpoint at Orellán or go to the village of Las Medulas. From the latter, you can explore the Roman gold mines 21 km (13 mi) west of Ponferrada, where jagged red cliffs rise out of oak and chestnut woods, and great pits lead to deep tunnels, canals, and caves. Bring a flashlight. *✉8 mi west of Ponferrad 🌐www.fundacionlasmedulas.com.*

VILLAFRANCA DEL BIERZO

80 *135 km (84 mi) west of León, 20 km (12 mi) west of Ponferrada.*

After crossing León's grape-growing region, where the complex and full-bodied Bierzo wines are produced, you'll arrive in this medieval village, dominated by a massive and still-inhabited feudal fortress. Villafranca was a destination in itself for some of Santiago's pilgrims: visit the Romanesque church of Santiago to see the Puerta del Perdón (Door of Pardon), a sort of spiritual consolation prize for exhausted worshippers who couldn't make it over the mountains. Stroll the streets and seek out the onetime home of the infamous Grand Inquisitor Torquemada. On the way out, you can buy wine at any of three local bodegas.

WHERE TO STAY & EAT

$$–$$$ **Parador de Villafranca del Bierzo.** This modern, two-story hotel overlooks the Bierzo valley. Rooms have heavy wood furniture, shuttered windows, and large baths. At the parador's restaurant ($$$$) dine on fresh Bierzo trout, *surtido de verduras naturales* (mixed fresh vegetables), or *tournedo con higos agridulces* (a plump, juicy steak wrapped in bacon and served with marinated figs and wild mushrooms). Try the local Bierzo wine, made primarily from the Mencia grape. ✉ *Av. de Calvo Sotelo 28, 24500* ☎ *987/540175* 🖷 *987/540010* 🌐 *www.parador.es* *38 rooms* *In-hotel: restaurant, bar* ▭ *AE, DC, MC, V.*

CASTILE ESSENTIALS

To research prices, get advice from other travelers, and book travel arrangements, visit www.fodors.com.

TRANSPORTATION

For more on travel to and in Castile, see the Getting There & Around section of the Castile Planner at the beginning of the chapter.

BY AIR

The only international airport in Castile is Madrid's Barajas; however, Salamanca, León, and Valladolid have domestic airports.

Contacts **Aeropuertos Españoles y Navegación Aérea (AENA)** (☎ *902/404704* 🌐 *www.aena.es*)—this is a central operations center providing information about flights and airports throughout Spain. Operators can speak English.

Aeropuerto de Barajas (✉ *Madrid* ☎ *902/353570*). **Aeropuerto de León** (✉ *León* ☎ *987/877700*). **Aeropuerto de Matacán** (✉ *Salamanca* ☎ *923/329600*). **Aeropuerto de Valladolid** (✉ *Valladolid* ☎ *983/415500*).

BY BUS

Bus connections between Madrid and Castile are excellent. There are several stations and stops in Madrid; buses to **Toledo** (1 hour) leave every half hour from the Estación del Sur, and buses to **Segovia** (1½ hours) leave every hour from La Sepulvedana's headquarters, which are near Príncipe Pío. Larrea sends buses to **Ávila** from the Méndez Alvaro Metro stop. Alsa travels to **León** (4½ hours) and **Valladolid** (2¼ hours), and Auto Res serves **Cuenca** (2¾ hours) and **Salamanca** (3 hours). Buses to **Soria** (3 hours), **El Burgo de Osma** (2½ hours), and **Burgos** (3½ hours) are run by Continental Auto.

From Burgos, buses head north to the Basque Country; from León, you can press on to Asturias. Services between towns are not as frequent as those to and from Madrid, so you may find it quicker to return to Madrid and make your way from there. Reservations are rarely necessary.

Bus Companies **Alsa** (☎ *902/422242* 🌐 *www.alsa.es*). **Auto Res** (✉ *Pl. Conde de Casal 6, Madrid* ☎ *902/020999* 🌐 *www.auto-res.net*). **Continental Auto** (✉ *Intercambiador Autobuses, Av. de América, Madrid* ☎ *91/7456300* 🌐 *www.continental-auto.es*). **La Sepulvedana/Larrea** (✉ *Paseo de la Florida 11, Madrid* ☎ *902/222282* 🌐 *www.lasepulvedana.es*).

Bus Stations **Madrid (Estación del Sur)** (✉ *Calle Méndez Alvaro s/n* ☎ *91/468–4200* 🌐 *www.estaciondeautobuses.com*). **Burgos** (✉ *C. Miranda 3* ☎ *947/265565*). **León** (✉ *C. Astorga s/n* ☎ *987/211000*).

BY CAR

Major divided highways—the A1 through A6—radiate out from Madrid, making Spain's farthest corners no more than five- to six-hour drives. The capital's outlying towns are only minutes away. If possible, avoid returning to Madrid on major highways at the end of a weekend or a holiday. The beginning and end of August are notorious for traffic jams, as is Easter week, which starts on Palm Sunday and ends on Easter Sunday. Side roads vary in quality but provide one of the great pleasures of driving around the Castilian countryside—surprise encounters with architectural monuments and wild and spectacular vistas.

Major National Agencies **Avis** (☎ *902/135531* 🌐 *www.avis.com*). **Europcar** (☎ *902/105030* 🌐 *www.europcar.es*). **Hertz** (☎ *902/402405* 🌐 *www.hertz.es*). **National/Atesa** (☎ *902/100101* 🌐 *www.atesa.com*). **Pepe Car** (☎ *902/36 05 35* 🌐 *www.pepecar.com*).

BY TAXI

All cities and most towns have taxi services, sometimes several. They must show a license number, and at the rear of the vehicle are the letters "SP" (*Servicio Público*). They usually have a sign on the roof reading TAXI and a sign on the windshield that reads either LIBRE in green or OCUPADO in red. If a green light on the roof is lighted, this means the car is for hire (libre). Taxis operate on meters within designated urban centers, and fees are negotiable for farther distances. The meter starts at a set figure, about €1.50, but should not be turned on until you start your journey. Drivers may charge more for extra luggage, night and holiday services, and going to and coming from airports or train stations. Give a tip based on service, with a minimum of €0.50.

BY TRAIN

Though it's often faster to travel by bus, all the main towns in Castile–León and Castile–La Mancha are accessible by train from Madrid. Several make feasible day trips: there are commuter trains from Madrid to Segovia (2 hours), Alcalá de Henares (45 minutes), Guadalajara (1 hour), and Toledo (1½ hours). Trains to Toledo depart from Madrid's Atocha station; trains to Salamanca, Burgos, and León depart from Chamartín; and both stations serve Ávila, Segovia, El Escorial, and Sigüenza, though Chamartín may have more frequent service. The one important town that's accessible only by train (and not bus) is

Sigüenza. Trains from Segovia go only to Madrid, but you can change at Villalba for Ávila and Salamanca.

Train Information RENFE (☎ *902/240202* 🌐 *www.renfe.es*).

CONTACTS & RESOURCES

EMERGENCIES

Emergency Services Fire, Police, or Ambulance (☎ *112*). **Información Toxicológica** (Poisoning ☎ *915/620420*). **Policía Local** (☎ *092*). **Policía Nacional** (☎ *091*).

INTERNET

All of the major cities in Castile–La Mancha have at least one internet café, or in cities like Toledo or Cuenca, many more. Wi-Fi is just starting to gain popularity but it certainly has a long way to go. You may not find Internet access in smaller spots like El Burgos de Osma or Numancia—in keeping with their medieval allure, they haven't yet connected themselves to the Web. They've lived for centuries without it and aren't in any rush to do so. The same applies to small villages anywhere in La Mancha.

VISITOR INFORMATION

Regional Tourist Offices Madrid (✉ *Duque de Medinaceli 2* ☎ *91/429–4951*). **Salamanca** (✉ *Casa de las Conchas, Rúa Mayor s/n* ☎ *923/268571*). **Toledo** (✉ *Puerta de Bisagra s/n* ☎ *925/220843*).

Local Tourist Offices Alcalá de Henares (✉ *Callejón de Santa María 1* ☎ *91/889–2694*). **Almagro** (✉ *Calle Bernardas 2* ☎ *926/860717*). **Aranjuez** (✉ *Pl. San Antonio 9* ☎ *91/891–0427*). **Astorga** (✉ *Calle Glorieta Eduardo de Castro 5* ☎ *987/618222*). **Ávila** (✉ *Pl. de Pedro Dávila 4* ☎ *920/211387*). **Burgos** (✉ *Pl. Alonso Martínez 7* ☎ *947/203125*). **Ciudad Real** (✉ *Av. Alarcos 31* ☎ ***926/216486***). **Ciudad Rodrigo** (✉ *Pl. Mayor 1* ☎ *926/216486*). **Consuegra** (✉ *Calle Molino de Viento/Bolero Windmill* ☎ *925/475731*). **Cuenca** (✉ *Pl. Mayor 1* ☎ *969/241050*). **Guadalajara** (✉ *Pl. de los Caídos 6* ☎ *949/211626*). **León** (✉ *Pl. de Regla 3* ☎ *987/237802*). **Ponferrada** (✉ *Calle Gil y Carrasco 4, next to castle* ☎ *987/424236*). **Salamanca** (✉ *Pl. Mayor 14* ☎ *923/218342*). **Segovia** (✉ Pl. Mayor 10 ☎ *921/460334*). **Sigüenza** (✉ *Paseo de la Alameda s/n* ☎ *949/347007*). **Soria** (✉ *Pl. Ramón y Cajal s/n* ☎ *975/212052*). **Toledo** (✉ *Puerta de Bisagra s/n* ☎ *925/220843*). **Valladolid** (✉ *Calle Acera de Recoletos s/n* ☎ *983/219310*). **Zamora** (✉ *C. Santa Clara 20* ☎ *980/531845*).

Galicia & Asturias

4

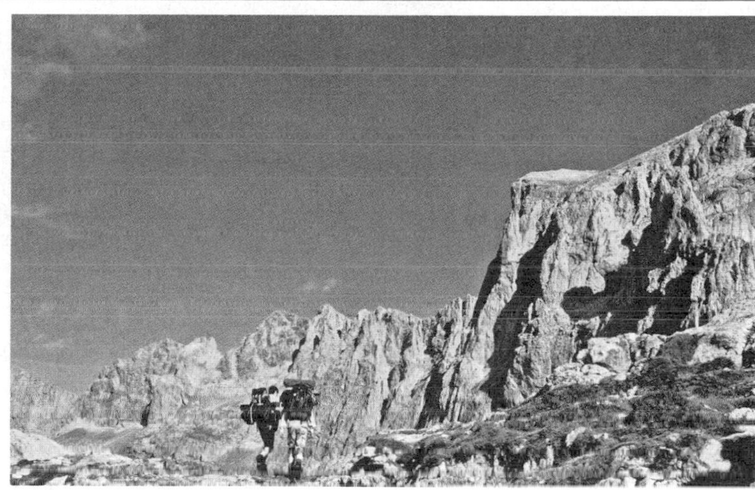

Picos de Europa, Asturias

WORD OF MOUTH

"I had read wonderful reviews of the Picos de Europa and was prepared to be underwhelmed. I wasn't. This area is divine and almost deserted, so see it before the tourists hordes descend upon it."

—OReilly

www.fodors.com/forums

WELCOME TO GALICIA & ASTURIAS

Òista del Arenal statue, by Francisco Leiro in Vigo.

TOP REASONS TO GO

★ **Gourmet Heaven:** Santiago is said to contain more restaurants and bars per square mile than any other city in Spain. Beautiful on the eye too.

★ **Sleeping Gracefully:** El Parador de Baiona is arguably Spain's most elegant parador.

★ **Rugged Turns:** Spend days in the spectacular Picos de Europa range getting lost in forgotten mountain villages.

★ **Getting on the Grapevine:** The Ribeira region, in the area between Vigo and Oursense, yields Spain's—if not Europe's—finest white wines.

★ **Waterfront Activity:** Watch the oyster hawkers at work while dining on a fresh catch on Vigo's Rúa Pescadería.

1 Picos de Europa. One of Spain's best-kept secrets, the "Peaks of Europe" lie across Asturias, Cantabria, and León, about 20 km (12.4 mi) inland from the coast. In addition to 2,700-meter (8,910-feet) peaks, the area has deep caves, excellent mountain refuges, and much wildlife. It's also known for its fine cheeses.

2 The A Coruña Coastline. Galicia has more coastline than any other region in Spain, and more unspoiled and untouristed beaches than anywhere else in the country, and perhaps even in Europe. You can opt for vast expands of sand facing the Atlantic ocean or tiny, tucked-away coves. Note that the water is colder than the Mediterranean and the weather more unreliable.

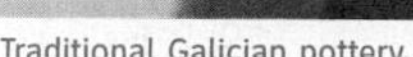

Traditional Galician pottery.

GETTING ORIENTED

In Spain's northwest reaches lie the bewitching provinces of Galicia and Asturias. These rugged Atlantic regions hide a corner of Spain so remote it was called *finis terrae* (end of the earth). It is Europe's westernmost point and, until 1492, as far as anyone knew, the world's. Galicia is famous for Santiago de Compostela, to which Christian pilgrims travel many miles to pay homage to St. James. In Asturias are verdant hills, sandy beaches, and the massive Picos de Europa.

3 The Senda Costera. Translated in English as the Coastal Way, this partly paved nature route between Pendueles and Llanes takes in some of Asturias's most spectacular coastal scenery, such as the noisy *bufones* (large water spouts created naturally by the erosion of the sea) and the Playa de Ballota.

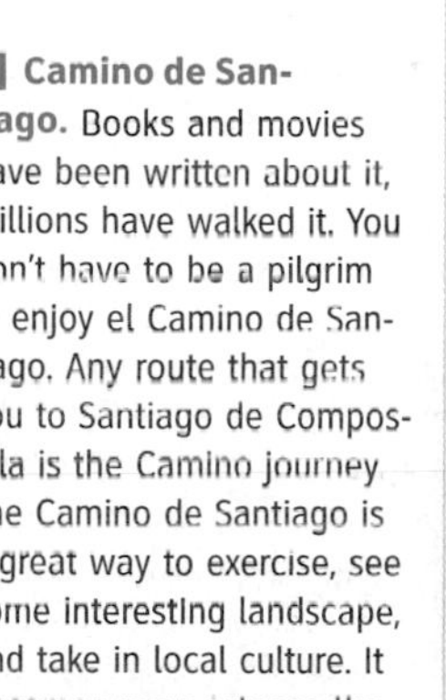

4 Camino de Santiago. Books and movies have been written about it, millions have walked it. You don't have to be a pilgrim to enjoy el Camino de Santiago. Any route that gets you to Santiago de Compostela is the Camino journey. The Camino de Santiago is a great way to exercise, see some interesting landscape, and take in local culture. It becomes more intense the closer you get to magnificent Santiago.

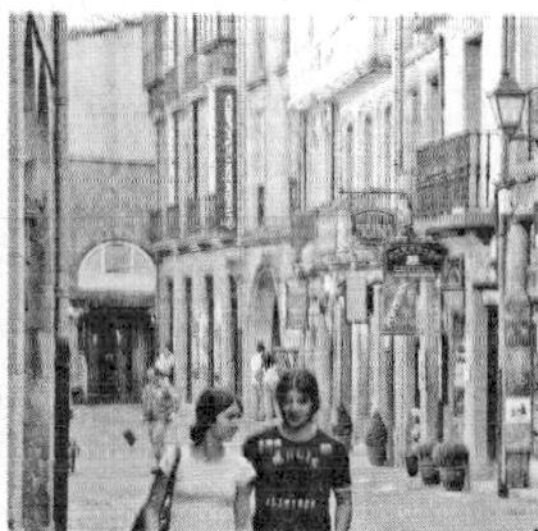

The lively town of Santiago de Compostela.

GALICIA & ASTURIAS PLANNER

When to Go

Galicia can get very hot (over 30°C/90°F) in the summer months between June and September. Summer is the best time for swimming and water sports, and Celtic music festivals—the **Ortigueira Festival** (www.festivaldeortigueira.com) in early July attracts leading Celtic musicians worldwide.

Due to its mountainous villages, Asturias is considerably cooler than Galicia, though Galicia can be rainy to the point of saturation—not for nothing is this region called Green Spain. Avoid traveling in the area in winter: the rain, wind, and freezing temperatures make driving an arduous experience.

Spring and fall may be the ideal time to explore, as the weather is reasonable and crowds are few.

Getting There & Around

The revolution in cheap airlines throughout Europe has had a twin effect of making some of the larger cities like Santiago and Oviedo accessible from other major cities in Europe as well as increasing domestic services between major towns. Galicia's main international airport is in Labacolla, 12 km (7 mi) east of Santiago de Compostela. Iberia flies daily from here to London, Paris, Zurich, Geneva, and Frankfurt, and the city is also accessible from various other cities in Europe on easyJet. Vueling Airlines connect Oviedo to a number of domestic and European cities. Iberia, Spanair, Air Europa, and Vueling all provide domestic connections with these cities from most major Spanish cities. The region's other domestic airports are in A Coruña, Vigo, and near San Estéban de Pravia, 47 km (29 mi) north of Oviedo, Asturias. Airport shuttles usually take the form of ALSA buses from the city bus station. Occasionally, Iberia runs a private shuttle from its office out to the airport; inquire when you book your ticket.

A car is the recommended means for travel within the region. The four-lane A6 expressway links the area with central Spain; it takes about five hours (650 km [403 mi]) to go from Madrid to Santiago. The expressway north from León to Oviedo and Gijón is the fastest way to cross the Cantabrian mountains. The AP9 north–south Galician ("Atlantic") expressway links A Coruña, Santiago, Pontevedra, and Vigo, and the A8 in Asturias links Santander to Ribadeo. Local roads along the coast or through the hills are more scenic but two or three times as slow.

Bus and train travel to smaller towns is in many instances irregular, sometimes unreliable or simply nonexistent. RENFE runs several trains a day from Madrid to Oviedo (7 hours) and Gijón (8 hours), and a separate line serves Santiago (11 hours). Daytime first- and second-class cars are available. RENFE has ticket windows at the stations in Santiago, A Coruña, Oviedo, and Gijón. Local RENFE trains connect the region's major cities with most of the surrounding small towns, but be prepared for dozens of stops. ALSA runs daily buses from Madrid to Galicia and Asturias.

See Galicia & Asturias Essentials at the end of the chapter for transportation contact information.

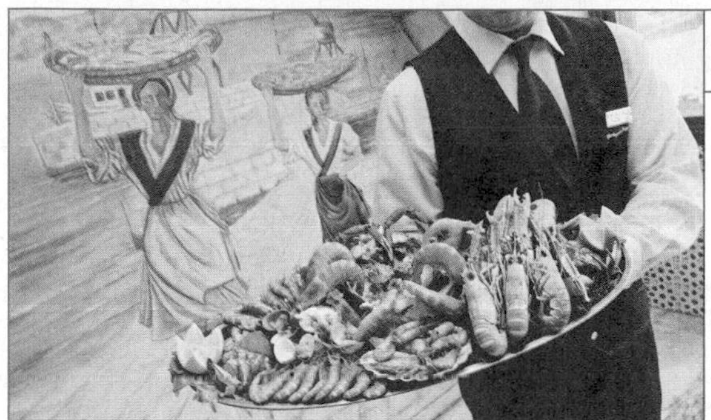

Discounts & Deals

In Galicia, visitors can get 20% off rural accommodations on certain days, and senior citizens and children get discounted or free tickets to museums and sights through **Turgalicia** (✉ *Ctra. Santiago–Noia Km 3, Santiago de Compostela* ☎ *981/542527* or *981/542511* 🌐 *www.turgalicia.es*).

Compostela 48 Horas (✉ *Rúa do Vilar 63, Santiago de Compostela* ☎ *981/555129* 🌐 *www.santiagoturismo.com*) is a €15 visitor's card providing discounts or free entry to key Santiago sites.

Galician Gastronomy

Ask anybody who's spent time in Galicia and they'll tell you that one of the highlights is the gastronomy. To get to know the cuisine here is akin to understanding the Galicians, so a visit to this region will surely be enhanced with good chunks of time spent in tapas bars and restaurants—and the less *salubrious* the better. Seafood in particular is a delight. It is cooked simply, with lots of respect, and served generously. The unstoppable *pulpo a Gallego* (tender octopus) and the second-to-none scallops are the best known. In Asturias, meat and dairy products are the best in Spain.

WHAT IT COSTS In Euros

	$$$$	$$$	$$	$	¢
Restaurants	over €20	€15–€20	€10–€15	€6–€10	under €6
Hotels	over €180	€100–€180	€60–€100	€40–€60	under €40

Prices are per person for a main course at dinner. Prices are for two people in a standard double room in high season, excluding tax.

Planning Your Time

Santiago de Compostela is a good option for flying into and can be covered easily in a few days. From there you may want to drive down the C550 to Cambados, stopping on the way at fishing villages along the Ría de Arousa. If you stick with the coast road to Pontevedra, you can spend time there exploring the medieval streets and tapas bars, then drive down to Vigo for a lunch of oysters on Rúa Pescadería. Continue south and arrive before dark at the Baiona parador. The more adventurous will want to explore the Camino villages of Samos, Sarria, Portomarín, Vilar de Donas, and Leboreiro—they embody all that is spiritual about Galicia.

Alternatively, travel to A Coruña, and from there head north to some of Spain's loveliest beaches and Viveiro. From here cross into Asturias and spend time in Luarca or Gijón. Another attractive option is getting lost in a small village in the Picos de Europa, spending some days there to walk, rest, and eat the local produce.

4

Updated by Michael Kessler
El Camino feature by Ben Curtis

SPAIN'S MOST ATLANTIC REGION IS en route to nowhere, an end in itself. Stretching northwest from the lonesome Castilian plains to the rocky seacoast, Asturias and Galicia incorporate lush hills and vineyards, gorgeous *rías* (estuaries), and the country's wildest mountains, the Picos de Europa. Northwestern Spain is a series of rainy landscapes, stretching from your feet to the horizon. Ancient granite buildings wear a blanket of moss, and even the stone *horreos* (granaries) are built on stilts above the damp ground. Swirling fog and heavy mist help keep local folktales of the supernatural alive. Rather than a guitar, you'll hear the *gaita* (bagpipe), legacy of the Celts' settlements here in the 5th and 6th centuries BC.

Though Galicia and Asturias are off the beaten track for many foreigners, they are not undiscovered. Spanish families flock to these cool northern beaches and mountains each summer. Santiago de Compostela, where a cathedral holds the remains of the apostle James, has drawn pilgrims over northern Spain's roads for 900 years, leaving churches, shrines, and former hospitals in their path. Asturias, north of the main pilgrim trail, has always maintained a separate identity, isolated by the rocky Picos de Europa. This and the Basque Country are the only parts of Spain never conquered by the Moors, so Asturian architecture shows little Moorish influence. It was from a mountain base at Covadonga that the Christians won their first decisive battle against the Moors and launched the Reconquest of Spain.

These magical, remote regions are sure to pull at your heart strings, so be prepared to fall in love. In Gallego they call the feeling *morriña,* a powerful longing for a person or place you've left behind.

EXPLORING GALICIA & ASTURIAS

Santiago de Compostela holds center stage in Spain's northwest corner, the final destination of the Camino de Santiago. To the south are the Rías Baixas, to the west are the beaches along the Atlantic coast. Farther north is the thriving port of A Coruña; the Bay of Biscay lies east, along the coast of Asturias. Oviedo is just inland, backed by the Picos de Europa.

ABOUT THE BEACHES

Galician and Asturian beaches include urban strands with all the amenities of big-city life a few steps from the sand as well as remote expanses that rarely become as crowded as the beaches of the Mediterranean. When the sun comes out, you can relax on the sand on the Asturian beaches of (from east to west) Llanes, Ribadesella, Cudillero, Santa Ana (by Cadavedo), Luarca, and Tapia de Casariego, among others. In Galicia, the beaches of Muros, Noya, O Grove, the Islas Cíes, Boa, and Testal are the top destinations. For surfers, Galicia's Montalvo, Foxos, and Canelas beaches, near Pontevedra, are tops. Others with good waves are Nerga and Punto de Couso, near Cangas, and farther south, El Vilar, Balieros, Rio Sieira, and Os Castros.

ABOUT THE RESTAURANTS

Galicia and Asturias are justly famous for seafood. The quality of the fish is so high that chefs frown on drowning inherent flavors in heavy sauces or pungent seasonings; expect simplicity rather than spice. Fish specialties are *merluza a la gallega,* steamed hake with sweet paprika sauce (Galicia), and *merluza a la sidra,* steamed hake in a tangy Asturian cider sauce (Asturias). Salmon and trout from Asturian rivers are additional treats. The scallop, a symbol of the pilgrimage to Santiago, is popular in Galicia, where you can also find bars serving nothing but wine and *pulpo a feira* (boiled and broiled octopus) or *berberechos* (cockles). Cheeses are delicious all over northwestern Spain: try the tangy *queso Cabrales* (Asturian blue cheese), and the Galician *queixo tetilla* (a semisoft cheese in the form of a woman's breast), a delicious dessert when served with *membrillo* (quince jelly). Valdeón cheese, from the Picos de Europa village of the same name, is one of the world's finest blue cheeses, made from cow's milk and fat, then perfumed with herbs. In Asturias, try *fabada* (butter beans and sausage), and in Galicia *caldo gallego* (white beans, turnip greens, chickpeas, cabbage, and potatoes). Those savory fish or meat pies called *empanadas* are native to Galicia, as is the famous *lacón con grelos* (cured ham with turnips and chorizo sausage). Asturians enjoy *entrecôte con queso Cabrales,* steak topped with a sauce made of the local blue cheese.

The best Galician wine is the fruity, full-bodied, white Albariño, perfect with seafood. The acidic Ribeiro wine is often served in a ceramic bowl. Brandy buffs should try Galicia's *queimada* (which superstitious locals claim is a witches' brew), made of potent, grappalike *orujo* mixed with lemon peel, coffee beans, and sugar in an earthenware bowl, then set aflame and stirred until the desired amount of alcohol is burned off. Asturias is known for its *sidra* (hard cider), served carbonated or still. Traditionally, cider is poured from overhead and tossed back immediately for full enjoyment of its effervescent flavor.

ABOUT THE HOTELS

There are nine charming paradores in Galicia alone: three in elegant mansions, two in ancient fortresses, and one in a former convent. The Rusticae chain is giving the paradores a run for their money with a series of graceful and affordable *pazos* (manor houses). Reservations are a good idea, especially between May and October.

Numbers in the text correspond to numbers in the margin and on chapter maps.

EASTERN GALICIA TO SANTIAGO

Entering Galicia from Castile-Leon puts travelers into the zone of Spain's famous pilgrimage: El Camino de Santiago. The main pilgrimage route, the *camino francés,* crosses the Pyrenees from France and heads west across northern Spain. If you drive into Galicia on the A6 expressway from Castile–León, you enter the homestretch.

O CEBREIRO

❶ *334 km (209 mi) southeast of Santiago.*

Deserted and haunting outside high season (and often fogged in or snowy to boot), O Cebreiro is a stark mountaintop hamlet built around a 9th-century church. Known for its round, thatched-roof stone huts called **pallozas,** the village has been perfectly preserved and is now an open-air museum showing what life was like in these mountains in the Middle Ages and, indeed, up until a few decades ago. One hut is now a **museum** of the region's Celtic heritage. Higher up, at 3,648 feet, you can visit a rustic 9th-century **sanctuary.**

WHERE TO STAY

$ **Hostal San Giraldo de Aurillac.** This rural budget hotel next provides home cooking and a good base for walking the mountains. The Santuario do Cebreiro next door is run by the same establishment. ✉ *O Cebreiro, Pedrafita do Cebreiro, 27670* ☎ *982/367125* 📠 *982/367115* *6 rooms* *In-room: no a/c. In-hotel: restaurant, bar* ▭ *MC, V.*

LUGO

❷ *35 km (22 mi) east of Santiago.*

Just off the A6 freeway, Galicia's oldest provincial capital is most notable for its 2½-km (1½-mi) **Roman wall.** Built in the year 260, these beautifully preserved ramparts completely surround the hidden granite streets of the old town. The walkway on top has good views. The baroque *ayuntamiento* (city hall) has a magnificent rococo facade overlooking the tree-lined **Praza Maior** (Plaza Mayor). There's a good view of the Río Miño valley from the **Parque Rosalía de Castro,** outside the Roman walls near the cathedral. Lugo's **cathedral,** open daily 8 AM to 8:30 PM, is a mixture of the Romanesque, Gothic, baroque, and neoclassical styles.

4

WHERE TO STAY & EAT

$$–$$$$ **Mesón de Alberto.** This cozy venue has excellent Galician fare and professional service. The bar and adjoining bodega (winery) serve plenty of cheap *raciónes* (appetizers). The *surtido de quesos Gallegos* provides generous servings of four local cheeses; ask for some *membrillo* (quince jelly) to go with them and the brown, crusty corn bread. The dining room upstairs has an inexpensive set menu. *Cruz 4* *982/228310* *www.mesondealberto.com* *AE, DC, MC, V* *Closed Sun.*

$$$ **Gran Hotel Lugo.** In a garden near the Praza Maior but outside the city walls, this spacious modern hotel has comfortable rooms done in shades of yellow and brown. Rooms overlook the garden swimming pool or a broad street. *Av. Ramón Ferreiro 21, 27002* *982/224152* *982/241660* *www.gh-hoteles.com* *156 rooms, 11 suites* *In-hotel: restaurant, pool, parking (fee)* *AE, DC, MC, V.*

$$ **Casa Grande da Fervenza.** This graceful 17th- to 19th-century manor house, on the banks of the Miño river 14 km (8 mi) south of Lugo, is filled with heavy ceiling beams, wooden columns, exposed stone, chestnut floors, and hand-painted sinks and crockery. Rooms are rustic but comfortable. *A Fervenza, O Corgo 27364* *982/150610* *982/151610* *www.fervenza.com* *8 rooms* *In-room: no a/c. In-hotel: restaurant, bar, pool, beachfront* *AE, DC, MC, V.*

VILAR DE DONAS

❸ *27 km (17 mi) southwest of Lugo.*

Southwest of Lugo, turn right in Ferradal onto the LU4005, pass the picnic grounds, and stop at the little **church** in Vilar de Donas to pay tribute to the knights of St. James, whose tombs line the inside walls. The afternoon sun spotlights carved-stone depictions, including the horizontal body of Christ. Portraits of the two medieval noblewomen who built the church are mixed with those of the apostles in the 15th-century frescoes on the apse. The church is open for visits April–October, Tuesday–Sunday 11–2 and 3–6; to arrange a visit off season, contact the **verger** (*982/153833*). Mass is held at 1 PM each Sunday.

LEBOREIRO

4 *38 km (23 mi) west of Vilar de Donas, 56 km (35 mi) east of Santiago.*

West of Vilar de Donas, the countryside flattens out. Just after the sign for Km 42 on the N547, turn left for Leboreiro, a farming hamlet with simple medieval stone houses surrounding a **Romanesque church.** On the west side of town, an old bridge and a stretch of the ancient pilgrims' road, paved with granite boulders, are surprisingly intact.

DID YOU KNOW?

Galicia, a major center of Celtic music, has produced arguably the world's finest musician of this genre, Carlos Nuñez. He has recorded with some of the globe's leading artists. As mournful as it is sweet and uplifting, Celtic music is intrinsic to the dark, cold nights draping Galician villages.

SANTIAGO DE COMPOSTELA

★ *650 km (403 mi) northwest of Madrid.*

A large, lively university makes Santiago one of the most exciting cities in Spain, and its cathedral makes it one of the most impressive. The building is opulent and awesome, yet its towers create a sense of harmony as a benign St. James, dressed in pilgrim's costume, looks down from his perch. Santiago de Compostela welcomes more than 4½ million visitors a year, with an extra 1 million during Holy Years (the next is in 2010), when St. James's Day, July 25, falls on a Sunday.

WHAT TO SEE

5 From the **Praza do Obradoiro,** climb the two flights of stairs to the main entrance to Santiago's **cathedral.** Although the facade is baroque, the interior holds one of the finest Romanesque sculptures in the world, the **Pórtico de la Gloria.** Completed in 1188 by Maestro Mateo (Master Mateo), this is the cathedral's original entrance, its three arches carved with figures from the Apocalypse, the Last Judgment, and Purgatory. On the left are the prophets; in the center, Jesus is flanked by the four evangelists (Matthew, Mark, Luke, and John) and, above them, the 24 elders of the Apocalypse playing celestial instruments. Just below Jesus is a serene St. James, poised on a carved column. Look carefully and you can see five smooth grooves, formed by the millions of pilgrims who have placed their hands here over the centuries. On the back of the pillar, people, especially students preparing for exams, lean forward to touch foreheads with the likeness of Maestro Mateo in the hope that his genius can be shared. In his jeweled cloak, St. James presides over the **high altar.** The stairs behind it are the cathedral's focal point, surrounded by dazzling baroque decoration, sculpture, and drapery. Here, as the grand finale of their spiritual journey, pilgrims embrace St. James and kiss his cloak. In the crypt beneath the altar lie the remains of St. James and his disciples, St. Theodore and St. Athenasius.

A pilgrims' mass is celebrated every day at noon. On special, somewhat unpredictable occasions, the *botafumeiro* (huge incense burner) is

Continued on page 250

Cathedral of Santiago de Compostela

EL CAMINO DE SANTIAGO

Traversing meadows, mountains, and villages across Spain, some 50,000 travelers embark each year on a pilgrimage to Galicia's Santiago de Compostela, the sacred city of St. James. Following one of seven main routes to this remote corner of Spain, the pilgrims log about 19 miles a day in a nearly 500-mile journey. Along the way, they encounter incredible hospitality by the Spaniards and trade stories with fellow adventurers. It is all part of a ritual that has been going on for centuries.

A SPIRITUAL JOURNEY

Puente La Reina, a town heavily influenced by the Pilgrim's Road to Santiago de Compostela, owes its foundation to the bridge that Queen Doña Mayor built over the Arga River.

The surge of spiritual seekers heading to Spain's northwest coast began as early as the 9th century, when news spread that the Apostle James's remains were there. By the middle of the 12th century, about 1 million pilgrims were arriving in Santiago each year. An entire industry of food hawkers, hoteliers, and trinket sellers awaited their arrival. They even had the world's first travel guide, the Codex Calixtinus (published in the 1130s), to help them on their way.

Some made the journey in response to their conscience, to do penance for their sins against God, while others were sentenced by law to make the long walk as payment for crimes against the state.

Legend claims that St. James's body was transported secretly to the area by boat after his martyrdom in Jerusalem in AD 44. The idea picked up steam in 814, when a hermit claimed to see miraculous lights in the sky, accompanied by the sound of angels singing, on a wooded hillside near Padrón. Human bones were quickly discovered at the site, and immediately—and perhaps somewhat conveniently—declared to be those of the apostle (the bones may actually have belonged to Priscillian, the leader of a 4th-century Christian sect).

Word of this important find quickly spread across a relic-hungry Europe. Within a couple of centuries, the road to Santiago had become as popular as the other two major medieval pilgrimages, to Rome and Jerusalem.

After the 12th century, pilgrim numbers began to gradually decline, due to the dangers of robbery along the route, a growing scepticism about the genuineness of St. James's remains, and the popular rise of science in place of religion. It was only in 1993, when the Galician government launched the *Xacobeo* initiative to increase the number of visitors to the region, that the pilgrimage's popularity experienced a massive resurgence. In holy years—years when July 25th, the feast of St. James Day, falls on a Sunday (the next is in 2010)—the annual number of people making the journey to Santiago doubles to 100,000. The determined bunch is composed of spiritual seekers as well as nature lovers—scenery along the route is wild and stunning, ranging from untouched beech forests in the Pyrenees to wildflower-covered plains in central Spain and verdant forests and empty peaks in Galicia.

SCALLOP SHELLS

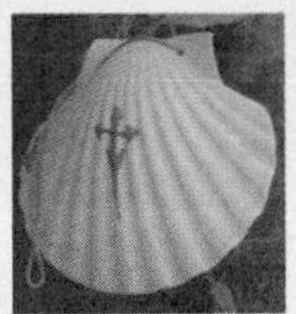

The scallop shell can be bought at most *albergues* along the route. After carrying it on the Camino, pilgrims take it home with them as a keepsake.

WHO WAS ST. JAMES?

After his martyrdom, the apostle James was revered even more by some and made a saint.

St. James the Great, brother of St. John the Evangelist (author of the Gospel of John and Revelation), was one of Jesus's first apostles. Sent by Jesus to preach that the kingdom of heaven had come, he crossed Europe and ended up in Spain. Along the way, he saved a knight from drowning in the sea. As legend goes, the knight resurfaced, covered in scallop shells. This is why Camino pilgrims carry this same type of seashell with them on their journey.

Beheaded by King Herod Agrippa on his return to Judea in AD 44, St. James, says the legend, was rescued by angels and transported in a rudderless boat to Spain, where his lifeless body was encased in stone. James is said to have resurfaced to aid the Christians in the Reconquista Battle of Clavijo, gaining him the title of Matamoros, or Moor Killer.

When the body of St. James (Santiago) was found, people came in droves to see his remains. The notion that their sins would be cleansed was developed to provide a kind of reward for walking so far, an idea no doubt subscribed to and encouraged by the church at the time.

THE PILGRIMAGE EXPERIENCE

A key Camino stop in La Rioja is the Romanesque-Gothic cathedral Santo Domingo de la Calzada, named for an 11th-century saint who had roads and bridges built along the route.

Not everyone does the route in one trip. Some split it into manageable chunks and take years to complete the whole course. Most, however, will walk an average of 19 miles (30 kilometers) a day to arrive in Santiago after a month-long trek. Though not as obvious as Dorothy's yellow-brick road to Oz, the Camino pathway, which sometimes follows a mountain trail or road and other times goes through a village or across a field, is generally so well marked that most travelers claim not to need a map (bringing one is highly recommended, however). Travelers simply follow the path's golden route markers—gold clamshell designs on blue backgrounds posted on buildings or painted on rocks and trail posts.

Walking is not the only option. Bicycles are common along the Camino and will cut the time needed to complete the pilgrimage in half. Arriving in Santiago on horseback is another option, as is walking with a donkey in tow, carrying the bags.

Your chosen mode of transport will have an effect on where you get to sleep for the night. Every town along the route has an official Camino *albergue*, or hostel, often housed in an ancient monastery or original pilgrim's hospice. (To learn where they are, ask each local tourist office.) They generally accommodate between 40 and 80 people. You can bunk down for free—though a token donation is expected—in the company of fellow walkers, but may only stay one night, unless severe Camino injuries prevent you from moving on at once. Beware that these places can fill up fast. Walkers get first priority, followed by cyclists and those on horseback, with organized walking groups at the bottom of the pecking order. Leave early every morning to ensure yourself a place for the night. (Sometimes you need to wait until after lunch for them to open.) If there is no room at the official albergues, there are plenty of paid hostels along the route. Wherever you stay, be sure to get your Pilgrims' Passport, or *credencial*, stamped, as it will provide proof along the way of just how far you've walked.

A typical day on the Camino involves setting off around 8 o'clock, walking hard through the morning—about 19 miles (30 kilometers)—then pressing on to the next village in the hope that you arrive in time to get a free bed. The afternoon is a time for catching up with fellow pilgrims, having a look around town, and doing a bit of washing. The Spanish people you meet along the way and the camaraderie with fellow pilgrims is a highlight of the trip for many.

Some albergues serve a communal evening meal, but there is always a bar in town that offers a lively atmosphere and a cheap (8–10 euros) Pilgrim's set menu (quality and fare varies; it consists of three courses plus bread and beverage). Sore feet are compared, local wine is consumed, and new walking partners are found for the following day's stage. Just make sure you get back to the albergue before curfew time around 10 or 11, or you may find a locked door awaits you at the end of the night!

On the Camino, all roads lead to the cathedral at Santiago de Compostela.

THE END OF THE LINE

Arriving at the end of the Camino de Santiago is an emotional experience. It is common to see small groups of pilgrims, hands clasped tightly together, tearfully approaching the moss- and lichen-covered cathedral in Santiago's Plaza del Obradoiro. After entering the building through the Pilgrim's Door and hugging the statue of St. James, a special mass awaits them at midday, the highlight of which is seeing the *Botafumeiro*, a giant incense-filled censer, swinging from the ceiling.

Those that have covered more than 62 miles (100 kilometers) on foot, or twice that distance on a bicycle—as evidenced by the stamped passport—can then collect their *Compostela* certificate from the Pilgrim's office (near the cathedral, at Rúa do Vilar 1). Each day, the first 10 pilgrims to request it are entitled to free meals for three days at the Hostal de los Reyes Catolicos, once a pilgrims' hospice, and now a five-star parador hotel next to the cathedral. Travelers who want to experience more scenery and gain the achievement of going to the "ends of the Earth" continue on to Finisterre at the western tip of Galicia's Atlantic coast, once thought to be the end of the world.

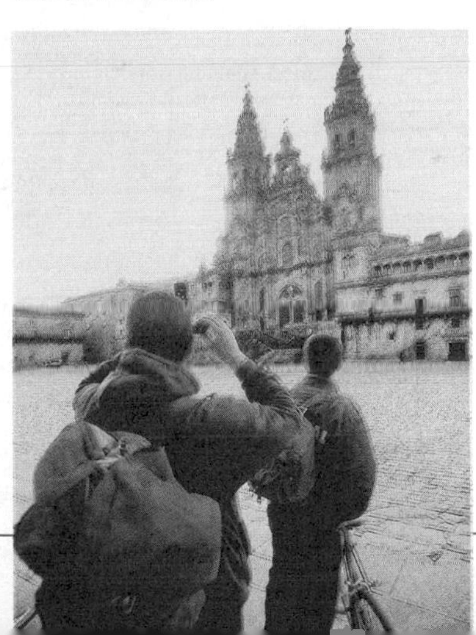

THE CAMINO FRANCÉS (FRENCH WAY)

The most popular of the seven main routes of the Camino de Santiago is the 497-mile (800-kilometer) Camino Francés (French Way), which starts in Spain, in Roncesvalles or Jaca, or in France, in St. Jean de Pied de Port, and

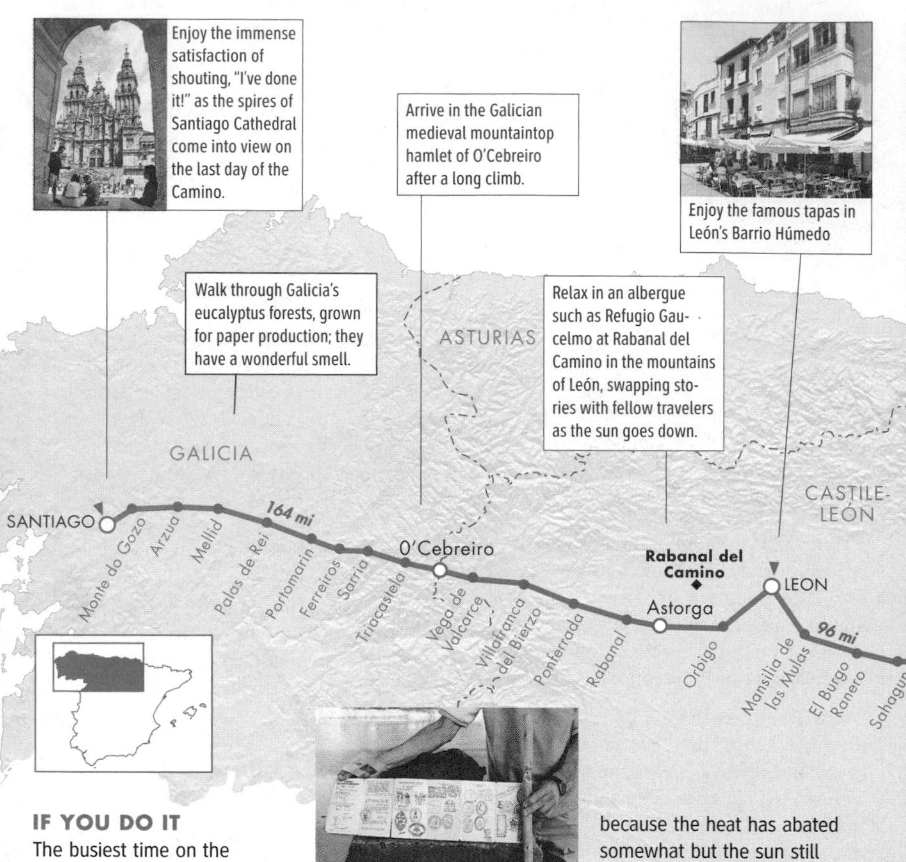

Take home a record of your trip.

IF YOU DO IT

The busiest time on the Camino is in the summer months, from June to September, when many of the Spanish make the most of their summer holidays to join the route. That means crowded paths and problems finding a room at night, particularly if you start the Camino on the first few days of any month. This time of year is also very hot. To avoid the intense heat and crowds, many pilgrims choose to start the Camino in April, May, or September. Some even make the journey in winter, but this is not at all advised, as Galicia and central Spain can get very cold at that time of year. The month of September is ideal because the heat has abated somewhat but the sun still rises early and stays out late.

You will need to be fully prepared for tough walking conditions before you set out. The single most important part of your equipment is your boot, which should be as professional as your budget allows and well worn in before you hit the trail. Other essentials include a good-quality—and

crosses the high Mesata plains into Galicia. The Camino Norte (Northern Way), which runs through the woodlands of Spain's rugged north coast, is also gaining in popularity.

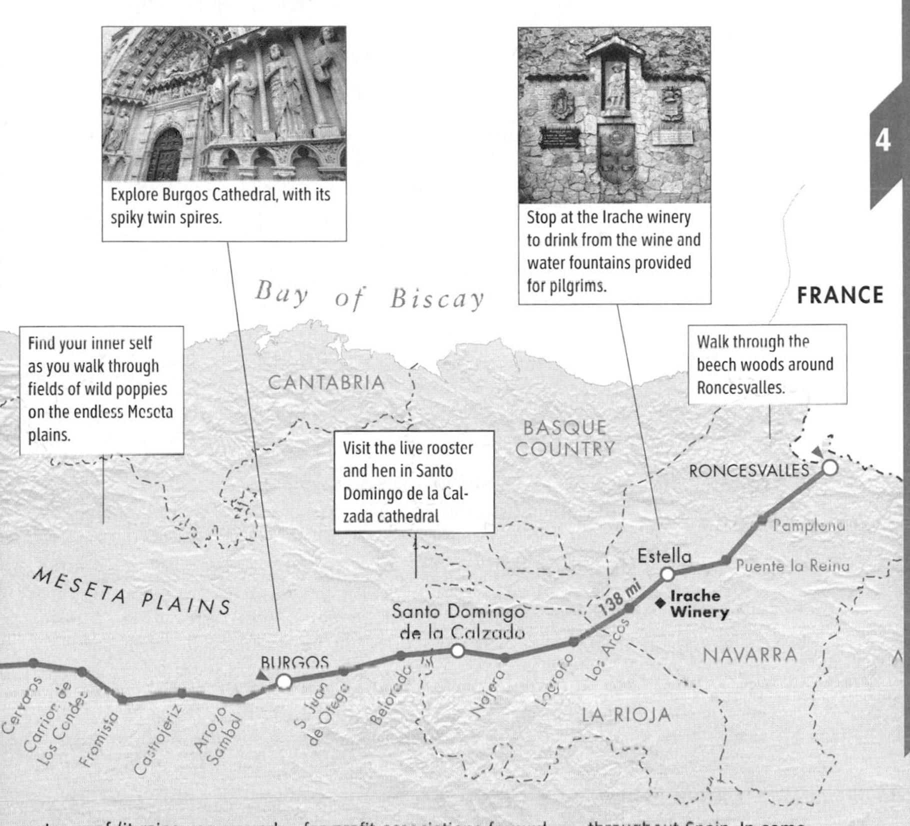

waterproof (it rains year-round in Galicia)—backpack, sleeping bag, sun cream, and a medical kit, including Vaseline and blister remedies for sore feet. Don't forget a set of earplugs as well, to keep out the sound of other pilgrims' snores and dawn departures.

To get hold of your *credencial,* or pilgrim's passport, contact one of the Camino confraternity groups. These are not-for-profit associations formed by previous pilgrims to help those in their own country who are thinking about doing the Camino (see *www.csj.org.uk/other-websites.htm* for a list of groups). You can also pick up a passport at many of the common starting points, such as the abbey in Roncesvalles, the cathedral in Le Puy, and local churches and Amigos del Camino de Santiago in villages throughout Spain. In some cases, even police stations and city halls have them.

Many albergues throughout Spain also can provide you with a valid *credencial* for a small fee.

HELPFUL WEB SITES

www.santiago-today.com
www.csj.org.uk
www.caminodesantiago.me.uk

attached to the thick ropes hanging from the ceiling and prepared for a ritual at the end of the pilgrims' mass: as small flames burn inside, eight strong laymen move the ropes to swing the vessel in a massive semicircle across the apse. In earlier centuries, this rite served as an air freshener—by the time pilgrims reached Santiago, they smelled a bit—well, you can imagine. Spanish national television broadcasts this ceremony live each July 25, St. James's Day. A botafumeiro and other cathedral treasures are on display in the **museums** downstairs and next door. On the right (south) side of the nave is the **Porta das Praterías** (Silversmiths' Door), the only purely Romanesque part of the cathedral's facade. The statues on the portal were cobbled together from parts of the cathedral. The double doorway opens onto the **Praza das Praterías,** named for the silversmiths' shops that used to line it. The fountain here is a popular place to rest in nice weather. ✉*Praza do Obradoiro* ☎*981/560527 museum, 981/583548 cathedral* 🎫*Cathedral free, combined museum ticket €5* ⏲*Cathedral daily 7* AM*–9* PM*; museums June–Oct., Mon.–Sat. 10–2 and 4–8, Sun. 10–2; Nov.–May, Mon.–Sat. 10–1:30 and 4–6:30, Sun. 10–1:30.*

For excellent views of the city, join a tour across the granite steps of the **cathedral roofs.** Pilgrims made the same 100-foot climb in medieval times to burn their travel-worn clothes below the *Cruz dos Farrapos* (Cross of Rags). ✉*Pazo de Xelmírez, Praza do Obradoiro* ☎*981/552985* 🎫*€10* ⏲*Tues.–Sun. 10–2 and 4–8.*

6 Step into the rich 12th-century **Pazo de Xelmírez** *(Palace of Archbishop Xelmírez)*, an unusual example of Romanesque civic architecture with a cool, clean, vaulted dining hall. The little figures carved on the corbels (supports) in this graceful, 100-foot-long space are lifelike, partaking of food, drink, and music with great medieval gusto. Each is different; stroll around for a tableau of mealtime merriment. ✉*Praza do Obradoiro* 🎫 *€5 combined museum ticket* ⏲*Tues.–Sun. 10–2 and 4–8.*

7 The **Hostal de los Reyes Católicos** *(Hostel of the Catholic Monarchs)*, facing the cathedral from the left, was built in 1499 by Ferdinand and Isabella to house the pilgrims who slept on Santiago's streets every night. Having lodged and revived travelers for nearly 500 years, it's the oldest refuge in the world and was converted from a hospital to a parador in 1953. The facade bears a Castilian coat of arms along with Adam, Eve, and various saints; inside, the four arcaded patios have gargoyle rainspouts said to be caricatures of 16th-century townsfolk. There's a small art gallery behind the lobby. Walk-in spectators without room keys risk being asked to leave, but for a negotiable cost, as part of a city tour, you can visit in the company of an official guide from the tourist office. ✉*Praza do Obradoiro 1* ☎*981/582200 hostel, 981/555129 tourist office* 🌐*www.parador.es* ⏲*Daily 10–1 and 4–6.*

Santiago de Compostela's streets hold many old *pazos* (manor houses), convents, and churches that in most towns would receive headline attention. But the best way to spend your remaining time here is simply to walk around the **casco antiguo** *(old town)*, losing yourself in its maze of stone-paved narrow streets and little plazas. The most beau-

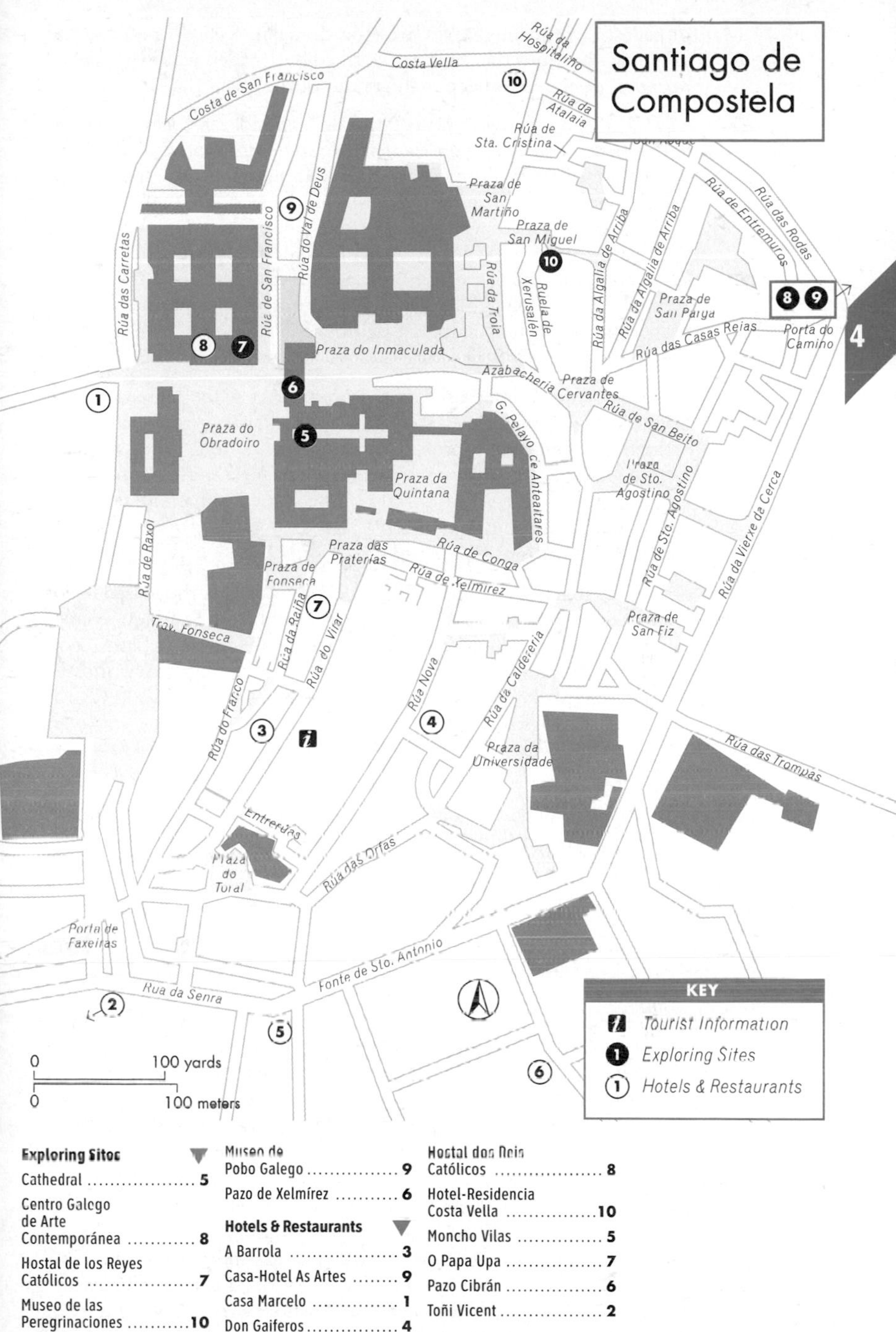

Exploring Sites

Cathedral **5**

Centro Galego de Arte Contemporánea **8**

Hostal de los Reyes Católicos **7**

Museo de las Peregrinaciones **10**

Museo do Pobo Galego **9**

Pazo de Xelmírez **6**

Hotels & Restaurants

A Barrola **3**

Casa-Hotel As Artes **9**

Casa Marcelo **1**

Don Gaiferos **4**

Hostal dos Reis Católicos **8**

Hotel-Residencia Costa Vella **10**

Moncho Vilas **5**

O Papa Upa **7**

Pazo Cibrán **6**

Toñi Vicent **2**

tiful pedestrian thoroughfares are Rúa do Vilar, Rúa do Franco, and Rúa Nova—portions of which are covered by arcaded walkways called *soportales,* designed to keep walkers out of the rain.

8 On the north side of town off the Porta do Camino, the **Centro Galego de Arte Contemporánea** *(Galician Center for Contemporary Art)* is a stark but elegant modern building that offsets Santiago's ancient feel. Portuguese designer Álvaro Siza built the museum of smooth, angled granite, which mirrors the medieval convent of San Domingos de Bonaval next door. Inside, a gleaming lobby of white Italian marble gives way to white-wall, high-ceiling exhibition halls flooded with light from massive windows and skylights. The museum has a good permanent collection and even better changing exhibits. ✉ *Rúa de Valle Inclán s/n* ☎ *981/546619* 🌐 *www.cgac.org* 🎟 *Free* 🕒 *Tues.–Sun. 11–8.*

9 Next door to the Center for Contemporary Art is the **Museo do Pobo Galego** *(Galician Folk Museum)*, in the medieval convent of Santo Domingo de Bonaval. Photos, farm implements, and other displays illustrate aspects of traditional Galician life. The star attraction is the 13th-century self-supporting spiral granite staircase that still connects three floors. ✉ *Rúa de Bonaval* ☎ *981/583620* 🌐 *www.museodopobo.es* 🎟 *Free* 🕒 *Tues.–Sat. 10–2 and 4–8, Sun. 11–2.*

10 North of Azabachería (follow Ruela de Xerusalén) is the **Museo de las Peregrinaciones** *(Pilgrimage Museum)*, with Camino de Santiago iconography from sculptures and carvings to *azabache* (compact black coal, or jet) items. For an overview of the history of the pilgrimage and the Camino's role in the development of the city itself, this is a key visit. ✉ *Rúa de San Miguel 4* ☎ *981/581558* 🎟 *€2.50* 🕒 *Tues.–Fri. 10–8, Sat. 10:30–1:30 and 5–8, Sun. 10:30–1:30.*

WHERE TO STAY & EAT

$$$$ ✕ **Casa Marcelo.** When it's open, this eruption into Santiago's culinary field is a find. Leek-and-potato soup with clams and other refined cooking based on local favorites are the rule. The €43 prix-fixe meal consists of a selection of six main dishes and two desserts. ✉ *Rúa Hortas 1* ☎ *981/558580* 💳 *AE, MC, V* 🕒 *Closed Sun.–Tues. and Feb.*

$$$–$$$$ ✕ **Toñi Vicent.** Galicia's most creative cuisine is concocted in this carefully furnished antiquary. *Marinada de lubina con ensalada amarga, aceite, limón, y eneldo* (marinade of sea bass with bitter salad, olive oil, lemon, and dill) is an example of the meeting of Galicia's finest produce with one of its most inventive chefs. ✉ *Rosalía de Castro 24* ☎ *981/594100* 💳 *AE, MC, V* 🕒 *Closed Sun. and Dec. 23–Jan. 7.*

$$–$$$$ ✕ **A Barrola.** Polished wooden floors, a niche with wine and travel books, and a lively terrace make this tavern a favorite with university faculty. The house salads, mussels with *santiaguiños* (crabmeat), *arroz con bogavante* (rice with lobster), and seafood empanadas are superb. ✉ *Rúa do Franco 29* ☎ *981/577999* 🌐 *www.restaurantesgrupobarrola.com* 💳 *AE, MC, V* 🕒 *Closed Mon. and Jan.–Mar.*

$$–$$$$ ✕ **Don Gaiferos.** One of Santiago's most distinguished restaurants, this tavern serves jumbo prawns stuffed with smoked salmon and white Ribeiro and Albariño wines. The spicy fish stew is enough for two,

and the *tarta de almendra* (almond tart) and the bilberry cheesecake are irresistible. ✉*Rúa Nova 23* ☎*981/583894* ▭*AE, DC, MC, V* ⊙*Closed Sun. and Dec. 24–31.*

$$$ ★ ✕**Moncho Vilas.** The owner of the eponymous restaurant reached a zenith when he prepared a banquet for the late Pope John Paul II (the pontiff visited Santiago in 1989). Specialties include salmon with clams, *merluza a la gallega* (hake with paprika sauce) or *a la vasca* (in a green sauce), and steak with garlicky potatoes. ✉*Av. Villagarcia 21* ☎*981/598637* ▭*AE, DC, MC, V* ⊙*No dinner Sun. Closed Mon.*

$$–$$$ ✕**O Papa Upa.** A luscious assortment of shellfish and the entrecôte Papa Upa, a massive T-bone steak, are specialties. Chase your meal as the locals do, with the "rite of burning firewater"—*queimada,* flaming brandy served in a ceramic bowl. ✉*Rúa da Raiña 18* ☎*981/566598* ▭*AE, DC, MC, V.*

4

$$$$ Fodor'sChoice ★ ✕**Hostal dos Reis Católicos.** This 15th-century masterpiece was originally built as a royal hospital designed to take care of sick pilgrims as they arrived in the city. A mammoth baroque doorway gives way to austere courtyards of box hedge and simple fountains, and to rooms furnished with antiques, some with canopy beds. Also known as the Parador de Santiago de Compostela, this hotel is one of the most highly regarded in the parador chain. Libredón, a restaurant ($$$–$$$$) in the grand, vaulted dining room, serves top-notch regional fare, including *lonchas de pulpo* (strips of octopus served with paprika and potato), foie gras, and *filloas de manzana y crema caramelizadas* (apple-and-caramel-cream pancakes), and is well worth a visit. The tapas bar, Enxebre, is lively and informal. ✉*Praza do Obradoiro 1, 15705* ☎*981/582200* 🖷*981/563094* 🌐*www.parador.es* *137 rooms* *In-hotel: 2 restaurants, bar, parking (fee)* ▭*AE, DC, MC, V.*

$$ ★ **Casa-Hotel As Artes.** A stone's throw from the cathedral, this little inn offers sunny quarters at great rates. Each room is named after a different artist and decorated accordingly—the Vivaldi room, for instance, has music-manuscript curtains. All rooms have recessed windows with beveled wood shutters, hardwood floors, and a wrought-iron double bed. ✉*Travesía de Dos Puertas 2, off Rúa San Francisco, 15707* ☎*981/572590 or 981/555254* 🖷*981/577823* 🌐*www.asartes.com* *7 rooms* *In-hotel: bar* ▭*AE, DC, MC, V* ⊙*Closed Jan. 8–31.*

$$ **Hotel-Residencia Costa Vella.** This inn snuggles up to Santiago's medieval wall at one of the city's highest points. The house is classically Galician, but the interior is awash in smooth blond wood and natural light from floor-to-ceiling windows—the better to behold the perfect little garden, stone wall, red tile rooftops, the baroque convent of San Francisco, and the green hills beyond. (Ask for a garden view.) Enjoy nice views from the airy breakfast room and reading area. ✉*Rúa Porta da Pena 17, 15704* ☎*981/569530* 🖷*981/569531* 🌐*www.costavella.com* *14 rooms* *In-hotel: bar* ▭*AE, DC, MC, V.*

$$ **Pazo Cibrán.** This 18th-century Galician farm mansion is 7 km (4 mi) from Santiago de Compostela. Owner Mayka Iglesias maintains six rooms in the main house and five large rooms in the old stable. The antiques-packed living room overlooks gardens with camellias, magnolias, palms, vines, and a bamboo walk. Breakfast is served in the *pazo* itself, with lunch

and dinner available in the nearby Casa Roberto. To get here, take the N525 toward Ourense from Santiago and turn right at Km 11, after the gas station. ✉*Rua San Xulián de Sales, 15885* ☎*981/511515* 📠*981/814766* 🌐*www.pazocibran.com* *11 rooms* *In-room: no a/c* 💳*AE, DC, MC, V.*

> **IT'S GALLEGO TO ME**
>
> In the Gallego language, the Castilian Spanish plaza (town square) is praza and the Castilian playa (beach) is praia. Closer to Portuguese than to Castilian Spanish, Gallego is the language of choice for nearly all road signs in Galicia.

TAPAS BARS

Adega Abrigadoiro. A five-minute walk behind the Colegio San Jerónimo, this tapas emporium serves one of the best selections of Galician delicacies in town. ✉*Carreira do Conde 5* ☎*981/563163.* **La Bodeguilla de San Roque.** One of Santiago's favorite spots for *tapeo* (tapas grazing) and *chiquiteo* (wine sampling), this tavern is a five-minute walk from the cathedral. ✉*Rua San Roque 13* ☎*981/564379.* **O Dezaseis.** Specialists in small servings of great products, this traditional favorite near the town's center is a must on any tapas crawl. ✉*Rúa de San Pedro 16* ☎*981/577633* 🌐*www.dezaseis.com.* **Prada a Tope.** This rustic spot behind the cathedral specializes in products from El Bierzo, either at the bar or in one of the dining rooms. ✉*Rua Troia 10* ☎*981/581909* 🌐*www.pradaatope.es.*

CAFÉS

Santiago is a great city for European-style coffee-nursing. Popular with students, **A Caldereria** (✉*Rua Caldereria 26* ☎*981/572045*) juxtaposes contemporary and traditional aesthetics. Try Clip Nougat, ice cream with pistachios and toasted almonds. Once a gathering place for Galician poets, the **Cafe Bar Derby** (✉*Rúa das Orfas 29* ☎*981/586417*) remains a serene place for coffee and pastries. Cozy **Iacobus** (✉*Rua Azibechería 5* ☎*981/582804* ✉*Rua Caldereria 42* ☎*981/583415*) blends stone walls with contemporary wood trim and light fixtures; see a glass cache of coffee beans in the floor.

NIGHTLIFE & THE ARTS

Santiago's nightlife peaks on Thursday night, as many students spend weekends at home with their families. For up-to-date information on concerts, films, and clubs, pick up the student-run *Compostelan* magazine at any newsstand; also check the monthly paper *Compostela,* available at the main tourist office on Rúa do Vilar. Bars and seafood-theme tapas joints line the old streets south of the cathedral, particularly **Rúa do Franco, Rúa da Raiña,** and **Rúa do Vilar.** A great first stop, especially if you haven't eaten dinner, is **Rúa de San Clemente,** off the Praza do Obradoiro, where three bars in a row offer two or three plates of tapas free with each drink, an astonishing value.

O Beiro (✉*Rúa da Raiña 3* ☎*981/581370*) is a rustic wine bar with a laid-back professional crowd. Galicia's oldest pub is also one of its most unusual: **Modus Vivendi** (✉*Praza Feixóo 1* 🌐*www.pubmodusvivendi.net*) is in a former stable. The old stone feeding trough is now a low table, and instead of stairs you walk on ridged stone inclines designed for the former occupants—horses and cattle. A thirtysomething crowd packs the low-ceiling bar nightly, and on weekends the bar hosts live music (jazz, ethnic, Celtic) and sometimes storytelling. Drink to Galicia's Celtic roots with live music at **Casa das Crechas** (✉ *Vía Sacra 3* ☎ *981/560751* 🌐 *www.casadascrechas.com*), where Celtic wood carvings hang from thick stone walls and dolls of playful Galician witches ride their brooms above the bar. **Retablo Concerto** (✉ *Rúa Nova 13* ☎ *981/564851* 🌐 *www.cafeconcertoretablo.com*) is cozy and has live music on weekends. **Blaster** (✉ *Av. República Argentina 6* ☎ *981/572809*) is a hot bar with, on occasion, a DJ spinning tunes.

The modern **Auditorio de Galicia** (✉ *Av. Burgo das Nacións* ☎ *981/573855* 🌐 *www.auditoriodegalicia.org*), north of town, has high-quality classical and jazz programs and a fine art gallery. In residence is the Royal Galician Philharmonic, which has hosted Il Giardino Armonico, the Academy of St. Martin-in-the-Fields, and the Leipzig Gewandhaus Orchestra. Players at Santiago's **Teatro Principal** (✉ *Rúa Nova 21* ☎ *981/528700*) stage plays in Spanish, as well as dance performances and film festivals.

SHOPPING

Galicia is known throughout Spain for its distinctive blue-and-white ceramics with bold modern designs, made in Sargadelos and O Castro. Peruse a wide selection at **Sargadelos** (✉ *Rúa Nova 16* ☎ *981/581905* 🌐 *www.sargadelos.com*)

SIDE TRIPS FROM SANTIAGO/PADRÓN

⓫ *20 km (12 mi) south of Santiago.*

Having grown up beside the Roman port of Iría Flavia, Padrón is where the body of St. James is believed to have washed ashore after its miraculous maritime journey. The town is known for its *pimientos de Padrón*, tiny green peppers fried and sprinkled with sea salt. The fun in eating these is that one in five or so is spicy-hot. Galicia's biggest **food market** is held here every Sunday.

Padrón was the birthplace of one of Galicia's heroines, the 19th-century poet Rosalía de Castro. The lovely **Casa-Museo Rosalía de Castro,** where she lived with her husband, a historian, now displays family memorabilia. ✉ *Ctra. de Herbón* ☎ *981/811204* 🌐 *www.rosaliadecastro.org* 🎫 *€1.50* ⏲ *May–Sept., Tues.–Sat. 10–2 and 4–8, Sun. 10–1:30; Oct.–Apr., Tues.–Sat. 10–1:30 and 4–7, Sun. 10–1:30.*

OFF THE BEATEN PATH

The barons who ruled over Galicia's peasants and the rest of its feudal society lived in *pazos* (country manor houses) like the one 27 km (17 mi) southeast of Santiago. At the Pazo de Oca (☎ *986/587435* 🎫 *€4, free Mon. 9–12:30* ⏲ *Daily 9–dusk*) stroll the gardens to the lily pond and lake, where a stone boat stays miraculously afloat.

SPORTS & THE OUTDOORS

With so much rugged wilderness, Spain's northwest has become the country's main outdoor-adventure region. The Picos de Europa and the green hills of Galicia beg to be hiked, trekked, climbed, or simply walked; other open-air diversions include horseback riding, canyon rappelling, bungee jumping, and spelunking. Ribadesella, Asturias, is Spain's white-water capital, with an international kayak race held in August on the Sella River from Arriondas to Ribadesella. Atlantic salmon, sea trout, and trout angling provides an excellent pretext for getting to know some of green Spain's finest river valleys and countryside.

BALLOONING

Stable weather conditions and outstanding mountain landscapes make the Picos de Europa ideal for year-round ballooning. Flights cost from €120 for a 30-minute introduction to €520 for a three-hour trip (prices are per person).

Contacts **Globoastur** (✉ *Gijón, Asturias* ☎ *985/355818* 🌐 *www.globoastur.com*).

GOLF

Asturias has golf courses in Llanes, Gijón, and Siero. Galician courses include Monte la Zapateira, near A Coruña; Domaio, in Pontevedra province; La Toja, on the island of the same name near O Grove; and Padrón. Santiago's links are near the airport, at Labacolla. Call the club a day in advance to reserve equipment.

Contacts **Campo de Golf del Aero Club Labacolla** (✉ *General Pardiñas, 34, Lugar de Mourena* ☎ *981/888276*). **Campo Municipal de Golf de las Caldas** (✉ *Av. La Premaña s/n, Las Caldas, Oviedo* ☎ *985/798132*). **Campo Municipal la Llorea** (✉ *N632, Km 62, La Llorea, Gijón* ☎ *985/333191*) **Club de Golf de Castiello** (✉ *N632, 5 km [3 mi] from Gijón toward Santander* ☎ *985/366313*).**Club de Golf La Cuesta** (✉ *Ctra. N634, Km 298, Llanes, 3 km [2 mi] east of Llanes, near Cué* ☎ *985/417230*). **Domaio** (✉ *San Lorenzo* ☎ *986/327051*). **La Barganiza** (✉ *San Martí de Anes-Siero, 12 km [7 mi] from Oviedo and 14 km [9 mi] from Gijón* 📬 *La Barganiza 33192–Carretera Siero-Asturias* ☎ *985/742468*). **La Toja** (✉ *El Grove* ☎ *986/730158*). **Monte la Zapateira** (✉ *C. Zapateira s/n, A Coruña* ☎ *981/285200*). **Padrón** (☎ *981/453910*).

HIKING

The tourist offices in Oviedo and Cangas de Onís can help you organize a Picos de Europa trek. The Picos visitor center in Cangas provides general information, route maps, and a useful scale model of the range. In summer, another reception center opens between Lakes Enol and Ercina, on the mountain road from Covadonga. The Centro de Aventuro Monteverde can organize canoeing, canyon rappelling, bungee jumping, spelunking, horseback riding, and jeep trips. Turismo y Aventura Viesca offers rafting, canoeing, jet skiing, climbing, trekking, bungee jumping, and archery. In A Coruña, Nortrek is a one-stop source for information and equipment pertaining to hiking, rock climbing, skiing, and bungee jumping.

Contacts **Centro de Aventuro Monteverde** (✉ *Calle Sargento Provisional 5, Cangas de Onís*

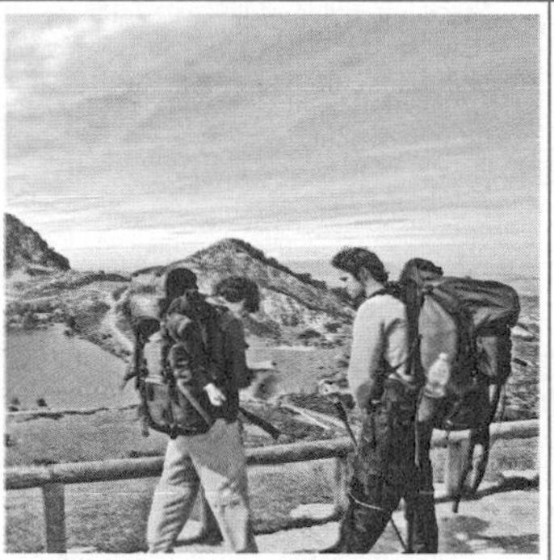

☎985/848079) is closed November–March. **Nortrek** (✉*Calle Inés de Castro 7, bajo, A Coruña* ☎*981/151674*). **Picos de Europa visitor center** (✉*Casa Dago, Av. Covadonga 43, Cangas de Onís* ☎*985/848614*). **Turismo y Aventura Viesca** (✉*Av. del Puente Romano 1, Cangas de Onís* ☎*985/357369* 🌐*www.aventuraviesca.com*).

HORSEBACK RIDING

Trastur leads wilderness trips on horseback through the remote valleys of western Asturias. The 5- to 10-day outings are designed for both beginners and experienced cowboys; mountain cabins provide shelter along the trail. Tours begin and end in Oviedo and cost about €108 a day, all-inclusive. The Centro Hípico de Turismo Ecuestre y de Aventuras/"Granjo O Castelo" conducts horseback rides along the pilgrimage routes to Santiago from O Cebreiro and Braga (Portugal). Federación Hípica Gallega has a list of all riding facilities in Galicia.

Contacts Centro Hípico de Turismo Ecuestre y de Aventuras/ "Granja O Castelo" (✉*Rúa Urzáiz 91–5D, Vigo* ☎*986/425937* 🌐*www.galicianet.com/castelo*). **Federación Hípica Gallega** (✉*Fotografo Luis Ksado 17, Edificio Federaciones Deportivas, Vigo* ☎*986/213800* 📠*986/201461* 🌐*www.fhgallega.com*). **Trastur** (✉*Muñalen-Cal Teso, Tineo* ☎*985/806036 or 985/806310*).

SKIING

The region's three small ski areas cater mostly to local families. The largest is San Isidro, in the Cantabrian Mountains, with 4 chairlifts, 8 drag lifts, and more than 22½ km (14 mi) of slopes. Just east of here is Valgrande Pajares, with two chairlifts, eight slopes, and cross-country trails. West of Ourense, in Galicia, Mazaneda has 2 chairlifts, 17 slopes, and 1 cross-country trail.

Contacts Mazaneda (✉*A Pobra de Trives* ☎*988/309747*). **San Isidro** (✉*Puerto San Isidro* ☎*987/731115*). **Valgrande Pajares** (✉*Brañillín* ☎*985/496123 or 985/957123*).

WATER SPORTS

In Santiago, contact diving experts Turisnorte for information on scuba lessons, equipment rental, guided dives, windsurfing, and parasailing. Courageous and experienced sailors might find yachting a spectacular way to discover hidden coastal sights; Yatesport Coruña (also in Santiago) rents private yachts and can arrange sailing lessons.

Contacts Turisnorte (✉*Raxoeira 14, Milladoiro, A Coruña* ☎*981/530009 or 902/162172*). **Yatesport Coruña** (✉*Puerto Deportivo, Marina Sada, Sada, A Coruña* ☎*981/620624*).

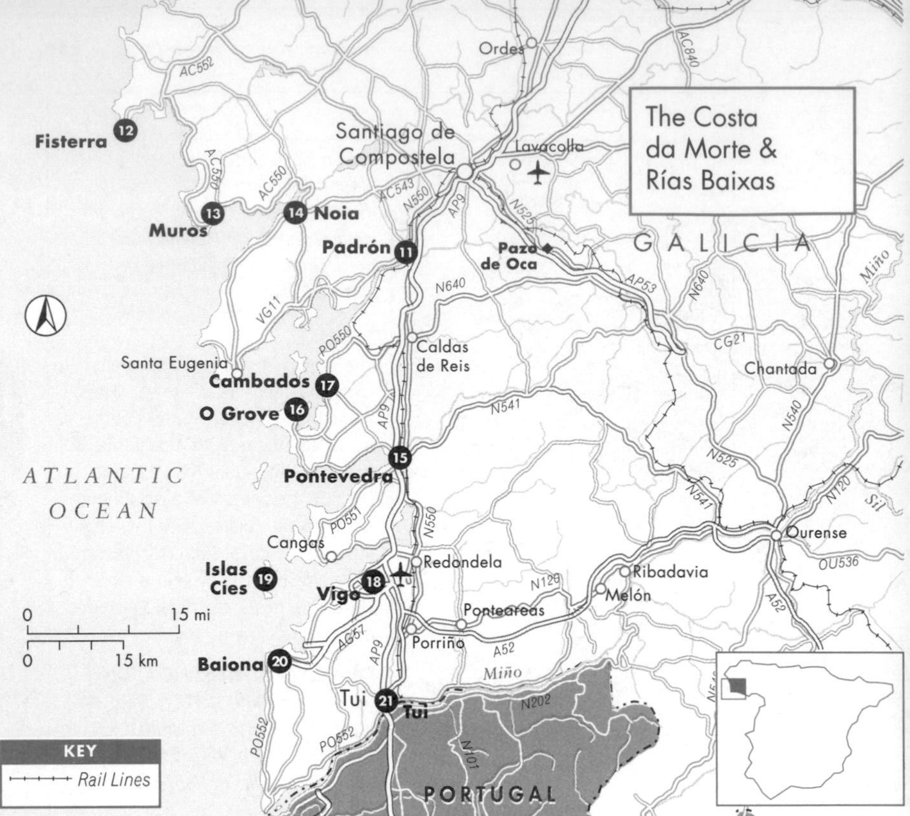

WHERE TO STAY & EAT

$$ ★ **A Casa Antiga do Monte.** This graceful manor house combines modern comfort and equipment with vintage furniture and Asturian architecture. The crackling fire in the dining room and the 18th-century *horreo* (granary) in the yard add up to perfect rustic comfort. Meals include local culinary delights such as *fabada* (bean stew) and *chorizo a la sidra* (chorizo sausage with cider). *Boca do Monte-Lestrove, 1½ km (1 mi) southwest of Padrón, 15916 981/812400 981/812401 www.susavilaocio.es 16 rooms In-room: no a/c. In-hotel: restaurant, bar, pool, gym, parking (fee) AE, DC, MC, V.*

THE COSTA DA MORTE & RÍAS BAIXAS

West of Santiago, scenic C543 leads to the coast. Straight west, the shore is windy, rocky, and treacherous—hence its name, the "Coast of Death." The series of wide, quiet estuaries south of here is called the Rías Baixas (Low Estuaries). The hilly drive takes you through a green countryside dappled with vineyards, tiny farms, and Galicia's trademark *horreos* (granaries), most with a cross at one or both ends.

FISTERRA

12 *50 km (31 mi) west of Santiago, 75 km (48 mi) southwest of A Coruña.*

There was a time when this lonely, windswept outcrop over raging waters was thought to be the end of the earth—the *finis terrae* (Cabo Finisterre in Castilian). The known Western world sank into the ocean here with a flourish of rocky beaches. All that's left is a rundown stone *faro* (lighthouse) perched on a cliff; though it's not officially open to the public, you might find the door open. Aside from legends, the only draw in this tiny seaside town is its pleasant (barring storms) main plaza and the 12th-century church of **Santa Maria das Areas.** Romanesque, Gothic, and baroque elements combine in an impressive but rather gloomy facade. ✉*Manuel Lago País s/n* *Free* *June–Sept., daily 9–2 and 3–6; Oct.–May, daily 10–2 and 4–6.*

4

MUROS

13 *55 km (34 mi) southeast of Fisterra, 65 km (40 mi) southwest of Santiago.*

Muros is a popular summer resort with lovely, arcaded streets framed by Gothic arches. The quiet back alleys of the old town reveal some well-preserved characteristic Galician granite houses. The real action here takes place when fishing boats return to dock from the mussel-breeding platforms that dot the bay. Wander the port on a weekday afternoon during the unloading and mussel-sorting and rinsing. At around 6 PM a siren signals the start of the *lonja* (fish auction), and anyone is welcome, though you need a special license to buy. Trays upon trays—some spilling over with more than a dozen slimy octopi, or cod with heaving gills—line the floor, which in turn is covered in a sheen of saltwater, jet-black squid ink, and fish blood—the favored footwear is knee-high rubber boots. Good nearby beaches include Praia de San Francisco and Praia de Area.

NOIA

14 *30 km (19 mi) east of Muros, 36 km (22 mi) west of Santiago.*

Deep within the Ría de Muros y Noia, the compact medieval town of Noia nuzzles up to the foot of the Barbanza mountain range. The Gothic church of **San Martín** rises over the old town's Praza do Tapal, facing resolutely out to sea. In the town center, **La Alameda** is a lovely sculpted park that gives way to a black-, white-, and red-tile pedestrian street lined with palm trees and stone and wrought-iron benches. You can catch glimpses of the ría through the trees; in the summer, the street fills with terrace cafés. Near Noia are Testal and Boa beaches.

PONTEVEDRA

15 *55 km (34 mi) southeast of Noia, 59 km (37 mi) south of Santiago.*

At the head of its ría, Pontevedra is the largest city on Spain's northwest coast after A Coruña. You approach through prefab suburbs, but Pontevedra's old quarter is well preserved and largely undiscovered. Speckled with bars, it's lively-to-wild on weekends.

The 16th-century seafarers' basilica of **Santa María Mayor,** with a 1541 facade, has lovely, sinuous vaulting and, at the back of the nave, a Romanesque portal. Above the door in the lower part of the basilica is a 16th-century image of Christ with the Virgin and St. John. At the end of the right nave is an 18th-century Christ by the Galician sculptor Ferreiro. ✉ *Av. de Santa María s/n* ☎ *986/866185* *Free* ⏲ *Daily 11–1 and 6–8.*

★ Pontevedra's **Museo Provincial** is in two 18th-century mansions connected by a stone bridge. Displays include exquisite Celtic jewelry, silver from all over the world, and several large model ships. The original kitchen, with stone fireplace, is intact; nearby, take the tiny, steep wooden stairs down to the reconstructed captain's chamber on the battleship *Numancia,* which limped back to Spain after the Dos de Mayo battle with Peru in 1866. Completing the loop, upstairs in the first building, are Spanish and Italian paintings and some inlay work. ✉ *Praza de Leña* ☎ *986/851455* *Free* ⏲ *Tues.–Sat. 10–2 and 4–7, Sun. 11–2.*

WHERE TO STAY & EAT

$$$–$$$$ ★ ✕ **Casa Solla.** Pepe Solla brings Galicia's bounty to his terrace garden restaurant, 2 km (1 mi) outside of town toward O Grove. Try the *menu desgustacion* (tasting menu) to sample a selection of regional favorites, such as *lomo de caballa* (grilled mackerel) and *jarrete de cordero* (sliced lamb shank). ✉ *Av. Sineiro 7, Ctra. de La Toja, Km 2, San Salvador de Poio* ☎ *986/872884* 🌐 *www.restaurantesolla.com* 💳 *AE, DC, MC, V* ⏲ *Closed Mon. and late Dec.–early Jan. No dinner Thurs. or Sun.*

$$$ ✕ **Casa del Barón.** A 16th-century manor house built on the foundations of an ancient Roman villa in the heart of the old quarter, the fairly dark Parador de Pontevedra has a baronial stone stairway winding up from the front lobby. Guest rooms have recessed windows with lace curtains and large wooden shutters; some face a small rose garden. The restaurant ($$–$$$$), which serves fine Galician food, is full of antique mirrors, candelabras, and portraits. ✉ *Barón 19, 36002* ☎ *986/855800* 📠 *986/852195* 🌐 *www.parador.es* *47 rooms* *In-room: Wi-Fi. In-hotel: restaurant, bar* 💳 *AE, DC, MC, V.*

TAPAS BARS

Jaqueyui. If you can cope with the lively, smoky atmosphere, then this cozy, central bar serves one of the most impressive slices of tortilla in Spain, ideally washed down with a glass of the fine house Rioja. ✉ *Rúa de Doña Tareixa 1* ☎ *986/861820.*

EN ROUTE **Driving west on the C550, you pass the vineyards of Albariño. As you wind your way through the small towns around here, you may come across the occasional donkey hauling wagons heaped with grapes.**

O GROVE

16 *31 km (19 mi) northwest of Pontevedra.*

O Grove (El Grove in Castilian) throws an illustrious shellfish festival the second week of October, but you can enjoy the day's catch in taverns and restaurants year-round. From here you can cross a bridge to the island of **A Toxa** (also called La Toja), famous for its spas—the waters are said to have healing properties. Legend has it that a man abandoned an ailing donkey here and found it up on all fours, fully rejuvenated, upon his return. The island's south side has a palm-filled garden anchored on one side by the **Capilla de San Sebastián,** a tiny church covered in cockleshells.

Nearby Reboredo is the home of **Acquarium/galicia,** one of Spain's finest aquariums, devised to showcase marine life endemic to Galicia in an original and interactive manner. *Punta Moreiras s/n 986/731515 www.acquariumgalicia.com €9 Mon. and Thurs. 10–5, Tues., Wed., and Fri.–Sun. 10–8.*

WHERE TO STAY & EAT

$$–$$$$ **El Crisol.** Photos of famous diners greet you as you enter this secluded spot. The menu has lobster, shrimp, spider crabs, scallops, and freshly caught fish. If you can't make up your mind, a house stew, *sopa de pescados mixtos* (mixed-fish soup), combines most of the above. Save room for the *torta de queso,* a rich cheesecake dessert. *Hospital 10 986/730029 AE, DC, MC, V Closed Mon. Sept.–June. No lunch Mon. July and Aug.*

$$$$ **Gran Hotel Hesperia La Toja.** Extravagant and exorbitant (for the region), this classic spa hotel is on the breezy island off O Grove, surrounded by pine trees. Guest rooms are simple, their charm slightly faded compared with the grandiose formality of the foyers and salons. Try to book a room with a sea view. *36991 Isla de la Toja 986/730025 986/730026 www.hesperia.com 197 rooms In-room: Wi-Fi. In-hotel: restaurant, bar, golf course, tennis court, pool, gym, spa, beachfront AE, DC, MC, V.*

CAMBADOS

17 *61 km (37 mi) southwest of Santiago.*

This breezy seaside town has a charming, almost entirely residential old quarter. The impressive main square, **Praza de Fefiñanes,** is bordered on almost two sides by an imposing Albariño bodega.

WHERE TO STAY & EAT

$$$ ✕🏨 **Parador de Cambados (El Albariño).** The bar of this airy mansion is large and inviting, with natural light and wooden booths. Rooms are warmly furnished with wrought-iron lamps, area rugs, and full-length wood shutters over small-pane windows. The kitchen's ($$–$$$$) *lenguado al vino albariño* (sole in Albariño wine sauce) is simply divine; order some Albariño wine in its purest form. ✉*Paseo de Cervantes s/n, 36630* ☎*986/542250* 📠*986/542068* 🌐*www.parador.es* *58 rooms* *In-hotel: restaurant, tennis court, pool* 💳*AE, DC, MC, V.*

SHOPPING

Cambados is the hub for Albariño wines, one of Spain's best white wines—full bodied and fruity, yet fresh. **A Casa do Albariño** (✉*Rúa Principe 3* ☎*986/542236* 🌐*www.vinosalbarino.com*) is a tiny, tasteful emporium of Galician wines and cheeses. Head to **Cucadas** (✉*Praza de Fefiñanes* ☎*986/542511*) for a particularly large selection of baskets, copper items, and Camariñas lace.

VIGO

18 *31 km (19 mi) south of Pontevedra, 90 km (56 mi) south of Santiago.*

Vigo's formidable port is choked with trawlers and fishing boats and lined with clanging shipbuilding yards. Its sights (or lack thereof) fall far short of its commercial swagger. The city's casual appeal lies a few blocks inland where the port commotion gives way to the narrow, dilapidated streets of the old town. From 8:30 to 3:30 daily, on **Rúa Pescadería** in the barrio called La Piedra, Vigo's famed *ostreras*—a group of rubber-glove fisherwomen who have been peddling fresh oysters to passersby for more than 50 years—shuck their way through bushels of oysters hauled into port that morning. Healthy rivalry has made them expert hawkers who cheerfully badger all who walk by, occasionally talking up the oyster-as-aphrodisiac. You buy a dozen (for about €6), the women plate them and plunk a lemon on top, and you can then take your catch into any nearby restaurant and turn it into a meal. A short stroll southwest of the old town brings you to the fishermen's barrio of **El Berbés.** Here the day starts as early as 5 AM with the pungent and cacophonous *lonja* (fish market), where fishermen sell their morning catch to vendors and restaurants. **Ribera del Berbés,** facing the port, has several seafood restaurants, most with outdoor tables in summer. South of Vigo's old town is the hilltop **Parque del Castro** (✉ 📠*etween Praza de España and Praza do Rei, beside Av. Marqués de Alcedo*), a quiet, stately park with sandy paths, palm trees, mossy embankments, and stone benches. Atop a series of steps are the remains of an old fort and a *mirador* (lookout) with fetching views of Vigo's coastline and the Islas Cíes.

WHERE TO EAT

$$–$$$$ ✕**El Mosquito.** Signed photos from the likes of King Juan Carlos and Julio Iglesias cover the walls of this elegant rose- and stone-wall restaurant, open since 1928. The brother-and-sister team of Manolo and Carmiña have been at the helm for the last few decades; their special-

ties include *lenguado a la plancha* (grilled sole) and *navajas* (razor clams). Try the *tocinillos*, a sugary, caramel flan. The restaurant's name refers to an era when wine arrived in wooden barrels: If mosquitoes gathered at the barrel's mouth, it held good wine. ✉ *Praza da Pedra 4* ☎ *986/224441* ▭ *AE, DC, MC, V* ⊗ *Closed weekends and Aug.*

$–$$$ ✕ **Bar Cocedero La Piedra.** This jovial tapas bar does a roaring lunch trade with Vigo locals. The chefs serve heaping plates of *mariscos* (shellfish) at market prices. Fresh and fruity Albariño wines are the beverage of choice; the chummy, elbow-to-elbow crowd sits at round tables covered with paper. ✉ *Rúa Pescadería 3* ☎ *986/223765* ▭ *AE, DC, MC, V.*

$ ✕ **Tapas Areal.** This ample and lively bar flanked by ancient stone and exposed redbrick walls is a good spot for tapas and beer or Albariños and Ribeiros. ✉ *México 36* ☎ *986/418643* ▭ *MC, V.*

4

SHOPPING

Traditional musical instruments, such as the bagpipes, are studied, displayed, and sold at the **La Escuela de Artes y Oficios** (*Universidade Popular do Vigo* ✉ *Av. García Barbón 5* ☎ *986/228087*).

ISLAS CÍES

19 *35 km (21 mi) west of Vigo in Atlantic Ocean.*

The Cíes Islands are a nature reserve and one of the last unspoiled refuges on the Spanish coast. From July to September, about eight boats a day leave Vigo's harbor, returning later in the day, for the round-trip fare of €12. The 45-minute ride brings you to white-sand beaches. Birds abound, and the only land transportation is your own two feet: it takes about an hour to cross the main island. For camping reservations (required), call **Camping Islas Cíes** (☎ *986/438358* 🌐 *www.campingislascies.com*), open Easter week and June 15 through September 15.

BAIONA

20 *12 km (8 mi) southwest of Vigo.*

At the southern end of the AP9 freeway and the Ría de Vigo, Baiona (Bayona in Castilian) is a summer haunt of affluent Gallegos. When Columbus's *Pinta* landed here in 1492, Baiona became the first town to receive the news of the discovery of the New World. Once a castle, **Monte Real** is one of Spain's most popular paradors; walk around the battlements for superb views. Inland from Baiona's waterfront, Paseo Marítima, a jumble of streets has seafood restaurants and lively cafés and bars. Calle Ventura Misa is one of the main drags. On your way into or out of town, check out Baiona's **Roman bridge.** The best nearby beach is Praia de América, north of town toward Vigo.

WHERE TO STAY & EAT

$$$ ✕🏨 **Parador de Baiona.** This baronial parador was built inside the walls of
Fodor's Choice ★ a medieval castle on a hilltop fortified since 200 BC. The rooms are plush, and some have balconies with ocean views toward the Islas Cíes. Try the *entremeses variados* (mixed appetizers) for a seafood sampler ($$$–

$$$$), or *parillada de pescados* (grilled swordfish, salmon, and cod). *✉Ctra. de Baiona at Monterreal, 36300 ☎986/355000 🖷986/355076 🌐www.parador.es 122 rooms In-room: Wi-Fi. In-hotel: restaurant, bar, tennis court, pool, gym, beachfront ▭AE, DC, MC, V.*

TUI

21 *14 km (9 mi) southeast of Baiona, 26 km (16 mi) south of Vigo.*

From Vigo, take the scenic coastal route PO552, which goes up the banks of the Miño River along the Portuguese border, or if time is short, jump on the inland A55; both routes lead to Tui, where steep, narrow streets rich with emblazoned mansions suggest the town's past as one of the seven capitals of the Galician kingdom. Today it's an important border town; the mountains of Portugal are visible from the cathedral. Across the river in Portugal, the old fortress town of Valença contains reasonable shops, bars, restaurants, and a hotel with splendid views of Tui.

Crucial during the medieval wars between Castile and Portugal, Tui has a 13th-century **cathedral** that looks like a fortress. The cathedral's majestic cloister surrounds a lush formal garden. *✉Pl. de San Fernando s/n ☎986/600511* €2 *Daily 9:30–1:30 and 4–7.*

WHERE TO STAY & EAT

$$$ **Parador de Tui.** This granite-and-chestnut hotel on the bluffs overlooking the Miño has lobbies filled with rural antiques and paintings by local artists. Guest rooms are furnished with convincing reproductions. Views of the woods surround the dining room ($$–$$$$), where specialties from the river Miño include Atlantic salmon, lamprey eel, sea trout, and river trout. For dessert, try the the *pececitos*, almond-flavor pastries made by local convent nuns. *✉Av. del Portugal s/n, 36700 ☎986/600300 🖷986/602163 🌐www.parador.es 32 rooms In-room: Wi-Fi. In-hotel: restaurant, bar, tennis court, pool, parking (no fee) ▭AE, DC, MC, V.*

A CORUÑA & RÍAS ALTAS

Galicia's gusty, rainy northern coast has inspired local poets to wax lyrical about raindrops falling continuously on one's head. Don't worry, the sun does shine here, and it suffuses town and country with a golden glow. North of A Coruña, the Rías Altas (Upper Estuaries) notch the coast as you head east toward the Cantabrian Sea.

A CORUÑA

22 *57 km (35 mi) north of Santiago.*

One of Spain's busiest ports, A Coruña (La Coruña in Castilian) prides itself on being the most progressive city in the region. The weather can be fierce, wet, and windy—hence the glass-enclosed, white-pane galleries on the houses lining the harbor.

WHAT TO SEE

To see why sailors once nicknamed A Coruña *la ciudad de cristal* (the glass city), stroll **Dársena de la Marina,** said to be the longest seaside promenade in Europe. Although the congregation of boats is charming, the real sight is across the street: a long, gracefully curved row of houses. Built by fishermen in the 18th century, the houses actually face *away* from the sea—at the end of a long day, these men were tired of looking at the water. Nets were hung from the porches to dry, and fish was sold on the street below. When Galicia's first glass factory opened nearby, someone thought to enclose these porches in glass, like the latticed stern galleries of oceangoing galleons, to keep wind and rain at bay. The resulting **glass galleries** ultimately spread across the harbor and eventually throughout Galicia.

Plaza de María Pita is the focal point of the *ciudad vieja* (old town). Its north side is given over to the neoclassical **Palacio Municipal,** or city hall, built 1908–12 with three Italianate domes. The **monument** in the center, built in 1998, depicts the heroine herself, Maior (María) Pita, holding her lance. When England's notorious Sir Francis Drake arrived to sack A Coruña in 1589, the locals were only half finished building the defensive Castillo de San Antón, and a 13-day battle ensued. When María Pita's husband died, she took up his lance, slew the Briton who tried to plant the Union Jack here, and revived the exhausted Coruñesos, inspiring women to join the battle as well.

The 12th-century church of **Santiago** (⊠*Pl. de la Constitución s/n*), the oldest church in A Coruña, was the first stop on the *camino inglés* (English route) toward Santiago de Compostela. Originally Romanesque, it's now a hodgepodge, with Gothic arches, a baroque altarpiece, and two 18th-century rose windows.

The **Colegiata de Santa María** (⊠*Pl. de Santa María*) is a Romanesque beauty from the mid-13th century, often called Santa María del Campo (St. Mary of the Field) because it was once outside the city walls. The facade depicts the Adoration of the Magi; the celestial figures include St. Peter, holding the keys to heaven. A quirk of this church is that, because of an architectural miscalculation, the roof is too heavy for its supports, so the columns inside lean outward, and the buttresses outside have been thickened. Couples who want to get married in the old town book this poetic church far in advance.

At the northeastern tip of the old town is the **Castillo de San Antón** *(St. Anthony's Castle)*, a 16th-century fort. Inside is A Coruña's **Museum of Archaeology**, with remnants of the prehistoric Celtic culture that once thrived in these parts. The collection includes silver artifacts as well as pieces of the Celtic stone forts called *castros.* ☎*981/189850* *€2* ⊙*July and Aug., Tues.–Sat. 10–8:30, Sun. 10–2:30; Sept.–June, Tues.–Sat. 10–7, Sun. 10–2.*

Across town, on a hill, is the **Casa de las Ciencias** *(Science Museum)*, a hands-on museum where children can learn the principles of physics and technology. ⊠*Parque de Santa Margarita* ☎*981/189844* ⊕*www.casaciencias.org* *Museum €2, planetarium €1* ⊙*Sept.–June, daily 10–7; July and Aug., daily 11–9.*

Much of A Coruña sits on a peninsula, on the tip of which is the **Torre de Hercules**—the oldest still-functioning lighthouse in the world. Originally built during the reign of Trajan, the Roman emperor born in Spain in AD 98, the lighthouse was rebuilt in the 18th century and looks strikingly modern; all that remains from Roman times are inscribed foundation stones. Scale the 245 steps for superb views of the city and coastline—and if you're here on a summer weekend, return at night, when the tower opens for views of city lights along the Atlantic. Lining the approach to the lighthouse are sculptures depicting figures from Galician and Celtic legends. At the base of the structure, a museum displays items dug up during the restoration of the lighthouse and area. ⊠*Ctra. de la Torre s/n* ☎*981/223730* *€2* ⊙*Sept.–June, daily 10–6; July and Aug., Sun.–Thurs. 10–6, Fri. and Sat. 10–11:45 PM.*

Designed in the shape of a ship's sail by Japanese architect Arata Isozaki, the **Domus/Casa del Hombre** *(Museum of Mankind)* is dedicated to the study of the human being, particularly the human body. Many exhibits are interactive. An IMAX film shows a human birth. ⊠*C. Santa Teresa 1* ☎*981/189840* ⊕*www.casaciencias.org* *Museum €2, IMAX €1* ⊙*July and Aug., daily 11–9; Sept.–June, daily 10–7.*

WHERE TO STAY & EAT

$$$–$$$$ ✕ **Casa Pardo.** Near the port, this chic, double-decker dining room has soft ocher tones, with perfectly matched wood furniture and cool lighting. Try the *rape a la cazuela* (bay leaf–scented monkfish and potatoes drizzled with oil and sprinkled with paprika, baked in a clay casserole). For dessert, there's flaky pastry with cream or chocolate soufflé. ✉ *Novoa Santos 15* ☎ *981/280021* ▭ *AE, DC, MC, V* ⊗ *Closed Sun.*

$$–$$$$ ★ ✕ **Adega o Bebedeiro.** Steps from the ultramodern Domus, this tiny restaurant is beloved by locals for its authentic food and low prices. It feels like an old farmhouse, with stone walls, floors, and fireplace; pine tables and stools; dusty wine bottles (*adega* means "wine cellar"); and rustic implements. Appetizers, such as *setas rellenas de marisco y salsa holandesa* (wild mushrooms with seafood and hollandaise sauce), are followed by fresh fish at market prices. ✉ *C. Ángel Rebollo 34* ☎ *981/210609* ▭ *AE, DC, MC, V* ⊗ *Closed Mon., no dinner Sun.; closed last 2 wks in June and last 2 wks in Dec.*

$–$$$ ★ ✕ **La Penela.** Try at least a few crabs or mussels with béchamel, for which this restaurant is locally famous. If shellfish isn't your speed, make sure you sample the equally popular roast veal. Enjoy the smart, contemporary, bottle-green dining room while feasting on fresh fish and sipping some Albariño. The restaurant occupies a corner of the lively Praza María Pita. ✉ *Praza María Pita 12* ☎ *981/209200* ▭ *AE, DC, MC, V* ⊗ *Closed Sun. and Jan. 10–25.*

$$$$ **Hesperia Finisterre.** This grande dame, where the old town joins the bay, is the oldest of A Coruña's top hotels. A favorite with businessfolk and families, it has large, carpeted rooms with modern wood furnishings and bright upholstery. Ask for a room overlooking the bay. ✉ *Paseo del Parrote 2, 15001* ☎ *981/205400* 📠 *981/208462* 🌐 *www.hesperia-finisterre.com* *92 rooms* *In-room: Ethernet, Wi-Fi. In-hotel: restaurant, bar, tennis courts, pools, gym* ▭ *AE, DC, MC, V.*

$$ **Tryp Coruña.** It's not charming, per se—fluorescent lighting abounds—but soft blues and nautical prints offset this high-rise's shortcomings while reinforcing the maritime feel. Convenient to the El Corte Inglés department store and bus and train stations, it runs like a well-oiled machine. ✉ *Ramón y Cajal 53, 15001* ☎ *981/242711* 📠 *981/236728* *181 rooms* *In-hotel: bar* ▭ *AE, DC, MC, V.*

NIGHTLIFE

Begin your evening in the **Plaza de María Pita**—bars, cafés, and tapas bars proliferate off the plaza's western corners and farther inland. **Calles Franja, Riego de Agua, Barrera,** and **Galera** and the **Plaza del Humor** have many bars, some of which serve Ribeiro wine in bowls. Night owls head for the posh and pricey clubs around **Praia del Orzán** (Orzán Beach), particularly along Calle Juan Canalejo. For lower key entertainment, the old town has cozy taverns where you can grab a nightcap even as the new day dawns. Try **A Roda 2** (✉ *Capitán Troncoso 8* ☎ *981/228671*) for tapas (such as octopus in its own ink and garlic garbanzo beans) and a lively evening crowd.

4

SHOPPING

Calle Real has boutiques with contemporary fashions. A stroll down **Calle San Andres,** two blocks inland from Calle Real, or **Avenida Juan Flórez,** leading into the newer town, may yield some sartorial treasures. Galicia has spawned some of Spain's top designers, notably **Adolfo Dominguez** (✉*Av. Finisterre 3* ☎*981/252539*). For hats and Galician folk clothing, stop into **Sastrería Iglesias** (✉*Rua Rego do Auga 14* ☎*981/221634*)—founded 1864—where artisan José Luis Iglesias Rodrígues sells his textiles. Authentic Galician *zuecos* (hand-painted wooden clogs) are still worn in some villages to navigate mud; the cobbler **José López Rama** (✉*Rúa do Muiño 7* ☎*981/701068*) has a workshop 15 minutes south of A Coruña in the village of Carballo. **Alfares de Buño** (✉*Plazuela de los Angeles 6* ☎*No phone*) sells glazed terra-cotta ceramics from Bunho, 40 km (25 mi) west of A Coruña on C552. These crafts are prized by aficionados—to see where they're made, drive out to Bunho itself, where potters work in private studios all over town. Stop into **Alfarería y Cerámica de Buño** (✉*C. Barreiros s/n, Bunho* ☎*981/721658*) to see the results. A wide selection of classic blue-and-white pottery is sold at **Cerámicas del Castro** (✉*O Castro s/n, Sada* ☎*981/620200*), north of Coruña in Sada.

> **BUY A BAGPIPE**
>
> Already own a kilt but need an instrument to complete the ensemble? Visit a bagpipe workshop and buy the real thing at Betanzos' **Sellas y Gaitas** (✉*Cerca s/n* ☎*No phone*), open weekdays 10–1 and 5–8. If you'd like to tour a bagpipe museum, head to the town of Gijón.

BETANZOS

23 ★ *25 km (15 mi) east of A Coruña, 65 km (40 mi) northeast of Santiago.*

The charming, slightly ramshackle medieval town of Betanzos is still surrounded by parts of its old city wall. It was an important Galician port in the 13th century but is now silted up. The 1292 monastery of **San Francisco** was converted into a church in 1387 by the nobleman Fernán Perez de Andrade, whose magnificent sepulchre, to the left of the west door, has him lying on the backs of a stone bear and boar, with hunting dogs at his feet and an angel receiving his soul by his head. The 15th-century church of **Santa María de Azougue** has 15th-century statues that were stolen in 1981 but subsequently recovered. It's a few steps uphill from the church of San Francisco.The tailors' guild put up the Gothic-style church of **Santiago,** which includes a Door of Glory inspired by the one in Santiago's cathedral. Above the door is a carving of St. James as the Slayer of the Moors.

VILALBA

24 *87 km (52 mi) east of A Coruña.*

Known as *Terra Cha* (Flat Land) or the Galician Mesopotamia, Vilalba is the source of several rivers, most notably the Miño, which flows down into Portugal. Hills and knolls add texture to the plain.

WHERE TO STAY & EAT

$$$$ **Parador Condes de Vilalba.** Part of the inn is in a massive 15th-century tower that was once a fortress. A drawbridge leads to the two-story lobby, hung with tapestries. The three large octagonal chambers in the tower have beam ceilings, wood floors, hand-carved Spanish furniture, and chandeliers. The restaurant ($$–$$$) offers empanada *de Rax,* made of beef loin, and empanada *de atún* (with tuna); for dessert, order the *San Simón,* a cone-shape, birch-smoked cheese served with apples or pears. ✉ *Valeriano Valdesuso s/n, 27800* ☎ *982/510011* 📠 *982/510090* 🌐 *www.parador.es* *48 rooms* *In-hotel: restaurant, bar, gym* *AE, DC, MC, V.*

4

MONDOÑEDO

25 *34 km (20 mi) northeast of Vilalba.*

Founded in 1156, this town was one of the seven capitals of the kingdom of Galicia from the 16th to early 19th century. The **cathedral,** consecrated in 1248, has a museum, a bishop's tomb with inlaid stone, and medieval murals showing the Slaying of the Innocents and St. Peter. The cathedral dominates the ancient **Plaza Mayor,** where a medieval pageant and market are held the first Sunday in August. The quiet streets and squares are filled with old buildings, monasteries, and churches, and include a medieval Jewish quarter.

The shop **El Rey de las Tartas** (✉ *Obispo Sarmiento 2* ☎ *982/521178*) is known for its dessert pies, or *tartas,* made with pastry, sponge cake, *cabello de ángel* ("angel's hair," a filling of pumpkin and syrup, composed of fine strands), and almonds.

VIVEIRO

26 *81 km (50 mi) northeast of Vilalba.*

★ The once-turreted city walls of this popular summer resort are still partially intact. Two festivals are noteworthy: the **Semana Santa** processions, in which penitents follow religious processions on their knees, and the **Rapa das Bestas,** a colorful roundup of wild horses the first Sunday in July (on nearby Monte Buyo).

WHERE TO STAY & EAT

$$ **Hotel Ego.** The view of the *ría* from this hilltop hotel outside Viveiro is unbeatable—you can even see the river's tiny islets—and every room has it. Rooms are carpeted and have enormous mirrors and vanity tables. The glassed-in breakfast room faces the ría and a cascade of trees; on a rainy day, you'd much rather be cooped up here than in

town. Adjoining the hotel is the elegant Nito restaurant ($$–$$$$), which serves excellent Galician cuisine, such as *percebes* (goose barnacles), spider crab, and lobster. ✉*Playa de Area, off N642, 27850* ☎*982/560987* 📠*982/561762* *29 rooms* *In-hotel: restaurant, bar* ▭*AE, MC, V.*

OFF THE BEATEN PATH

Distinctive blue-and-white-glazed contemporary ceramics are made at Cerámica de Sargadelos (✉*Ctra. Paraño s/n, Cervo* ☎*982/557841*), 21 km (13 mi) east of Viveiro. Watch artisans work weekdays 8:30–12:30 and 2:30–5:30. Shop hours are 11–2 and 4–7 on weekends and holidays.

RIBADEO

27 *50 km (31 mi) southeast of Viveiro.*

Perched on the broad *ría* of the same name, Ribadeo is the last coastal town before Asturias. The views up and across the estuary are marvelous—depending on the wind, the waves appear to roll *across* the ría rather than straight inland. Salmon and trout fishermen congregate upriver. Take the scenic walk or drive north of town to the **Illa de la Pancha** lighthouse (a 5-km [3-mi] round-trip), connected to the coastal cliffs by a small bridge. If the bridge is closed, savor the briny air around the grassy cliff top.

WHERE TO STAY & EAT

$$$ **Parador de Ribadeo.** Most rooms here have glassed-in sitting areas with views (Room 208 has the best) across the ría to Asturias. Parquet floors and harvest-yellow walls are accented by watercolors and etchings of the area. In the dining room ($$–$$$$) a cornucopia of shellfish is served, much of it swimming around in a holding tank. Try the *sopa de mariscos,* seafood soup with a light pastry top, and the ice cream that's been flavored with tetilla cheese and drizzled with honey. Fishing, horseback riding, and boating can be arranged. ✉*Amador Fernández 7, 27700* ☎*982/128825* 📠*982/128346* 🌐*www.parador.es* *46 rooms, 1 suite* *In-hotel: restaurant, bar* ▭*AE, DC, MC, V.*

WESTERN ASTURIAS

As you cross into the Principality of Asturias, the intensely green countryside continues, belying the fact that this is a major mining region once exploited by the Romans for its iron- and gold-rich earth. Asturias is bordered to the southeast by the imposing Picos de Europa.

LUARCA

28 *75 km (47 mi) east of Ribadeo, 92 km (57 mi) northeast of Oviedo.*

The A8 *autopista* (freeway) wanders along the entire Asturian coast toward Oviedo. The village of Luarca is tucked into a cove at the end of a final twist of the Río Negro, with a fishing port and, to the west, a sparkling bay. The town is a maze of cobblestone streets, stone stairways, and whitewashed houses, with a harborside decorated with

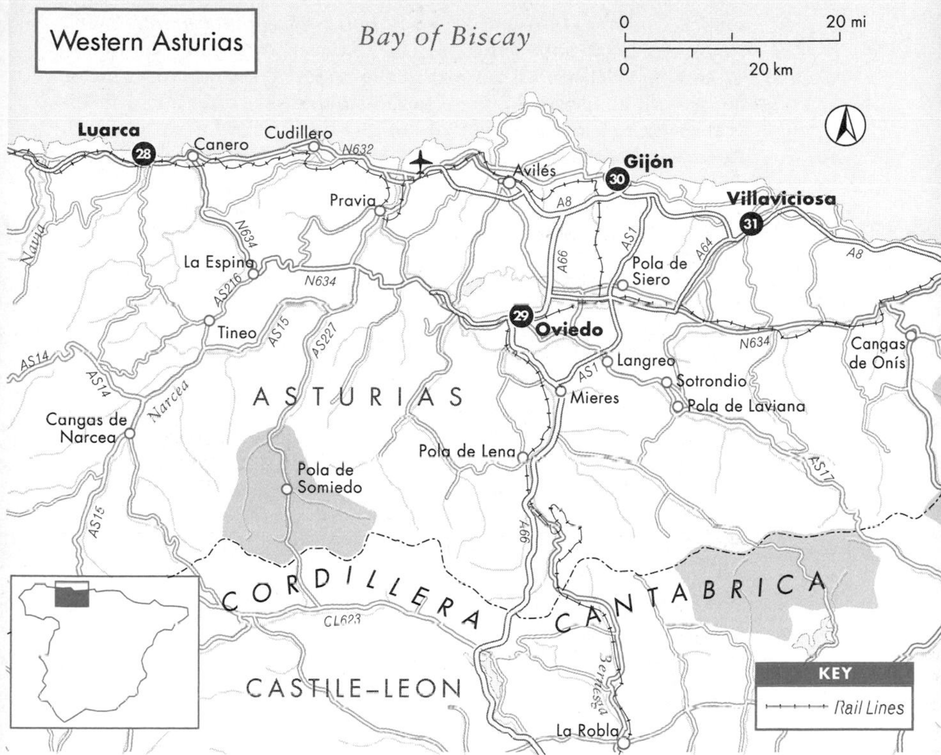

painted flowerpots. The aromas wafting from the restaurants may tempt you to stop for some freshly caught seafood.

WHERE TO STAY & EAT

$$–$$$$ ★ **Casa Consuelo.** Opened in 1935, Casa Consuelo, one of the most popular spots on Spain's northern coast, is famed for *merluza* (hake) with the northern Spanish delicacy *angulas* (baby eels) and blue cheese (at about €55 for two, depending on market prices). This dish and the busy restaurant itself are not to be missed. *Ctra. N634, Km 511, 6 km (4 mi) west of Luarca, Otur 985/641809 www.casaconsuelo.com Reservations essential AE, DC, MC, V Closed Mon.*

$–$$$ **El Barómetro.** This small, family-run seafood eatery in the middle of the harbor front has an inexpensive *menú del día* (daily menu) and a good choice of local fresh fish. For a bit more money, you can dig into *bogavante*, a large-claw lobster. *Paseo del Muelle 4 985/470662 MC, V Closed late Sept.–late Oct. No dinner Wed.*

$$ **Hotel Villa La Argentina.** This charming Asturian mansion on the hill above Luarca was built in 1899 by a wealthy "Indiano" (Spaniard who made his fortune in South America). On site is a small antiques museum. A restaurant is in the old coach house, surrounded by palm trees and imported shrubs. *Villar de Luarca s/n, 33700 985/640102 985/640973 www.villalaargentina.com 9*

rooms, 3 suites In-room: Wi-Fi. In-hotel: restaurant (summer only), bar, tennis court, pool DC, MC, V Closed early Jan.–mid-Mar.

$$ **Torre de Villademoros.** An artistically restored 18th-century manor house with an elevated *panera* (grain-storage structure) and a medieval tower, this lovely retreat 14 km (8½ mi) east of Luarca is a find. Rooms and both sea and meadow views are superb, as is the cuisine. *Villademoros, Valdés s/n, 33788 985/645264 985/645265 10 rooms In-room: no a/c. In-hotel: restaurant AE, DC, MC, V Closed weekdays Nov.–Mar.*

OVIEDO

29 *92 km (57 mi) southeast of Luarca, 50 km (31 mi) southeast of Cudillero, 30 km (19 mi) south of Gijón.*

Inland, the Asturian countryside starts to look a bit more prosperous. Wooden, thatch-roof horreos strung with golden bundles of drying corn replace the stark granite sheds of Galicia. A drive through the hills and valleys brings you to the capital city, Oviedo. Though primarily industrial, Oviedo has three of the most famous pre-Romanesque churches in Spain and a large university, giving it both ancient charm and youthful zest. Start your explorations with the two exquisite 9th-century chapels outside the city, on the slopes of Monte Naranco.

WHAT TO SEE

★ The church of **Santa María del Naranco,** with superb views, and its plainer sister, **San Miguel de Lillo** 300 yards uphill, are the jewels of an early architectural style called Asturian pre-Romanesque, a more primitive, hulking, defensive line that preceded Romanesque architecture by nearly three centuries. Commissioned as part of a summer palace by King Ramiro I when Oviedo was the capital of Christian Spain, these masterpieces have survived for more than 1,000 years. The **Reception Center** (*985/114901 Wed.–Mon. 11–1:30 and 4–6*) near the site provides videos that explain Asturian pre-Romanesque architecture. *Ctra. de los Monumentos, 2 km (1 mi) north of Oviedo 676/032087 €2.20 (includes guided tour), free Mon. (without guided tour) Apr.–Sept., Mon.–Sat. 9:30–1 and 3:30–7, Sun. 9:30–1; Oct.–Mar., Mon.–Sat. 10–12:30 and 3–4:30, Sun. 10–12:30.*

Oviedo's Gothic **cathedral** was built between the 14th- and the 16th centuries around the city's most cherished monument, the **Cámara Santa** (Holy Chamber). King Ramiro's predecessor, Alfonso the Chaste (792–842), built this chamber to hide the treasures of Christian Spain during the long struggle with the Moors. Heavily damaged during the Spanish civil war, it has since been rebuilt. Inside is the gold-leaf **Cross of the Angels,** commissioned by Alfonso the Chaste in 808 and encrusted with pearls and jewels. On the left is the more elegant **Victory Cross,** actually a jeweled sheath crafted in 908 to cover the oak cross used by Pelayo in the battle of Covadonga. The crosses and other treasures were stolen from the cathedral in 1977 but were recovered relatively intact as thieves tried to spirit them out of Europe through Portugal. *Pl. Alfonso II El Casto 985/221033 Cathedral free, Cámara*

Santa €1.25, museum €3 ⏲Sept.–June. Mon.–Sat. 10–1 and 4–7 (4–8 in July and Aug.), Sun. for mass only, at 10 AM *and 11* AM.

From the cathedral, look directly across the Plaza Alfonso for the still-inhabited 15th-century **Palacio de la Rúa,** the oldest palace in town. Near the Palacio de la Rúa, on Calle San Francisco, is the beautifully clean 16th-century **Antigua Universidad de Oviedo.** Behind the cathedral, the **Museo Arqueológico,** housed in the splendid Monastery of San Vicente, contains fragments of pre-Romanesque buildings. ✉*San Vicente 3* ☎*985/215405* *Free* ⏲*Tues.–Sat. 10–1:30 and 4–6, Sun. 11–1.*

WHERE TO STAY & EAT

$$$–$$$$ ★ ✕**Casa Fermín.** Skylights, plants, and an air of modernity belie the age of this sophisticated pink-and-granite restaurant, which opened in 1924. Founder Luis Gil introduced traditional Asturian cuisine at seminars around the world. Specialties include *fabada* (bean-and-sausage stew) and wild game in season. The wine cellar is well stocked. ✉*Calle San Francisco 8* ☎*985/216452* *www.casafermin.com* *AE, DC, MC, V* ⏲*Closed Sun.*

$$$ ★ ✕**La Máquina.** For the best *fabada* (bean-and-sausage stew) in Asturias, head 6 km (4 mi) outside Oviedo toward Avilés and stop at the farmhouse with the miniature locomotive out front. This L-shape, whitewashed dining room has attracted diners from across Spain for decades, some of whom think nothing of making a weekend trip solely for the purpose of eating here. ✉*Av. Conde de Santa Bárbara 59, Lugones* ☎*985/263636* *DC, MC, V* ⏲*Closed Sun. and mid-June–mid-July. No dinner.*

$$$$ Fodor's Choice ★ **Hotel de la Reconquista.** In an 18th-century hospice emblazoned with a huge, stone coat of arms, the ultraluxurious Reconquista costs almost twice as much as any other hotel in Asturias. The wide lobby, encircled by a balcony, is decked out with velvet upholstery and 18th-century paintings. A pianist entertains nightly. Guest rooms are large and modern, with comfortable beds and large armchairs. ✉*Calle Gil de Jaz 16, 33004* ☎*985/241100* *985/241166* *www.hoteldelareconquista.com* *132 rooms, 10 suites* *In-room: Wi-Fi. In-hotel: restaurant, bar* *AE, DC, MC, V.*

$$$ **NH Principado.** Try this hotel if you prize friendliness over flash. The NH chain is modern and functional, but this branch feels more distinguished than most. The hotel is conveniently located between the cathedral and the Plaza de la Escandalera. ✉*Calle San Francisco 6, 33003* ☎*985/217792* *985/213946* *www.nh-hoteles.com* *97 rooms* *In-room: Wi-Fi. In hotel: restaurant, bar* *AE, DC, MC, V.*

NIGHTLIFE & THE ARTS

The **Teatro Municipal** presents plays and concerts; check newspapers for schedules. The old town's main strip of dance clubs is on **Calle Canóniga.** A rather rowdy town after dark, Oviedo has plenty in the way of loud live music. **Calle Carta Puebla** is packed with pubs, many of which are Irish owing to the region's Celtic heritage. If you're still awake when the old town goes to sleep, try **Sir Lawrence** (✉*Calle Eugenio Tamayo 3* ☎*No phone*), where on the weekends you can dance into daylight.

4

SHOPPING

Some antiques shops are clustered together for a few blocks on **Calle de Mon.** On Thursday and Sunday mornings an outdoor market, **El Rastrillo,** which has some real finds (albeit amid some not-to-worthy items), is held in El Fontan. Shops throughout the city carry **azabache jewelry** made of jet. For handcrafted leather bags and belts, check out **Artesania Escanda** (✉ *Jovellanos 5* ☎ *985/210467*). Vacuum-packed *fabada* is sold at **Casa Veneranda** (✉ *Melquíades Álvarez 23* ☎ *985/212454*).

> **ROMAN BATHS**
>
> Western Asturias, a major mining region, was once a part of the Roman Gold Route. In Gijón you can view the Roman baths, *Termas Romanas.*

GIJÓN

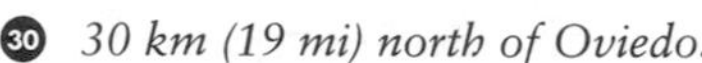

30 *30 km (19 mi) north of Oviedo.*

Full of hidden hot spots and friendly people, Gijón is part fishing port, part summer resort, and part university town, packed with cafés.

WHAT TO SEE

The promenade along **Praia San Lorenzo** extends from one end of town to the other. Across the narrow peninsula and the Plaza Mayor is the harbor, where the fishing fleet comes in with the day's catch. The steep peninsula is the old fishermen's quarter, **Cimadevilla,** now the hub of Gijón's nightlife. From the park at the highest point on the headland, beside Basque sculptor Eduardo Chillida's massive sculpture *Elogio del Horizonte* (In Praise of the Horizon), there's a panoramic view of the coast and city.

Termas Romanas (*Roman baths*), dating to the time of Augustus, are under the plaza at the end of the beach. ✉ *Campo Valdés* ☎ *985/345147* 🎫 *€2.35* ⏲ *Tues.–Sat. 10–1 and 5–8, Sun. 11–2 and 5–7.*

The **Museo de la Gaita** (*Bagpipe Museum*) is across the river on the eastern edge of town, past Parque Isabel la Católica. A collection of bagpipes from all over the world is augmented by workshops where you can see the instruments crafted. ✉ *Paseo del Doctor Fleming 877, La Güelga s/n* ☎ *985/332244* 🎫 *€2.35* ⏲ *Sept.–June, Tues.–Sat. 10–1 and 5–8, Sun. 11–2 and 5–7; July and Aug., Tues.–Sat. 10–1:30 and 5–9, Sun. 11–2 and 5–8.*

WHERE TO STAY & EAT

$$$–$$$$ ✕ **El Puerto.** This glass-enclosed dining room overlooks the harbor and serves fine, imaginative shellfish, seafood, and meats—a specialty is *merluza con bogavante en salsa verde* (hake and lobster with a parsley sauce). Feast on a four-plate menu or a *parillada de mariscos* (mixed platter of grilled shellfish). Game is served in season, and the wine list is substantial. ✉ *Calle Claudio Alvargonzález* ☎ *985/349096* ✍ *Reservations essential* 💳 *AE, DC, MC, V* ⏲ *No dinner Sun.*

$$$ ✕🏨 **Parador de Gijón.** In an old water mill in a park not far from the San Lorenzo Beach, this parador is one of the simplest and friendliest in Spain. Rooms in the newer wing are small, with bleached-wood floors and thick pine shutters, but most have wonderful views over the adjacent lake or

the park. In the restaurant ($–$$$), try the *tigres* (spicy stuffed mussels), *pimientos de piquillo rellenos* (green peppers stuffed with squid, mushrooms, and rice), or *oricios* (sea urchins), served raw or steamed with lemon juice or a spicy sauce. For dessert, try fresh figs (in season) with Cabrales cheese. ✉*Calle Torcuato Fernández Miranda 15, 33203* ☎*985/370511* 🖷*985/370233* 🌐*www.parador.es* *40 rooms* *In-room: Wi-Fi. In-hotel: restaurant* 💳*AE, DC, MC, V.*

CIDER HOUSE RULES

In order to aerate the cider, cider houses generally insist that either you or your waiter pour cider correctly—that is, from overhead to a glass held at knee level. This process is called the *escancio* (pouring), a much-valued skill around which entire tournaments are held. Give it a try. Spilling is allowed. The region's main cider center is in Villaviciosa.

4

EN ROUTE

East of Gijón is apple-orchard country, the source of the famous hard cider of Asturias. Rolling green hills against a highland backdrop, grazing cows, and white chalets add up to a remarkably Alpine landscape.

VILLAVICIOSA

31 *32 km (20 mi) east of Gijón, 45 km (28 mi) northeast of Oviedo.*

Cider-capital Villaviciosa has a big dairy and several bottling plants as well as an attractive old quarter. The Hapsburg Emperor Charles V first set foot in Spain just down the road from here. The town's annual five-day Fiesta de la Manzana (Apple Festival) begins the first Friday after September 8. To taste the regional hard cider, stop into **El Congreso** (✉*Pl. Generalísimo 25* ☎*No phone*), a popular *sidrería* (cider house) that also serves tasty tapas and shellfish straight from the tank. If time allows, check out the restored 15th-century **castle** (✉*3 km [2 mi] west of town on N632*). The beautiful sandstone walls, turrets, and archways now enclose a modern hotel and restaurant.

WHERE TO STAY

$ **Carlos I.** From the common-area wood floors, antique furniture, potted plants, and oil paintings to the cozy bar-cafeteria, this late-17th-century mansion is loaded with character. Guest rooms are spotless and relatively large. ✉*Pl. Carlos I 4, 33300* ☎*985/890121* 🖷*985/890051* *16 rooms* *In-hotel: bar* 💳*MC, V.*

THE PICOS DE EUROPA

With craggy peaks soaring up to the 8,688-foot Torre Cerredo, the northern skyline of the Picos de Europa has helped seafarers and fishermen navigate the Bay of Biscay for ages. To the south, pilgrims on their way to Santiago enjoy distant but inspiring views of the snowcapped range from the plains of Castile between Burgos and León. Over the years, regular, very heavy rain and snow have created canyons plunging 3,000 feet, natural arches, caves, and sinkholes (one of which is 5,213 feet deep). The Picos de Europa National Park, covering 413½-square km (257 square mi), is perfect for climbers and trekkers. Explore the main trails, hang glide, ride horses, cycle, or canoe. Two adventure-sports centers are in Cangas de Onís, near the Roman Bridge.

RIBADESELLA

32 *67 km (40 mi) east of Gijón, 84 km (50 mi) northeast of Oviedo.*

The N632 twists around green hills dappled with eucalyptus groves and allows you glimpses of the sea and sandy beaches down plunging valleys. The snowcapped Picos de Europa loom inland. This fishing village and beach resort is famous for copious fresh seafood, its cave, and the international canoe races held on the Sella River the first Saturday of August.

Discovered in 1968 by Señor Bustillo, the **Cueva Tito Bustillo** (Tito Bustillo Cave) has 20,000-year-old paintings on par with those in Lascaux, France, and Altamira. Giant horses and deer prance about the walls. To protect the paintings, no more than 375 visitors are allowed inside each day. The guided tour is in Spanish.There's also a museum of Asturian cave finds open year-round. ☎ *985/861120* ⊕ *www.titobustillo.com* 🎟 *€4* ⊙ *Museum and cave Apr.–Sept., Wed.–Sun. 10–5.*

LLANES

33 *40 km (25 mi) east of Ribadesella.*

This sprightly beach town is on a pristine stretch of the Costa Verde (Green Coast). Hug the shore in either direction outside town for vistas of cliffs looming over white-sand beaches and isolated caves.

WHAT TO SEE

The peaceful, well-conserved **Plaza Cristo Rey** marks the center of the old town, partially surrounded by the remains of its medieval walls. The 13th-century church of **Santa María** rises over the square. Nearby, off Calle Alfonso IX, a medieval tower houses the tourist office. A long canal, connected to a small harbor, cuts through the heart of Llanes, and along its banks rise yellow- and salmon-painted houses with glass galleries, against a backdrop of the Picos de Europa. At the daily portside fish market, usually held around 1 PM, vendors display heaping mounds of freshly caught seafood. Steps from the old town is **Playa del Sablón,** a little swath of sand that gets crowded on summer weekends. On the eastern edge of town is the larger **Playa de Toró.** Just 1 km (½ mi) east of Llanes is one of the area's most secluded beaches, the immaculate **Playa Ballota,** with private coves for picnicking and one of the few stretches of nudist sand in Asturias. West of Llanes, the most pleasant beaches lie between the towns of Barro and Celorio. Farther west (8 km [5 mi] from Llanes) is partially nudist **Playa de Torimbia,** a wild, virgin beach yet untouched by development. You can reach it only via footpath, roughly a 15-minute walk.

Dotting the Asturian coast east and west of Llanes are *bufones* (blowholes), cave like cavities, which occur nowhere else in Spain. Active blowholes shoot streams of water as high as 100 feet into the air;

unfortunately, it's hard to predict when this will happen, as it depends on the tide and the size of the surf. They are clearly marked so you can find them, and there are barriers to protect you when they expel water. There's a blowhole east of Playa Ballota; try to watch it in action from the **Mirador Panorámico La Boriza,** near the entrance to the golf course. If you miss it, the view is still worth a stop—on a clear day you can see the coastline all the way east to Santander.

WHERE TO STAY & EAT

$–$$$ ✕**Mirentxu.** Minutes from the fish market, near the small harbor bobbing with colorful fishing boats, this friendly Basque-influenced place serves heaping portions of grilled and fried fish. ✉*Calle Marinero 14* ☎*985/402236* ▭*DC, MC, V* ⊙*Closed Oct.–June.*

$$ **La Posada de Babel.** This exquisite family-run inn just outside Llanes has roaring fires in its public rooms. Expect plenty of personal attention here. One guest room is in a converted granary. ✉*La Pereda s/n, 33509* ☎*985/402525* 📠*985/402622* 🌐*www.laposadadebabel.com* *12 rooms* *In-hotel: restaurant, bar, bicycles* ▭*DC, MC, V* ⊙*Closed Nov.–Feb.*

4

SPORTS & THE OUTDOORS

Three kilometers (2 mi) east of Llanes, near the village of Cué, is the 18-hole **Club de Golf La Cuesta** (☎*985/403319* 🌐*www.golflacuesta.com*). You could hardly ask for a more beautiful location: atop a plateau 300 feet above sea level. Nine holes have views of the Asturian coastline, with all its misty coves and crashing waves; the other nine face the towering Picos de Europa.

CANGAS DE ONÍS

34 *25 km (16 mi) south of Ribadesella, 70 km (43 mi) east of Oviedo.*

The first capital of Christian Spain, Cangas de Onís is also the unofficial capital of the Picos de Europa National Park. Partly in the narrow valley carved by the Sella River, it has the feel of a mountain village. A high, humpback **medieval bridge** (also known as the Puente Romano, or Roman Bridge, because of its style) spans the Sella River gorge with a reproduction of Pelayo's Victory Cross, or the Cruz de la Victoria, dangling underneath. To help plan your rambles, consult the scale model of the park outside the **Picos de Europa visitor center** (✉*Casa Dago, Av. Covadonga 43* ☎*985/848614*). The store opposite (at No. 22), El Llagar, sells maps and guidebooks, a few in English.

WHERE TO STAY & EAT

$–$$$ ✕**Sidrería Los Arcos.** This busy tavern with lots of polished wood serves local cider, fine Spanish wines, and sizzling T-bone steaks. *Revuelto de morcilla* (scrambled eggs with blood sausage) is served on *torto de maiz* (a corn pastry base). ✉*Pl. del Ayuntamiento, enter on Av. Covadonga* ☎*985/849277* ▭*AE, MC, V.*

$$$ ★ ✕**Parador de Cangas de Onís.** On the banks of the Sella River, just west of Cangas, this friendly parador is part 8th-century Benedictine monastery and part modern wing. The older building, connected to

A GOOD TOUR: THE PICOS DE EUROPA

The best-known road trip in the Picos connects Cangas de Onís and Riaño along the twisting Sella Gorge, the **Ruta de los Beyos** on the N625 road, a two-hour drive up to the pass at **Puerto del Pontón** (Pontón Pass; 4,232 feet). Just beyond the pass, turn left (northeast) for a drive up to the **Puerto de Panderruedas** (4,757 feet) for a panoramic view of the peaks, especially in the early evening sun. From here you can descend northeast to the town of Posada de Valdeón and continue on to Caín for a look at the upper end of the famous Ruta del Cares.

For the **Ruta del Cares,** drive east on the AS114 from Cangas de Onís toward Panes, stopping just before Arenas de Cabrales: here the road descends a wide valley and reaches a *mirador* (lookout) onto the **Naranjo de Bulnes,** a huge tooth of rock way up in the peaks. The mountain was named for its occasional tendency to glow orange, *naranja,* at sunrise and sunset. Turn south in Arenas de Cabrales into the AS264 road to reach Poncebos, and leave the car near here for the four-hour Ruta de Cares walk to Caín through the **Garganta de Cares** gorge. The canyon presents itself fairly soon, so you can turn back without pangs if you don't want to make the full hike.

This route is popular, so arrive in Poncebos early in the day to avoid parking problems. You can also enter the Ruta at the other end—from **Puerto de Pontón,** a road leads to Puerto de Panderruedas, Posada de Valdeón, and Caín.

If you have another day, leave Cangas and drive via Panes and Potes around the entire park. Consider relocating to the southern side and staying at the **Parador de Fuente Dé.** South of Panes, turn right at Urdón's hydroelectric power station to Tresviso for unforgettable views and a chance to buy some local cheese. South of La Hermida on the N621 the **Garganta de La Hermida** cuts through sheer 600-foot limestone cliffs up to Potes.

West of Potes off the CA185 is the left turn for the **Monasterio de Santo Toribio de Liébana,** with a 13th-century Gothic church and 17th-century cloisters. The CA185 ends at Fuente Dé, where a cable car can whisk you to the top of the Picos. South of Potes the N621 continues south to Riaño, a two-hour drive. About halfway there, **Puerta de San Glorio** is the jumping-off point for the 2.2-km (1.3-mi) walk up to the Monumento al Oso, where a white stone bear marks another splendid view.

the newer one by a glass tunnel, has 11 period-style rooms, some with four-poster beds. Excellent local dishes ($$–$$$), such as *merluza del Cantabrica a la sidra* (hake cooked in cider) garnished with asparagus, are served in the bright dining room. ✉ *Monasterio de San Pedro de Villanueva, Ctra. N624, from N634, take right turn for Villanueva, 33550* ☎ *985/849402* 🖷 *985/849520* 🌐 *www.parador.es* *64 rooms* *In-hotel: restaurant, bar* 💳 *AE, DC, MC, V.*

$$ **Aultre Naray.** This 19th-century mansion overlooking the Escapa mountain range is a rare find. It's perfectly placed for hiking, camping, canoeing, and swimming (all of which the staff can help organize). It's not rustic, though—guest rooms have modern furniture, plenty of

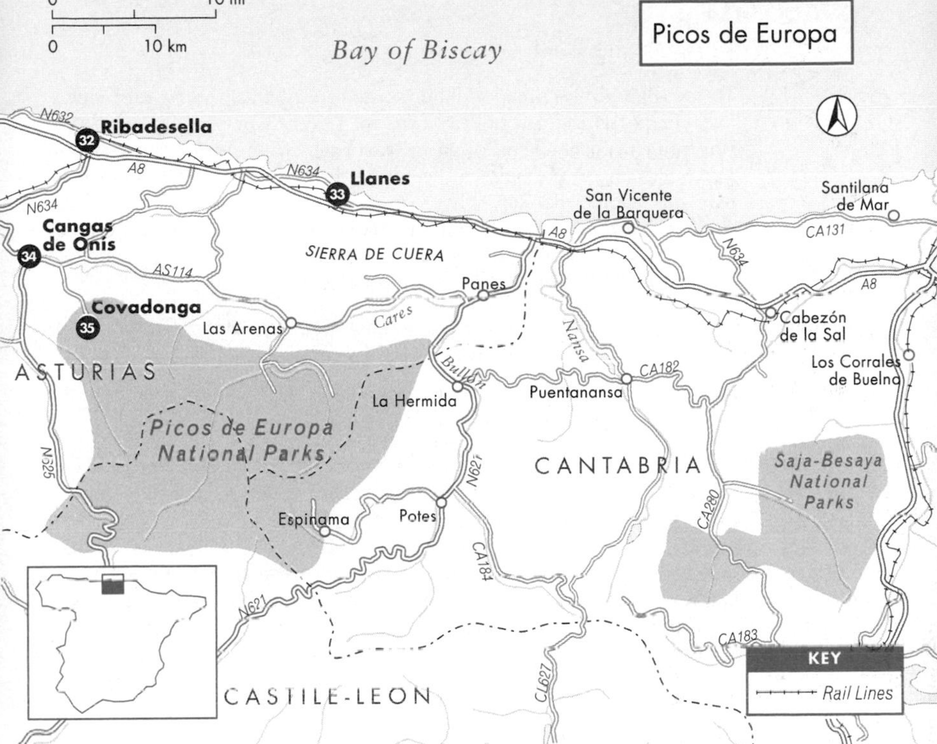

light, and, in some cases, pleasant sitting rooms. The hotel is 15 km (9 mi) east of town. ✉*N634, Km 335, Peruyes, 33547* ☎*985/840808* 🖷*985/840848* 🌐*www.aultrenaray.com* *10 rooms* *In-hotel: restaurant, bar* ▭*DC, MC, V.*

$$ **Hotel Los Lagos.** Each of the four floors of this bustling modern hotel has a different color scheme, ranging from cream to blue. Rooms have modern furniture and white-tile bathrooms. The hotel is in the center of town, near the tourist office. ✉*Jardines del Ayuntamiento 3, 33550* ☎*985/849421* 🖷*985/848405* 🌐*www.loslagos.as* *45 rooms* *In-room: no a/c, Wi-Fi. In-hotel: restaurant, bar* ▭*AE, MC, V.*

$ **Hospedería del Peregrino.** This simple but adequate hotel looks out at a magnificent nearby church. Rooms are small but cozy and decorated with abundant wood furnishings and checked curtains. ✉*AS 262 s/n, Covadonga 33589* ☎*985/846047* 🖷*985/846051* 🌐*www.picosdeuropa.net/peregrino* *7 rooms* *In-room: no a/c. In-hotel: restaurant, bar* ▭*AE, DC, MC, V* ⏲*Closed Dec.–Feb.*

¢ **La Naturaleza.** Poised at the foot of the Ruta del Cares, this place has views of Arenas de Cabrales and the Sella River. Four comfy rooms come with large, clean bathrooms. ✉*Calle La Segada, 33554* ☎*985/846487* 🖷*985/846101* *4 rooms* *In-room: no a/c. In-hotel: restaurant, bar* ▭*No credit cards* ⏲*Closed Dec. and Jan.*

COVADONGA

35 *14 km (9 mi) southeast of Cangas de Onís.*

To see high alpine meadowland, some rare Spanish lakes, and views over the peaks and out to sea (if the mist ever disperses), take the narrow road up past Covadonga to **Lake Enol**, stopping for the view en route. Starting to the right of the lake, a three-hour walk takes in views from the **Mirador del Rey**, where you can find the grave of pioneering climber Pedro Pidal. Farther up the road from Lake Enol are a summer-only tourist office and **Lake Ercina**, where Pope John Paul II picnicked during his 1989 tour of Asturias and Galicia.

NEED A BREAK?

Near Lake Enol is the Restaurante el Casín (✉ *Ctra. Santander–Oviedo s/n, Ribadesella* ☎ *985/860231*), with a small terrace bar overlooking the mountains and the lake. The set menu is €9; à la carte options include roasts and restorative *fabada* bean stews. It's closed January and February.

★ Covadonga's **shrine** is considered the birthplace of Spain. Here, in 718, a handful of sturdy Asturian Christians led by Don Pelayo took refuge in the Cave of St. Mary, about halfway up a cliff, where they prayed to the Virgin Mary to give them strength to turn back the Moors. Pelayo and his followers resisted the superior Moorish forces and set up a Christian kingdom that eventually led to the Reconquest. The cave has an 18th-century statue of the Virgin and Don Pelayo's grave. Covadonga itself has a **basilica,** and the **museum** has the treasures donated to the Virgin of the Cave, including a crown studded with more than 1,000 diamonds. ☎ *985/846096* *€3* *Daily 10:30–2 and 4–7:30.*

WHERE TO STAY & EAT

$$$ **Parador de Fuente Dé.** You can find this modern parador in a valley beside a cable car that ascends a soaring rock face to 2,705 feet in about four minutes. Somewhat spartan, it's a fine no-frills base for serious climbers and walkers and has a good restaurant ($$–$$$) with *cocido lebaniego* (a sturdy local stew) and steaks topped with Cabrales, the local blue cheese. The parador is east of the Cantabrian border, 23 km (14 mi) west of Potes. ✉ *Fuente Dé, 39588* ☎ *942/736651* *942/736654* *www.parador.es* *78 rooms* *In-hotel: restaurant, bar* *AE, DC, MC, V* *Closed Dec.–Feb.*

GALICIA & ASTURIAS ESSENTIALS

To research prices, get advice from other travelers, and book travel arrangements, visit www.fodors.com.

TRANSPORTATION

For more on travel to and in Galicia & Asturias, see the Galicia & Asturias Planner at the beginning of the chapter.

BY AIR

Airport Information **Aeropuerto de Alvedro** (✉ *A Coruña* ☎ *981/187200*). **Aeropuerto de Labacolla** (✉ *Santiago de Compostela* ☎ *981/547500*). **Aero-**

puerto de Peinador (✉ *Vigo* ☎ *986/268200*). **Aeropuerto de Ranon** (✉ *Oviedo* ☎ *985/127500*).

BY BIKE

The official *El Camino de Santiago en Bicicleta* leaflet available from **Información Xacobeo** or from the Santiago tourist office (⇨ Visitor Information) warns that the approximately 800 km (525 mi) route from the French border to Santiago is a very tough bike trip—bridle paths, dirt tracks, rough stones, and mountain passes. The best time of year to tackle it is late spring or early autumn. Tourist offices in Asturias sell the booklet *Rutas de Montaña, Senderismo, Montañismo y Bicicleta de Montaña*, which outlines different routes, for about €1.20. Bici Total rents out bicycles, as do some hotels and campsites.

4

Bike Routes **Información Xacobeo** (✉ *Pabellón de Galicia, San Lázaro s/n, Santiago de Compostela* 🌐 *www.xacobeo.es*). **Santiago bike route information** (🌐 *www.caminhodesantiago.com*).

Bike Rentals **Bici Total** (✉ *Av. de Lugo 221, Santiago de Compostela* ☎ *981/564562*).

BY BUS

Bus Company **ALSA** (✉ *Pl. Camilo Díaz Valiño s/n, Santiago de Compostela* ☎ *981/586133, 981/586453, or 902/422242* 🌐 *www.alsa.es*).

Bus Stations **A Coruña** (✉ *Caballeros 21* ☎ *981/184335*). **Lugo** (✉ *Pl. de la Constitución s/n* ☎ *982/223985*). **Oviedo** (✉ *Pl. Primo de Rivera 1* ☎ *902/422242*). **Pontevedra** (✉ *Calvo Sotelo s/n* ☎ *986/852408*). **Santiago** (✉ *Rúa de San Caetano s/n* ☎ *981/542416*). **Vigo** (✉ *Av. de Madrid 57* ☎ *986/373411*).

BY TRAIN

In addition to the RENFE trains to the area, there are narrow-gauge FEVE trains, which clatter slowly across northern Spain, connecting Galicia and Asturias with Santander, Bilbao, and Irún, on the French border. Buy tickets at local travel agencies, any FEVE train station, or the FEVE office in Oviedo or Madrid. FEVE's Transcantábrico narrow-gauge train tour (🌐 *www.transcantabrico.feve.es*) is an eight-day, 1,000-km (600-mi) journey through the Basque country, Asturias, and Galicia. English-speaking guides narrate, and a private bus takes the group from train stations to artistic and natural attractions. Passengers sleep on the train in suites and dine on local specialties. Trains run May–October, and the all-inclusive cost is €4,100 for two people in a suite.

Train Information **FEVE** (✉ *C. Monte Gamonal s/n, Oviedo* ☎ *985/297656 or 985/981700* ✉ *C. General Rodrigo 6, 2nd fl., Madrid* ☎ *91/453–3828*). **RENFE** (☎ *902/240202* 🌐 *www.renfe.es*).

CONTACTS & RESOURCES

BANKS & EXCHANGING SERVICES

Currency exchange offices are scarce, but there are branches of all of Spain's major banks in cities across Galicia and Asturias. They have 24-hour ATMs and offer currency exchange during business hours.

Currency Exchange **Cibernova** (*Rúa Nova 50, Santiago de Compostela No phone*). **El Corte Inglés** (*Ramón y Cajal 57, A Coruña 981/189400 www.elcorteingles.es*).

EMERGENCIES

Emergency Services **Fire, Police, or Ambulance** (*112*). **Policía Local** (*092*). **Policía Nacional** (*091*). **Cruz Roja** (Red Cross *913/354545*). **Guardia Civil** (*062*). **Insalud** (Public health service *061*). **Información Toxicológica** (Poison control *915/620420*).**Servicio Marítimo** (Air-sea rescue *902/107981*).

INTERNET, MAIL & SHIPPING

Internet cafés are easy to locate in tourist areas. Main post offices (*correos*) stay open until 8:30 weekdays; for urgent deliveries use Seur.

Internet Cafés **Cibercentro La Lila Street** (*La Lila 17, Oviedo 984/083400 www.lalila.org*). **Cibernova Street** (*Rúa Nova 50, Santiago de Compostela No phone*)

Post Offices **Correos** (*Alcalde Manuel Casas s/n, A Coruña 981/225175 Padre Ferrero 4, Oviedo 985/201306 Travesia Fonseca s/n, Santiago de Compostela 981/581252 Plaza de Compostela 3, Vigo 986/438144*).

Courier Services **Seur** (*Juan de Cierva 28–32A, Coruña 981/263600 Santa Susana 41 Oviedo 985/266005 Via Edison, Ciudad del Transporte, Poligono Industrial Tambre, Santiago de Compostela 981/566160 Fragosiño s/n, Vigo 986/411111*).

VISITOR INFORMATION

The Santiago tourist office has information on all of Galicia; the office in Oviedo covers Asturias.

Regional Tourist Offices **A Coruña** (*Av. Dársena de la Marina s/n 981/221822 www.turismocoruna.com*). **Gijón** (*Calle Rodriguez San Pedro s/n 985/341771 www.infogijon.com*).**Oviedo** (*Calle Cimadevilla 4 902/300202 www.ayto-oviedo.es*). **Pontevedra** (*Av. General Gutierrez Mellado 1 986/850814 www.turgalicia.com*). **Santiago de Compostela** (*Rúa do Vilar 63 981/555129 www.santiagoturismo.com*).

Local Tourist Offices **A Coruña** (*Edificio Sol, Sol s/n 981/184344*). **Cangas de Onís** (*Calle Camila Beceña 1 985/848005*). **Covadonga** (*Av. Covadonga s/n, Pl. del Ayuntamiento 985/846035*). **Gijón** (*Calle Rodriguez San Pedro s/n 985/341771*). **Llanes** (*Calle La Torre, Alfonso IX s/n 985/400164*). **Luarca** (*Calle Caleros 11 985/640083*). **Lugo** (*Praza Maior 27, Galerías 982/231361*). **O Grove** (*Pl. de Corgo 1 986/731415*) **Ourense** (*Calle Burgas 12, bajo 988/366064*). **Oviedo** (*Calle Marqués de Santa Cruz 1 985/227586*). **Pontevedra** (*Pl. de España 986/850814 La Herreria July–Sept., outdoor kiosks*). **Ribadeo** (*Pl. de España 982/128689*). **Ribadesella** (*Paseo de Muelle 985/860038 Closed Mon.*). **Santiago de Compostela** (*Rúa do Vilar 63 981/555129*). **Tui** (*Calle Colón s/n 986/601789*). **Vigo** (*Mercado, Pl. de la Piedra 986/810216*). **Villaviciosa** (*Parque Vallina 985/891759*).

Bilbao & the Basque Country

WITH CANTABRIA, NAVARRA & LA RIOJA

5

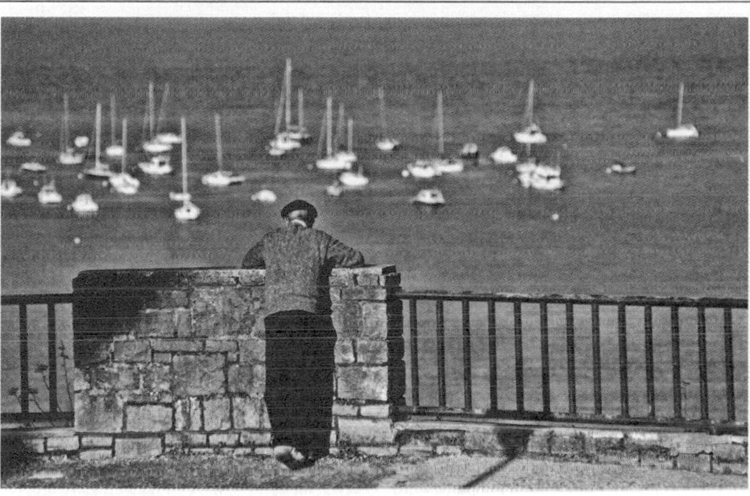
Hondarribia's fishing port

WORD OF MOUTH

"I would not argue that San Sebastian is a replacement for Barcelona, but I would say that it is a terrific place to understand the dynamism of northern Spain and begin to get a feel for . . . the "coolest" people in the world, the Basques."

—weber6560

www.fodors.com/forums

WELCOME TO BILBAO & THE BASQUE COUNTRY

TOP REASONS TO GO

★ **The Basque Coast:** From colorful fishing villages to tawny beaches to Europe's longest surfing wave, the Basque Coast always delights the eye.

★ **Tapas in San Sebastián:** For a sense of well-being, nothing matches San Sebastián's Parte Vieja, booming with the laughter of tavern-hoppers.

★ **Art & Architecture in Bilbao:** The Museo de Bellas Artes (Fine Arts Museum) and the titanium Guggenheim shimmer where steel mills and shipyards once stood, while verdant pastures loom above.

★ **Navarra's Sweeping Plains:** Contrasting with the emerald uplands of northern Navarra, the moonscape-like Bárdenas Reales southeast of Pamplona surround the Olite castle and parador.

★ **Rioja's Wine Country:** Spain's premier wine-growing region in La Rioja Alta and La Rioja Alavesa is filled with wine-tasting opportunities—and the fine cuisine to go with it.

Cantabria's countryside.

1 Cantabria. Santander's wide beaches and summer music and dance festival are the highlights of this mountain and maritime community. The Picos de Europa are spectacular. The Liébana Valley, the Renaissance town at Santillana del Mar, and ports and strands such as San Vicente de la Barquera are among Spain's finest treasures.

2 Bilbao & the Basque Country. The contrast between Bilbao and the rest of the Basque Country only makes each half of the equation better. A city famous for steel and shipbuilding, now an art and architecture hub, is surrounded by sylvan hillsides, tiny fishing ports, and beautiful beaches.

Bilbao's tramway.

GETTING ORIENTED

Bordering the coastline of the Bay of Biscay, Santander (Cantabria), and the Basque Country, and, farther inland, Navarra and La Rioja are a Spain apart—a land of moist green foothills, lush vineyards, and rolling meadowlands. A fertile slot between the Picos de Europa and the Pyrenees mountain ranges that stretch from the Mediterranean Cap de Creus all the way to Finisterre, (Land's End), on the Atlantic in northwestern Galicia, this northern Arcadia is an often rainy but always comforting reprieve from the bright, hot Spanish meseta to the south.

3 Navarra. Navarra offers much beyond Pamplona's running-with-the-bulls blowout. The moist green Pyrenean hills to the north contrast with the lunar Bárdenas Reales to the southeast, while the wine country south of Pamplona leads to lovely Camino de Santiago way stations Puente la Reina and Estella.

4 La Rioja. Spain's wine country is dedicated to tastes of all kinds. The Sierra de la Demanda offers such delicious detours as Francis Paniego's Echaurren or Viniegra de Abajo's Venta de Goyo, while the towns of Logroño, Haro, and Laquardia are well endowed with superb architecture and gastronomy.

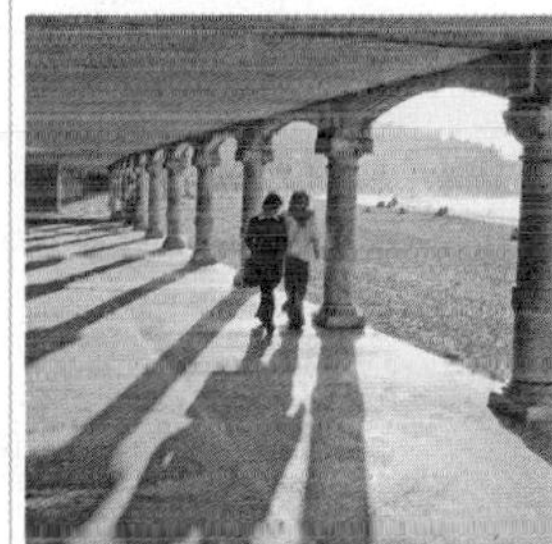
La Concha Beach. Donostia. San Sebastián.

5

BILBAO & THE BASQUE COUNTRY PLANNER

When to Go

Mid-April through June and then September and October are the best times to enjoy the temperate climate and both the coastal and upland landscapes of this wet and grassy corner of Spain, though any time of year except August, when Europeans are on vacation, is nearly as good. Pamplona in July is bedlam, but for party animals it's heaven. The Basque Country is rainy in winter, but the wet Atlantic weather is always invigorating and, as if anyone needed it in this culinary paradise, appetite-enhancing. Much of the classically powerful Basque cuisine evolved with the northern maritime climate in mind. The September film festival in San Sebastián coincides with the spectacular whaleboat regattas, while the beaches are still ideal and largely uncrowded.

Getting There & Around

Bilbao's airport at Sondika, 12 km (7 mi) outside the city, is the region's most important flight terminal with frequent international flights. Iberia has regular connections from Bilbao to Madrid, Barcelona, the United Kingdom, France, and Belgium. There are smaller airports at Santander, Hondarribia (serving San Sebastián), Vitoria, Logroño, and Pamplona, with twice-daily service to Madrid and Barcelona.

Santander and Bilbao are linked year-round to Plymouth, England, by twice-weekly car ferries run by Brittany Ferries. Book at least six weeks in advance in summer. A twice-weekly ferry between Bilbao and Portsmouth is operated by Ferries Golfo de Vizcaya. The trip takes about 24 hours. For ferries out to Vigo and points west, Vapores Suardiaz runs carriers during the summer.

Daily bus service connects the major cities to Madrid, Zaragoza, Barcelona (and with a layover or transfer to Spain's main destinations). From Madrid, call the bus company Continental Auto for details, or go right to the station at Calle Alenza 20. Even better, reserve online at www.alsa.es. Bus service between cities and smaller towns is comprehensive, but few have central bus stations; most have numerous bus lines leaving from various points in town.

Santander, Bilbao, San Sebastián, Pamplona, Vitoria, and Logroño are served by direct trains from Madrid's Chamartín or Puerta de Atocha stations and, with a transfer or two, virtually every major city in Spain. Trains are not the ideal way to travel here, but many cities are connected by RENFE trains. Also, the regional company FEVE runs a delightful narrow-gauge train that winds through stunning landscapes. From San Sebastián, lines west to Bilbao and east to Hendaye depart from Estación de Amara; most long-distance trains use Estación del Norte.

Explore destinations like a local by walking or, in the all-too-likely event of rain, taxi. Only Bilbao has a metropolitan transport system. *See Bilbao & the Basque Country Essentials at the end of this chapter for transportation contact information.*

Eat, Drink & be Merry

The concentration of celebrated chefs around San Sebastián is so dazzling that food is a natural rallying point here. Beyond the famous names such as Arzak, Subijana, Berasategui, and Aduriz, there are dozens of other rising stars in and around the Basque Country, from Bilbao to Hondarribia, not to mention the everyday excellence of ordinary food prepared with no gourmet pretensions beyond simple comforts. The mountain cooking of the Pyrenees and the inevitable symphony of food and wine in the winegrowing regions of Navarra and La Rioja are memorable, while Santander offers nonpareil seafood riches. Maintaining an appetite (and some semblance of a waistline) can become a problem on a food safari—and hiking is the answer. Walking the well-marked hiking trails of the Basque Country, Navarra, La Rioja, and Cantabria is the best way to succeed in wolfing down a significant portion of the terrific cuisine and surviving to tell the tale. Bring good walking shoes and check with local tourist offices for classic hikes such as the walk over the Pyrenees from St-Jean-Pied-de-Port to upper Navarra's Roncesvalles, a unique way to get a never-to-be-forgotten feel for the Pyrenean portal. The network of trails and ancient cobblestoned Roman roads up the Basque coast from Zumaya to Guetaria and Zarauz and on to San Sebastián and all the way to France will offer a look at corners of the Basque Country not seen from the freeways. From San Sebastián, the red and white GR (Gran Recorrido) markings at the end of the Zurriola beach will start you on a gorgeous three-hour hike to Pasajes de San Pedro, where a two-minute boat ride will whisk you across the Rentería shipping passage to Pasajes de San Juan (Pasaia Donibane in Euskera) and the town's several first-rate dining opportunities.

WHAT IT COSTS In Euros

	$$$$	$$$	$$	$	¢
RESTAURANTS	over €20	€15–€20	€10–€15	€6–€10	under €6
HOTELS	over €180	€100–€180	€60–€100	€40–€60	under €40

Prices are per person for a main course at dinner. Prices are for two people in a standard double room in high season, excluding tax.

Planning Your Time

A road trip through the entire region including Santander, the Basque Country, Navarra, and La Rioja would require at least a week's time. A glimpse, however brief, of Santillana del Mar's Renaissance town, Bilbao and its Guggenheim, San Sebastián and La Concha Beach, the Baztán Valley, Pamplona, Laguardia, and La Rioja's wine capital at Haro would constitute the top must-see elements in a classic whirlwind tour. If you doubled the time and spent two days in each of these destinations, the next tier of unmissable spots might include the Altamira Caves, Sardinero Beach at Santander, Mundaka and the Vizcayan Coast west of Bilbao, Guetaria, Pasajes de San Juan, and Hondarribia in and around San Sebastián, and Logroño in La Rioja. Even better, if you found a few weeks to wander in a relaxed fashion, you could make it up as you go along, counting on off-season space available in nearly all hotels and *paradores,* while crisscrossing the France-Spain border. The Cantabrican highlands in the Picos de Europa and La Rioja's Sierra de la Demanda both harbor some of the finest landscapes in Spain (not to mention culinary pilgrimages to Echaurren in Ezcaray or Venta de Goyo in Viiegra de Abajo), while the fishing villages and beaches between Santander and the French border offers ports or inlets so charming, you want to bottle them and take them home.

5

By George Semler

NORTHERN SPAIN IS A MISTY land of green hills, low russet rooflines, and colorful fishing villages, and is home to the formerly industrial city, Bilbao, reborn as a center of art and architecture. Santander, once the main seaport for Old Castile on the Bay of Biscay, is in a mountainous zone wedged between the Basque Country and, to the west, Asturias. Santander and the entire Cantabrian region are cool summer refuges for Madrileños, with sandy beaches, high sierra (including part of the Picos de Europa Mountains), and tiny highland towns. The semiautonomous Basque Country, with its steady drizzle (onomatopoetically called the *siri-miri*), damp verdant landscape, and rugged coastline, is a distinct national and cultural entity within the Spanish state. Navarra is considered Basque in the Pyrenees and merely Navarran in its southern reaches, along the Ebro River. La Rioja, tucked between the Sierra de la Demanda (a small-to-midsize mountain range that separates La Rioja from the central Castilian steppe) and the Ebro River, is Spain's premier wine country.

Called the País Vasco in Castilian Spanish, and Euskadi in the linguistically mysterious, non-Indo-European Basque language called Euskera, the Basque region is more a country within a country, or a nation within a state (the semantics are much debated). The Basques are known to love competition—it has been said that they will bet on anything that has numbers on it and moves (horses, dogs, runners, weight lifters—anything). Such traditional rural sports as chopping mammoth tree trunks, lifting boulders, and scything grass reflect the Basques' attachment to the land and to farm life as well as an ingrained enthusiasm for feats of strength and endurance. Even poetry and gastronomy become contests in Euskadi, as *bertsolaris* (amateur poets) improvise duels of sharp-witted verse, and male-only gastronomic societies compete in cooking contests to see who can make the best *sopa de ajo* (garlic soup) or *marmitako* (tuna stew).

The much-reported Basque separatist movement is made up of a small but radical sector of the political spectrum. The terrorist organization known as ETA, or Euskadi Ta Askatasuna (Basque Homeland and Liberty), has killed nearly 900 people in more than 35 years of activity. Conflict has waxed and waned over the years, though it has never affected travelers. When ETA declared a "permanent cease-fire" in April 2006, hope flared for an end to Basque terrorism until a late-December bomb that killed two brought progress to a halt. Batasuna, the (illegal) political wing of ETA, has, for the first time, split with the violent sector of the movement, which, in turn, has announced a formal termination of the cease-fire.

EXPLORING THE REGIONS

Northern Spain's Bay of Biscay area, at the western end of the Pyrenees and the border with France, is where the Cantabrian Cordillera and the Pyrenees nearly meet. The moist green foothills of the Basque Country and, to the west, Cantabria, gently fill this space between the otherwise unbroken chain of mountains that rises from the Iberian Peninsula's easternmost point at northern Catalonia's Cap de Creus and ends at western Galicia's Fisterra, or Finisterre, land's end. Navarra—part Basque and part Castilian-speaking Navarrese—lies just southeast and inland of the Basque Country, with the backdrop of the Pyrenees rising up to the north. La Rioja, below Navarra, nestles in the Ebro River valley under the Sierra de la Demanda to the south, and stretches east and downriver to Calahorra and the edge of Spain's central *meseta* (plains).

ABOUT THE BEACHES

Santander has excellent sandy beaches, and the beach at Laredo, between Santander and Bilbao, is one of Spain's best and relatively undiscovered. Another beach between Bilbao and San Sebastián, Lequeitio is particularly beautiful, and the smaller beaches at Zumaya, Getaria, and Zarauz are usually quiet. San Sebastián's best beach, La Concha, which curves around the bay along with the city itself, is scenic and clean, but packed in summer; Ondarreta, at the western end of La Concha, is often less crowded. Surfers gather at Zurriola on the northern side of the Urumea River. Hondarribia, the last stop before the French border, has a vast expanse of fine sand along the Bidasoa estuary.

ABOUT THE RESTAURANTS

Basque food in and around San Sebastián and Bilbao combines the fish of the Atlantic with a love of sauces that's rare south of the Pyrenees—a result, no doubt, of Euskadi's proximity to France. The now 30-year-old *nueva cocina vasca* (new Basque cooking), originally inspired by the Basque Country's neighbors to the north, invented lightened, streamlined versions of classic Basque dishes such as *marmitako* (tuna and potato stew). Traditional San Sebastián specialties include *chuleta de buey* (garlicky beefsteak grilled over coals), and firm, flaky *besugo a la parrilla* (sea bream grilled over coals), also wallowing in golden chips of crisped garlic. Around Bilbao, *bacalao al pil pil* is ubiquitous—cod-flank fillets cooked in a boiled emulsion of garlic and gelatin from the cod itself, so that the oil makes a popping noise ("pil-pil") and a white sauce is created. Other favorites are *kokotxas* (nuggets of cod jaw) and *pimientos de piquillo* (sweet red peppers stuffed with tuna or cod).

Cantabria's cooking is part mountain fare, such as roast kid and lamb or *cocidos* (bean stews) in the highlands, and part seafood on the coast. *Soropotun* is Santander's stew of bonito, potatoes, and vegetables. Navarra is famous for beef, lamb, and vegetable dishes, including *menestra de verduras* (a stew of artichokes, green beans, peas, lettuce, potatoes, onion, and chunks of cured ham). La Rioja has meaty stews and roasts in the mountains and vegetable dishes in the Ebro River basin.

La Rioja, south of the Basque Country, produces many of the finest wines in Spain; purists insisting on Basque wine with their Basque cuisine could choose a Rioja Alavesa, from the north side of the Ebro. Navarra also produces some fine vintages, especially rosés and reds—and in such quantity that some churches in Allo, Peralta, and other towns were actually built with a mortar mixed with wine instead of water.

Don't miss any chance to go to a *sidrería,* a cider house (in Astigarraga, near San Sebastián, there are no fewer than 17).

ABOUT THE HOTELS

The largely industrial and well-to-do north is an expensive part of Spain, which is reflected in room rates. San Sebastián is particularly pricey, and Pamplona rates double or triple during the San Fermín fiesta in July. Reserve ahead for Bilbao, where the Guggenheim Museum is filling hotels, and nearly everywhere else in summer. Another lodging option is the Agroturismo lodging network, which often offers rooms in a Basque *caserío* (farmhouse). Check with local tourist offices for details.

Numbers in the text correspond to numbers in the margin and on the chapter maps.

CANTABRIA

Historically part of Old Castile, the province of Cantabria was called Santander until 1984, when it became an Autonomous Community. The most direct route from Burgos to Santander is the slow but scenic N623 through the Cordillera Cantábrica, past the Ebro reservoir. For a memorable glimpse of Cantabria's section of the Picos de Europa Mountains, drive through La Liébana valley via Palencia and Potes, reaching the coast at San Vicente de la Barquera.

POTES

❶ *51 km (31 mi) south of San Vicente de la Barquera, 115 km (69 mi) west of Santander, 173 km (104 mi) north of Palencia.*

Known for its fine cheeses made of milk from cows, goats, and sheep, La Liébana is a highland domain well worth exploring. The region's main city, Potes, is named for and sprinkled with ancient bridges, surrounded with the stunning 9th-century **monasteries** of Santo Toribio de Liébana, Lebeña, and Piasca. The gorges of the Desfiladero de la Hermida pass are 3 km (2 mi) north, and the rustic town of Mogrovejo is on the way to the vertiginous cable car at Fuente Dé, 25 km (15 mi) west of Potes.

As you approach **Fuente Dé** by car or foot, you'll see a wall of gray stone rising 6,560 feet straight into the air. Visible at the top is the tiniest of huts: your destination. Get there via a little red-and-white funicular (€8 round-trip). Once at the top, you're hiking along the Ávila Mountain pasturelands, rich in native wildlife, between the central and eastern massifs of the Picos. There's an official entrance to Picos de Europa National Park up here.

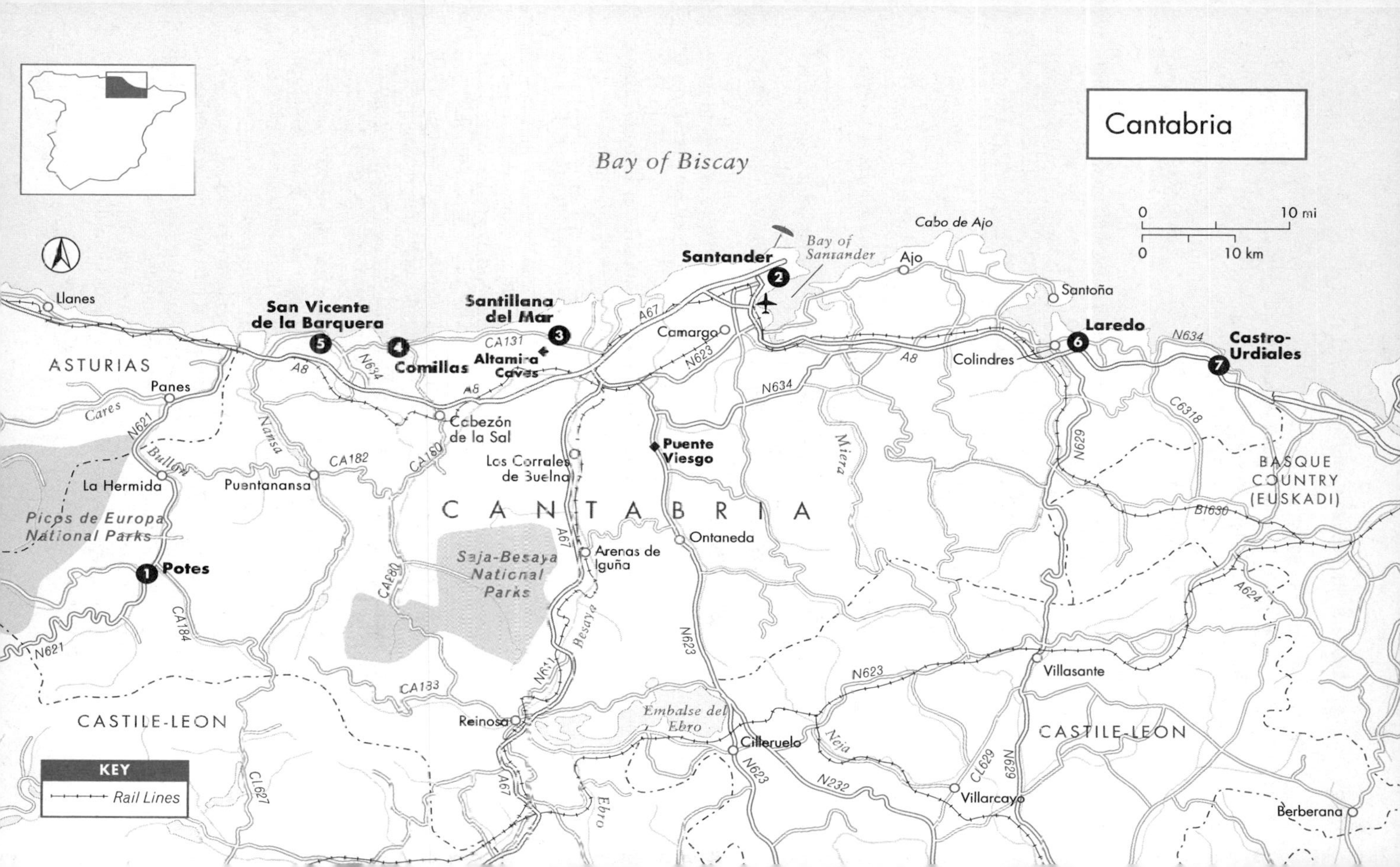

Cantabria
Bay of Biscay
0
10 mi
0
10 km
Cabo de Ajo
Bay of Santander
Santander
Ajo
Santoña
Llanes
San Vicente de la Barquera
Santillana del Mar
Camargo
Laredo
N634
Castro-Urdiales
ASTURIAS
Comillas
Altamira Caves
CA131
A67
N623
A8
Colindres
Panes
N634
C6318
Cares
N621
Bullón
Nansa
Cabezón de la Sal
CA182
CA180
Los Corrales de Buelna
Puente Viesgo
Miera
N629
BASQUE COUNTRY (EUSKADI)
La Hermida
Puentanansa
CANTABRIA
B1630
Picos de Europa National Parks
A67
Arenas de Iguña
Ontaneda
Potes
Saja-Besaya National Parks
CA280
A624
CA184
Besaya
N623
N621
N611
Villasante
CA183
N623
CASTILE-LEON
Reinosa
Embalse del Ebro
CASTILE-LEON
Cilleruelo
Neja
KEY
Rail Lines
CL627
A67
Ebro
N623
N232
CL629
N629
Villarcayo
Berberana

WHERE TO STAY & EAT

$–$$$ ✕ **El Bodegón.** A simple, friendly, cozy, and surprisingly contemporary space awaits behind an ancient stone facade. Here you can find a fine *cocido montañes* (mountain stew of sausage, garbanzo beans, and vegetables) at a rock-bottom price. The €8 lunch menu here is one of the best values for miles around. ✉ *San Roque 4* ☎ *942/730247* ▭ *AE, DC, MC, V* ⊗ *Closed Mon.*

$$ ✕ **Valdecoro.** You literally can't miss this family-run mountain house, which faces the main road through town. Rooms with modern appointments and an efficient staff make for a pleasant stay. The restaurant ($–$$$) is a town favorite for simple and authentic highland products and recipes prepared with care and wisdom. In winter, try the *cocido lebaniego,* a powerful mountain soup made of broth, beans, pork, chard, and chicken. ✉ *Roscabado 5, 39570* ☎ *942/730025* 📠 *942/730315* *41 rooms* *In-hotel: restaurant, parking (no fee)* ▭ *AE, DC, MC, V.*

SANTANDER

2 ★ *390 km (242 mi) north of Madrid, 154 km (96 mi) north of Burgos, 116 km (72 mi) west of Bilbao.*

Santander is one of the great ports on the Bay of Biscay. It's surrounded by beaches that are by no means isolated, but lack the sardinelike package-tour feel of so many Mediterranean resorts. A fire destroyed most of the old town in 1941, so the rebuilt city looks relatively modern, and although it has traditionally been a conservative stronghold loyal to the Spanish state (in contrast to its Basque neighbors), Santander is lively, especially in summer, when its university and music-and-dance festival fill the city with students and performers from abroad. Portus Victoriae, as Santander was then called, was a major port in the 1st- to 4th-century Roman Hispania Ulterior (and even earlier under the aboriginal Cántabros). Commercial life accelerated between the 13th and 16th centuries, but the waning of Spain's naval power and a series of plagues during the reign of Felipe II caused Santander's fortunes to plummet in the late 16th century. Its economy revived after 1778, when Seville's monopoly on trade with the Americas was revoked and Santander entered fully into commerce with the New World. In 1910 the Palacio de la Magdalena was built by popular subscription as a gift to Alfonso XIII and his queen, Victoria Eugenia, lending Santander prestige as one of Spain's royal watering spots.

Santander benefits from promenades and gardens, most of them facing the bay. Walk east along the Paseo de Pereda, the main boulevard, to the Puerto Chico, a small yacht harbor. Past the Puerto Chico, follow Avenida Reina Victoria, and you'll come to the tree-lined park paths above the first of the city's beaches, Playa de la Magdalena. Walk onto the Península de la Magdalena to the Palacio de la Magdalena, today the summer seat of the University of Menéndez y Pelayo, which conducts Spanish-language and Spanish-culture courses for foreigners. Beyond the Magdalena Peninsula, wealthy locals have built mansions facing the long stretch of shoreline known as El Sardinero, Santander's best beach.

Continued on page 297

BASQUE SPOKEN HERE

Bilbao
Bilbo
Saint-Sébastien
Donostia
BISCAYE
LABOURD
(FRANCE)
GUIPEÚZUOA
BASSE-NAVARRE
ÁLAVA
SOULE
Vitoria
Gasteiz
(SPAIN)
Pampelune
Irunea
NAVARRE

While the Basque Country's future as an independent nation-state has yet to be determined, the quirky, fascinating culture of the Basque people is not restricted by any borders. Experience it for yourself in the food, history, and sport.

Basque solar cross

The cultural footprints of this tiny corner of Europe, which straddles the Atlantic end of the border between France and Spain, have already touched down all over the globe. The sport of jai-alai has come to America. International magazines give an ecstatic thumbs-up to Basque cooking. Historians are pointing to Basque fishermen as the true discoverers of North America. And bestsellers, not without irony, proclaim *The Basque History of the World*. As in the ancient 4 + 3 = 1 graffiti equation, the three French (Labourd, Basse Navarre, and Soule) and the four Spanish (Guipúzcoa, Vizcaya, Alava, and Navarra) Basque provinces add up to a single people with a shared history. Although nationless, Basques have been Basques since Paleolithic times.

Stretching across the Pyrenees from Bayonne in France to Bilbao in Spain, the New Hampshire-sized Basque region retains a distinct culture, neither expressly French nor Spanish, fiercely guarded by its three million inhabitants. Fables stubbornly connect them with Adam and Eve, Noah's Ark, and the lost city of Atlantis, but a leading genealogical theory points to common bloodlines with the Celts. The most tenable theory is that the Basques are descended from aboriginal Iberian peoples who successfully defended their unique cultural identity from the influences of Roman and Moorish domination.

It was only in 1876 that Sabino Arana—a virulent anti-Spanish fanatic—proposed the ideal of a "pure" Basque independent state. That dream was crushed by Franco's dictatorial reign (1939–75, during which many Spanish Basques emigrated to France) and was immortalized in Pablo Picasso's *Guernica*. This famous painting, which depicts the catastrophic Nazi bombing of the Basque town of Gernika stands not only as a searing indictment of all wars but as a reminder of history's brutal assault upon Basque identity.

"THE BEST FOOD YOU'VE NEVER HEARD OF"*

*So said *Food & Wine* magazine. It's time to get filled in.

An old saying has it that every soccer team needs a Basque goaltender and every restaurant a Basque chef. Traditional Basque cuisine combines the fresh fish of the Atlantic and upland vegetables, beef, and lamb with a love of sauces that is rare south of the Pyrenees. Today, the *nueva cocina vasca* (new Basque cooking) movement has made Basque food less rustic and much more nouvelle. And now that *pintxos* (the Basque equivalent of tapas) have become the rage from Barcelona to New York City, Basque cuisine is being championed by foodies everywhere. Even superchef Alain Ducasse has gotten in on the action by opening his Ostapé inn in Bidarray in the heart of the Pays Basque.

WHO'S THE BEST CHEF?

Basques are so naturally competitive that meals often turn into comparative rants over who is better: Basque chefs based in France or in Spain. Some vote for Bayonne's Jean-Claude Tellechea (his L'Auberge du Cheval Blanc is famed for groundbreaking surf-and-turf dishes like hake roasted in onions with essence of poultry) or St-Jean-Pied-de-Port's Firmin Arrambide (based at his elegant Les Pyrénées inn). Others prefer the postmodern lobster salads found over the border in San Sebastián and Bilbao, created by master chefs José María Arzak and Martin Berasategui (at their eponymously named restaurants).

SIX GREAT DISHES

Angulas. Baby eels, cooked in olive oil and garlic with a few slices of guindilla pepper.

Bacalao al pil-pil. Cod cooked at a low temperature in an emulsion of olive oil and fish juices, which makes a unique pinging sound as it sizzles.

Besugo. Sea bream, or besugo, is so revered that it is a traditional Christmas dish. Enjoy it with sagardo, the signature Basque apple cider.

Marmitako. This tuna stew with potatoes and pimientos is a satisfying winter favorite.

Ttoro. Typical of Labourd fishing villages such as St-Jean-de-Luz, this peppery Basque bouillabaisse is known as *sopa de pescado* (fish soup) south of the French border.

Txuleta de buey. The signature Basque meat is ox steaks marinated in parsley and garlic and cooked over coals.

BASQUE SPORTS: JAI-ALAI TO OXCART-LIFTING

Sports are core to Basque society, and virtually none are immune from the Basque passion for competing, betting, and playing.

Over the centuries, the rugged physical environment of the Basque hills and the rough Cantabrian sea traditionally made physical prowess and bravery valued attributes. Since Basque mythology often involved feats of strength, it's easy to see why today's Basques are such rabid sports fans.

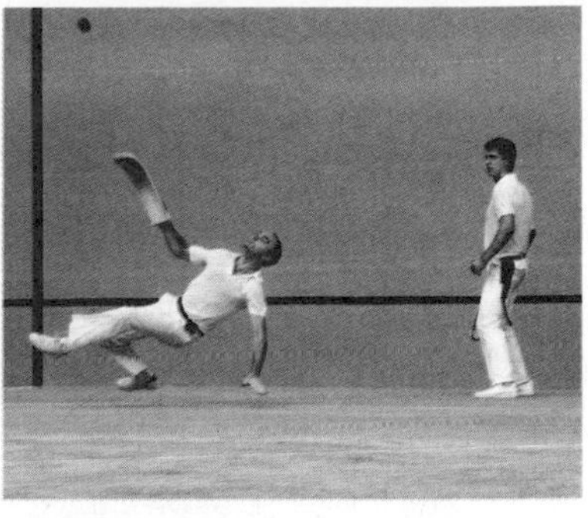

PELOTA

A Basque village without a frontón (pelota court) is as unimaginable as an American town without a baseball diamond. "The fastest game in the world," pelota is called *jai-alai* in Basque (and translated officially as "merry festival"). With rubber balls flung from hooked wicker gloves at speeds up to 150 mph—the impact of the ball is like a machine-gun bullet—jai-alai is mesmerizing. It is played on a three-walled court 175 feet long and 56 feet wide with 40-foot side walls.

Whether singles or doubles, the object is to angle the ball along or off of the side wall so that it cannot be returned. Betting is very much part of pelota and courtside wagers are brokered by bet makers as play proceeds. While pelota is the word for "ball," it also refers to the game. There was even a recent movie in Spain entitled *La Pelota Vasca*, used metaphorically to refer to the greater "ball game" of life and death.

HERRIKIROLAK

Herrikirolak (rural sports) are based on farming and seafaring. Stone lifters (*harrijasotzaileak* in Euskera) heft weights up to 700 pounds. *Aizkolari* (axe men) chop wood in various contests, *Gizon proba* (man trial) pits three-man teams moving weighted sleds; while *estropadak* are whaleboat rowers who compete in spectacular regattas (culminating in the September competition off La Concha beach in San Sebastián). *Sokatira* is tug of war, and *segalariak* is a scything competition. Other events include oxcart-lifting, milk-can carrying, and ram fights.

SOCCER

When it comes to soccer, Basque goaltenders have developed special fame in Spain, where Bilbao's Athletic Club and San Sebastián's Real Sociedad have won national championships with budgets far inferior to those of Real Madrid or FC Barcelona. Across the border, Bayonne's rugby team is a force in the French national competition; the French Basque capital is also home to the annual French pelota championship.

HABLA EUSKERA?

Although the Basque people speak French north of the border and Spanish south of the border, they consider Euskera their first language and identify themselves as the *Euskaldunak* (the "Basque speakers"). Euskera remains one of the great enigmas of linguistic scholarship. Theories connect it with everything from Sanskrit to Japanese to Finnish.

What is certain is where Euskera did not come from, namely the Indo-European family of languages that includes the Germanic, Italic, and Hellenic language groups. Currently used by about a million people in northern Spain and southwestern France, Euskera sounds like a consonant-ridden version of Spanish, with its five pure vowels, rolled "r," and palatal "n" and "l." Basque has survived two millennia of cultural and political pressure and is the only remaining language of those spoken in southwestern Europe before the Roman conquest.

The Euskaldunak celebrate their heritage during a Basque folk dancing festival.

A BASQUE GLOSSARY

Aurresku: The high-kicking *espata danza* or sword dance typically performed on the day of Corpus Christi in the Spanish Basque Country.

Akelarre: A gathering of witches that provoked witch trials in the Pyrenees. Even today it is believed that *jentilak* (magic elves) inhabit the woods and the Olentzaro (the evil Basque Santa Claus) comes down chimneys to wreak havoc—a fire is kept burning to keep him out.

Boina: The Basque beret or *txapela,* thought to have developed as the perfect protection from the siri-miri, the perennial "Scotch mist" that soaks the moist Basque Country.

Eguzki: The sun worship was at the center of the pagan religion that, in the Basque Country, gave way only slowly to Christianity. The Basque solar cross is typically carved into the east-facing facades of ancient *caserios* or farmhouses.

Espadrilles: Rope-soled canvas Basque shoes, also claimed by the Catalans, developed in the Pyrenees and traditionally attached by laces or ribbons wrapped up the ankle.

Etxekoandre: The woman who commands all matters spiritual, culinary, and practical in a traditional Basque farmhouse. Basque matriarchal inheritance laws remain key.

Fueros: Special Basque rights and laws (including exemption from serving in the army except to defend the Basque Country) originally conceded by the ancient Romans and abolished at the end of the Carlist Wars in 1876 after centuries of Castilian kings had sworn to protect Basque rights at the Tree of Gernika.

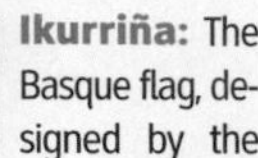

Ikurriña: The Basque flag, designed by the founder of Basque nationalism, Sabino Arana, composed of green and white crosses over a red background and said to have been based on the British Union Jack.

Lauburu: Resembling a four-leaf clover, *lau* (four) *buru* (head) is the Basque symbol.

Twenty: Basques favor counting in units of twenty (*veinte duros*—20 nickels—is a common way of saying a hundred pesetas, for example).

Txakolí: A slightly fizzy young wine made from grapes grown around the Bay of Biscay, this fresh, acidic brew happily accompanies tapas and fish.

The heart of El Sardinero is the Belle Epoque **Gran Casino del Sardinero,** an elegant casino and restaurant worth a quick visit even if gaming tables hold no charms for you. A white building fronted with red awnings and set in a park among sycamores, the casino lies at the center of the vacationer's Santander, surrounded by expensive hotels and several fine restaurants. ✉ *Plaza de Italia s/n* ☎ *942/276054* 🎫 *€4* ⏲ *Daily 8 PM–4 AM; slot machines open at 5 PM.*

In the old city, the center of life is the **Plaza Porticada,** officially called the Plaza Velarde. In August this unassuming little square is the seat of Santander's star event, the outdoor International Festival of Music and Dance.The blockish **Catedral de Santander** marks the transition between Romanesque and Gothic. Though largely rebuilt in the neo-Gothic style after serious damage in the 1941 fire, the cathedral retained its 12th-century crypt. The chief attraction here is the tomb of Marcelino Menéndez y Pelayo (1856–1912), Santander's most famous literary figure. The cathedral is across Avenida de Calvo Sotelo from the Plaza Porticada. ✉ *Somorrostro s/n* ☎ *942/226024* 🎫 *Free* ⏲ *Weekdays 10–1 and 4–7:30, weekends 8–2 and 4:30–8.*

5

The **Museo Municipal de Bellas Artes** *(Municipal Museum of Fine Arts)* has works by Flemish, Italian, and Spanish artists. Goya's portrait of absolutist king Fernando VII is worth seeking out; the smirking face of the lion at the king's feet clues you in to Goya's feelings toward his patron. The same building holds the **Biblioteca Menéndez y Pelayo** (☎ *942/234534*), a library with some 50,000 volumes, and the writer's study, kept as it was in his day. ✉ *C. Rubio s/n* ☎ *942/239485* 🎫 *Free* ⏲ *Museum Tues.–Fri. 10–1 and 5–8, Sat. 10–1. Library weekdays 9–2 and 4–9:30, Sat. 9–1:30.*

WHERE TO STAY & EAT

$$–$$$$ ✕ **Zacarías.** Whether you want tapas or dinner in full, try out this popular rustic and refined interior patio known for northern Spanish specialties. Owner and chef Zacarías Puente Herboso is a well-known food writer and an authority on Cantabrian recipes. Sample the *maganos encebollados* (calamari and caramelized onion) or the *alubias rojas estofadas* (red beans stewed with sausage). ✉ *General Mola 41* ☎ *942/212333* 💳 *AE, DC, MC, V.*

$$–$$$$ ★ 🏨 **Bahía.** Classical decor filled with state-of-the-art equipment and technology all make this Santander's finest hotel, with a front-and-center placement overlooking the bay. Rooms are spacious and filled with gauzy drapes and noble pieces of furniture and first-rate wood and stone. ✉ *Av. Alfonso XIII-6, 39000* ☎ *942/205000* 📠 *942/205001* 🌐 *www.hotelbahia.com* 🛏 *188 rooms* 👍 *In-hotel: restaurant, bar, parking (fee)* 💳 *AE, DC, MC, V.*

NIGHTLIFE & THE ARTS

Santander's big event is its International Festival of Music and Dance, which attracts leading artists, throughout August. To learn of current concert offerings, collect information at box offices in the Plaza Porticada and the Jardines de Pereda park.

SHOPPING

Men's fashions rule at **Golf** (✉*Plaza del Príncipe* ☎*942/312975*). Santander's ceramics emporium **La Muralla** (✉*Calle Arrabal 17* ☎*942/160301*) is known as the best in town. For footwear, **Loocky** (✉*Lealtad 6* ☎*942/211368*) is tops. Fine foods, including the Santanderino specialty *dulces pasiegos* (light and sugary cakes), can be tried and purchased at **Mantequerís Cántabras** (✉*Plaza de Italia s/n* ☎*942/272899*).

SANTILLANA DEL MAR

3 *29 km (18 mi) west of Santander.*

Fodor's Choice ★

This stunning ensemble of 15th- to 17th-century stone houses is one of Spain's greatest troves of medieval and Renaissance architecture.The town is built around the **Colegiata**, Cantabria's finest Romanesque structure, with a 17th-century altarpiece, the tomb of local martyr Santa Juliana, and sculpted capitals depicting biblical scenes. The adjoining Regina Coeli convent has a **Museo Diocesano** (☎*942/840317*) with liturgical art. ✉*Av. Le Dorat 2* ☎*942/818004* *Combined ticket for Colegiata and museum €3.50* *Daily 10–1 and 4–7; closed Mon. Oct.–May.*

The world-famous **Altamira Caves,** 3 km (2 mi) southwest of Santillana del Mar, have been called the Sistine Chapel of Prehistoric Art for the beauty of their drawings, believed to be some 20,000 years old. First uncovered in 1875, the caves are a testament to early man's admiration of aesthetic beauty and his surprising technical skill in representing it—especially in the use of rock forms to accentuate perspective. The caves are closed to visitors, but the reproduction in the **museum** is open to all. ✉*Museo de Altamira, 39330 Santillana del Mar, Cantabria* ☎*942/818005* *€3* *Daily 10–1 and 4–7; closed Mon. Oct.–May.*

WHERE TO STAY & EAT

$$$ Fodor's Choice ★ **Parador de Santillana Gil Blas.** Built in the 16th century, this lovely parador is in the erstwhile summer home of the Barreda-Bracho family. Rooms are baronial, with rich drapes and antique furnishings. The dining hall ($$–$$$$) serves good local fare. ✉*Pl. Ramón Pelayo 8, 39330* ☎*942/818000* *942/818391* *www.parador.es* *55 rooms, 1 suite* *In-hotel: restaurant, bar, parking (fee)* *AE, DC, MC, V.*

$$ **Casa del Organista.** A cozy 18th-century house with comfortable and tastefully appointed whitewashed rooms with lovely stone and wood details, this intimate hideaway offers a countrified base for exploring Spain's finest Renaissance town. ✉*Los Hornos 4, 39330* ☎*942/840352* *942/840191* *www.casadelorganista.com* *14 rooms* *No elevator* *AE, DC, MC, V* *Closed Dec. 15–Jan. 15.*

OFF THE BEATEN PATH

Puente Viesgo. In 1903 this 16th-century hamlet in the Pas Valley excavated four caves under the 1,150-foot peak of Monte del Castillo, two of which—the Cueva del Castillo, and the Cueva de las Monedas—are open to the public. Bison, deer, bulls, and even humanoid stick figures are depicted;

the oldest designs are thought to be 35,000 years old. Most arresting are the paintings of 44 (curiously, 35 of them left) hands, reaching out through time. The painters are thought to have blown red pigment around their hands through a hollow bone, leaving the negative image. Advance reservations are advised. ✉ ***N623, Km 28, from Santander*** ☎ ***942/598425*** 🌐 ***www.culturadecantabria.com*** 🎫 ***€4 per cave*** 🕐 ***May–Sept., Daily 10–1; Oct.–Apr., Wed.–Sun. 9:30–4.***

COMILLAS

❹ *49 km (30 mi) west of Santander.*

This astounding pocket of Catalan Art Nouveau architecture in the green hills of Cantabria will make you rub your eyes in disbelief. Why is it here? The Marqués de Comillas, a Catalan named Antonio López y López (1817–83)—the wealthiest and most influential shipping magnate of his time—was a fervent patron of the arts who encouraged the great Moderniste architects to use his native village as a laboratory. Antonio Gaudí's 1883–89 green-and-yellow-tile villa, El Capricho (a direct cousin of his Casa Vicens in Barcelona), is the main attraction. The town cemetery is filled with Art Nouveau markers and monuments, most notably an immense angel by eminent Catalan sculptor Josep Llimona**Palacio Sobrellano,** built in the late 19th century by Catalan architect Joan Martorell for the Marqués de Comillas, this exuberant neo-Gothic mansion contains surprising collections of everything from sculpture and painting to archaeology and ethnographical material. The chapel has benches and kneeling stalls that were designed by Gaudí. ☎ *942/720339* 🌐 *www.culturadecantabria.com* 🎫 *€3 palace, €6 palace and chapel* 🕐 *Sept.–May, Wed.–Sun. 10:30–2 and 4–7:30; June–Sept., daily 10–9.*

WHERE TO EAT

$$$–$$$$ ✕**El Capricho de Gaudí.** Dining in a Gaudí creation is all but an obligation, especially if the visual rush is accompanied by fresh turbot with young garlic or roast lamb from the moist Cantabrian hills. This unique spot is overpriced, but even for a cup of coffee or a bowl of soup it's an unforgettable and unique opportunity to break bread in the same space where the great Moderniste broke all the rules. ✉ *Barrio de Sobrellano* ☎ *942/720365* 🌐 *www.gaudiallgaudi.com* 💳 *AE, DC, MC, V* 🕐 *Closed Jan. 15–Feb. 15, and Mon. Oct.–May. No dinner Sun.*

SAN VICENTE DE LA BARQUERA

❺ *64 km (40 mi) west of Santander, 15 km (9 mi) west of Comillas.*

Important as a Roman port long before many other larger, modern shipping centers (such as Santander) were, San Vicente de la Barquera is one of the oldest and most beautiful maritime settlements in northern Spain. The 28 arches of the ancient bridge **Puente de la Maza,** which spans the *ría* (fjord), welcome you to town. Thanks to its exceptional Romanesque portals, the 15th-century church of **Nuestra Señora de los**

Angeles *(Our Lady of the Angels)* is among San Vicente's most memorable sights.Make sure you check out the arcaded porticoes of the **Plaza Mayor** and the view over the town from the Unquera road (N634) just inland.San Vicente celebrates **La Folía** in late April (the name translates roughly as "folly," and the exact date depends not only on Easter but on the high tide) with a magnificent maritime procession: the town's colorful fishing fleet accompanies the figure of La Virgen de la Barquera as she is transported (in part) by boat from her sanctuary outside town to the village church. There she is honored with folk dances and songs before being returned to her hermitage.

LAREDO

6 *49 km (30 mi) southeast of Santander, N635 southeast, N634 east.*

You would hardly know it today, but Laredo was a home port of the Spanish Armada and remained Spain's chief northern harbor until the French sacked it in the 18th century and Santander became the regional capital. This little town was thus visited by the Spanish royals, including Isabella the Catholic and Charles I, better known as the Holy Roman Emperor Carlos V. When Charles—the most powerful monarch in European history—stopped by in the mid-16th century, he donated two brass choir desks in the shape of eagles. Charles I's brass choir desks are on display in the parish church of **La Asunción** *(Church of the Assumption)*, in the center of the town's tiny old quarter, which you may want to walk through to see mansions with heraldic coats of arms.

WHERE TO STAY & EAT

$$ **El Risco.** *Risco* is Spanish for "cliff," which is appropriate for a hotel built into the craggy slope overlooking Laredo. The food at the restaurant ($$–$$$$) combines classical and contemporary Cantabrian fare; try the *pimientos rellenos de cangrejo* (peppers stuffed with crabmeat). Every room has a spectacular view of the town and cove below. Hotel reservations are essential in summer. *La Arenosa 2, 39770 942/605030 942/605055 www.hotelrisco.com 25 rooms In-hotel: restaurant, bar, no elevator AE, DC, MC, V.*

CASTRO-URDIALES

7 *34 km (21 mi) northwest of Bilbao.*

Behind Laredo, the N634 winds up into the hills, with views of the Bay of Santoña over your shoulder. A short drive, parts of it within sight of the coast, takes you into the fishing village of Castro-Urdiales, believed to be the oldest settlement on the Cantabrian coast. Castro-Urdiales (*castro* was the Celtiberian word for a fortified village) was the region's leading whaling port in the 13th and 14th centuries, when it had almost three times today's 13,000 residents. Now it's known mainly for its seafood. Overlooking the town is the mammoth, rose-color jumble of roofs and buttresses of the Gothic **Santa María** church.Behind the Santa María church is the medieval **castle,** to which a modern lighthouse has been appended.Aside from its arcaded **Plaza del Ayuntamiento** and the narrow streets of its **old quarter** (much of which burned on May 11, 1813), the main things to see in Castro-Urdiales are the Santa María church, looming Gothically over the town, the ruins of the fortress converted into a lighthouse beside it, and the harbor-front promenade flanked by a row of glass-gallery houses.

WHERE TO EAT

$$–$$$$ ✕**Mesón Marinero.** Local fishermen rub elbows with visiting elites at this pearl of a tavern and restaurant. The tapas on the bar will tempt you to forgo the main meal; if you manage not to *tapear*away the dinner hour, you're in for a treat in the second-floor dining room overlooking Castro's weathered fishing port. *Besugo* (sea bream) is unbeatable here. ✉*La Correría 23* ☎*942/860005* ▭*AE, DC, MC, V.*

EN ROUTE

The 45-minute drive on the N634 from Castro-Urdiales to Bilbao takes you through some of the sprawling industrial development that mars much of Vizcaya (Bizkaia, in Euskera, the Basque language), the westernmost of the three Basque provinces. The A8 freeway will get you to Bilbao in just 15 minutes. A tempting stop is Santurtzi, whose Hogar del Pescador **in the port is a popular spot for sardines.**

5

BILBAO & THE BASQUE COAST TO GETARIA

Starring Frank Gehry's titanium brainchild—the Museo Guggenheim Bilbao—Bilbao has established itself as one of Spain's 21st-century darlings. The loop around the coast of Vizcaya and east into neighboring Guipúzcoa province to Getaria and San Sebastián is a succession of colorful ports, ocher beaches, and green hills.

BILBAO

34 km (21 mi) southeast of Castro-Urdiales, 116 km (72 mi) east of Santander, 397 km (247 mi) north of Madrid.

Time in Bilbao (Bilbo, in Euskera) may soon need to be identified as BG or AG (Before Guggenheim, After Guggenheim). Never has a single monument of art and architecture so radically changed a city—or, for that matter, a nation, and in this case two: Spain and Euskadi. Frank Gehry's stunning museum, Norman Foster's sleek subway system, the glass Santiago Calatrava footbridge, and the leafy park and commercial complex in Abandoibarra, have all helped foment a cultural revolution in the commercial capital of the Basque Country. Greater Bilbao encompasses almost 1 million inhabitants, nearly half the total population of the Basque Country. Founded in 1300 by Vizcayan noble Diego López de Haro, Bilbao became an industrial center in the mid-19th century, largely because of the abundance of minerals in the surrounding hills. An affluent industrial class grew up here, as did the working-class suburbs that line the Margen Izquierda (Left Bank) of the Nervión estuary.

Bilbao's new attractions get more press, but the city's old treasures still quietly line the banks of the rust-color Nervión River. The Casco Viejo (Old Quarter)—also known as Siete Calles (Seven Streets)—is a charming jumble of shops, bars, and restaurants on the river's Right Bank, near the Puente del Arenal bridge. Throughout the old quarter are ancient mansions emblazoned with family coats of arms, noble wooden doors, and fine ironwork balconies. Carefully restored after devastating floods in August 1983, this is an upscale shopping district replete with excellent taverns, restaurants, and nightlife. The most interesting square is the 64-arch Plaza Nueva, where an outdoor market is pitched every Sunday morning. On the Left Bank, the wide, late-19th-century boulevards of the Ensanche neighborhood, such as Gran Vía (the main shopping artery) and Alameda Mazarredo, are the city's more formal face. Bilbao's cultural institutions include, along with the Guggenheim, a major museum of fine arts (the Museo de Bellas Artes) and an opera society (ABAO: Asociacion Bilbaina de Amigos de la Opera) with 7,000 members from all over Spain and parts of southern France. In addition, epicureans have long ranked Bilbao's culinary offerings among the best in Spain. Don't miss a chance to ride the speedy and quiet trolley line, the Euskotram, for a trip along the river from Atxuri Station to Basurto's San Mamés soccer stadium, reverently dubbed "La Catedral del Fútbol" (the Cathedral of Football).

WHAT TO SEE

8 The **Casco Viejo** *(Old Quarter)* is folded into an elbow of the Nervión River behind Bilbao's grand, elaborately restored theater. While exploring, don't miss the colossal food market **El Mercado de la Ribera** at the edge of the river, the Renaissance town house **Palacio Yohn** at the corner of Sant Maria and Perro, and the library and cultural center **Biblioteca Municipal Bidebarrieta** at Calle Bidebarrieta 4.Inaugurated in 1890, **Teatro Arriaga** was a symbol of Bilbao's industrial might and cultural vibrancy by the time it burned nearly to the ground in 1914. Styled after the Paris Opéra, the theater defies easy classification: although its symmetry and formal repetition suggest neoclassicism, its ornamentation defines the belle epoque style. Walk around to see the stained-glass windows in the back. ✉ *Plaza Arriaga 1* ☎ *94/479–2036* Ⓜ *Casco Viejo.*

9 Stop at Calle Esperanza 6 and take the elevator to Bilbao's iconic **Basílica de Begoña** overlooking the city. The church's three-naved Gothic hulk was begun in 1511 on a spot where the Virgin Mary had supposedly appeared long before. Partly destroyed in the First Carlist War of 1835, the facade, tower, and sacristy were rebuilt in the early 20th century. The 24-bell carillon, the largest of which weighs one ton, plays a series of hymns and traditional Basque melodies that change according to the season. On the occasion of the winter and summer solistices the carillon serenades Bilbao with a short concert that might include anything from Bach to local composer Juan Crisóstomo de Arriaga (1806–26), known as Spain's Mozart. ✉ *C/Virgen de Begoña 38* ☎ *94/412–7091* 🌐 *www.basilicadebegona.com* Ⓜ *Casco Viejo.*

10 Near the Ayuntamiento Bridge is the riverside **ayuntamiento** *(city hall)*, built in 1892. Ⓜ *Casco Viejo.*

11 Don't let the Guggenheim eclipse the **Museo de Bellas Artes** *(Museum of Fine Arts)*. Depending on your tastes, you may find the art here more satisfying. The museum's fine collection of Flemish, French, Italian, and Spanish paintings includes works by El Greco, Goya, Velázquez, Zurbarán, Ribera, and Gauguin. One large and excellent section traces developments in 20th-century Spanish and Basque art alongside those of their better-known European contemporaries, such as Léger and Bacon. The building sits on the rim of the pretty Doña Casilda Park, about a 30-minute walk from the Old Quarter. ✉ *Plaza del Museo 2* ☎ *94/439–6060* 🌐 *www.museobilbao.com* 🎟 *€5.50, free Wed., combined ticket with Guggenheim (valid 1 yr) €12 plus €2 additional on admittance to 2nd museum* ⏲ *Tues.–Sat. 10–1:30 and 4–7:30, Sun. 10–2* Ⓜ *Moyúa.*

Fodor's Choice ★

NEED A BREAK?

El Kiosko del Arenal (✉ ***Paseo del Arenal s/n, under the bandstand in Paseo del Arenal*** Ⓜ ***Casco Viejo*****) is an excellent place for coffee, beer, or tapas. Terrace tables offer views of the river in summer, and its spot underneath the bandstand is paradigmaticly clean and well-lit in winter.**

12 Covered with a dazzling 30,000 sheets of titanium, the **Museo Guggenheim Bilbao** opened in October 1997 and became Bilbao's main attraction overnight. The shimmering effect of this finned and fluted titanium whale next to the rusty waters of the Nervión is difficult to over-describe, especially for anyone familiar with the smoldering industrial heap that occupied this space not so long ago. Its 10th anniversary in 2007 was heralded with a series of exhibits featuring contemporary Basque artists, entitled "Cada uno a su gusto" ("Each to Their Own Taste"), is scheduled to last into 2008. An enormous atrium, more than 150 feet high, is connected to the 19 galleries by a system of suspended metal walkways and glass elevators. The ground floor is dedicated to large installations. The permanent collection and the excellent acoustiguide that accompanies it offer an entertaining and instructive survey of 20th-century art. ☎ *94/435–9080* 🌐 *www.guggenheim-bilbao.es* 🎟 *€10.50; €12 for special exhibits; combined ticket with Museo de Bellas Artes (valid 1 yr) €14 plus €2 additional on admittance to 2nd museum* ⏲ *July and Aug., daily 10–8; Sept.–June, Tues.–Sun. 10–8* Ⓜ *Moyúa.*

Fodor's Choice ★

13 Dubbed Bilbao's Eiffel Tower (albeit a horizontal version) the **Puente de Vizcaya** is commonly called the Puente Colgante (Hanging Bridge). Spanning the Nervión, this transporter hung from cables unites two distinct worlds: exclusive, quiet Las Arenas and Portugalete, a much older, working-class town that spawned Dolores Ibarruri, the famous Republican orator of the Spanish civil war, known as La Pasionaria for her ardor. Portugalete is a 15-minute walk from Santurce, where the quayside Hogar del Pescador serves simple and ample fish specialties. *Besugo* (sea bream) is the traditional choice, but the fresh grilled sardines are hard to pass up. To reach the bridge, take the subway to Areeta, or drive across the Puente de Deusto, turn left on Avenida

CLOSE UP

Glitzy Guggenheim

Described by Spanish novelist Manuel Vazquez Montalban as a "meteorite," Bilbao's Guggenheim may be the most celebrated building of all time. This eruption of light and titanium has reinvented this city. Perennially chided as the *barrio industrial* (industrial quarter) in contrast to San Sebastián's *barrio jardín* (garden quarter), Bilbao has long been perceived as a polluted steel and shipbuilding center.

The Guggenheim has changed all that. Frank Gehry's gleaming brainchild, alternately hailed as "the greatest building of our time" (architect Philip Johnson), "the best building of the 20th century" (Spain's King Juan Carlos), and "a miracle" (Herbert Muschamp, *New York Times*), has sparked a renaissance in the Basque Country. In its first year, the Guggenheim attracted 1.4 million visitors, three times the number expected and more than what both Guggenheim museums in New York received together that same period. Revenue in the first year alone exceeded the original investment. Incredibly, the Guggenheim already holds the Spanish record for single-day visits to a museum (9,300), and the crowds are not diminishing.

The museum itself is as superlative as the hoopla suggests. The smoothly rounded, asymmetrical, ship's-prow-like amalgam of limestone, glass, and titanium ingeniously recalls Bilbao's shipbuilding and steel-manufacturing past while using transparency and reflective materials to create a shimmering, futuristic luminosity. The final section of the Nervión's La Salve Bridge is almost part of the structure, rendering the Guggenheim the virtual doorway to Bilbao.

The collection, described by director Thomas Krens as "a daring history of the art of the 20th century," consists of 242 works, 186 from New York's Guggenheim and 50 acquired by the Basque government. Artists whose names are synonymous with the 20th century (Kandinsky, Picasso, Ernst, Braque, Miró, Calder, Malevich) and particularly artists of the '50s and '60s (Pollock, Rothko, De Kooning, Chillida, Tàpies, Iglesias) are joined by contemporary figures (Nauman, Muñoz, Schnabel, Badiola, Barceló, Basquiat). The huge ground-floor gallery is the largest in the world.

Lehendakari Aguirre, and follow signs for Las Arenas. ☎94/480–1012 🌐*www.puente-colgante.org* 🎫*€0.30 to cross on foot, €1.10 by car; €4 for visit to observation deck* Ⓜ*Areeta.*

14 **Catedral de Santiago** *(St. James's Cathedral).* Bilbao's earliest church, this was a pilgrimage stop on the coastal route to Santiago de Compostela. Work on the structure began in 1379, but fire destroyed most of it in 1571; it has a notable outdoor arcade. ✉*Plaza de Santiago* Ⓜ*Casco Viejo.*

The **Museo Arqueológico, Etnográfico e Histórico Vasco** *(Museum of Basque Archaeology, Ethnology, and History)* is in a lovely 16th-century convent. (Its Baroque elegance and lush green arcaded cloister more than justifies the visit.) The collection centers on Basque fishing, crafts, and agriculture. ✉*Pl. Miguel de Unamuno 4* ☎*94/415–5423* 🌐*www.euskal-museoa.org* 🎫*€3.50, free Thurs.* ⏰*Tues.–Sat. 10:30–1:30 and 4–7, Sun. 10:30–1* Ⓜ*Casco Viejo.*

The **Museo Diocesano de Arte Sacro** *(Diocesan Museum of Sacred Art)* occupies a carefully restored 16th-century cloister. The inner patio alone, ancient and intimate, is worth the visit. On display are religious silver works, liturgical garments, sculptures, and paintings dating back to the 12th century. ✉*Pl. de la Encarnación 9* ☎*94/432–0125* 🎫*€2* Ⓜ*Casco Viejo.*

15 **Palacio de Euskalduna.** In homage to the Astilleros Euskalduna (Basque Country shipbuilders) who operated shipyards here beside the Euskalduna Bridge into the mid-'80s, this music venue and convention hall resembles a rusting ship. Designed by Federico Soriano, Euskalduna opened in 1999 and is Bilbao's main opera venue and home of the Bilbao Symphony Orchestra. ✉*Abandoibarra 4, El Ensanche* ☎*94/403–5000* 🌐*www.euskalduna.net* 🎫*Tour €3* ⏰*Office weekdays 9–2 and 4–7; box office Mon.–Sat. noon–2 and 5–8:30, Sun. noon–2; guided tours Sat. at noon or by fax appointment* Ⓜ*San Mamés.*

16 **Museo Marítimo de Bilbao** *(Maritime Museum of Bilbao).* This interesting nautical museum on the left bank of the Ría de Bilbao reconstructs the history of the Bilbao waterfront and shipbuilding industry, beginning with medieval times. Temporary exhibits range from visits by extraordinary seacraft such as tall ships or traditional fishing vessels to thematic displays on 17th- and 18th-century clipper ships or the sinking of the *Titanic.* ✉*Muelle Ramón de la Sota* ☎*902/131000* 🌐*www.museomaritimobilbao.org* 🎫*€4* ⏰*Tues.–Sun. 10–8* Ⓜ*San Mamés.*

WHERE TO STAY & EAT

$$$–$$$$ ✕**Aizian.** Euskera for "in the wind," the Sheraton Bilbao restaurant—under the direction of chef José Miguel Olazabalaga—has in record time become one of the city's most respected dining establishments. Typically Bilbaino culinary classicism doesn't keep Mr. Olazabalaga from creating surprising reductions and contemporary interpretations of traditional dishes such as *la marmita de chipirón,* a stew of sautéed cuttlefish with a topping of whipped potatoes covering the sauce of squid ink. ✉*C. Lehendakari Leizaola 29, El Ensanche* ☎*94/428–0035*

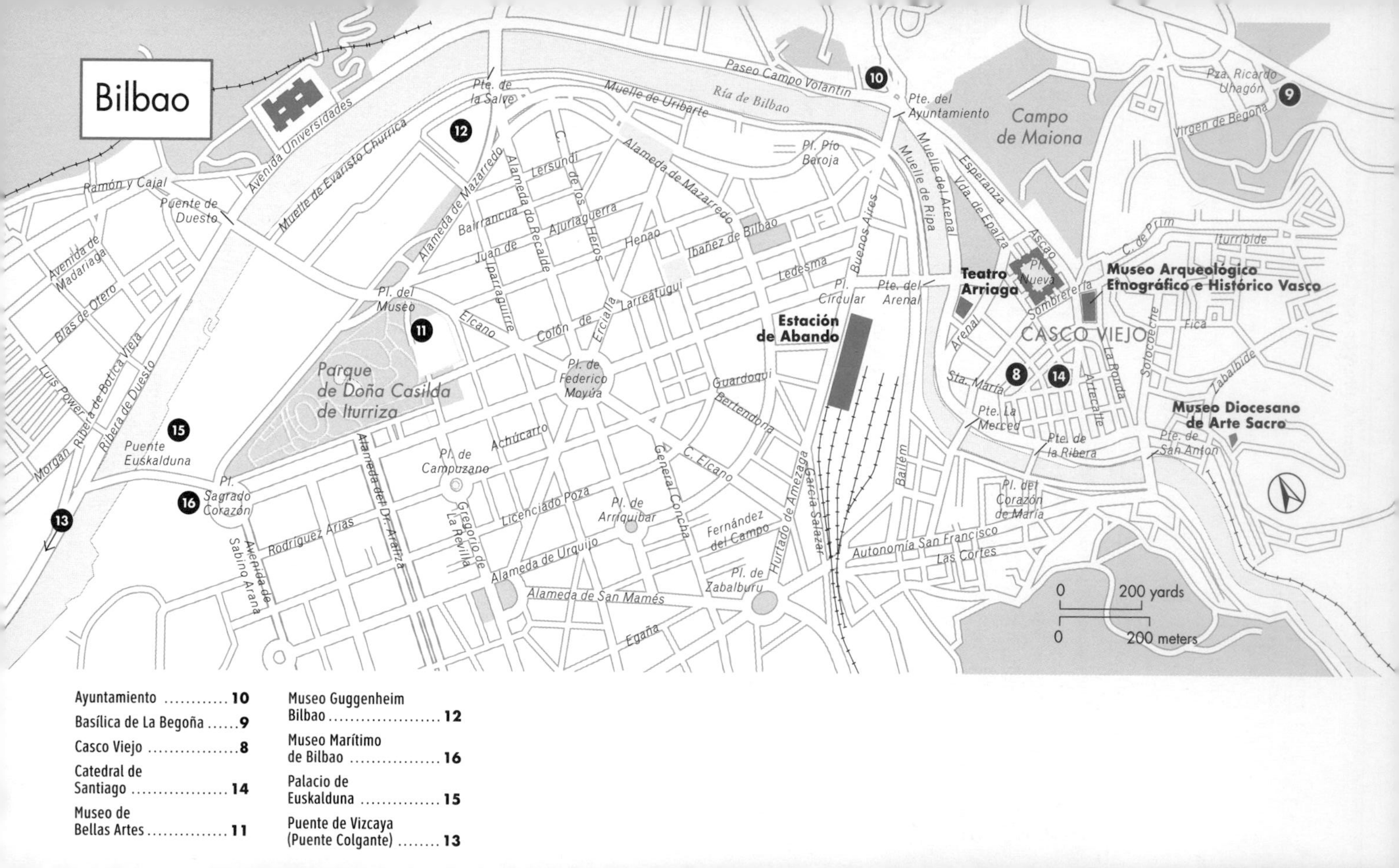
Bilbao
Campo de Maiona
Casco Viejo
Parque de Doña Casilda de Iturriza
Estación de Abando
Teatro Arriaga
Museo Arqueológico Etnográfico e Histórico Vasco
Museo Diocesano de Arte Sacro
Ría de Bilbao
Paseo Campo Volantín
Muelle de Uribarte
Muelle del Arenal
Muelle de Ripa
Muelle de Evaristo Churruca
Avenida Universidades
Pte. de la Salve
Pte. del Ayuntamiento
Pte. del Arenal
Pte. La Merced
Pte. de la Ribera
Pte. de San Antón
Puente de Deusto
Puente Euskalduna
Pl. Pío Baroja
Pl. Circular
Pl. Nueva
Pl. del Museo
Pl. de Federico Moyúa
Pl. de Campuzano
Pl. de Arriquibar
Pl. de Zabalburu
Pl. Sagrado Corazón
Pl. del Corazón de María
Pza. Ricardo Uhagón
Virgen de Begoña
Alameda de Mazarredo
Alameda do Recalde
Alameda de Urquijo
Alameda de San Mamés
Alameda del Dr. Areilza
Avenida de Sabino Arana
Avenida de Madariaga
Ramón y Cajal
Blas de Otero
Luis Power
Ribera de Botica Vieja
Ribera de Deusto
Morgan
Lersundi
C. de los Heros
Ajuriaguerra
Barrancua
Juan de Iparraguirre
Henao
Ibañez de Bilbao
Ledesma
Buenos Aires
Elcano
Colón de Larreátegui
Ercilla
Guardoqui
Bertendona
C. Elcano
General Concha
Achúcarro
Licenciado Poza
Gregorio de La Revilla
Rodríguez Arias
Fernández del Campo
Hurtado de Amezaga
García Salazar
Bailén
Autonomía
San Francisco
Las Cortes
Egaña
Esperanza
Vda. de Epalza
Ascao
Arenal
Sombrerería
Sta. María
Artecalle
La Ronda
Somera
Fica
Iturribide
C. de Prim
Tabalbide
0 200 yards
0 200 meters
Ayuntamiento 10
Basílica de La Begoña 9
Casco Viejo 8
Catedral de Santiago 14
Museo de Bellas Artes 11
Museo Guggenheim Bilbao 12
Museo Marítimo de Bilbao 16
Palacio de Euskalduna 15
Puente de Vizcaya (Puente Colgante) 13

AE, DC, MC, V Closed Sun. and Aug. 1–15 San Mamés.

$$$–$$$$ **El Perro Chico.** Named for the toll once charged here for crossing the footbridge below Bilbao's Mercado de la Ribera (a *perro chico* was the colloquial name for an ancient coin), this restaurant became a Frank Gehry favorite during his time in Bilbao supervising the construction of the Guggenheim. From owner Santiago Diez Ponzoa to chef Rafael García Rossi, everyone here genuinely enjoys preparing innovative and thoughtful cuisine without pretense. Try the *pato a la naranja* (duck à l'orange) or the *bacalao con berenjena* (salt cod with eggplant). *Aretxaga 2 94/415–0519 AE, DC, MC, V Closed Sun. No lunch Mon. Casco Viejo.*

BILBAO BLUE

The museum's offices, to the right of Jeff Koons's Puppy, are a bright, intense blue. Frank Gehry discovered this rich azure while working on his titanium opus and fell in love with it. Known locally as "Bilbao blue," the color comes from the vivid blue sky traditionally visible over Bilbao on the rare days when the persistent Atlantic drizzle lets up. Curiously, as a result of either the reflected light of the Guggenheim, the absence of industrial smog, or climate changes, Bilbao's blue skies are thought to be less intense. Now the offices are a tribute to this emblematic color.

$$$–$$$$ **Etxanobe.** Fernando Canales creates sleek, contemporary cuisine here on a par with the Basque Country's finest with seasonal offerings ranging from truffles in cream of potato and egg in winter to a superb crab salad in summer. This luminous corner of the Euskalduna palace overlooks the Nervión River, the hills of Artxanda above, and Bilbao. The panoramic elevator up to the restaurant is guaranteed to jump-start appetite-enhancing adrenaline. *Av. de Abandoibarra 4 94/442–1071 AE, DC, MC, V Closed Sun., Easter wk, and Aug. 1–20 San Mamés.*

$$$–$$$$ **Guggenheim Bilbao.** The museum's restaurant in residence has a lot to live up to, and easily succeeds. Famous for his eponymous restaurant outside San Sebastián, Martín Berasategui (or his staff) will install you at a table overlooking the Nervión and the green heights of Artxanda, then feed you such exciting creations as *pichón de Bresse* (wild pigeon) and *ensalada de bogavante* (lobster salad). *Av. Abandoibarra 2 94/423–9333 Reservations essential AE, DC, MC, V Closed Mon. and Jan. 1–19. No dinner Sun. or Tues. Moyúa.*

$$$–$$$$ ★ **Guria.** The late, great Genaro Pildain, born in what he called "the smallest village in Vizcaya Province," was the hands-down leader of Bilbao chefs, a genius of charm and simplicity. Having learned cooking from his mother, Don Genaro presided over one of Bilbao's finest tables for two decades. His business partner Carlos del Rey and chef Tomás Razquin carry on Don Genaro's tradition of generosity and hospitality. Everything's impeccable here, from the *crema de puerros con patatas* (cream of potato-and-leek soup) to the *perretxikos de Orduña* (small, wild spring mushrooms). *Gran Vía 66 94/441–5780 AE, DC, MC, V No dinner Sun. San Mamés.*

$$–$$$ ✕**Berton.** Dinner is served until 11:30 in this sleek, contemporary bistro in the Casco Viejo. Fresh wood tables with a green-tint polyethylene finish and exposed ventilation pipes give the dining room a designer look, and the classic cuisine ranges from Ibérico ham to smoked salmon, foie gras, cod, beef, and lamb. ✉*Jardines 11* ☎*94/416–7035* ▭*AE, DC, MC, V* ⊙*No dinner Sun. and holidays* Ⓜ*Casco Viejo.*

$–$$$ ✕**La Deliciosa.** For carefully prepared fare at friendly prices, this simple but cozy dining room is one of the best values in the Casco Viejo. The *crema de puerros* (cream of leeks) is as good as any in town, and the *dorada al horno* (roast gilthead bream) is fresh from the nearby La Ribera Market. ✉*Jardines 1* ☎*94/415–0944* ▭*AE, DC, MC, V* Ⓜ*Casco Viejo.*

$–$$ ✕**Arriaga.** The cider-house experience is a must in the Basque Country. Cider *al txotx* (straight from the barrel), sausage stewed in apple cider, codfish omelets, *txuletón de buey* (beef chops), and Idiazabal cheese with quince jelly are the classic fare. Reserving a table is a good idea, especially on weekends. ✉*Santa Maria 13* ☎*94/416–5670* ▭*AE, DC, MC, V* ⊙*No dinner Sun.* Ⓜ*Casco Viejo.*

$–$$ ✕**Kiskia.** A modern version of the traditional cider house, this rambling
Fodor's Choice ★ tavern near the San Mamés soccer stadium serves the classical *sidrería* menu of chorizo sausage cooked in cider, codfish omelet, *txuleta de buey*(beef chops), Idiazabal cheese with quince jelly and nuts, and as much cider as you can drink, all for €28. Actors, sculptors, writers, soccer stars, and Bilbao's (and Spain's) who's who frequent this boisterous marvel. ✉*Pérez Galdós 51, San Mamés* ☎*94/442–0032* ▭*AE, DC, MC, V* ⊙*No dinner Sun.–Tues.* Ⓜ*San Mamés.*

¢–$ ✕**Xukela.** Amid bright lighting and a vivid palette of greens and crimsons, chef Santiago Ruíz Bombin creates some of the tastiest and most eye-watering *pintxos* (morsels on toothpicks) in all of tapas-dom. The tavern has the general feel of a small library: lined with books and little nooks to enjoy them. ✉*El Perro 2* ☎*94/415–9772* ▭*AE, DC, MC, V* Ⓜ*Casco Viejo.*

$$$–$$$$ ★ ✕🏨**Lopez de Haro.** Because it's just five minutes from the Guggenheim, Bilbao's top hotel has become quite a scene. The converted 19th-century building has an English feel and all the comforts your heart desires. Club Náutico, a handy alternative on one of Bilbao's many rainy evenings, serves modern and classical Basque dishes, ranging from a simple *besugo* (sea bream) or one of the city's famous *bacalao* (codfish) preparations to sleek, contemporary interpretations of traditional favorites. ✉*Obispo Orueta 2, 48009* ☎*94/423–5500* 📠*94/423–4500* 🌐*www.hotellopezdeharo.com* *49 rooms, 4 suites* *In-room: dial-up. In-hotel: restaurant, bar, parking (fee)* ▭*AE, DC, MC, V* Ⓜ*Moyúa.*

$$$$ 🏨**Sheraton Bilbao Hotel.** This colossus, built over what was once the nerve center of Bilbao's shipbuilding industry, feels like a futuristic ocean liner. Designed by architect Ricardo Legorreta and inspired by the work of Basque sculptor Eduardo Chillida (1920–2002), the hotel is filled with contemporary art and models of Spanish ships. Rooms are high, wide, and handsome, with glass, steel, stone, and wood trimmings. The comforts and the views from upper floors are superb. The Chillida café and the restaurant, Aizian, are both excellent.

✉C. Lehendakari Leizaola 29, El Ensanche, 48001 ☎94/428–0000 📠94/428–0001 🌐www.sheraton-bilbao.com/esp ⇨199 rooms, 12 suites ♿In-room: dial-up. In-hotel: 2 restaurants, bar, gym, parking (fee) ▭AE, DC, MC, V Ⓜ San Mamés.

$$$–$$$$ ★ **Carlton.** Luminaries who have trod the halls of this grande dame include Orson Welles, Ava Gardner, Ernest Hemingway, Lauren Bacall, and most of Spain's great bullfighters. During the civil war it was the seat of the Republican Basque government; later it housed a number of Nationalist generals. It remains high-ceilinged and elegant, with creaky wooden floorboards and floor-to-ceiling windows swathed in heavy drapes. *✉Pl. Federico Moyúa 2, El Ensanche, 48009 ☎94/416–2200 📠94/416–4628 🌐www.aranzazu-hoteles.com ⇨137 rooms, 7 suites ♿In-room: dial-up. In-hotel: restaurant, bar, parking (fee) ▭AE, DC, MC, V Ⓜ Moyúa.*

$$$–$$$$ ★ **Gran Hotel Domine Bilbao.** Half modern design festival, half hotel, this member of the Silken chain, directly across the street from the Guggenheim, showcases the conceptual wit of Javier Mariscal, creator of Barcelona's 1992 Olympic mascot Cobi, and the structural know-how of Bilbao architect Iñaki Aurreroextea. With adjustable window-panes reflecting Gehry's titanium leviathan and every lamp and piece of furniture reflecting Mariscal's playful whimsy, this is the brightest star in Bilbao's design constellation. Comprehensively equipped and comfortable, it's the next best thing to moving into the Guggenheim. *✉Alameda de Mazarredo 61, El Ensanche, 48009 ☎94/425–3300 📠94/425 3301 🌐www.granhoteldominebilbao.com ⇨139 rooms, 6 suites ♿In-room: dial-up. In-hotel: restaurant, bar, parking (fee) ▭AE, DC, MC, V Ⓜ Moyúa.*

$$$ Fodor'sChoice ★ **Miró Hotel.** Across from the Guggenheim and one block away from Bilbao's Museo de Bellas Artes, this boutique hotel, refurbished by Barcelona interior designer Gabriel Miró, is extremely comfortable and daringly innovative. Rooms are quiet, spacious, and contemporary, with high-tech touches. Public rooms are done in blacks and beiges and are simple and unpretentious; the hip downstairs bar is punctuated with canary-yellow walls. Expect a free drink when you arrive, excellent service throughout your stay, and, if you opt for it, a lavish breakfast with fresh-squeezed orange juice, bacon, eggs, and more—enough to keep you full all day. There's also a CD and DVD library, in addition to plenty of books. *✉Alameda de Mazarredo 77, El Ensanche, 48001 ☎94/661–1880 📠94/425 5182 🌐www.mirohotelbilbao.com ⇨45 rooms, 5 suites ♿In-room: dial-up. In-hotel: restaurant, room service, bar, gym, spa, laundry service, airport shuttle, parking (fee) ▭AE, DC, MC, V Ⓜ Moyúa.*

$$–$$$ **Hotel Ercilla.** This modern hotel fills with bullfighting crowds during Bilbao's Semana Grande in early August, both because it's near the bullring and because it's the new place to see and be seen—not exactly the spot for a quiet getaway. Impeccable rooms, amenities, and service underscore its reputation. *✉C. Ercilla 37, El Ensanche, 48009 ☎94/470–5700 📠94/443–9335 🌐www.hotelercilla.es ⇨335 rooms, 10 suites ♿In-room: dial-up. In-hotel: restaurant, bar, parking (fee) ▭AE, DC, MC, V Ⓜ Moyúa.*

5

$–$$ **Iturrienea Ostatua.** Euskara (Basque) for "Hostal of the Fountain," this traditional Basque town house in Bilbao's old quarter has overhead wooden beams, stone floors, and ethnographical and historical objects adorning the walls. Management and staff are invariably smart, polite, and helpful. The only caveat is nocturnal noise on the front side, especially in summer. Try for a room in the back, or bring earplugs. ✉*Santa María Kalea 14, Casco Viejo, 48005* ☎*94/416–1500* *94/415–8929* *www.iturrieneaostatua.com* *21 rooms* *In-room: no a/c. In-hotel: no elevator* *AE, DC, MC, V* *Casco Viejo.*

CAFÉS

Bar los Fueros (✉*C. de los Fueros 4, Casco Viejo*), as much a watering hole as a café, is one of Bilbao's most authentic enclaves, perfect for an *aperitivo* (aperitif) or a nightcap. The **Café Bulevard** (✉*C. Arenal 3, Casco Viejo*) dates back to 1871. **Café El Tilo** (✉*C. Arenal 1, Casco Viejo*) may be the best in Bilbao, with wooden tables and original frescoes by Basque painter Juan de Aranoa (1901–73). It's open weekdays only. Refuel at the enormous **Café Iruña** (✉*Jardines de Albia, El Ensanche*), a turn-of-the-20th-century classic. Founded in 1926, **Café La Granja** (✉*Pl. Circular 3, El Ensanche*), near the Puente del Arenal, is a Bilbao classic for coffee, beer, and *tortilla de patata* (potato omelet).

NIGHTLIFE & THE ARTS

Bilbao holds a music festival in August; inquire at the main tourist office on Paseo de Arenal (☎94/479–5770), as venues change. The city's abundant nightlife breaks neatly down into ages and zones. Students and anyone else who can pass for being thirty-ish and under amass on and around Calle Licenciado Poza (known as Pozas, two blocks east of Gran Vía) and the Casco Viejo, where serious *poteo* (tippling) continues until late. Barring holidays, the first half of the week is quieter. **Flash** (✉*C. Telesforo Aranzadi 4, Near Hotel Carlton, El Ensanche*) has dinner, dancing, and cocktails. The bright **Palacio Euskalduna** (✉*Abandoibarra 4, El Ensanche* ☎*944/308372*), home of the Orquesta Sinfónica de Bilbao, has all but replaced the Arriaga as Bilbao's prime performing-arts venue. All ages meet for drinks at designer Javier Mariscal's playful **Splash & Crash** (✉*Alameda Mazarredo 61, El Ensanche*) cocktail lounge and pub in the Hotel Gran Domine.The historic **Teatro Arriaga** (✉*Pl. Arriaga s/n, Casco Viejo* ☎*94/416–3244*) still draws the world's top performers in ballet, theater, concerts, opera, and *zarzuela* (comic opera).

SHOPPING

Basque *txapelas* (berets) make charming gifts. **Basandere** (✉*C. Iparaguirre 4* ☎*94/423–6386*), near the Guggenheim, has artisanal Basque crafts and foods. Look for Elosegui, the best-known brand of txapelas, in the old quarter's **Sombreros Gorostiaga** (✉*C. Victor 9* ☎*94/416–1276*).

EN ROUTE

From Bilbao, drive west down the Nervión to Neguri and Getxo and follow the coast road around through Baquio, Bermeo, and Mundaka to Gernika before proceeding east. Depending on stops for lunch or sprawling on a breezy beach, this can be a two- to six-hour drive, all of it spectacularly scenic.

GETXO

17 *13 km (8 mi) northwest of Bilbao, 10 km (6 mi) southwest of Plentzia.*

Getxo, an early watering spot for the elite Bilbao industrial classes, has rambling mansions, five beaches, and an ancient fishing port. Restaurants and hotels along the beaches here make good hideaways—only a 20-minute ride from the center of Bilbao, on the British architect Norman Foster's designer subway line.

SAN JUAN DE GAZTELUGATXE

18 *12 km (7 mi) west of Bermeo.*

This tiny, gemlike hermitage clinging to its rocky promontory over the Bay of Biscay is exactly 231 steps up along a narrow corridor built into the top of a rocky ledge connecting what would otherwise be an island to the mainland. A favorite pilgrimage for Bilbainos on holidays, the Romanesque chapel is said to have been used as a fortress by the Templars in the 14th century.

A HEAVENLY STROLL

A walk around San Juan de Gaztelugatxe's chapel bell tower is said to cure nightmares and insomnia, as well as to make wishes come true.

WHERE TO STAY & EAT

$–$$ **Ostatua Gaztelubegi.** The views from this little hotel and restaurant overlooking the hermitage of San Juan de Gaztelugatxe are some of the most vertiginous of the Basque coast. The bar is always booming; the food is simple Basque cooking, from *alubias* to *besugo* (beans to sea bream). *Ctra. BI–3101, Km 3, from Bakio, 48130 94/619–4924 www.bakio.com 7 rooms In-room: no a/c. In-hotel: restaurant, bar, no elevator, parking (no fee)* AE, DC, MC, V.

BERMEO

19 *30 km (18 mi) east of Plentzia, 3 km (2 mi) west of Mundaka.*

Bermeo is easy to miss if you don't park and walk through the old part of town to the port. With the largest fishing fleet in Spain—some 60 long-distance tuna freezer ships of more than 150 tons, and nearly 100 smaller craft that specialize in hake, sea bream, gilthead, and other local species—Bermeo was long famous as a whaling port. In the 16th century, local whalers reportedly were obliged to donate the tongue of every whale to raise money for the church. Bermeo has one of only two wooden-boat shipyards on the northern coast, and the boats in its harbor make a colorful picture. Drive to the top of the windswept hill, where a cemetery overlooks the crashing waves below.

Bermeo's **Museo del Pescador** is the only museum in the world dedicated to the craft and history of fishermen and the fishing industry, from whales to anchovies. The tower was built by native son Alonso de Ercilla y Zuñiga (1533–94), poet and eminent soldier. Ercilla's "La

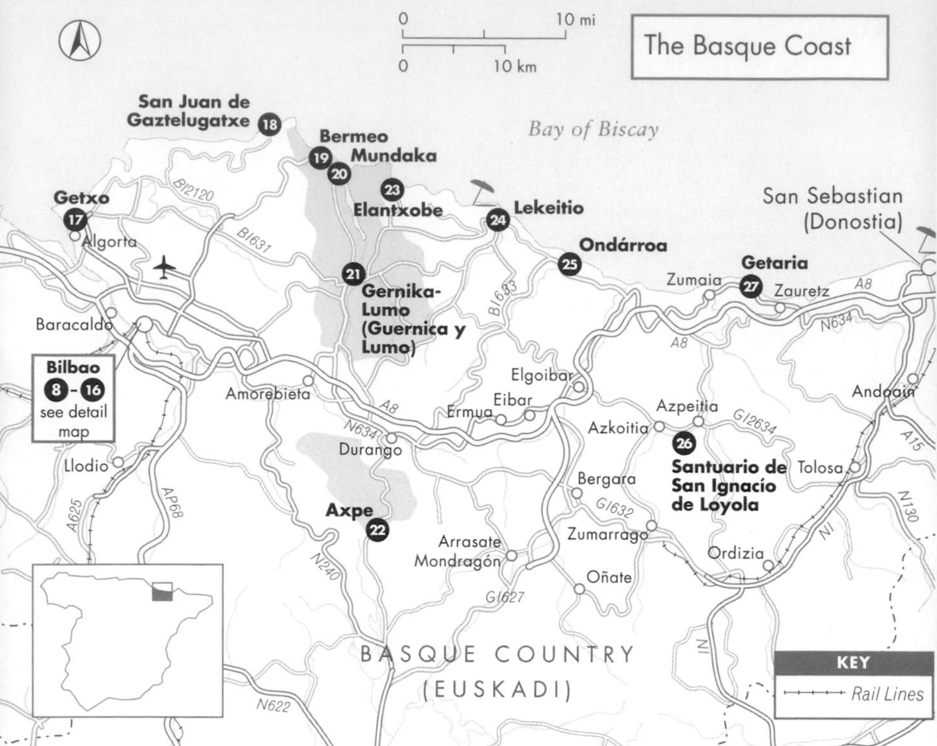

Araucana," an account of the conquest of Arauco (Chile), is considered one of the best Spanish epic poems. ✉ *Torre de Ercilla* ☎ *946/881171* 🎫 *Free* ⏲ *Tues.–Sat. 10–1:30 and 4–7:30, Sun. 10–1:30.*

WHERE TO EAT

$$–$$$$ ✕ **Jokin.** You'll have a good view of the *puerto viejo* (old port) from this cheerful, strategically located restaurant. The fish served comes directly off the boats in the harbor below. Try the *rape Jokin* (anglerfish in a clam and crayfish sauce) or *chipirones en su tinta* (small squid in its own ink) and, for dessert, the *tarta de naranja* (orange cake). ✉ *Eupeme Deuna 13* ☎ *94/688–4089* 💳 *AE, DC, MC, V* ⏲ *No dinner Sun.*

MUNDAKA

20 *45 km (28 mi) northeast of Bilbao.*

Tiny Mundaka, famous with surfers all over the world for its left-breaking roller at the mouth of the Ría de Guernica, has been in crisis since its wave mysteriously disappeared in 2004. October was prime time for Europe's longest wave until (according to one theory) a dredging displaced or altered the sandbar that created it. In 2005, studies were elaborated to determine where the wave has gone and how to get it back. As of early 2006, the wave was better, but not fully recovered, though signs are hopeful that it will be.

WHERE TO STAY & EAT

$$-$$$$ ✕ **Casino José Mari.** Built in 1818 as an auction house for the local fishermen's guild, this building, with wonderful views of Mundaka's beach, is now an eating club. The public is welcome, and it's a prime lunch stop in summer, when you can sit in the glassed-in, upper-floor porch. Very much a local haunt, the club serves excellent fish caught, more often than not, by members. ✉ *Parque Atalaya, center of town* ☎ *94/687–6005* ▭ *AE, MC, V.*

$$-$$$ **Atalaya.** Tastefully coverted from a private house, this 1911 landmark 37 km (22 mi) from Bilbao has become a big favorite for quick railroad-getaway overnights from Bilbao and the Guggenheim. (The train ride out is spectacular.) Guest rooms are charming and comfortable; those upstairs have balconies with marvelous views. Room No. 12 is the best in the house. The breakfast room is cheerful and light. ✉ *Paseo de Txorrokopunta 2, 48360* ☎ *94/617–7000* 📠 *94/687–6899* 🌐 *www.hotel-atalaya-mundaka.com* *11 rooms* *In-hotel: restaurant, bar* ▭ *AE, DC, MC, V.*

5

EN ROUTE

From Mundaka, follow signs for Gernika, stopping at the Mirador de Portuondo—a roadside lookout on the left as you leave town (BI-635, Km 43)—for an excellent view of the estuary.

GERNIKA-LUMO (GUERNICA Y LUMO)

21 *15 km (9 mi) east of Bilbao.*

On Monday, April 26, 1937—market day—Gernika suffered history's second terror bombing against a civilian population. (The first, much less famous, was against neighboring Durango, about a month earlier.) The planes of the Nazi Luftwaffe were sent with the blessings of General Francisco Franco to experiment with saturation bombing of civilian targets and to decimate the traditional seat of Basque autonomy. Since the Middle Ages, Spanish sovereigns had sworn under the ancient **oak tree of Gernika** to respect Basque *fueros* (special local rights—the kind of local autonomy that was anathema to the *generalísimo*'s Madrid-centered "National Movement," which promoted Spanish unity over local identity). More than 1,000 people were killed in the bombing, and today Gernika remains a symbol of independence in the heart of every Basque, known to the world through Picasso's famous canvas *Guernica* (now in Madrid's Centro de Arte Reina Sofía). The city was destroyed—though an oak tree miraculously emerged unscathed—and has been rebuilt as a modern, architecturally uninteresting town. The **Museo de la Paz** offers a closer look at the bombing heard around the world (thanks to the Picasso painting), and the **Museo de Euskalerria** provides insights into Basque culture, history, and ethnology. The stump of the sacred oak, which at last died several decades ago, can be found in the courtyard of the **Casa de Juntas** (a new oak has been planted alongside the old one)—the object of many a pilgrimage. Nearby is the

Continued on page 318

MINIATURE FOOD, MAXIMUM FLAVOR

An Introduction to TAPAS

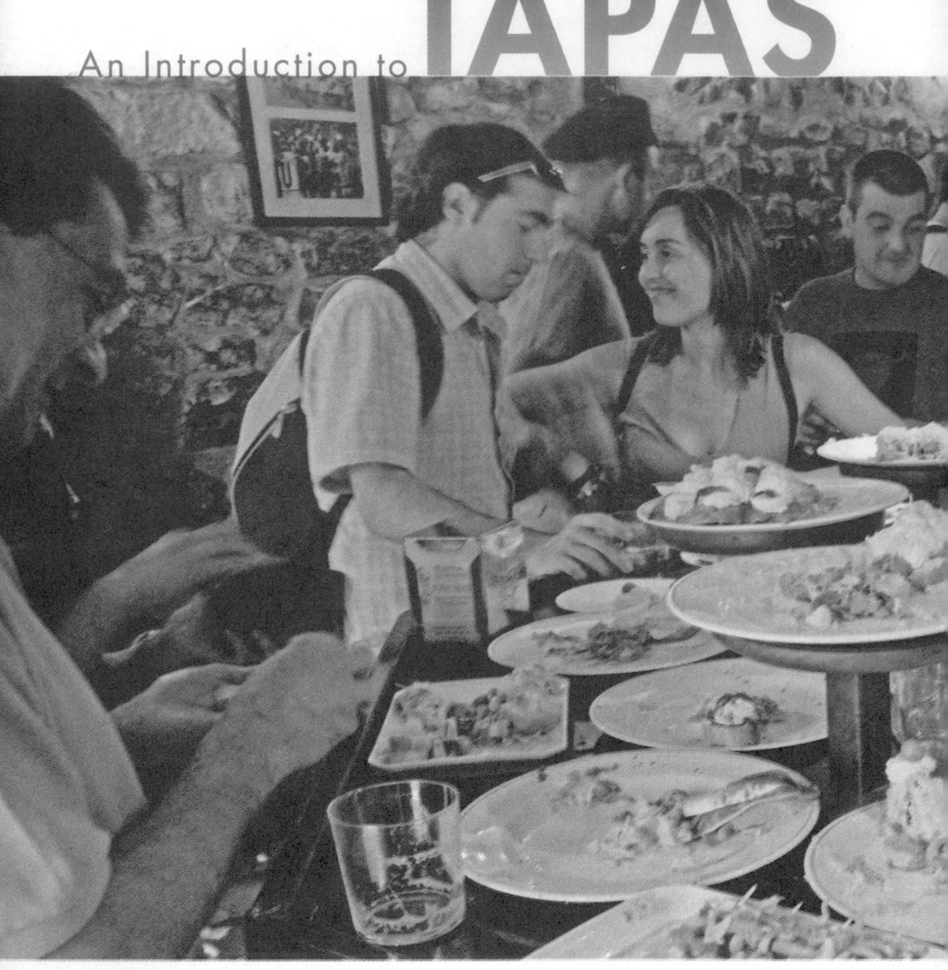

Virtually every day, coworkers head to a tapas bar after work for a *caña* (a 4–6 oz beer) that's almost always paired with a tapa or two. On weeknights, families crowd around tables with drinks and tapas, filling up on several *raciones* or small *cazuelas*. In the evenings, couples out on the town do "tapas crawls," the Spanish version of a pub crawl where *croquetas*

Defining tapas as merely a snack is, for a Spaniard, like defining air as an occasional breathable treat. If that sounds a little dramatic, consider how this bite-sized food influences daily life across all regions and classes throughout Spain.

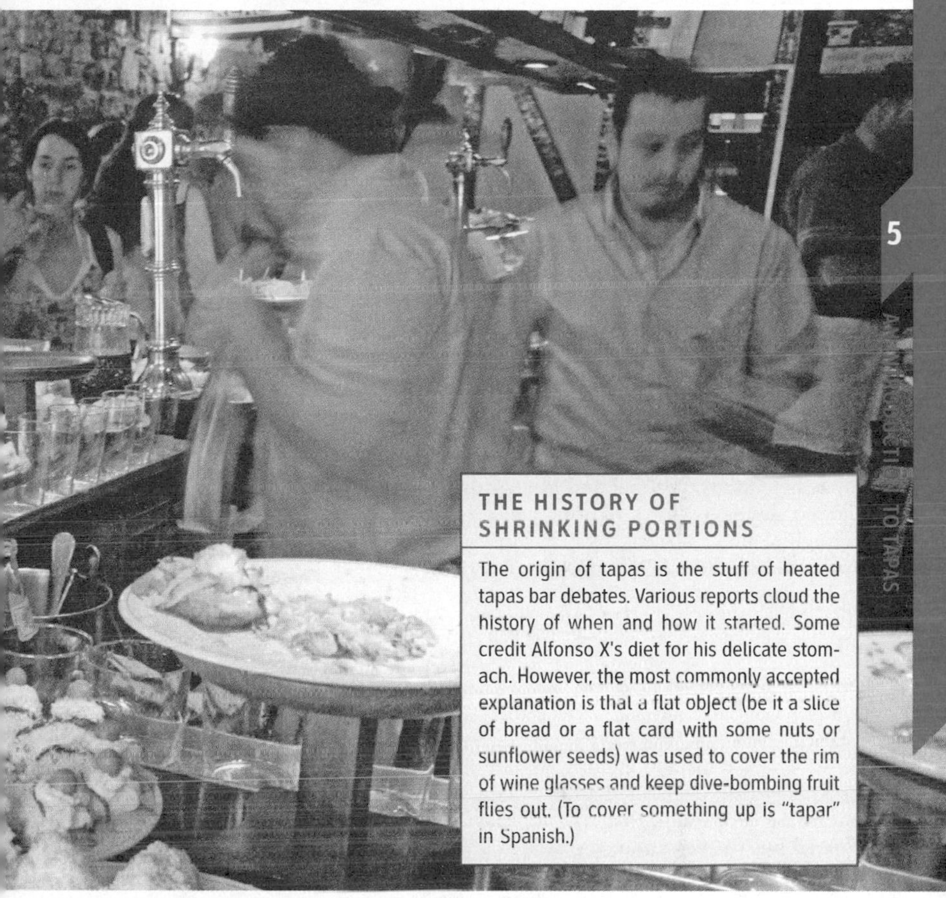

THE HISTORY OF SHRINKING PORTIONS

The origin of tapas is the stuff of heated tapas bar debates. Various reports cloud the history of when and how it started. Some credit Alfonso X's diet for his delicate stomach. However, the most commonly accepted explanation is that a flat object (be it a slice of bread or a flat card with some nuts or sunflower seeds) was used to cover the rim of wine glasses and keep dive-bombing fruit flies out. (To cover something up is "tapar" in Spanish.)

balance out rich wine. And sometimes the spread for a *pica-pica* (a nibbling marathon) with *tortilla de patata, aceitunas, chorizo,* and *jamon* will cause Spaniards to replace their lunch or dinner outright with tapas. These tiny dishes are such a way of life that a verb had to be created for them: *tapear* (to eat tapas) or "*ir a tapeo*" (to go eat tapas). The staff of life in Spain isn't bread. It's finger food.

TAPAS ACROSS SPAIN

MADRID

It is often difficult to qualify what is authentically from Madrid and what has been gastronomically cribbed from other regions thanks to Madrid's melting-pot status for people and customs all over Spain. While *croquetas, tortilla de patata,* and even *paella* can be served as tapas, *patatas bravas* and *calamares* can be found in almost any restaurant in Madrid. The popular *patatas* are a very simple mixture of fried or roasted potatoes with a "Brava" sauce. The sauce is slightly spicy, which is surprising given a country-wide aversion for dishes with the slightest kick. The *calamares*, fried in olive oil, can be served alone or with alioli sauce, mayonnaise, or—and you're reading correctly—in a sandwich. A slice of lemon usually accompanies your serving.

Tortilla de patata

Calamares

ANDALUSIA

Known for the warmth of its climate and its people, Andalusian bars tend to be very generous with their tapas—maybe in spite of the fact that they aren't exactly celebrated for their culinary inventiveness. But tapas here are traditional and among the best. Many times ordering a drink will bring you a sandwich large enough to make a meal, or a bowl of gazpacho that you could swim in. Seafood is also extremely popular in Andalusia, and you will find tapas ranging from sizzling prawns to small anchovies soaked in vinegar or olive oil.

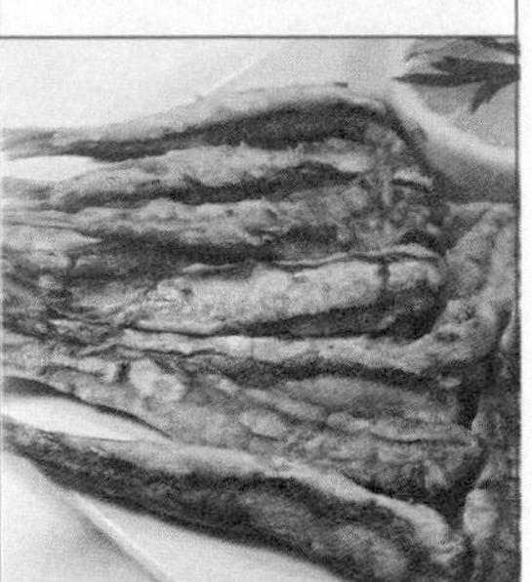

Fried anchovy fish

Pescado frito (fried fish) and *albondigas* (meatballs) are two common tapas for the region, and it's worth grazing multiple bars to try the different preparations. The fish usually includes squid, anchovies, and other tiny fish, deep fried and served as is. Since the bones are very small, they are not removed and considered fine for digestion. If this idea bothers you, sip some more wine. The saffron-almond sauce (*salsa de almendras* y *azafrán*) that accompanies the meatballs might very well make your eyes roll to the back of your head. And since saffron is not as expensive in Spain as it is in the United States, the meatballs are liberally drenched in it.

Not incidentally, Spain's biggest export, olives, grows in Andalusia, so you can expect many varieties among the tapas served with your drinks.

Albondigas

BASQUE COUNTRY

More than any other community in Spain, the Basque Country is known for its culinary originality. The tapas, like the region itself, tend to be more expensive and inventive. And since the Basques insist on doing things their way, they call their unbelievable bites *pintxos* (or *pinchos* in Spanish) rather than tapas. *Gildas*, probably the most ordered *pintxo* in the Basque Country, is a simple toothpick skewer composed of a special green pepper, (called *Guindilla Vasca*), an anchovy, and a pitted olive. All the ingredients must be of the highest quality, especially the anchovy, which should be marinated in the best olive oil and not be too salty. Pimientos *Rellenos* de *Bacalao* (roasted red peppers with cod) is also popular, given the Basque Country's adjacency to the ocean. The festive color of the red peppers and the savoriness of the fish make it a bite-sized Basque delicacy.

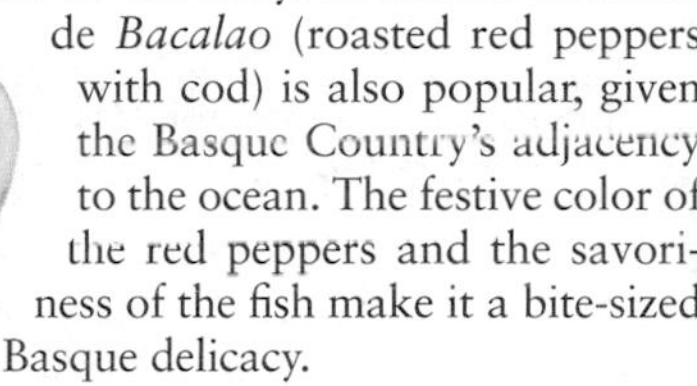

Red and green peppers pintxos

A spread of tapas selections

GET YOUR TAPAS ON

Madrid

El Bocaíto. Here you'll find the best *pescaito frito* (deep-fried whitebait) and a huge assortment of *tostas* (toast points with different toppings). ✉ *Libertad 6, Chueca.* ☎ *91/532-1219.*

Estay. You'll find delicious *tortilla Espanola con atun y lechuga* (Spanish omelet with tuna and lettuce) and excellent *rabas* (fried calamari). ✉ *Hermosilla 46, Salamanca* ☎ *91/578-0470.*

Andalusia

El Churrasco. With a name like this, you would expect the meats to be delicious, and they are. But don't miss the *berenjenas crujientes con salmorejo* (crispy fried eggplant slices with thick gazpacho). ✉ *Romero 16, Judería, Córdoba* ☎ *95/729-0819.*

El Rinconcillo. It's great for the view of the Iglesia de Santa Catalina and a *caldereta de venado* (venison stew). ✉ *C. Gerona 40, Barrio de la Macarena, Seville* ☎ *95/422-3183.*

The Basque Country

Aloña Berri Bar. The repeat winner of tapas championships, its *contraste de pato* (duck à l'orange) and *bastela de pichón* (pigeon pie) makes foodies swoon. ✉ *C. Bermingham 24, Gros, San Sebastián* ☎ *94/329-0818.*

Bernardo Etxea. Straight up, freshly prepared classics like fried peppers, octopus, and pimientos with anchovies are served here. ✉ *C. Puerto 7, Parte Vieja* ☎ *94/342-2055.*

Bite-sized food and drink

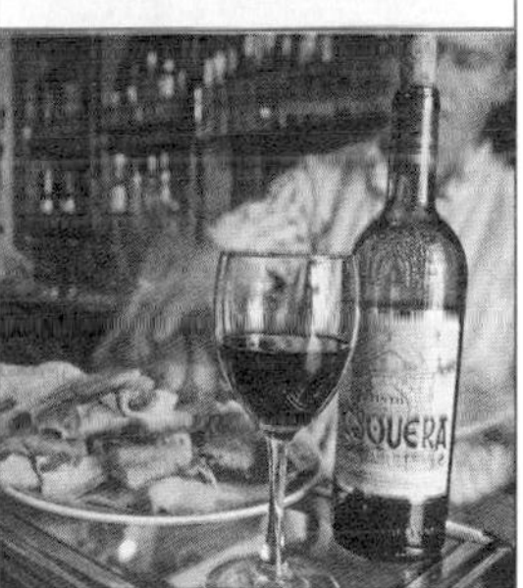

A wine pairing

stunning estuary of the **Ría de Gernika,** a stone's throw from some of the area's most colorful fishing towns.

WHERE TO STAY & EAT

$$–$$$$ ✕ **Baserri Maitea.** In the village of Forua 1 km (½ mi) northwest of Gernika, Basseri Maitea is in a stunning 250-year-old Basque caserío. Strings of red peppers and garlic hang from wooden beams in the cathedral-like interior. Entrées include the *pescado del día* (fish of the day) and *cordero de leche asado al horno de leña* (milk-fed lamb roasted in a wood-burning oven). ✉ *BI–635 to Bermeo, Km 2* ☎ *94/625–3408* ▭ *AE, DC, MC, V* ⊗ *No dinner Sun.–Thurs. Oct.–May.*

$–$$ **Boliña.** Not far from the famous oak site in downtown Gernika, the Boliña is pleasant and modern, a good base for exploring the Vizcayan coast. Rooms are small but comfortable. ✉ *Barrenkale 3, 48300* ☎ *94/625–0300* *94/625–0304* *16 rooms* *In-hotel: restaurant, bar, no elevator* ▭ *AE, DC, MC, V.*

OFF THE BEATEN PATH

Cuevas de Santimamiñe. On the Kortezubi road 5 km (3 mi) from Gernika, the Cuevas de Santimamiñe, also known as Santimamiñe Caverns, have important prehistoric cave paintings. Guided visits are offered weekdays at 10:30, noon, 4, and 5:30, except holidays. On your way out, look for signs for the nearby Bosque Pintado, rows of trees vividly painted by Basque artist Agustín Ibarrola, a striking and successful marriage of art and nature. ✉ ***Barrio Basondo, Kortezubi*** ☎ ***94/625–2975.***

EN ROUTE

For the Santimamiñe Caves, continue northeast from Gernika toward Kortezubi on the BI–638. For Elanchove (Elantxobe, in Euskera), turn left at Arteaga and follow the BI–3237 around the east side of the Ría de Gernika and the Urdaibai natural preserve. From there, the coast road through Ea and Ipaster leads to Lekeitio, one of the prettiest ports on the Basque coast. But if you long for a taste of Arcadian highlands 30 minutes inland, drive up to Axpe and see Amboto, Vizcaya's mythical limestone mountain.

AXPE

22 *47 km (28 mi) east of Bilbao, 46 km (27 mi) southeast of Gernika.*

The village of Axpe, in the valley of Atxondo, nestles under the limestone heights of 4,777-foot Amboto—one of the highest peaks in the Basque Country outside of the Pyrenees. Home of the legendary Basque mother of nature, Mari Urrika or Mari Anbotokodama (María, Our Lady of Amboto), Amboto, with its spectral gray rock face, is a sharp contrast to the soft green meadows running up to the very foot of the mountain. According to Basque scholar and ethnologist José María de Barandiarán in his *Mitología Vasca* (Basque Mythology), Mari was "a beautiful woman, well constructed in all ways except for one foot, which was like that of a goat."

To reach Axpe from Bilbao, drive east on the A8/E70 freeway toward San Sebastián. From Gernika, drive south on the BI635to the A6/E70 freeway and turn east for San Sebastián. Get off at the Durango exit 40 km (24 mi) from Bilbao and take the BI632 toward Elorrio. At Apatamonasterio turn right onto the BI3313 and continue to Axpe.

WHERE TO STAY & EAT

$$$–$$$$ Fodor's Choice ★ ✕ **Etxebarri.** All the rage around the Iberian Peninsula these days, Víctor Arguinzoniz has introduced cooking over coals to haute cuisine, tailoring woods and coals for different products and improvising equipment such as the pan to char-grill *angulas* (baby eels). Everything from clams and fish to the meats and even the rice with langoustines is healthful, flavorful, and exciting in this blocky stone house in the center of town. ✉ *Plaza San Juan 1* ☎ *94/658 3042* ▭ *AE, DC, MC, V* ⊙ *Closed Mon. No dinner Sun.*

$$–$$$ Fodor's Choice ★ ✕ **Mendigoikoa.** This handsome group of hillside farmhouses is among the province of Vizcaya's most exquisite hideaways. The lower farmhouse, Mendibekoa (lower mountain), has stunning rooms, an elegant breakfast room, and a glassed-in terrace overlooking the valley. At restaurant Mendigoikoa (Upper Mountain; $$–$$$$), heavy beams loom overhead and a fire usually crackles in the far corner. The *pichón de Navaz a la parrilla* (Navaz pigeon cooked over coals) or the *txuleta de buey* (beef chops) are memorable. ✉ *Barrio San Juan 33, 48290* ☎ *94/682–0833* 📠 *94/682–1136* 🌐 *www.mendigoikoa.com* *12 rooms* *In-hotel: restaurant, no elevator* ▭ *AE, DC, MC, V* ⊙ *Closed Dec. 22–Jan. 17. Restaurant closed Mon. No dinner Sun.*

5

ELANTXOBE

23 *27 km (17 mi) from Bermeo.*

The tiny fishing village of Elantxobe (Elanchove, in Spanish) is surrounded by huge, steep cliffs, with a small breakwater that protects its fleet from the storms of the Bay of Biscay. The view of the port from the upper village is breathtaking. The lower fork in the road leads to the port.

WHERE TO STAY & EAT

$–$$ ✕ **Casa Rural Arboliz.** On a bluff overlooking the Bay of Biscay about 2 km (1 mi) outside Elantxobe on the road to Lequeitio, this rustic inn is removed from the harborside bustle, offering a breath of the country life on the Basque coast. The modern rooms are simple and have balconies overlooking the sea. The restaurant serves simple Basque specialties with an emphasis on fresh fish and seafood. The *besugo la donostiarra* (sea bream covered in a garlic, oil, and vinegar sauce) is exceptional. ✉ *Arboliz 12, Ibarranguelua 48311* ☎ *94/627–6283* 🌐 *www.euskalnet.net/arboliz* *6 rooms* *In-hotel: restaurant, no elevator* ▭ *AE, DC, MC, V.*

LEKEITIO

24 *59 km (37 mi) east of Bilbao, 61 km (38 mi) west of San Sebastián.*

This bright little town is similar to Bermeo but has two wide, sandy beaches right by its harbor. Soaring over the Gothic church of Santa

María (open for mass only) is a graceful set of flying buttresses. Lequeitio is famous for its fiestas (September 1–18), which include a gruesome event in which men dangle for as long as they can from the necks of dead geese tied to a cable over the inlet while the cable is whipped in and out of the water by crowds of burly men at either end.

ONDÁRROA

25 *61 km (38 mi) east of Bilbao, 49 km (30 mi) west of San Sebastián.*

Farther east along the coast from Lekeitio, Ondárroa is a gem of a fishing town. Like its neighbors, it has a major fishing fleet painted various combinations of red, green, and white: the colors of the Ikurriña, the Basque national flag.

EN ROUTE

Continuing along the coastal road through Motrico and Deva, you'll approach some of the Basque Country's most colorful fishing ports and finest quayside restaurants. As you enter Zumaia, you'll see the turnoff for Azpeitia and the sanctuary of one of Spain's greatest religious figures, St. Ignatius of Loyola. A half-hour trip up the GI–631 takes you to this colossal structure.

SANTUARIO DE SAN IGNACIO DE LOYOLA

26 Cestona: 34 km (21 mi) southwest of San Sebastián.

The Sanctuary of St. Ignatius of Loyola, an exuberant baroque structure, was erected in honor of Iñigo Lopez de Oñaz y Loyola (1491–1556) after he was sainted as Ignacio de Loyola in 1622 for his defense of the Catholic Church against the tides of Martin Luther's Reformation. Almost two centuries later, Roman architect Carlos Fontana designed the basilica that would memorialize the saint. The ornate construction contrasts with the austere ways of Saint Ignatius himself, who took vows of poverty and chastity after his conversion. Polychrome marble, flamboyant altarwork, and a huge but delicate dome decorate the interior. The fortresslike tower house has the room where Ignatius (Iñigo, in Euskera) experienced conversion while recovering from his wound in a intra-Basque battle. Back on the coastal road is **Zumaia,** a cozy little port and summer resort with the estuary of the Urola River flowing (back and forth, according to the tide) through town. The **Museo Zuloaga** (☎*943/862341*), on N634 at the eastern edge of town, has an extraordinary collection of paintings by Goya, El Greco, Zurbarán, and others, in addition to works by the Basque impressionist Ignacio Zuloaga himself. The museum is open Easter–September 15, Wednesday–Sunday 4–8 PM. The rest of the year, it's open by prior arrangement only. Admission is €5.

WHERE TO STAY & EAT

$$ **Landarte.** For a taste of life in a Basque *caserio* (farmhouse), try this restored 16th-century country manor house an hour away in Getaria. The walk over will prime you for the pleasures of Basque dining; the walk back will prepare you for more. Stone walls, hand-hewn beams,

sea views, and happy and helpful hosts make this a top choice. ✉ *Crtra. de Artadi 1, Zumaia, 20750* ☎ *943/865358* 📠 *943/865358* 🌐 *www.landarte.net* 🛏 *6 rooms* 🛎 *In-room: no a/c. In-hotel: no elevator, parking (no fee)* 💳 *AE, DC, MC, V.*

GETARIA

27 *22 km (14 mi) west of San Sebastián.*

From Zumaia, the coast road and several good footpaths lead to Getaria (Guetaria, in Spanish), known as *la cocina de guipúzcoa,* the kitchen of Guipúzcoa province, for its many restaurants and taverns. Getaria was the birthplace of Juan Sebastián Elcano (1460–1526), the first circumnavigator of the globe and Spain's most emblematic naval hero. Elcano took over and completed Magellan's voyage after the latter was killed in the Philippines in 1521. The town's galleonlike **church** has sloping wooden floors resembling a ship's deck. **Zarautz,** the next town, has a wide beach and many taverns and cafés.

5

WHERE TO STAY & EAT

$$$–$$$$ ★ ✕ **Kaia Kaipe.** Suspended over Getaria's colorful fishing port and looking past Zarautz and San Sebastián all the way to Biarritz, this spectacular place puts together exquisite fish soups and serves fresh fish right off the boats—you can watch them being unloaded below. The town is the home of Txomin Etxaniz, the premier txakolí (tart young Basque white wine), and this is the place to drink it. ✉ *General Arnao 4* ☎ *943/140500* 💳 *AE, DC, MC, V* 🕓 *Closed Mar. 1–15 and Oct. 15–31.*

$ ✕🏨 **Iribar.** Iribar has been grilling fish and beef over coals for more than half a century. Just uphill from Getaria's singular church, the restaurant stands out for value, family-friendliness, and delicious fish and beef ($–$$$). The four rooms are impeccable, inexpensive, and the only berths available in the heart of this schoonerlike historic village. ✉ *Kale Nagusia 34* ☎ *943/140406* 📠 *943/140953* 🛏 *4 rooms* 🛎 *In-hotel: restaurant, bar, no elevator* 💳 *AE, DC, MC, V* 🕓 *Closed Thurs. and Oct. 1–15, Apr. 1–15. No dinner Wed.*

EN ROUTE

Heading east toward San Sebastián, the coast road to Zarautz is spectacular. In Zarautz, the shady terrace cafés around the central square, the bustling produce market, and the ample ocher beach are good reasons to stay, as is Karlo Arguiñano's famous restaurant. To get to San Sebastián, you have a choice of the A8 toll road or the coastal N634 highway. The former is a quick and scenic 20 km (12 mi), but the latter will take you through the village of Orio past a few more tempting inns and restaurants in Orio itself, or, in Usurbil, the Sidreria Ugarte.

OFF THE BEATEN PATH

For a look at an authentic Basque farmhouse, or *caserío,* where the Urdapilleta family farms pigs, sheep, cattle, goats, chickens, and ducks, take a detour up to the village of Bidegoian (8 km [5 mi] short of Tolosa on the Azpeitia–Tolosa road). Pello Urdapilleta (which means "pile of pigs" in Eus-

kara) sells artisanal cheeses and sausages and will show you how upland Basques have traditionally lived and farmed. ✉ *Elola Azpikoa Baserria, Bidegoian* ☎ *943/681006*

SAN SEBASTIÁN TO HONDARRIBIA

Graceful, chic San Sebastián invites you to slow down. Stroll the beach, or wander the streets. East of the city is Pasajes, where Lafayette set off to help the colonial forces in the American Revolution, and where Victor Hugo spent a winter writing. Just shy of the French border, you'll hit Hondarribia, a brightly painted, flower-festooned port town.

SAN SEBASTIÁN

28 *100 km (62 mi) east of Bilbao.*

Fodor's Choice ★

San Sebastián (Donostia, in Euskera) is an unusually sophisticated city arched around one of the finest urban beaches in the world, **La Concha** (The Shell), so named for its almost perfect resemblance to the shape of a scallop shell. The best way to see San Sebastián is to walk around: promenades and pathways lead up the hills that surround the city. The first records of San Sebastián date from the 11th century. A backwater for centuries, the city had the good fortune in 1845 to attract Queen Isabella II, who was seeking relief from a skin ailment in the icy Atlantic waters. The city is laid out with wide streets on a grid pattern, thanks mainly to the 12 different times it has been all but destroyed by fire. The last conflagration came after the French were expelled in 1813; English and Portuguese forces occupied the city, abused the population, and torched the place. Today, San Sebastián is a seaside resort on a par with Nice and Monte Carlo. It becomes one of Spain's most expensive cities in the summer, when French vacationers descend in droves. It is also, like Bilbao, a center of Basque nationalism.

WHAT TO SEE

Every corner of Spain champions its culinary identity, but San Sebastián's refined fare is in a league of its own. Many of the city's restaurants are in the **Parte Vieja** (Old Quarter), on the east end of the bay beyond the elegant **Casa Consistorial** (City Hall) and formal **Alderdi Eder** gardens. City Hall began as a casino in 1887; after gambling was outlawed early in the 20th century, the town council moved here from the Plaza de la Constitución, the Old Quarter's main square. The tiny **Isla de Santa Clara,** right in the entrance to the bay, protects the city from Bay of Biscay storms; this makes La Concha one of the calmest beaches on Spain's entire northern coast. A large hill dramatically dominates each side of the entrance to the bay, too.A visit to **Monte Igueldo,** on the western side of the bay, is a must. (You can drive up for a toll of €1 per person or take the funicular—cable car—for the same amount round-trip; it runs 10 to 8 in summer, 11 to 6 in winter, with departures every 15 minutes.) From the top, you get the remarkable panorama for which San Sebastián is famous: gardens, parks, wide tree-lined boulevards, Belle Epoque buildings, and, of course, the bay itself.

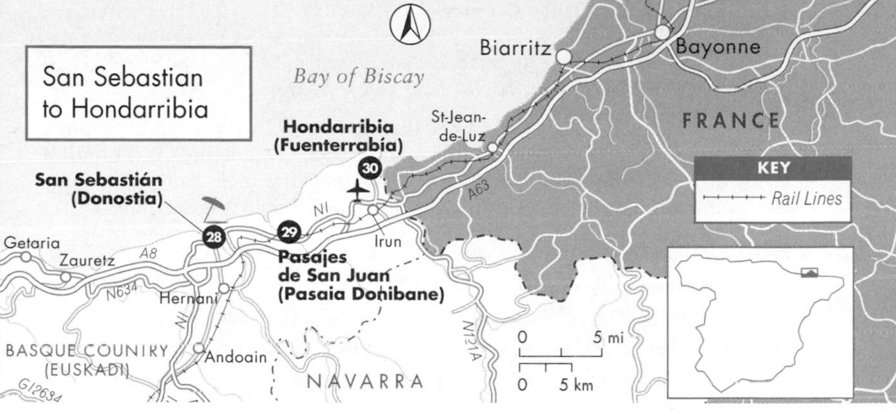

5

Designed by the world-renowned Spanish architect Rafael Moneo, and situated at the mouth of the Urumea River, the **Kursaal** is San Sebastián's postmodern concert hall, film society, and convention center. The gleaming cubes of glass that make up this bright, rationalist complex were conceived as a perpetuation of the site's natural geography, an attempt to "underline the harmony between the natural and the artificial" and to create a visual stepping-stone between the heights of Monte Urgull and Monte Ulía. It has two auditoriums, a gargantuan banquet hall, meeting rooms, exhibition space, and a sibling set of terraces overlooking the estuary. Martín Berasategui, director of his own restaurant in nearby Lasarte, is the creative force (and financier) behind the Kursaal dining room. ✉ *Av. de la Zurriola, Gros* ☎ *943/003000* 🌐 *www.kursaal.org* 🎫 *€3* 🕐 *Guided tours daily at 1:30. For guided tours in English make arrangements in advance.*

Just in from the harbor, in the shadow of Monte Urgull, is the baroque church of **Santa María,** with a stunning carved facade of an arrow-riddled Saint Sebastian. The interior is strikingly restful; note the ship above Saint Sebastian high on the altar.

Looking straight south from the front of Santa María, you can see the facade and spires of the **Catedral Buen Pastor** *(Cathedral of the Good Shepherd)* across town.

NEED A BREAK?

Steps from the facade of Santa María, in the heart of the old quarter, have a *chocolate con nata*—thick, dark hot chocolate with whipped cream—at the tiny café Kantoi (✉ *C. Mayor 10, Parte Vieja*).

The **Museo de San Telmo** is in a 16th-century monastery behind the Parte Vieja, to the right of the church of Santa María. The former chapel, now a lecture hall, was painted by José María Sert (1876–1945), author of notable works in Barcelona's city hall, London's Tate Gallery, and New York's Waldorf-Astoria hotel. Here, Sert's characteristic tones of gray, gold, violet, and earthy russets enhance the sculptural power of his work, which portrays events from Basque history. The museum displays Basque ethnographic items, such as prehistoric steles once used as grave markers, and paintings by Zuloaga, Ribera, and

El Greco. ✉*Pl. de Ignacio Zuloaga s/n, Parte Vieja* ☎*943/424970* *Free* ⏲*Tues.–Sat. 10:30–1:30 and 4–8, Sun. 10:30–2.*

San Sebastián is divided by the **Urumea River,** which is crossed by three bridges inspired by late-19th-century French architecture. At the mouth of the Urumea, the incoming surf smashes the rocks with such force that white foam erupts, and the noise is wild and Wagnerian.

OFF THE BEATEN PATH

Chillida Leku. In the Jáuregui section of Hernani, 10 minutes south of San Sebastián (suggestively close to both Martín Bersategui's restaurant in Lasarte *and* the cider houses of Astigarraga), the Eduardo Chillida Sculpture Garden and Museum, in a 16th-century farmhouse, is a treat for anyone interested in contemporary art. ✉***Caserío Zabalaga, Barrio Jáuregui 66, Lasarte*** ☎***943/336006*** ***www.museochillidaleku.com*** ***€8*** ⏲***Closed Tues. except July and Aug. and during wk before Easter.***

WHERE TO STAY & EAT

$$$$ Fodor'sChoice ★ **Arzak.** Renowned chef Juan Mari Arzak's little house at the crest of Alto de Miracruz on the eastern outskirts of San Sebastián is internationally famous, so reserve well in advance. Traditional Basque preparations are enhanced by Arzakian innovations designed to bring out the best in the natural products. The ongoing culinary dialogue between Juan Mari and his daughter Elena is one of the most endearing attractions here. They may not always agree, but it's all in the family, and the food just gets better and better. The sauces are perfect and every dish looks beautiful, but the prices (even of appetizers) are astronomical. Treat yourself to a remarkable dessert of chocolate with pine nuts. ✉*Alto de Miracruz 21, Alto de Miracruz* ☎*943/278465* *943/272753* *Reservations essential* *AE, DC, MC, V* ⏲*Closed Mon., last 2 wks in June, and Nov. 5–29. No dinner Sun.*

$$$$ Fodor'sChoice ★ **Martín Berasategui.** The sure bet here is the *lubina asada con jugo de habas, vainas, cebolletas y tallarines de chipirón* (roast sea bass with juice of fava beans, green beans, baby onions, and cuttlefish shaving), but go with whatever Martín suggests, especially if it's woodcock, *pichón de Bresse* (Bresse wood pigeon), or any other kind of game. The site of San Sebastián's racetrack, Lasarte is 8 km (5 mi) south of San Sebastián. ✉*Loidi Kalea 4, Lasarte* ☎*943/366471* *AE, DC, MC, V* ⏲*Closed Mon., Tues., and mid-Dec.–mid-Jan. No lunch Sat. No dinner Sun.*

$$$$ Fodor'sChoice ★ **Mugaritz.** This farmhouse in the hills above Errentería 8 km (5 mi) northeast of San Sebastián is surrounded by spices and herbs tended by boy-genius chef Andoni Luis Aduriz and his crew. In a rustic setting with a modern, open feeling, Aduriz demonstrates his mastery over vegetables, foie, and combining seafood with products of the nearby fields and forest. If you can resist the tasting menu and order carefully à la carte, Aduriz's inventive, contemporary cuisine is within reach of the non-tycoon budget at about €65 a head. ✉*Aldura Aldea 20-Otzazulueta Baserria, Errenteria* ☎*943/518343* *AE, DC, MC, V* ⏲*Closed Mon., wk before Easter, and Dec. 15–Jan. 15. No dinner Sun. No lunch Tues.*

$$$$ ★ **Urepel.** Too many cooks may spoil the broth, but not in this family enterprise. There's no head chef in this kitchen, where the staff, in prototypically Basque egalitarian fashion, works as a team. The cuisine balances classic and contemporary elements in a felicitous way. Typical Urepel inventions include a *chicharro al escama dorada* (a skinned, deboned mackerel served under a layer of golden-brown sliced potatoes) and the unbeatable and unusual dish of foie gras wrapped with veal. The appetizer of finely carmelized scallops with caviar is also excellent. *Paseo de Salamanca 3, Parte Vieja 943/424040 AE, DC, MC, V Closed Sun., Tues., Christmas and Easter wks, and 3 wks in July.*

TESTOSTERONE ASYLUM

The Basque Country's men-only eating societies may seem another example of Spain's stereotypical machismo. But ethnologists and sociologists have long defined Basque society as a powerful matriarchy wherein the authority of the *etxekoandre* (female house honcho) has been so absolute that men were kitchen exiles. The eating societies were initially drinking clubs for men kicked out of their homes. Food came later, and, with the Basque passion for competition, cooking contests and the pursuit of culinary excellence followed. At present, there are "co-ed" and even all-women's eating clubs.

$$$$ Fodor'sChoice ★ **Zuberoa.** Working in a 15th-century Basque farmhouse 9½ km (6 mi) northeast of San Sebastián just outside the village of Oiartzun, Hilario Arbelaitz has long been one of San Sebastián's most celebrated chefs. His original yet simple management of prime raw materials such as spring cuttlefish or woodcock has earned him a spot as one of Spain's top half-dozen culinary stars. Hilario manages to exude an unpretentious country atmosphere: nothing effete going on here, just a few friends sitting down to dine simply—but very, very well. *Plaza Bekosoro 1, Oiartzun 943/491228 AE, DC, MC, V Closed Sun., Wed., Dec. 1–15, Apr. 21–May 5, and Oct. 15–30.*

$–$$$ **Sidrería Petritegui.** For hearty dining and a certain amount of splashing around in hard cider, make this short excursion east of San Sebastián. Gigantic wooden barrels line the walls, and tables are piled with *tortilla de bacalao* (codfish omelet), *txuleta de buey* (beef chops), the smoky local sheep's-milk cheese from the town of Idiazabal, and, for dessert, walnuts and *membrillo* (quince jelly). *Ctra. San Sebastián–Hernani, Km 7, Astigarraga 943/457188 No credit cards No lunch weekdays.*

$$$–$$$$ ★ **Hotel María Cristina.** The graceful beauty of the belle epoque is embodied in San Sebastián's most luxurious hotel, which sits on the elegant west bank of the Urumea River. The grandeur continues in salons filled with Oriental rugs, potted palms, and Carrara marble columns, and in bedrooms to match—with gold fixtures and wood wardrobes. Marble bathrooms add still more style. A piano player pounds out an eclectic medley of tunes nightly at the bar. *Okendo 1, Centro, 20004 943/437600 943/437676 www.westin.com 108 rooms, 28 suites In-room: safe, dial-up. In-hotel: restaurant, room service, bar, laundry service, parking (fee), no-smoking rooms AE, DC, MC, V.*

$$$–$$$$ **Londres y de Inglaterra.** On the promenade above La Concha, this stately hotel has an old-world aesthetic that informs the bright, formal lobby and continues throughout the hotel. The bar and restaurant face the bay, and the guest rooms with views out to sea are the best in town. ✉ *Zubieta 2, La Concha, 20007* ☎ *943/440770* 🖷 *943/440491* 🌐 *www.hlondres.com* *139 rooms, 9 suites* *In-hotel: restaurant, bar, parking (fee)* 💳 *AE, DC, MC, V.*

$$$ **Europa.** A block from the beach and a 15-minute walk around La Concha from the booming Parte Vieja, this small Donosti hotel is staffed by savvy professionals eager to help you make the most of your time in town. Rooms are on the small side but comfortably furnished and equipped with essential items. ✉ *San Martín 52, Centro, 20007* ☎ *943/470880* 🖷 *943/471730* *68 rooms* *In-hotel: restaurant, bar, parking (fee)* 💳 *AE, DC, MC, V.*

$ **Aristondo.** A 15-minute drive above San Sebastián on Monte Igueldo, this comfortable farmhouse is a scenic and economical place to stay. Other nearby rural lodging options include farmhouses Izen Eder and Pilotegui. ✉ *Camino de Pilotegui 70, Igueldo, 20007* ☎ *943/215558* 🌐 *www.nekatur.net* *16 rooms* *In-hotel: no elevator, parking (no fee)* 💳 *No credit cards.*

TAPAS BARS

★ **Aloña Berri Bar.** Perennial winner of tapa championships, this place across the Urumea River in Gros is well worth the walk. José Ramon Elizondo's miniature creations, from *contraste de pato* (duck à l'orange) to his Moorish-based *bastela de pichón* (pigeon pie), are merely stupendous. Order the excellent crisp asparagus coated with burnt garlic. ✉ *C. Bermingham 24, Gros* ☎ *943/290818.*

★ **Astelena.** On the northeast corner of Plaza de la Constitución, this *bar de toda la vida* (lifetime favorite bar) is famous for its *pastel de pescado* (fish pudding). ✉ *C. Iñigo 1, Parte Vieja* ☎ *943/425245.*

Bar Ganbara. Near Plaza de la Constitución, morsels here range from shrimp and asparagus to Ibérico acorn-fed ham on croissants to anchovies, sea urchins, and wild mushrooms in season. ✉ *C. San Jerónimo 21, Parte Vieja* ☎ *943/422575.*

★ **Bar Gorriti.** Next to La Brecha Market, this traditional little pintxos bar is a classic, filled with good cheer and delicious tapas. ✉ *C. San Juan 3, Parte Vieja* ☎ *943/428353.*

Bar Ormazabal. You may not have *thought* you were starving, but when you catch a glimpse of the multicolor display that goes up on the Ormazabal bar at midday, hunger pangs will really kick in. ✉ *C. 31 de Agosto 22, Parte Vieja* ☎ *943/429907.*

Bergara Bar. Winner of many a miniature cuisine award, this rustic tavern just down the street from Aloñ Berri Bar on the corner of Arteche and Bermingham also serves roasts along with tapas and *pintxos.* ✉ *Arteche 8, Gros* ☎ *943/275026.*

Casa Vergara. This cozy bar, in front of the Santa María del Coro church, is always filled with reverent tapas devotees—and the counter is always piled high with morsels. ✉ *C. Mayor 21, Parte Vieja* ☎ *943/431073.*

★ **La Cepa.** This booming and boisterous tavern is one of the all-time standards. Everything from the Ibérico ham to the little olive, pepper, and anchovy combos called "penalties" will whet your appetite. ✉*C. 31 de Agosto 7, Parte Vieja* ☎*943/426394*.

NIGHTLIFE & THE ARTS

Glitterati descend on San Sebastián for its international film festival in the second half of September. Exact dates vary; ask the tourist office on Calle Fueros (☎943/426282). The same goes for the late-July jazz festival, which draws many of the world's top performers. At night, report in for *copas* or *potes* (both "drinks"), and general cruising in and around the Parte Vieja. The **Kursaal** (✉*Av. de la Zurriola* ☎*943/003000*) houses the Orquesta Sinfónica de Euskadi and is the favored venue for ballet, opera, theater, and jazz. There are varied programs of theater, dance, and more at **Teatro Victoria Eugenia** (✉*Reina Regente s/n, Centro* ☎*943/481155 or 943/481160*).

Akerbeltz (✉*Mari Kalea 10, Parte Vieja* ☎*943/460934*), at the corner over the port to the left of Santa María del Coro and the Gaztelubide eating society, is a cozy late-night refuge. San Sebastián's top disco is **Bataplan** (✉*Paseo de la Concha s/n, Centro* ☎*943/460439*), near the western end of La Concha. Filled with couples and night owls, **Bideluze** (✉*Pl. de Guipúzcoa 14, Centro* ☎*943/460219*) is always alive. **Discóbolo** (✉*Blvd. Zumardía 27, Centro* ☎*943/217678*), near the Parte Vieja, gets pretty incandescent. **Kabutzia** (✉*Paseo del Muelle s/n, Centro* ☎*943/429725*), above the Club Nautico seaward from the Casino, is a busy night haunt. **Ku** (✉*Ctra. Monte Igueldo s/n, Igueldo* ☎*943/212050*), up on the hill, has been going strong for three decades. **La Rotonda** (✉*Paseo de la Concha 6, Centro* ☎*943/429095*), across the street from Bataplan, below Miraconcha, is a top nightspot.

SHOPPING

San Sebastián is nonpareil for stylish home furnishings and clothing. Wander Calle San Martín and the surrounding pedestrian-only streets to see what's in the windows. **Bilintx** (✉*C. Fermín Calbetón 21, Parte Vieja* ☎*943/420080*) is one of Donosti's best bookstores. Stop into **Maitiena** (✉*Av. Libertad 32, Centro* ☎*943/424721*) for a fabulous selection of chocolates.**Ponsol** (✉*C. Narrica 4, Parte Vieja* ☎*943/420876*) is the best place to buy Basque berets; the Leclerq family has been hatting (and clothing) Donostiarras for three generations.

PASAJES DE SAN JUAN

29 *10 km (6 mi) east of San Sebastián.*

Generally marked as Pasaia Donibane, in Euskera, there are actually three towns around the commercial port of Rentería: **Pasajes Ancho,** an industrial port; **Pasajes de San Pedro,** a large fishing harbor, and historic **Pasajes de San Juan,** a colorful cluster of 18th- and 19th-century buildings along the channel to the sea. Best reached by driving into Pasajes de San Pedro, on the San Sebastián side of the strait, and catching a launch across the mouth of the harbor (about €0.50, depending on the time of day), this is too sweet a side trip to pass up. In 1777, at the age of 20, General Lafayette set out from Pasajes de San Juan to aid the American Revolution. Victor Hugo spent the summer of 1843 here writing his *Voyage aux Pyrenees.* The **Victor Hugo House** is the home of the tourist office and has an exhibit of traditional village dress. **Ontziola,** a research center for traditional wooden boat design, is directed by Xavier Agote, who taught boat-building in Rockland, Maine. Pasajes de San Juan can be reached via Pasajes de San Pedro from San Sebastián by cab or bus. Or, if you prefer to go on foot, follow the red-and-white-blazed GR trail that begins at the east end of the Zurriola beach—you're in for a spectacular three-hour hike along the rocky coast. By car, take N1 for France and, after passing Juan Mari Arzak's landmark restaurant at Alto de Miracruz, look for a marked left turn into Pasaia or Pasajes de San Pedro.

WHERE TO EAT

$$–$$$ FodorśChoice ★ ✕**Txulotxo.** Cozy and friendly, this exceptional restaurant sits on stilts at the edge of the Rentería ship passage, perpetually perched in the shadow of the occasional freighter passing only a dozen yards away. The *sopa de pescado* (fish soup), thick and piping hot, is nonpareil, as are the fresh grilled sole and monkfish and the pimiento-wrapped bacalao (codfish). Make sure you leave some time to stroll around town. ✉*Pasajes de San Juan* ☎*943/523952* 📠*943/519601* ✍*Reservations essential* ▭*AE, DC, MC, V* ⊗*Closed Tues. and Dec. 23–Jan. 15. No dinner Sun.*

HONDARRIBIA

30 *12 km (7 mi) east of Pasajes.*

Hondarribia (Fuenterrabía, in Castilian Spanish) is the last fishing port before the French border. Lined with fishermen's homes and small fishing boats, the harbor is a beautiful but touristy spot. If you have a taste for history, follow signs up the hill to the medieval bastion and onetime castle of Carlos V, now a parador.

WHERE TO STAY & EAT

$$$$ ✕**Alameda.** Hot young Hondarribia star chef Gorka Txapartegi opened this restaurant in 1997 after working with, among others, Martín Berasategui. The elegantly restored house in upper Hondarribia is a delight, as are the seasonally rotated combinations of carefully chosen ingredients, from duck to foie gras to vegetables. ✉*Minasoroeta 1* ☎*943/642789* ▭*AE, DC, MC, V* ⊗*Closed Mon., Dec. 24–Jan. 6, June 12–18, and Oct. 16–22. No dinner Sun.*

$$–$$$ ✕**La Hermandad de Pescadores.** This "brotherhood" is owned by the local fishermen's guild and serves simple, hearty fare at reasonable prices. Try the sopa de pescado or the *almejas a la marinera* (clams in a thick, garlicky sauce). If you come outside of peak hours (2–4 and 9–11), you'll find space at the long, communal boards. ✉*C. Zuloaga s/n* ☎*943/642738* ▭*AE, DC, MC, V* ⊗*Closed Wed. No dinner Tues.*

$$$–$$$$ **Parador de Hondarribia.** Replete with suits of armor and other chivalric bric-a-brac, this Parador El Emperador is in a superb medieval bastion that dates from the 10th century and housed Spain's founding Emperor Carlos V in the 16th century. Many rooms have views

of the Bidasoa River and estuary, rife with colorful fishing boats. Reserve ahead and ask for one of the three "special" rooms, with canopy beds and baronial appointments; they're worth the extra expense. ✉ *Pl. de Armas 14, 20005* ☎ *943/645500* 📠 *943/642153* 🌐 *www.parador.es* *36 rooms* *In-hotel: restaurant, bar, parking (fee)* 💳 *AE, DC, MC, V.*

$ **Caserío "Artzu"** This family barn and house, with its classic low, wide roofline, has been here in one form or another for some 800 years. Just west of the hermitage of Nuestra Señora de Guadalupe, 5 km (3 mi) above Hondarribia, Artzu offers modernized accommodations in an ancient caserío overlooking the junction of the Bidasoa estuary and the Atlantic. Better hosts than this warm, friendly clan are hard to find. ✉ *Barrio Montaña, 20280* ☎ *943/640530* 🌐 *www.euskalnet.net/casartzu* *6 rooms, 1 with bath* *In-room: no a/c, no TV. In-hotel: restaurant, bar, no elevator* 💳 *No credit cards.*

EN ROUTE

The fastest route from San Sebastián to Pamplona is the A15 Autovía de Navarra, which cuts through the Leizarán Valley and gets you there in about 45 minutes. Somewhat more scenic, if slower and more tortuous, is the 134-km (83-mi) drive on C133, which starts near Hondarribia and follows the Bidasoa River (the border with France) up through Vera de Bidasoa. When C133 meets N121, you can turn left up into the lovely Baztán Valley or right to continue through the Velate pass to Pamplona.

5

SOUTHERN NAVARRA & LA RIOJA

Bordering the French Pyrenees and populated largely by Basques, Navarra grows progressively less Basque toward its southern and eastern edges. Pamplona, the ancient Navarran capital, draws crowds with its annual feast of San Fermín, but medieval Vitoria, in the Basque province of Alava, is largely undiscovered by tourists. Olite, south of Pamplona, has a storybook castle, and the towns of Puente la Reina and Estella are visually indelible stops on the Camino de Santiago.

PAMPLONA

31 *79 km (47 mi) southeast of San Sebastián.*

Pamplona (Iruña, in Euskera) is known worldwide for its running of the bulls, made famous by Ernest Hemingway in his 1926 novel *The Sun Also Rises*. The occasion is the festival of San Fermín, July 6 to 14, when Pamplona's population triples (along with hotel rates), so reserve rooms months in advance. Tickets to the bullfights (*corridas*), as opposed to the running (*encierro*, meaning "enclosing"), to which access is free, can be difficult to get. Every morning at 8 sharp a sky-rocket is shot off, and the bulls kept overnight in the corrals at the edge of town are run through a series of closed-off streets leading to the bullring, a 902-yard dash. Running before them are Spaniards and foreigners feeling festive enough to risk a goring. The degree of peril in the *encierro*is difficult to gauge. Serious injuries occur nearly every day; deaths are rare but always a possibility. What's certain is the sense of danger, the mob hysteria, and the exhilaration.

Founded by the Roman emperor Pompey as Pompaelo, or Pameiopolis, Pamplona was successively taken by the Franks, the Goths, and the Moors. In 750, the Pamplonicas put themselves under the protection of Charlemagne and managed to expel the Arabs temporarily. But the foreign commander took advantage of this trust to destroy the city walls, so that when he was driven out once more by the Moors, the Navarrese took their revenge, ambushing and slaughtering the retreating Frankish army as it fled over the Pyrenees through the mountain pass of Roncesvalles in 778. This is the episode depicted in the 11th-century *Song of Roland,* although the French (anonymous) author chose to cast the aggressors as Moors. For centuries after that, Pamplona remained three argumentative towns until they were forcibly incorporated into one city by Carlos III (the Noble, 1387–1425) of Navarra.

WHAT TO SEE

Pamplona's **cathedral,** set near the portion of the ancient walls rebuilt in the 17th century, is one of the most important religious buildings in northern Spain, thanks to the fragile grace and gabled Gothic arches of its cloister. Inside are the tombs of Carlos III and his wife, marked by an alabaster sculpture. The **Museo Diocesano** (Diocesan Museum) houses religious art from the Middle Ages and the Renaissance. ✉ *C. Curia s/n* ☎ *948/210827* 🎫 *€4.50* ⏲ *Museum Weekdays 10–1:30 and 4–7, Sat. 10–1:30.*

On Calle Santo Domingo, in a 16th-century building once used as a hospital for pilgrims on their way to Santiago de Compostela, is the **Museo de Navarra,** with a collection of regional archaeological artifacts and historical costumes. ✉ *C. Jaranta s/n* ☎ *848/426492* 🎫 *€3.50* ⏲ *Tues.–Sat. 9–2 and 5–7, Sun. 9–2.*

Pamplona's most remarkable civil building is the ornate **ayuntamiento** *(town hall)* on the Plaza Consistorial, with its rich ochre facade setting off brightly gilded balconies. The interior is a lavish wood and marble display of wealth reminding visitors that Navarra was always a wealthy kingdom of its own. Originally a 15th-century courthouse, the present building was erected between 1753 and 1759.

NEED A BREAK?

Pamplona's gentry has been flocking to the ornate, French-style Café Iruña (✉ *Pl. del Castillo 44*) since 1888. Beyond the stand-up bar is a bingo hall (you must be 18 to play). The café is open daily 5 PM–3 AM.

One of Pamplona's greatest charms is the warren of small streets near the **Plaza del Castillo** (especially Calle San Nicolás), which are filled with restaurants, taverns, and bars. Pamplonicas are hardy sorts, well known for their eagerness and capacity to eat and drink.The central **Ciudadela,** an ancient fortress, is a parkland of promenades and pools. Walk through in late afternoon, the time of the *paseo* (traditional stroll), for a taste of everyday life here.

CLOSE UP

Running with the Bulls

In *The Sun Also Rises,* Hemingway describes the Pamplona *encierro* (bull-running, or, literally, "enclosing") in anything but romantic terms. Jake Barnes hears the rocket, steps out on his balcony and watches the crowd run by: men in white with red sashes and neckerchiefs, those behind running faster, then the bulls. "One man fell, rolled to the gutter, and lay quiet." It's a textbook move, and first-rate observation and reporting: An experienced runner who falls remains motionless (bulls respond to movement). In the next *encierro* in the novel, a man is gored through and through and dies. The waiter at the Iruña café mutters, "You hear? Muerto. Dead. He's dead. With a horn through him. All for morning fun. ..."

Despite this, generations of young Americans and other internationals have turned this barnyard bull-management maneuver into the Western world's most famous rite of passage. The idea is simple: 6 fighting bulls are guided through the streets by 8 to 10 *cabestros,* or steers (also known as *mansos,* meaning "tame"). The bulls are herded through the bullring to the holding pens from which they will emerge to be fought that afternoon. The course covers 924 yards. The Cuesta de Santo Domingo down to the corrals is the most dangerous part of the run, high in terror and low in elapsed time. The walls are sheer, and the bulls pass quickly. The fear here is that of a bull—as a result of some personal issue or idiosyncrasy—hooking along the wall of the Military Hospital on his way up the hill, forcing runners out in front of the speeding pack in a classic hammer and anvil movement. Mercaderes is next, cutting left for about 100 yards by the town hall, then right up Calle Estafeta. The outside of each turn and the centrifugal force of 10,000 kilos (22,000 pounds) of bulls and steers are to be avoided here.

Calle Estafeta is the bread and butter of the run, the longest (about 400 yards), straightest, and least complicated part of the course. The classic run, a perfect blend of form and function, is to remain ahead of the horns for as long as possible, fading to the side when overtaken. The long gallop up Calle Estafeta is the place to try to do it. The trickiest part of running with the bulls is splitting your vision so that with one eye you keep track of the bulls behind you and with the other you keep from falling over runners ahead of you.

At the end of Estafeta the course descends left through the *callejón,* the narrow tunnel, into the bullring. The bulls move more slowly here, uncertain of their weak forelegs, allowing runners to stay close and even to touch them as they glide down into the tunnel. The only uncertainty is whether there will be a pileup, in the tunnel. The most dramatic photographs of the *encierro* have been taken here, as the galloping pack slams through what occasionally turns into a solid wall of humanity. If all goes well—no bulls separated from the pack, no mayhem—the bulls will have arrived in the ring in less than three minutes.

The cardinal crime, punishable by a $1,000 fine, is to attempt to attract the bull, thus removing him from the pack and creating a deadly danger. There were 13 deaths during the 20th century, the last one on July 13, 1995. None in the 21st century—yet.

Edificio Baluarte. The Palacio de Congresos y Auditorio de Navarra, built in 2003 by local architectural star Patxi Mangado, is a sleek assemblage of black Zimbabwean granite with a concert hall of exquisite acoustical perfection made of beechwood from Navarra's famed Irati *haya* (beech) forest. Performances and concerts from opera to ballet are held in this modern venue built on the remains of one of the five bastions of Pamplona's 16th-century Ciudadela. ✉*Plaza del Baluarte* ☎*948/066066* 🌐*www.baluarte.com.*

OFF THE BEATEN PATH

Fundación–Museo Jorge Oteiza. Just 8 km (5 mi) east of Pamplona on the road toward France, this museum dedicated to the father of modern Basque art is a must-visit. Jorge Oteiza (1908–2003), in his seminal treatise *Quosque Tandem,* called for Basque artists to find an aesthetic of their own, instead of attempting to become part of the rich Spanish canon. Rejecting ornamentation in favor of essential form and a noninvasive use of space, Oteiza created a school of artists—of which Eduardo Chillida (1924–2002) was the most famous sculptor. The building itself, Oteiza's home for over two decades, is a large cube of red, earth-color concrete designed by Oteiza's longtime friend, Pamplona architect Francisco Javier Sáenz de Oiza. ✉*Alzuza, Ctra. N150, Km 8, from Pamplona* ☎*948/332074* 🌐www.museooteiza.org 🎫€4 ⏲*Tues.–Fri. 10–3, weekends 11–7.*

WHERE TO STAY & EAT

$$$–$$$$ ✕**Josetxo.** This warm, family-run restaurant in a stately mansion with classically elegant decorations is one of Pamplona's finest. Specialties include *hojaldre de marisco* (shellfish pastry), an *ensalada de langosta* (lobster salad) appetizer, and *muslo de pichón relleno de trufa y foie* (pigeon stuffed with truffles and foie gras). ✉*Príncipe de Viana 1* ☎*948/222097* 💳*AE, DC, MC, V* ⏲*Closed Sun. except during San Fermín, and Aug.*

$$–$$$ ✕**Erburu.** In the heart of the nightlife district, this dark, wood-beam restaurant is a true find, frequented by Pamplonans in the know. Come here to dine or just to sample tapas at the bar. Standouts are the Basque classic merluza con salsa verde (hake in green sauce) and any of the dishes made with *alcochofas* (artichokes). ✉*San Lorenzo 19–21* ☎*948/225169* 💳*AE, DC, MC, V* ⏲*Closed Mon. and last 2 wks in July.*

$$ ✕🏨**Casa Otano.** A friendly, tumultuous hotel and restaurant, Casa Otano is simple and well placed, right in the middle of the tapas-and-wine circuit and just a few paces from Pamplona's main square. The restaurant downstairs ($–$$$) serves hearty Basque fare. The general energy level is consistent with the madness that will be raging in the street if you come during San Fermín. ✉*San Nicolás 5, 31001* ☎*948/225095* 📠*948/212012* 🌐*www.casaotano.com* 🛏*15 rooms* 🛎*In-room: no a/c. In-hotel: restaurant, bar, no elevator* 💳*AE, DC, MC, V* ⏲*Closed last 2 wks in July.*

$$$–$$$$ 🏨**Los Tres Reyes.** Named for the three kings of Navarra, Aragón, and Castile—who, it was said, could meet at La Mesa de los Tres Reyes, in the Pyrenees, without stepping out of their respective realms—this

modern glass-and-stone refuge operates on the same principle: Come to Pamplona and find all the comforts of home. ✉*C. de la Taconera s/n, 31001* ☎*948/226600* 🖷*948/222930* 🌐*www.hotel3reyes.com* *152 rooms, 8 suites* *In-hotel: restaurant, bars, pool, gym, parking (fee)* 💳*AE, DC, MC, V.*

NIGHTLIFE & THE ARTS

The city has a thumping student life year-round, especially along the length of Calle San Nicolas. For an ultra-postmodern nightspot, try **Dodo Club** (✉*San Roque 7* ☎*948/198989*), where breakfast, lunch, free Wi-Fi Internet connection, and DJs keep things lively around the clock. **El Otro** (✉*Paulino Caballero 52* ☎*948/132543*) is perfect for a quiet libation, and known for its see-out bathrooms with one-way glass. In August, the **Festivales de Navarra** bring theater and other events to Pamplona. A varied summer program of concerts, ballet, and zarzuela is always in the offing; contact the **Teatro Gayarre** (✉*Av. Carlos III Noble 1* ☎*948/220139*) for information.

SHOPPING

The neckerchiefs worn for the running of the bulls are sold in various shops, as are *gerrikos,* the wide belts worn by Basque sportsmen during contests of strength, to hold in overstressed organs. You can buy botas in any Basque town, but Pamplona's **Anel** (✉*C. Comedías 7*) sells the best brand, Las Tres Zetas—"The Three Zs," written as ZZZ. For sweets, try **Salcedo** (✉*C. Estafeta 37*), open since 1800, which invented and still sells almond-based *mantecadas* (powder cakes), as well as *coronillas* (delightful almond-and-cream concoctions). **Hijas de C. Lozano** (✉*C. Zapatería 11*) sells *café y leche* (coffee and milk) toffees that are prized all over Spain.

OFF THE BEATEN PATH

Olite. 41 km (25 mi) south of Pamplona, you'll find a storybook castle marooned on the plains of Navarra. Olite offers an unforgettable glimpse into the life of Spain in the Middle Ages, including the 11th-century church of San Pedro, revered for its finely worked Romanesque cloisters and portal. But it's the town's castle, restored by Carlos III in the French style and brimming with ramparts, crenellated battlements, and watchtowers, that captures the imagination most. You can walk the ramparts. And should you get tired or hungry, part of the castle has been converted into a parador, making a fine place to catch a bite or a few Z's. *€3* *Daily 10–2 and 4–5.*

PUENTE LA REINA

32 *24 km (15 mi) south of Pamplona.*

Puente la Reina (Gares, in Euskera) is an important nexus on the Camino de Santiago: the junction of the two pilgrimage routes from northern Europe, one passing through Somport and Jaca and the other through Roncesvalles and Pamplona. A bronze sculpture of a pilgrim marks the spot. The graceful medieval bridge over the river Arga was built for pilgrims by Navarran King Sancho VII el Fuerte (the Strong) in the 11th century. The streets, particularly Calle Mayor, are lined with tiny, ancient houses. The church of **Santiago** (*St. James* ✉ *C. Mayor*) is known for its gold sculpture of the saint.The **Iglesia del Crucifijo** (*Church of the Crucifix* ✉ *Ctra. de Pamplona s/n*) has a notably expressive wooden sculpture of Christ on a Y-shape cross, gift of a 14th-century pilgrim.The octagonal church of **Santa María de Eunate** (✉ *5 km [3 mi] east of Puente la Reina*) was once used as a burial place for pilgrims who didn't make it.The church of **San Román** (✉ *6 km [4 mi] west of Puente la Reina*), in the restored village of Cirauqui, has an extraordinarily beautiful carved portal.

WHERE TO STAY & EAT

$$$–$$$$ **Hotel El Peregrino.** A time-honored haven for weary pilgrims on sound budgets, this handsome stone house north of town is hard to pass up. The rooms are small but charming. Roasts, *menestra de verduras* (Navarran vegetable stew), rack of suckling pig, and hearty bean-and-sausage-based soups are among the star offerings at the restaurant ($$–$$$$). ✉ *Ctra. Pamplona–Logroño, Km 23, 31100* ☎ *948/340075* *948/341190* *www.hotelelperegrino.com* *10 rooms, 3 junior suites* *In-hotel: restaurant, bar, pool* *AE, DC, MC, V.*

ESTELLA

33 *19 km (12 mi) south of Puente la Reina, 48 km (30 mi) north of Logroño.*

Once the seat of the Royal Court of Navarra, Estella (Lizarra, in Euskera) is an inspiring stop on the Camino de Santiago. Its heart is the arcaded Plaza San Martín, its chief civic monument the 12th-century **Palacio de los Reyes de Navarra** *(Palace of the Kings of Navarra)*. **San Pedro de la Rúa** (✉ *C. San Nicolás s/n*) has a beautiful cloister and a stunning carved portal.Across the River Ega from San Pedro, the doorway to the church of **San Miguel** has fantastic relief sculptures of St. Michael the Archangel battling a dragon.The **Iglesia del Santo Sepulcro** (*Church of the Holy Sepulchre* ✉ *C. Curtidores s/n*) has a beautiful fluted portal.**Santa María Jus del Castillo** (✉ *C. Curtidores s/n*), converted from a synagogue in 1145, is the only vestige of Estella's medieval Jewish quarter.The **Monasterio de Irache** (✉ *Ctra. de Logroño, Km 3*) dates from the 10th century but was later converted by Cistercian monks to a pilgrims' hospital; next door is the famous brass faucet that supplies pilgrims with free-flowing holy wine.

VITORIA & THE RIOJA ALAVESA

Medieval Vitoria, in the Basque province of Alava, is largely undiscovered by tourists, and the Rioja Alavesa and, in particular, Laguardia, rank among the Basque Country's most unforgettable destinations.

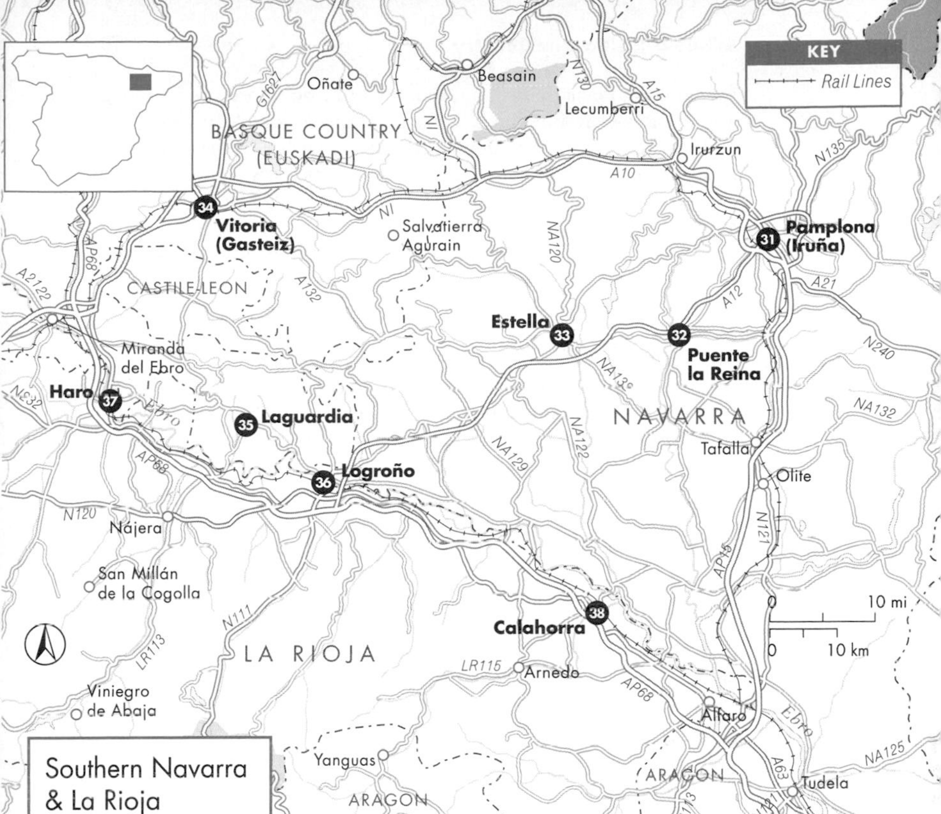

VITORIA

34 *93 km (56 mi) west of Pamplona, 115 km (71 mi) southwest of San Sebastián, 64 km (40 mi) southeast of Bilbao.*

Vitoria's standard of living has been rated the highest in Spain, based on such criteria as square meters of green space per inhabitant (14), sports and cultural facilities, and pedestrian-only zones. Capital of the Basque Country, and its second-largest city after Bilbao, Vitoria (Gasteiz, in Euskera) is in many ways Euskadi's least Basque city. Neither a maritime nor a mountain enclave, Vitoria occupies the steppelike *meseta de Alava* (Alava plain) and functions as a modern industrial center with a surprisingly medieval *Casco Antiguo* (Old Quarter).

Plaza de la Virgen Blanca, in the southwest corner of old Vitoria, is ringed by noble houses with covered arches and white-trim glass galleries. The monument in the center commemorates the Duke of Wellington's defeat of Napoléon's army here in 1813. For lunch, coffee, or tapas, look to the plaza's top left-hand corner for the Cafeteria de la Virgen Blanca, replete with giant wooden floorboards.The **Plaza de España,** across Virgen Blanca past the monument and the handsome El Victoria café, is an arcaded neoclassical square with the austere elegance typical of formal 19th-century squares all over Spain.The **Plaza del Machete,**

overlooking Plaza de España, is named for the sword used by medieval nobility to swear allegiance to the local fueros, or special Basque rights and privileges.A jasper niche in the lateral facade of the Gothic church of **San Miguel** (⊠*Plaza del Machete*) contains the Virgen Blanca (White Virgin), Vitoria's patron saint.The **Palacio de los Alava Esquivel** (⊠*C. de la Soledad*) is reached from the Plaza de la Virgen Blanca along Calle de Herrería, which follows the egg-shape outline along the west side of the old city walls.House **No. 27** (⊠*Across from Cantón Anorbin*) has elaborately sculpted engravings over the door and a giant coat of arms on the far corner. The house is past the church of San Pedro Apostol. The 15th-century **Torre de Doña Otxanda** (⊠*Calle Siervas de Jesús 24*) houses Vitoria's **Museo de Ciencias Naturales (Museum of Natural Sciences)**, which contains interesting botanical, zoological, and geological collections along with the museum's most prized items: pieces of amber from the nearby archeological site at Peñacerrada-Urizaharra.**El Portalón** (⊠*C. de la Correría 151*), the ancient brick-and-wood house at the corner across from the museum, a hostelry for 500 years, is an excellent restaurant and wine cellar.The **Museo de la Arqueología** (⊠*C. de la Correría*) has paleolithic dolmens, Roman art and artifacts, medieval objects, and the famous *stele del jinete* (stele of the horseback rider), an early Basque tombstone.Look at the door nearest the corner in the ocher house at **No. 14** (⊠*At C. Correría and Cantón Apaizgaitegi*) : its elaborate coat of arms depicts lions and castles, once painted gold and purple. Equally faded trim spirals around the corners of the house, and conch shells appear under scrolls below the windows.

The Torre de los Hurtado de Anda is across from the exquisitely sculpted Gothic doorway on the western facade of the **Catedral de Santa María** (⊠*C. Fray Zacarías Martinez s/n*). Go into the courtyard on the west side of this square; in the far right corner, you'll find the sculpted head of a fish protruding from the grass in front of an intensely ornate door. Walk through Calle Txikitxoa and up Cantón de Santa María behind the cathedral, noting the tiny accretions that have been added to the back of the apse over the centuries, clinging across corners and filling odd spaces.The lovely plateresque facade of the 16th-century **Palacio de Escoriaza-Esquibel** (⊠*C. Fray Zacarías Martinez*) overlooks an open space.Don't miss the austere **Palacio Villa Suso** (⊠*C. Fray Zacarías Martinez*), built in 1538. It's down toward the Plaza del Machete, across from the church of San Miguel.The **Casa del Cordón** (⊠*C. Cuchillería*), a 15th-century structure with a 13th-century tower, stands at No. 24, identifiable by the Franciscan *cordón* (rope) decorating one of the pointed arches on the facade.

★ The 1525 Palacio de Bendaña is home to one of Vitoria's main attractions, the **Museo Fournier de Naipes** *(Playing-Card Museum)*. In 1868 Don Heraclio Fournier founded a playing-card factory, started amassing cards, and eventually found himself with 15,000 sets, the largest and finest such collection in the world. As you survey rooms of hand-painted cards, the distinction between artwork and game piece quickly gets scrambled. The oldest sets date from the 12th century, making them older than the building, and the story parallels the history of printing.

The most unusual and finely painted sets come from Japan, India (the Indian cards are round), and the international practice of tarot. One German set has musical bars that can be combined to form hundreds of different waltzes. By the time you reach the 20th-century rooms, contemporary designs have been debunked as unoriginal. You'll never look at cards the same way again. ✉ *C. Cuchillería 54* ☎ *945/255555* *Free* ⏲ *Tues.–Fri. 10–2 and 4–6:30, Sat. 10–2, Sun. 11–2.*

Parque de la Florida (✉ *South of Plaza de la Virgen Blanca*) is nice respite during a tour of Vitoria.The **Museo Provincial de Armería** (*Provincial Arms Museum* ✉ *Paseo Fray Francisco de Vitoria*) has prehistoric hatchets, 20th-century pistols, and a sand-table reproduction of the 1813 battle between the Duke of Wellington's troops and the French. The museum is south of the Parque de la Florida. ✉ *Paseo de la Senda 8* ☎ *945/181925* *Free* ⏲ *Tues.–Fri. 10–2 and 4–6:30, Sat. 10–2, Sun. 11–2.*

The **Museo de Bellas Artes** (*Museum of Fine Arts* ✉ *Paseo Fray Francisco de Vitoria*) has paintings by Ribera, Picasso, and the Basque painter Zuloaga. Next door is the Palacio Ajuria-Enea, seat of the Basque government. ✉ *Paseo Fray Francisco 8* ☎ *945/181918* *Free* ⏲ *Tues.–Fri. 10–2 and 4–6:30, Sat. 10–2, 5–8, Sun. 11–2.*

OFF THE BEATEN PATH

Artium. Officially titled Centro-Museo Vasco de Arte Contemporáneo, this former bus station was opened in 2002 by King Juan Carlos I, who called it "the third leg of the Basque art triangle, along with the Bilbao Guggenheim and San Sebastián's Chillida Leku." The museum's permanent collection—including 20th- and 21st-century paintings and sculptures by Jorge Oteiza, Eduardo Chillida, Agustín Ibarrola, and Nestor Basterretxea, among many others—makes it one of Spain's finest treasuries of contemporary art. ✉ ***Calle de Francia 24*** ☎ ***945/209020*** ***www.artium.org*** ***€5*** ⏲ ***Tues.–Sun. 11–8.***

WHERE TO STAY & EAT

$$$–$$$$ ★ ✕ **El Portalón.** Between the dark, creaky wood floors and staircases and the ancient beams, pillars, and coats of arms, this famous 15th-century inn turns out classical Castillian and Basque specialties that reflect Vitoria's geography and social history. Try the *lomo de cebón asado en su jugo con puré de manzanas* (filet mignon with apple puree) or any of the *merluza* (hake) preparations. ✉ *C. Correría 151* ☎ *945/142755* *AE, DC, MC, V* ⏲ *Closed Sun., last 3 wks in Aug., wk before Easter, and Dec. 24–Jan. 4.*

$$$ ★ ✕ **Parador de Argómaniz.** Some 15 minutes east of Vitoria off N104 toward Pamplona, this 17th-century palace has panoramic views over the Alava plains and retains a powerful sense of mystery and romance, with long stone hallways punctuated by imposing antiques. Rooms have polished wood floors and huge, terra-cotta-floor bathrooms; some have glass-enclosed sitting areas and/or hot tubs. The wood-beam dining room ($$–$$$$) on the third floor makes each meal feel like a baronial feast. ✉ *N 1, Km 363, Argómaniz 01192* ☎ *945/293200*

945/293287 www.parador.es 53 rooms In-hotel: restaurant, bar, parking (no fee) AE, DC, MC, V.

EN ROUTE

Between Vitoria and Logroño, on the north bank of the Ebro River, is the wine-growing Rioja Alavesa region. Either sweep comfortably around on the Madrid road and approach from the west via Haro, Briones (with a lovely medieval bridge), and San Vicente de la Sonsierra, *or* drive south on the slower, curvier A2124 through the Puerto de Herrera pass to the Balcón de La Rioja for a view of the Ebro Valley.

LAGUARDIA

35 *66 km (40 mi) southeast of Vitoria, 17 km (10 mi) west of Logroño.*

Founded in 908 to stand guard, as its name suggests, over Navarra's southwestern flank, Laguardia is on a lofty promontory overlooking the Ebro River and the vineyards of the Rioja Alavesa—La Rioja wine country north of the Ebro in the Basque province of Alava. Flanked by the Sierra de Cantabria, the town rises shiplike, its prow headed north, over the savory sea of surrounding vineyards. Ringed with walls, Laguardia's dense cluster of emblazoned noble facades and stunning patios may have no equal in Spain. Relish the some 50 houses with coats of arms and medieval or Renaissance masonry.

Starting from the 15th-century Puerta de Carnicerías, or Puerta Nueva, the central portal off the parking area on the east side of town, the first landmark is the 16th-century *ayuntamiento,* (town hall) with its imperial shield of Carlos V. Farther into the square is the current town hall, built in the 19th century. A right down **Calle Santa Engracia** takes you past impressive facades—the floor inside the portal at No. 25 is a lovely stone mosaic, and a walk behind the triple-emblazoned 17th-century facade of No. 19 reveals a stagecoach, floor mosaics, wood beams, an inner porch, and, if you're lucky, the aroma of potato-and-leek soup. Nos. 15 and 9 have interesting reliefs and masonry. The Puerta de Santa Engracia, with an image of the saint in an overhead niche, opens out to the right, and on the left, at the entrance to Calle Víctor Tapia, house No. 17 bears a coat of arms with the Latin LAUS TIBI (Praise Be to Thee). Laguardia's crown architectural jewel is Spain's only Gothic polychrome portal, on the church of **Santa María de los Reyes.** Protected by a posterior Renaissance facade, the door centers on a lovely, lifelike effigy of La Virgen de los Reyes (Virgin of the Kings), sculpted in the 14th century and painted in the 17th by Juan Francisco de Ribera. Flanking the Virgin are the apostles and biblical scenes.

To the north of the ornate castle and hotel El Collado is the monument to the famous Laguardia composer of fables, Felix María Samaniego (1745–1801), heir to the tradition of Aesop and Lafontaine. Walk around the small, grassy park to the Puerta de Páganos and look right—you can see Laguardia's oldest civil structure, the late-14th-century **Casa de la Primicia,** at Calle Páganos 78 (so named as the place where fresh fruit was sold).If you walk left of the Casa de la Primicia, past several emblazoned houses to Calle Páganos 13, you can see the bodega (wine cellar) at the Posada Mayor de Migueloa, which is usually in full swing. Go through the corridor to the Posada's Calle Mayor entryway and walk up to the **Juanjo San Pedro** gallery at Calle Mayor 1, filled with antiques and artwork.

WHERE TO STAY & EAT

$$$$ **Hotel Marqués de Riscal.** Frank Gehry's latest explosion of genius looks as if a colony from outer space had taken up residence (or crashed) in the middle of La Rioja's oldest vineyards. This jumble of pink and gold titanium sheets and mirror finish stainless steel curves over and around rectilinear sandstone surfaces creating what looks from a distance like a gift-wrapped winery. With the winery's visitor center next door, the historic cellars and tasting rooms, the rolling hills of La Rioja offering activities from horseback riding to golf, and the Valdezcaray ski resort under an hour away, visitors here can catalog different ways to feel pampered. The Spa Caudalíe Vinothérapie complex provides new ways to make the most of grape juice, while Riojan star chef Francis Paniego's gourmet restaurant is sure to delight the palate. *C. Torrea 1, 01300 Elciego, 01340 945/180880 945/180881 www.luxurycollection.com 43 rooms, 11 suites In-hotel: restaurant, bar, meeting rooms, spa, parking (no fee) AE, DC, MC, V.*

$$–$$$ Fodor'sChoice ★ **Posada Mayor de Migueloa.** With a tavern at Calle Páganos 13 and a passageway leading to the stone reception area on Mayor de Migueloa, this 17th-century palace is a beauty. At the tavern ($$–$$$$), try *patatas a la riojana* (potatoes with chorizo) or *pochas con chorizo y costilla* (beans with sausage and lamb chop). Dinner ranges from beef with foie gras to *mollejas de cordero* (lamb sweetbreads) to *venado con miel y pomelo* (venison with a honey-and-grapefruit sauce). Guest rooms have beautiful, original, rough-hewn ceiling beams. *C. Mayor de Migueloa 20, 01300 945/621175 945/621022 www.mayordemigueloa.com 8 rooms In-hotel: restaurant, bar, no elevator AE, DC, MC, V Closed mid-Dec.–mid-Jan.*

$$ **Marixa.** Aficionados travel great distances to dine in Marixa's lovely restaurant, known for its excellent roasts, views, and value. The heavy, wooden interior is ancient and intimate, and the cuisine ($$–$$$) is Vasco-Riojano, combining the best of both worlds. Try the *menestra de riojana verduras,* a mixed-vegetable dish, or the *cordero asado a la parrilla,* lamb roasted over coals. Guest rooms are modern, cheery, and carpeted, with views over the medieval walls of Laguardia to the Ebro Valley beyond. *C. Sancho Abarca 8, 01300 945/600165 945/600202 www.hotelmarixa.com 10 rooms In-hotel: restaurant, bar, no elevator AE, DC, MC, V Closed mid-Dec.–mid-Jan.*

OFF THE BEATEN PATH

Herederos de Marqués de Riscal. The village of Elciego 6 km (4 mi) southeast of Laguardia is the site of the Hotel Marqués de Riscal, a daring contemporary design superimposed over a traditional winery by Frank Gehry. This wine-tasting facility, restaurant, hotel, and visitor center has quickly emerged as the flagship of Rioja's new push to reestablish its supremacy as Spain's top winemaking region. Tours of the vineyards—one of the most his-

toric in La Rioja—as well as the cellars are conducted in various languages, including English. ✉ *C. Torrea 1, Elciego* ☎ *945/606000* 🌐 *www.marques-deriscal.com* 🎫 *€6* ⏲ *Tours Mon.–Sat. 10, noon, and 4.*

LA RIOJA

A natural compendium of highlands, plains, vineyards, and the Ebro River basin, La Rioja has historically produced Spain's finest wines. The area's quarter of a million inhabitants live mainly along the Ebro, in the cities of Logroño, Haro, and Calahorra, but many of its treasures are in the mountains and river valleys. Drained by the Rivers Oja (hence the name *río oja*), Najerilla, Iregua, Leza, and Cidacos, La Rioja is composed of the Rioja Alta (Upper Rioja), the moist and mountainous western end, and the Rioja Baja (Lower Rioja), the flatter and dryer eastern end, more Mediterranean in climate. Logroño, the capital, lies between the two.

LOGROÑO

36 *92 km (55 mi) southwest of Pamplona on N-III.*

A busy city of 130,000 and a modern industrial center, Logroño retains a lovely old quarter between its two bridges, bordered by the Ebro and the medieval walls. Breton de los Herreros and Muro Francisco de la Mata are the quarter's most characteristic streets. An important wine- and tapas-tasting center, **Calle Laurel** and the neighboring streets are collectively known as *el sendero de los elefantes* (the path of the elephants)—an allusion to *trompas* (trunks), Spanish for a snootful. Order crianza and they'll break out the crystal. A *cosechero,* wine of the year, is served in small shot glasses, and *reserva* (made with specially selected grapes aged three years or more in oak and bottle) will elicit snifters for proper swirling, smelling, and tasting.

Near Logroño, the Roman bridge and the *mirador* (lookout) at **Viguera** are the main sights in the lower Iregua Valley. Santiago (St. James), according to legend, helped the Christians defeat the Moors at the **Castillo de Clavijo,** another panoramic spot. The **Leza (Cañon) del Río Leza** is La Rioja's most dramatic canyon.

Logroño's dominant landmarks are the finest sacred structures in Rioja. The 11th-century church of the **Imperial de Santa María del Palacio** (✉ *C. Ruavieja s/n*) is known as La Aguja (The Needle) for its pyramid-shape, 45-yard Romanesque-Gothic tower.The church of **Santiago el Real** (*Royal St. James* ✉ *Plaza de Santiago s/n*), reconstructed in the 16th century, is noted for its equestrian statue of the saint (also known as Santiago Matamoros–St. James the Moorslayer), which presides over the main door. **San Bartolomé** (✉ *C. San Bartolomé s/n*) is a 13th- to 14th-century French Gothic church with an 11th-century Mudejar tower and an elaborately sculpted 14th-century Gothic doorway.The **Catedral de Santa María de La Redonda** (✉ *Plaza de los Portales s/n*) is a landmark for its twin baroque towers.Many of Logroño's monuments, such as the elegant **Puente de Piedra** *(Stone Bridge)* , were built as part of the Camino de Santiago pilgrimage route.

WHERE TO STAY & EAT

$$–$$$$ ✕**Asador Emilio.** The Castilian rustic decor here includes a coffered wood ceiling, which merits a long look. Roast lamb cooked over wood coals is the specialty, but *aluvias* (kidney beans) and *migas de pastor* (bread crumbs with garlic and sausage) are hard to resist. ✉*Republica Argentina 8* ☎*941/233141* ▭*AE, DC, MC, V* ⏲*Closed Sun. June–Apr. and Aug..*

$$–$$$ ✕**El Cachetero.** Local fare based on vegetables is the rule here, but you can also tuck into roast goat or lamb. Though the dining room is classical and elegant, with antique furnishings and a serious look about it, the cuisine is homespun, its raw materials fresh and seasonally appealing. ✉*C. Laurel 3* ☎*941/228463* ▭*AE, DC, MC, V* ⏲*Closed Sun. and last wk in Aug. No dinner Wed.*

$–$$$ ★ ✕**La Rueda.** Cándida Calleja's upstairs perch over the Calle and Travesía del Laurel tapas-grazing scene is close enough to the action below but removed enough for a breath of fresh air. Memorable dishes include acorn-fed ham or *revuelto de gambas y puntas de espárragos trigueros* (eggs scrambled with shrimp and wild asparagus tips). The downstairs bar serves excellent sepia (cuttlefish) with chilling hits of Rojanda, La Rueda's own fresh young white wine. ✉*Travesía del Laurel 1* ☎*941/227986* ▭*AE, DC, MC, V* ⏲*Closed Sun. and Aug.*

$$–$$$ **Marqués de Vallejo.** Close to—but not overwhelmed by—the food- and wine-tasting frenzy of Calle del Laurel, this family-run hotel is near the best historic sites. Rooms are small but intimate. Stash your car in the garage beneath the nearby Plaza del Espolón. ✉*Marqués de Vallejo 8, 26005* ☎*941/248333* 📠*941/240288* 🌐*www.hotelmarquesdevallejo.com* *30 rooms* *In-hotel: restaurant, bar* ▭*AE, DC, MC, V.*

5

LA RIOJA ALTA

The Upper Rioja, the most prosperous part of La Rioja's wine country, extends from the Ebro River to the Sierra de la Demanda. La Rioja Alta has the most fertile soil, the best vineyards and agriculture, the most impressive castles and monasteries, a ski resort at Ezcaray, and the historical economic advantage of being on the Camino de Santiago. From Logroño, drive 12 km (7 mi) west on N120 to **Navarrete** to see its noble houses and the baroque altarpiece in Asunción church.

Nájera, 15 km (9 mi) west of Navarrete, was the court of the kings of Navarra and capital of Navarra and La Rioja until 1076, when La Rioja became part of Castile and the residence of the Castilian royal family. The monastery of **Santa María la Real** ✉*Calle de Monasterio s/n, Nájera* ☎*941/361083* 🌐*www.arteguias.com/monasterio/santamariarealnajera.htm* *€3* ⏲*Tues.–Sun. 10:30–1, 4–6.* (☎941/363650), "pantheon of kings," is distinguished by its 16th-century Claustro de los Caballeros (Cavaliers' Cloister), a flamboyant Gothic structure with 24 lacy plateresque Renaissance arches overlooking a grassy patio. The sculpted 12th-century tomb of Doña Blanca de Navarra is the monastery's best-known sarcophagus, and the 67 Flamboyant Gothic choir stalls, dating from 1495, are some of Spain's best.

Santo Domingo de la Calzada, 20 km (12 mi) west of Nájera on the N120, has always been a key stop on the Camino. Santo Domingo was an 11th-century saint who built roads and bridges for pilgrims and founded the hospital that is now the town's parador. The cathedral is a Romanesque-Gothic pile containing the saint's tomb, choir murals, and a walnut altarpiece carved by Damià Forment in 1541. The live hen and rooster in a plateresque stone chicken coop commemorate a legendary local miracle in which a pair of roasted fowl came back to life to protest the innocence of a pilgrim hanged for theft. Be sure to stroll through the town's beautifully preserved medieval quarter.

Enter the **Sierra de la Demanda** by heading south 14 km (8½ mi) on LO810. Your first stop is the town of **Ezcaray,** with its aristocratic houses emblazoned with family crests, of which the **Palacio del Conde de Torremúzquiz** (Palace of the Count of Torremúzquiz) is the most distinguished. Good excursions from here are the Valdezcaray winter-sports center; the source of the River Oja at Llano de la Casa; La Rioja's highest point, at the 7,494-foot Pico de San Lorenzo; and the Romanesque church of Tres Fuentes, at Valgañón.The town of **San Millán de la Cogolla** is southeast of Santo Domingo de la Calzada. Take LO809 southeast through Berceo to the Monasterio de Yuso, where a 10th-century manuscript on St. Augustine's *Glosas Emilianenses* has notes in what is considered the earliest example of the Spanish language, the vernacular Latin dialect known as Roman Paladino. The nearby Visigothic Monasterio de Suso is where Gonzalo de Berceo, recognized as the first Castilian poet, wrote and recited his 13th-century verse in the Castilian tongue, now the language of more than 300 million people.

WHERE TO STAY & EAT

$$–$$$ Fodor's Choice ★ ✕🏨 **Echaurren.** This rambling roadhouse in Ezcaray, 61 km (37 mi) southwest of Logroño, is 7 km (4 mi) below Valdezcaray, La Rioja's prime ski resort. Echaurren is famous for fine traditional cuisine ($$–$$$$) engineered by Marisa Sanchez and the original creations by her son, wunderkind Francis Paniego. Marisa's *patatas a la riojana* (potatoes stewed with peppers and chorizo) are as good as they get, and Francis, a youthful master chef with an immense future in the forefront of Spanish culinary art, experiments with wood coals and aromas. The rooms are comfortable and contemporary, and the staff and owners warm and engaging. ✉*Héroes del Alcázar 2, Ezcaray26280* ☎*941/354047* 📠*941/427133* 🌐*www.echaurren.com* *25 rooms* *In-hotel: restaurant, bar, parking (fee)* 💳*AE, DC, MC, V.*

HARO

37 *20 km (12 mi) west of Nájera on the N120, 49 km (29 mi) west of Logroño.*

Haro is the wine capital of La Rioja. Its **Casco Viejo** (Old Quarter) and best taverns are concentrated in the loop known as La Herradura (The

Horseshoe), with Santo Tomás at its curve, and the feet leading down San Martín and Santo Tomás to the open space at the upper left-hand (northeast) corner of Plaza de la Paz. Up the left side of the horseshoe, Bar La Esquina, on the left, is the first of many top-notch tapas bars. Bar Los Caños, behind a stone archway at San Martín 5, is built into the vaults and arches of the former church of San Martín.

Haro's century-old **bodegas** *(wineries)* have been headquartered in the *barrio de la estación* (train-station district) ever since the railroad opened in 1863. Guided tours and tastings, some in English, can be arranged at the facilities themselves or through the tourist office. Haro's June 29 Batalla del Vino (Wine Battle) is an epically wet and alcoholic brawl.

HARO'S WINE WAR

June 29 marks the Batalla del Vino in Haro. It's thought to have begun around 1710 as a jocular way to commemorate a millenary territorial dispute between the towns of Haro and Miranda de Ebro. In celebration of La Fiesta de San Pedro, hundreds of local revelers and visitors throw some 60,000 liters of not very good wine at each other using everything from buckets to vats, hoses, and water pistols. Traditional fiesta attire is white, which is quickly stained a permanent pink-purple color. By early afternoon, traditional dances are performed, and later wild cows are caped in the bullring.

The architectural highlight is the Flamboyant Gothic church of **Santo Tomás,** a single-nave church, with an intricately sculpted, reddish-tinge portal on the south side. The richly gilded 60-foot-high organ facade above the choir loft is stunning.

WHERE TO STAY & EAT

$$–$$$$ ✕**Terete.** A favorite with locals, this rustic place has been roasting lamb in wood ovens since 1877 and serves a hearty *minestra de verduras* (vegetables stewed with bits of ham). The wine cellar is stocked with some of the Rioja's best. ✉*C. Lucrecia Arana 17* ☎*941/310023* 💳*AE, DC, MC, V* ⊙*Closed Mon., 1st 2 wks in July, and last 2 wks in Aug.*

$$$ ★ **Hostería del Monasterio de San Millán.** Declared a World Heritage Site by UNESCO, this magnificent inn occupies a wing of the Monasterio de Yuso. Guest rooms are elegant and somewhat austere, but it has the comforts you need. ✉*Monasterio de Yuso San Millan de la Cogolla, 26326* ☎*941/373277* 📠*941/373266* 🌐*www.sanmillan.com* *22 rooms, 3 suites* *In-hotel: restaurant, bar* 💳*AE, DC, MC, V.*

$$–$$$ **Los Agustinos.** Haro's best hotel is built into a 14th-century monastery whose cloister (now a pleasant patio) is considered one of the best in La Rioja. Arches, a great hall, and tapestries complete the medieval look. ✉*San Agustín 2, 26200* ☎*941/311308* 📠*941/303148* 🌐*www.hotellosagustinos.com* *60 rooms* *In-hotel: restaurant, bar, parking (fee), minibar* 💳*AE, DC, MC, V.*

5

THE HIGHLANDS

The rivers forming the seven main valleys of the Ebro basin originate in the Sierra de la Demanda, Sierra de Cameros, and Sierra de Alcarama. **Ezcaray** is La Rioja's skiing capital in the **valley of the Rio Oja** just below the slopes at Valdezcaray in the Sierra de la Demanda. The upper **Najerilla Valley** is La Rioja's mountain sanctuary and wildest corner, an excellent hunting and fishing preserve. The Najerilla River, a rich, weed-choked chalk stream, is one of Spain's best trout rivers. Look for the Puente de Hiedra (Ivy Bridge), its heavy curtain of ivy falling to the surface of the water above Anguiano. The **Monasterio de Valvanera,** off C113 near Anguiano, is the sanctuary of the Virgen de Valvanera, a 12th-century Romanesque-Byzantine wood carving of the Virgin and child. **Anguiano** is renowned for its Danza de los Zancos (Dance of the Stilts), held July 22, when dancers on wooden stilts run downhill into the arms of the crowd in the main square..

The upper **Iregua Valley,** off N111, has the prehistoric Gruta de la Paz caves at Ortigosa. The artisans of **Villoslada del Cameros** make the region's patchwork quilts, called *almazuelas.* Climb to **Pico Cebollera** for a superb view of the valley. Work back toward the Ebro along the River Leza, through Laguna de Cameros and San Román de Cameros (known for its basket weavers), to complete a tour of the Sierra del Cameros. The upper **Cidacos Valley** leads to the **Parque Jurásico** (Jurassic Park) at Enciso, famous for its dinosaur tracks. The main village in the upper **Alhama Valley** is **Cervera del Rio Alhama,** a center for handmade *alpargatas* (rope-sole shoes).

WHERE TO STAY & EAT

$–$$$ ✕ **La Herradura.** High over the ancient bridge of Anguiano, this is an excellent place to try the local specialty, *caparrones colorados de Anguiano con sus sacramentos* (small, red kidney beans stewed with sausage and fatback). Unpretentious and family run, it's usually filled to the gills with Riojanos and fishermen. The house wine is an impressive Uruñuela *cosechero* (young wine of the year) from the Najerilla Valley. ✉ *Ctra. de Lerma, Km 14, Anguiano* ☎ *941/377151* ▭ *MC, V.*

$ ✕ ▣ **Hospedería Abadía de Valvanera.** Built into the former monks' quarters of a 16th-century monastery that was itself built over a 9th-century hermitage, this is an ideal base for hiking and getting away from it all. The church's 12th-century wood carving of the Virgin of Valvanera is the object of an overnight pilgrimage from Logroño every October 15 in celebration of the harvest. A crucial factor in Rioja's grape harvest, the Virgin is portrayed with a pomegranate (symbolizing fertility) and surrounded by vines. Rooms are simple (bordering on monastic) but comfortable and spotless, and the cuisine ($–$$), though undistinguished, offers local products and dishes at unbeatable prices. ✉ *Monasterio de Valvanera s/n, 5 km (3 mi) west of LR113, 26323* ☎ *941/377044* 🖷 *941/377194* 🌐 *www.abadiavalvanera.com* *28 rooms* *In-room: no a/c, no TV. In-hotel: restaurant, no elevator* ▭ *AE, DC, MC, V.*

LA RIOJA BAJA

La Rioja's eastern area is more Mediterranean than Atlantic or Castilian in climate and vegetation, bordering the plains of Navarra, Soria, and Aragón. Its main river, the Cidacos, joins the Ebro at Calahorra (population 20,000), the region's largest city.

Lower Rioja has a number of key sights, including **Alfaro**'s medieval houses and church of San Miguel; **Arnedo**'s Monasterio de Vico; **Cornago**'s castle, with its four towers (three conical, one rectangular); **Igea**'s Palacio del Marqués de Casa Torre; and **Enciso**'s Parque Jurásico (Jurassic Park), with dinosaur tracks 150 million years old. Ten kilometers (6 mi) from Calahorra, there are castle ruins at **Quel.Autol** is the site of rock formations known as El Picuezo y La Picueza (roughly, Mr. and Mrs. Rockpile) for their resemblance to man and wife.

CALAHORRA

38 *46 km (27½ mi) southeast of Logroño, 109 km (65½ mi) northwest of Zaragoza.*

The birthplace of Roman orator and rhetorician Quintilian (teacher of Tacitus), Calahorra was founded by the Romans 2,000 years ago. You can explore the town's Roman and medieval remains by following the tour posted near Calahorra's *ayuntamiento* (town hall)—it covers the Quintilian monument, the Jewish quarter, and the medieval quarter along with the churches of San Andrés, Santiago, and San Celedonio. Ask for a map inside.

WHERE TO EAT

$$–$$$$ ✕ **La Taberna de la Cuarta Esquina.** This simple provincial tavern exemplifies the best of Spain: excellent and unpretentious food and service in a family environment. Roasts and *menestra de verduras* (vegetable stewed with bits of ham) are irresistible here, especially in the dining room with the fireplace. ✉ *Cuatro Esquinas 16* ☎ *941/134355* ▭ *AE, DC, MC, V* ⊙ *Closed Tues. and last 2 wks of July.*

BILBAO & THE BASQUE COUNTRY ESSENTIALS

To research prices, get advice from other travelers, and book travel arrangements, visit www.fodors.com.

TRANSPORTATION

For more on travel to and in Bilbao and the Basque Country, see the planner at the beginning of this chapter.

BY AIR

Bilbao's airport serves much of this area, and smaller airports at Santander, Hondarribia (serving San Sebastián), Vitoria, Logroño, and Pamplona provide useful points of entry.

Airports **Aeropuerto de Bilbao (Sondika)** (☎ *94/486-9694*). **Aeropuerto de Logroño-Agoncillo** (☎ *941/277400*). **Aeropuerto de Pamplona** (☎ *948/168700*). **Aeropuerto de San Sebastián** (*Hondarribia* ☎ *943/643464*). **Aeropuerto de Santander** (☎ *942/202100*). **Aeropuerto de Vitoria** (☎ *945/163500*).

BY BIKE

Bike Maps **Bici Rent Donosti** (✉ *Paseo de la Zurriola 22, San Sebastián* ☎ *943/279260*). **Ciclos Larreki** (✉ *Av. de Guipúzcoa s/n, Pamplona* ☎ *948/150645*). **Comet** (✉ *Av. de la Libertad 6, San Sebastián* ☎ *943/422351*). **Fonfría** (✉ *General Dávila 206, Santander* ☎ *942/376563*).

BY BOAT & FERRY

Boat and ferries are link in various ways to England and other points.

Boat & Ferry Information **Brittany Ferries** (✉ *Paseo de Pereda 27, 39002 Santander* ☎ *942/220000 or 942/214500* ✉ *Millbay Docks, Plymouth PL1 3EW England* ☎ *0990/360360*). **Ferries Golfo de Vizcaya** (✉ *Cosme Etxevarrieta 1, 48009 Bilbao* ☎ *94/423-4477*). **Vapores Suardiaz** (✉ *Colon de Larreategui 30, 48009 Bilbao* ☎ *94/423-4300*).

BY BUS

From Madrid, daily buses go to all the major cities in this region. See the the chapter opening planner for more information.

Bus Company **Continental Auto** (✉ *C. Alenza 20, Madrid* ☎ *91/533-0400*).

Bus Stations **Bilbao** (✉ *Gurtubay 1* ☎ *94/439-5077*). **Logroño** (✉ *Av. España 1* ☎ *941/235983*). **Pamplona** (✉ *C. Conde Oliveto 8* ☎ *948/223854*). **San Sebastián** (✉ *C. Sancho el Sabio 33* ☎ *943/463974*). **Santander** (✉ *C. Navas de Tolosa s/n* ☎ *942/211995*). **Vitoria** (✉ *C. de los Herran 27* ☎ *945/258400*).

BY CAR

Even the remotest points are an easy one-day drive from Madrid, and the north is superbly covered by freeways. From the capital, it's 240 km (149 mi) on the N1 or the A1 toll road to Burgos, after which you can take the N623 to complete the 390 km (242 mi) to Santander. The drive from Madrid to Bilbao is 397 km (247 mi); follow the N1 or A1 past Burgos to Miranda del Ebro, where you pick up the A68. Car rentals are available in the major cities: Bilbao, Pamplona, San Sebastián,

Santander, and Vitoria. Cars can also be rented at Hondarribia, the San Sebastián airport.

Rental Agencies **Alquibilbo** (✉ *General Eguía 20, Bilbao* ☎ *94/441–2012*). **A-Rental** (✉ *C. Pérez Galdos 24, Bilbao* ☎ *94/427–0781*). **Avis** (✉ *C. Monasterio de la Oliva 29, Pamplona* ☎ *948/170036* ✉ *Aeropuerto de Pamplona* ☎ *948/168763* ✉ *Triunfo 2, San Sebastián* ☎ *943/461527* ✉ *Nicolás Salmerón 3, Santander* ☎ *942/227025*). **Europcar** (✉ *Av. Pio XII 43, Pamplona* ☎ *948/172523* ✉ *Aeropuerto de Pamplona* ☎ *948/312798* ✉ *Aeropuerto de Fuenterrabía [Hondarribia], San Sebastián* ☎ *943/668530* ✉ *Aeropuerto de Santander, Santander* ☎ *942/262546*).

BY TRAIN

Direct trains from Madrid run to Santander, Bilbao, San Sebastián, Pamplona, Vitoria, and Logroño. Bilbao's transport system stars the city's pride and joy subway line with stations designed by British architect Norman Foster. The Bilbao underground train, spotless and bright as a button, will also get you out to the beach at Getxo or Plentzia. Bilbao's Euskotram, running up and down the Nervion River past the Guggenheim to the Mercado de la Ribera, is an attraction in its own right: silent, swift, and panoramic as it glides up and down its grassy runway. The Euskotren leaving from Atxuri Station north of the Mercado de la Ribera runs along a spectacular route through Gernika and the Urdaibai Nature Preserve to Mundaka, probably the best way short of a boat to see this lovely wetlands preserve.

Railway Companies **Euskotren** (✉ *Estación de Atxuri, north of Mercado de la Ribera, Bilbao* ☎ *94/433–8007*). **FEVE** (☎ *902/100818*). **RENFE** (☎ *902/240202 general information San Sebastián office* ✉ *C. Camino 1* ☎ *943/426430 Santander office* ✉ *Paseo de Pereda 25* ☎ *942/212387 or 942/218567*).

Train Stations **Bilbao** (✉ *Estación de Abando, C. Hurtado de Amezaga* ☎ *94/423–8623 or 94/423–8636*). **Logroño** (✉ *Estación de Logroño, Plaza de Europa* ☎ *941/240202*). **Pamplona** (✉ *Estación de Pamplona, Road to San Sebastián* ☎ *948/130202*). **San Sebastián** (✉ *Estación de Amara, Plaza Easo 9* ☎ *943/450131 or 943/471852* ✉ *Estación del Norte, Av. de Francia* ☎ *943/283089 or 943/283599*). **Santander** (✉ *Estación de Santander, C. Rodríguez s/n* ☎ *942/210211*).

CONTACTS & RESOURCES

EMERGENCIES

Dial 091 for the police.

TOUR OPTIONS

Travel agents and tourist offices in major cities can suggest tours led by local guides. Bilbao Paso a Paso conducts fine tours of Bilbao.

Tour Operators **Bilbao Paso a Paso** (✉ *Cocherito de Bilbao 20, Ofic. 5* ☎ *94/473–0078*).

5

VISITOR INFORMATION

Information on the three Basque provinces (Alava, Vizcaya, and Guipúzcoa) is available at the government building in Vitoria and the tourist office in San Sebastián.

Regional Tourist Offices **Bilbao** (✉ *Gran Vía 441 Izquierda* ☎ *94/424–2277*). **San Sebastián** (✉ *C. Fueros 1* ☎ *943/426282*). **Vitoria** (✉ *Parque de la Florida* ☎ *945/131321*).

Local Tourist Offices **Bilbao** (✉ *Paseo de Arenal 1* ☎ *94/479–5760 or 94/416–5761*). **Comillas** (✉ *Aldea 6* ☎ *942/720768*). **Gernika** (✉ *Artekale 5* ☎ *946/255892*). **Getaria** (✉ *Parque Aldamar 2* ☎ *943/140957*). **Haro** (✉ *Pl. Monseñor Florentino Rodriguez* ☎ *941/303366*). **Hondarribia** (*Fuenterrabía* ✉ *Javier Ugarte 6* ☎ *943/645458*). **Laguardia** (✉ *Pl. San Juan* ☎ *945/600845*). **Logroño** (✉ *C. Miguel Villanueva 10* ☎ *941/291260*). **Mundaka** (✉ *Txorrokopunta 2* ☎ *946/177201*). **Pamplona** (✉ *C. Duque de Ahumada 3* ☎ *848/420420*). **Potes** (✉ *Independencia 30* ☎ *942/730787*). **San Sebastián** (✉ *C. Reina Regente s/n* ☎ *943/481166*). **Santander** (✉ *Jardines de Pereda* ☎ *942/216120* ✉ *Plaza de Velarde 5* ☎ *942/310708*). **San Vicente de la Barquera** (✉ *Generalísimo 20* ☎ *942/710797*). **Vitoria** (✉ *Edifício Europa, Av. Gasteiz* ☎ *945/161598*). **Zumaia** (✉ *Playa de Itzurun s/n* ☎ *943/143396*).

The Pyrenees

6

Rock outcroppings in Huesca, Aragón province

WORD OF MOUTH

"Very few people in Zaragoza speak English, but that should not deter you from visiting. You will just be playing charades for a lot of the time. [It's] one of my favorite cities in Spain . . . so respectable and beautiful."

—laclaire

www.fodors.com/forums

WELCOME TO THE PYRENEES

La Cerdanya's breathtaking landscape.

TOP REASONS TO GO

★ **Eagle-eye Views:** Hike up to Prat d'Aguiló (Eagle's Meadow) in the clouds over the Cerdanya for an unforgettable panorama over the sunniest and widest valley in the Pyrenees.

★ **Highland History:** Visit San Juan de Plan and the Gistaín Valley for a look at early-20th-century village life in one of the most remote central Pyrenean enclaves.

★ **Pyrenean Gems:** Stop at Taüll and see the Noguera de Tor Valley's exquisite miniaturesque Romanesque churches and their mural paintings.

★ **Spain's Grand Canyon:** Walk through the Parque Nacional de Ordesa y Monte Perdido for stunning scenery, complete with marmots and mountain goats.

★ **Basque Navarra:** Explore the lush and verdant Basque highlands in the Baztán Valley, and then follow the Bidasoa River down to colorful Hondarribia and the sparkling Bay of Biscay.

Hondarribia
2 Lesaka
Baztán Valley
Roncesvalles
Burguete
Irurtzun
Roncal Valley
PYRENEES
FRANCE
Aragues Valley
Anso Valley
Hecho Valley
Sanguesa
Jaca
Biescas
Bielsa
Gistaín
San Juan de Plan
Tafalla
Monasterio de San Juan de la Pena
1 Sabiñánigo
Ainsa
Campo
Parque Nacional de Ordesa y Monte Perdido
Ayerbe
ARAGÓN
Graus
Ejea de los Caballeros
Huesca
Tudela
Barbastro
3
Monzon
Tauste
Zuera
Binéfar
Alagon
Sarinena
Zaragoza
Fraga
Bujaraloz

1 Aragón and the Central Pyrenees. Aragón begins at Benasque, the jumping off point for Aneto, the highest peak in the Pyrenees. San Juan de Plan, Gistaín, and Bielsa are typical mountain enclaves. Parque Nacional de Ordesa y Monte Perdido is an unforgettable day-or-two-day trek. Jaca and the Hecho, Ansó, and Roncal valleys are steep and rocky Aragón at its purest.

Ordesa National Park

A medieval street in Zaragoza

2 The Western and Basque Pyrenees. Beginning in the Roncal Valley, the language you hear may be Euskera, the non–Indo-European language of the Basques. The highlands of Navarra, from Roncesvalles and Burguete down through the Baztán Valley to Hondarribia are a magical realm of rolling hillsides and emerald pastures.

GETTING ORIENTED

The Pyrenean valleys, isolated from each other and the world below for many centuries, retain a rugged mountain character, mixing distinct traditions with a common highland spirit of magic and mystery. Spain's natural border with France has also been seen as a nexus where medieval people took refuge and exchanged learning. A haven from the 8th-century Moorish invasion, the Pyrenees became an unlikely repository of Romanesque art and architecture, as well as a natural preserve of wildlife and terrain.

6

Basilica of Nuestra Señora del Pilar in Zaragoza.

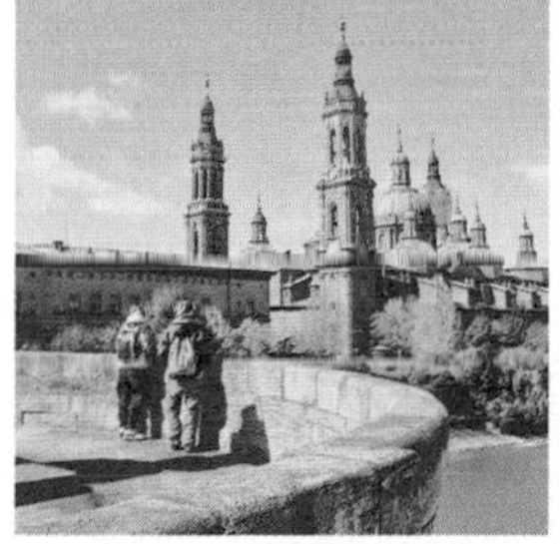

3 Lower Aragon: Zaragoza and Huesca. Should weather conditions drive you south and out of the Pyrenees, the Aragonese towns of Huesca and Zaragoza have much to offer. Huesca's early August Fiesta Mayor is a riotous outburst of joy, while Zaragoza's year-long 2008 Universal Exposition will keep the town abuzz for years to come.

THE PYRENEES PLANNER

When to Go

If you're a hiker, stick to the summer (June–September, especially July), when the weather is better and there's less chance of dense snow—not to mention blizzards or lightning storms at high altitudes. October is ideal for the still-green Pyrenean meadows and valleys and hillside hunts for wild mushrooms with comfortable daytime temperatures and fresh evening chills. November brings colorful leaves, the last mushrooms, and the first frosts. For skiing, come between December and April. The green springtime thaw, from mid-March to mid-April, is spectacular for skiing on the snowcaps and trout fishing or golfing on the valley floors. August is the only crowded month, when all of Europe is on summer vacation and the cooler highland air is at its best.

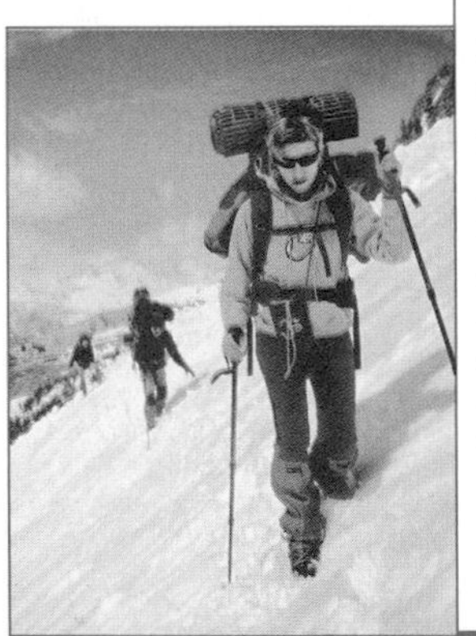

Getting There & Around

International flights to Barcelona, to Girona at the eastern end of the Pyrenees, to Bilbao, San Sebastián (Hondarribia), or to Biarritz-Bayonne at the western end put you in position for a Pyrenean adventure.

RENFE train connections up into the Pyrenees include lines from Barcelona to Puigcerdà at the eastern end, to Huesca and Jaca in the central Pyrenees, and Pamplona and San Sebastián at the western end of the cordillera. There is also a rail connection between Lleida and La Pobla de Segur in the western Catalan Pyrenees.

The most practical way to tour the Pyrenees is by car. The Eje Pirenaico (Pyrenean Axis), or N260, is a carefully engineered, safe cross-Pyrenean route that connects Cap de Creus, the Iberian Peninsula's easternmost point on the Mediterranean Costa Brava east of Girona and Cadaqués, with Cabo de Higuer, the lighthouse west of Hondarribia at the edge of the Atlantic Bay of Biscay.

The Collada de Toses (Tosses Pass) to Puigcerdà is the most difficult route into the Cerdanya Valley, but it's cost-free, the scenery is spectacular, and you get to include Camprodón, Olot, and Ripoll in your itinerary. Safer and faster, if more expensive (tolls total more than €25 from Barcelona to Bellver de Cerdanya) and somewhat less scenic, is the E9 through the Tuñel del Cadí (Cadí Tunnel). Once you're there, most of the Cerdanya Valley's two-lane roads are wide and well paved. As you move west, roads can be more difficult to navigate, winding dramatically through mountain passes.

Bus travel in the Pyrenees is the only way to cross from east to west (or vice versa) other than hiking or driving. This will require some zigzagging up and down from lowland hubs and busing back up the valleys. In most cases, four buses daily connect the main pre-Pyrenean cities (Barcelona, Zaragoza, Huesca, Pamplona) and the main highland distributors (Puigcerdà, La Seu d'Urgell, Vielha, Benasque, and Jaca). The time lost waiting for bus and planning your trip around departures makes this option a last resort. *See the Pyrenees Essentials at the end of this chapter for more information.*

Hiking the Pyrenees

There are many reasons to visit the Pyrenees: scenery, hiking, skiing, trout streams, art and architecture, or the opportunity to see what remains of a way of life that has endured largely unchanged. Hiking affords an ideal view of the scenery and remains one of the best ways to drink in the stunning landscape. No matter how spectacular they seem from paved roads, the mountainscapes are exponentially more stunning from upper hiking trails and high *pistas forestales* (forest tracks) that are best traveled in four-wheel drive vehicles. Day hikes or overnight two-day treks to mountain *refugios,* especially in the Ordesa or Aigüestortes national parks, will reveal the full splendor of the natural wonders of the Pyrenees. Local tourist offices can provide maps and recommended day hikes, while specialized bookshops such as Barcelona's Quera (Carrer Petritxol 2) have complete Pyrenean maps as well as books with detailed hiking instructions for the entire mountain range from the Atlantic to the Mediterranean. Hiking the Alberes range between Le Perthus and Cap de Creus on the well-marked GR (Gran Recorrido) 11 is a favorite two day spring or autumn hike, with an overnight stay at the Refugio de la Tanyareda just below Puig Neulós, the highest point in the Alberes. Hiking to the highest peak in the Pyrenees, the Aneto 11,168-foot Aneto is a one-day round-trip trek starting from the Refugio de la Renclusa above Benasque. Ordesa is another not-to-be-missed walk, with bed and dinner in the base camp town of Torla or a night up at the Refugio de Goriz at the head of the valley. Hiking in the Pyrenees should always be undertaken carefully. proper footwear, headwear, water supply, and weather forecast awareness are essential. Even in the middle of summer, a sudden snowstorm can turn a day hike to tragedy. See the **Pyrenees Hiking 101** box in this chapter for more details.

WHAT IT COSTS In Euros

	$$$$	$$$	$$	$	¢
RESTAURANTS	over €20	€15–€20	€10–€15	€6–€10	under €6
HOTELS	over €180	€100–€180	€60–€100	€40–€60	under €40

Restaurant prices are per person for a main course at dinner. Hotel prices are for a standard double room in high season, excluding tax.

Planning Your Time

With 43 days you can walk from Atlantic to Mediterranean. In 10 days to 2 weeks you can drive from sea to shimmering sea. A week is best for a single area—the Catalan Pyrenees, Baqueira-Beret and Vall d'Aran, Jaca and the central Pyrenees, or the Basque Pyrenees north of Pamplona. The classic sea-to-sea crossing begins with a wade in the Mediterranean at Cap de Creus, just north of Cadaqués, crossing westward to Hondarribia to do likewise at the Cabo Higuer lighthouse on the Bay of Biscay. A day's drive up through Figueres and Olot will bring you to **Camprodón**. Sant Joan de les Abadesses and Ripoll are important stops, especially for its famous sculpted Sant Maria de Ripoll portal. Puigcerdà, Llívia, and Bellver de Cerdanya are must-visits. To the west is **La Seu d'Urgell** on the way to **Parc Nacional d'Aigüestortes i Estany de Sant Maurici,** the **Vall d'Aran,** and the winter-sports center Baqueira-Beret. Stop at **Taüll** and the Noguera de Tor Valley's Romanesque churches. Farther west, **Benasque** is the jumping off point for Aneto, the highest peak in the Pyrenees. **San Juan de Plan and the Gistaín Valley, Bielsa** lead you to the remote valleys of Upper Aragón; **Parque Nacional de Ordesa y Monte Perdido** is Spain's grandest canyon, and **Jaca** the central Pyrenees' most important town. The Basque Pyrenees, the Irati beech forest, and the **Baztán Valley** bring you to the Bidasoa River.

By George Semler

THE SNOWCAPPED PYRENEES THAT SEPARATE the Iberian Peninsula from the rest of the European continent have always been a special realm, a source of legend and superstition. Along with the magic comes a surprising number of ancient cultures and languages, all Pyrenean and yet each profoundly different from the next. To explore the Pyrenees fully—appreciating the flora and fauna, the local gastronomy, the remote glacial lakes and streams, the Romanesque art in a thousand hermitages—could take a lifetime. Where to begin? Perhaps at Hemingway's beloved Irati beech forest and river above Pamplona, in the green hills of the Baztán Valley in Pyrenean Navarra, or at the Romanesque churches of the Noguera de Tor Valley and the lake country above at Sant Mauricio.

Each Pyrenean mountain system is drained by one or more rivers, forming some three dozen valleys between the Mediterranean and the Atlantic; these valleys were all but completely isolated until around the 10th century. Local languages still abound, with Castilian Spanish and Euskera (Basque) in upper Navarra; Grausín, Belsetán, Chistavino, Ansotano, Cheso, and Patués (Benasqués), in Aragón; Aranés, a dialect of Gascon French, in the Vall d'Aran; and Catalan at the eastern end of the chain from Ribagorça to the Mediterranean.

The earliest inhabitants of the Pyrenees, originally cave dwellers, later shepherds and farmers, saw their first invaders when the Greeks landed at Empúries, in Northern Catalonia, in the 6th century BC. The seagoing Carthaginians colonized Spain in the 3rd century BC, and their great general Hannibal surprised Rome by crossing the eastern Pyrenees in 218 BC. After defeating the Carthaginians, the Romans built roads through the mountains. The Iberian Peninsula was the last of the Roman Empire to be overtaken by the Visigoths in AD 409.

In the 8th century, the northern tribes then faced Moorish invaders from the south. Although Moorish influence was stronger in southern Spain, this region was nevertheless a meeting point for Arabic and European cultures at the end of the first millennium. The Moorish occupation sent Christianity fleeing to the hills, dotting the Pyrenees with Romanesque art and architecture. When Christian crusaders reconquered Spain, the Pyrenees were divided among three feudal kingdoms: Catalonia, Aragón, and Navarra, proud and independent entities with their respective spiritual "cradles" in the Romanesque mountain monasteries of Santa Maria de Ripoll, San Juan de la Peña, and San Salvador de Leyre.

Throughout the centuries, the Pyrenees have remained a strategic barrier and stronghold to be reckoned with. The Romans never completely subdued Los Vascones (as Greek historian Strabo (63-21 BC) called the Basques) in the western Pyrenean highlands. Charlemagne lost Roland and his rear guard at Roncesvalles in 778, and his Frankish heirs lost all of Catalonia in 988. Napoléon never completed his conquest of the peninsula after 1802, largely because of communications and supply problems posed by the Pyrenees, and Hitler, whether for geographical or political reasons, decided not to use post–civil war Spain to launch his African campaign in 1941. A D-Day option to make a landing on the beaches of northern Spain was scrapped because the Pyrenees looked too easily defendable (you can still see the south-facing bunkers on the southern flanks of the western Pyrenean foothills). Meanwhile, the mountainous barrier provided a path to freedom for downed pilots, Jewish refugees, and POWs fleeing the Nazis, just as it later meant freedom for political refugees running north from the Franco regime.

FOUR WAYS OF SAYING "GOOD DAY" IN THE PYRENEES

- In Spanish "Buenos días"
- In Catalan "Bon dia"
- In Euskera "Egun on"
- In Fabla Aragonesa "Buen Diya"

EXPLORING THE PYRENEES

For mountain worshippers, crossing the Pyrenees from the Mediterranean to the Atlantic (or vice versa) is a pilgrimage. It's a seven-week hike, but you can drive the route in anywhere from 2 to 14 days. As the crow flies, the Pyrenees stretch 435 km (270 mi) along Spain's border with France, though the sinuous borderline exceeds 600 km (370 mi). A drive across the N260 trans-Pyrenean axis connecting the destinations in this chapter would exceed 800 km (495 mi) in all. There are three main divisions: the Catalan Pyrenees from the Mediterranean to the Noguera Ribagorçana River south of Vielha, the central Pyrenees of Aragón extending west to the Roncal Valley, and the Basque Pyrenees falling gradually westward through the Basque Country to the Bay of Biscay and the Atlantic Ocean. The highest peaks are in Aragón—Aneto, in the Maladeta massif; Posets; and Monte Perdido, all of which are about 11,000 feet above sea level. Pica d'Estats (10,372 feet) is Catalonia's highest peak, and Pic d'Orhi (6,656 feet) is the highest in the Basque Pyrenees.

ABOUT THE RESTAURANTS

Pyrenean cuisine is characterized by thick soups, stews, roasts, and the use of local ingredients prepared differently in every valley, village, and kitchen from the Mediterranean to the Atlantic. The three main culinary schools correspond to the Pyrenees' three main regional and cultural identities—Catalan, Aragonese, and Basque—but within these are further subdivisions such as La Cerdanya, Vall d'Aran, Benasque, Roncal, and Baztán. Game is common throughout. Trout (now often raised in lakes and ponds fed by mountain streams), wild goat, deer, boar, partridge, rabbit, duck, and quail are roasted over coals or cooked in aromatic stews called *civets* in Catalonia and *estofadas* in Aragón and Navarra. Fish and meat are often seared on slabs of slate (*a la llosa* in Catalan, *a la piedra* in Castilian Spanish). Wild mushrooms are a local specialty in season, as are wild asparagus, leeks, and herbs such as marjoram, sage, thyme, and rosemary.

IF YOU LIKE

FISHING

Well populated with trout, the Pyrenees' cold-water streams provide excellent angling from mid-March to the end of August. Notable places to cast a line are the Segre, Aragón, Gállego, Noguera Pallaresa, Arga, Esera, and Esca rivers. Pyrenean ponds and lakes also tend to be rich in trout.

WINTER SPORTS

Skiing is the main winter sport in the Pyrenees, and Baqueira-Beret, in the Vall d'Aran, is the leading resort. Thanks to artificial-snow machines, there is usually fine skiing from December through March at more than 20 resorts—from Vallter 2000 at Setcases, in the Camprodón Valley, west to Isaba and Burguete, in Navarra. Although weekend skiing can be crowded in the eastern valleys, Catalonia's western Pyrenees tend to have more breathing room. Cerler-Benasque, Panticosa, Formigal, Astún, and Candanchú are the major ski areas in Huesca. Numerous resorts offer helicopter skiing and Nordic skiing. Leading Nordic areas include Lles, in the Cerdanya; Salardú and Beret in the Vall d'Aran; and Panticosa, Benasque, and Candanchú in Aragón. Jaca, Puigcerdà, and Vielha have public skating sessions, figure-skating classes, and ice-hockey programs. The newspapers *El País,El Periódico de Catalunya,* and *La Vanguardia Española* print complete ski information every Friday in winter. Ski conditions are available at 🌐 *www.pirineodigital.com/noticias-nieve.htm* or 🌐 *www.catski.net* (for Catalonia), 🌐 *www.aragob.es* (for Aragón), and 🌐 *www.aran.org* and 🌐 *www.baqueira.es* (for Baqueira and environs).

ABOUT THE HOTELS

Most hotels in the Pyrenees are informal and outdoorsy, with a large fireplace in one of the public rooms. They are usually built of wood and slate under a steep roof, blending with the surrounding mountains. Comfortable and protected, they reflect the tastes of the travelers, who are mostly skiers and hikers. Options include friendly family-owned establishments, rooms in Basque *caseríos* (farmhouses), and town houses. (Larger chain-type hotels are almost unheard of.)

Numbers in the text correspond to numbers in the margin and on the chapter maps.

EASTERN CATALAN PYRENEES

Catalonia's easternmost Pyrenean valley, the Vall de Camprodón, is still hard enough to reach that, despite pockets of Barcelona summer colonies, it has retained much of its agricultural culture and mountain wildness. It has several exquisite towns and churches and, above all, mountains, such as the Sierra de Catllar, thick with boar, mountain goat, wild trout, and snow partridge. Vallter 2000 and Núria are ski resorts at the eastern and western ends of the Pyrenees heights on the north side of the valley, but the middle reaches and main body of the valley have remained pasture for sheep, cattle, and horses, and de facto

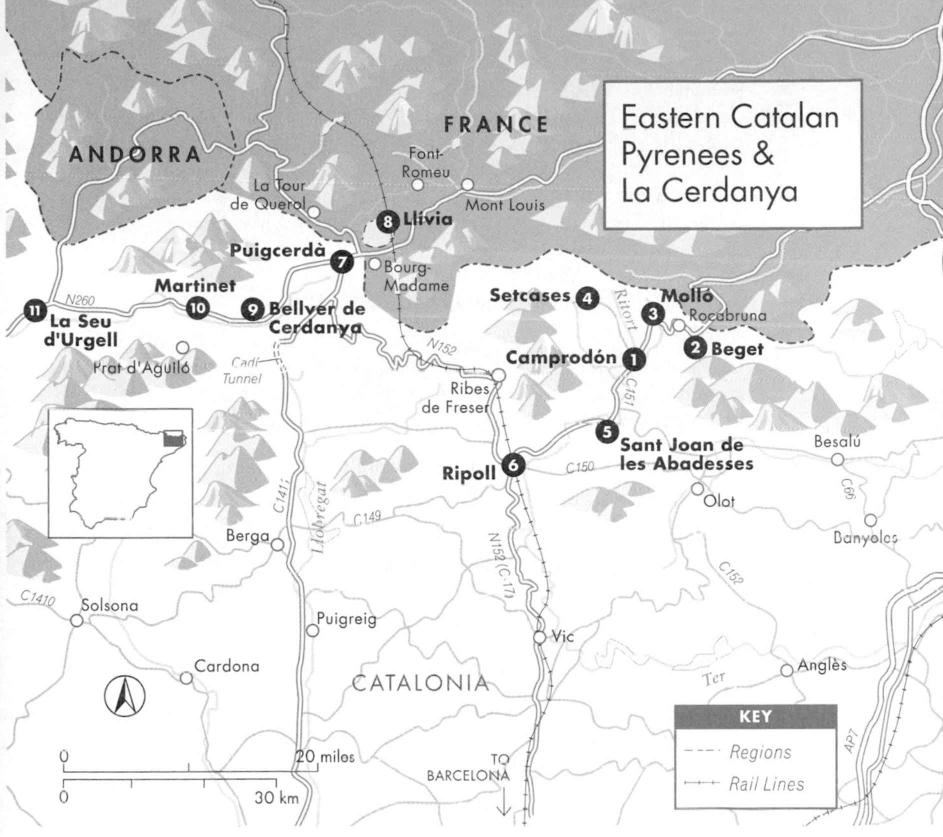

natural parks. To reach the Vall de Camprodón from Barcelona you can take the N152 through Vic and Ripoll; from the Costa Brava go by way of either Figueres or Girona, Besalú, and the Capsacosta tunnel. From France, drive southwest through the Col (Pass) d'Ares, which enters the head of the valley at an altitude of 5,280 feet from Prats de Molló.

CAMPRODÓN

❶ *127 km (80 mi) northwest of Barcelona.*

Camprodón, the capital of its *comarca* (county), lies at the junction of the Rivers Ter and Ritort—both excellent trout streams. The rivers flow by, through, and under much of the town, giving it a highland waterfront character (as well as a long history of flooding). The town owes much of its opulence to the summer folks from Barcelona who have built mansions along the leafy promenade, Passeig Maristany, at its northern edge. It's also known for its sausages of every imaginable size, shape, and consistency and for its two cookie factories, Birbas and Pujol, locked in eternal competition. (Birbas is better.)

Camprodón's best-known symbol is the elegant **12th-century stone bridge** that broadly spans the River Ter in the center of town.

WHERE TO STAY

$$ **Edelweiss.** This friendly and comfortable Pyrenean inn is a good base camp for skiers, hikers, wild-mushroom seekers, equestrian enthusiasts, and those interested in all manner of Camprodón Valley fauna. Rooms are simple but tasteful, with bright wood walls and a cheerful decor. The common rooms are low-key and informal, yet graceful spaces for socializing. ✉ *Ctra. de Sant Joan 28, 17867* ☎ *972/740614* 📠 *972/740605* 🌐 *www.edelweisshotel.net* *21 rooms* *In-hotel: bar, no elevator, parking (fee)* 💳 *AE, DC, MC, V.*

SHOPPING

Cal Xec (✉ *C. Isaac Albèniz 1* ☎ *972/740084*), the legendary sausage store at the end of the emblematic Camprodón Bridge, also sells the much-prized, shortbreadlike, vanilla-flavored Birbas cookies.

EN ROUTE

From Camprodón, take C151 north toward the French border at Col d'Ares and turn east toward Rocabruna, a village of crisp, clean Pyrenean stone houses at the source of the clear River Beget. The village is famous as a gastronomical pilgrimage to the excellent Can Po restaurant (⇨ Beget, *below*).

BEGET

2 ★ *17 km (11 mi) east of Camprodón.*

The village of Beget, considered Catalonia's *més bufó* (cutest), was completely cut off from motorized vehicles until the mid-1960s, when a *pista forestal* (a jeep track) was laid down; in 1980 Beget was finally fully connected to the rest of the world by an asphalt roadway. Beget's 30 houses are eccentric stone structures with heavy wooden doors and a golden tone peculiar to the Camprodón Valley. Graceful stone bridges span the stream in which protected trout feast. The 11th-century Romanesque church of **Sant Cristófol** has a diminutive bell tower and a rare 6-foot Majestat, a polychrome wood carving of Christ in a head-to-foot tunic, dating from the 12th or 13th century. The church is usually closed, but townsfolk can direct you to the keeper of the key.

WHERE TO EAT

$$$–$$$$ ✕ **Can Po.** This ancient, ivy-covered, stone-and-mortar farmhouse perched over a deep gully in nearby Rocabruna is carefully guarded semi-secret gastronomic wonderland famed for carefully prepared local dishes from *entrecot amb crema de ceps* (veal in wild-mushroom sauce) to the Catalan classic *anec amb peras* (duck prepared with stewed pears). Try the *civet de porc senglar* (stewed wild boar) in season (winter). ✉ *Ctra. de Beget s/n, Rocabruna* ☎ *972/741045* 💳 *AE, DC, MC, V* ⏲ *Closed Mon.–Thurs. mid-Sept.–mid-July, except Dec. 26–Jan. 6 and Easter wk.*

MOLLÓ

❸ *25 km (16 mi) northwest of Beget, 24 km (15 mi) south of Prats de Molló.*

Molló lies on route C151 on the Ritort stream toward Col d'Ares.The 12th-century Romanesque church of **Santa Cecilia** is a work of exceptional balance and simplicity, with a delicate Romanesque bell tower.

WHERE TO STAY

$$ **Calitxó.** Mountain views in all directions are spectacular at this small but comfortable family-run inn. Rooms are cozy and intimate rather than grand, welcome refuge from the wide open spaces outside. After breakfast in the lush garden, this is an ideal base for hiking excursions to Beget and other points in the valley. In a rustic chalet-type town house, the restaurant serves creative cuisine prepared with originality and fresh mountain ingredients. ✉*Passatge el Serrat,17868* ☎*972/740386* 🖷*972/740746* 🌐*www.hotelcalitxo.com* *23 rooms, 3 suites* *In-room: no a/c. In-hotel: restaurant, no elevator.* 💳*AE, DC, MC, V.*

SETCASES

❹ *11 km (7 mi) north of Camprodón, 15 km (9 mi) west of Molló, 91 km (56 mi) northwest of Girona.*

Although Setcases ("seven houses") is somewhat larger than its name would imply, this tiny village nestled at the head of the valley has a distinct mountain spirit and a gravelly roughness, as if washed by the torrents flowing through and over its streets en route to the River Ter. On the road back down the valley from Setcases, **Llanars,** just short of Camprodón, has a 12th-century Romanesque church, **San Esteban,** of an exceptionally rich shade of ocher. The wood and iron portal depicts the martyrdom of St. Stephen.

WHERE TO STAY

$$ **La Coma.** Don't fear oversleeping here—*coma* is Catalan Pyrenean dialect for "high and fertile meadow." The proprietors are kind country folk who know the mountains and can help you plan excursions. Rooms in the modern stone house are done in bright wood trim. The restaurant, with garden seating in summer, specializes in mountain *civets* (stews) and *escudellas* (thick vegetable, bean, pasta, and pork soup). ✉*Setcases 17869* ☎*972/136074* 🖷*972/136073* 🌐*www.hotellacoma.com* *20 rooms* *In-room: no a/c. In-hotel: restaurant, pool, gym, no elevator* 💳*AE, DC, MC, V.*

SPORTS & THE OUTDOORS

The **Vallter 2000 ski area** (☎*972/136057* 🌐*www.vallter2000.com*) above Setcases—built into a glacial cirque reaching a height of 8,216 feet—has a dozen lifts and, on very clear days at the top, views east all the way to the Bay of Roses on the Costa Brava.

SANT JOAN DE LES ABADESSES

5 *21 km (13 mi) southeast of Setcases, 14 km (9 mi) south of Camprodón.*

The site of an important church, Sant Joan de les Abadesses is named for the 9th-century abbess Emma and her successors. Emma was the daughter of Guifré el Pilós (Wilfred the Hairy), the founder of the Catalonian nation and medieval hero of the Christian Reconquest of Ripoll. The town's arcaded Plaça Major looks and feels plucked from medieval times, and the 12th-century bridge over the Ter is wide and graceful. The altarpiece in the 12th-century Romanesque church of **Sant Joan** (✉ *Plaça de la Abadía s/n* ☎ *972/720013*), a 13th-century polychrome wood sculpture of the Descent from the Cross, is one of the most expressive and human of that epoch.

RIPOLL

6 *10 km (6 mi) southwest of Sant Joan de les Abadesses, 105 km (62 mi) north of Barcelona, 65 km (40 mi) southeast of Puigcerdà.*

One of the first Christian strongholds of the Reconquest and a center of religious erudition during the Middle Ages, Ripoll is known as the *bressol* (cradle) of Catalonia's liberation from Moorish domination and the spiritual home of Guifré el Pelós (Wilfred the Hairy), first Count of Barcelona and legendary founder of the Catalan nation in the late 9th century. A dark, mysterious country town built around a **9th-century Benedictine monastery.** The town was a focal point of culture throughout French Catalonia and the Pyrenees, from the monastery's AD 879 founding until the mid-1800s, when Barcelona began to eclipse it.

The 12th-century doorway to the church of **Santa Maria** is one of Catalonia's great works of Romanesque art, crafted as a triumphal arch by stone masons and sculptors of the Roussillon school (that is, the school centered around French Catalonia and the Pyrenees). The sculptures portray the glory of God and of all his creatures from the Creation onward. You can pick up a guide to the figures on the portal either in the church or at the information kiosk nearby. *Cloister €3.50, museum €6* ⏲ *Tues.–Sun. 10–2 and 3–7.*

Fourteen kilometers (9 mi) north of Ripoll, the **cogwheel train** (☎ *972/732020*) ride from Ribes de Freser up to Núria provides one of Catalonia's most unusual excursions. Known as the *cremallera* (zipper), the line was completed in 1931 to connect Ribes with the Santuari de la Mare de Deu de Núria (Mother of God of Núria) and with mountain hiking and skiing. The ride takes 45 minutes and costs €17 round-trip.**Núria,** at an altitude of 6,562 feet at the foot of Puigmal, is a ski area, and in the 1950s it was the site of some of Spain's earliest ice-hockey activity.

The legend of the **Santuari de la Mare de Déu de Núria,** a Marian religious retreat, is based on the story of Sant Gil of Nîmes, who did penance in the Núria Valley during the 7th century. The saint left behind a wooden statue of the Virgin Mary, a bell he used to summon shepherds to prayer, and a cooking pot; 300 years later, a pilgrim found these treasures in this sanctuary. The bell and the pot came to have special importance to barren women, who were believed to be blessed with as many children as they wished by placing their heads in the pot and ringing the bell. *Núria Free Daily except during mass.*

WHERE TO STAY

$–$$ **Hotel Vall de Núria.** A simple barrackslike hybrid between a mountain refuge and a hotel, this alpine dormitory and the Alberg 100 yards higher up the slope offer comfortable lodging and dining at an altitude of 2,000 meters above sea level. For a day's outing or as jumping off point for a major hike (12 hours) to Ulldeter, above Setcases, or even a weeklong walk to the Mediterranean, this is a handy spot, accessible only by the cogwheel train from Ribes de Freser. *Estación de Montaña Vall de Núria, Queralbs, 17534 972/732030 972/732024 www.valldenuria.com 65 rooms In-hotel: restaurant, bar, tennis court, meeting rooms, no elevator AE, MC, V.*

EN ROUTE

From Ripoll, it's a 65-km (40-mi) drive on the N152 through Ribes de Freser and over the Collada de Toses (Tosses Pass) to Puigcerdà. Above Ribes, the road winds to the top of the pass over a sheer drop down to the Freser stream. Here, even during the driest months, emerald-green pastures remain moist in shaded corners. In early spring the climate can range from showers down in Ribes to a blizzard up on the Tosses Pass. This traditional approach to the Cerdanya has been all but replaced by the road through Manresa, Berga, and the Túnel del Cadí (Cadí Tunnel).

6

LA CERDANYA

The Pyrenees' widest, sunniest valley is said to be in the shape of the handprint of God. High pastureland bordered north and south by snow-covered peaks, La Cerdanya starts in France, at Col de la Perche (near Mont Louis), and ends in the Spanish province of Lleida, at Martinet. Split into two countries and subdivided into two more provinces on each side, the valley has an identity all its own. Residents on both sides of the border speak Catalan, a Romance language derived from early Provençal French, and regard the valley's political border with undisguised hilarity. Unlike any other valley in the upper Pyrenees, this one runs east–west and thus has a record annual number of sunlight hours.

PUIGCERDÀ

7 *170 km (105 mi) north of Barcelona, 65 km (40 mi) northwest of Ripoll.*

Puigcerdà (in Catalan, *puig* means "hill"; *cerdà* derives from "Cerdanya") is the largest town in the valley. From the promontory upon which it stands, the views down across the meadows of the valley floor and up into the craggy peaks of the surrounding Pyrenees give the town a schizophrenic sense of height and humility. The 12th-century Romanesque bell tower—all that remains of the town church destroyed in 1936 at the outset of the Spanish civil war—and the sunny sidewalk cafés facing it are among Puigcerdà's prettiest spots, as are the Gothic church of Santa Maria and its long square, the **Plaça del Cuartel.** On Sunday, markets sell clothes, cheeses, fruits, vegetables, and wild mushrooms to shoppers from both sides of the border.

CATALANS INSIDE AND OUT

Ceretanos (Cerdanya residents) have always scoffed at the relatively recently imposed borders that have separated families and geography since France and Spain became nation states. This popular verse ironizing Llívia's status as a Spanish "enclave" within France is an example: ... *Cerdanya dintre Cerdanya / fronteres inversemblants / dins de França un tros d'Espanya / dins i fora catalans* . . . (Cerdanya within Cerdanya / absurd borderlands / inside France a piece of Spain / in and outside Catalans) . . .

Plaça Cabrinetty, with its porticoes and covered walks, has a sunny northeastern corner where farmers in for the Sunday market gather. The square is protected from the wind and ringed by two- and three-story houses of various pastel colors, some with engraved decorative designs and all with balconies. Visit the font (spring) where a plaque of Magdalena Masip's poem "Voldria . . . " ("I wish . . . ") provides idyllic inspiration. It reads: " . . . i jo voldria tenir, la casa sota d'un avet, amb tot el bosc per jardí, i tot el cel per teulada . . . i fugirme del món d'aqui, pos em confundra i m'atabala, i quedar-me quieta així, bevent el bosc a glopades, amb gleves per coixí, i un jaç de fulles doradas." Translated: . . . And I wish that I could have / my house beneath a fir tree/ with all the woods for a garden / and all the sky for a roof. / And flee from the world around me / it overwhelms and confuses me / and stay quietly there / drinking the forest in gulps / with clods of earth for a pillow / and a bed of golden leaves . . .

From the balcony next to the **town hall** (✉ *Carrer Querol 1*), you get an ample view of the Cerdanya Valley that stretches all the way past Bellver de Cerdanya down to the sheer granite walls of the Sierra del Cadí, at the end of the valley. A 300-yard walk west from the fountain near Carrer Font d'en Llanas around the edge of town will bring you to the stairs leading up from the train station to the balcony. The verse on the corner of the town hall to your left as you look out is by the Catalan poet Joan Maragall (1860–1910). In English, the fragment reads ... *I love the balcony over the walls / When the townsfolk stroll there / and with nearly immobile eyes / follow the progress of the distant storm . . .*

Le petit train jaune (the little yellow train) leaves daily from Bourg-Madame and from La Tour de Querol, both simple walks into France from Puigcerdà. The border at La Tour, a longer but prettier walk, is marked only by a stone painted with the Spanish and French flags. This *carrilet* (narrow-gauge railway) is the last in the Pyrenees and is used for tours as well as transportation; it winds through the Cerdanya to the walled town of Villefranche de Conflent. The 63-km (39-mi) tour can take most of the day, especially if you stop to browse in Mont Louis or Villefranche. ✉ *Boarding at SNCF stations at Bourg-Madame or La Tour de Querol, France* ☎ *33 (0)4–68–30–85–02* 🌐 *www.le-rail.ch/text/projekt76.htm* 🎫 *€35 La Tour de Querol–Villefranche-de-Conflent round-trip* ⏲ *Schedule at Turismo office, Puigcerdà; or at RENFE station below Puigcerdà.*

WHERE TO STAY & EAT

$$–$$$$ ✕ **Josepmariamassó.** With sections of the medieval walls of Puigcerdà lining the downstairs dining rooms and postmodern cuisine emerging from the glass-walled kitchen, this is the town's top culinary showcase. The upstairs dining room is sleek and contemporary; the cellar is all ancient stone; and chef Josep Maria Massó is the most experimental chef in the Pyrenees—and English-speaking to boot. ✉ *Carrer d'Espanya 9* ☎ *972/884308* 💳 *AE, DC, MC, V* ⏲ *Closed June 15–30, Nov. 15–30, and Mon. No dinner Sun.*

$$–$$$$ ✕ **La Tieta.** This 500-year-old town house is two restaurants in one working out of a single kitchen. With separate entrances, half of the restaurant is a pizzeria and the other half serves classical Pyrenean fare such as *trinxat de Cerdanya* (a rib-sticking puree of cabbage and potatoes with bits of fried salt pork or bacon) or roasts cooked over coals. The garden is ideal for a late-night drink in summer. ✉ *Carrer dels Ferrers 20* ☎ *972/880156* 💳 *AE, DC, MC, V* ⏲ *Closed June 12–July 12 and Mon.–Wed. mid-Sept.–mid-June.*

$–$$$ ✕ **Madrigal.** The Pere Compte family has made this popular restaurant-bar near the town hall a Puigcerdà favorite for decades. The low-ceiling, wood-trim dining room is filled with tables and benches. Selections include tapas and meals of assorted specialties, such as *codorniz* (quail), *caracoles* (snails), *calamares a la romana* (calamari dipped in batter), *albóndigas* (meatballs), *esqueixada* (raw codfish with peppers and onion), and wild mushrooms in season. ✉ *Carrer Alfons I 3* ☎ *972/880860* 💳 *AE, DC, MC, V.*

$$$$ ✕🏨 **La Torre del Remei.** About 3 km (2 mi) west of Puigcerdà you can
Fodor'sChoice ★ find this splendid mansion, built in 1910 and brilliantly restored by José María and Loles Boix of the legendary restaurant Boix in Martinet, 26 km (16 mi) to the west. Everything is superb, from the belle epoque luxury of the manor house to the plush, tasteful suites, heated bathroom floors, huge bathtubs, and the bottle of Moët Chandon on your arrival. The restaurant serves fine international cuisine with an emphasis on local products such as lamb, trout, and game; reserve well in advance. ✉ *Camí Reial s/n, Bolvir de Cerdanya 17539* ☎ *972/140182* 📠 *972/140449* 🌐 *www.torredelremei.com* 🛏 *5 rooms, 17 suites* ♿ *In-hotel: restaurant, golf course, pool* 💳 *AE, DC, MC, V.*

$$$$ 🏨 **Fontanals Golf.** If you like being striking distance of ski slopes, trout streams, and a challenging golf course, this modern chalet-style ranch on the floor of the Cerdanya Valley will delight. Lavishly constructed with wood and glass, the resort has panoramic views into the Pyrenees on both sides of the valley. ✉ *C. Fontanals 2, Soriguerola, 17538* ☎ *972/891818* 📠 *972/891740* 🌐 *www.hotelfontanals.com* 🛏 *60*

rooms ♿ *In-hotel: restaurant, bar, golf course, tennis court, pool, no elevator* ▭ *AE, DC, MC, V.*

$$ **Hotel del Lago.** This comfortable old favorite near Puigcerdà's emblematic lake is a graceful, tastefully appointed series of buildings built around a central garden. A two-minute walk from the bell tower or the town market, it feels deceptively bucolic but it's actually almost in the center of town. ✉ *Av. Doctor Piguillem 7, 17520* ☎ *972/881000* 📠 *972/141511* 🌐 *www.hotellago.com* *15 rooms* ♿ *In-room: no a/c. In-hotel: pool, spa, no elevator* ▭ *AE, DC, MC, V.*

> **TIP**
>
> If you're planning a long-distance hiking trip, local bus connections will get you to your starting point and retrieve you from the finish line.

NIGHTLIFE

Young Spanish and French night owls fill the town's many clubs until dawn. **Le Clochard** (✉ *Carrer Major 54* ☎ *972/881615*) rocks in midtown Puigcerdá.H id="d2e1389"**No Ho Sé** (✉ *Ctra. 152, Km 170* ☎ *972/882248*), 5 km (3 mi) south of town on the Barcelona road, is the favored disco on weekend and holiday nights.

SPORTS & THE OUTDOORS

Pick up your **fishing license** after 7 PM, at the **Societat de Pesca de Puigcerdà** (✉ *Av. del Lago s/n* ☎ *972/141172*). With your Catalonia fishing license, you can buy a day pass (generally ranging from €4 to €9 though subject to change) for the Coto del Querol (reserved trout-fishing beat) on the Querol River (or the Segre) at **Tota Teca** (✉ *Ctra. N152, Km 169.5* ☎ *972/141027*); there's also good take-out food here. The town's **ice rink** (☎ *972/880243*) is worth checking out if you skate. The **Reial Club de Golf de la Cerdanya** (☎ *972/141408*) near Puigcerdà has 18 holes. Near Puigcerdà, the challenging **Club de Golf de Fontanals** (☎ *972/144374*), so called for its myriad water hazards, has 18 holes.

SHOPPING

Puigcerdà is one big shopping mall, and long a nexus for contraband clothes, cigarettes, and other items. **Carrer Major** is an uninterrupted row of stores selling what seems like everything, including books, jewelry, and sports equipment. The annual **equine fair,** in early November, is an unparalleled opportunity to study horses—and horse traders.

The **Sunday market** in Plaça del Cuartel, like those in most other Cerdanya towns, is a great place to look for local specialties such as herbs, goat cheese, wild mushrooms, honey, and basketry.

For the best *margaritas* in town (no, not those; these are crunchy-edged madeleines made with almonds), look for **Pasteleria Cosp** (✉ *Carrer Major 20* ☎ *972/880103*), founded in 1806.

6

LLÍVIA

8 *6 km (4 mi) northeast of Puigcerdà.*

A Spanish enclave in French territory, Llívia was marooned by the 1659 Peace of the Pyrenees treaty, which ceded 33 villages to France. Incorporated as a *vila* (town) by royal decree of Carlos V—who spent a night here in 1528 and was impressed by the town's beauty and hospitality—it managed to remain Spanish. At the upper edge of town, the fortified church **Mare de Deu dels Àngels** (✉*Carrer dels Forns 13* ☎*972/896301*) is an acoustic gem; check to see if any choral events are scheduled, especially in August and December, when the Llívia music festival schedules top classical groups.

Across from the church is the ancient pharmacy **Museu de la Farmacia** (✉*Carrer dels Forns 12* ☎*972/880103* ⏲*Daily Tues.–Fri. 10–4:20, weekends 10–1:50*), founded in 1415 and thought to be the oldest in Europe. Look for the **mosaic** in the middle of town commemorating Lampègia, *princesa de la pau i de l'amor* (princess of peace and of love), erected in memory of the red-haired daughter of the duke of Aquitania and lover of Munuza, a Moorish warlord who governed the Cerdanya during the Arab domination.

WHERE TO EAT

$$$–$$$$ ★ ✕ **Can Ventura.** Inside a flower-festooned 17th-century town house made of ancient stones, this handsome dining space is one of the Cerdanya's best for both cuisine and value. Trout and beef *a la llosa* (seared on slate) are house specialties, and the wide selection of *entretenimientos* (hors d'oeuvres) is delicious. ✉*Plaça Major 1* ☎*972/896178* ✍*Reservations essential* ▭*AE, DC, MC, V* ⏲*Closed June 20–July 15, Mon. July 16–Oct., and Tues.*

$$$–$$$$ Fodor's Choice ★ ✕ **La Formatgeria de Llívia.** Conveniently situated on Llívia's eastern edge (en route to Saillagousse, France), this restaurant is in a former cheese factory that still makes fresh mató cheese while you watch; there are tasting tables in the bar for those cheese-sampling. Juanjo Meya and his wife, master chef Marta Pous, have had great success with fine local cuisine, panoramic views looking south toward Puigmal and across the valley, and creating general charm and good cheer. The innovative taster's menu adds a new and creative dimension to the restaurant. An ample garden with swings and slides allows children to let off steam while their parents sample wines, cheeses, and Havana tobacco. ✉*Pla de Rô, Gorguja, 17527* ☎*972/146279* ✍*Reservations essential* ▭*AE, DC, MC, V* ⏲*Closed June 20–July 12, Tues., and Wed.*

BELLVER DE CERDANYA

9 ★ *31 km (19 mi) southwest of Llívia, 25 km (16 mi) west of Puigcerdà.*

Bellver de Cerdanya has preserved its slate-roof and fieldstone Pyrenean architecture more successfully than many of the Cerdanya's larger towns. Perched on a promontory over the **River Segre,** which winds around much of the town, Bellver is a mountain version of a fishing village—trout fishing, to be exact. Bellver's Gothic church of **Sant Jaume** and the arcaded **Plaça Major,** in the upper part of town, are lovely examples of traditional Pyrenean mountain-village design.

WHERE TO STAY & EAT

$$ ✕🏨 **Fonda Biayna.** A rustic retreat with woodsy furnishings that seems happily stuck in an early Pyrenean time warp, this hotel has simple, old-fashioned, and cozy guest rooms. The Catalan fare ($$–$$$) includes such dishes as roast rabbit *allioli* (a sauce of garlic and olive oil), *galtas de porc amb bolets* (pork cheeks with wild mushrooms), and *tiró amb naps i trumfes* (duck with turnips and potatoes). ✉ *Carrer Sant Roc 11, 25720* ☎ *973/510475* 🖷 *973/510853* 🌐 *www.fondabiayna.com* 🛏 *16 rooms* 👍 *In-room: no a/c, no phone, no TV. In-hotel: restaurant* 💳 *AE, DC, MC, V.*

SPORTS & THE OUTDOORS

Bar Blanch (✉ *Carrer San Roc 13* ☎ *973/510208*) is the town's de facto angling clubhouse, where, along with hearty mountain fare or a beer at the bar, you can buy licenses and day passes to the Coto from mid-March through August.The **Coto de Bellver,** a reserved section along the River Segre for trout fishing, was once one of Spain's best. Fishing pressure and reduced water volume due to global warming and the shrinking Pyrenean snow and ice cap have cut back on the trout population, but this is still a lovely place to spend time, fish or no fish.

MARTINET

❿ *10 km (6 mi) west of Bellver de Cerdanya.*

The town of Martinet hasn't much to offer except a few cozy watering spots that are hard to pass up in the heat of summer. For a course in trout economy and husbandry, have a close look over the railing along the River Segre just upstream from its junction with the Llosa River. Martinet's protected trout are famous in these parts: the fish dine from 1 to 4 in the afternoon, when the sun slants in and cooks off hatches of aquatic insects while illuminating every speckle and spot on the feeding trout.

For a spectacular excursion, drive or walk up the valley of the Llosa River into Andorra, or take the short but stunning walk from the village of **Aransa** to Lles: as you pull away from Aransa and onto an alpine meadow, the Cerdanya's palette changes with every twist of the trail. You'll even pass the ruins of a 10th-century hilltop hermitage. (The tourist office in La Seu d'Urgell has simple trail maps.) The village of **Lles** is a famous Nordic-skiing resort with 36 km (22 mi) of cross-country tracks.

WHERE TO STAY & EAT

$$ ✕🏨 **Cal Rei.** Built into former stables, this graceful and rustic country inn usually has a roaring fire in the common room and offers direct access to one of the Pyrenees' finest cross-country ski areas. The cuisine is powerful mountain fare ($$–$$$) designed to restore weary trekkers. Views of the Sierra del Cadí are spectacular. ✉ *Cadí 4 Lles de Cerdanya, 25726* ☎ *659/063915 mobile* 🖷 *973/515213* 🌐 www.cal.

rei@lles.net *8 rooms In-room: no a/c, no phone, no TV. In-hotel: restaurant, no elevator* *AE, DC, MC, V.*

OFF THE BEATEN PATH

The majestic Prat d'Aguiló, or Eagle's Meadow, 20 km (12 mi) south of Martinet, is one of the highest points in the Cerdanya that you can access without either a four-wheel-drive vehicle or a hike. The winding, bumpy drive up the mountain takes about an hour and a half (start with a full tank) and opens onto some excellent vistas of its own. From the meadow, the roughly three-hour climb to the top of the sheer rock wall of the Sierra del Cadí, directly above, reaches an altitude of nearly 8,000 feet. To get here from Martinet, take a dirt road that is rough but, barring new wash-outs, navigable by the average car. Follow signs for "Refugio Prat d'Aguiló."

LA SEU D'URGELL

11 *24 km (15 mi) west of Martinet, 20 km (12 mi) south of Andorra la Vella (in Andorra), 50 km (31 mi) west of Puigcerdà.*

Fodor'sChoice ★

La Seu d'Urgell is an ancient town facing the snowy rock wall of the Sierra del Cadí. As the seat (*seu*) of the regional archbishopric since the 6th century, it has a rich legacy of art and architecture. The Pyrenean feel of the streets, with their dark balconies and porticoes, overhanging galleries, and colonnaded porches—particularly **Carrer dels Canonges**—makes Seu mysterious and memorable. Look for the medieval **grain measures** at the corner of Carrer Major and Carrer Capdevila. The tiny food shops on the arcaded Carrer Major are intriguing places to assemble lunch for a hike.

6

★ The 12th-century **Catedral de Santa Maria** is the finest cathedral in the Pyrenees. One of the most moving sights in northern Spain is the cathedral's show of sunlight casting the rich reds and blues of Santa Maria's southeastern rose window into the deep gloom of the transept. The 13th-century cloister is known for the individually carved, sometimes whimsical capitals on its 50 columns. (They were crafted by the same Roussillon school of masons who carved the doorway on the church of Santa Maria in Ripoll.) Don't miss either the haunting, 11th-century chapel of **Sant Miquel** or the **Diocesan Museum**, which has a striking collection of medieval murals from various Pyrenean churches and a colorfully illuminated 10th-century Mozarabic manuscript of the monk Beatus de Liébana's commentary on the Apocalypse, along with a short film explaining the manuscript. *Plaça dels Oms* *973/350981* *Cathedral, cloister, and museum €4* *Daily 9–1 and 4–8.*

WHERE TO STAY & EAT

$$–$$$ **Cal Pacho.** Sample traditional local specialties at very reasonable prices in this dark, rustic spot, built in the typical Pyrenean style with stone and wood beams. Count on the filling *escudella* (mountain soup of vegetables, pork or veal, and noodles) in winter, and meat cooked over coals or on slate year-round. *Carrer La Font 11* *973/352719* *AE, DC, MC, V.*

$$$–$$$$ ★ **El Castell de Ciutat.** Just outside Seu, this tall wood-and-slate structure is one of the finest places in the Pyrenees. Rooms on the second floor have balconies overlooking the river; those on the third have slanted ceilings and dormer windows. Suites include a salon. The restaurant specializes in mountain cuisine, such as *civet de jabalí* (wild-boar stew) and *llom de cordet amb trinxat* (lamb cooked over coals and served with puree of potatoes and cabbage). Reserve in advance during summer or Easter week. *Ctra. de Lleida (N260), Km 229, 25700 973/350000 973/351574 www.hotelelcastell.com 32 rooms, 6 suites In-hotel: restaurant, pools, gym, no elevator AE, DC, MC, V.*

$$$ **Parador de la Seu d'Urgell.** These comfortable quarters right in town are built into the 12th-century church and convent of Sant Domènec. The interior patio—the cloister of the former convent—is a lush and tranquil hideaway. Rooms are simple but warm, and some face the mountains. *Carrer Sant Domènec 6, 25700 973/352000 973/352309 www.parador.es 77 rooms, 1 suite In-hotel: restaurant, pool, gym AE, DC, MC, V.*

OFF THE BEATEN PATH

Calbinyà. Ten minutes north of La Seu d'Urgell (off the road to Andorra), this Pyrenean village, with a Museu del Pagès (Farmer's Museum) and the 16th-century farmhouse and inn Cal Serni, is a place to find rustic charm, inexpensive meals, and a room for the night. ***Ctra. de Calbinyà s/n, Valls de Valira, 25798 973/352809 www.calserni.com 6 rooms AE, DC, MC, V.***

WESTERN CATALAN PYRENEES

"The farther from Barcelona, the wilder" is the rule of thumb, and this is true of the rugged countryside and chaotic fauna in the western part of Catalonia. Three of the greatest destinations in the Pyrenees are here: the Garonne-drained, Atlantic-oriented Vall d'Aran; the Noguera de Tor Valley with its matching set of gemlike Romanesque churches; and Parc Nacional d'Aigüestortes i Estany de Sant Maurici, which has a network of pristine lakes and streams. The main geographical units in this section are the valley of the Noguera Pallaresa River, the Vall d'Aran headwaters of the Atlantic-bound Garonne, and the Noguera Ribagorçana River valley, Catalonia's western limit.

SORT

12 *59 km (37 mi) west of La Seu d'Urgell.*

★ The capital of the Pallars Sobirà (Upper Pallars Valley) is a center for skiing, fishing, and white-water kayaking. Don't be fooled by with the town you see from the main road: one block back, Sort is honeycombed with tiny streets and protected corners built to stave off heavy winter weather. To get here from La Seu d'Urgell, take N260 toward Lleida, head west at Adrall, and drive 53 km (33 mi) over the Cantó Pass to

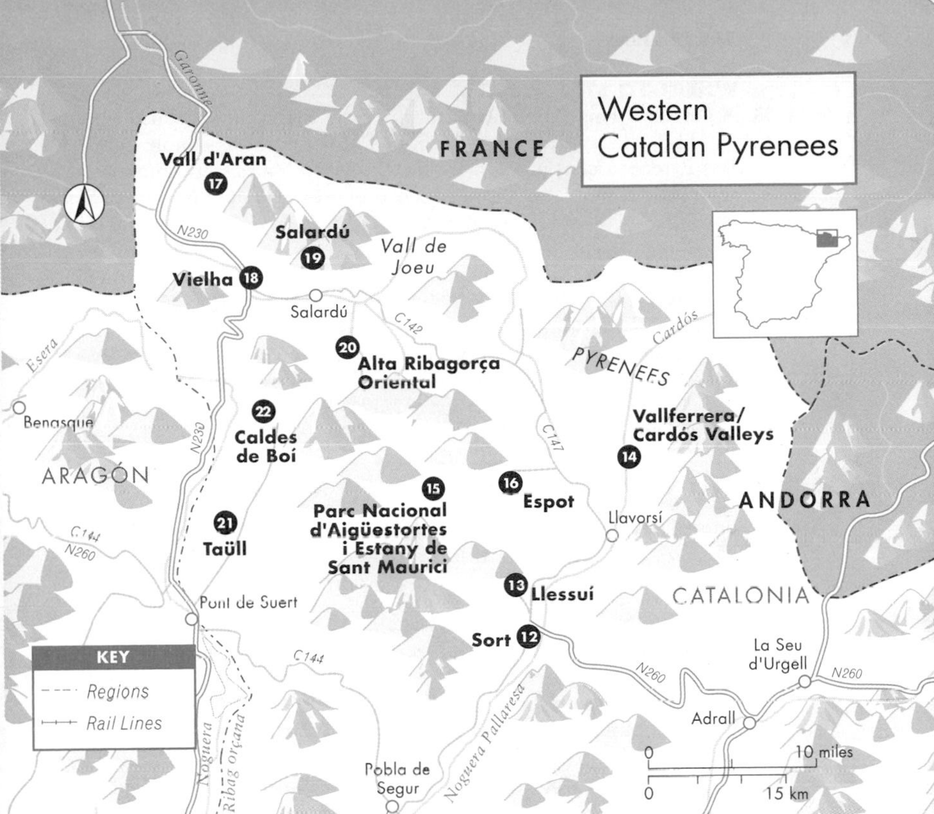

Sort. Sort is the origin of the road into the unspoiled **Assua Valley,** a hidden pocket of untouched mountain villages, including Saurí and Olp.

WHERE TO EAT

$$–$$$$ ★ **Fogony.** If you hit Sort at lunchtime, Fogony, one of the finest dining establishments in the Pyrenees, is a good reason to stop. Come here for local specialties such as *escudella* (a power stew with beans, pasta, pork, beef, fowl, and vegetables), roast lamb, or contemporary gems such as the *suquet de alcachofas* (stewed artichokes) before heading into the high country. ✉ *Av. Generalitat 45* ☎ *973/621225* ▭ *AE, DC, MC, V* ⊙ *Closed 2 wks in Jan. Closed Mon. except Christmas wk, Easter wk, and Aug. No dinner Sun.*

LLESSUÍ

13 *15 km (9 mi) north of Sort.*

Llessuí is at the head of the Upper Pallars Valley under the onetime ski slopes, now closed, of the Altars peak. The 12th-century Romanesque church of **Sant Pere** is topped with a typical conical Vall d'Aran bell tower resembling a pointed witch's hat. The village is now known for adventure sports such as rafting, mountain biking, hiking, or skiing in nearby Espot or Port Ainé.

WHERE TO STAY & EAT

$-$$ ✕ **Cal Kiko.** This little restaurant, a rustic Pyrenean spot also known as "El Pigal," is famous throughout Catalonia for its simple but peerless Pyrenean cooking and for its "Filiberto," a dessert composed of whipped cream, yogurt, and red currants. ✉ *Ctra. de Llessuí s/n, Llessui 25567* ☎ *973/621715* ▭ *No credit cards* ⏲ *Closed Oct. and Wed. No dinner Tues.*

$ ✕🏨 **Vall d'Àssua.** A cozy refuge, this little family-run and family-oriented place is a sure bet for simple Pyrenean home cooking ($–$$$) strong on thick stews and soups, and roasts cooked *a la brasa* (over coals). Guest rooms are small but comfortable. The family also rents out several apartments in country houses in the nearby village of Llagunes. ✉ *Ctra. de Llessuí, Altron, 25567* ☎📠 *973/621738* ↩ *11 rooms* 👍 *In-room: no TV. In-hotel: no elevator* ▭ *No credit cards* ⏲ *Closed Nov.*

VALLFERRERA & CARDÓS VALLEYS

⓮ *From Llavorsí—14 km (9 mi) from Sort on C14, at the junction of the Noguera Pallaresa and Cardós rivers—the road up to the Cardós and Vallferrera valleys branches off to the northeast.*

A trip up the Vallferrera Valley is a good way to penetrate some little-known countryside, explore icy trout streams, or browse through the Romanesque and Visigothic (pre-Romanesque) churches and chapels scattered in and around the village of **Alins** under Catalonia's highest mountain, the Pica d'Estats. In the neighboring Cardós Valley, the Romanesque bell tower of the church of **Santa Maria** rises amid green fields of alfalfa and early wheat and, in May, bright-red splashes of poppies.

PARC NACIONAL D'AIGÜESTORTES I ESTANY DE SANT MAURICI

⓯ ★ After Escaló, 12 km (7 mi) northwest of Llavorsí, the road to Espot and the park veers west.

Running water and the abundance of high mountain terrain are the true protagonists in this wild domain in the shadow of the twin peaks of Els Encantats. More than 300 glacial lakes and lagoons drain through flower-filled meadows and woods to the two Noguera River watercourses, the Pallaresa to the east and the Ribagorçana to the west. The ubiquitous water is surrounded by bare rock walls carved out by the glacier that left these jagged peaks and moist pockets. The land ranges from soft lower meadows below 5,000 feet to the highest crags at nearly double that height: the twin Encantats measure more than 9,000 feet, and surrounding peaks Beciberri, Peguera, Montarto, and Amitges hover between 8,700 feet and just under 10,000 feet.

The dozen Aigüestortes mountain refuges are the stars of the Pyrenees, ranging from the 12-bunk Beciberri, the highest bivouac in the Pyrenees at 9,174 feet, to the 80-bunk, 7,326-foot Ventosa i Calvell at the foot of Punta Alta. Between June and September these mountain accommodations fill with tired and hungry hikers sharing trail tips and lore.

CLOSE UP

Pyrenees Hiking 101

Walking the crest of the Pyrenees' range, with one foot in France and the other in Spain, is an exhilarating experience and well within reach of the moderately fit.

In fall and winter the Alberes Mountains between Cap de Creus, the Iberian Peninsula's easternmost point, and the border with France at Le Perthus is a sky-glide between the Côte Vermeille's curving strand to the north and the moist green patchwork of the Empordá to the south.

The eight-hour walk from Coll de Núria to Ulldeter over the Sierra Catllar, above Setcases, is a grassy corridor in good weather from April to October. The luminous Cerdanya Valley is a hiker's paradise year-round, while the summertime round-Andorra hike is a 360-degree tour of the Principality of Andorra.

The Parque Nacional de Aigüestortes y Lago San Mauricio is superb for trekking from spring through fall. The ascent of the 11,168-foot Aneto peak above Benasque is a full day's round-trip best approached in summer and only by fit and experienced hikers. Much of the hike is over the Maladeta glacier, from the base camp at the Refugio de La Renclusa, where you can rent crampons and ice axes.

In Parque Nacional de Ordesa y Monte Perdido you can take day trips up to the Cola de Caballo waterfall and back around the southern rim of the canyon or, for true mountain goats, longer hikes via the Refugio de Góriz to La Brèche de Roland and Gavarnie or to Monte Perdido, the Parador at La Pineta, and the village of Bielsa.

Farther west, the Irati Forest and the Basque hills between the 6,617-foot Pic D'Orhi and the Bay of Biscay at Hondarribia are snow-free for nine months of the year. The Camino de Santiago walk from Saint-Jean-Pied-de-Port to Roncesvalles is a marvelous 8–10-hour trek and manageable any time of year, though weather reports should be checked carefully from October to June.

Local *excursionista* (outing) clubs can help you get started; local tourist offices may also have brochures and rudimentary trail maps. Keep in mind that the higher reaches are safely navigable only in summer.

6

The park has strict rules: no camping, no fires, no vehicles beyond certain points, no unleashed pets. Entrance to the park is free. It is accessible from the Noguera Pallares and Ribagorçana valleys, and the Espot and Boí villages. For information and refuge reservations, contact the **park administration offices** (☎*973/694000 Barruera, 973/696189 Boí, 973/624036 Espot* 🌐*www.mma.es/parques/lared/*).

WHERE TO STAY

There are no hotels in the park, only refuges. The 66-bunk **Refugi d'Amitges** (☎*973/250109*) is near the Amitges lakes, at 7,920 feet. The 24-bunk **Refugi Ernest Mallafré** (☎*973/250118*) is at the foot of Els Encantats, near Lake Sant Maurici. **Refugi Josep Maria Blanc** (☎*973/250108*), at 7,755 feet, offers 40 bunks at the base of a peninsula reaching out into the Tort de Peguera Lake.

ESPOT

16 *15 km (9 mi) northwest of Llavorsí, 166 km (100 mi) north of Lleida.*

Espot is at the heart of the valley, along a clear, aquamarine stream, and next to the eastern entrance of Aigüestortes–Sant Maurici National Park. **Super-Espot** is the local ski area. The **Pont de la Capella** *(Chapel Bridge)*, a perfect, mossy arch over the flow, looks as though it might have grown directly from the Pyrenean slate.

EN ROUTE

From Esterri d'Aneu, C1412 reaches the sanctuary of Mare de Deu de Ares, a hermitage and shelter, at 4,600 feet, and the Bonaigua Pass, at 6,798 feet. The latter offers a dizzying look back at the Pallars Mountains and ahead to the Vall d'Aran and the Maladeta massif beyond.

VALL D'ARAN & ENVIRONS

17 *From Esterri d'Aneu, the valley runs 46 km (27 mi) east to Vielha over the Bonaigua Pass.*

The Vall d'Aran is at the western edge of the Catalan Pyrenees and the northwestern corner of Catalonia. North of the main Pyrenean axis, it's the Catalan Pyrenees' only Atlantic valley, opening northward into the plains of Aquitania and drained by the Garonne, which flows into the Atlantic Ocean above Bordeaux. The 48-km (30-mi) drive from Bonaigua Pass to the Pont del Rei border with France follows the riverbed.

The valley's Atlantic personality is evidenced by its climate—wet and cold—and its language: the 6,000 inhabitants speak Aranés, a dialect of Gascon French derived from the Occitanian language group. (Spanish and Catalan are also universally spoken.) Originally part of the Aquitanian county of Comminges, the Vall d'Aran maintained feudal ties to the Pyrenees of Spanish Aragón and became part of Catalonia-Aragón in the 12th century. In 1389 the valley was assigned to Catalonia.

Neither as wide as the Cerdanya nor as oppressively narrow and vertical as Andorra, the Vall d'Aran has a sense of well-being and order, an architectural harmony unique in Catalonia. The clusters of iron-gray slate roofs, the lush vegetation, and dormer windows (a sign of French influence) all make the Vall d'Aran a distinct geographic and cultural pocket that happens to have washed up on the Spanish side of the border.Hiking and climbing are popular here; guides are available year-round and can be arranged through the **tourist office** (☎*973/640110*) in Vielha.

VIELHA

18 *79 km (49 mi) northwest of Sort.*

Vielha (Viella, in Spanish), capital of the Vall d'Aran, is a lively crossroads vitally involved in the Aranese movement to defend and reconstruct the valley's architectural, institutional, and linguistic heritage. The octagonal, 14th-century bell tower on the Romanesque parish church of **Sant Miquel** is one of the town's trademarks, as is the 15th-century Gothic altar. The partly damaged 12th-century polychrome wood carving *Cristo de Mig Aran,* displayed under glass, evokes a sense of mortality and humanity with a power unusual in medieval sculpture.

North of Vielha, the tiny villages over the River Garonne hold intriguing little secrets, such as the sculpted Gallo-Roman heads (funeral stelae, or stone slabs, rehabilitated in the 12th century) carved into the village portal at **Gausac.**The bell tower in **Vilac** has an eccentric charm. **Vilamós**'s church, the oldest in the valley, is known for the three curious carved figures, thought to be Gallo-Roman funeral stelae, on its facade. Beautifully carved capitals on the supporting columns adorn the porticoed square in the border village of **Bossòst.**East of Vielha is the village of **Escunhau,** with steep alley-stairways.**Arties** makes a good stop, with its famous Casa Irene restaurant and historic parador.

WHERE TO STAY & EAT

$$–$$$$ ★ **Era Mola.** Also known as Restaurante Gustavo y María José, this former stable with whitewash walls serves French-inspired Aranese cuisine. The *confite de pato* (duck stewed with apple) and *magret de pato* (breast of duck served with *carradetas,* wild mushrooms from the valley) are favorites. *Carrer Marrec 14 973/642419 Reservations essential AE, DC, MC, V No lunch weekdays Dec.–Apr.*

$$$–$$$$ ★ **Casa Irene.** A rustic haven, this inn 6 km (4 mi) east of Vielha is known for fine mountain cuisine with a French flair. Three tasting menus and dishes such as poached foie gras in black truffles and roast wood pigeon in nuts and mint have made Irene a national treasure. The personal style and spacious and elegant rooms make this a highly recommendable address for lodging as well as food. *Carrer Major 3, 25599 Arties 973/644364 973/642174 www.hotelcasairene.com 22 rooms In-hotel: restaurant, parking (fee) Reservations essential AE, DC, MC, V Closed Nov.*

$$$ **Parador de Vielha.** This modern granite parador has a semicircular salon with huge windows and spectacular views over the Maladeta peaks of the Vall d'Aran. Rooms are furnished with traditional carved-wood furniture and floor-to-ceiling curtains. The restaurant ($$–$$$$) serves mainly Catalan cuisine, such as *espinacas a la catalana* (spinach cooked in olive oil with pine nuts, raisins, and garlic). *Ctra. del Túnel s/n, 25530 973/640100 973/641100 www.parador.es 118 rooms In-hotel: restaurant, pool AE, MC, V.*

$$$ **Parador de Arties.** Built around the Casa de Don Gaspar de Portolà, once home to the founder of the colony of California, this modern parador has sweeping views of the Pyrenees. Just 7 km (4 mi) from the Baqueira ski slopes and 2½ km (1½ mi) south of Vielha, it's big enough to seem festive, but small enough for intimacy. The cuisine specializes in sturdy Pyrenean soups and stews such as civet de jabalí (wild boar stew). *Ctra. Baqueira-Beret s/n, Arties, 25599 973/640801 973/641001 www.parador.es 54 rooms, 3 suites In-hotel: restaurant, pools, gym, parking (fee) AE, MC, V.*

6

$$ **Hotel Pirene.** You can find some of the best views in town from this modern hotel. Rooms are bright and simply furnished; sitting rooms are small but comfortable; and the helpful and friendly family running the hotel make each stay memorable. Book ahead during ski season: the place is 15 minutes from the slopes. It's on the left (or west) side of the N230 into Vielha. *Ctra. del Túnel s/n, 25530 973/640075 973/642295 www.hotelpirene.com 39 rooms In-room: no a/c. In-hotel: restaurant, bar AE, DC, MC, V.*

NIGHTLIFE

Bar Era Crin (*Carrer Sortaus 2, Escunhau 973/642061*) has live performances and pop rock to dance to. **Bar la Lluna** (*Carrer Major 10, Arties 973/641115*), a local favorite, occupies a typical Aranese house and has live performances on Wednesday. **Eth Clòt** (*Plaça Sant Orenç, Arties 973/642060*) is a hot *bar musicale.* **Glass** (*Centro Comercial Elurra, Betrén 973/640332*) is in a commercial complex near Vielha filled with a dozen music bars, pubs, and discos.

SALARDÚ

19 *9 km (6 mi) east of Vielha.*

Convenient to Tredós, the Montarto peak, the lakes and Circ de Colomers, Aigüestortes National Park, and the villages of Unha and Mongarri, Salardú is a pivotal point in the Vall d'Aran. The town itself, with just over 700 inhabitants, is known for its steep streets and its octagonal fortified bell tower. The 12th-century **Sant Andreu** church's Romanesque wood sculpture of Christ is said to have miraculously floated up the Garonne River.

The tiny village of **Unha** perches on a promontory 3 km (2 mi) above Salardú, with the elegant Ço de Brastet (Brastet House) at its entrance. Unha's 12th-century church of Santa Eulàlia has a curiously bulging 17th-century bell tower. East of Salardú is the village of **Tredós,** home of the Romanesque church of Santa Maria de Cap d'Aran—symbol of the Aranese independence movement and meeting place of the valley's governing body, the Conselh Generau, until 1827.

WHERE TO STAY & EAT

$$–$$$ **Casa Rufus.** Pine and checkered tablecloths cozily furnish this restaurant nestled in the tiny, gray-stone village of Gessa, between Vielha and Salardú. Rufus himself, who also runs the ski school at Baqueira, specializes in local country cooking; try the *conejo relleno de ternera* (rabbit stuffed with veal). *Sant Jaume 8, Gessa 973/645246 or 973/645872 MC, V Closed May–mid-July, Nov., and weekdays in Oct. No dinner Sun. No lunch weekdays mid-Sept.–Apr.*

$$$$ ★ **Meliá Royal Tanau.** This luxurious hotel 7 km (4 mi) east of Salardú is only a few steps from the lifts and offers services and amenities that include hydrotherapy massage and fine cuisine (with prices to match; $$$–$$$$). Considered one of the top skiing hotels in the Pyrenees, it is a refuge where you can count on being well pampered between assaults on the snowy heights. Top-floor rooms can be snug, with duplex apart-

ments and sleeping lofts with skylights opening directly out into the starry Pyrenean firmament. ✉ *Ctra. Baqueira-Beret, Km 7, 25598* ☎ *973/644446* 🖷 *973/644344* 🌐 *www.meliaroyaltanau.solmelia.com* *30 rooms, 15 apartments* *In-room: no a/c. In-hotel: restaurant, pool* ▭ *AE, MC, V.*

$$$–$$$$ **Val de Ruda.** For rustic surroundings light on luxury but long on comfort, and an outdoorsy, alpine feeling, this modern-traditional construction is a good choice. It was one of the first skiing hotels to go up here in the early '80s; it's just 660 feet from the slopes. This glass, wood, and stone refuge has a friendly staff and pine- and oak-beam warmth for après-ski wining and dining. ✉ *Ctra. Baqueira-Beret Cota 1500, 25598* ☎ *973/645258* 🖷 *973/645812* 🌐 *www.valderuda-bassibe.com* *34 rooms* *In-room: no a/c. In-hotel: restaurant, bar* ▭ *AE, DC, MC, V.*

SPORTS & THE OUTDOORS

Skiing, white-water rafting, hiking, climbing, horseback riding, and fly fishing are available throughout the Vall d'Aran. Consult the Vielha **tourist office** (☎ *973/640110*) for information.

DOGSLEDDING **La Pirena** (☎ *974/360098 tourist office in Jaca*), the Pyrenean version of the Iditarod, rages through the Vall d'Aran in early February. The race runs from Panticosa, above Jaca, to La Molina, near Puigcerdà, every winter in late January to early or mid-February.

SKIING The **Baqueira-Beret Estación de Esquí** *(Baqueira-Beret Ski Station)*, visited annually by King Juan Carlos I and the royal family, offers Catalonia's most varied and reliable skiing. The station's 87 km (57 mi) of *pistas* (slopes), spread over 53 runs, range from the gentle Beret slopes to the vertical chutes of Baqueira. The Bonaigua area is a mixture of steep and gently undulating trails with some of the longest, most varied runs in the Pyrenees. The internationally FIS-classified super-giant slalom run in Beret is Baqueira-Beret's star attraction, although the Hotel Pirene runs carefully guided helicopter outings to the surrounding peaks of Pincela, Areño, Parros, Mall de Boulard, Pedescals, and Bassibe, among others. A dozen restaurants and four children's areas are scattered about the facilities, and the thermal baths at Tredós are 4 km (2½ mi) away. ✉ *Salardú* ☎ *973/639000* 🖷 *973/644488* ✉ *Barcelona office: Av. Diagonal 656, Barcelona* ☎ *93/205–8292* 🖷 *93/205–8290* 🌐 *www.baqueira.es.*

OFF THE BEATEN PATH

The Vall de Joeu (Joeu Valley), above the town of Les Bordes 9 km (6 mi) northwest of Vielha, was for centuries the unsolved mystery of Vall d'Aran hydraulics. The Joeu River, one of the two main sources of the Garonne, appears to rise at Artiga de Lin, where it then cascades down in the Barrancs Waterfalls. On July 19, 1931, speleologist Norbert Casteret proved, by dumping 132 pounds of colorant into a cavern in neighboring Aragón, that this "spring" was actually glacier runoff from the Maladeta massif in the next valley to the southwest. The glacier melt flows into a huge crater, Els Aïgualluts, and reappears 4 km (3 mi) northeast at the Uelhs deth Joeu

(Eyes of Jupiter in Aranés, so named for the Roman deity's association with the heavens, weather, rainfall, and agriculture), where it flows north toward the Garonne, eventually emptying into the Atlantic.

ALTA RIBAGORÇA ORIENTAL

20 *From Vall d'Aran take the 6-km (4-mi) Vielha tunnel to the Alta Ribagorça Oriental.*

This valley includes the east bank of the Noguera Ribagorçana River and the Llevata and Noguera de Tor valleys. The latter has the Pyrenees' richest concentration of medieval art and architecture. The quality and unity of design apparent in the Romanesque churches along the Noguera de Tor River, in towns such as Durro, Boí, Erill la Vall, and Taüll, are the result of the sponsorship—and wives—of the counts of Erill. The Erill knights, away fighting Moors in distant battles of the Reconquest, left their spouses behind to supervise the creation of local houses of worship. The women then brought in Europe's leading masters of architecture, masonry, sculpture, and painting to build and decorate the churches. To what extent a single eye and sensibility was responsible for this extraordinarily harmonious and coherent set of churches may never be known, but it's clear that they all share certain distinguishing characteristics: a miniaturistic tightness combined with eccentric or irregular design, and slender rectangular bell towers that are light but forceful, perfectly balanced against the rocky background.

To get here from Vielha, route N230 runs south 33 km (20 mi) to the intersection with N260 (sometimes marked C144), which goes west over the Fadas Pass to Castejón de Sos. Four kilometers (2½ mi) past this intersection, the road up the Noguera de Tor Valley turns to the northeast, 2 km (1 mi) short of Pont de Suert.

TAÜLL

21 *58 km (36 mi) south of Vielha.*

Taüll is a town of narrow streets and tight mountain design—wooden balconies and steep slate roofs. The churches of Sant Climent and Santa Maria are lovely, and important churches near Taüll include Sant Feliu, at Barruera; Sant Joan Baptista, at Boí; Santa Maria, at Cardet; Santa Maria, at Col; Santa Eulàlia, at Erill-la-vall; La Nativitat de la Mare de Deu and Sant Quirze, at Durro; Sant Llorenç, at Sarais; and Sant Nicolau, in the Sant Nicolau Valley, at the entrance to Aigüestortes–Sant Maurici National Park. Taüll has a ski resort, **Bohí Taüll,** at the head of the Sant Nicolau Valley.

★ At the edge of town, the exquisite three-nave Romanesque church of **Sant Climent** was built in 1123. The six-story belfry has exceptionally harmonious proportions, Pyrenean stone that changes hues with the light, and a sense of intimacy that creates notable balance. In 1922 Barcelona's Museu Nacional d'Art de Catalunya became the home of the church's murals, including the famous *Pantocrator,* the work of the "Master of Taüll." The murals presently in the church are reproductions of the original. *€3 Daily 10–2 and 4–8.*

CALDES DE BOÍ

22 *6 km (4 mi) north of Taüll.*

The thermal baths in the town of Caldes de Boí include, between hot and cold sources, 40 springs. The caves inside the bath area are a singular natural phenomenon, with thermal steam seeping through the cracks in the rock. Take advantage of the baths' therapeutic qualities at either Hotel Caldes or Hotel Manantial—services range from a bath, at €7–€10, to an underwater body massage for €18. People with arthritis are frequent takers. *Hotel Caldes 973/696220 Hotel Manantial 973/696210 www.caldesdeboi.com Hotels and baths closed Oct.–May.*

WHERE TO STAY & EAT

$ **Fondevila.** Wooden trim and simple country furnishings warm the interior of this stone structure 3 km (2 mi) north of Taüll. The rooms are generously proportioned and cozy. The country cuisine ($–$$$) includes game in season and various Catalan specialties. *Carrer Única, 25528 Boí 973/696011 46 rooms In-room: no a/c, no TV (some) AE, DC, MC, V Closed Nov. 10–Dec. 26 and Jan. 7–Feb. 1.*

ARAGÓN & CENTRAL PYRENEES

The highest, wildest, and most spectacular range of the Pyrenees is the middle section, farthest from sea level. From Benasque on Aragón's eastern side to Jaca at the western edge are the great heights and most dramatic landscapes of Alto Aragón (Upper Aragón), including the Maladeta (11,165 feet), Posets (11,070 feet), and Monte Perdido (11,001 feet) peaks, the three highest points in the Pyrenean chain.

Communications between the high valleys of the Pyrenees were all but nonexistent until the 19th century. Four-fifths of the region had never seen a motor vehicle of any kind until well into the 20th century, and the 150-km (93-mi) border with France between Portalet de Aneu and Vall d'Aran had never had an international crossing. This combination of high peaks, deep defiles, and isolation has produced some of the Iberian Peninsula's best-preserved towns and valleys. Today, numerous ethnological museums bear witness to a way of life that has nearly disappeared since the 1950s. Residents of Upper Aragón speak neither Basque nor Catalan, but local dialects, such as Grausín, Chistavino, Belsetá, and Benasqués (collectively known as *fabla*), and have more in common with each other and with Occitanian or Langue d'Oc (the southwestern French language descended from Provençal) than with modern Spanish and French. Furthermore, each valley has its own variations on everything from the typical Aragonese folk dance, the *jota,* to

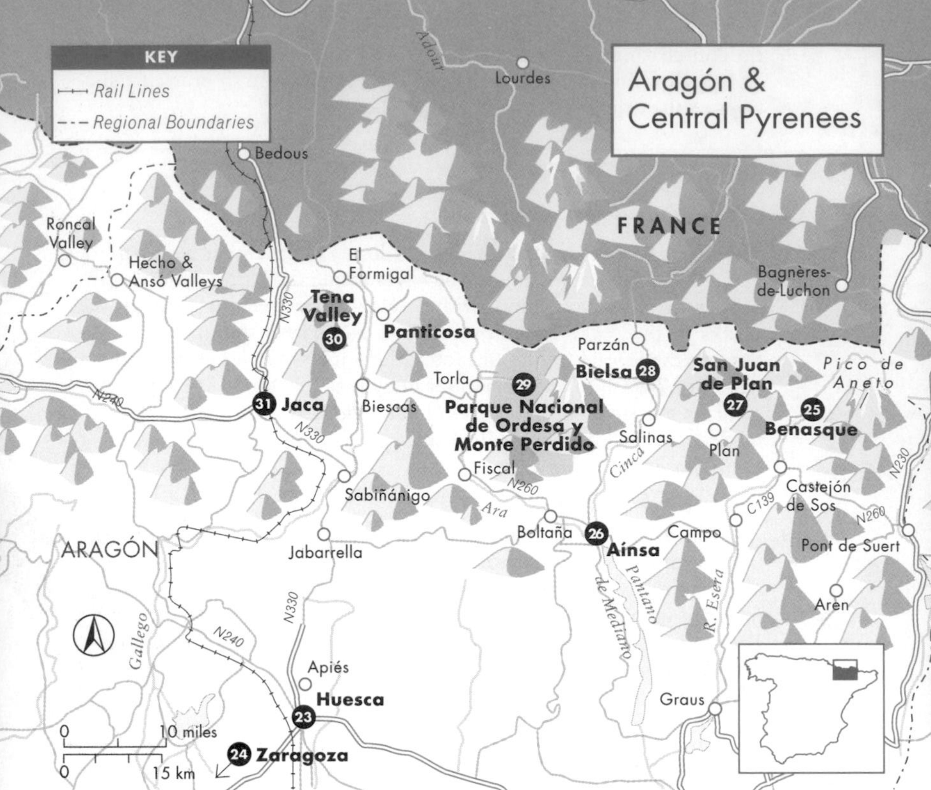

cuisine and traditional costume. Wildlife here includes several strains of mountain goat, deer, and, above Jaca between Somport and the French Vall d'Aspe, the Pyrenean brown bear.

The largely undiscovered cities of Huesca and Zaragoza are both useful Pyrenean gateways and destinations in themselves; Zaragoza is an unavoidable link between Barcelona and Bilbao. Both cities retain an authentic provincial character that is refreshing in today's cosmopolitan Spain. Huesca's lovely old quarter and Zaragoza's immense basilica, La Pilarica, are memorable places to explore.

HUESCA

23 *75 km (46 mi) southwest of Aínsa, 72 km (45 mi) northeast of Zaragoza, 123 km (74 mi) northwest of Lleida.*

Capital of Aragón until the royal court moved to Zaragoza in 1118, Huesca was founded by the Romans a millennium earlier. The city became an independent state with a senate and an excellent school system organized by the Roman general Sertorius in 77 BC. Much later, after centuries of Moorish rule, Pedro I of Aragón liberated Huesca in 1096. The town's university was founded in 1354 and now specializes in Aragonese studies.

An intricately carved gallery tops the eroded facade of Huesca's 13th-century Gothic **cathedral.** Damián Forment, a disciple of the 15th-century Italian master sculptor Donatello, created the alabaster altarpiece with scenes from the Crucifixion. ✉ *Pl. de la Catedral s/n* ☎ *974/292172* 💰 *Free* ⏲ *Mon.–Sat. 8–1 and 4–6:30.*

A PAMPLONA ALTERNATIVE

For an unspoiled Pamplona-like fiesta in another pre-Pyrenean capital, with bullfights, *encierros* (running of the bulls through the streets) and all-night revelry, try Huesca's San Lorenzo celebration August 9th–15th. Spain's top bullfighters are the main attraction, along with concerts, street dances, and liberal tastings of the excellent Somontano wines of upper Huesca. *Albahaca* (basil) is the official symbol of Huesca and the ubiquitous green sashes and bandannas will remind you that this is Huesca, not Pamplona (where red is the trimming).

Twice daily, the Huesca tourist office (in the former market at Plaza Luis Lopez Allué s/n) accompanies visitors into the Renaissance **ayuntamiento** *(town hall)* to see the 19th-century painting of the 12th-century beheading of a group of uncooperative nobles, ordered by Ramiro II. King Ramiro, having called a meeting for the purported pouring of a giant bell that would be audible throughout Aragón, proceeded to massacre the leading troublemakers; the expression *como la campana de Huesca* ("like the bell of Huesca") is still sometimes used to describe an event of surprising resonance. ✉ *Pl. de la Catedral 1* ☎ *974/292170* 💰 *Free* ⏲ *Mon.–Sat. at noon and 6.*

The **Museo Arqueológico Provincial** is an octagonal patio ringed by eight chambers, including the **Sala de la Campana** (Hall of the Bell), where the beheadings of 12th-century nobles took place. The museum is in parts of what was once the royal palace of the kings of Aragón and holds paintings by Aragonese primitives, including *La Virgen del Rosario* by Miguel Jiménez, and several works by the 16th-century Maestro de Sigena. ✉ *Pl. de la Universidad* ☎ *974/220586* 💰 *Free* ⏲ *Tues.–Sat. 10–2 and 5–8, Sun. 10–2.*

The church of **San Pedro el Viejo** has an 11th-century cloister with sculpted capitals. Ramiro II and his father, Alfonso I—the only Aragonese kings not entombed at San Juan de la Peña—rest in a side chapel. ✉ *Pl. de San Pedro s/n* ☎ *974/292164* 💰 *Free* ⏲ *Mon.–Sat. 10–2 and 6–8.*

Castillo de Loarre. This massively walled 11th-century monastery, 36 km (22 mi) west of Huesca off Route A132 on A1206, is nearly indistinguishable from the rock outcroppings that surround it. Inside the walls are a church, a tower, a dungeon, and even a medieval toilet with views of the almond and olive orchards in the Ebro basin.

WHERE TO STAY & EAT

$$$–$$$$ ✕ **Las Torres.** Huesca's top dining establishment makes inventive use of first-rate local Pyrenean ingredients ranging from wild mushrooms to lamb. The glass-walled kitchen is as original as the cooking that

6

emerges from it, and the wine list is strong in Somontanos, Huesca's own Denomination of Origin. Look for the *paticas de cordero deshuesados* (deboned lamb's trotters) for a taste of pure upper Aragón. ✉*María Auxiliadora 3* ☎*974/228213* ▭*AE, DC, MC, V* ⊙*Closed 2 wks at Easter, Aug. 16–31, and Sun.*

$$–$$$ **Pedro I de Aragón.** This modern structure over the leafy Parque Miguel Servet is lush with mirrors and marble in the lobby, and furnished with fresh and fragrant pine in the rooms. Comfort is the objective here, and the accommodations and service are the best in Huesca. ✉*Parque 34, 22003* ☎*974/220300* 📠*974/220094* 🌐*www.gargallo-hotels.com* *125 rooms, 4 suites* *In-room: no a/c. In-hotel: restaurant, bar, pool, minibar* ▭*AE, DC, MC, V.*

$ **San Marcos.** The building dates from 1890, and the rooms, though updated for comfort, remain tastefully decorated with traditional touches. Centrally located outside the 1st-century Roman walls, the hotel is a five-minute walk from Huesca's cathedral. ✉*San Orencio 10, 22001* ☎📠*974/222931* *29 rooms* ▭*AE, DC, MC, V.*

ZARAGOZA

24 *72 km (43 mi) southwest of Huesca, 138 km (86 mi) west of Lleida, 307 km (184 mi) west of Barcelona, 164 km (98 mi) southeast of Pamplona, 322 km (193 mi) northeast of Madrid.*

In high spirits amid the throes of its year-long 2008 Universal Exposition, which will be based on the theme of water and its own mighty river, Zaragoza is about as exciting as it has ever been. This traditionally provincial city is experiencing its greatest boom since the Romans established a thriving river port here in 25 BC. Rated one of Spain's most desirable places to live because of its air quality, cost of living, low-population density, and other qualities, Zaragoza seems full of self-contained well-being. Despite its hefty size (pop. 610,976), this sprawling provincial capital midway between Barcelona, Madrid, Bilbao, and Valencia is a detour from the tourist track connected by the AVE, Spain's high-speed railroad, with Madrid in under two hours (and after December 2007 with Barcelona on a new train line).

WHAT TO SEE

Straddling Spain's greatest river, the Ebro, 2,000-year-old Zaragoza was originally named Caesaraugusta, for Roman emperor Augustus. Its legacy contains everthing from Roman ruins and Jewish baths to Arab, Romanesque, Gothic-Mudéjar, Renaissance, baroque, neoclassical, and Art Nouveau architecture. Parts of the **Roman walls** are visible near the city's landmark Basílica de Nuestra Señora del Pilar. Nearby, the medieval **Puente de Piedra** (Stone Bridge) spans the Ebro. Checking out the **Lonja** (Stock Exchange), the Moorish **Aljafería** (Jewel Treasury), the **Mercado de Lanuza** (Produce Market), and the various **churches** in the old town—San Pablo, San Miguel, San Gil, Santa Engracia, San Carlos, San Ildefonso, San Felipe, Santa Cruz, and San Fernando—is a good way to navigate Zaragoza's jumble of backstreets.

Hulking on the banks of the Ebro, the **Basílica de Nuestra Señora del Pilar** *(Basilica of Our Lady of the Pillar)*, affectionately known as "La Pilarica," is Zaragoza's symbol and pride. An immense baroque structure with no fewer than 11 tile cupolas, La Pilarica is the home of the Virgen del Pilar, the patron saint not only of peninsular Spain but of the entire Hispanic world. The fiestas honoring this most Spanish of saints, held the week of October 12, are events of extraordinary pride and Spanish fervor, with processions, street concerts, bullfights, and traditional *jota* dancing. The cathedral was built in the 18th century to commemorate the appearance of the Virgin on a pillar (*pilar*), or pedestal, to St. James, Spain's other patron saint, during his legendary incarnation as Santiago Matamoros (St. James the Moorslayer) in the 9th century. La Pilarica herself resides in a side chapel that dates from 1754. The frescoes in the cupolas, some of which are attributed to the young Goya, are among the basilica's treasures. The **Museo Pilarista** holds drawings and some of the Virgin's jewelry. The bombs displayed to the right of the altar of La Pilarica chapel fell through the roof of the church in 1936 and miraculously failed to explode. ✉ *Pl. del Pilar s/n* 🎫 *Basilica free, museum €2* ⏲ *Basilica daily 5:45* AM–*9:30* PM, *museum daily 9–2 and 4–6.*

6

Zaragoza's cathedral, **La Seo** *(Catedral de San Salvador)*, at the eastern end of the Plaza del Pilar, is the city's bishopric, or diocesan *seo* (seat). An amalgam of architectural styles, ranging from the Mudéjar brick-and-tile exterior to the Gothic altarpiece to exuberant Churrigueresque doorways, the Seo nonetheless has an 18th-century baroque facade that seems to echo those of La Pilarica. The **Museo de Tapices** within contains medieval tapestries. The nearby medieval **Casa y Arco del Deán** form one of the city's favorite corners. ✉ *Pl. del Pilar* 🎫 *Cathedral €2, museum €2* ⏲ *Cathedral Mon.–Sat. 10–2 and 4–8, Sun. 5–8; museum Tues.–Sat. 10–2 and 4–6, Sun. 10–2.* The **Iglesia de la Magdalena**, next to the remains of the Roman forum, has an ancient brick Mudéjar bell tower. The church is usually open in the mornings. ✉ *Pl. de la Magdalena s/n* ☎ *976/299598.*

The **Museo del Foro** displays remains of the Roman forum and the Roman sewage system, though the presentation is in Spanish only. Two more Roman sites, the **thermal baths** at Calle de San Juan y San Pedro and the **river port** at Plaza San Bruno, are also open to the public. ✉ *Pl. de la Seo s/n* ☎ *976/399752* 🎫 *€2* ⏲ *Tues.–Sat. 10–2 and 5–8.*

The **Museo Camón Aznar** has a fine collection of Goya's works, particularly his engravings. ✉ *Carrer Espoz y Mina 23* ☎ *976/397328* 🎫 *Free* ⏲ *Tues.–Fri. 9–2 and 6–9, Sat. 10–2 and 6–9, Sun. 11–2.*

The **Museo del Centro de Historia** exhibits a wide range of memorabilia from Zaragoza's 2,000-year history, including audiovisual studies of different facets. The section on the River Ebro and the Roman exploitation of the port of Zaragoza are especially interesting. ✉ *Pl. San Agustín 2* ☎ *976/205640* 🎫 *Free* ⏲ *Tues.–Sat. 10–7:15, Sun. 10–1:15.* The **Museo Provincial de Bellas Artes** contains a rich treasury of Zaragoza's emblematic painter Francisco José Goya y Lucientes, including his portraits of Fernando VII, and his best graphic works: *Desastres de la guerra, Caprichos, and La tauromaquia.* ✉*Pl. de los Sitios 5* ☎*976/222181* 🎫*Free* ⊙*Tues.–Sat. 10–2 and 5–8, Sun. 10–2.*

The **Museo Pablo Gargallo** is one of Zarargoza's most treasured and admired gems, both for the palace as well as for the collection—Gargallo, born near Zaragoza in 1881, was one of Spain's greatest modern sculptors. ✉*Pl. de San Felipe 3* ☎*976/392058* 🎫*Free* ⊙*Tues.–Sat. 9–2 and 5–9, Sun. 9–2.*

The **Museo del Teatro Romano** showcases a restored Roman amphitheater as well as the objects recovered during the excavation process, including theatrical masks, platters, and even Roman hairpins. ✉*Calle San Jorge 12* ☎*976/205088* 🎫*€3.50* ⊙*Tues.–Sat. 10–9, Sun. 10–2.*

Palacio de La Aljafería is what remains of the Alhambra-esque original, which helps explain the importance of the nearly eight-century Moorish empire on the Iberian Peninsula. Originally an 11th-century fortress, the A former seat of the Spanish Inquisition, it's now the home of the Cortes (Parliament) de Aragón. The 9th-century Torre del Trovador (Tower of the Troubadour) appears in Giuseppe Verdi's opera *Il Trovatore.* ✉*Diputados s/n* ☎*976/289683* 🎫*€3.50* ⊙*Mon.–Wed. and weekends 10–2 and 4–7, Fri. 4–7.*

WHERE TO STAY & EAT

$$–$$$$ ✕ **La Venta del Cachirulo.** Outside Zaragoza, this roadhouse is worth a trip for authentic Aragonese cooking and folklore, including occasional *jota* dancing and singing. *Borrajas con almejas* (kale with clams) and *pato con cerezas* (duck with cherries) are among the local dishes served. ✉*Ctra. Logroño, N232, Km 1* ☎*976/460146* ▭*AE, DC, MC, V* ⊙*Closed Sun. and Mon. and 1st 2 wks in Aug.*

$–$$ ✕ **Casa Emilio.** One of the city's most popular restaurants among artists, journalists, and writers, this haven of straightforward cooking and conversation near the Aljafería and the train station offers excellent value and a friendly environment. Specialties include *verduras de temporada* (vegetables in season), *revuelto de bacalao al ajoarriero* (cod and scrambled eggs), *ventresca de bonito marinada* (marinated tuna belly) and *ternasco al horno de leña* (beef filet roasted in a wood oven). ✉*Av. Madrid 3–5* ☎*976/435839* ▭*AE, DC, MC, V.*

$ ★ ✕ **Los Victorinos.** This rustic tavern heavily adorned with bullfight-related paraphernalia—Victorinos are a much-feared breed of fighting bulls—offers an elaborate and inventive selection of tapas. Tucked in behind the Seo, this local secret opens at 7:30 every evening. ✉*Calle José de la Hera 6* ☎*976/394213* ▭*AE, DC, MC, V* ⊙*No lunch.*

$$$ 🏨 **Goya.** Smack in the city center, this hotel provides a balanced combination of comfort and proximity to the historic sights. It's a five-minute walk from the Basílica del Pilar and the Ebro River; here you can get the sense that you're part of the city's life. Rooms are modern, but not luxurious. ✉*Cinco de Marzo 5, 50004* ☎*976/229331* 📠*976/232154* 🌐*www.palafoxhoteles.com* 🛏*148 rooms* 🛎*In-hotel: restaurant, bar, parking (fee)* ▭*AE, DC, MC, V.*

$$ **Las Torres.** The rooms are small here, but the scenery is hard to beat. You may even be able to admire the domes of La Pilarica from your pillow. If you're a light sleeper, you may need earplugs to muffle the bonging of the bells—they ring every 15 minutes all through the night; interior rooms are much quieter. *Pl. del Pilar 11, 50003 976/394250 976/394254 www.hotellastorres.com 54 rooms In-hotel: parking (fee) AE, DC, MC, V.*

SHOPPING

El Tubo (*Cinegio 10 976/391177*) is Zaragoza's best store for handmade leather boots from all over Spain.

BENASQUE

25 *79 km (49 mi) southwest of Vielha.*

Fodor's Choice ★

Benasque, Aragón's easternmost town, has always been an important link between Catalonia and Aragón. This elegant mountain hub of a little more than 1,500 people harbors a number of notable buildings, including the 13th-century Romanesque church of **Santa Maria Mayor** and the ancient, dignified manor houses of the town's old families, such as the **palace of the counts of Ribagorza,** on Calle Mayor, and the **Torre Juste.** Take a walk around and peer into the entryways and patios of these palatial facades, left open just for this purpose.

Anciles, 2 km (1 mi) south of Benasque, is one of Spain's best-preserved and best-restored medieval villages, a collection of farmhouses and *palacetes* (town houses). The summer classical-music series is a superb collision of music and architecture, and the village restaurant, Ansils, combines modern and medieval motifs in both cuisine and design.

OFF THE BEATEN PATH

Pico De Aneto. Benasque is the traditional base camp for excursions to Aneto, which, at 11,168 feet, is the highest peak in the Pyrenees. You can rent crampons and a *piolet* (ice ax) for the two- to three-hour crossing of the Aneto glacier at any sports store in town or at the Refugio de la Renclusa—a way station for mountaineers—an hour's walk above the parking area, which is 17 km (11 mi) north of Benasque, off A139. The trek to the summit and back is not difficult, just long—some 20 km (12 mi) round-trip, with a 1,500-yard vertical ascent. Allow a full 12 hours.

WHERE TO STAY & EAT

$$–$$$$ **Asador Ixarso.** Roast goat or lamb cooked over a raised fireplace in the corner of the dining room is why this place is a fine refuge in chilly weather. The *revuelto de setas* (eggs scrambled with wild mushrooms) are superb, as are the salads. *Calle San Pedro 9 974/552057 AE, DC, MC, V Closed weekdays mid-Sept.–1st wk in Dec. and Easter–June.*

$$–$$$$ **Restaurante Ansils.** This rustic place, ingeniously designed in glass, wood, and stone, specializes in local Benasqués dishes, such as *civet de jabalí* (wild-boar stew) and *recau* (a thick vegetable broth). Lus-

cious holiday meals are served on Christmas and Easter. ✉*Anciles* ☎*974/551150* 💳*AE, DC, MC, V* ⏲*Closed weekdays Oct.–June.*

$$–$$$ ✕🏨 **Hospital de Benasque.** Some 13 km (8 mi) north of Benasque off the A139 road, this mountain retreat is an ideal base camp for hiking and cross-country skiing. Constructed and furnished in stone and fresh wood, rooms are simple and clean lined. The restaurant ($$–$$$) serves classical Pyrenean fare in a glassed-in dining room flooded with natural light. ✉*Camino Real de Francia s/n, 22440* ☎*974/552012* 📠*974/551052* 🌐*www.llanosdelhospital.com* *57 rooms* *In-room: no a/c. In-hotel: restaurant, parking (no fee)* 💳*AE, DC, MC, V.*

$$ ✕🏨 **Gran Hotel Benasque.** This spacious, modern hotel within walking distance from Benasque is bracketed by the highest crests in the Pyrenees (Aneto and Posets) and serves as an impeccably comfortable base for exploring them. The restaurant's mountain fare ($$–$$$$) includes *sopa Benasquesa* (a thick highland stew) and *crepas Aneto* (crepes with ham, wild mushroom, and béchamel sauce). ✉*Ctra. de Anciles s/n, 22440* ☎*974/551011* 📠*974/552821* 🌐*www.hoteles-valero.com* *69 rooms* *In-hotel: restaurant, bar, pools, gym* 💳*AE, MC, V* ⏲*Closed Nov.*

$$ ✕🏨 **La Casa del Río.** Just south of Benasque, this ramshackle Pyrenean house offers comfortable lodging and fly-fishing (guided excursions can be arranged) within casting distance of your pillow. The cuisine ($–$$$) includes mountain specialties and roasts cooked over coals. ✉*Crtra. Benasque Km 49.9, 22467 Vilanova* ☎📠*974/553493* 🌐*www.lacasadelrio.com* *8 rooms* *In-room: no a/c. In-hotel: restaurant, parking (no fee)* 💳*AE, DC, MC, V.*

SPORTS & THE OUTDOORS

The **Cerler ski area** (☎*974/551012* 🌐*www.cerler.com*), 6 km (4 mi) east of Benasque on the Cerler road, covers the slopes of the Cogulla peak. Built on a shelf over the valley at an altitude of 5,051 feet, Cerler has 26 ski runs, 3 lifts, and a guided helicopter service to drop you at the highest peaks. The outfitter **Danica Guías de Pesca** (☎*974/553493 or 659/735376* 🌐*www.danicaguias.com*) can show you the top spots and techniques for Pyrenean fly-fishing.

AÍNSA

26 *66 km (41 mi) southwest of Benasque.*

Aínsa's arcaded Plaza Mayor and old town are classic examples of medieval village design, with heavy stone archways and tiny windows. The 12th-century Romanesque church of **Santa María** has a quadruple-vaulted door. ✉*Old Quarter* *Free* ⏲*Daily 9–2 and 4–8.*

WHERE TO STAY & EAT

$$–$$$$ ✕ **Bodegas del Sobrarbe.** Superb lamb roasted in a wood oven is the specialty of this fine restaurant built into an 11th-century wine cellar. The setting is medieval: expect vaulted ceilings of heavy wood and stone. ✉*Pl. Mayor 2* ☎*974/500237* 💳*AE, DC, MC, V* ⏲*Closed Jan. and Feb.*

$ **Casa Cambra.** A once-abandoned village between Barbastro and Aínsa is home to this little inn, a perfect base for mountain sports of all kinds. The restored 18th-century house of stone and timber has rooms for two to four people and is part of a tourist complex that includes a restaurant. *Ctra. Barbastro–Aínsa, A138, Km 41.8, Morillo de Tou, 22395 974/500793 www.morillodetou.com 17 rooms In-room: no a/c, no TV MC, V.*

OFF THE BEATEN PATH **Añisclo gorges. On the road north from Aínsa, the Añisclo Canyon is 5 km (3 mi) north of the town of Escalona. A road to the west runs 14 km (9 mi) along the edge of the sheer rock divide to Urbez. As you drive into Urbez, you can see the ancient stone bridge. On the far bank of the river is the cave chapel named for St. Urbez, a hermit monk from Bordeaux who lived there in the 8th century.**

SAN JUAN DE PLAN & THE GISTAÍN VALLEY

27 *14 km (8½ mi) east of Salinas.*

This detour begins with a well-marked road heading east of Salinas, 25 km (15 mi) north of Aínsa. The Cinqueta River drains the Gistaín Valley, flowing by or through the mountain villages of Sin, Señes, Saravillo, Serveta, and Salinas. The town of San Juan de Plan presides at the head of the valley, where an ethnographic museum, a water-powered sawmill, and an early-music- and dance ensemble are the pride of the region. The mid-February carnival is among the most distinct and traditional celebrations in the Pyrenees. The **Museo Etnográfico** is a fascinating glimpse into a traditional way of life (dress, kitchen utensils, bedclothes, field tools) that endured largely intact until about 1975. *Pl. Mayor s/n 974/506052 €3 Daily 9–2 and 4–8.*

WHERE TO STAY & EAT

$–$$ ★ **Casa la Plaza.** Josefina Loste's pleasant inn has rustic and cozy rooms with antique furniture. Each room tucked into the eaves is different. The restaurant ($–$$$) serves excellent local dishes using fresh mountain products prepared lovingly, using traditional recipes in inventive ways. *Pl. Mayor s/n, 22367 974/506052 13 rooms In-room: no a/c AE, DC, MC, V Closed sporadically Oct.–May; call to confirm.*

BIELSA

28 *34 km (21 mi) northeast of Aínsa.*

Bielsa, at the confluence of the Cinca and Barrosa rivers, is a busy summer resort with some lovely mountain architecture and an ancient, porticoed town hall. Northwest of Bielsa the **Monte Perdido glacier** and the icy **Marboré Lake** drain into the **Pineta Valley** and the Pineta Reservoir. You can take three- or four-hour walks from the parador up to Larri, Munia, or Marboré Lake among remote peaks.

WHERE TO STAY & EAT

$$$ ✕🏨 **Parador de Bielsa.** Glass, steel, and stone define this modern structure overlooking the national park, the peak of Monte Perdido, and the source of the Cinca River. Rooms are done in bright wood, but the best part is your proximity to the park and the views. The restaurant ($$–$$$) specializes in Aragonese mountain dishes, such as *pucherete de Parzán* (a stew with beans, sausage, and vegetables). ✉ *Ctra. Valle de Pineta s/n, 22350* ☎ *974/501011* 📠 *974/501188* 🌐 *www.parador.es* *39 rooms* *In-room: no a/c. In-hotel: restaurant, bar* 💳 *AE, DC, MC, V.*

$$ ★ ✕🏨 **Hotel Valle de Pineta.** This corner castle overlooking the river junction is the most spectacular refuge in town. The restaurant ($$–$$$) is excellent, the views superb. Try for the top corner room, which looks across both the Pineta and Cinca valleys. ✉ *Calle Baja s/n, 22350* ☎ *974/501010* 📠 *974/501191* 🌐 *www.hotelvalledepineta.com* *26 rooms* *In-room: no a/c. In-hotel: restaurant, bar, pool* 💳 *AE, DC, MC, V* ⏲ *Closed Nov., Jan., and Feb.*

PARQUE NACIONAL DE ORDESA Y MONTE PERDIDO

29 Fodor'sChoice ★ *108 km (67 mi) west of Bielsa; from Aínsa, turn west on N260 for the 53-km (33-mi) drive to Torla (park entrance).*

Ordesa and Monte Perdido National Park is one of Spain's great but often overlooked wonders that some consider a junior version of North America's Grand Canyon. The entrance lies under the vertical walls of Monte Mondarruego, source of the Ara River and its tributary, the Arazas, which forms the famous Ordesa Valley. The park was founded by royal decree in 1918 to protect the natural integrity of the Central Pyrenees, and it has expanded from 4,940 to 56,810 acres as provincial and national authorities have added the Monte Perdido massif, the head of the Pineta Valley, and the Escuain and Añisclo canyons. Defined by the Ara and Arazas rivers, the Ordesa Valley is endowed with pine, fir, larch, beech, and poplar forests; lakes, waterfalls, and high mountain meadows; and protected wildlife, including trout, boar, chamois, and the *Capra pyrenaica* mountain goat.

Well-marked and well-maintained mountain trails lead to waterfalls, caves, and spectacular observation points. The standard tour, a full day's hike (eight hours), runs from the parking area in the Pradera de Ordesa, 8 km (5 mi) northeast of Torla, up the Arazas River, past the *gradas de Soaso* (Soaso risers; a natural stairway of waterfalls) to the *cola de caballo* (horse's tail), a lovely fan of falling water at the head of the Cirque de Cotatuero, a sort of natural amphitheater. A return walk on the south side of the valley, past the Refugio de los Cazadores (hunters' hut), offers a breathtaking view followed by a two-hour descent back to the parking area. A few spots, although not technically difficult, may seem precarious. Information and guidebooks are available at the booth on your way into the park at Pradera de Ordesa. The best time to come is May–mid-November, but check conditions with regional tourist offices before driving into a blizzard in May or missing out on *el veranillo de San Martín* ("Indian summer") in fall. ☎*974/243361 Pradera de Ordesa information office* 🌐*www.mma.es* *Free.*

EN ROUTE

Broto is a prototypical Aragonese mountain town with an excellent 16th-century Gothic church. Nearby villages, such as Oto, have stately manor houses with classic local features: baronial entryways, conical chimneys, and wooden galleries. Torla is the park's entry point and a popular base camp for hikers.

WHERE TO STAY & EAT

$–$$$ ✕ **El Rebeco.** In this graceful and rustic building in the upper part of town, the dining rooms are lined with historic photographs of Torla. The black marble and stone floor and the *cadiera*—a traditional open fireplace room with an overhead smoke vent—are extraordinary. In late fall, *civets* (stews) of deer, boar, and mountain goat are the order of the day. ✉*Calle Lafuente 55, Torla, 22376* ☎*974/486068* ▭*AE, DC, MC, V* ⊙*Closed Dec.–Easter.*

$$ **Villa de Torla.** This rustic gem has rooms in various shapes and sizes, all sharing typical Pyrenean décor featuring wood and stone. Sundecks and terraces and a private dining room make it easy to forget that "Spain's Grand Canyon" is just up the valley. ✉*Pl. Aragón 1, 22376* ☎*974/486156* 📠*974/486365* 🌐*www.hotelvilladetorla.com* *38 rooms* *In-hotel: restaurant, bar, pool, parking* ▭*AE, DC, MC, V.*

6

PANTICOSA & THE TENA VALLEY

30 *40 km (25 mi) west of Ordesa.*

The Valle de Tena, a north–south hexagon of 400 square km (154 square mi), is formed by the Gállego River and its tributaries, principally the Aguaslimpias and the Caldares. A glacial valley surrounded by peaks rising to more than 10,000 feet (such as the 10,900-foot Vignemale), Tena is a busy hiking and winter-sports center. **Sallent de Gállego,** at the head of the valley, has long been a jumping-off point for excursions to **Aguaslimpias, Piedrafita,** and the meadows of the Gállego headwaters at **El Formigal** (a major ski area) and **Portalet.** The lovely Pyrenean *ibon* (glacial lake) of **Respumoso** is accessible by a 2½-hour walk above the old road from Sallent to Formigal. The villages lining the valley are each unique, with Tramacastilla, Escarrilla, and Piedrafita especially representative of ancient Pyrenean village architecture. **Lanuza,** a ghost town since the reservoir built in 1975 flooded half the village, comes alive every summer when a floating stage hosts performers in the Pirineos Sur music festival.

WHERE TO STAY & EAT

$–$$ ✕ **Mesón Sampietro.** This cozy spot not far from Panticosa's lovely church blossoms after the skiing or hiking day ends. The house specialty, potatoes in olive oil, garlic, parsley, and vinegar is not to be missed. Take a seat at a traditional *susulia* bench—they have little fold-down tables between the two seats, making them good for dinner for two in front of a roaring fire. ✉*C. La Parra 5* ☎*974/487244* ▭*AE, DC, MC, V.*

$–$$ **Hotel Vicente.** Rooms here are simple but impeccable and look south over the town to Panticosa's ski area and the jagged peaks of the Sierra de Tendeñera mountains beyond. The lower access spills directly down into town, a five-minute walk from the gondola station. *Ctra. del Balneario 12, Panticosa22661 974/487022 974/487529 www.hotelvicente.com 16 rooms In-room: no a/c, no TV. In-hotel: restaurant AE, DC, MC, V.*

JACA

31 *24 km (15 mi) southwest of Biescas; down the Tena Valley through Biescas, a westward turn at Sabiñánigo onto N330 leaves a 14-km (9-mi) drive to Jaca.*

Jaca, the most important municipal center in Alto Aragón (with a population of more than 15,000), is anything but sleepy. Bursting with ambition, and blessed with the natural resources and first-rate facilities to express their relentless drive, Jacetanos are determined to make their city the site of a Winter Olympics someday. The town is already Spain's winter-sports capital, playing frequent host to major competitions, such as the World Figure Skating Championships and the national King's Cup in ice hockey.

Founded in 1035 as the kingdom of Jacetania, Jaca was an important stronghold during the Christian Reconquest of the Iberian Peninsula and proudly claims never to have bowed to the Moorish invaders. Indeed, the town still commemorates, on the first Friday of May, the decisive battle in which the appearance of a battalion of women, their hair and jewelry flashing in the sun, so intimidated the Moorish cavalry that they beat a headlong retreat.

An important stop on the pilgrimage to Santiago de Compostela, Jaca has the 11th-century **Catedral de Santa María,** one of the oldest in Spain. The **Museo Diocesano,** near the cloisters, is filled with excellent Romanesque and Gothic murals and artifacts. *974/356378 Museo €4 June–Sept., Tues.–Sun. 10–2 and 4–8; Oct.–May, Tues.–Sun. 11–1:30 and 4–7.*

The door to Jaca's **ayuntamiento** *(town hall)* (*Calle Mayor 24 974/355758*), has a notable Renaissance design. The massive **Ciudadella** *(Citadel)* is a good example of 17th-century military architecture. It has a display of thousands of military miniatures. *Av. Primer Viernes de Mayo s/n 974/363018 €4.50 Daily 11–noon and 4–6.*

In summer a free guided tour departs from the local RENFE station, covering the valley and the mammoth, semiderelict belle epoque railroad station at **Canfranc,** surely the largest and most ornate building in the Pyrenees. The train ticket costs €3; ask the tourist office for schedules.

WHERE TO STAY & EAT

$$–$$$$ ✕ **La Cocina Aragonesa.** This Jaca mainstay in the Hotel Conde Aznar, an elegant space decorated with local farming and mountaineering objects and centered around a mammoth fireplace, is known far and wide for fresh and innovative cuisine, especially game in season: venison, wild boar, partridge, duck. Try the partridge stuffed with foie gras. ✉ *Cervantes 5* ☎ *974/361050* ▭ *AE, DC, MC, V* ⏲ *Closed Nov. 15–30 and Wed. June–Sept.*

$–$$$ ✕ **La Tasca de Ana.** Ana's *tasca* (tavern) is one of Jaca's simplest and best. Nearly anyone in town will send you here for superb tapas of every kind. Invent your own meal by starting with a round of olives and working through, say, cured *jamó ibérico* (Iberian ham), *sepia* (cuttlefish), *albóndigas* (meatballs), and *civet de jabalí* (wild-boar stew), concluding with cheese from the neighboring Roncal Valley. ✉ *Pl. Ramiro I 3* ☎ *974/363621* ▭ *AE, DC, MC, V* ⏲ *Closed Mon.*

$–$$ ★ ✕ **El Fau.** Tucked next to the cathedral, El Fau overlooks Jaca's finest carved capitals and serves excellent *cazuelitas,* small earthenware casseroles containing anything from piping-hot garlic shrimp to wild mushrooms. In summer the cold beer here is legendary. ✉ *Pl. de la Catedral* ☎ *974/361719* ▭ *AE, DC, MC, V* ⏲ *Closed Mon.*

$$$ **Gran Hotel.** This rambling hotel, which serves as Jaca's official clubhouse, is central to both life and tourism here. Done up in wood, stone, and glass, it has a garden and a dining wing. The comfortable rooms have rich colors and practical wood furniture. ✉ *Paseo de la Constitución 1, 22700* ☎ *974/360900* 📠 *974/364061* 🌐 *www.inturmark.es* *165 rooms* *In-hotel: restaurant, pool* ▭ *AE, DC, MC, V.*

$–$$ **Hostal Somport.** A good budget option, this tidy little spot in the center of Jaca is halfway between the cathedral and the town hall. The rooms, beds, and baths are all well kept, and the location is an ideal crawling distance from the nearby taverns and music bars on Calle Gil Bergés. ✉ *Calle Echegaray 11, 22700* ☎📠 *974/363410* *17 rooms* *In-room: no a/c. In-hotel: restaurant* ▭ *AE, DC, MC, V.*

NIGHTLIFE

Discos such as **Dimensión** and **Oroel** are thronged with skiers and hockey players in season (October–April), but the main nocturnal attractions are Jaca's so-called *bares musicales* (music bars), usually less loud and smoky than the discos. Most of these are in the old town, around Plaza Ramiro I and along Calle Gil Bergés and Calle Bellido.

SPORTS & THE OUTDOORS

The **ski areas** of Candanchú and Astún are 32 km (20 mi) north of Jaca, on the road to Somport and the French border.

THE WESTERN & BASQUE PYRENEES

The Aragüés, Hecho, and Ansó valleys, drained by the Estarrún, Osia, Veral, and Aragón Subordán rivers, are the westernmost valleys in Aragón and rank among the most pristine parts of the Pyrenees. Today these sleepy hollows are struggling to generate an economy that will save this endangered species of Pyrenean life. With cross-country (Nor-

6

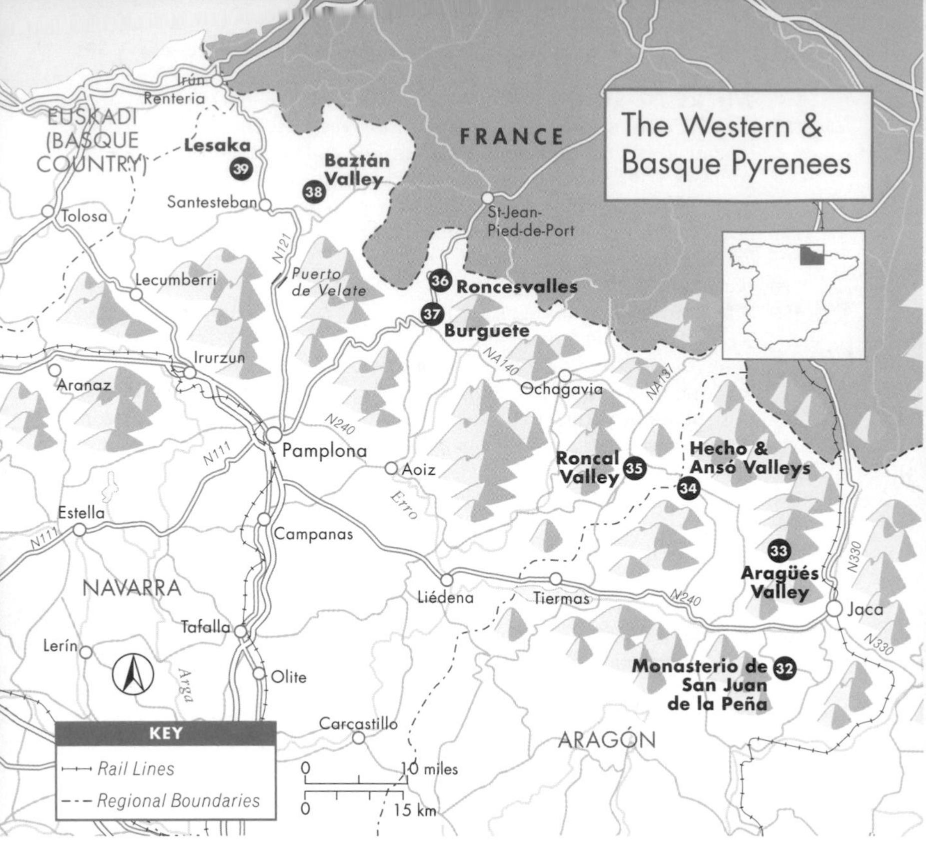

dic) skiing only, they are less frequented by tourists. As you move west into the Roncal Valley and the Basque Country, you will note smoother hills and softer meadows as the rocky central Pyrenees of Aragón begin to descend toward the Bay of Biscay. These wet and fertile uplands and verdant beech forests seem reflected in the wide lines and flat profiles of the Basque *caseríos* (farmhouses) hulking firmly into the landscape. The Basque highlands of Navarra, from Roncal through the Irati Forest to Roncesvalles, and along the Bidasoa River leading down to the Bay of Biscay, all seem like some Arcadian paradise with as the jagged Pyrenean peaks give way to sheep-filled pasturelands.

MONASTERIO DE SAN JUAN DE LA PEÑA

32 *22 km (14 mi) southwest of Jaca.*

★ South of the Aragonese valleys of Hecho and Ansó is the Monastery of San Juan de la Peña, a site connected to the legend of the Holy Grail and another "cradle" of Christian resistance during the 700-year Moorish occupation of Spain. Its origins can be traced to the 9th century, when a hermit monk named Juan settled here on the *peña* (cliff). A monastery was founded on the spot in 920, and in 1071 Sancho Ramirez, son of King Ramiro I, made use of this structure, which was built into the mountain's rock wall, to found the Benedictine Monasterio de San Juan de la Peña. The **cloister**, tucked under the cliff, dates from the 12th century and contains intricately carved capitals depicting biblical scenes. From Jaca, drive 11 km (7 mi) west on N240 toward Pamplona to a left turn clearly signposted for San Juan de la Peña. From there it's another 11 km (7 mi) to the monastery. ✉ *Off N240* ☎ *974/355119* 🌐 *www.monasteriosanjuan.com* 🎫 *€7* ⏲ *Oct.–mid-Mar., Tues.–Sun. 11–1:30 and 4–5:30; mid-Mar.–May, Tues.–Sun. 10–1:30 and 4–7; June–Sept., daily 10–noon and 4–8.*

EN ROUTE

To get to the westernmost Pyrenean valleys in Aragón from Jaca, head west on N240 for 20 km (12 mi), take a hard right at Puente de la Reina (after turning right to cross the bridge), and continue north along the Aragón-Subordán River. The first right after 15 km (9 mi) leads into the Aragüés Valley along the Osla River to Aisa and then Jasa.

ARAGÜÉS VALLEY

33 *Aragüés del Puerto is 2 km (1 mi) from Jasa.*

Aragüés del Puerto is a tidy mountain village with stone houses and lovely little corners, doorways, and porticoes. The distinctive folk dance in Aragüés is the *palotiau,* a variation of the *jota* performed only in this village. The **Museo Etnográfico** *(Ethnographic Museum),* in an ancient chapel in Aragüés del Puerto (ask for the caretaker at the town hall), offers a look into the past, from the document witnessing the 878 election of Iñigo Arista as king of Pamplona to the quirky manual wheat grinder. At the source of the River Osia, the Lizara **cross-country ski area** is in a flat expanse between the Aragüés and Jasa valleys. Look for 3,000-year-old megalithic dolmens sprinkled across the flat.

HECHO & ANSÓ VALLEYS

34 *Hecho Valley is 49 km (30 mi) northwest of Jaca; Ansó Valley is 25 km (15 mi) west of Hecho.*

You can reach the Valle de Hecho from the Aragüés Valley by returning to the valley of the Aragón-Subordan and turning north again on the A176.

The **Monasterio de San Pedro de Siresa,** above the town of Hecho, is the area's most important monument, a 9th-century retreat of which only the 11th-century church remains. *Cheso,* a medieval Aragonese dialect descended from the Latin spoken by the Siresa monks, is thought to be the closest to Latin of all Romance languages and dialects. Cheso has been kept alive in the Hecho Valley, especially in the works of the poet Veremundo Mendez Coarasa. ✉ *Calle San Pedro, Siresa* 🎫 *Free* ⏲ *July and Aug., daily 11–1 and 5–8; other months, call the Ayuntamiento de Siresa (☎ 974/375002) for key.*

The **Selva de Oza** *(Oza Forest),* at the head of the Hecho Valley, is above the **Boca del Infierno** (Mouth of Hell), a tight draw where road and river barely squeeze through.Beyond the Oza Forest is a **Roman road** used before the 4th century to reach France through the Puerto del Palo—one of the oldest routes across the border on the pilgrimage to Santiago de Compostela.

The **Valle de Ansó** is Aragón's western limit. Rich in fauna (mountain goats, wild boar, and even a bear or two), the Ansó Valley follows the Veral River up to Zuriza. The three **cross-country ski areas** above Zuriza are known as the Pistas de Linza. Near Fago is the sanctuary of the **Virgen de Puyeta,** patron saint of the valley. Towering over the head of the valley is Navarra's highest point, the 7,989-foot **Mesa de los Tres Reyes** *(Plateau of the Three Kings)*, named not for the Magi but for the kings of Aragón, Navarra, and Castile, whose 11th-century kingdoms all came to a corner here—allowing them to meet without leaving their respective realms. Try to be in the town of **Ansó** on the last Sunday in August, when residents dress in their traditional medieval costumes and perform ancestral dances of great grace and dignity.

WHERE TO STAY & EAT

$ **Gaby-Casa Blasquico.** This cozy inn, famed as Hecho's top restaurant ($–$$$), is known for its Aragonese mountain cuisine. Especially strong on game recipes from wild boar to venison to partridge or migratory pigeon, the menu also lists lamb and vegetable dishes. Make sure you call ahead: Gaby often opens for anyone who reserves in advance, even if the place is theoretically closed. *Pl. Palacio 1, Hecho 974/375007 Reservations essential 6 rooms In-room: no a/c. In-hotel: restaurant MC, V Closed 1st 2 wks in Sept.; restaurant closed weekdays Sept.–Holy Week.*

$$ **Usón.** For a base to explore the upper Hecho Valley or the Oza Forest, look no further. The staff at this friendly little Pyrenean inn will tell you where to rent a bike, get you a trout-fishing permit, or send you off in the right direction for a climb or hike. Rooms are simple and airy, decorated with colorful fabrics and quilts. *Ctra. Selva de Oza, HU2131, Km 7, Usón, 22720 974/375358 www.hoteluson.com 14 rooms In-room: no a/c. In-hotel: restaurant MC, V Closed Nov. 2–Mar. 15.*

RONCAL VALLEY

35 *17½ km (11 mi) west of Ansó Valley.*

The Roncal Valley, the eastern edge of the Basque Pyrenees, is famous for its sheep's-milk cheese, Roncal, and as the birthplace of Julián Gayarre (1844–90), the leading tenor of his time. The 34-km (21-mi) drive through the towns of **Burgui** and **Roncal** to **Isaba** winds through green hillsides and Basque *caseríos*, which house both farming families and their livestock. Burgui's red-tile roofs backed by rolling pastures contrast with the vertical rock and steep slate roofs of the Aragonese and Catalan Pyrenees; Isaba's wide-arched bridge across the Esca is a graceful reminder of Roman aesthetics and engineering techniques. To get to the valley from Jaca, take N240 west along the Aragón River; a right turn north on NA137 follows the Esca River from the head of the Yesa Reservoir up the Roncal Valley.

Try to be in the Roncal Valley for **El Tributo de las Tres Vacas** *(the Tribute of the Three Cows)*, which has been celebrated every July 13 since 1375. The mayors of the valley's villages, dressed in traditional gowns, gather near the summit of San Martín to receive the symbolic payment of three cows from their French counterparts, in memory of the settlement of ancient border disputes. Feasting and celebrating follow.

The road west (NA140) to **Ochagavia** through the Puerto de Lazar (Lazar Pass) has views of the Anie and Orhi peaks, towering over the French border. Two kilometers (1 mi) south of Ochagavia, at Escároz, a small secondary roadway winds 22 km (14 mi) over the Abaurrea heights to **Aribe,** known for its triple-arched medieval bridge and ancient *horreo* (granary). A 15-km (9-mi) detour north through the town of Orbaiceta up to the headwaters of the Irati River, at the Irabia Reservoir, gets you a good look at the **Selva de Irati** *(Irati Forest)*, one of Europe's major beech forests and the source of much of the timber for the fleet Spain commanded during her 15th-century golden age.

6

RONCESVALLES

36 ★ *2½ km (1½ mi) north of Burguete, 48 km (30 mi) north of Pamplona, 64 km (40 mi) northwest of Isaba in the Roncal Valley.*

Roncesvalles (often listed as Orreaga, in Euskera) is the site of the Colegiata, cloister, hospital, and 12th-century **chapel of Santiago,** the first Navarran church on the Santiago pilgrimage route.The **Colegiata** (*Collegiate Church* ✉ *Ctra. Pamplona–Francia, [N135], KM 48* 🌐 *www.roncesvalles.es*), built at the orders of King Sancho VII el Fuerte (the Strong), houses the king's tomb, which measures more than 7 feet long. The 3,468-foot **Ibañeta Pass,** above Roncesvalles, is a gorgeous route into France. A **menhir** (monolith) marks the traditional site of the legendary battle in *The Song of Roland* in which Roland fell after calling for help on his ivory battle horn. The well-marked eight hour walk to or from St-Jean-Pied-de-Port is one of the most beautiful and dramatic sections of the pilgrimage.

BURGUETE

37 *2½ km (1½ mi) south of Roncesvalles, 120 km (75 mi) northwest of Jaca.*

Burguete (Auritz in Euskera) lies between two mountain streams forming the headwaters of the Urobi River. The town was immortalized in Ernest Hemingway's *The Sun Also Rises*, with its evocative description of trout fishing in an ice-cold stream above a Navarran village.

WHERE TO STAY & EAT

$–$$ ✕🏨 **Hostal Burguete.** Hemingway's character Jake Barnes spends a few days here clearing his head before plunging back into the psychodrama of the San Fermín Festival and his impossible passion for Lady

Brett Ashley. The inn still works for this sort of thing, though there don't seem to be as many trout around these days. Good value and simple Navarran cooking ($–$$$) make this stalwart Basque town house a good stop for a meal or a night. With a little luck you can even sleep in Hemingway's bed; his room is kept exactly as it was when the novelist bunked here in the summer of 1924. ✉ *Calle Única 51, 31640* ☎ *948/760005* 📠 *948/790488* *22 rooms* *In-room: no a/c. In-hotel: restaurant, no elevator* 💳 *AE, DC, MC, V* ⏲ *Closed Feb. and Mar.*

EN ROUTE

To skip Pamplona and stay on the trans-Pyrenean route, continue 21 km (13 mi) southwest of Burguete on NA135 until you reach NA138, just before Zubiri. A right turn takes you to Urtasun, where the small NA252 leads left to the town of Iragui and over the pass at Col d'Egozkue (from which there are superb views over the Arga and Ultzana River valleys) to Olagüe, where it connects with NA121 some 20 km (12 mi) north of Pamplona. Turn right onto N121A and climb over the Puerto de Velate (Velate Pass)—or, in bad weather or a hurry, through the tunnel—to the turn for Elizondo and the Baztán Valley, N121B.

BAZTÁN VALLEY

38 *80 km (50 mi) north of Pamplona.*

Tucked neatly over the headwaters of the Bidasoa River and under the peak of the 3,545-foot Garramendi Mountain, which looms over the border with France, the rounded green hills of the Valle de Baztán make an ideal halfway stop between the central Pyrenees and the Atlantic. Each village in this enchanted Basque valley seems smaller and simpler than the next: tiny clusters of whitewashed, stone-and-mortar houses with red-tile roofs group around a central *frontón* (handball court).

WHERE TO STAY & EAT

$–$$$ ★ **Galarza.** The kitchen in this stone town house overlooking the Baztán River turns out excellent Basque fare, with a Navarran emphasis on vegetables. Try the *txuritabel* (roast lamb with a special stuffing of egg and vegetables), which is best in the spring (though available year-round), or *txuleta de ternera* (veal raised in the valley), good anytime of year. ✉ *Calle Santiago 1, Elizondo* ☎ *948/580101* 💳 *MC, V* ⏲ *Closed late Sept.–early Oct.*

$ ★ **Fonda Etxeberria.** In an old farmhouse with creaky floorboards and oak doors, this tiny in has small, handsome rooms. The palatial bathrooms are shared by guests (usually one bathroom per two to three rooms). The restaurant ($–$$) prepares simple country dishes such as *alubias de Navarra estofadas* (Navarran white beans stewed with chorizo) and roast lamb. ✉ *Kalea Antxitonea Trinketea (next to frontón court) s/n, 31700 Arizkun* ☎ *948/453013* 📠 *948/453433* *16 rooms without bath* *In-room: no a/c, no TV. In-hotel: restaurant, no elevator* 💳 *MC, V.*

LESAKA

 *21 km (13 mi) west of Elizondo in the Baztán Valley, 71 km (43 mi) northwest of Pamplona.*

If you're around for Pamplona's Festival of San Fermín (July 6–14), stop at Lesaka, just 2 km (1 mi) off the N121. Lesaka's patron saint is also San Fermín, and its *sanfermines txikos* (little San Fermín fests) may more closely resemble the one described in *The Sun Also Rises* than Pamplona's modern-day international beer brawl does.

THE PYRENEES ESSENTIALS

To research prices, get advice from other travelers, and book travel arrangements, visit www.fodors.com.

TRANSPORTATION

For more on travel to and in the Pyrenees, see the Pyrenees Planner at the beginning of the chapter.

6

BY AIR

Barcelona's international airport, El Prat de Llobregat (⇨chapter 7), is the largest gateway to the Catalan Pyrenees. Farther west, the airports at Zaragoza, Pamplona, and Hondarribia (Fuenterrabía) serve the Pyrenees of Aragón, Navarra, and the Basque Country. From Madrid, fly to Barcelona on Iberia's shuttle, or fly any of several airlines to Hondarribia or Pamplona.

Carrier **Iberia shuttle** (☎ *902/400500* ⊕ *www.iberia.com*).

BY BIKE

Because most roads do not include extra pavement for bicyclists, travel across the Pyrenees is challenging and somewhat dangerous. Experienced cyclists recommend "taking the road," that is, fully occupying a lane, as the safest way to travel. The best cycling options are local day trips and mountain-bike circuits on off-road tracks, trails, former railroad lines, and livestock paths. (Check with local tourist offices for details.) Generally, trans-Pyrenean biking is a series of long, grueling ascents and vertiginous, perilous descents that ought to be tackled only by experienced cyclists.

Bike Rentals **Ciclos Larequi** (✉ *Av. de Zaragoza 56, Pamplona* ☎ *948/150645*). **Deportes Aïgualluts** (✉ *Av. de los Tilos s/n, Benasque* ☎ *974/551215*). **Deportes Azus** (✉ *Villanúa, Jaca* ☎ *974/378217*). **El Baúl** (✉ *Av. de Francia, Benasque* ☎ *974/551030*). **Esports Iris** (✉ *Av. de Francia, Duana, near French border at Bourg Madame, Puigcerdà* ☎ *972/882398*). **Top Bike** (✉ *Pla d'Arenes, Ctra. Nacional 152, Puigcerdà* ☎ *972/882042*). **Vit's** (✉ *Pl. Mayor s/n, Benasque* ☎ *974/552088*).

BY BUS

Bus Lines **Ágreda La Oscense** (✉ *Paseo María Agustín 7, Zaragoza* ☎ *976/229343* ✉ *Estación Intermodal, Ronda de la Estación s/n, Huesca* ☎ *974/210700*). **Alsina Graells** (✉ *Calle Ali Bei 80, Barcelona* ☎ *93/265–6508* ✉ *Av. Garriga i Masó s/n,*

La Seu d'Urgell ☎ *972/350020* ✉ *Calle Saracibar s/n, Lleida* ☎ *973/271470*). **La Baztanesa** (✉ *Calle Conde Oliveta 6, Pamplona* ☎ *948/226712*). **La Roncalesa** (✉ *Estación de Autobuses, Calle Conde Oliveta 6, Pamplona* ☎ *948/222079*).

Bus Stations Barcelona Nord (✉ *Alí Bei 80, Barcelona* ☎ *902/260606*). **Huesca** (✉ *Ronda de la Estación s/n, Huesca* ☎ *974/210700*). **La Seu d'Urgell** (✉ *Av. Garriga i Masó s/n, La Seu d'Urgell* ☎ *973/350020*). **Lleida** (✉ *Saracibar s/n, Lleida* ☎ *973/271470*). **Pamplona** (✉ *Calle Conde Oliveta 6, Pamplona* ☎ *948/226712*).

Zaragoza (✉ *Paseo María Agustín 7, Zaragoza* ☎ *976/229343*).

BY CAR

Rental Agencies Avis (✉ *Carrer Casanova 209, Barcelona* ☎ *93/209–9533* 🌐 *www.avis.com*). **Europcar** (✉ *Carrer Viladomat 214, Barcelona* ☎ *93/439–8403 Estació de Sants 93/491–4822* 🌐 *www.europcar.com*). **Hertz** (✉ *Carrer Còrsega 293, Barcelona* ☎ *93/237–5680* 🌐 *www.hertz.com*). **Avis** (✉ *Calle Triunfo 2, San Sebastián* ☎ *943/461527* 🌐 *www.avis.com*). **Hertz** (✉ *Calle Zubieta 5, San Sebastián* ☎ *943/461084* 🌐 *www.avis.com*).

BY TRAIN

There are three small train stations deep in the Pyrenees: Puigcerdà, in the Cerdanya Valley; Pobla de Segur, in the Noguera Pallaresa Valley; and Canfranc, north of Jaca, below the Candanchú and Astún ski resorts. The larger gateways are Huesca and Lleida. From Madrid, connect through Barcelona for the eastern Pyrenees, Zaragoza and Huesca for the central Pyrenees, and Pamplona or San Sebastián for the western Pyrenees.

Contact RENFE (☎ *902/240202* 🌐 *www.renfe.es*).

SPORTS & THE OUTDOORS

FISHING

Ramón Cosiallf and Danica can take you fly-fishing anywhere in the world by horse or helicopter, but the Pyrenees are their home turf. For about €145 a day (depending on equipment), you'll be whisked to high Pyrenean lakes and ponds, streams, and rivers and armed with equipment and expertise. You can buy a fishing license for each autonomous region (Catalonia, Aragón, Navarra) at local rod-and-gun clubs, known as Asociaciones de Pesca and/or Caza. In Puigcerdà, licenses are available weekdays 9–2 at the office of Agricultura, Ramadería i Pesca.

Information Agricultura, Ramadería i Pesca (✉ *Calle de la Percha 17, Puigcerdà* ☎ *972/880515* 🌐 *www.gencat.net/darp* ✉ *Av. Meridiana 38, Barcelona* ☎ *93/409–2090*).

Danica (☎ *659/735376 or 974/553493* 🌐 *www.danicaguias.com*). **Departamento de Medio Ambiente** (✉ *Travessera de Gràcia 56, Barcelona* ☎ *93/567–0815* 🌐 *www.gencat.net/mediamb*).

SKIING

Spain's daily newspaper, *El País,* prints complete ski information every Friday in season (December–mid-April). For an up-to-the-minute ski report in Spanish or Catalan, call the ski-report hotline in Barcelona. For general information, contact the Catalan Winter Sports Federation.

Information **Federació Catalana Esports d'Hivern** (*Catalan Winter Sports Federation* ✉ *Carrer Casp 38, Barcelona* ☎ *93/415–5544* 🌐 *www.fceh.cat*). **Ski report** (☎ *93/416–0194* 🌐 *www.skiinfo.com/snowreport*).

CONTACTS & RESOURCES

EMERGENCIES

Emergency Services **General emergency** (☎ *091*). **Red Cross** (☎ *972/216400 in Girona, 974/221186 in Huesca, 973/267011 in Lleida, 948/203540 in Navarra*). **Police** (☎ *972/201381 in Girona, 974/244711 in Huesca, 973/245012 in Lleida, 948/237000 in Navarra*).

INTERNET, MAIL & SHIPPING

Most hotels, especially in the larger cities and towns of Puigcerdà, La Seu d'Urgell, Vielha, Benasque, Vielha, Zaragoza, and Jaca, provide free Internet access—getting online is now more the rule than the exception.

Federal Express and DHL Offices (local transporters are MRW and SEUR) are available only in larger Pyrenean destinations.

Internet Cafés **Change** (✉ *C. Jardiel s/n, Zaragoza* ☎ *976/297625*). **Ciberciva** (✉ *Av. Regimiento Galicia 2, Jaca* ☎ *974/356775*).

Cybercafé (✉ *Pl. Coto Marzo 1, Vielha* ☎ *973/641156*). **La Biblioteca de la Casa de la Cultura** (✉ *San Sebastián 5, Benasque* ☎ *974/551289*). **Oficina de Turismo del Consell Comarcal** (✉ *Pg. Joan Brudieu, La Seu d'Urgell* ☎ *973/353112*). **Online** (✉ *Carrer d'Espanya 23, Puigcerdà* ☎ *972/140820*). **Osc@.com** (✉ *C. San José de Calasanz 13, Huesca* ☎ *974/292166*).

Courier Services **MRW** ✉ *Calle Huesca 2, Jaca* ☎ *974/356031* ✉ *Av. de Francia Edificio Balbenus (bajos), Benasque* ☎ *974/551722* ✉ *Valles de Andorra s/n, La Seu d'Urgell* ☎ *973/354499* ✉ *Calle Breton 48, Zaragoza* ☎ *976/357600.* **SEUR** ✉ *C/Agricultura, Polígono Industrial Lucas Mayadas, Huesca* ☎ *974/229970* ✉ *Carrer Escoles Pies 9, Puigcerdà* ☎ *972/880602* ✉ *Polígono Industrial de Mig Aran, Vielha* ☎ *973/640588.*

TOUR OPTIONS

The Puigcerdà travel agency Touring Cerdanya can arrange guides, horses, or jeeps for treks to upper lakes, peaks, and meadows.

Contact **Touring Cerdanya** (✉ *Escuelas Pías 19, Puigcerdà* ☎ *972/880602 or 972/881450*).

6

VISITOR INFORMATION

Regional Tourist Offices **Barcelona** (✉ *Palau Robert, Passeig de Gràcia 107, at Av. Diagonal* ☎ *93/238–4000*). **Girona** (✉ *Rambla de la Llibertat 1* ☎ *972/202679*). **Huesca** (✉ *Calle Coso Alto 23* ☎ *974/225778*). **Lleida** (✉ *Pl. de la Paeria 11* ☎ *973/248120*). **Navarra** (✉ *Av. Duque de Ahumada 3, Pamplona* ☎ *948/211287*). **Zaragoza (Aragón)** (✉ *Calle Torreon de la Zuda, Glorieta de Pío XII* ☎ *976/393537*).

Local Tourist Offices **Aínsa** (✉ *Av. Pirenaica 1* ☎ *974/500767*). **Benasque** (✉ *Pl. Mayor 5* ☎ *974/551289*). **Bielsa** (✉ *Pl. del Ayuntamiento* ☎ *974/501000*). **Camprodón** (✉ *Pl. Espanya 1* ☎ *972/740010*). **Jaca** (✉ *Av. Rgto. Galicia* ☎ *974/360098*). **La Seu d'Urgell** (✉ *Av. Valira s/n* ☎ *973/351511*). **Panticosa** (✉ *C. San Miguel s/n* ☎ *974/487318*). **Puigcerdà** (✉ *Carrer Querol 1* ☎ *972/880542*). **Sant Joan de les Abadesses** (✉ *Pl. de la Abadía 9* ☎ *972/720599*). **Taüll** (✉ *Av. Valira s/n* ☎ *973/694000*). **Vielha** (✉ *Av. Castiero 15* ☎ *973/641196*).

Barcelona

The mid-13th century arcaded square Plaça Reial

7

WORD OF MOUTH

"Barcelona offers a staggering variety of pleasures, from early architecture in the Gothic Quarter to the Boqueria market's wealth of food products, to beach time and seafood in La Barceloneta."

—Billy M.

"A flamenco concert at the Palau de la Música Catalana with a tapa before and a light but delicious dinner at Cal Pep afterwards did it for me: Barcelona rocks."

—Susan

www.fodors.com/forums

WELCOME TO BARCELONA

★ **La Boqueria:** Barcelona's in-town produce market is the most exciting midcity cornucopia in the world. Try *Pinotxo* or *Quim de la Boqueria* for top tastes.

★ **Santa Maria del Mar:** Peerless Mediterranean Gothic style: a sweeping display of form and line. Hearing Renaissance polyphony in this architectural gem is the ultimate.

★ **La Sagrada Família:** Gaudí's stalagmites, stalactites, and cylindrical towers add up to the city's most surprising architectural marvel.

★ **El Palau de la Música Catalana:** Cavalry erupts from the wings, a stained-glass chandelier plummets from above: this Art Nouveau tour de force is alive with music before the first note sounds.

★ **Castellers & Sardanas:** Human castles and Catalonia's national dance, two of the beloved symbols for this nation-within-a-nation.

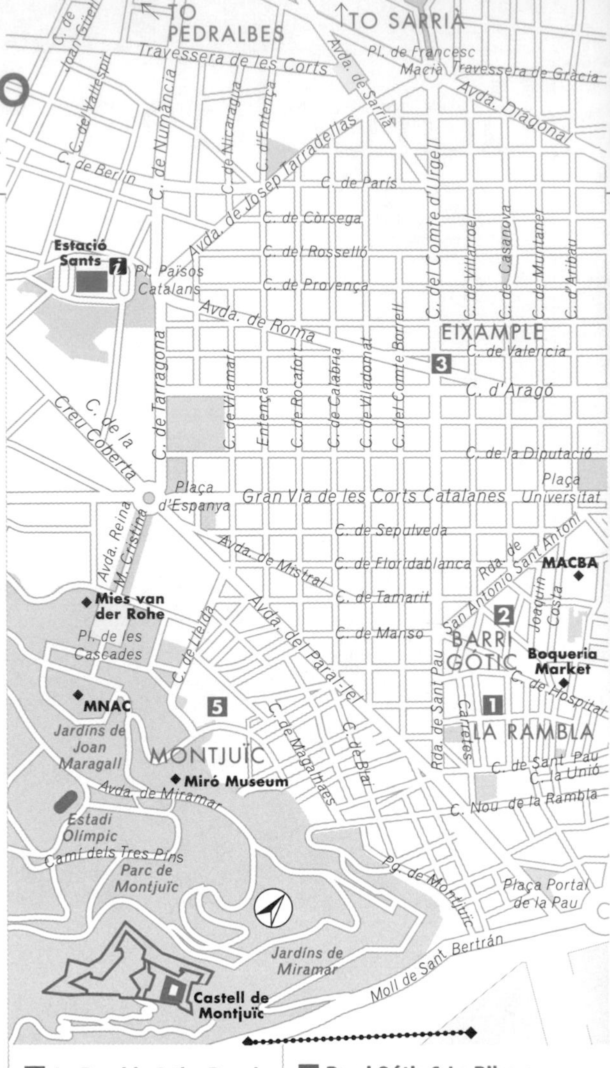

1 La Rambla & the Raval. La Rambla is the place to begin, home of the Boqueria market, the city's heart and soul (not to mention stomach). The Raval behind it holds everything from a medieval hospital to Gaudí buildings to the contemporary art museum MACBA.

2 Barri Gótic & La Ribera. Barcelona's Gothic Quarter lies north of the Rambla around the cathedral, a jumble of ancient streets filled with shops, cafés, and tiny squares. La Ribera, across Via Laietena farther north, centers on Santa Maria del Mar.

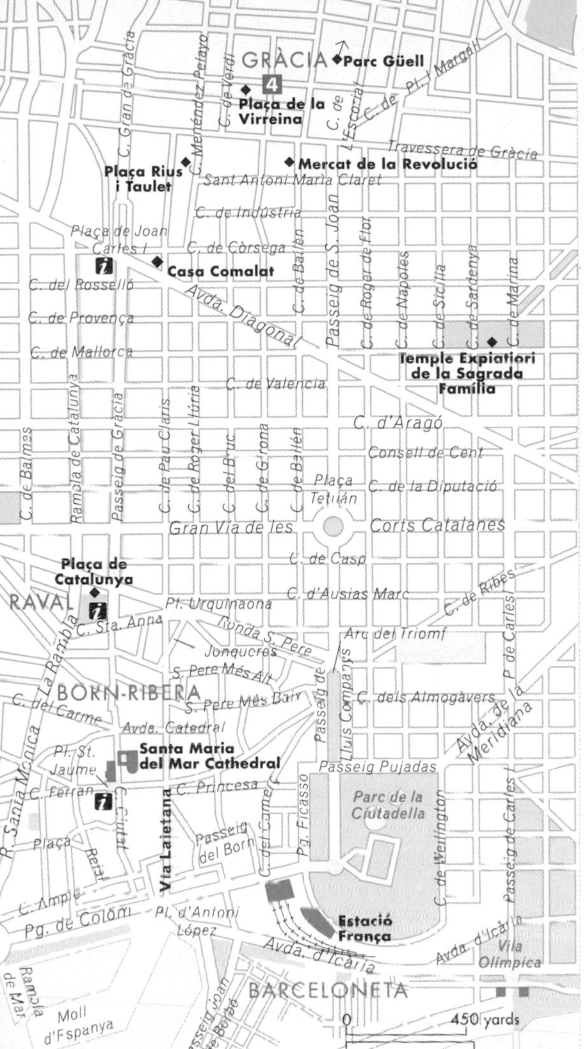

GETTING ORIENTED

Barcelona is a multi-sensory feast ranging from the Rambla's human variety show and the Boqueria market's celebration of fruit, fish, and food of all kinds, to the beaches, the steamy corners of the Born or the wide boulevards of the Eixample's Moderniste grid. Gaudí will take you into the onetime outlying villages of Gràcia and Sarrià, while paintings will lead you to the Montjuïc promontory and musical pursuits are held inside the city's finest architecture. In a city addicted to the avant-guard, uncommon originality is a common virtue.

7

3 The Eixample. The post 1860-Eixample spreads out above Plaça Catalunya and contains most of the city's Art Nouveau (In Spanish,"Modernista"; in Catalan, Moderniste) architecture, including Gaudí's iconic Sagrada Família church, along with hundreds of shops and places to eat.

4 Upper Barcelona. Mazelike Gràcia nestles above the rational Diagonal with Gaudí's Parc Güell at its upper edge. Sarrià and Pedralbes spread out farther west, with two Gaudí buildings, the city's finest monastery and cloister, and a rustic village trapped by urban encroachment in a pastoral time warp.

5 Montjuïc. The promontory over the south side of the city lacks the street vibe and excitement of the Rambla or the Gràcia, but the artistic treasures massed here are not to be missed: Miró, the MNAC, Mies van der Rohe, and Caixafòrum.

BARCELONA PLANNER

When to Go

Summer can be uncomfortably hot in Barcelona, and many of the finest restaurants and musical venues are closed. On the other hand, El Grec, the summer music festival, is a delight, and the August Gràcia Festa Major is a hoot, while the whole city becomes an extension of Barceloneta Beach, which is not without its attractions. October through June is the time to come to observe Barcelona's daily hum, with mid-November–early April pleasantly cool and the rest of the time ideally warm. Late September's Festa de la Mercé is a blowout not to miss; winter's Carnaval and calçot (long-stemmed onions) season are spectacular and delicious, and April and May are best of all: the Sant Jordi lovers' day on April 23 and the Sant Ponç celebration of natural produce in early May are the most magical moments of the year.

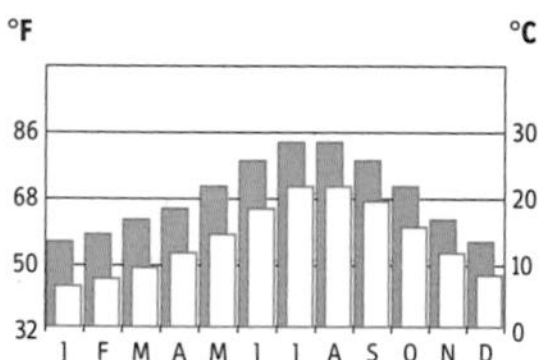

Getting There & Around

Barcelona's El Prat de Llobregat Airport, 7 km (4½ mi) south of the city, receives international flights from all over the world. Low-cost flights such as Ryanair land in Girona, an hour north of Barcelona. Getting to the city from the airport is easiest by taxi, but the bus to Plaça Catalunya (€4.75) leaves from directly in front of each terminal and is about as fast as a taxi and a fraction of the cost. From Plaça Catalunya a taxi to your hotel (€20–€25), can be easily flagged down. Car rental agencies in Barcelona are at the airport and at Sants train station. The T-10 ticket (€7), valid for metro or bus, is an essential resource. The FCG (Ferrocarril de la Generalitat) train from Plaça Catalunya through the center of town to Sarrià and outlying cities is a commuter train that gets you to within walking distance of nearly everything in Barcelona. Transfers to the regular city metro are free. A prime taxi stand is at the head of the Rambla on Plaça Catalunya, though lines often form there. A better choice is the one at Plaça Sant Jaume, at the center of the Gothic Quarter. Cabdrivers generally refuse to respond to a hail within 200 yards of a taxi stand, referring you to the line at the stand instead. Long-distance trains arrive and depart from Estació de Sants. En route to or from Sants, some trains stop at another station on Passeig de Gràcia at Carrer Aragó; this can be a good way to avoid the long lines that form at Sants during holidays, though even better is dealing directly with www.renfe.es. For schedules and fares, call RENFE at 902/240202. City buses run daily from 5:30 AM to 11:30 PM. The fare is €1.30. For multiple journeys purchase a Targeta T-10. Route maps are displayed at bus stops. Note that those with a red band always stop at a central square—Catalunya, Universitat, or Urquinaona—and blue indicates a night bus.

See the Barcelona Essentials at the end of this chapter for more transportation information.

Barcelona for Culture Vultures

Musical events in Barcelona's many venues are well worth pretrip plannning. Check schedules for the Liceu opera house, the Palau de la Música Catalana, the Auditori, or the many churches (especially Santa Maria del Mar) that hold concerts and recitals. Performances of Haendel's Messiah at Christmas and Mozart's Requiem at Easter, sometimes performed by top international ensembles such as London's The Sixteen, must be booked well in advance. Between early tapas and late-night restaurant options, there is rarely a need to choose between Orpheus and Epicurus in Barcelona; in fact, a 9 pm catharsis of Bach or Beethoven can leave you ravenous for dinner at 11.

El Pais and La Vanguardia have daily listings for art openings and concerts, many free, under their Agenda headings. Keeping an eye on these listings can guide you to some of Barcelona's best events, often with tapas and cava included. Performances of Castellers, the human pyramid squads unique to Catalonia, are announced in the weekend agenda section. La Guia del Ocio comes out every Thursday and lists the top musical and cultural events for the week along with all restaurants and different varieties of nocturnal activities. Many hotels hand out this guide gratis.

Foodies: reserve well in advance for Barcelona's top gourmet restaurants, including Àbac, Comerç 24, Arola, Neichel, Drolma, Moo, El Racó d'en Freixa, Alkimia, Caelis and, especially, Santi Santamariá's Can Fabes outside of town in Sant Celoni and Carmen Ruscalleda's Sant Pau in Sant Pol de Mar. Ferran Adrià's El Bulli in Roses is generally impossible to book, serves dinner only from April through September, and while an otherworldly experience is a pilgrimage for only the most devoted gourmand.

Futbol Club Barcelona, 2006 European Champions and Spain's one of Spain's top teams , plays every other week in Camp Nou.

WHAT IT COSTS In Euros

	$$$$	$$$	$$	$	¢
RESTAURANTS	over €25	€18–€25	€12–€18	€8–€12	under €8
HOTELS	over €225	€150–€225	€80–€150	€50–€80	under €50

Restaurant prices are per person for a main course at dinner. Hotel prices are for two people in a standard double room in high season, excluding tax.

Planning Your Time

The Rambla is the place to begin, starting from Plaça Catalunya and moving toward the Port. The Boqueria market captures the colors and aromas of Mediterranean life. Stop by the Liceu opera house, Plaça Reial, and Gaudí's Palau Güell. The Gothic Quarter is a warren of Roman and medieval alleys. Once the Roman Forum, Plaça Sant Jaume stretches between the municipal and Catalonian government palaces. Across Via Laietana, the neighborhoods of La Ribera and El Born are centered on the exquisite Mediterranean Gothic Santa Maria del Mar. The recently redesigned Picasso Museum is just a step away. A 20-minute walk gets you to Barceloneta, the traditional fisherman's quarter, with a dozen good seafood restaurants. El Raval is a good morning's walk, home of the medieval hospital, one of the city's finest Gothic spaces. Gràcia, and Sarrià are each good half-day explorations. Finally, hit Montjuïc to catch the Museu Nacional d'Art de Catalunya.

7

By George Semler

CAPITAL OF CATALONIA, 2,000-YEAR-OLD BARCELONA commanded a vast Mediterranean empire when Madrid was still a dusty Moorish outpost on the Spanish steppe. Relegated to second-city status only after Madrid became the seat of the royal court in 1561, Barcelona has long rivaled and often surpassed Madrid's supremacy. One of Europe's most visually stunning cities, Barcelona balances the medieval intimacy of its Gothic Quarter with the grace and distinction of the wide boulevards in the Moderniste Eixample—just as the Mediterranean Gothic elegance of the church of Santa Maria del Mar provides a perfect counterpoint to Gaudí's riotous Sagrada Família. Mies van der Rohe's pavilion seems even more minimalist after a look at the Art Nouveau Palau de la Música Catalana, and such exciting contemporary creations as Bofill's neoclassical, Parthenon-under-glass Teatre Nacional de Catalunya, Frank Gehry's waterfront goldfish, Norman Foster's Torre de Collserola, and Jean Nouvel's Torre Agbar all add spice to Barcelona's visual soup. Meanwhile, Barcelona's fashion industry is pulling even with those of Paris and Milan, and FC (Futbol Club) is Barcelona a perennial contender for European Championships and the world's most glamorous soccer club.

Barcelona has long had a frenetically active cultural life. It was the home of architect Antoni Gaudí, whose buildings are the most startling statements of Modernisme. Other leading Moderniste architects include Lluís Domènech i Montaner and Josep Puig i Cadafalch. The painters Joan Miró, Salvador Dalí, and Antoni Tàpies are also strongly identified with Catalonia. Pablo Picasso spent his formative years in Barcelona, and one of the city's treasures is a museum devoted to his works. Barcelona's opera house, the Liceu, is the finest in Spain; and the city claims such native Catalan musicians as cellist Pablo (Pau, in Catalan) Casals, opera singers Montserrat Caballé and José (Josep) Carreras, and early music master Jordi Savall.

In 133 BC the Roman Empire annexed the city. The Visigoths roared down from the north in the 5th century; the Moors invaded in the 8th; and in 801 the Franks under Charlemagne captured the city and made it their buffer zone at the edge of the Moors' Iberian empire. By 988, the autonomous Catalonian counties had gained independence from the Franks. Not until 1137 was Catalonia united through marriage with the House of Aragón, and yet another marriage, that of Ferdinand II of Aragón and Isabella of Castile (and queen of León) in 1474, brought Aragón and Catalonia into a united Spain. As the capital of Aragón's Mediterranean empire, Barcelona grew powerful between the 12th and the 14th centuries and began to falter only when maritime emphasis shifted to the Atlantic after 1492. Despite Madrid being the seat of Spain's Royal Court, Catalonia enjoyed autonomous rights and privileges until 1714, when, in reprisal for having backed the Austrian Hapsburg pretender to the Spanish throne, all institutions and expressions of Catalan identity were suppressed by Felipe V of the French Bourbon dynasty. Not until the mid-19th century would Barcelona's industrial growth bring about a renaissance of nationalism and a cultural flowering that recalled Catalonia's former opulence.

Catalan nationalism continued to strengthen in the 20th century. After the abdication of Alfonso XIII and the establishment of the Second Spanish Republic in 1931, Catalonia enjoyed autonomy and cultural freedom. Once again backing a losing cause, Barcelona was a Republican stronghold and hotbed of anti-fascist sentiment during the 1936–39 civil war, with the result that Catalan language and identity were suppressed under the 1939–75 Francisco Franco regime by such means as book burning, the renaming of towns, and the banning of the Catalan language in schools and the media. This repression had little lasting effect; Catalans jealously guard their language and culture and generally think of themselves as Catalans first, Spaniards second.

Catalonian home rule was granted after Franco's death in 1975, and Catalonia's governing body, the ancient Generalitat, was reinstated in 1980. Catalan is now Barcelona's co-official language, along with Castilian Spanish, and is eagerly promoted through free classes funded by the Generalitat. Street names are signposted in Catalan, and newspapers, radio stations, and a TV channel publish and broadcast in Catalan. The triumphant culmination of this rebirth, the definitive display of Catalan power, independence, business acumen, and creativity, was the staging of the Olympics in 1992. Using, in large part, funding from Madrid, Catalonia not only announced its existence to the world at large, but constructed ring roads and freeways, renovated stadiums and pools, created new harborside promenades, and moved an entire set of train tracks to make way for the Olympic Village. In the 21st century, innovative structures, such as Jean Nouvel's gherkin-like Torre Agbar or the Ricardo Bofill Vela (Sail) Hotel (still under construction), demonstrate Barcelona's insatiable appetite for novelty and progress.

EXPLORING BARCELONA

Barcelona is made up of four distinct areas. Between Plaça Catalunya and the port lies the Old City, or Ciutat Vella, including El Barri Gòtic (the Gothic Quarter), La Ribera (the waterfront, also known as Born-Ribera), and El Raval, the former slums or outskirts southwest of the Rambla. Above Plaça Catalunya is the grid-pattern expansion built after the city's third series of defensive walls were torn down in 1860. Known as the Eixample (the "Expansion"), this area contains most of Barcelona's Moderniste architecture. Farther north and west are the former outlying towns of Gràcia and Sarrià, the Pedralbes area, and, rising up behind the city to the northwest, the green hills of the Collserola nature reserve. Diagonal Mar, from Torre Agbar and Plaça de les Glòries east to the mouth of the River Besòs and the Mediterranean is the new Barcelona built for the 2004 Fòrum de les Cultures.

Numbers in the text correspond to numbers in the margins and on chapter maps.

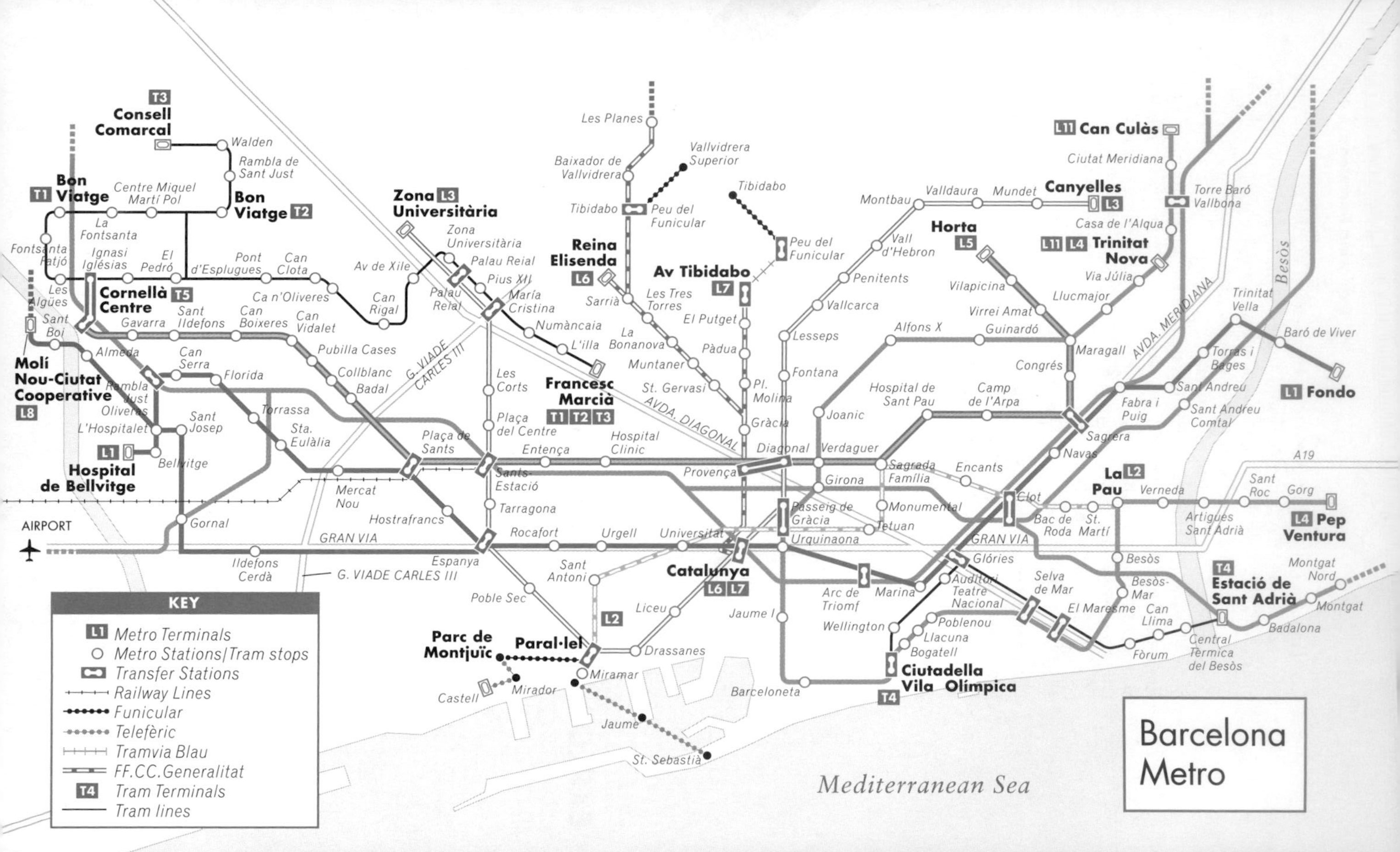
Barcelona Metro
Mediterranean Sea
KEY
L1 Metro Terminals
Metro Stations/Tram stops
Transfer Stations
Railway Lines
Funicular
Telefèric
Tramvia Blau
FF.CC.Generalitat
T4 Tram Terminals
Tram lines
T3 Consell Comarcal
Walden
Rambla de Sant Just
Bon Viatge T2
T1 Bon Viatge
Centre Miquel Martí Pol
La Fontsanta
Fontsanta Fatjó
Ignasi Iglésias
El Pedró
Pont d'Esplugues
Can Clota
Les Aigües
Cornellà Centre T5
Sant Boi
Molí Nou-Ciutat Cooperative L8
Gavarra
Sant Ildefons
Can Boixeres
Can Vidalet
Ca n'Oliveres
Av de Xile
Can Rigal
Zona Universitària L3
Zona Universitària
Palau Reial
Pius XII
Palau Reial
María Cristina
Numàncaia
L'illa
Francesc Macià T1 T2 T3
Almeda
Can Serra
Florida
Rambla Just Oliveras
L'Hospitalet
Sant Josep
L1 Hospital de Bellvitge
Bellvitge
Torrassa
Sta. Eulàlia
Pubilla Cases
Collblanc
Badal
G. VIADE CARLES III
Plaça de Sants
Les Corts
Plaça del Centre
Entença
Hospital Clínic
Sants-Estació
Tarragona
Mercat Nou
Hostafrancs
AIRPORT
Gornal
GRAN VIA
Ildefons Cerdà
G. VIADE CARLES III
Espanya
Rocafort
Urgell
Universitat
Sant Antoni
Poble Sec
L2
Parc de Montjuïc
Paral·lel
Castell
Mirador
Miramar
Jaume
St. Sebastià
Drassanes
Liceu
Catalunya L6 L7
Les Planes
Baixador de Vallvidrera
Vallvidrera Superior
Tibidabo
Peu del Funicular
Tibidabo
Peu del Funicular
Reina Elisenda L6
Sarrià
Les Tres Torres
La Bonanova
Muntaner
St. Gervasi
Av Tibidabo L7
El Putget
Pàdua
Pl. Molina
Gràcia
AVDA. DIAGONAL
Diagonal
Provença
Passeig de Gràcia
Urquinaona
Jaume I
Barceloneta
Montbau
Valldaura
Mundet
Canyelles L3
Vall d'Hebron
Penitents
Vallcarca
Lesseps
Fontana
Joanic
Verdaguer
Girona
Horta L5
Vilapicina
Virrei Amat
Alfons X
Guinardó
Hospital de Sant Pau
Camp de l'Arpa
Sagrada Família
Encants
Monumental
Tetuan
Arc de Triomf
Marina
L11 Can Culàs
Ciutat Meridiana
Torre Baró Vallbona
Casa de l'Alqua
L11 L4 Trinitat Nova
Via Júlia
Llucmajor
Maragall
Congrés
AVDA. MERIDIANA
Trinitat Vella
Baró de Viver
L1 Fondo
Torras i Bages
Sant Andreu
Sant Andreu Comtal
Fabra i Puig
Sagrera
Navas
Clot
Bac de Roda
St. Martí
La Pau L2
Verneda
Artigues Sant Adrià
Sant Roc
Gorg
L4 Pep Ventura
A19
Besòs
GRAN VIA
Glòries
Auditori Teatre Nacional
Selva de Mar
Besòs-Mar
El Maresme
Can Llima
Fòrum
Central Tèrmica del Besòs
T4 Estació de Sant Adrià
Badalona
Montgat
Montgat Nord
Besòs
Wellington
Poblenou
Llacuna
Bogatell
Ciutadella Vila Olímpica
T4

EL BARRI GÒTIC & LA RIBERA

This walk explores Barcelona's Gothic Quarter and spills across Via Laietana into the Barri de la Ribera, where the Picasso Museum, Santa Maria del Mar, and El Born are the main visits. Parts of the Barri Gòtic and the Barri Xinès (or Barrio Chino), Barcelona's notorious red-light district, have been much improved since the early 1990s; you'll happen on squares freshly begotten by the demolition of whole blocks and the planting of palm trees. Nonetheless, bag snatching is common in this part of town, so keep your wits about you, and if at all possible, carry nothing in your hands, while keeping any belongings on your person secure. The Barri de la Ribera, once the waterfront district, surrounds the basilica of Santa Maria del Mar and includes Carrer Montcada, Barcelona's poshest street in the 14th and 15th centuries. Much of the Barri de la Ribera was torn down in 1714 by the victorious Spanish and French army of Felipe V to create a glacis, an open no-man's land outside the walls of the occupying stronghold, La Ciutadella fortress.

A GOOD WALK

A good walk through the Barri Gòtic could begin at **Catedral de la Seu** ❶ and move through and around the cathedral to the **Museu Frederic Marès** ❷ (and its little terrace café, surrounded by Roman walls). Next, pass the patio of the Arxiu de la Corona d'Aragó (Archives of the House of Aragón); then turn left again and down into **Plaça del Rei** ❸. As you leave Plaça del Rei, the **Museu d'Història de la Ciutat** ❹ is on your left. Crossing Via Laietana, pass through the Plaça del Angel and walk down Carrer Princesa; this will take you to Carrer Montcada followed by a right turn to the **Museu Picasso** ❺. Walk along Carrer Montcada and see some of Barcelona's most elegant medieval palaces, before emerging into the Passeig del Born, with the giant steel hangar of the city's onetime main produce market, **El Born** ❻, looming at the far end. To your right is the back entrance of the church widely considered Barcelona's best, the Catalan Gothic **Santa Maria del Mar** ❼. After spending some time inside (note that the basilica closes each afternoon between 1:30 and 4:30), stop into La Vinya del Senyor, the excellent wine bar opposite the main door. Walk around the church's eastern side through the slight depression of the brick-cobbled square **Fossar de les Moreres** ❽. On the west side of Santa Maria del Mar are Carrer Sombrerers, the Gispert spice shop, and the entrance to Carrer Banys Vells, lined with interesting shops and restaurants. Walk to the far end of Banys Vells and go left through Barra de Ferro and Cotoners to Princesa. A walk back across Via Laietana into Carrer Ferran will take you to **Plaça Sant Jaume** ❾. From this square, once the Roman Forum, walk up Carrer Paradís (the second street to your right facing La Generalitat), take a sharp right, and have a look at the **Roman Columns** inside the entryway at Carrer Paradís 10. For a tour of Barcelona's *call* (from the Hebrew *qahal,* "meeting"), the medieval Jewish quarter, leave Plaça Sant Jaume on Carrer del Call, turn right on Sant Domènech del Call, and proceed to the next corner. Early Barcelona's **Sinagoga Major** (Main Synagogue) opens into Carrer Marlet across the intersection to your left. On the next corner—on the right is a stone

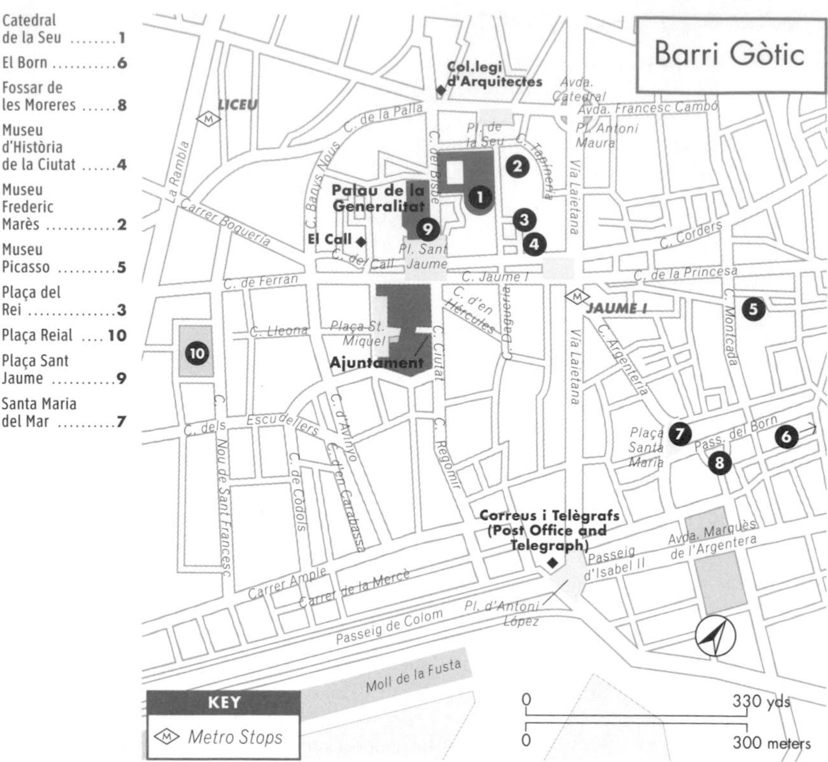

with Hebrew inscriptions, and a Spanish translation on a plaque—Arc de Sant Ramón del Call is another reminder of the Jewish community that prospered here until a 1391 pogrom decimated it a century before the 1492 expulsion. Take a left here, onto Carrer del Call, and then turn right on Carrer Ferran to reach the neoclassical square **Plaça Reial** ⑩.

TIMING This walk covers some 3 km (2 mi) and should take about three hours, depending on stops. Allow another hour for the Picasso Museum.

WHAT TO SEE: MAIN ATTRACTIONS

6 **El Born.** Once the site of medieval jousts, the Passeig del Born is at the end of Carrer Montcada behind the church of Santa Maria del Mar. The numbered cannonballs under the benches are in memory of the 1714 siege of Barcelona that concluded the 14-year War of the Spanish Succession. The Bourbon forces obliged local residents to tear down more than 900 of their own houses, about a fifth of the city at that time, to create an open no-man's land for the fortress built for the occupying army of the great villain of Barcelona history, Felipe V, grandson of Louis XIV. Walk down to the Born itself—a great iron hangar designed by Josep Fontseré in 1876. It was modeled after Les Halles, once Paris's beloved midcity produce market. Renovation of El Born uncovered the perfectly preserved lost city of 1714, complete with blackened fire-

places, taverns, wells, and the canal that brought water into the city. Sand dunes visible in the cellars attest to La Ribera's early position on the Barcelona waterfront before landfill created Barceloneta and the present harbor. Pending development of a history walk through the streets and houses, the Museu de Història de la Ciutat offers free visits overlooking the ruins of the 14th- to 18th-century Barri de la Ribera weekends 10–3. ✉ *Born-Ribera* ☎ *93/315–1111 Museu de Història de la Ciutat* Ⓜ *Jaume I.*

8 **Fossar de les Moreres** *(Cemetery of the Mulberry Trees)*. The inscription EN EL FOSSAR DE LES MORERES NO S'HI ENTERRA CAP TRAIDOR, or in the cemetery of the mulberry trees no traitor lies refers to the story of the graveyard keeper who refused to bury those who had fought on the invading side during War of the Spanish Succession, even when one of them turned out to be his son. This low marble monument is on the eastern side of the church of Santa Maria del Mar, honoring the defenders of Barcelona who gave their lives in the siege that, on September 11 1714, ended the war and established Felipe V on the Spanish throne. The torch-sculpture over the marble monument, often referred to as a *pebetero* (Bunsen burner), was erected in 2002. ✉ *Fossar de les Moreres, La Ribera.*

NEED A BREAK?

Mercat de Santa Caterina. This marketplace, a splendid carnival of colors and roller-coaster rooftops, was restored by the late Enric Miralles (though the project was finished in 2005 by his widow, architect Benedetta Tagliabue). Undulating wood and colored ceramic mosaic cellings, recalling both Gaudí and Miró, covers a glass floor through which sections of the original building here, a convent, is still visible. The spacious, clean-lined Santa Caterine Cuines restaurant offers an original menu with cuisine categories such as vegetarian, Mediterranean, Asian dishes cooked over coals (*carbo*). ✉ *Av. Francesc Cambo 16, Born-Ribera* ☎ *93/268–9918* 🌐 *www.mercatsbcn.com* Ⓜ *Catalunya.*

4 **Museu d'Història de la Ciutat** *(City History Museum)*. This fascinating museum traces the evolution of Barcelona from its first Iberian settlement to its alleged founding by the Carthaginian Hamilcar Barca in about 230 BC to Roman and Visigothic times and beyond. Antiquity is the focus here: Romans took the city during the Punic Wars, and the striking underground remains of their Colonia Favencia Julia Augusta Paterna Barcino, through which you can roam on metal walkways, are the museum's main treasure. Archaeological finds include parts of walls, fluted columns, and recovered busts and vases. Above ground, off the Plaça del Rei, the **Palau Reial Major**, the splendid **Saló del Tinell**, the chapel of **Santa Àgata**, and the **Torre del Rei Martí**, a lookout tower with views over the Barri Gòtic, complete the self-guided tour. ✉ *Palau Padellàs, Carrer del Veguer 2, Barri Gòtic* ☎ *93/315–1111* 🌐 *www.museuhistoria.bcn.es* 🎟 *€6 (includes admission to Monestir de Pedralbes, Park Güell Centre d'Interpretation, and Museu-Casa Verdaguer)* ⏲ *Oct.–May, Tues.–Sat. 10–2 and 4–8; June–Sept., Tues.–Sat. 10–8; Sun. 10–3* Ⓜ *Catalunya, Liceu, Jaume I.*

Continued on page 416

7

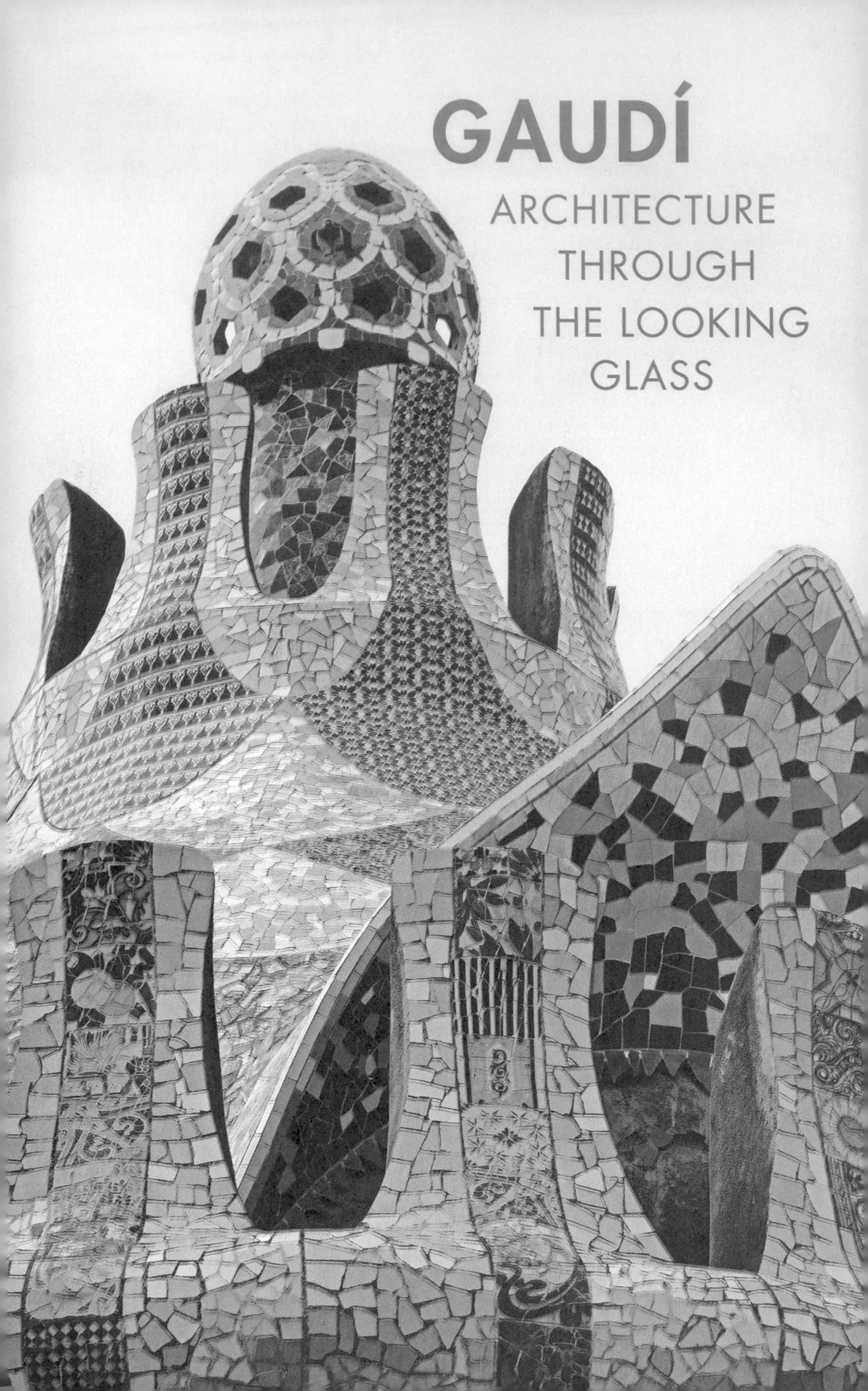
GAUDÍ
ARCHITECTURE
THROUGH
THE LOOKING
GLASS

(left) The rooftop of Parc Güell's gatehouse. (top) Construction continues on la Sagrada Família.

Shortly before his 75th birthday in 1926, Antonio Gaudí was hit by a trolley car while on his way to mass. The great architect–initially unidentified–was taken to the medieval Hospital de la Santa Creu in Barcelona's Raval and left in a pauper's ward, where he died two days later without regaining consciousness. It was a dramatic and tragic end for a man whose entire life seemed to court the extraordinary and the exceptional.

Gaudí's singularity made him hard to define. Indeed, eulogists at the time, and decades later, wondered how history would treat him. Was he a religious mystic, a rebel, a bohemian artist, a Moderniste genius? Was he, perhaps, all of these? He certainly had a rebellious streak, as his architecture stridently broke with tradition. Yet the same sensibility that created the avant-garde benchmarks Parc Güell and La Pedrera also created one of Spain's greatest shrines to Catholicism, the *Temple Expiatori de la Sagrada Família* (Expiatory Temple of the Holy Family), which architects agree is one of the world's most enigmatic structures (work on the cathedral continues to this day). And while most of Gaudí's works suggest a futurist aesthetic, he also reveled in the use of ornamentation, which 20th century architecture largely eschewed.

What is no longer in doubt is Gaudí's place among the great architects in history. Eyed with suspicion by traditionalists in the 1920s and '30s, vilified during the Franco regime, and ultimately redeemed as a Barcelona icon after Spain's democratic transition in the late '70s, Gaudí's work has finally gained universal admiration.

THE MAKING OF A GENIUS

Gaudí was born in 1852 the son of a boilermaker and coppersmith in Reus, an hour south of Barcelona. As a child, he helped his father forge boilers and cauldrons in the family foundry, which is where Gaudí's fascination with three-dimensional and organic forms began. Afflicted from an early age with rheumatic fever, the young architect devoted his energies to studying and drawing flora and fauna in the natural world. In school he was erratic: brilliant in the subjects that interested him, absent and disinterested in the others. As a seventeen-year-old architecture student in Barcelona, his academic results were mediocre. Still, his mentors agreed that he was brilliant.

Unfortunately being brilliant didn't mean instant success. By the late 1870s, when Gaudí was well into his twenties, he'd only completed a handful of projects, including the Plaça Reial lampposts, a flower stall, and the factory and part of a planned workers' community in Mataró. Gaudí's career got the boost it needed when, in 1878, he met Eusebi Güell, heir to a textiles fortune and a man who, like Gaudí, had a refined sensibility. (The two bonded over a mutual admiration for the visionary Catalan poet Jacint Verdaguer.) In 1883 Gaudí became Güell's architect and for the next three decades, until Güell's death in 1918, the two collaborated on Gaudí's most important architectural achievements, from high-profile endeavors like Palau Güell, Parc Güell, and Pabellones Güell to smaller projects for the Güell family.

(top) Interior of Casa Batlló. (bottom) Chimneys on rooftop of Casa Milà recall helmeted warriors or veiled women.

GAUDÍ TIMELINE

1883–1884

Gaudí builds a summer palace, *El Capricho* in Comillas, Santander for the brother-in-law of his benefactor, Eusebi Güell. Another gig comes his way during this same period when Barcelona ceramics tile mogul Manuel Vicens hires him to build his town house, *Casa Vicens*, in the Gràcia neighborhood.

El Capricho

1884–1900

Gaudí whips up the Güell Pabellones, Palau Güell, the Palacio Episcopal of Astorga, Barcelona's Teresianas school, the Casa de los Botines in León, Casa Calvet, and Bellesguard. These have his classic look of this time, featuring interpretation of Mudéjar (Moorish motifs), Gothic, and Baroque styles.

Palacio Episcopal

BREAKING OUT OF THE T-SQUARE PRISON

If Eusebi Güell had not believed in Gaudí's unusual approach to Modernisme, his creations may not have seen the light of day. Güell recognized that Gaudí was imbued with a vision that separated him from the crowd. That vision was his fascination with the organic. Gaudí had observed early in his career that buildings were being composed of shapes that could only be drawn by the compass and the T-square: circles, triangles, squares, and rectangles—shapes that in three dimensions became prisms, pyramids, cylinders and spheres. He saw that in nature these shapes are unknown. Admiring the structural efficiency of trees, mammals, and the human form, Gaudí noted ". . . neither are trees prismatic, nor bones cylindrical, nor leaves triangular." The study of natural forms revealed that bones, branches, muscles, and tendons are all supported by internal fibers. Thus, though a surface curves, it is supported from within by a fibrous network that Gaudí translated into what he called "ruled geometry," a system of inner reinforcement he used to make hyperboloids, conoids, helicoids, or parabolic hyperboloids.

These tongue-tying words are simple forms and familiar shapes: the femur is hyperboloid; the way shoots grow off a branch is helicoidal; the web between your fingers is a hyperbolic paraboloid. To varying degrees, these ideas find expression in all of Gaudí's work, but nowhere are they more clearly stated than in the two masterpieces La Pedrera and Parc Güell.

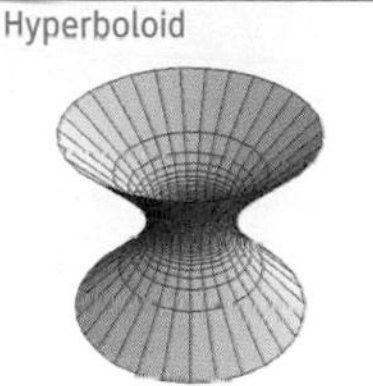

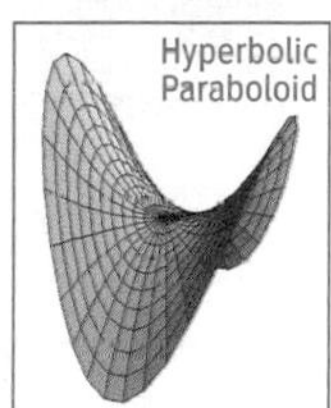

Casa Batlló's scaly dragon-back roof atop a structure composed of tibias, femurs, and skulls show Gaudí's interest in anatomy and organic forms.

1900–1917

Gaudí's Golden Years—his most creative, personal, and innovative period. Topping each success with another, he tackles Parc Güell, the reform of Casa Batlló, the Güell Colony church, Casa Milà (AKA La Pedrera), and the Sagrada Família school.

Casa Batlló's complex chimneys

1918–1926

A crushing blow: Gaudí suffers the death of his assistant, Francesc Berenguer. Grieving and rudderless, he devotes himself fully to his great unfinished opus, la Sagrada Família—to the point of obsession. On June 10th, 1926, he's hit by a trolley car. He dies two days later.

La Sagrada Família

HOW TO SEE GAUDÍ IN BARCELONA

Few architects have left their stamp on a major city as thoroughly as Gaudí did in Barcelona. Paris may have the Eiffel Tower, but Barcelona has Gaudí's still unfinished masterpiece, the Temple Expiatori de la Sagrada Família, the city's most emblematic structure. Dozens of other buildings, parks, gateways and even paving stones around town bear Gaudí's personal Art Nouveau signature, but the continuing progress on his last and most ambitious project makes his creative energy an ongoing part of everyday Barcelona life in a unique and almost spectral fashion.

(top) The serpentine ceramic bench at Parc Güell, designed by Gaudí collaborator Josep Maria Jujol, curves sinuously around the edge of the open square. (bottom) Sculptures byJosep María Subirachs grace the temple of the Sagrada Família.

In Barcelona, nearly all of Gaudí's work can be visited on foot or, at most, with a couple of metro or taxi rides. A walk from Palau Güell near the Mediterranean end of the Rambla, up past Casa Calvet just above Plaça Catalunya, and on to Casa Batlló and Casa Milà is an hour's stroll, which, of course, could take a full day with thorough visits to the sites. Casa Vicens is a half hour's walk up into Gràcia from Casa Milà. Parc Güell is another thirty- to forty-minute walk up from that. La Sagrada Família, on the other hand, is a good hour's hike from the next nearest Gaudí point and is best reached by taxi or metro. The Teresianas school, the Bellesguard Tower, and Pabellones Güell are within an hour's walk of each other, but to get out to Sarrià you will need to take the comfortable Generalitat (FGC) train.

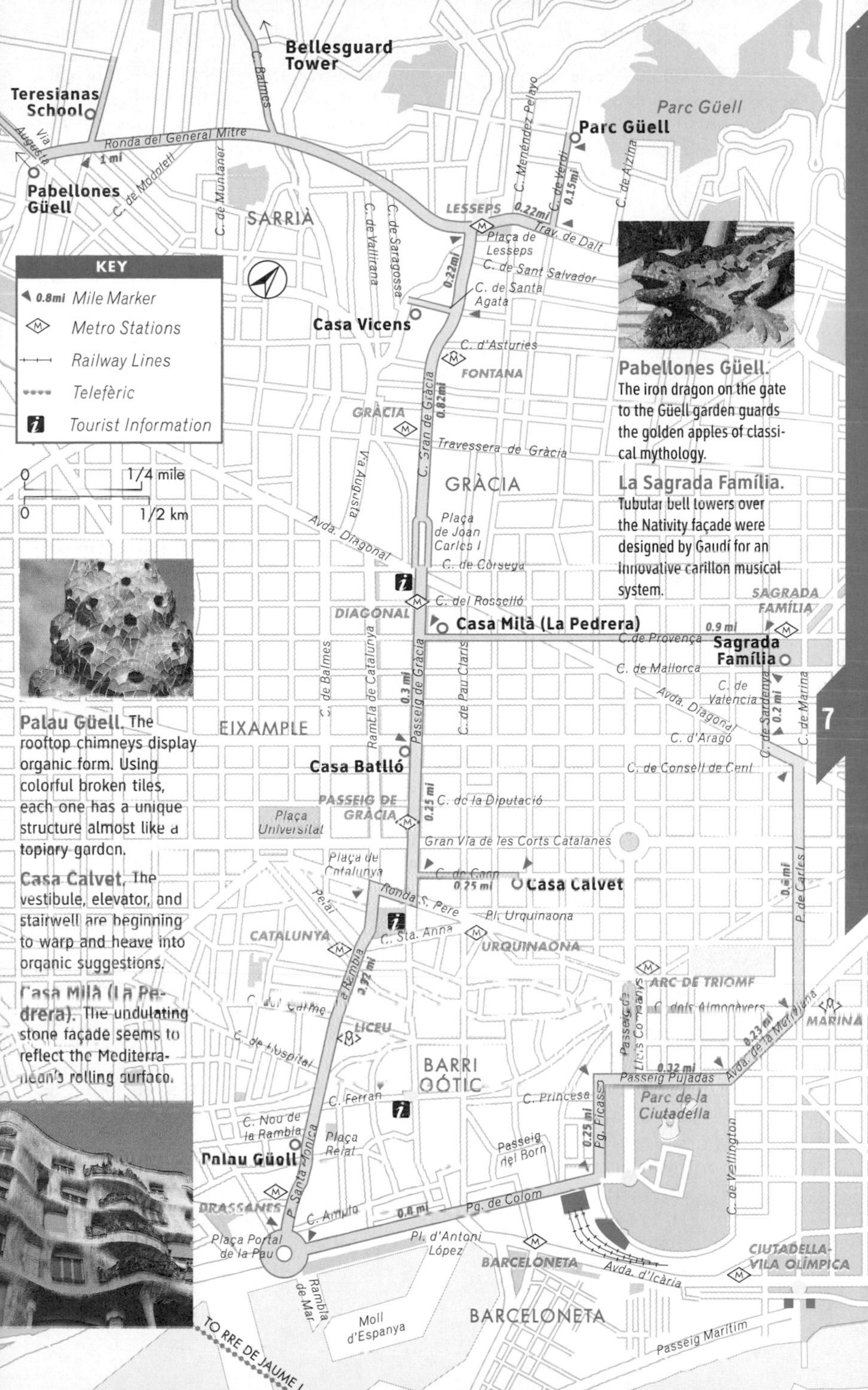

Pabellones Güell. The iron dragon on the gate to the Güell garden guards the golden apples of classical mythology.

La Sagrada Família. Tubular bell towers over the Nativity façade were designed by Gaudí for an innovative carillon musical system.

Palau Güell. The rooftop chimneys display organic form. Using colorful broken tiles, each one has a unique structure almost like a topiary garden.

Casa Calvet. The vestibule, elevator, and stairwell are beginning to warp and heave into organic suggestions.

Casa Milà (La Pedrera). The undulating stone façade seems to reflect the Mediterranean's rolling surface.

5 **Museu Picasso.** Picasso spent key formative years (1895–1904) in Barcelona and never forgot his salad days here as an irresistible young Bohemian. (His *Demoiselles d'Avignon* was, in fact, inspired by the eponymous Barcelona street known for its brothels, not by the French city.) A collection of his work can be found in Carrer Montcada, known for Barcelona's most elegant medieval and Renaissance palaces, five of which are occupied by the Picasso Museum. Though the 3,600-work permanent collection is strong on his early production, don't expect to find many of the artist's most famous works. Picasso's longtime crony and personal secretary Jaume Sabartés donated his private collection in 1960 to this museum, and Picasso himself donated another 1,700 works in 1970. Displays include childhood and adolescent sketches, works from Picasso's Blue and Rose periods, and the famous 44 cubist studies based on Velázquez's *Las Meninas*. The sketches, oils, schoolboy caricatures, and drawings from Picasso's early years in La Coruña and, later, in Barcelona are perhaps the most fascinating part of the museum, showing the facility the artist possessed from an early age. His *La Primera Communión (First Communion)*, painted at the age of 15, for which he was given a short review in the local press, was an important achievement for the young Picasso, and the Las Meninas studies and the bright *Pichones (Pigeons)* series provide a final explosion of color and light. *Suite 156*, a series of erotic and playful drawings on display when temporary exhibits allow space, may be the best of all. ✉ *Carrer Montcada 15–23, Born-Ribera* ☎ *93/319–6310* 🌐 *www.museupicasso.bcn.es* 🎫 *Permanent collection €7, temporary exhibits €6, combined ticket €9.50; free 1st Sun. of month* ⏲ *Tues.–Sat. 10–8, Sun. 10–3* Ⓜ *Catalunya, Liceu, Jaume I.*

Fodor'sChoice ★

3 **Plaça del Rei.** As chronicled in legend, song, and painting, this plaza has long been held to be the scene of Columbus's triumphal return from his first voyage to the New World, with Ferdinand and Isabella receiving "the discoverer" on the stairs fanning out from the corner. (As it eventually turned out, they were actually at a summer palace outside of town. Then again, Columbus thought he'd discovered the Indies.) The **Palau Reial Major** was the Catholic Monarchs' official residence in Barcelona. Its main room is the **Saló del Tinell,** a banquet hall built in 1362. Also around the square: the dark 15th-century **Torre Mirador del Rei Martí** (King Martin's Watchtower), above the Saló del Tinell; to the left, the **Palau del Lloctinent** (Lieutenant's Palace); the 14th-century **Capilla Reial de Santa Àgueda** (Royal Chapel of Saint Agatha), to the right of the stairway; and the **Palau Clariana-Padellàs** (Clariana-Padellàs Palace), moved here stone by stone from Carrer Mercaders in the early 20th century and now the entrance to the Museu d'Història de la Ciutat. The hulking bronze sculpture, *Topos* (Greek for "Place") by Basque sculptor Eduardo Chillida (1924–2002), the tiny shrine to St. Agatha behind glass above a 1638 Barcelona coat of arms, and, if you're lucky, the resonating notes of classical-guitar music on a quiet afternoon can all add up to a memorable Barcelona moment. Ⓜ *Catalunya, Liceu, Jaume I.*

10 **Plaça Reial.** Pungent and seedy around the edges but elegant and neoclassical in design, this symmetrical mid-19th-century arcaded square is bordered by ocher facades with balconies overlooking the **Fountain of the Three Graces** and lampposts designed by Gaudí. Restaurants and cafés, identifiable as tourist traps by the photo-menus (the only good one is Taxidermista), line the square. On Sunday morning, crowds gather to sell and trade stamps and coins. After dark the square is a nightlife hot spot starring Jamboree for jazz and boogy, Los Tarantos for flamenco, and Glaciar for young beer-drinking internationals. Ⓜ *Catalunya, Liceu.*

9 **Plaça Sant Jaume.** Two thousand years ago, this formal square was the center of the Roman forum, which seems fitting for the modern-day site of both Catalonia's and Barcelona's government seats. The Plaça was cleared in the 1840s, but the two imposing buildings facing each other across it are much older, their original Gothic facades on their respective north sides facing Carrer del Bisbat and Carrer Ciutat. The 15th-century *Ajuntament* (City Hall) contains impressive black-and-burnished-gold murals (1928) by Josep Maria Sert and the historic Saló de Cent, where the Council of One Hundred, Europe's earliest proto-democratic body founded in 1372, governed until Felipe V abolished Catalonia's autonomous institutions in 1715. Filled with art, the ajuntament is open to the public on Sunday morning (10–1) and on special holidays. During the week, check listings for free concerts or events here. The **Palau de la Generalitat**, seat of the Catalan government, is a majestic 15th-century palace—through the front windows you can see the gilded ceiling of the Saló de Sant Jordi (Hall of St. George), named for Catalonia's dragon-slaying patron saint. Normally you can visit the Generalitat only on certain holidays, such as the Día de Sant Jordi (St. George's Day), April 23; check with the *protocolo* (protocol office). The Generalitat hosts carillon concerts, open to the public, on occasional Sundays at noon. ✉ *Pl. Sant Jaume 1, Barri Gòtic* ☎ *93/402–7000* 🌐 *www.bcn.es* ⏲ *Sun. 10–1* Ⓜ *Catalunya, Liceu, Jaume I.*

7 **Santa Maria del Mar.** The most breathtakingly symmetrical and graceful of all Barcelona's churches is on the Carrer Montcada end of Passeig del Born, an early Gothic basilica with Romanesque echoes and overtones. Simple and spacious, this pure and classical space enclosed by soaring columns is something of an oddity in ornate and complex Moderniste Barcelona. Santa Maria del Mar (Saint Mary of the Sea) was built from 1329 to 1383, an extraordinarily prompt construction time in that era, in fulfillment of a vow made a century earlier by Jaume I to build a church to watch over all Catalan seafarers. The architect in charge of the construction, a mere stonemason named Montagut de Berenguer, designed a bare-bones basilica (an oblong Roman royal hall used for public meetings and later adapted for early Christian or medieval churches) that is now considered the finest existing example of Catalan (or Mediterranean) Gothic architecture. The number eight (or multiples thereof)—the medieval numerological symbol for the Virgin Mary—runs through every element of the basilica's construction: 16 octagonal pillars rising 16 meters before arching out another 16 meters to the painted

Fodor's Choice ★

7

keystones at the apex of the arches 32 meters overhead. The sum of the lateral aisles, 8 meters each, equals the width of the center aisle, and the difference in height between the central and lateral naves, 8 meters, equals their width. The result of all this proportional balance is a tonic sense of peace and uplift, an almost mystical poise enhanced by a lovely rose window whose circular mass in blues and crimsons perfectly offsets the golden sandstone verticality of the columns. Any excuse to spend time in Santa Maria del Mar, from eavesdropping on a wedding, to hearing a concert, to using it merely as a shortcut through to the Passeig de Born, is valid. The haunting "Cant de la Sibil.la" ("Song of the Sibyl"), performed on Christmas Eve before the midnight Mass, is a concert not to miss, and Handel's *Messiah* at Christmas and Haydn's *Creation* at Easter are also annual events. Any chance to hear Renaissance choral music here—performing the works of such composers as Tomás Luís de Victoria, Guerrero, Tallis, and Byrd—especially if performed by the Sixteen or the Tallis Scholars, is an unmissable treat. Check out the diminutive organ loft for a glimpse of Neil Crowley, the Texas-born Santa Maria del Mar organ master. ✉ *Pl. de Santa Maria, Born-Ribera* ☎ *93/310–2390* ⏲ *Daily 9–1:30 and 4:30–8* Ⓜ *Catalunya, Jaume I.*

VISCA SANTA MARIA !

"Santa Maria!" was the battle cry of the Catalan sailors of the Catalano-Aragonese alliance that conquered the Balearic Islands from the Moors in 1229 and went on to extend Catalonia's Mediterranean empire as far as Athens by 1311. Athens was governed by the so-called Catalan Grand Company, a group of Barcelona mercenaries nominally under the flag of the House of Aragón. Present-day vestiges of Catalonia's Mediterranean empire include the Catalan street names on the island of Sardinia.

ALSO WORTH SEEING

❶ **Catedral de la Seu.** On Saturday afternoons, Sunday mornings, and occasional evenings, Barcelona folk gather in the Plaça de la Seu to dance the *sardana*, a somewhat demure circular dance and a great symbol of Catalan identity. The Gothic cathedral was built between 1298 and 1450, with the spire and neo-Gothic facade added in 1892. Architects of Catalan Gothic churches strove to make the high altar visible to the entire congregation, hence the unusually wide central nave and slender side columns. The first thing you see upon entering are the high relief sculptures on the choir stalls, telling the story of **Santa Eulàlia** (Barcelona's co-patron along with La Mercé, Our Lady of Mercy). To the right of this high relief is a sculpture of St. Eulàlia, standing with her emblematic cross, resurrected as a living saint. Other highlights are the beautifully carved choir stalls; St. Eulàlia's tomb in the crypt; and the battle-scarred crucifix in the Lepanto Chapel to the right of the main entrance. The tall cloisters surround a tropical garden, and outside, at the building's front right corner, is the intimate Santa Llúcia chapel. The cathedral is floodlighted in striking yellows at night, and the stained-glass windows are backlighted. ✉ *Pl. de la Seu* ☎ *93/342–8260* 🌐 *www.catedralbcn.org* 🎫 *1–5* PM *€6, the rest of the time free* ⏲ *Daily 7:45* AM*–7:45* PM *1–5, visitors can* *see entire cathedral, museum, bell tower, and rooftop* Ⓜ *Catalunya, Liceu, Jaume I.*

❷ **Museu Frederic Marès** *(Frederic Marès Museum).* You can browse for hours among the miscellany assembled by the early-20th-century sculptor-collector Frederic Marès in this trove of art and odds and ends. Everything from paintings and polychrome wood carvings, such as Juan de Juní's 1537 masterpiece *Pietà* and the Master of Cabestany's late-12th-century *Apparition of Christ to His Disciples at Sea,* to Marès's collection of pipes and walking sticks is stuffed into this rich potpourri. ✉ *Pl. Sant Iu 5, Barri Gòtic* ☎ *93/310–5800* 🌐 *www.museumares.bcn.es* 🎫 *€4; free 1st Sun. of month and Wed. afternoon* ⏲ *Tues., Wed., Fri., and Sat. 10–7, Thurs. 10–5, Sun. 10–3* Ⓜ *Catalunya, Liceu, Jaume I.*

THE RAMBLA & THE RAVAL

Barcelona's best-known promenade is a constant and colorful flood of humanity past flower stalls, bird vendors, mimes, musicians, newspaper kiosks, and outdoor cafés. Federico García Lorca called this street the only one in the world that he wished would never end; traffic plays second fiddle to the endless *paseo* (stroll) of locals and travelers alike. The whole avenue is referred to as Las Ramblas (Les Rambles, in Catalan) or La Rambla, but each section has its own name: Rambla Santa Monica is at the southeastern, or port, end; Rambla de les Flors in the middle; and Rambla dels Estudis at the top, near Plaça de Catalunya. El Raval is the area to the west of the Rambla, originally a slum outside Barcelona's second set of walls, which ran down the left side of the Rambla. Alas, Rambla-happy tourists are tempting prey for thieves and scam artists. Do *not* play the shell game (Barcelona's local three-card monte), dress conservatively, keep maps and guidebooks hidden, conceal cameras, and leave wallets and passports in your hotel safe.

A GOOD WALK

Start on the Rambla opposite the Plaça Reial and wander down toward the sea, to the **Monument a Colom** ⓫ and the Rambla de Mar. From here you might make a brief probe into the unprepossessing modern **Port** ⓬. As you move back to the Columbus Monument, investigate the **Museu Marítim** ⓭ and its medieval Drassanes Reials shipyards. Gaudí's **Palau Güell** ⓮ on Carrer Nou de la Rambla is the next stop before the **Gran Teatre del Liceu** ⓯, and along the way take a peek at Barcelona's red-light district, the **Barri Xinès** ⓰. At the Miró mosaic at Pla de la Boqueria, cut right to the Plaça del Pi and the church of **Santa Maria del Pi** ⓱. Back on the Rambla, take in the facade and perhaps some savories at **Antigua Casa Figueres** ⓲, stroll through the **Boqueria** ⓳ food market and the **Palau de la Virreina** ⓴ exhibition center next door, and then cut around to the courtyards of the medieval **Antic Hospital de la Santa Creu** ㉑. Next, visit the **Museu d'Art Contemporani de Barcelona** (MACBA) ㉒ and the **Centre de Cultura Contemporànea de Barcelona** (CCCB) ㉓, on Carrer Montalegre, before returning to the Rambla. Finish your walk along Carrer Tallers, ending up in **Plaça de Catalunya** ㉔.

TIMING This walk covers 3 km (2 mi). With stops, allow three hours.

CLOSE UP

Picasso's Barcelona

Barcelona's claim to Pablo Picasso (1881–1973) has been contested by Málaga, the painter's birthplace, as well as by Madrid, where *Guernica* hangs, and even by the town of Gernika itself, victim of the 1937 Luftwaffe saturation bombing that inspired the famous canvas. Picasso, a staunch anti-Franco opponent after the war, refused to return to Franco's Spain. In turn, the Franco regime allowed no public display of Picasso's work until 1961, when the artist's Sardana frieze at Barcelona's Architects' Guild was unveiled. Picasso never set foot on Spanish soil for the last 39 years of his life.

Picasso spent a sporadic but formative period of his youth in Barcelona between 1895 and 1904, after which he moved to Paris to join the fertile art scene in the French capital. Picasso's father had been appointed art professor at the Reial Acadèmia de les Belles Arts in La Llotja. Picasso, a precocious draftsman, began advanced classes in the academy at the age of 15. Working in different studios between academic stints in Madrid, the 19-year-old Picasso first exhibited at Els Quatre Gats, a tavern still thriving on Carrer Montsió. Much intrigued with the Bohemian life of Barcelona's popular neighborhoods, Picasso's early cubist painting, *Les Demoiselles d'Avignon,* was inspired not by the French town but by the Barcelona street Carrer d'Avinyó, then known for its brothel. After his move to Paris, Picasso returned occasionally to Barcelona until his last visit in summer of 1934.

Considering Picasso's off-and-on tenure in Barcelona, followed by a 36-year residence in Paris and a 39-year self-imposed exile, it's remarkable that Barcelona and Picasso should be so intertwined in the world's perception of the city. The Picasso Museum, although an excellent visit, is only the fourth-most important art venue on any art connoisseur's list of Barcelona galleries. The museum was the brainchild of the artist's longtime friend Jaume Sabartés, who believed that his vast private collection of Picasso works should be made public. After much wrangling with the Franco regime, who were loath to publicly recognize such a prominent anti-Franco figure and author of a work titled *The Dream and the Lie of Franco* (1937), the Picasso Museum finally opened in 1963. **Iconoserveis Culturals** (✉ *C. Muntaner 185 Eixample* ☎ *93/410–1405* 🌐 *www.iconoserveis.com*) gives walking tours through the key spots in Picasso's Barcelona life, covering studios, galleries, taverns, Picasso family apartments, and the painter's favorite haunts and hangouts.

WHAT TO SEE: MAIN ATTRACTIONS

21 Fodor's Choice ★ **Antic Hospital de la Santa Creu.** The 15th-century medieval hospital, now housing the Biblioteca de Catalunya (the "Library of Catalunya") cultural institutions, and the Escola Massana art school, is one of the four finest Gothic spaces in Barcelona (along with Drassanes, Santa Maria del Mar, and La Llotja). Approach it from the back door of the Boqueria starting at the Carrer del Carme end, where, across from the **Reial Acadèmia de Cirurgia i Medecina,** the courtyard of the Casa de Conva-

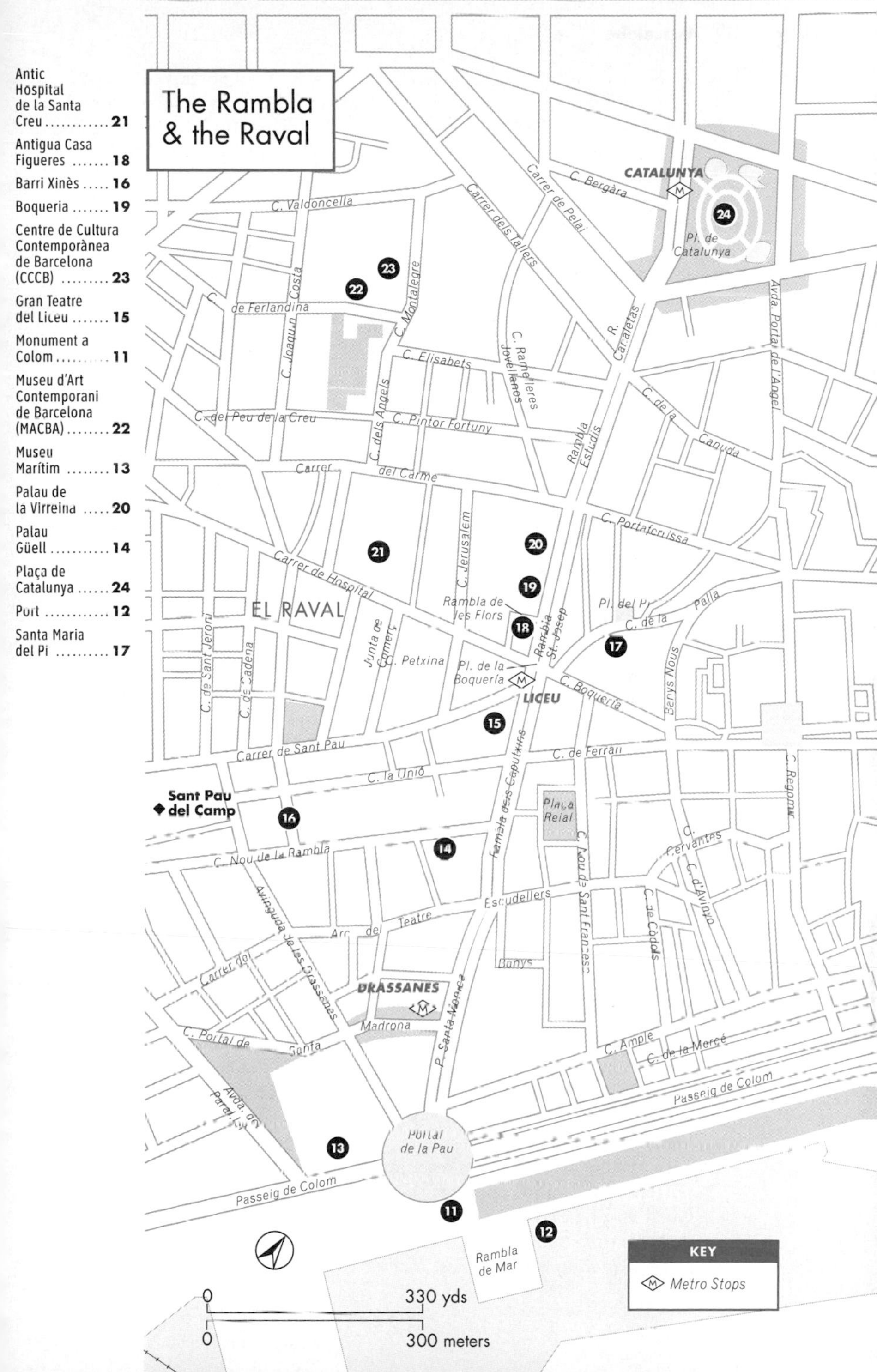

The Rambla & the Raval
Antic Hospital de la Santa Creu 21
Antigua Casa Figueres 18
Barri Xinès 16
Boqueria 19
Centre de Cultura Contemporània de Barcelona (CCCB) 23
Gran Teatre del Liceu 15
Monument a Colom 11
Museu d'Art Contemporani de Barcelona (MACBA) 22
Museu Marítim 13
Palau de la Virreina 20
Palau Güell 14
Plaça de Catalunya 24
Port 12
Santa Maria del Pi 17
CATALUNYA
C. Bergara
Carrer de Pelai
Carrer dels Tallers
Pl. de Catalunya
C. Valdoncella
C. Joaquín Costa
de Ferlandina
C. Montalegre
C. Elisabets
C. Ramelleres
Jovellanos
R. Canaletas
Avda. Portal de l'Angel
C. de la Canuda
C. del Peu de la Creu
C. dels Angels
C. Pintor Fortuny
Rambla Estudis
Carrer del Carme
C. Jerusalem
C. Portaferrissa
Carrer de Hospital
EL RAVAL
Rambla de les Flors
Rambla St. Josep
Pl. del Pi
C. de la Palla
Banys Nous
C. de Sant Jeroni
C. Petxina
Pl. de la Boqueria
LICEU
C. Boqueria
Carrer de Sant Pau
C. de Ferran
C. la Unió
Rambla dels Caputxins
Plaça Reial
C. Regomir
Sant Pau del Camp
C. Nou de la Rambla
C. Cervantes
C. d'Avinyo
Escudellers
Teatre
C. Nou de Sant Francesc
C. de Còdols
Avinguda de les Drassanes
Banys
DRASSANES
P. Santa Mònica
Madrona
C. Ample
C. de la Mercé
Passeig de Colom
Avda. de Paral.lel
Portal de la Pau
Passeig de Colom
Rambla de Mar
KEY
Metro Stops
0
330 yds
0
300 meters

lescència leads in past scenes from the life of St. Paul portrayed in lovely blue-and-white ceramic tiles hand-painted by master craftsman Llorenç Passolas in 1680–81. The green-and-white-tiled patio houses the Institut d'Estudis Catalans inside. The second-floor garden behind the clock is dedicated to Catalan novelist Mercé Rodoreda. Turn right as you leave the entryway, take a look into the beautifully vaulted reading rooms on either side down the stairs, and continue through the orange grove in the hospital patio to the stairs leading up to the right for a look at the wide Gothic arches inside the Biblioteca de Catalunya. Out on Carrer Hospital to the left is **La Capella,** once the hospital chapel and now a gallery with contemporary art. ✉ *Carrer del Carme 45, or Carrer Hospital 56, Raval* 🌐 *www.gencat.es/bc* Ⓜ *Catalunya, Liceu.*

16 **Barri Xinès.** As you walk from Plaça Reial toward the sea, Barcelona's red-light district, the Barri Xinès (traditionally called the Barrio Chino in Castilian Spanish) is on your right. Though literally translatable as Chinatown, China had nothing to do with this; the name is a generic reference to foreigners of all kinds. The area is ill-famed for prostitutes, drug pushers, and street thieves, but it's not as dangerous as it looks; the reinforced police presence here may make it safer than other parts of the Gothic Quarter.

19 ★ **Boqueria.** Barcelona's most spectacular food market, also known as the Mercat de Sant Josep, is an explosion of life and color sprinkled with delicious little bar-restaurants. **Pinotxo** has long been a sanctuary for food lovers; **Quim de la Boqueria** is hot on its heels. **El Kiosco Universal** on the northeast corner has great atmosphere but only fairground goods. Don't miss mushroom expert and author Petràs and his Fruits del Bosc (Fruits of the Forest), a mad display of wild mushrooms, herbs, nuts, and berries at the very back. ✉ *La Rambla 91, Rambla* 🌐 *www.boqueria.info* ⏲ *Mon.–Sat. 8–8* Ⓜ *Liceu.*

13 **Museu Marítim.** The superb Maritime Museum is in the 13th-century **Drassanes Reials** (Royal Shipyards), to the right at the foot of the Rambla. This vast medieval space, one of Barcelona's finest Gothic structures, seems more like a cathedral than a boatyard and is filled with ships, including a life-size reconstructed galley, figureheads, and early navigational charts. Take the self-guided tour. ✉ *Av. de les Drassanes s/n, Rambla* ☎ *93/342–9920* 🌐 *www.museumaritimbarcelona.org* 🎫 *€6; free 1st Sat. of month after 3* ⏲ *Daily 10–7* Ⓜ *Drassanes.*

14 **Palau Güell.** Antoni Gaudí built this mansion during the years 1886–89 for his patron, textile baron Count Eusebi de Güell, and soon found himself in the international limelight. The dark facade is a dramatic foil for the treasure house inside, where spear-shape Art Nouveau columns frame the windows and prop up a series of intricately coffered wood ceilings. Gaudí is most himself on the roof, where his playful, polychrome ceramic chimneys fit right in with later works such as Parc Güell and La Pedrera. All visits are guided by groups. ✉ *Carrer Nou de la Rambla 3–5, Rambla* ☎ *93/317–3974* ⏲ *Closed until late 2007; call for update* Ⓜ *Drassanes, Liceu.*

OFF THE BEATEN PATH

Sant Pau del Camp. Barcelona's oldest church was originally outside the city walls (*del camp* means "in the fields") and was a Roman cemetery as far back as the 2nd century, according to archaeological evidence. What you see now was built in 1127 and is the earliest Romanesque structure in Barcelona, redolent of the pre-Romanesque Asturian churches or of the pre-Romanesque Sant Michel de Cuxà in Prades, Catalunya Nord (Catalonia North, aka southern France). Elements of the church (the classical marble capitals atop the columns in the main entry) are thought to be from the 6th and 7th centuries. The hulking mastodonic shape of the church is a reflection of the defensive mentality of Barcelona's early Christians, for whom the bulwark of the church served as a spiritual, if not physical, refuge during an era of Moorish sackings and invasions. Check carefully for musical performances here, because the church is an acoustical gem. Note the tiny stained-glass window high on the facade facing Carrer Sant Pau. If Santa Maria del Pi's rose window is Europe's largest, this is quite probably the smallest. The tiny cloister, the only way in during afternoon opening hours, is Sant Pau del Camp's best feature, one of Barcelona's semisecret treasures. From inside the church, the right side of the altar leads out into this patio surrounded by porches or arcades. Sculpted Corinthian capitals portraying biblical scenes support triple Mudéjar arches. ✉ *Sant Pau 101, Raval* ☎ *93/441–0001* ⏲ *Cloister weekdays 4:30–7:30. Sun. mass at 10:30, 12:30, and 8* PM Ⓜ *Catalunya, Liceu, Paral.lel.*

ALSO WORTH SEEING

18 **Antigua Casa Figueres.** This Moderniste café, grocery, and pastry store on the corner of Carrer Petxina has a splendid mosaic facade and exquisite Art Nouveau fittings. The best way to get a close look at them is to sit down for a hot chocolate, tea, or coffee. The fluffy (if oversweet) *ensaimadas,* a spiraling Mallorcan pastry sprinkled with confectioner's sugar are hard to resist. ✉ *La Rambla 83, Rambla* ☎ *93/301–6027* 🌐 *www.escriba.es* Ⓜ *Catalunya, Liceu* ⏲ *Daily 8:30* AM*–9* PM.

23 **Centre de Cultura Contemporànea de Barcelona** *(CCCB).* Formerly a medieval convent and hospital, the renovated Casa de la Caritat holds the CCCB, a combination museum, exhibition space, lecture hall, and concert hall. A bonus to coming here is the reflecting wall, which allows you to see over the rooftops to Montjuïc and beyond. ✉ *Carrer Montalegre 5, Raval* ☎ *93/306–4100* 🌐 *www.cccb.org* 🎫 *€5; entry to patio and bookstore free* ⏲ *Tues., Thurs., and Fri. 11–2 and 4–8, Wed. and Sat. 11–8, Sun. 11–7* Ⓜ *Catalunya.*

15 **Gran Teatre del Liceu.** Along with Milan's La Scala, Barcelona's opera house has long been considered one of the most beautiful in Europe. First built in 1848, this cherished landmark was torched in 1861, bombed in 1893, and once again gutted by a blaze of mysterious origins in early 1994. Barcelona's soprano Montserrat Caballé stood on the Rambla in tears as her beloved venue was consumed. Five years later, a restored and renewed Liceu, equipped for modern produc-

tions, opened anew. Even if you don't see an opera, don't miss the 45-minute tour of the building; some of the Liceu's oldest and most spectacular rooms were untouched by the fire. For an extra charge, a 75-minute visit includes Círculo del Liceu, with the extraordinary Ramon Casas collection of paintings. Express tours are 20 minutes and less comprehensive. Under the opera house, with entrances on Carrer Sant Pau and the Rambla, Espai Liceu features a cafeteria; a shop specializing in opera-related gifts, books, and recordings; an intimate 50-person-capacity circular concert hall; and a Mediateca with recordings and films of past opera productions. ✉ *La Rambla 51–59, Rambla* ☎ *93/485–9900* 🌐 *www.liceubarcelona.com* 🎫 *Guided tours €6, 75-min tour €9, 20-min express tour €4* ⏲ *Tours daily at 10* AM *in English, express tours daily at 11* AM*, noon, and 1* PM Ⓜ *Liceu.*

11 **Monument a Colom** *(Columbus Monument)*. At the foot of the Rambla, take an elevator to the top of this monument for a bird's-eye view over the city. (The entrance is on the harbor side.) ✉ *Portal de la Pau s/n, Rambla* ☎ *93/302–5224* 🎫 *€3* ⏲ *Daily 9–8:30* Ⓜ *Drassanes.*

22 **Museu d'Art Contemporani de Barcelona** *(Barcelona Museum of Contemporary Art, MACBA)*. Designed in 1992 by American architect Richard Meier, this controversial white explosion of planes and glass around a cylindrical three-story reception hall contains 20th-century masters including Calder, Rauschenberg, Oteiza, Chillida, and Tàpies. The optional guided tour takes visitors through the philosophy behind abstract art. ✉ *Pl. dels Àngels 1, Raval* ☎ *93/412–0810* 🌐 *www.macba.es* 🎫 *€7.50, Wed. €3* ⏲ *Mon. and Wed.–Fri. 11–7:30, Sat. 10–8, Sun. 10–3; free guided tours daily at 6, Sun. at noon* Ⓜ *Catalunya.*

20 **Palau de la Virreina.** The neoclassical Virreina Palace, built by a viceroy to Peru in 1778, is now an exhibition center for paintings, photography, and historical items usually dedicated to social and environmental issues and honoring Catalonia's struggle of "internal exile." The building also has a bookstore and a municipal tourist office. ✉ *La Rambla 99, Rambla* ☎ *93/316–1000* 🌐 *www.bcn.es/virreinaexposicions* 🎫 *Free; €3 charge for some exhibits* ⏲ *Mon.–Sat. 11–8, Sun. 11–3* Ⓜ *Liceu.*

24 **Plaça de Catalunya.** Barcelona's main transport hub, the Plaça de Catalunya is the frontier between the old city and the post-1860 Eixample. Café Zurich, at the head of the Rambla and the mouth of the metro, is a classic rendezvous point.

12 **Port.** Beyond the Columbus Monument—behind the Duana, or former customs building, now site of the Barcelona Port Authority—is the **Rambla de Mar,** a boardwalk with a drawbridge. The Rambla de Mar extends out to the **Moll d'Espanya,** with its Maremagnum shopping center, IMAX theater, and aquarium. Next to the Duana, you can board a Golondrina boat for a tour of the port or take a boat to the end of the *rompeolas,* 3 km (2 mi) out to sea, and walk back into the old fishing village of Barceloneta, now Barcelona's beachfront section. From the Moll de Barcelona's Torre de Jaume I, farther to the right, you can catch a cable car to Montjuïc or Barceloneta.

17 **Santa Maria del Pi** *(St. Mary of the Pine)*. Like Santa Maria del Mar, the church of Santa Maria del Pi is another example of Mediterranean Gothic architecture, though its bulky, somber interior makes its soaring and elegant sister ship seem even more astounding by comparison. The gigantic rose window is best seen from inside in the late afternoon. The adjoining squares, **Plaça del Pi** and **Plaça de Sant Josep Oriol**, are two of the liveliest, most appealing spaces in the Gothic Quarter. ✉ *Pl. del Pi s/n, Rambla* ☎ *93/318–4743* ⏲ *Daily 9–1:30 and 4:30–8* Ⓜ *Liceu.*

THE EIXAMPLE

North of Plaça de Catalunya is the checkerboard known as the Eixample. With the dismantling of the city walls in 1860, Barcelona embarked upon an expansion scheme fueled by the return of rich colonials, by an influx of provincial aristocrats who had sold their country estates after the debilitating second Carlist War (1847–49), and by the city's growing industrial power. The street grid was the work of urban planner Ildefons Cerdà; much of the building here was done at the height of Modernisme. The Eixample's principal thoroughfares are Rambla de Catalunya and Passeig de Gràcia, where the city's most elegant shops vie for space among its best Art Nouveau buildings.

A GOOD TOUR

Starting in the Plaça de Catalunya, walk up Passeig de Gràcia until you reach the corner of Consell de Cent. Enter the Bermuda Triangle of Moderniste architecture, the **Manzana de la Discòrdia** **25**. The **Casa Montaner i Simó–Fundació Tàpies** **26** is around the corner on Carrer Aragó. Gaudí's **Casa Milà** **27**, known as La Pedrera, is three blocks farther up Passeig de Gràcia; after touring the interior and rooftop, walk up Passeig de Gràcia to Vinçon for a look through one of Barcelona's top design stores, with views into the back of Casa Milà. Just around the corner, at Diagonal 373, is Puig i Cadafalch's intricately sculpted **Palau Baró de Quadras** **28**, now housing the Casa Asia cultural center. Two minutes farther is his Nordic castlelike **Casa de les Punxes** **29** at No. 416–420. From here it's a 10-minute hike to yet another Puig i Cadafalch masterpiece, **Casa Macaia** **30**. Finally, take a taxi to Gaudí's emblematic **Temple Expiatori de la Sagrada Família** **31**. If you've still got energy and curiosity to burn, stroll over to Domènech i Montaner's **Hospital de Sant Pau** **32**.

TIMING Depending on how many taxis you take, this is a four- to five-hour tour.

WHAT TO SEE: MAIN ATTRACTIONS

27 ★ **Casa Milà.** Gaudí's Casa Milà, usually referred to as **La Pedrera** (The Stone Quarry), has a curving stone facade that bobs around the corner of the block. When the building was unveiled, in 1905, residents weren't enthusiastic about those cavelike balconies. Don't miss Gaudí's rooftop chimney park, especially in late afternoon, when the sunlight slants over the city into the Mediterranean. The handsome **Espai Gaudí** (Gaudí Space) in the attic has excellent critical displays of Gaudí's works, theories, and techniques, including an upside-down model of the Sagrada

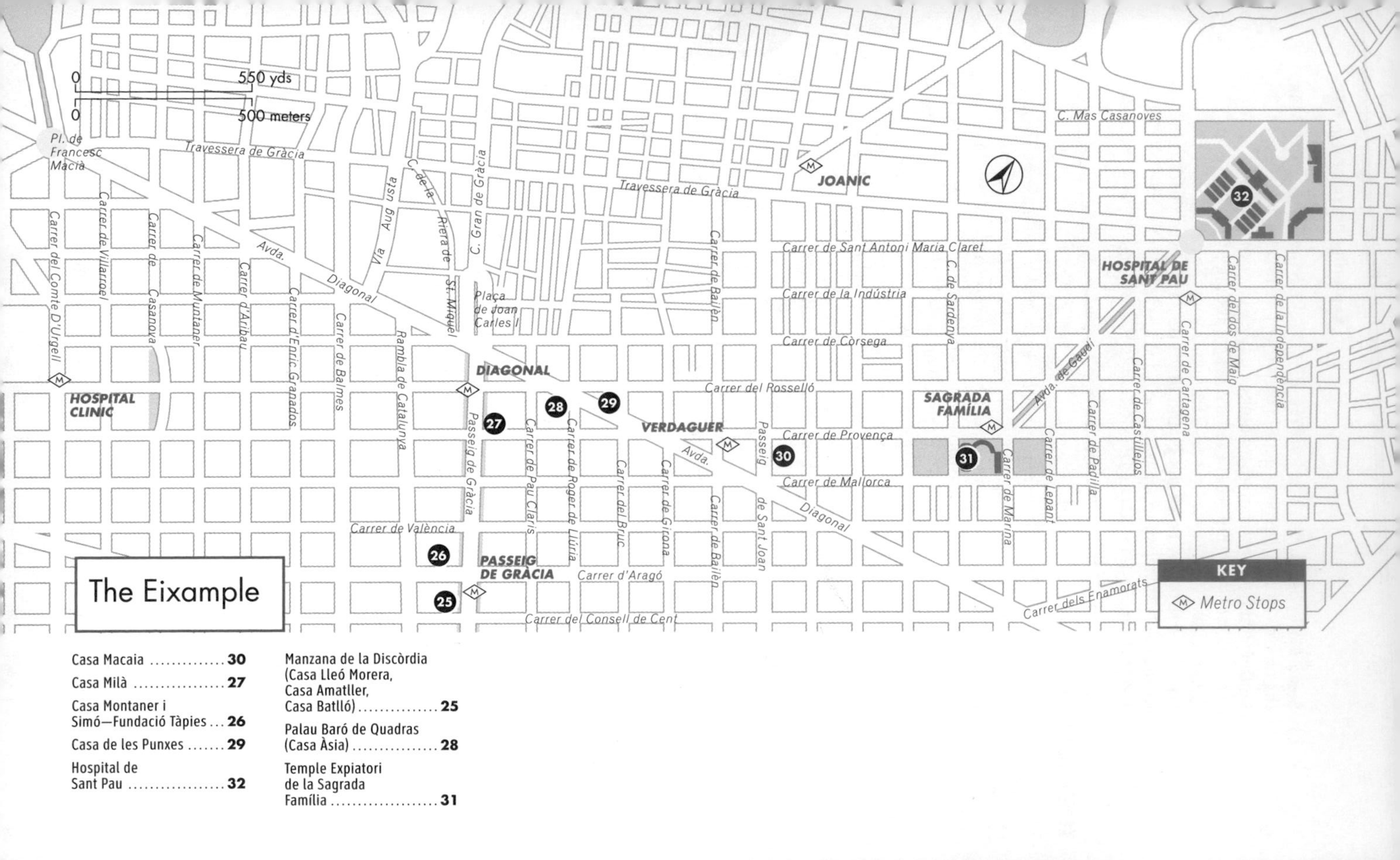

The Eixample
KEY
Metro Stops
0 550 yds
0 500 meters
Pl. de Francesc Macià
Travessera de Gràcia
C. Mas Casanoves
JOANIC
HOSPITAL DE SANT PAU
SAGRADA FAMÍLIA
VERDAGUER
DIAGONAL
PASSEIG DE GRÀCIA
HOSPITAL CLINIC
Carrer de Sant Antoni Maria Claret
Carrer de la Indústria
Carrer de Còrsega
Carrer del Rosselló
Carrer de Provença
Carrer de Mallorca
Carrer de València
Carrer d'Aragó
Carrer del Consell de Cent
Carrer dels Enamorats
Carrer del Comte D'Urgell
Carrer de Villarroel
Carrer de Casanova
Carrer de Muntaner
Carrer d'Aribau
Carrer d'Enric Granados
Carrer de Balmes
Rambla de Catalunya
Passeig de Gràcia
Carrer de Pau Claris
Carrer de Roger de Llúria
Carrer del Bruc
Carrer de Girona
Carrer de Bailèn
Passeig de Sant Joan
Carrer de Marina
Carrer de Lepant
Carrer de Padilla
Carrer de Castillejos
Carrer de Cartagena
Carrer del dos de Maig
Carrer de la Independència
C. de Sardenya
Avda. de Gaudí
Avda. Diagonal
Via Augusta
C. de la Riera de St. Miquel
C. Gran de Gràcia
Plaça de Joan Carles I
Casa Macaia 30
Casa Milà 27
Casa Montaner i Simó—Fundació Tàpies ... 26
Casa de les Punxes 29
Hospital de Sant Pau 32
Manzana de la Discòrdia (Casa Lleó Morera, Casa Amatller, Casa Batlló) 25
Palau Baró de Quadras (Casa Àsia) 28
Temple Expiatori de la Sagrada Família 31

Família made of hanging beads. The **Pis de la Pedrera,** a restored apartment, gives an interesting glimpse into the life of its resident family in the early 20th century. Guided tours are offered weekdays at 6 PM and weekends at 11 AM. ✉ *Carrer Provença 261–265, Eixample* ☎ *902/400973* 🎫 *Espai Gaudí €5, Pis de la Pedrera €4, combined ticket €8* ⏲ *Daily 10–8; guided tours weekdays at 6 PM, weekends at 11 AM. Espai Gaudí roof terrace open for drinks evenings June–Sept.* Ⓜ *Diagonal, Provença.*

CATALAN FOR BEGINNERS

Catalan is derived from Latin and Provençal French, whereas Spanish has a heavy payload of Arabic vocabulary and phonetics. For language exchange *(intercambios)*, check the bulletin board at the central university Philosophy and Letters Faculty on Gran Via or any English bookstore for free half-hour exchanges of English for Catalan (or Spanish), a great way to get free private lessons and meet locals. Who knows? With the right chemistry intercambios at times lead to cross-cultural flings. Who said the language of love is French?

25 Fodor's Choice ★ **Manzana de la Discòrdia.** A pun on the Spanish word *manzana,* meaning both city block and apple, the reference is to the classical myth of the Apple of Discord, in which Eris, goddess of strife, drops a golden apple with the inscription "to the fairest." Hera, Athena, and Aphrodite all claim the apple; Paris is chosen to settle the dispute and awards the apple to Aphrodite, who promises him Helen, the most beautiful of women, triggering the Trojan War. On this block you can find the architectural counterpoint, where the three main Moderniste architects go hand to hand, drawing steady crowds of architecture buffs. Of the three, Casa Batlló is clearly the star.

Casa Lleó Morera (No. 35) was extensively rebuilt (1902–06) by Palau de la Música Catalana architect Domènech i Montaner and is a treasure chest of Modernisme. The facade is covered with ornamentation and sculptures of female figures using the modern inventions of the age: the telephone, the telegraph, the photographic camera, and the Victrola. The inside is currently closed to the public, but a quick glimpse into the entryway on the corner will give an idea of what's upstairs.

The pseudo-Flemish **Casa Amatller** (No. 41) was built by Josep Puig i Cadafalch in 1900 when the architect was 33 years old. Puig i Cadafalch's architectural historicism sought to recover Catalonia's proud past, in combination with eclectic elements from Flemish or Netherlandish architectural motifs. The Eusebi Arnau sculptures range from St. George and the dragon to the figures of a handless drummer with his dancing bear. The flowing-haired "Princesa" is thought to be Amatller's daughter, and the animals up above are pouring chocolate, a reference to the source of the Amatller family fortune. Casa Amatller is closed to the public (call or ask about any change in this), but an office on-site dispenses tickets for the Ruta del Modernisme tour.

At No. 43, the colorful and bizarre **Casa Batlló** —Gaudí at his most spectacular—with its mottled facade resembling anything from an abstract pointillist painting to rainbow sprinkles on an ice-cream cone, is usually easily identifiable by the crowd of tourists snapping photographs on the sidewalk. Nationalist symbolism is at work here: the scaly roofline represents the Dragon of Evil impaled on St. George's cross, and the skulls and bones on the balconies are the dragon's victims. These motifs are allusions to Catalonia's Middle Ages, with its codes of chivalry and religious fervor. The interior design follows a gently swirling maritime motif in stark contrast to the terrestrial strife represented on the facade. ✉*Passeig de Gràcia 43, between Carrer Consell de Cent and Carrer Aragó, Eixample* ☎*93/216–0306* 🌐*www.casabatllo.es* 🎫*€17* ⏲*Daily 9–8* Ⓜ*Passeig de Gràcia.*

31 Fodor's Choice ★ **Temple Expiatori de la Sagrada Família.** Barcelona's most unforgettable landmark, Antoni Gaudí's Sagrada Família was conceived as nothing short of a Bible in stone. This landmark is one of the most important architectural creations of the 19th to 21st centuries. No building in Barcelona, and few in the world, is more deserving of half-a-day's scrutiny. Consider bringing binoculars.

Start at the **Nativity facade,** where Gaudí addresses the fundamental mystery of Christianity: why does God the Creator become, through Jesus Christ, a creature? Gaudí's answer-in-stone is that God wanted to free man from the slavery of selfishness, symbolized here by the iron fence around the serpent at the base of the central column. The column depicts the genealogy of Christ. Overhead are the constellations in the Christmas sky at Bethlehem. Higher up is the Crowning of the Virgin under an overhang, atop which is a pelican feeding its young with its blood, a symbol of the eucharistic sacrifice. Below, two angels adore the initials of Christ (JHS) under the symbols of the cross, the Alpha and Omega. The cypress at the top is the evergreen symbol of eternity pointing to heaven; the white doves, souls seeking eternity.

To the right, the Portal of Faith, above Palestinian flora and fauna, shows scenes from the youth of Jesus, including his preaching at the age of 13. Higher up are grapes and wheat, symbols of the eucharist, and a sculpture of a hand and eye, symbols of divine providence. The left-hand Portal of Hope begins at the bottom with flora and fauna from the Nile; the Slaughter of the Innocents; the flight of the Holy Family into Egypt; Joseph, surrounded by his carpenter's tools, contemplating his son; and the marriage of Joseph and Mary. Above this is a sculpted boat with anchor (representing the church), piloted by St. Joseph assisted by the Holy Spirit. Overhead is a typical spire from the Montserrat massif. Gaudí intended these towers to house a system of tubular bells capable of playing more complex music than standard bell systems. The towers' peaks represent the apostles' successors in the form of miters, the official headdress of bishops of the Western church.

The **Passion facade** on the southwestern side, at the entrance to the grounds, is a dramatic contrast to the Nativity facade. Josep Maria Subirachs, the sculptor chosen in 1986 to execute Gaudí's plans—initially an atheist, and author of statements such as "God is one of man's greatest creations"—now confesses to a respectful agnosticism.

Known for his distinctly angular, geometrical interpretations of the human form, Subirachs boasted that his work "has nothing to do with Gaudí." When in 1990 artists, architects, and religious leaders called for his resignation after he sculpted an anatomically complete naked Christ on the cross, Subirachs defended the piece as part of the stark realism of the scene he intended to portray. Subirachs pays double homage to Gaudí in the Passion facade: over the left side of the main entry is the blocky figure of Gaudí making notes or drawings, and the Roman soldiers are modeled on Gaudí's helmeted chimneys on the roof of La Pedrera.

Framed by leaning tibialike columns representing the bones of the dead, the scenes begin at the left with the Last Supper. The faces of the disciples are contorted in confusion and dismay, especially that of Judas, who clutches a bag of money behind his back over the figure of a reclining hound (a symbol of fidelity contrasting with the treachery of Judas). The next sculptural group represents the prayer in the Garden of Gethsemane and Peter awakening, followed by the kiss of Judas. The numerical cryptogram behind this contains 16 numbers that can be added 310 different ways for a total of 33, the age of Christ at his death.

In the center, Jesus is lashed to a pillar during his flagellation, a tear track carved into his expressive countenance. The column's top stone is off kilter, a reminder of the stone to be removed from Christ's sepulchre. The knot and broken reed at the base of the pillar symbolize Jesus' physical and psychological suffering. To the right of the door is a rooster, with Peter lamenting his third denial of Christ "before the cock crows." Farther to the right are Pilate and Jesus with a crown of thorns, and just above, back on the left, is Simon of Cyrene helping Jesus with the cross after his first fall. Over the center, where Jesus consoles the women of Jerusalem ("Don't cry for me; cry for your children"), is a faceless Veronica—faceless because her story is considered apocryphal, holding the veil with which she wiped Christ's face, only to find his likeness miraculously imprinted upon it. To the left is a sculpture of Gaudí making notes, the evangelist in stone, and farther left the equestrian figure of a centurion piercing the side of the church with his spear, the church representing the body of Christ. Above are the soldiers rolling dice for Christ's clothing and the naked, crucified Christ. The moon to the right of the cross refers to the darkness at the moment of Christ's death and to the full moon of Easter; to the right are Peter and Mary at the sepulchre, the egg above Mary symbolizing the Resurrection. At Christ's feet is a figure with a furrowed brow, perhaps suggesting the agnostic's anguished search for certainty, thought to be a self-portrait of Subirachs characterized by the sculptor's giant hand and an "S" on his right arm. High above is a gold figure of the resurrected Christ.

Future of the project. Architect Jordi Bonet, 81, director of the work on the Sagrada Família, celebrated the 125th anniversary of the laying of the first stone on March 19, 2007 (Saint Joseph's day), appropriate as the project began by a society dedicated to the figure of Saint Joseph. Predictions on the completion of the apse and the construction of the east-facing main facade range from 20 to 30 years, depending on donations and advances in construction technology. This covered apse will have space for 15,000 people, a choir loft for 1,500, and occupy an area large enough to encompass the entire Santa Maria del Mar basilica. The towers still to be completed over the apse include those dedicated to the four evangelists (Matthew, Mark, Luke, and John), the Virgin Mary, and the highest of all, dedicated to Christ. The main facade will face east across Carrer Mallorca and a wide esplanade that will be created by the demolition of an entire city block of apartment houses built during the 1960s. ✉ *Mallorca 401, Eixample* ☎ *93/207–3031* 🌐 *www.sagradafamilia.org* 🎫 *€10, bell tower elevator €2.* ⏲ *Oct.–Mar., daily 9–6; Apr.–Sept., daily 9–8* Ⓜ *Sagrada Família.*

ALSO WORTH SEEING

28 **Casa Àsia–Palau Baró de Quadras.** The neo-Gothic and plateresque (intricately carved in silversmithlike detail) house built by Puig i Cadafalch in 1904 for Baron Quadras displays, on its facade, some of the most spectacular Eusebi Arnau sculptures in town. Look for St. George slaying the dragon, and don't miss the alpine chaletlike windows across the top floor. Casa Àsia, with an excellent library for Asia-related cultural and business research, offers free visits to its main floors and art gallery. ✉ *Av. Diagonal 373, Eixample* ☎ *93/238–7337* 🌐 *www.casaasia.es* 🎫 *Free* ⏲ *Tues.–Sat. 10–8, Sun. 10–2* Ⓜ *Diagonal.*

29 **Casa de les Punxes** *(House of the Spikes).* Also known as Casa Terrades for the family that commissioned it, this cluster of six conical towers ending in impossibly sharp needles is one of several Puig i Cadafalch inspirations rooted in the Gothic architecture of northern Europe, an ur-Bavarian or Danish castle in downtown Barcelona. It is one of the few freestanding Eixample buildings visible from 360 degrees. ✉ *Av. Diagonal 416–420, Eixample* Ⓜ *Diagonal.*

30 **Casa Macaia.** Built in 1901, this graceful Puig i Cadafalch building was until recently the seat of the Centre Cultural Fundació "La Caixa," a far-reaching cultural entity funded by the Caixa Catalana (Catalan Savings Bank). The Eusebi Arnau sculptures over the door depict, somewhat cryptically, a man mounted on a donkey and another on a bicycle, reminiscent of the similar Arnau sculptures on the facade of Puig i Cadafalch's Casa Amatller on Passeig de Gràcia. ✉ *Passeig de Sant Joan 108, Eixample* Ⓜ *Verdaguer.*

26 **Casa Montaner i Simó–Fundació Tàpies.** This former publishing house was converted to a modern, airy, split-level showcase for the work of contemporary Catalan painter Antoni Tàpies, as well as temporary exhibits. The bookstore is strong on Tàpies and Asian art. ✉ *Carrer Aragó 255, Eixample* ☎ *93/487–0315* 🎫 *€4.50* ⏲ *Tues.–Sun. 10–8.*

32 **Hospital de Sant Pau.** Certainly one of the most beautiful hospital complexes in the world, a 10-minute walk down Avinguda Gaudí from the Sagrada Família, the Hospital de Sant Pau is notable for its Mudejar motifs and sylvan plantings. The hospital wards are set among gardens under exposed brick facades intensely decorated with mosaics and polychrome ceramic tile. Begun in 1900, this monumental production

won Lluís Domènech i Montaner his third Barcelona "Best Building" award, in 1912. (His previous two prizes were for the Palau de la Música Catalana and Casa Lleó Morera.) The Moderniste enthusiasm for nature is apparent here; the architect believed patients are more apt to recover if they are surrounded by trees and flowers than in sterile hospital wards. Domènech i Montaner also believed in the therapeutic properties of form and color and decorated the hospital with Pau Gargallo sculptures and colorful mosaics. ✉ *Carrer Sant Antoni Maria Claret 167, Eixample* ☎ *93/291–9000* 🌐 *www.santpau.es* 🎫 *Free; tour €5* ⏲ *Daily 9–8; tours weekends 10–2, weekdays by advance arrangement* Ⓜ *Hospital de Sant Pau.*

UPPER BARCELONA: GRÀCIA, PARC GÜELL, PEDRALBES & SARRIÀ

Barcelona's upper reaches begin with Pedralbes, a neighborhood of graceful mansions grouped around a stunning Gothic monastery. Parc Güell is Gaudí's Art Nouveau urban garden. Sarrià and Gràcia were outlying villages swallowed up by the expanding metropolis. The Monestir de Pedralbes closes at 2, so start with Pedralbes and Sarrià, then visit Parc Güell and Gràcia. Tibidabo, with its amusement park and Norman Foster's Torre de Collserola should be considered only on an (increasingly unusual) unsmoggy day.

7

A GOOD TOUR

From the **Monestir de Pedralbes** 33, a 20-minute walk gets you to the main square of **Sarrià** 34. After exploring Sarrià, another short walk downhill through the Jardins de la Villa Amèlia leads past Gaudí's Finca Güell gate and gatehouse (now the Cátedra Gaudí research center) to the **Palau Reial de Pedralbes** 35, which, in turn, is a short walk downhill to the FC Barcelona soccer stadium. **Tibidabo** 36 has wonderful vistas on clear days, and the restaurant La Venta is a fine place for lunch in the sun. A truly fantastic photo op awaits at **Torre de Collserola** 37. Free transportation is provided to the tower from Plaza Tibidabo. Gaudí's **Parc Güell** 38 is most easily reached by taxi. While there, don't miss the **Casa-Museu Gaudí** 39. After the park, walk down through **Gràcia** 40 to **Casa Vicens** 41. Parc Güell and Tibidabo are best seen in mid- to late afternoon, when the sun backs around to the west and illuminates the Mediterranean.

TIMING If you do it all at once, this is a five- to six-hour outing. Add another two hours if you want to go up to the Collserola Tower.

WHAT TO SEE: MAIN ATTRACTIONS

41 **Casa Vicens.** Gaudí's first important commission as a young architect was built between 1883 and 1885, at which time he had not yet thrown away his architect's tools, particularly the T-square. The historical eclecticism of the early–Art Nouveau movement is evident in the Orientalist themes and Mudejar details lavished on the facade. The house was commissioned by a ceramics merchant, which may explain the eye-catching color ceramic tiles that render most of the facade a striking checkerboard—Barcelona's first example of this now-omnipresent

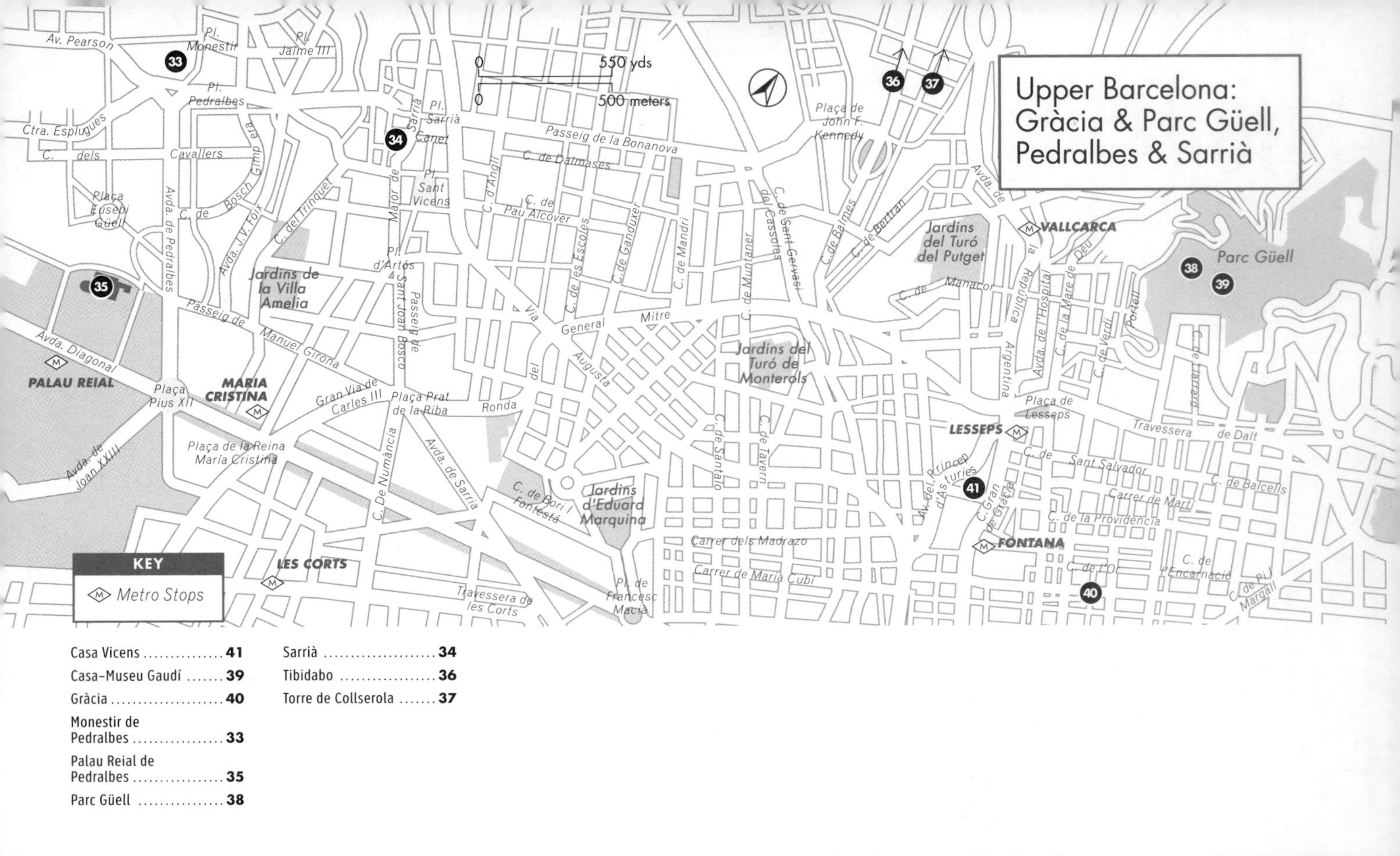
Upper Barcelona:
Gràcia & Parc Güell,
Pedralbes & Sarrià
KEY
Metro Stops
0 550 yds
0 500 meters
PALAU REIAL
MARIA CRISTINA
LES CORTS
VALLCARCA
LESSEPS
FONTANA
Parc Güell
Jardins de la Villa Amelia
Jardins del Turó del Putget
Jardins del Turó de Monterols
Jardins d'Eduard Marquina
Avda. Diagonal
Avda. de Pedralbes
Passeig de la Bonanova
Passeig de Manuel Girona
Plaça Pius XII
Plaça de la Reina María Cristina
Plaça Prat de la Riba
Plaça de John F. Kennedy
Plaça de Lesseps
Pl. de Francesc Macià
Via Augusta
Ronda del General Mitre
Travessera de Dalt
Travessera de les Corts
Avda. de Sarrià

technique. The palm leaves on the gate and surrounding fence have been attributed to Gaudí assistant, Francesc Berenguer, and the comic iron lizards and bats oozing off the facade are Gaudí's playful nod to the Gothic gargoyle. ✉ *Carrer de les Carolines 24–26, Gràcia.*

40 **Gràcia.** Along with being a neighborhood, Gràcia is a state of mind, a virtual village republic that has periodically risen in rebellion against city, state, and country. The street names (Llibertat, Fraternitat, Progrès, Venus) reveal the ideological history of this nucleus of working-class sentiment. Barcelona's first collectivized manufacturing operations (i.e., factories) were clustered here—a dangerous precedent, as workers organized into radical groups ranging from anarchists to feminists to esperantists. Once an outlying town, Gràcia joined Barcelona only under duress and attempted to secede from the Spanish state in 1856, 1870, 1873, and 1909. Lying above the Diagonal from Carrer de Còrsega up to Parc Güell, this jumble of streets is filled with appealing bars and restaurants, movie theaters, and outdoor cafés, usually thronged by hip couples. The August Festa Major fills the streets with the rank-and-file residents of this lively yet intimate little pocket of resistance to Organized Life.

From Parc Güell, dig out your city map and follow Carrer Larrard across Travessera de Dalt and down Carrer Torrent de les Flors through upper Gràcia to **Plaça Rovira i Trias,** where a bronze effigy of architect Antoni Rovira i Trias sits on a bench. Continue downhill and west to **Plaça de la Virreina** to see the work of Francesc Berenguer at Carrer del Or 44. (If Barcelona was Gaudí's sandbox, Gràcia was Berenguer's—nearly every major building in this neighborhood is his creation.) Cut over to **Plaça del Diamant** to see in bronze the heroine of Mercé Rodoreda's famous 1962 novel *La Plaça del Diamant.* Moving through Plaça Trilla, cross Gran de Gràcia to Carrer de les Carolines to see Gaudí's very first house, **Casa Vicens.**

Your next stop is the produce market **Mercat de la Llibertat,** an uptown Boqueria. Cut east along Cisne, cross Gran de Gràcia, and pass another Berenguer creation on Ros de Olano, the Mudejar-style **Centre Moral Instructiu de Gràcia. Plaça del Sol,** one of Gràcia's most popular squares, is downhill. From here, continue east to Gràcia's other market, the **Mercat de la Revolució.** Walk three blocks back over to Grácia's main square, **Plaça Rius i Taulet,** with its emblematic clock tower. From Plaça Rius i Taulet, cut out to **Gran de Gràcia** for a look at some more Art Nouveau buildings by Berenguer (Nos. 15, 23, 35, 49, 51, 61, and 77). For lunch, consider Galician seafood at Botafumeiro, Basque fare at Ipar Txoko just below Plaça Rius i Taulet.

33 **Monestir de Pedralbes.** One of Barcelona's hidden treasures, this monastery (in fact, a convent) was founded by Reina Elisenda, widow of Catalonia's Sovereign Count Jaume II, for Clarist nuns in 1326. The unusual, three-story Gothic cloister is the finest in Barcelona. The abess's day cell, the Capella de Sant Miquel, has famous murals painted in 1346 by Ferrer Bassa, a Catalan master much influenced by the Italian Renaissance. Scratched into the painting, on the right side

between Saints Francis and Clare, you can make out what is widely considered Barcelona's earliest graffito: *Joan no m'oblides* (John, don't forget me), proof that not all of the novotiates were there by their own choice. You can also visit the medieval living quarters and kitchen. Look for the ruts broken into the arcaded walkways by Napoléonic cannon during the 1809 French occupation. The museum shows religious paintings and artifacts collected over the centuries. ✉ *Baixada Monestir 9, Pedralbes* ☎ *93/203–9282* 🌐 *www.museuhistoria.bcn.es* 🎟 *€5; free 1st Sun. of month. €6 also includes admission to Museu Històrica de la Ciutat, Parc Güell Centre d'Interpretation, and Museu-Casa Verdaguer* ⏲ *Oct.–May, Tues.–Sun. 10–2; June–Sept., Tues.–Sun. 10–5* Ⓜ *Reina Elisenda.*

38 Fodor's Choice ★ **Parc Güell.** Güell Park is one of Gaudí's, and Barcelona's, most pleasant and stimulating places to spend a few hours; it's light and playful, alternately shady, green, floral, and sunny. Named for and commissioned by Gaudí's main patron, Count Eusebio Güell, the park was intended as a hillside garden suburb on the English model. Barcelona's bourgeoisie seemed happier living closer to "town," however, so only two of the houses were ever built. The Güell family eventually turned the land over to the city as a public park. Gaudí highlights include an Art Nouveau extravaganza with gingerbread gatehouses topped with a hallucinogenic red-and-white fly ammanite wild mushroom (rumored to have been a Gaudí favorite) on the right and a *phallus impudicus* mushroom (no translation necessary) on the left. The gatehouse on the right holds the **Center for the Interpretation and Welcome to Parc Güell,** with plans, scale models, photos, and suggested routes analyzing the park in detail. Other highlights include the ⇨ **Gaudí Casa–Museu** (the house where Gaudí lived with his niece for 20 years), the Room of a Hundred Columns—a covered market supported by tilted Doric-style columns and mosaic-encrusted buttresses, and guarded by a patchwork lizard—and the fabulous serpentine, polychrome bench that snakes along the main square. ✉ *Carrer d'Olot s/n; take Metro to Lesseps; then walk 10 min uphill or catch Bus 24 to park entrance, Gràcia* ⏲ *Oct.–Mar., daily 10–6; Apr.–June, daily 10–7; July–Sept., daily 10–9* Ⓜ *Lesseps.*

ALSO WORTH SEEING

39 The **Casa-Museu Gaudí,** within Parc Güell, is in a pink, Alice-in-Wonderland house designed by Gaudí's assistant and right hand, Francesc Berenguer (1866–1914); this is where Gaudí lived with his niece from 1906 to 1926. Exhibits include Gaudí-designed furniture, decorations, drawings, portraits, and a bust of the architect. ✉ *Parc Güell, up hill to right of main entrance, Gràcia* ☎ *93/219–3811* 🎟 *€4* ⏲ *May–Sept., daily 10–8; Oct.–Feb., daily 10–6; Mar. and Apr., daily 10–7.*

OFF THE BEATEN PATH

CosmoCaixa–Museu de la Ciència Fundació "La Caixa" Young scientific minds work overtime in this ever-more-interactive science museum, just below Tibidabo. Among the many displays designed for children seven and up are Geological Wall, a history of rocks and rock formations studied through a transversal cutaway section; and the Underwater Forest, show-

casing the climate and species of an Amazonian rain forest in a large greenhouse. Expositions of sustainable exploitation techniques such as "The Red Line: How to Make Wood Without Damaging the Forest" are accompanied by explanations of environmental problems and how to correct them. ✉ ***Teodor Roviralta 55, Sant Gervasi*** ☎ ***93/212–6050*** 🌐 ***www.cosmocaixa.com*** 🎫 ***€4 (€2 per interactive activity inside)*** ⏲ ***Tues.–Sun. 10–8*** Ⓜ ***Avinguda de Tibidabo and Tramvía Blau halfway.***

35 **Palau Reial de Pedralbes** *(Royal Palace of Pedralbes)*. Built in the 1920s for King Alfonso XII, the palace houses the **Museu de Ceràmica,** covering Spanish ceramic art from its Moorish beginnings up through medieval work from Manises and Paterna to Talavera de la Reina and Puente del Arzobispo. Catalan tile work, porcelain from Alcora, and Picasso and Miró creations complete the exhibit. The **Museu de les Arts Decoratives** exhibits household and design objects from medieval times through the Industrial Revolution and Spanish civil war up to contemporary design. ✉ *Av. Diagonal 686, Pedralbes* ☎ *93/280–5024 decorative arts museum, 93/280–1621 ceramic museum* 🌐 *www.museuceramica.bcn.es* 🎫 *€4 includes both museums; free 1st Sun. of month* ⏲ *Tues.–Sat. 10–6, Sun. 10–3* Ⓜ *Palau Reial.*

34 **Sarrià.** This intimate, bite-size 1,000-year-old village was once a cluster of farms and country houses overlooking Barcelona from the hills. Start at the main square, Plaça Sarrià, which holds an antiques market on Tuesday morning, a book market on Friday, occasional *sardana* dances on Sunday morning, and Christmas fairs in season. The Romanesque church tower, lighted a warm ocher at night, looms overhead. Across Passeig Reina Elisenda from the church, wander through the brick-and-steel **produce market** and the tiny **Plaça Sant Gaietà** behind it. Back in front of the church, cut through the Placeta del Roser to the left of the main door and you'll come to the elegant **town hall** in the Plaça de la Vila; note the buxom bronze sculpture of Pomona, goddess of fruit and the harvest, by famed Sarrià sculptor Josep Clarà (1878–1958). After a peek at the massive ceiling beams (and tempting prix-fixe lunch menu) in the restaurant Vell Sarrià, at the corner of Major de Sarrià, go back to the Pomona bronze and turn left toward Carrer dels Paletes (with its tiny Sant Antoni, patron saint of workers, or *paletes*, overhead to the right). Back on Major de Sarrià, continue down this pedestrian-only street and turn left onto **Carrer Canet,** with its cottagelike artisans' quarters, formerly factory workers' housing provided by a nearby 19th-century textile mill. The house at No. 15 is an original two-story village house. No. 21 has unusual floral ornamentation on the facade, and No. 23 is a rustic village dwelling painted a characteristic earthy Mediterranean orange.

Turn right on Carrer Cornet i Mas and walk two blocks down to Carrer Jaume Piquet. A quick probe to the left will take you to No. 30, Barcelona's most perfect small-format **Moderniste house,** complete with faux-medieval upper windows, wrought-iron grillwork, floral and fruit ornamentation, and organically curved and carved wooden doors. Don't miss the restored wooden door at No. 9, or the Falangist eagle

7

over the entrance of what was until 1976 the local telegraph office. Farther down at No. 15 is a fascist symbol left over from the 1951 Instituto Nacional de Vivienda (National Housing Institute). The tiny pink house down at No. 36 is another typical Sarrià village house. The next stop down Cornet i Mas is Sarrià's most picturesque square, **Plaça Sant Vicens,** a leafy space ringed by early village houses and centered on a statue of Sarrià's patron saint. Note the other renditions of the saint over the square's upper right corner. The café Can Pau is the local hangout, once a haven for such authors as Gabriel García Marquez and Mario Vargas Llosa, who lived in Sarrià in the early 1970s, on the cusp of their fame. Check out the Gouthier oyster-, salmon-, *foie-* (duck or goose liver-), caviar-, and wine-tasting bar on the lower corner of the square. To get to the Monestir de Pedralbes from Plaça Sant Vicens, walk back up Mayor de Sarrià and through the market to the corner of Sagrat Cor and Ramon Miquel Planas; then turn left and walk straight west for 15 minutes, past the splendid upper-city mansions of Pedralbes. Other Sarrià landmarks include the two **Foix** pastry stores, one at Plaça Sarrià 9–10 and the other on Major de Sarrià 57, above Bar Tomás. Both have excellent pastries, artisanal breads, and cold cava. The late J.V. Foix, son of the store's founders, was one of the great Catalan poets of the 20th century, a key player in keeping the Catalan language alive during the 40-year Franco regime. The store in Plaça Sarrià—a good place for homemade ice cream—has a bronze bust of the poet, and the Major de Sarrià shop has a plaque identifying the house with one of the poet's most memorable verses: *Tota amor és latent en l'altra amor / tot llenguatge és saó d'una parla comuna / tota terra batega a la pàtria de tots / tota fe serà suc d'una mes alta fe.* (Every love is latent in the other love / every language is part of a common tongue / every country touches the fatherland of all / every faith will be the lifeblood of a higher faith.) ✉ *Pl. Sarrià, Sarrià; take Bus 22 from bottom of Av. de Tibidabo, or U-6 train on FFCC subway to Reina Elisenda.*

NEED A BREAK?

Bar Tomás (✉ *Major de Sarrià 49, Sarrià* ☎ *93/203–1077* Ⓜ *Sarrià*), home of the finest potatoes in town and a Barcelona institution, is on the corner of Jaume Piquet. Order the *doble mixta* of potatoes with *allioli* (garlic and olive oil) and a splash of fiery hot sauce. Draft beer (ask for a *caña*) is the de rigueur drink.

36 **Tibidabo.** On a windy, cleary day, the views from this hill are legendary, particularly from the 850-foot communications tower, Torre de Collserola. There's not much to see here except the vista, particularly from the tower. Breezy, smog-free days are few and far between in 21st-century Barcelona, but if (and only if) you hit one, this excursion is worth considering. The restaurant **La Venta,** at the base of the funicular, is excellent, a fine place to sit in the sun in cool weather (don't fret over sunburn; the establishment provides straw sun hats). The bar **Mirablau** is a popular hangout for evening drinks. ✉ *Plaça del Doctor Andreu s/n Take Tibidabo train (U-7) from Pl. de Catalunya or buses 24 and 22 to Pl. Kennedy. At Av. Tibidabo, catch Tramvía Blau (Blue Trolley), which connects with funicular to summit* Ⓜ *Tibidabo.*

37 **Torre de Collserola.** Created by Norman Foster, the Collserola Tower was erected for the 1992 Olympics amid controversy over defacement of the traditional mountain skyline. As an immense communications mast with a cylindrical midsection housing an observation deck and a restaurant, it's now considered the best piece of contemporary architecture in the city's upper reaches. ✉ *Av. de Vallvidrera; take the funicular up to Tibidabo; from Pl. Tibidabo there is free transport to the tower. Tibidabò* ☎ *93/406–9354* 🌐 *www.torredecollserola.com* *€6* ⏲ *Wed.–Fri. 11–2:30 and 3:30–6, weekends 11–6* Ⓜ *Tibidabo.*

SANT PERE, LA RIBERA, LA CIUTADELLA & BARCELONETA

Barcelona's old textile neighborhood, around the church of Sant Pere, includes the flagship of the city's Moderniste architecture, the Palau de la Música Catalana. Barceloneta, once the open sea, silted in and became a salt marsh until 1753, when French military engineer Prosper de Verboom designed a housing project for families who had lost their homes in La Ribera. Together, these areas form a good walk within and around what were once Barcelona's 13th-century walls.

A GOOD WALK

These neighborhoods northeast of the Gothic Quarter begin with the **Palau de la Música Catalana** 42, a 10-minute walk from Plaça Catalunya. After the Palau, continue along Carrer Sant Pere Més Alt past the church of **Sant Pere de les Puelles** 43 and out to the **Arc del Triomf** 44, on Passeig de Sant Joan. From there, walk through the **Parc de la Ciutadella** 45, past the **Castell dels Tres Dragons** 46, the **Museu de la Geologia** 47, and **La Cascada** 48 (a waterfall with rocks by Gaudí) until unmistakable aromas announce the zoo. The Barcelona **Zoo** 49 has dolphins, rhinos, and an albino gorilla. Leaving the zoo, pass the **Estació de França** 50, and continue on to the edge of **Port Vell** 51 next to the Palau de Mar. For a look at Catalonia's version (for once) of its own history, check out the interactive **Museu d'Història de Catalunya** 52. Then walk around the port to **El Transbordador Aeri del Port** 53 for a ride over the harbor, or walk through **Barceloneta** 54 and along the beach to the **Port Olímpic** 55.

TIMING Depending on the number of stops, this walk can take a full day. Count on at least four hours of actual walking time.

WHAT TO SEE: MAIN ATTRACTIONS

54 **Barceloneta.** Once Barcelona's pungent fishing port, Barceloneta retains much of its maritime flavor. It's an exciting and colorful walk through narrow streets with lines of laundry snapping in the breeze. Stop in Plaça de la Barceloneta to see the baroque church of **Sant Miquel del Port,** with its oversize sculpture of the winged archangel himself. Look for the Barceloneta market and the restaurant Can Ramonet on Carrer de la Maquinista, and for the original two-story houses and the restaurant Can Solé on Carrer Sant Carles. Barceloneta's surprisingly clean and sandy **beach,** though overcrowded in midsummer, offers swimming, surfing, and a lively social scene from late May through September.

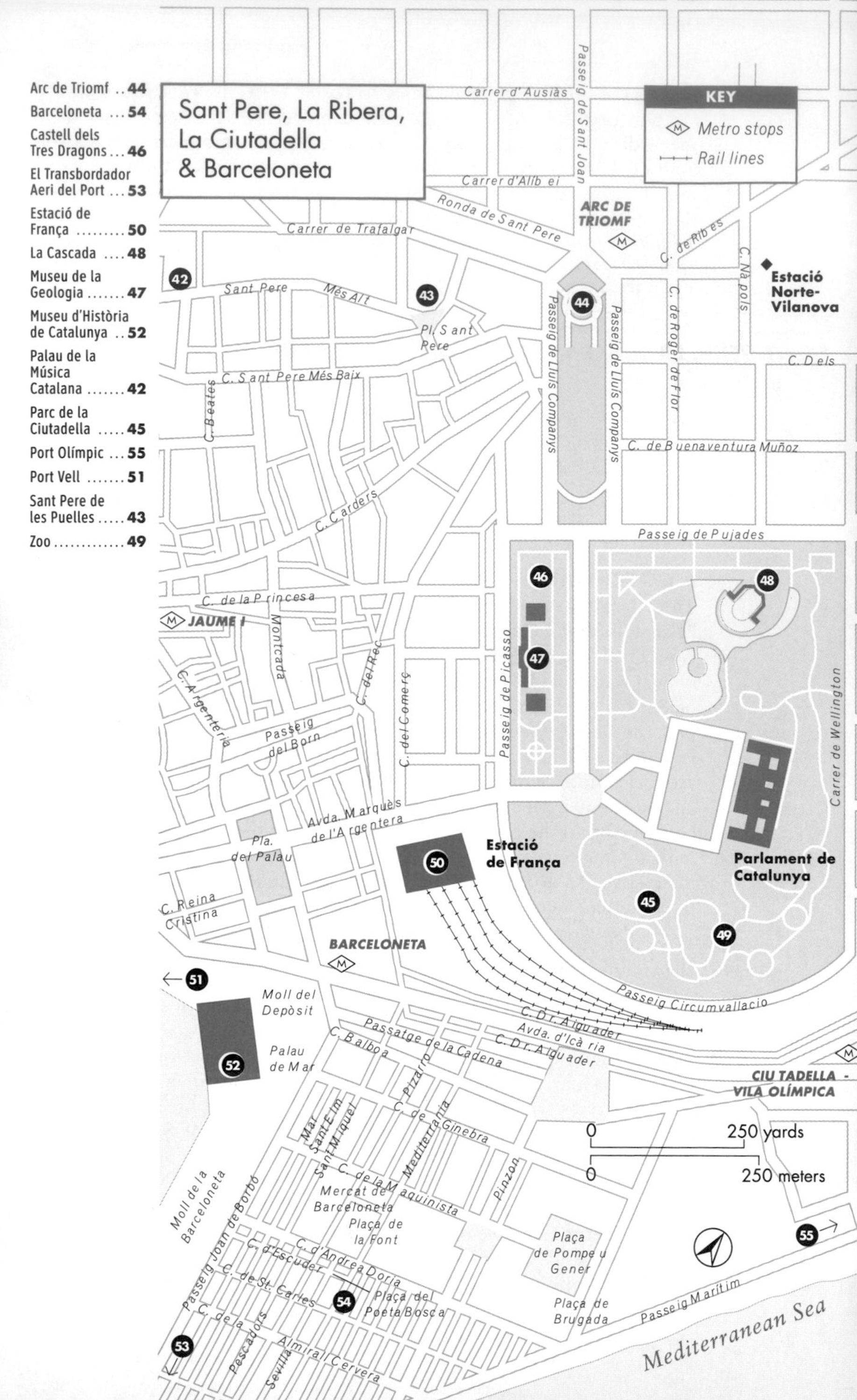

Arc de Triomf .. 44
Barceloneta ... 54
Castell dels Tres Dragons ... 46
El Transbordador Aeri del Port ... 53
Estació de França 50
La Cascada 48
Museu de la Geologia 47
Museu d'Història de Catalunya .. 52
Palau de la Música Catalana 42
Parc de la Ciutadella 45
Port Olímpic ... 55
Port Vell 51
Sant Pere de les Puelles 43
Zoo 49
Sant Pere, La Ribera, La Ciutadella & Barceloneta
KEY
Metro stops
Rail lines
Carrer d'Ausiàs
Passeig de Sant Joan
Carrer d'Alib ei
Ronda de Sant Pere
Carrer de Trafalgar
ARC DE TRIOMF
C. de Rib es
C. Nàpols
Estació Norte-Vilanova
Sant Pere Més Alt
Pl. Sant Pere
C. Sant Pere Més Baix
C. Beates
Passeig de Lluís Companys
C. de Roger de Flor
C. Dels
C. de Buenaventura Muñoz
C. Carders
Passeig de Pujades
C. de la Princesa
JAUME I
Montcada
C. del Rec
C. Argenteria
C. del Comerç
Passeig de Picasso
Carrer de Wellington
Passeig del Born
Avda. Marquès de l'Argentera
Pla. del Palau
Estació de França
Parlament de Catalunya
C. Reina Cristina
BARCELONETA
Moll del Depòsit
Passeig Circumvallacio
C. Dr. Aiguader
Avda. d'Icària
Passatge de la Cadena
C. Balboa
Palau de Mar
CIUTADELLA - VILA OLÍMPICA
C. Pizarro
C. de Ginebra
Mar
Sant Elm
Sant Miquel
Mediterrània
0
250 yards
0
250 meters
C. de la Maquinista
Mercat de Barceloneta
Pinzon
Moll de la Barceloneta
Passeig Joan de Borbó
Plaça de la Font
C. d'Escuder
C. d'Andrea Doria
Plaça de Pompeu Gener
C. de St. Carles
Plaça del Poeta Bosca
Plaça de Brugada
Passeig Marítim
C. de la
Pescadors
Sevilla
Almiral Cervera
Mediterranean Sea

42 **Palau de la Música Catalana.** A riot of color and form, Barcelona's Music Palace is the flagship of the city's Moderniste architecture. Designed by Lluís Domènech i Montaner in 1908, it was originally conceived by the Orfeó Català musical society as a vindication of the importance of music at a popular level—as opposed to the Liceu opera house's identification with the Catalan (often Castilian-speaking monarchist) aristocracy. The Palau's exterior is remarkable in itself, albeit hard to see because there's no room to back up and behold it. Above the main entrance are busts of Palestrina, Bach, Beethoven, and (around the corner on Carrer Amadeu Vives) Wagner. Look for the colorful mosaic pillars on the second upper level, a preview of what's inside. The Miquel Blay sculptural group over the corner of Sant Pere Més Alt and Amadeu Vives depicts everyone from St. George the dragon slayer (at the top) to fishermen with oars over their shoulders.

Fodor'sChoice ★

The interior is an uproar. Wagnerian cavalry erupts from the right side of the stage over a heavy-browed bust of Beethoven, and Catalonia's popular music is represented by the flowing maidens of Lluís Millet's song "Flors de Maig" ("Flowers of May") on the left. Overhead, an inverted stained-glass cupola seems to offer the divine manna of music; painted rosettes and giant peacock feathers explode from the tops of the walls. Even the stage is populated with muselike Art Nouveau musicians, each half bust, half mosaic. The visuals alone make music sound different in here, and at any important concert the excitement is palpably thick. If you can't attend one, take a tour of the hall. *Ticket office ✉ Carrer Sant Francesc de Paula 2, just off Via Laietana, around corner from hall, Sant Pere ☎ 902/442–882 🌐 www.palaumusica.org 🎫 Tour €8 ⏲ Sept.–June, tours daily 10–3:30, July and Aug. tours daily 10–7 Ⓜ Catalunya.*

7

ALSO WORTH SEEING

44 **Arc del Triomf.** This imposing, exposed-redbrick arch on Passeig de Sant Joan was built by Josep Vilaseca as the grand entrance for the Universal Exposition of 1888. Similar in size and sense to the triumphal arches of ancient Rome, this one refers to Jaume I El Conqueridor's 1229 conquest of the Moors in Mallorca—as suggested by the bats, always part of Jaume I's coat of arms, on either side of the arch.

NEED A BREAK?

Friendly Can Manel la Puda (☎ *93/221–5013*), at Passeig de Joan de Borbó 60–61 in Barceloneta, is always good for an inexpensive feast in the sun. Serving lunch until 4 and starting dinner at 7, it's a popular place for *suquets* (fish stew), paella, and *arròs a banda* (rice with de-shelled seafood). It's closed Monday, and they accept all major plastic. On Monday or if Can Manel is booked solid, La Mar Salada next door is just as good.

46 **Castell dels Tres Dragons** *(Castle of the Three Dragons)*. Built by Domènech i Montaner as a restaurant for the Universal Exposition of 1888, this arresting structure was named in honor of a popular mid-19th-century comedy by the father of the Catalan theater, Serafí Pitarra. Greeting you on the right as you enter the Ciutadella from Passeig Lluí Companys, the building has exposed brickwork and visible iron supports, both

CLOSE UP

Moderniste Barcelona

Characterized by intense ornamentation and the use of natural or organic lines and forms, Modernisme (aka Art Nouveau) swept Europe between 1880 and 1914, though nowhere did it proliferate as it did in Barcelona, beginning with the Universal Exposition of 1888. Here it tapped into the playful Catalan artistic impulse (as evidenced in the works of Gaudí) because it coincided with Barcelona's late-19th-century industrial prosperity.

A cultural movement that went beyond architecture, Barcelona's Modernisme affected the design of everything from clothes to hairstyles to tombstones. Painters such as Ramón Casas and Santiago Russinyol, sculptors such as Miquel Blay and Eusebi Arnau, stained-glass artisans, ceramicists, acid engravers, and wood-carvers all played a part in the explosion of artistic exuberance.

Barcelona's Palau de la Música Catalana by Lluís Domènech i Montaner, the flagship of the movement, is a stunning compendium of Art Nouveau decorative techniques, including acid-etched glass and stained glass, polychrome ceramic ornamentation, carved wooden arches, and sculptures. Antoni Gaudí is the most famous of the Moderniste architects. Josep Puig i Cadafalch's Casa Amatller and Casa de les Punxes are examples of Modernisme's eclectic, historical tendencies. Josep Graner i Prat's Casa de la Papallona, Joan Rubió Bellver's Casa Golferichs, Gaudí's Casa Batlló, and Salvador Valeri i Pupurull's Casa Comalat are Moderniste mansions that make Barcelona's Eixample a living architecture museum.

The Ruta del Modernisme is an itinerary through the Barcelona of Gaudì, Domènech i Montaner, and Puig i Cadafalch, the architects who, along with others, made Barcelona the world capital of Modernisme in the late 19th and early 20th centuries: palaces, private houses, the temple that has become a symbol of the city, and a huge hospital join pharmacies, lampposts, and benches—115 works in all—tracing Art Nouveau's explosion in Barcelona.

There are three Modernisme Centers (☎902/076621), which sell items related to the route, including a route pack with discount vouchers, a map showing all 115 works, a guide to Moderniste bars and restaurants, a pencil, a notebook, and a bag in which to carry it all. The *Modernisme Route* guidebook—the most comprehensive Modernisme study in Barcelona—is available for €12 in most local bookstores and at all three Modernisme Centers. ■ **TIP→The Modernisme Route offers discount vouchers good for up to 50% on all Moderniste monuments in the city and in another 13 towns.**

radical innovations of their time. Moderniste architects later met here to exchange ideas and experiment with traditional crafts; the castle now holds Barcelona's **Museum of Zoology.** ✉*Passeig Picasso 5, La Ciutadella* ☎*93/319–6912* 🌐*www.bcn.es/medciencies* 💶*€3.75* 🕓*Tues., Wed., Fri.–Sun. 10–2:30, Thurs. 10–6:30* Ⓜ*Arc de Triomf.*

53 **El Transbordador Aeri del Port** *(cable car)*. The creaky looking but recently refurbished cable car leaving from the tower at the end of Passeig Joan de Borbó connects the Torre de San Sebastián on the Moll de Barce-

RECOMMENDED MODERNISTE MONUMENTS

■ Casa Amatller	■ CosmoCaixa, Museu de la Ciència
■ Casa Batlló	■ Hidroelèctrica
■ Casa Calvet	■ Hospital de la Santa Creu i Sant Pau
■ Casa Comalat	■ Museu Nacional d'Art de Catalunya (MNAC)
■ Casa de les Punxes (Casa Terrades)	■ Museu de Zoologia
■ Casa Lleó Morera	■ Observatori Fabra
■ Casa Milà (La Pedrera)	■ Palau de la Música Catalana
■ Casa Fuster	■ Palau del Baró de Quadras
■ Casa Macaya	■ Palau Montaner
■ Casa Planells	■ Pavellons Güell
■ Casa Thomas	■ Temple Expiatori de la Sagrada Família
■ Casa Vicens	■ Torre Bellesguard
■ Conservatori Municipal de Música	

loneta, the tower of Jaume I in the boat terminal, and the Torre de Miramar on Montjuïc. The Torre de Altamar restaurant in the tower at the Barceloneta end serves excellent food and wine and has nonpareil views. ✉ *Passeig Joan de Borbó s/n, Barceloneta* ☎ *93/225–2718* 🎟 *€9 round-trip, €7.50 one-way* ⏲ *Daily 10:45–7* Ⓜ *Barceloneta.*

50 **Estació de França.** Once Barcelona's main train station, the gracefully restored Estació de França is outside the west gate of the Ciutadella. Wander in for a rush of European railroad nostalgia. ✉ *Marquès de l'Argentera s/n, Born-Ribera* Ⓜ *Barceloneta.*

48 **La Cascada.** Take a break by the Ciutadella's lake, and, behind it, you'll find the monumental *Cascada,* (Falls) by Josep Fontseré, designed for the Universal Exposition of 1888. The waterfall's rocks were the work of a young architecture student named Antoni Gaudí—his first public work, appropriately natural and organic, a hint of things to come. ✉ *La Ciutadella* Ⓜ *Arc de Triomf, Ciutadella.*

47 **Museu de la Geologia.** The Museum of Geology is next to the Castell dels Tres Dragons and the Umbracle, the black slats of which help create jungle lighting for a valuable collection of tropical plants. Barcelona's first public museum, it has rocks, minerals, and fossils from Catalonia and the rest of Spain. ✉ *Off Passeig de Picasso, La Ciutadella* ☎ *93/319–6895* 🌐 *www.bcn.es/museuciencies* 🎟 *€3.50; free 1st Sun. of month* ⏲ *Tues., Wed., Fri.–Sun. 10–2, Thurs. 10–6:30* Ⓜ *Arc de Triomf, Ciutadella.*

52 **Museu d'Història de Catalunya.** Built into what used to be a port warehouse, this state-of-the-art museum is interactive (visitors can try on armor or ride a mechanical horse along with activating computerized displays) making you part of Catalonian history. Beginning from prehistoric times, the emergence of the language and identity of Catalonia is traced through more than 3,000 years into the contemporary democratic era. Explanations of the exhibits appear in Catalan, Castilian, and English. Guided tours are available on Sunday at noon and 1 PM. The rooftop cafeteria, open to the general public, has excellent views over the harbor. ✉ *Pl. Pau Vila 3, Barceloneta* ☎ *93/225–4700* 🌐 *www.mhcat.net* 🎫 *€4; free 1st Sun. of month* ⏲ *Tues. and Thurs.–Sat. 10–7, Wed. 10–8, Sun. 10–2:30* Ⓜ *Barceloneta.*

45 **Parc de la Ciutadella** *(Citadel Park).* Once a fortress designed to consolidate Madrid's military occupation of Barcelona, the Ciutadella is now the city's main downtown park. The clearing dates from shortly after the War of the Spanish Succession, when Felipe V demolished some 2,000 houses in what was then the Barri de la Ribera (Waterfront Neighborhood) to build a fortress and barracks for his soldiers and fields of fire for his artillery. The fortress walls were pulled down in 1868 and replaced by gardens laid out by Josep Fontserè. Within the park are a cluster of museums, the Catalan parliament, and the city zoo. ✉ *Passeig Picasso/Passeig Pujades/Carrer de Wellington, Born-Ribera* Ⓜ *Barceloneta.*

55 **Port Olímpic.** Choked with yachts, restaurants, and tapas bars of all kinds, the Olympic Port is 2 km (1 mi) up the beach, marked by the mammoth Frank Gehry goldfish sculpture in front of Barcelona's first real skyscraper, the Hotel Arts. The port rages on Friday and Saturday night, especially in summer, with hundreds of young people circling and grazing until daybreak. ✉ *Carrer de la Marina/Passeig Marítim, Born-Ribera* Ⓜ *Ciutadella, Vila Olimpica.*

51 **Port Vell** *(Old Port).* From Pla del Palau, cross to the edge of the port, where the Moll d'Espanya, the Moll de la Fusta, and the Moll de Barceloneta meet. Just beyond the Lichtenstein sculpture *Barcelona Head,* in front of the post office, the modern Port Vell complex stretches up the grassy hill to the wood-panel *Ictineo II* reproduction of the submarine created by Narcis Monturiol (1819–85). The submarine was the world's first, launched in the Barcelona port in 1862. Beyond are the IMAX theater, the aquarium, and the Maremagnum shopping mall along the Moll d'Espanya. The Moll de Barceloneta, with its five (somewhat pricey and impersonal) quayside terrace restaurants, stretches along the sport marina across the way. ✉ *Passeig d'Ítaca s/n, Barceloneta-Port Vell* Ⓜ *Barceloneta.*

43 **Sant Pere de les Puelles** *(St. Peter of the Novices).* One of the oldest medieval churches in Barcelona, this one has been destroyed and restored so many times that there's little left to see except the beautiful stained-glass window, which illuminates the stark interior. *Puelles* comes from the Latin *puella* (girl)—the convent here was known for the beauty and

nobility of its young women. ✉ *Lluís El Piadós 1, Sant Pere* ☎ *93/268–0742* ⏲ *Open for mass only* Ⓜ *Catalunya, Jaume I.*

49 **Zoo.** Barcelona's zoo (scheduled to be moved out to the Fòrum at the mouth of the River Besòs by 2009) presently occupies the bottom part of the Parc de la Ciutadella. Reptiles, and a full complement of African animals reside in this colony squeezed in between the Catalan Parliament and the Universidad Pompeu Fabra. Look for the statue of *La Senyoreta del Paraigua* (*Lady with Umbrella*) near the dolphins. ✉ *La Ciutadella* ☎ *93/225–6780* 🌐 *www.zoobarcelona.com* *€15* ⏲ *Daily 10–7* Ⓜ *Arc de Triomf, Ciutadella.*

MONTJUÏC

This far-flung, leafy park on a hill to the south of town requires some tedious hiking between sites and lacks the intensity and color of Barcelona street life, but the art is world class. Named for the Jewish cemetery once on its slopes (or for the Roman deity Jove, take your pick), Montjuïc is best reached by taxi, by Bus 61, on foot from Plaça Espanya, or by the funicular that operates from the Paral.lel. The cross-harbor cable car from Barceloneta or from the Jaume I midstation in the port is another, spectacular, approach (acrophobes, be warned). Ⓜ *Paral.lel.*

A GOOD WALK

Walking from sight to sight on Montjuïc is possible but not recommended. You'll want fresh feet to see the sights here, especially the vast art displays in the Palau Nacional and the Miró Foundation.

The El Transbordador Aeri del Port cable car drops you at the Jardins de Miramar, a 10-minute walk from the Plaça de Dante. From here, another small cable car takes you up to the **Castell de Montjuïc** 56. From the bottom station, the **Fundació Miró** 57 is a few minutes' walk, and beyond it is the **Estadi Olímpic** 58. From the stadium, walk straight down to the Palau Nacional and its **Museu Nacional d'Art de Catalunya** 59. From here, a wide stairway leads down toward Barcelona's convention fairgrounds; the Plaça de Espanya, behind the so-called Venetian Towers, was built as the grand entrance to Barcelona's 1929 World's Fair. As you descend this stairway past the **Plaça de les Cascades** 60, the **Mies van der Rohe Pavilion** 61 is on your left, and across the street is Casaramona (1913), now the **CaixaForum** 62. Uphill to the left is **Poble Espanyol** 63, a miniature-scale sampling of architecture from all over Spain, and the **Museu d'Arqueologia de Catalunya** 64 is around to the right of the stairs.

TIMING With unhurried visits to the Miró Foundation and the Romanesque exhibit in the Palau Nacional, this is a four- to five-hour excursion. Have lunch afterward in the Poble Espanyol.

WHAT TO SEE: MAIN ATTRACTIONS

57 ★ **Fundació Miró.** The Miró Foundation was a gift from the artist Joan Miró to his native city and is one of Barcelona's most exciting showcases of contemporary art. The airy, white building was designed by Josep Lluís Sert and opened in 1975; an extension was added by Sert's

CaixaForum (Casaramona) **62**

Castell de Montjuïc **56**

Estadi Olímpic **58**

Fundació Miró **57**

Mies van der Rohe Pavilion **61**

Museu d'Arqueologia de Catalunya **64**

Museu Nacional d'Art de Catalunya **59**

Plaça de les Cascades **60**

Poble Espanyol **63**

pupil Jaume Freixa in 1988. Miró's unmistakably playful and colorful style, filled with Mediterranean light and humor, seems a perfect match for its surroundings, and the exhibits and retrospectives that open here tend to be progressive and provocative, from Moore to Mapplethorpe. Look for Alexander Calder's mercury fountain. Miró himself rests in the cemetery on Montjuïc's southern slopes. During the Franco regime, which he strongly opposed, Miró first lived in self-imposed exile in Paris, then moved to Majorca in 1956. When he died in 1983, the Catalans gave him a send-off amounting to a state funeral. ✉ *Av. Miramar 71, Montjuïc* ☎ *93/443–9470* 🌐 *www.bcn.fjmiro.es* 🎫 *€8* 🕓 *Tues., Wed., Fri., and Sat. 10–7, Thurs. 10–9:30, Sun. 10–2:30.*

61 **Mies van der Rohe Pavilion.** The reconstructed Mies van der Rohe Pavilion (the German contribution to the International Exposition of 1929) is a "less is more" study in interlocking planes of white marble, green onyx, and glass: the aesthetic opposite of the Moderniste Palau de la Música. The pavilion occasionally hosts cultural events, cocktail parties, and book releases/signings. ✉ *Av. Marquès de Comillas s/n, Montjuïc* ☎ *93/423–4016* 🌐 *www.miesbcn.com* 🎫 *€4* 🕓 *Daily 10–8.*

59 **Museu Nacional d'Art de Catalunya** *(MNAC, Catalonian National Museum of Art).* Housed in the imposingly domed, towered, frescoed, and columned **Palau Nacional,** built in 1929 as the centerpiece of the World's Fair, this superb museum was renovated in 1995 by Gae Aulenti, architect of the Musée d'Orsay in Paris. In 2004 the museum's three collections—Romanesque, Gothic, and the Cambó Collection, an eclectic trove, were joined by the 19th- and 20th-century collection of Catalan impressionist and Moderniste painters. Also now on display is the Thyssen-Bornemisza collection of early masters, with works by Zurbarán, Rubens, Tintoretto, Velázquez, and others. With this influx of artistic treasure, the MNAC becomes Catalonia's grand central museum. Pride of place goes to the Romanesque exhibition, the world's finest collection of Romanesque frescoes, altarpieces, and wood carvings, most of them rescued from chapels in the Pyrenees during the 1920s to save them from deterioration, theft, and art dealers. Many, such as the famous *Cristo de Taüll* fresco (from the church of Sant Climent de Taüll in Taüll), have been reproduced and replaced in their original settings. ✉ *Mirador del Palau 6, Montjuïc* ☎ *93/622–0375* 🌐 *www.mnac.es* 🎫 *€9* 🕓 *Tues.–Sat. 10–7, Sun. 10–2:30.*

Fodor's Choice ★

ALSO WORTH SEEING

62 **CaixaForum** *(Casaramona).* Top art exhibits and concerts in a cleverly restored Art Nouveau factory make this relative newcomer a popular weekend culture magnet. Built by architect Josep Puig i Cadafalchto in 1911 to house a textile factory, this redbrick Art Nouveau fortress opened in early 2002 as a center for cultural events. Casaramona has come back to life as one of Barcelona's hottest new art venues. The contemporary entryway was designed by Arata Isozaki, architect of the nearby Palau Sant Jordi. ✉ *Av. Marquès de Comillas 6–8, Montjuïc* ☎ *93/476–8600* 🌐 *www.fundacio.lacaixa.es* 🎫 *Free; charge for evening concerts* 🕓 *Tues.–Sun. 10–8; later for concerts.*

56 **Castell de Montjuïc.** Built in 1640 by rebels against Felipe IV, the star-shape pentagon has been stormed several times, most famously in 1705 by Lord Peterborough for Archduke Carlos of Austria. In 1808, during the Peninsular War, it was seized by the French under General Dufresne. During an 1842 civil disturbance, Barcelona was bombed from its heights by a Spanish artillery battery. During the 1939–75 Franco regime, the castle was notorious as a dungeon for political prisoners. Executions were carried out in the gardens with frequency. Catalonian President Lluís Companys was shot by firing squad here in 1940. The moat has lush green gardens, with one side given over to an archery range, while the terraces have sweeping views over the city and the Mediterranean. The fortress houses, for the moment, the Museu Militar. Plans are in the works to convert the castle, which the Spanish government has formally returned to Catalunya, into a museum dedicated to peace. ✉ *Ctra. de Montjuïc 66, Montjuïc* ☎ *93/329–8613* 🎫 *€3* 🕓 *Tues.–Sun. 9:30–8.*

58 **Estadi Olímpic.** The Olympic Stadium was originally built for the International Exposition of 1929, with the idea that Barcelona would then be the site of the 1936 Olympics (ultimately staged in Hitler's Berlin). After failing twice, Barcelona celebrated the attainment of its long-cherished goal by renovating the semi-derelict stadium in time for 1992, providing seating for 70,000. The **Galeria Olímpica,** a museum about the Olympic movement in Barcelona, displays objects and shows audiovisual replays from the 1992 games. An information center traces the history of the modern Olympics from Athens in 1896 to the present. Next door and just downhill stands the futuristic **Palau Sant Jordi Sports Palace,** designed by the noted Japanese architect Arata Isozaki. The Isozaki structure has no pillars or beams to obstruct the view. The roof was built first, then hydraulically lifted into place. ✉ *Passeig Olímpic 17–19, Montjuïc* ☎ *93/426–0660* 🌐 *www.fundaciobarcelonaolimpica.es* 🎫 *Gallery €4* 🕓 *Tues.–Sat. 10–2 and 4–7.*

64 **Museu d'Arqueologia de Catalunya.** Just downhill to the right of the Palau Nacional, the Museum of Archaeology holds important finds from the Greek ruins at Empúries, on the Costa Brava. These are shown alongside fascinating objects from, and explanations of, Megalithic Spain. ✉ *Passeig Santa Madrona 39–41, Montjuïc* ☎ *93/424–6577* 🌐 *www.mac.es* 🎫 *€2.50* 🕓 *Tues.–Sat. 9:30–7, Sun. 10–2:30.*

60 **Plaça de les Cascades.** At night near the Mies van der Rohe Pavilion is a multicolor fountain in the Plaça de les Cascades. For a scenic stroll, meander down the esplanade past the exhibition halls, to the large and frenetic **Plaça d'Espanya.** Across the square is Les Arenes bullring, no longer used for bullfights, its neo-Mudéjar facade of exposed brick horseshoe arches containing an ultramodern shopping, leisure, and performance complex. From here, you can take the metro or Bus 38 back to the Plaça de Catalunya.

63 **Poble Espanyol.** The Spanish Village was created for the International Exposition of 1929. A sort of artificial Spain-in-a-bottle, with reproductions of Spain's architectural styles, it takes you from the walls of

Ávila to the wine cellars of Jerez de la Frontera amid shops, houses, and crafts workshops en route. The liveliest time to come is at night, and a reservation at one of the half-dozen restaurants gets you in free, as does the purchase of a ticket for the two discos or the Tablao del Carmen flamenco club. ✉*Av. Marquès de Comillas s/n* ☎*93/508–6300* 🌐*www.poble-espanyol.com* 🎫*€8* ⏲*Mon. 9–8, Tues.–Thurs. 9–2 am, Sat. 9–4 am, Sun. 9–midnight.*

BEACHES

Ever since Barcelona revamped its beaches for the 1992 Olympics, the summer beach scene has been multitudinous. Five kilometers (3 mi) of beaches now run from the Platja (Beach) de Sant Sebastià, a nudist enclave, northward through the Barceloneta, Port Olímpic, Nova Icària, Bogatell, Mar Bella, Nova Mar Bella, and Novíssima Mar Bella beaches to the Fòrum complex and the rocky Illa Pangea swimming area. Next to the mouth of the Besòs River is Platja Nova. Topless bathing is common. The beaches immediately north of Barcelona include Montgat, Ocata, Vilasar de Mar, Arenys de Mar, Canet, and Sant Pol de Mar, all accessible by train from the RENFE station in Plaça de Catalunya. Especially worthy is **Sant Pol** (✉*Passeig Maritim 59* ☎*93/665–1347*), with clean sand in Sant Pol de Mar. Also in this handsome old part of town is Carme Ruscalleda's famous **Sant Pau,** one of the top three restaurants in Catalonia. The farther north you go, toward the Costa Brava, the better the beaches. Ten kilometers (6 mi) south is **Castelldefels,** with a long, sandy beach and a series of bars and restaurants. A 15-minute train ride from Passeig de Gràcia's (or Plaça de Catalunya's) RENFE station to Gavà or Castelldefels deposits you on the 10-km-long (6-mi-long) beach for a (usually) windy walk in the sand. From October to March the sun sets into the Mediterranean here, thanks to the westward slant of the coastline. There are several good places for lamb chops, *calçots* (spring onions), and paella; the best, Can Patricio, serves lunch until 4:30. **Sitges Beach,** another 25 minutes south, has better sand and clearer water than Castelldefels.

BARS & CAFÉS

Barcelona may have more bars and cafés per capita than any other place in the world. Here you can find a wide selection of colorful tapas places, sunny outdoor cafés, tearooms, chocolaterias, and, of course, *coctelerías* (cocktail bars), *whiskerias* (often singles bars filled with professional escorts), *xampanyerias* (serving champagne and cava), and beer halls. Most stay open until about 2:30 AM.

CAFÉS

Café de l'Opera. Opposite the opera house, this high-ceiling Art Nouveau space has welcomed operagoers and performers grabbing a cup of tea or coffee for more than 100 years. For locals, it's a central point on

7

the Rambla traffic pattern. ✉ *La Rambla 74, Rambla* ☎ *93/317–7585* ⏲ *Daily 9:30* AM*–2:15* AM Ⓜ *Liceu.*

Café Paris. This café is a lively place to kill time. Everyone from Prince Felipe, heir to the Spanish throne, to poet and pundit James Townsend Pi Sunyer can be spotted here in season. The tapas are excellent, the beer is cold, and the place is open 365 days a year. ✉ *Carrer Aribau 184, at Carrer Paris, Eixample* ☎ *93/209–8530* ⏲ *Daily 8* AM*–2:30* AM Ⓜ *Provença.*

Café Viena. The rectangular perimeter of this bar is always packed with travelers in a party mood. The pianist upstairs lends a cabaret touch. Draft beer and an Iberico ham *flauta* (thin sandwich) always hit the spot. ✉ *La Rambla dels Estudis 115, Rambla* ☎ *93/349–9800* ⏲ *Daily 8* AM*–2:30* AM Ⓜ *Catalunya.*

Café Zurich. Ever of key importance to Barcelona society, this classic spot at the top of the Rambla is the city's prime meeting place. The outdoor tables offer peerless people-watching; the elegant interior has a high ceiling. ✉ *Pl. de Catalunya 1, Rambla* ☎ *93/317–9153* ⏲ *Daily 8* AM*–2:30* AM Ⓜ *Catalunya.*

Els Quatre Gats. Picasso staged his first exhibition here, in 1899, and Gaudí and the Catalan impressionist painters Ramón Casas and Santiago Russinyol held meetings of their Centre Artistic de Sant Lluc in the early 20th century. The restaurant is undistinguished, but the café is a good place to read and people-watch. ✉ *Carrer Montsió 3, Barri Gòtic* ☎ *93/302–4140* ⏲ *Daily 8* AM*–2:30* AM Ⓜ *Catalunya.*

Espai Barroc. Filled with baroque embellishments and music, this unusual *espai* (space) is on Carrer Montcada's most beautiful patio, the 15th-century Palau Dalmases. The stairway, with a bas-relief of the rape of Europa, leads up to the Omnium Cultural, a center for the study and diffusion of Catalan history and culture. The patio merits a look even if you find the café too lugubrious. ✉ *Carrer Montcada 20, La Ribera* ☎ *93/310–0673* ⏲ *Tues.–Sat. 8* PM*–midnight* Ⓜ *Jaume I.*

La Bodegueta. If you can locate this dive (literally, it's two steps down from the sidewalk), you'll find a cluttered space with a dozen small tables, a few places at the marble counter, and happy couples having coffee or beer—and maybe some ham or *tortilla española de patatas* (a typically Spanish, omeletlike potato-and-onion delicacy). ✉ *La Rambla de Catalunya 100, Eixample* ☎ *93/215–4894* ⏲ *Daily 8* AM*–1* AM Ⓜ *Provença.*

Schilling. Near Plaça Reial, the hip and penumbral Schilling is always packed. Have coffee by day, drinks and tapas by night. ✉ *Carrer Ferran 23, Barri Gòtic* ☎ *93/317–6787* ⏲ *Daily 10* AM*–2:30* AM Ⓜ *Catalunya, Liceu.*

Travel Bar. With entrances on Carrer de la Boqueria and Placeta del Pi, and tables in the shady square behind Sant Maria del Pi, this hot spot for young travelers offers everything from Internet access to walking tours. ✉ *Carrer de la Boqueria 27, Barri Gòtic* ☎ *93/342–5252* ⏲ *Daily 8* AM*–2:30* AM Ⓜ *Catalunya, Liceu.*

COCTELERÍAS

Almirall. This Moderniste bar in the Raval is quiet, dimly lit, and dominated by an Art Nouveau mirror and frame behind the marble bar. It's an evocative spot, romantic and mischievous. ✉ *Carrer Joaquín Costa 33, Raval* ☎ *93/302–4126* ⏲ *Daily 11* AM*–2:30* AM Ⓜ *Catalunya, Liceu, Sant Antoni.*

Dry Martini Bar. The eponymous specialty is the best bet at this spot, which exudes a kind of genteel wickedness. This seems to be a popular hangout for mature romantics, husbands, and wives, though not necessarily each other's. The speakeasy restaurant through the kitchen is excellent, too. ✉ *Carrer Aribau 162, Eixample* ☎ *93/217–5072* ⏲ *Daily 11* AM*–2:30* AM Ⓜ *Provença.*

El Born. This former codfish emporium is now a charming and intimate haven for drinks, raclettes, and fondues. The marble cod basins in the entry and the spiral staircase to the second floor are the quirkiest details. ✉ *Passeig del Born 26, La Ribera* ☎ *93/319–5333* ⏲ *Daily 7* PM*–2:30* AM Ⓜ *Jaume I.*

El Copetín. Right on Barcelona's best-known cocktail avenue, this bar has good drinks and Irish coffee. Dimly lighted, it has a romantic South Seas motif. ✉ *Passeig del Born 19, La Ribera* ☎ *93/319–4496* ⏲ *Daily 7* PM*–2:30* AM Ⓜ *Jaume I.*

El Paraigua. Behind the *ajuntament* (city hall), this pricey but stylish bar serves cocktails and classical-music recordings in an elegant Art Nouveau space. ✉ *Pas de l'Ensenyança 2, Barri Gòtic* ☎ *93/302–1131* ⏲ *Daily 11* AM*–2:30* AM Ⓜ *Jaume I, Liceu.*

Miramelindo. The bar has a range of herbal liquors, fruit cocktails, mojitos, and Brazilian specialties such as *caipirinhas* (crushed lime and sugar with *cachaça,* a sugar-cane liquor), served in a Caribbean wood and wicker setting. Recorded music is usually jazz, bossa nova, or quiet salsa. ✉ *Passeig del Born 15, La Ribera* ☎ *93/310–3727* ⏲ *Daily 7* PM*–2:30* AM Ⓜ *Jaume I.*

TAPAS BARS

As a result of Catalonia's distinct social mores, tapas have historically never been an important part of Barcelona life. But stand by: astute Catalans and Basque chefs are busy transforming Barcelona into an emerging tapas capital (until now, San Sebastian, Sevilla, Cadiz, or perhaps Madrid led the tapas charge). Especially around Santa Maria del Mar and the Passeig del Born area, nomadic wine tippling and tapa tasting are proliferating. Beware of the tapas places along Passeig de Gràcia: although the tapas here are a lot better than Big Macs, the tapas here are microwaved and far from Barcelona's best.

Fodor's Choice ★ **Cal Pep.** A two-minute walk east from Santa Maria del Mar toward the Estació de França, Pep's has Barcelona's best and freshest selection of tapas, cooked and served piping hot in this boisterous space. ✉ *Pl. de les Olles 8, Born-Ribera* ☎ *93/319–6183* ⏲ *Tues.–Sat. 1–4* PM *and 8–midnight, Mon. 8* PM*–midnight* Ⓜ *Jaume I.*

7

Fodor'sChoice ★ **Casa Lucio.** With preserved and fresh ingredients and original dishes flowing from the kitchen, this handsome (though expensive) little gem just two blocks south of the Mercat de Sant Antoni is well worth tracking down. Lucio's wife, Maribel, is relentlessly inventive. Try the *tastum albarole* (cured sheep cheese from Umbria) or the *pochas negras con morcilla* (black beans with black sausage). ✉*Carrer Viladomat 59, Eixample* ☎*93/424–4401* ⏲*Mon.–Sat. 1–4* PM *and 8–11* PM Ⓜ*Sant Antoni.*

Fodor'sChoice ★ **Cata 1.81.** Small delicacies such as truffle omelets and foie gras make this a taste treat as well as a wine-tasting *(cata)* sanctuary. The wine selections are thoughtfully and carefully worked out, and the industrial steel tables with center bottle wells are contemporary and chic. ✉*Carrer Valencia 181, Eixample* ☎*93/323–6818* ⏲*Tues.–Sat. 1–4* PM *and 8–midnight, Mon. 8* PM*–midnight* Ⓜ*Provença.*

Cerveseria La Catalana. This booming bar is filled for a reason: excellent food at fair prices. Try the small *solomillo* (filet mignon)—a mini-morsel that will take the edge off your carnivorous instincts without undue damage to your wallet. ✉*Mallorca 236, Eixample* ☎*93/216–0368* ⏲*Daily 8* AM*–1:30* AM Ⓜ*Provença.*

Ciudad Condal. A Barcelona hot spot, this restaurant and grazing ground serves fine tapas to a well-heeled crowd in a classical wooden tavern. ✉*La Rambla de Catalunya 18, Eixample* ☎*93/318–1997* ⏲*Daily 7:30* AM*–1:30* AM Ⓜ*Passeig de Gràcia.*

El Irati. Between Plaça del Pi and the Rambla, this roaring brawl of a Basque bar has only one drawback: it's hard to squeeze into. If there's space, take it; if not, move on. Try coming around 1 PM or 7:30 PM. The standard beverage here is *txakolí,* a white Basque wine. The restaurant in back is excellent. ✉*Carrer Cardenal Casañas 17, Barri Gòtic* ☎*93/302–3084* ⏲*Tues.–Sun. 12:30* PM*–midnight.*

El Vaso de Oro. At the uptown edge of Barceloneta, this bar has become more and more popular over the last few years with young, polished professionals. If you can catch it when it's not crammed with customers, you're in for some of the best beer and tapas in town. ✉*Carrer Balboa 6, Barceloneta* ☎*93/319–3098* ⏲*Daily 9* AM*–midnight* Ⓜ*Barceloneta.*

Euskal Etxea. The tapas and canapés speak for themselves here at this Basque cultural enclave (Euskal Etxea means "Basque House") just down from the Picasso Museum. ✉*Placeta Montcada 13, Born-Ribera* ☎*93/310–2185* ⏲*Mon.–Sat. 9* AM*–1* AM*, Sun. 9* AM*–4:30* PM Ⓜ*Jaume I.*

Inòpia Clàssic Bar. Albert Adrià, younger brother and chief culinary researcher for his hyper-famous brother Ferran Adrià of El Bulli fame has opened his own tapas bar just a few blocks west of the Mercat de Sant Antoni. Products and preparations are uniformly interesting and excellent here, from the fragrant Torta del Casar cheese, to the olive sampler served in a ceramic flute. ✉*Carrer Tamarit 104, Eixample* ☎*93/424–5231* ⏲*Tues.–Sat. 7:30* PM*–11* PM*, Sun. 1–4* PM Ⓜ*Rocafort, Poble Sec.*

Mantequeria Can Ravell. Lovers of exquisite wines, hams, cheeses, oils, whiskies, cigars, caviars, baby eels, and any other delicacy you can think of—this is your spot. The backroom table, where strangers share tastes, is open from about 10 AM to 8 PM; it's first-come, first-served. ✉ *Carrer Aragó 313, Eixample* ☎ *93/457–5114* ⏲ *Tues.–Sat. 8* AM*–9* PM Ⓜ *Passeig de Gràcia.*

Sagardi. This attractive, wood-and-stone cider house comes close to re-creating its Basque prototype, with cider shooting from mammoth (fake) barrels and piping-hot tapas out front, and *txuletas de buey* (beefsteaks) prepared over coals in the restaurant out back. ✉ *Carrer Argenteria 62, La Ribera* ☎ *93/319–9993* ⏲ *Daily 10* AM*–1* AM Ⓜ *Jaume III.*

Taller de Tapas. Next to Plaça del Pi, facing the eastern lateral facade of Santa Maria del Pi, this fine tapas specialist has it all: cheery young staff, traditional Catalan dishes in bite-size format, and service from midday to midnight. The other Taller de Tapas on Carrer Argenteria 51 near Santa Maria del Mar is equally excellent. ✉ *Pl. de Sant Josep Oriol 9, Barri Gòtic* ☎ *93/302–6243* ⏲ *Daily 10* AM*–2* AM Ⓜ *Liceu.*

XAMPANYERIAS & WINE BARS

El Xampanyet. Just down Carrer Montcada from the Picasso Museum, hanging *botas* (wineskins) mark one of Barcelona's liveliest saloons, usually stuffed to the gills. Caveat: The sparkling wine served here is not cava but a sweet brew of indeterminate origin. Stick with beer or one of their excellent wines. ✉ *Carrer Montcada 22, La Ribera* ☎ *93/319–7003* ⏲ *Closed Mon.*

La Vinya del Senyor. Ambitiously named "The Lord's Vineyard," this excellent wine bar across from the entrance to Santa Maria del Mar changes its savvy by-the-glass wine selections every fortnight. ✉ *Pl. de Santa Maria 5, La Ribera* ☎ *93/310–3379* ⏲ *Closed Mon.*

El Bitxo. An original wine list and ever-changing choices of interesting cava selections accompany creative tapas and small dishes from *foie* (duck or goose liver) to Ibérico (native Iberian pigs fattened on acorns) hams and cheeses, all in a rustic wooden setting 50 yards from the Palau de la Música. ✉ *Verdaguer i Callis 9, Sant Pere* ☎ *93/268–1708.*

La Taverna del Palau. Behind a glass facade facing the Palau de la Música, this sleek little tavern is perfect for a hit of cava during intermission or a beer and a *flauta* (thin, flutelike sandwich) of cured ham. ✉ *Carrer Sant Pere Més Alt 8, Sant Pere* ☎ *93/268–8481.*

7

WHERE TO EAT

Barcelona's restaurant scene is an ongoing surprise. Between the cutting-edge of avant-garde culinary experimentation and the cosmopolitan and rustic dishes of traditional Catalan fare is a fleet of inventive chefs producing some of Europe's finest Mediterranean cuisine.

THE CUISINE

Catalans are legendary lovers of fish, vegetables, rabbit, duck, lamb, game, and natural ingredients from the Pyrenees or the Mediterranean. The *mar i muntanya* (sea and mountain—that is, surf and turf), a recipe combining seafood with upland products, is a standard. Rabbit and prawns, cuttlefish and meatballs, chickpeas and clams are just a few examples. Combining salty and sweet tastes—a Moorish legacy—is another common theme, as in duck with pears, rabbit with figs, or lamb with olives.

The Mediterranean diet, which is based on olive oil, seafood, fibrous vegetables, onions, garlic, and red wine, is at home in Barcelona, and food tends to be seasoned with Catalonia's four basic sauces—*allioli* (pure garlic and olive oil), *romescu* (almonds, hazelnuts, tomato, garlic, and olive oil), *sofregit* (fried onion, tomato, and herbs), and *samfaina* (a ratatouillelike vegetable mixture).

Typical entrées include *habas a la catalana* (a spicy broad-bean stew), *bullabesa* (fish soup-stew similar to the French bouillabaisse), and *espinacas a la catalana* (spinach cooked with oil, garlic, pine nuts, raisins, and bits of bacon). Bread is often doused with olive oil and spread with tomato to make *pa amb tomaquet,* delicious on its own or as a side order.

MEAL TIMES

Lunch is served from 1 to 4, dinner 9 to 11. Certain restaurants serve continuously from 1 PM to 1 AM.

DEALS & DISCOUNTS

Menús del día (menus of the day), served only at lunchtime, are good values. Beware of the *advice* of hotel concierges and taxi drivers, who have been known to warn that the place you are going is either closed or no good anymore and to recommend places where they get kickbacks.

AND TO DRINK

Catalan wines from the nearby Penedès region, especially the local *méthode champenoise* (sparkling white wine known in Catalonia as cava), adequately accompany regional cuisine. Meanwhile, winemakers from the Priorat, Ampurdan, and Costers del Segre regions are producing some of Spain's most exciting new wines.

CIUTAT VELLA (OLD CITY)

Ciutat Vella comprises the Rambla, Barri Gòtic, Ribera, and Raval districts between Plaça de Catalunya and the port. Chic new restaurants and cafés seem to open daily in Barcelona's Old City.

$$$$ Fodor's Choice ★ ✕ **Àbac.** In the tradition of Catalonia's finest restaurants, Xavier Pellicer leaves no detail to chance here, preparing carefully selected ingredients in innovative recipes based on culinary canons learned from Europe's top chefs. The taster's menu is the only reasonable choice here: trust Xavi (any attempt at economy is roughly analagous to quibbling about deck chairs on the Titanic). Located until October 2007 on Carrer del Rec in the Ribera-Born neighborhood, Àbac is now an uptown boutique hotel as well as a gourmet pilgrimage. For fine feasting no more than a convenient crawl from your luxury suite with the latest spa facilities on hand to repair the damage, this is one of Barcelona's most exciting new combinations of superb dining and impeccable accomodations. ✉ *Avenida del Tibidabo 1–7, Tibidabo* ☎ *93/319–6600* ℻ *93/319–4519* 🌐 *www.restaurantabac.com* *14 rooms* *In-hotel: restaurant, bar, spa, public Wi-fi, parking (fee)* *Reservations essential* ▭ *AE, DC, MC, V* ⊙ *Closed Sun. and Aug. No lunch Mon.* Ⓜ *Tibidabo.*

$$$$ Fodor's Choice ★ ✕ **Ca l'Isidre.** Gourmets, gourmands, cognoscenti, and epicureans of all stripe recognize Ca l'Isidre as the finest restaurant in Barcelona. Just off Avinguda del Paral.lel in the darkest Raval, this is a favorite with Barcelona's art crowd. Paintings and engravings by Miró, Dalí, Joan Pere Viladecans and other stars line the walls. The traditional yet contemporary Catalan cooking draws on fresh produce from the Boqueria and has a slight French accent. Isidre's wines are invariably novelties from all over the Iberian Peninsula; ask for his advice and you will get a great wine as well as an oenology, geography, and history course delivered with charm, brevity, and wit. The homemade foie gras is superb. Come and go by cab at night; the area can be shady. ✉ *Carrer de les Flors 12, Raval* ☎ *93/441–1139* *Reservations essential* ▭ *AE, MC, V* ⊙ *Closed Sun., Easter wk, and mid-July–mid-Aug.* Ⓜ *Paral.lel.*

$$$$ ✕ **Comerç 24.** Artist, aesthete, and chef Carles Abellan playfully reinterprets traditional Catalan favorites at this sleek, designer dining spot. Try

7

BEST BETS FOR BARCELONA DINING

Need a cheat sheet for Barcelona's thousands of restaurants? Fodor's writers have selected some of their favorites by price, cuisine, and experience in the lists shown here. You can also search by neighborhood or find specific details about a restaurant in our full reviews—just peruse the following pages. Happy dining in Catalonia's capital by the sea. ¡Bon profit!

FODOR'S CHOICE

Àbac, $$$$, Tibidabo

Ca L'Isidre, $$$$, Raval

Cal Pep, $$, Born-Ribera*

Casa Leopoldo, $$$, Raval

Casa Lucio, $$$, Eixample*

Cata 1.81, $$, Eixample*

Comerç 24, $$$$, Born-Ribera

Drolma, $$$$, Eixample

El Racó de Can Fabes, $$$$, Sant Celoni

For tapas bar listings, marked with *, see previous section of chapter.

HIGHLY RECOMMENDED

Can Gaig, $$$$, Eixample

Can Majó, $$$, Barceloneta

Manairó, $$$, Eixample

Neichel, $$$$, Pedralbes

Sant Pau, $$$$, Sant Pol de Mar

Silvestre, $$, Sant Gervasi

Taktika Berri, $$$$, Eixample

Tram-Tram, $$$, Sarrià

By Price

$

Agut, Barri Gòtic

Ca l'Estevet, Raval

Can Manel la Puda, Barceloneta

Folquer, Gràcia

$$

Café de l'Acadèmia, Barri Gòtic

Cometacinc, Barri Gòtic

El Mató de Pedralbes, Pedralbes

Silvestre, Sant Gervasi

Taxidermista, Rambla

$$$

Can Majó, Barceloneta

Cinc Sentits, Eixample

Manairó, Eixample

Suquet de l'Almirall, Barceloneta

Tram-Tram, Sarrià

Vivanda, Sarrià

$$$$

Àbac, Tibidabo

Ca l'Isidre, Raval

Can Gaig, Eixample

Comerç 24, Born-Ribera

Drolma, Eixample

El Racó de Can Fabes, Sant Celoni

By Cuisine

TRADITIONAL SPANISH

El Asador de Aranda, $$$, Tibidabo

TRADITIONAL CATALAN

Antiga Casa Solé, $$$$, Barceloneta

Ca l'Isidre, $$$$, Raval

Can Gaig, $$$$, Eixample

Casa Leopoldo, $$$, Raval

Drolma, $$$$, Eixample

Neichel, $$$$, Pedralbes

Tram-Tram, $$$, Sarrià

CONTEMPORARY CATALAN

Àbac, $$$$, Tibidabo

Andaira, $$$$, Barceloneta

L'Olivé, $$$, Eixample

Mey Hofmann, $$$$, Born Ribera

Sant Pau, $$$$, Sant Pol de Mar

EXPERIMENTAL

Cinc Sentits, $$$, Eixample

Comerç 24, $$$$, Born-Ribera

El Racó d'en Freixa, $$$$, Sant Gervasi

Manairó, $$$, Eixample

TAPAS

Cal Pep, $$, Born-Ribera*

Casa Lucio, $$$, Eixample*

El Vaso de Oro, $$, Barceloneta*

Inòpia Classic Bar, $$, Eixample*

Mantequeria Can Ravell, $$, Eixample*

Sagardi, $$, Born-Ribera*

STEAK HOUSE

El Asador de Aranda, $$$, Tibidabo

Gorría, $$$, Eixample

PAELLA

Can Majó, $$$, Barceloneta

Suquet de l'Almirall, $$$, Barceloneta

SEAFOOD

Antiga Casa Solé, $$$$, Barceloneta

Botafumeiro, $$$$, Gràcia

By Experience

BEST BANG FOR YOUR BUCK

Barceloneta, $$, Barceloneta

Cal Pep, $$, Born-Ribera*

Mantequeria Ya Ya Amelia, $$, Eixample

Silvestre, $$, Sant Gervasi

Vivanda, $$$, Sarrià

QUAINT & COZY

Agut, $, Barri Gòtic

Antiga Casa Solé, $$$$, Barceloneta

Ca l'Estevet, $, Raval

Casa Lucio, $$$, Eixample*

YOUNG & HAPPENING

Cinc Sentits, $$$, Eixample

Comerç 24, $$$$, Born-Ribera

Manairó, $$$, Eixample

Nonell, $$$, Barri Gòtic

Shunka, $$, Barri Gòtic

SUMMER DINING

Can Majó, $$$, Barceloneta

Torre d'Alta Mar, $$$$, Barceloneta

Tram-Tram, $$$, Sarrià

Vivanda, $$$, Sarrià

the deconstructed *tortilla de patatas* (potato omelet), or the *huevo kinder* (an egg with surprises inside, based on a popular children's toy). For dessert, prepare for a postmodern version of the traditional after-school snack of chocolate, olive oil, salt, and bread. Abellán's cuisine is always original and, though sometimes flirting with the border between fine dining and playing with your food, unfailingly delicious. ✉*Carrer Comerç 24, Born-Ribera* ☎*93/319–2102* ✍*Reservations essential* ▭*AE, DC, MC, V* ⊗*Closed Sun.* Ⓜ*Jaume I.*

WORD OF MOUTH

"The food in Barcelona is great, the culture is quite off-beat, and there is a general air of revelry and youth all over town."

–nessundorma

$$$$ ✕**El Passadís d'en Pep.** This lively bistro hidden away at the end of a passadis (corridor) off Pla del Palau serves a rapid-fire succession of delicious seafood tapas and wine as soon as you appear. Sometime late in the proceedings you may be asked to make a decision about your main course, usually fish of one kind or another. You're free to stop at this point. Avoid *bogavante* (lobster) unless you're on an expense account. ✉*Pl. del Palau 2, Born-Ribera* ☎*93/310–1021* ▭*AE, DC, MC, V* ⊗*Closed Sun. and last 2 wks of Aug.* Ⓜ*Jaume I.*

$$$$ ✕**Mey Hofmann.** Superb fare in a romantic upstairs dining room overlooking Santa Maria del Mar distinguish this cooking academy and first-rate restaurant specializing in Mediterranean cuisine. The young waiters and waitresses are chefs-in-training and are usually encyclopedic about ingredients and preparations, from aperitif wines to cheeses and desserts. ✉*Carrer Argenteria 74–78, Born-Ribera* ☎*93/319–5889* ▭*AE, DC, MC, V* ⊗*Closed weekends* Ⓜ*Jaume I.*

$$$–$$$$ Fodor'sChoice ★ ✕**Casa Leopoldo.** Rosa Gil and her family receive guests warmly at this superb seafood and Catalan cuisine specialist in the Raval west of the Rambla. To get here, approach along Carrer Hospital, take a left on the wide new Rambla del Raval down to Carrer Sant Rafael and take another left 50 feet to the front door of this clean, well-lit, ceramic-tiled gem. Try the *revuelto de ajos tiernos y gambas* (eggs scrambled with young garlic and shrimp) or the famous *cap-i-pota* (stewed head and hoof of pork). Albariños and Priorats are Rosa Gil's favorites. ✉*Sant Rafael 24, Raval* ☎*93/441–3014* ▭*AE, DC, MC, V* ⊗*Closed Mon. No dinner Sun.* Ⓜ*Liceu.*

$$$–$$$$ ✕**Nonell.** Chef Oliver Balteo draws from his experiences as a culinary professor in Venezuela as well as on his Lebanese roots to produce excellent, eclectic cuisine in this recent addition to the city's gastronomic scene. Dishes range from classical Mediterranean to Castilian roast suckling pig to Middle Eastern creams and sauces. The wine list is entirely original, featuring labels you may have never heard of but will be glad to get to know; the service is impeccable and delivered with panache and wit—and in perfect English. ✉ *Pl. Isidre Nonell, Barri Gòtic* ☎*93/301–1378* ▭*AE, DC, MC, V* Ⓜ*Catalunya, Liceu.*

$$–$$$ ✕**Café de l'Acadèmia.** With wicker chairs, stone walls, and background classical music, this place is sophisticated-rustic, and the excellent Catalan cuisine makes it much more than a mere café. It's frequented by

politicians and functionaries from the nearby Generalitat and is always boiling with life. Be sure to reserve at lunchtime. ✉*Lledó 1, Barri Gòtic* ☎*93/319–8253* 💳*AE, DC, MC, V* Ⓜ*Jaume I.*

$$–$$$ ✕ **Cometacinc.** This stylish place in the Barri Gòtic, an increasingly chic neighborhood of artisans and antiquers, is a fine example of Barcelona's taste and technology with new-over-old architecture and interior design. Although the 30-foot floor-to-ceiling wooden shutters are already a visual feast, the carefully prepared interpretations of old standards, such as the *carpaccio de toro de lidia* (carpaccio of fighting bull) with basil sauce and pine nuts, are also brilliant. ✉*Carrer Cometa 5, Barri Gòtic* ☎*93/310–1558* 💳*AE, DC, MC, V* ⏲*Closed Tues.* Ⓜ*Jaume I.*

$$–$$$ ✕ **Shunka.** Widely regarded as Barcelona's finest Japanese restaurant, this cozy hideaway behind the Hotel Colón serves straight across the counter from the burners to the diners. Mediterranean and Japanese cuisines have much in common (raw fish dishes, for starters). ✉*Sagristans 5, Barri Gòtic* ☎*93/412–4991* 💳*AE, DC, MC, V* Ⓜ*Liceu.*

$$–$$$ ✕ **Taxidermista.** Don't worry: no road kill is served here. Once a natural-science museum and taxidermy shop (from which Dalí once purchased 200,000 ants and a stuffed rhinoceros), this is the only recommendable restaurant in the sunny Plaça Reial. Interior decorator Beth Gali designed the interior around original beams and steel columns. Delicacies such as *bonito con escalivada y queso de cabra* (white tuna with braised eggplants, peppers, and goat cheese) are served at outside tables best enjoyed in the winter sun. ✉*Pl. Reial 8, Rambla* ☎*93/412–4536* 💳*AE, DC, MC, V* ⏲*Closed Mon.* Ⓜ*Liceu.*

7

$–$$$ ✕ **Agut.** This is no-frills classical Catalan fare at a fantastic value. Wood paneling and oil paintings provide the background for the mostly Catalan crowd in this homey restaurant in the lower reaches of the Gothic Quarter. Agut was founded in 1924, and its popularity has never waned, despite the enormous changes in Barcelona's dining scene. In season (September through May), try the *pato silvestre agridulce* (sweet-and-sour wild duck). There's a good selection of wine, but no frills such as coffee or liqueur. ✉*Gignàs 16, Barri Gòtic* ☎*93/315–1709* 💳*AE, MC, V* ⏲*Closed Mon. and July. No dinner Sun.* Ⓜ*Jaume I.*

$–$$$ ✕ **Ca l'Estevet.** Estevet and his family are in charge of everything from the kitchen to the front door here, and the carefully elaborated Catalan cuisine sparkles, especially at these prices. Facing the journalism school and around the block from the former home of Barcelona's *La Vanguardia* daily, this romantic little spot near the MACBA (Contemporary Art Museum) is popular with journalists, students, and artists. Try the asparagus cooked over coals, the *chopitos gaditanos* (deep-fried baby octopus), or the *magret de pato* (duck breast). The house wine is inexpensive and perfectly drinkable. ✉*Valdoncella 46, Raval* ☎*93/302–4186* 💳*AE, DC, MC, V* ⏲*Closed Sun.* Ⓜ*Catalunya.*

$–$$$ ✕ **El Foro.** This hot spot near the Born is always full to the rafters with lively young and young-at-heart people. Painting and photographic exhibits line the walls, and the menu is dominated by pizzas, salads, and meat cooked over coals. Flamenco and jazz performances downstairs are a good postdinner option. ✉*Princesa 53, Born-Ribera* ☎*93/310–1020* 💳*AE, DC, MC, V* ⏲*Closed Mon.* Ⓜ*Jaume I.*

Where to Eat in Barcelona
Estació Central-Sants
Palau Nacional
Castell de Montjuïc
Boqueria Market
Plaça Universitat
Plaça d'Espanya
Pl. de Francesc Macià
Avda. Diagonal
Gran Via de les Corts Catalanes
Travessera de les Corts
Travessera de Gràcia
Ronda del General Mitre
Passeig de Manuel Girona
Avda. de J. Tarradellas
Avda. de Roma
Avda. de Mistral
Avda. del Paral·lel
Ronda Sant Antoni
Rda. de Sant Pau
Pg. de Montjuïc
Pg. de Colom
Moll de la Fusta
Moll d'Espanya
Moll de Sant Bertrán
Portal de la Pau
Plaça Reial
Pl. de Catalunya
Rambla de Catalunya
Pg. de Gràcia
Jardins de Joan Maragall
Jardins de Miramar
Estadi Olímpic
TORRE DE JAUME I

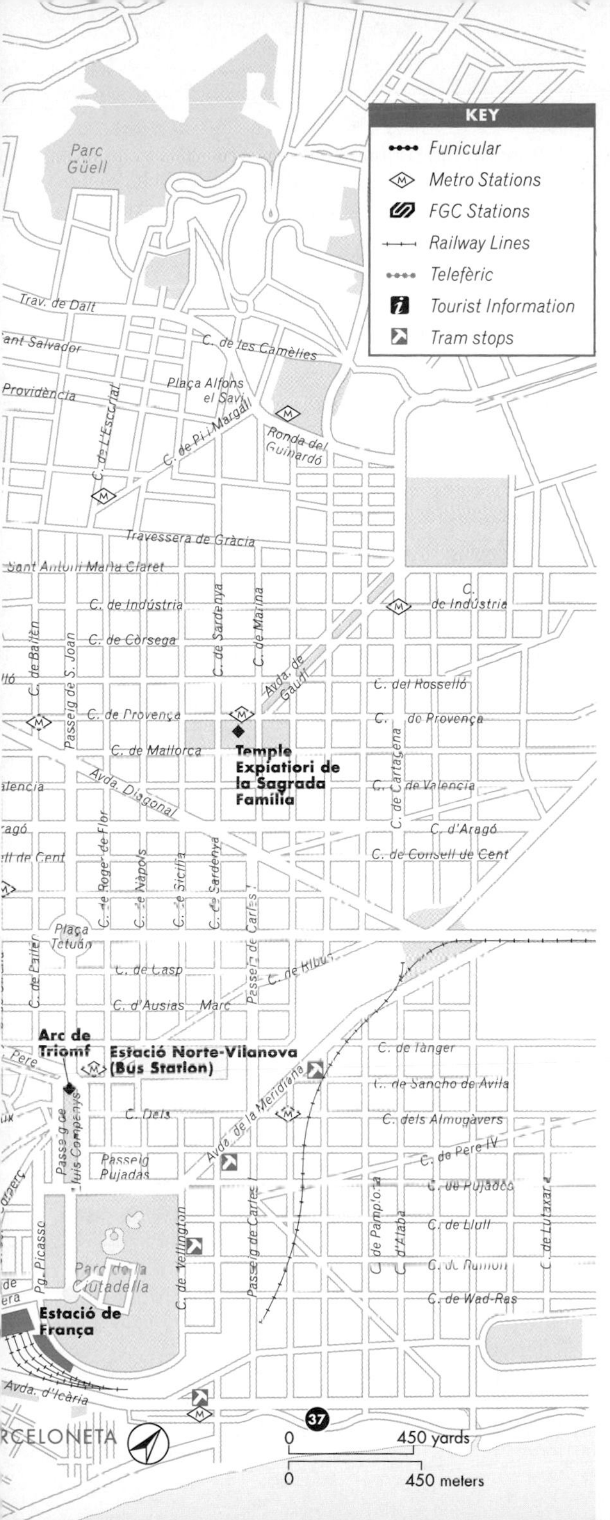
KEY
Funicular
Metro Stations
FGC Stations
Railway Lines
Telefèric
Tourist Information
Tram stops
Parc Güell
Trav. de Dalt
C. de les Camèlies
Plaça Alfons el Savi
C. de Pi i Margall
Ronda del Guinardó
Travessera de Gràcia
C. de Indústria
C. de Còrsega
C. de Sardenya
C. de Marina
Avda. de Gaudí
C. del Rosselló
C. de Provença
C. de Mallorca
Temple Expiatiori de la Sagrada Família
Avda. Diagonal
C. de Cartagena
C. de Valencia
C. d'Aragó
C. de Consell de Cent
Passeig de S. Joan
Plaça Tetuán
C. de Casp
C. d'Ausias Marc
Passeig de Carles I
Arc de Triomf
Estació Norte-Vilanova (Bus Station)
C. de Tànger
Avda. de la Meridiana
C. dels Almogàvers
C. de Pere IV
Passeig Pujadas
C. de Pujades
Pg. Picasso
Parc de la Ciutadella
C. de Wellington
C. de Llull
C. de Wad-Ras
Estació de França
Avda. d'Icària
37
0 450 yards
0 450 meters

BARCELONETA & THE PORT OLÍMPIC

Barceloneta and the Port Olímpic (Olympic Port) have little in common beyond their seaside location, the former a traditional fishermen's quarter and the latter a crazed disco strip with thousand-seat restaurants.

$$$$ ✕**Torre d'Altamar.** Seafood of every stripe, spot, fin, and carapace emanates from the kitchen here, but the filet mignon, under a colossal slab of *foie* (duck or goose liver), is a tour de force, too. The restaurant is in the cable-car tower over the far side of the port and has spectacular views of Barcelona as well as far out into the Mediterranean. ✉*Passeig Joan de Borbó 88 –Torre de San Sebastián, Barceloneta* ☎*93/221–0007* ▭*AE, DC, MC, V* ⏲*Closed Sun. No lunch Mon.* Ⓜ*Barceloneta.*

$$$–$$$$ ✕**Andaira.** New flavors and innovative, contemporary cooking distinguish this young couple's contribution to the Barceloneta dining panorama. It's not that Andaira doesn't do the traditional waterfront rice and fish dishes, but that they do them with a sleek, modern flair, all within sight of the Mediterrenean. ✉*Vila Joiosa 52–54, Barceloneta* ☎*93/221–1616* ▭*AE, DC, MC, V* Ⓜ*Barceloneta.*

$$$–$$$$ ✕**Antiga Casa Solé.** The open kitchen and its aromas, sights, sounds, and warmth match the fine fish and rice dishes served here. Two blocks from the sea side of Plaça de Sant Miquel, Barceloneta's prettiest square, you can find this traditional midday-Sunday pilgrimage site, which occupies an original Barceloneta fisherman's house and serves fresh, well-prepared, piping-hot seafood. Whether it's *lenguado a la plancha* (grilled sole) or the exquisite *arroç negre amb sepia en su tinta* (black rice with squid in its ink), everything here comes loaded with flavor. ✉*Sant Carles 4, Barceloneta* ☎*93/221–5012* ▭*AE, DC, MC, V* ⏲*Closed Mon. and last 2 wks of Aug. No dinner Sun.* Ⓜ*Barceloneta.*

$$$–$$$$ ★ ✕**Can Majó.** One of Barcelona's premier seafood restaurants, Can Majó combines fine cooking and a cosmopolitan, this-is-the-place-to-be vibe. House specialties include *caldero de bogavante* (a cross between paella and lobster bouillabaisse) and *suquet* (fish stewed in its own juices), but whatever you choose will be excellent. In summer the terrace overlooking the Mediterranean is the closest you can come to beachside dining. ✉*Almirall Aixada 23, Barceloneta* ☎*93/221–5455* ▭*AE, DC, MC, V* ⏲*Closed Mon. No dinner Sun.* Ⓜ*Barceloneta.*

$$$–$$$$ ✕**Reial Club Marítim.** For sunset or harbor views, excellent maritime fare, and a sense of escape from the city, try Barcelona's yacht club, just around the harbor through Barceloneta. Highlights are paella *marinera* (seafood paella), *rodaballo* (turbot), *lubina* (sea bass), and *dorado* (sea bream). Ask for the freshest fish they have and you won't be disappointed. ✉ *Moll d'Espanya, Barceloneta* ☎*93/221–7143* ▭*AE, DC, MC, V* ⏲*No dinner Sun.* Ⓜ*Barceloneta.*

$$$–$$$$ ✕**Suquet de l'Almirall.** Specialists in rice dishes and *caldoso de bogavante,* a brothy rice dish with lobster, this is one of Barceloneta's finest seafood havens. With an intimate terrace for alfresco dining in summer, "The Admiral's Fish Stew" indeed serves fare fit for the admiralty. ✉*Passeig Joan de Borbó 65, Barceloneta* ☎*93/221–6233* ▭*AE, DC, MC, V* ⏲*Closed Mon. No dinner Sun.* Ⓜ*Barceloneta.*

$$–$$$$ ✕**Barceloneta.** This rollicking, riverboatlike dining room at the end of the yacht marina in Barceloneta doesn't provide an intimate space for a romantic dinner a deux. On the other hand, the food is delicious, the service impeccable, the hundreds of fellow diners make the place feel like a cheerful New Year's Eve celebration. All in all, a bad time is rarely had here. Rice and fish dishes are the specialty, and the salads are excellent. ✉*L'Escar 22, Barceloneta* ☎*93/221–2111* ▭*AE, MC, V* Ⓜ*Barceloneta.*

$–$$$ ✕**Can Manel la Puda.** The first choice for paella in the sun, year-round, Can Manel is near the end of the main road out to the Barceloneta beach. Any time before 4 PM will do; it then reopens at 7. *Arròs a banda* (rice with peeled shellfish) and paella marinera (seafood and rice) or *fideuá* (with noodles instead of rice) are all delicious. ✉*Passeig Joan de Borbó 60, Barceloneta* ☎*93/221–5013* ▭*AE, DC, MC, V* ⊙*Closed Mon.* Ⓜ*Barceloneta.*

EIXAMPLE

Eixample dining, invariably upscale and elegant, ranges from traditional cuisine in Moderniste houses to designer fare in sleek minimalist-experimental spaces.

$$$$ ★ ✕**Can Gaig.** Market-fresh ingredients and original combinations here are solidly rooted in traditional recipes from Catalan home cooking. The menu balances seafood and upland specialties, game, and homegrown products of all kinds. This longtime Barcelona favorite, recently relocated to the city center, is famous for mingling superb design and carefully prepared cuisine. Try the *perdiz asada con jamón ibérico* (roast partridge with Iberian ham), or, if it's available, *becada* (woodcock), one of Carles Gaig's signature dishes. ✉*Carrer Aragó 214, Eixample* ☎*93/429–1017* 📠*93/429–7002* ✍*Reservations essential* ▭*AE, DC, MC, V* ⊙*Closed Mon., Easter wk, and Aug.* Ⓜ*Passeig de Gràcia*

$$$$ Fodor'sChoice ★ ✕**Drolma.** Chef Fermin Puig's blend of tradition, innovation, and inspiration produces classical Mediterranean excellence based on peerless products and painstakingly perfect execution. Named (in Sanskrit) for Buddha's female side, this intimate refuge has been a success since the first day they opened their doors. The *menú de degustaciò* (tasting menu) might have pheasant cannelloni in foie-gras sauce with fresh black truffles or giant prawn tails with *trompettes de la mort* (black wild mushrooms) with *sôt-l'y-laisse* (literally "fool leaves it there"; in fact, chicken nuggets). Fermin's foie gras *a la ceniza con ceps* (cooked over wood coals with wild mushrooms) is a typical example of a childhood favorite reinvented in the big city. ✉ *Majestic Hotel, Passeig de Gràcia 70, Eixample* ☎*93/496–7710* ✍*Reservations essential* ▭*AE, DC, MC, V* ⊙*Closed Sun. and Aug.* Ⓜ*Provença, Passeig de Gràcia.*

$$$$ ✕**Lasarte.** Martin Berasategui's landing in the Catalan capital comes at a moment when Spain's great chefs are in general expansion mode around the peninsula. Alex Garés, chief cook in Berasategui's absence, trained with the best (Pellicer of Àbac and Manolo de la Osa in Cuenca's Las Rejas) and serves an eclectic selection of Basque, Mediterranean, market, and personal interpretations and creations. Expect whimsical

and playful aperitifs to deepen to surprising and serious combinations such as *foie* and smoked eel or simple wood pigeon cooked to perfection. For a lighter, more economical Berasategui-directed experience, try Loidi, recently opened next door, with a prix-fixe €32 four-course menu of appetizer, fish, meat, and dessert. ✉ *Mallorca 259, Eixample* ☎ *93/445–0000* ▭ *AE, DC, MC, V* ⊙ *Closed weekends* Ⓜ *Provença.*

$$$$ ★ ✕ **Taktika Berri.** At this Basque restaurant specializing in San Sebastián's favorite dishes, the only drawback is that a table is hard to come by unless you call weeks (yes, weeks) in advance. The tapas served over the bar, however, are of such a high quality that you can barely do better à table, though there is a theory extant that dining well precludes seeing your feet. The charming family that owns and runs this semisecret nugget will take good care of you. ✉ *Valencia 169, Eixample* ☎ *93/453–4759* ✍ *Reservations essential* ▭ *AE, DC, MC, V* ⊙ *No dinner Sat. Closed Sun.* Ⓜ *Provença.*

$$$–$$$$ ✕ **Casa Calvet.** This Art Nouveau space in Antoni Gaudí's 1898–1900 Casa Calvet just a block down from the Palace (the hotel formerly known as the Ritz) is an opportunity to break bread in one of the great Moderniste's creations. The dining room is a graceful and spectacular design display featuring signature Gaudí ornamentation from looping parabolic door handles to polychrome stained glass, acid engravings, and wood carved in floral and organic motifs. The menu is Mediterranean, with an emphasis on light, contemporary fare. ✉ *Casp 48, Eixample* ☎ *93/412–4012* ▭ *AE, DC, MC, V* ⊙ *Closed Sun. and last 2 wks of Aug.* Ⓜ *Urquinaona.*

$$$–$$$$ ✕ **Cinc Sentits.** The engaging Artal family—maître d' and owner Rosa, server and eloquent food narrator Amy, and chef Jordi—a Catalan family that clocked a couple of decades in Canada and the United States, offers a unique Barcelona experience: cutting-edge, creative, original cuisine explained in detail in perfect English, all in a minimalist, contemporary design setting. Three tasting menus—light, tasting, and *omakase* (a "trust the chef" menu, including wine pairings of the chef's choice)—provide a wide range of tastes and textures. At the end of the meal, a printout reprises the nine minicourses and seven wines that have just crossed your plate and palate. ✉ *Aribau 58, Eixample* ☎ *93/323–9490* ▭ *AE, DC, MC, V* ⊙ *Closed Sun. No dinner Mon.* Ⓜ *Provença.*

$$$–$$$$ ✕ **El Tragaluz.** *Tragaluz* means skylight—literally, "light-swallower"—and this is an excellent choice if you're still on a design high from Gaudí's Pedrera. The sliding roof opens to the stars in good weather, and the chairs, lamps, and fittings by Javier Mariscal (creator of 1992 Olympic mascot Cobi) reflect Barcelona's passion for whimsy and playful design. The Mediterranean cuisine is light and innovative. ✉ *Passatge de la Concepció 5, Eixample* ☎ *93/487–0196* ▭ *AE, DC, MC, V* ⊙ *Closed Jan. 5. No lunch Mon.* Ⓜ *Diagonal.*

$$$–$$$$ ✕ **Gorría.** One of the two best Basque restaurants in Barcelona (the other is Taktika Berri—near impossible to get into), this establishment serves everything from the stewed *pochas* (white beans) to the heroic *chuletón* (steak), which is as pure as the Navarran Pyrenees. The Castillo de Sajazarra reserva '95, a brick-red Rioja, provides per-

fect accompaniment at this delicious pocket of Navarra in the Catalan capital. ✉ *Diputació 421, Eixample* ☎ *93/245–1164* ▭ *AE, DC, MC, V* ⏲ *Closed Sun.* Ⓜ *Monumental.*

$$$–$$$$ ✕ **L'Olivé.** Urban and cosmopolitan chic, L'Olive specializes in contemporary interpretations of traditional Catalan home cooking drawing the faithful to this midtown favorite. This sleek, contemporary Eixample space decorated in soothing, clean-lined tans and mauves is always filled with savvy diners having a great time. You soon see why: excellent fare, smart service, and some of the best *pa amb tomaquet* (toasted bread with olive oil and squeezed tomato) in town. ✉ *Carrer Balmes 47, Eixample* ☎ *93/452–1990* ▭ *AE, DC, MC, V* ⏲ *No dinner Sun.* Ⓜ *Provença.*

$$$–$$$$ ★ ✕ **Manairó.** A *manairó* is a mysterious Pyrenean (obviously culinary) elf who helps make things happen, and Jordi Herrera may be one. A demon for everything from blow torch–fried eggs to meat cooked *al clavo ardiente* (à la burning nail—fillets warmed from within by red-hot spikes producing meat both rare and warm and never undercooked), Jordi also cooks cod under a lightbulb at 220 degrees (*bacalao iluminado*—illuminated codfish) and serves a palate-cleansing gin and tonic with liquid nitrogen, gin, and lime. The intimate though post-modern-edgy design of the dining room is a perfect reflection of the cuisine. ✉ *Diputació 424, Eixample* ☎ *93/231–0057* ⌂ *Reservations essential* ▭ *AE, DC, MC, V* ⏲ *Closed Sun., Mon., and last 3 wks of Aug.* Ⓜ *Monumental.*

$$–$$$$ ✕ **Mantequeria Ya Ya Amelia.** Lovingly prepared and intelligent dishes ranging from warm goat-cheese salad to *foie* (duck or goose liver) to beef distinguish this delicatessen and *mantequeria* (literally, "buttery") two blocks uphill from Gaudí's Sagrada Família. The wine list is exquisite and the service is cheerful. Ask for the chef's table by the kitchen. The original Ya Ya Amelia (*Ya Ya* is an affectionate Spanish nickname for "grandmother") around the corner at Sardenya 364 (☎ 93/456–4573) is closed on Sunday, but open on Monday (so one or the other is always available). Both restaurants serve continuously from 1 PM to midnight. The Mantequeria is usually fresher, less smoky, and less crowded. ✉ *Carrer Còrsega 537, Eixample* ☎ *93/435–8048* ▭ *AE, DC, MC, V* ⏲ *Closed Mon.* Ⓜ *Sagrada Família.*

GRÀCIA

This exciting yet intimate neighborhood has everything from the most sophisticated cuisine in town to Basque taverns in a lively context.

$$$$ ✕ **Botafumeiro.** Fleets of waiters in white outfits flash by at the speed of light in Barcelona's best Galician restaurant, a seafood medley from shellfish to finfish to cuttlefish to caviar. An assortment of *media ración* (half-ration) selections is available at the bar, where *pulpo a feira* (squid on potato) and *jamón bellota de Guijuelo* (acorn-fed ham) make peerless late-night fare. People-watching is tops, and the waiters are better than stand-up comics. ✉ *Carrer Gran de Gràcia 81, Gràcia* ☎ *93/218–4230* ▭ *AE, DC, MC, V* Ⓜ *Gràcia.*

$–$$$ ✕ **Folquer.** With one of the best-value taster's menus in Barcelona, Folquer serves creatively prepared traditional Catalan specialties using first-rate ingredients. This little hideaway in the bottom of Gràcia is a good way to end a tour of this village within a city. ✉ *Torrent de l'Olla 3, Gràcia* ☎ *93/217–4395* ▭ *AE, DC, MC, V* ⊙ *Closed Sun. and last 2 wks of Aug. No lunch Sat.* Ⓜ *Diagonal.*

SARRIÀ-PEDRALBES & SANT GERVASI

Take an excursion to the upper reaches of town for an excellent selection of restaurants, along with cool summer evening breezes and a sense of village life in Sarrià.

$$$$ ✕ **El Racó d'en Freixa.** Chef Ramón Freixa's original riffs on traditional recipes, all using peerless ingredients, have established his work as *cuina d'autor* (designer cuisine). A typical specialty is *peus de porc en escabetx de guatlle* (pig's trotters with quail in a garlic-and-parsley gratin). Four textures (raw, frozen, stewed, transparent) of tomato with Palamós jumbo shrimp is another original creation. The minimalist, clean-lined design of the dining room perfectly matches the aesthetic of Freixa's cuisine. ✉ *Sant Elíes 22, Sant Gervasi* ☎ *93/209–7559* ▭ *AE, DC, MC, V* ⊙ *Closed Mon., Easter wk, and Aug. No dinner Sun.* Ⓜ *Sant Gervasi.*

$$$$ ★ ✕ **Neichel.** Alsatian chef Jean-Louis Neichel masterfully manages a wide variety of exquisite ingredients such as *foie,* truffles, wild mushrooms, herbs, and the best seasonal vegetables. His flawless Mediterranean delicacies include *ensalada de gambas de Palamós al sésamo con puerros* (shrimp from Palamós with sesame-seed and leeks) and *espardenyes amb salicornia* (sea slugs and sea asparagus) on sun-dried-tomato paste. The formal dining room may seem a trifle over-carpeted and staid, but the hush allows the other senses to kick in with authority. ✉ *Carrer Bertran i Rózpide 1, off Av. Pedralbes, Pedralbes* ☎ *93/203–8408* ✍ *Reservations essential* ▭ *AE, DC, MC, V* ⊙ *Closed Sun., Mon., and Aug.* Ⓜ *Maria Cristina.*

$$$–$$$$ ✕ **Le Quattro Stagioni.** For excellent, streamlined Italian cuisine that will remind you more of postmodern Catalan cooking than of *The Godfather,* this chic spot just down from the Bonanova metro stop on the Sarrià line is a winner. It's always filled with intriguing-looking bons vivants (evenly balanced between hip locals and clued-in tourists), and the garden is cool and fragrant on summer nights. ✉ *Dr. Roux 37, Sant Gervasi* ☎ *93/205–2279* ▭ *AE, DC, MC, V* Ⓜ *Tres Torres.*

$$$–$$$$ ★ ✕ **Tram-Tram.** Isidre Soler and his wife, Reyes, have put together one of Barcelona's finest culinary offerings at what was once the end of the old tram line above the village of Sarrià. Try the *menú de degustaciò* and you might score marinated tuna salad, cod medallions, and venison filets mignons. Perfect portions and a streamlined reinterpretation of space within this traditional Sarrià house—especially in or near the garden out back—make this a memorable dining experience. ✉ *Major de Sarrià 121, Sarrià* ☎ *93/204–8518* ▭ *AE, DC, MC, V* ⊙ *Closed Sun. and late Dec.–early Jan. No lunch Sat.* Ⓜ *Reina Elisenda.*

$$$–$$$$ ✕ **Vivanda.** This leafy garden just above Plaça de Sarrià is especially wonderful between May and mid-October, when outside dining is a delight. The menu has Catalan specialties such as *espinacas a la catalana* (spinach with raisins, pine nuts, and garlic) and inventive combinations of seafood and inland products. ✉ *Major de Sarrià 134, Sarrià* ☎ *93/203–1918* ▭ *AE, DC, MC, V* ⊙ *Closed Sun.* Ⓜ *Reina Elisenda.*

$$–$$$$ ✕ **Acontraluz.** This stylish covered terrace in the leafy upper-Barcelona neighborhood of Tres Torres has a strenuously varied menu ranging from game in season, such as *rable de liebre* (stewed hare) with chutney, to the more northern *pochas con almejas* (beans with clams). Dishes are prepared with care and flair; the lunch menu is a bargain. ✉ *Milanesat 19, Tres Torres* ☎ *93/203–0658* ▭ *AE, DC, MC, V* Ⓜ *Tres Torres.*

$$–$$$ ★ ✕ **Silvestre.** Modern cuisine at extraordinary value has made a roaring success of this attractive dining spot in upper Barcelona. Just below Via Augusta 50 yards from the Muntaner train stop, a series of intimate dining rooms and cozy corners are carefully tended by chef Guillermo Casañé and Marta Cabot, his charming (and perfect-English-speaking) partner and maître d'. Look for fresh market produce lovingly prepared and dishes such as tuna tartare or noodles and shrimp. ✉ *Santaló 101, Sant Gervasi* ☎ *93/241–4031* ▭ *AE, DC, MC, V* ⊙ *Closed Sun., 2 wks in Aug., and Easter wk. No lunch Sat.* Ⓜ *Muntaner.*

$$ ✕ **El Mató de Pedralbes.** Named for the *mató* (cottage cheese) traditionally prepared by the Clarist nuns across the street in the Monestir de Pedralbes, this is a fine stop after touring the monastery, which closes at 2. The restaurant has one of the most typically Catalan, best-value menus in town. Look for *sopa de ceba gratinée* (onion soup), *trinxat* (chopped cabbage with bacon bits), and *truite de patata i ceba* (potato-and-onion omelet). ✉ *Obispo Català, Pedralbes* ☎ *93/204–7962* ▭ *AE, DC, MC, V* ⊙ *Closed Sun.* Ⓜ *Reina Elisenda.*

TIBIDABO

$$$–$$$$ ✕ **El Asador de Aranda.** Designed by Art Nouveau architect Rubió i Bellver, this immense palace 1,600 feet above the Avenida Tibidabo metro station is a hike—but worth remembering if you're in upper Barcelona. The kitchen specializes in *cordero lechal* (roast lamb); try *pimientos de piquillo* (hot, spicy peppers) on the side. The dining room has a terra-cotta floor and a full complement of Art Nouveau ornamentation ranging from intricately carved wood trimmings to stained-glass partitions, acid-engraved glass, and Moorish archways. ✉ *Av. del Tibidabo 31, Tibidabo* ☎ *93/417–0115* ▭ *AE, DC, MC, V* ⊙ *Closed Easter wk and Sun. in Aug. No dinner Sun.* Ⓜ *Av. Tibidabo.*

OUTSKIRTS OF BARCELONA

With the many fine in-town dining options available in Barcelona, any out-of-town recommendations should rank somewhere in the uppermost stratosphere of excellence. These two, both among the top five or six establishments below the Pyrenees, undoubtedly do.

7

$$$$ ★ ✕ **Sant Pau.** Carme Ruscalleda's nonpareil restaurant in Sant Pol de Mar is a delight from soup to nuts, or, more accurately, from amuse-bouches to petits fours. Spain's top-ranked female chef is a pixie-ish powerhouse whose menu changes often, but star dishes may include *vieiras* (scallops) with crisped artichoke flakes on roast potato, or *lubina* (sea bass) on baby leeks and chard in *garnatxa* (sweet Catalan wine) sauce. If you're lucky enough to be there for Valentine's Day or, even better, the 23 April Sant Jordi lover's fest, order the *misiva de amor* (love letter), a pastry envelope with slivers of raspberries, wild strawberries, blueberries, and julienned peaches. Sant Pol de Mar is a scenic 40-minute train ride along the beach from Plaça Catalunya's RENFE station: the Calella train stops at the door. (The last evening train is too early for dinner, so attempt this only for lunch.) ✉*Nou 10, Sant Pol de Mar* ☎*93/760–0662* ▭*AE, DC, MC, V* ⊙*Closed Mon., 2 wks in Mar., and 2 wks in Nov. No dinner Sun.*

$$$$ Fodor'sChoice ★ ✕🏨 **El Racó de Can Fabes.** Santi Santamaria's master class in Mediterranean cuisine merits the 45-minute train ride (or 30-minute drive) north of Barcelona to Sant Celoni. One of the top three restaurants ($$$$) in Spain, this is a must for anyone interested in fine dining. Every detail, from the six flavors of freshly baked bread to the cheese selection, is superb. The taster's menu is the wisest solution. The RENFE stations are at Passeig de Gràcia or Sants—the last train back is at 10:24 PM, so this is a lunchtime-only transport solution. However, El Racó has five sleek rooms so you can always reach a bed just a short crawl from the dinner table. ✉*Sant Joan 6, Sant Celoni* ☎*93/867–2851* 📠*93/867–3861* 🌐*www.canfabes.com* 🛏*5 rooms* 👍*In-hotel: restaurant, parking (fee)* ▭*AE, DC, MC, V* ⊙*Closed Mon., 1st 2 wks of Feb., and late June–early July. No dinner Sun.*

WHERE TO STAY

Barcelona's hotels offer clear distinctions. Hotels in the Ciutat Vella (Old City)—the Gothic Quarter and along the Rambla—are charming and convenient for sightseeing, though sometimes short on peace and quiet. Relative newcomers such as the Neri, the Duquesa de Cardona, the Banys Orientals, and the Casa Camper Barcelona are contemporary design standouts inhabiting medieval architecture, a combination at which Barcelona architects and decorators are peerless. Eixample hotels (including most of the city's best) are late-19th- or early-20th-century town houses restored and converted into exciting modern environments.

Downtown hotels, including the Palace (former Ritz), the Claris, the Majestic, the Condes de Barcelona, and the Hotel Omm best combine style and luxury with a sense of place, and the peripheral palaces (the Hotel Arts, the Eurostar Grand Marina, and the Rey Juan Carlos I) are less about Barcelona and more about generic luxury. Sarrià and Sant Gervasi upper city hotels get you up out of the urban crush, and Olympic Port and Diagonal Mar hotels are in high-rise towers (requiring transport to and from the real Barcelona). Smaller budget hotels are less than half as expensive as some of the luxury addresses and more a part of city life.

CIUTAT VELLA (OLD CITY)

$$$$ Fodor'sChoice ★ **Duquesa de Cardona.** This refurbished 16th-century town house overlooking the port has ultracontemporary facilities with designer touches, all in an early-Renaissance structure. The exterior rooms, though small, have views of the harbor, the World Trade Center, and the passenger-

WHERE TO STAY IN BARCELONA

	Neighborhood Vibe	Pros	Cons
Rambla	A solid stream of humanity around the clock, the Rambla is always alive and palpitating. A promenade that is chock full of every type of street life, this is where you can feel the city's pulse.	The Rambla is the city's most iconic runway and always an exciting strip. The Boqueria market, the flower stalls, the opera house, and Plaça Reial are all quintessential Barcelona.	The incessant crush of humanity can be overwhelming, especially if FC Barcelona wins a championship and the entire city descends upon the Rambla.
Gothic Quarter & Ribera-Born	With 19th-century gaslight-type lamps glowing in the corners of Roman and Gothic areas, this is a romantic part of town. The Picasso Museum and Santa Maria del Mar basilica sit nearby.	The architecture of the Gothic Quarter is tangible evidence of the city's past. Plaça Sant Jaume, the cathedral, Plaça del Rei, and the Born-Ribera district are the main reasons to visit the city.	Echoes reverberate around this ancient sound chamber and, while there is little serious noise, what there is goes a long way.
Raval	The Raval has always been a rough and tumble part of town. But the nightlife is exciting and the diversity of the neighborhood is exemplary. Bonus: living behind the Boqueria market.	For the closest thing to Marrakesh in Barcelona, the Raval has a buzz all its own. A contemporary art museum, the medieval hospital, and the Mercat de Sant Antoni offer plenty to explore.	The Raval can seem dangerous, whether it is or not. Certain corners teem with prostitutes, drug dealers, and Barcelona's seamiest elements.
Eixample	Some of Gaudí's best buildings line the sidewalks and many of the city's finest hotels and restaurants are right around the corner. And then there's the shopping ...	Eixample remains the world's only Art Nouveau neighborhood, constantly rewarding to the eye. Gaudí's unfinished masterpiece La Sagrada Família is within walking distance.	A bewildering grid without numbers or alphabetization, the Eixample can seem hard-edged compared to the older, quirkier, parts of Barcelona.
Barceloneta & Olympic Port	The onetime fisherman's quarter, Barceloneta retains its informal and working-class ambience, with laundry flapping over the streets and sidewalk restaurants lining Passeig Joan de Borbó.	Living near the beach gives the city a laid-back feel. The Olympic Port is a world apart, but Barceloneta is brimming with the best seafood dining spots in town.	Barceloneta offers few hotel opportunities, while the Olympic Port offers only one: the monolithic Hotel Arts, which, for all its quality, seems a tourist colony away from the rest of town.
Pedralbes, Sarrià & Upper Barcelona	Upper Barcelona is leafy and residential and the air is always a few degrees cooler. Pedralbes holds Barcelona's finest mansions; Sarrià is a rustic village suspended in the urban sprawl.	Getting above the madding fray and into better air has distinct advantages and the upper reaches of Barcelona offers them. A 15-minute train ride connects Sarrià with the Rambla.	The only drawback to staying in upper Barcelona is the 15-minute commute to the most important monuments and attractions. After midnight on weeknights this will require a taxi.

boat terminals. The hotel is a 10-minute walk from everything in the Gothic Quarter or Barceloneta, and no more than a 30-minute walk from the main Eixample attractions. The miniature rooftop pool, more a plunge than a swimming venue, provides relief in summer. ✉ *Passeig de Colom 12, Rambla, 08002* ☎ *93/268–9090* 📠 *93/268–2931* 🌐 *www.hduquesadecardona.com* *44 rooms* *In-room: dial-up. In-hotel: restaurant, pool* 💳 *AE, DC, MC, V* Ⓜ *Drassanes.*

LODGING TIP

Hotels will negotiate room rates if they're not full. Ask about weekend rates, which are often half; faxing for reservations may also get you a good deal. Business travelers may get a 40% break.

$$$$ **Grand Hotel Central.** Recently opened in the famous Cambó house on the edge of the Gothic Quarter very near the Barcelona cathedral, this hot new midtown hideaway is becoming a magnet for the hip and swashbuckling from around Europe and beyond. Rooms are flawlessly furnished and equipped with high-tech design features, from flat-screen TVs to DSL hookups. The restaurant, supervised by internationally acclaimed chef Ramón Freixa, is bound for glory, and the top-floor pool offers a unique perch over the city's 2,000-year-old Roman and Gothic central nucleus. Via Laietana is noisy; go by the rule: the higher the better. ✉ *Via Laietana 30, Barri Gòtic , 08003* ☎ *93/295–7900* 📠 *93/268–1215* 🌐 *www.grandhotelcentral.com* *147 rooms* *In-room: Ethernet. In-hotel: restaurant, bar, pool, gym, parking (fee)* 💳 *AE, DC, MC, V* Ⓜ *Catalunya.*

$$$$ **Hotel Neri.** Owner Bruno Figueras and designer Cristina Gabà have created a unique oasis of taste in the heart of the Gothic Quarter. Built into a 17th-century palace over one of the Gothic Quarter's smallest and most charming squares, Plaça Sant Felip Neri, the Neri is a singular counterpoint of ancient and avant-garde design. The rooms are medievalesque yet clean lined, hard edged, and equipped with great facilities. Noise from the echo-chamber square can be a problem on summer nights and winter mornings when kindergarten convenes. ✉ *Carrer Sant Sever 5, Barri Gòtic, 08002* ☎ *93/304–0655* 📠 *93/304–0337* 🌐 *www.hotelneri.com* *22 rooms* *In-room: dial-up. In-hotel: restaurant, bar* 💳 *AE, DC, MC, V* Ⓜ *Liceu, Catalunya.*

$$$$ **Le Meridien.** The top Rambla hotel, this supremely luxurious giant offers a variety of characterless but impeccable rooms and suites, many of which overlook Barcelona's most emblematic promenade. Painted in pastel hues with brightly colored bedding and curtains, rooms include complete laptop and fax hookups. Rooms over the Rambla are completely soundproofed. Ask to have a look at the presidential suite for a peek at one of Barcelona's greatest hideaways (for clients with an extra two grand per night on their hands). ✉ *La Rambla 111, Rambla, 08002* ☎ *93/318–6200, 800/543–4300 reservations in U.S. and Canada* 📠 *93/301–7776* 🌐 *www.lemeridien-barcelona.com* *390 rooms* *In-room: safe. In-hotel: restaurant, bar, parking (fee)* 💳 *AE, DC, MC, V* Ⓜ *Catalunya.*

$$$–$$$$ Fodor'sChoice ★ **Colón.** Surprisingly charming and intimate for such a sizable hotel, this slightly ramshackle Barcelona standby is directly across the plaza from the cathedral, overlooking weekend *sardana* dancing, Thursday antiques markets, and, of course, the floodlighted cathedral by night. Rooms are comfortable and tasteful; try to get one with a view of the cathedral. The Colón was a favorite of Catalan painter Joan Miró. Considering its combination of comfort, style, and location, it may be the best place to stay in Barcelona, though it is far from the most luxurious. *Av. Catedral 7, Barri Gòtic, 08002 93/301–1404 93/317–2915 www.hotelcolon.es 140 rooms, 5 suites In-room: dial-up. In-hotel: restaurant, bar AE, DC, MC, V Catalunya.*

$$$–$$$$ **Eurostars Grand Marina Hotel.** A tower built around a central patio, this ultracontemporary monolith offers maximum luxury two minutes from the Rambla over Barcelona's port. With stunning views of the city or Mediterranean, the Grand Marina is in the middle of, though well above, Barcelona's best sights. Rooms are bright and comfortable, albeit somewhat generic, and the public spaces are geometrical expanses of sleek glass and steel. Guests tend to be conventioneers and business travelers. *Moll de Barcelona s/n, World Trade Center, Port Olímpic, 08039 93/603–9000 93/603–9090 www.grandmarinahotel.com 291 rooms In-hotel: 3 restaurants, bar, pool, gym, parking (fee) AE, DC, MC, V Drassanes.*

$$$–$$$$ **H1898.** This elegant, if somewhat impersonal, hotel overlooking the Rambla occupies a building with an illustrious history as the headquarters of the Compañia de Tabacos de Filipinas, a prestigious Barcelona business concern for nearly 100 years. Named for the fateful year when Spain was stripped of its final colonial possesions, the Philippines among them, the hotel's elegance is an homage to bygone glories as well as a sign of the city's present opulence. Rooms are superbly equipped with state-of-the-art appliances (such as flat-screen plasma TVs), and the location is unbeatable. *La Rambla 109, Rambla, 08002 93/552–9552 93/552–9550 www.nnhotels.es 166 rooms, 3 suites In-room: Ethernet. In-hotel: restaurant, bar, pool, gym, parking (fee) AE, DC, MC, V Catalunya.*

$$$–$$$$ **Montecarlo.** The ornate, illuminated entrance takes you from the Rambla through an enticing marble hall; upstairs, you enter a sumptuous reception room with a dark-wood Art Nouveau ceiling. Guest rooms, though not spacious, are modern, bright, and functional, and many overlook the Rambla. *La Rambla 124, Rambla, 08002 93/412–0404 93/318–7323 www.montecarlobcn.com 55 rooms, 1 suite In-hotel: restaurant, bar, parking (fee) AE, DC, MC, V Catalunya.*

$$–$$$$ **Rivoli Ramblas.** Behind this upper-Rambla facade lies an imaginative interior adorned with faux–Art Nouveau details, soothing lighting, and elegant marble floors. The rooms are pastel in hue and contemporary in design. The roof-terrace bar has panoramic views. *La Rambla 128, Rambla , 08002 93/481–7676 93/317–5053 www.rivolihotels.com 81 rooms, 9 suites In-hotel: restaurant, bar, gym, parking (fee) AE, DC, MC, V Catalunya.*

$$$ **Casa Camper Barcelona.** This revolutionary new hotel halfway between the Rambla and the MACBA (Museum of Contemporary Art) is the mutual brainchild of the Camper footwear empire and Barcelona's nonpareil Vinçon design store. No smoking, no tips, a free 24-hour snack facility to which you can invite your friends, ecologically recycled residual waters, children up to 12 staying free of charge, and the Foodball restaurant next door serving spheroids of natural ingredients such as garbanzo beans and spinach all add up to a dazzling new address in the formerly dark and scary Raval. *C. Elisabets 11, Raval, 08001 93/342–6280 93/342–7563 www.casacamper.com 20 rooms, 5 suites In-hotel: restaurant, parking (fee), no-smoking rooms AE, DC, MC, V BP Catalunya.*

$$$ **Nouvel.** Centrally located below Plaça de Catalunya, this hotel blends white marble, etched glass, elaborate plasterwork, and carved, dark woodwork in its handsome Art Nouveau interior. The rooms have marble floors, firm beds, and smart bathrooms. The narrow street is pedestrian-only and therefore quiet, but views are nonexistent. *Carrer Santa Anna 18–2, Rambla, 08002 93/301–8274 93/301–8370 www.hotelnouvel.com 71 rooms In-room: safe. In-hotel: restaurant, bar AE, DC, MC, V Catalunya.*

$$$ **Racó del Pi.** This sleek, modern space on a bustling Gothic Quarter street offers first-rate service and flawless if somewhat characterless accommodations. Equidistant from the cathedral, the Boqueria market, Plaça Catalunya, and the Palau de la Musica, this cozy *racó* (corner) is as practical as it is spotless. *Carrer del Pi 7, Rambla, 08002 93/342–6190 93/342–6191 www.h10.es 37 rooms In-hotel: bar AE, DC, MC, V Catalunya, Liceu.*

7

$$–$$$ **Citadines.** This Rambla *aparthotel* (a hotel that rents apartments with kitchens) offers a good value with a prime location. Impeccably bright and modern, soundproof, and generally well equipped, the hotel has rooms with kitchenettes and small dining areas, especially convenient for families with small children. The rooftop solarium with views over the Mediterranean and the Rambla may be the hotel's best feature. *La Rambla 122, Rambla, 08002 93/270–1111 93/412–7421 www.citadines.com 115 studios, 16 apartments In-room: kitchen. In-hotel: bar AE, DC, MC, V Catalunya.*

$$ **Continental.** This modest hotel stands at the top of the Rambla, below Plaça de Catalunya. Space is tight, but rooms manage to accommodate large, firm beds. It's high enough over the Rambla to escape street noise, so ask for a room overlooking Barcelona's most emblematic promenade. George Orwell stayed here with his wife in 1937 immediately after recovering from a gunshot wound through the throat. *La Rambla 138, Rambla, 08002 93/301–2570 93/302–7360 www.hotelcontinental.com 35 rooms In-room: safe AE, DC, MC, V Catalunya.*

$$ **Hostal Gat Xino.** A cheery space in what was once one of the Raval's darker corners Gat Raval's sister ship places the adventurous traveler in the middle of what may seem more like a North African souk than a modern design metropolis. Near the intersection of Carrers Carmen and Hospital, the Gat Xino gives you an up-close look at one of Bar-

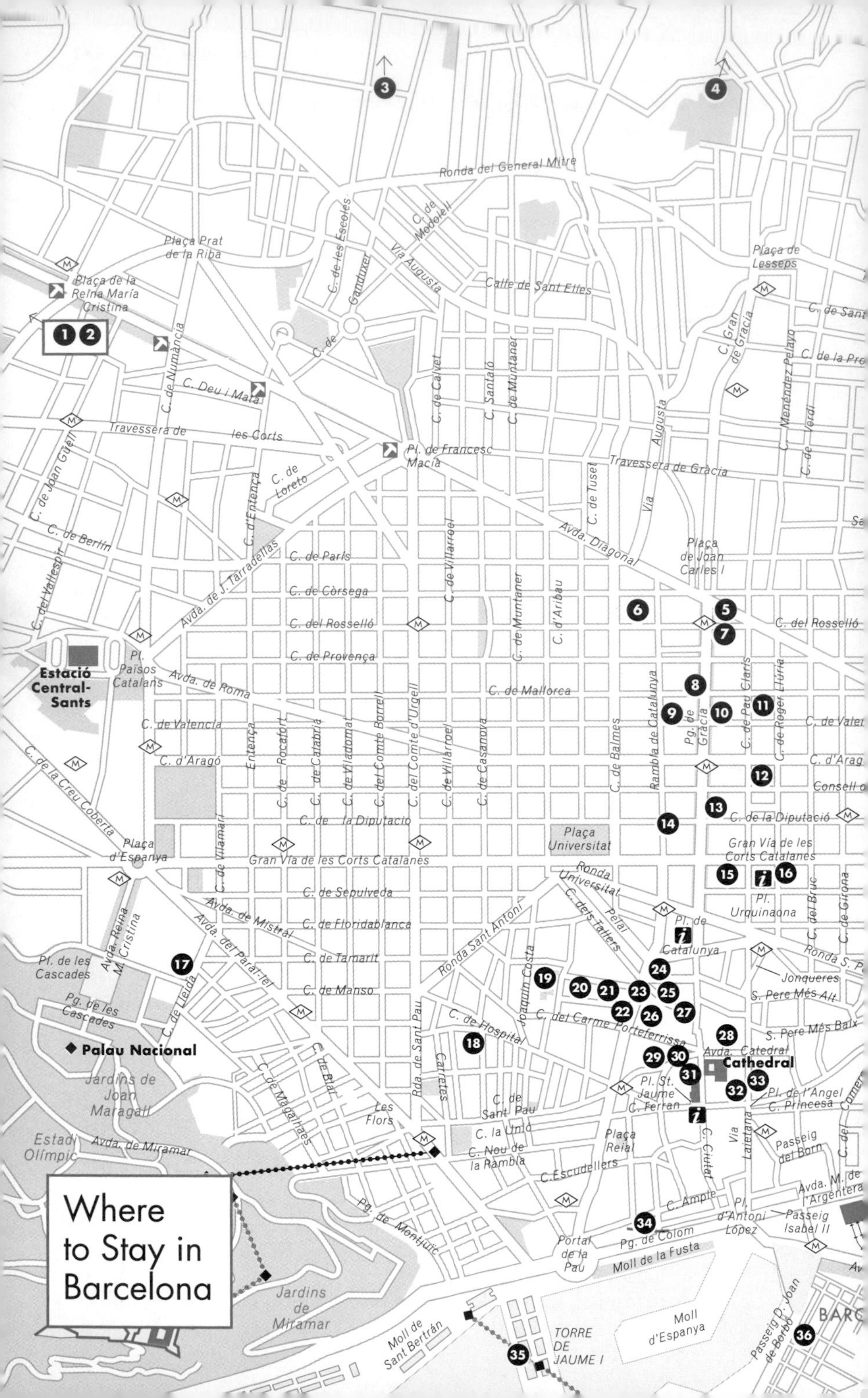

Where to Stay in Barcelona
Ronda del General Mitre
Avda. Diagonal
Gran Via de les Corts Catalanes
Estació Central-Sants
Palau Nacional
Cathedral
Plaça Universitat
Plaça d'Espanya
Pl. de Catalunya
Pl. de Francesc Macià
Plaça Reial
Jardins de Joan Maragall
Jardins de Miramar
Estadi Olímpic
Moll de la Fusta
Moll d'Espanya
Moll de Sant Bertrán
TORRE DE JAUME I

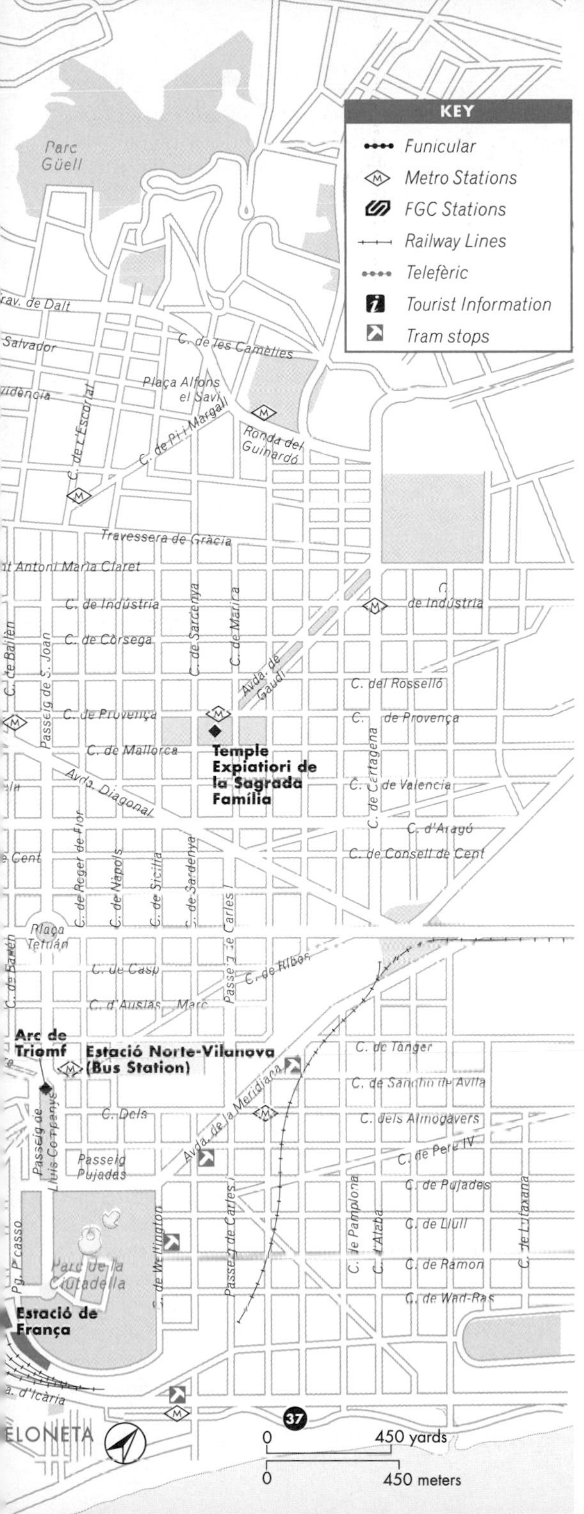

AC Diplomatic 12
Calderón 14
Casa Camper Barcelona 20
Citadines 27
Claris 11
Colón 28
Condes de Barcelona 8
Continental 24
Continental Palacete 13
Duquesa de Cardona 34
Eurostars Grand Marina Hotel 35
Fira Palace 17
Gallery 6
Grand Hotel Central 33
Gran Hotel la Florida 4
Gran Vía 15
H1898 22
Hostal Gat Raval 19
Hostal Gat Xino 18
Hotel Arts 37
Hotel Neri 31
Hotel Omm 5
Hotel Palace 16
Jardí 29
Le Meridien 21
Majestic 10
Marina Folch 36
Montecarlo 26
Nouvel 25
Paseo de Gràcia 7
Princesa Sofía 1
Racó del Pi 30
Regente 9
Rey Juan Carlos I 2
Rivoli Ramblas 23
Suizo 32
Turó de Vilana 3

celona's most cosmopolitan and traditionally tumultuous neighborhoods. Rooms, though tiny, are decorated in bright colors, and the value is unbeatable. In the bargain, you may discover that the Raval and its raucous street life are inhabited by some of Barcelona's friendliest citizens. ✉*Carrer Hospital 155, Raval, 08001* ☎*93/324–8833* 📠*93/324–8834* 🌐*www.gataccommodation.com* *35 rooms* *In-hotel: restaurant* 💳*AE, DC, MC, V* Ⓜ*Sant Antoni.*

$$ **Jardí.** Perched over the traffic-free and charming Plaça del Pi and Plaça Sant Josep Oriol, this budget hotel has rooms with views of the Gothic church of Santa Maria del Pi. All rooms have pine furniture and small bathrooms. The in-house breakfast is excellent, and the alfresco tables at the Bar del Pi, downstairs, are ideal in summer. With five floors and an elevator, this is not the Ritz: beds and furniture are flimsy, and the square can be noisy in summer, but it's still a great value. ✉*Pl. Sant Josep Oriol 1, Barri Gòtic, 08002* ☎*93/301–5900* 📠*93/342–5733* 🌐*www.hoteljardi-barcelona.com* *40 rooms* 💳*AE, DC, MC, V* Ⓜ*Liceu, Catalunya.*

$$ **Suizo.** Location and value are the main reasons this undistinguished but functional and comfortable hotel has faithfully served Barcelona for the better part of a century. The public rooms have elegant, modern seating and good views over the bustling square overlooking Via Laietana and the Jaume I subway stop at the front door. The guest rooms, though cramped, have bright walls, wood or tile floors, and miniscule but up-to-date bathrooms. ✉*Pl. del Àngel 12, Barri Gòtic, 08002* ☎*93/310–6108* 📠*93/315–0461* 🌐*www.gargallo-hotels.com* *59 rooms* *In-room: safe. In-hotel: bar, laundry service* 💳*AE, DC, MC, V* Ⓜ*Jaume I.*

$–$$ Fodor's Choice ★ **Hostal Gat Raval.** This hip little hole-in-the-wall opens into a surprisingly bright and sleekly designed modern space with rooms that come in different shapes, styles, and number of beds, all cheerily appointed and impeccably maintained. Just around the corner from the MACBA, the Gat Raval seems to have been influenced by Richard Meier's shining contemporary structure, though you'd never guess it from the street. Rooms are small and far from luxurious but the value is among Barcelona's best. ✉*Carrer Joaquín Costa 44, Raval, 08001* ☎*93/481–6670* 📠*93/342–6697* 🌐*www.gataccommodation.com* *22 rooms* 💳*AE, DC, MC, V* Ⓜ*Universitat.*

BARCELONETA & THE PORT OLÍMPIC

$$$$ ★ **Hotel Arts.** This luxurious Ritz-Carlton monolith overlooks Barcelona from the Olympic Port, providing unique views of the Mediterranean, the city, and the mountains behind. The hotel's main drawback is that it's somewhat in a world of its own, a short taxi ride from the center of the city. That said, its world is an exciting one. True to its name, fine art—from Chillida drawings to Susana Solano sculptures—hangs everywhere. Sergi Arola's restaurant is a chic, postmodern culinary playground. ✉*Calle de la Marina 19, Port Olímpic, 08005* ☎*93/221–1000* 📠*93/221–1070* 🌐*www.harts.es* *397 rooms, 59 suites, 27 apartments* *In-hotel: 3 restaurants, room service, bar, pool, beachfront, parking (fee)* 💳*AE, DC, MC, V* Ⓜ*Ciutadella–Vila Olímpica.*

$–$$ **Marina Folch.** Crisp, clean, and contemporary, this budget Barceloneta hideaway is five minutes from the beach, with views over the port. The restaurant (Peru) downstairs, and the generous and caring family at the helm make this a winner for the economy-minded traveler. ✉ *Carrer Mar 16 pral., Barceloneta, 08003* ☎ *93/310–3709* 📠 *93/310–5327* *11 rooms* *In-hotel: restaurant* ▭ *AE, DC, MC, V* Ⓜ *Barceloneta.*

EIXAMPLE

$$$$ **Claris.** Widely considered Barcelona's best hotel, this midtown refuge is a fascinating mélange of design and tradition. The rooms come in 60 modern layouts, some with restored 18th-century English furniture and some with contemporary furnishings from Barcelona's endlessly playful legion of lamp and chair designers. Lavishly endowed with wood and marble, the hotel also has a Japanese water garden. The restaurant, East 47, is stellar. ✉ *Carrer Pau Claris 150, Eixample, 08009* ☎ *93/487–6262* 📠 *93/215–7970* 🌐 *www.derbyhotels.es* *80 rooms, 40 suites* *In-hotel: 2 restaurants, bar, pool, gym, laundry service, parking (fee)* ▭ *AE, DC, MC, V* Ⓜ *Passeig de Gràcia.*

Fodor's Choice ★

$$$$ **Fira Palace.** Built in the early '90s, this hotel has established itself as one of Barcelona's most popular business and convention havens. Close to the Fira de Barcelona convention facility, it offers easy access to Montjuïc and its attractions. Impeccably modern, it's also a solid choice for generic creature comfort rather than local color. ✉ *Av. Rius i Taulet 1, Eixample, 08004* ☎ *93/426–2223* 📠 *93/424–8679* 🌐 *www.fira-palace.com* *258 rooms, 18 suites* *In-room: dial-up. In-hotel: restaurant, bar, pool, gym, parking (fee)* ▭ *AE, DC, MC, V* Ⓜ *Poble Sec.*

7

$$$$ **Gallery.** In the upper part of the Eixample, just below the Diagonal, this modern hotel offers impeccable comfort and service and a central location for middle and upper Barcelona. (In the other direction, you're only a half-hour walk from the waterfront.) It's named for its proximity to the city's prime art-gallery district, a few blocks away on Rambla de Catalunya and Consell de Cent. Rooms are small and charmless though comfortable and efficient. ✉ *Carrer Rosselló 249, Eixample, 08008* ☎ *93/415–9911* 📠 *93/415–9184* 🌐 *www.galleryhotel.com* *108 rooms, 5 suites* *In-room: dial-up. In-hotel: restaurant, bar, gym, parking (fee)* ▭ *AE, DC, MC, V* Ⓜ *Provença.*

$$$$ **Hotel Omm.** Another member of Barcelona's lengthening list of design hotels, this postmodern architectural tour de force created by a team of designers seeks to create, in a playful way, a mystic sense of peace consonant with its eponymous mantra. The rooms, reception area, pool, and upper rooms overlooking the roof terrace of Gaudí's Casa Milá all contribute to this aura. The restaurant, Moo, is an oasis of modern cuisine orchestrated by the Roca brothers—Joan, Josep, and Jordi—who have achieved international prestige with their Celler de Can Roca near Girona. Roca offerings range from the bizarre to the classical, but one word to the wise: unless the idea of swallowing a cigar appeals to you, avoid the chocolate stogie. ✉ *Carrer Rosselló 265, Eixample, 08008* ☎ *93/445–4000* 📠 *93/445–4004* 🌐 *www.hotelomm.es* *58 rooms, 1 suite* *In-hotel: restaurant, bar, pool, parking (fee)* ▭ *AE, DC, MC, V* Ⓜ *Diagonal, Provença.*

$$$$ ★ **Hotel Palace.** Founded in 1919 by Caesar Ritz, this grande dame of Barcelona hotels has been restored to the splendor of its earlier years. The imperial lobby is at once rambling and elegant; guest rooms contain Regency furniture, and some have Roman baths and mosaics. The restaurant, Diana, serves superb French and Catalan cuisine. *Gran Via de les Corts Catalanes 668, Eixample, 08010 93/510–1130 93/318–0148 www.hotelpalacebarcelona.com 122 rooms In-hotel: restaurant, bar, gym AE, DC, MC, V Passeig de Gràcia.*

$$$$ Fodor'sChoice ★ **Majestic.** On Barcelona's most stylish boulevard, surrounded by fashion emporiums, you can find this near-perfect place to stay. The building is part Eixample town house and part modern extension, but pastels and Mediterranean hues warm each room and the furnishings are all state-of-the-art contemporary. The superb restaurant, Fermin Puig's internationally acclaimed Drolma, is a destination in itself. *Passeig de Gràcia 68, Eixample, 08008 93/488–1717 93/488–1880 www.hotelmajestic.es 273 rooms, 30 suites In-room: dial-up. In-hotel: 2 restaurants, bar, pool, gym, parking (fee) AE, DC, MC, V Passeig de Gràcia.*

$$$–$$$$ **AC Diplomatic.** Well placed in the middle of the Eixample, within walking distance of nearly everything in town, this newly outfitted, high-tech hotel offers much more value than many of its more expensive neighbors. From flat-screen TVs to free minibars, everything in the building, even the service, seems a little better than its neighbors, especially if you can negotiate a weekend, low-season bargain. Spare, wood-paneled rooms, the outside pool, and the Mediterranean market-driven cuisine at Nichte, the hotel restaurant, can make this refuge a hard place to leave. *Carrer Pau Claris 122, Eixample, 08009 93/272–3810 93/272–3811 www.ac-hotels.com 211 rooms In-room: dial-up. In-hotel: restaurant, bar, pool, gym, parking (fee) AE, DC, MC, V Diagonal.*

$$$–$$$$ Fodor'sChoice ★ **Condes de Barcelona.** Reserve well in advance—this is one of Barcelona's most popular hotels. The pentagonal lobby has a marble floor and the original columns and courtyard from the 1891 building. The newest rooms have hot tubs and terraces overlooking interior gardens. An affiliated fitness club nearby has golf, squash, and swimming. The hotel's two restaurants, Lasarte and the less formal bistrolike Loidi, are directed by Martin Berasategui and serve excellent Basque-influenced cuisine. *Passeig de Gràcia 75, Eixample, 08008 93/445–0000 93/445–3232 www.condesdebarcelona.com 181 rooms, 2 suites In-room: safe. In-hotel: restaurant, bar, pools, gym, parking (fee) AE, DC, MC, V Passeig de Gràcia.*

$$$–$$$$ **Regente.** Moderniste furnishings and copious stained glass lend style and charm to this smallish hotel. The public rooms are carpeted in a mix of patterns; guest rooms, fortunately, are restrained. The verdant roof terrace and the prime position on the Rambla de Catalunya seal the positive verdict. *La Rambla de Catalunya 76, Eixample, 08008 93/487–5989 93/487–3227 www.hcchotels.com 79 rooms In-room: safe. In-hotel: restaurant, bar, pool AE, DC, MC, V Passeig de Gràcia.*

$$$ **Calderón.** On leafy Rambla de Catalunya, this modern high-rise has facilities normally found in hotels farther out of town. Public rooms are huge, with cool, white-marble floors, and the bedrooms follow suit. For stunning views, ask for a higher floor. *La Rambla Catalunya 26, Eixample, 08007 93/301–0000 93/412–0120 www.nh-hoteles.com 224 rooms, 29 suites In-hotel: restaurant, bar, pools, gym, parking (fee) AE, DC, MC, V Passeig de Gràcia.*

$$–$$$ ★ **Continental Palacete.** This former in-town mansion, or *palacete*, provides a splendid drawing room, two elegant suites swathed in lush carpets, velvet curtains, and tapestry wall decoration, and a location nearly dead center between all of Barcelona's main attractions. The views over the leafy tree-lined tunnel of Rambla Catalunya offer people watching from your balcony, while the 24-hour free buffet is handy but unnecessary in food-obsessed Barcelona. Ask specifically for one of the exterior rooms; the interior rooms on the elevator shaft can be noisy. *La Rambla de Catalunya 30, Eixample, 08007 93/445–7657 93/445–0050 www.hotelcontinental.com 17 rooms, 2 suites In room: refrigerator. In-hotel: free buffet AE, DC, MC, V Passeig de Gràcia.*

$$–$$$ **Gran Via.** A Moderniste enclave with an original chapel, a hall-of-mirrors breakfast room, and a sweeping staircase, this slightly down-at-the-heel 19th-century town house has an antique charm that compensates for missing technology and comforts. Guest rooms have plain alcoved walls, bottle-green carpets, and Regency-style furniture; those overlooking Gran Via itself have better views but are quite noisy. *Gran Via 642, Eixample, 08007 93/318–1900 93/318–9997 www.nnhotels.com 53 rooms In-hotel: public Internet, parking (fee) AE, DC, MC, V Passeig de Gràcia.*

$$ **Paseo de Gràcia.** Formerly a hostel, the Paseo has soft-color bedrooms with plain, good-quality carpets and sturdy wooden furniture. Add the location, on a handsome Eixample boulevard, and you have a good budget option. Some rooms, though not necessarily the newest, have balconies with views west over the city and the Collserola hills beyond. *Passeig de Gràcia 102, Eixample, 08008 93/215–5828 93/215–3724 33 rooms AE, DC, MC, V Passeig de Gràcia.*

7

SARRIÀ-PEDRALBES & SANT GERVASI

$$$$ **Princesa Sofía.** This modern high-rise has numerous business facilities and meeting rooms and everything from beauty salons and shops to three different restaurants. The staff is highly professional and efficient, catering primarily to business travelers and convention guests. FC Barcelona's soccer stadium is 200 yards away, while the upper Barcelona destinations of Sarrià and Pedralbes are a 15-minute walk away. The rooms, decorated in soft colors, are ultracomfortable. *Pl. Pius XII 4, Diagonal, 08028 93/508–1000 93/508 1001 www.expogrupo.com 475 rooms, 25 suites In-hotel: 3 restaurants, bar, pools, gym, parking (fee) AE, DC, MC, V Maria Cristina.*

$$$$ ★ **Rey Juan Carlos I.** Towering over the western end of Barcelona's Avinguda Diagonal, this luxury hotel is also an exciting commercial complex where you can even buy or rent a fur or limousine. The lush

garden, which includes a pond with swans, has an Olympic-size swimming pool, and the green expanses of Barcelona's finest in-town country club, El Polo, are beyond. The restaurant Chez Vous serves French cuisine, and Café Polo has a sumptuous buffet. Rooms are spacious, comfortable, and flawlessly equipped with cutting-edge technology from Internet access to flat screen TV to Jacuzzis. ✉ *Av. Diagonal 661–671, Diagonal, 08028* ☎ *93/364–4040* 🖷 *93/364–4264* 🌐 *www.hrjuancarlos.com* *375 rooms, 37 suites* *In-room: dial-up. In-hotel: 2 restaurants, bars, tennis court, pool, gym, spa, parking (fee)* 💳 *AE, DC, MC, V* Ⓜ *Zona Universitària.*

$$–$$$ Fodor's Choice ★ **Turó de Vilana.** Surrounded by bougainvillea-festooned villas and mansions above Barcelona's Passeig de la Bonanova, this shiny hotel has a hot tub in every room; immaculate and gleaming halls and public areas of stone, steel, and glass; and a pleasant staff. Rooms are luminous. In summer, upper Barcelona is noticeably cooler, not to mention quieter at night. The Turó de Vilana is a 10-minute walk from the Sarrià train that connects you with the city center in 15 minutes. ✉ *Carrer Vilana 7, Sant Gervasi, 08017* ☎ *93/434–0363* 🖷 *93/418–8903* 🌐 *www.turodevilana.com* *20 rooms* *In-hotel: restaurant, room service* 💳 *AE, DC, MC, V* Ⓜ *Sarrià.*

TIBIDABO

$$$$ **Gran Hotel la Florida.** This David Stein Group gem provides unaparalleled views over Barcelona, water sculptures everywhere but in your bed, a superb restaurant (L'Orangerie), and designer suites that are difficult to leave behind. Twenty minutes (and euros) from the port, this design hotel first opened in 1925 has roared back to the forefront of Barcelona's most stylish lodgings. ✉ *Ctra. Vallvidrera al Tibidabo 83–93, Tibidabo, 08035* ☎ *93/259–3000* 🖷 *93/259–3001* 🌐 *www.hotellaflorida.com* *74 rooms, 22 suites* *In-room: safe. In-hotel: restaurant, bar, pool, gym, spa, parking (fee)* 💳 *AE, DC, MC, V* Ⓜ *Tibidabo.*

NIGHTLIFE & THE ARTS

Barcelona's art and nightlife scenes start early and never quite stop. To find out what's on, look in newspapers or the weekly *Guía Del Ocio*, which has a section in English, available at newsstands all over town. *Activitats*, available at the Palau de la Virreina (La Rambla 99) or the Centre Santa Monica (La Rambla 7) lists cultural events.

THE ARTS

CLASSICAL MUSIC

The basilica of Santa Maria del Mar, the church of Santa Maria del Pi, the Monestir de Pedralbes, Drassanes Reials, and the Saló del Tinell, among other ancient and intimate spaces, hold concerts. Barcelona's music festival brings a long series of concerts in June and July. In late September, the **International Music Festival** is part of the feast of Nostra Senyora de la Mercè (Our Lady of Mercy), Barcelona's patron saint. Pop concerts are held in the Palau Sant Jordi on Montjuïc.

Barcelona's most famous concert hall is the Moderniste **Palau de la Música Catalana** (✉*Sant Francesc de Paula 2, Sant Pere* ☎*93/295–7200*), with performances September–June. Tickets range from €6 to €100 and are best purchased well in advance, though a last-minute *palco sin vistas* (box seat with no sight of the stage) is a good way to get into the building for a concert. The contemporary **Auditori de Barcelona** (✉*Carrer Lepant 150, near Plaça de les Glòries, Eixample* ☎*93/247–9300*) has classical music, with occasional jazz and pop thrown in. Barcelona's **Gran Teatre del Liceu** (✉*La Rambla 51–59 [box office: La Rambla de Capuchinos 63], Rambla* ☎*93/485–9900 box office*) stages operas and recitals.

DANCE

L'Espai de Dansa i Música de la Generalitat de Catalunya (✉*Travessera de Gràcia 63, Eixample* ☎*93/414–3133*)—generally listed as L'Espai, or "The Space"—is the prime venue for ballet and modern dance, as well as some musical offerings. **El Mercat de les Flors** (✉*Carrer Lleida 59, Eixample* ☎*93/426–1875*), near Plaça de Espanya, is a traditional venue for modern dance and theater.

FILM

Though many foreign films are dubbed, Barcelona has a full complement of original-language cinema; look for listings marked "v.o." (*versión original*). **Verdi** (✉*Carrer Verdi 32, Gràcia*) screens current releases with original-version sound tracks in a fun neighborhood for pre- and post-movie eating and drinking. The **Icaria Yelmo** (✉*Salvador Espriu 61, Port Olímpic*) complex in the Olympic Port has the city's largest selection of English-language films. **Renoir Les Corts** (✉*Eugeni d'Ors 12, behind Diagonal's El Corte Inglés, Diagonal*) is a good choice for recently released English-language features of all kinds. **Casablanca** (✉*Passeig de Gràcia 115, Eixample*) plays original-language movies, generally art flicks.

FLAMENCO

Barcelona is not richly endowed with flamenco haunts, because Catalans consider flamenco—like bullfighting—a foreign import from Andalusia. On the Plaça Reial, **Los Tarantos** (✉*Pl. Reial 17, Barri Gòtic* ☎*93/318–3067*) spotlights Andalusia's best flamenco. **El Patio Andaluz** (✉*Aribau 242, Eixample* ☎*93/209–3378*) has rather touristy flamenco shows twice nightly (at 10 and midnight) and a karaoke section upstairs. Tour groups in search of flamenco gravitate to **El Cordobés** (✉*La Rambla 35, Rambla* ☎*93/317–6653*). **El Tablao de Carmen** (✉ *Poble Espanyol, Av. Marquès de Comillas s/n Montjuïc* ☎*93/325–6895*) hosts touring flamenco troupes up on Montjuïc. **La Taberna Flamenca** (✉*Art 12, Horta-Guinardó* ☎*93/351–8757*) is a *sala rociera,* meaning they sing a salve to La Virgen del Rocío every night and welcome amateur flamencos.

THEATER

Most plays are performed in Catalan, though some are in Spanish. Barcelona is known for avant-garde theater and troupes that specialize in mime, large-scale performance art, and special effects (La Fura dels

7

Baus, Els Joglars, Els Comediants). **Teatre Lliure** has English subtitles on Wednesday, to make theater accessible for visitors. Other theaters are beginning to follow this lead. Call ahead for details. Several theaters along Avinguda Parallel specialize in musicals. The **Teatre Nacional de Catalunya** (✉ *Pl. de les Arts 1* ☎ *93/306–5700*), near Plaça de les Glories at the eastern end of the Diagonal, is a glass-enclosed classical temple designed by Ricardo Bofill, architect of Barcelona's airport. Programs cover everything from Shakespeare to ballet to avant-garde theater. The **Teatre Poliorama** (✉ *La Rambla Estudios 115, Rambla* ☎ *93/317–7599*) is below Plaça de Catalunya. The **Teatre Romea** (✉ *Carrer Hospital 51, Raval* ☎ *93/301–5504*) is behind the Boqueria. The **Teatre Tívoli** (✉ *Carrer Casp 8, Eixample* ☎ *93/412–2063*), above Plaça de Catalunya, has theater and dance performances. Gràcia's **Teatre Lliure** (✉ *Carrer Montseny 47, Gràcia* ☎ *93/218–9251*) stages theater, dance, and musical events. The **Mercat de les Flors** (✉ *Lleida 59, Montjuïc* ☎ *93/426–1875*), near Plaça de Espanya, is the city's most traditional dance and theater venue.

NIGHTLIFE

CABARET

Near the bottom of the Rambla, the minuscule **Bar Pastis** (✉ *Carrer Santa Mònica 4, Rambla* ☎ *93/318–7980*) has both live performances and LPs of every Edith Piaf song ever recorded. **Arnau** (✉ *Av. Paral. lel 60, Eixample* ☎ *93/242–2804*) is an old-time music hall that's still going strong. **Starlets** (✉ *Av. Sarrià 44, Eixample* ☎ *93/430–9156*) has a combination cabaret and disco program. **Joy's** (✉ *Carrer Rocafort 231, Eixample* ☎ *93/430–9156*) hosts a floor show, cabaret, and dancing.

CASINO

The **Gran Casino de Barcelona** (✉ *Carrer de la Marina, Port Olímpic* ☎ *93/225–7878*), under the Hotel Arts, is open daily 1 PM–5 AM.

JAZZ & BLUES

The Palau de la Música Catalana holds an **international jazz festival** in November. The Gothic Quarter's **Harlem Jazz Club** (✉ *Carrer Comtessa Sobradiel 8, Barri Gòtic* ☎ *93/310–0755*) is small but atmospheric, with good jazz and country bands. **Jamboree-Jazz & Dance-Club** (✉ *Pl. Reial 17, Rambla* ☎ *93/301–7564*) is a center for jazz, rock, and flamenco. **Luz de Gas** (✉ *Carrer Muntaner 246, Eixample* ☎ *93/209–7711*) hosts every genre from Irish fusion to Cuban sounds. **Luna Mora** (✉ *Port Olímpic, next to Hotel Arts, Port Olímpic* ☎ *93/221–6161*) stages the gamut, from country blues to salsa and soul. **Nao Colón/Club Bamboo** (✉ *Av. Marques de l'Argentera 19, Born-Ribera* ☎ *93/268–7633*) combines the sounds and the cuisine of the Mediterranean followed by jazz, blues, flamenco, fusion, hard rock, and house after midnight. The bustling **Zacarías** (✉ *Av. Diagonal 477, Eixample* ☎ *93/207–5643*) stages live music from a variety of musical genres, including jazz, rock, folk, and blues.

LATE-NIGHT BARS

Bar musical is Spanish for any bar with music loud enough to drown out conversation. **Port Olímpic** and the Port Vell's **Maremagnum.** are wildly active but, compared to other options, better to *avoid*. Especially in summer and on weekends, these are far from Barcelona's best nightlife options.

Universal (✉ *Carrer Marià Cubí 182–184, Eixample* ☎ *93/200–7470*) has been the hottest bar in town for 30 years. **Mas i Mas** (✉ *Carrer Marià Cubí 199, Eixample* ☎ *93/209–4502*), across the street from Universal, is so crowded that social intimacy is guaranteed. **Nick Havanna** (✉ *Carrer Roselló 208, Eixample* ☎ *93/215–6591*) has, along with a consistently hot program of live music, Barcelona's most entertaining urinals. **L'Ovella Negra** (✉ *Carrer Sitjàs 5, Raval* ☎ *93/317–1087*) is the top student tavern. **Glaciar** (✉ *Pl. Reial 13, Rambla* ☎ *93/302–1163*) is *the* spot for young out-of-towners. For a more laid-back scene, with high ceilings, billiards, tapas, and hundreds of students, visit the popular **Velodrom** (✉ *Carrer Muntaner 211–213, Eixample* ☎ *93/230–6022*), below the Diagonal. Two blocks from Velodrom is the intriguing *bar-museo* (bar-cum-museum) **La Fira** (✉ *Carrer Provença 171, Eixample* ☎ *93/323–7271*). Downtown, deep in the Barrio Chino, try the **London Bar** (✉ *Carrer Nou de la Rambla 34, Raval* ☎ *93/302–3102*), an Art Nouveau circus haunt with a trapeze suspended above the bar. **Bar Almirall** (✉ *Carrer Joaquin Costa 33, Raval* ☎ *93/412–1535*) has an Art Nouveau chicness. **Bar Muy Buenas** (✉ *Carrer del Carme 63, Raval* ☎ *93/442–5053*) is an Art Nouveau gem. Over by the Sagrada Família, the **Michael Collins Irish Pub** (✉ *Pl. Sagrada Família 4, Eixample* ☎ *93/459–1964*) has a strong Anglo following. Above Via Augusta in upper Barcelona, the **Sherlock Holmes** (✉ *Carrer Copernic 42–44, Eixample* ☎ *93/414–2184*) is an ongoing Brit-fest with live musical performances and darkly intimate corners. Above Via Augusta, **Opiniao** (✉ *Carrer Ciutat de Balaguer 67, below Bonanova, La Bonanova* ☎ *93/418–3399*) is another upper-Barcelona dive, a hot local club. **George & Dragon** (✉ *Carrer Diputació 269, Eixample* ☎ *93/488–1765*), named for Barcelona's ubiquitous symbols of good and evil, is a rollicking English pub just off Passeig de Gràcia. Café-restaurant-bar **Salero** (✉ *Carrer del Rec 60, Eixample* ☎ *93/488–1765*) is always packed with young miscreants.

NIGHTCLUBS & DISCOS

Most clubs have a discretionary cover charge and like to inflict it on foreigners, so dress up and be prepared to talk your way past the bouncer. Any story can work; for example, you own a chain of nightclubs and are on a world tour. Don't expect much to happen until 1:30 or 2.

Tops for some time now has been the prisonesque nightclub **Otto Zutz** (✉ *Carrer Lincoln 15, Eixample* ☎ *93/238–0722*), off Via Augusta. The nearly classic **Up and Down** (✉ *Carrer Numancia 179, Eixample* ☎ *93/280–2922*), pronounced "Pen- *dow*," is a good choice for elegant carousers. A line forms at **Bikini** (✉ *Carrer Deu i Mata 105, at Entença, Eixample* ☎ *93/322–0005*) on festive Saturday nights. **Torres de Avila** (✉ *Av. Marquès de Comillas 25, Montjuïc* ☎ *93/424–9309*), in

7

Pueblo Espanyol, is wild and woolly until broad daylight on weekends. **Danzatoria** (✉ *Av. Tibidabo 61, Tibidabo* ☎ *93/211–6261*), a fusion of Salsitas and Partycular (two former clubs), is a "multispace" with five venues (disco, hall, dance, chill-out, garden) and fills with models and hopeful guys. **Sala Razzmatazz** (✉ *Carrer Almogavers 122, Poble Nou* ☎ *93/320–8200*) offers Friday and Saturday disco madness until dawn. Weeknight concerts have international stars such as Ani DiFranco and Enya. **Bucaro** (✉ *Carrer Aribau 195, Eixample* ☎ *93/209–6562*) rocks until dawn, albeit largely for the extremely young. **Buda Barcelona** (✉ *Carrer Pau Claris 92, Eixample* ☎ *93/318–4252*) is the hottest nightspot in the Eixample, with celebrities and glamour galore. The beachfront **CDLC** (✉ *Passeig Maritim 32, Port Olímpic* ☎ *93/224–0470*) has compartmentalized *sofa-camas* (sofa beds of a sort) for prime canoodling. **DosTrece** (✉ *Carrer del Carme 40, Raval* ☎ *93/443–0341*) packs in young internationals for dancing and carousing and general hooking up. **It Café** (✉ *Carrer Joaquin Costa 4, Raval* ☎ *93/443–0341*) is a design oasis not far from the MACBA in the Raval. The **Loft** (✉ *Carrer Pamplona 88, Poble Nou* ☎ *93/272–0910*), an offshoot of Sala Razzmatazz, is dedicated to electronic music. **Row Club** (✉ *Carrer Rosselló 208, Eixample* ☎ *93/237–5405*) is big on techno. **Sala Cibeles** (✉ *Carrer de Córsega 363, Eixample* ☎ *93/272–0910*) has big sound system and singing DJs. Salsa sizzles at the exuberantly Caribbean **Antilla BCN Latin Club** (✉ *Carrer Aragó 141, Eixample* ☎ *93/451–4564*). **Luz de Luna** (✉ *Carrer Comerç 21, La Ribera* ☎ *93/310–7542*) lays down wall-to-wall salsa; oxygen masks are advised. **Agua de Luna** (✉ *Carrer Viladomat 211, Eixample* ☎ *93/410–0440*) is a torrid salsa scene in the western Eixample. **Pachá** (✉ *Carrer Dr. Marañon 17, Pedralbes-Les Corts* ☎ *93/204–0412*) offers two raging discos and a restaurant.

Costa Breve (✉ *Carerr Aribau 230, Eixample* ☎ *93/200–7346*) accepts postgraduates with open arms. **El Otro** (✉ *Carrer Valencia 166, Eixample* ☎ *93/323–6759*) is kind to aging (over-thirty) miscreants. For big-band tango in an old-fashioned *sala de baile* (dance hall), head to **La Paloma** (✉ *Carrer Tigre 27, Raval* ☎ *93/301–6897*), with kitschy 1950s furnishings.

SPORTS & THE OUTDOORS

GOLF

Call ahead to reserve tee times. Weekday greens fees range from about €36 at most courses to €72 on weekends and holidays. San Cugat's **Club de Golf de San Cugat** (✉ *Carrer Villa s/n* ☎ *93/674–3908*) has hilly greens and 18 holes. Greens fees are €65 on weekdays and €130 on weekends. Sitges' **Club de Golf Terramar** (✉ *Passeig Maritim s/n* ☎ *93/894–0580*) offers 18 holes along the beach. Greens fees are €75 during the week and €90 on weekends.

HEALTH CLUBS

For specifics, look in the *Páginas Amarillas/Pàgines Grogues* (*Yellow Pages*) under "Gimnasios/Gimnasis." The **DiR** (☎ *901/304030 general information Main branch* ✉ *DiR Diagonal, Carrer Ganduxer 25–27,*

Eixample ☎*93/202–2202*) network of fitness centers is worthy, with addresses all over Barcelona. A day membership, €11, includes aerobics classes and the use of a sauna, a steam room, a swimming pool, squash courts, and MTV.

HIKING

The **Collserola** hills behind the city offer well-marked trails, fresh air, and lovely views. Take the San Cugat, Sabadell, or Terrassa FFCC train from Plaça de Catalunya and get off at Baixador de Vallvidrera; the information center, 10 minutes uphill next to **Vil.la Joana** (now the Jacint Verdaguer Museum), has maps of this mountain woodland 20 minutes from downtown. The walk back into town can take from two to five hours, depending on your speed and the trails you pick. **Club Excursionista de Catalunya** (✉*Carrer Paradís 10, Barri Gòtic* ☎*93/315–2311*) has information on hiking in Barcelona's outskirts. Ask the **Asociació Excursionista, Etnográfica i Folklorica** (✉*Carrer d'Avinyó 19, Barri Gòtic* ☎*93/302–2730*) about hikes, including treks in the Pyrenees.

SOCCER

If you're in Barcelona between September and June, go see the celebrated FC Barcelona play soccer (preferably against Real Madrid, if you can score a ticket) at Barcelona's gigantic stadium, **Camp Nou** (✉*Carrer Arístides Maillol, Les Corts* ☎*93/496–3608* 🌐*www.fcbarcelona.com* 🎫*Museum €5.30, combined ticket including tour of museum, field, and sports complex €9.50* ⏲*Museum Mon.–Sat. 10–6:30, Sun. 10–2* Ⓜ*Collblanc, Palau Reial*). Games are played Saturday night at 9 or Sunday afternoon at 5, though there may be international Champion's League games on Tuesday or Wednesday evening as well. Ask your hotel concierge how to get tickets, or call the club in advance. The stadium seats 98,000 and fills to capacity for big games. If FC Barcelona is touring, rival team Espanyol may be playing. Ticket prices are usually less expensive and the ticket availability tends to be a bit easier. A worthwhile alternative to seeing a game is the guided tour of the FC Barcelona museum and facilities. The museum has a five-screen video showing the club's most memorable goals, along with player biographies and displays chronicling the history of one of Europe's most colorful soccer clubs.

SWIMMING

Piscines Bernat Picornell (✉*Av. del Estadi 30–40, Montjuïc* ☎*93/423–4041*) comprises indoor and outdoor pools plus a sauna, gymnasium, and fitness equipment. Overlooking the beach from Barceloneta, the **Club Natació de Barceloneta** (✉ *Passeig Joan de Borbó, Barceloneta* ☎*93/221–0010*), also known as Complex Esportiu Municipal Banys Sant Sebastiá, has an indoor pool.

TENNIS

Vall d'Hebron (✉*Passeig Vall d'Hebron 178–196, Passeig Vall d'Hebron* ☎*93/427–6500* 🎫*Clay courts €15/hr, hard courts €17/hr* ⏲*8 AM–11 PM*) has Olympic tennis facilities. **Complejo Deportivo Can Caralleu** (*Can Caralleu Sports Complex* ✉*Calle Esports 2–8* ☎*93/203–7874* 🎫*€8/hr day, €10/hr night* ⏲*Daily 8 AM–11 PM*), above Pedralbes, a 30-

CLOSE UP

Move Over, Milan

Ever since the 1992 Olympic Games blew the lid off any lingering doubts about Barcelona's contemporary creative potential, new clothing designers and boutiques have been proliferating. Barcelona Fashion Week (BFW) has now taken its place as one of Europe's most important fashion meets alongside those of Paris, London, and Milan. Meanwhile, the Pasarel. la Gaudí, formerly Barcelona's main event, has become Barcelona Bridal Week. The late September Barcelona Fashion Week, largely stripped of public financing, has forged a path of its own relying largely on young local designers as well as traditional heavyweights such as Antonio Miró, Armand Basi, Gonzalo Comellas, and Adolfo Domínguez. Even top-name Madrid designers such as Victorio & Lucchino, Miriam Ocáriz, and Soul Aguilar, citing the Catalan capital's innovative image, prefer to show in Barcelona instead of at Madrid's own Cibeles fashion event.

Meanwhile, those hot street styles admired around town for so long have jumped to center stage. Bread & Butter Barcelona (BBB), begun in Berlin and described as a street-fashion trade show, has been so successful in Barcelona that winter and summer events are now built into the city calendar for the foreseeable future. The July 2006 conclave brought 800 designers from 95 countries and over 50,000 visitors to multifaceted proceedings encompassing art, architecture, music, dance, catwalks, tastings, piercings, body art, and frenzied spates of sponsored parties. The B&B Brand Bible lists more than 1,000 designers from Custo and Desigual to undergrounders such De Puta Madre, Kult, and System5.

Not without a sense of humor, some events take on *Zoolander* proportions, with ever-zanier happenings such as Antonio Miró's BFW 2006 catwalk held in Barcelona's infamous Carcel Modelo, the model prison constructed in the early 20th century. Miró's January 2007 runway featuring illegal immigrants addressed a serious contemporary social issue. The semi-spontaneous fringe Fashion Freak gatherings held during the Bread & Butter event in different venues around town culminate with the Freak Boutique in the Café Noir. "Coolhunters," undercover style sleuths, prowl the back alleys looking for details of urban chic that could go from Raval to runway to rack in a matter of weeks.

Oh, and the shops! From local clothing stars Zara and Custo to whimsical design objects at BD (Barcelona Design) or Vinçon, to old crafts standbys such as La Manual Alpargatera or Cerería Subirà, Barcelona is becoming as famous for shopping as for architecture and design.

minute walk uphill from the Reina Elisenda subway stop (FFCC de la Generalitat), has hard courts and clean air. **Club Vall Parc** (✉ *Ctra. de la Rabassada 79, Tibidabo* ☎ *93/212–6789* 💰 *€15/hr day, €19/hr night* ⏲ *Daily 8* AM*–midnight*) is upscale.

SHOPPING

Between the surging fashion scene, a host of young clothing designers, clever home furnishings, rare and delicious foodstuffs, and art and antiques, Barcelona is the best place in Spain to unload extra ballast from your wallet. True, bargains are few outside saffron and rope-sole shoes, but quality and selection are excellent. Most stores are open Monday–Saturday 9–1:30 and 5–8, but some close in the afternoon. Virtually all close on Sunday.

SHOPPING DISTRICTS

For high fashion, browse along Passeig de Gràcia and the Diagonal between Plaça Joan Carles I and Plaça Francesc Macià. There are two-dozen antiques shops in the Gothic Quarter, another 70 shops off Passeig de Gràcia on Bulevard dels Antiquaris, and still more in Gràcia and Sarrià. Barcelona's prime shopping districts are the Passeig de Gràcia, Rambla de Catalunya, Plaça de Catalunya, Porta de l'Àngel, and Avinguda Diagonal up to Carrer Ganduxer. For old-fashioned Spanish shops, prowl the Gothic Quarter, especially **Carrer Ferran.** The area surrounding **Plaça del Pi,** from the Boqueria to Carrer Portaferrissa and Carrer de la Canuda, is thick with boutiques, jewelry, and design shops. The **Barri de la Ribera,** around Santa Maria del Mar, especially El Born area, has a cluster of design, fashion, and food shops. Design, jewelry, and knickknack shops cluster on Carrer Banys Vells and Carrer Flassaders, near Carrer Montcada. The shopping colossus **L'Illa,** on the Diagonal beyond Carrer Ganduxer, includes the department store FNAC and other temptations. **Carrer Tuset,** north of the Diagonal, has lots of small boutiques. The **Maremagnum** mall, in Port Vell, is convenient to downtown. **Diagonal Mar,** at the eastern end of the diagonal, along with the **Fòrum 2004** complex offer many shopping options in a mega-shopping-mall environment.

SPECIALTY STORES

ANTIQUES

The headquarter of antiques shopping is the Gothic Quarter, where **Carrer de la Palla** and **Carrer Banys Nous** are lined with shops full of prints, maps, books, paintings, and furniture. An antiques market is held in front of the **cathedral** every Thursday from 10 to 8. In upper Barcelona, the entire village of **Sarrià** is becoming an antiquer's destination, with shops along Cornet i Mas, Pedró de la Creu, and Major de Sarrià. The Eixample's **Centre d'Antiquaris** (✉ *Passeig de Gràcia 55, Eixample*) contains 75 antiques stores. Moderniste aficionados should check out **Gothsland** (✉ *Carrer Consell de Cent 331, Eixample*). **La Maison Colo-**

niale (✉ *Carrer Sant Antoni Abat 61, Raval*) has 15th-century stone vaulting and colonial treasures. **Novecento** (✉ *Passeig de Gràcia 75, Eixample*) has antique art and jewelry. **Alcanto** (✉ *Passeig de Gràcia 55–57, Eixample*) is a clearinghouse for buying and selling. **Antiguedades J. Pla** (✉ *Carrer Aragó 517, Eixample*) buys and sells antiques.

ART

There's a cluster of art galleries on Carrer Consell de Cent between Passeig de Gràcia and Carrer Balmes, and around the corner on Rambla de Catalunya. The Born–Santa Maria del Mar quarter is another art destination, along Carrer Montcada and the parallel Carrer Bany Vells. **Galeria Joan Prats** (✉ *La Rambla de Catalunya 54 , Eixample*) is a veteran, known for the quality of its artists' works. **Eude** (✉ *Carrer Consell de Cent 278, Eixample*) showcases young artists. **Sala Dalmau** (✉ *Carrer Consell de Cent 347, Eixample*) is an established art outlet. **Sala Rovira** (✉ *La Rambla de Catalunya 62, Eixample*) has shown top artists Tom Carr and Blanca Vernis. The **Joan Gaspar** (✉ *Pl. Letamendi 1, Eixample*) started with Picasso and Miró. Carrer Petritxol, which leads down into Plaça del Pi, is lined with galleries, notably **Sala Parès** (✉ *Carrer Petritxol 5, Barri Gòtic*).

BOOKS

La Central (✉ *Carrer Mallorca 237, Eixample*) is Barcelona's best bookstore. **La Central del Raval** (✉ *Carrer Elisabets 6, Eixample*), in the former chapel of the Casa de la Misericòrdia, sells books on architecture. **Altair** (✉ *Gran Via de les Corts Catalanes 616, Eixample*) is Barcelona's premier travel and adventure bookstore, with many titles in English. **BCN Books** (✉ *Carrer Roger de Llúria 118, Eixample*) is a top store for books in English. **Casa del Llibre** (✉ *Passeig de Gràcia 62, Eixample*) is a book feast with English titles. **Laie** (✉ *Carrer Pau Claris 85, Eixample*) is a book lover's sanctuary, with cultural events as well as stacks. The bookstore in the **Palau de la Virreina** (✉ *La Rambla 99, Rambla*) has books on art, design, and Barcelona in general. **El Corte Inglés,** especially the branch in Porta del Àngel, sells English guidebooks and novels.

BOUTIQUES & JEWELRY

Chanel, Armani, Loewe, and the other big names have stores on Passeig de Gràcia. **El Bulevard Rosa** (✉ *Passeig de Gràcia 53–55, Eixample*) is a collection of boutiques with the latest outfits. The stretch of Avinguda Diagonal between Passeig de Gràcia and Carrer Ganduxer is lined with high-end shops. **Adolfo Domínguez** (✉ *Passeig de Gràcia 35, Av. Diagonal 570, Eixample*) is one of Spain's leading designers. The two locations of Toni Miró's **Groc** (✉ *C. Muntaner 382, Eixample* ✉ *La Rambla de Catalunya 100, Eixample*) have the latest looks for men, women, and children. **David Valls** (✉ *C. Valencia 235, Eixample*) represents new, young Barcelona fashion design. **May Day** (✉ *C. Portaferrissa 16, Barri Gòtic*) carries cutting-edge clothing, footwear, and accessories. **Joaquim Berao** (✉ *C. Rosselló 277, Eixample*) is a top jewelry designer. Beatriz Würsch displays her unusual jewelry designs in **Forum Ferlandina** (✉ *Ferlandina 31, Raval*), next to the MACBA. **El Ingenio** (✉ *Carrer Rauric 6, Barri Gòtic*) has one of the prettiest antique storefronts in town and, inside, costumes, puppets, carnival masks, and gadgets for all ages. **Janina**

(✉*Rambla Catalunya 94 , Eixample*) sells trendy and stylish lingerie and women's intimate articles by La Perla, Eres, Dolce & Gabbana and others. **No Te Nom** (✉*Carrer Pau Claris 159, Eixample*) means "it has no name" in Catalan and sells new fabrics and design accessories. **On Land** (✉*Valencia 273, Eixample*) is all street fashion designed by the hottest young designers in town. **Custo Barcelona** (✉*Plaça de les Olles 7, Born-Ribera*) is becoming a city icon and *the* place for colorful, whimsical, tops that you can try immediately out at the feeding frenzy going on next door at Cal Pep. **Majoral** (✉*Carrer Argenteria 66, Born-Ribera*) makes and sells organic, almost edible-looking rings, earrings, brooches, pins, and assorted bling.

SHOPPING HOT SPOTS

Antiques Center: Carrer de la Palla

Bling: Majoral

Bookstore: La Central

Ceramics Studio: Art Escudellers

Cobbler: La Manual Alpargartera

Gourmet Food Market: Mantequeria Can Ravell

Music Store: Discos Castelló

Spice Shop: Casa Gispert

Stationery Boutique: Papirum

Top: Custo Barcelona

CERAMICS

Art Escudellers (✉*Carrer Escudellers 23–25 , Barri Gòtic*) has ceramics from all over Spain, with more than 200 different artisans represented and maps showing where the work is from. In addition, the art gallery and the wine-, Ibérico ham–, and cheese-tasting bar downstairs makes this the best studio in town. **Ítaca** (✉*Carrer Ferrán 26, Barri Gòtic*) has ceramic plates, bowls, and pottery from Talavera de la Reina and La Bisbal. For Lladró, try **Pla de l'Os** (✉*Carrer de la Boqueria 3, Barri Gòtic*) , off the Rambla. In Sarrià, behind the market on your way into bougainvillea-choked Plaça Sant Gaietà, check out the ceramics store **Nica & Bet** (✉*Carrer Pare Miquel de Sarrià 10, Sarrià*); don't miss the beautifully restored wooden doors. Although perusing smaller establishments is always worthwhile, one of Barcelona's big department stores, **El Corte Inglés,** at Plaça Catalunya or Diagonal, is a good bet for ceramics shoppers.

DEPARTMENT STORES

The ubiquitous **El Corte Inglés** has four locations: Plaça de Catalunya 14, Porta de l'Angel 19–21, Avinguda Francesc Macià 58, and Avinguda Diagonal 617. Among other emporiums, Plaça de Catalunya includes **FNAC** and **Habitat,** which also has stores on Tuset at the Diagonal.

DESIGN & INTERIORS

The area around the church of Santa Maria del Mar, an artisans' quarter since medieval times, is full of cheerful design stores and art galleries.

Vinçon (✉*Passeig de Gràcia 96, Eixample*) occupies a rambling Moderniste house and carries everything from Filofaxes to handsome kitchenware. You can also find one of Barcelona's most spectacular Art

Nouveau fireplaces, complete with a stylized face for a hearth. Upscale **Gimeno** (✉*Passeig de Gràcia 102, Eixample*) has everything from clever suitcases to the latest in furniture design. **bd** (*Barcelona Design* ✉*Carrer Mallorca 291–293, Eixample*) is a spare, cutting-edge home-furnishing store in another Moderniste gem, Domènech i Montaner's Casa Thomas. **Vientos del Sur** (✉*Carrer Argenteria 78, La Ribera*), part of the Natura chain, has a good selection of crafts. **Ici et Là** (✉*Pl. Santa Maria del Mar 2, La Ribera*) is across the square and has an eclectic selection of clothing, gifts, and knickknacks. **Fem** (✉*Palau 6, behind ajuntament, Barri Gòtic*) has interesting artifacts and artisanship. **Papers Coma** (✉*Carrer Montcada 20, La Ribera*) has inventive knickknacks. **Estudi Pam2** (✉*Sabateret 1–3, La Ribera*), behind Carrer Montcada, sells ingenious design items. **Suspect** (✉*Carrer Comerç 29, La Ribera*), north of the Born, specializes in clothes and furniture made by Spastor, a group of Barcelona designers. **Gotham** (✉*Cervantes 7, Barri Gòtic*), behind Town Hall, restores furniture from the '50s and '60s. It's a perennial set for Almodóvar movies. Amid mouthwatering interior design, **La Comercial** (✉ *Carrer del Rec 52 and 73, La Ribera*) off Passeig del Born has clothes by Paul & Joe, Paul Smith, and Isabel Marant. **Sita Murt** (✉*Carrer d'Avinyó 18, Barri Gòtic*) is a stunning subterranean space with a clever play of mirrors and collections from Antik Batik, Save the Queen, and Esteve Sita Murt.

BOOKS & ROSES

Barcelona's day of Sant Jordi (April 23) is something of a Valentine's Day, Catalan-style. Ladies receive roses, and men receive books. On that day, Barcelona becomes one huge rose-scented bookstore, with kiosks full of books lining the streets next to flower sellers. The rose tradition stems from Barcelona's medieval rose festival. Then international book day was appended to April 23, and the tradition of bestowing a book on your rose-giving sweetheart was born.

FINE FOODS

Casa Gispert (✉*Carrer Sombrerers 23, La Ribera*), on the inland side of Santa Maria del Mar, is one of the most aromatic and esthetically perfect shops in Barcelona, bursting with spices, saffron, chocolates, and nuts. **Jobal** (✉*C. Princesa 38, La Ribera*) is a charming and fragrant saffron and spice shop. **La Barcelonesa** (✉*Carrer Comerç 27, La Ribera*) specializes in dry goods, spices, tea, and saffron. **Tot Formatge** (✉*Passeig del Born 13, La Ribera*) has cheeses from all over Spain and the world. **Vila Viniteca** (✉*C. Agullers 7, La Ribera*), near Santa Maria del Mar, is one of the best wine shops in Barcelona, and the produce store across the way sells some of the best cheeses around. **La Botifarreria de Santa Maria** (✉*Carrer Santa Maria 4, La Ribera*), next to the church of Santa Maria, has excellent cheeses, hams, pâtés, and homemade *sobrassadas* (pork pâté with paprika). **El Magnífico** (✉*Carrer Argenteria 64, La Ribera*) is famous for its coffees. Behind the Picasso Museum, **Born Cooking** (✉*Corretger 9, La Ribera*) is a work of art in itself, serving delicious cakes, quiches, and all manner of sweets and savories.

La Casa del Bacalao (✉ *Condal 8, off Portal del Angel, Barri Gòtic*) specializes in salt cod and books of codfish recipes. **La Palmera** (✉ *C. Enric Granados 57, Eixample*) has a superb collection of wines, hams, cheeses, and olive oils. **Caelum** (✉ *C. de la Palla 8, Barri Gòtic*) sells crafts and such foods as honey and preserves, made in convents and monasteries all over Spain. **Mantequeria Can Ravell** (✉ *Carrer Aragó 313, Eixample*) restaurant and delicatessen is Barcelona's number one all-around wine, cheese, ham, and fine foods specialist. **La Cave** (✉ *Av. J. V. Foix 80, Sarrià*) is a wine cellar with a flair. Polyglot Claude Cohen and company not only sell wine, but teach it. **Vilaplana** (✉ *C. Francesc Perez Cabrero, Eixample*) is famous for its pastries, cheeses, hams, pâtés, caviars, and fine deli items. **Tutusaus** (✉ *C. Francesc Perez Cabrero 5, Sant Gervasi*) specializes in fine Ibérico hams and superb cheeses from all over Europe. **OroLíquido** (✉ *C. de la Palla 8, Barri Gòtic*) sells the finest olive oils from Spain and the world at large.

FOOD & FLEA MARKETS

Spectacular food markets include the Mercat de la Llibertat, near Plaça Gal.la Placidia, and Mercat de la Revolució, on Travessera de Gràcia, both in Gràcia. On Thursday, a natural-produce market (honeys, cheeses) fills Plaça del Pi with interesting tastes and aromas. On Sunday morning, a stamp and coin market fills Plaça Reial; also on Sunday, the Plaça Sant Josep Oriol holds a painter's market, along with another general crafts and flea market near the Columbus Monument at the port end of the Rambla. The **Boqueria** (✉ *La Rambla 91, Rambla*) is Barcelona's most colorful food market and the oldest of its kind in Europe. Open Monday–Saturday 8–8, it's most active before 3 PM. Barcelona's biggest flea market, **Els Encants** (✉ *Dos de Maig, on Plaça de les Glòries, Eixample* Ⓜ *Glòries*) is held Monday, Wednesday, Friday, and Saturday 8–7. The **Mercat Gòtic** (✉ *Pl. de la Seu, Barri Gòtic*) fills the area in front of the Catedral de la Seu on Thursday. The **Mercat de Sant Antoni** (✉ *Ronda Sant Antoni, Eixample*) is an old-fashioned food, clothing, and used-book (many in English) market that's best on Sunday.

GIFTS & MISCELLANY

Stationery lovers will want to linger in the Gothic Quarter's **Papirum** (✉ *Baixada de la Llibreteria 2, Barri Gòtic*), a tiny, medieval-tone shop with exquisite hand-printed papers and writing implements. **La Manual Alpargartera** (✉ *Carrer d'Avinyó 7, Barri Gòtic*), off Carrer Ferran, specializes in handmade rope-sole sandals and espadrilles. **Solé** (✉ *C. Ample 7, Barri Gòtic*) makes shoes by hand and sells others from all over the world. **La Lionesa** (✉ *C. Ample 21, Barri Gòtic*) is an old-time grocery store. Barcelona's best music store is **Discos Castelló** (✉ *Carrer Tallers 3, Raval*). For textiles, try **Teranyina** (✉ *C. Notariat 10, Raval*). **Baclava** (✉ *C. Notariat 10, Raval*) shares an address with Teranyina and sells artisanal products. **Otman** (✉ *Carrer Cirera 4, La Ribera*) has light and racy frocks, belts, blouses, and skirts. Cutlery flourishes at the stately **Ganiveteria Roca** (✉ *Pl. del Pi 3, Barri Gòtic*), opposite the giant rose window of the Santa Maria del Pi church.

SIDE TRIPS FROM BARCELONA

Numbers in the margin correspond to points of interest on the Side Trips from Barcelona map.

MONTSERRAT

1 *50 km (30 mi) west of Barcelona.*

A favorite side trip from Barcelona is a visit to the shrine of La Moreneta, the Black Virgin of Montserrat, Catalonia's patron saint, in a Benedictine monastery high in the Serra de Montserrat west of town. These dramatic, sawtooth peaks have given rise to countless legends: here St. Peter left a statue of the Virgin Mary carved by St. Luke, Parsifal found the Holy Grail, and Wagner sought inspiration for his opera. Montserrat is as memorable for its strange, pink hills as it is for its religious treasures, so be sure to explore the area. The monastic complex is dwarfed by the grandeur of the jagged peaks, and the crests above are bristling with chapels and hermitages. The hermitage of **Sant Joan** can be reached by funicular. The views over the mountains to the Mediterranean and, on a clear day, to the Pyrenees are breathtaking; the rugged, boulder-strewn terrain makes for dramatic walks and hikes.

Although a monastery has stood on the same site in Montserrat since the early Middle Ages, the present 19th-century building replaced the rubble left by Napoléon's troops in 1812. The shrine is world-famous, and one of Catalonia's spiritual sanctuaries—honeymooning couples flock here by the thousands seeking La Moreneta's blessing on their marriages, and twice a year, on April 27 and September 8, the diminutive statue of Montserrat's Black Virgin becomes the object of one of Spain's greatest pilgrimages. To get here, follow the A2/A7 *autopista* on the upper ring road (Ronda de Dalt), or from the western end of the Diagonal as far as Salida (Exit) 25 to Martorell. Bypass this industrial center and follow signs to Montserrat. Alternatively, you can take a train from the Plaça Espanya metro station (hourly 8:36–6:36, connecting with the funicular leaving every 15 minutes) or go on a guided tour with Pullmantur or Julià (⇨ Tour Options *in* Barcelona Essentials).

Only the basilica and museum are regularly open to the public. The **basilica** is dark and ornate, its blackness pierced by the glow of hundreds of votive lamps. Above the high altar stands the famous polychrome statue of the Virgin and Child, to which the faithful can pay their respects by way of a separate door. ☎ *93/877–7777* ⊙ *Daily 6* AM*–10:30* AM *and noon–6:30* PM.

The monastery's **museum** has two sections: the Secció Antiga has old masters, among them works by El Greco, Correggio, and Caravaggio, and the amassed gifts to the Virgin; the Secció Moderna concentrates on recent modern Catalan painters. ☎ *93/877–7766 abbey and museum* ⊙ *Secció Antiga Tues.–Sat. 10:30–2, Secció Moderna Tues.–Sat. 3–6.*

SITGES, SANTES CREUS & POBLET

This trio of attractions south and west of Barcelona can be seen comfortably in a day. Sitges is the prettiest and most popular resort in Barcelona's immediate environs, flaunting an excellent beach, a whitewashed and flowery old quarter. It's also one of Europe's premier gay resorts. The Cistercian monasteries west of here, at Santes Creus and Poblet, are characterized by monolithic Romanesque architecture and beautiful cloisters. By car, head southwest along Gran Via or Passeig Colom to the freeway that passes the airport on its way to Castelldefels. From here, the freeway and tunnels will get you to Sitges in 20 to 30 minutes. From Sitges, drive inland toward Vilafranca del Penedès and the A7 freeway. The A2 (Lleida) leads to the monasteries. Regular trains leave Sants and Passeig de Gràcia for Sitges; the ride takes a half hour. To get to Santes Creus or Poblet from Sitges, take a Lleida-line train to L'Espluga de Francolí, 4 km (2½ mi) from Poblet. For Poblet, you can also stay with the train to Tarragona and catch a bus to the monastery (Autotransports Perelada ☎973/202058).

SITGES

2 *43 km (27 mi) southwest of Barcelona.*

The Sitges beach is well provided with fine sand that is carefully maintained in pristine condition, and the human flora and fauna usually found sun-worshipping on it are dazzling specimens for every taste and preference, lending the display of sea, sand, and celebrants a nearly catwalk-like intensity. The eastern end of the strand is dominated by an albaster statue of the 16th-century painter El Greco, usually more at home in Toledo, where he spent most of his professional career. The artist Santiago Rusinol is to blame for this surprise, as he was such an El Greco fan that he not only installed two El Greco paintings in his Museu Cau Ferrat but had this sculpture planted on the beach.

The most interesting museum here is the **Cau Ferrat**, founded by Santiago Rusiñol (1861–1931) and containing some of his own paintings together with two El Grecos. Connoisseurs of wrought iron will love the beautiful collection of *cruces terminales*, crosses that once marked town boundaries. Next door is the **Museu Maricel de Mar,** with more artistic treasures, and **Casa Llopis,** a romantic villa offering a tour of the house and local wine tasting is a short walk across town. ✉*Fonollar s/n* ☎*93/894–0364* 🌐*www.diba.es* 🎟*€4, valid for all three museums; free 1st Wed. of month* ⏰*June 14–Sept. 30., Tues.–Sat. 9:30–2 and 4–7, Sun. 10–2; Oct. 1–June 13, Tues.–Sat. 9:30–2 and 3:30–6:30, Sun. 10–2.*

NEED A BREAK?

Linger over excellent Mediterranean products and cooking with a nonpareil sea view at **Vivero** (✉*Passeig Balmins* ☎*93/894–2149*). The clean-lined contemporary style enhances both the seascapes and the seafood. The restaurant is closed Tuesday February–April.

EN ROUTE

After leaving Sitges, make straight for the A2 *autopista* by way of Vilafranca del Penedès. Wine buffs may want to stop here to taste some excellent Penedès wines; you can tour and sip at the **Bodega Miguel Torres** (✉*Carrer Comerç 22* ☎*93/890–0100*). There's an interesting **Museu del**

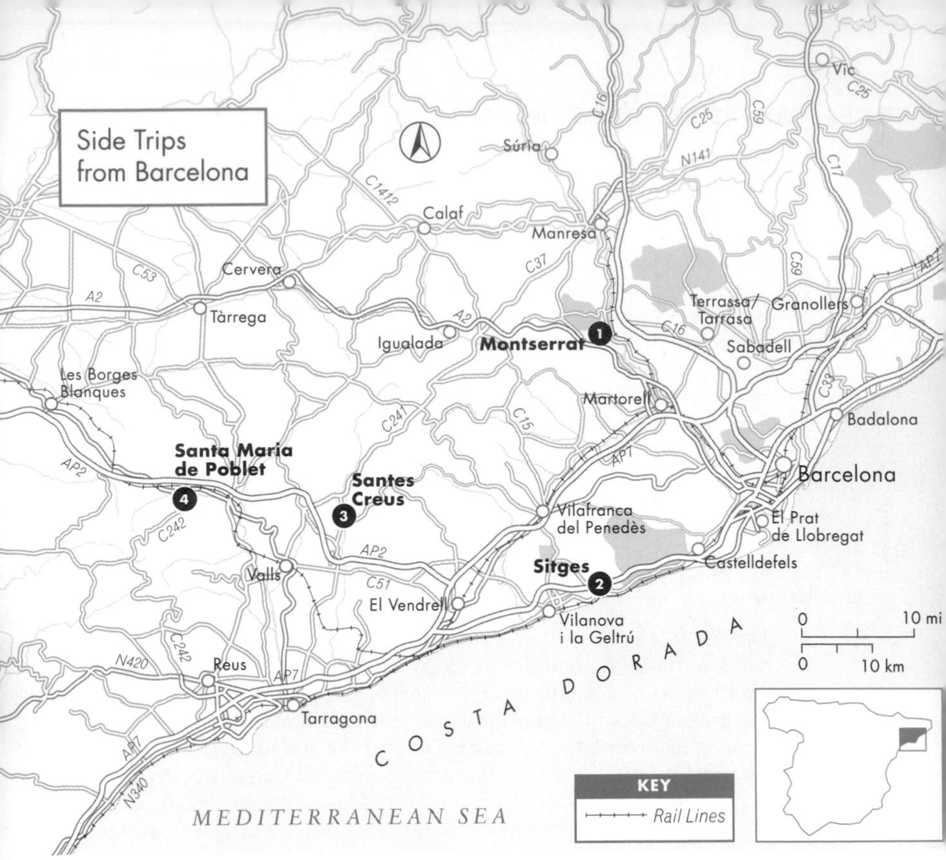

Vi (✉ *Plaça Jaume I, 1* ☎ *93/890–0582*) (*Wine Museum*) in the Royal Palace, with descriptions of wine-making history. Admission is €4; it's open Tuesday–Sunday 10–2 and 4–7.

SANTES CREUS

❸ 95 km (59 mi) west of Barcelona.

Founded in 1157, Santes Creus is the first of the monasteries you'll come upon as A2 branches west toward Lleida. Three austere aisles and an unusual 14th-century apse combine with the newly restored cloisters and the courtyard of the royal palace. ✉*Off A2* ☎*977/638329* 🎫*€4* ⏲*Mid-Mar.–mid-Sept., Tues.–Sun. 10–1:30 and 3–7; mid-Sept.–mid-Jan., Tues.–Sun. 10–1:30 and 3–5:30; mid-Jan.–mid-Mar., Tues.–Sun. 10–1:30 and 3–6.*

Montblanc is off A2 at Salida (Exit) 9, its ancient gates too narrow for cars. A walk through its tiny streets reveals Gothic churches with stained-glass windows, a 16th-century hospital, and medieval mansions.

SANTA MARIA DE POBLET

❹ *8 km (5 mi) west of Santes Creus.*

This splendid Cistercian foundation at the foot of the Prades Mountains is one of the great masterpieces of Spanish monastic architecture. The cloister is a stunning combination of lightness and size; on sunny days the shadows on the yellow sandstone are extraordinary. Founded in 1150 by Ramón Berenguer IV in gratitude for the Christian Reconquest, the monastery first housed a dozen Cistercians from Narbonne. Later, the Crown of Aragón used Santa Maria de Poblet for religious retreats and burials. The building was damaged in an 1836 anticlerical revolt, and monks of the reformed Cistercian Order have managed the difficult task of restoration since 1940. Today, monks and novices again pray before the splendid retable over the tombs of Aragonese rulers, restored to their former glory by sculptor Frederic Marès; they also sleep in the cold, barren dormitory and eat frugal meals in the stark refectory. You can join them if you'd like—18 very comfortable rooms are available (for men only). Call **Padre Benito** (☎*977/870089*) to arrange a stay of up to 15 days within the stones and silence of one of Catalonia's gems. ✉*Off A2* ☎*977/870254* *€4* *Guided tours by reservation Apr.–Sept., daily 10–12:30 and 3–6; Oct.–Mar., daily 10–12:30 and 3–5:30.*

OFF THE BEATEN PATH

Valls. The town of Valls, famous for its early spring *calçotada* (long-stem onion roast) held on the last Sunday of January, is 10 km (6 mi) from Santes Creus and 15 km (9 mi) from Poblet. Even if you miss the big day, *calçots* are served from November to April at rustic and rambling farmhouses such as Cal Ganxo (☎*977/605960*) in nearby Masmolets, and the Xiquets de Valls, Catalonia's most famous *castellers* (human castlers), might be putting up a human skyscraper.

7

BARCELONA ESSENTIALS

To research prices, get advice from other travelers, and book travel arrangements, visit www.fodors.com.

TRANSPORTATION

For more on travel to and in Barcelona, see the Barcelona Planner at the beginning of this chapter.

Modern Barcelona, above the Plaça de Catalunya, is built on a grid system. The old town, however, from the Plaça de Catalunya to the port, is a labyrinth of narrow streets, so you'll need a good street map. Most sightseeing can be done on foot—you won't have any choice in the Barri Gòtic—but you'll have to use the metro, buses, or taxis to link sightseeing areas. The Dia T-1 pass is valid for one day of unlimited travel on all subway, bus, and FFCC lines. Maps showing bus and metro routes are available free from booths in the Plaça de Catalunya; for general information on public transport, call 93/412–0000. Turisme de Barcelona sells two-, three-, four-, and five-day versions of the very worthwhile Barcelona Card. For €24, €29, €33, and €36 (these are 2007 prices; expect a €2 hike for 2008), you get unlimited travel on all public transport as well as discounts at 27 museums, 10 restaurants, 14 leisure sites, and 20 stores. Caveat: the restaurants and shops covered are uniformly mediocre and the only important museum savings is 20% at the very expensive Casa Batlló. Travel cards, covering transport only, cost €9.60, €13.70, €17.50, and €20.80 for two-, three-, four-, and five-day passes. Other services include walking tours of the Gothic Quarter, an airport shuttle, a bus to Tibidabo, and the Tombbus, which connects key shopping areas.

Barcelona's new tramway system is divided into two subsectors: **Trambaix** serves the western end of the Diagonal between Plaça Francesc Macià and destinations in the Baix Llobregat, L'Hospitalet de Llobregat, Cornellà, Sant Joan Despí, Esplugues de Llobregat, Sand Just Desvern, and Sand Feliu de Llobregat; **Trambesòs** serves the eastern end of the Diagonal between Plaça de les Glories, Diagonal Mar, and the Fòrum 2004 area in the delta of the river Besòs.

Contact Turisme de Barcelona (✉ *Pl. de Catalunya 17 bis, Eixample* ☎ *93/285-3834*).

BY AIR

All international and domestic flights arrive at the spectacular glass, steel, and marble El Prat de Llobregat Airport, 14 km (9 mi) south of Barcelona.

Most flights from the United States connect in Madrid or at other European points such as London, Amsterdam, Paris, or Frankfurt; only Continental, Delta, and Iberia fly nonstop to Barcelona.

The Aerobus leaves the airport for Plaça de Catalunya every 15 minutes (6 AM–11 PM) on weekdays and every 30 minutes (6:30 AM–10:30 PM) on weekends. From Plaça de Catalunya, it leaves for the airport every 15 minutes (5:30 AM–10 PM) on weekdays and every 30 minutes (6:30 AM–10:30 PM) on weekends. The fare is €3.85.

Cab fare from the airport into town is about €23. If you're driving your own car, follow signs to the Centre Ciutat and you'll enter the city along Gran Via. For the port area, follow signs for the Ronda Litoral. The journey to the center of town can take anywhere from 15 to 45 minutes, depending on traffic *(see Traffic, in By Car)*.

The RENFE airport train is a good way to avoid surface gridlock and works economically and flawlessly as long as you leave plenty of time at either end, since trains run only every half hour. From the airport, the RENFE station is a 10- to 15-minute walk (with moving walkway) from your gate through the terminal and over an overpass. Trains leave the airport every 30 minutes between 6 AM and 12 midnight, stopping at the Estació de Sants, then at the Plaça de Catalunya, later at the Arc de Triomf, and finally at Clot. Trains going to the airport leave every 30 minutes from 6 AM to midnight. The one-way fare is €2.35.

Contacts Aeroport del Prat (☎ *902/404704*). **Airport Lost and Found** (☎ *900/100405*).

BY BIKE

Bicitram is a bike-rental outfit that stays open on weekends and holidays. Los Filicletos rents bikes, skates, and scooters. Un Menys—"One Less," in Catalan, meaning one less car on the streets of Barcelona—

organizes increasingly popular outings that tack drinks, dinner, and dancing on to a gentle, guided bike ride for a total price of about €30 (which includes bike rental).

Bike Rentals **Bicitram** (✉ *Marquès de l'Argentera 15* ☎ *636/401997*). **Los Filicletos** (✉ *Passeig de Picasso 38* ☎ *93/319–7811*). **Un Menys** (✉ *Esparteria 3* ☎ *93/268–2105* 📠 *93/319–4298*).

BY BUS

Barcelona's main bus station is Estació del Nord, east of the Arc de Triomf. Buses also depart from the Estació de Sants as well as from the depots of Barcelona's various private bus companies. Rather than pound the pavement (or the telephone, usually futile because of overloaded lines) trying to sort out Barcelona's complex and confusing bus system, reserve online or go through a travel agent, who can quickly book you the best bus passage to your destination.

City buses run daily 5:30 AM–11:30 PM. The fare is €1.35. For multiple journeys purchase a Targeta T-10 (valid for bus or metro), which buys you 10 rides for €7. Route maps are displayed at bus stops. Note that those with a red band always stop at a central square—Catalunya, Universitat, or Urquinaona—and blue indicates a night bus. Schedules are available at bus and metro stations or at 🌐*www.bcn.es/guia/welcomea.htm*

BY CABLE CAR & FUNICULAR

The Montjuïc Funicular is a cog railroad that runs from the junction of Avinguda Paral.lel and Nou de la Rambla to the Miramar station on Montjuïc (Paral.lel). It operates daily 11 AM–9:30 PM in summer, and weekends and holidays 11 AM–8 PM in winter; the fare is €1.20. A *telefèric* then takes you up to Montjuïc Castle. In winter the telefèric runs weekends and holidays 11–2:45 and 4–7:30; in summer, daily 11:30–9. The fare is €3.85. A Transbordador Aeri Harbor Cable Car runs between Miramar and Montjuïc across the harbor to Torre de Jaume I, on Barcelona's *moll* (quay), and on to Torre de Sant Sebastià, at the end of Passeig Joan de Borbó in Barceloneta. You can board at either stage. The fare is €9.50 round-trip (€7.50 one-way), and the car runs October–June, weekdays noon–5:45, weekends noon–6:15, and July–September, daily 11–9. To reach the summit of Tibidabo, take the metro to Avinguda de Tibidabo, then the Tramvía Blau (€2.30 one-way, €3 round-trip) to Peu del Funicular, and finally the Tibidabo Funicular (€2 one-way, €3 round-trip) from there to the Tibidabo fairground. It runs every 30 minutes, 7:05 AM–9:35 PM ascending, 7:25 AM–9:55 PM descending.

BY CAR

Getting around Barcelona by car is generally more trouble than it's worth. The *rondas* (ring roads) make entering and exiting the city easy, unless it's rush hour, in which case traffic comes to a halt. Between parking, navigating, *alcoholemia* (alcohol blood-level) patrols, and the general wear and tear of driving in the city, the subway, taxis, buses, and walking are your best bets in Barcelona.

For travel outside of Barcelona, the freeways to Girona, Figueres, Sitges, Tarragona, and Lleida are surprisingly fast. Routine cruising speed on Spanish freeways is 140 km/h (84 mph) or more. If you drive at the official speed limit of 120 km/h (72 mph), you seriously risk high-speed rear-ending. The distance to Girona, 97 km (58 mi), is a 45-minute shot. The French border is an hour away. Perpignan is, at 188 km (113 mi), an hour and 20 minutes.

On freeways (possibly because official driving-school manuals date before the invention of Spain's excellent network of freeways), do not expect motorists coming down the inside lane to move left and give way. The "merging" concept does not exist in Spain. Expect to come to a full stop at the red yield triangle at the end of the on-ramp and wait for a break in traffic.

Spanish highway engineers have discovered the British roundabout. Remember that the motorist *in* the roundabout has the right of way, even if you're the vehicle to the right (which is the normal rule of thumb elsewhere, where vehicles coming from your right have right of way).

Note that National Car Rental is affiliated with the Spanish agency Atesa, or Avis. Europcar has good weekend deals. Vanguard rents motorcycles as well as cars.

PARKING You can often find a legal and safe parking place on the street, and underground public parking is plentiful, easy, and cheap.

TRAFFIC Barcelona's rush hours take place from 8:30 to 9:30 AM, from 2 to 3 PM, and, intermittently, from 5 to 9 PM.

Major Agencies **Avis** (✉ *Carrer Casanova 209, Eixample* ☎ *93/209–9533* ✉ *Carrer Aragó 235, Eixample* ☎ *93/487–8754* 🌐 *www.avis.com*). **Europcar** (✉ *Viladomat 214, Eixample* ☎ *93/439–8403* ✉ *Estació de Sants* ☎ *93/491–4822* 🌐 *www.europcar.com*). **Hertz** (✉ *Carrer Còrsega 293, Eixample* ☎ *93/237–5680* ✉ *Tuset 10, Eixample* ☎ *93/217–3248* 🌐 *www.hertz.com*).

Local Agencies **Atesa** (✉ *El Prat Airport, El Prat* ☎ *93/298–3433* ✉ *Muntaner 45, Eixample* ☎ *93/323–0266*). **Vanguard** (✉ *Londres 31, Eixample* ☎ *93/439–3880*).

BY SUBWAY

The subway is the fastest, cheapest, and easiest way to get around Barcelona. You pay a flat fare of €1.30 no matter how far you travel (with free transfers for up to an hour and 15 minutes), but it's more economical to buy a 10-ride Targeta T-10 for €7 valid for Metro and FGC Generalitat trains, the Tramvía Blau blue tram, and the Montjuïc Funicular. This card can be shared by up to ten people. Fares are scheduled to increase by up to 15 *centimes* after January 1, 2008. Metro lines are color coded, and the FGC trains are marked with a reclining S-like blue and white icon. Lines 2, 3, and 5 run weekdays 5 AM–midnight. Lines 1 and 4 close at 1 AM. On Friday, Saturday, and holiday evenings all trains run until 2 AM. The FGC Generalitat trains run until 12:30 on weekdays and 2:15 AM on weekends and eves of holidays. Sunday trains run on weekday schedules.

Information **Transports Metropolitans de Barcelona (TMB)** (✉ *Número 60 [Zona Franca] 21–23, Zona Franca* ☎ *93/298–7000* 🌐 *www.tmb.net*).

BY TAXI

Taxis are black and yellow and show a green rooftop light when available for hire. The meter starts at €1.50 (€1.60 at night and on weekends and holidays). There are supplements for luggage, night travel, Sunday and holidays, rides from a station or to the airport, and for trips to or from the bullring or a soccer *(fútbol)* match. There are cab stands all over town, and you can also hail cabs on the street. One of the prime taxi stands is at the head of the Rambla on Plaça Catalunya, though lines often form there. Another handy one is at Plaça Sant Jaume, dead center in the Gothic Quarter. Within 200 yards of a taxi stand, cab drivers generally refuse to respond to a hail, referring you to the line at the stand.

Information **City Taxis** (☎ *93/387–1000, 93/490–2222, or 93/357–7755 24 hours a day*).

BY TRAIN

Long-distance trains arrive and depart from Estació de Sants. En route to or from Sants, some trains stop at another station on Passeig de Gràcia at Carrer Aragó; this can be a good way to avoid the long lines that form at Sants during holidays, though even better is dealing directly with www.renfe.es. For schedules and fares, call RENFE at 902/240202.

7

Almost all long-distance trains arrive and depart from Estació de Sants. En route to or from Sants, some trains stop at another station on Passeig de Gràcia at Carrer Aragó; this can be a good way to avoid the long lines that form at Sants during holidays. The Estació de França, near the port, now handles only a few long-distance trains within Spain. For schedules and fares, call RENFE. Although overnight train travel is convenient, time efficient, and easy if you like to sleep on trains, beware: unless you have a fairly pricey compartment for two (or four), you will be packed in with strangers in a four-person compartment with often suffocating heat and windows that do not open. The air shuttle (or a scheduled flight) between Madrid and Barcelona can, if all goes well, get you door to door in less than three hours for only about €40 more.

Train Information & Stations **Estació de Sants** (✉ *Pl. dels Països Catalans s/n, Eixample*). **RENFE** (☎ *902/240202, 902/243402 international information in Spain and worldwide*).

CONTACTS & RESOURCES

CHILDREN IN BARCELONA

Check listings in daily newspapers for children's activities on Saturday and Sunday morning. The Fundació Miró is one of Barcelona's most child-friendly venues, with clowns, storytellers, and events of all kinds from 10 to 2 on weekends. The Barcelona Zoo—especially the dolphin show—are great favorites with small *barcelonins*. The Museu de la Ciència offers excellent interactive scientific games and virtual experiences. Drassanes Reials and the Museu Marítimo have superb displays designed for children. Last of all is the amusement park up on Tibidabo, a once-popular children's event that has simply been eclipsed by superior activities.

EMERGENCIES

Tourist Attention, a service provided by the local police department, can help if you're the victim of a crime or need medical or psychological assistance. English interpreters are on hand. To find out which pharmacies are open late at night or 24 hours on a given day, look on the door of any pharmacy or in any local newspaper under "Farmacias de Guardia." Alternatively, dial 010.

Emergency Services **Ambulance** (☎ *93/300–2020 Creu Roja, Red Cross*). **Hospital Clinic** (✉ *Villarroel 170, Eixample* ☎ *93/454–6000 or 93/454–7000* Ⓜ *Blue line to Hospital Clinic*). **Medical assistance** (☎ *061*). **Police** (☎ *091 or 092 Main police station* ✉ *Via Laietana 43, Barri Gòtic* ☎ *93/301–6666*). **Tourist Attention** (✉ *Guardia Urbana, La Rambla 43, Rambla* ☎ *93/290–3440*). **24-Hour Pharmacies** (☎ *010*).

INTERNET

Surrounded by medieval stone, the art gallery–cum–Internet café bcnet offers everything from e-mail checking to video conferences until 1 AM. Another venue, Idea, which also has a bookstore, is perfect for e-mail. Easy Internet offers over 200 computers in each location from 8 am to 2:30 am seven days week.

Internet Cafés **Bar Travel** (✉ *Carrer de la Boqueria 27, Barri Gòtic* ☎ *93/410–8592*). **bcnet** (✉ *Carrer Barra de Ferro 3, La Ribera* ☎ *93/268–1507*). **Cafe Internet Navego** (✉ *Carrer Provença 546, Eixample* ☎ *93/436–8459*). **Easy Internet Café** (✉ *Ronda Universitat 35, Eixample* ☎ *93/310–3218*). **Easy Internet Café** (✉ *Rambla 31a 546 , Ciutat Vella* ☎ *93/319–5954*). (✉ *Pl. Comercial 2, El Born* ☎ *93/268–8787*).

TOUR OPTIONS

BOAT TOURS Golondrina harbor boats make short trips around the harbor from the Portal de la Pau, near the Columbus Monument. The fare is €5 for a 40-minute tour. The 90-minute ride in a glass-bottom catamaran that parallels the coast up past Barcelona's Olympic Port to the Fòrum complex at the northeastern end of the Diagonal costs €12. For an interesting amphibean loop, get off at the Fòrum and take the grassy tramway line back for a look at the new Diagonal Mar neighborhood and Barcelona's new architecture from the low triangular Fòrum building itself, past the Oscar Tusquets–designed Hotel Princess, Jean Nouvel's Torre Agbar, Ricardo Bofill's Teatre Nacional de Catalunya, the Diposit de les Aigues, to the Ciutadella-Vila Olímpica tram and metro stop behind the zoo.

Depending on the weather, the catamarans leave every hour on the half hour 11:30–5:30 (to 6:30 from Holy Week through September). Regular Golondrina departures are spring and summer (Holy Week–September), daily 11–7; fall and winter, weekends and holidays only, 11–5. It's closed mid-December–early January.

Contact Golondrina (☎ *93/442–3106* 🌐 *www.lasgolondrinas.com*)

BUS TOURS From mid-June to mid-October, the Bus Turistic (9:30–7:30 every 30 minutes) runs on a circuit that passes all the important sights. A day's ticket, which you can buy on the bus, costs €9 (€6 half day) and also covers the fare for the Tramvía Blau, funicular, and Montjuïc cable car across the port. The ride starts at the Plaça de Catalunya. Julià Tours and Pullmantur run day and half-day excursions outside the city. The most popular trips are those to Montserrat and the Costa Brava resorts, the latter including a cruise to the Medes Isles.

Contacts Julià Tours (✉ *Ronda Universitat 5, Eixample* ☎ *93/317–6454*). **Pullmantur** (✉ *Gran Via 635, Eixample* ☎ *93/318–5195*).

WALKING TOURS The **Barcelona Tourist Office (Turisme de Barcelona)** offers weekend walking tours of the Gothic Quarter (at 10 AM) for €9. **Ruta Gourmet** walking tours through emblematic points of the city's gastronomic life are also available, with tastings, for €11. The **Aula Gastronómica del Mercat de la Boqueria** (Cooking Lessons at the Boqueria Market) includes tours of the market with breakfast, cooking classes, and tastings. **Urbancultours** has English-language walking tours covering Gaudí's Sagrada Família, the medieval Jewish quarter, and other sights. For Thursday afternoon boat tours of the harbor and the fishermen's quarter (€10), and visits to the daily fish auction (€7), reserve ahead with **Consorci El Far de Barcelona.**

Contacts Aula Gastronómica del Mercat de la Boqueria (✉ *La Rambla 91, Rambla* ☎ *93/304–0272* 🌐 *www.barcelonaculinaria.com*). **Consorci El Far de Barcelona** (✉ *L'Escar 6, Barceloneta* ☎ *93/217–7457* 🌐 *www.elfar.diba.es*). **Palau de la Virreina** (✉ *La Rambla 99, Rambla*) . **Turisme de Barcelona** (✉ *Pl. de Catalunya 17 bis, Eixample* ☎ *93/285–3832* 🌐 *www.barcelonaturisme.com*). **Urbancultours** (☎ *93/417 1191*).

DISCOUNTS & DEALS

The Barcelona Card offers discounts in nearly all of Barcelona's major museums and stores, access to public transport gratis, and discounts on theater and music events. It is obtainable in Turisme de Barcelona offices in Plaça de Catalunya and Plaça Sant Jaume (both open Monday–Saturday 9–9 and Sunday 10–2), as well as in the Sants train station (open daily 8–8) and the El Prat airport.

Turisme de Barcelona sells the multi-attraction Barcelona Card in single-day through five-day versions. For €17 up to €30, you get unlimited travel on all public transport as well as discounts at 27 museums, 10 restaurants, 14 recreational sites, and 20 stores, as well as additional services. You can buy the card at all tourist offices, the El Corte Inglés department store, and the Barcelona Aquarium, among other sites.

Contacts Estació de Sants (✉ *Pl. dels Països Catalans s/n, Eixample*). **Turisme de Barcelona** (✉ *Pl. de Catalunya 17 bis, Eixample* ☎ *906/301282* 🌐 *www.barcelonaturisme.com* ✉ *Pl. Sant Jaume 1, Barri Gòtic* ☎ *906/301282*).

7

VISITOR INFORMATION

Turisme de Barcelona has two main locations, both open Monday through Saturday 9–9 and Sunday 10–2: Plaça de Catalunya, in the center of town, and Plaça Sant Jaume, in the Gothic Quarter. There are smaller facilities at the Sants train station, open daily 8–8; the Institut de Cultura (at La Rambla 99 and La Rambla 7) open Monday–Saturday 9–9 and Sunday 10–2, has cultural information only. The Palau de Congressos is open daily 10–8 during trade fairs and conventions only. For general information in English, dial 010 between 8 AM and 10 PM any day but Sunday. El Prat Airport has two offices (in terminals A and B) with tourist information, open Monday–Saturday 9:30–8 and Sunday 9:30–3. The tourist office in Palau Robert, open Monday–Saturday 10 to 7, specializes in provincial Catalonia. From June to mid-September, tourist information aides patrol the Gothic Quarter and La Rambla area 9 AM to 9 PM. They travel in pairs and are recognizable by their uniforms of red shirts, white trousers or skirts, and badges.

City Tourist Offices **Institut de Cultura** (✉ *La Rambla 99, Rambla* ☎ *93/316-1000*). **Institut de Cultura Centro de Arte Santa Mónica** (✉ *La Rambla 7, Rambla* ☎ *93/316-2811*).

Palau de Congressos (✉ *Av. María Cristina s/n, Eixample* ☎ *902/233200*). **Turisme de Barcelona** (✉ *Pl. de Catalunya 17 bis, Eixample* ☎ *807/117222* 🌐 *www.barcelonaturisme.com* ✉ *Pl. Sant Jaume 1, Barri Gòtic* ☎ *906/301282*).

Regional Tourist Offices **El Prat Airport** (☎ *93/478-4704*). **Palau Robert** (✉ *Passeig de Gràcia 107, at Diagonal, Eixample* ☎ *93/238-4000*).

Catalonia & the Levante

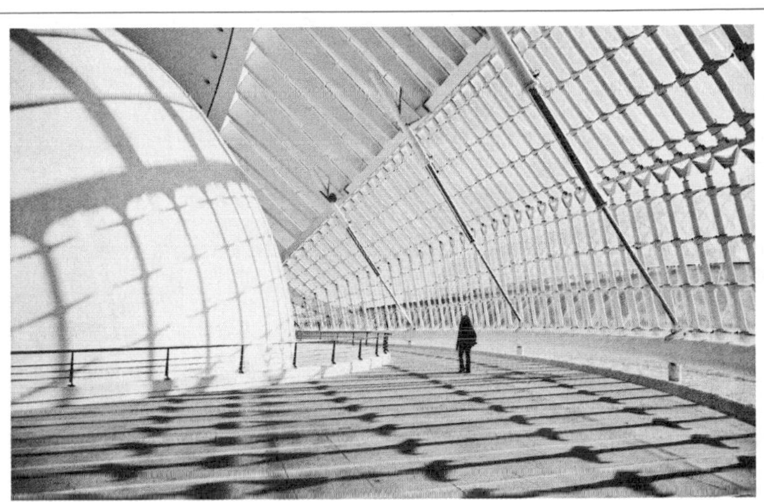

Valencia's Ciutat de les Arts i les Ciències

8

WORD OF MOUTH

"In the Barrio del Carmen, you will find a favorite longtime hang-out called 'Bar el Pilar.' Mussels are a specialty here, but *patatas bravas*, and dozens more tapas and plates of yummy treats will be brought to you quickly if you are lucky to secure some space at one of the teeny tables or at the long bar."

—Lin

www.fodors.com/forums

WELCOME TO CATALONIA & THE LEVANTE

TOP REASONS TO GO

★ **Seeing Valencia from atop the Miguelete Tower:** The best panoramic view of the city.

★ **Visiting Barrio Carmen:** If you want to get a feel for the city's energy, this is the place to do it—Valencians of all walks of life eat, drink, and party here.

★ **Dining on Seafood at Joan Gatell's in Cambrils:** Simply, the best in town.

★ **Bird-watching at Delta de l'Ebre:** If you're looking for some tranquillity in beautiful surroundings.

★ **Celebrating into the Wee Hours with the Crowd at Las Fallas:** In mid-March, one of the most visible and preeminent festivals in all of Europe turns into an all-night party long after the effigies are burned.

Woman in traditional dress during the Fallas festival in Valencia.

1 La Garroxta. This is one of Catalonia's most attractive regions, and still largely unknown. The land around Olot contains some 40 well-preserved volcanic cones at Croscat, and the volcano of Santa Margarida. The nearby villages of Vall d'En Bas, with lush green plains, provide a sharp contrast.

Cervera
Tarrega
Mequinenza
Montblanch
Valls
ZARAGOZA
Reus
Tarragona
Gandesa
La Ametlla De Mar
Tortosa
4
Delta de l'Ebre
Morella
San Carlos De La Rapita
Vinaroz
Peniscola
Torreblanca
0 20 mi
0 30 km
Los Mases
Alcora
Borriol
Jerica
Burriana
Segorbe
Vall De Uxo
COSTA DEL AZAHAR
El Puerto
Valencia
Albufera Nature Park
Cullera

2 Costa Brava. While much of the coastline along this rugged stretch has now been over-exploited, the spectacularly robust land and marine park of Parc Cap De Creus, the mystical presence of Salvador Dali in towns like Figueres, and the stunning whitewashed town of Cadaqués still make any visit exhilarating.

The Salvador Dali Museum at Fiqueres with its humorous enlarged eggs.

3 Sitges & the wine country. The beautiful gay-friendly seaside town of Sitges remains a major attraction. But just as worthy is the Penedes area, the heart of Spain's *cava* production, producing excellent white wine. El Priorat is also making a name for itself with wineries in the stunning mountainous terrain.

4 The Ebro Delta. Resplendent with an array of animals and birdlife, the 20,000-acre Parc Natural de Delta de l'Ebre is one of Catalonia's, and Spain's, most treasured resources. It's a great place to take a relaxing break before dropping in and out of either romantic Tarragona or cosmopolitan Valencia.

GETTING ORIENTED

It's not without reason that Catalonia is the most visited of Spain's provinces. The Pyrenees that separate it from France provide some of the country's best skiing and its rugged Costa Brava in the north and Costa Dorada to the south are havens for sun worshippers. Its interior is full of surprises too: stunning Romanesque villages in the Girona region, volcanoes in La Garrotxa, *cava* and wine-growing towns in and around Tarragona, an expanding growing rural tourism industry, and the region's growing international reputation for its cuisine make Catalonia attractive to to all tastes.

Ciutat de les Arts i les Ciències, Valencia.

8

CATALONIA & THE LEVANTE PLANNER

When to Go

Catalonia and the Levante is a diverse area. If it's beaches you want then by all means come in the hot summer months but expect crowds and oppressive heat—up to 40°C (104°F). The coastline is more comfortable in May and September. If it's skiing in the Pyrenees that you're after, then February and March are your peak months. Winter traveling in the region also has its advantages—places like Valencia still have plenty of sunshine and if you're visiting villages and wineries in the countryside you might find you've got the run of the place! A word of warning: many restaurants outside the major towns may close during weekdays during winter. Always phone ahead. The same goes for most centers of interest—opening hours tend to be shorter, with some locations closing at around 6 PM.

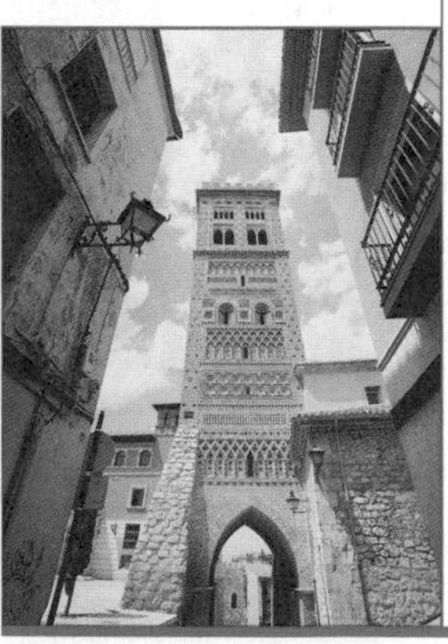

Getting There & Around

El Prat de Llobregat in Barcelona, 62 mi north of Tarragona, is the main international airport. Girona is the closest airport to the northern end of this terrain and a good option if you're flying to Spain via the United Kingdom. Low cost airline Ryanair runs regular services from London. Valencia has an international airport with direct flights to London, Paris, Brussels, Lisbon, Zurich, and Milan. Reus Airport also receives international flights from London.

Spain and Catalonia have excellent roads, if you're in the driver's seat the only drawback is high toll fees on the *autopistas* (highways). Barcelona is surrounded by a network of *rondas,* or ring roads, with quick access from every corner of the city. Look for signs for these rondas, then follow signs to France (Francia), Girona, and the A7 autopista, which goes all the way to France. The Girona turn off is clearly marked. Simlarly, the A7 *autopista* also runs down south to Tarragona and Valencia.

The major car-hire operators such as Avis, Hertz, and Europcar have numerous offices in the larger cities. In recent years though the competitive edge of these international firms is seeing stiff competition from local outfit Pepecar, which does most of its business through online bookings: the earlier you book, the cheaper your car.

Barcelona's urban RENFE train system is an efficient and cheap way of discovering both inland and coastal Catalonia. From Placa Catalunya and Sants, RENFE accesses all the major towns like Viç and even skiing towns like Puigcerda in the north. If it's beach you want up north or south, RENFE trains will literally leave you on the sand. To head up toward the Costa Brava, trains can be caught again, at both Sants and Placa Catalunya.

Leaving Valencia, you can connect to Madrid (via Cuenca) or Alicante (via Játiva). Within the region, trains run more or less down the coast: Tarragona to Salou, Cambrils to Tortosa, Vinaròs to Peñíscola, Benicàssim to Castellón, and Sagunto to Valencia. A line also goes from Valencia to Zaragoza by way of Sagunto and Teruel; local lines go around Valencia from the Cronista Rivelles station.

See the Catalonia & the Levante Essentials at the end of this chapter for more transportation information.

Rural Tourism: Getting in Touch with the Land

While the beaches of the Costa Brava, the wonders of the Delta del'Ebre, and the marvels of Valencia rate high on anyone's list on a visit to Catalonia and the Levante, the appeal of a more relaxed and authentic trip that rural tourism offers is fast attracting international visitors.

First, search out rural tourism accommodation—depending on your tastes you can opt for a luxury farmhouse where the local family will cook, pamper, and indulge you. Or you might decide on something more rustic where you rent out a fully equipped farmhouse and cook for yourself and your family. Many of the *masías* (farmhouses) are still part of working farms (in fact they are obliged to be to qualify as an agri-tourism accommodation) and most are in small villages around the countryside. Many have swimming pools for the hot summer months and each one offers its own unique services. The kids can milk the cows, ride the horses, rent quads to go off the beaten track, play in the pool or games room. The adults can visit local villages (most of the masías owners are happy to provide a family member to act as a guide), try the local produce, visit nearby wineries, or just chill out.

Two areas that are well equipped for agri-tourism are La Garrotxa and Cerdanya. La Garrotxa allows you to rest up in quiet locations close to the Parc Natural de la Zona Volcánica de la Garrotxa, where you can take walks or book a hot-air-balloon ride to the stunning town of Santa Pau or the equally pretty towns of Valle En Bas nearby.

The Cerdanya region boasts some of the most scenic villages in all of Catalonia, some of them abandoned. The countryside here is another universe—snow-capped mountains contrast with deep valleys. What's more, it's in the center of the regions' biggest skiing area (which is surprisingly cheap).

The following tourist office Web sites have excellent English-language information: *www.turismerural.com* *www.turismegarrotxa.com* *www.cadimoixero.com*

WHAT IT COSTS In Euros

	$$$$	$$$	$$	$	¢
RESTAURANTS	over €20	€15–€20	€10–€15	€6–€10	under €6
HOTELS	over €180	€100–€180	€60–€100	€40–€60	under €40

Prices are per person for a main course at dinner. Prices are for two people in a standard double room in high season, excluding tax.

Planning Your Time

Outside of Barcelona, the beautiful towns of Vic, Ripoll, Girona, and Cadaqués are easily reachable from the city by bus or train in a couple of hours. Figueres is also a must if you want to catch the Dalí museum. If you want to explore the Pyrenees or La Garrotxa, hiring a car is a better option for exploring. Heading down south, Tarragona is much easier to get to on the RENFE train—the roads from Barcelona are invariably clogged with traffic, especially on weekends and during summer. Tarragona and its environs are definitely worth a few days. The city's Romanic wonders are best seen on foot at a leisurely pace broken up with a meal at any of its fine seafood restaurants in the Serallo fishing quarter. A day trip to the nature reserve at Delta de L'Ebre is a must. Alternatively, if you have a car, a day visit to the wineries in the Penedes region on the way to Tarragona is well worth the trip. Most of Spain's cava comes from here. A short drive to the picturesque seaside town of Sitges for lunch is also an option. From Tarragona it's a comfortable train ride or car trip to Valencia. A car will allow you to stop off at the coastal towns of Gandesa, Morella and Peñíscola. Valencia and its old town, great markets, the Santiago Calatrava–designed City of Arts and Sciences, and historical buildings can be covered in a few days but those wishing to sample its food and get a sense of local life might want to spend more time in the Barrio del Carmen.

Updated by Michael Kessler

STRADDLING CATALONIA (CATALUNYA) AND VALENCIA, this region allows you to sample the differences and similarities between these two feuding Mediterranean cousins.

Often ignored by travelers who bolt from its airport to the resorts of the Costa Brava, Girona is in many respects the gateway to Northern Catalonia and its attractions—the Pyrenees, the volcanic region of La Garrotxa, and of course the pristine beaches of the upper Costa Brava. Northern Catalonia is memorable for the soft, green hills of the Ampurdan farm country, the Alberes mountain range at the eastern end of the Pyrenees, and the rugged Costa Brava. Sprinkled across the landscape are *masías* (farmhouses) with austere, grayish or pinkish staggered-stone rooftops and ubiquitous square towers that make them look like fortresses. Even the tiniest village has its church, arcaded square, and *rambla,* where villagers take their evening *paseo.*

The Valencia region was part of the House of Aragón, Catalonia's medieval Mediterranean empire, after Jaume I conquered it in the 13th century. Along with Catalonia, Valencia was incorporated into a united Spanish state in the 15th century, but the most energetic cultivators of its separate cultural and linguistic identity still resent their centuries of Catalan domination. The Catalan language prevails in Tarragona, a city and province of Catalonia, but Valenciano, widely considered a dialect of Catalan (many valencianos consider it a language proper), is spoken and written on street signs in the Valencian provinces. You may notice the subtle difference in dialect as you move south.

The *huerta* (a fertile, irrigated coastal plain) is devoted mainly to citrus and vegetable farming, which lends color to the landscape and fragrance to the air. Grayish, arid mountains form a stark backdrop to the lush coast. Over the years these shores have entertained Phoenician, Greek, Carthaginian, and Roman visitors—the Romans stayed several centuries and left archaeological reminders all the way down the coast, particularly in Tarragona, the capital of Rome's Spanish empire by 218 BC. Rome's dominion did not go uncontested, however; the most serious challenge came from the Carthaginians of North Africa. The three Punic Wars, fought over this territory between 264 BC and 146 BC, led to the immortalization of the Carthaginian general Hannibal.

The same coastal farmland and beaches that attracted the ancients now call to modern-day tourists, though a chain of ugly developments has marred much of this shore. Inland, however, local culture has survived intact. The rugged and often beautiful territory is dotted with small fortified towns, several of which bear the name of Spain's 11th-century national hero, El Cid, as proof of the battles he fought here against the Moors 900 years ago. Each town has a porticoed Plaza Mayor, a warren of whitewashed houses, and countless coats of arms.

Founded by the Greeks, the city of Valencia was in Moorish hands from 712 to 1238, apart from a brief interlude from 1094 to 1102, when El Cid reconquered it. Colorful *azulejos* (glazed, patterned tiles) and bright-blue church cupolas reflect Moorish traditions here. Spain's golden age left striking souvenirs of the 15th century as well: the Gothic

Lonja (Silk Exchange) and mansions, and the primitive paintings of Jacomart and Juan Reixach in the Museum of Fine Arts. The flamboyant Palacio del Marqués de Dos Aguas embodies the vitality of Churrigueresque, the early Spanish baroque.

EXPLORING THE COSTA BRAVA TO VALENCIA

Named for its wild and rugged coastline, the Costa Brava contains some of the most pristine water in Spain. Volcanic cliffs tower over bays dotted with yachts and snorkelers. There's no secret this is where Salvador Dalígot his inspiration. His birthplace, Figures, is home to his wacky museum, and the whitewashed sea town of Cadaques is home to his even wackier residence.

The ancient city of Tarragona—with a Roman amphitheater and aqueduct—infuses the northern wedge of Southern Catalonia with a medieval flavor. Southwest of Tarragona are the wetlands of the Ebro Delta, rich in birdlife. Inland lies the rugged Sierra de Beceite mountains and the walled town of Morella. The Ebro River snakes its way through the interior, passing through the historical town of Tortosa. Southern Catalonia's interior is best accessed by car, as the bus and trains have limited routes. South of Tortosa, lively resort towns—including Benicarló, Peñíscola, and Benicàssim—dot the Costa del Azahar. The region's crown jewel is artistic Valencia, perched on the southern end of the Costa del Azahar.

ABOUT THE BEACHES

Beaches here are endless swaths of fine-grain sand. At the northern end of the region, are the pristine bays and beaches of the Costa Brava. San Pol has plenty of space and tranquillity. Roses can often get too crowded but Palafrugell offers a nice hidden away alternative. If it's tucked away coves you're after, head up to the Cap de Creus national park.

8

Salou has the best beaches, along with a lively, palm-lined promenade. More tranquil are the beaches of the Delta de l'Ebre (Ebro Delta), the best of which is Playa de los Eucaliptos, reached by a scenic road from Amposta via Montells. There are views of the wetlands and, as you approach the beach, of the sea. Peñíscola's beach seems to go on forever—the sand is soft, and the old city rises out of the sea at one end. Alcocéber has a series of small uncrowded sandy crescents, and just to its north is the sophisticated marina at Las Fuentes. Benicàssim's long, crescent-shape beach is the most dramatic, with mountains rising steeply in the background. Valencia itself has a long beach that's wonderful for sunning and has numerous restaurants, but it's not the best place to swim; for cleaner water, head south to El Saler near Valencia.

ABOUT THE RESTAURANTS

The Alt Amporda region, taking in the Costa Brava and its surrounding inland areas, has a justifiably renowned reputation for food. It's home to some of the country's premier restaurants and—in the case of super chef Ferran Adrià's El Bulli—the world's greatest restaurant. The seafood in this region is excellent and it has a deserved reputation for the best anchovies in Spain.

In and around Valencia, indeed all along the Mediterranean coast, you're in the homeland of *paella valenciana*—a hearty rice dish flavored with saffron and embellished with seafood, poultry, meat, peas, and peppers. Prepared to order in a *caldero* (shallow pan), paella takes a full 20 minutes to cook, so it's not for when you're in a hurry. Good paella is fabulous, but it's often overpriced because of tourist demand, and it's usually best not to choose paella from a *menú del día*—it'll probably be bland and disappointing. For the optimum experience, find a restaurant that specializes in paella, one where you can be sure of the freshest ingredients. A variant is *arroz a la banda,* in which the fish and rice are cooked separately; the fish is fried in garlic, onion, and tomato, and the rice is boiled in the resulting stock. *Romesco,* a spicy blend of almonds, peppers, and olive oil, is used as a fish and seafood sauce in Tarragona, especially during the *calçotada* (spring onion) feasts of February. If you're here for September's Santa Tecla festival, look for *espineta amb cargolins* (tuna with snails), perhaps accompanied by some excellent wine from the nearby Penedés or Priorato vineyard. The Ebro Delta is renowned for its fresh fish and eels, as well as specialties such as *rossejat* (fried rice in a fish broth, dressed with garlic sauce). *Jamones* (hams), *cecinas* (smoked meats), and *carnes a la brasa* (meats cooked over coals) are all staples of cooking in the Maestrazgan mountain range, along with good *trucha* (trout), *conejo* (rabbit), and local *trufas* (truffles).

ABOUT THE HOTELS

In Girona, boutique hotels are springing up everywhere and generally offer a good value alternative to the more impersonal larger hotels. Accommodations in beach resorts on the Costa Brava like Roses are often more expensive. A good alternative if you're planning on driving around and exploring inland Northern Catalonia is to seek out masias, adapted farmhouses that are often more kid-friendly and located in less touristy areas. Antique, one-of-a-kind lodgings are in gratifying abundance on the Ebro Delta and in the Maestrazgo Mountains. On the shore, hotels are more mundane, with modern high-rises predominating. Tarragona has several standard hotels. Just north and south of Valencia, the towns of Puzol and El Saler have some famous luxury properties; the city itself offers a reasonable mix of hotels. Book your room months in advance if you plan to be in Valencia during Las Fallas (mid-March).

Numbers in the text correspond to numbers in the margin and on the chapter maps.

NORTHERN CATALONIA

Northern Catalonia is for many *the* reason to visit Spain. Girona plays little sister to Barcelona and is these days for many travelers an obligatory stopover for those arrving from the United Kingdom on cheap

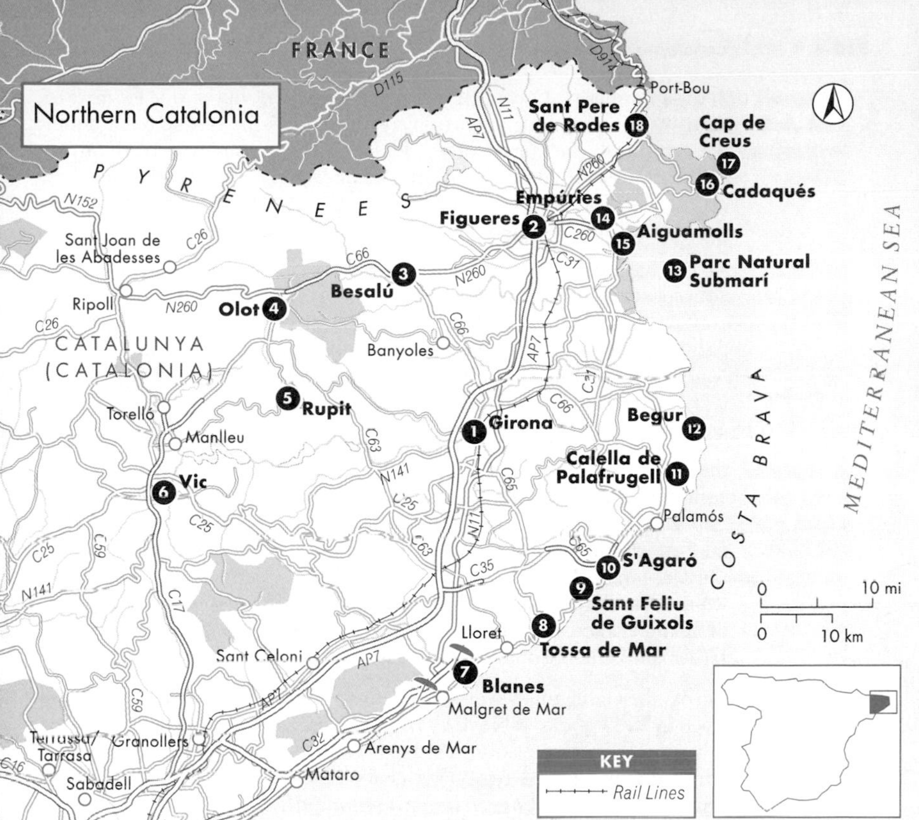

flights. With a Jewish quarter that rivals Mallorca's, Girona's old center is remarkeably well preserved. Restaurants lose nothing in comparison with Barcelona and the new influx of immigration into the city over the past 15 years is diversifying its cuisine.

The nearby towns of Besalu and Figueres couldn't be more different. Figueres is an unexceptional town made exceptional by the Dali Musuem. Besalu is a jewel of a town a Romanic cluster that protrudes on a cliff and leaves you gaping at its beauty. It also happens to have some of the most prestigous restaurants in all of Catalonia. Eating in them won't come cheap, but you'll eat well.

Less well known are the medieval towns in and around La Garrtotxa areas. Ripoll, Rupit, and Olot all hold wonderful surprises and probably boast the best produce in the region.

GIRONA

1 *97 km (60 mi) northeast of Barcelona.*

Walk along the river to Plaça de la Independencia and admire Girona's best-known view of pastel yellow, pink, and orange waterfront facades, their windows draped with a colorful mix of drying laundry reflected in the shimmering Onyar. (If you drive here, park in the free lot next to the River Onyar, under the train trestle.) Cross the bridge from under the arcades in the corner of the Plaça and find your way to the tourist office, to the right at La Rambla Llibertat 1. Then work your way up through the labyrinth of steep streets, using the cathedral's huge baroque facade as a guide, leading to the stunning Jewish quarter.

At the base of the Girona cathedral's 90 steps and left through the Sobreportes gate are the **Banys Arabs,** or Arab Baths. Built by Morisco craftsmen in the late 12th century, long after Girona's Islamic occupation (795–1015) had ended, the baths are both Romanesque and Moorish in design. *€2.50 Apr–Sept., Mon.–Sat. 10–7, Sun. 10–2; Oct.–Mar., Tues.–Sun. 10–2.*

A five-minute walk from the cathedral leads to the **Torre de Gironella,** the highest point in the Jewish quarter. It was here that Girona's Jewish community took refuge in August 1391, emerging 17 weeks later to find their houses in ruins. Even though Spain's expulsion decree didn't take effect until 1492, this attack ended the Girona Jewish community. On December 20, 1998, the first Hanukkah celebration in 607 years was held in the gardens, with representatives of the Jewish communities of Spain, France, Portugal, Germany, and the United States present and Jerusalem's chief Sephardic rabbi, Rishon Letzion, presiding.

Across the Galligants River is the church of **Sant Pere** *(Holy Father)*, finished in 1131 and notable for its octagonal belfry and the detailed capitals atop the cloister columns. Next door is the **Museu Arqueològic,** which documents the region's archaeological history since Paleolithic times. *€1.,80 Church and museum daily 10:30–1:30 and 4–5.*

To see the inside of Girona's **cathedral,** designed by Guillem Bofill in 1416, do a loop around it. The cathedral is known for its immense, uncluttered Gothic nave, which, at 75 feet, is the widest in the world and the epitome of the spatial ideal of Catalan Gothic architects. The **museum** contains the famous *Tapis de la Creació* (*Tapestry of the Creation*) and a 10th-century copy of Beatus's manuscript *Commentary on the Apocalypse*. The stepped Passeig Arqueològic runs below the walls of the Old City; climb through the Jardins de la Francesa to the highest ramparts for a view of the 11th-century Romanesque **Torre de Carlemany** (Charlemagne Tower), the oldest part of the cathedral. *€3 Oct.–June, daily 9:30–1:15 and 3:30–7; July–Sept., daily 9:30–7.*

Next door to Girona's cathedral is the **Palau Episcopal** (Bishop's Palace), which houses the **Museu d'Art,** a good mix of Romanesque, Catalan Gothic, and modern art. *€3 Tues.–Sat. 10–7, Sun. 10–1.*

What was once the cramped and squalid center of the 13th-century *Call,* or Jewish quarter, is the sight of the **Centre Bonastruc ça Porta,** the lifeblood of the activities that refer to the recuperation of the Jewish heritage of Girona. Its **Museu de Història dels Jueus** (Museum of Jewish History) has 21 stone tablets, one of the finest collections in the world of medieval Jewish funerary slabs. *Carrer de la Força 8 972/216761 €3 Tues.–Sat. 10–2 and 4–7, Sun. 10–2.*

The **Museu d'Història de la Ciutat,** on Carrer de la Força, is filled with memorabilia from Girona's long and embattled past, from pre-Roman objects to paintings and drawings from the notorious siege at the hands of Napoléonic troops to the early municipal lighting system and the medieval printing press. ✉*Carrer de la Força 27* ☎*972/222229* 🌐*www.ajuntament.gi/museu_ciutat* 🎫*€3* ⏲*May–Sept., Mon.–Sat. 10–8, Sun. 10–3; Oct.–Apr., Mon.–Sat. 10–6, Sun. 10–3.*

The interactive **Museu del Cinema** has artifacts and movie-related paraphernalia going all the way back to Chinese shadows, the first rudimentary moving pictures. Look for the Cine Nic toy filmmaking machines, originally developed in 1931 by the Nicolau brothers of Barcelona and now being relaunched commercially. ✉*Carrer Sèquia 1* ☎*972/412777* 🌐*www.museudelcinema.org* 🎫*€4* ⏲*May–Sept., Mon.–Sat. 10–8, Sun. 10–3; Oct.–Apr., Mon.–Sat. 10–6, Sun. 10–3.*

WHERE TO STAY & EAT

$$$–$$$$ Fodor'sChoice ★ ✕**El Celler de Can Roca.** Girona's best restaurant and one of Catalonia's top six, this unusual, spacious, and elegantly simple spot west of town might serve anything from steak tartare with mustard ice cream to simple *vieiras* (scallops) with peas or a surf and turf of *pies de porc amb espardenyes* (trotters with sea slugs). ✉*Ctra. Taialà 40, 2 km (1½ mi) west of Girona, Sant Gregori first roundabout to Taialà* ☎*972/222157* 🌐*www.cellercanroca.com* 💳*AE, DC, MC, V* ⏲*Closed Dec. 23–Jan. 15, 1st 2 wks in July, and Sun. and Mon.*

$$–$$$ ★ ✕**Cal Ros.** Tucked under the arcades just behind the north end of Plaça de la Llibertat, this perennial favorite combines ancient stone arches with a crisp, contemporary interior and cheerful lighting. The cuisine is gamy and delicious: hot goat-cheese salad with pine nuts and *garum* (black-olive-and-anchovy paste dating back to Roman times), *oca amb naps* (goose with turnips), and a blackberry sorbet not to miss. ✉*C. Cort Reial 9* ☎*972/217379* 💳*AE, DC, MC, V* ⏲*Closed Mon. No dinner Sun.*

$$$ ★ 🏨**Hotel Històric y Apartaments Històric Girona.** This snappy boutique hotel has one room (the suite) with views of the cathedral and Gothic vaulting overhead. The apartments, in a 9th-century house, include parts of a 3rd-century Roman wall and a Roman aqueduct on the ground floor and in one of the apartments. One dining room even contains a wall made in the pre-Romanesque *opus spicatum* herringbone pattern. Casilda Cruz rents these good-value apartments in the old quarter for as many days as you'd like, from one day to one month. ✉*Carrer Bellmirall 4A, 17004* ☎*972/223583* 📠*972/200932* 🌐*www.hotelhistoric.com* *8 rooms, 7 apartments, 1 suite* *In-room: kitchen. In-hotel: restaurant* 💳*AE, DC, MC, V.*

$$ 🏨**Bellmirall.** Gorgeously cute, this inn across the Onyar in the Jewish quarter offers top value in the heart of Girona's most historic section. ✉*Carrer Bellmirall 3, 17001* ☎*972/204009* *7 rooms* *In-room: no a/c* 💳*AE, DC, MC, V* ⏲*Closed Jan. and Feb.*

8

CLOSE UP

Catalonia's National Dance

The *sardana*, Catalonia's national dance, is often perceived as anything but exuberant, a solemn and dainty affair usually danced by senior citizens in front of the Barcelona Cathedral at midday on weekends. Look for an athletic young *colla* (troupe), though, and you will see the grace and fluidity the sardana can create. The long faces and intense concentration are the result of the mathematical precision of a dance consisting of 76 steps in sets of four, each dancer needing to know exactly where he or she is at all times. The Basque fandango or the Aragonese jota are athletic explosions of joy, whereas the sardana is melancholic, reflective, and subtle.

Said to be a representation of the passing of time, a choreography of the orbits and revolutions of the moon and stars, the circular sardana is recorded in Greek chronicles dating back 2,000 years. The name of the dance may have come from the 14th-century Catalan colony on the Mediterranean island of Sardinia, though the alternate spelling *cerdana* suggests it may have originated in the Pyrenean Cerdanya valley.

Pep Ventura, famous *tenora* (oboe) master and sardana composer, made his debut in 1837; the sardana's popularity skyrocketed with Ventura's own. Performed in circles of all sizes and of dancers of all ages, the sardana is accompanied by the *cobla* (sardana combo), five wind instruments, five brass, and the director, who plays a three-holed flute called the *flabiol* and a small drum, the *tabal,* which he wears attached to his flute arm, normally the right. The sardana, for all its delicate primness and numerical rigor, never fails to communicate a strong emotion, a combination of nostalgia and *enyorança,* a sense of longing for old traditions and glories past and future.

FIGUERES

2 *37 km (23 mi) north of Girona on the A7.*

This bustling country town is the capital of the Alt Empordà (Upper Ampurdan). Take a walk along the Figueres Rambla, scene of the *passeig* (*paseo* in Castilian; the constitutional midday or evening stroll), and have a coffee in one of several traditional cafés. The **Teatre-Museu Dalí** pays spectacular homage to a unique artist. The museum is installed in a former theater next to the bizarre, ocher-color Torre Galatea, where Dalí lived until his death in 1989. The remarkable Dalí collection includes a vintage Cadillac with ivy-cloaked passengers whom you can water for less than a euro. Dalí himself is entombed beneath the museum. ✉ *Pl. Gala-Salvador Dalí 5* ☎ *972/677500* 🌐 *www.salvador-dali.org* 🎟 *€10* ⏲ *Nov.–Feb., Tues.–Sun. 10:30–6; Mar.–May, Tues.–Sun. 9:30–6; June, daily 9:30–6, July–Sept., daily 9–8, Oct., Tues.–Sun. 9:30–6.*

WHERE TO STAY & EAT

$$$ Fodor'sChoice ★ ✕🏨 **Hotel Empordà.** A mile north of town, this hotel and elegant restaurant run by Jaume Subirós is hailed as the birthplace of modern Catalan cuisine and has become a pilgrimage destination for foodies

seeking superb French, Catalan, and Spanish cooking ($$$–$$$$). Try the *terrina calenta de lluerna a l'oli de cacauet* (hot pot of gurnard fish in peanut oil) or, if it's winter, *llebre a la Royal* (boned hare cooked in red wine). Guest rooms have parquet floors and sparkling bathrooms, and you can sit in the sun and have a drink on the terrace. The hotel is 1½ km (1 mi) north of town. ✉*Antiga Carretera de França s/n, 17600* ☎*972/500562* 📠*972/509358* 🌐*www.hotelemporda.com* *42 rooms* *In-hotel: restaurant, bar, some pets allowed* ▭*AE, DC, MC, V.*

SALVADOR DALI SITES

Artist Salvador Dalí is entombed beneath the Teatre-Museu Dalí, in Figueres. His former home, a castle in Pubol, is where his wife, Gala, is buried. His summer home in Port Lligat Bay, north of Cadaqués, is now a museum focused on the surrealist's life and work.

$$–$$$ ✕ **Hotel Duràn.** Once a stagecoach relay station, the Duràn is now a hotel and restaurant ($–$$) open every day of the year. Salvador Dalí had his own private dining room here, and you can take a meal amid pictures of the great surrealist. Try the *mandonguilles amb sepia al estil Anna* (meatballs and cuttlefish), a *mar i muntanya* (surf-and-turf) specialty of the house. ✉*C. Lasauca 5, 17600* ☎*972/501250* 📠*972/502609* 🌐*www.hotelduran.com* *65 rooms* *In-hotel: restaurant, bar, parking (fee)* ▭*AE, MC, V.*

BESALÚ

❸ *34 km (21 mi) north of Girona.*

Once the capital of a feudal county as part of Charlemagne's 8th- and 9th-century Spanish March, Besalú is 25 km (15 mi) west of Figueres on C260. This ancient town's most emblematic sight is its **fortified bridge,** complete with crenellated battlements. **Sant Vicenç** (✉*Carrer de Sant Vicenç s/n*) is Besalú's best Romanesque church. The church of **Sant Pere** (✉*Pl. de Sant Pere s/n*) is all that remains of the 10th-century Benedictine monastery torn down in 1835. The ruins of the convent of **Santa Maria** on the hill above town are a panoramic vantage point over Besalú. The **tourist office** (☎*972/591240*) in the arcaded Plaça de la Llibertat can provide opening hours for Sant Pere as well as keys to the *miqwe*, the rare **Jewish baths** discovered in the 1960s. A **Tren Turistic** leaves from the bridge every 45 minutes and visits the baths and the two churches for a cost of €3. The extraordinary town of **Castellfollit de la Roca** perches on its prowlike basalt cliff over the Fluvià River 16 km (10 mi) west of Besalú.

WHERE TO EAT

$$–$$$$ ★ ✕ **Els Fogons de Can Llaudes.** A faithfully restored 11th-century Romanesque chapel holds proprietor Jaume Soler's outstanding restaurant, one of Catalonia's best. A typical main dish is *confitat de bou amb patates al morter i raïm glacejat* (beef confit with glacé grapes, served with mashed potatoes with nutmeg). The *menú de degustación* (tasting menu) is recommended; call at least one day in advance to reserve this

menu. ✉Prat de Sant Pere 6 ☎972/590858 ⚠Reservations essential ▭AE, MC, V ⊙Closed Tues. and Nov.

OLOT

❹ *21 km (13 mi) west of Besalú, 55 km (34 mi) northwest of Girona, 130 km (78 mi).*

Capital of the Garrotxa area, Olot is famous for its 19th-century school of landscape painters and has several excellent Art Nouveau buildings, including one with a facade by Moderniste master Lluís Domènech i Montaner. The **Museu Comarcal de la Garrotxa** *(County Museum of La Garrotxa)* has an assemblage of Moderniste art and sculptures by Miquel Blai, creator of the long-tressed maidens who support the balconies on Olot's main boulevard. ✉*Carrer Hospici 8* ☎*972/279130* 🎟*€3* ⊙*Mon. and Wed.–Sat. 11–2 and 4–7 Closed Tues. and public holidays.*

The villages of **Vall d'En Bas** lie south of Olot off A153. The twisting old road goes past farmhouses whose dark wooden balconies are bedecked with bright flowers. Turn off for **Sant Privat d'En Bas** for a step back in time. The village of **Els Hostalets d'En Bas** eloquently defines rustic. A modern freeway cuts across this countryside to Vic, but you'll miss a lot by taking it.

WHERE TO STAY & EAT

$$–$$$$ ✕ **Restaurante Ramón.** Ramon's eponymous restaurant is the opposite of rustic: sleek, modern, refined, and international. Samples of the *cuina de la terra* (home cooking of regional specialties) include *patata de Olot* (potato stuffed with veal) and *cassoleta de judias amb xoriç* (white haricot with sausage). ✉*Carrer Bolós 22* ☎*972/261001* ⚠*Reservations essential* ▭*AE, DC, MC, V* ⊙*Closed Thurs.*

$$–$$$ 🏨 **Mas les Comellas.** One of the new breed of agri-tourism lodgings that are booming in the Garrotxa area, Mas de Comellas has set the bar very high since it opened in late 2006. The 15th-century farmhouse is set in the rolling green plains of La Vall d'en Bas outside of Olot, and from the moment you arrive owner Maria Angeles and the Casals family greet you with kisses and hugs, going out of their way to ensure you have a five-star experience. The five double rooms are superbly decorated; the common areas by the open fire, in the lounge room, and by the pool are cleverly thought out; and the food is five-star value but at much more accessible prices. It's a great place to bring kids of all ages—there's horseback riding, cow milking, trekking, and hot air ballooning nearby. A nice touch is the minicinema complex in the entertainment room with a DVD player and English-language TV channels. ✉*Joanetes s/n, Vall d'en Bas, La Garrotxa, Girona, 17176* ☎*628/617759* 📠*972/270774* *5 rooms* *In room: Wi-Fi, DVD. In-hotel: pool* ▭*AE, DC, MC, V.*

(Margin: Fodor's Choice ★)

RUPIT

5 *33 km (20 mi) south of Olot, 97 km (60 mi) north of Barcelona.*

Rupit is a spectacular stop for its medieval houses and its food, the highlight of which is beef-stuffed potatoes. Built into a rocky promontory over a stream in the rugged Collsacabra region (about halfway from Olot to Vic), the town has some of the most aesthetically perfect **stone houses** in Catalonia, some of which were reproduced for Barcelona's "Spain-in-a-bottle" miniature architectural sampler, Poble Espanyol, for the 1929 International Exposition.

WHERE TO STAY & EAT

$–$$ Fodor's Choice ★ **El Repòs.** Hanging over the river that runs through Rupit, this restaurant ($–$$$) serves the best meat-stuffed potatoes around. Ordering a meal is easy: just learn the word *patata.* Other specialties include duck and lamb. Rooms are rustic but cozy. *C. Barbacana 1 93/852–2100 11 rooms AE, DC, MC, V Closed weekdays Oct.–Easter. Will open by arrangement.*

VIC

6 *66 km (41 mi) north of Barcelona.*

Known for its conservatism and Catalan nationalism, Vic rests on a 1,600-foot plateau at the confluence of two rivers and serves as the area's commercial, industrial, and agricultural hub. The wide **Plaça Major,** surrounded by Gothic arcades and well supplied with bars and cafés, perfectly expresses the city's personality. Vic's religiosity is demonstrated by its 35 churches, of which the largely neoclassical **cathedral** (*Pl. de la Catedral s/n 93/886–4449 €1 Daily 10–1 and 4–7*) has a fine collection of religious relics.

8

WHERE TO EAT

$$–$$$$ **Art de Coch.** Named for Catalonia's first medieval cookbook, this central location a few steps from Vic's Plaça Major serves modern versions of antique recipes, as the early Catalan would suggest. The interior patio is intimate and quiet, and the cuisine is carefully elaborated with fresh market products. *Sant Miquel dels Sants 1 93/886–4033 AE, DC, MC, V Closed Mon. and 1st 2 wks in Sept. No dinner Sun.*

$$–$$$ **Ca l'U.** Translated as "The One," Ca l'U is in fact *the* place in Vic for hearty local cuisine with a minimum of pretense. Try the *llangostinos i llenguado* (prawns and sole) or the regional standard, *botifarra i mongetas* (sausage and beans). *Pl. Santa Teresa 4–5 93/886–3504 MC, V Closed Mon. No dinner Sun.*

THE COSTA BRAVA

The Costa Brava (Wild Coast) is a rocky stretch of shoreline that begins at Blanes and continues north through 135 km (84 mi) of coves and beaches to the French border at Port Bou. This tour concentrates on selected pockets—Tossa, Cap de Begur, Cadaqués—where the rocky terrain has discouraged the worst excesses of real-estate speculation. Here, on a good day, the luminous blue of the sea still contrasts with red-brown headlands and cliffs; the distant lights of fishing boats reflect on wine-color waters at dusk; and umbrella pines escort you to the fringes of secluded *calas* (coves) and sandy white beaches.

COSTA BRAVA BEACHES & SITES

7 The beaches closest to Barcelona are at **Blanes** (✉*Crucetours* ☎*972/314969*), where small boats can take you to Cala de Sant Francesc or the double beach at Santa Cristina between May and October.

8 The next stop north from Blanes on the coast road is **Tossa de Mar,** christened "Blue Paradise" by painter Marc Chagall, who summered here in 1934. The only Chagall painting in Spain, Celestial Violinist, is in Tossa's **Museu Municipal** (*Municipal Museum* ☎*972/340709*), open Tuesday–Sunday 10–1 and 5–8. Admission is €3.50. Tossa's walled **medieval town** and pristine beaches are among Catalonia's best.

9 **Sant Feliu de Guixols** follows Tossa de Mar, after 23 km (15 mi) of hairpin curves over hidden inlets. Tiny turnouts or parking spots on this route nearly always lead to intimate coves with stone stairways winding down from the road. Visit Sant Feliu's two fine beaches, church and monastery, Sunday market, and lovely **Passeig del Mar.**

10 **S'Agaró,** one of the Costa Brava's best clusters of seaside mansions, is 3 km (2 mi) north of Sant Feliu. The 30-minute walk along the **sea wall** from Hostal de La Gavina to Sa Conca Beach is a delight. Likewise, the one-hour hike from Sant Pol Beach over to Sant Feliu de Guixols for lunch and back is a superb look at the Costa Brava at its best.

11 Up the coast from S'Agaró, a road leads east to **Llafranc,** a small port with quiet waterfront hotels and restaurants, and forks right to **Calella de Palafrugell,** a pretty fishing village known for its July Habaneras festival. (*Habaneras* are Catalan-Cuban sea chanties inspired by the Spanish-American War.) Just south is the panoramic promontory **Cap Roig,** with views of the barren Formigues (Ants) Isles and a fine botanical garden that you can tour with a guide March–December, daily 9–9, for €4. The left fork drops down to **Tamariu,** one of the Costa's prettiest inlet towns. A climb over the bluff leads down to the parador at **Aiguablava,** a modern eyesore overlooking magnificent cliffs and crags.

12 From **Begur,** north of Aiguablava, you can go east through the *calas* or take the inland route past the rose-color stone houses and ramparts of the restored medieval town of **Pals.** Nearby **Peratallada** is another medieval town with fortress, castle, tower, palace, and well-preserved walls. North of Pals there are signs for **Ullastret,** an Iberian village dating from the 5th century BC.

Continued on page 522

El Bulli's Letter Soup

SPAIN'S FOOD REVOLUTION

If milkshake waterfalls, bite-sized soup squares, and smoking cocktails sound like mouthwatering menu items, you may be ready to pull up a chair at the adventurous table of *la nueva cocina*. You won't be sitting alone: Foodies worldwide are lining up for reservations at Spain's hottest restaurants.

The movement, variously termed "*la nueva cocina*" (the new kitchen), "molecular gastronomy," or "avant-garde cooking," is characterized by the exploration of new techniques, resulting in dishes that defy convention. By playing with the properties of food, chefs can turn solids into liquid, and liquid into air. Olive oil "caviar," hot ice cream, and carrot-juice noodles are just a few of the alchemic manifestations of taste, texture, and temperature that have emerged. Ferran Adrià of El Bulli in Roses is widely credited as the creative force behind Spain's new culinary movement, but chefs throughout the country have followed his lead. Beyond Spain, the movement is already having a seismic impact on the international culinary scene. Chefs from other European countries and the Americas have shifted their focus, looking beyond France—long esteemed as the world's culinary vanguard—to Spain for new techniques and inspiration.—*Erica Duecy*

FERRAN ADRIÀ—*LA NUEVA COCINA'S* VISIONARY

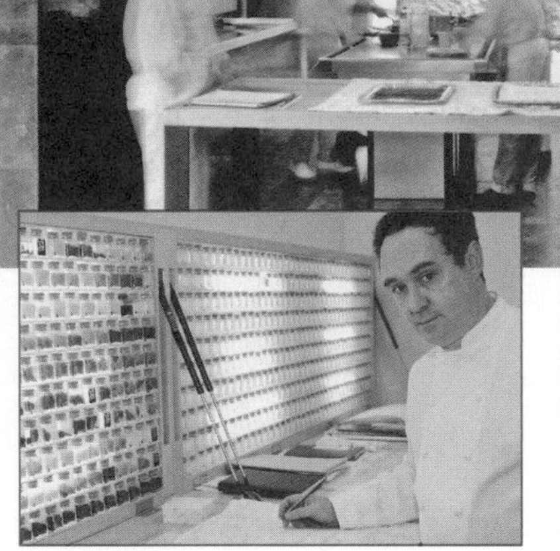

(clockwise from top left): Adrià's spiral of black sesame-seed crunch with coconut ice cream; razor-clam sushi with ginger spray; curry-glazed kaffir lime leaves; beet chips with vinegar powder; the El Bulli kitchen; Adrià in his Barcelona workshop.

Adrià has often been called the world's top chef, but his rise to fame didn't happen overnight. Adrià was an emerging talent in 1987 when he attended a cooking demonstration by legendary French chef Jacques Maximin who spoke about his belief that "creativity means not copying." By Adrià's account, that statement transformed his approach to cooking.

The changeover to conceptual cuisine—where techniques and concepts became the driving force for Adrià's creativity—occurred in 1994, when he developed a technique for producing dense foam from various liquids. A handful of new techniques emerged in those early years, but "nowadays, that process is accelerated," he says. "Within one year, I am working with several types of techniques."

Some of Adrià's most famous dishes include puffed rice paella, Parmesan marshmallows, a cocktail of frozen gin and hot lemon fizz, mini cuttlefish ravioli with bursting pockets of coconut and ginger, and almond ice cream swirled with garlic oil and balsamic vinegar. These creative concoctions are served at El Bulli in meals of 25 to 30 courses, with each course no more than a few bites.

GETTING THERE

Reservations are booked a year in advance for Ferran Adrià's El Bulli restaurant in Roses, located about 175 km north of Barcelona, set on an isolated beach. The El Bulli Web site features a comprehensive photo catalog of Ferran Adrià's creations from 1985 to present: www.elbulli.com El Bulli, Cala Montjoi. Ap. 30 17480. Girona. 972/150457.

TRICKS OF THE TRADE

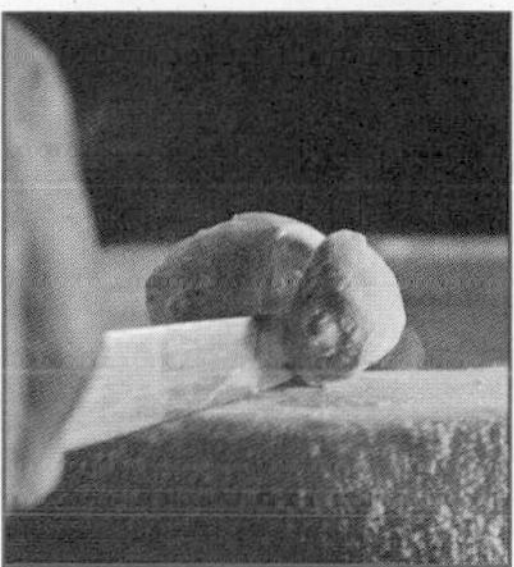

(clockwise from top left): Dry ice changes from a solid directly to a gas without becoming liquid; liquid nitrogen boils in a glass container at room temperature; a nitro-cooled pistachio truffle; a nitro-cooled caipirinha with tarragon essence.

Many techniques of *la nueva cocina* are borrowed from the food processing industry, including the use of liquid nitrogen, dry ice, and gellifying agents. This technological approach to cooking may seem like a departure from Spain's ingredient-driven cuisine, but avant-garde chefs say their creations are no less rooted in Spanish culture than traditional fare like paella.

One leading chef, Juan Mari Arzak, describes his approach as "not traditional Basque cooking, but rather culturally influenced cooking from the region, using the products of the region," he says. "We are doing things that haven't been done before." Using *lyophilization*, a freeze-drying technique, Arzak makes powders from peanuts and licorice. "You use the powder to add flavor to things," he says. "If you dust tuna with peanut powder and salt, it concentrates the underlying flavors to make the tuna taste like a more intense version of tuna."

Additionally, an unprecedented spirit of collaboration has defined the movement. "It is true that in other culinary movements chefs have been reluctant to share their knowledge," Adrià says. "Some people ask us, why do you share everything? Why do you share your secrets? The answer is that that's the way we understand cooking—that it's meant to be shared."

HOW DO THEY DO IT?

Daniel Garcia at El Calima using liquid nitrogen.

Liquid nitrogen: Just a small amount of this cryogenic fluid can be used to make instant ice cream from any liquid, including olive oil. Because liquid nitrogen can cause frostbite if it touches exposed skin, excess amounts of the substance must be allowed to evaporate before the food is served.

Dry ice: Bubbling sauces and cascading milk shakes can be made by adding dry ice to a liquid so it bubbles over the rim of its container.

Gellifiers: Fruit and vegetable juices can be used to make noodles with this technique. When juice is mixed with methylcellulose, a thickening compound derived from cellulose, it solidifies and can be extruded through a thin tube to form noodles.

Freeze-drying: The technique behind freeze-dried ice cream and soups is used to create concentrated powders from items like ham and berries. First, the substance is frozen in a controlled environment. Then, the pressure is lowered while applying heat so the frozen water in the substance becomes a gas.

THE SPANISH ARMADA

Among the most recognized contributors to *la nueva cocina* are Juan Mari Arzak, Martín Berasategui, Alberto Chicote, Quique Dacosta, Daniel García, Joan Roca, and Paco Roncero.

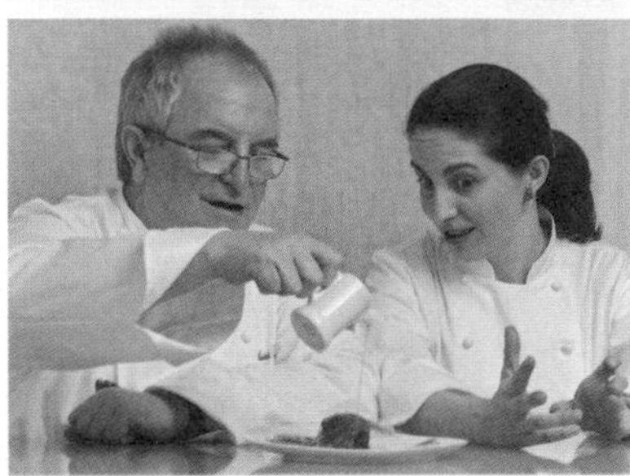

Chef Juan Mari Arzak and his daughter Elena.

Juan Mari Arzak is recognized for modernizing and reinvigorating Basque cuisine at Restaurante Arzak in San Sebastián, which he now operates with his daughter Elena, who represents the fourth generation of Arzak restaurateurs. Despite his deep culinary roots and decades-long career, Arzak says he works to maintain a fresh perspective. "It's important to look at the world through a cook's eyes, but to think like a little kid," he says. "Because when you are a boy, you have the capacity to be amazed and surprised." Restaurante Arzak, ✉ Avda. Alcalde Jose Elosegui, 273 / 20015 Donostia / San Sebastian. ☎ 943/278465. 🌐 www.arzak.info.

At his eponymous fine-dining restaurant in Lasarte, **Martín Berasategui** is known for his dedication to local products and fresh flavors. Notable dishes have included foie gras, smoked eel, and apple terrine; and *percebes,* goose barnacles served with fresh peas in vegetable broth. Martín Berasategui, ✉ Calle Loidi, 4 / E-20160 Lasarte-Oria. ☎ 943/366471. 🌐 www.martinberasategui.com.

The cuisine at **Alberto Chicote's** Nodo fuses Spanish and Japanese ingredients and techniques. His version of tuna tataki, for example, features seared tuna, which is macerated in soy sauce and rice vinegar then chopped and served with chilled garlic cream, and garnished with drops of olive oil and black olive powder. Nodo, ✉ Calle Velázquez 150, Retiro/Salamanca, Madrid. ☎ 915/644044.

Quique Dacosta is the inventive self-taught chef at the helm of El Poblet in Dénia, a coastal town in the Alicante region. The restaurant specializes in contemporary seafood but can veer also into highly conceptual fare like his "Guggenheim Bilbao oysters," a dish of shimmering oysters in barnacle stock, glazed with a sauce made from aloe vera, agar agar (a seaweed-based gellifier), and powdered silver. El Poblet, ✉ Ctra Les Marines, km. 3, Dénia. ☎ 965.784179. 🌐 www.elpoblet.com.

IT'S AN ADVENTURE

Puffed-rice paella may not be a dish that appeals to every diner. But try to view the experience as an exploration of the palate, and a teaser for the mind. Practitioners of *la nueva cocina* typically serve their creative concoctions in small servings over several courses, a presentation style meant to stimulate a thoughtful, conscious eating experience. Sure, customers may not like everything they put into their mouths, but still they come to be dazzled by the bold flavors and unexpected textures. Don't be surprised to see diners exclaim in delight and awe as they dive into these new sensory experiences.

In his early 30s, **Daniel García** is one of the younger practitioners of *la nueva cocina*, as well as head chef at El Calima, the restaurant in the Hotel Don Pepe in Marbella. "My cultural inspiration comes from the area where I work, in Andalusia, the south of Spain," he says. Acclaimed dishes include gazpacho with anchovies and *queso fresco* snow, and a passion fruit flan with herb broth and eucalyptus-thyme essence. Hotel Gran Meliá Don Pepe, ✉ Ave. José Meliá, Marbella. ☎ 952/764252.

Joan Roca is chef at El Celler de Can Roca in Girona, which he runs with his two brothers, Josep and Jordi. Roca is known for his work exploring the intersection between aroma and flavor, with dishes such as his "Adaptation of the Perfume *Angel* by Thierry Mugler," featuring cream of toffee, chocolate, gelée of violet and bergamot, and red fruits ice cream with vanilla. Savories include smoked lemon prawn with green peas and liquorice, and white and green asparagus with cardamom oil and truffles. El Celler de Can Roca, ✉ Carretera de Taialá. ☎ 972/222157. 🌐 www.cellercanroca.com.

Chefs in action, demonstrating their creativity in the kitchen: (top) Alberto Chicote with his assistants; (bottom) Martín Berasategui.

Paco Roncero is chef at La Terraza del Casino in Madrid, one of the city's most acclaimed establishments. He is considered one of Ferran Adrià's most outstanding students. "When I started working with Ferran (in 1998), my whole concept of cuisine changed," he says. "I started researching and trying to do new things. Now my cuisine is modern, *vanguardia*, without losing sight of tradition."

13 L'Estartit is the jumping-off point for the spectacular **Parc Natural Submarí** *(Underwater Natural Park)* by the Medes Isles, famous for diving and for underwater photography.

14 The Greco-Roman ruins at **Empúries** are Catalonia's most important archaeological site. This port, complete with breakwater, is one of the most monumental ancient engineering feats on the Iberian Peninsula. As the Greeks' original point of arrival in Spain, Empúries was also where the Olympic Flame entered Spain for Barcelona's 1992 Olympic Games.

15 The **Aiguamolls** *(Marshlands)*, a nature reserve with migratory waterfowl from all over Europe, lies mainly around **Castelló d'Empúries,** but the main information center is at El Cortalet, on the road in from Sant Pere Pescador. Follow the road from Empúries, crossing the Fluvià River at Sant Pere Pescador, and proceed north through the wetlands to Castelló. From Castelló d'Empúries, a series of roadways and footpaths traverses the marshes, the latter well marked on the information center's maps.

16 **Cadaqués,** Spain's easternmost town, still has the whitewashed charm that made this fishing village into an international artists' haunt in the early 20th century. The Marítim is the central hangout both day and night; after dark, you might also enjoy the Jardí, across the square. Salvador Dalí's house, now a museum, still stands at Port Lligat, a 30-minute walk north of town.

The **Casa Museu Salvador Dalí** was Dalí's summerhouse and a site long associated with the artist's notorious frolics with everyone from poets such as Federico García Lorca and Paul Eluard (whose wife, Gala, became Dalí's muse and spouse) to filmmaker Luis Buñuel. Filled with bits and pieces of the surrealist's daily life, it's an important point in the "Dalí triangle," completed by the castle at Pubol and the Museu Dalí, in Figueres. ✉ *3-km (2-mi) walk north from Cadaqués town center, along beach Port Lligat* ☎ *972/251015* 🌐 *www.salvador-dali.org* 🎫 *€10* ⏲ *By appointment, Mar. 15–Jan. 7, Tues.–Sun.*

The **Castillo Pubol,** Dalí's former castle-home, is now the resting place of Gala, his perennial model and mate. It's a chance to wander through yet more Dalíesque landscape: lush gardens, fountains decorated with masks of Wagner (the couple's favorite composer), and distinctive elephants with giraffe's legs and claw feet. Two lions and a giraffe stand guard near Gala's tomb. ✉ *Rte. 255 toward La Bisbal, 15 km (9 mi) east of A7* ☎ *972/488655* 🎫 *€10* ⏲ *Mar. 15–June 14 and Sept. 16–Jan. 6, Tues.–Sun. 10:30–5:15; June 15–Sept. 15, daily 10:30–8.*

17 **Cap de Creus,** north of Cadaqués, Spain's easternmost point, is a fundamental pilgrimage, if only for the symbolic geographical rush. The hike out to the lighthouse—through rosemary, thyme, and the salt air of the Mediterranean—is unforgettable. The Pyrenees officially end (or rise) here. New Year's Day finds mobs of revelers awaiting the first emergence of the "new" sun from the Mediterranean.

18 The monastery of **Sant Pere de Rodes,** 7 km (4½ mi) by car (plus a 20-minute walk) above the pretty fishing village El Port de la Selva, is the last site on the Costa Brava, and one of the most spectacular. Built in the 10th and early 11th centuries by Benedictine monks—and sacked and plundered repeatedly since—this Romanesque monolith, now being restored, commands a breathtaking panorama of the Pyrenees, the Empordà plain, the sweeping curve of the Bay of Roses, and Cap de Creus. (Topping off the grand trek across the Pyrenees, Cap de Creus is a spectacular six-hour walk from here on the well-marked GR-11 trail.)

WHERE TO STAY & EAT

$$$$ Fodor'sChoice ★ **El Bulli.** A gastronomic wonderland, this pleasant seaside hideaway has become a foodie's mecca—just don't show up without reservations: getting a table requires calling months in advance. If you do manage to get to the front of the 12-month waiting list, be prepared for a culinary spectacle you'll never forget. Without question it's become the world's most famous restaurant, and not without reason. El Bulli has revolutionized gastronomy around the world and put Spanish cuisine at the global cutting edge. Chef Ferran Adrià will make your palate his playground with a 35-course taster's menu that began with concepts such as *espuma de humo* (foam of smoke), progressed through rosewater bubbles and *aire de zanahoria con coco amargo* (air of carrot with bitter coconut), and has moved on past Ferran's recent passion in culinary chemistry: "freeze-frying" eggs in liquid nitrogen. Cala Montjoi is 7 km (4½ mi) southeast of Roses, the same distance from Cadaqués by boat or footpath and 22 km (14 mi) by car. *Cala Montjoi, Roses, Girona 972/150457 972/150717 www.elbulli.com Reservations essential AE, DC, MC, V Closed Oct.–Mar. No lunch.*

$$–$$$ **Can Pelayo.** This tiny, no-frills, family-run restaurant serves the best fish in Cadaqués. It's hidden behind Plaça Port Alguer, a few minutes' walk south of the town center. *Carrer Pruna 11, Cadaqués 972/258356 AE, DC, MC, V Closed weekdays Oct.–May.*

$$–$$$ **La Xicra.** Somewhat of an institution, this rustic, almost kitschy restaurant provides local fare that includes, in winter, *es niu*, a powerful combination of game fowl, fish tripe, pork meatballs, and cuttlefish, stewed in a rich sauce. *C/ Sant Antoni 17, Palafrugell 972/305630 www.restaurantlaxicra.com AE, DC, MC, V Closed Wed. and Nov. No dinner Tues.*

$–$$$ **Royal.** This sunny, beachside spot serves fisherman-style creations of impressive freshness and quality. The *suquet* (fish cooked slowly to create its own juice, or *suc*) is especially commendable. *Passeig de Mar 9, Tamariu 972/620041 MC, V.*

$$$–$$$$ **El Hostal de la Gavina.** At the eastern corner of Sant Pol beach in S'Agaró, La Gavina is a superb display of design and food founded in 1932 by Josep Ensesa, who invented S'Agaró itself. Fine comforts and dining ($$$–$$$$) are augmented by nearby tennis, golf, and horseback riding. *Pl. de la Rosaleda s/n, S'Agaró 17248 972/321100 972/321573 www.lagavina.com 58 rooms, 16 suites In-hotel: restaurant, bar, tennis courts, pool, gym AE, DC, MC, V Closed Nov.–Easter except Dec. 30–Jan. 2.*

8

$$–$$$ ★ ✕🏨 **Bar Cap de Creus.** Right next to the Cap de Creus lighthouse, this excellent Indian/Catalan restaurant ($–$$$) has spectacular views. It's open every day of the year, 9 AM–1 AM. The proprietor also rents three self-contained apartments (four beds each) upstairs. In Cadaqués itself, the owner can direct you to his very good Moroccan restaurant, Can Shelabi. ✉ *Cap de Creus, Carretera Cap De Creus, Cadaqués, 17488* ☎ *972/199005* 🌐 *www.cardamon.es* *3 apartments* *In-room: kitchen* ▭ *MC, V.*

$$ ✕🏨 **La Riera.** Built into a medieval house, this rustic hotel and restaurant ($–$$$) is a quiet hideaway in lovely Peratallada, near Begur. The dining room is in the former wine cellar, and the rooms have ceiling beams over painted ceramic tiles. Food includes such local specialties as *peu de porc amb cargols* (pig's feet with snails). ✉ *Pl. de les Voltes 3, Peratallada 17113* ☎ *972/634142* 📠 *972/635040* *8 rooms* *In-hotel: restaurant, bar* ▭ *AE, DC, MC, V.*

$$$ 🏨 **Playa Sol.** Open for more than 40 years, this hotel has the experience that comes with age. The rooms are done tastefully in red and ocher; some overlook the sea. The Playa Sol is in the cove of Es Pianc on the left side of the bay of Cadaqués as you face the sea, a five-minute walk from the village center. Boaters will love this place—all types of craft tie up here, thanks to Catalan writer Josep Pla who spread its fame as the best place to drop anchor in Cadaqués. ✉ *Platja Pianc 3, Cadaqués, Girona, 17488* ☎ *972/258100* 📠 *972/258054* 🌐 *www.playasol.com* *49 rooms* *In-hotel: restaurant, bar, pool* ▭ *AE, DC, MC, V* ⏲ *Closed mid-Dec.–mid-Feb.* 🍽 *BP.*

$$–$$$ 🏨 **Mar Menuda.** This modern Costa Brava hideaway offers as much peace and quiet—*and* as many varieties of water sports—as you can possibly handle. Equipment and instruction are available for windsurfing, sailing, swimming, and scuba diving. The hotel terrace overlooks the coast and the town of Tossa de Mar, with a medieval castle and an old quarter full of cobble streets. ✉ *Platja Mar Menuda s/n, Tossa de Mar 17320* ☎ *972/341000* 📠 *972/340087* 🌐 *www.marmenuda.com* *50 rooms* *In-hotel: restaurant, bar, tennis court, pool* ▭ *AE, DC, MC, V* ⏲ *Closed Nov.–Dec. 26.*

TARRAGONA

⑲ *98 km (60 mi) southwest of Barcelona, 251 km (155 mi) northeast of Valencia.*

Just over an hour from Barcelona, Tarragona gives you a mix of activities in a fresh provincial capital. An ancient outpost of the Roman Empire, it remains a fishing port, busy shipping harbor, and vibrant cultural center. As capital of the Roman province of Tarraconensis (from 218 BC), Tarraco, as it was then called, formed the empire's principal stronghold in Spain, and by the 1st century BC the city was regarded as one of the empire's finest urban creations. Its wine was already famous, and its people were the first in Spain to become Roman citizens. The apostle Paul preached here in AD 58, and Tarragona became the seat of the Christian church in Spain until it was superseded by Toledo in the 11th century. Tarragona was selected by UNESCO in 2000 as a

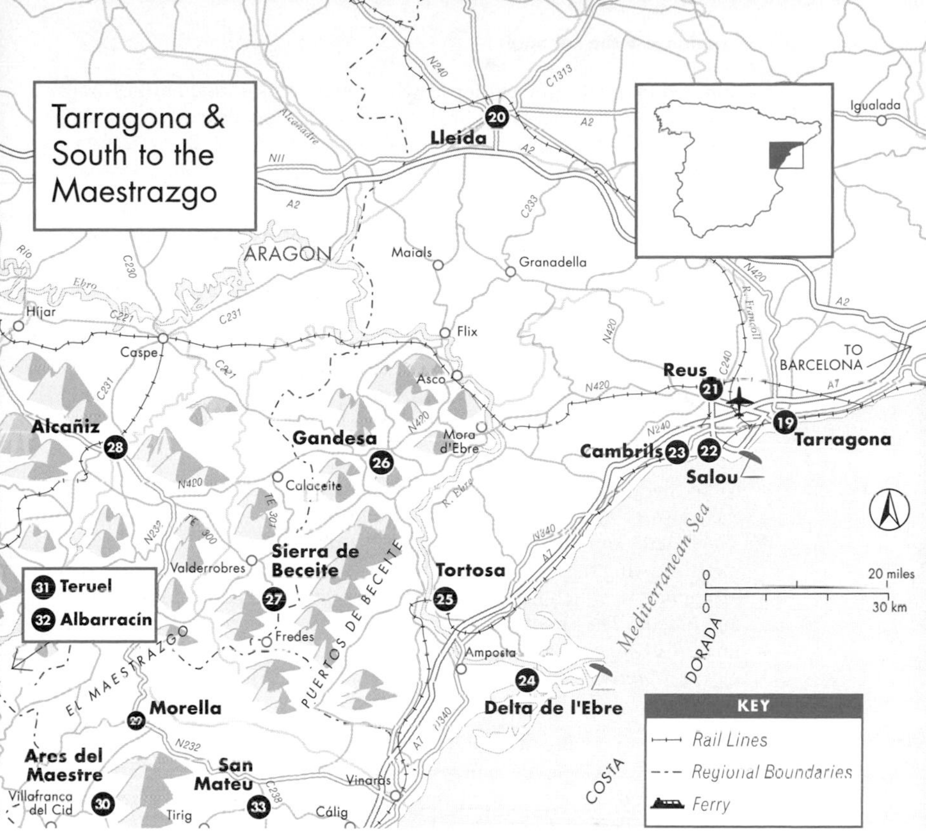

World Heritage Site for its extensive Roman remains and exceptional and ongoing excavations. Check out the €8 combination ticket, which includes admission to the amphitheater, Circus Maximus, Praetorium, and Casa Castellarnau. Valid for one year, the pass is a good deal if you plan to explore several of the major sites.

WHAT TO SEE

Approaching the city from Barcelona, 19 km (12 mi) north of Tarragona, you pass the **triumphal arch of Berà,** dating from the 3rd century BC. From the Lleida (Lérida) road, or *autopista,* you can see the 1st-century **Roman aqueduct** that helped carry fresh water 32 km (19 mi) from the River Gayo. Tarragona is divided clearly into old and new by the Rambla Vella—the old town and most of the Roman remains are to the north, and modern Tarragona spreads toward the south.

★ Start your tour at the acacia-lined Rambla Nova, at the end of which is a balcony overlooking the sea, the Balcó del Mediterràni. Walking uphill along Passeig de les Palmeres, you arrive at the remains of Tarragona's **amphitheater,** sitting in the shadow of the modern, semicircular Hotel Imperial Tarraco, artfully echoing the amphitheater's curve. Walk down the steps to the amphitheater to see just how well preserved it is—you're free to wander through the access tunnels and along the seating rows. In the center of the theater are the remains of two superimposed churches, the earlier of which was a Visigothic basilica built to mark the martyrdom of St. Fructuosus and his deacons in AD 259 (they were burned alive). ✉*Parc de Miracle* ☎*977/242579* 🎫*€2 or €8 combination ticket* ⏲*Wk after Easter–Sept., Tues.–Sat. 9–9, Sun. 9–3; Oct.–Holy Easter wk, Tues.–Sat. 9–5, Sun. 9–3.*

Explore the excavated vaults from the 1st-century Roman **Circus Maximus.** The plans just inside the gate show that these formed only a small corner of a vast arena (350 yards long), where 23,000 spectators gathered to watch chariot races. As medieval Tarragona grew, the city gradually swamped the Circus. The Circus is across the Rambla Vella from the Tarragona amphitheater. ☎*977/241952* 🎫*€2, joint entry with Praetorium, or €8 combination ticket* ⏲*Wk after Easter–Sept., Tues.–Sat. 9–9, Sun. 9–3; Oct.–Easter wk, Tues.–Sat. 9–7, Sun. 9–3.*

The former **Praetorium** served as Augustus's town house and is said to be the birthplace of Pontius Pilate. In the Middle Ages, it housed the kings of Catalonia and Aragón during their visits to Tarragona. The Praetorium now has a **Museu d'Història** (History Museum), with plans showing the evolution of the city; the highlight is the **Hippolytus sarcophagus,** which has a bas-relief depicting the legend of Hippolytus and Fraeda. The Praetorium is around the corner from the Circus Maximus. ✉*Passeig Sant Antoni* ☎*977/221736* 🎫*€2, joint entry with Circus Maximus, or €8 combination ticket* ⏲*Wk after Easter–Sept., Tues.–Sat. 9–9, Sun. 9–3; Oct.–Easter wk, Tues.–Sat. 9–7, Sun. 9–3.*

★ Next door to the Praetorium, in a 1960s neoclassical building, is **Museu Nacional Arqueològic.** It includes Roman statuary, keys, bells, and belt buckles, and the Head of Medusa, with its piercing stare. There's an excellent video on Tarragona's history. ✉*Pl. del Rei 5* ☎*977/221736* 🌐*www.mnat.es* 🎫*€2.40, free Tues.* ⏲*June–Sept., Tues.–Sat. 10–8, Sun. 10–2; Oct.–May, Tues.–Sat. 10–1:30 and 4:30–7, Sun. 10–2.*

Under the arcade on the Carrer de la Merceria is a stairway leading to Tarragona's **cathedral.**If no mass is in progress, enter through the cloister. The main attraction is the **altarpiece** of St. Tecla, a detailed depiction of the life of Tarragona's patron saint. ✉*Plaça de la Seu* ☎*977/238685* 🎫*€2.40* ⏲*June–mid-Oct., Mon.–Sat. 10–7; mid-Oct.–mid-Nov., Mon.–Sat. 10–5; mid-Nov.–mid-Mar., Mon.–Sat. 10–2; mid-Mar.–May, Mon.–Sat. 10–1 and 4–7.*

Built by Tarragona nobility in the 18th century, **Casa Castellarnau,** a Gothic *palacete,* or town house, is now a museum with furnishings from the 18th and 19th centuries. The last member of the Castellarnau family vacated the house in 1954. ✉*Carrer Cavallers 14* ☎*977/242220* 🎫*€2 or €8 combination ticket* ⏲*June–Sept., Tues.–Sat. 9–9, Sun. 9–3; Oct.–May, Tues.–Sat. 9–7, Sun. 9–3.*

Les Voltes (✉*End of Carrer Cavallers at Plaça Pallol*), is a Roman forum with a Gothic upper story and also one of the prettiest corners in Tarragona. The **Passeig Arqueològic** (✉*Through Portal del Rose*) is a path that skirts the 3rd-century BC Ibero-Roman ramparts and is built on even earlier walls of giant rocks. The glacis was added by English military engineers in 1707, during the War of the Spanish Succession. Look for the rusted bronze of Romulus and Remus. At the **Serallo** fishing quarter, boats unload their catch at the quayside. Peek inside the market, where fish are swiftly auctioned off to fishmongers and restaurateurs. The market is accessible by Bus 2 if you happen to be traveling from the Portal del Rose. Near the fish market is the **Necròpolis i Museu Paleocristià** *(Tomb and Paleochristian Museum).* ✉ *Av. Ramón y Cajal 80* ✉ *Paseo de la Independencia 15* ☎ *977/211175* *€2.40 combination ticket with Museu Arqueològic, free Tues.* ⏲ *June–Sept., Tues.–Sat. 10–1 and 4:30–8, Sun. 10–2; Oct.–May, Tues.–Sat. 10–1:30 and 3–5:30, Sun. 10–2.*

WHERE TO STAY & EAT

$$$$ ✕ **La Puda.** The prime quayside location guarantees fresh seafood, including a mixed platter of hake, sole, and monkfish with spicy *salsa Romesco.* Locals love this place, even though the menu is written in several languages. The restaurant is simply decorated: a tile floor, salmon-color walls, and white tablecloths. ✉ *Muelle Pescadores 25* ☎ *977/211511* ▭ *AE, DC, MC, V* ⏲ *No dinner Sun. Oct.–May.*

$$$–$$$$ ★ ✕ **Les Coques.** If you have time for only one meal in Tarragona, take it at this elegant little restaurant in the heart of the old town. Both mountain and Mediterranean food are served, from hearty *cordero* (lamb) to *calamarsets* (baby calamari sautéed in olive oil, garlic, and secret seasonings) and *lubina* (sea bass). ✉ *Carrer San Lorenzo 15* ☎ *977/228300* *Reservations essential* ▭ *AE, DC, MC, V* ⏲ *Closed Sun. Closed 1st 2 wks in Feb. and late July–mid-Aug.*

$$$ ★ ✕ **Les Voltes.** Built into the vaults of the Roman Circus Maximus, this out-of-the-way spot is a combination of 2,000-year-old chiseled stone, contemporary polished steel, and thick plate glass. The hearty menu of fish dishes and international fare includes oven-baked sea bass with vegetables and the specialty of the house, *rap al all cremat* (monkfish in fried garlic). In winter, *calçotadas* (spring onions) are available; it's best to order them a day in advance. The bar is a popular late-night spot. ✉ *Carrer Trinquet Vell 12* ☎ *977/230651* ▭ *MC, V* ⏲ *Closed Mon. No dinner Sun.*

$ ✕ **El Tiberi.** Just steps off the Rambla Nova sits this bustling, rustic restaurant. Here you can graze on a buffet of Catalan dishes, from *butifarra* (Catalan sausage) to *pa amb tomaquet* (toasted bread smeared with tomato and drizzled in olive oil). Finish off with *crema catalana,* Catalonia's answer to crème brûlée. ✉ *Carrer Martí d'Ardenya 5* ☎ *977/235403* 🌐 *www.eltiberi.com* ▭ *MC, V* ⏲ *Closed Mon.*

$$$ **Imperial Tarraco.** Overlooking the Mediterranean, this large, white, half-moon-shape hotel has plain but comfortable guest rooms, and each has a private balcony. Ask for a sea view. The large public rooms have cool marble floors and black leather furniture. The hotel caters to business travelers and conferences during the week, so off-season weekend rates (Fri.–Sun., Sept.–May) are a steal at half the regular price. ✉ *Passeig Palmeres s/n 43003* ☎ *977/233040* 📠 *977/216566* 🌐 *www.hotelhusaimperialtarraco.com* *170 rooms* *In-hotel: restaurant, bar, tennis court, pool* ▭ *AE, DC, MC, V* *BP.*

$–$$ **Hotel Lauria.** Guest rooms are basic, but the old-style wooden furnishing make them agreeable. The hotel's terraces overlook the serene pool and patio area, the Rambla Nova, or the sea. This is the most pleasant place to stay downtown. ✉*Rambla Nova 20, 43004* ☎*977/236712* 📠*977/236700* 🌐*www.hlauria.es* *72 rooms* *In-hotel: bar* 💳*AE, DC, MC, V* 🍽*CP.*

¢–$ **Pensión La Noria.** Rising above the spirited Plaça de la Font, this small place sports a cheery yellow facade with wrought-iron balconies. The interior is drab and institutional, but the basic, functional rooms (linoleum floors, simple furnishings) are clean and fresh-smelling, and some have small balconies, making this one of Tarragona's better budget digs. The entrance is through the bar-cafeteria. ✉*Pl. de la Font 53, 43003* ☎*977/238717* *24 rooms* *In-hotel: bar* 💳*MC, V.*

NIGHTLIFE & THE ARTS

The **Teatro Metropol** (✉*Rambla Nova 46* ☎*977/244795*) is Tarragona's center for music, dance, theater, and cultural events ranging from *castellers* (human-castle formations), usually performed in August and September, to folk dances. Castellers is a centuries-old Catalan tradition. Dressed in typical Catalan dress, participants climb atop one another to create a towering human castle. On Rambla Nova, near Plaça Imperial Tarraco, is a life-size paean to Tarragona's gravity-defying castellers. At the very top of this bronze sculpture is a child with his hand in the air, the official gesture that signals the dismantling of the tower.

Nightlife in Tarragona takes two forms: older and quieter in and around the Casco Viejo, and younger and more raucous in the southern, newer part of town, south of Rambla Nova. There's a row of restaurants and dance spots in the Puerto Deportivo, a pleasure-boat harbor separate from the working port.

SHOPPING

Expect to haggle for bargains; **Carrer Major** has some exciting antiques stores. Rummage thoroughly, as the gems are often hidden away. You might also try the shops in front of the cathedral. **Poblet** (✉*Carrer Major 27–29* ☎*977/23492*) has antique furniture, lamps, fans, watches, porcelain, and bronze busts. **Mercat d'Antiguitats** *(antiques market)* fills the Plaça de la Seu on Sunday 9 to 3. For Tarragona crafts, browse the ceramics and Roman-style candleholders and plates at **Mosaic** (✉*Carrer Major 19* ☎*977/234246*).

LLEIDA

20 *150 km (90 mi) south of Taüll, 150 km (90 mi) east of Zaragoza.*

The pleasant provincial capital of Lleida (Lérida in Castilian) borders the banks of the River Segre in the heart of Catalonia's agricultural and farm country. The Romans settled here around 200 BC, and the Arabs took control of the city in the 8th century.

The landmark **La Seu Vella,** the old cathedral, was built between the 13th and 15th centuries in a transitional Romanesque-Gothic style and was converted to a military barracks after the 1707 siege of Felipe V. That explains its Vauban-style walls and esplanades, which makes it seem like a fortress. It's especially panoramic in late afternoon, when the low light spotlights the city, the Segre River, and the countryside beyond. Open daily 10–1:30 and 4–7:30, it can be reached by escalator and elevator from Plaça Sant Joan or on foot via Carrer Cavallers. The medieval chapel of **Sant Jaume Peu de Rome** is on the Catalan route of the Camino de Santiago pilgrimage. Lleida's sculptor Jaume Gort fashioned the Sculpture of Saint James, and local artist Miquel Roig Nadal painted a work hung in the altar.

One block inside the old town, the most vital pedestrian artery, **Carrer Major,** runs parallel to the river. After 8 PM the newer area around Plaça Ricard Viñas is the hub of café, terrace, and restaurant life. Two key architectural sights here are **La Paeria,** a 13th-century Gothic mansion distinguished by massive stone archways, and the immense arched entrance to the **Antic Hospital de Santa Maria,** now the city's Cultural Center. Worth checking out while you're here is the **Arc del Pont,** opposite the Pont Vell (Old Bridge), the bridge leading across the Segre just upstream from La Paeria. This arch was the ancient gateway into the walled city; the bronze figures depict the two fallen heroes of the local Ilergetes tribe, Indíbil and Mandoni. The 14th-century church of **Sant Llorenç,** has a slender bell tower and porticoed doorway.

8

SOUTH TO THE MAESTRAZGO

This segment goes from the purely recreational, such as the Port Aventura theme park, to the sublime, encompassing the extraordinary natural resources from the Ebro Delta to the Sierra de Beceite. The wildly varied route takes you from below sea level (in parts of the delta) to high stone villages in the hills; from wetlands to the arid hinterlands of Tarragona.

REUS

21 *13 km (8 mi) northwest of Tarragona.*

Reus is an industrial town with the distinction of having been the birthplace of Antoni Gaudí, as well as the longtime home of his fellow Moderniste architect Lluís Domènech i Montaner. If you're into Moderniste buildings, Lluís Domènech's **Casa Navàs** is well worth the short detour. Follow the signs to the center of Reus and you arrive at the Plaça del Mercadal; the Casa Navàs is beside the *ajuntament* (town hall). The rich interior decoration includes mosaics, stained glass, tiles with characteristic Moderniste floral motifs, and oddly shaped leather chairs. There are no formal visiting hours, but the house is usually open Thursday–Saturday 10–1. (It's generally closed December–February. Stop by the **tourist office** (⊠*Pl. de la Llibertad s/n* ☎*977/778149*) to arrange a visit; they only allow groups with a minimum of six people to tour the house. Admission is €5. **Teatre Fortuny** (✉ *Pl. Prim 4* ☎ *902/332211*) is the Reus's primary theater and opera showcase.

SALOU

22 *11 km (7 mi) south of Reus.*

If you're starting to crave a sunny afternoon on the beach, stop in Salou, a modern resort with a long esplanade of young palms. The town itself is long on glitz but short on charm. History buffs might appreciate that the conquerors of Mallorca set out from the old port here in 1229.

On the edge of Salou, the **Universal Port Aventura** (✉ *Autovéia Salou/Vila-Seca, Km 2, Apartat 90/43480 Vila-Seca, Tarragona* ☎ *902/202220 or 977/779000* 🌐 *www.portaventura.es*) boldly offers "the adventure of your life" to anyone brave enough to shell out €35 or €28 per child under 11 for rides, waterslides, and steam engines. Prices rise €2 during the peak summer months of July and August; the park is closed from early January to late March. Port Aventura's hotel offers reasonably budgeted lodging aimed at families.

CAMBRILS

23 *7 km (4½ mi) west of Salou, 18 km (11 mi) southwest of Tarragona.*

Food lovers come to Cambrils to dine in the Joan Gatell restaurant. Refreshingly less developed than Salou, Cambrils has a marina and a bustling fishing port. The fine-sand beaches draw Spanish families, who stroll the town's cobbled streets.

WHERE TO EAT

$$$$ Fodor'sChoice ★ ✕ **Joan Gatell.** Since 1970, Joan Pedrell Font—assisted by wife Fanni and now son Jordi too—has been preparing exquisite local meals starring the freshest seafood from the Costa Daurada. Try the baby eels, *fideos negros amb sepionets* (paella in baby-squid ink), or the superb *suquet,* a traditional Catalan fish stew. Increasingly popular with international visitors, Joan Gatell is a total eating experience—the modern fittings and clean lines inside the beautiful restored stone building makes it welcoming, the sevice is attentive and the loving cooking brings out the best in the local seafood produce. Bring your wallet! ✉ *Miramar 26* ☎ *977/360057* 💳 *AE, DC, MC, V* ⊗ *Closed Mon., mid-Dec.–mid-Jan., and 1st 2 wks of May. No dinner Sun.*

DELTA DE L'EBRE

24 *77 km (48 mi) southwest of Tarragona, 60 km (37 mi) south of Cambrils.*

The Ebro Delta, a flat piece of wetland à la the Netherlands, juts into the Mediterranean on land deposited over the years by the Ebro River. The largest wetland park in Catalonia, the 20,000-acre **Parc Natural del Delta de l'Ebre** has endless salt marshes, sand dunes, reed beds, and rice paddies. The delta's waters teem with fish (largemouth bass, pike, black bullheads), and frogs, toads, and spiny-footed lizards populate the marshlands and beaches. The park is a major stopping and breeding place for more than 200,000 birds of more than 300 species—an impressive 60% of Europe's bird species can be seen here during the year. A vast variety of waterbirds (shoveler ducks, mallards, coots) descend by the thousands in October and November, when the rice has been harvested but the fields are still full of water. Morning and early evening in autumn and winter yield the best bird-watching. Unfortunately, the delta's most widespread critter is the mosquito, so you'll need a strong repellent to explore the wetlands. To get to the park, take N230 and follow signs to Sant Jaume d'Enveja; at Sant Jaume, take a ferry to the town of Deltebre. Staff at the **Park Information Office** (☒ *Carrer Doctor Martí Buera 22* ☎ *977/489679* 🌐 *www.parcsdecatalunya.net*) can tell you how to visit the reserve proper—which occupies the delta's northern, eastern, and southern tips—and give you the required permit. The information office is open Monday through Saturday 10 to 2 and 3 to 6 and Sunday 10 to 1.

WHERE TO STAY

$ **Lo Molí de Rosquilles.** Once an olive-oil mill, this old stone building with original furnishings functions as a charming and cozy hotel. A library stocked with regional books invites you to delve into the history, geography, and ecology of the Ebro Delta. Food is served for guests only; don't miss the excellent bread, cooked in a wood-burning oven. The hotel is in Masdenverge, 20 km (12 mi) west of Deltebre and 5 km (3 mi) north of Amposta (en route to Santa Barbara). ☒ *C. Catalunya 6, Masdenverge 43878* ☎ *977/718052 or 629/358929* *8 rooms* *In-room: no TV (some). In-hotel: restaurant* *MC, V.*

TORTOSA

25 *80 km (50 mi) southwest of Tarragona.*

Tortosa, straddling the Ebro River 10 km (6 mi) inland, was successively Roman, Visigothic, Moorish, and Christian. The town was the scene of one of the Spanish civil war's bloodiest battles. The Republicans, loyal to the democratically elected government and already in control of Catalonia, crossed the Ebro in July 1936 to attack the rebel Nationalists' rear guard. They got no farther than Tortosa, and were pinned down in trenches until they were forced to retreat, having lost 150,000 lives. You can cover the city's sights in a few hours.

Tortosa's local parador, in the ruined hilltop **Castillo de la Zuda,** is worth visiting even if you don't stay the night. Originally a Templar fortress, the castle (and town) passed into the hands of the Moors around the year 713, where it remained until its reconquest in 1153 by Ramón Berenguer IV, count of Barcelona. From the castle walls are views across the fertile Ebro Valley to the Sierra de Beceite. ☒ *Parador Castillo de la Zuda* ☎ *977/444450.*

The Renaissance **Colegio Sant Lluís** has an arcaded patio, embellished with a frieze depicting the kings of Aragón. It houses an impressive archival collection, including a population map of Tortosa dated 1149 and signed by Ramón Berenguer IV. The 13th-century *El Llibre de les Costums de Tortosa* is the first judicial text written in Catalan. ✉*Sant Domènec s/n.*

Tortosa's **cathedral** looks baroque, but if you enter through the cloister you can see that the building itself is purely Gothic. It was common in 18th-century Spain to tack these exuberant stuccos on to Gothic structures; the style is called Churrigueresque, after its first practitioner, José Churriguera. ✉*Croera s/n* ⏲*Cloister daily, cathedral for mass only.*

WHERE TO STAY & EAT

$$–$$$ ✕ **Rosa Pinyol.** Following in his mother's illustrious footsteps, chef and owner Joan Pinyol concocts regional dishes based on the Ebro Delta's teeming underwater population, from sea bass to sole, and fresh seasonal vegetables, including asparagus. His careful preparation of each dish may delay your food—but it's worth the wait. Try the *rape asado con calcots* (grilled monkfish with calcots, a springtime green onion native to this region). The restaurant is just west of the old town, across the Pont de l'Estat (Estat Bridge). ✉*Hernan Cortés 17* ☎*977/502001* ▭*AE, DC, MC, V* ⏲*Closed Sun. No dinner Mon.*

$$$ ★ **Parador de Tortosa.** Few sights around Tortosa can equal the superb view from the old Arab Castillo de la Zuda across the Ebro Valley to the Sierra de Beceite. Dark shades of mahogany and copious tapestries evoke the past. Guest rooms have heavy wood furniture, and have terra-cotta floors, rugs, and plain walls. The restaurant serves Catalan fare, including *bacalao con espinacas y allioli* (cod with spinach and garlic mayonnaise) and *pato del Delta con mandarinas* (Delta duck with mandarins). ✉*Castillo de la Zuda s/n, Tortosa 43500* ☎*977/444450* 📠*977/444458* 🌐*www.parador.es* *72 rooms* *In-hotel: restaurant, bar, pool, parking (no fee)* ▭*AE, DC, MC, V.*

NIGHTLIFE & THE ARTS

October marks the **Felip Pedrell Musical Festival,** when classical and chamber music concerts are showcased at the **Teatre Auditori Felip Pedrell** (✉*Pl. Salvador Videllet* ☎*977/510144*).

GANDESA

26 *87 km (54 mi) west of Tarragona.*

The terrain surrounding Gandesa is rugged, and some of the mountainsides are covered in pine trees. There are views of the fields and orchards in the valleys below. Renowned for its strong wine (up to 16% alcohol), Gandesa also has two architectural landmarks. The extraordinary **Cooperativa Agrícola** *(Wine Cooperative)* was designed by the Moderniste architect Cèsar Martinell in 1919. The white, Islamic-looking facade does little to prepare you for the remarkable vaulting inside, constructed entirely of small bricks ingeniously arranged to allow for expansion and contraction. This is a working building (open weekdays 9–1 and 3–7, Saturday 9–1, Sunday 10–2), and you can buy some local wine here for a sleepy picnic on the way to Alcañiz or Beceite. ✉ *Av. Catalunya 28, Gandesa* ☎ *977/420017.*

WHERE TO STAY & EAT

¢ ✕🏨 **Hostal Piqué.** Though uninviting from the outside, this modern roadhouse has a large, smart dining room with white tablecloths and professional service. The menu mixes everyday local options with rarer, pricier delicacies. The *menú del día* (menu of the day) is an excellent bargain ($), and may include *ensalada de queso de cabra* (salad with goat cheese), *sopa de cebolla* (onion soup), peppers stuffed with seafood, and steak. Rooms are comfortable and economical. ✉ *Via Catalunya 68, 43780* ☎ *977/420068* 📠 *977/420329* *48 rooms* *In-room: no a/c, no TV (some). In-hotel: restaurant* 💳 *AE, MC, V.*

SIERRA DE BECEITE

27 *15 km (9 mi) southwest of Gandesa on N420.*

The mountains of the Sierra de Beceite offer a beautiful excursion near Gandesa, as long as you and your car can handle some bumpy roads. Just after you enter the Aragonese province of Teruel is **Calaceite** on your right: explore its ancient, labyrinthine streets, which converge at the arcaded Plaza Porticada. For a closer inspection of the Beceite massif, turn left at the Calaceite crossroads and drive along TE301. Turn right after 18 km (11 mi) at a T junction to reach **Valderrobres,** with a fortified palace and a Renaissance town hall that served as the model for Barcelona's Poble Espanyol. Continue to **Beceite** and follow PANORAMA signs for a bumpy drive culminating in an impressive vista. Depending on the condition of these forest roads, you can drive all the way to **Fredes,** due south of Beceite. The kings of Catalonia, Aragón, and Valencia are said to have met near here, on the Tossal dels Tres Reis (4,450 feet), to iron out disputes. The best way to explore these hills is on foot (or on horseback); a sign on the way into Beceite points you toward the tourist office, which has trail maps and can arrange horseback rides. From Valderrobres, you can cut back to the Alcañiz road via TE300, which follows the Matarraña River.

8

ALCAÑIZ

28 *62 km (38 mi) west of Gandesa, 74 km (46 mi) north of Morella.*

Alcañiz lies on a plain, encircled by the River Guadaloupe and surrounded by ugly, modern apartment blocks, the result of a population explosion following the success of the nearby olive and almond orchards. The highway (N420) enters the town along a street that bustles with ongoing construction. For the old town, turn left at the end of this street to the Plaza Mayor. The **Lonja** (✉ *Exchange, Pl. Mayor*) has pointed arches defining its Gothic origin. The galleries and overhanging eaves on both buildings of the Renaissance **ayuntamiento** (*Town Hall* ✉ *Pl. Mayor, adjoining the Lonja*) mark them as Aragonese. The **Colegiata** (✉ *Pl. Mayor*) church has a baroque facade and an impressively ornate portal; by comparison, the painted interior is simple and rather dull. Alcañiz's hilltop **castle** (✉*Castillo de Calatrava* ☎*978/830400*) was the seat of the Calatrava Knights in the 14th century and is now a parador.

WHERE TO STAY & EAT

$$$ ★ **Parador de Alcañiz.** Installed in the sturdy castle of the Calatrava Knights, this hotel grandly surveys the olive-growing plain and the foothills of the Maestrazgo. Guest rooms have terra-cotta tile floors, patterned rugs, dark furniture, generous beds, and good views. The traditional restaurant ($–$$$) is spacious and warm, and serves Aragonese fare, such as *ternasco asado* (grilled lamb) and sweet *almendrandos* (small almond cakes). ✉*Castillo de Calatrava, 44600* ☎*978/830400* *978/830366* *www.parador.es* *37 rooms* *In-hotel: restaurant, bar* *AE, DC, MC, V.*

MORELLA

29 ★ *74 km (46 mi) south of Alcañiz, 64 km (40 mi) northwest of Benicarló.*

The walled town of Morella stands on a towering crag in Castellón, the northernmost Valencian province. It's not immediately evident if you approach from the north, but from the south and east the land drops away sharply, creating a natural fortress—the scene of several bloody battles. Morella's main thoroughfare is the arcaded **Calle Don Blasco de Alagón.** The numerous bars here are packed on weekends. Morella's **castle** is accessible through the gate on the Plaza de San Francisco, on the uppermost of the town's contoured streets. Just inside the gate is the ruined cloister and small church of an old Franciscan monastery; inside the church vault are several polychrome reliefs of Saint Francis. In 1088 El Cid scaled these walls and wreaked havoc on the occupying Moors. During the Carlist Wars of the 16th century, the castle became a stronghold for General Cabrera, who captured Morella in 1838 for Don Carlos, pretender to the Spanish throne. The walk up to the castle takes a good 15 minutes. ☎*964/173128* *www.morella.net or www.morella.net* *€1.50* *Oct.–Mar., daily 10:30–6:30; Apr.–Sept., daily 9–9.*

The blue-tile dome on the beautiful church of **Santa María la Mayor** lends an exotic note to this otherwise Gothic structure. The larger of the church's two doorways, depicting the Apostles, dates from the 14th century. A spiral marble staircase leads to the raised, flat-vaulted choir. The sanctuary got the full baroque treatment, as did the high altar. The **museum** has a painting by Francisco Ribalta and some 15th-century Gothic panels. The church is near Morella's castle on Calle Hospital. *€1.50* *June–Sept., daily 11–2 and 4–7; Oct.–May, daily noon–2 and 4–6.*

WHERE TO STAY & EAT

$$$ ★ **Restaurante El Mesón del Pastor.** In a restored 14th-century stone mansion on a side street off Calle Don Blasco de Alagón, chef José Ferrer specializes in Maestrazgan fare such as *conejo relleno trufado* (rabbit stuffed with truffles) and dishes with wild and farmed mushrooms. Des-

serts include *buñuelos con miel* (fried dumplings with honey), *tarta de almendras* (almond tart), and homemade *cuajada,* a firm curd yogurt. In November the restaurant hosts a mushroom specialty week. Next door is a simple 12-room inn ($$). ✉*Cuesta Jovaní 5–7* ☎*964/160249* 🌐*www.hoteldelpastor.com* 💳*AE, DC, MC, V* ⊗*Closed Wed. Sept.–July. No dinner weekdays. No lunch Sat. Sept.–July.*

$$ Fodor'sChoice ★ ✕🏨 **Cardenal Ram.** As the name suggests, this is a hotel rich in history—a former ancestral home to the famous Spanish prelate Cardnial Ram. Its stone walls and ubiquitous coats of arms set the tone. The lobby's huge tapestry depicts the 1414 visit of Antipope Papa Luna. Rooms have pine floors, bare white walls, high-beamed ceilings, and magnificent heavy furniture. The fine restaurant ($$–$$$) serves a succulent *solomillo* (sirloin) and fragrant *perdiz* (partridge). ✉*Cuesta Suñer 1, 12300* ☎*964/173085* 🌐*www.cardenalram.com* 📠*964/173218* *19 rooms* *In-room: no a/c. In-hotel: restaurant* 💳*MC, V.*

SHOPPING

The Maestrazgo region produces brightly colored handwoven woolens. The best buys are striped *mantas morellanas* (Morellan bedspreads), available along Calle Blasco de Alagón and around Plaza Arciprestal.

ARES DEL MAESTRE

30 *50 km (31 mi) southwest of Morella on N232, the main road to Villafranca del Cid, and CS802 toward Albocácer.*

Ares del Maestre is on the most dramatic site of any village in this area—like Morella, it rests on a crag, but here the drop is more severe and the vistas are more rewarding. Lush valleys dotted with well-tended fields unfold far below, in marked contrast to the surrounding terrain of stark mountains and craggy cliffs. A very steep climb, windy in winter and scorching in summer, takes you to a ruined **castle.**

8

TERUEL

31 *110 km (68 mi) southwest of Ares del Maestre, backtrack on CS802 toward Morella, then get on TE811 at Villafranca del Cid, 148 km (92 mi) northwest of Valencia.*

This provincial Aragonese capital is famous for its Mudejar architecture, its medieval lovers of lore, and its cured ham—displayed proudly in grocery stores throughout town. Once part of the city walls, Teruel's **Mudejar towers** were built between the 12th and 16th centuries in a style more reminiscent of Muslim minarets than Christian belfries. The highlight of the **cathedral** is its coffered ceiling with 13th-century court and hunting scenes, visible from the upper gallery.

The church of **San Pedro** has a Mudejar tower but is best known for its adjoining **Mausoleo de los Amantes** (Lovers' Mausoleum). Here lie the tombs of Diego and Isabel, two 13th-century Teruel lovers who died, it's said, of broken hearts. A wealthy merchant's daughter named Isabel de Segura fell in love with a young man named Diego de Marcilla, who had no means to marry a woman of Isabel's status. Her father naturally forbade the match. Determined to marry his true love and prove himself worthy in her father's eyes, Diego set out to seek his fortune. He returned five years later in triumph to ask for Isabel's hand—only to find that she was being married that very day to the son of a wealthy merchant from the nearby town of Albarracín. Overcome with grief, Diego died on the spot; the next day, at his funeral, Isabel, devastated, also died. Their story—Spain's version of Romeo and Juliet—captured the imagination of 16th-century European artists, including Tirso de Molina and Hartzenbusch. ✉ *North of Pl. Bretón* 🌐 *www.teruel.com.*

WHERE TO STAY & EAT

$$–$$$ ✕🏨 **Parador de Teruel.** Teruel's parador was built in 1956 to match the town's famous Mudejar-style architecture. The spacious rooms have parquet floors and floral wallpaper befitting an Aragonese palacete. The flower and herb gardens are beautifully maintained, as are the pool and tennis courts. The restaurant ($$–$$$) serves both regional and national cuisine—everything from paella valenciana to *caldereta de cordero* (lamb stew). ✉ *Ctra. Sagunto–Burgos, N234, Km 124, 44080* ☎ *978/601800* 📠 *978/608612* 🌐 *www.parador.es* *58 rooms, 2 suites* *In-hotel: restaurant, tennis courts, pool* 💳 *AE, DC, MC, V.*

ALBARRACÍN

32 *37 km (23 mi) west of Teruel, 185 km (116 mi) northwest of Valencia.*

West of Teruel are the grand Sierras de Albarracín, a vast massif carved into spectacular ravines by the powerful Guadalaviar and Curvo rivers. Rocky mountain plateaus loom above fertile valleys rich with wild vegetation, hulking pine and fir trees, and a population of deer and wild boar—which often end up as succulent dishes on the menus of mountain restaurants. Trekking trails cross the region, much of which remains refreshingly untamed, and there are 30-odd delightful villages, with ancient stone-and-wood houses and cobblestone streets. The area's natural and cultural riches all seem to come together in the small town of Albarracín. Perched at 3,840 feet above a luxuriant gorge with the Guadalaviar rushing below, the village makes an eye-catching picture of ancient stone houses and crenellated walls, against a gorgeous backdrop of evergreen hills and craggy cliffs. Climb the steep cobblestone streets past tiny old-fashioned *carnicerías* (butcher shops) and groups of old men leaning on their canes, and you really start feeling like you're deep in Spain. Rising above the Plaza Mayor is the **cathedral,** with a beautiful 16th-century *retablo* (altarpiece) featuring St. Peter.

WHERE TO STAY & EAT

$$ ★ ✕🏨 **Casa de Santiago.** At the top of an ancient staircase near the Plaza Mayor is this family-run hotel in a beautifully restored country house. The rooms are all individually decorated, and there are ample sitting rooms on every floor; one is outfitted with oversize brown-leather sofas that you can sink into, a rope-woven rocking chair, and big baskets of

magazines. One flight up is a sunlighted attic suite with a wrought-iron writing desk and splendid views of the valley and the red-tile roofs of town. The small restaurant ($$–$$$) serves excellent Aragonese fare, including roast veal and *migas,* fried spiced-bread crumbs with chopped pork and onions. ✉*Subida a las Torres 11, 44100* ☎*978/700316* 🌐*www.casadesantiago.net* *8 rooms, 1 suite* *In-room: no a/c, no TV. In-hotel: restaurant* ▭*MC, V* ⏲*Closed Feb.*

SAN MATEU

33 *26 km (16 mi) west of Benicarló, take CS802 southeast from Ares del Maestre to Albocácer, and then turn left.*

The small town of San Mateu proudly bears the subtitle Capital del Maestrazgo because it was from here that King Jaume I set out on his decisive reconquering raids in the 13th century, freeing the region finally from Moorish control. Sturdy Gothic mansions near the Plaza Mayor attest to San Mateu's regal past. Visit the Iglesia Arciprestal (Archpriest's Church) on the corner of the plaza—its nave is a fine example of the Catalan Gothic style, and the vault covers a wide expanse, dispensing with the need for columns.

THE COSTA DEL AZAHAR

Named for the orange blossom and its all pervading fragrance along this sweet coastal plain, the Costa del Azahar was transformed by the tourist-inspired building boom of the 1960s and '70s. Benicarló and Peñíscola are, with Vinaròs, the northernmost towns on the Costa del Azahar (in Castellón de la Plana province), and Sagunto marks the start of the Costa de Valencia.

8

BENICARLÓ

34 *55 km (34 mi) south of Tortosa.*

Benicarló has become a major tourist center. The harbor is a lively confusion of fishing and pleasure craft, and the beaches are jammed with locals and northern European sunseekers most of the year.

WHERE TO STAY & EAT

$$$–$$$$ ✕**Casa Pocho.** Literally translated as "The Tubby One's House"—owner Paco Puchal is affectionately known as El Pocho (tubby)—this maritime-theme restaurant is famous for turning out good seafood. *Langostinos* (prawns) are a good choice, as are the *almejas* (clams), *lubina* (sea bass), and fillet of sole. ✉*San Gregorio 49, Vinaròs* ☎*964/451095* ▭*MC, V* ⏲*Closed Mon. No dinner Sun.*

$$$ ✕🏨**Parador de Benicarló.** The main attraction here is the large, semiformal garden, which runs down to the sea—a perfect place to rest, away from the crowded beaches. Public rooms are huge and bright, with white-wicker furniture and white walls. Guest rooms have tile floors and functional furniture; ask for a seaside view. Travelers with disabilities are well accommodated. The parador's restaurant

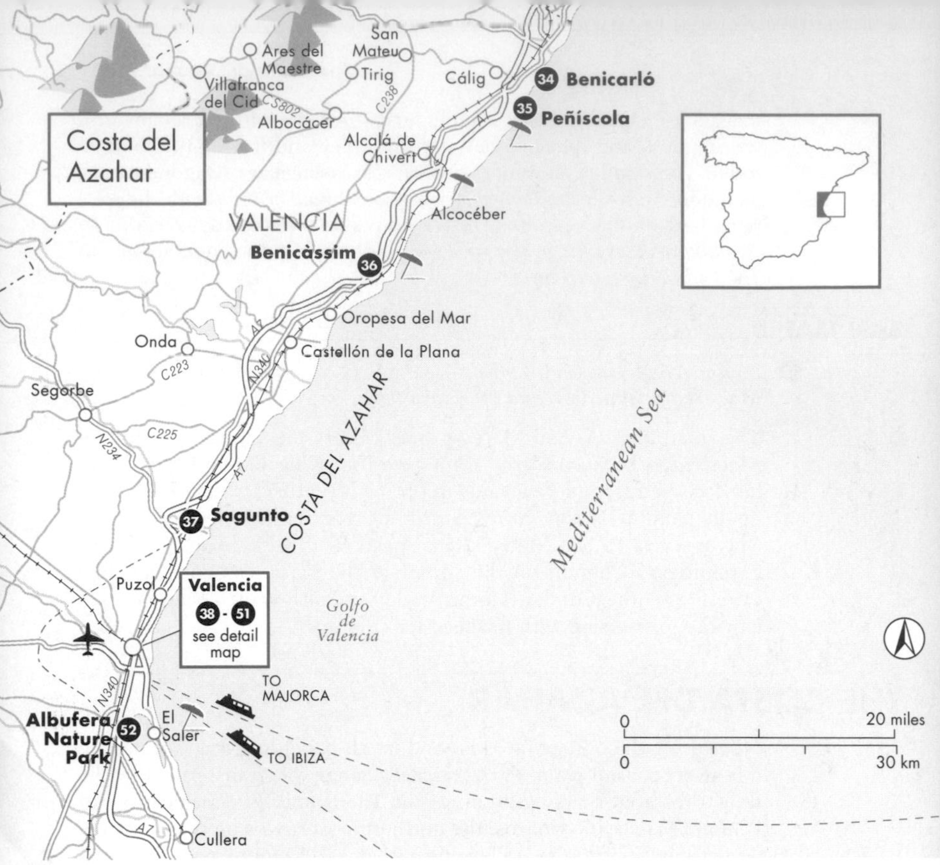

($$$–$$$$) is well known for its generous fish and seafood dishes. ✉ *Av. Papa Luna 5, 12580* ☎ *964/470100* 📠 *964/470934* 🌐 *www.parador.es* *108 rooms* *In-hotel: restaurant, bar, tennis court, pool* 💳 *AE, DC, MC, V.*

PEÑÍSCOLA

35 *7 km (4½ mi) south of Benicarló, 60 km (37 mi) northeast of Benicàssim.*

Peñíscola owes its foundation to the Phoenicians. It later became the bridgehead by which the Carthaginian Hamilcar (father of Hannibal) imported his elephants and munitions to wage the first of the three Punic Wars. Carthaginian influence in Iberia reached its zenith some 20 years later, in 230 BC, but was eventually eroded by that of Rome.

Fodor'sChoice ★ Peñíscola's **old town** is a cluster of white houses and tiny narrow streets leading up to the castle on a promontory, which gave people perfect surveillance of the coast. The beach here is one of the best in the area.

You can drive up to the **castle**, but in summer the traffic makes it smarter to leave your car by the town walls and walk. Of chief interest are the chapel and study of the antipope Papa Luna, to whom the 14th-century castle passed in the 15th century. Hardly any of Papa Luna's effects remain, but while you're in his drafty quarters, try to imagine this 90-year-old Frenchman (the former Pope Benedict XIII) passing the last six years of his life attending mass and composing schismatic bulls while surrounded by hostile Moorish townsfolk. ☎964/480021 €2 ⏲*Apr.–mid-June and mid-Sept.–mid-Oct., daily 9–8:30; mid-June–mid-Sept. 9:30–2 and 4:30–9:30; mid-Oct.–Mar., daily 9:30–1 and 3:15–6.*

WHERE TO STAY & EAT

$$$ **Hostería del Mar.** Officially a "semiparador," this modern, white hotel next to Peñíscola's long beach meets the paradores' high standards. Most guest rooms have balconies; some overlook the old town and others the beach. Inside, they have white walls, tile floors, and Castilian-style dark-wood and leather furniture. The rustic, beamed public rooms surround a leafy pool terrace. The Los Ficus restaurant—named after a regional tree—serves fish in season, including *rape,merluza* (hake) and tasty *chuletas* (pork chops). ✉*Av. Papa Luna 18, 12598* ☎*902/480600* 🌐*www.hosteriadelmar.net* 📠*964/481363* *86 rooms* *In-hotel: restaurant, bar, tennis court, pool, some pets allowed (fee)* 💳*AE, DC, MC, V.*

BENICÀSSIM

36 *60 km (37 mi) southwest of Peñíscola, 13 km (8 mi) northeast of Castellón de la Plana.*

Geographically blessed, the coastal town of Benicàssim is backed by the dramatic shapes of the Desierto de las Palmas mountain range, and the Mediterranean laps the town's long, sandy swimming beaches. Early vacationers—mostly wealthy Valencians—were suitably charmed, and the first vacation villa was built here in 1887. By 1900, Benicàssim was a genteel getaway, prompting its nickname: the Biarritz of the Costa de Azahar. This all changed during Spain's tourist boom in the early 1960s, when package tours arrived en masse along the coast; resorts replaced rusticity, and the local flavor of many coastal towns faded in the face of high-rise concrete jungles and quadrilingual menus. Although Benicàssim has its share of characterless apartment blocks, it was spared the worst resort-style excesses. Pleasant pedestrian promenades run alongside its clean, sandy beaches, and today most summer visitors are vacationing Spanish families. The well preserved 16th-century **Torre de San Vicente,** a watchtower (not open to the public), once guarded against marauding pirates and looms over a popular beach of the same name.

Seven kilometers (4 mi) inland from Benicàssim and set against the soothing backdrop of silent mountain peaks is the **Monasterio del Desierto de las Palmas,** a Carmelite monastery founded in 1694. The small museum houses Carmelite religious figurines and clothing from centuries past. ✉*Carretera Desierto de las Palmas s/n* ☎*964/300950* €2 ⏲*Monastery daily 10:30–1, museum Sun. noon–2.*

8

WHERE TO STAY & EAT

$$$ ✕ **Villa del Mar.** This secluded old country manor house has a dining terrace ringed by palms and pines. The food international and regional; try the *arroces valencianos* (Valencian rice dishes). On summer evenings a barbecue is held in the garden. ✉ *Paseo Marítimo Pilar Coloma 24* ☎ *964/302852* ▭ *AE, MC, V* ⊗ *Closed Nov.*

$$–$$$ **Voramar.** On the beach at the north end of town, this small neoclassical hotel is encircled by ample balconies. Ask for a room overlooking the sea, and you'll have a large balcony to yourself, with the sand directly below and gorgeous vistas of the Mediterranean. Prices dip considerably if you opt for a mountain-facing room, and even more so for a room with no balcony, just a window with a view (if you can call it that) of the parking lot. Rooms are plain and functional, with tile floors, white walls, and 1970s furniture. ✉ *Paseo Pilar Coloma 1, 12560* ☎ *964/300150* 📠 *964/300526* 🌐 *www.voramar.net* *58 rooms* *In-hotel: restaurant, bar, tennis court, some pets allowed* ▭ *AE, DC, MC, V* *CP.*

NIGHTLIFE & THE ARTS

Since 1995 Benicàssim has made a name for itself on the indie-music circuit. Thousands descend for the annual **Festival Internacional de Benicàssim** (*FIB* 🌐 *www.fiberfib.com*) held in August, which has headlined such artists as Nick Cave, Mouse on Mars, and Björk. On a more traditional note, late July brings the **Festival de Habaneras,** featuring sorrowful sailor songs on the guitar, often with Cuban rhythms. In summer, Benicàssim pulsates with the liveliest *marcha* (night "scene") on the Costa de Azahar. The city center is the nocturnal hot spot; **Plaza de los Dolores** and **Calle Santo Tomás** are packed with pubs and clubs. Enjoy the Mediterranean's balmy nights on Benicàssim's seaside promenade, **Paseo del Pilar Coloma,** where graceful 19th-century villas have been converted into classy terrace bars and restaurants.Groove to rock and pop at **K'asim** (✉ *Av. Gimeno Tomás*), a happening nightclub that swarms with locals and foreigners in the summer.

SAGUNTO

37 *65 km (40 mi) southwest of Benicàssim, 23 km (14 mi) northeast of Valencia.*

Sagunto will ring a bell if you've read Caesar's history: Saguntum, as the Romans called it, was the sparking point for the Second Punic War. When Hannibal laid siege to the town (at that time a port, from which the sea has since receded), the people heroically held out, faithfully expecting a Roman relief force, and eventually burned the town rather than surrender to the Carthaginians. Rambling Moorish fortifications dominate Sagunto from the hilltops, and within this citadel earlier **Roman remains** are now being excavated. In the citadel (on Plaza de San Fernando) is the **Antiquarium Epigráfico,** a collection of inscriptions on marble and epigraphs dedicated to various Roman emperors, and Roman funeral stones. Visit the well-restored **amphitheater.** More complete than Tarragona's, it went up during the Roman rebuilding five years after Hannibal's siege. ✉*Next to Placa de San Fernando* 🎫*Free* ⏲*Amphitheater and citadel: May–Sept., Tues.–Sat. 10–8, Sun. 10–2; Oct.–Apr., Tues.–Sat. 10–6, Sun. 10–2. Epigraph collection: May–Sept., Tues.–Sat. 10–2 and 5–8, Sun. 10–2; Oct.–Apr., Tues.–Sat. 10–2 and 4–6, Sun. 10–2.*

NIGHTLIFE & THE ARTS

The month of August brings **Sagunto a Escena** (✉*Pl. Cronista Chabret* ☎*962/662213* 🌐*www.aytosagunto.es*), a festival of classical Mediterranean drama for which theater groups perform ancient plays in Sagunto's Roman amphitheater.

VALENCIA & ENVIRONS

Spain's third-largest city and the capital of the Levante, Valencia is nearly equidistant from Barcelona and Madrid. If you have time for a day trip (or you decide to stay in the coastal town of El Saler), make your way to the Albufera, a scenic coastal wetland teeming with native wildlife, especially migratory birds. Tourist buses leave from Plaza de la Reina daily.

VALENCIA

362 km (224 mi) south of Barcelona, 351 km (218 mi) southeast of Madrid.

Valencia is a defiantly proud city. It was the last city in Spain to stand up to the Republicans against General Franco before the country fell to 40 years of dictatorship. Today it represents the essence of contemporary Spain—daring design and cutting-edge cuisine, while still deeply bowing to tradition.

Despite its proximity to the Mediterranean, Valencia's history and geography have been defined most significantly by the River Turia and the fertile floodplain (*huerta*) that surrounds it. The city has been fiercely contested ever since it was founded by the Greeks. El Cid captured Valencia from the Moors in 1094 and won his strangest victory here in 1099: he died in the battle, but his corpse was strapped to his saddle and so frightened the waiting Moors that it caused their complete defeat. In 1102, his widow, Jimena, was forced to return the city to Moorish rule; Jaume I finally drove them out in 1238. Modern Valencia was best known for its flooding disasters until the River Turia was diverted to the south in the late 1950s. Since then the city has been on a steady course of urban beautification. The lovely *puentes* (bridges) that once spanned the Turia look equally graceful spanning a wandering municipal park, and the spectacular futuristic Ciudad de las Artes y de las Sciencias (City of Arts and Sciences) designed by Valencian-born architect Santiago Calatrava has at long last created an exciting architectural link between this river town and the Mediterranean. Valencia's port, and parts of the city itself, underwent major structural refurbishment in anticipation of the 2007 America's Cup sailing classic.

A GOOD WALK

Begin your stroll through Valencia's historic center at the **cathedral** 38 in the Plaza de la Reina (climb the Miguelete Tower for good city views). Cross the Plaza de la Virgen and before you to the left stands the Gothic **Palau de la Generalitat** 39. Continuing down Calle Caballeros, you pass Valencia's oldest church, **San Nicolás** 40. After spending time inside, walk to the Plaza del Mercado and the 15th-century **Lonja de la Seda** 41. Travel down Avenida María Cristina to the **Plaza del Ayuntamiento** 42, one of the city's liveliest areas. After a five-minute walk down Avenida Marqués de Sotelo, you'll find the Moderniste **Estación del Tren (Train Station)** 43. Next to it is the **Plaza de Toros** 44. Head back to the city center via the bustling Plaza del Ayuntamiento and then walk along Calle Poeta Querol to the wedding-cake facade of the **Palacio del Marqués de Dos Aguas** 45. Cross the Calle Poeta Querol to Plaza Patriarca and enter the **Real Colegio del Patriarca** 46. Wander old town's streets on your way north toward the Turia River—cross by Puente de la Trinidad to see the **Museo de Bellas Artes** 47, adjoined by the Jardines del Real (Royal Gardens). Walk up Calle San Pio V to the Puente de Serranos and cross back to the 14th-century **Torre de Serranos,** which once guarded the city's entrance. Turn right for the **Casa Museo José Benlliure** 48, and continue west to the **Institut Valencià d'Art Modern (IVAM)** 49. On a separate outing, cross the Turia and stroll south to the **Palau de la Música** 50 and **Ciutat de les Arts i les Ciències** 51.

TIMING Allow a full day for a tour of the old quarter, the Museo de Bellas Artes, and the IVAM. Tack on a few hours the next day for the Palau de la Música and Ciutat de les Arts i les Ciències.

WHAT TO SEE

48 **Casa Museo José Benlliure.** Cross the Puente de Serranos, turn right down Calle Blanquerías, and stop at No. 23. The modern Valencian painter-sculptor Jose Benlliure is known for his portraits and large-scale historical and religious paintings, many of which hang in Valencia's Museo de Bellas Artes (Museum of Fine Arts). Here in his elegant house and studio are 50 of his works, including paintings, ceramics, sculptures, and drawings. On display are also works by his son, Pepino, who painted in the small, flower-filled garden in the back of the house, and iconographic sculptures by Benlliure's brother, the well-known sculptor Mariano Benlliure. ☎ *963/919103* *Free* *Tues.–Sat. 9:30–2 and 4:30–8, Sun. 9:30–2.*

38 **Cathedral.** Valencia's 13th- to 15th-century cathedral is the heart of the city. The building has three portals—Romanesque, Gothic, and rococo, respectively. Inside, Renaissance and baroque marble were removed in a successful restoration of the original Gothic style, as is now the trend in Spanish churches. The Capilla del Santo Cáliz (Chapel of the Holy Chalice) displays a purple agate vessel once said to be the Holy Grail (Christ's cup at the Last Supper) and thought to have been brought to Spain in the 4th century. Behind the altar you can see the left arm of **St. Vincent,** who was martyred in Valencia in 304. Stars of the cathedral **museum** are Goya's two famous paintings of St. Francis de Borja, Duke of Gandia. To the left of the cathedral entrance is the octagonal tower

Casa Museo José Benlliure 48
Cathedral 38
Ciutat de les Arts i les Ciències................51
Estación del Tren 43
Institut Valencià d'Art Modern (IVAM) 49
Lonja de la Seda 41
Museo de Bellas Artes......47
Palacio del Marqués de Dos Aguas (Ceramics Museum) 45
Palau de la Generalitat 39
Palau de la Música 50
Plaza del Ayuntamiento 42
Plaza de Toros 44
Real Colegio del Patriarca 46
San Nicolás 40

CLOSE UP

America's Cup in Valencia

In 2007 the 32nd America's Cup was held in Valencia, from June 23 through July 7. Team Allinghi from Switzerland won the cup. The last time the America's Cup was held on European waters, the year was 1851.

Reliable wind conditions and the promise of a new sailing village helped Valencia take the honor of hosting the world's oldest sporting trophy event.

Spain's third-largest city was the first non-English-speaking nation to hold the sailing competition since the mid-19th century; races have been held only in Britain, the United States, Australia, and New Zealand. The 2007 event was also the first Cup not to be staged in the home waters of the title-holders.

The Cup delivered major infrastructure improvements to the city, including an airport expansion, a subway line from the airport to the transformed port (with a new 700-berth marina), a competitor's village, and vantage points.

Spanish King Juan Carlos was over the moon—he's a yachting freak and devoted competitor in Majorca's sailing season. Apparently he continues to have cause to rejoice: the 33rd America's Cup in 2009 will be in Valencia again. For more information, go to 🌐*www.americascup.com*

El Miguelete, which you can climb: the roofs of the old town create a kaleidoscope of orange and brown terra-cotta, and the sea appears in the background. It's said that you can see 300 belfries from here, including bright-blue cupolas made of ceramic tiles from nearby Manises. The tower was built in 1381, and the final spire added in 1736. ✉*Pl. de la Reina* ☎*963/918127* 🎟*Cathedral free, museum €1.20, tower €1.20* ⏲*Cathedral Mon.–Sat. 7:30–1 and 4:30–8:30, Sun. 7:30–1 and 5–8:30. Museum and chapel Dec.–Feb., Mon.–Sat. 10–1; Mar.–May, Oct., and Nov., Mon.–Sat. 10–1 and 4:30–6; June–Sept., Mon.–Sat. 10–1 and 4:30–7. Tower weekdays 10–12:30 and 4:30–6:30, weekends 10–1:30 and 5–6:30.*

51 **Ciutat de les Arts i les Ciències.** Designed by native son Santiago Calatrava, this sprawling futuristic complex is the home of Valencia's **Museu de les Ciències Príncipe Felipe** (Prince Philip Science Museum), **L'Hemisfèric** (Hemispheric Planetarium), **L'Oceanogràfic** (Oceanographic Park), and **Palau de les Arts** (Palace of the Arts). With resplendent buildings resembling combs and crustaceans, the Ciutat is a favorite of architecture buffs and curious kids. The Science Museum has soaring platforms filled with lasers, holograms, simulators, and hands-on lab experiments. The eye-shape planetarium projects 3-D virtual voyages on its huge IMAX screen. At the Oceanographic Park you can take a submarine ride through a coastal marine habitat. New additions include an amphitheater, an indoor theater, and a chamber-music hall. ✉*Av. Autovía del Saler 7* ☎*902/100031* 📠*961/974505* 🌐*www.cac.es* 🎟*Museu de les Ciències €7.50, L'Hemisfèric €7.50, €11.20 for admission to both, L'Oceanogràfic €22, €29.90 for admission to all 3* ⏲*Museum mid-Sept.–June, Sun.–Fri. 10–8, Sat. 10–9; July–mid-Sept.,*

Fodor's Choice ★

daily 10–9. L'Oceanogràfic mid-Sept.–June, Sun.–Fri. 10–6, Sat. 10–8; July–mid-Sept. 10–midnight. L'Hemisfèric daily shows generally every hr on the hr 11–8; Fri. and Sat., additional show at 9.

43 **Estación del Tren.** Designed by Demetrio Ribes Mano in 1917, the train station is a splendid Moderniste pile replete with citrus motifs. ✉ *Down Av. Marqués de Sotelo from the ayuntamiento.*

49 **Institut Valencià d'Art Modern (IVAM).** Dedicated to modern and contemporary pieces, the art institute has a permanent collection of 20th-century avant-garde works, European Informalism (including the Spanish artists Saura, Tàpies, and Chillida), pop art, and photography. The museum is out near the Turia riverbed's elbow. ✉ *Guillem de Castro 118* ☎ *963/863000* 🌐 *www.ivam.es* 🎫 *€2, free Sun.* ⏲ *June–Aug., Tues.–Sun. 10–10; Sept.–May, Tues.–Sun. 10–8.*

41 **Lonja de la Seda** *(Silk Exchange)*. Downhill from San Nicolás, on the Plaza del Mercado, is the 15th-century Lonja. It is a product of Valencia's golden age, when the arts came under the patronage of Ferdinand I. Widely regarded as one of Spain's finest Gothic buildings, it has a perfect Gothic facade decorated with ghoulish gargoyles, complemented inside by high vaulting and twisted columns. Opposite the Lonja stands the **Iglesia de los Santos Juanes** (Church of the St. John), whose interior was destroyed during the civil war, and, next door, the Moderniste **Mercado Central** (Central Market), built entirely of iron and glass. The bustling food market is open Monday to Saturday, 8 AM to 2 PM, with stall after stall of fresh fruits and vegetables, meat, fish, and dried fruits and nuts. ✉ *Plaça Ciudad de Brujas s/n 46001* 🎫 *Free* ⏲ *Tues.–Fri. 9:30–2 and 4:30–8, weekends 9:30–1:30.*

8

47 **Museo de Bellas Artes** *(Museum of Fine Arts)*. Valencia was a thriving center of artistic activity in the 15th century, and the city's Museum ★ of Fine Arts is one of the best in Spain. To get here, walk behind the cathedral and cross the Puente de la Trinidad (Trinity Bridge) to the river's north bank; the museum is at the edge of the **Jardines del Real** (Royal Gardens), with fountains, rose gardens, tree-lined avenues, and a small zoo. The Royal Gardens are open daily 8–dusk. Many of the best paintings by Jacomart and Juan Reixach, two of several artists known as the Valencian Primitives, are here, as is work by Hieronymus Bosch—or El Bosco, as they call him here. The ground floor has the murky, 17th-century Tenebrist masterpieces of Francisco Ribalta and his pupil José Ribera, together with a Velázquez self-portrait and a room devoted to Goya. Upstairs, look for Joaquín Sorolla (Gallery 66), the luminous Valencian painter of everyday Spanish life in the 19th century. ✉ *C. San Pío V s/n* ☎ *963/932046* 🌐 *www.cult.gva.es/mbav* 🎫 *Free* ⏲ *Tues.–Sun. 10–8.*

45 **Palacio del Marqués de Dos Aguas.** This building, near the Plaza Patriarca ★ and across Calle Poeta Querol, has a fascinating baroque alabaster facade. Embellished with fruits and vegetables, it centers on the figures of the *Dos Aguas* (*Two Waters*), carved by Ignacio Vergara in the 18th century. The palace contains the **Museo Nacional de Cerámica,** with a magnificent collection of mostly local ceramics. Look for the Valen-

cian kitchen on the second floor. ✉ *C. Poeta Querol 2* ☎ *963/516392* 🎫 *Palace and museum €2.40, free Sat. afternoon and Sun. morning* ⏲ *Tues.–Sat. 10–2 and 4–8, Sun. 10–2.*

39 **Palau de la Generalitat.** On the left side of the Plaza de la Virgen, fronted by orange trees and box hedges, is the elegant eastern facade of what was once the Gothic home of the Valencia Cortés (Parliament), until it was suppressed by Felipe V for supporting the wrong (losing) side during the War of the Spanish Succession in the 18th century. The two *salones* (reception rooms) in the older of the two towers have superb woodwork on the ceilings. Call in advance for permission to enter. ☎ *963/863461* ⏲ *Weekdays 9–2.*

50 **Palau de la Música** *(Concert Hall).* On one of the nicest stretches of the Turia riverbed, a pond is backed by a huge glass vault: Valencia's Palace of Music. Supported by 10 porticoed pillars, the dome gives the illusion of a greenhouse, both from the street and from within its sun-filled, tree-landscaped interior. Home of the Orquesta de Valencia, the main hall also hosts performers on tour from around the world, including chamber and youth orchestras, opera, and an excellent concert series featuring early, baroque, and classical music. For concert schedules, pick up a *Turia* guide or one of the local *periodicos* (newspapers) at any newsstand. To see the building without concert tickets, pop into the **art gallery,** which is host to free changing exhibits. ✉ *Paseo de la Alameda 30* ☎ *963/375020* 🌐 *www.palauvalencia.com* ⏲ *Gallery daily 10:30–1:30 and 5:30–9.*

42 **Plaza del Ayuntamiento.** Down Avenida María Cristina from the market, this plaza is the hub of city life, a fact well conveyed by the massiveness of its baroque facades. The **ayuntamiento** *(Town Hall)* itself contains the city tourist office and a museum on the history of Valencia. ⏲ *ayuntamiento weekdays 8:30–2:30.*

Plaza de la Virgen. From the cathedral's Gothic Puerta de los Apóstoles (Apostle Door), emerge on this pedestrian plaza, a lovely place for a refreshing *horchata* (tiger-nut milk) in the late afternoon. Next to its portal, market gardeners from the *huerta* bring their irrigation disputes before the Water Tribunal, which has met every Thursday at noon since 1350. It is said that it is the oldest surviving legal system in the world. Verdicts are given on the spot, and sentences have ranged from fines to deprivation of water.

44 **Plaza de Toros.** Adjacent to the train station is the bullring, one of the oldest in Spain. The best bullfighters are featured during the Fallas in March, particularly March 18 and 19. Just beyond, down Pasaje Dr. Serra, the **Museo Taurino** *(Bullfighting Museum)* has bullfighting memorabilia, including bulls' heads and matadors' swords. 🎫 *Free* ⏲ *Bullring and museum Mon. 10–2, Tues.–Sun. 10–8.*

46 **Real Colegio del Patriarca** *(Royal College of the Patriarch).* The colegio stands on the far side of Plaza Patriarca, toward the center of town. Founded by San Juan de Ribera in the 16th century, it has a lovely Renaissance patio and an ornate church, and its museum holds works

by Juan de Juanes, Francisco Ribalta, and El Greco. ✉*Entrance off C. de la Nave* 🎫*€1.20* ⏲*Daily 11–1:30.*

40 **San Nicolás.** A small plaza contains Valencia's oldest church, once the parish of the Borgia Pope Calixtus III. The first portal you come to, with a tacked-on, rococo bas-relief of the Virgin Mary with cherubs, hints well at what's inside: every inch of the originally Gothic church is covered with Churrigueresque embellishments. ✉*C. Abadía San Nicolás* 🎫*Free* ⏲*Open for mass daily 8–9* AM *and 7–8* PM; *Sat. 6:30–8:30* PM; *Sun. various masses 8–1:15.*

WHERE TO EAT

$$$$ ✕**Civera.** This restaurant, is run by the well-known Civera seafood merchants family. It enjoys local renown for its fresh fish and seafood, especially the *langosta* (lobster), either *a la plancha* (grilled), *hervidos* (boiled), or *a la sal* (baked in salt). A marine theme is underscored by white walls, beams, and sumptuous displays of fish, fruit, and vegetables. Just three blocks northwest of the Museo de Bellas Artes. ✉*C. Lérida 11* ☎*963/475917* ▭*AE, DC, MC, V* ⏲*Closed Mon., Easter wk, and Aug. No dinner Sun.*

$$$$ ✕**Eladio.** West of the city center is this welcoming restaurant decorated with oak and marble. The many Galician fish dishes here are prepared with a mixture of tradition and invention—and some Swiss influences by chef Eladio Rodríguez, who spent some formative years in Switzerland. Try the *rape* (monkfish) or *lubina* (sea bass) *a la brasa* (grilled), or *rodaballo a la Gallega* (turbot with sweet paprika oil), and finish up with a mouthwatering *tarta* (cake) of *almendras* (almonds). ✉*Chiva 40* ☎*963/842244* ▭*AE, DC, MC, V* ⏲*Closed Sun. and Aug.*

8

$$$$ Fodor's Choice ★ ✕**La Sucursal.** La Sucursal is solid proof that Valencia can match the the cutting-edge contemporary cuisine of its big brother Barcelona. A thoroughly modern but also very cozy spot within the IVAM (Institut Valencía d'Modern Art), it is simply a taste sensation. You won't leave with a full wallet, but then again it's unlikely you'll sample deer carpaccio anywhere else or partake of an *arroz caldoso de bogavante* (rice soup with lobster) as good. At times the food veers toward the indescribable, but there's barely a weakness. Best to let the attentive staff make suggestions and go with it. ✉*Guillén de Castro 188* ☎*963/746655* 🌐*www.restaurantelasucursal.com* ✍*Reservations essential* ▭*AE, DC, MC, V* ⏲*Closed Sun.*

$$$ ✕**El Timonel.** Decorated like the inside of a yacht, this central restaurant (two blocks east of the bullring) serves outstanding shellfish. The cooking is simple using the freshest ingredients; try the *pescado de roca* (rockfish), grilled *lenguado* (sole), or *lubina* (sea bass). Also top-notch are the eight different kinds of *arrozes* ("rice dishes," a Spaniard term for paella), including paella with lobster and peeled *mariscos* (shellfish) For a sweet finale, delve into the house special *naranjas a la reina,* oranges spiced with rum and topped with *salsa de fresa* (strawberry sauce). Lunch attracts businesspeople, and dinner brings in a crowd of locals and foreigners. ✉*Félix Pizcueta 13* ☎*963/526300* 🌐*www.eltimonel.com* ▭*AE, DC, MC, V* ⏲*Closed Mon.*

$$$ ✕**La Pepica.** For the best in Valencia's seafood paella, head to the waterfront. At this bustling longtime family restaurant, dig into *arroz marinero* (seafood paella) topped with shrimp and mussels or hearty platters of *calamare* (squid) and *langostinos* (prawns). Save room for the delectable tarts made with fruit in season. ✉*Paseo Neptuno 6* ☎*963/710366* ▭*AE, DC, MC, V* ⊙*Closed last 2 wks of Nov. No dinner Mon.–Thurs. Sept.–May.*

$$ ✕**Patos.** Small, cozy, and very popular with locals, this restored 18th-century town house has an earthy look, thanks to the terra-cotta tiles, wood-panel walls, and overhead beams. On weekdays, the set lunch menu is a real bargain at €10 and usually includes *ternera* (veal) and *lomo* (pork loin). The set dinner (and weekend) menu is €18 and sometimes includes *cordero* (lamb) and *solomillo* (pork sirloin). Get here by 9:30 PM to snag a table; you can also dine outside in summer. The restaurant is just north of Calle de la Paz, in the old quarter. ✉*C. del Mar 28* ☎*963/921522* ▭*MC, V* ⊙*No dinner Sun. and Mon.*

WHERE TO STAY

$$–$$$ ✕**Ad Hoc.** Small and beautifully designed, this 19th-century town house offers immediate access to the old quarter and the Turia gardens. Owner Luis García Alarcón is an antiquarian, and the hotel reflects his eye for ancient design and architectural elegance. Weekend rates (a third less than weekday prices) are a great value. A buffet breakfast is included on weekends only. The excellent restaurant ($$$–$$$$) draws a pleasant mix of Valencian locals and hotel guests; tuck into paellas or one of the creative meat dishes, including duck with pine nuts, lentils and shrimp, cod with spinach, and a divine passion-fruit sorbet. ✉*Boix 4, 46003* ☎*963/919140* ⎙*963/913667* 🌐*www.adhoc hoteles.com* *28 rooms* *In-hotel: restaurant, some pets allowed* ▭*AE, DC, MC, V.*

$$$–$$$$ ★ **Reina Victoria.** Valencia's grande dame is an excellent choice if you want timeworn charm and a good location, next to the Plaza del Ayuntamiento. The spacious reception rooms have cool marble floors (with rugs to take the chill off), as does the smart, classy restaurant. The smallish guest rooms are clothed in green or burgundy chintz and deep-pile carpets. A buffet breakfast is included on the weekends only. ✉*Barcas 4, 46002* ☎*963/520487* ⎙*963/522721* 🌐*www.husa.es* *97 rooms* *In-hotel: restaurant, bar* ▭*AE, DC, MC, V.*

$$$–$$$$ **Sidi Saler.** The stretch of coastline just south of Valencia suffers from ongoing construction, but this hotel, surrounded by the Saler Nature Park, is an oasis of luxury. Many of the modern and bright guest rooms have views of the sea. Breakfast is included in the price—fill up on a buffet of *revueltos* (scrambled eggs), a variety of breads, and fresh fruit. Ask about weekend rates, which are often considerably less than on weekdays. ✉*Playa del Saler, 46012* ☎*961/610411* ⎙*961/610838* 🌐*www.hotelessidi.es* *276 rooms* *In-hotel: restaurant, bars, tennis courts, pools, spa, some pets allowed (fee)* ▭*AE, DC, MC, V* *BP.*

$$–$$$ ★ **Holiday Inn Valencia.** The Holiday Inn is great value compared with may other similar establishments. Close to the city center, its rooms are light and spacious, and have high-speed Internet access. The staff is attentive, and the Mezzo & Mezzo restaurant serves good Italian and

international fare—a real bonus is that kids under 12 can eat for free. The bar at the rooftop pool is a bonus. ✉*Paseo de La Alameda 38, 46023* ☎*963/032100* 🌐*www.valencia.holiday-inn.com* *200 rooms* *In-hotel: restaurants, bar, pool, gym* *AE, DC, MC, V.*

$–$$ **Villarreal.** Rustic on the outside, modern on the inside, this little family-friendly hotel is between the Mercado Central and Plaza del Ayuntamiento. In a neighborhood where a moderately priced room is a scarce commodity, this is your very best bet. The neutral-hue rooms are spotless. Breakfast is included on the weekends. ✉*Ángel Guimerá 58, 46008* ☎*963/824633* *963/840247* *25 rooms* *In-hotel: restaurant* *AE, DC, MC, V.*

FABULOUS FIESTAS

In Valencia, **Las Fallas** fills an entire week in March, reaching their climax on March 19, El Día de San José (St. Joseph's Day), the Spanish Father's Day. Las Fallas grew from the fact that St. Joseph is the patron saint of carpenters; in medieval times, carpenters' guilds celebrated by making huge bonfires with wood shavings. Today it's a weeklong celebration of fireworks, flower-strewn floats, carnival processions, and bullfights. On March 19, huge effigies of popular and not-so-popular figures are ceremoniously burned. Tarragona's most important fiestas are **St. Magí** (August 19) and **St. Tecla** (September 23).

NIGHTLIFE & THE ARTS

Sleep seems to be anathema here. You can experience Valencia's nocturnal way of life at any time except summer, when locals disappear on vacation and the international set moves to the beach. Nightlife in the old town centers around Barrio del Carmen, a lively web of streets that unfolds north of Plaza del Mercado. A string of bars and pubs dot Calle Caballeros, leading off Plaza de la Virgen—these establishments are very popular, if not a little tired; the Plaza del Tossal also has some popular cafés, as does Calle Alta, leading off Plaza San Jaime. Some of the funkier and newer places are to be found in and around Plaza del Carmen. Across the river in the new town, look for appealing hangouts along Avenida Blasco Ibáñez and on Plaza de Cánovas del Castillo and Plaza Zuquer. Out by the sea, Paseo Neptuno and Calle de Eugenia Viñes are lined with loud clubs and bars. Castellón and Valencia jointly publish *Que y Donde*, the major listings magazine; *Turia* focuses on Valencia.

Fodor's Choice ★ If you want nonstop nightlife at its frenzied best, come during **Las Fallas** (🌐*www.fallas.com*) in March, when revelers throng the streets and last call at many of the bars and clubs isn't until the wee hours of morning, if at all. The **Feria de Julio** (☎*963/520694*), is July's monthlong festival of theater, film, dance, and music.

The **Filmoteca** (✉*Pl. del Ayuntamiento 17* ☎*963/539300*) has changing monthly programs of films in their original language (look for *v.o.—versión original*) and an artsy haunt of a café. An 11th-century Arab wall is incorporated into the 18th-century palace that is **Carmen** (✉*C. Caballeros 38* ☎*963/925273*), a sleek bar-club whose many floors are connected by ramps. There are several art installations, and the music is always sharp. The airy, perennially popular, bar-club-performance-space **Radio City** (✉*Santa Teresa 19* ☎*963/914151*) offers an eclectic nightly showcase from flamenco (on Tuesday at 11 PM) and Afro-jazz fusion to theater. For quiet after-dinner drinks, try the jazzy, lighthearted bar **Café de la Seu** (✉*Santo Cáliz 7* ☎*963/915715*), with contemporary art and animal-print chairs. For a taste of *el ambiente andaluz* (Andalusian atmosphere) tuck into tapas and cocktails at **El Albero** (✉*Ciscar 12* ☎*963/337428*). At 11 PM Thursday through Saturday, there's Andalusian singing. Locals out for a cocktail before hitting the clubs start their evening at **Xuquer Palace** (✉*Pl. Xuquer 8* ☎*963/615811*), with Barcelona-style Moderniste furnishings. **Casablanca** (✉*Eugenia Viñes 152* ☎*963/713366*) has an elegant postwar look; it's open Thursday through Sunday and has everything from waltz to swing music. Valencia has a lively gay nightlife, with a string of bars and clubs on Calle Quart and around the Plaza del Mercado. Follow the trendsters to the hopping **Venial** (✉*Quart 26* ☎*963/917356*), where you can enjoy a tipple or two, groove on the packed dance floor, or just take in the *gran espectaculos* of sequinned and/or muscled performers strutting their stuff on stage.

SHOPPING

A flea market is held every Sunday morning by the cathedral. Another crafts and flea market takes place on Sunday morning in Plaza Luis Casanova, near the *campo de fútbol* (soccer stadium). If it's great local designer wear you're after, then head straight to the Barrio Carmen.

ALBUFERA NATURE PARK

52 *11 km (7 mi) south of Valencia.*

This beautiful freshwater lagoon was named by Moorish poets—*albufera* means "the sun's mirror." Dappled with rice paddies, the Parque Natural de la Albufera is a nesting site for more than 250 bird species, including herons, terns, egrets, ducks, and gulls. Admission is free, and there are miles of lovely walking trails.

From Valencia, buses depart from the corner of Sueca and Gran Vía de Germanías on the hour (every half hour in summer) daily 7 AM to 9 PM. ☎*961/627345* 🌐*www.albufera.com.*

WHERE TO EAT

$$$–$$$$ ★ ✕**La Matandeta.** With its white garden walls, this engaging restaurant appears from a distance to be a shining island in a sea of rice paddies. Thanks to the local birdlife—snowy egrets, gray herons—a lunchtime drive to La Matandeta can be almost as eye-opening as the culinary creations of its proprietors, Maria Dolores Baixauli and Rafael Galvez. A traditional main dish is the *paella de pato, pollo, y conejo* (paella with duck, chicken, and rabbit). Don't forget to specify which of the 50 types of olive oil you'd like on your whole-wheat bread or salad. ✉*Ctra. Alfafar, Km 4* ☎*962/112184* ▭*MC, V* ⊙*Closed Mon.*

CATALONIA & THE LEVANTE ESSENTIALS

To research prices, get advice from other travelers, and book travel arrangements, visit www.fodors.com.

TRANSPORTATION

For more on travel to and in Catalonia & the Levante, see the Catalonia & the Levante Planner at the beginning of this chapter.

BY AIR

See the Catalonia planner at the beginning of this chapter for more information.

Airports Aeropuerto de Valencia (☎ *961/598500*). **Aeropuerto de Girona** (☎ *902/404704* 🌐 *www.aena.es*). **Aeropuerto del Prat** (☎ *93/298–3838*). **Aeropuerto del Reus** (☎ *902/404704* 🌐 *www.aena.es*).

Carriers Easyjet (🌐 *www.easyjet.com*) .**Iberia** (☎ *902/400500* 🌐 *www.iberia.es*).**Ryanair** (☎ *In Spain 807/220032* 🌐 *www.ryanair.com*).**Vueling** (☎ *In Spain 902/333933* 🌐 *www.vueling.com*).

BY BOAT & FERRY

Transmediterránea ferries leave both Barcelona and Valencia for Majorca and Ibiza Monday through Sunday.

Contacts Trasmediterránea (✉ *Estación Marítima, Valencia* ☎ *902/454645, 977/225506 Tarragona shuttle* 🌐 *www.trasmediterranea.es*).

BY BUS

Sarfa operates buses from Barcelona to Blanes, Lloret, Sant Feliu de Guixols, Platja d'Aro, Palamos, Begur, Roses, and Cadaqués.

The trip from Barcelona to Tarragona is easy; 8 to 10 buses leave Barcelona's Estación Vilanova-Norte every day. Connections between Tarragona and Valencia are frequent, and from Valencia buses continue down the coast and on to Madrid. Valencia's bus station is across the river from the old town; take Bus 8 from the Plaza del Ayuntamiento. Transport inland to Morella and Alcañiz can be arranged from Vinaròs, and Castellón and Sagunto have bus lines that head west to Teruel. Within Valencia, buses are the main mode of public transport; central lines begin at the Plaza del Ayuntamiento. Buses to the beaches and suburbs leave from the Plaza Puerta del Mar. The tourist office has more details.

If you want to go to Vic, contact **Segalés** (☎ *93/889-2577*). For Ripoll, call **Teisa** (✉ *Pau Claris 118* ☎ *93/488–2837*).

Bus Information Bacoma SA bus line (✉ *Pl. Imperial Tarraco s/n, Tarragona* ☎ *977/222072*). **Sarfa** (✉ *Estació Norte–Vilanova C. Alí Bei 80, Barcelona* ☎ *93/265–1158* Ⓜ *Arc de Triomf*)**Valencia bus station** (✉ *Av. Menendez Pidal 13* ☎ *963/497222*).

8

BY CAR

The A7 *autopista* leads into this region at both ends. The coastal N340 can get clogged, so you're often better off paying to use the autopista. A car is extremely valuable, even necessary, if you want to explore the inland Maestrazgo mountains, where much of the driving is smooth, uncrowded, and scenic.

In Tarragona, Avis works out of the travel agency Viajes Vibus. In Valencia you have a choice of Avis, Hertz, or Europcar.

National Agencies Avis (✉ *Pin Soler 10, Tarragona* ☎ *977/219156* 🌐 *www.avis.com* ✉ *Gran Vía Ramón y Cajal, 2, Valencia* ☎ *963/168019*). **Europcar** (✉ *Antiguo Reino de Valencia 7, Valencia* ☎ *963/741512* 🌐 *www.europcar.es* ✉ *Airport, Valencia* ☎ *961/521872* ✉ *Estación RENFE, Játiva 24, Valencia* ☎ *963/3519055*). **Hertz** (✉ *Segorbe 7, Valencia* ☎ *963/415036* 🌐 *www.hertz.es* ✉ *Airport, Valencia* ☎ *961/523791*).

BY TRAIN

RENFE operates trains, which leave Sants and Passeig de Gràcia every 1½ hours for Girona, Figueres, and Port Bou (France). Some trains for northern Catalonia and France also leave from the França Station. For Vic and Ripoll, catch a Puigcerdà train (every hour or two) from Sants or Plaça de Catalunya.

The local train to the Costa Brava pokes along the coast to Blanes every 30 minutes, departing Sants at 13 and 43 minutes after every hour and Plaça de Catalunya 5 minutes later.

The AVE train travels from Madrid to Lleida (with a stop in Zaragoza). The trip to Zaragoza is just under two hours and starts at €45 each way; to Lleida, the trip is just under three hours and starts at €55 each way. By December 2007 it is expected that the AVE will be expanded to continue to Barcelona. From Lleida, there are numerous train connections to the rest of Catalonia, especially north to the Pyrenees.

Trains bound for Tarragona (via Zaragoza) leave Barcelona's Passeig de Gràcia and Sants stations every half hour or so. Tarragona's RENFE station is downhill from the Mediterranean Balcony, south toward the port. Leaving Valencia, you have a choice of train connections to Madrid (via Cuenca) or Alicante (via Játiva). The main station, Estación del Norte, is on Calle Játiva next to the bullring, a short walk or cab ride from most hotels. Within the region, trains run more or less down the coast: Tarragona to Salou, Cambrils to Tortosa, Vinaròs to Peñíscola, Benicàssim to Castellón, and Sagunto to Valencia. A line also goes from Valencia to Zaragoza by way of Sagunto and Teruel; local lines go around Valencia from the Cronista Rivelles station. Contact the tourism office for information on specific routes.

Train Information RENFE ☎ *902/240202* 🌐 *www.renfe.es*). **RENFE Valencia–Cronista Rivelles** (☎ *902/240202*). **Valencia–Estación del Norte** (✉ *Plaza de Toros, Valencia* ☎ *902/240202*).

SPORTS & THE OUTDOORS

SAILING

The safe waters off Spain's eastern coast make for good sailing conditions. Ask the local tourist office about procuring a boat, contact one of the clubs below, or just chance upon rental outfits.

Contacts **Club Náutico Castellón** (✉ *Escollera de Poniente* ☎ *964/280354*). **Club Náutico Salou** (✉ *Port Salou* ☎ *977/382166*). **Club Náutico Valencia** (✉ *Camino del Canal 91* ☎ *963/679011*). **Real Club Náutico Tarragona** (✉ *Puerto Deportivo* ☎ *977/240360*).

CONTACTS & RESOURCES

EMERGENCIES

Emergency Services **Ambulance** (☎ *964/211253 in Castellón, 977/244728 in Gandesa, 964/160962 in Morella, 977/252525 in Tarragona, 963/677375 in Valencia*). **Hospital Clínico** (☎ *963/862600*). **Hospital Joan XXIII** (☎ *977/295800*). **Hospital Provincial** (☎ *964/210522*). **Police** (☎ *091 national toll-free*).

LODGING

APARTMENT & VILLA RENTALS

Throughout Catalonia are farmhouses (called a *casa rural* in Spanish and a *casa de pagès* in Catalan and Valenciano). Accommodations vary widely, from small rustic homes with a few rooms to spacious farmhouses with wood-beam ceilings, fireplaces, and outdoor pools. The high-end farmhouses are called Gîtes. Most tourist offices have a pamphlet, called *Gîtes de Catalunya*, with color photos, and also sell a book on the *Cases de Pagès de Catalunya*. You can also peruse listings of farmhouses on the Catalunya Tourist Office Web site (🌐 *www.gencat.es/probert*).

Local Agents **Federació d'Agroturisme i Turisme Rural Comarques de Tarragona** (✉ *Sant Francesc 1, 43360Cornudella de Montsant* ☎ *977/821082* 🌐 *www.agroturisme.org*).**Torrecorinto Apartamentos Turísticos** (✉ *Av. de Corinto 1, Playa de Canet, Sagunto* ☎ *962/608911*).

TOUR OPTIONS

Bus and boat tours from Barcelona to the Costa Brava, Girona, and Figueres are run by Julià Travel. Buses leave Barcelona at 9 and return at 6. The prices range from €80 per person with lunch for the Costa Brava to €90 for Girona and Figueres. Pullmantur runs tours to several main points on the Costa Brava.

In Tarragona, the city tourist office (just below the cathedral) leads a tour of the cathedral and archaeological sites. The Tarraco Guide Bureau runs guided tours through the Roman sights of Tarragona (€10 per person). They also conduct day tours to the Ebro Delta and Peñíscola. Throughout the year, the double-decker Valencia Bus Turistic (daily 10:30–7:30, until 9 in summer; departing every hour) travels on a circuit throughout the city that passes all the main sights. A 24-hour ticket (€10) allows you to get on and off when you wish at four main boarding points: Plaza de la Reina, Institut Valencià d'Art Modern (IVAM), Museo de Bellas Artes, and Ciutat de les Arts i les

Ciències. The Valencia Bus Turistic company also offers a two-hour guided trip (€12) to and around the Albufera Nature Park. The bus departs from the Plaza de la Reina in the center of Valencia. In the summer (and during the rest of the year, depending on demand) Valencia's regional tourist office also organizes tours of the Albufera Nature Park. You tour the port area before continuing south to the lagoon itself, where you can visit a traditional *barraca* (thatch farmhouse). You'll end up in the Devesa Gardens, where you can hire a boat to explore the rice paddies.

Tour Operators **Julià Travel** (✉ *Ronda Universitat 5* ☎ *93/317–6454* 🌐 *www.juliatravel.com*). **Pullmantur** (✉ *Gran Vía 635* ☎ *93/318–5195*). **Tarraco Guide Bureau** (✉ *Rambla Nova 21* ☎ *977/248866*). **Valencia Bus Turistic** (☎ *96/341–4400* 🌐 *www.valenciabusturistic.com*).

VISITOR INFORMATION

Regional tourist offices—in Castellón, Tarragona, and Valencia—have area-wide information. There are local tourist offices in Albarracín, Benicàssim, Morella, Peñíscola, Reus, Sagunto, Tarragona, Teruel, Tortosa, and Valencia. Castellón and Valencia also have information phone lines.

Local Tourist Offices **Albarracín** (✉ *Diputación 4* ☎ *978/710251*). **Benicàssim** (✉ *Médico Segarra 4* ☎ *964/300962* 🌐 *www.benicassim.org*). **Morella** (✉ *Pl. San Miguel* ☎ *964/173032* 🌐 *www.morella.net*). **Peñíscola** (✉ *Paseo Marítimo* ☎ *964/480208*). **Reus** (✉ *San Juan s/n* ☎ *977/778149* 🌐 *www.reus.net*). **Sagunto** (✉ *Pl. Cronista Chabret* ☎ *962/662213* 🌐 *www.sagunt.com/turismo*). **Tarragona** (✉ *Carrer Major 39* ☎ *977/245203*). **Teruel** (✉ *Tomás Nogués 1* ☎ *978/602279* 🌐 *www.teruel.net*). **Tortosa** (✉ *Pl. España* ☎ *977/442567*). **Valencia** (✉ *Pl. Ayuntamiento 1* ☎ *963/510417* ✉ *Estación RENFE, Játiva 24* ☎ *963/528573*).

Regional Tourist Offices **Castellón** (✉ *Pl. María Agustina 5* ☎ *964/358688* 🌐 *www.castellon-costaazahar.com*). **Tarragona** (✉ *Rambla Nova 118* ☎ *977/238033*). **Valencia** (✉ *Paz 48* ☎ *963/986422* 🌐 *www.comunidad-valenciana.com*).

The Balearic Islands

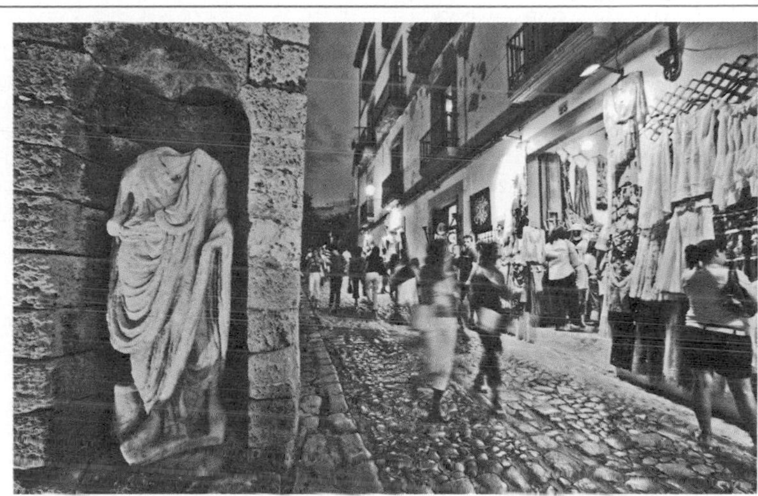

The cobblestoned streets of Ibiza Town (Eivissa)

9

WORD OF MOUTH

"Both Ibiza and Majorca have lovely parts, and it's great if you can hire a car and go explore the islands. In the north of Majorca there are [resorts] with great beaches . . . ."

—Chloe

"Ibiza is two different worlds. When the mad party scene is over for the summer, people relax, take quiet long weekends in the great countryside, and hang out with friends."

—John

www.fodors.com/forums

WELCOME TO THE BALEARIC ISLANDS

TOP REASONS TO GO

★ **Stop Me Before I Pamper Myself Again:** Luxurious boutique hotels on restored and redesigned rural estates are *the* hip accommodations in the Balearics. Many have their own holistic spas: restore and redesign yourself at one of them.

★ **Spines & All:** Seafood specialties like Minorca's *caldereta de langosta* (spiny lobster stew) come straight from the boat to portside restaurants all over the islands.

★ **Hard Day's Night:** Ibiza has clubs that don't even *open* until 5 AM.

★ **On the Rocks:** The rugged coast of Majorca's Tramuntana, from Valldemossa to Sóller, is one of the most beautiful unspoiled settings in the world.

★ **In the Swim:** The islands abound with small sandy coves called *calas,* like Cala'n Turqueda, on Minorca's south coast—many so isolated you can reach them only by boat.

1 Mahón. Minorca's capital city commands the largest and deepest harbor in the Mediterranean. Many of the houses above the port date to the 18th-century occupation by the Imperial British navy.

Woman wearing a traditional outfit in Ibiza.

2 Palma. Majorca's capital is a trove of art and architectural gems, from its magnificent cathedral and Gothic quarter, to the art deco buildings of the Catalan modernists, to the works of Joan Miró.

3 The Tramuntana. Few landscapes in the world can match the forested peaks and steep seacliffs of the Sierra del Norte, in Majorca's northwest—a region still unspoiled and undeveloped.

Hiking the Tramuntana.

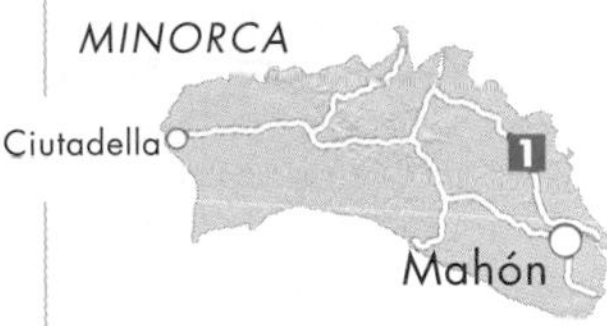

GETTING ORIENTED

The Balearic islands lie 50–190 mi (approximately 80–300 km) off the Spanish mainland, roughly between Valencia and Barcelona. In the center, Majorca, with its rolling eastern plains and mountainous northwest, is the largest of the group. Minorca, its closest neighbor, is virtually flat—but like Ibiza and tiny Formentera to the west, it's blessed with a rugged coastline of small inlets and sandy beaches.

4 Eivissa. Sleepy from November to May, the capital of Ibiza is transformed in summer into Party Central for retro hippies and nonstop clubbers. Dalt Vila, the medieval quarter on the hill overlooking the town, is a UNESCO World Heritage site.

Eivissa in full swing.

THE BALEARIC ISLANDS PLANNER

When to Go

July and August are peak season in the Balearics; it's hot, and even the most secluded beaches are crowded. Weatherwise, May and October are ideal, with June and September just behind. Winter is quiet, too cold for the beach, but fine for hiking, golfing, and exploring. The clubbing season on Ibiza begins in June, but beat the crowds with a visit in mid-May, for the Medieval Festival in Dalt Vila. Late February is a good time to be on Majorca, for *Sa Rua,* the carnival season in Palma in the week before Lent. Plan to be on Minorca in the last weekend of June, for the spectacular displays of horsemanship at the Festival of Sant Joan in Ciutadella. Note: between November and February many hotels and restaurants are closed for their own holidays or seasonal repairs.

Getting There & Around

Each of the islands is served by an international airport, all of them within 15 or 20 minutes by car or bus from the capital city. There are daily domestic connections to each from Barcelona, Madrid, and Valencia: no-frills and charter operators fly to Palma, Mahón, and Elvissa from many European cities, especially during the summer. There are also interisland flights. In high season, book early.

For die-hard romantics, the best way to get to the Balearic Islands is by overnight ferry from Barcelona. Sailings to Palma depart around 11 PM; you can watch the lights of Barcelona sinking into the horizon for hours—and when you arrive in Palma, around 6 AM, see the spires of the cathedral bathed in the morning sun. Ferries serve Minorca and Ibiza as well. There are also fast ferries and catamarans, which take about 4½ hours. Overnight ferries have both lounges and private cabins; the fast ferries and catamarans have only lounges.

By far, the best way to get around the islands is by car. Car rental agencies have offices at the airports and seaports, in the capital cities, and in many of the seaside resorts. (Reserving a car from home with a major agency can save you money, but don't count out the local companies, which often have better rates.) A car is essential if you want to beach-hop, especially to the isolated coves, or visit any of the islands' archaeological sites. The only trains in the Balearics are on Majorca, connecting Palma to Inca and Sóller; buses provide most of the public transportation. Bus services are good from Palma to towns throughout Majorca, and on Minorca between Mahón and Ciutadella and the towns in between. On Ibiza, hourly or half-hourly buses link Elvissa to the major beach resorts; routes to other parts of the island run less frequently. Service on Formentera is very limited: rent a car—or better yet, a scooter.

See the Balearic Islands Essentials at the end of this chapter for more transportation information.

Dig In

One thing you should be able to count on, from any self-respecting Mediterranean island, is great seafood—and the Balearics deliver. Majorcans revel in their *sopas i panades de peix* (fish soups and pies). On Minorca, the harbor restaurants of Mahón, Ciutadella, and Fornells are famous for their *llagosta* (spiny lobster), grilled or served in a *caldereta*—a stew with peppers, onion, tomato, and garlic; another Minorcan specialty is the ugly but succulent *cap roig* (scorpion fish.) From Ibiza's little coves and inlets, fishermen venture out for sea bass, bream, grouper, and *dorada* (John Dory); they sell the catch directly to beach shacks and family restaurants celebrated for *bullit* (fish casserole), *guisat de peix* (a kind of hotpot dish that can also include varieties of shellfish), and *burrida de ratjada* (ray poached with almonds).

The Balearic farms and forests yield another sort of bounty: traditional dishes like *sofrit pagès* (country-style sausage with potatoes and red peppers stewed in olive oil and garlic), *rostit* (oven-roasted pork with liver, eggs, bread, and apples), and *tumbet* (fried zucchini, potatos, eggplant, and bell peppers baked in tomato sauce). Restaurants in the Ibizan countryside serve wonderful lamb and goat chops *a la brasa* (on a wood-fired outdoor grill); Minorcan free-range beef is lean and tender; any Majorcan chef worth his or her salt has a recipe for rabbit; and no meal should begin without *sopas mallorquinas*, a rich vegetable soup in meat stock, usually served over pieces of thinly sliced bread. Delicatessen specialties are also traditional, like *sobrasada*, the pork-and-red-pepper Majorcan sausage paste. Even the fluffy, sweet *ensaimada*—a powdery spiral pastry—is based on *saim* (pork fat).

Meat, fish, and noodle dishes are usually served with a helping of garlic mayonnaise called allioli (Legend has it that mayonnaise itself was invented on Minorca during the French occupation and named after Mahón.) Minorca also has one of the 12 *denominacion de origin* officially designated cheese-producing regions in Spain. The *curado* (fully cured) cheese is the best.

WHAT IT COSTS In Euros

	$$$$	$$$	$$	$	¢
RESTAURANTS	over €20	€15–€20	€10–€15	€6–€10	under €6
HOTELS	over €180	€100–€180	€60–€100	€40–€60	under €40

Prices are per person for a main course at dinner. Prices are for two people in a standard double room in high season, excluding tax.

Planning Your Time

Start in Majorca with **Palma.** Begin early at the Cathedral and explore the city's monuments: the Llotja, the Almudaina Palace, the Placa Major. The churches of Santa Eulalia and Sant Francesc, and the Arab Baths are a must. Staying overnight in Palma means you can sample the nightlife, and have time to visit the museums (Es Baluard, Miró). Take the old train to **Sóller,** and rent a car for a trip over the Sierra de Tramuntana to **Deià,Son Marroig,** and **Valldemossa.** The roads are twisty; give yourself a full day. Spend the night in Sóller, and you can drive from there in less than an hour, via **Lluc** and **Pollença** to the Roman and Arab remains at **Alcúdia.** By hydrofoil it's just over three hours from Port d'Alcúdia to **Ciutadella,** on Menorca; the port, the **Cathedral,** and the narrow streets of the old city can be explored in half a day. Make your way across the island to **Mahón,** and devote an afternoon to the highlights there. The local bus takes about an hour. From Mahón, you can take a 30 minute interisland flight to **Eivassa.** On Ibiza, plan a full day for the World Heritage site of **Dalt Vila** and the shops of **Sa Penya,** and the better part of another for **Santa Gertrudis** and the north coast. But if you've come to Ibiza to party, of course, time has no meaning.

Updated by Jared Lubarsky

COULD ANYTHING GO WRONG IN a destination that gets, on average, 300 days of sunshine a year? True, the water is only warm enough for a dip May through October—but the climate does seem to give the residents of the Balearics a year-round sunny disposition. They are a remarkably *hospitable* people, not merely because tourism accounts for such a large chunk of their economy, but because history and geography have combined to put them in the crossroads of so much Mediterranean trade and traffic.

The Balearic Islands were outposts, successively, of the Phoenician, Carthaginian, and Roman empires before the Moors invaded in 902 and took possession for some 300 years. In 1235, the Moors were ousted by Jaume I of Aragón, and the islands became part of the independent kingdom of Majorca until 1343, when they returned to the Crown of Aragón under Pedro IV. Upon the marriage of Isabella of Castile to Ferdinand of Aragón in 1469, the Balearics were joined to a united Spain. Great Britain occupied Minorca in 1704, during the War of the Spanish Succession, to secure the superb natural harbor of Mahón as a naval base. The British stayed for almost a century, interrupted only by an invasion in 1756, which gave the French control for 12 years, and a shorter reoccupation by the Spanish 20 years later. Under the Treaty of Amiens, Britain finally returned Minorca to Spain in 1802.

During the Spanish civil war, Minorca remained loyal to Spain's democratically elected Republican government, while Majorca and Ibiza sided with Franco's insurgents. Majorca became a home base for the Italian fleet supporting the fascist cause. This topic is still broached delicately on the islands; they remain fiercely independent of one another in many ways. Even Mahón and Ciutadella, at opposite ends of Minorca—all of 44 km (27 mi) apart—remain estranged over differences dating from the war.

The tourist boom, which began during Francisco Franco's regime (1939–75), turned great stretches of Majorca's and Ibiza's coastlines into strips of high-rise hotels, fast-food restaurants, and discos.

In 1983 the Balearics became an Autonomous Community. One result has been the replacement of Castilian Spanish by the Catalan language (banned for official use by Franco) in its Mallorquín, Menorquín, and Ibizencan dialects. This guide uses Catalan for place names wherever they appear so in maps and pamphlets: *avinguda* (avenue), *Carrer* (street), and *plaça* (square) are Catalan; *cala* is the local word for "cove" or "inlet."

EXPLORING THE BALEARIC ISLANDS

Majorca and Ibiza are the most heavily developed of the islands, in terms of resorts and tourist infrastructure, and draw the lion's share of foreign visitors, especially from Germany and Great Britain. The north coasts of both have spectacular rocky coastlines, undeveloped areas, and wonderfully clear waters. Minorca, the preferred destination of Spanish and Catalan families on holiday, prides itself on being a protected biosphere; much of it is still farms and pastures, checkerboarded with low stone walls, and nature reserves. Formentera has virtually no tourism outside the summer months.

ABOUT THE BEACHES

MAJORCA The closer a beach is to Palma, the more crowded it's likely to be. West of the city is Palma Nova; behind the lovely, narrow beach rises one of the most densely developed resorts on the island. Paguera, with several small beaches, is the only sizable local resort not overshadowed by high-rises. Camp de Mar, with a good beach of fine white sand, is small and relatively undeveloped but is sometimes overrun with day-trippers from other resorts. Sant Elm, at the end of this coast, has a pretty little bay and a tree-shaded parking lot. East of Palma, a 5-km (3-mi) stretch of sand runs along the main coastal road from C'an Pastilla to Arenal, forming a package-tour nexus also known collectively as Playa de Palma. The crowded beach is long with fine white sand.

On the northwest coast, there's a popular beach at Port de Sóller. Farther north, the lovely Sa Calobra Beach, with its fine white sand and quiet cove, draws lots of day visitors in the summer. Moderately developed Cala St. Vicenç has fine, soft sand in two narrow bays. At Port de Pollença, on the north coast, the sand is imported, but the resort is attractive and has good water sports. There's frequent water-taxi service from Port de Pollença to Formentor, one of the finest beaches on Majorca. The north coast also has the island's longest sand beach; it stretches 8 km (5 mi) from Port de Alcúdia to beyond C'an Picafort. Ses Casetes, near Port des Pins, is the best stretch.

Majorca's east coast has numerous beaches and coves, though few are easily reachable by car. Canyamel, near the Caves of Artà, is a large, undeveloped strand. Farther south, Costa d'es Pins is an extensive development, with a good sandy stretch backed by a thin line of pines. Tourist buses, which look like train engines, run from here to Cala Millor, where the beach is accessible only on foot. Still farther south, Cala d'Or is a pleasant resort, and Cala Gran, a short walk away, is even more attractive. Cala Mondrajó is a tiny, sandy bay with little development; it's most easily reached by boat from Portopetre or Cala Figuera. On the south coast, the dune-backed beach at Es Trenc, near Colònia de Sant Jordi, is a quiet seaside patch. The 10-km (6-mi) walk along the beach from Colònia de Sant Jordi to the Cap Salines lighthouse is one of Majorca's treasures.

MINORCA Cala Sa Mesquida, north of Mahón, is a popular beach with limited access by road. Farther north, Es Grau, a sandy stretch with dunes behind it, lies at the edge of the S'Albufera nature reserve. Before the lighthouse at the end of Cap Favàritx are the nudist beaches Cala Presili and Playa Tortuga. Arenal d'en Castell, a sheltered circular bay, and Arenal de Son Saura (Son Parc) are the north's biggest sandy beaches. At the junction of the Mahón–Fornells and Mercadal–Fornells roads, take the small lane leading west and follow signs to Binimellà, an excellent sandy beach. It's often deserted, and the caves in the tiny coves to the west provide welcome shade in the summer.

9

The only reasonable and open-to-the-public beach north of Ciutadella is Cala Morell. Minorcans claim that the inlets and beaches at Cala Algaiarens are the nicest. Son Saura, Cala en Turqueta, Macarella, and Cala Galdana at the west end of the south coast are all reached by driving southeast from Ciutadella toward Son Saura. All three are classic Minorcan beaches with trees down to the water's edge, horseshoe coves, and white sand. To the east, Cala Mitjana, Cala Trebaluger, Cala Fustam, and Cala Escorxada are accessible by land only on foot, but you can rent boats with outboard engines to reach them or Son Saura. You can get to the long, straight, sandy stretches of Binigaus, Sant Adeodato, and Santo Tomas from Mercadal, and to Son Bou, the island's longest beach (with a nudist section), from Alaior. Cala'n Porter is a British enclave sheltered by cliffs. On the southeastern tip of the island is the windswept, white-sand beach at Punta Prima.

IBIZA Immediately south of Ibiza Town (aka Eivissa) is a long, sandy beach, the nearly 3-km (2-mi) Playa d'en Bossa. Farther on, a left turn at Sant Jordi on the way to the airport leads across the salt pans to Cavallet and Ses Salines, two of the best beaches on the island. Topless bathing is accepted all over Ibiza, but Es Cavallet is the official nudist beach. The remaining beaches on this part of the island are accessible from the Ibiza–Sant Josep–Sant Antoni highway, down side roads that often end in rough tracks. North of Sant Antoni, there are no easily accessible beaches until you reach Puerto San Miguel, an almost rectangular cove with relatively restrained development. Next along the north coast, accessible via San Juan, is Portinatx, a series of small coves with sandy beaches, of which the first and last, Cala Xarraca and Caló d'Es Porcs, are the best. East of San Juan is the long, curved cove beach of Cala San Vicente. Popular with families, it has a more leisurely pace than Ibiza's other resorts. The beaches on the east coast have been developed, but Santa Eulalia remains attractive. The resort has a narrow, sloping beach in front of a pedestrian promenade that is much less frenetic than Sant Antoni.

FORMENTERA Wild and lonely beaches are the rule on Formentera. The undeveloped Playa de Mitjorn stretches for 7 km (4 mi) along the south of the island. Trucadors, a long, thin spit at the north, has 2 km (1 mi) of sand on each side, and in summer you can wade to Es Palmador, where you can find more sandy beaches and a preponderance of nude bathers.

ABOUT THE HOTELS

Many hotels on the islands include a continental or full buffet breakfast in the price of a room.

MAJORCA Majorca's newer resorts—more than 1,500 of them—are concentrated mainly on the southern coast, and mainly serve the package-tour industry. Perhaps the best accommodations on the island are the number of grand old country estates and town houses that have been converted into boutique hotels, ranging from simple and relatively inexpensive *agroturismos* to stunning outposts of luxury.

MINORCA Apart from a few hotels and hostels in Mahón and Ciutadella, almost all of Minorca's tourist lodgings are in beach resorts. As on the other

CELEBRATIONS FROM ISLAND TO ISLAND

MAJORCA FIESTAS

Sant Joan Pelós is celebrated June 23–24 in Felanitx; a man dressed in sheepskins represents John the Baptist. The **Romería de Sant Marçal** (Pilgrimage of St. Mark), held June 30 in Sa Cabaneta.

MINORCA FIESTAS

Ciutadella's feast of **Sant Joan** (June 23–24) has townspeople dancing on horseback, trying to keep the horses up on their hind legs while the crowd gathers beneath. **Sant Lluís,** at the end of August, spotlights equestrian activities. Mahón's **Fiestas de Gràcia** (September 7–8) are the season's final celebrations.

IBIZA FIESTAS

Ibiza's patron saint, **Mare de Déu dels Neus** (Our Lady of the Snows), is honored on August 8 in memory of the conquest of Ibiza. **Sant Antoni d'Abat** (January 17) has processions of pets, cavalry, and livestock. On February 12 the **Festes de Santa Eulalia** is a boisterous winter carnival with folk dancing and live music. **Sant Josep** (March 19) is known for folk dancing, which you can also see in Sant Joan every Thursday evening. On June 23 and 24, witness the islandwide **Festa Major de Sant Joan** (Feast of St. John the Baptist). The **Festa del Mar,** honoring the Mare de Déu del Carme (Our Lady of Carmen), is held July 15–16 in Eivissa, Santa Eulalia, Sant Antoni, and Sant Josep, and on Formentera.

FORMENTERA FIESTAS

On July 15 and 16 islanders honor the **Virgen del Carmen,** patron saint of sailors, with processions of boats and anything else that floats. On July 25, Sant Francesc dances in honor of **Sant Jaume** (St. James), Spain's male patron saint.

islands, many of these are fully reserved by travel operators in the high season and often require a week's minimum stay, so it's generally most economical to book a package that combines airfare and accommodations. Alternatively, inquire at the tourist office about boutique and country hotels, especially in and around Sant Lluis.

9

IBIZA Ibiza's hotels are mainly in coastal Sant Antoni and Playa d'en Bossa. Many of these are excellent, but unless you're eager to be part of a mob, Sant Antoni has little to recommend it. Playa d'en Bossa, close to Eivissa, is prettier, but it lies under the flight path to the airport. To get off the track and into the island's largely pristine interior, look for *agroturismo* lodgings in Els Amunts (The Uplands) and in villages such as Santa Gertrudis or Sant Miquel de Balanzat.

FORMENTERA If July and August are the only months you can visit, reserve well in advance. To get the true feel of this smallest major member of the archipelago, look for the most out-of-the-way *calas* and fishing villages.

Numbers in the text correspond to numbers in the margin and on the chapter maps.

MAJORCA

Saddle-shaped Majorca is more than five times the size of either Minorca or Ibiza. The Sierra de Tramuntana, a dramatic mountain range soaring to nearly 5,000 feet, runs the length of its northwest coast, and a ridge of hills borders the southeast shores; between the two lies a flat plain that in early spring becomes a sea of almond blossoms, "the snow of Majorca." The island draws more than 10 million visitors a year—Palma's international airport is bigger than Barcelona's—many of them bound for summer vacation packages in the coastal resorts. The beaches are beautiful, but save time for the charms of the northwest and the interior: caves, bird sanctuaries, monasteries and medieval cities, local museums, outdoor cafés, and village markets.

PALMA DE MAJORCA

❶ *40-min flight, 8-hr overnight ferry, or 4 ½-hr catamaran from Barcelona.*

If you look north of the cathedral (La Seu, or the "seat" of the Bishopric, to Majorcans) on a map of the city of Palma, you can see around the Plaça Santa Eulalia a jumble of tiny streets that made up the earliest settlement. Farther out, a ring of wide boulevards, known as the Avenues, follow a path made from walls built by the Moors to defend the larger city that emerged by the 12th century. The zigzags mark the bastions that jutted out at regular intervals. By the end of the 19th century the walls were largely torn down; the only place where you can still see the massive defenses is Ses Voltes, along the seafront west of the cathedral.

A streambed (*torrent*) used to run through the middle of the old city, dry for most of the year but often a raging flood in the rainy season. In the 17th century it was diverted to the east, along the moat that ran outside the city walls. The stream's natural course is now followed by La Rambla and the Passeig d'es Born, two of Palma's main arteries. The traditional evening *paseo* (promenade) takes place on the Born.

If you come to Palma by car, park in the garage beneath the Parc de la Mar (the ramp is just off the highway from the airport, as you reach the cathedral) and stroll along the park. Beside it run the huge bastions guarding the Almudaina Palace; the cathedral, golden and massive, rises beyond. Where you exit the garage, there's a **ceramic mural** by the late Catalan artist and Majorca resident Joan Miró, facing the cathedral across the pool that runs the length of the park.

If you begin early enough, a walk along the ramparts at Ses Voltes from the *mirador* (lookout) beside the Palma cathedral is spectacular. The first rays of the sun turn the upper pinnacles of La Seu bright gold and begin to work their way down the sandstone walls. From the Parc de la Mar, follow Avinguda Antoni Maura past the steps to the palace. Just below the Plaça de la Reina, where the **Passeig d'es Born** begins, turn left on Carrer de la Boteria into the Plaça de la Llotja (don't miss a chance to visit the Llotja itself, the Mediterranean's finest civic Gothic build-

ing, if it's open), and stroll from there through the Plaça Drassana to the **Museu d'Es Baluard,** at the end of Carrer Sant Pere.

9

Retrace your steps to Avinguda Antoni Maura. Walk up the Passeig d'es Born to Plaça Joan Carles I, then left on Avenida de La Unió and up Carrer de Sant Joan. About 110 yards west of the Plaça Joan Carles I, on the Plaça del Mercat, is **San Nicolau** (✉ *Plaça del Mercat*), a 14th-century church with a hexagonal bell tower. The ornate facades of the **Casas Casasayas** (✉ *Plaça del Mercat, 13, 14*), on opposite corners of Carrer Santa Cilia, were designed by Moderniste architect Francesc Roca Simó in 1908; the ground floors are occupied by a bank and a boutique. Although brilliant examples of the Moderniste style, the Casas Casasayas are outshone by the **Gran Hotel** (✉ *Pl. Weyler 3*), across the square, built between 1901 and 1903 by Luis Domènech i Montaner, author of Barcelona's Palau de la Música Catalana. The alabaster facade is sculpted like a wedding cake, with floral motifs, angelic heads, and coats of arms; the original interiors, alas, have been "refurbished." No longer a hotel, the building is owned by the Fundació "La Caixa," a cultural and social organization funded by the region's largest bank. Don't miss the permanent exhibit of Majorcan impressionist Anglada Camarassa.

Take time to appreciate the neoclassical symmetry of the **Teatre Principal,** at the top of the Plaça Weyler (☎*971/7725548*), Palma's chief venue for opera and classical music, which reopened in April 2007 after extensive renovation. Near the steps leading up to the right of the Teatre Principal is the **Forn des Teatre** (✉*Pl. Weyler 12*), a unique bakery known for its *ensaimadas* (a typically Spanish fluffy pastry) and *cocas* (meat pies). From the Forn des Teatre, climb the steps to the **Plaça Major.** A crafts market fills this elegant neoclassical square on Monday, Friday, and Saturday between 10 and 2. A flight of steps on the east side of the Plaça Major leads down to the **Rambla,** a pleasant promenade lined with flower stalls.

★ A few steps from the north archway of the Plaça Major is the **Museu d'Art Espanyol Contemporani.** This fine little museum was established by the Joan March Foundation to display what had been a private collection of modern Spanish art; the building itself was a sumptuous private home dating to the 18th century. The second and third floors were redesigned to accommodate a series of small galleries, with one or two works at most—by Picasso, Miró, Juan Gris, Dalí, Antoni Tàpies, Miguel Barceló, among others—on each wall. ✉*Carrer Sant Miguel 11* ☎*971/713515* 🌐*www.march.es/museupalma* *Free* ⏲Weekdays *10–6:30, Sat. 10:30–2.*

Walk south from the Plaça Major on Carrer Colom, and above the Cacao Sampaka chocolate shop on the right, at the next small square, contemplate another Art Nouveau delight: the **Can Forteza Rei** (✉*Plaça Marqués Palmer 1*), designed by the original owner, Luis Forteza Rei, in 1909. The building has twisted wrought-iron railings and surfaces inlaid with bits of polychrome tile, signature touches of Gaudí and his contemporaries. A wonderful carved stone face, in a painful grimace, flanked by dragons, ironically frames the stained-glass windows of a third-floor dental clinic. Carrer Colom brings you to the 17th-century **Ajuntament** (*Town Hall* ✉*Plaça Cort*); stop in to see the collection of *gigantes*—the huge painted and costumed mannequins paraded through the streets at festivals—on display in the lobby. The olive tree on the right side of the square is one of Majorca's so-called *olivos milenarios*—thousand-year-old olives—and may be even older.

Turn right at the olive tree for a brief detour to the end of the Plaça Cort. On the left at the corner of Carrer de Jaume II is yet another gem of Palma's early Modernist architecture: the **Can Corbella** (✉*Plaça Cort 3*), designed in the 1890s by the Nicolás Lliteras.

A few steps along the Carrer de la Cadena bring you to the imposing Gothic church of **Santa Eulalia.** In 1435, 200 Jews were converted to Christianity in this church after their rabbis were threatened with being burned at the stake. ✉*Plaça Santa Eulalia, Barrio Antiguo.*

From the Plaça de Sant Eulalia, take the Carrer del Convent de Sant Francesc to the beautiful 13th-century monastery church of **Sant Francesc,** established by Jaume II when his eldest son took monastic orders and gave up rights to the throne. Fra Junípero Serra, the missionary who founded San Francisco, California, was later educated here; his statue stands to the left of the main entrance. The basilica houses the tomb of the eminent 13th-century scholar Ramón Llull. Enter the church and cloisters through the collegiate buildings on the east side. ✉ *Plaça Sant Francesc, Barrio Antiguo* ⏲ *Mon.–Sat. 9:30–1 and 3–6, Sun. 9:30–1* 🎫 *€1.*

From the Plaça Sant Francesc, take Carrer Pere Nadal south toward the bay; the street changes names as it descends, crossing Carrer del Call (in many Spanish cities and towns, the term *call* indicates the site of the medieval Jewish quarter) to become Carrer Santa Clara, then Carrer de Can Pont i Vic. On the left as it turns to Carrer de la Portella is the **Museu de Majorca**. Housed in the 18th-century ducal palace of the Condes de Ayamans, the museum exhibits the findings of all the major archeological research on Majorca, from prehistory to the Roman, Vandal, and Moorish occupations: pottery, bronzes, stone burial chambers, tools, and ornaments. Wall panels are in English. ✉ *Carrer de la Portella 5, Barrio Antiguo* ☎ *971/717540* 🎫 *€2.40* ⏲ *Tues.–Sat. 10–7, Sun. 10–2.*

From the Museu de Majorca, walk down Carrer de la Portella and turn left before the archway at the bottom of the street; follow the signs to one of Palma's oldest monuments, the 10th-century **Banys Arabs** *(Arab Baths)*, in a wonderful walled garden of tall palms, palmettos, and lemon trees. In its day, it was not merely a public bathhouse but a social institution, an oasis where you could soak, relax, and gossip with your neighbors. ✉ *Serra 7, Barrio Antiguo* ☎ *971/721549* 🎫 *€1.50* ⏲ *Dec.–Mar., daily 9–6; Apr.–Nov., daily 9–7:30.*

Fodor'sChoice ★ Palma's **cathedral** is an architectural wonder that took almost 400 years to build (1230–1601). The extraordinarily wide (63-foot) expanse of the nave is supported on 14 extremely slender 70-foot-tall columns, which fan out at the top like palm trees. The nave is dominated by an immense rose window, 40 feet in diameter, from 1370. Over the main altar (consecrated in 1346) is the almost surrealistic **baldoquí** by Antoni Gaudí completed in 1912: an enormous canopy, lamps suspended from it like elements of a mobile, rising to a Crucifixion scene at the top. To the right of it, in the Chapel of the Santisima, is an equally remarkable work, by the modern sculptor Miquel Barceló: a painted ceramic tableau that covers the walls of the chapel like a skin. Unveiled in 2007, the tableau is based on the New Testament account of the miracle of the loaves and fishes; Barceló renders this story in a bizarre composition of rolling waves, gaping cracks, protruding fish heads, and human skulls. The **bell tower** above the cathedral's Plaça Almoina door holds nine bells, the largest of which is known as N'Eloi, meaning "Praise." N'Eloi was cast in 1389, weighs 5½ tons, needs six men to ring it, and has shattered stained-glass windows with its sound. ✉ *Pl. Almoina s/n, Barrio Antiguo* ☎ *971/723130* 🎫 *€4* ⏲ *Apr.–May, weekdays 10–5:15; June–Sept., weekdays 10–6:15; Nov.–Mar., weekdays 10–3:15; year-round, Sat 10–2:15, Sun. for worship only, 8:30–1:45, 6:30–7:45.*

Opposite Palma's cathedral is the **Palau de l'Almudaina** *(Almudaina Palace)*, residence of the royal house of Majorca during the Middle Ages and

9

originally an Arab citadel. It's now a military headquarters. Guided tours generally depart hourly during open hours. ✉*Carrer Palau Reial s/n, Barrio Antiguo* ☎*971/214134* 🎫*€3.20; €4 with a guided tour; audioguide €2* ⏲*Weekdays 10–2 and 4–6, Sat. 10–2.*

DID YOU KNOW?

It's no small measure of modern-day Majorca's openness and liberality that the most important commission in Palma's cathedral in nearly a century was entrusted to Miquel Barceló—a self-proclaimed atheist.

The **Llotja** *(Exchange)*, on the seafront west of the Plaça de la Reina, was built in the 15th century and is connected by an interior courtyard to the **Consolat de Mar** (Maritime Consulate). With its decorative turrets, battlements, fluted pillars, and Gothic stained-glass windows—part fortress, part church—it attests to the veneration of wealth Majorca achieved in its heyday as a Mediterranean trading power. It can be visited inside only when there are special exhibitions in the Merchants Chamber. ✉*Pl. de la Llotja 5, La Llotja* ☎*971/711705* ⏲*During exhibits, Tues.–Sat. 11–2 and 5–9, Sun. 11–2.*

★ Inaugurated in January 2004, the **Museu d'Es Baluard** *(Museum of Modern and Contemporary Art of Palma)* rises on a long-neglected archaeological site at the western end of the city, parts of which date back to the 12th century. The building itself is an outstanding convergence of old and new: the exhibition space uses and merges into the surviving 16th-century perimeter walls of the fortified city, with a stone courtyard facing the sea and a promenade along the ramparts. There are three floors of galleries; the collection includes work by Miró, Picasso, Magritte, Tapiès, Calder, and other major artists. The café-terrace Restaurant del Museu (Tuesday–Sunday 1–4 and 8–11), in the courtyard, affords a fine view of the marina. ✉*Pl. Porta de Santa Catalina s/n, Puig Sant Pere* ☎*971/908200* 🌐*www.esbaluard.org* 🎫*€6* ⏲*Oct.–May, Tues.–Sun. 10–8; June–Sept., Tues.–Sun. 10 AM–10 PM.*

The **Castell de Bellver** *(Bellver Castle)* overlooks the city and the bay from a hillside. It was built at the beginning of the 14th century, in Gothic style but with a circular design—the only one of its kind in Spain. An archaeological **museum** of the history of Majorca and a small collection of classical sculpture sit inside. ✉*Camilo José Cela s/n* ☎*971/730657* 🎫*€2, free Sun.* ⏲*Castle and museum: Oct.–Mar., Mon.–Sat. 8–8; Apr.–Sept., Mon.–Sat. 8–9. Castle only: Sun. 10–5.*

The permanent collection in the **Museu Fundació Pilar y Joan Miró** *(Pilar and Joan Miró Foundation Museum)* includes a great many drawings and studies by the Catalan artist, who spent his last years on Majorca, but shows far fewer finished paintings and sculptures than the Fundació Miró in Barcelona. Don't miss the adjacent studio, built for Miró by his friend the architect Josep Lluis Sert. The artist did most of his work here from 1957 on. ✉*Carrer Joan de Saridakis 29, Cala Major, Marivent* ☎*971/701420* 🌐*http://miro.palmademallorca.es/english/index.htm* 🎫*€5* ⏲*Sept. 16–May 15, Tues.–Sat. 10–6, Sun. 10–3; May 16–Sept. 15, Tues.–Sat. 10–7, Sun. 10–3.*

WHERE TO STAY & EAT

> **WORD OF MOUTH**
>
> "Palma and the little towns in the north have lots of foreign residents, but they're still very Spanish. The weather is great, and the people are very friendly."
>
> –Fiona

$$$–$$$$ ★ ✕ **Koldo Royo.** Crowded with modern art, this chic yellow dining room overlooks the marina. Chef-owner Koldo Royo conjures up Basque specialties such as lamprey eel, salt cod, tripe, and stuffed quail; try the *cochinillo confitado con salsa de miel* (roast suckling pig with honey sauce). ✉ *Av. Gabriel Roca 3, Paseo Marítimo* ☎ *971/732435* ▭ *AE, MC, V* ⊙ *Closed Sun. and Mon.*

$–$$ ✕ **La Bóveda.** Within hailing distance of the Llotja, this bustling, popular eatery serves tapas and inexpensive platters such as chicken or ham croquettes, grilled cod topped with tomato sauce, garlic shrimp, and *revuelto con setas y jamón* (scrambled eggs with mushrooms and ham). Tables are always at a premium; there's additional seating at the counter, or on stools around upended wine barrels. Nothing fancy here: just ample portions of good food. ✉ *Carrer de la Botería 3, La Llotja* ☎ *971/714863* ▭ *AE, MC, V* ⊙ *Closed Sun.*

$$$$ Fodor's Choice ★ ✕ **Read's Hotel & Spa.** A 15-minute drive from Palma, this peaceful retreat centers on a restored 18th-century estate house, with its own vineyard—a favorite with British honeymooners and haven-seekers. Detached suites have private gardens. The rooms are each furnished in a different, fanciful style, from Moorish-exotic to traditional and modern; lobby and lounge areas are filled with antiques from the owner's collection. The "Vespasian" spa, new in 2007, has an indoor pool with Greek motifs, and rooms for esthetic and deep relaxation treatments. Chef-Director Marc Fosh garnered top honors for his superb restaurant; serious eaters will book the "chef's table" in the evening–an alcove in the kitchen. ✉ *Ctra. Santa María–Alaró s/n, 07320* ☎ *971/140261* 📠 *971/140762* ⊕ *www.readshotel.com* *8 rooms, 15 suites* *In-room: safe, DVD, Wi-Fi. In-hotel: 2 restaurants, room service, bar, tennis court, 2 pools, gym, spa, bicycles, no elevator, laundry service, concierge, public Internet, public Wi-Fi, airport shuttle, parking (no fee), no children under 14* ▭ *AE, DC, MC, V* *BP.*

$$$$ ★ ✕ **Gran Hotel Son Net.** This restored estate house—parts of which date back to 1672—is one of Majorca's most luxurious hotels. Poplars and palms shade the terrace above the 30-meter pool, with the village of Puigpunyent and the surrounding countryside spread out below. Room decors can be a bit over the top—a lot of red and rose pink—but the bathrooms are truly palatial. The restaurant, L'orangerie, set in an ancient olive press, is an ideal showcase for the creations of chef Christian Rullan, trained at Le Nôtre in Paris but fiercely proud of his Majorcan roots; try his lamb in rosemary sauce with sauteed artichokes and wild mushrooms. (A sister hotel, Son Julia, opened in 2006 near Llucmajor, to the southeast.) ✉ *Carrer Castillo de Son Net, Puigpunyent 07194* ☎ *971/147000* 📠 *971/147001* ⊕ *www.sonnet.es* *26 rooms, 4 suites* *In-room: safe, refrigerator, DVD, some Ethernet, Wi-Fi. In-hotel: 2 restaurants, room service, 2 bars, 2 pools, gym, spa,*

9

bicycles, laundry service, concierge, public Internet, public Wi-Fi, airport shuttle, parking (no fee), no-smoking rooms ▭*AE, DC, MC, V.*

$$$ ★ **Palau Sa Font.** Warm Mediterranean tones and crisp, clean lines give this boutique hotel an atmosphere very different from anything else in Palma, and draw a predominately young European clientele. A 16th-century Episcopal palace (the bishop's residence), restored as a hotel in 2000, it has ample rooms with linen curtains and plump comforters. The light, airy breakfast room has chairs in pastel yellow, lime green, and orange. From the terrace in the tower, you have 360-degree views of Palma's old quarter. ✉*Carrer Apuntadores 38, Barrio Antiguo, 07012* ☎*971/712277* 📠*971/712618* 🌐*www.palausafont.com* *19 rooms* *In-room: refrigerator, Ethernet. In-hotel: bar, pool, some pets allowed* ▭*AE, MC, V* *BP.*

$$ **Born.** Romanesque arches and a giant palm tree spectacularly cover the central courtyard and reception area of this hotel, which occupies the former mansion of a noble Majorcan family. Guest rooms are modest, though some have the original coffered and painted ceilings, and the rates are more than reasonable. A buffet breakfast is included in the price. ✉*Carrer Sant Jaume 3, Centro, 07012* ☎*971/712942* 📠*971/718618* 🌐*www.hotelborn.com* *30 rooms* *In-hotel: restaurant, bar, no elevator, laundry service, airport shuttle, no-smoking rooms* ▭*AE, DC, MC, V* *BP.*

$ **Hostal Apuntadores.** It's easy to see why this is Palma's hostal of choice among budget travelers. It's cheap; the rooftop terrace has arguably the city's best view—overlooking the cathedral and the sea; and it's in the heart of the old town, within strolling distance of the bustling Passeig d'es Born. Rooms are basic (and some are cramped) but clean; ask for a room with a balcony. There is one dormitory-style room that sleeps six. ✉*Carrer Apuntadores 8, Barrio Antiguo, 07012* ☎*971/713491* 🌐*www.palma-hostales.com* *29 rooms, 15 with bath* *In-room: no phone, safe, refrigerator, Wi-Fi. In-hotel: restaurant, bar, laundry service, public Internet, public Wi-Fi* ▭*MC, V.*

NIGHTLIFE & THE ARTS

THE ARTS Outside in summer, the City of Palma Symphony Orchestra performs about twice a month at the **Auditorium** (✉*Passeig Marítim 18, Paseo Marítimo* ☎*971/734735* 🌐*www.auditoriumdepalma.com*), which also hosts performances by guest soloists and chamber orchestras, rock concerts, musicals, and plays. The neoclassical **Teatre Principal** (✉*laça Weiler s/n, Centro* ☎*971/713346* 🌐*www.teatreprincipal.com*) is the city's venue for opera, choral music, and drama.

NIGHTLIFE With some 200 discos and music bars scattered throughout the city and across the island, Majorca's nightlife is never hard to find. Many of the hot spots are concentrated 6 km (4 mi) west of Palma at **Punta Portals,** in Portals Nous, where King Juan Carlos I often moors his yacht when he's in Majorca in early August for the Copa del Rey—an international regatta and a magnet for Europe's beautiful people. In Palma, the section of the Passeig Marítim known as **Avinguda Gabriel Roca** is a nucleus of taverns, pubs, and clubs. The ever-popular **Pacha** (☎*971/455908*) thumps to house music until the wee hours. Once a week (usually Sunday) they host gay night, "Pacha Loca," with an infectious anything-goes vibe; the cover charge can be pricey (€10–€20). Outdoor elevators transport you from Avinguda Gabriel Roca to a large, packed-with-foreigners dance floor at the sleek and futuristic **Tito's** (☎*971/730017*).

★ The **Plaça de la Llotja** and surrounding streets are where to go for *copas* (drinking, tapas sampling, and general carousing). Elegant **Abaco** (✉*Carrer de Sant Joan 1, La Llotja* ☎*971/714939*) offers baroque music amid fragrant flowers and fruit.

Carrer Apuntadores, a street on the Born's west side in the old town, is lined with casual bars that appeal especially to night owls in their twenties and thirties. On the weekends, you can often come across impromptu live rock and pop acts performed on small back stages. Some of Palma's best jazz acts play the small, smoky jazz club **Barcelona** (✉*Carrer Apuntadores s/n, La Llotja* ☎*No phone*) on weekends. Relax over cocktails at the low-lighted, genteel **Golden Door.**

Join the after-work crowd basking in the Palma of yesteryear at **Grand Café Capuccino** (✉*Carrer Sant Miquel 53, Barrio Antiguo* ☎*971/719764*), an elegant bar-restaurant in a traditional Majorcan town house. **Bluesville** (✉*Carrer Ma de Morro 3, Barrio Antiguo* ☎*No phone*) is a laid-back bar popular with both locals and foreigners. You can listen to rock and blues on Saturday nights.In summer (June–September), head to the nearby suburb of Magalluf and dance the night away at the gargantuan disco **BCM Planet Dance** (✉*Av. S'Olivera s/n, Magalluf* ☎*No phone*), popular with a pan-European crowd.

Palma's **Gran Casino de Majorca** is a short distance from the harbor. There's an admission charge of €4, and you'll need your passport to enter; dress is informal, but T-shirts, shorts, and sandals are considered inappropriate. ✉*Urb. Sol de Majorca s/n, Calvià* ☎*971/130000* 🌐*www.casinodemallorca.com* ⏲*Daily 5–5.*

9

SPORTS & THE OUTDOORS

Turisme Actiu, a leaflet that details all sports clubs, describes everything from sea diving to skydiving, and is available at tourist offices.

BICYCLING The Majorca tourist board has an excellent series of leaflets on bike routes with maps, details about the terrain, sights, and distances. The tourist office of Cala Ratjada, in northeast Majorca, has a 12 page brochure that includes maps and photographs.

BIRD-WATCHING Majorca has two notable nature reserves, ideal for bird-watchers. **S'Albufera de Majorca** (✉*Ctra. Port d'Alcúdia–Ca'n Picafort, Hotel Parc Natural* ☎*971/892250* 🌐*www.mallorcaweb.net/salbufera* ⏲*Apr.–Sept., daily 9–7; Oct.–Mar., daily 9–5*) is the largest wetlands zone in Majorca, with binoculars for rent. **Sa Dragonera** (✉*Llista de Correus E-07458 Can Picafort, Majorca* ☎*971/180632* ⏲*Apr.–Sept., daily 9–5; Oct.–Mar., daily 9–4*) has a large colony of sea falcons and is accessible by boats from Sant Elm, the western tip of Majorca. **Cruceros Margarita** (☎*639/617545*) excursion boats to Sa Dragonera leave from the port of Sant Elm, at the western tip of the island, and from

Port d'Andratx, Monday–Saturday (except in January) at 10:15, 11:15, 12:15, and 1:15. The fare is €10.

GOLF Majorca has more than a score of 18-hole golf courses, among them PGA championship venues of fiendish difficulty. For more information, contact the **Federación Balear de Golf** (*Balearic Golf Federation* ☒*Av. Jaime III 17, Palma* ☎*971/722753* 🌐*www.fbgolf.com*).

HANG GLIDING For memorable views of the island, glide above it on an ultralight. Arrange a trip at **Escuela de Ultraligeros "El Cruce"** (☒*Ctra. Palma–Manacor, Km 42, Petra* ☎*629/392776*). For hang gliding, contact **Parapente Alfàbia** (☎*971/891366 or 687/626536* 🌐*www.parapentealfabia.com*). **Club Vol Lliure Majorca** (☎*655/766443* 🌐*www.cvlmajorca.com*) conducts weekend and intensive hang-gliding courses.

HIKING-WALKING Majorca is an excellent destination for hiking. In the Sierra de Tramuntana, you can easily arrange to trek one way and take a boat, bus, or train back. Ask the tourist office for the free booklet *20 Hiking Excursions on the Island of Majorca,* with detailed maps and itineraries. For excellent drawings and maps, track down *12 Classic Hikes Through Majorca,* by the German author Herbert Heinrich, available in the bookstores at key sights. For more hiking information contact the **Grup Excursionista de Majorca** (*Majorcan Hiking Association* ☒*Carrer Andreu Feliu 20, Palma* ☎*871/947900* 🌐*www.gemweb.org*). A useful outfit for foreign trekkers is **Explorador** (☎*600/557770* 🌐*www.exploradors.com*).

SAILING For information on sailing, call the **Federación Balear de Vela** (*Balearic Sailing Federation* ☒*Carrer Joan Miró s/n [San Agustin], Palma* ☎*971/402412* 🌐*www.federacionbalearvela.org*). The **Escuela Nacional de Vela de Calanova** (*National Sailing School* ☒*Av. Joan Miró 327, Palma* ☎*971/402512*) can clue you in about sailing in the Balearics. The **Club de Mar** (☒*Muelle de Pelaires, south end of Passeig Marítim, La Llotja, Palma* ☎*971/403611* 🌐*www.clubdemar-Majorca.com*) is famous among yachties. It has its own hotel, bar, disco, and restaurant. Charter a yacht at **Cruesa Majorca Yacht Charter** (☒*Passeig Marítim 16, Edificio Tròpic, Palma* ☎*971/282821* 🌐*www.cruesa.com*).

SCUBA DIVING Ask about scuba diving at **Escuba Palma** (☒*Via Rey Jaume I 84, Santa Ponsa* ☎*971/694968*). **Big Blue** (☒*Marti Ros García 6, Edificio Ski Club, Palma Nova, Calvià* ☎*971/681686*) is a scuba resource.

WATER SPORTS You can rent windsurfers and dinghies at most beach resorts; both skin- and scuba diving are excellent; and the island has some 30 yacht marinas. On the northwest coast at Port de Sóller, canoes, windsurfers, dinghies, motor launches, and waterskiing gear are available for rent from Easter to October at **Escola d'Esports Nàutics** (☒*Calle Marina s/n, Port de Sóller* ☎*609/354132* 🌐*www.nauticsoller.com*).

SHOPPING

Majorca's specialties are leather shoes and clothing, porcelain, souvenirs carved from olive wood, handblown glass, artificial pearls, and espadrilles. Top-name fashion boutiques line **Avinguda Jaume III** and the nearby Plaça Joan Carles I. Several antiques shops line the Plaça

Almoina. Less-expensive shopping strips are **Carrer Sindicat** and **Carrer Sant Miquel**—both pedestrian streets running north from the Plaça Major—and the small streets south of the Plaça Major. The **Plaça Major** itself has a modest crafts market Monday, Thursday, Friday, and Saturday 10 to 2. In summer the market is open daily 10 to 2; January and February, it's open weekends only. Another crafts market is held May 15 through October 15, 8 PM to midnight in **Plaça de les Meravelles.**

Leather is best in the high-end **Loewe** (✉*Av. Jaime III 1, Centro* ☎*971/715275*), a branch of the famed Spanish firm founded in 1846. Bags, jackets, and the like are artfully displayed in classy, perfumed surroundings; the expert staff provides personal attention. **Rampel** (✉*Av. Jaime III 21, Centro* ☎*971/715139*) sells high-quality leather coats and bags. **Barrats** (✉*Av. Jaime III 5, Centro* ☎*971/213024*) specializes in leather coats and shoes for women. Majorca's most popular footwear export—in summer, it seems like every Spaniard sports a pair—are its simple, comfortable slip-on espadrilles (usually with a leather front over the first half of the foot and a strap across the back of the ankle). They come in every color of the rainbow. Look for a pair at **Alpargatería La Concepción** (✉*Concepción 17, Barrio Antiguo* ☎*971/710709*).

Mediterráneo (✉*Av. Jaume III 11, Centro* ☎*971/712159*) sells high-quality artificial pearls in its elegant sit-down showroom. **Persépolis** (✉*Av. Jaume III 23, Centro* ☎*971/724539*) carries high-quality antiques. **Las Columnas** (✉*C. Sant Domingo 24, Barrio Antiguo*) has ceramics from all over the Balearic Islands. Visit **Gordiola** (✉*Carrer de la Victoria 8–12, Centro* ☎*971/711541*), glassmakers since 1719, for a variety of original bowls, bottles, plates, and decorative objects. The company's workshop is in Alguida, on the Palma-Manacor road, where you can watch the glass being blown and even try your hand at making a piece. Stop by **La Casa del Olivo** (✉*Carrer Pescateria Vella, Centro* ☎*971/727025*), just off Carrer Jaume II, for olive-wood crafts, from bowls to cutting boards.Local, national, and foreign wines are on sale at **La Vinoteca** (✉*Plaza Virgen de la Salud 3, Plaza de España* ☎*971/728829*).The **Colmado Santo Domingo** (✉*Carrer Santo Domingo 1* ☎*971/714887* 🌐*www.colmadosantodomingo.com* ⏲*Mon.–Sat. 10–8*), a wonderful little shop for the *artesenal* food specialities of Majorca: *sobresada* (soft salami) of black pork, sausages of all sorts, cheeses, jams and honeys and preserves.

JARDINS D'ALFÀBIA

❷ *17 km (10½ mi) north of Palma.*

Here's a sound you don't often hear in the Majorcan interior: the sound of falling water. The Moorish viceroy of the island developed the springs and hidden irrigation systems here sometime in the 12th century, to create this remarkable oasis on the road to Sóller, with its 40-odd varieties of trees, climbers, and flowering shrubs. The 17th-century manor house, furnished with antiques and painted panels, has a collection of original documents that chronicle the history of the estate.

✉Ctra. Palma–Sóller, Km. 17 ☎971/613123 🎫€4.50 ⏲Nov.–Mar., weekdays 9–5:30, Sat. 9–1; Apr.–Oct., Mon.–Sat. 9–6:30.

SÓLLER

3 ★ *13 km (8 ½ mi) north of Jardins d'Alfàbia, 30 km (19 mi) north of Palma.*

All but the briefest visits to Majorca should include at least an overnight stay in Sóller, for it's own sake—this is one of the most beautiful towns on the island. Sóller is thick with palatial homes built in the 19th and early 20th centuries by the owners of agricultural estates in the Sierra de Tramuntana, and the merchants who thrived on the export of the region's oranges, lemons, and almonds. Many of the buildings here, like the **Church of Sant Bartomeu** and the **Bank of Sóller,** on the Plaça Constitució, and the nearby **Can Prunera,** are gems of the Modernist style, designed by contemporaries of Antoni Gaudí. The tourist information office in the **Town Hall,** next to Sant Bartomeu, has a walking tour map of the important sites.

■**TIP➜ If you're driving to Sóller from Palma, take the tunnel (€4) at Alfàbia, rather than the road over the mountains. The latter is spectacular—lemon and olive trees on stone-walled terraces, farmhouses perched on the edges of forested cliffs—but demanding. Save your strength for even better mountain roads ahead.** Travel retro to Sóller from Palma on one of the six daily trains (round-trip: €14) from Pla[cd]a d'Espanya: a string of wooden coaches with leather-covered seats dating from 1912.

Sóller's **Station Building Galleries** (✉*Pl. Espanya 6* ☎*971/630301* 🎫*Free* ⏲*Daily 10:30–6:30*) have two small collections, one of engravings by Joan Miró, the other of ceramics by Picasso.

Catch the charming old blue-and-brass trolly (€3) that threads its way through town, down to Port de Sóller.

WHERE TO STAY & EAT

$$ ✕🏨 **El Guía.** Built in 1880, El Guía ("The Guide") is furnished in a comfortable mix of rustic and Modernist styles, with nothing fancy in the way of services or amenities. A few steps from the railroad station, it has a pretty courtyard with wrought-iron gates, rooms with a view of the mountains, and a restaurant popular for Majorcan specialties. ✉*Carrer Castanyer 2, 07100* ☎*971/630227* 📠*971/632634* 🌐*www.sollernet.com/elguia* *18 rooms* *In-room: no TV. In-hotel: restaurant, no elevator* 💳*MC, V* ⏲*Closed Nov.–Mar.* 🍽*BP.*

$$$$ 🏨 **L'Avenida.** Opened in March 2007, this boutique hotel was a stately private home, built in 1910 by Joan Rubio, a disciple of Gaudí, for a wealthy local merchant. The transformation retains some of the original Modernist features—frescoed ceilings, a marble staircase with wrought-iron railing—but from there it goes ultramodern, with white fiber rugs and black furniture, animal-print fabrics, designer lamps, and jet chandeliers, set off by shimmery taupe drapes. The house blends its own toiletries, with orange, juniper, and black pepper. ✉*Gran Via 9, 07100* ☎*971/634075* 🌐*www.avenida-hotel.com* *8 rooms* *In-*

room: safe, refrigerator, DVD, Ethernet, Wi-Fi. In-hotel: restaurant, bar, pool, bicycles, no elevator, laundry service, concierge, public Wi-Fi, no children under 14, no-smoking rooms ▭*MC, V.*

DEIÀ

4 ★ *9 km (5½ mi) southwest of Sóller.*

Deià is perhaps best known as the adopted home of the English poet and writer Robert Graves, who lived here off and on from 1929 until his death in 1985. The village is still a favorite haunt of writers and artists, including Graves's son Tomás, author of *Pa amb oli (Bread and Olive Oil)*, a guide to Majorcan cooking, and British painter David Templeton. The setting is unbeatable; all around Deià rise the steep cliffs of the Sierra de Tramuntana. There's live jazz on summer evenings. On warm afternoons, literati gather at the beach bar in the rocky cove at Cala de Deià, 2 km (1 mi) downhill from the village. Walk up the narrow street to the village church; the small **cemetery** behind it affords views of mountains terraced with olive trees and of the coves below. It's a fitting spot for Graves's final resting place, in a quiet corner.

In 2007, the Fundació Robert Graves opened a museum dedicated to Deià's most famous resident, in **Ca N'Alluny,** the house he built in 1932, overlooking the sea. The museum might be better described as a shrine: Graves' furniture and books, he personal effects and the press he used to print many of his works, are all preserved. ✉*Ctra. Deià-Sóller s/n* ☎*971/636185* 🌐*www.fundaciorobertgraves.com* *€5* ⏲*Tues.–Sat. 10–5, Sun. 10–3.*

WHERE TO STAY & EAT

¢–$ ✕**Restaurante Xelini El Barrigón.** The Dèians' favorite tapas bar is a cluttered, friendly place with stone floors and high-beamed ceilings, and resident artwork on whitewashed walls. In good weather, there are tables out in the back garden. Specialties include spicy sausage with onions and red peppers, fried goat cheese, and lamb tacos. ✉*Carrer Arxiduc Luis Salvador 19* ☎*971/639139 or 627/907310* 🌐*www.xelini.com* ▭*MC, V* ⏲*Closed Mon.*

$$$$ Fodor's Choice ★ ✕**La Residencia.** Two 16th- to 17th-century manor houses have been artfully combined to make this exceptional hotel on a hill facing the village of Deià, superbly furnished with Majorcan antiques, modern canvases, and canopied four-poster beds. Herbs, olives, fruit, and flowers come straight to the kitchen and guest rooms from the hotel's lush landscaped gardens. El Olivo, the restaurant ($$$–$$$$), offers an inventive Spanish and continental menu. The hotel has its own shuttle to the sea at Lluc al Cari. ✉*Son Canals s/n, 07179* ☎*971/639011* 📠*971/639370* 🌐*www.hotel-laresidencia.com* *67 rooms* *In-room: safe, refrigerator, DVD, Ethernet, Wi-Fi. In-hotel: 3 restaurants, room service, bar, 2 tennis courts, 3 pools, gym, spa, bicycles, children's programs, laundry service, public Internet, public Wi-Fi, airport shuttle, parking (no fee), no kids under 10 during July 1–Aug. 17, Oct. 20–31, Christmas, and New Year, no-smoking rooms* ▭*AE, DC, MC, V* *BP.*

9

SON MARROIG

5 *4 km (2½ mi) west of Deià.*

West of Deià is Son Marroig, one of the estates of Austrian archduke Luis Salvador (1847–1915), who arrived in Majorca as a young man and fell in love with the place. Speaker of 14 languages and a prolific writer, the archduke acquired estates and built great houses, mostly along the northwest coast, which he then furnished with miradors at each spectacular viewpoint. Now a museum, Son Marroig contains the archduke's collections of Mediterranean pottery and ceramics, old Majorcan furniture, and paintings. From April through early October, the Deià International Festival holds classical concerts here.

From the mirador you can see, nearly 1,000 feet below, **Sa Foradada,** a spectacular rock peninsula pierced by a huge archway, beneath which the archduke moored his yacht. A pathway, beginning near the café in the parking area, leads down to Sa Foradada (1 hour down, 1½ hours up). Four kilometers (2½ mi) farther, behind the restaurant C'an Costa, on the right, is another of the archduke's miradors, **Ses Pites,** named for the spiky cactus plants that surround it. ☒*Ctra. Deià–Valldemossa s/n* *€3* *May–Sept., Mon.–Sat. 10–8; Oct.–Apr., Mon.–Sat. 10–5:30.*

On the road south from Deià to Valldemossa is the **Monestir de Miramar,** founded in 1276 by Ramón Llull, who established a school of Asian languages here. It was bought in 1872 by the Archduke Luis Salvador and restored as a mirador. Explore the garden and the tiny cloister, then walk below through the olive groves to a spectacular lookout. ☒*Ctra. Deià–Valldemossa s/n* ☎*971/616073* *€3* *Mon.–Sat. 10–5.*

VALLDEMOSSA

6 *18 km (11 mi) north of Palma.*

The **Reial Cartuja** *(Royal Carthusian Monastery)* was founded in 1339, but when the monks were expelled in 1835, it was privatized, and the cells became apartments for travelers. The most famous lodgers were Frédéric Chopin and his lover, the Baroness Amandine Dupin—a French novelist who used the pseudonym George Sand. The two spent three difficult months here in the cold, damp winter of 1838–39. The tourist office, in the plaza next to the church, sells a ticket good for all of the monastery's attractions.

In the **church,** note the frescoes above the nave—the monk who painted them was Goya's brother-in-law. The **pharmacy,** in the cloisters, was made by the monks in 1723 and is almost completely preserved; from here, a long corridor leads to the apartments occupied by Chopin and Sand, furnished in period style. The piano is original. Nearby, another set of apartments houses the local **museum,** with mementos of Archduke Luis Salvador and a collection of old printing blocks. From here you return to the ornately furnished **King Sancho's palace,** a group of rooms originally built by King Jaume II for his son Sancho. ☒*Pl. de la*

Cartuja s/n ☎971/612106 📠971/612514 🌐www.valldemossa.com 🎫€8 ⏲Dec. and Jan., Mon.–Sat. 9:30–5; Feb., Mon.–Sat. 9:30–5, Sun. 10–1; Mar. and Oct., Mon.–Sat. 9:30–5:30, Sun. 10–1; Apr.–Sept., Mon.–Sat. 9:30–6:30, Sun. 10–1; Nov. 9:30–4:30, Sun. 10–1.

WHERE TO STAY

$$$$ ★ **Valldemossa Hotel.** The breathtaking vistas alone are worth a stay. Once part of the Valldemossa Carthusian monastery, this beautifully restored Majorcan stone house–turned–luxury hotel sits on a hill amid acres of olive trees and has sweeping views of the Bay of Palma and the Tramuntana mountains. Modern rooms have snowy white curtains and comforters, and antique bedsteads. You can relax on rattan chairs shaded by palms in the sunny patio and then ease into the evening at the elegant restaurant, which serves Mediterranean and international dishes. Between June 15 and August 20, a minimum stay of three nights is required. ✉*Ctra. Valldemossa s/n, 07170* ☎*971/612626* 📠*971/612625* 🌐*www.valldemossahotel.com* *3 rooms, 9 suites* *In-room: safe, refrigerator, DVD, Ethernet. In-hotel: restaurant, cafeteria, bar, 2 pools, spa, laundry service, airport shuttle, parking (no fee), no-smoking rooms* 💳*AE, MC, V* *BP.*

BANYALBUFAR

7 *23 km (14 mi) northwest of Palma.*

Originally terraced by the Romans, this tiny town overlooks its tiny harbor from high on a cliff. A 1½-km (1-mi) walk southwest leads to the **Mirador Ses Animes** observation point.

WHERE TO STAY

$$–$$$ ★ **Mar i Vent.** This small family-run hotel is at the north end of Banyalbufar. Paths lead down to two small, rocky coves for sea swimming. All guest rooms have balconies with sea or mountain views, and are furnished in traditional style with simple blond-wood furniture and red-brown tile floors. ✉*Carrer Major 49, Banyalbufar, 07191* ☎*971/618000* 📠*971/618201* 🌐*www.hotelmarivent.com* *29 rooms* *In-room: some a/c, safe, Ethernet. In-hotel: restaurant, room service, bar, tennis court, pool, bicycles, laundry service, public Internet, public Wi-Fi, airport shuttle, parking (no fee), no-smoking rooms* 💳*MC, V* ⏲*Closed Dec. and Jan.* *BP.*

BINISSALEM

8 *18 km (11 mi) northeast of Palma.*

Binissalem is the center of one of the island's two D.O. (Denominación de Orígen) registered wine regions and has a riotous harvest festival in mid-September, when surplus grapes are dumped by the truckload for participants to fling at each other. The town is a good base, not just for visits to the local **bodegas** *(wineries)*, but for forays around the island: Palma remains a half an hour by car.

INCA

9 *28 km (17 mi) northeast of Palma.*

Inca is known for its leather factories and its Thursday open-air market, the largest on Majorca (making parking a nightmare). If you don't find what you want among the stalls, hunt for crafts, leather, and pottery at the emporium outside town, on the left side of the road to Alcúdia. Be sure to try some *galletas* (a local kind of cookies).

WHERE TO EAT

$$–$$$ ✕ **Celler C'an Amer.** A *celler* is a uniquely Majorcan combination of wine cellar and restaurant, and Inca has no fewer than six. C'an Amer is the best, with heavy oak beams and huge wine vats lining the walls behind the tables and banquettes. Antonia, the dynamic chef-owner, serves some of the best *lechona* (suckling pig) and *tumbet* (vegetables baked in layers) on the island. Portions here are heroic. Winter specialties include a superb oxtail soup prepared with red wine and seasonal mushrooms. ✉ *Carrer Pau 39* ☎ *971/501261* ▭ *AE, MC, V* ⊙ *Closed weekends, Mar.–Sept. No dinner Sun.*

MANACOR

10 *50 km (30 mi) east of Palma.*

Majorca's second-largest town, Manacor is known primarily for its Majórica artificial-pearl industry; from here, it's only a few minutes' drive to any of the beaches on the island's eastern coast. Prehistoric settlement sites abound in this area; later, the Romans moved in, followed by the Moors, who built a mosque where the Gothic parish church of **Nostra Senyora de les Dolores** (Our Lady of Sorrows) now stands.

WHERE TO STAY & EAT

$$$$ ✕ **La Reserva Rotana.** This luxury hotel is in a beautifully restored manor house 3 km (2 mi) north of Manacor. The ornate coffered ceiling in the main sitting room is from a medieval convent in Cordoba. Double rooms with private terraces by the pool have ceiling fans, wrought-iron four-poster beds, walk-in closets. The 500-acre Rotana estate has its own heliport, golf course, orchards, and kitchen gardens, which supply the restaurant with fresh produce for its excellent Mediterranean cuisine. Hotel rates include greens fee. ✉ *Camí de S'Avall, Km 3, Manacor, 07500* ☎ *971/845685* 🖷 *971/555258* 🌐 *www.reservarotana.com* *13 doubles, 9 suites* *In-room: safe, refrigerator, DVD (some). In-hotel: 2 restaurants, room service, bar, 9-hole golf course, tennis court, pool, gym, bicycles, laundry service, concierge, public Internet, public Wi-Fi, airport shuttle, parking (no fee)* ▭ *AE, MC, V* ⊙ *Closed Jan.* *BP.*

SHOPPING

The weekly market in Manacor is held on Monday morning.

ALCÚDIA

11 *54 km (34 mi) northeast of Palma.*

The first city on the site of Alcúdia was a Roman settlement, in 123 BC. The Moors reestablished a town here, and after the Reconquest it became a feudal possession of the Knights Templars; the first ring of city walls dates to the early 14th century. Begin your visit at the **Church of Sant Jaume,** and walk through the maze of narrow streets inside to the **Porta de Xara,** with its twin crenelated towers.

The **Museu Monogràfic de Pollentia** has an excellent collection of Roman items. ✉ *Carrer Sant Jaume 30* ☎ *971/547004* *Joint ticket for museum and Roman ruins €2* ⏲ *Tues.–Fri. 10–3:30, weekends 10:30–1.*

Just outside Alcúdia, off the port road, a signposted lane leads to the small, 1st-century BC **Teatre Romà** *(Roman Amphitheater).*

POLLENÇA

12 *5 km (3 mi) inland of the port.*

The history of this pretty little town goes back at least as far as the Roman occupation of the island; the only trace of that period is a small **stone bridge** at the edge of town. In the 13th century Pollença and much of the land around it was owned by the Knights Templars—who built the imposing **Church of Nuestra Senyora de Los Ángeles,** on the west side of the present-day Plaça Major. The church looks east to the 330-meter peak of the Puig de Maria, with the 15-century **Sanctuary** at the top. The **Calvari** of Pollença is a flight of 365 stone steps to a tiny **chapel,** and a panoramic view as far as Cap de Formentor. There's a colorful weekly **market** here on Sunday mornings.

OFF THE BEATEN PATH

★ **Cap de Formentor. The winding road north from Port de Pollença to the tip of the island is spectacular. Stop at the Mirador de la Cruete: here, the rocks crest into the sea to form deep narrow inlets of multishaded blue; off to the right, a winding road leads to a stone tower called the Talaia d'Albercuix, at the highest point on the peninsula.**

WHERE TO STAY

$$$ **Hotel Juma.** In March 2007 this little hotel on Pollença's main square marked its 100th birthday. Rooms are small and simply but comfortably furnished with traditional Majorcan pieces and hand-embroidered drapes. The Juma is a good choice for a weekend stay to enjoy the Sunday market in the square. The owners have another seven-room property, L'Hostal, around the corner (✉ *Carrer Mercat, 18, 07460* ☎ *971/535282* *www.hostalpollensa.com*) in an old stable that's been converted to a modern boutique hotel. ✉ *Pl. Major 9, 07460* ☎ *971/535002* *971/534155* *www.hoteljuma.com* *7 rooms* *In-room: safe, Ethernet, Wi-Fi. In-hotel: bar, laundry service, public Wi-Fi, no-smoking rooms* *MC, V* *BP.*

9

$$$ **Hotel Son Sant Jordi.** Tucked up next to the Iglésia Sant Jordi, on a small terraced square in Pollença, this small hotel emerged in 2002 from the conversion of a pair of abandoned houses. Its particular charm is the garden in back: a pool and pavilion set among lemon, almond, and orange trees. Rooms are simply furnished, with canopied four-poster beds, red-brown tile floors, and cupboard closets. Open year-round, the Son Sant Jordi has a three-course Sunday brunch (€12.90) from 1 to 4 PM, with live jazz. ✉*Carrer Sant Jordi 27, 07460* ☎*971/530389 or 629/307473* 📠*971/535109* 🌐*www.hotelsonsantjordi.com* *8 rooms* *In-room: safe, refrigerator, Wi-Fi. In-hotel: restaurant, room service, bar, pool, bicycles, laundry service, public Wi-Fi, airport shuttle, parking (no fee), no-smoking rooms* *MC, V* *BP.*

THE ARTS

★ Pollença hosts an acclaimed international **music festival** in July and August. Founded in 1961, it has brought in such performers as Mstislav Rostropovic, Jessye Norman, the St. Petersburg Philharmonic, the Camerata Köln and the Alban Berg Quartet. Concerts are held in the cloister of the **Convent of Sant Domingo.** Contact the Festival ticket office (☎*971/535077 or 971/534012* 🌐*www.festivalpollenca.org*).

LLUC

13 *20 km (12 mi) southwest of Pollença.*

The **Santuari** in the remote mountain village of Lluc is widely considered Majorca's spiritual heart. La Moreneta, also known as La Virgen Negra de Lluc (the Black Virgin of Lluc), is here in the 17th-century **church.** The **museum** has an eclectic collection of ceramics, paintings, clothing, folk costumes, and religious items. A boys' choir sings psalms in the chapel August–May, weekdays at 11:15 AM and around 4:45 PM, and at 11 AM for Sunday mass; hours change during holidays and the summer. The Christmas Eve performance of Cant de la Sibila (Song of the Sybil) is an annual choral highlight. ☎*971/871525* *Museum €2.60; admission to the monastery free* *Daily 10–1:15 and 2:30–5:15.*

WHERE TO STAY & EAT

¢ **Santuari de Lluc.** The Lluc monastery offers simple, clean, and cheap accommodation, mostly in cells once occupied by priests. Although the vast building has one bar and three Majorcan restaurants ($–$$$), nightlife is restricted, and guests are asked to be silent after 11 PM. ✉*Santuari de Lluc, Pl. Pelegrins s/n, 07315* ☎*971/871525* 📠*971/517096* *110 rooms* *In-room: no a/c, some kitchenettes, no TV. In-hotel: 3 restaurants, bar* *V.*

TORRENT DE PAREIS

14 *2 km (1 mi) east of Sa Calobra.*

From Escorca's church of Sant Pere, you can hike down the Torrent de Pareis, a ravine that drops dramatically to the sea. Use proper footwear, carry a cellphone if you can, don't go alone, and don't go at all if rain is forecasted. Rescue bridages have been called out for hikers lost or trapped and suffering from hypothermia or exhaustion.

ANDRATX

15 *23 km (14 mi) southwest of Banyalbufar.*

Andratx is a charming cluster of white and ocher hillside houses, rather like cliff dwellings, with the 3,363-foot Mt. Galatzó behind it. Many of the towns on Majorca are at some distance from their seafronts; from Andratx you can take a 4-km (1½-mi) drive through S'Arracó to Sant Elm and on to the rocky shore opposite Sa Dragonera—an island shaped indeed like the long-armored back of a dragon. Local history has it that the tiny island of Pantaleu, just to the west of it, was where Jaume I chose to disembark in September 1200, on his campaign to retake Majorca from the Moors.

WHERE TO STAY & EAT

$$$–$$$$ **Villa Italia.** This ornate, rose-color hideaway, once a 1920s *palacito,* was built in a Florentine style, with marble floors and faux-classical columns. It has fine views over the port from the main building. The rococo suites in pink and salmon are truly palatial; doubles, with antique oak beams and rough plaster walls, all have comfortable private terraces. The elegant restaurant, Club Royal, serves Mediterranean cuisine. *C. San Carlos 13, Port D'Andratx, 07157 971/674011 971/673350 www.hotelvillaitalia.com 10 rooms, 7 suites In-room: safe, refrigerator, dial-up. In-hotel: restaurant, room service, bar, pool, gym, spa, laundry service, concierge, public Internet, airport shuttle, some pets allowed AE, MC, V BP.*

MINORCA

9

Minorca, the northernmost Balearic island, is a knobby, cliff-bound plateau with a single central hill—El Toro—from whose 1,100-foot summit you can see the whole island. Prehistoric monuments— *taulas* (huge stone T-shapes), *talayots* (spiral stone cones), and *navetes* (stone structures shaped like overturned boats)—left by the first Neolithic settlers are everywhere on the island. Tourism came late to Minorca, as it was traditionally more prosperous than its neighbors, and Franco punished the island—which aligned with the Republic in the Civil War—by restricting development here. Having sat out the early Balearic boom, Minorca has avoided many of the other islands' industrialization troubles: there are no high-rise hotels, and the herringbone road system, with a single central highway, means that each resort is small and separate. There's less to see and do on Minorca, and more unspoiled countryside, than on the other Balearics; it's where Spaniards and Catalans tend to take their families on holiday.

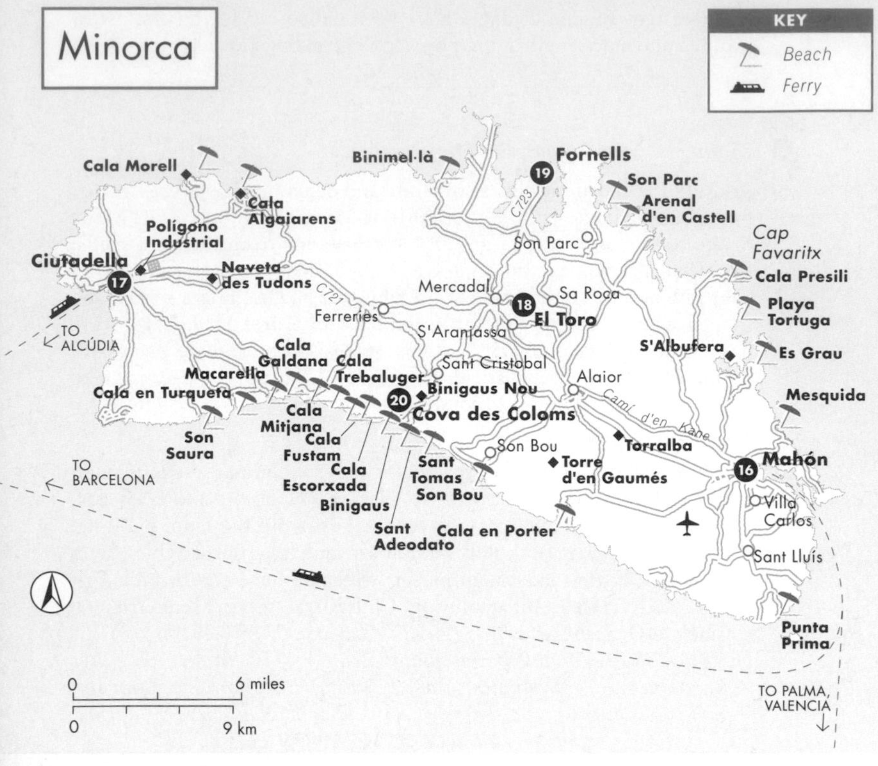

MAHÓN (MAÓ)

16 *Overnight ferry, fast hydrofoil (about 3 hours), or 40-min flight from Barcelona; 6-hr ferry from Palma.*

Established as the island's capital in 1722, when the British began their nearly 80-year occupation, Mahón stills bears the stamp of its former rulers. The streets nearest the port are lined with four-story Georgian town houses in various states of repair; the Mahónese still nurse a craving for Chippendale furniture, and drink gin; English is widely spoken. Mahón is quiet for much of the year, but between June and September the waterfront pubs and restaurants swell with foreigners.

Stop in at No. 25 on the Carrer de Sa Rovellada de Dalt, the **Ateneo,** a cultural and literary society with wildlife, seashells, seaweed, minerals, and stuffed birds. Side rooms include paintings and mementos of Minorcan writers, poets, and musicians. ✉ *Carrer Rovellada de Dalt 25* ☎ *971/360553* 🎟 *Free* ⏲ *Weekdays 10–2 and 4–10, Sat. 5–9.*

From Sa Rovellada de Dalt, turn left on Carrer de ses Moreres, then right on Carrer Bastió to where it becomes Carrer Costa d'en Deià, and—if it's open—have a look at the **Teatre Principal** (✉ *Carrer Costa d'en Deia s/n* ☎ *971/355776*). The theater was built in 1824 as an opera house, with five tiers of boxes, red plush seats, and gilded woodwork—a La Scala in miniature. Fully restored in 2005, the Principal still hosts a brief opera season; if you're visiting in the first week of December or June, get tickets at all costs.

> **THE TENOR'S TEST RUN**
>
> Opera companies from Italy en route to Spain made the Teatre Principal in Mahón their first port of call; if the Mahónese gave it a poor reception, it would get cut from the repertoire.

Carrer Costa d'en Deaià descends to the Plaça Reial (a bit grandiosely named, for an unimposing little rectangle), where it becomes the Carrer sa Ravaleta. Ahead is the church of **La Verge del Carme** (✉*Pl. del Carme* ☎*971/362402*), which has a fine painted and gilded altarpiece. Adjoining the church are the cloisters, now used as a **public market,** the intervals between the massive stone arches filled with stalls selling fresh produce and a variety of local specialties such as cheeses and sausages.

A few steps north from the Cloister del Carme bring you to the church of **Santa María** (✉*Pl. de la Constitució* ☎*971/363949*), which dates from the 13th century but was rebuilt during the British occupation and restored after being sacked during the civil war. The church's pride is its 3,200-pipe baroque organ, imported from Austria in 1810. There are concerts (€3) here weekdays 11:30–12:30.

Behind the church of Santa María is the **Plaça de la Conquesta,** with a statue of Alfons III of Aragón, who wrested the island from the Moors in 1287. From the Plaça de la Conquesta, walk up Carrer Alfons III and turn right at the The **Ajuntament** (✉*Pl. de la Constitució 1* ☎*971/369800*) to Carrer Isabel II, a street lined with many Georgian homes. Turn west from Carrer Isabel II on Carrer Rector Mort, and at the far end of the street is the massive gate of **Puerta de San Roque,** the only surviving portion of the 14th-century city walls, rebuilt in 1587 to protect Mahón from the pirate Barbarossa (Redbeard).

9

WHERE TO STAY & EAT

$$$$ ★ ✕ **Marivent.** Mahónese generally agree this is the best kitchen in town. Chef Lydia Barben does wonders with a seasonal menu that always features fresh fish and Minorcan free-range beef. The sea bream with black rice risotto and Mahón cheese is wonderful. Marivent has a second-floor patio for dining alfresco; the third-floor main room, with a harbor view, is done in understated elegance with white walls and uprights, and narrow black beams. The staff is attentive, and the wine list has some 200 Spanish and French labels. August is the busiest month. ✉*Moll de Llevant 314* ☎*971/369801 or 699/062117* *Reservations essential* ▭*AE, MC, V* ⊗*Closed Tues. and Christmas–3rd wk of Jan. No dinner Feb.–May, Mon., Wed., and Sun.*

$$$–$$$$ Fodor'sChoice ★ ✕ **Es Moli de Foc.** The two-story red building where chef Vicente Vila holds court was originally a flour mill; it's the oldest building in the little village of Sant Climent, about 3 km (2 mi) from the airport. Es Moli doesn't look like much inside, but the food is exceptional. Don't miss the prawns carpaccio with cured Mahón cheese and artichoke oil, or the black paella with monkfish and squid. Order off the menu for

the *carrilleras de ternera* (boiled beef cheeks) with potato purée. Top off with ice cream of Minorcan cheese and figs. In summer, book a table on the terrace. ✉ *Carrer Sant Llorenç 65, Sant Climent* ☎ *971/153222* ▭ *MC, V* ⊙ *Closed Jan. and Mon. Oct.–May. No dinner Sun.*

$–$$ ✕ **Itake.** On the port since 1994, Itake is an amiable clutter of 12 tables, a chalkboard listing specials of the day, ceiling fans, paper place mats, and frosted-glass lamps. This is arguably the best place in Mahón for an inexpensive, informal meal with a different touch. Where neighboring eateries pride themselves on fresh fish, Itake serves warm goat cheese, burgers, kangaroo steaks in mushroom sauce, and ostrich breast with strawberry coulis. That said, nothing here is made with any real elaboration: orders come out of the kitchen at nearly the rate of fast food. ✉ *Moll de Llevant 317* ☎ *971/354570* ▭ *AE, DC, MC, V* ⊙ *Closed Mon. No dinner Sun. Sept.–June.*

$$$$ Fodor'sChoice ★ **Biniarroca Country House Hotel.** Floral print duvets, shelves with knickknacks, comfy chairs: this is an English vision of a secluded rural retreat. The real glory of Biniarroca is the garden, planted with irises, lavender, flowering trees: enter from the terrace of the Roman-style main pool, through an Alice-in-Wonderland iron gate. One ground-floor room has wheelchair access. The hotel's fine restaurant (Continental, with a Minorcan accent) has a summer terrace. ✉ *Cami Vell 57, Sant Lluis, 07710* ☎ *971/150059 or 619/460942* 🖷 *971/151250* 🌐 *www.biniarroca.com* *17 rooms, 2 suites* *In-room: safe, refrigerator (some rooms), Wi-Fi. In-hotel: restaurant, coffee shop, room service, 2 bars, 2 pools, no elevator, laundry service, concierge, public Internet, public Wi-Fi, parking (no fee), some pets allowed, no chilren under 16, no-smoking rooms* ▭ *MC, V* ⊙ *Closed Nov.–Mar.*

$$$$ **Sant Joan de Binissaida.** Approach this lovely restored farmhouse, some 15 km (9 mi) from Mahón, on an avenue lined with chinaberry and fig trees. There's an excellent restaurant, with meals on the deck in good weather; a row of adjoining stables has been converted to additional guest accommodations, with individual terraces. All the rooms at Sant Joan are named for composers (owner Josep Maria Quintana is a serious opera fan); the first-floor "Rossini" is fully wheelchair-accessible. The decor is antique, including a wonderful common room with deep leather chairs, a baize-topped card table—and an oratory. ✉ *Camí de Binissaida 108, Es Castell, 07720* ☎ *971/355598 or 618/874381* 🖷 *971/355001* 🌐 *www.binissaida.com* *10 rooms, 2 suites* *In-room: a/c (some rooms), safe, refrigerator (some rooms), Wi-Fi. In-hotel: restaurant, room service, bar, pool, no elevator, laundry service, public Wi-Fi, parking (no fee)* ▭ *MC, V* ⊙ *Closed Jan.–Mar.*

$$$ **Casa Albertí.** The most centrally located of the Mahón hotels, the Casa Alberti was built in 1740 as a private home, during the British occupation, and is registered as a *patrimonio historico-cultural*. The house had been empty some 15 years when Dani Crespo and his partners bought it and turned it into a friendly, comfortable boutique hotel in 2004. The house has 15-foot ceilings, the original marble staircases, and tile floors; the rooms are furnished in rustic style from local and Barcelona antiques shops. Rates include breakfast in the big commu-

nal kitchen and adjoining interior patio. ✉ *Carrer Isabel II, 9, 07701* ☎ *971/354210 or 686/393569* 📠 *971/354210* 🌐 *www.casalberti.com* *4 rooms, 2 suites* *In-room: no phone, safe, refrigerator, Ethernet. In-hotel: no elevator, public Internet, no-smoking rooms* 💳 *MC, V.*

NIGHTLIFE

Akelarre (✉ *Anden de Poniente 41* ☎ *971/368520*) is a smart drinking venue near the port with live concerts (jazz and blues) on Thursday and Friday nights. Catch live jazz Tuesday (May–September) at the **Casino** (✉ *Sant Jaume 4, Sant Climent* ☎ *971/153418* *€10*) bar and restaurant. It's closed Wednesday. Sant Climent is 4 km (2½ mi) southwest of Mahón.The hottest spot in relatively staid Minorca is the **Cova d'en Xoroi** (✉ *C. Cova s/n* ☎ *971/377236* *€6*), in the beach resort of Cala en Porter, about a 20-minute drive from Mahón. The setting is a series of caves in a cliff high above the sea that, according to local legend, was once the refuge of a castaway Moorish pirate. By day (11–7) it's a tourist attraction, with bars and café terraces; by night, it's a dance-until-dawn disco. In Mahón itself, the bars opposite the ferry terminal fill with locals and visitors late at night. **Latitude 40** (✉ *Moll de Llevant 265* ☎ *971/364176*) is where yachtsmen and their chic companions enjoy evening cocktails and tapas; it's closed Sunday. The longtime favorite **Mambo** (✉ *Moll de Llevant 209* ☎ *971/351852*) has rustic stone walls and tasty cocktails.

SPORTS & THE OUTDOORS

DIVING The clear Mediterranean waters here are ideal for diving. Equipment and lessons are available at Cala En Bosc, Son Parc, Fornells, and Cala Tirant. For scuba diving, compressed air is available at **Club Marítimo** (✉ *Moll de Llevant, 287, Mahón* ☎ *971/365022*). For exploring the waters off the western end of the island, equipment and services are available at **Club Náutico** (✉ *Camí del Baix s/n, Ciutadella* ☎ *971/383918* 🌐 *www.cnciutadella.com*).

GOLF Minorca's sole golf course is **Golf Son Parc** (✉ *Urb. Son Parc s/n* ☎ *971/188875* 🌐 *www.golfsonparc.com*), 9 km (6 mi) east of Mercadal.

WALKING In the south, each cove is approached by a *barranca* (ravine or gully), often from several miles inland. The head of **Barranca Algendar** is down a small, unmarked road immediately on the right of the Ferreries–Cala Galdana Road; the barranca ends at the local beach resort, and from there you have a lovely walk north along the sea to an unspoiled half-moon of sand at **Cala Macarella**. Extend your walk north, if time allows, through the forest along the riding trail to **Cala Turqueta**, where you find some of the island's most impressive sea grottoes.

WINDSURFING & SAILING Charter a yacht from **Nautica Technimar** (✉ *Ctra. de Cal'n Blanes s/n, Ciutadella* ☎ *971/380538* 🌐 *www.nauticatecnimar.com*) Monday–Saturday. For charters and trips around the island, contact **Blue Mediterraneum** (✉ *Moll de Llevant s/n, Mahón* ☎ *609/305314* 🌐 *www.chartermenorca.com*) Tuesday–Sunday.

9

SHOPPING

Minorca is known for shoes and leather wear, as well as cheese, gin, and, recently, wine. In Mahón, buy leather goods at **Marks** (✉*Sa Ravaleta 18* ☎*971/322660*). **Musupta** (✉*Sa Ravaleta 26* ☎*971/364131*) is another source in the capital for leather. Inland, the showroom of **Pons Quintana** (✉*Calle San Antonio 120, Alaior* ☎*971/371050*) has a full-length window overlooking the factory where they make their ultrachic women's shoes. It's closed weekends. The company also has a shop in Mahón, at Sa Ravaleta 21 that stays open on Saturday. The showroom of **Jaime Mascaro** (✉*Poligon Industrial s/n, Ferreries* ☎*971/373837*), on the main highway from Alaior to Cuitadella, features not only shoes and bags but fine leather coats and belts for men and women. Mascaro also has a shop in Mahón, at Carrer ses Moreres.

A good place to buy the tangy, Parmesan-like Mahón cheese is **Hort de Sant Patrici** (✉*Camí Ruma-Sant Patrici s/n, Ferreries* ☎*971/373702* 🌐*www.santpatrici.com*). You can't visit the dairy itself, but Sant Patrici has a shop, beautiful grounds with a small vineyard and botanical garden, and a display of traditional cheese-making techniques and tools.

In the 18th century, wine was an important part of the Minorcan economy: the British, who knew a good place to grow wine when they saw one, planted the island thick with vines. Viticulture was simply abandoned when Minorca returned to the embrace of Spain, and it has emerged again only in the past few years. The most promising of the small handful of new Minorcan wineries is **Bodegas Binifadet** (✉*Ses Barraques s/n, Sant Lluis* ☎*971/150715* 🌐*www.binifadet.com*), which began as a hobby for founder Carlos Angles and his son Lluis, a labor of love that evolved into a determination to produce high-quality local wines in market volume. They did a creditable job of it, now making 5,000 bottles a year of white (Chardonnay, Muscat) and 20,000 of red (Merlo-Cabernet, Syrah). The robust young Binifada wines are on the shelves all over Minorca; the winery is open for tastings May–October, Monday–Saturday 10–1 and 4–8, and well worth a visit.

The other gastronomic legacy of the British occupation was gin. Visit the **Xoriguer distillery** (✉*Anden de Poniente 91* ☎*971/362197*), on Mahón's quayside, near the ferry terminal, and take a guided tour, sample various types of gin, and buy some to take home.

CIUTADELLA

⑰ *44 km (27 mi) west of Mahón.*

Ciutadella was Minorca's capital before the British settled in Mahón, and its history is richer. As you arrive via the Me-1, the main artery across the island from Mahón, turn left at the second roundabout and follow the ring road to the Passeig Maritim; at the end, near the **Castell de Sant Nicolau** watchtower (visits daily, June–October 10–1 and 5–10) is a **monument to David Glasgow Farragut,** the first admiral of the U.S. Navy, whose father emigrated from Ciutadella to the United States. From here, take Passeig de Sant Nicolau to the **Plaça de s'Esplanada,** and park near the Plaça d'es Born. From a passage on the left side of Ciutadella's columned and crenelated **Ajuntament** (✉*Pl. d'es Born*), on the west side of the Born, steps lead up to the **Mirador d'es Port,** a lookout from which you can survey the harbor. The local **Museu Municipal** houses artifacts of Minorca's prehistoric, Roman, and medieval past, including records of land grants made by Alfons III to the local nobility after defeating the Moors. It's in an ancient defense tower, the Bastió de Sa Font (Bastion of the Fountain), at the east end of the harbor. ☎*971/380297* 🌐*www.ciutadella.org/museu* 🎫*€2.20, free Wed.* ⏲*Nov.–Apr., Tues.–Sat. 10–2; May–Oct., Tues–Sat. 10–2 and 6–9.*

The monument in the middle of the Plaça d'es Born commemorates the citizens' resistance of a Turkish invasion in 1588. South from the plaza along the east side of the Born is the block-long 19th-century **Palau Torresaura** (✉*Carrer Major del Born 8*), built by the Baron of Torresaura, one of the many noble families from Aragón and Catalonia that repopulated Minorca after it was captured from the Moors in the 13th century. The interesting facade faces the plaza, though the entrance is on the side street (it is not open to the public). The **Palau Salort,** on the opposite side of the Carrer Major, is the only noble home regularly open to the public. The coats of arms on the ceiling are those of the families Salort (a salt pit and a garden: *sal* and *ort,* or *huerta*) and Martorell (a marten). ✉*Carrer Major des Born* 🎫*€2* ⏲*May–Oct., Mon.–Sat. 10–2.*

The Carrer Major leads to the Gothic **Cathedral** (✉*Pl. de la Catedral at Plaça Píus XII*), which has some beautifully carved choir stalls. The side chapel has round Moorish arches, remnants of the mosque that once stood on this site; the bell tower is a converted minaret.

Follow the arcade of Carrer de Quadrado north from the cathedral and turn right on Carrer del Seminari, lined on the west side with some of the city's most impressive historic buildings. Among them is the **Seminari of the 17th-century Convent and Eglésia del Socors** (✉*Carrer del Seminari at Carrer Obispo Vila*), which hosts Ciutadella's summer festival of classical music.

Ciutadella's **port** is accessible from steps that lead down from Carrer Sant Sebastià. The waterfront here is lined with seafood restaurants, some of which burrow into caverns far under the Born.

WHERE TO STAY & EAT

$$–$$$$ ✕ **Cafe Balear.** Seafood doesn't get much fresher than this. The owners' boat docks nearby every day—except Sunday—and the restaurant fish tank is seldom empty. The house special, *arroz caldoso de langosta* (lobster and rice stew), is a masterpiece, as are *pulpo a la gallega* (octopus in paprika and olive oil), *cigalas* (crayfish), lobster with onion, and grilled *navajas* (razor clams). ✉*Paseo San Juan 15* ☎*971/380005* 💳*AE, DC, MC, V* ⏲*No dinner Mon. and Sun. Nov.–June.*

$$$ ★ 🏨 **Hotel Rural Sant Ignasi.** Ciutadella is not especially well endowed with hotels, but 10 minutes by car from the central square, in the Minorcan countryside, is this comfortable and reasonably priced little delight. The main building is a manor house dates to 1777; the original barn

now accommodates five large suites. Rooms have stone arches, cupboard closets, English and Minorcan antiques; rugs, drapes, and sofas are color-coordinated in teal and black or beige and brown. Ask for a ground-floor double with a private garden. Es Loc, the hotel's excellent restaurant, specializes in Minorcan seafood; in summer, meals are served on the tree-shaded poolside terrace. The Sant Ignasi is a favorite with young Spanish families. ✉*Ctra. Cala Morell s/n, Ciutadella, 07760* ☎*971/385575* 🖷*971/480537* 🌐*www.santignasi.com* *17 doubles, 9 suites* *In-room: safe, refrigerator, Ethernet (some rooms). In-hotel: restaurant, room service, bar, pool, bicycles, no elevator, laundry service, public Internet, parking (no fee), some pets allowed, no-smoking rooms* 💳*MC, V.*

SHOPPING

Gin, shoes, leather, costume jewelry, and cheese are the items to shop for here; try the Ses Voltes area, the Es Rodol zone near Plaça Artrutx and Ses Voltes, and along the Camí de Maó between Plaça Palmeras and Plaça d'es Born. **Nadia Rabosio** (✉*Carrer Santissim 4* ☎*971/384080*) is an inventive designer with an original selection of jewelry and hand-painted silks. **Maria Juanico** (✉*Carrer Seminari 31* ☎*971/480879* ⏲*Mon.–Sat. 10:30–2 and 5:30–8*) has an atelier in the back of the shop, where she makes her interesting plated and anodized silver jewelry and accessories.The industrial complex *(polígono industrial)* on the right as you enter Ciutadella has shoe factories, each with shops. Prices may be the same as in stores, but the selections are greater. In Plaça d'es Born, a market is held on Friday and Saturday. For Mahón cheeses and sausages, go to **Ca Na Riera** (✉*Hospital de Santa Magdalena 7* ☎*971/380748*). Visit **ARTEME** (*Artesanos de Minorca* ✉*Carrer Comerciants 9* ☎*971/381550*) for the town's only *alferería* (pottery maker).

EL TORO

18 *24 km (15 mi) northwest of Mahón.*

Follow signs in Es Mercadal (the crossroads at the island's center) to the peak of El Toro, Minorca's highest point, at all of 1,555 feet. From the monastery on top you can see the whole island and across the sea to Majorca.

WHERE TO EAT

$$–$$$ ✕**Ca N' Olga.** It's hard to find, but the inventive country cuisine served here—local snails, quail in sherry—is worth it. Off the Camino de Tramuntana, in central Es Mercadal, Olga's is under an archway to the left (ask for directions if you don't see it). Make for the small patio. ✉*Pont Na Macarrana s/n, Es Mercadal* ☎*971/375459* 💳*AE, DC, MC, V* ⏲*Closed Tues. Apr.–June. No lunch June–Oct., or Mon. and Wed. Nov.–Dec. and Mar.–May.*

$$–$$$ ✕**Molí d'es Reco.** You know it's gotta be good: the truck drivers stop here for lunch, on the route from Mahón to Ciutadella. This restaurant is in an old windmill just off the highway, at the west end of Es Mercadal; it has fortress-thick whitewashed stone walls and low vaulted

ceilings, and a constant air of cheerful bustle. On warm summer days there are tables on the terrace. Minorcan specialties here include squid stuffed with anglerfish and shrimps, and chicken with *centollo* (spider crab). The thick vegetable soup called *sopas menorquinas* is excellent. ✉ *Carrer Major 53, Mercadal* ☎ *971/375392* 💳 *AE, DC, MC, V* ⊗ *Closed Jan. 17–Feb. 17.*

FORNELLS

⓳ *35 km (21 mi) northwest of Mahón.*

The first fortifications built here to defend the Bay of Fornells from pirates date to 1625. A little village (full-time population: 500) of whitewashed houses with red tile roofs, Fornells comes alive in the summer high season, when the Spanish and Catalan families arrive in droves to open their holiday chalets at the edge of town and in the nearby beach resorts; the bay—Minorca's second largest and deepest—offers ideal conditions for windsurfing, sailing and scuba diving.

WHERE TO EAT

$$$–$$$$ ✕ **Es Pla.** The modest wooden exterior of this waterside restaurant in Fornells' harbor, on the north coast, is misleading. King Juan Carlos is said to make regular detours here during Balearic jaunts to indulge in the *Es Pla caldereta de langosta* (lobster stew)—which at market price/weight skews an otherwise reasonably priced menu. Excellent fish dishes include scallops "Gallega" style, anglerfish with *maresco* (seafood) sauce, and grilled scorpion fish—a local specialty. ✉ *Pasaje Es Pla, Puerto de Fornells* ☎ *971/376655* 💳 *AE, DC, MC, V.*

WINDSURFING & SAILING

Several miles long and a mile wide, but with a narrow entrance to the sea and virtually no waves, the Bay of Fornells gives the beginner a feeling of security and the expert plenty of excitement.

Wind Fornells (✉ *Ctra. Mercaval Fornells s/n, Es Mercadal* ☎ *971/188150 or 659/577760* 🌐 *www.windfornells.com*) rents boards, dinghies, and catamarans, and gives lessons in English or Spanish; they're open May–October.

9

COVA DES COLOMS

⓴ *40 km (24 mi) west of Mahón.*

The massive Cova Des Coloms (Cave of Pigeons), also known as the Cathedral, is the most spectacular cave on Minorca. Eerie rock formations rise up to a 77-foot-tall ceiling. To reach the cave, take the Ferreries road at San Cristobal and turn up to the primary school, beyond the school the paved road continues for about 3 km (2 mi) toward Binigaus Nou. Leave the car in the designated parking area, climb over the stile, and take the path that follows the right-hand side of the barranca (ravine or gully) toward the sea; you'll come to a well-trodden path bearing down into the bottom of the barranca and up the other side. The entrance to the cave is around an elbow, camouflaged by a tree. A flashlight helps.

IBIZA

Settled by the Carthaginians in the 5th century BC, Ibiza managed to maintain its unique character through successive waves of invasion and occupation until the 1960s, when it became a tourist destination. With a full-time population of barely 140,000, it gets some 2 million visitors a year. Blessed with beaches—50 of them, by one count—it also has the world's largest disco, Privilege, with a capacity of 10,000. About 25% of the people who live on Ibiza year-round are foreigners.

Efforts to promote Ibiza as a year-round destination have been to little avail; from October to April, the pace of life here is decidedly slow, and most of the island's hotels and restaurants are closed. More successful has been the recent transformation to "quality tourism." In the 1960s and early '70s Ibiza was discovered by sun-seeking hippies, eventually emerging as an icon of counter-culture chic. Ibizans were—and still are—friendly and tolerant of their eccentric visitors. In the late 1980s and 1990s, club culture took over. Young ravers flocked here from all over the world, to dance all night and pack the sands of built-up beach resorts like Sant Antoni. That party-hardy Ibiza is still alive and well, but a new wave of luxury rural hotels, offering oases of peace and privacy, with spas and gourmet restaurants is emblematic of the future.

IBIZA TOWN (EIVISSA)

40-min flight or 9-hr ferry from Barcelona.

★

Hedonistic and historical, Eivissa (Ibiza, in Catalan), is a city jam-packed with cafés and nightspots and trendy shops; looming over it are the massive stone walls of **Dalt Vila**—the medieval city declared a UNESCO World Heritage site in 1999—and its Gothic cathedral. Squeezed between the north walls of the old city and the harbor is **Sa Penya,** a long labyrinth of stone-paved streets that offer the city's best exploring. What would the fishermen who used to live here have thought, to see so many of their little whitewashed houses transformed into bars and off-beat restaurants and boutiques with names like the Kabul Sutra Tantra Shop and Bitch?

Enter Sa Penya from the west end of Passeig Vara de Rey. Across from the Hotel Montesol, take **Carrer Rimbau** and turn right on Carrer Guillem Montgri to the **Plaça de la Constitució,** where a little building that looks something like a miniature Greek portico houses the local open-air produce market. Beyond it, a ramp leads up to the **Portal de Ses Taules,** the main gate of **Dalt Vila,** the walled upper town. On each side stands a statue, Roman in origin and now headless: Juno on the right, an armless male on the left.

Inside Dalt Vila, the ramp continues to the right between the outer and inner walls and opens into a long, narrow plaza lined with stalls and

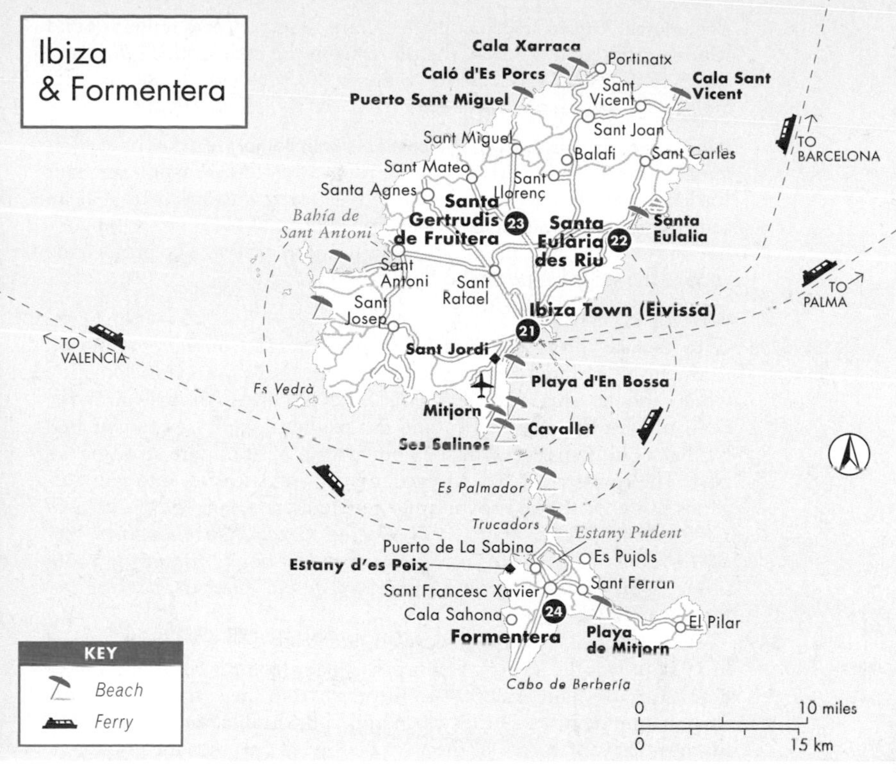

sidewalk cafés. Don't worry about losing your way: aim uphill for the cathedral, downhill for the gate. A little way up Sa Carroza, a sign on the left points back toward the **Museu d'Art Contemporani,** housed in the gateway arch. ✉ *Ronda Pintor Narcis Putget s/n* ☎ *971/302723* 🎫 *€1.20, Sun. free* ⏲ *Oct.–Apr., Tues.–Fri. 10–1:30 and 4–6, weekends 10–1:30; May–Sept., Tues.–Fri. 10–1:30 and 5–8, weekends 10–1:30.*

Uphill from the museum is a sculpture of a priest sitting on one of the stone seats in the gardens. On the left, the wide **Bastió de Santa Llúcia** *(Bastion of St. Lucia)* has a panoramic view.

Wind your way up past the 16th-century church of **Sant Domingo** (✉ *Carrer de Balanzat*), its roof an irregular landscape of tile domes, and turn right in front of the ajuntament housed in the church's former monastery. From the church of San Domingo, follow any of the streets or steps leading uphill to Carrer Obispo Torres (Carrer Major). The **cathedral** is on the site of religious structures from each of the cultures that have ruled Ibiza since the Phoenicians. Built in the 13th and 14th centuries and renovated in the 18th century, the cathedral has a Gothic tower and a baroque nave. ✉ *Carrer Major* ☎ *971/312774* ⏲ *Weekdays 10–1, Sun. 10:30–noon.*

The **Museu Arqueològic** has Phoenician, Punic (Carthaginian), and Roman artifacts. It's across the plaza from the cathedral. ✉*Pl. Catedral 3* ☎*971/301231* *€2.40, free Sun.* ⏲*Oct.–Mar., Tues.–Sat. 9–3, Sun. 10–2; Apr.–Sept., Tues.–Sat. 10–2 and 6–8, Sun. 10–2.*

Behind the cathedral, from the **Bastió de Sant Bernat** *(Bastion of St. Bernard)*, a promenade with sea views runs west to the bastions of Sant Jordi and Sant Jaume, past the **Castell**—a fortress formerly used as an army barracks, turned over to the city of Ibiza in 1973. In 2006 work began to transform it into a 70-room luxury parador. The promenade ends at the steps to the **Portal Nou** (New Gate).

WHERE TO STAY

$$$–$$$$ **La Ventana.** From the dainty, green-shuttered *ventanas* (windows) to the lushly painted rooms with handsome beds draped in romantic white canopies, this intimate hillside hotel is a breath of fresh air in the heart of Dalt Vila. Tucked behind the medieval walls, it's surrounded by the cobbled streets of history but within a 10-minute stroll of the port. The roof terrace has Morrocan-style sofas to sink into and gorgeous vistas of the old town and the Mediterranean. ✉*Sa Carrossa 13, 07800* ☎*971/390857* *971/390145* *www.laventanaibiza.com* *14 rooms* *In-room: safe, refrigerator. In-hotel: restaurant, room service, bar, no elevator, laundry service, public Internet, parking (no fee)* *AE, MC, V.*

$$$ **Hotel Montesol.** Location, location, location. The Montesol opened in 1934 (it was the island's first hotel), and still hasn't done anything—despite an overhaul in 2000—to lift itself from the category of a one-star accommodation. But it's clean and comfortable, and it sits smack on the northwest corner of the Vara de Rey, the promenade in the center of Eivissa, where everyone comes to see and be seen—steps from the port, at the foot of the Dalt Vila. Rooms are simple and spare, with bare white tile floors and flower-print bedspreads mismatched to plaid drapes. Only four rooms have double beds: the rest are twins and singles. Fashion photographers love the balconies facing the promenade. ✉*Paseo Vara de Rey 2, 07800* ☎*971/310161* *971/310602* *www.hotelmontesol.com* *55 rooms* *In-room: safe. In-hotel: cafeteria* *MC, V* *BP.*

$$$ **Los Molinos.** A brisk 10-minute walk from Ibiza brings you to this beachfront hotel, over the hill that separates the city from neighboring Figueretas. Rooms are fairly large, with blue bedspreads and blue-beige curtains, but the furniture is warehouse-quality; be sure to specify if you want a (more expensive) room with a balcony facing the water. A good buffet breakfast is billed separately at €9.50. ✉*Carrer Ramón Muntaner 60, Figueretas, 07800* ☎*971/302250* *971/302504* *www.thbhotels.com* *165 rooms, 3 suites* *In-room: safe, refrigerator. In-hotel: 2 restaurants, room service, bar, pool, gym, spa, bicycles, coin laundry, parking (no fee)* *AE, DC, MC, V* *BP.*

NIGHTLIFE

Fodor's Choice ★ **Ibiza's discos** are famous throughout Europe. Keep your eyes open during the day for free invitations to discos, handed out on the street. This will save you a sometimes expensive (€10–€50) entry fee. Also note that a handy, all-night "Discobus" service (☎971/192456) runs between Ibiza, Sant Antoni, Santa Eulalia, and the major discos. Almost all of these clubs—Pacha, Amnesia, Privilege, El Divino, Space—open in mid-June and close in late September, though some will have special parties on New Year's Eve.

Down in the town, the trendy place to start the evening is **Keeper** (✉*Paseo Marítimo, Ibiza Nueva* ☎*971/310509*), where you can sip your drink sitting on a carousel horse. A lively, very young scene rocks **El Divino Café** (✉*Carrer Vara De Ray* ☎*971/119–0177*). In summer, boats depart between 1 AM and 4 AM from in front of El Divino Café for the marina and **El Divino Disco** (✉*Puerto de Ibiza Nueva* ☎*971/190176* 🌐*www.eldivino-ibiza.com*), which is a typical Ibiza disco with throbbing dance music (and spectacular views of Ibiza Town). The "in" place for older nighthawks is the stylish bar in the foyer of the former **Teatre Pereira** (✉*Carrer Comte Roselló 3* ☎*971/191468*). A young, international crowd dances to techno at **Pacha** (✉*Av. 8 de Agosto s/n* ☎*971/313612* 🌐*www.pacha.com*). The popular **Amnesia San Rafael** (✉*Ctra. Sant Antoni, opposite Km 5 marker* ☎*971/198041*) has several ample dance floors that throb to house and funk. **Privilege** (✉*Ctra. Ibiza–Sant Antoni, Km 7, San Rafael* ☎*971/198477*) is the grande dame of Ibiza's nightlife, with a giant dance floor, a swimming pool, and more than a dozen bars. **Space** (✉*Playa d'en Bossa* ☎*971/396793* 🌐*www.space-ibiza.es*), which doesn't even open until other discos have closed, is where the serious clubbers come to dance "after hours."

The **Casino de Ibiza** is a small gaming club with roulette tables, blackjack and slots. You will need your passport to enter. ✉*Ctra. Sant Antoní, junto a Rotonda Juan XXIII s/n* ☎*971/313312* 🌐*www.casinoibiza.com* 🎫*€5 1st visit. Free subsequent visits* 🕒*Daily 6 PM–5 AM.*

Gay nightlife converges on **Carrer de la Verge,** in **Sa Penya,** where a multinational crowd bar-hops until the wee hours. The ever-popular gay bar **Dome** (✉*Carrer Alfonso XII* ☎*No phone*) has a leafy terrace that overflows with revelers in summer.

9

SPORTS & THE OUTDOORS

For information on sports on Ibiza and Formentera, obtain a free copy of the magazine *Touribisport* (🌐*www.touribisport.com*), available locally.

BICYCLING **Mr. Bike** (✉*Av. Isidoro Nacabich 63A bajo* ☎*971/392300*) rents bicycles in Ibiza Town.

BOATING Explore Ibiza by sea with **Coral Yachting** (✉*Marina Botafoc* ☎*971/313521*). **Cruiser Ibiza** (✉*Puerto Deportivo, Marina Botafoc s/n* ☎*971/316170* 🌐*www.cruiseribiza.com*) runs charters.

GOLF Ibiza's only 18-hole course is **Golf de Ibiza** (✉*Ctra. Jesús–Cala Llonga, Km 6, Santa Eulària* ☎*971/196118* 🌐*www.golfibiza.com*). Greens fees are €90 a day.

HORSEBACK RIDING **Centro Ecuestre Easy Rider** (*Easy Rider Equestrian Center* ✉*Camí del Sol d'en Serra, Cala Llonga, Santa Eulalia des Riu* ☎*971/339192*) offers a two-hour ride along the coast and inland.

SCUBA DIVING Year-round a team with a decompression chamber is on standby at the **Policlinica de Nuestra Señora del Rosario** (✉*Via Romana s/n* ☎*971/301916*).

Go scuba diving in Sant Antoni with **Centro de Buceo Sirena** (✉*Balanzat 21 bajo, Sant Antoni* ☎*971/342966*). Dive in Sant Joan with **Centro Subfari** (✉*Portinatx, San Joan* ☎*971/333067*). **Diving Center San Miguel** (✉*Puerto de San Miguel* ☎*971/334539* 🌐*www.diving-center-sanmiguel.com*) also offers diving. **Active Generation** (✉*Edifici Faro II, Local 10. Pasea Marítimo, San Antoní* ☎*971/341344* 🌐*www.active-generation.com*) offers instruction and guided dives, as well as kayaking, parasailing and boat rentals. Dive in Sant Josep with **Orca Sub** (✉*Club Hotel Tarida Beach, Sant Josep* ☎*971/806307*). Rent scuba gear in Eivissa at **Vellmari** (✉*Marina Botafoc, Local 101–102* ☎*971/192884* 🌐*www.vellmari.com*).

TENNIS **Ibiza Club de Campo** (✉*Ctra. Sant Josep, Km 4* ☎*971/300088* 🌐*www.ibiza-spotlight.com/clubdecampo*), with six clay and two composition courts, is the largest tennis club on the island. Nonmembers can play here for €6 per hour during the day and €3.60 per hour at night. There are public tennis courts at **Port Sant Miquel,** available to all.

WALKING **Ecoibiza** (✉*C. Abad y Lasierra 35, Ibiza Ciutat, 07800* ☎*971/302347* 🌐*www.ecoibiza.com*) has lots of ecologically friendly countryside hikes, and can also arrange horseback riding, sailing, and sea fishing.

SHOPPING

In the late 1960s and '70s, Ibiza built a reputation for extremes of fashion. Little of this phenomenon survives, though the softer designs of Smilja Mihailovich (under the Ad Lib label) still prosper. Along Carrer d'Enmig is an eclectic collection of shops and stalls selling fashion and crafts. Although the Sa Penya area of Eivissa still has a few designer boutiques, much of the area is now called the Mercat dels Hippies (Hippie Market), with more than 80 stalls of knickknacks. For trendy casual gear, sandals, belts, and bags, try **Ibiza Republic** (✉*Carrer Antoni Mar 15* ☎*971/314175*).For wines and spirits, visit **Enotecum** (✉*Av. d'Isidoro Macabich 43* ☎*971/399167*).

SANTA EULÀRIA DES RIU

❷❷ *15 km (9 mi) northeast of Ibiza.*

At the edge of this town on the island's eastern coast, to the right below the road, a Roman bridge crosses what is claimed to be the only permanent river in the Balearics (hence "des Riu," or "of the River"). Ahead, on the hilltop, are the cubes and domes of the church—to reach it, look for a narrow lane to the left, signed PUIG DE MISSA, itself so named for the hill where regular mass was once held. A stoutly arched, cryptlike covered area guards the entrance; inside are a fine gold reredos and blue-tile stations of the cross.

WHERE TO STAY & EAT

$–$$$ ✕ **Mezzanotte.** Opened in March 2006, this charming little portside restaurant is a branch of the popular Mezzanotte in Eivissa. There are just 12 tables inside, softly lighted with candles and track lights; in summer, seating expands to an interior patio and tables on the sidewalk. The kitchen prides itself on hard-to-find fresh ingredients flown in from Italy. The linguine with jumbo shrimp, saffron, and zucchini—or with *bottarga* (dried and salted mullet roe from Sardinia)—is wonderful. Value for price here is excellent; the €15 prix-fixe lunch menu is an absolute bargain. ✉ *Paseo de s'Alamera 22, Santa Eulària* ☎ *971/319498* ▭ *MC, V* ⊗ *Closed Jan. and Mon.*

$$$$ **Atzaró.** The label *agroturismo*—a farm inn—is a misnomer for this upscale boutique hotel, which counts supermodels and European nobility among its visitors. The original building was a 300-year-old family farmhouse; as the hotel grew, it added separate suite cottages, a pool, and a luxurious spa. Rooms are huge, with natural wood beams, stone walls, terra-cotta-tile floors, and rustic furniture. The spacious grounds are laid out like a Balinese retreat, with accent pools and fountains, stone lanterns and wood sculptures, and small private pavilions with hand-carved ceilings and deep, inviting divans. ✉ *Ctra. Sant Joan, Km 15, Santa Eulària, 07840* ☎ *971/338838* 🖷 *971/331650* 🌐 *www.atzaro.com* *7 rooms, 9 suites* *In-room: safe, refrigerator, DVD, Ethernet, Wi-Fi. In-hotel: restaurant, room service, 2 bars, 2 pools, gym, spa, bicycles, no elevator, laundry service, public Ethernet, public Wi-Fi, parking (no fee)* ▭ *AE, MC, V* *BP.*

$$$$ **Can Curreu.** The traditional Ibizan architecture here feels a lot like a
Fodor'sChoice ★ Greek island village: a cluster of low buildings with thick whitewashed walls, the edges and corners gently rounded off. Each accommodation at Can Curreu has one of these buildings to itself, with a private patio, artfully separated from its neighbors. Rooms have comfortable, deep sofas, upholstered in orange-red and yellow, built-in pine cupboard closets, red-brown tile floors: the overall effect is supremely *soothing*. Suites have fireplaces and Jacuzzi tubs. The hotel has its own stables, and orange and lemon groves. The excellent Can Curreu restaurant (closed Mon. in winter) serves an excellent five-course tasting menu. Mick Jagger stayed here. No satisfaction? Hard to believe. ✉ *Ctra. de Sant Carles, Km 12, Santa Eulària, 07840* ☎ *971/335280* 🖷 *971/335280* 🌐 *www.cancurreu.com* *3 rooms, 9 suites* *In-room: safe, refrigerator, kitchen (some), Wi-Fi. In-hotel: restaurant, bar, room service, pool, gym, bicycles, no elevator, public Wi-Fi, parking (no fee)* ▭ *AE, MC, V* *BP.*

SANTA GERTRUDIS DE FRUITERA

23 *15 km (9 mi) north of Eivissa.*

Blink and you miss it: that's true of most of the small towns in the island's interior—and especially so of Santa Gertrudis, not much more

9

than a bend in the road. But don't blink: Santa Gertrudis is strategic, and it's cute. From here, you are only a few minutes' drive from some of the island's flat-out best resort hotels and spas. You are minutes from the most beautiful secluded north coves and beaches: **S'Illa des Bosc, Benirrás** (where they have drum circles to salute the setting sun), **S'Illot des Renclí, Portinatx, Caló d'En Serra.** Santa Gertrudis itself has offbeat shops, and laid-back sidewalk cafés, and good food. Artists and expats like it here: they've given it an appeal that now makes for listings of half a million dollars for a modest three-bedroom flat.

WHERE TO STAY & EAT

$$$$ ★ **Cas Gasí.** With splendid views of Ibiza's one and only mountain, the 1,567-foot Sa Talaiassa, this lovely late-19th-century manor house is surrounded by hills of olive trees, redolent of Tuscany. Privacy—the sort that draws people like Richard Gere and Claudia Schiffer—is the keynote here: there's a monitored gate at the foot of the driveway; the restaurant and spa are exclusively for guests. Airy, rustic rooms with wood-beam ceilings are gracefully furnished with canopied beds and contemporary designer chairs: bathrooms have Moroccan-style tiling. One hitch: a minimum five-night stay is required. ✉ *Cami Vell a Sant Mateu s/n, Santa Gertrudis, 07814* ☎ *971/197700* 🖷 *971/197899* 🌐 *www.casgasi.com* *10 double rooms, 2 suites* *In-room: safe, kitchenettes (some), refrigerators, DVD, Ethernet. In-hotel: restaurant, cafeteria, bar, 2 pools, gym, spa, bicycles, no elevator, laundry service, public Internet, public Wi-Fi, airport shuttle, parking (no fee), some pets allowed* 💳 *AE, DC, MC, V* *BP.*

$$$$ **Hacienda Na Xamena.** Ibiza's showcase five-star hotel is on a rocky headland in Sant Miquel, in the northern part of the island, at the end of a rutted dirt road. A pair of Thai Buddhas flanking the main entrance introduce the Hacienda's fascination with Oriental and African motifs; the note is repeated in the rooms with carved headboards and mirror frames, saffron orange drapes, teak and mahogany furniture. All the bathrooms have Jacuzzis, some with panoramic vistas of Na Xamena inlet and the sea. From the huge main pool, and the terraced restaurants and lounges above it, you get an utterly breathtaking sunset view. ✉ *Apdo. 423, San Miguel, 07815* ☎ *971/334500* 🖷 *971/334514* 🌐 *www.hotelhacienda-ibiza.com* *50 rooms, 15 suites* *In-room: safe, refrigerator, Ethernet, Wi-Fi. In-hotel: 4 restaurants, room service, 2 bars, tennis court, 2 pools, gym, spa, bicycles, laundry service, concierge, public Internet, public Wi-Fi, parking (no fee), some pets allowed, no-smoking rooms* 💳 *AE, MC, V* ⏲ *Closed Nov.–Apr.*

$–$$ ✕ **Can Caus.** Ibiza might pride itself—justly—on its seafood, but there comes a time for meat and potatoes. When that time comes, take the 20-minute drive from Eivissa to the outskirts of Santa Gertrudis, to this informal, family-style roadside restaurant, and feast on skewers of barbecued *sobrasada* (soft pork sausage), goat chops, lamb kebabs, or grilled sweetbreads with red peppers, onions, and eggplant. Most people eat at the long wooden tables on the terrace. Can Caus also has a "Centre Artesanal" for the production of traditional Ibizen specialties, for sale in the little market next to the restaurant. ✉ *Ctra. Sant Miquel,*

Km 3.5, Santa Gertrudis ☎ *971/197516* 💳 *AE, MC, V* 🕒 *Tues.–Sun. noon–midnight, year-round.*

SHOPPING

te Cuero (✉ *Pl. de la Iglesia s/n, Santa Gertrudis* ☎ *971/197100* 🕒 *Weekdays 11–2 and 6–8*) specializes in hand-tooled leather bags and belts with great designer buckles. **Casi Todo** (✉ *Pl. de la Iglesia s/nSanta Gertrudis* ☎ *971/197023* 🌐 *www.casitodo.com* 🕒 *Weekend 10–2, Sat. noon–2*) is an antiques shop that buys interesting items from homes all over the island, posts the items on its Web site, and sells them at auction on Saturday mornings.

FORMENTERA

24 *90 min by ferry from Ibiza, 30–40 min by fast boat.*

For a calm respite from Ibiza's dance-until-you-drop madness, sleepy little Formentera is the answer. Just south of Ibiza, Formentera has managed to sidestep rampant overdevelopment. Though it can still get crowded in the summer, many of the island's long white-sand beaches are generally unspoiled, and you can pedal along quiet country roads in relative solitude.

You can begin this tour from Eivissa, Sant Antoni, or Santa Eulalia, as all have ferries to La Sabina—though the fast boats all connect from Eivissa. Formentera is mostly beach and countryside; there are relatively few places to stay, but lots of visitors from Ibiza who come for lunch and a few afternoon hours in the sun, and go back for the nightlife. If you want to picnic, buy supplies in Eivissa. It's worth standing on deck during the short passage for the excellent views of Dalt Vila and the smaller islands en route. Look for Trucadors, the stretch of sand that almost links Formentera with Es Palmador.

La Sabina has several car-, bicycle-, and moped-rental agencies, and most people rent bikes to explore this flat little island. From La Sabina, it's only 3 km (2 mi) to Formentera's tiny capital, **Sant Francesc Xavier,** a few yards off the main road. There's an active hippie market in the small plaza before the church. At the main road, turn right toward Sant Ferran, 2 km (1 mi) away. Beyond Sant Ferran the road travels for 7 km (4 mi) along a narrow isthmus, keeping slightly closer to the rougher, northern side, where waves come crashing over the rocks when a wind is blowing.

The plateau on the island's east side ends at the lighthouse **Faro de la Mola.** Nearby is a **monument to Jules Verne,** who set part of his novel *Journey Through the Solar System* in Formentera. The rocks around the lighthouse are carpeted with purple thyme and sea holly in spring and fall.

Back on the main road, turn right at Sant Ferran toward Es Pujols. The few hotels here are the closest Formentera comes to beach resorts, even if the beach is not the best. Beyond Es Pujols the road skirts **Estany Pudent,** one of two lagoons that almost enclose La Sabina. Salt was once extracted from Pudent, hence its name, which means "stinking pond," although the pond now smells fine. At the northern tip of Pudent, a road to the right leads to a footpath that runs the length of **Trucadors,** a narrow sand spit. The long, windswept beaches here are excellent.

WHERE TO STAY & EAT

$–$$$ ✕ **Sa Palmera.** On the beachfront in Es Pujols, Sa Palmera is known for paella and extremely fresh fish, such as the grilled *dorada* (sea bream) and *lubino* (sea bass). The locals' favorite is the *parrillada,* a platter of three types of grilled fish (depending on the catch of the day) served with potatoes and a salad. ✉ *Calle Aguadulce 15–31, Es Pujols* ☎ *971/328356* ▭ *MC, V* ⊗ *Closed last Fri. of Oct.–1st Fri. of Mar.*

$–$$ ★ ✕▣ **Fonda C'an Rafalet.** This simple inn is a few steps from the water at the tiny fishing cove of Es Caló; stay here, and one of the fishing boats drawn up on the rocky strand is likely to have come in that morning with your lunch. Paellas are the specialties here; don't miss the rice with *bogavante* (a type of lobster). The lack of a sandy beach has saved Es Caló from rampant development, but the setting is lovely: the brilliant blue-green of the water is bounded on the east by a long, dramatic line of cliffs. The hotel is 12 km (7 mi) from La Sabina. ✉ *Ctra. La Mola, Km 12 Apdo. de Correos 225, Es Caló de Sant Agustí, Sant Francesc Xavier, 07860* ☎🖷 *971/327016* ↩ *15 rooms* 👍 *In-room: no phone, no TV. In-hotel: restaurant, bar, beachfront, no elevator* ▭ *MC, V* ⊗ *Closed Nov.–Mar.*

$$$ ▣ **Sa Volta.** Near the beach in Es Pujols, one of the island's busiest villages, this is a cozy and, if you choose one of the more modest rooms, economical lodging choice. Standard rooms have geometric print bedspreads and matching drapes in blue and orange, and mass-production furniture; demi-suites have four-posters with gauzy bedcurtains. Family-run, it's a favorite with young couples on budget vacations. ✉ *Miramar 94, Es Pujols, 07860* ☎ *971/328125* 🖷 *971/328228* ⊕ *www.savolta.com* ↩ *22 rooms, 3 suites* 👍 *In-room: safe, refrigerator. In-hotel: restaurant, bar, pool, beachfront, bicycles, coin laundry, public Internet, no-smoking rooms* ▭ *MC, V* ⊗ *Closed Jan.–Mar.*

SHOPPING

El Pilar is the chief crafts village here. Stores and workshops sell handmade items, including bags, ceramics, jewelry, and leather goods. El Pilar's crafts market draws shoppers on Sunday afternoon, May–September. From June through August, the market is also on Wednesday afternoon. From May through September, crafts are sold in the morning at the San Francesc Xavier market and in the evening in Es Pujols.

SPORTS & THE OUTDOORS

You can rent bikes and motorcycles in La Sabina at **Moto Rent Mitjorn** (✉ *Playa de Migjorn* ☎ *971/328611* ⊕ *www.guiaformentera.com/mitjorn*).

BOATING The graceful sloop *Princesa de Mar* (☎ *971/390068* ⊕ princesadelmar@insotel.com) travels around and between Ibiza and Formentera daily. The young crew provides plenty of laughs, and lovely views await aboard the sunset cruise. The boat departs from Ibiza's port or La Sabina in Formentera and costs €35 per person. Boats are for hire at **Náutica Pins** (✉*Av. Mediterráneo 15–19, La Sabina* ☎*971/322651* 🌐*www.guiaformentera.com/nauticapins*).

DIVING You can take diving courses at **Vell Marí** (✉*Puerto Deportivo Marina de Formentera s/n, La Sabina* ☎*971/322105*).

THE BALEARIC ISLANDS ESSENTIALS

To research prices, get advice from other travelers, and book travel arrangements, visit www.fodors.com.

TRANSPORTATION

For more on travel to and in the Balearic Islands, see the Planner at the beginning of this chapter.

BY AIR

Iberia, Spanair, and Air Europa have daily direct flights between Palma and Barcelona, Madrid, Alicante, Valencia, Minorca, and Ibiza, as well as direct flights two or three times a week to Bilbao and Vitoria. Interisland flights should be booked well in advance for summer travel. Iberia and a large number of charter operators also serve other European cities. Iberia flies direct to Mahón from Barcelona and Palma three or four times daily, and most of these flights start and end in Madrid. Air Europa and Spanair also fly to Mahón. Iberia has direct daily flights to Ibiza from Barcelona, Madrid, Valencia, and Palma.

TRANSFERS Bus 1 runs between Palma's airport and the bus station on Plaça d'Espanya, next to the Inca train station. The last bus from town is around 2:30 AM; the last bus from the airport leaves at 2:15 AM. The fare is €1.80, and the trip takes 30 minutes. A taxi is about €20. A meter taxi to Mahón from the airport costs about €12. An hourly bus service runs between Ibiza's airport and Eivissa from 7 AM to 10:30 PM (on the hour from town, on the half hour from the airport; fare €2.70, journey time is about 20 minutes). By taxi, the same trip costs about €16.

Airports **Aeropuerto de Ibiza (IBZ)** (☎*971/809000*). **Aeropuerto de Minorca (MAH)** (☎*971/157000*). **Aeropuerto de Palma de Majorca (PMI)** (☎*971/789099*).

Carriers **Air Europa** (☎*902/401501* 🌐*www.air-europa.com*). **British Airways** (☎*971/787737* 🌐*www.britishairways.com*). **British Midland** (☎*971/789269* 🌐*www.flybmi.com*). **Easyjet** (☎*902/299992* 🌐*www.easyjet.com*). **Iberia** (☎*902/400500* 🌐*www.iberia.com*). **Spanair** (☎*902/131415* 🌐*www.spanair.com*).

BY BOAT & FERRY

BARCELONA Overnight ferries to the Balearic Islands leave from the Terminal Drassanes, at the foot of the Ramblas. Depending on the line and the season, the Trasmediterránea, Balearia, and Iscomar car ferries to Palma, Majorca, sail between 11 and 11:30 PM; all three lines serve Minorca and Ibiza as well. Fast ferries and 43-knot catamarans, also operated by Trasmediterránea and Balearia, with passenger lounges only, speed from Barcelona to Palma and Alcúdia (Majorca), to Ciutadella (Minorca), and to Eivissa (Ibiza). Depending on the destination, the trip takes between three and five hours.

Round-trip fares on the overnight ferries vary with the line, the season, and the points of departure and destination, but are around €140 for lounges and about €280–€360 for a double cabin. In the high summer season, it's wise to reserve a cabin well in advance. Major credit cards are accepted for all mainland–Balearic and most interisland fares.

DENIA Balearia runs a daily two-hour "Super Fast Ferry" service for passengers and cars between Denia (Alicante) and Eivissa, and a similar three-hour service between Denia and Palma on weekends. Iscomar runs a slower car-and-truck ferry service between Denia and Sant Antoni, Ibiza.

IBIZA Trasmediterránea sails to Barcelona and Valencia from Ibiza, and once a week (Sunday) to Palma, and from May to October they run a daily hydrofoil service from Palma and Denia, as well as less frequent service from Valencia and Barcelona. Balearia runs a "Super Fast Ferry" to Denia daily, which takes two hours. In summer, Flebasa runs a daily 2½-hour hovercraft between Sant Antoni (Ibiza) and mainland Benidorm; contact Coral Travel. Flebasa also runs a car ferry and a fast hydrofoil between Sant Antoni (Ibiza) and mainland Denia, with bus connections from Denia to Madrid and Valencia.

INTERISLAND Boats from Palma, Majorca, to neighboring beach resorts leave from the jetty opposite the Auditorium, on the Passeig Marítim. The tourist office has a schedule. In summer, excursions to Minorca's remotest beaches leave daily from the jetty next to the Nuevo Muelle Comercial, in Mahón's harbor. Daily ferries connect Alcúdia (Majorca) and Ciutadella (Minorca) in three to four hours, depending on the weather; a hydrofoil makes the same journey in about an hour. From May to October, a daily hydrofoil service connects Palma and Ibiza; call Naviera Mallorquina. There are frequent car and fast ferry services between Ibiza and Formentera operated by Balearia, Mediterránea Pitiusa, and other local lines.

MAJORCA Trasmediterránea sails daily (and twice on Sunday) from Palma to Barcelona, daily from Palma to Valencia, and weekly (Sunday) from Palma to Mahón and Ibiza. Balearia has a daily "Super Fast Ferry" car ferry service between Palma and Denia, direct on weekends but via Ibiza on weekdays. From June to September, a twice-weekly Euromer service connects Palma with Sète, France.

MINORCA Trasmediterránea sails between Mahón and Barcelona six days a week in summer (mid-June to mid-September) and to Palma and Valencia every Sunday.

VALENCIA Trasmediterránea ferries leave Valencia in midmorning for Palma, arriving early evening. There are also ferries from Valencia to Ibiza and Minorca: departure days and times vary with the season; service is more frequent in summer.

Boat & Ferry Information Balearia (✉ *Estación Marítima, Drasanes s/n, Barcelona* ☎ *902/160180* 🌐 *www.balearia.com*). **Coral Travel** (✉ *Carrer Mar 11, Sant Antoni, Ibiza* ☎ *971/343711 or 971/343752* ✉ *Carrer Isadoro Macabich 14, Santa Eulalia, Ibiza* ☎ *971/330512 or 971/330561*). **Flebasa** (✉ *Estación Marítim, Ibiza* ☎ *971/310711* ✉ *Edificio Faro, Sant Antoni, Ibiza* ☎ *971/342871* ✉ *Madrid* ☎ *91/473–2055* ✉ *Denia* ☎ *96/784011*). **Formentera port information** (☎ *971/195900*). **Inserco** (☎ *971/322210*). **Iscomar** (✉ *Estación Marítima, Muelle 9, Barcelona* ☎ *902/119128* 🌐 *www.iscomar.com*). **Mediterránea Pitiusa** (☎ *971/32244*). **Naviera Mallorquina** (☎ *971/710153*). **Pitra** (☎ *971/191068*). **Trasmapi** (☎ *971/322930, 971/322703 on Formentera*). **Trasmediterránea** (✉ *Estación Marítima, Barcelona* ☎ *902/454645* 🌐 *www.trasmediterranea.es* ✉ *Estación Marítima, Valencia* ☎ *963/164850* ✉ *Estación Marítima 2, Muelle de Paraires, Palma de Majorca* ☎ *971/70745* ✉ *Nuevo Muelle Comercial, Mahón, Minorca* ☎ *971/366050* ✉ *Estación Marítima, Ibiza* ☎ *971/315050*). **Umafisa Lines** (☎ *902/191068*).

BY BUS

A good network of bus service fans out from Palma to towns throughout Majorca: the various suburban bus routes carry some 35 million passengers a year. Most buses leave from the city station, next to the Inca railway terminus on the Plaça d'Espanya; a few terminate at other points in Palma. The tourist office on the Plaça d'Espanya has schedules. Several buses a day run the length of Minorca between Mahón and Ciutadella, stopping at Alaior, Mercadal, and Ferreries en route. From smaller towns there are daily buses to Mahón and connections, though often indirect, to Ciutadella. A regular bus service from the west end of Ciutadella's Plaça Explanada shuttles beachgoers between town and the resorts to the south and west. On Ibiza, buses run every half hour from Eivissa (Avinguda Isidoro Macabich) to Sant Antoni and Playa d'en Bossa, roughly hourly to Santa Eulalia. Buses from Ibiza to other parts of the island are less frequent, as is the cross-island bus between Sant Antoni and Santa Eulalia. The schedule is published in newspapers. A very limited bus service connects Formentera's villages, shrinking to one bus each way between San Francisco and Pilar on Saturday and disappearing altogether on Sunday and holidays.

Bus Stations Ciutadella (✉ *Pl. de S'Esplanada, across from tourist office*). **Eivissa** (✉ *Av. Isidoro Macabich and Extremadura* 🌐 *www.ibizabus.com*). **Palma de Majorca** (✉ *Estación Central* ☎ *971/752224*).

BY CAR

Majorca's main highways are well surfaced, and a fast, 25-km (15-mi) motorway penetrates deep into the island between Palma and Inca. Palma is ringed by an efficient beltway, the Vía Cintura. For destinations in the north and west, follow the ANDRATX and OESTE signs on the beltway; for the south and east, follow the ESTE signs. Driving in the mountains that parallel the northwest coast and descend to a cliff-side corniche is a different matter; you'll be slowed not only by winding roads but by tremendous views and tourist traffic.

A car is essential if you want to beach-hop on Minorca, as few of the beaches and *calas* are served by public transport. However, most historic sights are in Mahón or Ciutadella, both of which have reasonable bus service from other parts of the island, and once you're in town, everything is within walking distance. You can see the island's archaeological remains in a day's drive, so you may want to rent a car for just part of your visit. Ibiza is best explored by car or motor scooter: many of the beaches lie at the end of rough, unpaved roads.

In 2005, work began on Ibiza on a six-lane divided highway connecting the capital with the airport and Sant Antoni to be finished sometime in 2008. It's still a bit confusing to get in and out of Eivissa, but once you're past the construction sites, driving is easy, and remains the only feasible way of getting to some of the island's smaller coves and beaches. Tiny Formentera can almost be covered on foot, but renting a car at La Sabina is an obvious time-saver. ⚠ **Finding a legal parking space on the street—indicated by painted blue lines—can be a nightmare anywhere in the Balearics; The meter maids are super-vigilant, so don't forget to find a nearby parking ticket dispenser, feed it coins for the time you want (dispensers won't take paper money), then take the ticket back to the car and lock it inside, on the dashboard. The fine for parking overtime is also payable at the dispensers.**

BY TAXI

Taxis in Palma are metered. For trips beyond the city, charges are posted at the taxi stands. On Minorca, you can pick up a taxi at the airport or in Mahón and Ciutadella; on Ibiza, taxis are available at the airport and in Eivissa, Figueretas, Santa Eulalia, and Sant Antoni. On Formentera, there are taxis in La Sabina and Es Pujols. Most taxis in Minorca, Ibiza, and Formentera are not metered.

Taxi Companies **Majorca Associación Fono-Taxi** (✉ *Palma* ☎ *971/728081*). **Radio-Taxi** (✉ *Palma* ☎ *971/755440*). **Taxi-Palma-Radio** (✉ *Palma* ☎ *971/401414*).**Minorca Radio-Taxi** (✉ *Mahón* ☎ *971/367711* ✉ *Ciutadella* ☎ *971/381896*). **Ibiza** (✉ *Aeropuerto de Ibiza* ☎ *971/305230* ✉ *Eivissa* ☎ *971/307000 or 971/306602* ✉ *Figueretas* ☎ *971/301676*). **Radio-Taxi** (✉ *Sant Joan* ☎ *971/333033*). **Associación Sindical de Taxistas de Sant Antoni** (✉ *Sant Antoni* ☎ *971/340074*). **Formentera** (✉ *La Sabina* ☎ *971/322002*). **Radio-Taxi** (✉ *Es Pujols* ☎ *971/332016* ✉ *Es Pujols* ☎ *971/322080*).

BY TRAIN

The public *Ferrocarils de Mallorca* railway line plies between Palma and Inca, with stops at about half a dozen villages en route. A journey on the privately owned Palma–Sóller railway is a must: completed in 1912, it still uses the carriages of that era. The line trundles across the plain to Bunyola, then winds through tremendous mountain scenery to emerge high above Sóller. An ancient tram connects the Sóller terminus to Port de Sóller, leaving every hour on the hour, 9–6; the Palma terminal is near the corner of the Plaça d'Espanya, on Calle Eusebio Estada next to the Inca rail station.

Train Information **Palma Train Station** (✉ *Ferrocarrils de Mallorca, Plaça d'Espanya, Palma* ☎ *971/752245*). **Sóller tram** (✉ *Eusebi Estada 1, Sóller* ☎ *971/752051*).

CONTACTS & RESOURCES

EMERGENCIES

Emergency Services **Fire, Police or Ambulance** (☎ *112*). **Guardia Civil** (☎ *062*). **Insalud** (*Public Health Service* ☎ *061*). **Policía Local** (*Local Police* ☎ *092*). **Policía Nacional** (*National Police* ☎ *091, Mallorca 971/225200, Minorca 971/381090, Ibiza 971/398831*). **Información Toxicológica** (*Poisoning Information* ☎ *915/620420*).

LODGING

There are hundreds of real estate agents offering properties for short-term rentals. Contact the tourist offices or check the local papers for listings, but also consider booking through a travel agent, who can usually put together an attractive lodging package that includes transportation. **Kuhn and Partner** (✉ *Pl. de la Lonja 1, Palma, 07001* ☎ *971/228880* 🌐 *www.kuhn-partner.com*) is a major Majorca real estate agency with numerous branches. For information on more than 75 small country hotels away from the crowds, contact **Associació Agroturisme Balear** (✉ *Av. Gabriel Alomar i Villalonga 8A, 2A, Palma de Majorca 07006* ☎ *971/721508* 📠 *971/717317*).

TOUR OPTIONS

In Palma, take in the sights from an open-top **City Sightseeing** (☎ *902/101081*) bus that departs from various stops throughout the town, including Plaça de la Reina, and travels along the Passeig Marítim and up to the Castell de Bellver. Tickets (€13) are valid for 24 hours, and you can get on and off as many times as you wish along the way. All of Palma's tourist offices have information and details. Also in Palma, groups of up to four or five can hire a horse-drawn carriage with driver at the bottom of the Born; on Avinguda Antonio Maura; in the nearby cathedral square; and on the Plaça d'Espanya, at the side farthest from the railway station. A tour of the city costs about €25.

9

Most Majorca hotels offer guided tours. Typical itineraries are the Caves of Artà or Drac, on the east coast, including the nearby Auto Safari Park and an artificial pearl factory in Manacor; the Chopin museum in the old monastery at Valldemossa, returning through the writers' and artists' village of Deià; the port of Sóller and the Arab gardens at Alfàbia; the Thursday market and leather factories in Inca; Port de Pollença; Cape Formentor; and northern beaches. Nearly every Majorcan resort runs excursions to neighboring beaches and coves—many inaccessible by road—and to the islands of Cabrera and Dragonera. Starting in summer 2007, visitors to Cabrera can take a self-guided tour of the island's underwater ecosystem—using a mask and snorkel with a sound system incorporated; the recording explains the main points of interest as you swim along. Contact **Excursions a Cabrera** (☎ *971/657012* 🌐 *www.excursionsacabrera.com*) or the **National Park Office** in Palma (✉ *Plaza de España 8* ☎ *971/725 010* 🌐 *cabrera@mma.es*) or in Colònia de Sant Jordi (✉ *Carrer Burguesa 2*). On Minorca, sightseeing trips leave Mahón's harbor from the quayside near the Xoriguer gin factory; several boats have glass bottoms. Fares average around €10. Departure times vary; check with the Tourist Information office on the Moll de Ponent, at the foot of the winding stairs from the old city to the harbour. Every Ibiza resort runs trips to neighboring beaches and to smaller islands off the coast. Trips from Ibiza to Formentera include an escorted bus tour. In Sant Antoni, which has little to offer in the way of beaches, a whole flotilla advertises trips.

VISITOR INFORMATION

The regional tourist office for the Balearic Islands is the Consellaria de Turismo de Balear. Several tourist offices in Palma's airport have information on Majorca and towns nearby. The offices in Mahón and Ciutadella have local information.

Local Tourist Offices–Majorca **Oficina de Turismo de Majorca** (✉ *Aeropuerto de Palma* ☎ *971/789556*). **Alcúdia** (✉ *Passeig Marítim s/n* ☎ *971/547257* ⏲ *Apr.–Oct.*). **Manacor** (✉ *Plaça Ramon Llull s/n* ☎ *971/847241*). **Palma** (✉ *Pl. de la Reina 2* ☎ *971/712216* ✉ *Passeig d'es Born 27* ☎ *971/729634* ✉ *Parc de Ses Estacions, across from train station and near Plaça España* ☎ *971/292758*). **Pollença** (✉ *Carrer Sant Domingo 2* ☎ *971/535077*). **Sóller** (✉ *Pl. de Espanya s/n* ☎ *971/638008* ✉ *Carrer Canónigo Oliver* ☎ *971/633042*). **Valldemossa** (✉ *Av. de Palma 7* ☎ *971/612019*).

Local Tourist Offices–Minorca **Ciutadella** (✉ *Pl. de la Catedral 5* ☎ *971/382693*). **Mahón** (✉ *Moll de Llevant 2* ☎ *902/329015*). **Minorca** (✉ *Aeropuerto de Minorca Ctra. de San Clemente s/n Mahón* ☎ *971/157115*).

Local Tourist Offices–Ibiza (Eivissa) & Formentera **Aeropuerto de Ibiza** (✉ *Ctra. Sa Caleta s/n Sant Josep* ☎ *971/809118*). **Formentera** (✉ *Carrer Calpe s/n Port de La Sabina* ☎ *971/322057* 🌐 *www.formentera.es/en/turismo*). **Eivissa** (✉ *Carrer Antonio Riquer 2* ☎ *971/301900*). **Santa Eulalia** (✉ *Carrer Mariano Riquer Wallis 4* ☎ *971/330728*). **Sant Antoni** (✉ *Passeig de Ses Fonts s/n* ☎ *971/343363*). **Sant Joan** (✉ *Carrer de l'Ajuntament 4* ☎ *971/333003*).

Regional Tourist Office **Consellaria de Turismo de Balear** (✉ *Carrer Montenegro 5, Palma de Majorca, 07012* ☎ *971/176191* 🌐 *www.illesbalears.es*).

The Southeast

Balconies in Cartagena, Murcia region

10

WORD OF MOUTH

"Don't forget Benidorm . . . It's 'party central' for British, German, and Spanish people all together. (Young, not so young, and retired people . . . everybody seems to find a place to have fun there). [However] I very much prefer other little villages not far from Benidorm that don't have such a 'festive' feel."

—kenderina

www.fodors.com/forums

WELCOME TO THE SOUTHEAST

TOP REASONS TO GO

★ **Castillo de Santa Barbara, Alicante:** This grande dame of a castle dates from the 16th century and is the city's must-see main attraction. The best approach is via an elevator within the mountainside.

★ **Cartagena, Murcia:** Hannibal's namesake city—after his Carthage in North Africa—the historic center is the place to roam tangles of medieval streets.

★ **Guadalest, Alicante:** This town is pure drama. Dating from the 16th century, the Moorish influence is evocatively reflected in buildings seemingly sculptured out of the rock's face.

★ **Altea:** This historic hilltop village is picturesque and unspoiled; the narrow cobbled lanes are delightful for strolling.

★ **La Manga, Murcia:** The place to come to if you feel like a dip in the warm therapeutic waters of the Mar Menor followed by a mildly more energetic round of golf at the magnificently landscaped La Manga Resort.

1 Costa Blanca North. Think lush coastal plans with orchards of citrus trees that scent the air and produce an Impressionist painting of blossoms and fruit. The rice paddies stretching south give rise to Valencia's culinary specialty, paella.

2 Central Costa Blanca. This is the place to come for sandcastles, sea, and fun in the sun. The flip side is atmospheric villages that still reflect their seafaring heritage with superb fish restaurants.

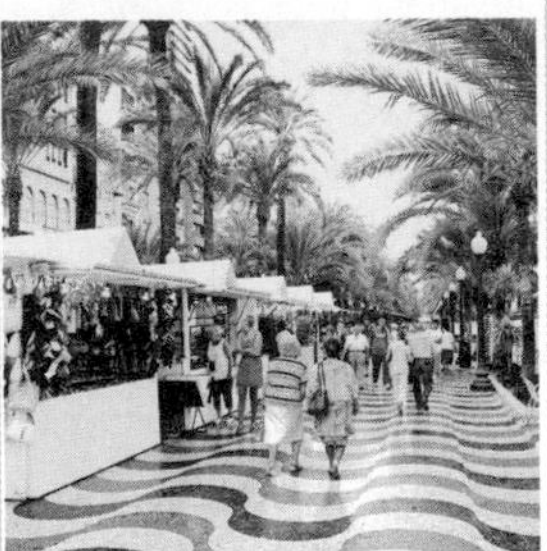

Esplanada de Espana, Alicante City.

3 Alicante Region. This city has ample charm, a fascinating historic center, and a vibrant night owl scene. The region is surrounded by a rich agricultural area punctuated by towns like Elche; a fascinating World Heritage site.

4 La Manga del Mar Menor. A long "sleeve" of sandy beach surrounded by still salt water makes this a historically therapeutic getaway.

TERUEL
Segorbe
Vall De Uxo
El Puerto
COSTA DEL AZAHAR
Utiel
Requena
Valencia
Burjasot
Gulf of Valencia
1
VALENCIA
Sueca
Alcira
Tabernes De Valldigna
Gandia
Jativa
Denia
Almansa
Onteniente
Guadalest
Cabo De La Nao
2
Altea
Villena
Alcoy
Yecla
Benidorm
Jumilla
ALICANTE
3
Elche
Alicante
COSTA BLANCA
Orihuela
Murcia
Torrevieja
Mediterranean Sea
San Javier
4
La Manga del Mar Menor
La Union
Mazzaron
Cartagena
COSTA CALIDA

GETTING ORIENTED

Culturally and geographically diverse, the region's most populated coastal resorts stretch north from the provincial capital of Alicante. Benidorm has the uneviable reputation of being the largest resort in the world, yet it has magnificent sweeping beaches and a something-for-everyone nightlife. South of here are such traditional working cities as Alicante and Murcia while, heading inland, the scenery is dramatically diverse with flat scrubland, olive and citrus groves, craggy mountain ranges, nature reserves, and stuck-in-a-time-warp villages where you will still need to speak Spanish to order a beer.

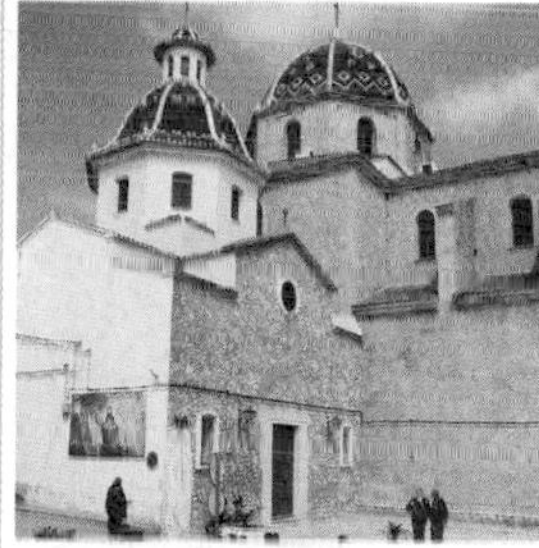

The church square of Nuestra Señora del Consuelo in Altea.

10

THE SOUTHEAST PLANNER

When to Go

Try to visit this region between late September and November or between April and June. Summer is crowded, oppressively hot, and more expensive with accommodation at a premium. In contrast, springtime is mild and an excellent time to tour the region, particularly the rural areas where blossoms hang on the branches and wild flowers dazzle the landscape. Easter is also entertaining, with parades and traditional ceremonies throughout the province. The early fall is still warm enough for a dip in the sea, but pack your umbrella as there may be rain. Winter can be chilly with central heating still a rarity, but with many clear, sunny days, it's an ideal season for outdoor activities, such as hiking.

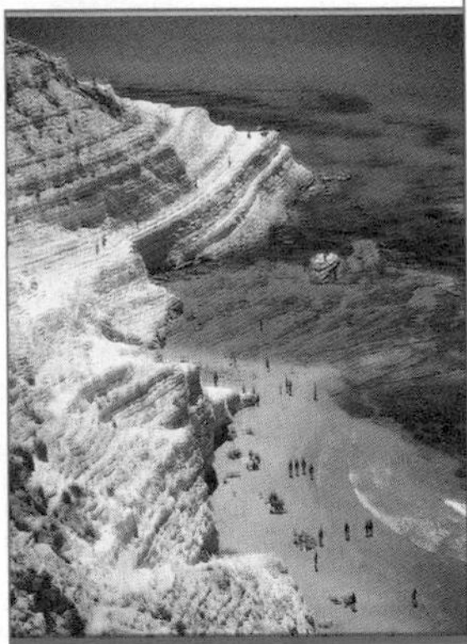

Getting There & Around

Iberia has the most flights to this part of Spain. However if you are arriving from the United States, it may be more economical for you to fly to London and then catch one of the no-frills airlines like easyjet, which has frequent flights to Alicante. There are three airports serving the region: Valencia, Alicante, and San Javier (for Mar Menor and Murcia). If you are traveling here from other parts of Spain, catching a bus is a reliable option although few travelers use the service, preferring trips organized by local travel agencies and hotels. Private companies run buses down the coast and from Madrid to Valencia, Benidorm, and Alicante. Bus travel is generally inexpensive and comfortable.

Arriving by train lands you in Alicante, which has two train stations: the main Estación de Madrid and the local Estación de la Marina, from where the the local FGV line (not affiliated with RENFE) runs along the Costa Blanca from Alicante to Denia. The Estación de la Marina is at the far end of Playa Postiguet and can be reached by buses C1 and C2 from downtown.

The *autopista* (toll highway) A7 runs from Barcelona through Valencia and Alicante as far as Murcia, with the A37 branching off just south of Elche to Cartagena. Tolls, though high, are often worth it for the time saved and the safer conditions. The other main links with the region are the A3 from Madrid to Valencia and the N111/A31 from Madrid to Murcia via Albacete. The N332 offers a nontoll (but slower) alternative down the coast from Valencia to Águilas, but between Denia and Calpe it's necessary to take smaller, slower roads if you want to be near the sea.

There are numerous car-rental companies, from all the major firms to local operations. Always shop around for the best price. Reservations are generally essential only during the Christmas and Easter holidays.

Balearia and Iscomar offer ferry services from Denia to Ibiza and Palma de Mallorca. In summer you can cross from Santa Pola to the tiny island of Tabarca. Boat excursions leave from most resorts along the coast, including some with underwater viewing areas.

See the Southeast Essentials at the end of this chapter for more transportation information.

Outdoor Activities

Although many visitors to the Costa Blanca seek nothing more energetic than lying on the beach while skimming a summer paperback, others may seek something mildly more bracing. For visitors in the cooler months, for example, the region offers some excellent walking and hiking opportunities, particularly around the Sierra Mariola and Sierra Aitana regions, both easily accessible from the Costa Blanca resorts. There are many companies that offer "walking vacations," most based in the United Kingdom. Check the following Web sites for information: *www.waymarkholidays.com*, *www.fell-walker.co.uk/costa-blanca.htm*, *www.spanish-fiestas.com/walking/alicante.htm*. This area is also suitably mountainous for climbers. The most obvious rock is Calpes Peñon de Ifach although this is a perilous peak and only recommended for advanced climbers. The best known area is northwest of Valencia in the Turia Valley.

Equestrian enthusiasts can find plenty of riding schools, which provide classes as well as trekking opportunities. Pick up brochures at the local tourist offices. Water sports are also widely available and you can learn to sail in most of the major resorts. Benidorm has a multilingual cableski and water-sports center, check the *www.surf.to/cableski* Web site for more details. Kitesurfing is becoming increasingly popular with the necessary gear is available for rent direct from several beaches, including Santa Pola, Benidorm, and Cullera; the same applies to windsurfing. If pedal power is more your thing, several companies offer a range of cycling holidays. Check *www.realholidays.com* and *www.ciclocostablanca.com*.

This region is also a birdwatcher's paradise. The main coastal plain is a migratory highway for thousands of birds winging their way between Europe and Africa. The salt pans of Santa Pola and Albufera Lake are particular hot spots.

WHAT IT COSTS In Euros

	$$$$	$$$	$$	$	¢
RESTAURANTS	over €20	€15–€20	€10–€15	€6–€10	under €6
HOTELS	over €180	€100–€180	€60–€100	€40–€60	under €40

Prices are per person for a main course at dinner. Prices are for two people in a standard double room in high season, excluding tax.

Planning Your Time

Alicante's town hall and travel agencies arrange tours of the city and bus and train tours to Guadalest, the Algar waterfalls, Benidorm, the Peñón de Ifach (Calpe), and Elche. In Benidorm, large hotels arrange similar excursions. Elche's town hall organizes tours of the city and environs. Alicante's town hall runs tours to Jijona, where you can visit one of the turrón factories before ogling the stalactites and stalagmites at the Cueva de Canalobre (Cave of Canalobre). If you prefer to go it alone you can choose from three different coastal experiences (the lagoon, the populous beaches of the Costa Blanca, and the less populated Mojácar), two distinct inland trips (the steppe around Albacete and the mountains near Murcia), and three major cities (Alicante, Albacete, and Murcia). For a real taste of the area in just a few days, start with the lakeside village of El Palmar and La Albufera. Continue south through Cullera and the elegant coastal town of Denia to the curved bay at Cabo de la Nao, before hitting Jávea. Travel on to the stylish small village of Altea, then head to Alicante before moving inland through Elche. Next stop is Murcia, with its superb cathedral, then Cartagena to explore there. If you have longer there is no shortage of additional places to see, including the playground of La Manga del Mar Menor and a boat trip to Tabarca Island.

Updated by Mary McLean

SPAIN'S SOUTHEASTERN CORNER IS A holiday brochure cliché of contrasts, best known for its sand, sunshine—and planes full of tourists. Inland the region's varied terrain ranges from the coastal plains of the far north to the peaceful soft sands and still waters of La Manga del Mar Menor. Literary buffs can contemplate the inland province of Albacete, historically part of Murcia, and the scene of Don Quijote's exploits in the Castilian expanse of La Mancha. Fertile river valleys wiggle their way between the mountains here like a silk cord, while the villages are simple and traditional; you'll probably need Spanish to order a beer or ask for directions. There's a heady sense of history throughout the region, especially in the southeastern towns where the architecture reflects the area's long Moorish occupation. Alicante was in Moorish hands from 718 to 1249; Murcia, from 825 to 1243.

During the civil war, many towns were bombarded and churches looted throughout these provinces. The ensuing reconstruction was painfully slow—a situation that continued until the 1960s, when the Spanish coasts saw the first package-tour vacationers. Benidorm is a perfect example of how small fishing villages grew into leading tourist resorts in less than a generation. Agriculture and industry have also continued to grow, and Alicante is now the fourth-wealthiest province in Spain.

Despite the large number of foreign residents and the annual swell of summer visitors, locals have remained fiercely protective of their regional culture. The traditional fiestas here are wonderfully colorful and exuberant, as are the distinctive local cuisine and craftsmanship.

EXPLORING THE SOUTHEAST

From Valencia's Albufera to the beginning of the Costa Blanca and down the coast through Alicante then on through the Murcia coastline, this part of Spain is rich in beaches, salt lagoons, steppes, mountain villages, and Mediterranean port cities. The Costa Blanca coastline of coves and white-sand beaches stretches from just north of Denia all the way south to the border with the Murcia coastline. It's peppered with resorts—Benidorm being far and away the splashiest and most crowded—and the resulting onslaught of summer tourists. Just tucked inland from the coast is a sprinkling of interesting villages, attractions, and larger towns, including Elche, Murcia, and Lorca.

ABOUT THE RESTAURANTS

Rice grows better in the Valencian provinces than anywhere else in Spain, which explains why paella was born here. Remember that paella should be eaten immediately after it's cooked—don't order it from a *menú del día* (menu of the day) unless you can be sure it's fresh. Another rice dish to try is *arroz a la banda* (rice and vegetables with meat or fish, cooked over a wood fire). Alicante and Jijona are known for their *turrón*, nougat made with almonds and flavored with honey. In Elche you can savor fresh dates. Murcian cooking uses products of the *huerta* (floodplain) and the sea, with a marked Arab influence in preparation. *Caldero de Mar Menor*, a traditional fisherman's rice dish, is cooked in huge iron pots, has a distinctly oily consistency, and is flavored by fish cooked in its own juices. Delicious as tapas or a first course are *muchirones* (broad beans in a spicy sauce, similar to the Catalan *habas a la catalana*) and *cocas* (meat pies akin to empanadas).

ABOUT THE HOTELS

Many hotels on this coast are modern high-rises. There are also some very tasteful independent hotels. A few coastal hotels close for the winter.

Numbers in the text correspond to numbers in the margin and on the chapter maps.

SOUTH OF VALENCIA TO THE COSTA BLANCA

This short drive takes you through the Albufera wetlands and into the northern end of the Costa Blanca, known as La Marina Alta (the High Shore). Compared with the sunbathers' strip south of Denia, these lonely marshlands and deserted beaches are wonderfully undiscovered.

LA ALBUFERA

1 *16 km (10 mi) south of Valencia.*

One of the largest bodies of freshwater in Spain, the **Parque Natural de La Albufera** supports four main environments: a sandbar, a marsh, the Albufera lagoon, and (to a lesser extent) hills and woodlands. More than 250 species of birds have been identified here—90 species breed here regularly. ✉*Centre d'Informació Raco del'Olla, El Palmar* ☎*96/162–7345* ⏲*Mon., Wed., and Fri. 9–2, Tues., Thurs., and weekends 9–2 and 3:30–5:30.*

El Palmar, the major village in the area, is home to numerous restaurants specializing in paella Valenciana, made with game birds and seafood.

WHERE TO STAY

$$$ **Hotel Sidi Saler.** On the edge of La Albufera, and just south of the city of Valencia, this slick, modern hotel has comfortable carpeted rooms and is a Frisbee-throw-away from miles of unspoiled beaches. With a free shuttle bus to and from Valencia, it makes a good base from which to explore the city as well as the nature park and El Palmar. ✉*Playa el Saler, Valencia, 46012* ☎*96/161–0411* *96/161–0838* *www.sidi-saler.com* *256 rooms, 16 suites* *In-hotel: 2 restaurants, bar, tennis courts, pools, gym, spa, children's programs (ages 6–12), beachfront, parking (no fee), airport shuttle, public Internet, public Wi-Fi, some pets allowed* *AE, DC, MC, V.*

CULLERA

2 *39 km (24 mi) south of Valencia, 27 km (17 mi) north of Gandía.*

Past the lighthouse and around the rocky point is modern Cullera, a resort with futuristic high-rises. The gasping climb up to the **Ermita de Nuestra Señora del Castillo** (Hermitage of Our Lady of the Castle) and **castle ruins** rewards you with views of the sea, huerta, and mountains.

10

GANDÍA

3 *30 km (19 mi) northwest of Denia.*

Fodor'sChoice ★

Gandía is a prosperous commercial town with a lively nightlife enjoyed, particularly, by visiting madrileños on the weekends. The town also has a coastal resort, Playa de Gandia, with a long sandy beach recognized as being one of the best on the Costa Blanca. The old town lies 4 km (2½ mi) inland and is best known for its sumptuous former palace of the Borja dynasty. Gandía became the Borgia fief after King Ferdinand granted the duchy to the family in 1485. The canny Borgia pope Alexander VI was one of the most notorious of all Renaissance prelates, but the family's reputation was later redeemed by the local Jesuit St. Francis Borgia (1510–72), who was canonized in 1671. The **Palau Ducal dels Borja** *(Ducal Palace)* , signposted from the city center, was founded by St. Francis in 1546 and serves as a Jesuit college. Elaborate ceilings and bright-color *azulejos* (glazed tiles) adorn the 17th-century state rooms. ☎*96/287–1465* 🌐*www.palauducal.com* 🎫*€ 5* 🕓*Guided tours June–Aug., Tues.–Sat. hourly 10–2 and 5–9, Sun. 10–2; Sept.–May, Tues.–Sat. hourly 10–2 and 4–8, Sun. 10–2.*

WHERE TO EAT

$$–$$$ **Gamba Marisqueria.** Justifiably famous around these parts, this restaurant is a family-run affair and a local favorite. The food is attractively presented, and only the freshest ingredients are used. The menu varies, but try the *fideuà de mariscos* (seafood paella made with noodles instead of rice), which feeds two, if it's available. *Carretera Nazaret-Oliva s/n 96/284–1310 Reservations essential AE, DC, MC, V Closed Mon. No dinner Oct.–June.*

$–$$ **Mesón Gallego.** This Galician restaurant dishes up hearty typical dishes like *pulpo a la gallega* (octopus) cooked over coals and dressed with oil and paprika and plenty of meat and game. The surroundings are unpretentious and rustic with tables spilling out onto the bustling port area. Ask for Galician *culcas,* shallow ceramic bowls for drinking the young Ribeiro wines. *Levante 37, Grao de Gandía 96/284–1892 AE, MC, V Closed Wed. No dinner Tues.*

THE COSTA BLANCA

The White Coast is best known for that magic vacation combo of sand, sea, and sun. This stretch of coastline begins between Gandía and Denia and ends near Murcia's border, just north of the Mar Menor. There are some excellent, albeit crowded, beaches here, as well as more secluded coves and stretches of sand. Alicante is the largest city and still largely overlooked by visitors who typically head straight for the better known coastal resorts, like Benidorm.

DENIA

4 *100 km (62 mi) south of Valencia, 8 km (5 mi) north of Jávea and east of Ondara.*

Infamous as the gastronomic capital of the Costa Blanca, Denia is a good place to sample Mediterranean seafood—try *picaetes de sepia y calamar* (squid and cuttlefish) or *suquet de rape* (stewed monkfish).

The northernmost beach resort on the Costa Blanca, Denia is a busy tourist town known for its fishing boats and fiestas, which culminate in the midsummer St. John's Day bonfires (June 23). Backed by the Montgó massif, rising to more than 2,100 feet to the west, Denia's beaches to the north—Les Marines, Les Bovetes, and Les Deveses—are smooth and sandy, whereas the coast to the south is rocky, forming *calas* (tiny secluded inlets that recall the Costa Brava, north of Barcelona).

Denia's most interesting architectural attraction is the **Palau del Governador,** the Governor's Palace, within a Moorish-era castle. Overlooking the town, the castle has an interesting archaeological museum as well as a Renaissance bastion and a Moorish portal with a lovely horseshoe arch. (*€2.15 Daily 10–1:30 and 3–6*). One notable church is **Iglesia de la Asunción** *(Church of the Assumption).*

IF YOU LIKE

BEACHES

The southeastern coastline varies from the long stretches of sand dunes north of Denia and south of Alicante to the coves and crescents of the Costa Blanca. The benign climate permits lounging on the beach almost year-round.

Altea, popular with families, is busy and pebbly, but the old town has retained a traditional *pueblo* feel with narrow cobbled streets and attractive squares. **Benidorm's** two white, crescent-shape beaches, packed in summer, extend for more than 5 km (3 mi) and are widely considered the best in Spain. **Calblanque** is on the road between Los Belones and Cabo de Palos, which takes you down a longish, rough track to a succession of nearly deserted sands frequented mainly by young murcians. **Calpe's** beaches have the scenic advantage of the sheer outcrop Peñón de Ifach (Cliff of Ifach), which stands guard over stretches of sand to either side. **Denia** and **Jávea** both have family beaches where children paddle in relatively safe waters. **Gandía's** sandy beach is well kept, its promenade lined with bars and restaurants.

FIESTAS & FESTIVALS

Denia throws a **mini Fallas** March 16 to 19. Alcoy's spectacular **Moros y Cristianos** (Moors and Christians) festival, held April 21 to 24, includes a reenactment of clashes from the Christian Reconquest, the battle to dislodge the Moors at the end of the 15th century. Murcia's **Semana Santa** (Holy Week) processions are among the most illustrious in Spain; those in Lorca are known for the opulent costumes of both Christian and Roman participants and for the penitents' solemn robes. Altea's **Moros y Cristianos** spectacle, staged the third Sunday in May, is a combination of battle reenactment and pageantry, complete with elaborate costumes and local kids dressed up as knights in shining armor. Alicante's main festival is **Hogueras de San Juan** (St. John's Day Bonfires), June 21 to 24. **El Misteri** (the Mystery Play) is performed in Elche in two parts, August 14 to 15, preceded by a public dress rehearsal.

The closest ferry connections to the Balearic Islands are in Denia. **Balearia** (☎*902/160180* 🌐*www.balearia.net*) sails to Ibiza, Formentera, and Mallorca and **Iscomar** (☎*902/119128* 🌐*www.iscomar.com*) sails to Ibiza, and then onward to Palma de Mallorca.

★ Inland from Denia, the **Cueva de las Calaveras** (*Cave of Canalobre* ☎*96/640–4235* 🎫*€ 3.50* ⏲*June–Sept., daily 9–8; Oct.–May, daily 9–6*), near Benidoleig, was inhabited by prehistoric humans some 50,000 years ago. The Cave of Skulls has numerous bones from that period. More than 300 yards long, the cave of stalactites and stalagmites has a dome rising to more than 60 feet. **Safari Park Vergel** (✉*Carretera CV700, Vergel-Pego, El Verger* ☎*96/643–9808* 🎫*€13.50* ⏲*Mar.–May, daily 10–6; June–Sept., daily 10–7; Oct.–Feb., daily 10–5*) is a zoo with 145 species of animals, including lions, Bengal tigers, yaks, elephants, and exotic birds.

WHERE TO STAY & EAT

$-$$ Fodor'sChoice ★ **Drassanes.** Built into Denia's original medieval shipyards (for which it's named), Drassanes is a well-known place for fresh local seafood. Informal and spread over two levels, the food here is authentic and flat-out good. *Arroz a la banda* (rice with seafood) is the house specialty. *C. Puerto 15 96/578–1118 AE, MC, V Closed Mon. and Nov.*

$ Fodor'sChoice ★ **El Port.** Found in the old seamen's quarter, just across from the port, this is one of those classic Denia spots that features all kinds of fish and shellfish dishes, as well as rice specialties, tapas, and mouthwatering desserts. *Esplanada Bellavista 12 96/578–4973 AE, MC, V Closed Mon.*

$$$ **Denia Marriott La Sella Golf Resort & Spa.** This large hotel, about 15 minutes west of Denia and 1½ km (1 mi) past the small town of La Xara, is ideal if you want to combine sporting facilities and a fine spa with sightseeing and the beaches of the coast. The rooms are larger than in most other places, and it's a child-friendly hotel, with on-site babysitting and a seasonal Kids Club. *Alqueria Ferrando, Jesus Pobre, 03749 96/645–4054 96/575–7880 www.marriott.com 178 rooms, 8 suites In-hotel: 2 restaurants, bar, golf course, tennis court, pool, gym ,children's programs (ages 4–12), laundry facilities, laundry service, parking (no fee), no-smoking rooms, public Wi-Fi, business services, some pets allowed AE, DC, MC, V.*

$$$ **La Posada del Mar.** Directly under Denia castle, and a few steps across from the harbor, this hotel is housed in the former 13th-century customs post and has been renovated with style and innovation. The rooms are individually decorated with a nautical them and most have balconies and views over the harbor and sea. La Posada's rooftop terrace is particularly inviting. *Plaça de les Drassanes s/n, 03700 96/643–2966 96/642–0155 www.laposadadelmar.com 20 rooms, 5 suites In-room: safe, Ethernet. In-hotel: bar, laundry facilities, parking (no fee), public Internet, public Wi-Fi AE, DC, MC, V.*

$$ **Hotel Chamarel.** Inside a 19th-century mansion in the town center, this eclectic hotel is a charming one-of-a-kind find. Expect art deco–style furniture, a bold mix and match of colors, modern art, high-tech facilities, and a tranquil patio surrounded by lush greenery. There are two standards of rooms, the superior with four-poster beds, beamed ceilings and shiny wooden floors. *Calle Cavallers 13, 03700 96/643–5007 96/643–5600 www.hotelchamarel.com 9 rooms, 5 suites In-room: Ethernet. In-hotel: restaurant, bar, cafeteria, meeting room, parking (fee), no elevator AE, DC, MC, V.*

10

JÁVEA

5 *108 km (67 mi) southeast of Valencia, 92 km (57 mi) northeast of Alicante, 8 km (5 mi) south of Denia.*

A labyrinth of tiny streets and houses with arched portals and Gothic windows, Jávea has an antique aspect contrasted only (ironically) by its modern church, **Santa María de Loreto.** The church-fortress of **San Bar-**

tolomé is the town's architectural gem. Restaurants around the port's **Aduanas del Mar** area serve *arroz a la marinera* (seafood paella).

The **Soler Blasco,** an ethnological and archaeological museum, has a superb set of Iberian gold jewelry discovered in 1904 during building excavation works. ✉*Calle Primicies s/n* ☎*96/579–1098* *Free* ⏲*Mar.–Oct., Tues.–Fri. 10–1 and 6–8, weekends 10–1; Nov.–Feb., Tues.–Sun. 10–1.*

WHERE TO STAY & EAT

$$$–$$$$ ✕**Restaurante Puerto.** On the first floor of a delightful building and with a nifty terrace, right between the beach and the harbor, this has the best location in Jávea. The cuisine is Valenciana, and the specialties here are paellas, *zarzuela con mariscos,* (shellfish) and rice dishes. There are special lunchtime *menú del días* for €10 and €16. ✉*Aduanas del Mar* ☎*96/579–1064* ▭*AE, DC, MC, V.*

$$$–$$$$ **El Rodat.** This hotel is a chic comfortable option providing all the extras you expect at the price, including an extensive health and beauty center and the option of renting your very own villa with private garden. The interior is plush, if conservative, with a gold, gray, and cream color scheme and the whole hotel is surrounded by lush tropical gardens with lofty palms, pine trees and brilliantly colored bourgainvillea. The restaurant terrace has panoramic views of the adjacent Montgó Natural Park. ✉*Ctra. al Cabo de la Nao s/n, 03730* ☎*96/647–0710* *96/647–1550* *www.elrodat.com* *34 suites, 8 rooms, 12 villas* *In-hotel: cable TV, restaurant, bar, pool, spa, public Internet, public Wi-Fi, parking (no fee)* ▭*AE, DC, MC, V.*

$$$ **Parador de Jávea.** Ensconced in a lush palm grove, with terrific views of the bay and white-sand beach below, this modern parador is four stories tall and far more tasteful than the high-rise hotels elsewhere on the Costa Blanca. The oak-trim, ceramic-tile guest rooms are airy and pleasant. ✉*Av. del Mediterráneo 7, 03730* ☎*96/579–0200* *96/579–0308* *www.parador.es* *70 rooms* *In-room: Wi-Fi. In-hotel: restaurant, bar, pool, gym* ▭*AE, DC, MC, V.*

$$ **Hotel Miramar.** This small, unpretentious hotel is a little basic when it comes to facilities but Miramar makes up for that with its location right on the promenade by the bay. Rooms with sea views cost slightly more. ✉*Plaza Almirante Bastareche 12, 03730* ☎*96/579–0100* *96/579–0102* *26 rooms* *In-hotel: bar, restaurant, no elevator* ▭*MC, V.*

CABO DE LA NAO

❻ *10 km (6 mi) southeast of Jávea.*

Cabo de la Nao (Cape Nao) is a great spur of land jutting into the Mediterranean toward Ibiza, barely 100 km (62 mi) away. As you round the point, you turn from a coast that looks toward Italy to one that faces Africa. In the same few miles, you pass from an agriculture of oranges and rice to one of olives and palms, and from a benign (if variable) climate to one of tawny aridity.

MORAIRA

7 *12 km (7 mi) northeast of Calpe, 20 km (12 mi) southeast of Jávea.*

Narrow streets leading down to Moraira's harbor preserve an air of seclusion. The *casco viejo* (old town) has a good selection of bars and restaurants, and the outskirts give way to chalets and private homes. Built in the Middle Ages, the **castle** and watchtower overlooking the port warded off Mediterranean pirates.

WHERE TO STAY

$$$  **Swiss Moraira.** Reopened in April 2006 and secluded in a pine forest above Moraira (off the road to Calpe), this low-rise luxury hotel is ideal if you're looking for peace and comfort. The rooms are large and light—three of the superior ones have hot tubs—are arranged around lush tropical gardens with palm trees surrounding the swimming pool. The beach and marina are 3 km (2 mi) away. ✉ *C. Haya 175, Urb. Club Moraira, 03724* ☎ *965/747104* 🖷 *965/747074* 🌐 *www.swisshotelmoraira.com* *33 rooms* *In-hotel: restaurant, bar, tennis court, pool, public Wi-Fi, parking (no fee)* 💳 *AE, DC, MC, V.*

EN ROUTE

The Cabo de Sant Antoni promontory, just north of Jávea, rises to 525 feet and is much steeper on its northern side than the southern. After the reconquest in the early 13th century, religious hermits made their home here. Later, fortifications were added to protect against the Barbary Pirates. Toward the end of the 19th century, these fortifications were replaced by the lighthouse that now stands here. The views to the south are best, encompassing the bay across to the Cap de Sant Marti.

CALPE

8 ★ *15 km (9 mi) southwest of Jávea, 8 km (5 mi) north of Altea.*

The road from Moraira to Calpe is very scenic, winding through the cliffs and hills covered in villas and passing small, rocky, and pebbly bays. Calpe has an ancient history, and its strategic location has attracted Phoenicians, Greeks, Romans, and Moors, with the latter dedicated to agriculture and fishing. After the reconquest by Jaume I, the Christians and Moors lived together peacefully, but between the 14th and 17th century they were under almost constant threat from the Barbary Pirates. This led to the construction of numerous fortifications such as the Torreó de la Peça, a defense tower named after an artillery piece used to defend the city. (Two of these cannons can be seen next to the Torreó.) Today the Old Town, full of striking small streets and squares, is a delightful place to wander.

Calpe has always been dominated by the **Peñón d'Ifach,** a huge calcareous rock more than 1,100 yards long, 1,090 feet high, and joined to the mainland by a narrow isthmus. The area is rich in flora and fauna, with more than 300 species of plant life and 80 species of land and marine birds identified here. A visit to the top is not for the fainthearted; wear shoes with traction for the hike, which includes a trip through a tunnel to the summit. The views are spectacular, reaching to the island of Ibiza on a clear day.

CASTLES GALORE

There are close to 100 castles in the Costa Blanca region, most originate from the days of the Moors and were built between the 8th and 13th centuries. Built as a defense against such predictable outside threats as pirates and outside invadors, they also protected the city against tax collectors!

The fishing industry is still very important in Calpe, and every evening the fishing boats return to port with their catch. The subsequent auction at the **Fish Market** can be watched from the walkway of La Lonja de Calpe. *Port* *Weekdays 5–7.*

Close to the port is another connection to the fish industry in Calpe. The **Baños de la Reina,** a group of six rooms, was built into the sea in the late-Roman period, around the 5th century. Legend says that it was reminiscent of a Moorish queen's spa; in fact, the rooms were hatcheries, used by the Romans to dry and salt fish. *South of port.*

The **Mundo Marino** company offers a complete range of sailing trips, including cruises between the towns up and down the coast. Some of the vessels have glass bottoms, so you can keep an eye on the abundant marine life here. *Port* *www.mundomarino.es.*

WHERE TO STAY & EAT

$$–$$$$ **Playa.** Quite simply, this (and its adjacent sister restaurant La Lonja) is a seafood and shellfish lovers' paradise. Just opposite the fishing port, it has an array of sample dishes that is staggering, from a few oysters for a handful of euros up to family-style combination plates at €100 each. You may even get treated to a free sample and glass of sangria just for looking. *Explanada del Puerto* *96/583–0032* *MC, V.*

$$$ **Hotel Bahía.** One of the latest hotels to grace the seafront, the slick, modern Bahía provides all the creature comforts accentuated by stylish décor and exceptional service. The rooms are classy in an understated way with splashes of bright color complimenting the more neutral overall color scheme and design. Bedroom terraces overlook the Playa Arenal but the hotel is equally well located for sidewalk cafés and a stroll around town. The spa provides a wide range of treatments for those seeking a spot of self pampering in between a plunge in the pool. *Av. de Valenica 24, 03710* *96/583–9702* *www.bahiacalpe-hotel.com* *284* rooms *In-hotel: restaurant, room service, bar, pool, gym, spa, beachfront, public Wi-Fi, parking (fee)* *MC, V* *BP.*

$ **Pensión el Hidalgo.** A pleasant family-run pensión near the beach. The rooms are small but cozy with a friendly spare-room feel; several have private balconies. A major perk is the breakfast terrace with a sea view you normally have to pay a premium for. *Av. Rosa de los Vientos 19, edificio Santa Maria, 03710* *96/583–9317* *www.pensionelhidalgo.com* *9 rooms* *MC, V* *BP.*

ALTEA

9 *10 km (6 mi) south of Calpe, 11 km (7 mi) north of Benidorm.*

Altea is an old fishing village with white houses and a striking church with a blue ceramic-tile dome. One of the best-conserved towns on the Costa Blanca, it serves as a foil to the skyscraping tourist towers of Benidorm. The beach here is pebbly. North of town, the Altea Hills area is more built up, with pretty villas lining the hills and cliffs.

WHERE TO STAY & EAT

$$$–$$$$ ✕ **La Costera.** This extremely popular restaurant mixes excellent Swiss cooking with bizarre furnishings and a nightly show. Specialties include the delicious, typically Swiss dish *rostit con carne troceada y champiñon* (chopped meat with mushrooms and potatoes) and fondues. ✉ *Costera del Mestre la Música 8* ☎ *96/584–0230* *Reservations essential* ▭ *MC, V* ⊗ *Closed Nov.–Feb. No lunch.*

$ **Hostal Fornet.** Rooms are modest but squeaky clean with white walls and pine furnishings at this pleasant small hotel in the historic center. The friendly owners are multilingual, but the real *piece de resistance* is the roof terrace with its stunning view of the church's distinctive blue tiled cupola and surrounding tangle of streets with a Mediterranean backdrop. ✉ *C. Beniardá 1, 03590* ☎ *96/584–3005* *35 rooms* *In-hotel: restaurant, bar, no elevator* ▭ *MC, V* ⊗ *Closed in January* *EP.*

BENIDORM

10 *11 km (7 mi) south of Altea, 42 km (26 mi) northeast of Alicante.*

Benidorm is an overdeveloped resort with tens of thousands of hotel beds and a seemingly bottomless capacity for tourists. Thanks to its twin, white crescent-shape beaches, Benidorm first became popular with mass tourism from northern Europe in the 1960s, and they're still a great attraction today. The city hasn't looked back since those early tourism days, and hundreds of thousands still flock here annually. As a consequence, the numerous karaoke clubs and British-run pubs offering all-day breakfasts and satellite soccer games give it a decidedly un-Spanish feel—and it's certainly not the place for those seeking a quiet vacation by the Mediterranean. Those with children, though, may appreciate the nearby famous Terra Mítica theme park and animal and water parks as well as the available boat trips. For a fantastic view, follow signs to Club Sierra Dorada at the eastern edge of town and climb up to the **Rincón de Loix** (Loix Corner).

Mundomar. This park's variety of marine and exotic animals includes colorful parrots. In addition to a children's playground there are dolphin, sea lion, and parrot shows. ✉ *Sierra Helada s/n, Rincón de Loix* ☎ *96/586–9101* *www.mundomar.es* *€20.*

Excursiones Marítimas Benidorm. Of the many boat trips offered by this company, the excursion to the Isla de Benidorm is one of the best. Here you can swim and look at the local birdlife. Boats depart every hour

10–5. The fare is €12 for adults. If you want to see more of the beautiful coastline here, opt for the one-hour cruise up to Calpe; this allows a little time for sightseeing there. These trips depart Monday–Saturday at 11, with a return sail to Calpe at 3.30 ☎*96/585–0052* ⊕*www.excursionesmaritimasbenidorm.com.*

Terra Mítica. Owned by Paramount, this is one of Europe's largest theme parks. In addition to many rides, there are shows that include pirate battles, chariot races, and fighting gladiators. ✉*Just outside Benidorm, Carretera de Benidorm a Finestrat, da de Moralet s/n* ☎*902/020220* ⊕*www.terramiticapark.com* *€33* *Apr., May, and Sept., daily 10–8; June–Aug., daily 10–midnight; Oct.–Dec. and mid- to late-Mar., weekends 10–8.*

WHERE TO STAY & EAT

$$$ ✕ **Tiffany's.** At this old timer of a restaurant, you can enjoy such classic French-inspired dishes as lobster thermidor and steak with Roquefort cheese. The atmosphere is formal without being stuffy and diners are treated to live piano music. There's an excellent list of French and Spanish wines. ✉*Av. Mediterráneo, Edifício Coblanca 3* ☎*96/585–1680* *AE, DC, MC, V* *Closed Jan. No lunch.*

$ ✕ **I Fratelli.** Reliable Italian with a soupçon of French country cooking is the calling card of this restaurant. Neapolitan music complements the stylish Moderniste touches: sleek black chairs, white tablecloths, and exotic potted plants. Best bets are pasta and *pescados a la sal* (fish baked in salt). ✉*Dr. Orts Llorca* ☎*96/585–3979* *AE, DC, MC, V* *Closed Nov.*

$$$$ **Montiboli.** A few miles south of Benidorm, this hotel sits on a cliff, overlooking a beautiful bay. Surrounded by luxuriant vegetation and the blue Mediterranean waters, it is, undoubtedly, the hotel of choice for many miles around. The rooms are totally luxurious with reflective marble floors—as are the public rooms and the gourmet restaurant. ✉*Partida Montiboli s/n, Villajoysa, 03570* ☎*96/589–0250* *96/589–3857* ⊕*www.montiboli.com* *89 rooms* *In-hotel: restaurant, bar, tennis court, pools, gym, spa, beachfront, laundry service, public Wi-Fi, parking (no fee)* *MC, V.*

$$$ **Gran Hotel Bali.** Housed in two futuristic buildings, one with 19 floors and the other with 43, this hotel wouldn't look out of place in Manhattan. There are marvelous views from the upper floors and the terrace. Rooms have a slick corporate appearance with modern furniture and fittings. The hotel is 400 yards from the beach and a little more than a mile from both the center of town and the Terra Mítica theme park. ✉*Calle Luis Prendes s/n, 03502* ☎*96/681–5200* *96/681–5208* ⊕*www.granhotelbali.com* *688 rooms, 84 suites* *In-hotel: 2 restaurants, bars, pools, spa, gym, laundry facilities, public Internet, public Wi-Fi* *AE, DC, MC, V.*

$$ **Hotel Colón.** This is one of Benidorm's oldest hotels, dating from 1961, but totally revamped in 2002. Positioned on the front line of Pontiente Beach, near the old town, the rooms are decorated in classic Mediterranean blue with sparkling white tiled bathrooms. Half-board is available for a minimal extra cost. ✉*Paseo Colón 3,*

03502 ☎96/585–0412 🌐www.hotelcolon.net 60 rooms In-hotel: restaurant, bar, beachfront, some pets allowed ▭MC, V ⊗Closed Nov. BP.

NIGHTLIFE

Countless bars and discos with names such as Jockey's and Harrods (reflecting Benidorm's popularity with Brits and Germans) line Avenida de Europa and the Ensanche de la Playa de Levante. The **Benidorm Palace** (*✉Av. Severo Ochoa ☎96/585–1661 🌐www.benidorm-palace.com*) offers a cabaret Tuesday–Saturday, with Spanish dance and an international musical show. Dinner starts at 8:30; the show at 10. Since its opening in 1977 this has been one of the major tourist attractions for the region, with capacity for 1,500. Admission for dinner and show is €40; for the show only, €25.

ALICANTE

11 *82 km (51 mi) northeast of Murcia, 183 km (113 mi) south of Valencia by coast road, 42 km (26 mi) south of Benidorm.*

The Greeks called it Akra Leuka (White Summit) and the Romans named it Lucentum (City of Light), since as a crossroads for inland and coastal routes, Alicante has always been known for its luminous skies. The city is dominated by the Castillo de Santa Bárbara, but also memorable is its grand **Explanada,** lined with date palms. Directly under the castle is the city beach, the Playa del Postiguet. The city's pride is the long, curved Playa de San Juan, which runs north from the Cap de l'Horta to El Campello. The small TRAM train (*🌐www.tram-alicante.com*) runs from the city center on the beach to El Campello. From the same open-air station in Alicante the FGV train departs to Denia, with stops in El Campello, Benidorm, Altea, Calpe, and elsewhere.

OLD TOWN

Concatedral of San Nicolás de Bari. Built between 1616 and 1662 on the site of a former mosque, this church has an austere facade that was designed by Agustín Bernardino, an admirer of Herrera (of Escorial fame). Inside, it's dominated by a dome nearly 150 feet high, a pretty cloister, and a lavish baroque side chapel. Its name comes from the day that Alicante was reconquered, December 6, 1248—the feast day of St. Nicolás. *✉Pl. del Abad Penalva 1 ☎96/521–2662 ⊗Daily 7:30–12:30 and 5:30–8:30.*

Iglesia de Santa María. Constructed in a Gothic style over the city's main mosque between the 14th and 16th centuries, this is Alicante's oldest church. The main door is flanked by beautiful baroque stonework by Juan Bautista Borja while the interior highlights are the golden rococo high altar, a Gothic image in stone of St. Mary, and a sculpture of the Sants Juanes by Rodrigo de Osona. *✉Pl. de Santa María ☎96/521–6026 ⊗Tues.–Sun. 4–8:30.*

Museo de Bellas Artes Gravina. Inside a beautiful palace, MUBAG, as it's known, has art collections from the 16th to early 20th centuries. *✉Gravina 13–15 ☎96/514–6780 🌐www.mubag.org Free*

May–Oct., Tues.–Sat. 10–2 and 5–9; Nov.–Apr., Tues.–Sat. 10–2 and 4–8.

Ayuntamiento. Constructed between 1701 and 1780, the town hall is a beautiful example of baroque civic architecture. Take a look inside and ask gate officials for permission to explore the ornate halls and rococo chapel on the first floor. *Pl. de Ayuntamiento 96/514–9100.*

OUTSIDE OLD TOWN

Santa Bárbara Castle (*Castillo de Santa Bárbara*). Benacantil Mountain, rising to a height of 545 feet, forms a strategic position overlooking not just the city but the sea and the whole Alicante plain for many miles. Remains from civilizations dating from the Bronze Age onward have been found here, and the oldest parts, at the highest level, are from the 9th to 13th centuries. Most of the work was undertaken between 1562 and 1580 during the reign of Felipe II. This is one of the largest existing medieval fortresses in Europe. The castle is named after a virgin martyr whose saint's day coincided with the date that the castle was reconquered, December 4, 1248. The castle is most easily reached by first walking through a 200-yard tunnel entered from Av. Jovellanos 1, along Postiguet Beach by the pedestrian bridge, then taking the elevator up 472 feet to the entrance. *Near Postiguet Beach 96/516–2128 Free, elevator €2.40 Elevator and castle daily 10–7; last elevator up at 6:30.*

Capa Collection. Professor Eduardo Capa donated this collection of contemporary Spanish sculpture, the largest such collection in the world. Some 250 of the total of 700 works are permanently displayed here, including pieces by Benlliure, Pérez Comendador, and Alberto Sánchez. *Castillo de Santa Bárbara 96/515–2969 Free Tues.–Sat. 10:30–2:30 and 4–6:30, Sun. and holidays 10:30–2:30.*

Museo Arqueológico Provincial (*MARQ*). Inside the old hospital of San Juan de Dios, this museum has exhibits dating from the Palaeolithic era to modern times, with a particular emphasis on Iberian art. *Plaza Dr. Gómez Ulla s/n 96/514–9000 www.marqalicante.com €3 Tues.–Sat. 10–7, Sun. and holidays 10–2.*

Museo Taurino. In the Plaza de Toros, the Bullfighting Museum is a must for aficionados of the sport. There are fine examples of costumes (the "suits of lights"), bulls' heads, posters, capes, and sculptures. *Pl. de España s/n 96/521–9930 Free Tues.–Fri. 10:30–1:30 and 5–8, Sat. 10:30–1:30.*

Museo de Fogueres. Bonfire festivities are popular in this part of Spain, and the effigies can be elaborate and funny, including satirized political figures and entertainment stars. Every year the best *ninots* (effigies) are saved from the flames and placed in this museum, which also has an audiovisual presentation of the festivities, scale models, photos, and costumes. *Av. Rambla de Méndez Núñez 29 96/514–6828 Free May–Oct. Tues.–Sat. 10–2 and 6–9, Sun. and holidays 10–2.*

WHERE TO STAY & EAT

$$–$$$ ✕ **Dársena.** The Marina Deportiva, a stretch of harbor front lined with restaurants and cafés, is the location of this old Alicante standard that, in 2006, celebrated its 45th anniversary. Mediterranean rice dishes (more than 150 options) are the house specialty, but pay close attention to the outstanding fish specials, which vary depending on the season and the luck of the local fishermen. Highlights include paella *con bogavante* (with lobster) and *arroz de caracoles y calamares* (short-grain rice with escargots and calamari). ✉ *Marina Deportiva–Muelle de Levante 6* ☎ *96/520–7399* 🌐 *www.darsena.com* ▭ *AE, DC, MC, V.*

$ ✕ **Nou Manoulin.** This inviting brick-walled restaurant is generally packed out with locals, here for the excellent value daily menu. This is a superb place to tuck into an authentic paella or other rice concoctions. If you can't find a bench, head for the tapas bar, which serves generous platefuls of healthy, filling tapas, ideally washed down with a glass of ice cold *fino* (sherry). ✉ *C. Villegas 3* ☎ *965/200368* ▭ *MC, V.*

$$$$ 🏨 **Amérigo.** This former Dominican convent is right in the historic center of Alicante. The building has been tastefully refurbished to blend its historic tendencies with the best of modern features and technology to become one of the newest and best luxury hotels in the city center. It also incorporates a fashionable tapas bar, a rooftop terrace and pool, and on-site private parking—a real luxury in Alicante. From here it is a short walk to nearby places of interest, including Postiguet Beach. ✉ *Rafael Altamira 7, 03002* ☎ *96/514–6570* 📠 *96/514–6571* 🌐 *www.hospes.es* *81 rooms* *In-hotel: restaurant, bars, pool, gym, public Wi-Fi, parking (fee)* ▭ *MC, V.*

$$ 🏨 **Hotel Mediterránea Plaza.** This elegant hotel is under the arches in the central Plaza del Ayuntamiento, with its magnificent baroque town hall. The lobby sets the tone for the hotel with its acres of glossy marble and refined décor. The rooms have parquet floors and a soothing blue-and-white color scheme with luxurious marble-clad bathrooms with tubs. There is a roof terrace with stunning views and plenty of extras for the price. ✉ *Pl. del Ayuntamiento 6, 03002* ☎ *965/210188* 🌐 *www.hotelmediterraneaplaza.com* *50 rooms* *In-hotel: bar, gym, spa, public Wi-Fi* ▭ *MC, V* 🍴 *EP.*

10

$ 🏨 **Hostal Les Monges Palace.** In a restored 18th-century building, this family-run pension is behind the ayuntamiento in Alicante's central old quarter. Rooms are furnished with eccentric artwork and quirky charm. The Japanese Suite (*Suite Japonés*) is equipped with hot tub and sauna. ✉ *C. San Agustín 4, 03002* ☎ *96/521–5046* 📠 *96/514–7189* 🌐 *www.lesmonges.net* *16 rooms, 2 suites* *In-room: dial-up. In-hotel: parking (fee)* ▭ *MC, V.*

Fodor'sChoice ★

NIGHTLIFE

Run-down bars populate the streets behind the ayuntamiento. In summer the liveliest places are along the water, on the Ruta del Puerto and Ruta de la Madera. Among the slicker pubs and discos is **Z-Club** (✉ *Calle San Fernando s/n* ☎ *96/521–0646*), where Alicante twentysomethings groove to house and techno. Thirtysomething couples gather at **Byblos Disco** (✉ *C. San Francisco s/n* ☎ *647/654298* 🌐 *www.byblosdisco.com*).

SHOPPING

Local **crafts** include basketwork, embroidery, leatherwork, and weaving, each specific to a single town or village. You can find these in the major resorts, though their prices may be inflated. The most satisfying places to shop are often neighborhood markets, so inquire about market days. For **ceramics** travel to the town of Agost, 20 km (12 mi) inland from Alicante. Potters here make jugs and pitchers from the local white clay, with porosity that is ideal for keeping liquids cool.

SANTA POLA

12 *19 km (11.8 mi) south of Alicante.*

This fishing town, which has nearly 15 km (10 mi) of mainly fine-sand and safe beaches with shallow, clear water, is an ideal location for families with children. The closest mainland city to Tabarca Island, Santa Pola has the port for several boats that make regular trips here.

There are records showing that people have lived in this area since the 4th century BC, when a fortified city was built to protect the settlers who fished and traded with other Mediterranean societies. The population increased with the coming of the Romans in the 1st century BC, who made it one of their main ports. Many of the fortifications seen today, including the town's castle, date from the 16th century and were built to defend the town from raids by the Barbary Pirates, who had taken over nearby Tabarca Island.

WHAT TO SEE

Exhibits at **Museo del Mar** detail Santa Pola's history and its close relationship with the sea, from prehistoric times through the fortification of the coast. ✉*Santa Pola Castle* ☎*96/669–1532* 🎫*€1.50* ⏲*May–Sept., Tues.–Sat. 11–1 and 6–10, Sun. 11–1:30; Oct.–Apr., Tues.–Sat. 11–1 and 4–7, Sun. 11–1:30.*

The eight rooms of **Museo de la Pesca** detail the life of fishermen in Santa Pola. There are models of boats, historic documents, and even the reconstruction of a fisherman's house. ✉*Santa Pola Castle* ☎*96/541–3351* 🎫*€1.50* ⏲*Tues.–Sat. 11–1 and 6–10 (4–7 in off-season, Oct.–May), Sun. 11–1:30.*

Inside an old salt mill within the natural park, **Museo de la Sal** tells the story of salt production, including all aspects of the actual extraction, as well as the salt's uses and characteristics. There are also bird-watching observatories. ✉*Av. Zaragoza 45* ☎*96/669–3546* 🎫*Free* ⏲*Fri.–Mon. and Wed. 9–2:30, Tues. and Thurs. 9–2:30 and 4–6.*

Acuario. This aquarium has nine large tanks with creatures native to the local Mediterranean environment—including *musolas* (a type of shark), crossbow fish, conger eels, octopi, and morays. ✉*Plaza Fernández Ordoñez s/n* ☎*96/541–6916* 🎫*€2.40* ⏲*Apr.–Oct., daily 11–1 and 6–10; Nov.–Mar., Tues.–Sat. 10–1 and 5–7, Sun. 10–1.*

Parque Natural de Les Salines de Santa Pola. This natural park of 6,103 acres overlaps with an old early 18th-century hunting and fishing reserve. It wasn't until a salt factory was opened in 1890 that the area was transformed. By making the seawater flow through a circuit of ponds to precipitate out the salt, the area has developed its own ecosystem. The park supports about 8,000 flamingos, one of the few places on the Iberian Peninsula with a permanent flock, as well as many other species, including sandpipers, osprey, and herons. The old Tamarit Tower, dating from the 16th century, stands in an isolated position by the side of N332. ✉ *South of Santa Pola, on either side of N332 Rd.*

Rio Safari Elche. Surrounded by more than 4,000 palm trees, you can take a small train to view large animals; visit smaller ones, such as crocodiles, reptiles, and birds; take in the animal shows; and even take a dip in the pool. ✉ *Ctra. Santa Pola-Elche* ☎ *96/663–8288* 🌐 *www.riosafari.com* *€18* *May–Oct., daily 10:30–8 with shows at 1, 5, and 8; Nov.–Apr., daily 10:30–6 with shows at 1 and 6.*

La Lonja. Every evening the fishing boats come back home, and their catch is auctioned off at the fish market here. It's a fascinating sight. ✉ *Puerto Pesquero.*

ISLA DE TABARCA

13 *4½ km (3 mi) east of Santa Pola.*

Fans of Pirates of the Caribbean and treasure map tales will enjoy the pirate connection of this small island off the Valenciano coast that became a base for the Barbary Pirates in the Middle Ages. In 1760 Carlos III fortified it and populated it with about 600 Genoan fishermen after an agreement with the king from the Tabarka Peninsula (between Tunisia and Algeria). These ancestors account for the Italian surnames of many of today's island dwellers. A little more than a mile long and 437 yards wide, and car free, the small fortified enclosure was listed as a National Historic Artistic Complex in 1964. The few restaurants specialize in seafood; the secluded beaches are great for snorkeling or simply sunbathing.

Cruceros Baeza-Parodi (☎ *608/330422 or 639/893920*) and **Cruceros La Gola de Guadarmar** (☎ *689/123623*) operate glass-bottom catamarans between Santa Pola and Tabarca. Crossings, which run four times a day, take around 25 minutes, and cost €13 each way.

10

INLAND FROM THE COSTA BLANCA

GUADALEST

14 *24 km (15 mi) north of Benidorm.*

The old town of Guadalest, originally Moorish, perches atop a crag within the walls of a castle ruined in a 1644 earthquake. Because of the steep terrain here, the tiny streets are stepped. To the north are splendid views over a large reservoir. The population is only 200, but this tiny village is the second-most-visited place in Spain, after the Prado

Museum. People are drawn here for the seven museums in town and the one just outside it.

Built after the earthquake of 1644 by a family of nobility, the **Museo Municipal Casa Orduña** was plundered during the War of Succession in 1708. All the furnishings on display here belong to the family and demonstrate how the affluent lived in the 19th century. The museum also serves as the entrance to the castle itself. ✉ *Iglesia 2* ☎ *96/588–5393* *€3.50* *May–Oct., daily 10:15–1:45 and 3:15–8; Nov.–Apr., daily 10:15–1:45 and 3:15–6.*

Attached to a natural rock, the **Antonio Marco Museum** contains miniature models of churches and homes made by Antonio Marco. On the top floor is a huge nativity scene, weighing 12 tons. ✉ *Calle de la Virgen 2* ☎ *96/588–5323* *€3* *May–Oct., daily 10–9; Nov.–Apr., daily 10–6.*

The name says it all. At the **Museo de Tortura Medieval** you can see torture methods used from the Spanish Inquisition through the 20th century here. All kinds of instruments are displayed on the four floors, including finger screws and whips. History buffs, horror fans, and older kids who watch *Scream* at sleepovers seem to get a kick out of the gory details. ✉ *Honda 2* ☎ *61/005–1001* *€3* *May–Oct., daily 10:30–9; Nov.–Apr., 10:30–6.*

The **Museo Ribera Girona,** the first of its kind in the province, exhibits contemporary art from numerous artists, including those of the founder, Ribera Girona. Many of the works here have been displayed in famous museums around the world. ✉ *Peña 1* ☎ *96/588–5062* *€4* *May–Oct., daily 10–8; Nov.–Apr., daily 10–6.*

WHERE TO EAT

$ ★ **El Tossal.** Just outside the pedestrian-only area of the old town, El Tossal, has a wood-beam dining room and outside terraces. On weekdays there's a set meal with a selection of tapas, main course, dessert, wine, and bread—all for less than €9. ✉ *Aitana* ☎ *96/588–5352* *MC, V.*

OFF THE BEATEN PATH

Just 10 km (6 mi) northwest of Altea, the hilltop town of Polop has two interesting features: a castle and the Plaza Fuente de la Provincia, which holds a collection of 221 taps for water, each donated by a different town in the province. Villagers armed with jugs can obtain free, constant mountain water from this square.

JIJONA

15 *24 km (15 mi) north of Alicante.*

Jijona is the home of *turró,* an almond-and-honey-based nougat of Moorish origin, still produced by more than 25 family-run businesses.

Museo del Turrón. This museum is in the old Turrones El Lobo carpentry works, in a business park on the outskirts of Jijona on the road to Busot. Guided tours (in Spanish, along with brochures in English) of this three-floored museum explain the production of *turrón,* marzipan, and other confections that have been the economic foundation of this town since the early 20th century. ✉*Poligon industrial "Ciutat del Turrón," sector 10, 2, Ctra. Xixona-Busot, Km 1* ☎*96/561–0225* ⊕*www.museodelturron.com* *€1* ⏲*Weekdays guided tours hourly 10–7, weekend tours hourly 10–1.*

EN ROUTE

Caves of Candelabra, one of the most spacious caves in Spain, has a length of 50 feet and a high ceiling. The stalagtites have created weird shapes, and the acoustic properties are put to use with musical shows. At an elevation of 2,300 feet on the slopes of the Cabezón de Oro (Golden Head) mountain, the location offers impressive views across the Mediterranean and the plain of Alicante. ✉***3 km (2 mi) north of Busot*** ☎***96/569–9250*** ***€4*** ⏲***July–Sept., daily 10:30–7:50; Oct.–June daily 11–5:50.***

ELCHE

16 *24 km (15 mi) southwest of Alicante, 34 km (21 mi) northeast of Orihuela, 58 km (36 mi) northeast of Murcia.*

If Alicante is torrid in summer, Elche is even hotter. The largest palm forest in Europe surrounds Elche, however, granting some escape from the worst of the heat. The Moors first planted the palms for dates, Europe's most reliable crop, and the trees still produce these as well as yellow fronds. (Throughout Spain the fronds are blessed on Palm Sunday and hung on balconies to ward off evil during the coming year.) Colonized by ancient Rome, Elche was later ruled by the Moors for 500 years. The remarkable stone bust known as *La Dama de Elche,* one of the earliest examples of Iberian sculpture (now in Madrid's Museum of Archaeology), was discovered here in 1897.

Elche's history dates back to the Neolithic period, when it was a mile south of the present town—it was at this site, L'Alcudia, that La Dama de Elche was discovered. The site includes the Museo Arqueológico with exhibits from the Copper and Bronze ages, as well as pieces from the Iberian and Roman eras. ✉*Ctra. Dolores, Km 2* ☎*96/661–1506* *€2.50* ⏲*Apr.–Sept., Tues.–Sat. 10–2 and 4–8, Sun. 10–2; Oct.–Mar., Tues.–Sat. 10–5, Sun. 10–2.*

Fodor's Choice ★ **Elche Palm Grove.** The Moors originally irrigated the land and started planting palm trees here, and these days there are more than 200,000 palm trees growing within the city. Many of the plantations have been turned into public parks, and efforts are being made to bring back traditional crafts. The blanched palm leaves are used in Elche's two most important cultural events—the Palm Sunday procession and the Mystery Play of Elche. The latter, dating from the Middle Ages and performed every year, represents the last days of Mary's life, her death, assumption, and coronation. ✉*Porta de la Morera* ☎*96/545–1936* *€4* ⏲*Apr.–Sept., daily 9–8:30; Oct.–Mar., daily 9–6.*

In the cellar of the 16th-century **Arab Baths Convent of Our Lady of Mercy** is an intriguing complex of Arab baths, with tiled walls and ceilings. ☒ *Passeig de les Eres de Santa Llúcia 13* ☎ *96/545–2887* *Free.*

WHERE TO STAY & EAT

$$–$$$ ✕ **Els Capellans.** This restaurant in the Huerto del Cura hotel is exceptional. Cold appetizers might include spider crab and avocado cake with green apples or creamed asparagus with salmon croquettes. For a main dish you might find lamb kebab on a bed of eggplant or grilled fillets of sole with razor clams in an artichoke cream sauce. ☒ *Porta de la Morera 14* ☎ *96/661–0011* *AE, DC, MC, V.*

$$$ ★ **Huerto del Cura.** A subtropical location and a large, private garden in Elche's palm grove make this modern hotel perfect for relaxation. The bedrooms, in bungalow huts, are gloomy because of the shady location but are tastefully decorated. ☒ *Porta de la Morera 14, 03203* ☎ *96/661–0011* *96/542–1910* *www.huertodelcura.com* *81 rooms, 10 suites* *In-hotel: restaurant, bar, tennis court, pool, gym, public Wi-Fi* *AE, DC, MC, V.*

THE MURCIA COAST

The Murcia Coast is markedly different from the coastline to the north. Here you are met by the curious Mar Menor, an inland sea hemmed in by La Mangor, the narrow strip of land that has beaches on either side. These days, La Manga is famous for its numerous hotels, particularly the huge La Manga complex on the mainland, just before the Cabo de Palos. The main town along the coast is Cartagena, which has a long and glorious history and is well worth a visit. Águilas, almost at the border with Andalusia, is a pleasant surprise, with a mild climate and fine beaches.

LA MANGA DEL MAR MENOR

17 *45 km (28 mi) southeast of Murcia.*

The advance of rocks and sand from two headlands into the Mediterranean Sea transformed what was once a bay into the Mar Menor (Smaller Sea), a famously calm expanse of water about 20 feet deep. The Mar Menor is Europe's largest saltwater lake (170 square km [105 square mi]), and, because of its high salt and iodine content, it's used as a therapeutic health resort for rheumatism patients. The Manga ("sleeve") is the 21-km (13-mi) spit of sand averaging some 990 feet wide that separates it from the Mediterranean. Four canals, called *golas,* connect the Mar Menor with the Mediterranean. The Manga has 42 km (26 mi) of immense, sandy beaches on both the Mediterranean and the Mar Menor sides, allowing swimmers to choose more or less exposed locations and warmer or colder water according to season and weather.

Museo de Carruajes y Motocicletas Zamar *(Museo de Carruajes y Motocicletas Zamar).* Just before the exit to the Hyatt Regency La Manga, this

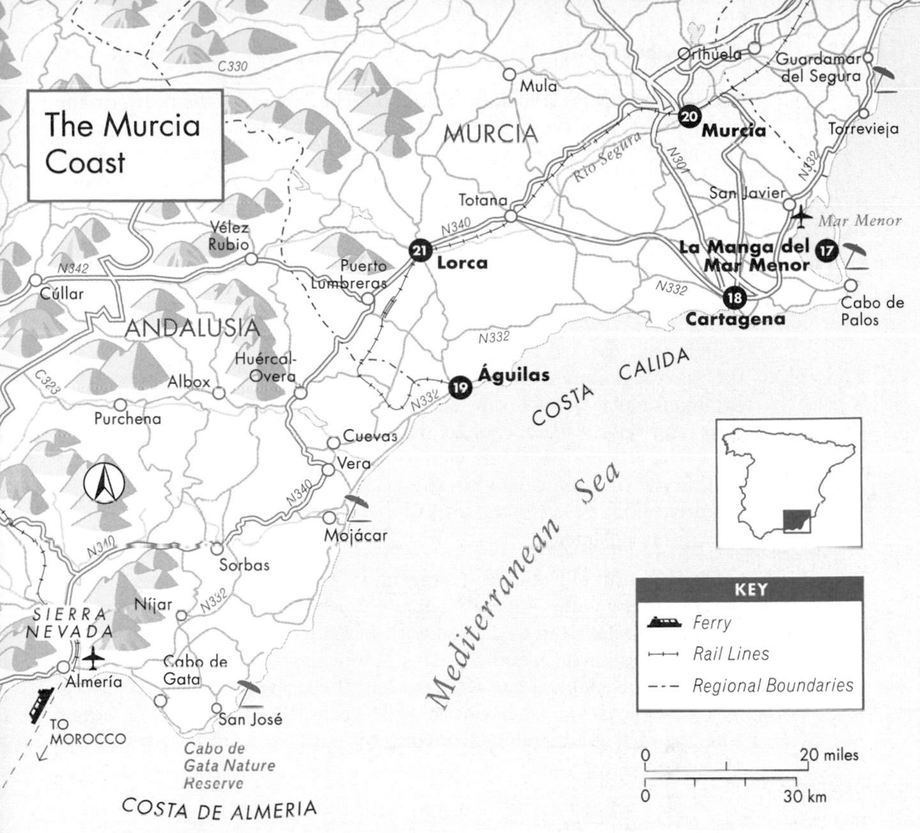

museum has an interesting collection of carriages from the 17th century to the present, as well as one of the largest collections of motorcycles in Spain. ✉*Ctra. La Unión, Km 2, El Algar* ☎*96/813–6656* 🌐*www.museodecarruajeszamar.com* ⏲*Tues.–Sun. 10–2 and 4–9.*

10

WHERE TO STAY & EAT

$ ✕**D'Bistro.** This is where the locals go—nothing fancy, but great food in good quantities. The prix-fixe lunch, at €9,is a great value, especially with a bottle of wine thrown in. ✉*C. Zoco D'Levante, 1st fl.* ☎*96/814–0370* 💳*MC, V.*

$$$$ **Hyatt Regency La Manga.** Golf pervades this superbly situated luxury clubhouse-hotel, just above the Mar Menor. For nongolfers, the resort has no fewer than 22 tennis courts and a regulation cricket pitch, the latter of which may account for the surfeit of British-registered Range Rovers in the parking lot. You can also rent apartments or villas. ✉*Los Belones, Murcia, 30385* ☎*96/833–1234* 📠*96/833–1235* 🌐*www.lamanga.hyatt.com* *192 rooms* *In-hotel: restaurant, bars, golf courses, tennis courts, pool, public Wi-Fi* 💳*AE, DC, MC, V.*

SPORTS & THE OUTDOORS

Notable for its absence of waves of any kind, the Mar Menor is a serious sailing destination. Various schools offer windsurfing, waterskiing, catamaran sailing, and other marine diversions.

Socaire Watersports School. In Santiago de la Ribera, to the north on the mainland side of the Mar Menor, this school offers sailing and windsurfing courses using a variety of vessels, and rents out equipment to qualified adults who wish to sail around the lake. ✉ *Playa del Castillico* ☎ *606/111813* 🌐 *www.socaire.com.*

CARTAGENA

18 *48 km (29 mi) south of Murcia.*

Founded in the 3rd century BC by the Carthaginians, this is Spain's principal naval base. From Cartagena you have easy access to the resort La Manga del Mar Menor and the twisty, scenic 100-km (62-mi) drive along N332 to the start of the Costa de Almería.

WORD OF MOUTH

"Cartagena is a very cute old Roman/Carthaginian seaport."

–WishIwasthere

General Asdrúbal founded Cartagena in 227 BC. Even then its natural harbor surrounded by five hills made it a busy port. It was from here that Hannibal set out in 218 BC with a mighty army and his elephants crossing the Pyrenees and the Alps before narrowly failing to destroy the Roman Republic. The Romans had their revenge in 209 BC, when they conquered Cartagena during the Second Punic War. This began a period of splendor under Roman rule that lasted until the beginning of the 2nd century AD.

In 44 BC Cartagena was honored with the title of Colony—Colonia Urbs lulia Nova Carthago—and it prospered because of its mines and its easily defended natural harbor and the inland sea, Mar Menor then known as El Almarjal, directly to the north. As elsewhere, when the Romans left there was a long period of decadence and troubles, with the Visigoths controlling for long periods before being replaced by the Moors in 734 AD. The reconquest came early here, in 1245 led by a prince who later became Alfonso X "The Wise." The Catholic monarchs began fortifications around the hills of the harbor to defend the city against the Moors, who retained power in nearby Granada until 1492. After that the Spanish Armada was stationed here for defensive purposes and to support military attacks on North Africa and the Mediterranean. At this time, in the early 16th century, castles and the huge city walls—both still visible today—were constructed, but they couldn't stop Sir Francis Drake from sacking Cartagena in 1585. The city was named capital of the Mediterranean Maritime Department in 1728, resulting in a large population growth to support the construction of arsenals, barracks, and castles. Mining remained economically important at this time, and remained so until the end of the 1920s. After the Cantonal Revolution in 1873 many of the buildings seen today were constructed. During the Spanish Civil War Cartagena remained steadfastly loyal to the Republican government, and was one of the last cities in Spain to surrender to Generalissimo Francisco Franco's troops.

A **tour bus** departs from outside the tourist office, directly across from the Punic Wall. With commentary about the city's attractions, the tour is a good introduction to Cartagena. ✉ *Tourist Office* €4.

WHAT TO SEE

Most of what can be seen of the **Castillo de la Concepción** today was built by Enrique III in the 14th century, using the remains of nearby Roman ruins. The views from here are astounding, reaching out over the town, harbor, and the Mediterranean. A **panoramic lift** (elevator) on Calle Gisbert rises nearly 150 feet to a gangway that leads to the Concepción Castle. Besides saving a strenuous walk, the gangway also offers great views on the way up. The lift costs €1. ✉ *Concepción Hill* ☎ *96/852–5326* *€3.50* *Mid-June–mid-Sept., daily 10:30–8:30.*

Cartagena suffered through much aerial bombardment during the Spanish civil war, since it was the base for most the Republican fleet. For the safety of its citizens, shelters with a capacity of 5,500 were built into the sides of the Concepción hill. At the **Refugio Museo de la Guerra Civil,** visitors today can see the conditions people had to endure during those harrowing days. ✉ *Gisbert 10* ☎ *96/850–0093* *€3.50* *Mon.–Sat. 10–2:30 and 4–6:30.*

The **Pabellón de Autopsias,** near the panoramic lift, was a part of the naval hospital when it was built in 1768. Autopsies and anatomy lessons were held here as part of the research into the constant epidemics that swept Cartagena in the late 18th century. Exhibits cover the anatomy sessions of those days. Across the road, and under Plaza de Toros, are some remains of the Roman Amphitheatre. Dating from the 1st century BC, it's one of the oldest of its kind on the Iberian Peninsula. ✉ *Calle Gisbert* ☎ *96/852–9582* *€1.50* *Tues.–Sun. 10–2:30 and 4–6:30.*

Across from the tourist office on the San José hill, the **Muralla Púnica** *(Punic Wall)* dates from 227 BC. The walls enclosed and helped defend the Punic city that became the capital of the Carthaginians on the Iberian Peninsula. ✉ *San Diego 25* ☎ *96/852–5477* *€3.50* *Tues.–Sun. 10–2:30 and 4–6:30.* At the remains of the **Casa de la Fortune,** which belonged to a wealthy family of the 1st century BC, the most attractive feature is the fresco painted on the dining-room walls. It's to the south of the tourist office, down the main road. ✉ *Pl. del Risueño* *€2.50* *Tues.–Sun. 10:30–2:30.*

10

On display at the **Decumano Calzada Romana** is a section of the Roman road known as the Decumano Maximo, which joined the harbor to the Forum. ✉ *Plaza de los Tres Reyes s/n* *€2* *July–Sept., Tues.–Sun. 4–6; Oct.–June, Tues.–Sun. 12:30–2:30.* Discovered in 1987, the **Teatro Romano** dates from the late 1st century BC. It was built into the northern slopes of the Cocepción hill. ✉ *Plaza Condesa Peralta s/n.*

A little distance outside the old town, and built over the 4th-century Roman necropolis of San Antón, the **Museo Arqueológico** is the headquarters for all archaeological study in this area. ✉ *Ramón y Cajal 45* ☎ *96/853–9027* *Free* *Tues.–Fri. 10–2:00 and 5–8, weekends 11–2.*

With all of Cartagena's maritime influences, it's appropriate to take to the water and find out more about this natural harbor. Guides on the **Barco Turístico** (*Tourist Catamaran*) talk about the harbor's system of fortifications, as well as intriguing legends and stories about the town's trading and military role of Cartagena. ✉*Muelle Alfonso XII* 🎫*€5.50.*

WHERE TO EAT

$$$–$$$$ ✕ **Mare Nostrum.** On the ground floor is a welcoming bar for snacks and tapas, and upstairs is a more formal dining room offering seafood, shellfish, and meat entrées, accompanied by such rice dishes as *arroz caldero* (fish and rice stew) and *arroz con Bogavante* (rice with lobster). ✉*Paseo Alfonso XII s/n, at the Puerto Deportivo* ☎*968/522131* 💳*AE, DC, MC, V.*

ÁGUILAS

19 *96 km (60 mi) southwest of Cartagena.*

Águilas, the last town of any size in Murcia, sits in a privileged position between two fine beaches and under the 16th-century Castillo de San Juan, which dominates a 280-foot-tall promontory in the center of town. The crystal-clear waters along the coastline hold fascinating, colorful underwater life. **Centro de Buceo–Águilas** leads dives between Águilas and Cabo Cope, rents all necessary equipment, and runs diving courses. ✉*Isaac Peral 13* ☎*968/493215* 🌐*www.buceoaguilas.com.*

WHERE TO STAY & EAT

$$–$$$ ✕ **Delicias del Mar.** This large restaurant has an equally large terrace, with both having delightful views across the bay over the marina to the commanding castle. The menu offers a wide range of typical dishes with an emphasis on meat and seafood. ✉*Aire 145* ☎*968/410015* 💳*MC, V* ⏲*No dinner Mon.–Wed.*

$$$ 🏨 **Don Juan Spa & Resort.** Enjoying an ace position, right on the beach at Playa Poniente, this hotel is considered the fanciest place to stay in town. The rooms are large and modern with plush furnishings and unparalleled views of the Mediterranean. Facilities include the Mondariz Spa & Beauty center. ✉*Playa Poniente, Av. del Puerto Deportivo 1, 30880* ☎*968/493493* 📠*968/414949* 🌐*www.hoteldonjuan.es* *128 rooms* *In-room: Ethernet. In-hotel: restaurant, bar, pools, gym, spa, concierge, public Internet* 💳*AE, DC, MC, V.*

INLAND FROM THE MURCIA COAST

There are only two towns inland that are worth venturing away from the coast to explore: the capital, Murcia, these days a busy, modern city; and Lorca, a considerably smaller community to the southwest.

MURCIA

20 *82 km (51 mi) southwest of Alicante, 146 km (91 mi) southeast of Albacete, 219 km.*

A provincial capital and university town of more than 300,000, Murcia was first settled by Romans. Later, in the 8th century, the conquering Moors used Roman bricks to build the city proper. The result was reconquered and annexed to the crown of Castile in 1243. The Murcian dialect contains many Arabic words, and many Murcians clearly reveal Moorish ancestry.

★ Murcia's **cathedral** is a masterpiece of eclectic architecture. Begun in the 14th century, the cathedral received its magnificent facade—considered one of Spain's fullest expressions of the Churrigueresque style—as late as 1737. The 19th-century English traveler Richard Ford described it as "rising in compartments, like a drawn out telescope." The 15th century brought the Gothic **Door of the Apostles** and, inside, the splendid chapel of **Los Vélez,** with a beautiful, star shape stone vault. Carvings by the 18th-century Murcian sculptor Francisco Salzillo were added later. The **museum** has been undergoing restoration; call ahead before planning to visit. The **bell tower,** built between 1521 and 1792, is also undergoing repairs and is sometimes closed to the public. ☎ *96/821–6344* *€1.20* *Daily 10–1 and 5–8, (4–7 in off-season).*

Wander north on the pedestrian shopping street Calle Trapería and you soon reach the 19th-century **Casino,** which retains the aura of a British gentleman's club. Despite the name, this has never been a gambling center—murcians come to read the newspaper and play billiards. The **Casino** has been undergoing restoration; call ahead before planning to visit. ✉ *C. Trapería.*

The **Museo Salzillo,** by the bus station, has the main collection of Francisco Salzillo's disturbingly realistic polychrome *pasos* (carvings), carried in Easter processions. ✉ *Plaza San Agustín 1* ☎ *96/829 1893* *www.museosalzillo.es* *€3* *Tues.–Sat. 9:30–2 and 5–8, Sun. 11–2.*

WHERE TO STAY & EAT

$$–$$$ ★ ✕ **Hispano.** For a typically Spanish brand of rusticity, look no further than this establishment run by a well-known Murcian family of restaurateurs-hoteliers named Abellán, who opened the Hispano in 1979. It is popular for Murcian and nouvelle cuisine, and traditional fare such as paella and *solomillo* (veal). ✉ *Arquitecto Cerdá 3* ☎ *96/821–6152* *AE, DC, MC, V* *Closed Sun. in July and Aug.*

$$ ★ ✕ **Rincón de Pepe.** In the center of the old town, this comfortable hotel is 50 yards from the cathedral's apse. Guest rooms are bright and modern, and the lobby and reception rooms have cool marble floors. The fine restaurant ($$–$$$) serves a good selection of *tapeo murciano,* samples of favorite Murcian dishes. Chef Francisco Gonzáles uses produce from the hotel's own organic farm, plus fish from the nearby Mar Menor and lamb from Segura. Highlights on the extensive menu include *cordero segureño asado a la murciana* (local lamb roasted Murcian-style). ✉ *Apóstoles 34, 30002* ☎ *96/821–2239* *96/822–1744*

🌐*www.nh-hoteles.com* 148 *rooms* *In-room: Wi-Fi. In-hotel: restaurant, parking (fee)* *AE, DC, MC, V* *No dinner Sun.*

$ **Hispano 1.** Rooms at this central budget hotel are basic but comfortable, and the public sitting area is large and tasteful. Ask for an exterior room, with a view of the pedestrian street below. There is a sister fancier hotel (Hispano 11) just around the corner if you want a little more luxury; the excellent restaurant is shared between the two. ✉*Trapería 8–10, 30001* ☎*96/821–6152* *96/821–6859* 46 *rooms* *In-hotel: restaurant, parking (fee), no elevator* *AE, DC, MC, V.*

NIGHTLIFE

Bars come and go, but you can always find action on both edges of the university, especially **Calle Doctor Fleming.** West of campus, a well-dressed young set gathers on the streets in front of the Teatro Romea; **Los Claveles** (✉*C. Alfaro 10* ☎*No phone*) is the center of action in this zone. It's closed Sunday through Tuesday. When the university bars close, there's always the main disco in the city center, **DNC Dance Club** (✉*Centrofama, C. Puerta Nueva s/n* ☎*No phone* 🌐*www.dnc-danceclub.com*).

LORCA

21 ★ *62 km (39 mi) southwest of Murcia, 37 km (23 mi) inland from Mediterranean at Águilas.*

Leave the highway for a glimpse of Lorca, an old market town and the scene of some of Spain's most colorful Holy Week celebrations. The Casa de los Guevara, on Lope Gisbert, houses the tourist office; from here head down Alamo to the elegant **Plaza de España,** ringed by rich baroque buildings, including the ayuntamiento, law courts, and Colegiata (collegiate church). Follow signs from the plaza up to the **castle.**

WHERE TO EAT

$ ★ ✕ **Casa Cándido.** A happy mix of Lorcans and travelers partake of the locally inspired food here; try the classic *trigo con conejo y caracoles* (bulgar wheat with rabbit and snails). With a location just outside the town center, this rustic, relaxed, old-fashioned restaurant has been going strong on home cooking for more than half a century. ✉*Santo Domingo 13* ☎*96/846–6907* *MC, V* *No dinner Sun.*

THE SOUTHEAST ESSENTIALS

To research prices, get advice from other travelers, and book travel arrangements, visit www.fodors.com.

TRANSPORTATION

For more on travel to and in the Southeast, see the Southeast Planner at the beginning of this chapter.

BY AIR

Airports **Aeropuerto de Valencia** (☎ *96/159–8500*). **Alicante** (✉ *El Altet, 12 km (7 mi) south of town* ☎ *96/691–9000*). **San Javier** (✉ *Mar Menor north shore, off N332* ☎ *96/857–0073*).

Carriers **Easyjet** (🌐 *www.easyjet.com*).**Iberia** (☎ *902/400500* 🌐 *www.iberia.com*).

BY BOAT & FERRY

Ferries **Balearia** (☎ *902/160–180* 🌐 *www.balearia.net*). **Iscomar** (☎ *902/119–128* 🌐 *www.iscomarferrys.com*).

BY BUS

Alsa is the main bus line in this region; check the Web site for timetables and bus stations, or contact the respective local tourist office.

Bus Lines **Alsa** (☎ *902/422242* 🌐 *www.alsa.es*).

BY CAR

There are several car rental agencies at Alicante airport, as well as in the larger towns. Hotels also have car-hire information and can book you a car with advance notice.

Rental Agencies **Autoeurope** (☎ *888/223–5555* 🌐 *www.autoeurope.com*). **Europa Rent-a-Car** (✉ *Av. de la Comunidad Valenciana 10, Benidorm* ☎ *96/680–2902* 🌐 *www.europa-rentacar.es* ✉ *Aeropuerto de Alicante, Alicante* ☎ *96/568–3362*). **Hertz** (✉ *Av. de la Estacíon 22, Alicante* ☎ *96/513–1123* 🌐 *www.hertz.com*).

10

BY TAXI

Taxi Companies **Cooperativa de Taxis** (☎ *96/578–6565 in Denia*). **Radio Taxi** (☎ *96/525–2511 in Benidorm*).

BY TRAIN

Rail Lines **RENFE** (☎ *902/240202* 🌐 *www.renfe.es*).

Train Stations **Alicante-FGV** (☎ *96/585–1895* 🌐 *www.fgv.es*). **Alicante-RENFE** (☎ *902/240202*). **FGV Station, Alicante** (☎ *96/526–2731*). **Murcia** (☎ *902/240202*).

Tour Operators **Alicante Ayuntamiento** (✉ *Plaza del Ayuntamiento* ☎ *96/514–9100* 🌐 *www.comunitat-valenciana.com*). **Elche Ayuntamiento** (✉ *Plaça de Baix* ☎ *96/665–8000* 🌐 *www.ayto-elche.es*).

CONTACTS & RESOURCES

EMERGENCIES

In an emergency, call one of the Spain-wide emergency numbers for police, ambulance, or fire services. The local Red Cross (Cruz Roja) can also dispatch an ambulance in case of an emergency. The Hospital General Univeritario in Alicante has a 24-hour emergency department. For nonemergencies, there are private medical clinics throughout the Costa del Sol, which often have staff members who can speak some English.

Emergency Services **Fire, Police or Ambulance** (☎ *112*). **Guardia Civil** (☎ *062*). **Insalud** (*Public health service* ☎ *061*). **Policía Local** (*Local police* ☎ *092*). **Policía Nacional** (*National police* ☎ *091*). **Hospital General Universitario** (*Hospital* ☎ *96/593-8300*).

Información Toxicológica (*Poisoning* ☎ *915/620420*).

INTERNET, MAIL & SHIPPING

Internet Cafés **Internet Cafe** (✉ *Intorrepc, Edificio Lomas Playa 111, Torrevieja* ☎ *966/920788*). **Internet Center Calpe** (✉ *Calle Navio Edificio Navio 7, Calpe* ☎ *96/5874712*).

Post Office (✉ *Calle Calle de Alemania 7, Alicante* ☎ *96/5200000*).

Courier Service **DHL** (✉ *Calle Marco Parc 1VA-4R, Alicante* ☎ *902/122424* 🌐 *www.dhl.es*).**MRW** (✉ *Pl. Balmis 3, Alicante* ☎ *96/5230638* 🌐 *www.mrw.es*).

VISITOR INFORMATION

Local Tourist Offices **Aguilas** (✉ *Plaza Antonio Cortijo s/n* ☎ *96/849-3173* 🌐 *www.aguilas.org*). **Albacete** (✉ *Posada del Rosario/del Tinte 2* ☎ *96/758-0522* 🌐 *www.albacity.org*). **Alicante** (✉ *Rambla Mendez Nuñez 23* ☎ *96/520-0000* 🌐 *www.costablanca.org*). **Benidorm** (✉ *Av. Martínez Alejos 16* ☎ *96/585-3224* 🌐 *www.benidorm.org*). **Calpe** (✉ *Av. Ejércitos Españoles s/n* ☎ *96/583-6920*). **Cartagena** (✉ *Plaza Almirante Bastarreche* ☎ *968/506483* 🌐 *www.cartagena.es*). **Denia** (✉ *Plaza Oculista Builges 9* ☎ *96/642-2367*). **Elche** (✉ *Parque Municipal* ☎ *96/665-8140* 🌐 *www.turismedelx.com*). **Gandía** (✉ *Marqués de Campo s/n* ☎ *96/287-7788* 🌐 *www.gandia.org*). **Jávea** (✉ *Plaza Almirante Bastarreche 11* ☎ *96/579-0736* 🌐 *www.xabia.org*).

Lorca (✉ *López Gisbert* ☎ *96/846-6157 or 968/479700* 🌐 *www.ayuntalorca.es*). **Murcia** (✉ *Plaza Cardenal Belluga* ☎ *96/835-8749* 🌐 *www.murciaciudad.com*). **Santa Pola** (✉ *Plaza Diputación* ☎ *96/669-2276* 🌐 *www.santapola.com*).

Regional Tourist Offices **Alicante** (✉ *Rambla de Mendez Nuñez 23* ☎ *96/520-0000* 🌐 *www.comunidad-valenciana.com*). **Murcia** (✉ *Plaza Julian Romea 4* ☎ *902/101070* 🌐 *www.murciaturistica.com*).

Andalusia

The Mosque of Cordoba

WORD OF MOUTH

"Andalusia feels, looks, sounds, and tastes so different from Catalonia that I thought I had arrived in another world. Until you hear flamenco and see the Moorish architecture and taste the cumin seed in the cooking, you don't fully understand how diverse Spain is."

—Eyecandy

www.fodors.com/forums

WELCOME TO ANDALUSIA

Cordoba's Great Mosque.

TOP REASONS TO GO

★ **Arabian Romance:** Soak in the history and drama of the mighty Alhambra in Granada.

★ **Enchanted Dancing:** Olé the night away at a heel-stomping flamenco show. Jerez de la Frontera is the "cradle of flamenco."

★ **Priceless Paintings:** Bask in the golden age of Spanish art at Seville's Museo de Bellas Artes.

★ **Exquisite Architecture:** Marvel at the jasper, marble, granite, and onyx of Córdoba's Mezquita.

★ **Tempting Tapas:** Try a little bit of everything on an evening tapas crawl.

★ **Tumultuous Fiestas:** Celebrate Semana Santa (Holy Week) with rich festivities in Granada, Cordóba, or Seville.

★ **Matador Moves:** Witness a bullfight in the historic bullrings of Seville or Ronda.

1 Seville. Long Spain's chief riverine port, the captivating town of Seville sits astride the Guadalquivir River that launched Columbus to the New World and Magellan around the globe. South of the capital is fertile farmland; in the north are highland villages.

2 Huelva. Famed as live oak-forested grazing grounds for the treasured *cerdo ibérico* (Iberian pig), the province's Sierra de Aracena is a fresh and leafy mountain getaway on the border of Portugal. Huelva's Doñana National Park is one of Spain's greatest national treasures.

Holy Week procession in Granada.

3 Cádiz. Cádiz is to Spain what Havana is to Cuba, but with less salsa and more charm. It is well known for its sherries and sherrylike Manzanilla.

4 Córdoba. A center of world culture in the 9th and 10th centuries, Códoba is a living monument to its past glory. Its prized building is the Mezquita (mosque). In the countryside, acorns and olives thrive.

5 Málaga. Pablo Picasso was born in this maritime province, known for its tapas taverns, bullring, and tourist beaches, but also the mountain town of Ronda.

6 Jaén. Andalusia's northwesternmost province is a striking contrast of olive groves, pristine wilderness, and Renaissance towns with elegant palaces and churches.

7 Granada. The blend of Christian and Moorish cultures are dramatically counterposed in Granada, especially in the sultry enclave of the Alhambra.

8 Almería. Once a textile and commercial giant, Almería today showcases architectural reminders of this past, as well as colorful cave dwellings.

GETTING ORIENTED

Andalusia is infinitely varied and diverse within its apparent unity. Seville and Granada are like feuding sisters, one vivaciously flirting, the other darkly brooding. Córdoba and Cádiz are estranged cousins, one landlocked, the other virtually under sail. Huelva and Almería are universes apart, the first a verdant Atlantic Arcadia and the second a parched Mediterranean sunbelt. And Jaén is an upland country bumpkin—albeit with Renaissance palaces—compared with the steamy cosmopolitan seaport of Málaga.

ANDALUSIA PLANNER

When to Go

The best months to go to Andalusia are October and November, and April and May.

Andalusia is blisteringly hot in the summer. If summer is your only chance to come, plan time in the Sierra de Aracena in Huelva, the Pedroches of northern Córdoba province, Granada's Sierra Nevada and Alpujarra highlands, or the Sierra de Cazorla in Jaén. Autumn catches the cities going about their business, the temperatures are moderate, and you will rarely see a line form. The months between December and April tend to be cool, uncrowded, and quiet. But come spring, it's fiesta time, with Seville's Semana Santa (Holy Week) the most moving and multitudinous. April showcases whitewashed Andalusia at its floral best, every patio and facade covered with everything from bougainvillea to honeysuckle.

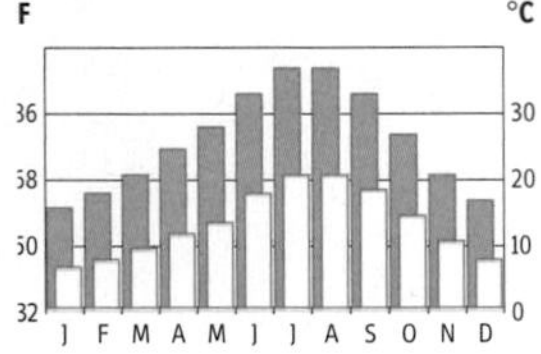

Getting There & Around

Seville is easily reached by air, although from the U.S. you need to connect in Madrid or London. Domestically, airlines such as Air Europa, Spanair, and Vueling connect Madrid, Barcelona, Valencia, and other major Spanish cities with Seville, Granada, Málaga, and Gibraltar, while Iberia flies from Jerez de la Frontera to Almería, Madrid, Barcelona, Bilbao, Valencia, Ibiza, and Zaragoza.

From Madrid, the best approach to Andalusia is via the high-speed railroad connection, the AVE. In under three hours, the spectacular ride winds from Madrid's Atocha Station through the olive groves and rolling fields of the Castilian countryside to Córdoba and on to Seville. Another option, especially if you plan to go outside Seville, Granada, and Córdoba, is to travel by car. The main road south from Madrid is the A4/E5.

Once in the region, buses are the best way (other than driving) to get around Andalusia. Buses serve most small towns and villages and are faster and more frequent than trains. From Granada, Alsina Gräells serves Alcalá la Real, Almería, Almuñecar, Cazorla, Córdoba, Guadix, Jaén, Lanjarón, Motril, Órgiva, Salobreña, Seville, and Úbeda.

Autocares Bonal operates buses between Granada and the Sierra Nevada. Granada's bus station is on the highway to Jaén. Buses serve Córdoba as well, but the routes are covered by myriad companies. For schedules and details, go to Córdoba's bus station (next to the train station) and inquire with the appropriate company. Alsina Gräells connects Córdoba with Granada, Seville, Cádiz, Badajoz, and Málaga. Alsa long-distance buses connect Seville with Madrid; with Cáceres, Mérida, and Badajoz in Extremadura; and with Córdoba, Granada, Málaga, Ronda, and Huelva in Andalusia. Regional buses connect the towns and villages in this region. The coastal route links Granada, Málaga, and Marbella to Cádiz. From Ronda, buses run to Arcos, Jerez, and Cádiz.

See Andalusia Essentials at the end of this chapter for transportation contact information.

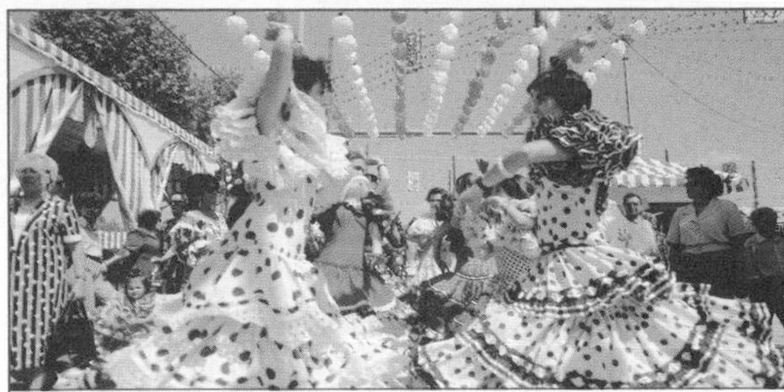

Planning Your Time

A week in Andalusia should include visits to Córdoba, Seville, and Granada to see, respectively, the Mezquita, the Cathedral and Giralda, and the Alhambra. Two days in each city nearly fills the week, though the extra day would be best spent in Seville, by far Andalusia's most vibrant concentration of art, architecture, culture, and excitement.

A week or more in Seville alone would be well spent, especially during the *Semana Santa* celebration when the city, though crowded, becomes a giant street party. With more time on your hands, Cádiz, Jerez de la Frontera, and Sanlucar de Barrameda form a three- or four-day cruise through flamenco, sherry, Andalusian equestrian culture, and tapas emporiums.

A three-day trip through the Sierra de Aracena will introduce you to a lovely Atlantic upland, filled with Mediterranean black pigs deliciously fattened on acorns, while the Alpujarra Mountains east of Granada offer anywhere from three days to a week of hiking and trekking opportunities in some of Iberia's highest and wildest reaches. For nature enthusiasts, there's also the highland Cazorla National Park and the wetland Doñana National Park—Andalusia's highest and lowest outdoor treasures. The Pueblos Blancos, whitewashed villages in the mountains, provide a dazzling two-day exploration with a night in Ronda.

WHAT IT COSTS In Euros

	$$$$	$$$	$$	$	¢
RESTAU-RANTS	over €20	€15–€20	€10–€15	€6–€10	under €6
HOTELS	over €180	€100–€180	€60–€100	€40–€60	under €40

Prices are per person for a main course at dinner. Prices are for two people in a standard double room in high season, excluding tax.

Fiesta Fun

Fiestas, which fill the calendar in Andalusia, can be a great way to combine the themes for which this region is known: flamenco, bullfighting, gastronomy, nature, wines, golf, skiing, and water-based activities.

Cádiz is famous for its January *Carnaval*, while Seville throws the most spectacular fiesta in all of Spain during *Semana Santa* (Holy Week), followed by the decidedly more secular *Feria de Abril*, starring beautiful horses and bountiful bullfights. Córdoba's *Cruces de Mayo* fiesta and its floral patio competition fills the month of May. Early June is the gypsy favorite, the Romería del Rocío festival in Huelva, a multitudinous pilgrimage on horseback and carriage to the hermitage of la Virgen del Rocío, Our Lady of the Dew. Early August showcases horse races on the beaches of Sanlúcar de Barrameda, while Málaga's mid-August *feria* (fair) offers top bullfights and flamenco. The second week of October Jaén celebrates the olive harvest.

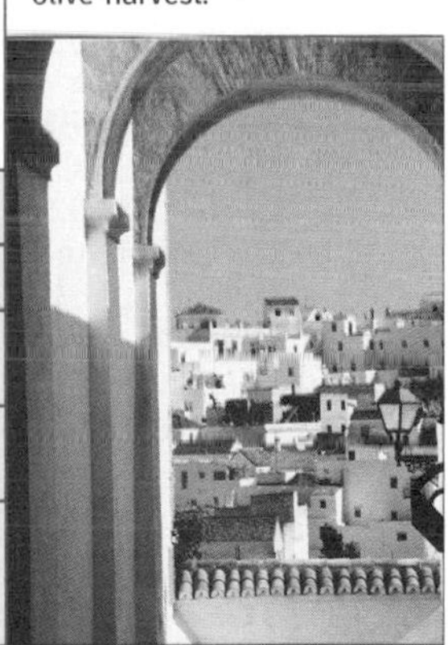

By George Semler

GYPSIES, BULLS, FLAMENCO, HORSES—ANDALUSIA IS the Spain of story and song, the one Washington Irving romanticized in the 18th century. Andalusia is, moreover, at once the least and most surprising part of Spain: least surprising because it lives up to the hype and stereotype that long confused all of Spain with the Andalusian version, and most surprising because it is, at the same time, so much more.

To begin with, five of the eight Andalusian provinces are maritime, with colorful fishing fleets and a wealth of seafood usually associated with the north. Secondly, there are snowcapped mountains and ski resorts in Andalusia, the kind of high sierra resources long thought most readily available in the Alps, or even the Pyrenees, yet the Sierra Nevada is within sight of North Africa. Thirdly, there are wildlife-filled wetlands and highland pine and oak forests rich with game and trout streams, not to mention free-range Iberian pigs. And lastly, there are cities such as Seville that somehow manage to combine all of this natural plenty with the creativity and cosmopolitanism of London or Barcelona.

Andalusia—for 781 years (711–1492) a Moorish empire and named for Al-Andalus (Arabic for "Land of the West")—is where the authentic history and character of the Iberian Peninsula and Spanish culture are most palpably, visibly, audibly, and aromatically apparent.

Though church- and Franco regime–influenced historians endeavor to sell a sanitized, Christians-versus-infidels portrayal of Spanish history, what most distinctively imprinted and defined Spanish culture—and most singularly marked the art, architecture, language, thought, and even the cooking and dining customs of most of the Iberian Peninsula—was the almost eight-century reign of the Arabic-speaking peoples who have become known collectively as the Moors.

All the romantic images of Andalusia, and Spain in general, spring vividly to life in Seville. Spain's fourth-largest city is a cliché of matadors, flamenco, tapas bars, gypsies, geraniums, and strolling guitarists. So tantalizing is this city that many travelers spend their entire Andalusian time here. It's a good start, for an exploration of Andalusia must begin with the cities of Seville, Córdoba, and Granada as the fundamental triangle of interest and identity. But there's so much more than these urban treasures. A more thorough Andalusian experience includes such unforgettable natural settings as Huelva's Sierra de Aracena and Doñana wetlands, Jaén's Parque Natural de Cazorla, Cádiz's *pueblos blancos* (white villages), and Granada's Alpujarras. The smaller cities of Cádiz—the Western world's oldest metropolis, founded by Phoenicians more than 3,000 years ago—and Jerez, with its sherry cellars and purebred horses, have much to recommend themselves as well. And in between the urban and rural attractions is another entire chapter of Andalusian life: the noble towns of the countryside, ranging from Carmona—Alfonso X's "Lucero de España" (Morning Star of Spain)—to Jaén's Renaissance gems of Úbeda and Baeza, Córdoba's Priego de Córdoba, Málaga's Ronda, and Cádiz's Arcos de la Frontera.

EXPLORING ANDALUSIA

ABOUT THE RESTAURANTS

Spaniards drive for miles to sample the succulent seafood of Puerto de Santa María and Sanlúcar de Barrameda and to enjoy *fino* (a dry and light sherry from Jerez) and Manzanilla (a dry and delicate Sanlúcar sherry with a hint of saltiness). Others come to feast on tapas in Seville or Cádiz. The village of Jabugo, in Huelva, is famous for its cured ham from the free-ranging Iberian pig. Look for Spain's top dining delicacy *jamon ibérico de bellota* (Ibérico acorn-fed ham) on the menu. Córdoba's specialties are *salmorejo* (a thick version of gazpacho topped with hard-boiled egg) and *rabo de toro* (bull's-tail or oxtail stew). A glass of *fino de Moriles,* a dry, sherrylike wine from the Montilla-Moriles district, makes a good aperitif.

Moorish dishes such as *bstella* (from the Moorish *bastilla,* a salty-sweet puff pastry with pigeon or other meat, pine nuts, and almonds) and spicy *crema de almendras* (almond cream soup) are not uncommon on Granada menus. *Habas con jamón de Trevélez* (broad beans with ham from the Alpujarran village of Trevélez) is Granada's most famous regional dish, with *tortilla al Sacromonte* (an omelet made of calf's brains, sweetbreads, diced ham, potatoes, and peas) just behind. *Sopa sevillana* (tasty fish and seafood soup made with mayonnaise), surprisingly named for Granada's most direct rival city, is another staple, and *choto albaicinero* (braised kid with garlic, also known as *choto al ajillo*), is also a specialty.

Note that many restaurants are closed on Sunday evenings, and several close for all of August.

ABOUT THE HOTELS

Seville has grand old hotels, such as the Alfonso XIII, and a number of former palaces converted into sumptuous hostelrie. The Parador de Granada, next to the Alhambra, is a magnificent way to enjoy Granada. Hotels on the Alhambra hill, especially the parador, must be reserved long in advance. Lodging establishments in Granada's city center, around the Puerta Real and Acera del Darro, are unbelievably noisy, so ask for a room toward the back. Though Granada has plenty of hotels, it can be difficult to find lodging during peak tourist season—Easter to late October. In Córdoba, several pleasant hotels occupy houses in the old quarter, close to the mosque. Other than during Holy Week and the May Patio Festival, it's easy to find a room in Córdoba, even if you haven't reserved one.

In all three cities, hotels fill up fast for Holy Week and major festivals, so book early—six to eight months in advance. Also note that prices in hotels can rise by at least 50% during fiesta time.

Outside the main cities, bed-and-breakfasts and rural lodgings give good access to the countryside and its rich folk traditions.

Numbers in the text correspond to numbers in the margin and on chapter maps.

SEVILLE

550 km (340 mi) southwest of Madrid.

Seville's whitewashed houses, bright with bougainvillea, its ocher-colored palaces, and its baroque facades have long enchanted both sevillanos and travelers. Lord Byron's well-known line, "Seville is a pleasant city famous for oranges and women," may be true, but is far too tame. Yes, the orange trees are pretty enough, but the fruit is too bitter to eat except as Scottish-made marmalade. As for the women, stroll down the swankier pedestrian shopping streets and you can't fail to notice just how good-looking *everyone* is. Aside from being blessed with even features and flashing dark eyes, sevillanos exude a cool sophistication of style about them that seems more Catalan than Andalusian.

This bustling city of almost 800,000 has its downsides: traffic-choked streets, high unemployment, a notorious petty-crime rate, and at times the kind of impersonal treatment you won't find in the smaller cities of Granada and Córdoba.

EXPLORING SEVILLE

The layout of the historic center of Seville makes exploring easy. The central zone—**Centro**—around the cathedral, the Alcázar, Calle Sierpes, and Plaza Nueva is splendid and monumental, but it's not where you'll find Seville's greatest charm. **El Arenal,** home of the Maestranza bullring, the Teatro de la Maestranza concert hall, and a concentration of picturesque taverns, still buzzes the way it must have when stevedores (ship loaders) loaded and unloaded ships from the New World. Just north of Centro, the medieval Jewish quarter, **Barrio de Santa Cruz,** is a lovely, whitewashed tangle of alleys. The **Barrio de la Macarena** to the west is rich in sights and authentic Seville atmosphere. The fifth and final neighborhood to explore, on the far side of the river Guadalquivir, is in many ways the best of all—**Triana,** the traditional habitat for sailors, Gypsies, bullfighters, and flamenco artists, as well as the main workshop for Seville's renowned ceramics artisans.

CENTRO

1 ★ **Cathedral.** The cathedral can be described only in superlatives: it's the largest and highest cathedral in Spain, the largest Gothic building in the world, and the world's third-largest church, after St. Peter's in Rome and St. Paul's in London. After Ferdinand III captured Seville from the Moors in 1248, the great mosque begun by Yusuf II in 1171 was reconsecrated to the Virgin Mary and used as a Christian cathedral. But in 1401 the people of Seville decided to erect a new cathedral, one that would equal the glory of their great city. They promptly pulled down the old mosque, leaving only its minaret and outer court, and set about constructing the existing building in just over a century—a remarkable feat for the time.

When visiting, head first for the **Patio de los Naranjos** (Courtyard of Orange Trees), on the northern side and part of the original mosque. The fountain in the center was used for ablutions before people entered the mosque. Near the Puerta del Lagarto (Lizard's Gate), in the corner near the Giralda, try to find the wooden crocodile—thought to have been a gift from the emir of Egypt in 1260 as he sought the hand of the daughter of Alfonso the Wise—and the elephant tusk, found in the ruins of Itálica. The cathedral's exterior, with its rose windows and flying buttresses, is a monument to pure Gothic beauty. the dimly illuminated interior, aside from the well-lighted high altar, can be disappointing: Gothic purity has been largely submerged in ornate baroque decoration. Enter the cathedral through the Puerta de la Granada or the Puerta Colorada. In the central nave rises the **Capilla Mayor** (Main Chapel) and its intricately carved altarpiece, begun by a Flemish carver in 1482. This magnificent *retablo* (altarpiece) is the largest in Christendom (65 feet by 43 feet). It depicts some 36 scenes from the life of Christ, with pillars carved with more than 200 figures.

A CRAZY CHURCH?

In building Seville's cathedral, the clergy renounced their incomes for the cause, and a member of the chapter is said to have proclaimed, "Let us build a church so large that we shall be held to be insane."

Make your way to the opposite (southern) side of the cathedral to see the **monument to Christopher Columbus.** The great explorer's coffin is borne aloft by the four kings representing the medieval kingdoms of Spain: Castile, León, Aragón, and Navarra. Columbus's son Hernando Colón (1488–1539), is also interred here; his tombstone is inscribed with the words A CASTILLA Y A LEÓN, MUNDO NUEVO DIO COLÓN (to Castile and León, Columbus gave a new world).

Between the elder Columbus's tomb and the Capilla Real, at the eastern end of the central nave, the cathedral's treasures include gold and silver, relics, and other works of art. In the **Sacristía de los Cálices** (Sacristy of the Chalices) look for Martínez Montañés's wood carving *Crucifixion, Merciful Christ*; Valdés Leal's *St. Peter Freed by an Angel*; Zurbarán's *Virgin and Child*; and Goya's *St. Justa and St. Rufina*. The **Sacristía Mayor** (Main Sacristy) holds the keys to the city, which Seville's Moors and Jews presented to their conqueror, Ferdinand III. Finally, in the dome of the **Sala Capitular** (Chapter House), in the cathedral's southeastern corner, is Murillo's *Immaculate Conception*, painted in 1668.

One of the cathedral's highlights, the **Capilla Real** (Royal Chapel), is reserved for prayer and concealed behind a ponderous curtain, but you can duck in if you're quick, quiet, and properly dressed (no shorts or sleeveless tops). To do so, enter from the Puerta de los Palos, on Plaza Virgen de los Reyes (signposted ENTRADA PARA CULTO—entrance for worship). Along the sides of the chapel are the tombs of the wife of 13th century's Ferdinand III, Beatrix of Swabia, and his son Alfonso X, called the Wise; in a silver urn before the high altar rest the relics of Ferdinand III himself, Seville's liberator. Canonized in 1671, he was said to have died from excessive fasting. In the (rarely open) vault below lie the tombs of Ferdinand's descendant Pedro the Cruel and Pedro's mistress, María de Padilla.

Before you duck into the Capilla Real, climb to the top of the **Giralda,** which dominates Seville's skyline. Once the minaret of Seville's great mosque, from which the faithful were summoned to prayer, it was built between 1184 and 1196, just 50 years before the reconquest of Seville. The Christians could not bring themselves to destroy this tower when they tore down the mosque, so they incorporated it into their new cathedral. In 1565–68 they added a lantern and belfry to the old minaret and installed 24 bells, one for each of Seville's 24 parishes and the 24 Christian knights who fought with Ferdinand III in the Reconquest. They also added the bronze statue of Faith, which turned as a weather vane—*el giraldillo,* or "something that turns," thus the name Giralda. To give it a rest after 400 years of wear and tear, the original statue was replaced with a copy in 1997. With its baroque additions, the slender Giralda rises 322 feet. Inside, instead of steps, 35 sloping ramps—wide enough for two horsemen to pass abreast—climb to a viewing platform 230 feet up. It is said that Ferdinand III rode his horse to the top to admire the city he had conquered. If you follow his route, you'll be rewarded with a view of tile roofs and the Guadalquivir shimmering beneath palm-lined banks. ✉ *Pl. Virgen de los Reyes, Centro* ☎ *95/421–4971* 🎫 *Cathedral and Giralda €7.50* ⏲ *Cathedral Mon.–Sat. 11–5, Sun. 2:30–6, and for mass (8:30, 9, 10, noon, 5).*

❸ ★ **Alcázar.** The Plaza Triunfo forms the entrance to the Mudejar palace built by Pedro I (1350–69) on the site of Seville's former Moorish *alcázar* (fortress). Don't mistake the Alcázar for a genuine Moorish palace, like Granada's Alhambra—it may look like one, and it was indeed designed and built by Moorish workers brought in from Granada, but it was commissioned and paid for by a Christian king more than 100 years after the reconquest of Seville. In its construction, Pedro the Cruel incorporated stones and capitals he pillaged from Valencia, from Córdoba's Medina Azahara, and from Seville itself. The palace serves as the official Seville residence of the king and queen.

You enter the Alcázar through the Puerta del León (Lion's Gate) and the high, fortified walls. You'll first find yourself in a garden courtyard, the **Patio del León** (Courtyard of the Lion). Off to the left are the oldest parts of the building, the 14th-century **Sala de Justicia** (Hall of Justice) and, next to it, the intimate **Patio del Yeso** (Courtyard of Plaster), the only part of the original 12th-century Almohad Alcázar. Cross the **Patio de la Montería** (Courtyard of the Hunt) to Pedro's Mudejar palace, arranged around the beautiful **Patio de las Doncellas** (Court of the Damsels), resplendent with delicately carved stucco. Opening off this patio, the **Salón de Embajadores** (Hall of the Ambassadors), with its cedar cupola of green, red, and gold, is the most sumptuous hall in the palace. It was here that Carlos V married Isabel of Portugal in 1526.

Other royal rooms include the three baths of Pedro's powerful and influential mistress, María de Padilla. María's hold over her royal lover—and his courtiers, too—was so great that legend says they all lined up to drink her bathwater. The **Patio de las Muñecas** (Court of the Dolls) takes its name from two tiny faces carved on the inside of one of its arches, no doubt as a joke on the part of its Moorish cre-

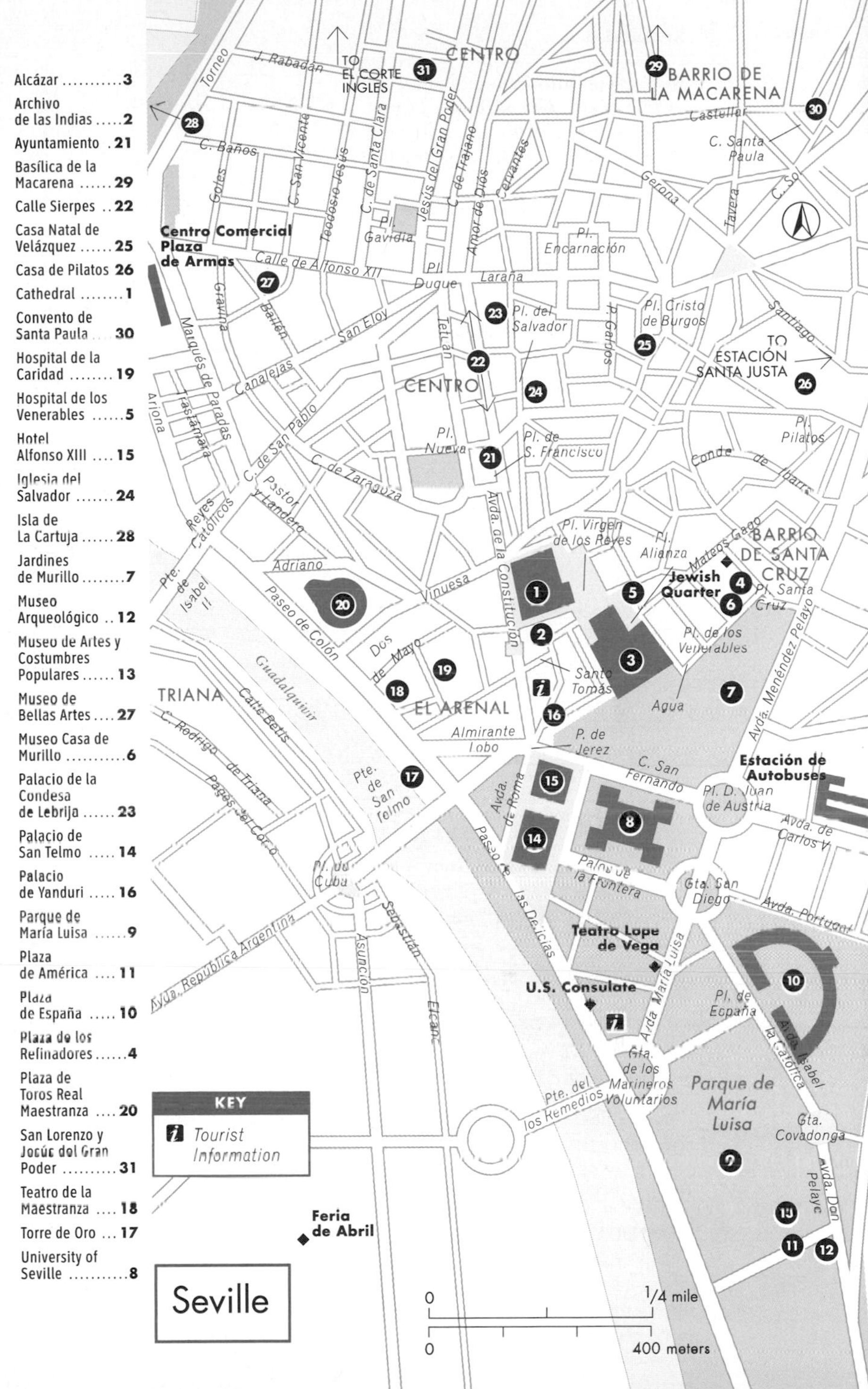

Alcázar 3
Archivo de las Indias 2
Ayuntamiento 21
Basílica de la Macarena 29
Calle Sierpes 22
Casa Natal de Velázquez 25
Casa de Pilatos 26
Cathedral 1
Convento de Santa Paula 30
Hospital de la Caridad 19
Hospital de los Venerables 5
Hotel Alfonso XIII 15
Iglesia del Salvador 24
Isla de La Cartuja 28
Jardines de Murillo 7
Museo Arqueológico 12
Museo de Artes y Costumbres Populares 13
Museo de Bellas Artes 27
Museo Casa de Murillo 6
Palacio de la Condesa de Lebrija 23
Palacio de San Telmo 14
Palacio de Yanduri 16
Parque de María Luisa 9
Plaza de América 11
Plaza de España 10
Plaza de los Refinadores 4
Plaza de Toros Real Maestranza 20
San Lorenzo y Jesús del Gran Poder 31
Teatro de la Maestranza 18
Torre de Oro 17
University of Seville 8
CENTRO
TO EL CORTE INGLES
BARRIO DE LA MACARENA
Centro Comercial Plaza de Armas
TO ESTACIÓN SANTA JUSTA
BARRIO DE SANTA CRUZ
Jewish Quarter
TRIANA
EL ARENAL
Estación de Autobuses
Teatro Lope de Vega
U.S. Consulate
Parque de María Luisa
Feria de Abril
Guadalquivir
KEY
Tourist Information
Seville
0
1/4 mile
0
400 meters

ators. Here Pedro reputedly had his half brother, Don Fadrique, slain in 1358; and here, too, he murdered guest Abu Said of Granada for his jewels—one of which is now among England's crown jewels. (The huge ruby came to England by way of the Black Prince—Edward, Prince of Wales [1330–76], eldest son of Edward III. Pedro gave the ruby to him for helping in the revolt of his illegitimate brother in 1367.)

Next is the Renaissance **Palacio de Carlos V** (Palace of Charles V), endowed with a rich collection of Flemish tapestries depicting Carlos's victories at Tunis. Look for the map of Spain: it shows the Iberian Peninsula upside down, as was the custom in Arab mapmaking. There are more goodies—rare clocks, antique furniture, paintings, and tapestries—on the upper floor, in the **Estancias Reales** (Royal Chambers), used by King Juan Carlos I and his family when in town.

In the **gardens**, inhale jasmine and myrtle, wander among terraces and baths, and peer into the well-stocked goldfish pond. From the gardens, a passageway leads to the **Patio de las Banderas** (Court of the Flags), which has a classic view of the Giralda.

Tours depart in the morning only, every half hour in summer and every hour in winter. ✉*Pl. del Triunfo, Santa Cruz* ☎*95/450–2323* 🌐*www.patronato-alcazarsevilla.es* 🎫*€7* ⏲*Tues.–Sat. 9:30–7, Sun. 9:30–5.*

WHERE'S COLUMBUS?

Christopher Columbus knew both triumph and disgrace, yet he found no repose—he died, bitterly disillusioned, in Valladolid in 1506. No one knows for certain where he is buried; he was reportedly laid to rest for the first time in the Dominican Republic and then moved over the years to other locations. His remains are thought to be in Seville's Cathedral.

2 **Archivo de las Indias** (Archives of the Indies). Opened in 1785 in the former Lonja (Merchants' Exchange), this dignified Renaissance building stores archives of more than 40,000 documents, including drawings, trade documents, plans of South American towns, even the autographs of Columbus, Magellan, and Cortés. ✉*Av. de la Constitución, Santa Cruz* ☎*95/421–1234* 🎫*Free* ⏲*Mon.–Sat. 10–4, Sun. 10–2.*

21 **Ayuntamiento** (City Hall). This Diego de Riaño original, built between 1527 and 1564, is in the heart of Seville's commercial center. A 19th-century, plateresque facade overlooks the Plaza Nueva. The other side, on the Plaza de San Francisco, has Riaño's work. ✉*Pl. Nueva 1, Centro* ☎*95/459–0101* 🎫*Free* ⏲*Tours Tues.–Thurs. at 5:30.*

22 **Calle Sierpes.** This is Seville's classy main shopping street. Near the southern end, at No. 85, a plaque marks the spot where the Cárcel Real (Royal Prison) once stood (now a bank). Miguel de Cervantes began writing *Don Quijote* in one of its cells.

25 **Casa Natal de Velázquez.** Spanish painter Diego de Velázquez was born in this *casa de vecinos* (town house shared by several families) in 1599. The house fell into ruin, but was bought in the 1970s by fashion designers Victorio and Lucchino, who restored it for use as their studio. It is not open to the public. ✉*Calle Padre Luis María Llop 4, Centro.*

A GOOD WALK: SEVILLE

Allow at least a day to tour Seville.

Start with the **cathedral** ❶ and a climb up the Giralda, the earlier Moorish mosque's minaret. Down Avenida de la Constitución is the **Archivo de las Indias** ❷, with the walled **Alcázar** ❸ fortress and palace behind.

From the Giralda, plunge into the Barrio de Santa Cruz, a tangle of narrow streets and squares that was Seville's medieval Jewish Quarter, near the **Plaza de los Refinadores** ❹. Don't miss the baroque **Hospital de los Venerables** ❺, a hospice with a leafy patio and several notable paintings. On Calle Santa Teresa is the **Museo Casa de Murillo** ❻ and the **Jardines de Murillo** ❼. At the far end of the gardens is the **University of Seville** ❽, once the tobacco factory where Bizet's Carmen rolled stogies.

Across the Glorieta de San Diego is the **Parque de María Luisa** ❾, with **Plaza de España** ❿ at its northwest end and **Plaza de América** ⓫ on its southeast flank, site of the **Museo Arqueológico** ⓬, displaying Roman sculpture and mosaics. Opposite is the **Museo de Artes y Costumbres Populares** ⓭.

Back toward the center along the Paseo de las Delicias on Avenida de Roma is the baroque **Palacio de San Telmo** ⓮, seat of Andalusia's autonomous government, with the neo-Mudéjar **Hotel Alfonso XIII** ⓯ behind it. On the north side of Puerta de Jerez is **Palacio de Yanduri** ⓰, birthplace of the Nobel Prize–winning poet Vicente Aleixandre (1898–1984).

South along Calle Almirante Lobo, stands the riverside **Torre de Oro** ⓱ opposite the **Teatro de la Maestranza** ⓲. Behind the theater is the **Hospital de la Caridad** ⓳, exhibiting Seville's leading painters. Downriver is the **Plaza de Toros del Real Maestranza** ⓴. Finally, head away from the river toward the Plaza Nueva, in the heart of Seville to see the **Ayuntamiento** ㉑.

North of the town hall is **Calle Sierpes** ㉒, Seville's famous shopping street. Backtrack down Calle Cuna, parallel to Sierpes, to No. 8 to see the **Palacio de la Condesa de Lebrija** ㉓. Continue down Calle Cuna to Plaza del Salvador and the **Iglesia del Salvador** ㉔, a former mosque. Walk up Alcaicería to Plaza de la Alfalfa and along Sales y Ferrer toward Plaza Cristo del Burgos—in an alley off the square is the **Casa Natal de Velázquez** ㉕, the painter's 1599 birthplace. From Plaza Cristo de Burgos follow Descalzos and Caballerizas to the **Casa de Pilatos** ㉖, modeled on Pontius Pilate's house in Jerusalem.

Several Seville visits may require separate trips: if you're an art lover, set aside half a day for the **Museo de Bellas Artes** ㉗. Across the Pasarela de la Cartuja bridge is the island of **La Cartuja** ㉘, a Carthusian monastery now the Andalusian Center of Contemporary Art. To visit the **Basílica de la Macarena** ㉙, home of the beloved Virgen de la Macarena, either walk an hour or taxi from the center.

Other key sites in the Macarena area are the Gothic **Convento de Santa Paula** ㉚ and the church of **San Lorenzo y Jesús del Gran Poder** ㉛, where Holy Week floats are on display.

24 **Iglesia del Salvador.** Built between 1671 and 1712, the Church of the Savior stands on the site of Seville's first great mosque, and remains can be seen in the Courtyard of the Orange Trees. Also of note are the sculptures of *Jesus de la Pasión* and St. Christopher by Martínez Montañés. In 2003 archaeologists discovered an 18th-century burial site here; digs are still being carried out with walkways installed to facilitate visits. ✉ *Pl. del Salvador, Centro* ☎ *95/459–5405* 🎫 *€2 with guide* ⏲ *Weekends only 10–2 and 4–8.*

23 **Palacio de la Condesa de Lebrija.** This lovely palace has three ornate patios, including a spectacular courtyard graced by a Roman mosaic taken from the ruins in Itálica, surrounded by Moorish arches and fine azulejos. The side rooms house a collection of archaeological items. ✉ *Calle Cuna 8, Centro* ☎ *95/422–7802* 🎫 *€7, €4 for ground floor only* ⏲ *Weekdays 10:30–1:30 and 4:30–7:30, Sat. 10–2.*

BARRIO DE SANTA CRUZ

★ The twisting alleyways and traditional ocher houses add to the tourist charm of this barrio, which is the old **Jewish Quarter.** On some streets, bars alternate with antiques stores and souvenir shops, but most of the quarter is quiet and residential. The Callejón del Agua, beside the wall of the Alcázar's gardens, has some of the quarter's finest mansions and patios. On the Plaza Alianza, pause to enjoy the antiques shops and outdoor cafés. In the Plaza de Doña Elvira, with its fountain and *azulejo* (painted tile) benches, young sevillanos gather to play guitars. Just around the corner from the hospital, at Callejón del Agua and Jope de Rueda, Rossini's Figaro serenaded Rosina on her Plaza Alfaro balcony. Adjoining the Plaza Alfaro, in the Plaza Santa Cruz, flowers and orange trees surround a 17th-century filigree iron cross, which marks the site of the erstwhile church of Santa Cruz, destroyed by Napoléon's General Soult. The painter Murillo was buried here in 1682, though his current resting place is unknown.

26 **Casa de Pilatos.** This palace was built in the first half of the 16th century by the dukes of Tarifa, ancestors of the present owner, the Duke of Medinaceli. It's known as Pilate's House because Don Fadrique, first marquis of Tarifa, allegedly modeled it on Pontius Pilate's house in Jerusalem, where he had gone to on a pilgrimage in 1518. With its fine patio and superb azulejo decorations, the palace is a beautiful blend of Spanish Mudejar and Renaissance architecture. The upstairs apartments, which you can see on a guided tour, have frescoes, paintings, and antique furniture. ✉ *Pl. Pilatos 1, Santa Cruz* ☎ *95/422–5298* 🎫 *€8; lower floor only, €5* ⏲ *Daily 9–6.*

5 **Hospital de los Venerables.** Once a retirement home for priests, this baroque building now has a cultural foundation that organizes on-site art exhibitions. The required 20-minute guided tour takes in a splendid azulejo patio with an interesting sunken fountain (designed to cope with low water pressure) and upstairs gallery, but the hospital's highlight is its chapel, featuring frescoes by Juan Valdés Leal. ✉ *Pl. de los Venerables 8, Santa Cruz* ☎ *95/456–2696* 🎫 *€4.75 with guide* ⏲ *Daily 10–1:30 and 4–7:30.*

DON JUAN: LOVER OF LEGENDS

Originally brought to literary life by the Spanish Golden Age playwright Fray Gabriel Téllez (better known as Tirso de Molina) in 1630, the figure of Don Juan has been portrayed in countless variations through the years, usually changing to reflect the moral climate of the times. As interpreted by such notables as Molière, Mozart, Goldoni, Byron, and Bernard Shaw, Don Juan has ranged from voluptuous hedonist to helpless victim, fiery lover to coldhearted snake. The plaques around his effigy in Plaza de los Refinadores can be translated: "Here is Don Juan Tenorio, and no man is his equal. From haughty princess to a humble fisherwoman, there is no female he doesn't desire, nor affair of gold or riches he will not pursue. Seek him ye rivals; surround him players all; may whoever values himself attempt to stop him or be his better at gambling, combat, or love."

7 **Jardines de Murillo** (Murillo Gardens). From the Plaza Santa Cruz you can embark on a stroll through these shady gardens, where you'll find a statue of Christopher Columbus. ✉ *Pl. Santa Cruz, Santa Cruz.*

6 **Museo Casa de Murillo.** Bartolomé Estéban Murillo (1617–82) lived here for a time; there's a small museum here dedicated to the painter's life, but it's open only for special exhibitions. ✉ *C. Santa Teresa 8, Santa Cruz* ☎ 🖷 *95/422–9415* 🎫 *Free* ⏲ *Weekdays 10–2 and 4–7.*

16 **Palacio de Yanduri.** Nobel Prize–winning poet Vicente Aleixandre was born here. ✉ *Puerta de Jerez (north side) s/n, Santa Cruz.*

4 **Plaza de los Refinadores.** This shady square filled with palms and orange trees is separated from the Murillo gardens by an iron grillwork and ringed with stately glass balconies. At its center is a monument to Don Juan Tenorio, the famous Don Juan known for his amorous conquests. ✉ *Santa Cruz.*

EL ARENAL & PARQUE MARIA LUISA

Parque María Luisa is part shady midcity forestland and part monumental esplanade. El Arenal, named for its sandy riverbank soil, was originally a neighborhood of shipbuilders, stevedores, and warehouses. The heart of Arenal lies between the Puente de San Telmo just upstream from the Torre de Oro and the Puente de Isabel II (Puente de Triana). El Arenal extends as far north as Avenida Alfonso XII to include the Museo de Bellas Artes. Between the park and Arenal is the university.

19 **Hospital de la Caridad.** Behind the Maestranza Theater is this almshouse for the sick and elderly, where six paintings by Murillo (1617–82) and two gruesome works by Valdés Leal (1622–90) depicting the Triumph of Death are displayed. The baroque hospital was founded in 1674 by Seville's original Don Juan, Miguel de Mañara (1626–79). A nobleman of licentious character, Mañara was returning one night from a riotous orgy when he had a vision of a funeral procession in which the partly

decomposed corpse in the coffin was his own. Accepting the apparition as a sign from God, Mañara renounced his worldly goods and joined the Brotherhood of Charity, whose unsavory task was to collect the bodies of executed criminals and bury them. He devoted his fortune to building this hospital and is buried before the high altar in the chapel. ✉ *C. Temprado 3, El Arenal* ☎ *95/422–3232* 🎫 *€5* ⏲ *Mon.–Sat. 9–1:30 and 3:30–7:30, Sun. 9–1.*

15 Fodor'sChoice ★ **Hotel Alfonso XIII.** Seville's most emblematic hotel, this grand, Mudejar-style building next to the university was built—and named—for the king's visit to the 1929 fair. Nonguests are welcome to admire the gracious Moorish-style courtyard, best appreciated while sipping an ice-cold *fino* (dry sherry) from the adjacent bar. ✉ *Calle San Fernando 2, El Arenal* ☎ *95/491–7000.*

12 **Museo Arqueológico** (Museum of Archaeology). This fine Renaissance-style building has artifacts from Phoenician, Tartessian, Greek, Carthaginian, Iberian, Roman, and medieval times. Displays include marble statues and mosaics from the Roman excavations at Itálica and a faithful replica of the fabulous Carambolo treasure found on a hillside outside Seville in 1958: 21 pieces of jewelry, all 24-karat gold, dating from the 7th and 6th centuries BC. ✉ *Pl. de América, El Arenal/Porvenir* ☎ *95/423–2401* 🎫 *€1.50, free for EU citizens* ⏲ *Tues. 2:30–8:30, Wed.–Sat. 9–8:30, Sun. 9–2:30.*

13 **Museo de Artes y Costumbres Populares** (Museum of Folklore). The Mudejar pavilion opposite the Museum of Archaeology is the site of this museum of mainly 19th- and 20th-century Spanish folklore. The first floor has re-creations of a forge, a bakery, a wine press, a tanner's shop, and a pottery studio. Upstairs, exhibits include 18th- and 19th-century court dress, stunning regional folk costumes, carriages, and musical instruments. ✉ *Pl. de América 3, El Arenal/Porvenir* ☎ *95/423–2576* 🎫 *€1.50, free for EU citizens* ⏲ *Tues. 3–8, Wed.–Sat. 9–8, Sun. 9–2.*

27 Fodor'sChoice ★ **Museo de Bellas Artes** (Museum of Fine Arts). This museum is second only to Madrid's Prado in Spanish art. It's in the former convent of La Merced Calzada, most of which dates from the 17th century. The collection includes Murillo, Zurbarán, Valdés Leal, and El Greco; outstanding examples of Seville Gothic art; and baroque religious sculptures in wood (a quintessentially Andalusian art form). In the rooms dedicated to Sevillian art of the 19th and 20th centuries, look for Gonzalo Bilbao's *Las Cigarreras,* a group portrait of Seville's famous cigar makers. ✉ *Pl. del Museo 9, El Arenal/Porvenir* ☎ *95/478–6482* 🌐 *www.museosdeandalucia.es* 🎫 *€1.50, free for EU citizens* ⏲ *Tues. 2:30–8:15, Wed.–Sat. 9–8:15, Sun. 9–2:15.*

14 **Palacio de San Telmo.** This splendid baroque palace is largely the work of architect Leonardo de Figueroa. Built between 1682 and 1796, it was first a naval academy and then the residence of the Bourbon dukes of Montpensier, during which time it outshone Madrid's royal court for sheer brilliance. The palace gardens are now the Parque de María Luisa, and the building itself is the seat of the Andalusian government. The main portal, vintage 1734, is a superb example of the fanciful

Churrigueresque style. ■**TIP→ Call in advance if you want to arrange a visit.** ✉*Av. de Roma, El Arenal* ☎*95/503–5500.*

9 **Parque de María Luisa.** Formerly the garden of the Palacio de San Telmo, the park is a blend of formal design and wild vegetation. In the burst of development that gripped Seville in the 1920s, it was redesigned for the 1929 Exhibition, and the impressive villas you see now are the fair's remaining pavilions, many of them consulates or schools. Note the **statue of El Cid** by Rodrigo Díaz de Vivar (1043–99), who fought both for and against the Muslim rulers during the Reconquest. ✉*Main entrance: Glorieta San Diego, El Arenal.*

11 **Plaza de América.** Walk to the south end of the Parque de María Luisa, past the Isla de los Patos (Island of Ducks), to find this plaza, typically carpeted in white doves and designed by Aníbal González. It's a blaze of color, with flowers, shrubs, ornamental stairways, and fountains tiled in yellow, blue, and ocher. The three impressive buildings surrounding the square—in neo-Mudejar, Gothic, and Renaissance styles—were built by González for the 1929 fair. Two of them now house Seville's museums of archaeology and folklore.

10 **Plaza de España.** This grandiose half-moon of buildings on the eastern edge of the Parque de María Luisa was Spain's centerpiece pavilion at the 1929 Exhibition. The brightly colored azulejo pictures represent the 50 provinces of Spain, while the four bridges symbolize the medieval kingdoms of the Iberian Peninsula. You can rent small boats for rowing along the arc-shape canal.

20 **Plaza de Toros Real Maestranza** (Royal Maestranza Bullring). Sevillanos have spent many a thrilling Sunday afternoon in this bullring, built between 1760 and 1763. Painted a deep ocher, the stadium is the one of the oldest and loveliest *plazas de toros* in Spain. An adjoining museum has prints and photos. ✉*Paseo de Colón 12, El Arenal* ☎*95/422–4577* 🎫*Plaza and bullfighting museum €5 with English-speaking guide* ⏲*Daily 9:30–7 (bullfighting days 9:30–3).*

18 **Teatro de la Maestranza** (Maestranza Theater). Opposite the Torre de Oro is Seville's opera house. One of Europe's leading halls, the Maestranza presents opera, zarzuela (Spanish light opera), classical music, and jazz. ✉*Paseo de Colón 22, El Arenal* ☎*95/422–6573 or 95/422–3344* 🌐*www.teatromaestranza.com*

17 **Torre de Oro** (Tower of Gold). A 12-sided tower on the banks of the Guadalquivir built by the Moors in 1220 to complete the city's ramparts, it served to close off the harbor when a chain was stretched across the river from its base to another tower on the opposite bank. In 1248, Admiral Ramón de Bonifaz broke through this barrier, and Ferdinand III captured Seville. The tower houses a small naval museum. ✉*Paseo Alcalde Marqués de Contadero s/n, El Arenal* ☎*95/422–2419* 🎫*€1* ⏲*Tues.–Fri. 10–2, Sat.–Sun. 11–2.*

8 **University of Seville.** At the far end of the Jardines de Murillo, opposite Calle San Fernando, stands what used to be the **Real Fábrica de Tabacos** (Royal Tobacco Factory). Built in the mid-1700s, the fac-

CLOSE UP

Seville's Long and Noble History

Conquered in 205 BC by the Romans, Seville gave the world two great emperors, Trajan and Hadrian. The Moors held Seville for more than 500 years and left it one of their greatest works of architecture—the iconic Giralda tower that served as the minaret over the main city mosque. Saint King Ferdinand (Fernando III) lies enshrined in the glorious cathedral; and his rather less saintly descendant, Pedro the Cruel, builder of the Alcázar, is buried here as well.

Seville is justly proud of its literary and artistic associations. The painters Diego Rodríguez de Silva Velázquez (1599–1660) and Bartolomé Estéban Murillo (1617–82) were sons of Seville, as were the poets Gustavo Adolfo Bécquer (1836–70), Antonio Machado (1875–1939), and Nobel Prize–winner Vicente Aleixandre (1898–1984). The tale of the ingenious knight of La Mancha was begun in a Seville jail—Don Quixote's creator, Miguel de Cervantes, twice languished in a debtors' prison. Tirso de Molina's Don Juan seduced in Seville's mansions, and Rossini's barber, Figaro, was married in the Barrio de Santa Cruz. It was at the old tobacco factory where Bizet's sultry Carmen first met Don José.

tory employed some 3,000 *cigarreras* (female cigar makers) less than a century later, including Bizet's opera heroine *Carmen,* who reputedly rolled her cigars on her thigh. ✉*C. San Fernando s/n, Parque Maria Luisa* ☎*95/455–1000* *Free* ⏲*Weekdays 9–8:30.*

BARRIO DE LA MACARENA

This immense neighborhood covers the entire northern half of historic Seville and deserves to be walked not once but many times. Most of the best churches, convents, markets, and squares are concentrated around the center of this barrio in an area delimited by the Arab ramparts to the north, the Alameda de Hercules to the west, the Santa Catalina church to the south, and the Convento de Santa Paula to the east. The area between the Alameda de Hercules and the Guadalquivir is known to locals as the Barrio de San Lorenzo, a Barrio de la Macarena subdivision that's ideal for an evening of tapas grazing.

29 **Basílica de la Macarena.** This church holds Seville's most revered image, the Virgin of Hope—better known as La Macarena. Bedecked with candles and carnations, her cheeks streaming with glass tears, the Macarena steals the show at the procession on Holy Thursday, the highlight of Seville's Holy Week pageant. She's the patron of gypsies and the protector of the matador. So great are her charms that young Sevillian bullfighter Joselito spent half his personal fortune buying her emeralds. When he was killed in the ring in 1920, the Macarena was dressed in widow's weeds for a month. There's a small adjacent museum devoted to her costumes and jewels. ✉*C. Bécquer 1, La Macarena* ☎*95/490–1800* *Basilica free, museum €3.50* ⏲*Basilica daily 9:30–2 and 5–9, museum daily 9:30–2 and 5–8.*

30 Fodor'sChoice ★ **Convento de Santa Paula.** This 15th-century Gothic convent has a fine facade and portico, with ceramic decoration by Nicolaso Pisano. The chapel has some beautiful azulejos and sculptures by Martínez Montañés. There's a small museum and shop selling delicious cakes and jams made by the nuns. ✉ *C. Santa Paula 11, La Macarena* ☎ *95/453–6330* 💶 *€2* ⏲ *Tues.–Sun. 10:30–1.*

31 **San Lorenzo y Jesús del Gran Poder.** This 17th-century church has many fine works by such artists as Montañés and Pacheco, but its outstanding piece is Juan de Mesa's *Jesús del Gran Poder (Christ Omnipotent).* ✉ *C. Jesús del Gran Poder, La Macarena* ☎ *95/438–4558* 💶 *Free* ⏲ *Daily 8–1:30 and 6–9.*

FIESTA TIME!

Seville's color and vivacity is most intense during Semana Santa, when lacerated Christs and bejeweled, weeping Mary statues are paraded through town on floats borne by often barefooted penitents. A week later, sevillanos throw April Fair, featuring midday horse parades with men in broad-brim hats and Andalusian riding gear astride prancing steeds, and women in ruffled dresses riding sidesaddle behind them. Bullfights, fireworks, and all-night singing and dancing complete the spectacle.

TRIANA

Across the Guadalquivir from central Seville, Triana used to be the gypsy quarter. Today it has a tranquil, neighborly feel by day, while its atmospheric clubs and flamenco bars throb at night. Enter Triana by the **Puente Isabel II** (better known as the Puente de Triana), built in 1852, the first bridge to connect the city's two sections. Walk across Plaza Altozano up Calle Jacinto and turn right at **Calle Alfarería** (Pottery Street) to see a slew of pottery stores and workshops. Return to Plaza Altozano and walk down Calle Pureza as far as the small **Capilla de los Marineros** (Seamen's Chapel), home to a venerated statue of Mary called the Esperanza de Triana. Head back toward the river and **Calle Betis** for some of the city's most colorful bars, clubs, and restaurants.

28 **Isla de La Cartuja.** Named after its 14th-century Carthusian monastery, this island, across the river from northern Seville, was the site of the decennial Universal Exposition (Expo) in 1992. The island has the Teatro Central, used for concerts and plays; Parque del Alamillo, Seville's largest and least known park; and the Estadio Olímpico, a 60,000-seat covered stadium. The best way to get to La Cartuja is by walking across one or both (one each way) of the superb Santiago Calatrava bridges spanning the Guadalquivir. The Puente de la Barqueta crosses to La Cartuja while, downstream, the Puente del Alamillo connects la Isla Mágica with Seville. Buses C1 and C2 also serve La Cartuja. ✉ *Av. Americo Vespucci 2, La Cartuja* ☎ *95/503–7070* 💶 *€3.30* ⏲ *Daily 10–8.*

The eastern shore holds the **Isla Mágica,** (☎ *902/161716* 🌐 *www.islamagica.es* 💶 *Apr. and May €21, June–Oct. €23.50* ⏲ *Apr. and May, weekends 11* AM*–midnight; June–Oct., daily 11* AM*–midnight*) with 14 attractions, including the hair-raising Jaguar roller coaster. The

14th century **Monasterio de Santa María de las Cuevas** (Monasterio de La Cartuja, ✉*Isla de la Cartuja* ☎*95/503–7070* *€3, free Tues. for EU citizens* ⏲*Tues.–Fri. 10–7:30, Sat. 11–8, Sun. 10–2:30*) was regularly visited by Christopher Columbus, who was buried here for a few years. Part of the building houses the Centro Andaluz de Arte Contemporáneo, which has an absorbing collection of contemporary art.

WHERE TO STAY & EAT

TAPAS BARS

Bar Estrella. This prizewinning tapas emporium does excellent renditions of everything from *paté de esparragos trigueros* (wild asparagus paté) to *fabas con pringá* (stewed broad beans). ✉*C. Estrella 3, Santa Cruz* ☎*95/422–7535.*

Bar Gran Tino. Named for the giant wooden wine cask that once dominated the bar, this busy spot on the funky Plaza Alfalfa serves an array of tapas, including *calamares fritos* (fried squid) and wedges of crumbly Manchego cheese. ✉*Pl. Alfalfa 2, Centro* ☎*95/421–0883.*

Bar Rincón San Eloy. This place is always heaving with a happy mix of shoppers and students. You can buy stacked mini-sandwiches, as well as tapas and sherry from the barrel. If no tables are left, grab a pew on the tiled steps. ✉*Calle San Eloy 2, Centro* ☎*95/421–8079.*

Bodega Santa Cruz. A young college crowd frequents this spot in Seville's famous former Jewish quarter. There's an excellent selection of traditional tapas, including a mini-tortilla. Your bill is chalked up at your place at the bar. ✉*Calle Mateo Gago 8, Santa Cruz* ☎*95/421–3246.*

Bodega San Jose. At this funky old 1893 bar decorated with faded Semana Santa posters and shelves of dusty bottles, the wine and sherry is served straight from the barrel and accompanied by *gambas* (prawns), the house specialty, prepared in several delicious ways. ✉*Calle Adriano 10, El Arenal* ☎*95/422–4105.*

El Rinconcillo. Founded in 1670, this lovely spot serves a classic selection of dishes, such as the *caldereta de venado* (venison stew), a superb *salmorejo* (thick gazpacho-style soup), and *espinacas con garbanzos* (creamed spinach with chickpeas). The views of the Iglesia de Santa Catalina out the front window are unbeatable. Your bill is chalked up on the wooden counters. ✉*C. Gerona 40, La Macarena* ☎*95/422–3183* ⏲*Closed Wed.*

WHERE TO EAT

$$$$ ★ ✕**Egaña-Oriza.** Owner José Mari Egaña is Basque, but he is considered one of the fathers of modern Andalusian cooking. The restaurant, on the edge of the Murillo Gardens opposite the university, has spare contemporary decor with high ceilings and wall-to-wall windows. The menu might include *lomos de lubina con salsa de erizos de mar* (sea bass with sea urchin sauce) or *solomillo con foie natural y salsa de ciruelas* (fillet steak with foie gras and plum sauce). On the downside, the service can be slow. You can always drop into the adjoining Bar España for an hors d'oeuvre tapa such as stuffed mussels with béchamel sauce. ✉*San Fernando 41, Santa Cruz Jardines de Murillo* ☎*95/422–7211* 💳*AE, DC, MC, V* ⏲*Closed Sun. and Aug. No lunch Sat.*

$$$–$$$$ ★ **La Albahaca.** Overlooking one of Seville's prettiest small plazas in the Barrio de Santa Cruz, this wonderful old family manor house was built by the celebrated architect Juan Talavera as a home for his own family; inside, four dining rooms are decorated with tiles, antique oil paintings, and leafy plants. There's a Basque twist to many of the dishes—consider the *lubina al horno con berenjenas y yogur al cardamomo* (baked sea bass with eggplant in a yogurt-and-cardamom sauce) or *foie de oca salteado* (lightly sautéed goose liver) followed by the delicious fig mousse. There's an excellent €27 daily menu. *Pl. Santa Cruz 12, Santa Cruz 95/422–0714 Reservations essential AE, DC, MC, V Closed Sun.*

$$$–$$$$ Fodor'sChoice ★ **Poncio.** In the three small, comfortable dining rooms, diners enjoy dishes based on Andalusian tradition with a French flair. Chef Willy Moya trained in Paris and blends local and cosmopolitan cuisine flawlessly. Try the *salmorejo encapotado* (thick, garlic-laden gazpacho topped with diced egg and ham), or the *besugo con gambitas* (sea bream with shrimp). Desserts include a delectable version of French toast, showered with slivered almonds and garnished with rich cinnamon ice cream. The restaurant is around the corner from the Iglesia de Santa Ana, Seville's oldest church. *C. Victoria 8, Triana 95/434–0010 AE, DC, MC, V Closed Sun. No dinner Mon.*

$$–$$$$ **Becerrita.** The affable Jesus Becerra runs this cozy—verging on cramped—establishment. Diligent service and tasty modern treatments of such classic Spanish dishes as *lomo de cordero a la miel* (loin of lamb in a honey sauce) and *rape con salsa de manzana* (monk fish with applesauce) have won the favor of sevillanos. *Calle Recaredo 9, Santa Cruz/Santa Catalina 95/441–2057 www.becerrita.com Reservations essential AE, MC, V No dinner Sun. and Aug.*

$$–$$$$ ★ **Enrique Becerra.** Excellent tapas and a lively bar await at this restaurant run by the fifth generation of a family of celebrated restaurateurs (Enrique's brother Jesus owns Becerrita). The menu focuses on traditional, home-cooked Andalusian dishes, such as *pez espada al amontillado* (swordfish cooked in dark sherry) and *cordero a la miel con espinacas* (honey-glazed lamb stuffed with spinach and pine nuts). Don't miss the cumin seed–laced *espinacas con garbanzos* (spinach with chickpeas). *Calle Gamazo 2, El Arenal 95/421–3049 AE, DC, MC, V Closed Sun. and last 2 wks of July.*

$$$ **San Marco.** In a 17th-century palace in the shopping district, this Italian restaurant has original frescoes, a gracious patio, and a menu that combines Italian, French, and Andalusian cuisine. Pasta dishes, such as ravioli stuffed with shrimp and pesto sauce, are notable. The restaurant has four satellites, but this one, the original, is the most charming. *Calle Cuna 6, Centro 95/421–2440 Reservations essential AE, DC, MC, V.*

$$–$$$ **La Isla.** Using fresh fish from Cádiz and Huelva, La Isla serves wonderful *parrillada de mariscos y pescados,* a fish and seafood grill for two people. *Zarzuela,* the Catalan seafood stew, is another favorite, and simple meat dishes are also served. The dining room and tapas bar are adorned with traditional Sevillano tiles. *Calle Arfe 25, El Arenal 95/421–2631 AE, DC, MC, V Closed Aug.*

$-$$$ ✕ **El Corral del Agua.** Abutting the outer walls of the Alcázar on a narrow pedestrian street in the Santa Cruz neighborhood is a restored 18th-century palace, with a patio filled with geraniums and a central fountain. Andalusian specialties, such as *cola de toro al estilo de Sevilla* (Seville-style bull's tail), are prepared with contemporary flair. ✉ *Callejón del Agua 6, Santa Cruz* ☎ *95/422–4841* ▭ *AE, DC, MC, V* ⊗ *Closed Sun. and Jan. and Feb.*

$-$$$ ✕ **Modesto.** The downstairs is a lively, crowded tapas bar; upstairs is the dining room, which has stucco walls decorated with blue-and-white tiles. The house specialty is a crisp *fritura Modesto* (a selection of small fish fried in top-quality olive oil); another excellent choice is the *cazuela al Tío Diego* (Uncle Diego's casserole—ham, mushrooms, and shrimp simmering in an earthenware dish). You can dine cheaply here, but beware: *mariscos* (shellfish) take the bill to another level. ✉ *Calle Cano y Cueto 5, Santa Cruz* ☎ *95/441–6811* ▭ *AE, DC, MC, V.*

$-$$ ✕ **Habanita.** A vegetarian restaurant in the buzzing Alfalfa barrio is a rarity. The vast menu emphasizes Mediterranean and Cuban fare. Dishes might include yucca with garlic, black beans with rice, tamales, and strict vegan fare. There are girth-expanding desserts and a good wine list. Some meat dishes are available. ✉ *Calle Golfo 3, Santa Cruz/Alfalfa* ☎ *606/716456* ▭ *MC, V* ⊗ *No dinner Sun.*

$-$$ ✕ **Mesón Don Raimundo.** Tucked into an alleyway off Calle Argote de Molina near the cathedral, this former 17th-century convent with its eclectic decor of religious artifacts tends to attract the tour buses. Still, it's worth the trip for its generous portions of traditional fare, including Mozarab-style wild duck (braised in sherry) and solomillo *a la castellana* (Castilian-style steak). Start with the crisp *tortillitas de camarones* (batter-fried shrimp pancakes) or stuffed peppers. ✉ *Argote de Molina 26, Santa Cruz* ☎ *95/422–3355* ▭ *AE, DC, MC, V.*

WHERE TO STAY

$$$$ ★ ✕🏨 **El Bulli Hotel Hacienda Benazuza.** This five-star luxury hotel is in a rambling country palace near Sanlúcar la Mayor, 15 km (9 mi) outside Seville off the main road to Huelva. Surrounded by olive and orange trees and in a courtyard with towering palms, the building incorporates an 18th-century church. The interior has clay-tile floors and ocher walls. The acclaimed restaurant, La Alquería, serves Spanish and international dishes, creative variations on the recipes of superstar Catalan chef (and hotel owner) Ferrán Adrià. ✉ *C. Virgen de las Nieves, Sanlúcar la Mayor 41800* ☎ *95/570–3344* 📠 *95/570–3410* 🌐 *www.elbullihotel.com* ⇨ *41 rooms, 3 suites* ♿ *In-room: public Wi-Fi. In-hotel: 2 restaurants, tennis court, pool, Wi-Fi, public Internet, parking (no fee), some pets allowed* ▭ *AE, DC, MC, V* ⊗ *Closed Jan.*

$$$$ Fodor'sChoice ★ 🏨 **Alfonso XIII.** Inaugurated by King Alfonso XIII in 1929, this grand hotel is a splendid, historical Mudejar-style palace, built around a huge central patio and surrounded by ornate brick arches. The public rooms have marble floors, wood-panel ceilings, heavy Moorish lamps, stained glass, and ceramic tiles in the typical Seville colors. There is a Spanish and Japanese restaurant, as well as an elegant bar. ✉ *San Fernando 2, El Arenal, 41004* ☎ *95/491–7000* 📠 *95/491–7099* 🌐 *www.westin.*

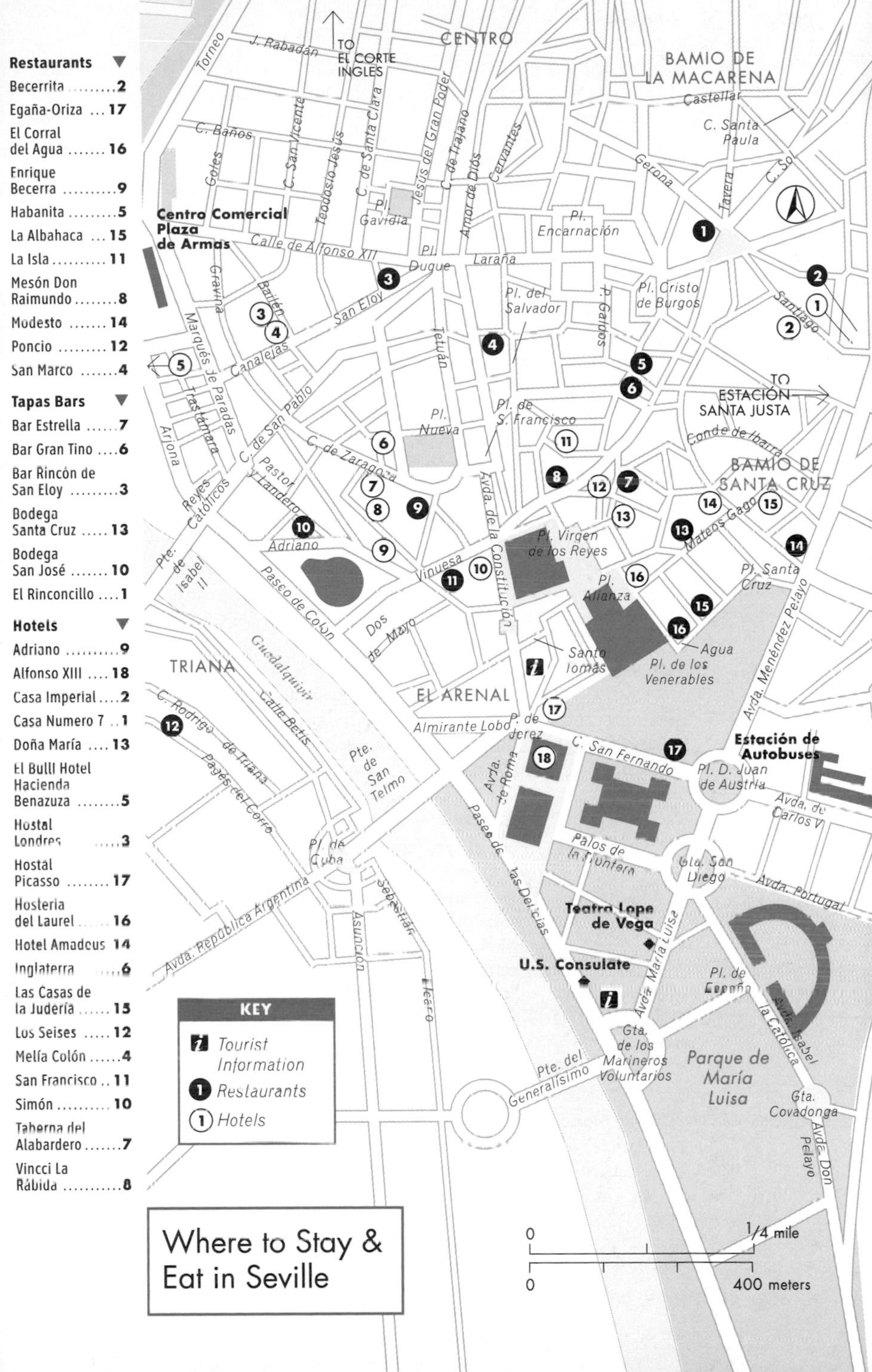

Where to Stay & Eat in Seville
Restaurants
Becerrita 2
Egaña-Oriza 17
El Corral del Agua 16
Enrique Becerra 9
Habanita 5
La Albahaca 15
La Isla 11
Mesón Don Raimundo 8
Modesto 14
Poncio 12
San Marco 4
Tapas Bars
Bar Estrella 7
Bar Gran Tino 6
Bar Rincón de San Eloy 3
Bodega Santa Cruz 13
Bodega San José 10
El Rinconcillo 1
Hotels
Adriano 9
Alfonso XIII 18
Casa Imperial 2
Casa Numero 7 1
Doña María 13
El Bulli Hotel Hacienda Benazuza 5
Hostal Londres 3
Hostal Picasso 17
Hosteria del Laurel 16
Hotel Amadeus 14
Inglaterra 6
Las Casas de la Judería 15
Los Seises 12
Melía Colón 4
San Francisco 11
Simón 10
Taberna del Alabardero 7
Vincci La Rábida 8
KEY
Tourist Information
Restaurants
Hotels
CENTRO
TO EL CORTE INGLES
BAMIO DE LA MACARENA
BAMIO DE SANTA CRUZ
TO ESTACIÓN SANTA JUSTA
Centro Comercial Plaza de Armas
TRIANA
EL ARENAL
Estación de Autobuses
Teatro Lope de Vega
U.S. Consulate
Parque de María Luisa
Guadalquivir
Pl. Encarnación
Pl. del Salvador
Pl. Nueva
Pl. de S. Francisco
Pl. Virgen de los Reyes
Pl. Alianza
Pl. de los Venerables
Pl. Santa Cruz
Pl. Cristo de Burgos
Pl. Gavidia
Pl. Duque
Pl. D. Juan de Austria
Pl. de Cuba
Pl. de España
Gta. San Diego
Gta. de los Marineros Voluntarios
Gta. Covadonga
Pte. de Isabel II
Pte. de San Telmo
Pte. del Generalísimo
Paseo de Colón
Paseo de las Delicias
Avda. de la Constitución
Avda. de Roma
Avda. María Luisa
Avda. Isabel la Católica
Avda. Menéndez Pelayo
Avda. de Carlos V
Avda. Portugal
Avda. República Argentina
Calle de Alfonso XII
Calle Betis
C. San Fernando
0 1/4 mile
0 400 meters

com/hotelalfonso ⇒*127 rooms, 19 suites* ♿*In-room: Wi-Fi. In-hotel: 2 restaurants, bar, Wi-Fi, pool, parking (fee)* ▭*AE, DC, MC, V.*

$$$$ **Casa Imperial.** Adjoining the Casa de Pilatos, and once connected to it via underground tunnel, this 16th-century palace is the former residence of the marquis of Tarifa. Public areas surround four plant-filled patios. The 24 suites are approached by a stairway adorned with trompe l'oeil tiles. Each suite is different—one has a private courtyard with a trickling fountain—but all have kitchenettes. There's a roof terrace with gorgeous views. ✉*Calle Imperial 29, Santa Cruz/Santa Catalina, 41003* ☎*95/450–0300* 📠*95/450–0330* 🌐*www.casaimperial.com* ⇒*24 suites* ♿*In-room: kitchen, Wi-Fi. In-hotel: restaurant, bar, public Wi-Fi, parking (no fee)* ▭*AE, DC, MC, V* 🍽*BP.*

$$$$ **Casa Numero 7.** Voted by *Tatler* magazine as Best Small Hotel in Europe, this exquisite mansion-hotel is owned by a director of González Byass, the famous sherry producer. Dating from 1847, the interior retains a homey, lived-in feel with family-owned antiques, original oil paintings, and plush furnishings throughout. Each room is individually designed, and there is an elegant salon with fireplace and comfy chairs. The roof terrace has Giralda views, and breakfast is excellent, with fluffy scrambled eggs an agreeable option. ✉*C. Virgenes 7, Santa Cruz, 41003* ☎*95/422–1581* 📠*95/421–4527* 🌐*www.casanumero7.com* ⇒*6 rooms* ♿*In-hotel: bar* ▭*AE, V* 🍽*BP.*

$$$$ ★ **Los Seises.** This hotel is in a section of Seville's 16th-century Palacio Episcopal (Bishop's Palace), and the combination of modern and Renaissance architecture is striking: Room 219, for instance, is divided by a 16th-century brick archway, and breakfast (for an extra €16) is served in the old chapel. A pit in the center of the basement restaurant reveals the building's foundations and some archaeological finds, including a Roman mosaic. The rooftop pool and summer restaurant are in full view of the Giralda. ✉*Calle Segovias 6, Santa Cruz, 41004* ☎*95/422–9495* 📠*95/422–4334* 🌐*www.hotellosseises.com* ⇒*42 rooms, 2 suites* ♿*In-room: Wi-Fi. In-hotel: restaurant, pool, public Wi-Fi, parking (fee)* ▭*AE, DC, MC, V* 🍽*BP.*

$$$$ **Meliá Colón.** A white-marble staircase leads up to the central lobby, which has a magnificent stained-glass dome and crystal candelabra. Downstairs is the El Burladero restaurant, with a bullfight theme, and La Tasca tavern, packed midday with slick local businessmen. The old-fashioned rooms are elegantly furnished with silk drapes and bedspreads, and wood fittings. ✉*Calle Canalejas 1, El Arenal/San Vicente, 41001* ☎*95/450–5599* 📠*95/422–0938* 🌐*www.solmelia.com* ⇒*204 rooms, 14 suites* ♿*In-room: public Wi-Fi. In-hotel: restaurant, bar, Wi-Fi, public Internet* ▭*AE, DC, MC, V* 🍽*BP.*

$$$–$$$$ **Doña María.** In a 14th-century former mansion, one of Seville's most charmingly old-fashioned hotels is near the cathedral. Some rooms have been refurbished in minimalist contemporary chic, but most are more ornate and furnished with antiques. Bathrooms throughout are spacious. There's also a rooftop pool with a view of the Giralda. ✉*Calle Don Remondo 19, Santa Cruz, 41004* ☎*95/422–4990* 📠*95/421–9546* 🌐*www.hdmaria.com* ⇒*64 rooms* ♿*In-room: Wi-Fi. In-hotel: pool, public Wi-Fi* ▭*AE, DC, MC, V.*

$$$–$$$$ **Inglaterra.** This longtime favorite with British visitors to Seville is elegantly run by third generation owner Manolo Otero. The downstairs Trinity pub is a fine hotel bar in the grand tradition, while Galería, the gourmet restaurant upstairs in the mezzanine serves traditional Seville cuisine with creative and contemporary touches. The rooms are traditionally decorated but extremely comfortable. ✉ *Pl. Nueva 7, Centro, 41001* ☎ *95/422–4970* 🖷 *95/456–1336* 🌐 *www.hotelinglaterra.es* *94 rooms* *In-room: Wi-Fi* ▭ *AE, DC, MC, V.*

$$$–$$$$ **Vincci La Rábida.** Rooms in this 18th-century palace are elegant yet traditional, with terra-cotta tiling and wrought-iron bed frames with en suite marble bathrooms. The lounge areas and stunning central patio are sumptuous, and the large sun terrace—complete with outdoor hot tub—has superb city and cathedral views. ✉ *Castelar 24, Santa Cruz, 41001* ☎ *95/450–1280* 🖷 *95/421–6600* 🌐 *www.vinccihoteles.com* *79 rooms, 2 suites* *In-room: dial-up, Wi-Fi. In-hotel: restaurant, public Wi-Fi, parking (fee)* ▭ *AE, MC, V.*

$$$ **Hostería del Laurel.** A small tree-lined square in the heart of the Barrio de Santa Cruz is an unbeatable position for this hotel. It's known for its bodega, which is mentioned in Zorilla's popular 19th-century play *Don Juan Tenorio*, as well as for the adjoining restaurant, which specializes in traditional local cuisine, such as *pollo a la Sevillana* (chicken in a rich gravy sauce) and *espinacas* (spinach) and squid in garlic. The rooms are a relatively recent addition, spread between two floors. They are spotlessly clean and simply furnished. ✉ *Pl. de los Venerables 5, Santa Cruz, 41004* ☎ *95/422–0295* 🖷 *95/421–0450* 🌐 *www.hosteriadellaurel.com* *21 rooms* *In-hotel: restaurant, bar* ▭ *MC, V* 🍽 *BP.*

$$$ **Las Casas de la Judería.** This labyrinthine hotel occupies three of the barrio's old palaces, each arranged around inner courtyards. The spacious guest rooms are painted in subdued pastel colors and decorated with prints of Seville. The hotel is tucked into a passageway off the Plaza Santa María. ✉ *Callejón de Dos Hermanas 7, Santa Cruz, 41004* ☎ *95/441–5150* 🖷 *95/442–2170* 🌐 *www.casasypalacios.com* *103 rooms, 3 suites* *In-room: dial-up. In-hotel: restaurant, bar, parking (fee)* ▭ *AE, DC, MC, V.*

$$$ ✕ **Taberna del Alabardero.** Near the Plaza Nueva, this highly regarded mansion-hotel and restaurant is a superb mid-Seville retreat in a traditional setting. A courtyard and bar precede the dining area, which is decorated in Sevillian tiles. Modern dishes include *bacalao a la parrilla triija de hongos sobre pil-pil y aceite de jamón* (grilled cod with mushrooms in a spicy chili-and-ham sauce). ✉ *Calle Zaragoza 20, El Arenal* ☎ *95/456–0637* 🖷 *95/456–3666* 🌐 *www.tabernadelalabardero.com* *7 rooms* ▭ *AE, DC, MC, V* ⊙ *Closed Aug.*

$$–$$$ **Adriano.** Opened in 2004 in an 18th-century mansion, this small hotel has good-size rooms centered around three patios. A short stroll from the cathedral, the river, and the sophisticated shops on Calle Sierpes, Adriano has rooms decorated in a straightforward style with striped burgundy-and-cream fabrics and shiny marble on the floors and in the bathroom. There's a bar downstairs, just one of many on the street. ✉ *Calle Adriano 12, El Arenal, 41001* ☎ *95/4293800* 🌐 *www.hoteladriano.net* *34 rooms* *In-hotel: bar, parking (fee).*

$$–$$$ ★ **Hotel Amadeus.** With pianos in the soundproof rooms and a music room off the central patio and lobby, this acoustical oasis is ideal for touring professional musicians and music fans in general. Classical concerts are regularly held on the patio. The 18th-century manor house has been equipped with such modern amenities as in-room data ports and a small glass-wall elevator that whips quietly up and down a corner of the central patio. You can enjoy breakfast (an extra €7) on the roof terrace overlooking the Judería and Giralda. ✉ *Calle Farnesio 6, Santa Cruz, 41004* ☎ *95/450–1443* 📠 *95/450–0019* 🌐 *www.hotelamadeussevilla.com* *14 rooms* *In-room: ethernet. In-hotel: restaurant, parking (fee)* 💳 *AE, DC, MC, V.*

$$ **Hostal Londres.** Near the Museo de Bellas Artes and in the thick of the lively Barrio de San Lorenzo nightlife, this simple, comfortable place is a real find. Rooms are plain but clean and cheery, and some have balconies. ✉ *San Pedro Mártir 1, El Arenal, 41001* ☎ *95/421–2896* 📠 *95/450–3830* *22 rooms* 💳 *MC, V.*

$$ **Hostal Picasso.** You can't beat this situation for the price, within confessional distance of the cathedral and a few minutes' walk from the shopping district in the center of town and the Barrio de Santa Cruz. In this traditional building festooned with potted plants, the rooms vary in size but they are all bright and tidy, with sunny yellow paintwork. Several have small balconies. The same management owns the nearby Van Gogh, of comparable quality and price. ✉ *C. San Gregorio 1, El Arenal, 41001* ☎ *95/4210864* 🌐 *www.grupo-piramide.com* *17 rooms* 💳 *AE, V.*

$$ **San Francisco.** An 18th-century town house near the cathedral and the main shopping area houses this modest hotel. A central patio enlivens the entrance, and the simple rooms have en suite marble bathrooms. The upstairs terrace has five-star cathedral views. The friendly owner speaks some English. ✉ *Calle Álvarez Quintero 38, Santa Cruz, 41004* ☎ *95/450–1541* *17 rooms* 💳 *MC, V.*

$$ **Simón.** In a rambling turn-of-the-19th-century town house, this hotel is a good choice for inexpensive, comfortable accommodations near the cathedral. The spacious, fern-filled, azulejo-tile patio makes a fine initial impression; the marble stairway and high-ceiling and pillared dining room are cool, stately spaces. The rooms are less grand, but the mansion's style permeates the house. ✉ *Calle García de Vinuesa 19, El Arenal, 41001* ☎ *95/422–6660* 📠 *95/456–2241* 🌐 *www.hotelsimonsevilla.com* *29 rooms* *In-hotel: restaurant, some pets allowed* 💳 *AE, DC, MC, V.*

NIGHTLIFE & THE ARTS

Seville has lively nightlife and plenty of cultural activity. The free monthly magazine *El Giraldillo* (🌐 *www.elgiraldillo.es*) lists classical and jazz concerts, plays, dance performances, art exhibits, and films in Seville and all major Andalusian cities. (For American films in English, look for the designation *v.o.*, for *versión original.*)

NIGHTLIFE

FLAMENCO CLUBS

Seville has a handful of commercial *tablaos* (flamenco clubs), patronized more by tourists than locals. They offer, generally, somewhat mechanical flamenco at high prices, with mediocre cuisine as the icing on the cake. Check local listings and ask at your hotel for performances by top artists. Spontaneous flamenco is often found for free in *peñas flamencas* (flamenco clubs) and flamenco bars in Triana.

Casa Anselma is a semi-secret (unmarked) bar on the corner of Antillano Campos where Anselma and her friends sing and dance for the pure joy and catharsis that is at the heart of flamenco. ✉*Calle Pagés del Corro 49, Triana* ☎*No phone* *Free* *Shows nightly after 11.*

★ **Casa de la Memoria de Al-Andaluz,** housed in an 18th-century palace, has a nightly show plus classes for the intrepid. ✉*Calle Ximenez de Enciso 28, Santa Cruz* ☎*95/456–0670* *€12* *Shows nightly at 9.*

Casa del Carmen is a newcomer to the Seville flamenco scene. The flamenco here is generally as passionate and raw as it needs to be to retain credibility. ✉*Calle Marqués de Paradas 30, Santa Cruz* ☎*95/421–2889* *€12* *Shows nightly at 8:30 and 10.*

El Tamboril is a late-night bar in the heart of the Barrio de Santa Cruz noted for its great glass case in which the Virgin of Rocío sits in splendor. At 11 each night, locals pack in to sing the *Salve Rociera,* an emotive prayer to her. Afterward everything from flamenco to salsa continues until the early hours. ✉*Pl. Santa Cruz, Santa Cruz* *Free.*

La Carbonería—when it gets packed, which is most Thursdays, the flamenco is spontaneous. ✉*C. Levíes 18, Santa Cruz* ☎*95/421–4460.*

Los Gallos is an intimate club in the heart of the Barrio de Santa Cruz. Performances are good and reasonably authentic. ✉*Pl. Santa Cruz 11, Santa Cruz* ☎*95/421–6981* *www.tablaolosgallos.com* *€30 with 1 drink* *Shows nightly at 8 and 10:30. Closed Jan.*

THE ARTS

Long prominent in the opera world, Seville is particularly proud of its opera house, the **Teatro de la Maestranza** (✉*Paseo de Colón 22, Arenal* ☎*95/422–3344* *www.teatromaestranza.com*). Classical music and ballet are performed at the **Teatro Lope de Vega** (✉*Av. María Luisa s/n, Parque de María Luisa* ☎*95/459–0853*). The modern **Teatro Central** (✉*José de Gálvez s/n, Isla de la Cartuja* ☎*95/503–7200* *www.teatrocentral.com*) stages theater, dance, and classical and contemporary music.

BULLFIGHTING

Bullfighting season is Easter through Columbus Day; most *corridas* (bullfights) are held on Sunday. The highlight is the April Fair, with Spain's leading toreros; other key dates are Corpus Christi (date varies; about seven weeks after Easter), Assumption (August 15), and the last weekend in September. Bullfights take place at the **Maestranza Bullring** (✉*Paseo de Colón 12, Arenal* ☎*95/422–4577*). Bullfighting tickets are expensive; buy them in advance from the official *despacho de entradas* (*ticket office* ✉*Calle Adriano 37, Arenal* ☎*95/450–1382*), alongside the bullring. Other despachos sell tickets on Calle Sierpes, but these are unofficial and charge a 20% commission.

Continued on page 670

FLAMENCO

THE HEARTBEAT OF SPAIN

Palmas, the staccato clapping of flamenco.

Rule one about flamenco: You don't see it. You feel it. There's no soap opera emoting here. The pain and yearning on the dancers' faces and the eerie voices—typically communicating grief over a lost love or family member—are real. If the dancers manage to summon the supernatural *duende* and allow this inner demon to overcome them, then they have done their jobs well.

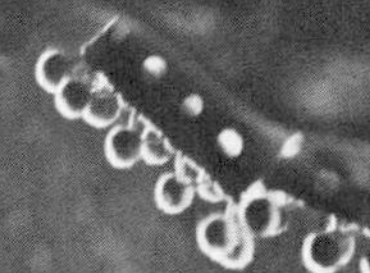

11

FLAMENCO: THE HEARTBEAT OF SPAIN

DUENDE HEAD TO TOE

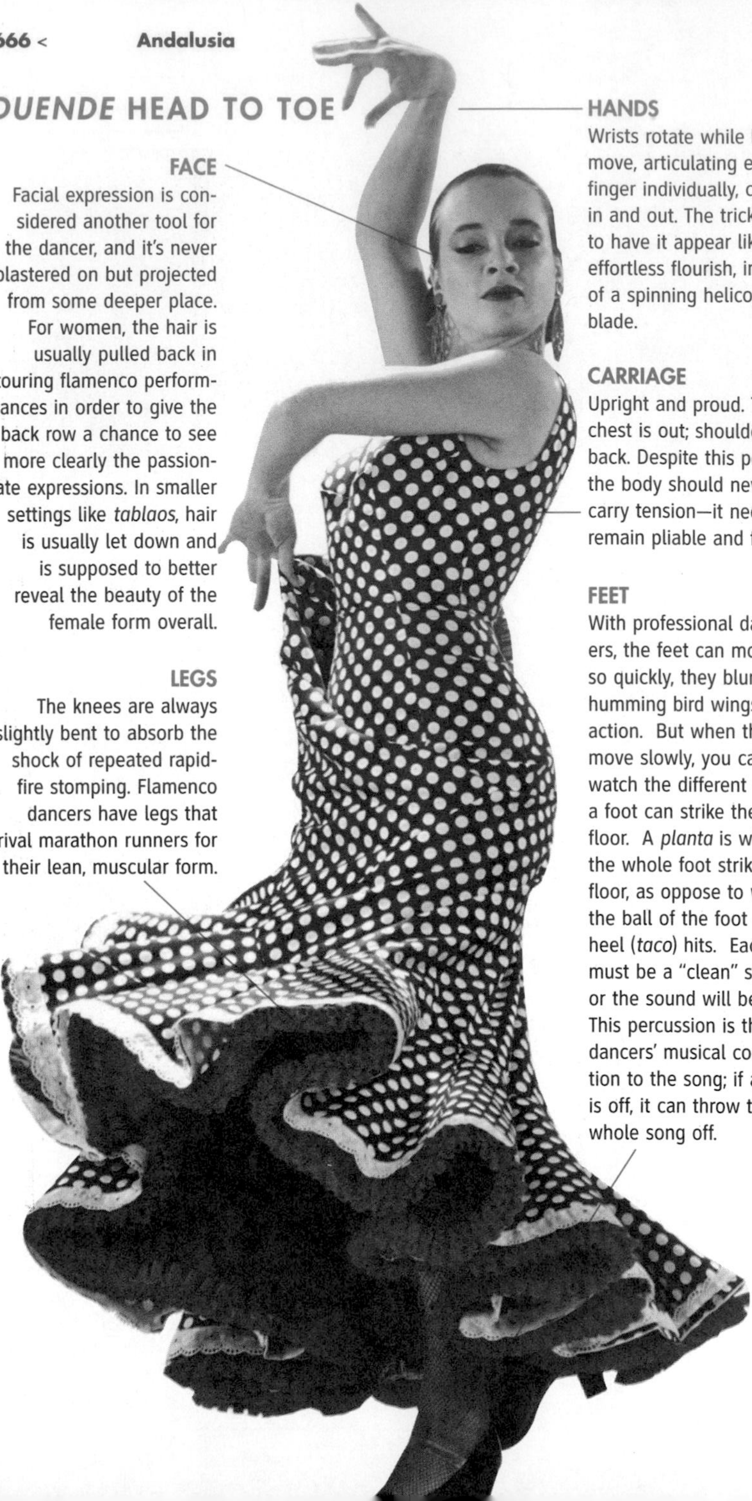

FACE

Facial expression is considered another tool for the dancer, and it's never plastered on but projected from some deeper place. For women, the hair is usually pulled back in touring flamenco performances in order to give the back row a chance to see more clearly the passionate expressions. In smaller settings like *tablaos*, hair is usually let down and is supposed to better reveal the beauty of the female form overall.

LEGS

The knees are always slightly bent to absorb the shock of repeated rapid-fire stomping. Flamenco dancers have legs that rival marathon runners for their lean, muscular form.

HANDS

Wrists rotate while hands move, articulating each finger individually, curling in and out. The trick is to have it appear like an effortless flourish, instead of a spinning helicopter blade.

CARRIAGE

Upright and proud. The chest is out; shoulders back. Despite this position, the body should never carry tension—it needs to remain pliable and fluid.

FEET

With professional dancers, the feet can move so quickly, they blur like humming bird wings in action. But when they move slowly, you can watch the different ways a foot can strike the floor. A *planta* is when the whole foot strikes the floor, as oppose to when the ball of the foot or the heel (*taco*) hits. Each one must be a "clean" strike or the sound will be off. This percussion is the dancers' musical contribution to the song; if a step is off, it can throw the whole song off.

FLAMENCO 101

All the elements of flamenco working in harmony.

ORIGINS

The music is largely Arabic in its beginnings, but you'll detect echoes of Greek dirges and Jewish chants, with healthy doses of Flemish and traditional Castillian thrown in. Hindu sways, Roman mimes, and other movement informs the dance, but we may never know the specific origins of flamenco.

The dance, along with the nomadic Gypsies, spread throughout Andalusia and within a few centuries had developed into many variations and styles, some of them named after the city where they were borne (such as Malagueñas, Sevillanas) and others taking on the names after people, emotions, or bands. In all, there are over 50 different styles (or *palos*) of flamenco, four of which are the stylistic pillars others branch off from—differing mainly in rhythm and mood: *Toná*, *Soleá*, *Fandango,* and *Seguiriya.*

CLAPPING AND CASTANETS

The sum of its parts are awe-inspiring, but if you boil it down, flamenco is a combination of music, singing, and dance. Staccato hand-clapping almost sneaks in as a fourth part—the sounds made from all the participants' palms, or *palmas* is part of the *duende*—but this element remains more of a

continued on following page

THE FLAMENCO HOOK-UP

When *duende* leads to love.

That cheek-to-cheek chemistry that exists between dance partners isn't missing in flamenco—it's simply repositioned between the dancer and the musicians. In fact, when you watch flamenco, you may feel what seems like an electric wire connecting the dancer to the musicians. In each *palo* (style) of music there are certain *letras* (lyrics) inherent within the song that tip off dancers and spark a change in rhythm. If the cues are off, the dancer may falter or simply come off flat. At its best, the dancer and the guitarist are like an old married couple that can musically finish each other's sentences. This interconnectedness has been known to lead into the bedroom, and it's not unusual for dancers and musicians to hook up offstage as well. Two famous couples include dancer Eva La Yerbabuena with guitarist Paco Jarano and dancer Manuela Carrasco with guitarist Joaquín Amador.

connector that all in the performance take part in when their hands are free.

Hand-clapping was likely flamenco's original key instrument before the guitar, *cajón* (wooden box used for percussion), and other instruments arrived on the scene. Perhaps the simplest way to augment the clapping is to add a uniquely designed six string guitar, in which case you've got yourself a *tablao*, or people seated around a singer and clapping. Dance undoubtedly augments the experience, but isn't necessary for a *tablao*. These exist all throughout Andalusia and are usually private affairs with people who love flamenco. One needn't be a Gypsy in order to take part in it. But it doesn't hurt.

Castanets (or *palillos*) were absorbed by the Phoenician culture and persevered by the Spanish, now part of their own folklore. They accompany other traditional folk dances in Spain and are used pervasively throughout flamenco (though not always present in some forms of dance). Castanets can be secured in any number of ways. The most important thing is that they are securely fastened to the hand (by thumb or any combination of fingers) so that the wrist can snap it quickly and make the sound.

FLAMENCO NOW

Flamenco's enormous international resurgence has been building for the past few decades. Much of this revival can be attributed to pioneers like legendary singer Camarón de la Isla, guitarist Paco de Lucía, or even outsiders like Miles Davis fusing flamenco with other genres like jazz and rock. This melding brought forth flamenco pop—which flourished in the 80s and continues today—as well as disparate fusions with almost every genre imaginable, including heavy metal and hip-hop. Today the most popular flamenco fusion artists include Ojos de Brujo and Chambao—all of which have found an audience outside of Spain.

IT'S A MAN'S WORLD

Joaquín Cortés

In the U.S., our image of a flamenco dancer is usually a woman in a red dress. So you may be surprised to learn that male dancers dominate flamenco and always have. In its beginnings, men did all the footwork and only since the 40s and 50s have women started to match men step-for-step and star in performances. And in the tabloids, men usually get the sex symbol status more than women (as seen through Farruquito and Cortés). Suits are the traditional garb for male dancers, and recent trends have seen female dancers wearing them as well—presumably rebelling against the staid gender roles that continue to rule Spain. Today, male dancers tend to wear a simple pair of black trousers and a white button-down shirt. The sex appeal comes for unbuttoning the shirt to flash a little chest and having the pants tailor-made to a tightness that can't be found in any store. In traditional *tablaos*, male dancers perform without accessories, but in touring performances—upping the razzle dazzle—anything goes: canes, hats, tuxedos, or even shirtless (much to the delight of female fans).

DANCING WITH THE STARS

SEX, MANSLAUGHTER, EVEN MONOGAMY

Farruquito was born into a flamenco dynasty. He started dancing when he was 8 years old and rose very high in the flamenco and celebrity world (*People* magazine named him one of the 50 most beautiful people in the world) until September 2003 when he ran two lights in an unlicensed, uninsured BMW, hitting and killing a pedestrian.

FARRUQUITO, The Wild Child

EVA LA YERBABUENA, The Pro

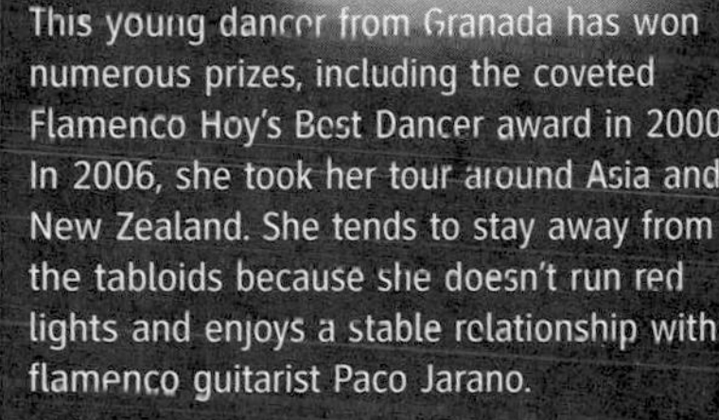

This young dancer from Granada has won numerous prizes, including the coveted Flamenco Hoy's Best Dancer award in 2000. In 2006, she took her tour around Asia and New Zealand. She tends to stay away from the tabloids because she doesn't run red lights and enjoys a stable relationship with flamenco guitarist Paco Jarano.

JOAQUÍN CORTÉS, The Lady's Man

Stateside, we're still swooning over her Oscar-nominated sister, Penélope, but in Spain, Mónica also captures the spotlight. With the same dark hair and pillowy lips as her sibling, Mónica works as a flamenco dancer and actress. Most recently she stared in a Soap Opera in Spain called *Paso Adelante*, a Spanish version of *Fame*.

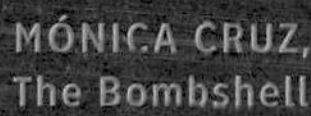

MÓNICA CRUZ, The Bombshell

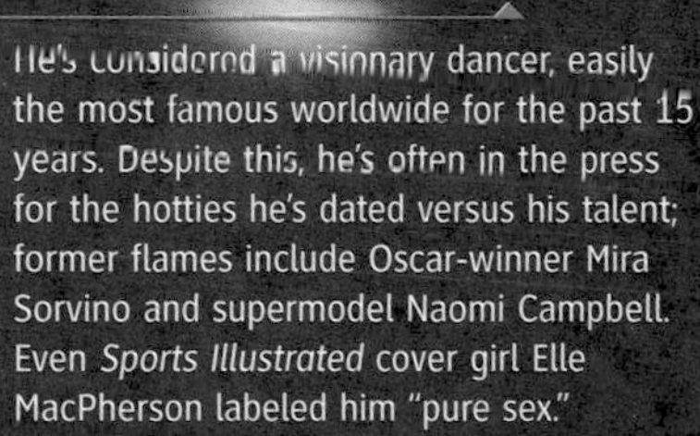

He's considered a visionary dancer, easily the most famous worldwide for the past 15 years. Despite this, he's often in the press for the hotties he's dated versus his talent; former flames include Oscar-winner Mira Sorvino and supermodel Naomi Campbell. Even *Sports Illustrated* cover girl Elle MacPherson labeled him "pure sex."

SHOPPING

Seville is the region's main shopping area and the place for archetypal Andalusian souvenirs, most of which are sold in the Barrio de Santa Cruz and around the cathedral and Giralda, especially on Calle Alemanes. The shopping street for locals is Calle Sierpes, along with neighboring Cuna, Tetuan, Velázquez, Plaza Magdalena, and Plaza Duque—boutiques abound here. A permanent arts-and-crafts market near the cathedral is **El Postigo** (✉ *Calle Arfe s/n, Arenal* ☎ *95/456–0013*).

ANTIQUES

For antiques, try Mateos Gago, opposite the Giralda, and in the Barrio de Santa Cruz on Jamerdana and Rodrigo Caro, off Plaza Alianza.

CERAMICS

In the Barrio de Santa Cruz, browse along Mateos Gago; Romero Murube, between Plaza Triunfo and Plaza Alianza, on the edge of the barrio; and between Plaza Doña Elvira and Plaza de los Venerables. Look for traditional azulejo tiles and other ceramics in the Triana **potters' district,** on Calle Alfarería and Calle Antillano Campos. **Cerámica Santa Isabel** (✉ *Calle Alfarería 12, El Zurraque* ☎ *95/434–4608*) is one of a string of Triana ceramics shops. In central Seville, **Martian Ceramics** (✉ *Calle Sierpes 74, Centro* ☎ *95/421–3413*) has high-quality dishes, especially the flowers-on-white patterns native to Seville.

FLAMENCO WEAR

Flamenco wear can be expensive; local women will gladly spend a month's grocery money, or more, on their frills, with dresses ranging from €100 to €400 and up. Try recommended shops **María Rosa** (✉ *Calle Cuna 13, Centro* ☎ *95/422–2143*) and **Molina** (✉ *Sierpes 11, Centro* ☎ *95/422–9254*), which also sells the traditional foot-tapping shoes. For privately fitted and custom-made flamenco dresses, try **Juan Foronda** (✉ *Calle Virgen de los Reyes 3, Centro* ☎ *95/421–1856*).

PASTRIES

Seville's most celebrated pastry outlet is **La Campana** (✉ *Sierpes 1, Centro* ☎ *95/422–3570*), founded in 1885. Andalusia's convents are known for their homemade pastries—sample sweets from several convents at **El Torno** (✉ *Pl. del Cabildo s/n, Santa Cruz* ☎ *95/421–9190*).

STREET MARKETS

A few blocks north of Plaza Nueva, **Plaza del Duque** has a crafts market on Friday and Saturday. The flea market **El Jueves** is held on Calle Feria in the Barrio de la Macarena on Thursday morning. A Sunday morning crafts market is a weekly happening at the northern Barrio de la Macarena's **Alameda de Hercules.** There's a Sunday pet market in the upper Barrio de Santa Cruz's **Plaza Alfalfa.**

TEXTILES

You can find blankets, shawls, and embroidered tablecloths woven by local artisans at the three shops of **Artesanía Textil** (✉ *Calle García de Vinuesa 33, Arenal* ☎ *95/456–2840* ✉ *Sierpes 70, Centro* ☎ *95/422–0125* ✉ *Pl. de Doña Elvira 4, Santa Cruz* ☎ *95/421–4748*).

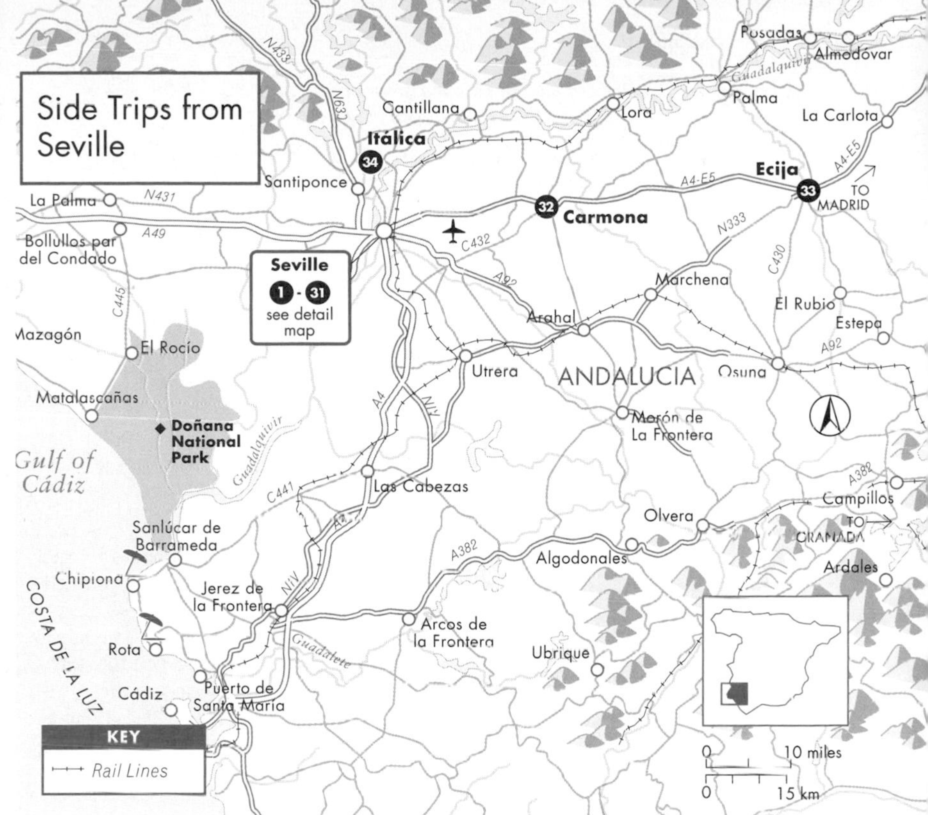

SIDE TRIPS FROM SEVILLE

CARMONA

32 *32 km (20 mi) east of Seville off NIV.*

Claiming to be one of the oldest inhabited places in Spain (the Phoenicians and Carthaginians had settlements here), Carmona, on a steep, fortified hill, became an important town under both the Romans and the Moors. As you wander its ancient, narrow streets, you can see many Mudejar and Renaissance churches, medieval gateways, and simple whitewashed houses of clear Moorish influence, punctuated here and there by a baroque palace. Local fiestas are held in mid-September.

WHAT TO SEE

Park your car near the Puerta de Sevilla in the imposing **Alcázar de Abajo** (Lower Fortress), a Moorish fortification built on Roman foundations. Grab a map at the tourist office, in the tower beside the gate. On the edge of the "new town," across the road from the Alcázar de Abajo, is the church of **San Pedro** (✉ *Calle San Pedro*), begun in 1466. Its interior is an unbroken mass of sculptures and gilded surfaces, and its baroque tower, erected in 1704, is an unabashed imitation of Seville's Giralda.

Up Calle Prim is the **Plaza San Fernando,** in the heart of the old town; its 17th-century houses have Moorish overtones.

The Gothic church of **Santa María** (✉ *Calle Martín*) was built between 1424 and 1518 on the site of Carmona's former Great Mosque. It retains its beautiful Moorish courtyard, studded with orange trees. Behind Santa María is the **Museo de la Ciudad,** with exhibits on Carmona's history. There's plenty for children; interactive exhibits are labeled in English and Spanish. ✉ *Calle San Ildefonso 1* ☎ *954/140128* *€2* *Mon. 11–2, Tues.–Sun. 11–7.*

Stroll down to the **Puerta de Córdoba** (Córdoba Gate) on the eastern edge of town. This old gateway was first built by the Romans around AD 175, then altered by Moorish and Renaissance additions. The Moorish **Alcázar de Arriba** (Upper Fortress) was built on Roman foundations and later converted by King Pedro the Cruel into a fine Mudejar palace. Pedro's summer residence was destroyed by a 1504 earthquake, but the parador amid its ruins has a breathtaking view.

★ At the western end of town lies the splendid **Roman necropolis.** Here, in huge underground chambers, some 900 family tombs were chiseled out of the rock between the 2nd and 4th centuries BC. The walls, decorated with leaf and bird motifs, have niches for burial urns. The most spectacular tombs are the **Elephant Vault** and the **Servilia Tomb,** which resembles a complete Roman villa with its colonnaded arches and vaulted side galleries. ✉ *C. Enmedio* ☎ *95/414–0811* *€2* *Mid-Sept.–mid-June, Tues.–Fri. 9–4:45, weekends 10–1:45; mid-June–mid-Sept., Tues.–Fri. 8:30–1:45, Sat. 10–2.*

WHERE TO STAY & EAT

$$–$$$ ✕ **San Fernando.** You enter from a side street, but this second-floor restaurant looks out onto the Plaza de San Fernando. Set in an 18th-century palace, the beige dining room is pleasant in its simplicity. The kitchen serves Spanish dishes with flair—as in cream of apple soup or light fried potato slivers shaped like a bird's nest. Game, including partridge, are perennial favorites. ✉ *Calle Sacramento 3* ☎ *95/414–3556* *AE, DC, MC, V* *Closed Mon. and Aug. No dinner Sun.*

$$$–$$$$ ✕ **Alcázar de la Reina.** Stylish and contemporary, this hotel has public areas that incorporate three bright and airy courtyards, with marble floors and pastel walls. Guest rooms are spacious and comfortable. The elegant Ferrara ($$–$$$) serves a tasty combination of Italian and Spanish dishes, served à la carte or on a *menú de degustación* (gourmet menu) with four courses and dessert. ✉ *Pl. de Lasso 2, 41410* ☎ *95/419–6200* *95/414–0113* *www.alcazar-reina.es* *66 rooms, 2 suites* *In-room: Ethernet (some). In-hotel: restaurant, bar, pool, parking (fee), some pets allowed* *AE, DC, MC, V* *BP.*

$$$ ★ **Parador Alcázar del Rey Don Pedro.** The Parador de Carmona has superb views from its hilltop position among the ruins of Pedro the Cruel's summer palace. The public rooms surround a central, Moorish-style patio, and the vaulted dining hall and adjacent bar open onto an outdoor terrace overlooking the sloping garden. Spacious rooms have rugs and dark furniture. All but six, which face onto the front

courtyard, look south over the valley; the best rooms are on the top floor. ✉ *Calle del Alcázar s/n, 41410* ☎ *95/414–1010* 📠 *95/414–1712* 🌐 *www.parador.es* *63 rooms* *In-room: dial-up, Wi-Fi. In-hotel: restaurant, bar, pool, Wi-Fi, public Internet* 💳 *AE, DC, MC, V.*

ÉCIJA

33 *48 km (30 mi) northeast of Carmona.*

Écija is dubbed the "the frying pan," "furnace," or "oven" of Andalusia for midsummer temperatures often reaching 100°F/37°C. On a more positive note, it has more ceramic-tiled baroque church towers per capita (11) than any other town in Spain.

WHAT TO SEE

Écija's most famous ornamented church is the **Iglesia de Santa María** in the palm tree–shaded Plaza de España, an important meeting point on infernally hot summer evenings. The **Iglesia de San Juan** has an intricate and harmoniously crafted Mudéjar bell tower. The **Iglesia de Santiago** assembles Mudéjar windows from an earlier structure with an 18th-century patio and 17th-century nave and side aisles. Important civil structures in Écija begin with the baroque **Palacio de Peñaflor** (✉ *Calle Emilio Castelar 26* ☎ *95/483–0273* *Free* *Patio only: weekdays 10–1 and 4:30–7:30, weekends 11–1*) with its concave facade and its *trampantojo* (trompe l'oeil) faux-relief paintings. Note the presentation of the stable windows below the false wrought-iron balcony, which is the noblest feature in the facade. The Renaissance **Valdehermoso Palace** (✉ *Calle Emilio Castelar 37*) near the Iglesia de San Juan is an elegant and aristocratic structure. The **Palacio de Benamejí** (✉ *Plaza de la Consitución s/n*) with its two watchtowers is another of Écija's finest houses. The **Palacio del Conde de Aguilar** (✉ *Calle Sor Angela Cruz s/n*) has a lovely baroque portal and a wrought-iron gallery.

WHERE TO STAY & EAT

$$ **Platería.** This little hideaway in the old silversmiths' quarter has breezy rooms with plenty of space and a good restaurant ($–$$$) that serves regional and national dishes. The building is modern, and the rooms are decorated in sleek, spare lines and tones that exert a cooling influence in this hottest of Andalusian towns. Air-conditioned. ✉ *C. Platería 4, 41400* ☎ *95/590–2754* 📠 *95/590 4553* 🌐 *www.hotelplateria.net* *18 rooms* *In hotel: Restaurant, bar* 💳 *AE, DC, MC, V.*

ITÁLICA

34 *12 km (7 mi) north of Seville, 1 km (½ mi) beyond Santiponce.*

Fodor's Choice ★

One of Roman Iberia's most important cities in the 2nd century with a population of over 10,000, Itálica today is a monument of Roman ruins, complete with admission charge. Founded by Scipio Africanus in 205 BC as a home for veteran soldiers, Itálica gave the Roman world two great emperors, Trajan (52–117) and Hadrian (76–138). About 25% of the site has been excavated, with work still in progress. You can find traces of city streets, cisterns, and the floor plans of several

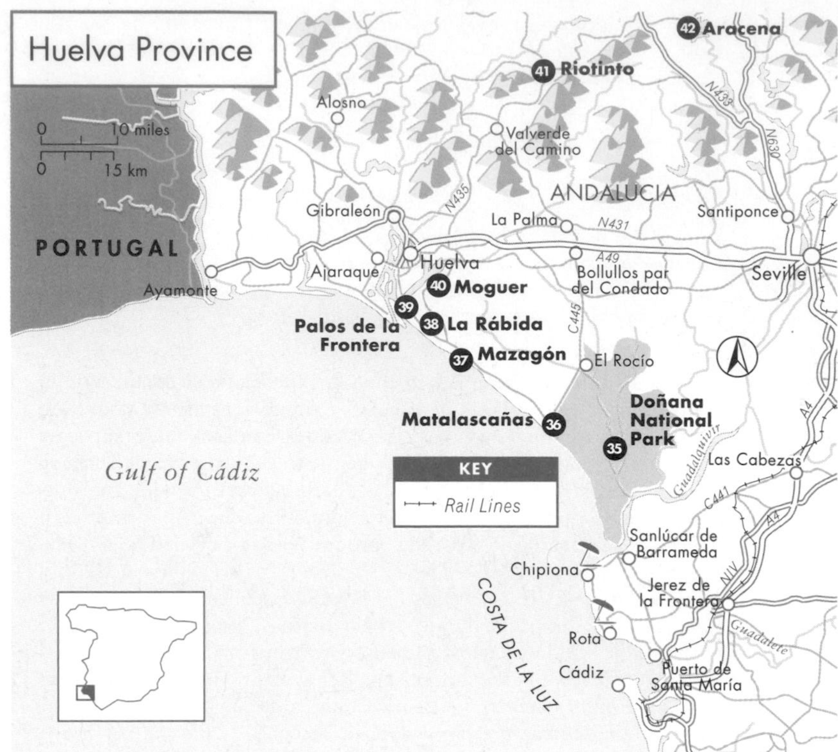

villas, some with mosaic floors, though all the best mosaics and statues have been removed to Seville's Museum of Archaeology. Itálica was abandoned and plundered as a quarry by the Visigoths, who preferred Seville. It fell into decay around AD 700. The remains you can see include the huge, elliptical **amphitheater**, which held 40,000 spectators, a **Roman theater**, and **Roman baths.** The small town of Santiponce has sprung up nearby. ☎ *95/599–7376 or 95/599–6583* 🎫 *€1.50, free for EU citizens* ⏲ *Tues.–Sat. 9–5:30, Sun. 10–4.*

WESTERN ANDALUSIA'S GREAT OUTDOORS: PROVINCE OF HUELVA

When you've had enough of Seville's urban bustle, nature awaits in Huelva—from the Parque Nacional de Doñana to the oak forests of the Sierra de Aracena, nothing is much more than an hour's drive from Seville. If you prefer history, hop on the miners' train at Riotinto, or visit Aracena's spectacular caves. Columbus's voyage to the New World was sparked near here, at the monastery of La Rábida and in Palos de la Frontera. The visitor center at La Rocina has Doñana information.

DOÑANA NATIONAL PARK

35 *100 km (62 mi) southwest of*
Fodor'sChoice ★ *Seville.*

One of Europe's last swaths of wilderness, these wetlands are beside the Guadalquivir estuary. The site was named for Doña Ana, wife of a 16th-century duke, who, prone to bouts of depression, one day crossed the river and wandered into the wetlands, never to be seen alive again. The 188,000-acre park sits on the migratory route from Africa to Europe and is the winter home and breeding ground for as many as 150 species of rare birds. Habitats range from beaches and shifting sand dunes to marshes, dense brushwood, and sandy hillsides of pine and cork oak. Two of Europe's most endangered species, the imperial eagle and the lynx, make their homes here, and kestrels, kites, buzzards, egrets, storks, and spoonbills breed among the cork oaks. A good base of exploration is the hamlet of **El Rocío,** on the park's northern fringe. In spring, during the Romería del Rocío pilgrimage (40 days after Easter Sunday), up to a million people converge on the local *santuario* (shrine) to worship the Virgen del Rocío. The rest of the year, many of El Rocío's pilgrim-brotherhood houses are empty. Most of the streets are unpaved to make them more comfortable for horses, as many of the yearly pilgrimage events are on horseback or involve horse-drawn carts. At the Doñana **La Rocina visitor center** (☎*959/442340*), less than 2 km (1 mi) from El Rocío, you can peer at the park's many bird species from a 3½-km (2-mi) footpath. It's open daily 9–7. Five kilometers (3 mi) away, an exhibit at the **Palacio de Acebrón** (✉*Ctra. de la Rocina s/n* ☎*959/448 711*) explains the park's ecosystems. It's open daily 9–6:30; last entrance is one hour before closing.

DOÑANA TOURS

Jeep tours of the reserve depart twice daily (Tuesday–Sunday at 8:30 and 3) from the park's Acebuche reception center, 2 km (1 mi) from Matalascañas. Tours are limited to 125 people and should be booked well in advance. Passengers can often be picked up from hotels in Matalascañas. Contact **Parque Nacional de Doñana,** ✉*Cooperativa Marisma del Rocío, Centro de Recepción, Matalascañas, 21760* ☎*959/430432* 🌐*www.donana.es.*

Two kilometers (1 mi) before Matalascañas, you can find **Acebuche** (✉*El Acebuche s/n* ☎*959/448640* 🌐*www.parquenacionaldonana.com*), the park's main interpretation center and the departure point for jeep tours, which must be reserved in advance. The center is open June–September, daily 8 AM–9 PM and October–May, daily 9–7. Tours leave daily June–September at 8:30 and 5 and October–May at 8:30 and 3 and last four hours; they cover a 70-km (43-mi) route across beaches, sand dunes, marshes, and scrub. Cost is €24. Off-season (November–February) you can usually book a tour with just a day's notice; at other times, book as far in advance as possible.

WHERE TO STAY

$$$ **El Cortijo de Los Mimbrales.** On the Rocío–Matalascañas road, this convivial, one-story Andalusian farm-hacienda is perched on the park's edge, a mere 1 km (½ mi) from the visitor center at La Rocina. Spend

a relaxed evening with fellow nature lovers in comfy chairs by the fireplace in the large common lounge. Pick a colorfully decorated room, or a bungalow that sleeps two to four, with a kitchenette and small private garden. Some rooms and bungalows have fireplaces. There are stables on the premises, and the hotel can arrange horseback rides on the fringes of the park. ✉*Ctra. del Rocío a Matalascañas (A483), Km 30, 21750* ☎*959/442237* 📠*959/442443* 🌐*www.cortijomimbrales.com* *24 rooms, 2 suites, 5 bungalows* *In-room: no a/c. In-hotel: restaurant, bar, pool, some pets allowed* 💳*AE, DC, MC, V* *BP.*

$$ **Toruño.** Despite its location behind the famous Rocío shrine, the theme at this simple, friendly hotel is nature: it's run by the same cooperative that leads official park tours and has become a favorite of birdwatchers. Each room is named after a local bird species. Those on the first floor have balconies and priceless views over the marshes. ✉*Pl. del Acebuchal 22, 21750* ☎*959/442323* 📠*959/442338* *30 rooms* *In-hotel: restaurant* 💳*MC, V* *BP.*

MATALASCAÑAS

36 *3 km (2 mi) south of Acebuche, 85 km (53 mi) southwest of Seville.*

Its proximity to Acebuche, Doñana's main reception center, makes Matalascañas a convenient lodging base for park visitors. In general though, it's a rather incongruous and ugly sprawl of hotels and vacation homes, very crowded at Easter and in summer, and eerily deserted the rest of the year (most hotels close November–March). There are some nice beaches for relaxation, and the local ocean waters good for windsurfing.

WHERE TO STAY

$$$ **Hotel Tierra Mar Golf.** Try this large beachfront hotel if you want to combine Doñana with the seashore. The nearby 18-hole Dunes golf course (€30 greens fee) is windy and challenging year-round; the more gentle prospect of lawn bowling is available within the hotel's grounds. The rooms are modern, spacious, and have balconies. ✉*Matalascañas Parcela 120, Sector M, 21760* ☎*959/440300* 📠*959/440720* 🌐*www.atlanticclub-hoteles.com* *250 rooms* *In-room: dial-up. In-hotel: restaurant, tennis court, pool, gym* 💳*AE, DC, MC, V.*

MAZAGÓN

37 *22 km (14 mi) northwest of Matalascañas.*

There isn't much to see or do in this coastal town, but its parador makes a good base for touring La Rábida, Palos de la Frontera, and Moguer. Mazagón's beautiful beach is among the region's nicest, because of its sweeping sandy beach sheltered by steep cliffs.

WHERE TO STAY & EAT

$$$ ✕ **Parador de Mazagón.** This peaceful modern parador stands on a cliff surrounded by pine groves, overlooking a sandy beach 3 km (2 mi) southeast of Mazagón. Most rooms have balconies overlooking the garden. The restaurant serves Andalusian dishes and local seafood

specialties, such as stuffed baby squid and hake medallions. ✉*Playa de Mazagón, 21130* ☎*959/536300* 📠*959/536228* 🌐*www.parador.es* *63 rooms* *In-room: Wi-Fi. In-hotel: restaurant, bar, tennis courts, pool, public Wi-Fi, bicycles, parking (no fee)* 💳*AE, DC, MC, V.*

LA RÁBIDA

38 *8 km (5 mi) northwest of Mazagón.*

You may want to extend your Doñana tour to see the monastery of **Santa María de La Rábida,** "the birthplace of America." In 1485 Columbus came from Portugal with his son Diego to stay in this Mudejar-style Franciscan monastery. Here he discussed his theories with friars Antonio de Marchena and Juan Pérez, who interceded on his behalf with Queen Isabella. The early 15th-century church holds a much-venerated 14th-century statue of the **Virgen de los Milagros** (Virgin of Miracles). The **frescoes** in the gatehouse were painted by Daniel Vázquez Díaz in 1930. ✉*Camino del Monasterio, Ctra. de Huelva* ☎*959/350411* 🎫*€3 with audio guide, €2.50 without* ⏲*Tues.–Sun. 10–1 and 4–7.*

Two kilometers (1 mi) from the monastery, on the seashore, is the **Muelle de las Carabelas** (Caravels' Wharf), a reproduction of a 15th-century port. The star exhibits here are the full-size models of Columbus's flotilla, the *Niña, Pinta,* and *Santa María,* built using the same techniques as in Columbus's day. Board each one and learn more about the discovery of the New World in the adjoining museum. ✉*Paraje de la Rábida* ☎*959/530597 or 959/530312* 🎫*€3.50* ⏲*Tues.–Sun. 9–7.*

PALOS DE LA FRONTERA

39 *4 km (2½ mi) northwest of La Rábida, 12 km (7 mi) northeast of Mazagón.*

On August 2, 1492, the *Niña,* the *Pinta,* and the *Santa María* set sail from Palos de la Frontera. At the door of the church of **San Jorge** (1473), the royal letter ordering the levy of the ships' crew and equipment was read aloud, and the voyagers took their water supplies from the fountain known as La Fontanilla (fountain) at the town's entrance.

MOGUER

40 *12 km (7 mi) northeast of Palos de la Frontera.*

The residents of this old port town now spend more time growing strawberries than seafaring, as you can see from the surrounding fields. While in Moguer, see the **Casa Museo Zenobia y Juan Ramón Jiménez,** former home of the Nobel Prize–winning poet who penned the much-loved *Platero y Yo.* At this writing, the Casa-Museo was closed for renovations with plans to reopen soon. Guided tours are offered hourly. ✉*C. Juan Ramón Jiménez 10* ☎*959/372148* 🌐*www.fundacion-jrj.es* 🎫*€2.50* ⏲*Tues.–Sat. 10:15–2 and 5–8, Sun. 10–2*

RIOTINTO

 *74 km (46 mi) northeast of Huelva.*

Heading north from Palos and Huelva on the N435, you can reach the turnoff to Minas de Riotinto, the mining town near the source of the Riotinto (literally, "Red River"). The waters are the color of blood because of the minerals leached from the surrounding mountains; this area has some of the richest copper deposits in the world, as well as gold and silver. In 1873 the mines were taken over by the British Rio Tinto Company Ltd., which started to dig an open-pit mine and build a 64-km (40-mi) railway to the port of Huelva to transport mineral ore. The British left in 1954, but mining activity continues today, albeit on a smaller scale. Riotinto's landscape, scarred by centuries of intensive mining, can be viewed as part of a **tour** conducted by the Fundación Riotinto. The tour's first stop, the **Museo Minero** (Museum of Mining), has archaeological finds and a collection of historical steam engines and rail coaches. Next comes the **Corta Atalaya,** one of the largest open-pit mines in the world (4,000 feet across and 1,100 feet deep), and **Bellavista,** the elegant English quarter where the British mine managers lived. The tour ends with an optional ride on the **Tren Minero** (Miners' Train), which follows the course of the Riotinto along more than 24 restored km (15 mi) of the old mining railway. Opt for the full tour as described (offered the first Sunday of each month, October–May), or just visit individual sights. ☎ *959/590025 Fundación Riotinto* 🌐 *www.parquemineroderiotinto.com* 🎫 *Full tour €15* ⏲ *Museum daily 10:30–3 and 4–8. Miners' Train mid-Apr.–mid-May and mid-Sept.–mid-Oct., weekends at 5* PM*; mid-June–mid-July and mid-Oct.–mid-Apr., weekends at 4* PM*; mid-July–mid-Sept., daily at 1:30* PM.

ARACENA

 *105 km (65 mi) northeast of Huelva, 100 km (62 mi) northwest of Seville.*

Stretching north of the Riotinto mines is the 460,000-acre Sierra de Aracena nature park, an expanse of hills cloaked in cork and holm oak. This region is known for its cured Ibérico hams, which come from the prized free-ranging Iberian pigs that gorge on acorns in the autumn months before slaughter; the hams are buried in salt and then hung in cellars to dry-cure for at least two years. The best Ibérico hams have traditionally come from the village of **Jabugo.** The capital of the region is Aracena, whose main attraction is the spectacular cave known as the **Gruta de las Maravillas** (Cave of Marvels). The 12 caverns hide long corridors, stalactites and stalagmites arranged in wonderful patterns, and stunning underground lakes. ✉ *Pl. Pozo de Nieves, Pozo de Nieves* ☎ *959/128355* 🎫 *€8* ⏲ *Guided tours, if sufficient numbers, weekdays hourly 10:30–3 and 4–6; weekends hourly 10:30–1:30 and 3–6.*

WHERE TO STAY & EAT

$-$$ **Casas.** There's not much wall space left in the intimate beamed dining room of this typical Sierra Morena restaurant: plates, pots, pans, mirrors, and religious pictures cover every inch. Specializing in the region's famous ham and pork, the honest, home-style cooking is at its best with dishes prepared according to what is in season. *Calle Colmenetas 41 959/128044 MC, V No dinner.*

$$–$$$ **Finca Buenvino.** This lovely country house inn, nestled in 150 acres of woods, is run by a charming British couple, Sam and Jeannie Chesterton. The room price includes a big breakfast; dinner with tapas is available for a moderate extra sum. Jeannie also conducts Spanish cookery and tapas courses for groups of up to six people. Three woodland self-catering cottages are available, each with its own pool. The house is 6 km (4 mi) from Aracena. *N433, Km 95, 21293 Los Marines 959/124034 959/501029 www.fincabuenvino.com 5 rooms, 3 cottages In-room: no a/c, no phone, kitchen (some), no TV. In-hotel: restaurant, bar, pools MC, V Closed mid-July–mid-Sept. MAP.*

$ **Galaroza Sierra.** The common areas in this stone-clad hotel are done in light wood with rustic furnishings and woven textiles. Rooms have small balconies and views of the mountains, and the four bungalows face the swimming pool. Pork dishes are the restaurant's specialty. Galaroza Sierra is on the outskirts of the village of Galaroza, 3 km (2 mi) from Jabugo; the surrounding countryside is ideal for walking. *Ctra. Sevilla–Lisboa, Km 69.5, Galaroza, 21291 959/123237 959/123236 www.hotelgalaroza.com 22 rooms, 7 bungalows In-hotel: restaurant, pool DC, MC, V.*

THE LAND OF SHERRY: JEREZ DE LA FRONTERA & CÁDIZ PROVINCE

A trip through Cádiz is a trip back in time. Winding roads take you through scenes ranging from flat and barren plains to seemingly endless vineyards, and the rolling countryside is carpeted with blindingly white soil known as *albariza*—unique to this area, and the secret to the grapes used in sherry. Throughout the province, *los pueblos blancos* (the white villages) provide striking contrasts with the terrain, especially at Arcos de la Frontera, where the village sits dramatically on a crag overlooking the gorge of the Guadalete River. In Jerez de La Frontera, you can savor the town's internationally known sherry or delight in the skills and forms of purebred Carthusian horses. Finally, in the city of Cádiz, absorb about 3,000 years of history in what is generally considered the oldest continuously inhabited city in the Western world.

JEREZ DE LA FRONTERA

43 *97 km (60 mi) south of Seville.*

★ Jerez, world headquarters for sherry, is surrounded by vineyards of chalky soil, whose Palomino grapes have funded a host of churches and noble mansions. Names such as González Byass, Domecq, Harvey, and Sandeman are inextricably linked with Jerez. The word "sherry," first used in Great Britain in 1608, is an English corruption of the town's old Moorish name, Xeres. Both sherry and horses are the domain of Jerez's Anglo-Spanish aristocracy, whose Catholic ancestors came here from England centuries ago. At any given time, more than half a million barrels of sherry are maturing in Jerez's vast aboveground cellars.

WHAT TO SEE

The 12th-century **Alcázar** was once the residence of the caliph of Seville. Its small, octagonal **mosque** and **baths** were built for the Moorish governor's private use. The baths have three sections: the *sala fria* (cold room), the larger *sala templada* (warm room), and the *sala caliente* (hot room), for steam baths. In the midst of it all is the 17th-century **Palacio de Villavicencio,** built on the site of the original Moorish palace. A camera obscura, a lens-and-mirrors device that projects the outdoors onto a large indoor screen, offers a 360-degree view of Jerez. ✉ *Alameda Vieja* 🎫 *€1.50, €3.50 including camera obscura* ⏲ *Mid-Sept.–Apr., daily 10–6; May–mid-Sept., daily 10–8.*

Across from the Alcázar and around the corner from the González Byass winery, the **cathedral** (✉ *Pl. de la Encarnación* ⏲ Weekdays *11–1, 6–8; Sat.11–2 and 6–8, Sun. 11–2*) has an octagonal cupola and a separate bell tower, as well as Zurbarán's canvas *La Virgen Niña* (the Virgin as a young girl). On the **Plaza de la Asunción,** one of Jerez's most intimate squares, you can find the Mudejar church of **San Dionisio** and the ornate **cabildo municipal** (city hall), whose lovely plateresque facade dates from 1575.

The **Centro Andaluz de Flamenco** is a flamenco museum; it includes an audio-and-visual library, and a multimedia show. ✉ *Palacio Pemartín, Pl. San Juan 1* ☎ *956/322711* 🎫 *Free* ⏲ *Weekdays 9–2.*

Diving into the maze of streets that form the scruffy San Mateo neighborhood east of the town center, you come to the **Museo Arqueológico,** one of Andalusia's best archaeological museums. The collection is strongest on the pre-Roman period. The star item, found near Jerez, is a Greek helmet dating from the 7th century BC. ✉ *Pl. del Mercado s/n* ☎ *956/341350* 🎫 *€2* ⏲ *Sept.–mid-June, Tues.–Fri. 10–2 and 4–7, weekends 10–2:30; mid-June–Aug., Tues.–Sun. 10–2:30.*

NEED A BREAK?

Bar Juanito (✉ *Pescadería Vieja 8 and 10* ☎ *956/334838*) has a flowery patio and is a past winner of the national Best Tapas Bar in Spain award. Jolly Faustino Rodríguez and his family serve 50 different tapas and larger-portion raciones. It's closed Monday and during El Rocó pilgrimage.

Just west of the town center the **Parque Zoológico** is set within lush botanical gardens where you can usually spy up to 33 storks' nests. Primarily a place for the rehabilitation of injured or endangered animals native to Spain, the zoo also houses white tigers, elephants, and a giant red panda. ✉ *C. Taxdirt* ☎ *956/153164* 🌐 *www.zoobotanicojerez.com* 🎫 *€7.50* ⏲ *June–Sept, Tues.–Sun. 10–8, Oct.–May, Tues.–Sun. 10–6.*

A TOAST TO JEREZ: WINERY TOURS

On a **bodega** (winery) visit, your guide will explain the *solera* method of blending old wine with new, and the importance of the *flor* (a sort of yeast that forms on the surface of the wine as it ages) in determining the kind of sherry.

Most bodegas welcome visitors, but it's advisable to phone ahead for an appointment, if only to make sure you join a group that speaks your language. Cellars usually charge an admission fee of €3–€6, and some close in August. Tours, about an hour, go through the aging cellars, with their endless rows of casks. (You won't see the actual fermenting and bottling, which take place in more modern, less romantic plants outside town.) Finally, you'll be invited to sample generous amounts of pale, dry *fino*; nutty *amontillado*; or rich, deep *oloroso*, and, of course, to purchase a few robustly priced bottles in the winery shop.

If you have time for only one bodega, tour the González Byass (✉ *Calle Manuel María González* ☎ *956/357000* 🌐 *www.gonzalez-byass.com*), home of the famous Tío Pepe. This tour is well organized and includes La Concha, an open-air aging cellar designed by Gustave Eiffel. Jerez's oldest bodega is **Domecq** (✉ *Calle San Ildefonso 3* ☎ *956/151500*), founded in 1730. Aside from sherry, Domecq makes the world's best-selling brandy, Fundador. **Harveys** (✉ *Calle Pintor Muñoz Cebrián s/n* ☎ *956/319650*) is the source of Harvey's Bristol Cream. **Sandeman** (✉ *Calle Pizarro 10* ☎ *956/301100* 🌐 *www.sandeman.com*) is known for its man-in-a-cape logo. **Museo de Vino** (✉ *Calle Cervantes 3, La Atalaya* ☎ *956/182100* 🎫 *€6* ⏲ *Tues.–Sun. 10–2*), a sherry museum, offers a multimedia show twice daily at 10 and noon, plus a sherry pouring exhibition, a bar, a restaurant, and a shop.

Fodor's Choice ★ The **Real Escuela Andaluza del Arte Ecuestre** *(Royal Andalusian School of Equestrian Art)* operates on the grounds of the Recreo de las Cadenas, a 19th-century palace. This prestigious school was masterminded by Alvaro Domecq in the 1970s. Every Thursday (and at various other times throughout the year) the Cartujana horses—a cross between the native Andalusian workhorse and the Arabian—and skilled riders in 18th-century riding costume demonstrate intricate dressage techniques and jumping in the spectacular show "Cómo Bailan los Caballos Andaluces" (roughly, "The Dancing Horses of Andalusia"). Reservations are essential. Admission price depends on how close to the arena you sit; the first two rows are the priciest. The rest of the week, you can visit the stables and tack room, watch the horses being schooled, and see rehearsals. ✉ *Av. Duque de Abrantes s/n* ☎ *956/319635* 🌐 *www.realescuela.org* 🎫 *€17–€25, €8 for rehearsals* ⏲ *Shows, Nov.–Feb., Thurs. at noon; Mar.–July 14, Tues. and Thurs. at noon; July 15–Oct., Fri. at noon; Mar., fair nightly at 10:30. Rehearsals, Mon.–Wed. and Thurs. 10–1.*

Just outside Jerez de la Frontera is **Yeguada de la Cartuja,** the largest state-run stud farm in Spain, specializing in Carthusian horses. In the 15th century, a Carthusian monastery on this site started the breed for which Jerez and the rest of Spain are now famous. Every Saturday at 11 AM a full tour and show begin. Book ahead. ✉ *Finca Fuente El Suero, Ctra. Medina–El Portal, Km 6.5* ☎ *956/162809* 🌐 *www.yeguada-cartuja.com* 🎫 *€13–€18, according to seating* ⏲ *Shows Sat. at 11 AM.*

SPRING IN JEREZ

May and September are the most exciting times to visit Jerez, as spectacular fiestas transform the town. For the Feria del Caballo (Horse Fair), in early May, carriages and riders fill the streets, and purebreds from the School of Equestrian Art compete in races and dressage displays. September brings the Fiesta de Otoño (Autumn Festival), when the first of the grape harvest is blessed on the steps of the cathedral.

Jerez's **bullring** is on Calle Circo, northeast of the city center. Tickets are sold at the official ticket office on Calle Porvera, though only about five bullfights are held each year, in May and October. Six blocks from the bullring is the **Museo Taurino,** a bullfighting museum where admission includes a drink. ✉ *Calle Pozo del Olivar 6* ☎ *956/319000* 🎫 *€3* ⏲ *Weekdays 9–2.*

WHERE TO STAY & EAT

$$–$$$ ✕ **La Carboná.** This cavernous restaurant in a former bodega has a suitably rustic atmosphere with arches, original beams, and a central fireplace for winter nights. During the summer you can often enjoy live music, and sometimes flamenco, too, while you dine. The chef has worked at several top-grade restaurants; his menu provides an innovative twist to classic dishes, such as *pechuguitas de cordorniz rellenas de pétalos de rosa y foié* (quail stuffed with rose petals and liver pâté). There's an excellent wine list as well. ✉ *C. San Francisco de Paula 2* ☎ *956/347475* 💳 *MC, V* ⏲ *Closed Tues.*

$–$$$ ✕ **El Bosque.** Housed in a modern villa with contemporary paintings of bullfighting themes, this is one of the most stylish dining spots in town. Most tables are round and seat four; the smaller of the two dining rooms has picture windows overlooking a park. The food is contemporary Spanish. *Sopa de galeras* (soup of mantis shrimp) makes a rich appetizer; follow up with *confit de pato de laguna* (leg of wild duck) or *perdiz estofado con castañas* (stewed partridge with chestnuts). ✉ *Av. Alcalde Alvaro Domecq 26* ☎ *956/307030* 💳 *AE, DC, MC, V* ⏲ *Closed Mon. No dinner Aug.*

$–$$$ ✕ **Gaitán.** Within walking distance of the riding school, this restaurant has brick arches and white walls decorated with colorful ceramic plates and photos of famous guests. It's crowded with businesspeople at lunchtime. The menu is Andalusian, with a few Basque dishes thrown in. When in season, *setas* (wild mushrooms) make a delicious starter; follow with *cordero asado* (roast lamb) in a sauce of honey and brandy. ✉ *Calle Gaitán 3* ☎ *956/168021* 💳 *AE, DC, MC, V* ⏲ *Closed Sun.*

$–$$ ✕ **Venta Antonio.** Crowds come to this roadside inn for superb, fresh seafood cooked in top-quality olive oil. You enter through the busy bar, where lobsters await their fate in a tank. Try the specialties of the Bay of Cádiz, such as *sopa de mariscos* (shellfish soup) followed by succulent *bogavantes de Sanlúcar* (local lobster). ✉*Ctra. de Jerez–Sanlúcar, Km 5* ☎*956/140535* 💳*AE, DC, MC, V* ⊗*No dinner Sun.*

$–$$ ★ ✕ **La Mesa Redonda.** Owner José Antonio Valdespino spent years researching the classic recipes once served in aristocratic Jerez homes, and now his son, José, presents them in this small, friendly restaurant off Avenida Alcalde Alvaro Domecq, around the corner from the Hotel Avenida Jerez. Don't be put off by the bland exterior—within, the eight tables are surrounded by watercolors and shelves are lined with cookbooks. Ask the chef's mother, Margarita—who has an encyclopedic knowledge of Spanish wines—what to order. ✉*Calle Manuel de la Quintana 3* ☎*956/340069* 💳*AE, DC, MC, V* ⊗*Closed Sun. and mid-July–mid-Aug.*

$$$–$$$$ **Montecastillo Hotel and Golf Resort.** Outside Jerez near the racetrack, the sprawling, modern Montecastillo adjoins a golf course designed by Jack Nicklaus—ask for a room with a terrace overlooking the course. The common areas are spacious and have marble floors. Rooms are cheerfully decorated, with bright floral bedspreads and rustic clay tiles. ✉*Ctra. de Arcos, Km 9.6, 11406* ☎*956/151200* 🖷*956/151209* 🌐*www.montecastillo.com* *119 rooms, 2 suites, 20 villas* *In-room: dial-up, Wi-Fi. In-hotel: restaurant, golf course, tennis court, pools, gym, spa* 💳*AE, DC, MC, V* *BP.*

$$$ ★ **Hotel Sherry Park.** Set back from the road in an unusually large, tree-filled garden, this modern hotel is designed around several patios filled with exotic foliage. The sunny hallways are hung with contemporary paintings. Rooms are bright and airy and decorated in sunny peach and blue; most have balconies overlooking the garden and pool. There are good deals out of season, as well as special weekend packages. ✉*Av. Alvaro Domecq 11, 11407* ☎*956/317614* 🖷*956/311300* 🌐*www.hipotels.com* *172 rooms* *In-hotel: restaurant, bar, pools, gym* 💳*AE, DC, MC, V* *BP.*

$$$ **Hotel Villa Jerez.** This hacienda-style, tastefully furnished hotel has luxury to offer in the historic part of town. The mature gardens surround a traditional courtyard and are lushly landscaped with palm trees and a dazzle of colorful plants and flowers. Facilities include an elegant restaurant with terrace, a saltwater swimming pool, and a gym. Bedrooms are plush and well equipped, and the staff is friendly and efficient. ✉*Av. de la Cruz Roja 7, 11407* ☎*956/153100* 🖷*956/304300* 🌐*www.villajerez.com* *14 rooms, 4 suites* *In-room: ethernet. In-hotel: restaurant, bar, pool* 💳*AE, DC, MC, V.*

$$ **Ávila.** This friendly, inexpensive hotel on a side street off Calle Arcos offers affordable central lodgings. The rooms have basic furnishings and tile floors; beds are European twin-size. A TV lounge and a small bar/breakfast room adjoin the lobby. ✉*Calle de Ávila 3, 11401* ☎*956/334808* 🖷*956/336807* *32 rooms* *In-hotel: bar, parking (fee)* 💳*AE, DC, MC, V.*

$–$$ **El Ancla.** With yellow-and-white paintwork, wrought-iron balconies, and wooden shutters, El Ancla's architecture is classic Jerez. The hotel doubles as a popular bar, which is good for atmosphere but means it can be noisy at night. Rooms are plainly furnished but comfortable. The underground parking lot across the street is a bonus. ✉*Pl. del*

Mamelón, 11405 ☎956/321297 📠956/325005 20 rooms In-hotel: parking (fee).

SPORTS

Formula One Grand Prix races—including the Spanish motorcycle Gran Prix on the first weekend in May—are held at Jerez's racetrack, the **Circuito Permanente de Velocidad** (✉*Ctra. Arcos, Km 10* ☎*956/151100* 🌐*www.circuitodejerez.com*).

SHOPPING

Browse for wicker and ceramics along **Calle Corredera** and **Calle Bodegas.** **Duarte** (✉*Calle Lancería 15* ☎*956/342751*) is the best-known saddle shop in town. It sends its beautifully wrought leather all over the world, including even to the British royal family.

ARCOS DE LA FRONTERA

31 km (19 mi) east of Jerez.

★ Its narrow and steep cobblestone streets, whitewashed houses, and finely crafted wrought-iron window grilles make Arcos the quintessential Andalusian *pueblo blanco* (white village). Make your way to the main square, the Plaza de España, the highest point in the village; one side of the square is open, and a balcony at the edge of the cliff offers views of the Guadalete Valley. On the opposite end is the church of **Santa María de la Asunción,** a fascinating blend of architectural styles: Romanesque, Gothic, and Mudejar, with a plateresque doorway, a Renaissance retablo, and a 17th-century baroque choir. The *ayuntamiento* (town hall) stands at the foot of the old castle walls on the northern side of the square; across from here is the Casa del Corregidor, onetime residence of the governor and now a parador. Arcos is the most western of the 19 pueblos blancos, whitewashed towns dotted around the Sierra de Cádiz.

WHERE TO STAY & EAT

$$–$$$ ✕ **El Convento.** With tables set around a graceful Andalusian patio, this rustic-style restaurant (owned by but separate from the hotel on Calle Maldonado) is known for its fine regional cooking. The *sopa de tagarninas* (wild asparagus soup) is one of the town treasures, as are the *garbanzos con tomillo* (chickpeas with thyme) and the *abajado* (wild rabbit or lamb stew). ✉*Calle Marqués de Torresoto 7* ☎*956/703222* 💳*AE, DC, MC, V* ⊗*Closed Jan.*

$$$ ★ ✕🏨 **Parador Casa del Corregidor.** Expect a spectacular view from the terrace—the parador clings to the cliff side, overlooking the rolling valley of the Guadalete River. Public rooms include a popular bar and restaurant that opens onto the terrace, and an enclosed patio. Spacious guest rooms are furnished with dark Castilian furniture, *esparto* (reed) rugs, and abundant tiles. The best are rooms 15–18, which overlook the valley. At the restaurant, try a local dish such as *berenjenas arcenses* (spicy eggplant with ham and chorizo) or sample 10 regional specialties with the *menú degustacíon* (tasting menu; €25). ✉*Pl. del Cabildo, 11630* ☎*956/700500* 📠*956/701116* 🌐*www.parador.es* *24 rooms*

In-room: dial-up, Wi-Fi. In-hotel: restaurant, bar, public Wi-Fi, public Internet *AE, DC, MC, V.*

$$ **El Convento.** Perched atop the cliff behind the town parador, this tiny hotel (a former convent) shares the same amazing view, though the rooms are much smaller—and cheaper. Some rooms have balconies, and there's a large rooftop terrace on the edge of the cliff. *Calle Maldonado 2, 11630* *956/702333* *957/704128* *www.webdearcos.com/elconvento* *11 rooms* *In-hotel: restaurant* *AE, DC, MC, V* *Closed Jan.*

$$ Fodor's Choice ★ **La Casa Grande.** Built in 1729, this extraordinary 18th-century mansion encircles a lushly vegetated central patio and is perched on the edge of the 400-foot cliff to which Arcos de la Frontera clings. Each room has been restored by Catalan owners Elena Posa and Ferran Grau. The artwork, the casually elegant design of the living quarters, and inventive bathrooms are all a delight. The breakfast terrace allows you to look down on falcons circling hundreds of feet above the riverbed below. The rooftop rooms, in El Palomar (The Pigeon Roost) and El Soberao (The Attic), are the best. *C. Maldonado 10, 11630* *956/703930* *956/703930* *www.lacasagrande.net* *5 rooms, 2 suites* *In-room: Wi-Fi. In-hotel: breakfast terrace, no elevator.* *AE, DC, MC, V* *BP.*

$–$$ **Real de Veas.** This tastefully converted 19th-century town house is home to this gem of a hotel. Rooms are set around a central glass-covered patio and are decorated in neutral tones agreeably coupled with rustic furniture. The marble-clad bathrooms have all the extras, including whirlpool baths and hair dryers. The congenial Spanish owners also dish up a more-generous-than-most breakfast, which includes cheese and cold cuts. *C. Corredera 12, 11630* *956/717370* *956/717269* *www.hotelrealdeveas.com* *12 rooms* *In-room: dial-up. In-hotel: restaurant* *MC, V* *BP.*

SANLÚCAR DE BARRAMEDA

45 *24 km (15 mi) northwest of Jerez.*

Columbus sailed from this harbor on his third voyage to the Americas, in 1498. Twenty years later, Magellan began his circumnavigation of the globe from here. Today this fishing town has a crumbling charm and is best known for its *langostinos* (jumbo shrimp) and Manzanilla, an exceptionally dry sherry. The most popular restaurants are in the **Bajo de Guía** neighborhood, on the banks of the Guadalquivir. Here, too, is a visitor center for Doñana National Park.

Boat trips can take you up the river, stopping at various points in the park; the *Real Fernando*, with bar and café, does a four-hour cruise up the Guadalquivir to the Coto de Doñana. *Bajo de Guía, Sanlúcar de Barrameda* *956/363813* *www.visitasdonana.com* *€15.50* *Cruises Apr., May, and Oct., daily at 10 AM and 4 PM; Nov.–Mar., daily at 10 AM; June–Sept., daily at 10 AM and 5 PM.*

WHERE TO STAY & EAT

$\$\$–\$\$\$ **Casa Bigote.** Colorful and informal, this spot on the beach is known for its fried *acedias* (a type of small sole) and langostinos, which come from these very waters. The seafood paella is also catch-of-the-day fresh. Reservations are essential in summer. *Bajo de Guía 956/362696 AE, DC, MC, V Closed Sun. and Nov.*

$\$\$–\$\$\$ **Mirador de Doñana.** This Bajo de Guía landmark overlooking the water serves delicious *chocos* (crayfish), shrimp, and the signature dish *mi barca mirador* (white fish in a tomato sauce). The dining area overlooks the large, busy tapas bar. *Bajo de Guía 956/364205 MC, V Closed Jan.*

$–$$ **Casa Balbino.** After the sunset at Bajo de Guía Beach, the serious tapas and tippling begins in the Plaza del Cabildo, Sanlúcar's party nerve center. Balbino is the best of these taverns—though the *patatas aliñá* (potatoes dressed in an olive oil vinaigrette) at nearby Bar Barbiana are noteworthy as well. *Pl. del Cabildo 14 956/362647 AE, DC, MC, V Closed Jan.*

$–$$ **Los Helechos.** Named for the ferns *(los helechos)* that dominate the patio and entryway, this breezy place with a lovely rooftop terrace has the distinct advantage of being out of earshot but within stumbling distance of the Plaza del Cabildo. *Pl. Madre de Dios 9, 11540 956/361349 956/369650 www.hotelloshelechos.com 56 rooms In-hotel: restaurant, bar, parking (fee) AE, DC, MC, V.*

PUERTO DE SANTA MARÍA

46 *12 km (7 mi) southwest of Jerez, 17 km (11 mi) north of Cádiz.*

This attractive, if somewhat dilapidated, little fishing port on the northern shores of the Bay of Cádiz, with lovely beaches nearby, has white houses with peeling facades and vast green grilles covering the doors and windows. The town is dominated by the Terry and Osborne sherry and brandy bodegas. Columbus once lived in a house on the square that bears his name (Cristóbal Colón), and Washington Irving spent the autumn of 1828 at Calle Palacios 57. The marisco bars along the Ribera del Marisco (Seafood Way) are Puerto de Santa María's current claim to fame. Casa Luis, Romerijo, La Guachi, and Paco Ceballos are among the most popular, along with Er Beti, at Misericordia 7. The tourist office has a list of six tapas routes that take in 39 tapas bars.

The **Castillo de San Marcos** was built in the 13th century on the site of a mosque. Created by Alfonso X, it was later home to the Duke of Medinaceli. Among the guests were Christopher Columbus—who tried unsuccessfully to persuade the duke to finance his voyage west—and Juan de la Cosa, who, within these walls, drew up the first map ever to include the Americas. The red lettering on the walls is a 19th-century addition. *Pl. del Castillo 965/851751 €5, free Tues. Tues., Thurs., and Sat. 10–2.*

This stunning neo-Mudejar **Plaza de Toros** was built in 1880 thanks to a donation from the winemaker Thomas Osborne. It originally had seating for exactly 12,816 people, the population of Puerto at that time.

✉Los Moros 🎫Free ⏲Apr.–Oct., Thurs.–Tues. 11–1:30 and 6–7:30; Nov.–Mar., Thurs.–Tues. 11–1:30 and 5:30–7. Closed bullfight days plus 1 day before and after each bullfight.

WHERE TO STAY & EAT

$$–$$$ ✕**El Faro de El Puerto.** In a villa outside town, the "Lighthouse in the Port" is run by the same family that established the classic El Faro in Cádiz. Like its predecessor, it serves excellent fish; also available are such delicacies as veal rolls filled with foie gras in a sweet sherry sauce and several vegetarian options. *✉Ctra. Fuentebravia–Rota, Km 0.5 ☎956/858003 or 956/870952 🌐www.elfarodelpuerto.com 💳AE, DC, MC, V ⏲No dinner Sun. Sept.–July.*

$$$–$$$$ ★ **Monasterio San Miguel.** Dating from 1733, this monastery is a few blocks from the harbor. There's nothing spartan about the former cells; they're now air-conditioned rooms with all the trappings. The restaurant is in a large, vaulted hall (formerly the nuns' laundry); the baroque church is now a concert hall; and the cloister's gardens provide a peaceful refuge. Beam ceilings, polished marble floors, and huge brass lamps enhance the 18th-century feel. If you're traveling out of season, check the Web site for discounts. *✉C. Virgen de los Milagros 27, 11500 ☎956/540440 📠956/542604 🌐www.jale.com 139 rooms, 11 suites In-room: Wi-Fi. In-hotel: restaurant, bar, pool, public Wi-Fi, public Internet, parking (fee) 💳AE, DC, MC, V.*

CÁDIZ

47 ★ *32 km (20 mi) southwest of Jerez, 149 km (93 mi) southwest of Seville.*

Surrounded by the Atlantic Ocean on three sides, Cádiz was founded as Gadir by Phoenician traders in 1100 BC and claims to be the oldest continuously inhabited city in the Western world. Hannibal lived in Cádiz for a time, Julius Caesar first held public office here, and Columbus set out from here on his second voyage, after which the city became the home base of the Spanish fleet. In the 18th century, when the Guadalquivir silted up, Cádiz monopolized New World trade and became the wealthiest port in Western Europe. Most of its buildings—including the cathedral, built in part with gold and silver from the New World—date from this period. The old city is African in appearance and immensely intriguing—a cluster of narrow streets opening onto charming small squares. The golden cupola of the cathedral looms above low white houses, and the whole place has a slightly dilapidated air. Spaniards flock here in February to revel in the carnival celebrations, but in general it's not very touristy.

WHAT TO SEE

Begin your explorations in the Plaza de Mina, a large, leafy square with palm trees and plenty of benches. The tourist office is in the northwestern corner. On the square's western flank, the ornamental facade of the **Colegio de Arquitectos** (College of Architects) is especially beautiful.

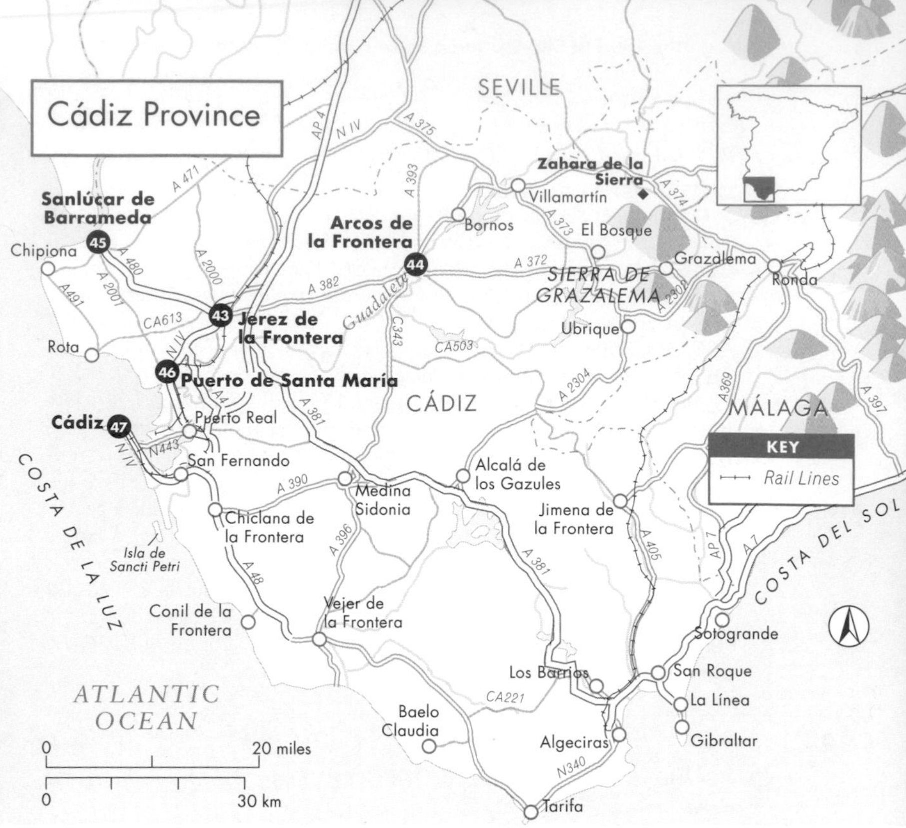

On the east side of the Plaza de Mina, is the **Museo de Cádiz** (Provincial Museum). Notable pieces include works by Murillo and Alonso Cano as well as the *Four Evangelists* and set of saints by Zurbarán, which have much in common with his masterpieces at Guadalupe, in Extremadura. The archaeological section contains Phoenician sarcophagi from the time of this ancient city's birth. ✉ *Pl. de Mina* ☎ *956/212281* 🎟 *€1.50, free for EU citizens* ⏲ *Tues. 2:30–8, Wed.–Sat. 9–8, Sun. 9–2.*

A few blocks east of the Plaza de Mina, next door to the Iglesia del Rosario, is the **Oratorio de la Santa Cueva,** an oval 18th-century chapel with three frescoes by Goya. ✉ *C. Rosario 10* ☎ *956/222262* 🎟 *€2.50* ⏲ *Tues.–Fri. 10–1 and 4:30–7:30, weekends 10–1.*

Farther up Calle San José from the Plaza de la Mina is the **Oratorio de San Felipe Neri.** Spain's first liberal constitution was declared at this church in 1812, and here the Cortes (Parliament) of Cádiz met when the rest of Spain was subjected to the rule of Napoléon's brother, Joseph Bonaparte (more popularly known as Pepe Botella, for his love of the bottle). On the main altar is an *Immaculate Conception* by Murillo, the great Sevillian artist who in 1682 fell to his death from a scaffold while working on his *Mystic Marriage of St. Catherine* in Cádiz's Chapel of Santa Catalina. ✉*Calle Santa Inés 38* ☎*956/211612* 🎟*€2.50* ⏲*Mon.–Sat. 10–1:30.*

Next door to the Oratorio de San Felipe Neri, the small but pleasant **Museo de las Cortes** has a 19th-century mural depicting the establishment of the Constitution of 1812. Its real showpiece, however, is a 1779 ivory-and-mahogany model of Cádiz, with all of the city's streets and buildings in minute detail, looking much as they do now. ✉*Santa Inés 9* ☎*956/221788* 🎟*Free* ⏲*Oct.–May, Tues.–Fri. 9–1 and 4–7, weekends 9–1; June–Sept., Tues.–Fri. 9–1 and 5–8, weekends 9–1.*

Four blocks west of Santa Inés is the Plaza Manuel de Falla, overlooked by an amazing neo-Mudejar redbrick building, the **Gran Teatro Manuel de Falla.** The classic interior is impressive as well; try to attend a performance. ✉*Pl. Manuel de Falla* ☎*956/220828.*

Backtrack along Calle Sacramento toward the city center to **Torre Tavira.** At 150 feet, this tower, attached to an 18th-century palace that's now a conservatory of music, is the highest point in the old city. More than a hundred such watchtowers were used by Cádiz ship owners to spot their arriving fleets. A camera obscura gives a good overview of the city and its monuments; the last show is a half hour before closing time. ✉*Calle Marqués del Real Tesoro 10* ☎*956/212910* 🎟*€4* ⏲*Mid-June–mid-Sept., daily 10–8; mid-Sept.–mid-June, daily 10–6.*

Five blocks southeast of the Torre Tavira are the gold dome and baroque facade of Cádiz's **cathedral,** begun in 1722, when the city was at the height of its power. The Cádiz-born composer Manuel de Falla, who died in 1946 at the age of 70, is buried in the **crypt.** The cathedral **museum,** on Calle Acero, displays gold, silver, and jewels from the New World, as well as Enrique de Arfe's processional cross, which is carried in the annual Corpus Christi parades. The cathedral is known as the New Cathedral because it supplanted the original 13th-century structure next door, which was destroyed by the British in 1592, rebuilt, and renamed the church of **Santa Cruz** when the New Cathedral came along. The entrance price includes the crypt, museum, and church of Santa Cruz. ✉*Pl. Catedral* ☎*956/259812* 🎟*€4* ⏲*Mass Sun. at noon; museum Tues.–Fri. 10–2 and 4:30–7:30, Sat. 10–1.*

Next door to the church of Santa Cruz are the remains of a 1st-century BC **Roman theater** (✉*Campo del Sur s/n, Barrio del Pópulo* 🎟*Free* ⏲*Daily 10–2*); it is still under excavation.

The impressive *ayuntamiento (city hall)* (✉*Pl. de San Juan de Dios s/n*) overlooks the Plaza San Juan de Diós, one of Cádiz's liveliest hubs. The building is attractively illuminated at night. The **Plaza San Francisco,** near the ayuntamiento, is a pretty square surrounded by white-and-yellow houses and filled with orange trees and elegant street lamps. It's especially lively during the evening *paseo* (promenade).

WHERE TO STAY & EAT

$$–$$$$ Fodor'sChoice ★ ✕**El Faro.** This famous fishing-quarter restaurant is deservedly known as the best in the province. Outside, it's one of many low-rise, white houses with bright-blue flowerpots; inside it's warm and inviting, with

half-tile walls, glass lanterns, oil paintings, and photos of old Cádiz. Fish dominates the menu, but alternatives include *cebón al queso de cabrales* (venison in blue-cheese sauce). If you don't want to go for the full splurge, there's an excellent tapas bar as well. ✉ *Calle San Felix 15* ☎ *956/211068* ▭ *AE, DC, MC, V.*

$$–$$$ ★ ✕ **El Ventorrillo del Chato.** Standing on its own on the sandy isthmus connecting Cádiz to the mainland, this former inn was founded in 1780 by a man ironically nicknamed "El Chato" (pug-nosed) for his prominent proboscis. Run by a scion of El Faro's Gonzalo Córdoba, the restaurant serves tasty regional specialties in charming Andalusian surroundings. Seafood is a favorite, but meat, stews, and rice dishes are also well represented on the menu, and the wine list is very good. ✉ *Vía Augusta Julia s/n* ☎ *956/250025* ▭ *AE, DC, MC, V* ⊗ *Closed Sun.*

$–$$ ✕ **Casa Manteca.** Cádiz's most quintessentially Andalusian tavern is just down the street from El Faro restaurant and a little deeper into the La Viña barrio (named for the vineyard that once grew here). *Chacina* (Iberian ham or sausage) served on waxed paper and Manzanilla (sherry from Sanlúcar de Barrameda) are standard fare at this low wooden counter that has served bullfighters and flamenco singers, as well as dignitaries from around the world since 1953. ✉ *Corralón de los Carros 66* ☎ *956/213603* ▭ *AE, DC, MC, V* ⊗ *Closed Mon. No lunch Sun.*

$$$ **Parador de Cádiz.** Cádiz's modern Parador Atlántico has a privileged position on the headland overlooking the bay and is the only hotel in its class in the old part of Cádiz. The spacious indoor public rooms have gleaming marble floors, and tables and chairs surround a fountain on the small patio. The cheerful, bright-green bar, decorated with ceramic tiles and bullfighting posters, is a popular meeting place for Cádiz society. Most rooms have small balconies facing the sea. ✉ *Av. Duque de Nájera 9, 11002* ☎ *956/226905* 🖷 *956/214582* ⊕ *www.parador.es* *143 rooms, 6 suites* *In-room: dial-up, Wi-Fi. In-hotel: restaurant, bar, pool, gym, parking (no fee), some pets allowed* ▭ *AE, DC, MC, V* *BP.*

$$ **Bahía.** Just off the bustling Plaza de San Juan de Dios, on a tree-lined pedestrian street, this is a budget winner. The beds are firm, and most rooms have small balconies. The lack of dining room is compensated for by the variety and proximity of bars and restaurants. ✉ *Calle Plocia 5, 11002* ☎ *956/259061* 🖷 *956/254208* *21 rooms* ▭ *MC, V.*

NIGHTLIFE & THE ARTS

The **Gran Teatro Manuel de Falla** (✉ *Pl. Manuel de Falla* ☎ *956/220828*) is Cádiz's cultural hub; the tourist office has performance schedules.

CÓRDOBA

166 km (103 mi) northwest of Granada, 407 km (250 mi) southwest of Madrid, 143 km (86 mi) northeast of Seville.

Once a medieval city famed for the peaceful and prosperous coexistence of its three religious cultures—Islamic, Jewish, and Christian—Córdoba is a perfect analogue for the cultural history of the Iberian Peninsula. Strategically located on the north bank of the Guadalquivir

River, Córdoba was the Roman and Moorish capital of Spain, and its old quarter, clustered around its famous mosque (Mezquita), remains one of the country's grandest and yet most intimate examples of its Moorish heritage.

The Romans invaded in 206 BC, later making it the capital of Rome's section of Spain. Nearly 800 years later, the Visigoth king Leovigildus took control. The tribe was soon supplanted by the Moors, whose emirs and caliphs held court here from the 8th century to the early 11th century. At that point Córdoba was one of the greatest centers of art, culture, and learning in the Western world; one of its libraries had a staggering 400,000 volumes. Moors, Christians, and Jews lived together in harmony within Córdoba's walls. Chroniclers of the day put the city's population at around a million, making it the largest city in Europe, though historians believe the real figure was closer to half a million (there are fewer than 300,000 today). In that era, it was considered second in importance only to Constantinople. However, in 1009 Prince Muhammad II and Omeyan led a rebellion that broke up the Caliphate, leading to power flowing to separate Moorish kingdoms.

Córdoba remained in Moorish hands until it was conquered by King Ferdinand in 1236 and repopulated with people from the north of Spain. Later the Catholic Monarchs used the city as a base from which to plan the conquest of Granada. In Columbus's time, the Guadalquivir was navigable as far upstream as Córdoba, and great galleons sailed its waters. Today, the river's muddy water and marshy banks evoke little of Córdoba's glorious past, but the city's bridge—of Roman origin, though much restored by the Arabs and successive generations—and an old Arab waterwheel recall a far grander era.

Córdoba today, with its modest population of just over 300,000, offers a cultural depth and intensity—a direct legacy from the great emirs, caliphs, philosophers, physicians, poets, and engineers of the days of the caliphate—that far outstrips the city's current commercial and political power. The city's artistic and historical treasures begin with the *mezquita-catedral* (mosque-cathedral), as it is ever-more-frequently called, and continue through the winding, whitewashed streets of the Judería (the medieval Jewish quarter); the jasmine-, geranium-, and orange blossom–filled patios; the Renaissance palaces; and the two dozen churches, convents, and hermitages, nearly all of them Mudéjar (built by Moorish artisans) built directly over former mosques.

EXPLORING CÓRDOBA

Córdoba is a very manageable city. It is densely packed with beautiful patios, doorways, streets, rooftops, windows bursting with flowers, and twisting alleyways with surprises around every corner. In general, neighborhoods are known by the parish churches at their center. The main city subdivisions used in this book are the **Judería,** including the Mezquita, the San Basilio neighborhood behind the Jardines de los Reales Alcázares, and the Torre de la Calahorra across the river; the **Plaza de la Corredera,** a historic gathering place for everything from horse

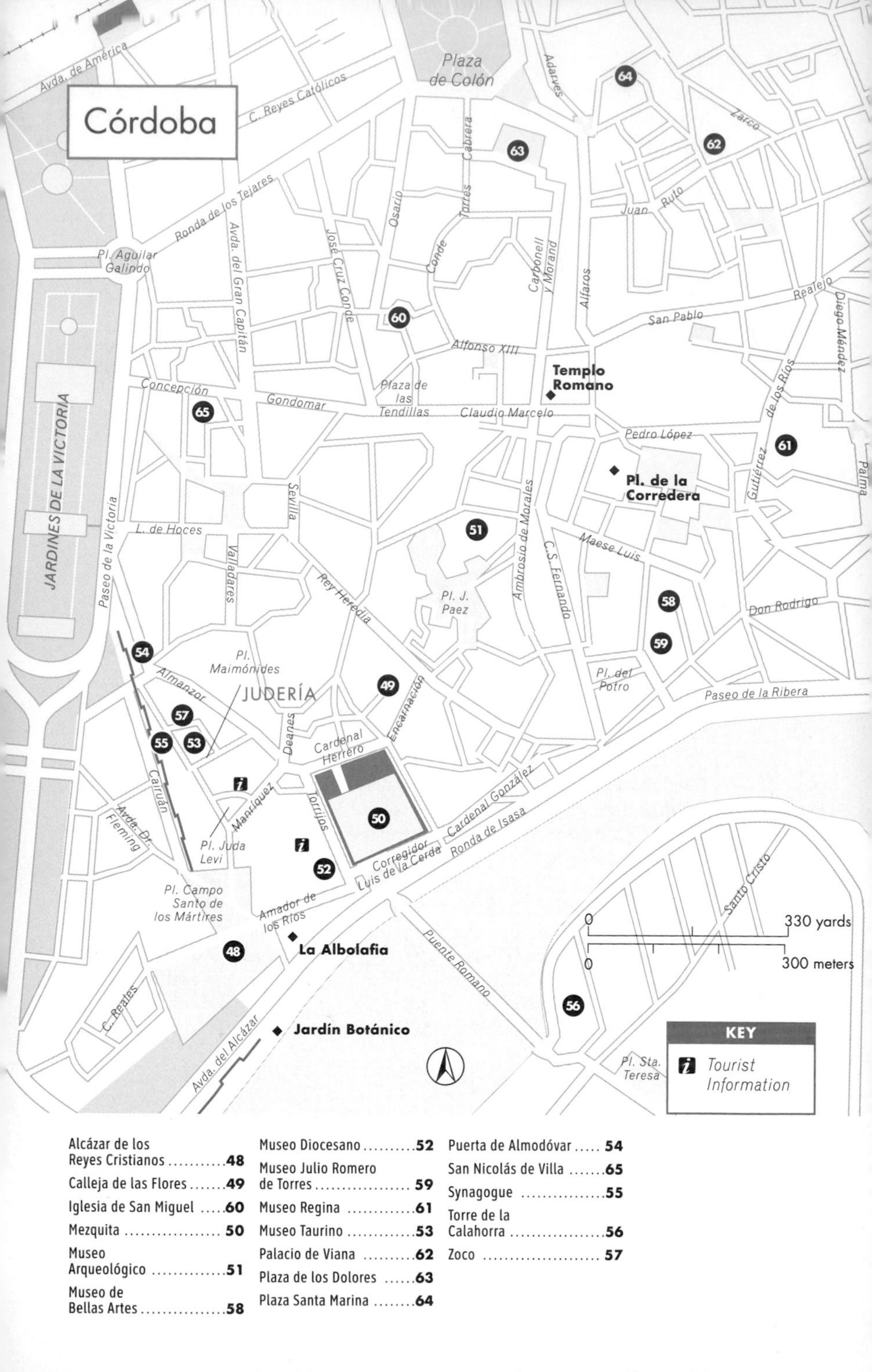
Córdoba
Avda. de América
C. Reyes Católicos
Plaza de Colón
Adarves
Zarco
Ronda de los Tejares
Pl. Aguilar Galindo
Avda. del Gran Capitán
José Cruz Conde
Osario
Conde
Torres Cabrera
Carbonell y Morand
Alfaros
Juan Rufo
Realejo
Diego Méndez
San Pablo
Alfonso XIII
Templo Romano
Concepción
Gondomar
Plaza de las Tendillas
Claudio Marcelo
de los Ríos
Gutiérrez
Pedro López
Pl. de la Corredera
Palma
JARDINES DE LA VICTORIA
Paseo de la Victoria
L. de Hoces
Sevilla
Valladares
Ambrosio de Morales
C.S. Fernando
Maese Luis
Rey Heredia
Pl. J. Paez
Don Rodrigo
Pl. Maimónides
Almanzor
JUDERÍA
Deanes
Encarnación
Pl. del Potro
Paseo de la Ribera
Cardenal Herrero
Manríquez
Torrijos
Cairuán
Avda. Dr. Fleming
Pl. Juda Levi
Cardenal González
Ronda de Isasa
Corregidor Luis de la Cerda
Pl. Campo Santo de los Mártires
Amador de los Ríos
La Albolafia
Santo Cristo
Puente Romano
0
330 yards
0
300 meters
C. Reales
Avda. del Alcázar
Jardín Botánico
Pl. Sta. Teresa
KEY
Tourist Information
48
49
50
51
52
53
54
55
56
57
58
59
60
61
62
63
64
65
Alcázar de los Reyes Cristianos 48
Calleja de las Flores 49
Iglesia de San Miguel 60
Mezquita 50
Museo Arqueológico 51
Museo de Bellas Artes 58
Museo Diocesano 52
Museo Julio Romero de Torres 59
Museo Regina 61
Museo Taurino 53
Palacio de Viana 62
Plaza de los Dolores 63
Plaza Santa Marina 64
Puerta de Almodóvar 54
San Nicolás de Villa 65
Synagogue 55
Torre de la Calahorra 56
Zoco 57

races to bullfights and a neighborhood that, for the purposes of this book, stretches from the Paseo de la Ribera along the Guadalquivir, through the artistically important Plaza del Potro, past the Plaza de la Corredera to the ruins of the Roman Temple; and the **Centro,** from the area around Plaza de las Tendillas to the Iglesia de Santa Marina and the Torre de la Malmuerta. Incidentally, this *centro comercial* (commercial center) is much more than a succession of shops and stores. The town's real life, the everyday hustle and bustle, takes place here, and the general ambience is very different from that of the tourist center around the Mezquita. Some of the city's finest Mudéjar churches and best taverns, as well as the Palacio de los Marqueses de Viana, are in this pivotal part of town well back from the Guadalquivir waterfront.

CÓRDOBA BY BIKE

Never designed to support modern motor traffic, Cordoba's medieval layout is ideal for bicycles. **Cordoba La Llana en Bici** (✉ *Calle Lucano 20* ☎ *639/425884* 🌐 *www.cordobaenbici.com*) offers a variety of tours including half-day excursions, gastronomical tours, rides out to the ruins of the Medina-Azahara palace 8 km (5 mi) outside town, or, farther afield in the Sierra Morena, cycling tours of the Cardeña–Montoro and Hornachuelos nature parks.

Some of the most characteristic and rewarding places to explore in Córdoba are the parish churches and the taverns that inevitably accompany them. The *iglesias fernandinas* (so-called for their construction after Saint-King Fernando III's conquest of Córdoba) are nearly always built over mosques with stunning horseshoe arch doorways and Mudéjar towers. Taverns tended to spring up around these populous hubs of city life. Examples are the Taberna de San Miguel (aka Casa el Pisto) next to the church of the same name, and the Bar Santa Marina (aka Casa Obispo) next to the Santa Marina Church. Most neighborhoods are built around their parish churches and have a well-known tavern, if not several, nearby, providing an excellent way to explore neighborhoods, see churches, and taste *finos* (montilla-moriles sherry) and *tentempies* (tapas –literally, "keep you on your feet").

■ TIP→ Córdoba's council authorities and private institutions frequently change the hours of the city's sights; before visiting an attraction, confirm hours with the tourist office or the sight itself.

WHAT TO SEE

48 **Alcázar de los Reyes Cristianos** *(Fortress of the Christian Monarchs).* Built by Alfonso XI in 1328, the Alcázar is a Mudejar-style palace with splendid gardens. (The original Moorish Alcázar stood beside the Mezquita, on the site of the present Bishop's Palace.) This is where, in the 15th century, the Catholic Monarchs held court and launched their conquest of Granada. Boabdil was imprisoned here in 1483, and for nearly 300 years the Alcázar served as the Inquisition's base. The most important sights here are the Hall of the Mosaics and a Roman stone sacrophagus from the 2nd or 3rd century. ✉ *Pl. Campo Santo de los Mártires, Judería* ☎ *957/420151* 🎫 *€4, free Fri.* ⏲ *May–Sept.,*

Tues.–Sat. 10–2 and 6–8, Sun. 9:30–3; Oct.–Apr., Tues.–Sat. 10–2 and 4:30–6:30, Sun. 9:30–2:30.

49 **Calleja de las Flores.** You'd be hard pressed to find prettier patios than those along this tiny street, a few yards off the northeastern corner of the Mezquita. Patios, many with ceramics, foliage, and iron grilles, are key to Córdoba's architecture, at least in the old quarter, where life is lived behind sturdy white walls—a legacy of the Moors, who honored both the sanctity of the home and the need to shut out the fierce summer sun. Between the second and the third week of May, right after the early May **Cruces de Mayo,** (Crosses of May) competition when neighborhoods compete at setting up elaborate crosses decorated with flowers and plants, Córdoba throws a **Patio Festival,** during which private patios are filled with flowers, opened to the public, and judged in a municipal competition. Córdoba's council publishes a map with an itinerary of the best patios in town—note that most are open only in the late afternoon during the week and all day on weekends.

OFF THE BEATEN PATH

Jardín Botánico *(Botanical Garden)*. Across from Córdoba's modest zoo is its modern botanical garden, with outdoor spaces—including a section devoted to aromatic herbs—as well as greenhouses full of plants from South America and the Canary Islands. The Museo de Etnobotánica explores the way in which humans interact with the plant world. ✉ *Av. de Linneo s/n, Parque Zoológico* ☎ *957/200018* 🎫 *€2* ⏲ *Apr.–Oct., Tues.–Sun. 10–2:30 and 5:30–7:30; Nov.–Mar., Tues.–Sat. 10:30–2:30 and 4:30–6:30, Sun. 10:30–6:30.*

50 Fodor's Choice ★ **Mezquita** *(Mosque)*. Built between the 8th and 10th centuries, Córdoba's mosque is one of the earliest and most transportingly beautiful examples of Spanish Muslim architecture. The plain, crenellated walls of the outside do little to prepare you for the sublime beauty of the interior. As you enter through the **Puerta de las Palmas** (Door of the Palms), some 850 columns rise before you in a forest of jasper, marble, granite, and onyx. The pillars are topped by ornate capitals taken from the Visigothic church that was razed to make way for the mosque. Crowning these, red-and-white-stripe arches curve away into the dimness. The ceiling is carved of delicately tinted cedar. The Mezquita has served as a cathedral since 1236, but its origins as a mosque are clear. Built in four stages, it was founded in 785 by Abd ar-Rahman I (756–88) on a site he bought from the Visigoth Christians. He pulled down their church and replaced it with a mosque, one-third the size of the present one, into which he incorporated marble pillars from earlier Roman and Visigothic shrines. Under Abd ar-Rahman II (822–52), the Mezquita held an original copy of the Koran and a bone from the arm of the prophet Mohammed and became a Muslim pilgrimage site second only to Mecca in importance.

Al Hakam II (961–76) built the beautiful **Mihrab** (prayer niche), the Mezquita's greatest jewel. Make your way over to the **Qiblah,** the south-facing wall in which this sacred prayer niche was hollowed out. (Muslim law decrees that a Mihrab face east, toward Mecca, and that worshippers do likewise when they pray. Because of an error in calculation, the Mihrab here faces more south than east. Al Hakam II spent hours agonizing over a means of correcting such a serious mistake, but he was persuaded by architects to let it be.) In front of the Mihrab is the **Maksoureh,** a kind of anteroom for the caliph and his court; its mosaics and plasterwork make it a masterpiece of Islamic art. A last addition to the mosque as such, the Maksoureh was completed around 987 by Al Mansur, who more than doubled its size.

After the Reconquest, the Christians left the Mezquita largely undisturbed, dedicating it to the Virgin Mary and using it as a place of Christian worship. The clerics did erect a wall closing off the mosque from its courtyard, which helped dim the interior and thus separate the house of worship from the world outside. In the 13th century, Christians had the **Capilla de Villaviciosa** built by Moorish craftsmen, its Mudejar architecture blending with the lines of the mosque. Not so the heavy, incongruous baroque structure of the **cathedral,** sanctioned in the very heart of the mosque by Charles V in the 1520s. To the emperor's credit, he was supposedly horrified when he came to inspect the new construction, exclaiming to the architects, "To build something ordinary, you have destroyed something that was unique in the world" (not that this sentiment stopped him from tampering with the Alhambra to build his Palacio Carlos V). Rest up and reflect in the **Patio de los Naranjos** (Orange Court), perfumed in springtime by orange blossoms. The **Puerta del Perdón** (Gate of Forgiveness), so named because debtors were forgiven here on feast days, is on the north wall of the Orange Court. It's the formal entrance to the mosque. The **Virgen de los Faroles** (Virgin of the Lanterns), a small statue in a niche on the outside wall of the mosque along the north side on Cardenal Herrero, is behind a lantern-hung grille, rather like a lady awaiting a serenade. The **Torre del Alminar,** the minaret once used to summon Moorish faithful to prayer, has a baroque belfry.

Wheelchairs are available, and audio guides can be rented for €3 Monday–Saturday. ✉ *Calle Torrijos and Cardenal Herrero, Judería* ☎ *957/470512* 🎫 *€8* ⏲ *Jan. and Dec., daily 10–5:30; Feb. and Nov., daily 10–6; Mar. and July–Oct., daily 10–7; Apr.–June, daily 10–7:30.*

NEED A BREAK?

The lively Plaza Juda Levi, surrounded by a maze of narrow streets and squares, lies at the heart of the Judería and makes a great spot for indulging in a little people-watching. Sit outside here with a drink or, better still, an ice cream from Helados Juda Levi.

51 **Museo Arqueológico.** In the heart of the old quarter, the Museum of Archaeology has finds from Córdoba's varied cultural past. The ground floor has ancient Iberian statues, and Roman statues, mosaics, and artifacts; the upper floor is devoted to Moorish art. By chance, the ruins of a Roman theater were discovered right next to the museum in 2000—have a look from the window just inside the entrance. The alleys and steps along Altos de Santa Ana make for great wandering. ✉ *Pl. Jerónimo Paez, Judería* ☎ *957/474011* 🎫 *€1.50, free for EU citizens* ⏲ *Tues. 2:30–8:30, Wed.–Sat. 9–8:30, Sun. 9–2:30.*

52 **Museo Diocesano.** Housed in the former Bishop's Palace, facing the mosque, the Diocesan Museum is devoted to religious art, with illustrated prayer books, tapestries, paintings (including some Julio Romero de Torres canvases), and sculpture. The medieval wood sculptures are the museum's finest treasures. *Note that the museum was closed in 2007. At the time of this writing it was due to open soon.* ✉ *Calle Torrijos 12, Judería* ☎ *957/496085* 🎫 *€2, free with ticket for Mezquita* ⏲ *June–Sept., weekdays 9:30–3, Sat. 9:30–1:30; Oct.–Mar., weekdays 9:30–1:30 and 3:30–5:30, Sat. 9:30–1:30.*

53 **Museo Taurino** (Museum of Bullfighting). Two adjoining mansions on the Plaza Maimónides (or Plaza de las Bulas) house this museum. It's worth a visit, as much for the chance to see a restored mansion as for the posters, Art Nouveau paintings, bull's heads, suits of lights (bullfighter outfits), and memorabilia of famous Córdoban bullfighters including the most famous of all, Manolete. To the surprise of the nation, Manolete, who was considered immortal, was killed by a bull in the ring at Linares in 1947. ✉ *Pl. Maimónides, Judería* ☎ *957/201056* 🎫 *€3, free Fri.* ⏲ *Tues.–Sat. 10–2 and 6–8 (4:30–6:30 Oct.–May), Sun. 9:30–3.*

54 **Puerta de Almodóvar.** Outside this old Moorish gate at the northern entrance of the Judería is a statue of **Seneca,** the Córdoban-born philosopher who rose to prominence in Nero's court in Rome and was forced to commit suicide at his emperor's command. The gate stands at the top of the narrow and colorful Calle San Felipe.

55 **Synagogue.** The only Jewish temple in Andalusia to survive the expulsion and inquisition of the Jews in 1492, Córdoba's synagogue is also one of only three ancient synagogues left in all of Spain (the other two are in Toledo). Though it no longer functions as a place of worship, it's a treasured symbol for Spain's modern Jewish communities. The outside is plain, but the inside, measuring 23 feet by 21 feet, contains some exquisite Mudejar stucco tracery. Look for the fine plant motifs and the Hebrew inscription saying that the synagogue was built in 1315. The women's gallery, not open for visits, still stands, and in the east wall is the ark where the sacred scrolls of the Torah were kept. ✉ *C. Judíos, Judería* ☎ *957/202928* 🎫 *€0.30, free for EU citizens* ⏲ *Tues.–Sat. 9:30–2 and 3:30–5:30, Sun. 9:30–1:30.*

56 **Torre de la Calahorra.** The tower on the far side of the Puente Romano (Roman Bridge) was built in 1369 to guard the entrance to Córdoba. It now houses the **Museo Vivo de Al-Andalus** (Museum of Al-Andalus), with films and audiovisual guides (in English) on Córdoba's history. Climb the narrow staircase to the top of the tower for the view of the Roman bridge and city on the other side of the Guadalquivir. *The museum was closed at the time of this writing but was due to open by press time.* ✉ *Av. de la Confederación, Sector Sur* ☎ *957/293929* 🎫 *€5, €5.50 with audiovisual show* ⏲ *May–Sept., daily 10–2 and 5:30–8:30 with audiovisual shows at 10:30, 11:30, noon, 5, 6, and 7; Oct.–Apr., daily 10–6 with audiovisual shows at 11, noon, 1, 3, and 4.*

57 **Zoco.** *Zoco* is the Spanish word for the Arab souk, the onetime function of this courtyard near the synagogue. It now is the site of a daily crafts

market, where you can see artisans at work, and evening flamenco in summer. ✉*Calle Judíos 5, Judería* ☎*957/204033* 🎫*Free.*

NEED A BREAK?

Wander over to the Plaza de las Tendillas, which is halfway between the Mezquita and Plaza Colón. The terraces of the Café Boston and Café Siena are both enjoyable places to relax with a coffee when the weather is warm.

58 **Museo de Bellas Artes.** Hard to miss because of its deep-pink facade, Córdoba's Museum of Fine Arts, in a courtyard just off the Plaza del Potro, belongs to a former Hospital de la Caridad (Charity Hospice). It was founded by Ferdinand and Isabella, who twice received Columbus here. The collection includes paintings by Murillo, Valdés Leal, Zurbarán, Goya, and Sorolla. ✉*Pl. del Potro, 1 San Francisco* ☎*957/473345* 🌐*www.juntadeandalucia.es/cultura/museos/MBACO* 🎫*€1.50, free for EU citizens* ⏲*Tues. 2:30–8:30, Wed.–Sat. 9–8:30, Sun. 9–2:30.*

59 ★ **Museo Julio Romero de Torres.** Across the courtyard from the Museum of Fine Arts, this museum is devoted to the early-20th-century Córdoban artist Julio Romero de Torres (1874–1930), who specialized in surreal and erotic portraits of demure, partially dressed Andalusian temptresses. Romero de Torres was also a flamenco *cantaor* (singer), died at the age of 56, and is one of Córdoba's greatest folk heroes. ✉*Pl. del Potro 1, San Francisco* ☎*957/491909* 🌐*www.museojulioromero.com* 🎫*€4, free Fri.* ⏲*Tues.–Sat. 10–2 and 4:30–6:30, Sun. 9:30–2:30.*

60 ★ **Iglesia de San Miguel.** Complete with Romanesque doors built around Mudéjar horseshoe arches, the San Miguel Church, the square and café terraces around it, and its excellent tavern, Taberna San Miguel-Casa El Pisto, form one of the city's finest combinations of art, history, and gastronomy. ✉*Pl. San Miguel Centro.*

61 ★ **Museo Regina.** You can watch craftsmen at work here creating the delicate silver filigree pieces for which Córdoba is famous. Construction unearthed the Roman and Moorish archaeological remains that are on display on the ground floor. ✉*Pl. Luís Venegas 1, Centro* ☎*957/496889* 🌐*www.museoregina.com* 🎫*€3* ⏲*June–mid-Sept., daily 9–2 and 5:30–9; mid-Sept.–May., daily 10–3 and 5–8.*

62 **Palacio de Viana.** This 17th-century palace is one of Córdoba's most splendid aristocratic homes. Also known as the **Museo de los Patios,** it contains 12 interior patios, each one different; the patios and gardens are planted with cypresses, orange trees, and myrtles. Inside the building are a carriage museum, a library, embossed leather wall hangings, filigree silver, and grand galleries and staircases. As you enter, note that the corner column of the first patio has been removed to allow the entrance of horse-drawn carriages. ✉*Pl. Don Gomé, Centro* ☎*957/496741* 🎫*Patios only €3, patios and interior €6* ⏲*Mid-June–Sept., Mon.–Sat. 9–2; Oct.–Apr., Mon.–Sat. 10–1 and 4–6.*

63 **Plaza de los Dolores.** The 17th-century Convento de Capuchinos surrounds this small square north of Plaza San Miguel. The square is where you feel most deeply the city's languid pace. In its center, a statue

CÓRDOBA FIESTAS

Córdoba parties hard during **Carnival,** on the days leading up to Ash Wednesday, and **Semana Santa** (Holy Week) is always intensely celebrated with dramatic religious processions.

May brings **Las Cruces de Mayo** (The Crosses of May) during the first week of the month, the **Festival de los Patios** (Patio Festival) during the second, and the **Concurso Nacional de Flamenco** (National Flamenco competition) during the second week of May every third year. Córdoba's annual **Feria de Mayo** is the city's main street party, held during the last week of May.

The **International Guitar Festival** brings major artists to Córdoba in early July. Córdoba celebrates **Nuestra Señora de Fuensanta** on the last Sunday in September and the **Romería de San Miguel** (Procession of St. Michael) on September 29.

of **Cristo de los Faroles** (Christ of the Lanterns) stands amid eight lanterns hanging from twisted wrought-iron brackets. ✉*Centro.*

64 **Plaza Santa Marina.** At the edge of the **Barrio de los Toreros,** a quarter where many of Córdoba's famous bullfighters were born and raised, stands a statue of the famous bullfighter Manolete (1917–47) opposite the lovely *fernandina* church of Santa Marina de Aguas Santas (St. Marina of Holy Waters). Not far from here, on the Plaza de la Lagunilla, is a Manolete bust. ✉*Pl. Conde Priego Centro.*

65 **San Nicolás de Villa.** This classically dark Spanish church displays the Mudejar style of Islamic decoration and art forms. Córdoba's well-kept city park, the **Jardínes de la Victoria,** with tile benches and manicured bushes, is a block west of here. ✉*C. San Felipe, Centro.*

WHERE TO EAT

$$$–$$$$ Fodor'sChoice ★ **El Caballo Rojo.** This is one of the most famous traditional restaurants in Andalusia, frequented by royalty and society folk. The interior resembles a cool, leafy Andalusian patio, and the dining room is furnished with stained glass, dark wood, and gleaming marble. The menu mixes traditional specialties, such as *rabo de toro* (oxtail stew) and *salmorejo* (a thick version of gazpacho), with dishes inspired by Córdoba's Moorish and Jewish heritage, such as *alboronia* (a cold salad of stewed vegetables flavored with honey, saffron, and aniseed), *cordero a la miel* (lamb roasted with honey), and *rape mozárabe* (grilled monkfish with Moorish spices). ✉*Calle Cardenal Herrero 28, Judería* ☎*957/475375* 🌐*www.elcaballorojo.com* 💳*AE, DC, MC, V.*

$$$–$$$$ ★ **El Churrasco.** The name suggests grilled meat, but this restaurant in the heart of the Judería serves much more than that. Try tapas such as the *berenjenas crujientes con salmorejo* (crispy fried eggplant slices with thick gazpacho) in the colorful bar. The grilled fish is also supremely fresh, *and* the steak is the best in town. On the inner patio, there's alfresco dining when it's warm outside (covered in winter). ✉*Calle*

Romero 16, Judería ☎*957/290819* 🌐*www.elchurrasco.com* ▭*AE, DC, MC, V* ⊙*Closed Aug.*

$$–$$$$ ✕**Los Marqueses.** Los Marqueses is in the heart of the Judería area, inside a delightful 17th-century palace. It specializes in Mediterranean and Andalusian cuisine; dishes may include fried eggplant with honey, wild mushroom risotto with prawns, and turbot fillets with potato and mascarpone sauce. The lunch menu, served Monday–Saturday, is a bargain at under €30. ✉*Calle Tomás Conde 8, Judería* ☎*957/202094* ▭*AE, DC, MC, V* ⊙*Closed Mon. and 15 days in Sept.*

$$$ ★ ✕**Bodegas Campos.** A block east of the Plaza del Potro, this restaurant in a traditional old wine cellar is the epitome of all that is great about Andalusian cuisine and service. The dining rooms are in barrel-heavy and leafy courtyards. Regional dishes include *ensalada de bacalao y naranja* (salad of salt cod and orange with olive oil) and *solomillo con salsa de setas* (sirloin with a wild mushroom sauce). The *menu degustacíon* (taster's menu) is a good value at €35. ✉*Calle Los Lineros 32, San Pedro* ☎*957/497643* ▭*AE, MC, V* ⊙*No dinner Sun.*

$$–$$$ ✕**Casa Pepe de la Judería.** Antiques and some wonderful old oil paintings fill this three-floors' labyrinth of rooms just around the corner from the mosque, near the Judería. The restaurant is always packed, noisy, and fun. From May through October, the rooftop opens for barbecues, and there is live Spanish guitar music most nights. A full selection of tapas and house specialties includes *presa de paletilla ibérica con salsa de trufa* (pork shoulder fillet with a truffle sauce). The restaurant also has a fixed-price menu. ✉*Calle Romero 1, off Deanes, Judería* ☎*957/200744* ▭*AE, DC, MC, V.*

$$–$$$ ✕**El Blasón.** In an old inn one block west of Avenida Gran Capitán, El Blasón has a Moorish-style entrance bar leading onto a patio enclosed by ivy-covered walls. Downstairs there is a lounge with a red tile ceiling and old polished clay plates on the walls. Upstairs are two elegant dining rooms where blue walls, white silk curtains, and candelabras evoke early 19th-century luxury. The menu includes *salmón fresco al cava* (fresh salmon in cava, Spanish sparkling wine) and *muslos de pato al vino dulce* (leg of duck in sweet wine sauce). ✉*José Zorrilla 11, Centro* ☎*957/480625* ▭*AE, DC, MC, V.*

$$–$$$ ✕**El Burlaero.** A block from the front of the Mezquita, El Burlaero—so-named for a bullring's wooden barrier—has wood-beamed ceilings and an antique, traditional charm. The seven different rooms, all decorated with bullfight memorabilia and hunting trophies, can serve as many as 200 diners. There's also a terrace for outdoor dining. Typical dishes include grilled swordfish, meat-and-vegetable brochette, Iberian pork, and partridge with onions. ✉*Calleja de la Hoguera 5, Judería* ☎*957/472719* ▭*MC, V.*

$$–$$$ ✕**Taberna Casas Salinas.** This has been an established favorite in Córdoba since 1879; the tiles, paintings, wooden furniture, glassed-in patio, bodega with barrels, and small bar all reflect this era. The cuisine, typical of the Córdobese mountains, might include goat's cheese, meatballs, blood sausage, and lamb chops. ✉*Calle Tundidores 3, Plaza de la Corredera* ☎*957/480135* ▭*AE, DC, MC, V* ⊙*Closed Sun.*

$$–$$$ Fodor'sChoice ★ ✕ **Taberna San Miguel-Casa El Pisto.** This central Córdoba hotspot behind Plaza de las Tendillas is always booming with happy diners, most of them Córdobans, enjoying a wide range of typical pinchos and raciones accompanied by chilled glasses of Moriles, the excellent local sherrylike wine. The heavy wooden bar is as good a spot as any, but the tables in the back rooms crackle with conviviality. ✉ *Pl. de San Miguel 1, Centro* ☎ *957/470166* ▭ *AE, DC, MC, V* ⊙ *Closed Sun.*

$–$$$ ✕ **Los Alarifes.** This delightful restaurant serves a fine selection of typical Spanish dishes, including leek salad with Iberian ham, smoked salmon and carrot vinaigrette, cod with red peppers, and partridge. The daily set menu is less than €18. ✉ *Hotel Alfaros, Calle Alfaros 18, Centro* ☎ *957/491920* ▭ *AE, DC, MC, V.*

$–$$ ✕ **Comedor Árabe Andalussí.** This tiny restaurant is perfect for a romantic dinner for two, in part because of the lack of space but also because of the atmosphere—it's warm and cozy, with Oriental carpets and ornate drapes and cushions. All the Moroccan favorites are here, including tabbouleh, falafel, and couscous, which makes it especially apt for vegetarians. The *tagines* (earthenware vessels with conical tops used for stewing meat and vegetables in Morocco) for two are excellent and will easily feed four, but beware: no wine is served here, in accordance with Islamic religious law. If you ask nicely, the management will allow you to bring in your own wine—try this phrase: *¿Por favor, podemos traer una botella de vino para acompañar nuestra comida?* (May we please bring in a bottle of wine to accompany our meal?) ✉ *Pl. Abades 4, Judería* ☎ *957/475162* ▭ *No credit cards.*

$–$$ ✕ **El Tablón.** Opened in 1890 as a bodega, El Tablón became a restaurant with simple decor in 1985. From inside or on the pleasing columned patio, you can select from a typical Córdoba-style menu that includes a good choice of two courses plus drink and dessert for just €10.50. Pizzas, tapas, and sandwiches are also available. The small bar, with no seats and a marble counter, retains a 19th-century feel. ✉ *Calle Cardenal González 69, Judería* ☎ *957/476061* ▭ *MC, V.*

$–$$ ✕ **La Abacería.** By the west side of the Mezquita, close to the tourist office, La Abacerí has a large bar, a pleasing open central patio, and, usually, a full restaurant. It has homemade tapas: *patatas allioli* (potatoes in allioli sauce), *berenjenas fritas* (fried eggplant), *calamares fritos* or *plancha* (squid fried or grilled), and *tortilla de patatas* (Spanish potato omelet), all sold in half or full portions. ✉ *Corregidor Luis de la Cerda 73, Judería* ☎ *957/487050* ▭ *MC, V.*

¢ ✕ **Bar Santos.** This very small, quintessentially Spanish bar, with no seats and numerous photos of matadors and flamenco dancers, seems out of place surrounded by the tourist shops and overshadowed by the Mezquita. Its appearance—and its prices—are part of its charm. Tapas, such as *morcillo Iberico* (Iberian blood sausage) and *bocadillos* (sandwiches; literally "little mouthfuls") are excellent in quality and value while the Santos *tortilla de patata* (potato omelet) is renowned and celebrated both for its taste and heroic thickness. ✉ *Calle Magistral González Francés 3, Judería* ☎ *957/479360* ▭ *MC, V.*

WHERE TO STAY

$$$$ **Palacio del Bailío.** Open and thriving since summer 2006, the beautiful 17th-century mansion is built over the ruins of a Roman house in the heart of the historical center of Córdoba. The company specializes in carefully and tastefully renovating impressive and historic buildings to the highest of expected modern standards, and this is another exemplary example of its work. Archaeological remains, mixed with high-tech features (such as Internet access), and a relaxing spa complete the enticing cocktail. ✉ *Calle Ramírez de las Casas Deza 10–12, Plaza de La Corredera, 14001* ☎ *957/498993* 📠 *957/498994* 🌐 *www.hospes.es* *53 rooms* *In-room: Ethernet, Wi-Fi. In-hotel: restaurant, bar, pools, spa, bicycles, laundry facilities, public Wi-Fi, public Internet* 💳 *MC, V.*

$$$ Fodor's Choice ★ **Amistad Córdoba.** Two 18th-century mansions that look out on the Plaza de Maimónides in the heart of the Judería are now a stylish hotel. (You can also enter through the old Moorish walls on Calle Cairuán.) There's a cobblestone Mudejar courtyard, carved-wood ceilings, and a plush lounge area; the newer wing across the street is done in blues and grays and Norwegian wood. Guest rooms are large and comfortable. ✉ *Pl. de Maimónides 3, Judería, 14004* ☎ *957/420335* 📠 *957/420365* 🌐 *www.nh-hoteles.com* *84 rooms* *In-room: dial-up. In-hotel: restaurant, room service, bar, laundry service, parking (fee)* 💳 *AE, DC, MC, V.*

$$$ **Casa de los Azulejos.** Although renovated in 1934, this 17th-century house still has its underground rooms with vaulted ceilings. Decorated with colorful tiles, it mixes Andalusian and Latin American influences. All rooms, painted in warm, pastel colors and filled with antique furnishings, open onto the central patio. There's an Andalusian–Latin American restaurant and a Mexican cantina on the premises. ✉ *Calle Fernando Colón 5, Centro, 14002* ☎ *957/470000* 📠 *957/475496* 🌐 *www.casadelosazulejos.com* *7 rooms, 1 suite* *In-hotel: 2 restaurants, public Internet* 💳 *MC, V.*

$$$ **Conquistador.** Ceramic tiles and inlaid marquetry adorn the bar and public rooms at this contemporary, Andalusian-Moorish-style hotel next to the Mezquita. The reception area overlooks a colonnaded patio, fountain, and small enclosed garden. Rooms are comfortable and classically Andalusian; those at the front have small balconies overlooking the mosque, which is floodlighted at night. ✉ *Magistral González Francés 17, Judería, 14003* ☎ *957/481102 or 957/481411* 📠 *957/474677* 🌐 *www.hotelconquistadorcordoba.com* *99 rooms, 3 suites* *In-room: dial-up. In-hotel: room service, bar, laundry service, parking (fee)* 💳 *AE, DC, MC, V.*

$$$ **La Hospedería de El Churrasco.** As should be expected from a place associated with the nearby restaurant of the same name, this small hotel is one of the town's most beautiful and tasteful places to stay. Each room is individually furnished with fine antiques, but also comes with such modern facilities as plasma TVs. The terrace-solarium has fine views of the Mezquita. ✉ *Calle Romero 38, Judería, 14003* ☎ *957/294808* 📠 *957/421661* 🌐 *www.elchurrasco.com* *9 rooms* *In-room: dial-up. In-hotel: parking (no fee)* 💳 *AE, DC, MC, V* 🍽 *BP.*

$$$ **Lola.** Lola, the owner, has decorated the rooms in this former 19th-century palace with decorative flair and attention to detail. There are original beams, woven rugs, antique wardrobes, and art deco decorative pieces. The bathrooms are airy, modern, and marbled. Tucked down a side street, Lola is away from the tour groups, but a short stroll away from all the big-city sights. The roof terrace has Mezquita tower views. There's parking on nearby Plaza Vallinas. ✉ *Calle Romero 3, Judería, 14003* ☎ *957/200305* 🖷 *957/422063* 🌐 *www.hotelconencantolola.com* *8 rooms* 💳 *AE, MC, V* 🍽 *CP.*

$$$ **Maciá Alfaros.** One of the advantages of this elegant hotel is that it's in a quieter part of the city but just a 15-minute walk from the Mezquita. The rooms are large, with modern furnishings and a terrace or balcony. The rooms opening onto the inner patio overlook the pool. ✉ *Alfaros 18, Centro, 14001* ☎ *957/491920* 🖷 *957/492210* *133 rooms* *In-room: dial-up. In-hotel: restaurant, bar, pool, laundry service, parking (no fee)* 💳 *AE, D, MC, V.*

$$$ **Maimónides.** The lobby here has a colonnaded sand-color hall with tile floors and a remarkable *mocárabe* (ornamental wood) ceiling. Outside there's a small patio with wrought-iron tables and chairs. Rooms and bathrooms have marble floors and are decorated in light tones. Some of the rooms make you feel like you're so close to the Mezquita you can touch it. ✉ *Torrijos 4, Judería, 14003* ☎🖷 *957/471500* 🌐 *www.hotusa.es* *82 rooms* *In-room: dial-up. In-hotel: restaurant, public Internet, parking (fee)* 💳 *MC, V.*

$$$ **Parador de Córdoba.** A peaceful, leafy garden surrounds this modern parador on the slopes of the Sierra de Co Córdoba, 5 km (3 mi) north of town. Rooms are sunny, with wood or wicker furnishings, and the pricier ones have balconies overlooking the garden or facing Córdoba. ✉ *Av. de la Arruzafa, El Brillante, 14012* ☎ *957/275900* 🖷 *957/280409* 🌐 *www.parador.es* *89 rooms, 5 suites* *In-room: dial-up. In-hotel: restaurant, room service, tennis court, pool, parking (no fee)* 💳 *AE, DC, MC, V.*

$$ **Gonzalez.** A few minutes from the Mezquita, Gonzalez was originally built as a 16th-century palace and has been converted into a small hotel with an elegant marble entrance and a typical Córdobese central patio. Many of the single, double, twin, and triple rooms here overlook the patio. ✉ *Calle Manrique 3, Judería, 14003* ☎ *957/479819* 🖷 *957/486187* *17 rooms* 💳 *AE, DC, MC, V.*

$$ **Mezquita.** Across from the mosque, this hotel in a restored 16th-century home is filled with bronze sculptures depicting Andalusian themes, and the public areas are filled with antiques collected by the owner. The best rooms face the interior patio, and one of them is what used to be the house's old chapel. All have elegant dark wooden headboards and matching pink curtains and bedspreads. The only real drawback is the lack of parking; your best bet is nearby Plaza Vallinas. ✉ *Pl. Santa Catalina 1, Judería, 41003* ☎ *957/475585* 🖷 *957/476219* *21 rooms* *In-room: dial-up. In-hotel: bar* 💳 *AE, DC, MC, V.*

$–$$ **El Tablón.** Close to the Mezquita, this comfortable hostel has pleasantly decorated rooms in a traditional old-fashioned Spanish style. There's a restaurant and bar across the street. ✉ *Cardenal González 69, Judería, 14003* ☎ *957/476061* ⊕ *www.hostaleltablon.com* ⎙ *957/486240* ⇨ *8 rooms, 1 suite* ♁ *In-hotel: restaurant, bar* ▭ *MC, V.*

$ **Hotel Maestre.** Rooms here overlook a gracious inner courtyard framed by arches. The Castilian-style furniture, gleaming marble, and high-quality oil paintings add elegance to excellent value. The hotel is around the corner from the Plaza del Potro. The management also runs an even cheaper lodging, the Hostal Maestre, and two types of apartments down the street; the best are large and clean and offer one of the best deals in town. ✉ *Calle Romero Barros 4–6, San Pedro, 14003* ☎ *957/472410* ⎙ *957/475395* ⊕ *www.hotelmaestre.com* ⇨ *26 rooms* ♁ *In-hotel: parking (fee)* ▭ *AE, MC, V.*

NIGHTLIFE & THE ARTS

NIGHTLIFE

Córdoba locals hang out mostly in the areas of Ciudad Jardín (the old university area), Plaza de las Tendillas, and the Avenida Gran Capitán.

Café Málaga (✉ *Calle Málaga 3, Centro*), a block away from Plaza de las Tendillas, is a laid-back hangout. **Salón de Té** (✉ *Calle del Buen Pastor 13, Judería*), a few blocks away from the Mezquita, is a beautiful place for tea, with a courtyard, side rooms filled with cushions, and a shop selling Moroccan clothing. It closes at midnight. **Sojo** (✉ *Calle Benito Pérez Galdós 3, off Av. Gran Capitán, Centro* ☎ *957/487211* ✉ *José Martorell 12, Judería*) has a trendy crowd. The branch in the Judería has DJs on weekends. **O'Donoghue's** (✉ *Av. Gran Capitán 38, Centro* ☎ *957/481678*) is an Irish pub favored by locals. For some of the best views of Córdoba, drop by **Hotel Hesperia** (✉ *Av. de la Confederación 1, Sector Sur* ☎ *957/421042* ⊕ *www.hesperia-cordoba.com*), across the Guadalquivir. The hotel has a rooftop bar, open only in summer.

Córdoba's most popular flamenco club, the year-round **Tablao Cardenal** (✉ *Calle Torrijos 10, Judería* ☎ *957/483320* ⊕ *www.tablaocardenal.com*) is worth the trip just to see the courtyard of the 16th-century building, which was Córdoba's first hospital. Admission is €20.

THE ARTS

During the **Patio Festival,** on the second and third weeks of May, the city is invaded by flamenco dancers and singers. The **Festival de Córdoba-Guitarra** attracts Spanish and international guitarists for more than two weeks of great music in July, and orchestras perform in the Alcázar's garden on Sunday throughout summer. The **Feria de Mayo** (the last week of May) draws popular performers to the city. See concerts, ballets, and plays year-round in the **Gran Teatro** (✉ *Av. Gran Capitán 3, Centro* ☎ *957/480644* ⊕ *www.teatrocordoba.com*).

SPORTS & OUTDOORS

The top golf course near Córdoba is the 18-hole **Club de Campo y Deportivo de Córdoba** (✉ *Crta. Antigua de Córdoba–Obejo Km 9, Av. del Brillante* ☎ *957/350208*). For swimming, try the **Piscina Municipal** (✉ *Av. del Brillante, Polideportivo Ciudad Jardín, Alcalde Sanz Noguer s/n, Av. del Brillante* ☎ *957/484846*).

SHOPPING

Córdoba's main shopping district is around Avenida Gran Capitán, Ronda de los Tejares, and the streets leading away from Plaza Tendillas. **Artesanía Andaluza** (✉ *Calle Tomás Conde 3, Judería* ☎ *957/203781*), near the Museo Taurino, sells Córdoban crafts, including fine embossed leather (a legacy of the Moors) and jewelry made of filigree silver from the mines of the Sierra Morena. Córdoba's artisans sell their crafts in the **Zoco** (✉ *C. Judíos, opposite synagogue, Judería* ☎ *957/204033*); note that many stalls are open May–September only. **Meryan** (✉ *Calleja de las Flores 2 and Encarnación, 12* ☎ *957/475902* 🌐 *www.meryancor.com*) is one of Córdoba's best workshops for embossed leather.

EN ROUTE

Begun in 936, **Medina Azahara** (sometimes spelled Madinat Al-Zahra) was built in the foothills of the Sierra Morena—about 8 km (5 mi) west of Córdoba on C431—by Abd ar-Rahman III for his favorite concubine, az-Zahra (the Flower). Historians say it took 10,000 men, 2,600 mules, and 400 camels 25 years to erect this fantasy of 4,300 columns in dazzling pink, green, and white marble and jasper brought from Carthage. Here, on three terraces, stood a palace, a mosque, luxurious baths, fragrant gardens, fishponds, an aviary, and a zoo. In 1013 the place was sacked and destroyed by Berber mercenaries. In 1944 the Royal Apartments were rediscovered, and the Throne Room was carefully reconstructed. The outline of the mosque has also been excavated. The only covered part of the site is the Salon de Abd Al Rahman III; the rest is a sprawl of foundations, defense walls, and arches that hint at the splendor of the original city-palace. There is no public transport out to here, but the authorities run a daily tourist bus, so check with the tourist offices for hours and place of departure. ✉ *Off C431; follow signs en route to Almodóvar del Río* ☎ *957/355506* 🎫 *€1.50, free for EU citizens* ⏲ *Tues.–Sat. 10–8:30, Sun. 10–2.*

SIDE TRIPS FROM CÓRDOBA

If you have time to go beyond Córdoba, head west to the ruins and partial reconstruction of the Muslim palace Medina Azahara, site of a once-magnificent complex, or south to the wine country around Montilla, olive oil–rich Baena, and the Subbética mountain range, a cluster of small towns virtually unknown to travelers.

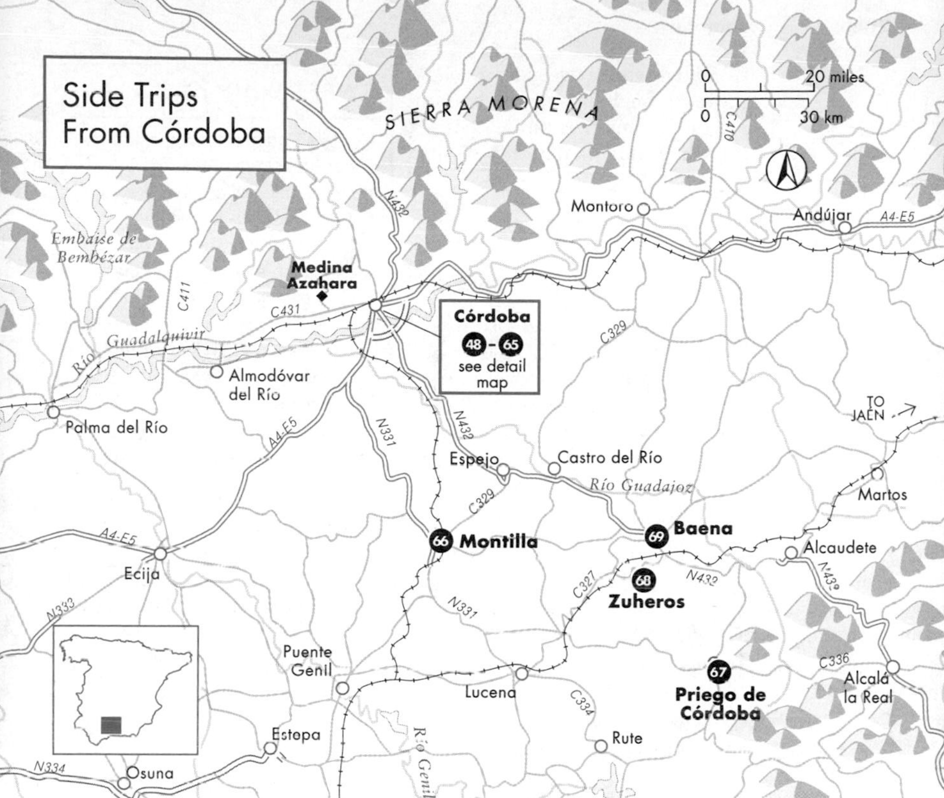

The enitre Subbética region is protected as a natural park. The mountains, canyons, and wooded valleys are stunning. You'll need a car to explore the area, and in some parts, the roads are rather rough. To reach these meriting-a-visit towns in *la Campiña* (the countryside), take the low road (N331) through Montilla, cutting north to Baena via Zuheros, or take the high road (N432) through Espejo and Baena, cutting south through Cabra. For park information or hiking advice, contact the **Mancomunidad de la Subbética** (✉ *Ctra. Carcabuey–Zagrilla, Km 5.75, Carcabuey* ☎ *957/704106* 🌐 *www.subbetica.org*). You can also pick up handy information, including a pack of maps titled *Rutas Senderistas de la Subbética,* from any local tourist office. The packet details 10 walks on handy cards with sketched maps.

Southern Córdoba is also the province's main olive-producing region, with the town of **Lucena** at its center. By following the Ruta del Aceite (olive oil route) you pass by some of the province's most picturesque villages. In Lucena is the Torre del Moral, where Granada's last Nasrid ruler Boabdil was imprisoned in 1483 after launching an unsuccessful attack on the Christians; and the Parroquia de San Mateo, a small but remarkable Renaissance–Gothic cathedral. The town makes furniture and brass and copper pots. Southeast of Lucena, C334 crosses the **Embalse de Iznájar** (Iznájar Reservoir) amid spectacular scenery. On

C334 halfway between Lucena and the reservoir, in **Rute**, you can sample the potent *anís* (anise) liqueur for which this small, whitewashed town is famous.

> **SWEET WINE**
>
> Montilla's grapes contain so much sugar (transformed into alcohol during fermentation) that they are not fortified with the addition of extra alcohol. For this reason, the locals claim that Montilla wines do not give you a hangover.

MONTILLA

66 *46 km (28 mi) south of Córdoba.*

Heading south from Córdoba to Málaga through hills ablaze with sunflowers in early summer, you reach the Montilla-Morilés vineyards of the Córdoban campiña. Every fall, 47,000 acres' worth of Pedro Ximénez grapes are crushed here to produce the region's rich Montilla wines, which are similar to sherry. Recently, Montilla has started developing a young white wine similar to Portugal's Vinho Verde.

Bodegas Alvear. Founded in 1729, this bodega in the center of town is Montilla's oldest. Besides being informative, the fun tour and wine tasting gives you the chance to buy a bottle or two of Alvear's tasty version of the sweet Pedro Ximenez aged sherry. ✉ *Calle María Auxiliadora 1* ☎ *957/652939* 🌐 *www.alvear.es* 🎫 *Tour €2, with wine tasting €3–€4.50* 🕙 *Guided tour and wine tasting Mon.–Sat. 12:30; shop Mon. 4:30–6:30, Tues.–Fri. 10–2 and 4:30–6:30, Sat. 11–1:30.*

WHERE TO STAY & EAT

$$–$$$ ★ ✕ **Las Camachas.** The best-known restaurant in southern Córdoba Province is in an Andalusian-style hacienda outside Montilla—near the main road toward Málaga. Start with tapas in the attractive tiled bar, and then move to one of six dining rooms. Regional specialties include *alcachofas al Montilla* (artichokes braised in Montilla wine), *salmorejo* (a thick version of gazpacho), *perdiz campiña* (country-style partridge), and *cordero a la miel* (lamb with honey). You can also buy local wines here. ✉ *Av. Europa 3* ☎ *957/650004* 💳 *AE, DC, MC, V.*

$$ 🏨 **Don Gonzalo.** Just 3 km (2 mi) southwest of Montilla is one of Andalusia's better roadside hotels. The wood-beam covered common areas have a mixture of decorative elements; note the elephant tusks flanking the TV in the lounge. The clay-tile rooms are large and comfortable; some look onto the road, others onto the garden and pool. Ask to see the wine cellar; it's a beauty. ✉ *Ctra. Córdoba–Málaga, Km 47, 14550* ☎ *957/650658* 📠 *957/650666* 🌐 *www.hoteldongonzalo.com* 🛏 *35 rooms, 1 suite* 👍 *In-room: dial-up. In-hotel: restaurant, bar, tennis court, pool* 💳 *AE, DC, MC, V.*

SHOPPING

On the outskirts of town, coopers' shops produce barrels of various sizes, some small enough to serve as creative souvenirs. On Montilla's main road, **Tonelería J. L. Rodríguez** (✉ *Ctra. Córdoba–Málaga, Km 43.3* ☎ *957/650563* 🌐 *www.toneleriajlrodriguez.com*) is well worth a stop not just to see the barrels and other things for sale—such as local wines—but also to pop in the back and see them being made.

PRIEGO DE CÓRDOBA

67 ★ *103 km (64 mi) southeast of Córdoba and 37 km (23 mi) northeast of Lucena via C334 going north to Cabra, then east on C340.*

The jewel of Córdoba's countryside is **Priego de Córdoba,** a town of 14,000 at the foot of Mt. Tinosa. Wander down Calle del Río opposite the town hall to see 18th-century mansions, once the homes of silk merchants. At the end of the street is the Fuente del Rey (King's Fountain), with some 130 water jets, built in 1803. Don't miss the lavish baroque churches of La Asunción and La Aurora or the Barrio de la Villa, an old Moorish quarter with a maze of narrow streets of white-wall buildings.

WHERE TO STAY

$$ **Villa Turística de Priego.** Clustered to form an Andalusian pueblo, the semidetached units of this gleaming-white complex sleep between two and six people each. Some have a terrace or balcony. It's in the heart of the Subbética nature park—near Zagrilla, 6 km (4 mi) from Priego de Córdoba. *Aldea de Zagrilla, 14816 957/703503 957/703573 www.villadepriego.com 47 apartments/villas, 5 rooms In-hotel: restaurant, bar, pool AE, DC, MC, V Closed Jan.*

OFF THE BEATEN PATH

Barceló La Bobadilla—Standing on its own 1,000-acre estate amid olive and holm-oak trees, this complex ($$$$) 14 km (9 mi) west of the town of Loja resembles a Moorish village, or a rambling *cortijo* (ranch). It has white walls, tile roofs, patios, fountains, and an artificial lake. Guest buildings center around a 16th-century-style chapel that houses a 1,595-pipe organ. Each room has either a balcony, a terrace, or a garden. One restaurant serves highly creative international cuisine, and the other serves more down-to-earth regional items. The hotel is just south of the La Subbética region, technically in Granada Provice, but it has by far the best accommodations in the area. *Finca La Bobadilla, Apdo 144 E, Loja18300 958/321861 958/321810 www.la-bobadilla.com 52 rooms, 10 suites In-hotel: 2 restaurants, tennis courts, pools, gym AE, DC, MC, V.*

ZUHEROS

68 *80 km (50 mi) southeast of Córdoba.*

At the northern edge of the Subbética and at an altitude of 2,040 feet, Zuheros is one of the most attractive villages in the province of Córdoba. From the road up, it's hidden behind a dominating rock face topped off by the dramatic ruins of a castle built by the Moors over a Roman castle. The view from here back over the valley is immense. Next to the castle is the Iglesia de Santa María, built over a mosque. The base of the minaret is the foundation for the bell tower.

WHAT TO SEE

The **Museo Histórico-Arqueológico Municipal** displays archaeological remains found in local caves and elsewhere; some date back to the Middle Palaeolithic period some 35,000 years ago. You can also visit the remains of the Renaissance rooms in the castle, across the road. Call ahead for tour times. ⊠*Pl. de la Paz 2* ☎*957/694545* *€2* *Apr.–Sept., Tues.–Fri. 10–2 and 5–7; weekends 10–7; Oct.–Mar., Tues.–Fri. 10–2 and 4–6; weekends 10–6.*

Opened in 2002, and housed in an impressive square mansion from 1912, the **Museo de Costumbres y Artes Populares Juan Fernandez Cruz** is at the edge of the village. Exhibits here detail the way of life and local customs and traditions. ⊠*Calle Santo s/n* ☎*957/694690* *€2* *Tues.–Sun. 11–2 and 4–7.*

Found some 4 km (2½ mi) above Zuheros along a windy, twisty road, the **Cueva de los Murciélagos** *(Cave of the Bats)* runs for about 2 km (1¼ mi), although only about half of that expanse is open to the public. The main attractions are the wall paintings dating from the Neolithic Age (6,000–3,000 BC) and Chalcolithic Age (3,000–2,000 BC), but excavations have identified that the cave was already inhabited 35,000 years ago. Items from the Copper and Bronze ages as well as from the Roman period and the Middle Ages have also been found here. ⊠*Information and reservations: Calle Nueva 1* ☎*957/694545 weekdays 10–2:30 and 5–7* informacion@cuevadelosmurcielagos.com *€5.30* *By appointment only: Apr.–Sept., weekdays noon–5:30, weekends 11–6:30; Oct.–Mar., weekdays 12:30–4:30, weekends 11–5:30.*

WHERE TO STAY & EAT

$–$$$ ✕ **Los Palancos.** Literally built into the cliff face of the towering mountain that Zuheros is built upon, this is a small restaurant and tavern of some charm. Expect local mountain-style cuisine featuring roast young goat, rabbit, partridge, and suckling pig, and choose from many items of local produce to take home with you. ⊠*Calle Llana 43* ☎*957/694538* *MC, V.*

$–$$ **Señorios de Zuheros.** In a central location, Señorios de Zuheros offers 10 apartments with three or four beds as well as six studios with sleeping accommodations for two people. All rooms are modern and well equipped. ⊠*Calle Horno 3, 14870* ☎*957/694527* *www.zuherosapartamentos.com* *10 apartments, 6 rooms* *In-hotel: restaurant, bar, laundry facilities* *MC, V.*

$–$$ **Zuhayra.** On a narrow street in Zuheros, this small hotel has comfortable large rooms with views over the village rooftops to the valley below. There's a cozy bar and dining room with original beams and an open fireplace. Groups of artists on organized trips often stay here. ⊠*C. Mirador 10, 14870* ☎*957/694693* *957/694702* *18 rooms* *In-hotel: restaurant, bar* *AE, DC, MC, V.*

BAENA

69 *66 km (43 mi) southeast of Córdoba.*

Outside the boundaries of Subbética and surrounded by chalk fields producing top-quality olives, Baena is an old town of narrow streets, whitewashed houses, ancient mansions, and churches clustered beneath Moorish battlements.

The **Museo del Olivar y el Aceite** is housed in the old olive mill owned and operated by Don José Alcalá Santaella until 1959. The machinery on display dates from the middle of the 19th century, when the mill was capable of processing up to 3 tons a day. The museum aims to demonstrate the most important aspects of olive cultivation, olive-oil production, and the way of life of workers in this most important industry in this region. ✉ *Calle Cañada 7* ☎ *957/691641* 🌐 *www.museoaceite.com* 💳 *€3* 🕒 *May–Sept., Tues.–Sat. 11–2 and 6–8, Sun. 11–2; Oct.–Apr., Tues.–Fri. 11–2 and 4–6, Sun. 11–2.*

WHERE TO STAY & EAT

$$–$$$ **La Casa Grande.** In the center of town just a few steps from the famous Nuñez de Prado olive oil mill, this is the top hotel in Baena and for miles around. The reception hall is high-celilinged and elegant, the restaurant a good reason for stopping in for a meal, and the professional and friendly staff always helpful. Rooms have antiques and a breezy, comfortable feel to them. ✉ *Av. De Cervantes 35, 14850* ☎ *957/671905* 📠 *957/692189* 🌐 *www.lacasagrande.es* *38 rooms* *In-hotel: restaurant, bar, pool, laundry facilities, laundry service, parking (no fee)* 💳 *AE, DC, MC, V.*

$$ **Fuente las Piedras.** This stylish hotel 25 km (15 mi) northeast of Baena in the town of Cabra on the A316 road to Jaén is on the edge of the Parque Natural Sierra Subbética. Its rooms are modern and generous in size. A large pool is surrounded by gardens. ✉ *Av. Fuente de las Piedras s/n, Cabra, 14940* ☎ *957/529740* 📠 *957/521407* 🌐 *www.mshoteles.com/fuentelaspiedras* *61 rooms* *In hotel: restaurant, bar, pool, laundry facilities, laundry service, parking (no fee)* 💳 *MC, V.*

LAND OF OLIVES: JAÉN PROVINCE

Jaén is dominated by its *alcázar* (fortress). To the northeast are the olive-producing towns of Baeza and Úbeda. Cazorla, the gateway to the Parque Natural Sierra de Cazorla Segura y Las Villas, lies beyond.

JAÉN

70 *107 km (64 mi) southeast of Córdoba, 93 km (58 mi) north of Granada.*

Nestled in the foothills of the Sierra de Jabalcuz, Jaén is surrounded by towering peaks and olive-clad hills. The Arabs called it Geen (Route of the Caravans) because it formed a crossroad between Castile and Andalusia. Captured from the Moors by Saint King Ferdinand III in 1246, Jaén became a frontier province, the site of many a skirmish

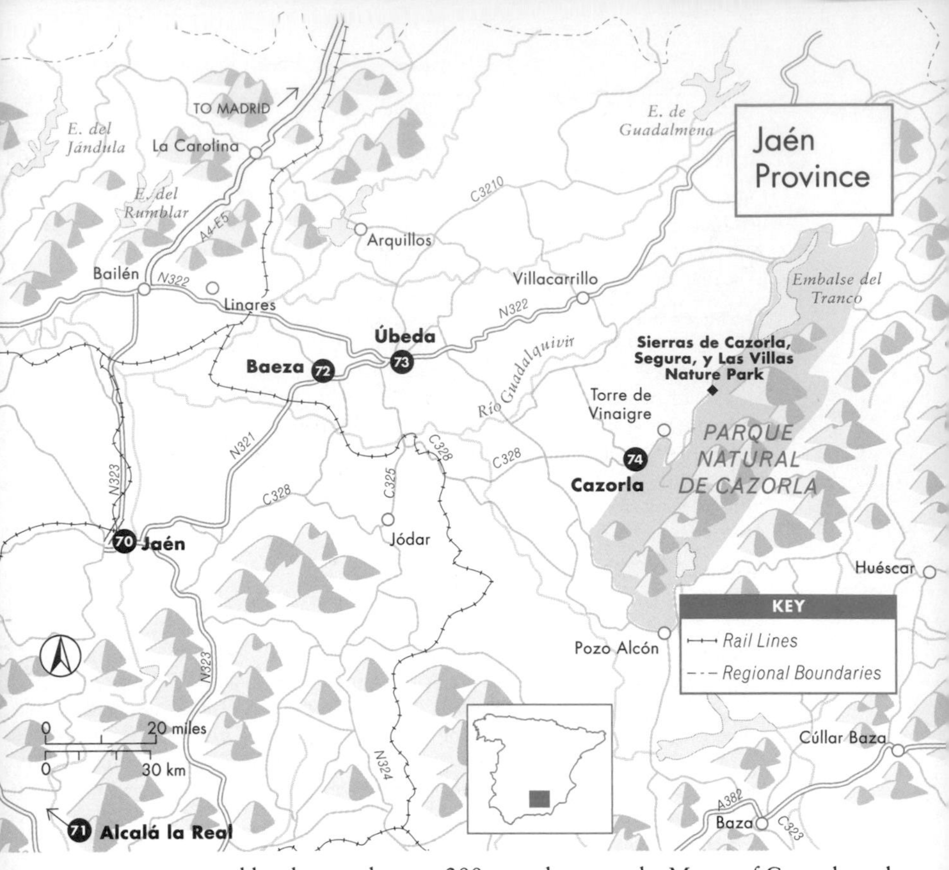

and battle over the next 200 years between the Moors of Granada and Christians from the north and west. Today the province earns a living from its lead and silver mines and endless olive groves.

★ The **Castillo de Santa Catalina,** perched on a rocky crag 400 yards above the center of town, is Jaén's star monument. The castle may have originated as a tower built by Hannibal; the site was fortified continuously over the centuries. The Nasrid king Alhamar, builder of Granada's Alhambra, constructed an *alcázar* here, but King Ferdinand III captured it from him in 1246 on the feast day of Santa Catalina (St. Catherine). Catalina consequently became Jaén's patron saint, so when the Christians built a castle and chapel here, they dedicated both to her. ✉ *Ctra. del Castillo de Santa Catalina* ☎ *953/120733* 🎫 *€3* ⏲ *June–Sept., Thurs.–Tues. 10–2 and 4:30–7; Oct.–May, Thurs.–Tues. 10–2 and 3:30–6.*

Jaén's **cathedral** is a hulk that looms above the modest buildings around it. Begun in 1492 on the site of a former mosque, it took almost 300 years to build. Its chief architect was Andrés de Vandelvira (1509–75); many more of Vandelvira's buildings can be seen in Úbeda and Baeza. The ornate facade was sculpted by Pedro Roldán, and the figures on top of the columns include San Fernando (King Ferdinand III) surrounded by the four evangelists. The cathedral's most treasured relic is the **Santo Rostro** (Holy Face), the cloth with which, according to tradition, St. Veronica cleansed Christ's face on the way to Calvary, leaving his image imprinted on the fabric. The *rostro* (face) is displayed every Friday. In the underground **museum,** look for *San Lorenzo,* by Martínez Montañés; the *Immaculate Conception,* by Alonso Cano; and a Calvary scene by Jácobo Florentino. ✉*Pl. Santa María* ☎*953/234233* *Cathedral free, museum €3* ⏲*Cathedral Mon.–Sat. 8:30–1 and 5–8, Sun. 9–1 and 6–8; museum Tues.–Sat. 10–1 and 5–8.*

Explore the narrow alleys of old Jaén as you walk from the cathedral to the **Baños Árabes** (Arab Baths), which once belonged to Ali, a Moorish king of Jaén, and probably date from the 11th century. Four hundred years later, in 1592, Fernando de Torres y Portugal, a viceroy of Peru, built himself a mansion, the **Palacio de Villardompardo,** right over the baths, so it took years of painstaking excavation to restore them to their original form. The palace contains a small museum of folk crafts and a larger museum devoted to native art. There are guided tours of the baths, one of the largest and best conserved in Spain, every 30 minutes. ✉*Palacio de Villardompardo, Pl. Luisa de Marillac* ☎*953/248068* *Free (bring ID or passport)* ⏲*Tues.–Fri. 9–8, weekends 9:30–2:30.*

Jaén's **Museo Provincial** has one of the best collections of Iberian (pre-Roman) artifacts in Spain. The newest wing has 20 life-size Iberian sculptures discovered by chance near the village of Porcuna in 1975. The museum proper is in a 1547 mansion, on a patio with the facade of the erstwhile Church of San Miguel. The fine-arts section has a roomful of Goya lithographs. ✉*Paseo de la Estación 29* ☎*953/2313339* *€2, free for EU citizens* ⏲*Sun. 9–2:30; Wed. and Thurs.–Sat. 9–8:30, Tues. 3–8 and 2:30–8:30.*

WHERE TO STAY & EAT

$$$–$$$$ ✕ **Casa Vicente.** Locals typically pack this family-run restaurant around the corner from the cathedral. You can have drinks and tapas in the colorful tavern, then move to the cozy courtyard dining room. The traditional Jaén dishes—game casseroles, Jaén-style spinach, and *cordero Mozárabe* (Mozarab-style roast lamb with a sweet-and-sour sauce)—are especially good. ✉*Calle Francisco Martín Mora 1* ☎*953/232222* *AE, MC, V* ⏲*Closed Aug. and Wed. No dinner Sun.*

$$–$$$ ✕ **Casa Antonio.** Exquisite Andalusian food is served at this somber yet elegant restaurant with three small dining rooms, all with cherrywood-panel walls, dark plywood floors, and a few modern-art paintings. Try the *foie y queso en milhojas de manzana verde caramelizada en aceite de pistacho* (goose or duck liver and cheese in julienned green apples caramelized in pistachio oil) or *salmonetes de roca en caldo tibio de molusco y aceite de vainilla* (red mullet in a warm mollusk broth and vanilla oil). ✉*Calle Fermín Palma 3* ☎*953/270262* *AE, MC, V* ⏲*Closed Aug. and Mon. No dinner Sun.*

$$$ Fodor's Choice ★ **Parador de Jaén.** Built amid the mountaintop towers of the Castillo de Santa Catalina, this is one of the showpieces of the parador chain and a reason in itself to visit Jaén. The parador's grandiose exterior echoes the castle next door, as do the lofty ceilings, tapestries, baro-

nial shields, and suits of armor inside. Comfortable bedrooms, with canopy beds, have balconies overlooking fields stretching toward a dramatic mountain backdrop. ✉*Calle Castillo de Santa Catalina, 23001* ☎*953/230000* 📠*953/230930* 🌐*www.parador.es* *45 rooms* *In-room: dial-up. In-hotel: restaurant, pool* *AE, DC, MC, V.*

ALCALÁ LA REAL

71 *75 km (46.5 mi) south of Jaén on N432 and A316.*

This ancient city, known to the Iberians and Romans, grew to prominence under the Moors who ruled here for more than 600 years. And it was they who gave it the first part of its name, Alcalá, which originated from a word meaning "fortified settlement."

The **Fortaleza de la Mota.** as it's known today, was started by the Moors in 727 and sits imperiously at an elevation of 3,389 feet, dominating not only the town but the whole area for miles around. From here, you can see spectacular views of the towering peaks of the Sierra Nevada on the southern horizon. During the 12th century the city changed hands frequently as the Moors fought to keep their control of the area. Finally, in 1341 Alfonso XI reconquered the town for good, adding Real (Royal) to its name. It remained of strategic importance until the Catholic Monarchs reconquered Granada—indeed, it was from here that they rode out to accept the keys of the city and the surrender. Hundreds of years later, the French forces left the town in ruins after their retreat in the early 19th century. The town itself was gradually rebuilt, but the fortress, consisting of the *alcazaba* (citadel) and the abbey church that Alfonso XI built, were more or less ignored. Up until the late 1990s, it was possible just to drive up and look around—exposed skeletons were visible in some open tombs on the floor of the church.

These days, things are more organized. To view it, you need a ticket. Then you face a long, uphill climb to the complex, which also has a small archaeology museum. ☎*639/647796* *€2* *July–Sept. 10:30–1:30 and 5–8; Oct.–June 10:30–1:30 and 3:30–6:30.*

WHERE TO STAY

$ **Hospedería Zacatín.** This smallish hideaway in the center of town is an inexpensive and cozy way station for visitors to Alcalá la Real. Rooms are simple but well equipped and outfitted with contemporary facilities. The restaurant is rustic and comfortable. ✉*Calle Pradillo 2, 23680* ☎*953/580568* 📠*953/580301* 🌐*www.hospederiazacatin.com* *15 rooms* *In-hotel: restaurant, bar, parking (no fee)* *MC, V.*

BAEZA

72 *48 km (30 mi) northeast of Jaén on N321.*

Fodor's Choice ★

The historic town of Baeza is nestled between hills and olive groves. Founded by the Romans, it later housed the Visigoths and became the capital of a *taifa* (kingdom) under the Moors. The Saint King Ferdinand III captured Baeza in 1227, and for the next 200 years it stood on the frontier of the Moorish kingdom of Granada. In the 16th and 17th centuries, local nobles gave the city a wealth of Renaissance palaces.

WHAT TO SEE

The **Casa del Pópulo,** in the central paseo—where the Plaza del Pópulo (or Plaza de los Leones) and Plaza de la Constitución (or Plaza del Mercado Viejo) merge to form a cobblestone square—is a beautiful circa 1530 structure. The first Mass of the Reconquest was supposedly celebrated on its curved balcony; it now houses Baeza's tourist office.

In the center of the town square is an ancient Iberian-Roman statue thought to depict Imilce, wife of Hannibal; at the foot of her column is the **Fuente de los Leones** *(Fountain of the Lions).*

To find Baeza's **university,** follow the steps on the south side of the Plaza del Pópulo. The college opened in 1542, closed in 1824, and later became a high school, where the poet Antonio Machado taught French from 1912 to 1919. The building now functions as a cultural center (a new school has been built next door). You can visit Machado's classroom—request the key—and the patio. ✉*Calle Beato Juan de Ávila s/n* ☎*953/740154* ⏲*Thurs.–Tues. 10–2 and 4–6.*

Baeza's **cathedral** was originally begun by Ferdinand III on the site of a former mosque. The structure was largely rebuilt by Andrés de Vandelvira, architect of Jaén's cathedral, between 1570 and 1593, though the west front has architectural influences from an earlier period. A fine 14th-century rose window crowns the 13th-century Puerta de la Luna (Moon Door). Don't miss the baroque silver monstrance (a vessel in which the consecrated Host is exposed for the adoration of the faithful), which is carried in Baeza's Corpus Christi processions—the piece is kept in a concealed niche behind a painting, but you can see it in all its splendor by putting a coin in a slot to reveal the hiding place. Next to the monstrance is the entrance to the clock tower, where a small donation and a narrow spiral staircase take you to one of the best views of Baeza. The remains of the original mosque are in the cathedral's Gothic cloisters. Entrance to the cloister and small museum is €2. ✉*Pl. de Santa María* ☎*953/744157* ⏲*May–Sept., daily 10–1 and 5–7; Oct.–Apr., daily 10:30–1 and 4–6.*

Plaza de Santa María. The main square of the medieval city is surrounded by not just the cathedral but also other palaces. The highlight is the fountain, built in 1564 and resembling a triumphal arch.

Iglesia de Santa Cruz. This rather small and plain church dates from the early 13th century. Not only was it one of the first built here after the Reconquest, but it's also one of the earliest Christian churches in all of Andalusia. It has two Romanesque portals and a curved stone altar. ✉*Pl. de Santa Cruz s/n* ⏲*Mon.–Sat. 11–1 and 4–5:30, Sun. noon–2.*

Casa Museo de Vera Cruz. Found immediately behind the Santa Cruz Church, and housed in a building dating from 1540, this museum has religious artifacts from the 16th, 17th, 18th, and 19th centuries. There's also a small shop selling local products. ✉*Pl. de Santa Cruz s/n* 🎟*€1.50* ⏲*Daily 11–1 and 4–6.*

Palacio de Jabalquinto. Built between the 15th and 16th centuries by Juan Alfonso de Benavides as a palatial home, this palace has a flamboyant Gothic facade and a charming marble colonnaded Renaissance patio. It's a perfect example of how the old can be retained and incorporated into the new. ✉*Pl. de Santa Cruz s/n* ⊙*Weekdays 9–2.*

The ancient student custom of inscribing names and graduation dates in bull's blood (as in Salamanca) is still evident on the walls of the seminary of **San Felipe Neri** (✉*Cuesta de San Felipe*), built in 1660. It's opposite Baeza's cathedral.

Baeza's **ayuntamiento** (*town hall* ✉*Pl. Cardenal Benavides, just north of Pl. del Pópulo*) was designed by cathedral master Andrés de Vandelvira. The facade is ornately plateresque; look between the balconies for the coats of arms of Felipe II, the city of Baeza, and the magistrate Juan de Borja. Arrange for a visit to the *salón de plenos,* a major hall with painted, carved woodwork. A few blocks west of the ayuntamiento, the 16th-century **Convento de San Francisco** (✉*C. de San Francisco*) is one of Vandelvira's architectural religious masterpieces. You can see its restored remains—the building was spoiled by the French army and partially destroyed by a light earthquake in the early 1800s.

WHERE TO STAY & EAT

$$–$$$ ✕**Vandelvira.** Seldom do you have the chance to eat in a 16th-century convent. The restaurant, within two galleries on the first floor of the Convento de San Francisco, has lots of character and magnificent antiques. Specialties include the *pâté de perdiz con aceite de oliva virgen* (partridge pâté with olive oil) and the *manitas de cerdo rellenas de perdiz y espinacas* (pig's knuckles filled with partridge and spinach). It has a summer terrace that doubles as a tavern. ✉*C. de San Francisco 14* ☎*953/748172* ▭*AE, DC, MC, V* ⊙*Closed Mon. No dinner Sun.*

$ ✕▣ **Juanito.** Rooms in this small, unpretentious hotel are simple and comfortable. The restaurant's ($–$$$) proprietor is a champion of Andalusian food, and the chef has revived such regional specialties as *alcachofas Luisa* (braised artichokes), *ensalada de perdiz* (partridge salad), and *cordero con habas* (lamb and broad beans); desserts are based on old Moorish recipes. The hotel is next to a gas station on the edge of town, toward Úbeda. ✉*Paseo Arca del Agua, 23440* ☎*953/740040* 🖷*953/742324* ⊕*www.juanitobaeza.com* *36 rooms, 1 suite* *In-hotel: restaurant, tennis court, pool* ▭*MC, V* ⊙*No dinner Sun. and Mon.*

ÚBEDA

73 *9 km (5½ mi) northeast of Baeza on N321.*

Fodor's Choice ★

Úbeda is in the heart of Jaén's olive groves, and olive oil is indeed the main concern here. Although this modern town of 30,000 is relatively dull (it has a reputation as being a serious, religious place), the *casco antiguo* (old town) is one of the most outstanding enclaves of 16th-century architecture in Spain. Follow signs to the *Zona Monumental*

(Monumental Zone), where there are countless Renaissance palaces and stately mansions, most closed to the public.

The Plaza del Ayuntamiento is crowned by the privately owned **Palacio de Vela de los Cobos.** It was designed by Andrés de Vandelvira (1505–75), a key figure in the Spanish Renaissance era for Úbeda's magistrate, Francisco de Vela de los Cobos. The corner balcony has a central white-marble column that's echoed in the gallery above.

WHAT TO SEE

Vandelvira's 16th-century Palacio Juan Vázquez de Molina is better known by its nickname, the **Palacio de las Cadenas** (House of Chains), because decorative iron chains were once affixed to the columns of its main doorway. It's now the town hall and has entrances on both Plaza Vázquez de Molina and Plaza Ayuntamiento. Molina was a nephew of Francisco de los Cobos, and both served as secretaries to emperor Carlos V and king Felipe II.

The Plaza Vázquez de Molina, in the heart of the old town, is the site of the **Sacra Capilla del Salvador.** This building is photographed so often that it has become the city's unofficial symbol. Sacra Capilla was built by Vandelvira, but he based his design on some 1536 plans by Diego de Siloé, architect of Granada's cathedral. Considered one of the masterpieces of Spanish Renaissance religious art, the chapel was sacked in the frenzy of church burnings at the outbreak of the civil war. However, it retains its ornate west front and altarpiece, which has a rare Berruguete sculpture. ✉*Pl. Vázquez de Molina* ☎*953/758150* *€3* *Mon.–Sat. 10–2 and 4:30–7, Sun. 10:45–2 and 4:30–7.*

The **Ayuntamiento Antiguo** (Old Town Hall), begun in the early 16th century but restored as a beautiful arcaded baroque palace in 1680, is now a conservatory of music. From the hall's upper balcony, the town council watched celebrations and *autos-da-fé* ("acts of faith"—executions of heretics sentenced by the Inquisition) in the square below. On the north side is the 13th century church of San Pablo, with an Isabelline south portal. ✉*Pl. Primero de Mayo, off C. María de Molina* *1-hr tour at 7 PM.*

The **Hospital de Santiago,** sometimes jokingly called the Escorial of Andalusia (in allusion to Felipe II's monolithic palace and monastery outside of Madrid), is a huge, angular building in the modern section, and yet another one of Andrés de Vandelvira's masterpieces in Úbeda. The plain facade is adorned with ceramic medallions, and over the main entrance is a carving of Santiago Matamoros (St. James the Moorslayer) in his traditional horseback pose. Inside are an arcaded patio and a grand staircase. Now a cultural center, it holds some of the events at the International Spring Dance and Music Festival. ✉*Av. Cristo Rey* ☎*953/750842* *Daily 8–3 and 4–10.*

WHERE TO STAY & EAT

¢–$$ ✕**Libra.** A very pleasant and comfortable combination of cafeteria, pub, and bar, Libra is on a busy plaza on the edge of the older part of town. Combination plates consist of *huevos fritos, calamares, y patatas fritas* (fried eggs, squid, and french fries) and *bacon, huevos fritos, patatas fritas, y asadillo* (bacon, fried eggs, french fries, and red peppers) as well as a tempting selection of sandwiches. ✉*Pl. Andalucía 3–5* ☎*953/757480* ▭*MC, V.*

$$$ Fodor'sChoice ★ ✕🏨**Parador de Úbeda.** This splendid parador is in a 16th-century ducal palace on the Plaza Vázquez de Molina, next to the Capilla del Salvador. A grand stairway, decked with tapestries and suits of armor, leads up to the guest rooms, which have tile floors, lofty wood ceilings, dark Castilian-style furniture, and large bathtubs. The dining room, specializing in regional dishes, serves perhaps the best food in Úbeda; try one of the *perdiz* (partridge) entrées. There's a bar in the vaulted basement. ✉*Pl. Vázquez de Molina s/n, 23400* ☎*953/750345* 🖷*953/751259* 🌐*www.parador.es* *35 rooms, 1 suite* *In-hotel: restaurant, bar, no elevator* ▭*AE, DC, MC, V.*

$$$ 🏨**Palacio de la Rambla.** In old Úbeda, the wonderfully beautiful 16th-century mansion has been in the same family since it was built, and part of it still hosts the regal Marquesa de la Rambla when she's in town. Eight of the rooms are open to overnighters; each is unique, but all are large and furnished with original antiques, tapestries, and works of art; some have chandeliers. The palace is arranged on two levels, around a cool, ivy-covered patio. ✉*Pl. del Marqués 1, 23400* ☎*953/750196* 🖷*953/750267* *7 rooms, 1 suite* *In-hotel: parking (fee), no elevator* ▭*AE, MC, V.*

$$–$$$ 🏨**María de Molina.** In the heart of the Monumental Zone (Zona Monumental), this hotel is in a large town house formerly known as La Casa de los Curas (The Priests' House), because it once housed two priests who were twins. Each room is different, but all are done in warm pastels and elegant Andalusian furnishings; some have balconies. Rooms 204–207 have the best views over the town's rooftops. The rates go up on weekends and holidays. ✉*Pl. del Ayuntamiento s/n, 23400* ☎*953/795356* 🖷*953/793694* 🌐*www.hotel-maria-de-molina.com* *27 rooms* *In-hotel: restaurant, bar* ▭*AE, DC, MC, V.*

$$–$$$ 🏨**Rosaleda de Don Pedro.** This beautiful 16th-century mansion, in the city's Monumental Zone (Zona Monumental), blends the best of the old with all the comforts a modern traveler would expect. The rooms and public areas are spacious, and the pool offers relief from the summer heat. A unique feature is its parking facility—you drive your car into an elevator to be taken down to the car park. ✉*Calle Obispo Toral 2, 23400* ☎*953/795147* 🖷*953/795149* 🌐*www.rosaledadedonpedro.com* *30* *In-hotel: restaurant, bar, pool, public Internet, parking (no fee)* ▭*AE, DC, MC, V.*

$$ 🏨**Hospedería El Blanquillo.** This hotel is in a small palace from the 16th century, and it's close to the walls and the Hospital Salvador. The simply furnished rooms surround a central patio. The restaurant's specialty is Mediterranean cuisine. ✉*Pl. del Carmen 1, 23400* ☎*953/795405* 🖷*953/795406* *16 rooms, 1 suite* *In-hotel: restaurant, bar, laundry facilities* ▭*MC, V.*

SHOPPING

Little Úbeda is the crafts capital of Andalusia, with workshops devoted to carpentry, basket weaving, stone carving, wrought iron, stained glass, and, above all, the city's distinctive green-glaze pottery. Calle Valencia is the traditional potters' row, running from the bottom of town to Úbeda's general crafts center, northwest of the old quarter (follow signs to Calle Valencia or Barrio de Alfareros). Úbeda's most famous potter was Pablo Tito, whose craft is carried on at three different workshops run by two of Tito's sons (Paco and Juan) and a son-in-law, Melchor, each of whom claims to be the sole true heir to the art.

All kinds of ceramics are sold at **Alfarería Góngora** (⊠ *Calle Cuesta de la Merced 32* ☎ *953/754605*). **Antonio Almazara** (⊠ *Calle Valencia 34* ☎ *953/753692* ⊠ *Calle Fuenteseca 17* ☎ *953/753365*) is one of several shops specializing in Úbeda's green-glaze pottery. The extrovert **Juan Tito** (⊠ *Pl. del Ayuntamiento 12* ☎ *953/751302*) can often be found at the potter's wheel in his rambling shop, which is packed with ceramics of every size and shape. **Melchor Tito** (⊠ *Calle Valencia 44* ☎ *953/753365*) focuses on classic green-glaze items. **Paco Tito** (⊠ *Calle Valencia 22* ☎ *953/751496*) devotes himself to clay sculptures of characters from *Don Quixote,* which he fires in an old Moorish-style kiln. His shop has a small museum as well as a studio.

CAZORLA

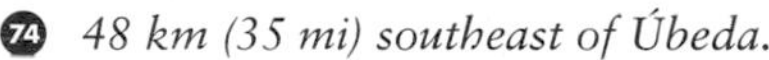

74 *48 km (35 mi) southeast of Úbeda.*

Unspoiled and remote, the village of Cazorla is at the east end of Jaén province. The pine-clad slopes and towering peaks of the Cazorla and Segura sierras rise above the village, and below it stretch endless miles of olive groves. In spring, purple jacaranda trees blossom in the plazas.

WHAT TO SEE

For a break from human-made sights, drink in the scenery or watch for wildlife in the **Parque Natural Sierra de Cazorla, Segura y Las Villas** *(Cazorla, Segura and Las Villas Nature Park).* Try to avoid the summer and late spring months, when the park teems with tourists and locals. It's almost impossible to get accommodations in fall, particularly when it's deer season (September and October). For information on hiking, camping, canoeing, horseback riding, or guided excursions, contact the **Agencia de Medio Ambiente** (⊠ *Tejares Altos, Cazorla* ☎ *953/720125* ⊠ *Fuente de Serbo 3, Jaén* ☎ *953/012400*), or the park visitor center. For hunting or fishing permits, apply to the Jaén office well in advance. Deer, wild boar, and mountain goats roam the slopes of this carefully protected patch of mountain wilderness 80 km (50 mi) long and 30 km (19 mi) wide, and hawks, eagles, and vultures soar over the 6,000-foot peaks. Within the park, at **Cañada de las Fuentes** (Fountains' Ravine), is the source of Andalusia's great river, the Guadalquivir. The road through the park follows the river to the shores of **Lago Tranco de Beas.** Alpine meadows, pine forests, springs, waterfalls, and gorges make Cazorla a perfect place to hike. A short film shown in the **Centro de Interpretación Torre del Vinagre** (⊠ *Ctra. del Tranco, Km 37.8*

953/713040 *Daily 11–2 and 4–6*), in Torre de Vinagre, introduces the park's main sights. Displays explain the park's plants and geology and the staff can advise you on camping, fishing, and hiking trails.

There's also a **hunting museum,** with such "cheerful" attractions as the interlocked antlers of bucks who clashed in autumn rutting season, became helplessly trapped, and died of starvation. Nearby are a **botanical garden** and a **game reserve.** Between June and October the park maintains seven well-equipped **campsites.** Past Lago Tranco and the village of Hornos, a road goes to the **Sierra de Segura** mountain range, the park's least crowded area. At 3,600 feet, the spectacular village of **Segura de la Sierra,** on top of the mountain, is crowned by an almost perfect castle with impressive defense walls, a Moorish bath, and a nearly rectangular bullring.

Déjate Guiar-Excursiones organizes four-wheel-drive trips into restricted areas of the park to observe the flora and fauna and photograph the larger animals. *Paseo del Santo Cristo 17, Bajo, Edificio Parque 953/721351 www.turisnat.org.*

EN ROUTE

Leave Cazorla Nature Park by an alternative route—the spectacular gorge carved by the Guadalquivir River, a rushing torrent beloved by kayak enthusiasts. At the El Tranco Dam, follow signs to Villanueva del Arzobispo, where N322 takes you back to Úbeda, Baeza, and Jaén.

WHERE TO STAY & EAT

$$–$$$ **Parador de Cazorla.** Isolated in a valley at the edge of the nature reserve, 26 km (16 mi) above Cazorla village, lies this white, modern parador with red-tile roof. It's a quiet place, popular with hunters and anglers. The restaurant serves regional dishes such as *pipirrana* (a salad of finely diced peppers, onions, and tomatoes) and, in season, game. *Calle Sierra de Cazorla, 23470 953/727075 953/727077 www.parador.es 33 rooms In-hotel: restaurant, pool, parking (no fee) AE, DC, MC, V Closed Dec. and Jan.*

$$ **Villa Turística de Cazorla.** On a hill with superb views of the village of Cazorla, this leisure complex rents semidetached apartments sleeping one to six. Each has a balcony or terrace as well as a kitchenette—some have a full kitchen—and fireplace. The restaurant ($–$$), done in welcoming warm ocher tones, specializes in trout, lamb, and game. *Ladera de San Isicio s/n, 23470 953/710100 953/710152 www.villacazorla.com 32 apartments In-room: kitchen. In-hotel: restaurant, bar, pool MC, V.*

$ **La Hortizuela.** Deep in the heart of Cazorla Nature Park, in what was once a game warden's house, is a small hotel that's the perfect base for exploring the wilderness. Guest rooms are in the back, beyond the central courtyard, and most have unhindered views of the forest-clad mountainside (a few look onto the patio). Wild boar, game, deer, and fresh trout are usually available in the restaurant ($–$$). *Ctra. del Tranco, Km 50.5, 2 km (1 mi) east of visitor center up dirt track, Coto Ríos23478 953/713150 www.lahortizuela.com 23 rooms In-hotel: restaurant, pool, parking (no fee) MC, V CP.*

$$ **Casa Rural La Calerilla.** Tucked into the mountainside, on the road leading down to Cazorla away from the valley and almost hidden from the road itself, is this rather charming and new stone *casa rural.*(rural house) The rooms are bright with a traditional decor, and the garden and pool area is a great place to wind down. *Ctra. de la Sierra, Km 24.5, Burunchel, 23479 953/727326 953/727034 www.casaruralcalerilla.com 11 rooms In-hotel: restaurant, bar, pool, parking (no fee), no elevator MC, V.*

$$ **Coto del Valle.** This delightful new hotel in Cazorla's foothills is easily recognized by the huge fountain outside. Built in traditional highland stone architecture, the hotel has rooms with a mountain decor and a restaurant with a fireplace and mounted game ranging from mountain goats to redleg partridges. *Ctra. del Tranco, Km 34.3, 23470 953/124067 www.hotelcotodelvalle.com 59 rooms In-hotel: restaurant, bar, pool, parking (no fee) AE, DC, MC, V.*

GRANADA

430 km (265 mi) south of Madrid, 261 km (162 mi) east of Seville, and 160 km (100 mi) southeast of Córdoba.

The Alhambra and the tomb of the Catholic Monarchs are the pride of Granada. The city rises majestically from a plain onto three hills, dwarfed—on a clear day—by the Sierra Nevada. Atop one of these hills perches the pink gold Alhambra palace. The stunning view from its mount takes in the sprawling medieval Moorish quarter, the caves of the Sacromonte, and, in the distance, the fertile *vega* (plain), rich in orchards, tobacco fields, and poplar groves.

Split by internal squabbles, Granada's Moorish Nasrid dynasty gave Ferdinand of Aragón an opportunity in 1491; spurred by Isabella's religious fanaticism, he laid siege to the city for seven months, and on January 2, 1492, Boabdil, the "Rey Chico" (Boy King), was forced to surrender the keys of the city to the Catholic Monarchs. As Boabdil fled the Alhambra via the Puerta de los Siete Suelos (Gate of the Seven Floors), he asked that the gate be sealed forever.

EXPLORING GRANADA

Granada can be characterized by its major neighborhoods. East of the Darro River and up the hill is **La Alhambra.** South of it and around a square and a popular hangout area, Campo del Príncipe, is **Realejo.** To the west of the Darro and going from north to south are the two popular neighborhoods, **Sacromonte** and **Albayzín** (also spelled Albaicín). The latter is the young and trendy part of Granada, full of color, flavor, and charming old architecture and narrow, hilly streets. On either side of Gran Vía de Colón and the streets that border the cathedral (Reyes Católicos and Recogidas—the major shopping areas) is the area generally referred to as **Centro,** the city center. These days much of the Alhambra and Albayzín areas are closed to cars, but starting from

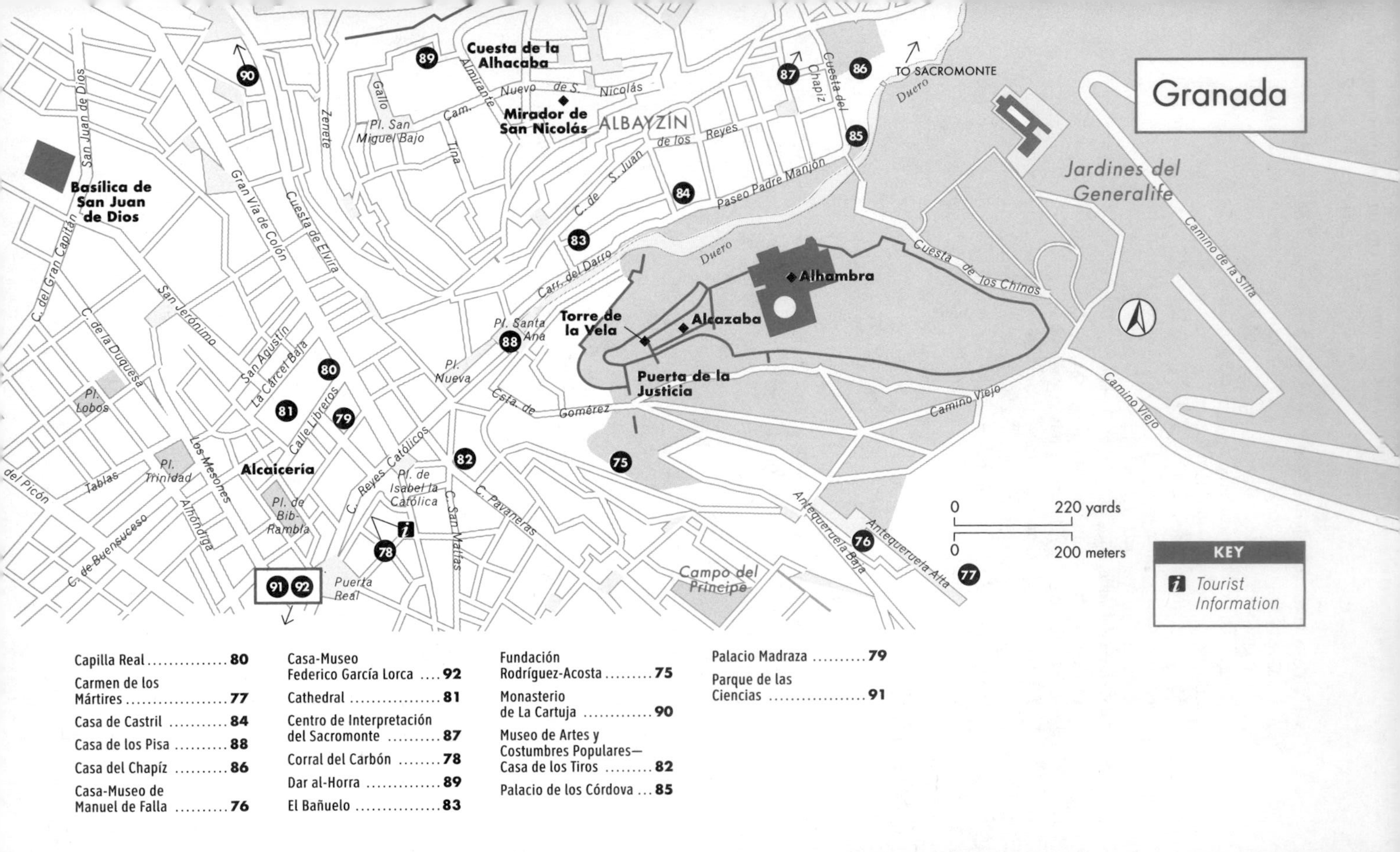

Granada
Jardines del Generalife
Camino de la Silla
TO SACROMONTE
Duero
Cuesta del Chapiz
Cuesta de la Alhacaba
Mirador de San Nicolás
ALBAYZÍN
Nuevo de S. Nicolás
Almirante
Cam.
Gallo
Pl. San Miguel Bajo
Tina
Zenete
de los Reyes
C. de S. Juan
Paseo Padre Manjón
Carr. del Darro
Cuesta de los Chinos
Alhambra
Alcazaba
Torre de la Vela
Puerta de la Justicia
Camino Viejo
Cuesta de Elvira
Gran Vía de Colón
San Juan de Dios
Basílica de San Juan de Dios
C. del Gran Capitán
San Jerónimo
C. de la Duquesa
Pl. Lobos
San Agustín
La Cárcel Baja
Calle Libreros
Pl. Santa Ana
Pl. Nueva
Csta. de Gomérez
Alcaicería
Pl. Trinidad
Los Mesones
Tablas
del Picón
Alhóndiga
C. de Buensuceso
Pl. de Bib-Rambla
C. Reyes Católicos
Pl. de Isabel la Católica
C. San Matías
C. Pavaneras
Puerta Real
Campo del Príncipe
Antequeruela Baja
Antequeruela Alta
0 220 yards
0 200 meters
KEY
Tourist Information
Capilla Real ... 80
Carmen de los Mártires ... 77
Casa de Castril ... 84
Casa de los Pisa ... 88
Casa del Chapíz ... 86
Casa-Museo de Manuel de Falla ... 76
Casa-Museo Federico García Lorca ... 92
Cathedral ... 81
Centro de Interpretación del Sacromonte ... 87
Corral del Carbón ... 78
Dar al-Horra ... 89
El Bañuelo ... 83
Fundación Rodríguez-Acosta ... 75
Monasterio de La Cartuja ... 90
Museo de Artes y Costumbres Populares—Casa de los Tiros ... 82
Palacio de los Córdova ... 85
Palacio Madraza ... 79
Parque de las Ciencias ... 91

the Plaza Nueva there are now minibuses—numbers 30, 31, 32, and 34—that run frequently to these areas.

LA ALHAMBRA

Fodor's Choice ★ With more than 2 million visitors a year, the Alhambra is Spain's most popular attraction. The complex has three main parts: the Alcazaba, the Palacios Nazaríes (Nasrid Royal Palace), and the Generalife. *See the Alhambra in-focus feature for details on visiting the attraction.*

77 **Carmen de los Mártires.** Up the hill from the Hotel Alhambra Palace, this turn-of-the-20th-century Granada *carmen* (private villa), and its gardens—the only area open to tourists—are like a Generalife in miniature. ✉ *Paseo de los Mártires, Alhambra* ☎ *958/227953* 🎫 *Free* ⏲ *Apr.–Oct., weekdays 10–2 and 5–7, weekends 10–7; Nov.–Mar., weekdays 10–2 and 4–6, weekends 10–6.*

76 **Casa-Museo de Manuel de Falla.** The composer Manuel de Falla (1876–1946) lived and worked for many years in this rustic house, tucked into a charming little hillside lane with lovely views of the Alpujarra Mountains. In 1986 Granada paid homage to Spain's classical-music composer by naming its new concert hall (down the street from the Carmen de los Mártires) the Auditorio Manuel de Falla—and from this institution, fittingly, you have a view of his little white house. Note the bust in the small garden: it stands where the composer once sat to enjoy the sweeping view. ✉ *C. Antequeruela Alta 11, Alhambra* ☎ *958/228318* 🎫 *€3* ⏲ *Open by guided 30-min tour only, Tues.–Sat. 10–1:30.*

REALEJO

75 **Fundación Rodríguez-Acosta/Instituto Gómez Moreno.** A few yards from the impressive Alhambra Hotel, this nonprofit organization was founded at the bequeath of the painter José Marí Rodríguez-Acosta. Inside a typical Granadino *carmen* (private villa), it houses works of art, archaeological findings, and a library collected by the Granada-born scholar Manuel Gómez-Moreno Martínez. Other exhibits include valuable and unique objects from Asian cultures and the prehistoric and classical eras. ✉ *Callejón Niños del Rollo 8, Realejo* ☎ *958/227497* 🌐 *www.fundacionrodriguezacosta.com* 🎫 *€4* ⏲ *Wed.–Sun. 10–2; last entrance 30 min before closing.*

82 **Museo de Artes y Costumbres Populares–Casa de los Tiros.** This 16th-century palace, adorned by the coat-of-arms of the Grana Venegas family who owned it, was named House of the Shots for the musket barrels that protrude from its facade. The stairs to the upper-floor displays are flanked by portraits of miserable-looking Spanish royals, from Ferdinand and Isabella to Philip IV. The highlight is the carved wooden ceiling in the Cuadra Dorada (Hall of Gold), adorned with gilded lettering and portraits of royals and knights. Old lithographs, engravings, and photographs show life in Granada in the 19th and early 20th centuries. ✉ *Calle Pavaneras s/n, Realejo* ☎ *958/221072* 🎫 *Free* ⏲ *Tues. 2:30–8:30, Wed.–Sat. 9–8:30, Sun. 9–2:30.*

A GOOD WALK: GRANADA

Save a full day for the Alhambra and the Alhambra hill sites: the Alcazaba, Generalife, Alhambra Museum, **Fundación Rodríguez-Acosta** 75, **Casa-Museo de Manuel de Falla** 76, and **Carmen de los Mártires** 77. The following walk covers the other major Granada sights.

Begin at Plaza Isabel la Católica (corner of Gran Vía and Calle Reyes Católicos), with its statue of Columbus presenting the Queen with his New World maps. Walk south on Calle Reyes Católicos and turn left into the **Corral del Carbón** 78—the oldest building in Granada.

Cross back over Calle Reyes Católicos to the Alcaicería, once the Moorish silk market and now a maze of alleys with souvenir shops and restaurants. Behind the Alcaicería is Plaza Bib-Rambla, with its flower stalls and historic Gran Café Bib-Rambla, famous for hot chocolate and churros (a deep-fried flour fritter). Calle Oficios leads to **Palacio Madraza** 79, the old Moorish University, and the **Capilla Real** 80, next to the **cathedral** 81.

Off the cathedral's west side is the 16th-century Escuela de las Niñas Nobles, with its plateresque facade. Next to the cathedral, just off Calle Libreros, are the Curia Eclesiástica, an Imperial College until 1769; the Palacio del Arzobispo; and the 18th-century Iglesia del Sagrario. Behind the cathedral is the Gran Vía de Colón. Cross Gran Vía and head right to Plaza Isabel la Católica.

Make a detour to the **Casa de los Tiros** 82 (on Calle Pavaneras, across Calles Reyes Católicos) before returning to Plaza Isabel la Católica. Follow Reyes Católicos to Plaza Nueva, and the ornate 16th-century Real Cancillería (Royal Chancery), now the Tribunal Superior de Justicia (High Court). Just north is Plaza Santa Ana, and the church of Santa Ana, designed by Diego de Siloé.

Walk through Plaza Santa Ana into Carrera del Darro—recently renovated, with new hotels and restaurants—and you come to the 11th-century Arab bathhouse, **El Bañuelo** 83 and the 16th-century **Casa de Castril** 84, site of Granada's Archaeological Museum.

Follow the river along the Paseo del Padre Manjón (Paseo de los Tristes)—to the **Palacio de los Córdoba** 85. Climb Cuesta del Chapíz to the Morisco **Casa del Chapíz** 86. To the east are the caves of Sacromonte and the **Centro de Interpretación del Sacromonte (Cuevas)** 87. Turn west into the streets of the Albayzín, with the interesting **Casa de los Pisa** 88 and **Dar al-Horra** 89 nearby. Best reached by taxi are the 16th-century **Monasterio de La Cartuja** 90, the interactive science museum **Parque de las Ciencias** 91, and **Casa-Museo Federico García Lorca** 92.

SACROMONTE

The third of Granada's three hills, the Sacromonte rises behind the Albayzín. The hill is covered with prickly pear cacti and riddled with caverns. These caves may have sheltered early Christians; 15th-century treasure hunters found bones inside and assumed they belonged to San Cecilio, the city's patron saint. Thus the hill was sanctified—*sacro monte* (holy mountain)—and an abbey built on its summit, the **Abadía de**

Continued on page 731

ALHAMBRA

Floating mirage-like on its promontory overlooking Granada, the mighty and mysterious Alhambra shimmers vermilion in the clear mountain air, with the white peaks of the Sierra Nevada rising behind it. This sprawling palace-fortress, named from the Arabic for "red citadel" *(al-Qal'ah al-Hamra)*, was the last bastion of the 800-year Moorish presence on the Iberian Peninsula. Composed of royal residential quarters, court chambers, baths, and gardens, surrounded by defense towers and massive walls, the Alhambra is an architectual gem where Moorish kings worked and played—and even murdered their enemies.

LOOK UP

Among the stylistic elements you can see in the Alhambra are **Arabesque** geometrical designs, and elaborate **Mocárabe** arches.

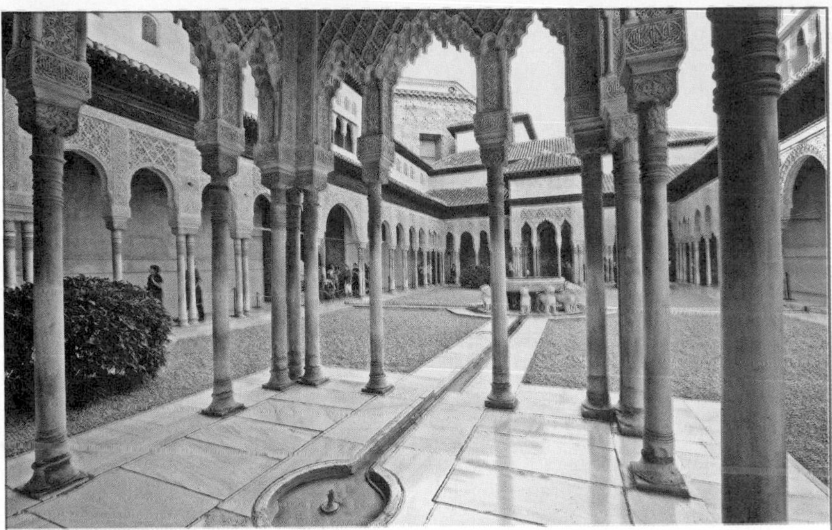

Built of perishable materials, the Alhambra was meant to be forever replenished and replaced by succeeding generations. Currently, it is the Patio de los Leones's (above) season for restoration.

INSIDE THE FORTRESS

More than 2 million annual visitors come to the Alhambra today, making it Spain's top attraction. Vistors revel in the palace's architectural wonders, most of which had to be restored after the alterations made after the Christian reconquest of southern Spain in 1492 and the damage from an 1821 earthquake. Incidentally, Napoléon's troops commandeered the site in 1812 with intent to level it; their attempts were foiled.

The courtyards, patios, and halls offer an ethereal maze of Moorish arches, columns, and domes containing intricate stucco carvings and patterned ceramic tiling. The intimate arcades, fountains, and light-reflecting pools throughout are identified in the ornamental inscriptions as physical renderings of paradise taken from the Koran and Islamic poetry. The contemporary visitor to this dream like space feels the fleeting embrace of a culture that brought its light to a world emerging from medieval darkness.

ARCHITECTURAL TERMS

Arabesque: An ornament or decorative style that employs flower, foliage, or fruit, and sometimes geometrical, animal, and figural outlines to produce an intricate pattern of interlaced lines.

Mocárabe: A decorative element of carved wood or plaster based on juxtaposed and hanging prisms resembling stalactites. Sometimes called *muquarna* (honeycomb vaulting), the impression is similar to a beehive and the honey has been described as light.

Mozárabe: Sometimes confused with Moçárabe, the term Mozárabe refers to Christians living in Moorish Spain. Thus, Christian artistic styles or recourses in Moorish architecture (such as the paintings in the Sala de los Reyes) also are identified as *mozárabe*, or, in English, mozarabic.

Mudéjar: This word refers to Moors living in Christian Spain. Moorish artistic elements in Christian architecture, such as horseshoe arches in a church, also are referred to as Mudéjar.

ALHAMBRA'S ARCHITECTURAL HIGHLIGHTS

Court of the Lions

The **columns** used in the construction of the Alhambra are unique, with extraordinarily slender cylindrical shafts, concave base moldings, and carved rings decorating the upper extremities. The capitals have simple cylindrical bases under prism-shaped heads decorated in a variety of vegetal motifs. Nearly all of these columns support false arches constructed purely for decorative purposes. The 124 columns surrounding the Patio de los Leones (Court of the Lions) are the best examples.

Cursive epigraphy

Cursive epigraphy is used to quote the Koran and Arabic poems. Considered the finest example of this are the Ibn-Zamrak verses that decorate the walls of the Sala de las Dos Hermanas.

Ceramic tiles

Glazed ceramic tiles covered with geometrical patterns in primary colors cover the walls of the Alhambra with a profusion of styles and shapes. Red, blue, and yellow are the colors of magic in Sufi tradition, while green is the life-giving color of Islam.

Gate of Justice

The **horseshoe arch**, widening before rounding off with lower ends extending around the circle until they begin to converge, was the quintessential Moorish architectural innovation, used not only for aesthetic and decorative purposes but because it allowed greater height than the classical, semicircular arch inherited from the Greeks and Romans. The horseshoe arch also had a mystical significance in recalling the shape of the *mihrab*, the prayer niche in the *qibla* wall of a mosque indicating the direction of prayer and suggesting a door to Mecca or to paradise. Horseshoe arches and arcades are found throughout the Alhambra.

Alhambra fountains

The Koran describes paradise as "gardens underneath which rivers flow," and **water** is used as a practical and ornamental architectural element throughout the Alhambra. Whether used musically, as in the canals in the Patio de los Leones or visually, as in the reflecting pool of the Patio de los Arrayanes, water is used to enhance light, enlarge spaces, or provide musical background for a desert culture in love with the beauty and oasis-like properties of hydraulics in all its forms.

The Alcazaba was built chiefly by Nasrid kings in the 1300s.

LAY OF THE LAND

The complex has three main parts: the Alcazaba, the Palacio Nazaríes (Nasrid Royal Palace), and the Generalife. Across from the main entrance is the original fortress, the **Alcazaba**. Here, the watchtower's great bell was once used to announce the opening and closing of the irrigation system on Granada's great plain.

A wisteria-covered walkway leads to the heart of the Alhambra, the **Palacios Nazaríes**. Here, delicate apartments, lazy fountains, and tranquil pools contrast vividly with the hulking fortifications outside. It is divided into three sections: the *mexuar*, where business, government, and palace administration were headquartered; the *serrallo*, a series of state rooms where the sultans held court and entertained their ambassadors; and the harem, which in its time was entered only by the sultan, his family, and their most trusted servants, most of them eunuchs. Nearby is the Renaissance Palacio de Carlos V (Palace of Charles V), featuring a perfectly square exterior but a circular interior courtyard. Designed by Pedro Machuca, a pupil of Michelangelo, it is where the sultan's private apartments once stood. Part of the building houses the free **Museo de la Alhambra**, devoted to Islamic art. Upstairs is the more modest **Museo de Bellas Artes**.

Over on Cerro del Sol (Hill of the Sun) is **Generalife**, ancient summer palace of the Nasrid kings.

TIMELINE

1238 First Nasrid king, Ibn el-Ahmar, begins Alhambra.

1391 Nasrid Palaces is completed.

1492 Boabdil surrenders Granada to Ferdinand and Isabella, parents of King Henry VIII's first wife, Catherine of Aragon.

1524 Carlos V begins Renaissance Palace.

1812 Napoléonic troops arrive with plans to destroy Alhambra.

1814 The Duke of Wellington sojourns here to escape the pressures of the Peninsular War.

1829 Washington Irving lives on the premises and writes *Tales of the Alhambra*, reviving interest in the crumbling palace.

1862 Granada municipality begins Alhambra restoration that continues to this day.

2006 The Patio de los Leones undergoes a multiyear restoration.

ALHAMBRA'S PASSAGES OF TIME

From Columbus's commissioning to a bloody murder, historic events as well as everyday affairs happened between these walls.

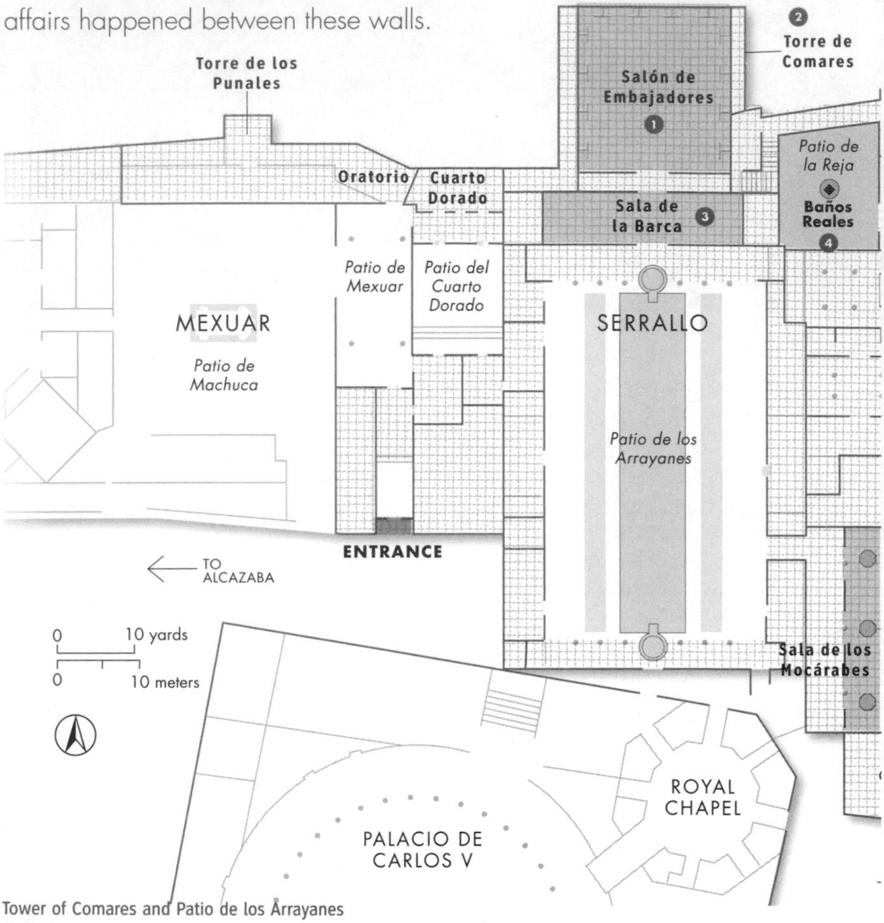

PALACIOS NAZARIÁES (NASRID ROYAL PALACE)

Torre de los Punales

Salón de Embajadores 1

2 Torre de Comares

Oratorio

Cuarto Dorado

Sala de la Barca 3

Patio de la Reja

Baños Reales 4

Patio de Mexuar

Patio del Cuarto Dorado

MEXUAR

Patio de Machuca

SERRALLO

Patio de los Arrayanes

ENTRANCE

TO ALCAZABA

0 10 yards

0 10 meters

Sala de los Mocárabes

ROYAL CHAPEL

PALACIO DE CARLOS V

Tower of Comares and Patio de los Arrayanes

1 In **El Salón de Embajadores**, Boabdil drew up his terms of surrender, and Christopher Columbus secured royal support for his historic voyage in 1492. The carved wooden ceiling is a portrayal of the seven Islamic heavens, with six rows of stars topped by a seventh-heaven cupulino or micro-cupola.

2 **Torre de Comares**, a lookout in the corner of this hall is where Carlos V uttered his famous line, "Ill-fated the man who lost all this."

3 Mistakenly named from the Arabic word *baraka* (divine blessing), **Sala de la Barca** has a carved wooden ceiling often described as an inverted boat.

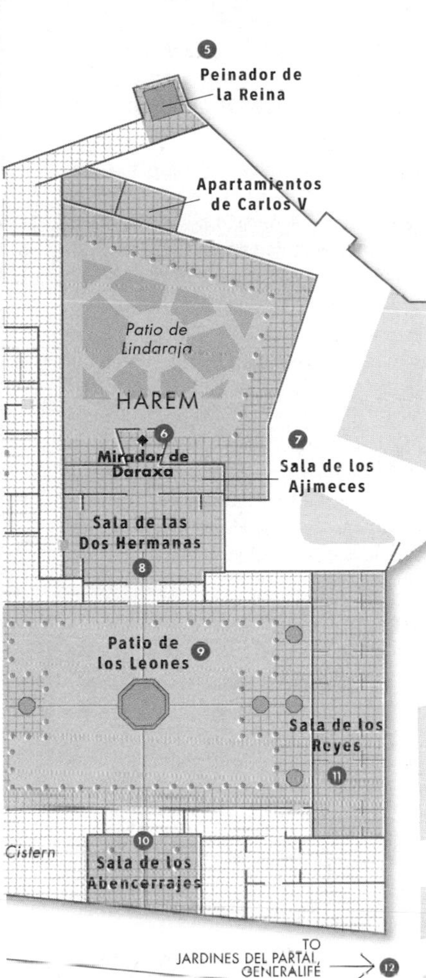

Sala de los Reyes

❹ The **Baños Reales** is where the sultan's favorites luxuriated in brightly tiled pools beneath star-shape pinpoints of light from the ceiling above. It is open to visitors on certain days. An up-to-date timetable can be obtained from the tourist office.

❺ **El Peinador de la Reina**, a nine-foot-square room atop a small tower was the Sultana's boudoir. The perforated marble slab was used to infiltrate perfumes while the queen performed her toilette. Washington Irving wrote his *Tales of the Alhambra* in this romantic tree house-like perch.

❻ Sultana Zoraya often found refuge in this charming little balcony (**Mirador de Daraxa**) overlooking the Lindaraja garden.

❼ Shhh, don't tell a secret here. In the **Sala de los Ajimeces**, a whisper in one corner can be clearly heard from the opposite corner.

❽ In the **Sala de las Dos Hermanas**, twin slabs of marble embedded in the floor are the "sisters," though Washington Irving preferred the story of a pair of captive Moorish beauties.

❾ In the **Patio de Los Leones** (Court of the Lions), a dozen crudely crafted lions support the fountain at the center of this elegant courtyard, representing the signs of the zodiac sending water to the four corners. (The lions are currently not on display while the court undergoes restoration through 2008.)

❿ In the **Sala de los Abencerrajes**, Muley Hacen (father of Boabdil) murders the male members of the Abencerraje family in revenge for their chief's seduction of his daughter Zoraya. The rusty stains in the fountain are said to be bloodstains left by the pile of Abencerraje heads.

The star-shaped cupola, reflected in the pool, is considered the Alhambra's most beautiful example of stalactite or honeycomb vaulting.

The octagonal dome over the room is best viewed at sunset when the 16 small windows atop the dome admit sharp, low sunlight that refracts kaleidoscopically through the beehive-like prisms.

⓫ In the **Sala de los Reyes**, the ceiling painting depicts the first 10 Nasrid rulers. It was painted by a Christian artist since Islamic artists were not allowed to usurp divine power by creating human or animal figures.

The overhead painting of the knight rescuing his lady from a savage man portrays chivalry, a concept introduced to Europe by Arabic poets.

⓬ The terraces of **Generalife** grant incomparable views of the city.

Generalife gardens

PLANNING YOUR VISIT

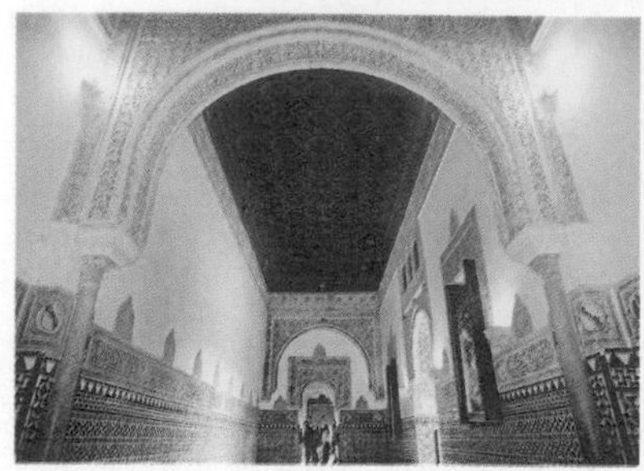

The acoustics in the Palace of Charles V are ideal for the summer symphony concerts at the Alhambra.

GETTING THERE & AROUND

The best approach to the Alhambra is straight up the Cuesta de Gomérez from Plaza Nueva to the Puerta de la Justicia. From hotels up the river Darro in the Albayzín, the walk around the back walls of the palace along the Cuesta de los Chinos is a good hike. Buses 30 and 32 run from Plaza Nueva to the Alhambra. If you're driving, don't park on the street (it leaves your car vulnerable to a break-in). Instead, use the Alhambra parking lot or park underground on Calle San Agustín, just north of the cathedral, and take a taxi or the minibus from Plaza Nueva.

The entrance to the Nasrid Royal Palace is behind Carlos V's Renaissance Palace and leads into the *mexuar*, the chambers of state. The best route through the Alhambra traces an s-shaped path through the *mexuar*, the *serrallo*, and the harem, starting with the Patio de los Leones and ending with the Peinador de la Reina.

Wheelchairs are available on request; inquire at the Entrance Pavilion.

WHEN TO GO

Winter's low, slanting sunlight is best for seeing the Alhambra, and the temperatures are ideal for walking. Spring brings lush floral colors to the gardens. Fall is also sharp, cooler, and clear. July and August are crowded and hot.

The **Festival Internacional de Música y Danza de Granada** (☎ 34 958/276241 🌐 www.granadafestival.org) held annually from mid-June to mid-July offers visitors an opportunity to hear a concert in the Alhambra or watch a ballet in the Generalife amphitheater.

GETTING TICKETS

Entrance to the Alhambra complex of the Alcazaba, Nasrid Palaces, Mosque Baths, and Generalife is strictly controlled by quotas. There are three types of timed tickets: morning, afternoon, and evening; note that the evening ticket is valid only for the Nasrid Palaces.

Tickets for the Alhambra complex and the Nasrid Palaces cost €12. Tickets can be obtained online at 🌐 www.alhambratickets.com, by phone at ☎ 902/224460 in Spain or ☎ 34 91/537–9178 outside Spain, or at any BBVA (Banco Bilbao Vizcaya Argentaria) branch.

You can visit the Palace of Charles V and its two museums (Museo de la Alhambra and Museo de Bellos Artes) independently of the Alhambra. They're open Tues.–Sat. 9–2:30

HOURS OF OPERATION

The Alhambra is open every day except December 25 and January 1.

November through February, morning visits are daily from 8:30 to 2, with a maximum capacity of 3,300; afternoon visits are daily from 2 to 6, with a maximum capacity of 2,100; and evening visits are Friday and Saturday from 8 to 9:30, with a maximum capacity of 400.

March to October, morning visits are daily from 8:30 to 2, with a maximum capacity of 3,300; afternoon visits are daily from 2 to 8, with a maximum capacity of 3,300; and evening visits are Tuesday through Saturday from 10 to 11:30, with a maximum capacity of 400.

Visits to the main gardens are allowed daily, from 8:30 to 6 year-round; from March through October access is until 8.

CONTACT INFORMATION

Patronato de la Alhambra ☎ 34 958/027900 ✉ informacion.alhambra.pag@juntadeandalucia.es 🌐 www.alhambra-patronato.es.

Sacromonte (✉*C. del Sacromonte, Sacromonte* ☎*958/221445* 💳*€3* ⏲*Tues.–Sat. 11–1 and 4–6, Sun. 4–6; guided tours every ½ hr*). The Sacromonte has long been notorious as a domain of Granada's gypsies and a den of pickpocketing, but its reputation is largely undeserved. The quarter is more like a quiet Andalusian *pueblo* (village) than a rough neighborhood. Many of the quarter's colorful *cuevas* (caves) have been restored as middle-class homes, and some of the old spirit lives on in a handful of *zambras*—flamenco performances in caves garishly decorated with brass plates and cooking utensils. These shows differ from formal flamenco shows in that the performers mingle with you, usually dragging one or two onlookers onto the floor for an improvised dance lesson. Ask your hotel to book you a spot on a cueva tour, which usually includes a walk through the neighboring Albayzín and a drink at a tapas bar in addition to the zambra.

BICYCLING IN GRANADA

At the foot of the Iberian Peninsula's tallest mountain—the 11,427-foot Mulhacén peak—Granada offers challenging mountain cycling opportunities, while spinning through the hairpin turns of the Alpujarra mountain range east of Granada is both scenic and hair-raising. For more information about cycling tours around Granada, contact **Cycling Country** (✉*C/Salmerones 18, Alhama de Granada* ☎*958/360655* 🌐*www.cyclingcountry.com*) run by husband-and-wife team Maggi Jones and Geoff Norris in a town about 55 km (33 mi) away.

87 **Centro de Interpretación del Sacromonte.** A word of warning: even if you take the 30 or 32 minibus or the city sightseeing bus to get here, you will still be left with a steep, arduous walk to reach the center. The Museo Etnográfico shows how people lived here, and other areas show the flora and fauna of the area as well as cultural activities. ✉*Calle Barranco de los Negros s/n* ☎*958/215120* 🌐*www.sacromontegranada.com* 💳*€4 museum, €1 for other areas* ⏲*Apr.–Oct., Tues.–Fri. 10–2 and 5–9; Nov.–Mar., Tues.–Fri. 10–2 and 4–7, weekends 11–7.*

ALBAYZÍN

Fodor's Choice ★ Covering a hill of its own, across the Darro ravine from the Alhambra, this ancient Moorish neighborhood is a mix of dilapidated white houses and immaculate *carmenes* (private villas in gardens enclosed by high walls). It was founded in 1228 by Moors who fled Baeza after Saint King Ferdinand III captured the city. Full of cobblestone alleyways and secret corners, the Albayzín guards its old Moorish roots jealously, though its 30 mosques were converted to baroque churches long ago. A stretch of the Moors' original city wall runs beside the Cuesta de la Alhacaba. If you're walking—the best way to explore—you can enter the Albayzín from either the Cuesta de Elvira or the Plaza Nueva. Alternatively, on foot or by taxi (parking is impossible), begin in the Plaza Santa Ana and follow the Carrera del Darro, Paseo Padre Manjón, and Cuesta del Chapíz. One of the highest points in the quarter, the plaza in front of the church of San Nicolás—called the **Mirador de San Nicolás**—has one of the finest views in all of Granada: on the hill opposite, the turrets and towers of the Alhambra form a dramatic silhouette against the snowy peaks of the Sierra Nevada. The sight is most magical at dawn, dusk, and on nights when the Alhambra is floodlighted. Interestingly, given the area's Moorish history, the two sloping, narrow streets of Calderería Nueva and Caldería Vieja that meet at the top by the Iglesia San Gregorio have developed into something of a North African bazaar. They are full of shops and stalls selling clothes, bags, crafts, and trinkets. The numerous little teahouses and restaurants here have a decidedly Moroccan flavor. Be warned that there have been some thefts in the Albayzín area, so keep your money and valuables out of sight.

88 **Casa de los Pisa.** Originally built in 1494 for the Pisa family, this house's claim to fame is its relationship to San Juan de Dios, who came to Granada in 1538 and founded a charity hospital to take care of the poor and abandoned. Befriended by the Pisa family, he was taken into the Pisa home when he fell ill in February 1550. A month later, he died there, at the age of 55. Since that time, devotees of the saint have traveled from around the world to this house with a stone Gothic facade, now run by the Hospital Order of St. John. Inside are numerous pieces of priceless religious works of art, an extensive collection of paintings and sculptures depicting St. John, jewelry, and furniture. ✉ *Calle Convalecencia 1, Albayzín* ☎ *958/222144* 🎫 *€3* ⏲ *Mon.–Sat. 10–1.*

84 **Casa de Castril.** Bernardo Zafra, secretary to Queen Isabella, once owned this richly decorated 16th-century palace. Before you enter, notice the exquisite portal, and the facade carvings depicting scallop shells and a phoenix. Inside is the **Museo Arqueológico** (Archaeological Museum), where you can find artifacts from provincial caves and from Moorish times, Phoenician burial urns from the coastal town of Almuñécar, and a copy of the *Dama de Baza* (Lady of Baza) a large Iberian sculpture discovered in northern Granada Province in 1971 (the original is in Madrid). ✉ *Carrera del Darro 41, Albayzín* ☎ *958/225640* 🎫 *€1.50, free for EU citizens* ⏲ *Tues. 2:30–8, Wed.–Sat. 9–8:30, Sun. 9–2:30.*

86 **Casa del Chapíz.** There's a delightful garden in this fine 16th-century Morisco house (built by Moorish craftsmen under Christian rule). It houses the School of Arabic Studies and is not generally open to the public, but if you knock, the caretaker might show you around. ✉ *C. Cuesta del Chapíz at C. del Sacromonte, Albayzín.*

89 **Dar al-Horra.** Hidden in the back of the upper Albayzín this semi-secret gem was built in the 15th century for the mother of Boabdil, last Nasrid ruler of Granada. After the 1492 conquest of Granada, Dar al-Horra—House of the Honest Woman—was ceded to royal secretary Don Hernando de Zafra. Isabella la Católica later founded the Convent of Santa Isabel la Real here, which continued until the 20th century. Typical of Nasrid art, the interior resembles that of the Alhambra. The north side is the most interesting, with two floors and a tower. The bottom floor is covered with an exquisite flat wooden ceiling decorated with geometric figures. ✉ *Callejón de las Monjas s/n Albayzín* ☎ *958/077800* 🎫 *Free* ⏲ *Weekdays 10–2.*

83 **El Bañuelo** *(Little Bath House)*. These 11th-century Arab steam baths might now be a little dark and dank, but try to imagine them filled, some 900 years ago, with Moorish beauties. The dull brick walls were then backed by bright ceramic tiles, tapestries, and rugs. Light comes in through star-shape vents in the ceiling, à la the bathhouse in the Alhambra. ✉*Carrera del Darro 31, Albayzín* ☎*958/227938* 🎫*Free* ⏲*Tues.–Sat. 10–2.*

NEED A BREAK?

The park at Paseo Padre Manjón, along the Darro River—also known as the Paseo de los Tristes (Promenade of the Sad) because funeral processions once passed this way—is a terrific place for a coffee break at one of the cafés or bars along the paseo. Dappled with fountains and stone walkways, the park has a stunning view of the Alhambra's northern side.

85 **Palacio de los Córdova.** At the end of the Paseo Padre Manjón, this 17th-century noble house today holds Granada's municipal archives and is used for municipal functions and art exhibits. You're free to wander about the large garden. ✉*Cuesta del Chapiz 4, Albayzín.*

CENTRO

80 **Capilla Real** *(Royal Chapel)*. Catholic Monarchs Isabella of Castile and Ferdinand of Aragón are buried at this shrine. The couple originally planned to be buried in Toledo's San Juan de los Reyes, but Isabella changed her mind when the pair conquered Granada in 1492. When she died in 1504, her body was first laid to rest in the Convent of San Francisco (now a parador), on the Alhambra hill. The architect Enrique Egas began work on the Royal Chapel in 1506 and completed it 15 years later, creating a masterpiece of the ornate Gothic style now known in Spain as Isabelline. In 1521 Isabella's body was transferred to a simple lead coffin in the Royal Chapel crypt, where it was joined by that of her husband, Ferdinand, and later her unfortunate daughter, Juana la Loca (Joanna the Mad), and son-in-law, Felipe el Hermoso (Philip the Handsome). Felipe died young, and Juana had his casket borne about the peninsula with her for years, opening the lid each night to kiss her embalmed spouse good night. A small coffin to the right contains the remains of Prince Felipe of Asturias, a grandson of the Catholic Monarchs and nephew of Juana la Loca who died in his infancy. The underground **crypt** containing the five lead coffins is quite simple, but it's topped by elaborate marble **tombs** showing Ferdinand and Isabella lying side by side (commissioned by their grandson Charles V and sculpted by Domenico Fancelli). The **altarpiece**, by Felipe Vigarini (1522), comprises 34 carved panels depicting religious and historical scenes; the bottom row shows Boabdil surrendering the keys of the city to its conquerors and the forced baptism of the defeated Moors. The **sacristy** holds Ferdinand's sword, Isabella's crown and scepter, and a fine collection of Flemish paintings once owned by Isabella. ✉*Calle Oficios, Centro* ☎*958/229239* 🌐*www.capillarealgranada.com* 🎫*€3* ⏲*Apr.–Oct., Mon.–Sat. 10:30–1 and 4–7, Sun. 11–1 and 4–7; Nov.–Mar., Mon.–Sat. 10:30–1 and 3:30–5:30, Sun. 11–1 and 3:30–6:30.*

81 **Cathedral.** Granada's cathedral was commissioned in 1521 by Charles V, who considered the Royal Chapel "too small for so much glory" and wanted to house his illustrious late grandparents someplace more worthy. Charles undoubtedly had great designs, as the cathedral was created by some of the finest architects of its time: Enrique Egas, Diego de Siloé, Alonso Cano, and sculptor Juan de Mena. Alas, his ambitions came to little, for the cathedral is a grand and gloomy monument, not completed until 1714, and never used as the crypt for his grandparents (or parents). You enter through a small door at the back, off the Gran Vía. Old hymnals are displayed throughout, and there's a museum, which includes a 14th-century gold-and-silver monstrance (used for communion) given to the city by Queen Isabella. Audio guides are available for €3. ✉ *Gran Vía s/n, Centro* ☎ *958/222959* 🎫 *€3* ⏲ *Apr.–Oct., Mon.–Sat. 10:30–1:30 and 4–8, Sun. 4–8; Nov.–Mar., Mon.–Sat. 10:45–1:30 and 4–7, Sun. 4–7.*

78 **Corral del Carbón** *(Coal House)*. This building was used to store coal in the 19th century, but its history goes further back. Dating from the 14th century, it was used by Moorish merchants as a lodging house, and then later by Christians as a theater. It's one of the oldest Moorish buildings in the city, and is the only Arab structure of its kind in Spain. ✉ *Pl. Mariana Pineda s/n, Centro* ☎ *958/221118* 🎫 *Free* ⏲ *Weekdays 10–1:30 and 5–8, weekends 10:30–2.*

79 **Palacio Madraza.** This building conceals the old Islamic seminary built in 1349 by Yusuf I. The intriguing baroque facade is elaborate; inside, across from the entrance, an octagonal room is crowned by a Moorish dome. There are occasional free art and cultural exhibitions. ✉ *C. Zacatín s/n, Centro* ☎ *958/223447.*

OUTSKIRTS OF TOWN

92 **Casa-Museo Federico García Lorca.** Granada's most famous native son, the poet Federico García Lorca, gets his due here, in the middle of a park devoted to him on the southern fringe of the city. Lorca's onetime summer home, **La Huerta de San Vicente,** is now a museum—run by his niece Laura García Lorca—with such artifacts as his beloved piano and changing exhibits on specific aspects of his life. ✉ *Parque García Lorca, Virgen Blanca s/n, Arabial* ☎ *958/258466* 🌐 *www.huertadesanvicente.com* 🎫 *€3, free Wed.* ⏲ *July and Aug., Tues.–Sun. 10–3; Apr., May, June, and Sept., Tues.–Sun. 10–1 and 5–8; Oct.–Mar. Tues.–Sun. 10–1 and 4–7. Guided tours every 45 min until 30 min before closing.*

90 **Monasterio de La Cartuja.** This Carthusian monastery in northern Granada (2 km [1 mi]) from the center and reached by the number 8 bus) was begun in 1506 and moved to its present site in 1516, though construction continued for the next 300 years. The exterior is sober and monolithic, but inside are twisted, multicolor marble columns; a profusion of gold, silver, tortoiseshell, and ivory; intricate stucco; and the extravagant sacristy—it's easy to see why Cartuja has been called the Christian answer to the Alhambra. ✉ *C. de Alfacar, Cartuja* ☎ *958/161932* 🎫 *€4* ⏲ *Apr.–Oct., Mon.–Sat. 10–1 and 4–8, Sun. 10–noon and 4–8; Nov.–Mar., Mon.–Sun. 10–1 and 3:30–6.*

91 **Parque de las Ciencias** *(Science Park)*. Across from Granada's convention center, and easily reached on either a number 1 or 5 bus, this museum has a planetarium and interactive demonstrations of scientific experiments. The 165-foot observation tower has views to the south and west. This is the most-visited museum in Andalusia. ✉ *Av. del Mediterráneo, Zaidín* ☎ *958/131900* 🌐 *www.parqueciencias.com* *Park €4.50, planetarium €2* ⏲ *Tues.–Sat. 10–7, Sun. and holidays 10–3. Closed Sept. 15–30.*

WHERE TO STAY & EAT

WHERE TO EAT

$$$–$$$$ ★ ✕ **Ruta del Veleta.** It's worth the short drive 5 km (3 mi) out of town to this Spanish restaurant, which serves some of the best food in Granada. House specialties include *carnes a la brasa* (succulent grilled meats) and fish dishes cooked in rock salt, as well as seasonal dishes such as *Solomillo de jabalí con frutos de otoño y salsa de vinagre* (wild boar fillet with autumn fruits in a vinegar-and-honey sauce). Dessert might be *morito de chocolate templado con helado de gachas* (warm chocolate sponge cake with ice cream). ✉ *Ctra. de la Sierra 136, on road to Sierra Nevada, Cenes de la Vega* ☎ *958/486134* 🌐 *www.rutadelveleta.com* ▭ *AE, DC, MC, V* ⏲ *No dinner Sun.*

$$–$$$$ ✕ **Azafrán.** It is rather a charming surprise when entering this restaurant, nestled at the foot of the Albayzín by the side of the Darro River and in the shadow of the Alhambra, to find such a bright and modern decor. It is newly opened, and you can expect an interesting and varied menu with fish and meat dishes as well as pasta, couscous, and an enticing rice-and-fish casserole. ✉ *Paseo de los Tristes 1, Albayzín* ☎ *958/226882* ▭ *MC, V.*

$$–$$$$ ✕ **La Ermita en la Plaza de Toros.** As the name implies, this classy restaurant is under the seats of the Plaza de Toros; the decor, with *carteles* (bullfighting posters), bulls' heads, and bullfighter suits, reflects that fact. Meat selections such as *rabo de toro estofado al vino tinto* (bull's tail cooked in red wine) and *lomo de buey Gallego a la parrilla* (grilled beef tenderloin) dominate, but there are also seafood dishes and daily specials. ✉ *Calle Dr. Olóriz 25, Centro* ☎ *958/290257* ▭ *MC, V.*

$$$ ✕ **La Yedra Real.** This is a very modern-style restaurant with a terrace that has a good selection of typical Spanish dishes at reasonable prices. Because it is very close to the Alhambra's main entrance, it's an ideal stop for those visiting this amazing monument. ✉ *C. Viejo del Cementerio s/n, Alhambra* ☎ *958/229145* ▭ *MC, V* ⏲ *Closed Mon.*

$$–$$$ ✕ **Bodegas Castañeda.** A block from the Cathedral across Gran Vía, this is a delightfully typical Granadino bodega. In addition to its wines, the specialties here are *jamón ibérico* (acorn fed Ibérico ham) and *embutidos* (sausages). The extensive list of tapas includes the likes of *queso viejo en aceite* (cured cheese in olive oil), bacon with Roquefort cheese, and *jamón de Trevélez* (ham from the Alpujarran village of Trevélez). Combination plates and *raciónes* (family-style platters) come in two sizes. ✉ *Calle Almireceros 1–3, Centro* ☎ *958/223222* ▭ *MC, V.*

$$–$$$ ✕ **Carmen Verde Luna.** This intriguingly named restaurant, Carmen (Arabic for "summer cottage") Green Moon, a reference to Federico García Lorca's famous poem "Romance Somnámbulo" (Sleepwalking Ballad), has a terrace with marvelous views across to the Alhambra and Sierra Nevada. Regional dishes here might include toasted and stuffed eggplants with pâté, stuffed sea bass and vegetables, and hake with prawns. ✉ *Calle Nuevo de San Nicolás 16, Albayzín* ☎ *958/291794* ▭ *MC, V.*

$$–$$$ ✕ **Cunini.** Around the corner from the cathedral is Granada's best fish house, where seafood, often fresh from the boats at Motril, is displayed in the window at the front of the tapas bar. Both the *pescaditos fritos* (fried) and the *parrillada* (grilled) fish are good choices, and if it's chilly, you can warm up with *caldereta de arroz, pescado y marisco* (rice, fish, and seafood stew). There are tables outdoors in warm weather. ✉ *Calle Pescadería 14, Centro* ☎ *958/250777* ▭ *AE, DC, MC, V* ⊙ *Closed Mon. No dinner Sun.*

$$–$$$ ✕ **Jardines Alberto.** Spacious and well located near the Alhambra, this restaurant has two outside patios with stunning views of the Generalife, plus a summer bar and barbecue. The interior is cozy and rustic, and the food, classically *granadino* with a choice of five-course menu, includes dishes such as *lomo de cerdo ibérico confitado al ajo y hierbas serranas con puré de castañas* (preserved Ibérico pork with garlic, wild herbs, and chestnut sauce) followed by the diet-defying *mousse de turron y crema de cafe* (nougat mousse with coffee cream). ✉ *Av. Alixares del Generalife s/n, Alhambra* ☎ *958/224818* ▭ *AE, MC, V* ⊙ *Closed Sun. No dinner Mon.*

$$–$$$ ★ ✕ **Mirador de Morayma.** Buried in the Albayzín, this place is hard to find and might appear to be closed (ring the doorbell). Once inside, you'll have unbeatable views across the gorge to the Alhambra, particularly from the wisteria-laden outdoor terrace. The adequate menu has some surprises, such as smoked *esturión* (sturgeon) from Riofrío, served cold with cured ham and a vegetable dip, and the *ensalada de remojón granadino,* a salad of cod, orange, and olives. ✉ *Calle Pianista García Carrillo 2, Albayzín* ☎ *958/228290* ▭ *AE, MC, V* ⊙ *No dinner Sun.*

$$–$$$ ★ ✕ **Sevilla.** Since 1930 this colorful, central two-story restaurant has fed the likes of the composer de Falla and the poet García Lorca. There are four dining rooms and an outdoor terrace overlooking the Royal Chapel and Cathedral. There's a small but superb tapas bar; the dinner menu includes Granada favorites such as *sopa sevillana* (soup with fish and shellfish) and *tortilla al Sacromonte* (with bull's brains and testicles) as well as more elaborate dishes. ✉ *Calle Oficios 12, Centro* ☎ *958/221223* ▭ *AE, DC, MC, V* ⊙ *No dinner Sun.*

$$–$$$ ✕ **Velázquez.** Tucked into a side street one block west of the Puerta de Elvira and Plaza del Triunfo, this cozy, very Spanish restaurant has long been popular with locals. At street level, the brick-wall bar is hung with hams; the intimate, wood-beam dining room is upstairs. House specialties include *zancarrón cordero a la miel* (lamb with honey) and *lomitos de rape* (braised monkfish medallions). ✉ *Calle Emilio Orozco 1, Centro* ☎ *958/280109* ▭ *MC, V* ⊙ *Closed Sun.*

$–$$$ ✕ **Taberna Tendido 1.** Also found under the Plaza de Toros, this is next to the La Ermita but more informal. Dishes on the menu of salads, cheeses, smoked fish, and popular tapas are served in three sizes—tapa, half-*ración* (half portion) and *ración* (full portion)—and fit neatly onto the barrel tops. Fixed-price menus are also available. ✉*Calle Dr. Olóriz 25, Centro* ☎*958/203136* 🌐*www.tendido1.com* ▭*MC, V.*

$-$$ ✕**Antigua Bodega Castañeda.** This typical and traditional-style bodega, close to Plaza Nueva, is the ideal place to pop into for a snack and a quick drink. It features salads, sandwiches—made with toasted slipper bread—smoked fish, cheeses, pates, stews, tapas, stuffed baked potatoes, and desserts, and an interesting range of wines. ✉*Calle Elvira 5, Centro* ☎*958/226362* ▭*MC, V.*

$-$$ ✕**Kasbah Tetería.** On a sloping street that feels very North African, Kasbah Tetería has a menu that's fairly short. Dishes include couscous with chicken, lamb, and vegetables, as well as tasty *pasteles árabes* (cakes). ✉*Calle Caldereria Nueva 4, Centro* ☎*958/227936* ▭*MC, V.*

$-$$ ✕**Meknes Rahma.** This Moroccan restaurant has an unusual location—on the edge of the Albayzín at the junction of the road to Sacromonte—but can be easily reached on the minibus numbers 31 or 32 from Plaza Nueva. In addition to dishes such as Moroccan soup and shish kebab, there's a selection of Eastern teas, and, for entertainment, belly dancing. ✉*Peso de la Harina 1, Albayzín* ☎*958/227430* ▭*MC, V.*

$-$$ ✕**Mesón Blas Casa.** In the choicest square in the Albayzín, this restaurant serves solidly traditional cuisine that includes *rabo de toro* (oxtail) and habas con jamón (ham with broadbeans). There's a cheap and filling *menú del día* (daily menu) and a fireplace for warming the toes when there's snow on the Sierras. ✉*Pl. San Miguel Bajo 15, Albayzín* ☎*958/273111* ▭*MC, V* ⏲*Closed Mon.*

WHERE TO STAY

$$$$ ★ **Palacio de los Patos.** This beautiful palace is unmissable, as it sits proudly on its own in the middle of one of Granada's busiest shopping streets. While retaining its 19th-century classical architecture, it also, thanks to remodeling and renovation, incorporates absolutely everything—including a gastronomic restaurant and spa—that even the most discriminating 21st-century traveler could desire. Some consider this Granada's finest hotel. ✉*Calle Solarillo de Gracia 1, Centrón, 18002* ☎*958/536516* 📠*958/536517* 🌐*www.hospes.es* *42 rooms* *In-room: Ethernet. In-hotel: restaurant, bar, pool, spa, parking (fee)* ▭*AE, DC, MC, V.*

$$$$ Fodor'sChoice ★ **Parador de Granada.** This is Spain's most expensive and popular parador, and it's right in the Alhambra precinct. The building, a former Franciscan monastery built by the Catholic Monarchs after they captured Granada, is soul-stirringly gorgeous. If possible, go for a room in the old section where there are beautiful antiques, woven curtains, and bedspreads. The rooms in the newer wing are also charming but simple. Reserve four to six months in advance. ✉*Calle Real de la Alhambra s/n, Alhambra, 18009* ☎*958/221440* 📠*958/222264* 🌐*www.parador.es* *34 rooms, 2 suites* *In-room: dial-up. In-hotel: restaurant, bar, parking (no fee)* ▭*AE, DC, MC, V.*

$$$-$$$$ **Casa de los Migueletes.** This very attractive 17th-century mansion with patios and galleries is found close to the popular Plaza Nueva. Expect to find antique or handmade furnishings in the individually dec-

orated rooms—some with Alhambra views. It comes by its name from the fact that it was once the headquarters of the Migueletes, a 19th-century rural police force. It is 100% no-smoking. Parking arrangements are at the Plaza Puerta Real garage some distance away. ✉ *Benalua 11, Albayzín, 18010* ☎ *958/210700* 🖷 *958/210702* 🌐 *www.casamigueletes.com* 24 *rooms, 1 suite* *In-room: Ethernet. In-hotel: bar, parking (fee)* 💳 *AE, DC, MC, V.*

$$$ Fodor's Choice ★ **Alhambra Palace.** Built by a local duke in 1910, this neo-Moorish hotel is on leafy grounds at the back of the Alhambra hill. The interior is very Arabian Nights, with orange-and-brown overtones, multicolor tiles, and Moorish arches and pillars. Even the bar is decorated as a mosque. Rooms overlooking the city have incredible views, as does the terrace, a perfect place to watch the sun set on Granada and its fertile plain. ✉ *Calle Peña Partida 2, Alhambra, 18009* ☎ *958/221468* 🖷 *958/226404* 🌐 *www.h-alhambrapalace.es* *124 rooms, 11 suites* *In-room: dial-up. In-hotel: restaurant, bars, parking (no fee)* 💳 *AE, DC, MC, V.*

$$$ **Carmen.** This hotel has a prized city-center location on a busy shopping street, and is directly across from the El Corte Inglés department store. The rooms are spacious and have a mix of modern and classic decor. The rooftop terrace and pool offer stunning views of the city. ✉ *Acera del Darro 62, Centro, 18005* ☎ *958/258300* 🖷 *958/256462* 🌐 *www.hotelcarmen.com* *270 rooms, 13 suites* *In-hotel: restaurant, bar, pool, parking (fee)* 💳 *AE, DC, MC, V.*

$$$ **Carmen de la Alcubilla del Caracol.** In a traditional Granadino *carmen*–style house, on the slopes of the Alhambra, this is one of Granada's most stylish hotels. The rooms are bright, airy, and furnished with antiques; they also have views over the city and the Sierra Nevada. The traditional terraced garden, with water troughs fed by an irrigation system from the Alhambra itself, is a peaceful oasis. ✉ *Calle Aire Alta 12, Alhambra, 18009* ☎ *958/215551* 🌐 *www.alcubilladelcaracol.com* *7 rooms* *In-room: Wi-Fi. In-hotel: restaurant, bar, parking (no fee), public Wi-Fi* 💳 *MC, V* ⏲ *Closed Aug.*

$$$ ★ **Casa Morisca Hotel.** The architect-owner of this 15th-century building transformed it into a hotel and received the 2001 National Restoration Award for the project. The brick building has many original architectural elements, three floors, and a central courtyard with a small pond and well. The rooms aren't large, but they get a heady Moorish feel through wonderful antiques and views of the Alhambra and Albayzín. ✉ *Cuesta de la Victoria 9, Albayzín, 18010* ☎ *958/221100* 🖷 *958/215796* 🌐 *www.hotelcasamorisca.com* *12 rooms, 2 suites* *In-room: dial-up. In-hotel: restaurant* 💳 *AE, DC, MC, V.*

$$$ **El Ladrón de Agua.** Situated by the side of the Darro River, in an interesting area directly under the imposing shadow of the Alhambra, this 16th-century mansion is called the Water Thief—a name inspired from a poem by Juan Ramón Jiménez (winner of the Nobel Prize for Literature in 1956). The rooms, traditionally decorated, are all named after poems by Federico García Lorca and Manuel deFalla, and are found around the galleries of the two floors, with the best found in the tower; eight of the rooms overlook the Alhambra, There is no nearby

parking. ✉ *Carrera del Darro 13, Albayzín, 18010* ☎ *958/215040* 🖷 *958/224345* 🌐 *www.ladrondeagua.com* *15 rooms* *In-room: Wi-Fi. In-hotel: restaurant, bar* 💳 *AE, DC, MC, V.*

$$$ **Palacio de los Navas.** In the center of the city, this was built by aristocrat Francisco Navas in the 16th century and later became the Casa de Moneda (The Mint). It retains original architectural features while also blending in new features with the old to become a particularly charming hotel. ✉ *Calle Navas 1, Centro, 18009* ☎ *958/215760* 🖷 *958/215760* 🌐 *www.palaciodelosnavas.com* *19 rooms* *In-hotel: parking (fee)* 💳 *AE, DC, MC, V.*

$$$ ★ **Reina Cristina.** In the former Rosales family residence, where the poet Lorca was arrested after taking refuge when the Spanish civil war broke out, the Reina Cristina is near the lively and central Plaza de la Trinidad. Plants trail from the windowsills of the reception area and a covered patio with a small marble fountain. A marble stairway leads to the simply but cheerfully furnished (red fabrics on a white background) guest rooms. ✉ *Calle Tablas 4, Centro, 18002* ☎ *958/253211* 🖷 *958/255728* 🌐 *www.hotelreinacristina.com* *43 rooms* *In-hotel: restaurant, bar, parking (fee)* 💳 *AE, DC, MC, V* *BP.*

$$–$$$ **Alojamientos con Encanto.** A bargain for groups and families, these elegant, comfortable, and large apartments are on the slopes of the Albayzín. Tiles, wrought-iron headboards, and other local crafts accent the apartments; quarters in the upper reaches of the Albayzín share a pebble patio crowded with plants and a terrace with magnificent views of the Alhambra. ✉ *C. Cuesta del Chapiz 54, Albayzín, 18010* ☎ *958/222428* 🖷 *958/222810* 🌐 *www.granada-in.com* *In-room: Ethernet. In-hotel: parking (no fee)* 💳 *AE, DC, MC, V.*

$$–$$$ **Guadalupe.** This charming hotel is close to the Alhambra. The rooms, in single, double, and triple sizes, are traditionally styled and of a generous size. ✉ *Paseo de la Sabica 30, Alhambra, 18009* ☎ *958/223423* 🖷 *958/223494* 🌐 *www.hotelguadalupe.es* *58 rooms* *In-hotel: restaurant* 💳 *AE, DC, MC, V.*

$$–$$$ **Inglaterra.** The interior of this 19th-century house in the heart of town (two blocks east of the Gran Vía de Colón) is comfortable and modern. Guest rooms are painted in pastel tones and have functional furniture and polished-wood floors. ✉ *Calle Cetti Meriem 4, Centro, 18010* ☎ *958/221558* 🖷 *958/227100* 🌐 *www.nh-hoteles.com* *36 rooms* *In-hotel: restaurant, parking (fee)* 💳 *AE, DC, MC, V.*

$$–$$$ **Palacio de Santa Inés.** It's not often you stay in a 16th-century palace, and this one in particular has a stunning location in the heart of the Albayzín. Rooms on the two upper floors are centered on a courtyard with frescoes painted by a disciple of Raphael. Each room is magnificently decorated with antiques and modern art; some have balconies with Alhambra views. ✉ *Cuesta de Santa Inés 9, Albayzín, 18010* ☎ *958/222362* 🖷 *958/222465* 🌐 *www.palaciosantaines.com* *15 rooms, 20 suites* *In-hotel: restaurant, parking (fee)* 💳 *AE, DC, MC, V.*

$$ **Hotel Los Tilos.** With a comfortable modern interior and a central location overlooking a pleasant square with a daily flower market, this good-value no-frills hotel is worth a try. Best of all is the fourth-

floor terrace where you can sip a drink, read a book, or just enjoy the panoramic view of the skyline. ✉ *Pl. Bib-Rambla 4, Centro, 18001* ☎ *958/266712* 📠 *958/266801* 🌐 *www.hotellostilos.com* *30 rooms* *In-hotel: parking (fee)* ▭ *MC, V.*

¢–$ **Britz.** If you plan on spending considerable time at the Alhambra and don't have wads of cash, consider this hostel, which is within walking distance. Rooms are more than adequate, and some have terraces and brightly tiled bathrooms. Its location on the bustling Plaza Nueva means noise can be a problem, but on the other hand there is also a wide choice of sidewalk cafés a short stroll away. ✉ *Cuesta de Gomérez 1, Centro, 18010* ☎ *958/223652* 🌐 *www.lisboaweb.com* *22 rooms, some with bath* *In-room: no TV* ▭ *MC, V.*

NIGHTLIFE & THE ARTS

THE ARTS

Get the latest on arts events at the **Diputacíon de Cultura** (Department of Culture), in the **Palacio de los Condes de Gabia** (✉ *Pl. de los Girones 1, Centro* ☎ *958/247383*); free magazines at the tourist offices also have schedules of cultural events. Granada's orchestra performs in the **Auditorio Manuel de Falla** (✉ *Paseo de los Mártires, Realejo* ☎ *958/222188*). Plays are staged at the **Teatro Alhambra** (✉ *Calle Molinos 56, Realejo* ☎ *958/220447*). Granada's **Festival Internacional de Teatro** fills 10 days with drama each May; contact the **tourist office** (✉ *Pl. Mariana Pineda 10, Centro* ☎ *958/247128*) for details. The **Festival Internacional de Música y Danza de Granada** (☎ *958/220691, 958/221844 tickets* 🌐 *www.granadafestival.org*) is held annually from mid-June to mid-July, with some events in the Alhambra itself. Contact the tourist office or visit the Web site for information on November's **Festival Internacional de Jazz de Granada** (🌐 *www.jazzgranada.net*).

FLAMENCO

Flamenco is played throughout the city, especially in the *cuevas* (caves) of the Albayzín and Sacromonte, where *zambra* shows—informal performances by gypsies—take place almost daily. The most popular cuevas are along the Camino de Sacromonte, the major street in the neighborhood of the same name. For any Sacromonte show, prepare to part with lots of money (€18–€20 is average). In August free shows are held at the delightful El Corral del Carbón square—home of the tourist office. The annual Encuentro Flamenco festival held during the first days of December typically attracts some of the country's best performers. If you do not want to show up randomly at the flamenco clubs, join a tour through a travel agent or your hotel, or contact **Los Tarantos** (✉ *Calle del Sacromonte 9, Sacromonte* ☎ *958/224525*), which has lively nightly shows with midnight performances on Friday and Saturday. **Sala Alhambra** (✉ *Parque Empresarial Olinda, Edif. 12* ☎ *958/412269 or 958/412287*) runs well-organized, scheduled performances. **La Rocío** (✉ *Calle del Sacromonte 70, Albayzín* ☎ *958/227129*) is a good spot for authentic flamenco shows. **María La Canastera** (✉ *Calle del Sacromonte 89, Sacromonte* ☎ *958/121183*) is another one of the cuevas on Camino de Sacromonte with unscheduled zambra shows.

TAPAS BARS

Poke around the streets between the Carrera del Darro and the Mirador de San Nicolás, particularly around the bustling Plaza San Miguel Bajo, for Granada's most colorful twilight hangouts. Also try the bars and restaurants in the arches underneath the Plaza de Toros (Bullfighting Ring), on the west of the city and a bit farther from the city center. For a change, check out some Moroccan-style tea shops, known as *teterías*—these first emerged in Granada and are now equally popular in Seville and Málaga, particularly among students. Tea at such places can be expensive, so be sure to check the price of your brew before you order. The highest concentration of teterías is in the Albayzín, particularly around Calle Caldererría Nueva where, within a few doors from each other, you find Tetería Kasbah, Tetería Oriental, and El Jardín de los Sueños, which also sells delicious milk shakes—try the almond and pistachio.

La Trastienda (✉*Calle Cuchilleros 11, Centro* ☎*958/226985*) is named "The Backroom" because of where you eat the tapas—after you get your tapas and drink, take them to the dining area in back. **Le Gran Taberna** (✉*Pl. Nueva 12, Centro* ☎*958/228846*) serves unusual tapas, such as trout with cottage cheese, Roquefort with beets, and goat's-cheese canapés, as well as the more standard selections. **Taberna Salínas** (✉*Elvira 13, Centro* ☎*958/221411*) has a brick-and-beam decor and great wine to accompany its delicious tapas. More filling fare is also available. Off Calle Navas in Plaza Campillo is **Chikito** (✉*Pl. del Campillo 9, Puerta Real* ☎*958/223364*), best known for its tasty sit-down meals, but the bar is an excellent place for tapas. The place is usually packed, so additional tables are set up on the square in summer. Moroccan-run **Al-Andalus** (✉*Elvira 12,, Centro*) serves tasty tapas, including bite-size falafel and other vegetarian options. **La Taberna de Baco** (✉*Campo del Príncipe 22, Realejo* ☎*958/226732*) fuses Ecuadoran and Andalusian flavors. **El Pilar del Toro** (✉*C. Hospital de Santa Ana 12, Albayzín* ☎*958/225170*) is a bar and restaurant with a beautiful patio. The popular **Bodegas Castañeda** (✉*Elvira 6, Centro* ☎*958/226362*) serves classic tapas, as well as baked potatoes with a choice of fillings. **Bodega Peso La Harina** (✉*Placeta del Peso de la Harina, Sacromonte*), on a square right at the entrance of Camino de Sacromonte, prepares reliably good tapas. Southeast of Granada's cathedral, **Café Botánico** (✉*Calle Málaga 3, Centro* ☎*958/271598*) is a modern hot spot with a diverse menu that serves twists on traditional cuisine for a young, trendy crowd.

NIGHTLIFE

Granada's ample student population makes for a lively bar scene. Some of the trendiest bars are in converted houses in the Albayzín and Sacromonte and in the area between Plaza Nueva and Paseo de los Tristes. Calle Elvira and Caldería Vieja, and Nueva are crowded with laid-back coffee and pastry shops. In the modern part of town, Pedro Antonio de Alarcón and Martinez de la Rosa have larger but less glamorous offerings. Another nighttime gathering place is the Campo del Príncipe, a large plaza surrounded by typical Andalusian taverns.

El Eshavira (✉*Calle Postigo de la Cuna 2, Albayzín* ☎*958/290829*) is a smoky, dimly lighted club where you can hear sultry jazz and occasional flamenco. **Planta Baja** (✉*C. Horno de Abad 11, Centro* ☎*958/207607*) is a funky late-night club that hosts bands playing everything from exotic pop to garage and soul. **Fondo Reservado** (✉*Calle Santa Inés 4, Albayzín* ☎*958/222375*) is a hip hangout for mainly students, and has late-night dance music. **Granada 10** (✉*Calle Carcel Baja 10, Centro* ☎*958/224001*), with an upscale crowd, is a discotheque in a former theater. **La Industrial Copera** (✉*Calle de la Paz 7, Ctra. de la Armilla* ☎*958/258449*) is a popular disco, especially on Friday night. **Zoo** (✉*C. Mora 2, Puerta Real* ☎*No phone*) is one of the longest-established and largest discos in town.

SHOPPING

A Moorish aesthetic pervades Granada's silver-, brass- and copperware, ceramics, marquetry (especially the *taraceas,* wooden boxes with inlaid tiles on their lids), and woven textiles. The main shopping streets, centering on the Puerta Real, are the Gran Vía de Colón, Reyes Católicos, Zacatín, Ángel Ganivet, and Recogidas. Most antiques stores are on Cuesta de Elvira, and Alcaicería—off Reyes Católicos—and Cuesta de Gomérez, on the way up to the Alhambra, also has many handicraft shops. **Cerámica Fabre** (✉*Pl. Pescadería 10, Centro*), near the cathedral, has typical Granada ceramics: blue-and-green patterns on white, with a pomegranate in the center. For wicker baskets and esparto-grass mats and rugs, head off the Plaza Pescadería to **Espartería San José** (✉*C. Jaudenes 22, Centro*).

SIDE TRIPS FROM GRANADA

The fabled province of Granada spans the Sierra Nevada mountains, with the beautifully rugged Alpujarras, and the highest peaks on mainland Spain—Mulhacén at 11,407 feet and Veleta at 11,125 feet. This is where you can find some of the prettiest, most ancient villages; it is one of the foremost destinations for Andalusia's increasingly popular rural tourism. Granada's plain (known as *la vega*), covered with orchards and tobacco and poplar groves, is covered in snow half the year.

EN ROUTE

Eight miles (12 km) south of Granada on N323, the road reaches a spot known as the Suspiro del Moro *(Moor's Sigh)*. Pause here a moment and look back at the city, just as Granada's departing "Boy King," Boabdil, did 500 years ago. As he wept over the city he'd surrendered to the Catholic Monarchs, his scornful mother pronounced her now legendary rebuke: "You weep like a boy for the city you could not defend as a man."

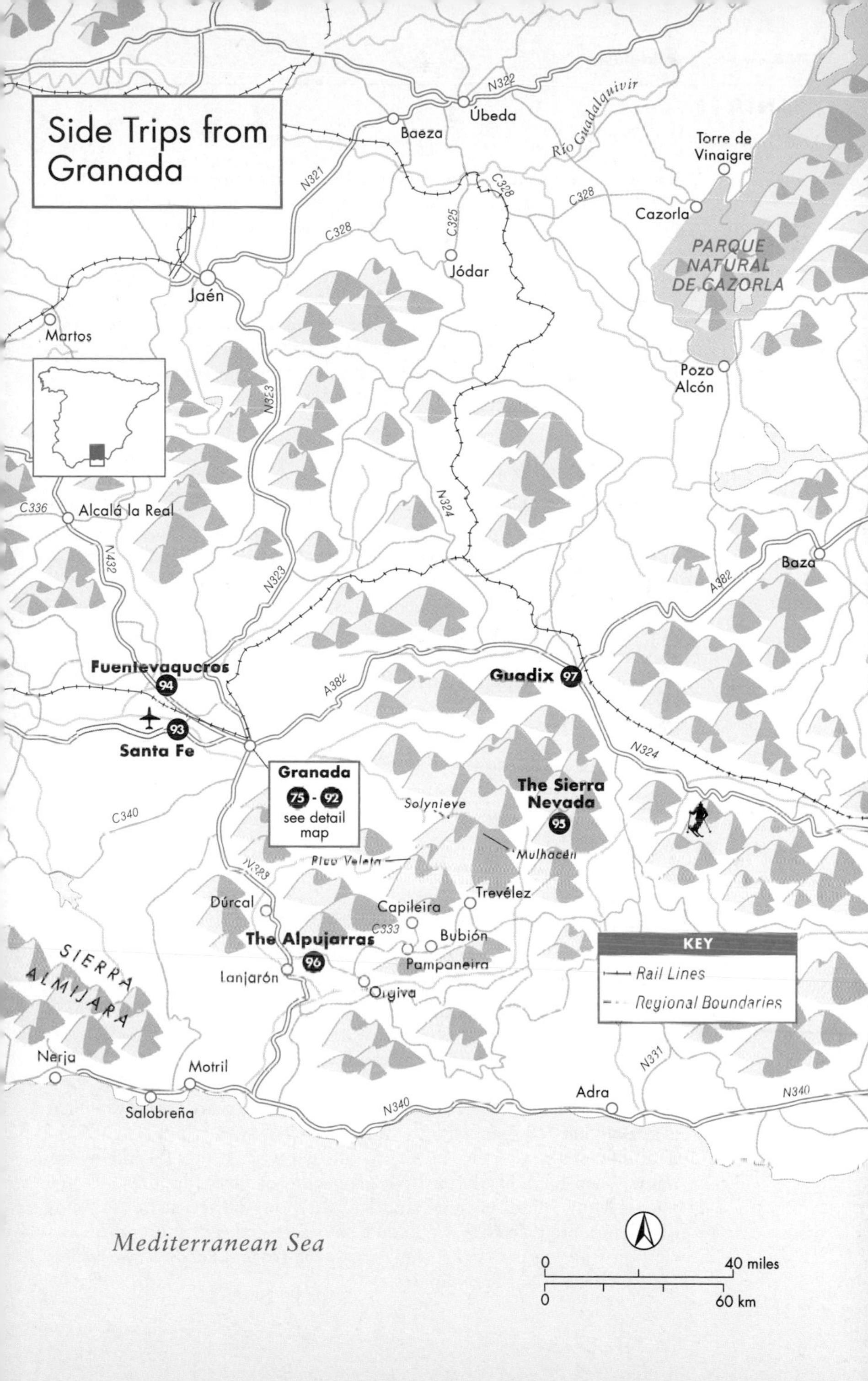

Side Trips from Granada
Úbeda
Baeza
N322
Río Guadalquivir
Torre de Vinaigre
Cazorla
C328
N321
C325
Jódar
Jaén
Martos
PARQUE NATURAL DE CAZORLA
Pozo Alcón
N323
N324
C336
Alcalá la Real
N432
Baza
A382
Fuentevaqueros
94
Guadix
97
93
Santa Fe
Granada
75 - 92
see detail map
The Sierra Nevada
95
Solynieve
C340
Mulhacén
Pico Veleta
N323
Dúrcal
Trevélez
Capileira
C333
Bubión
The Alpujarras
96
Pampaneira
Lanjarón
Orgiva
SIERRA ALMIJARA
KEY
Rail Lines
Regional Boundaries
N331
Nerja
Motril
Adra
N340
Salobreña
Mediterranean Sea
0
40 miles
0
60 km

SANTA FE

93 *8 km (5 mi) west of Granada just south of N342.*

Santa Fe was founded in winter 1491 as a campground for Ferdinand and Isabella's 150,000 troops as they prepared for the siege of Granada. It was here, in April 1492, that Isabella and Columbus signed the agreements that financed his historic voyage, and thus the town has been called the Cradle of America. Santa Fe was originally laid out in the shape of a cross, with a gate at each of its four ends, inscribed with Ferdinand and isabella's initials. The town has long since transcended those boundaries, but the gates remain—to see them all at once, stand in the square next to the church at the center of the old town.

FUENTEVAQUEROS

94 *10 km (6 mi) northwest of Santa Fe.*

The **Museo Casa Natal Federico García Lorca,** the poet's childhood home, opened as a museum in 1986, when Spain commemorated the 50th anniversary of Lorca's assassination and celebrated his reinstatement as a national figure after 40 years of nonrecognition during the Francisco Franco regime. The house has been restored with original furnishings, and the former granary, barn, and stables have been converted into exhibition spaces, with temporary art shows and a permanent display of photographs, clippings, and other memorabilia. A two-minute video shows the only existing footage of Lorca. Tour hours vary; call ahead. ✉ *Calle del Poeta García Lorca 4* ☎ *958/516453* 🌐 *www.museogarcialorca.org* 🎫 *€2* ⏲ *Closed Mon.*

THE SIERRA NEVADA

95 The drive southeast from Granada to Pradollano along the N420/A395—Europe's highest road, by way of Cenes de la Vega—takes about 45 minutes. It's wise to carry snow chains from mid-November even as late as April or May. The mountains here make for an easy and worthwhile excursion, especially for those keen on trekking.

The **Pico de Veleta,** Spain's third-highest mountain, is 11,125 feet, and the view from its summit across the Alpujarra range to the sea, at distant Motril, is stunning; on a very clear day you can see the coast of North Africa. In July and August you can drive or take a minibus to within hundreds of yards of the summit—a trail takes you to the top. ■ **TIP→ It's cold up here, so bring a warm jacket and scarf, even if Granada is sizzling hot.** To your left, the mighty **Mulhacén,** the highest peak in mainland Spain, soars to 11,427 feet. Legend has it that it came by its name when Boabdil, the last Moorish king of Granada, deposed his father, Muly Abdul Hassan, and had the body buried at the summit of the mountain so that it couldn't be desecrated. For more information on trails to the two summits, call the **Natural Park's Service office** (☎ *958/763127*) in Pampaneira.

The Sierra Nevada ski resort's two stations—Pradollano and the higher Borreguiles—draw crowds from December to May. In winter, **buses** (✉ *Autocares Bonal* ☎*958/465022*) to Pradollano leave Granada's bus station three times a day on weekdays, and four times on weekends and holidays. Tickets are €6 round-trip. As for Borreguiles, you can get there only on skis.

SKIING

The **Estación de Esquí Sierra Nevada** is Europe's southernmost ski resort and one of its best equipped. At the Pradollano and Borreguiles stations there's good skiing from December through May. Both stations have a special snowboarding circuit, floodlighted night slopes, a children's ski school, and après-ski sun and swimming in the Mediterranean less than an hour (33 km [20 mi]) away. There's an **information center** (☎*958/249100*) at Plaza de Andalucía 4 *www.cetursa.es*.

WHERE TO STAY

$$$–$$$$ **El Lodge.** A fantastic slope-side location and friendly, professional service adds up to the best hotel in the Sierra Nevada. It's built of Finnish wood—unusual for southern Spain, but perfectly appropriate in this alpine area—and has a warm, cozy quality. Know, however, that accommodations are not particularly large. Rooms are entirely wood—ceiling, walls, and floors. ✉*C. Maribel 8, 18196* ☎*958/480600* *958/481314* *www.ellodge.com* *16 rooms, 4 suites* *In-hotel: restaurant, bar, gym* *AE, DC, MC, V* *Closed May–Oct.* *BP.*

THE ALPUJARRAS

96 ★ *Village of Lanjarón: 46 km (29 mi) south of Granada.*

A trip to the Alpujarras, on the southern slopes of the Sierra Nevada, takes you to one of Andalusia's highest, most remote, and most scenic areas, home for decades to painters, writers, and a considerable foreign population. The Alpujarras region was originally populated by Moors fleeing the Christian Reconquest (from Seville after its fall in 1248, then from Granada after 1492). It was also the final fiefdom of the unfortunate Boabdil, conceded to him by the Catholic Monarchs after he surrendered Granada. In 1568 rebellious Moors made their last stand against the Christian overlords, a revolt ruthlessly suppressed by Philip II and followed by the forced conversion of all Moors to Christianity and their resettlement farther inland and up Spain's eastern coast. The villages were then repopulated with Christian soldiers from Galicia, who were granted land in return for their service against the Moors. To this day the Galicians' descendants continue the Moorish custom of weaving rugs and blankets in the traditional Alpujarran colors of red, green, black, and white, and they sell their crafts in many of the villages. Be on the lookout for handmade basketry and pottery as well.

Houses here are squat and square; they spill down the southern slopes of the Sierra Nevada, bearing a strong resemblance to the Berber homes in the Rif Mountains, just across the sea in Morocco. If you're driving, the road as far as Lanjarón and Orgiva is smooth sailing; after that come steep, twisting mountain roads with few gas stations. Beyond sightseeing, the area is a haven for outdoor activities such as hiking and horseback riding. Inquire at the **Information Point** at Plaza de la Libertad s/n, at Pampaneira.

EN ROUTE

Lanjarón, the western entrance to the Alpujarras some 46 km (29 mi) from Granada, is a spa town famous for its mineral water, collected from the melting snows of the Sierra Nevada and drunk throughout Spain. Orgiva, the next and largest town in the Alpujarras, has a 17th-century castle. Here you can leave C348 and follow signs for the villages of the Alpujarra Alta (High Alpujarra), including Pampaneira, Capileira, and especially Trevélez, which lies on the slopes of the Mulhacén at 4,840 feet above sea level. Reward yourself with a plate of the locally produced *jamón serrano* (cured ham). Trevélez has three levels, the Barrio Alto, Barrio Medio, and Barrio Bajo; the butchers are concentrated in the lowest section (Bajo). The higher levels have narrow cobblestone streets, whitewashed houses, and shops.

WHERE TO STAY & EAT

If you're looking for the unusual—or a slightly longer stay—rural houses scattered throughout the region are an affordable alternative. For information, contact the tourist office of Granada or **Rustic Blue** (✉*Barrio de la Ermita, Bubión* ☎*958/763381* 🌐*www.rusticblue.com*), which also organizes walking and riding excursions.

$$ **Taray Botánico.** This hotel has its own farm and makes a perfect base for exploring the Alpujarras. Public areas and guest rooms are in a low, typical Alpujarran building. The sunny quarters are decorated with Alpujarran handwoven bedspreads and curtains; three rooms have rooftop terraces, and there's a pleasant common terrace. Most of the restaurant's ($–$$) food comes from the estate, including trout and lamb; in season, you can even pick your own raspberries or oranges for breakfast. ✉*Ctra. Tablate–Albuñol, Km 18, Órgiva, 18400* ☎*958/784525* *958/784531* 🌐*www.turgranada.com/hotel-taray* *15 rooms* *In-hotel: restaurant, pool* *AE, DC, MC, V.*

$ **La Fragua.** Spotless rooms with baths (and some with balconies), fresh air, and views over the rooftops of Trevélez to the valley beyond are the perks at this small, friendly hotel in a typical village house behind the town hall. The restaurant is in a separate house up the street, serving regional dishes such as *arroz liberal* (hunter's rice with sausage and salami), *lomo a los aromas de la sierra* (pork loin with herbs), and *choto al ajillo* (piglet meat in garlic sauce). ✉*Calle de San Antonio 4, Barrio Medio, Trevélez18417* ☎*958/858626* *958/858614* *14 rooms* *In-hotel: restaurant* *MC, V* *Closed Mid-Jan.–mid-Feb.*

GUADIX

97 *47 km (30 mi) east of Granada on A92.*

Guadix was an important mining town as far back as 2,000 years ago and has its fair share of monuments, including a cathedral (built 1594–1706) and a 9th-century Moorish *alcazaba* (citadel). But Guadix and the neighboring village of Purullena are best known for their cave

SPORTS TOURS

Based in the Alpujarras, **Nevadensis** (✉ *Pl. de la Libertad, Pampaneira* ☎ *958/763127* 🌐 *www.nevadensis.com*) leads guided tours of the region on foot, horseback, and mountain bike.

In Granada, **Sólo Aventura** (✉ *Pl. de la Romanilla 1, Centro, Granada* ☎ *958/804937* 🌐 *www.soloaventura.com*) offers one- to seven-day outdoor sports—trekking, mountaineering, climbing, mountain biking, and other activities—around the Alpujarras, Sierra Nevada, and the rest of the province.

Kayak Sur (✉ *Calle Arabial, Urbanizació Parque del Genil, Edificio Topacio, Sur, Granada* ☎ *958/523118* 🌐 *www.kayaksur.com*) organizes kayaking and canoeing trips to the River Guadalfeo. **Granada Romántica/Grupo Al Andalus** (✉ *Calle Santa Ana 16, Granada* ☎ *958/805481* 🌐 *www.grupoalandalus.com*) takes up to five people in balloon trips above the city and its surroundings. **Excursiones Bujarkay** (☎ *953/721111* 🌐 *www.guiasnativos.com*) leads guided hikes as well as horseback and four-wheel-drive tours. In Zuheros, the **Alúa** (✉ *Calle Horno 3, Zuheros* ☎ *957/694527* 🌐 *www.aluactiva.com*) can help you with planning and getting the equipment for hiking, rock climbing, mountain biking, caving, and other active sports. Horseback-riding tours, some with English-speaking guides, are offered in the villages of the Alpujarras, Sierra Nevada, and in the Sierra de Cazorla; **Cabalgar Rutas Alternativas** (✉ *Calle Bubión, Alpujarras* ☎ *958/763135* 🌐 *www.ridingandalucia.com*) is one established Alpujarras agency. **Dallas Love** (✉ *Ctra. de la Sierra, Bubión, Alpujarras* ☎📠 *958/763038* 🌐 *www.spain-horse-riding.com*) offers trail rides for up to 10 days in the Alpujarras. The price includes overnight stays and most meals.

communities. Around 2,000 caves were carved out of the soft, sandstone mountains, and most are still inhabited. Far from being troglodytic holes in the wall, they are well furnished and comfortable, with a pleasant year round temperature; a few serve as hotels. A small cave museum, **Cueva Museo,** is in Guadix's cave district. Toward the town center, the **Cueva la Alcazaba** has a ceramics workshop. A number of private caves have signs welcoming you to inspect the premises, though a tip is expected if you do. Purullena, 6 km (4 mi) from Guadix, is also known for ceramics.

WHERE TO STAY & EAT

$$ ✕🏨 **Comercio.** In the historic center of Guadix is this enchanting little family-run hotel. Rooms in the 1905 building have dark-wood classic furniture, modern bathrooms, and, except for the few that are carpeted, marble floors. The public areas include an art gallery, a jazz concert room, and the best restaurant ($–$$$) in town, with such local specialties as roast lamb with raisins and pine nuts. ✉ *C. Mira de Amezcua 3, 18500* ☎ *958/660500* 📠 *958/665072* 🌐 *www.hotelcomercio.com* *40 rooms, 2 suites* *In-hotel: restaurant, parking (no fee)* 💳 *AE, DC, MC, V.*

$$ **Cuevas Pedro Antonio de Alarcón.** If you're looking for a so-called authentic experience, consider staying in a cave. In a "suburb" outside Guadix, this unique lodging consists of 19 adjoining caves and one suite. Each cave sleeps two to five and has a kitchenette; the honeymoon cave has a whirlpool bath. The whitewashed walls and polished clay-tile floors are decorated with charming Granadian crafts and colorful rugs; handwoven Alpujarran tapestries serve as doors between the rooms. The restaurant, also subterranean, serves regional dishes. *Barriada San Torcuato, 18500 958/664986 958/661721 www.andalucia.com/cavehotel 19 rooms, 1 suite In-room: no a/c, kitchen. In-hotel: restaurant, pool AE, MC, V EP.*

ANDALUSIA ESSENTIALS

To research prices, get advice, and book travel arrangements, visit www.fodors.com.

TRANSPORTATION

For information on travel to and in Andalusia, see the Andalusia Planner at the beginning of the chapter.

BY AIR

Ryanair operates inexpensive no-frills flights from London to Seville or Jerez de la Frontera for less than €40 round-trip. Air connections to Seville also can be had from other major European cities, including such as Frankfurt, Paris, and Amsterdam. Low-cost flights to Granada from the U.K. include connections on Ryanair and Monarch from London and Liverpool for less than €40. Iberia flies from the U.K. to Granada, Jerez de la Frontera, Seville, and Málaga for about €200. Cheap flights from England and Ireland to Málaga include connections via easyJet, Monarch, First Choice, Air Scotland, Jet2, Excel Airways, Ryanair, and Aer Lingus, flying from such airports as: Manchester, Luton, Gatwick, Birmingham, Dublin, and Shannon.

Andalusian cities you can reach via air include Granada, Jerez de la Frontera, Málaga, and Seville. The region's main airport is in Seville, 7 km (3 mi) east of the city on the A4/E5 highway to Córdoba. There's a bus from the airport to the center of Seville every half hour on weekdays (6:30 AM–8 PM), and every hour on weekends and holidays. It costs €4 one-way. The smaller Aeropuerto de Jerez is 7 km (4 mi) northeast of Jerez on the road to Seville. There's no public transport into Jerez, you will need to take a taxi (approximately €18). Málaga Airport is one of Spain's major hubs (especially for travelers from other European countries) and therefore a possible access point for Granada, Córdoba, and Almería. (These cities are approximately two hours apart by car.)

In Granada, **J. González** buses (€6) run between the center of town and the airport, leaving every 30 minutes from the Palacio de Congresos, and making a few other stops along the way to the airport. Times are listed at the bus stop; service is reduced in winter. **Line 14**

(☎950/221422) municipal bus service (€1) operates between the airport and the city center with buses every 30 minutes.

Airports Aeropuerto de Almería (☎*950/213700*). **Aeropuerto de Granada** (Aeropuerto Federico Garcí Lorca) (☎*958/245200*). **Aeropuerto Internacional de Málaga** (☎*95/204-8484*). **Aeropuerto Jerez de la Frontera** (☎*956/150000*). **Aeropuerto de Sevilla** (Aeropuerto San Pablo) (☎*95/444-9000*).

Airport Tranfers J. González (☎*958/490164*).

Airlines Air Europa (✉*Aeropuerto de Sevilla, Seville* ☎*95/444-9179* 🌐*www.aireuropa.com*). **British Airways** (✉*Aeropuerto de Sevilla, Seville* ☎*902/111333* 🌐*www.ba.com*). **Iberia** (✉*Av. Buhaira 8, Seville* ☎*95/498-7357, 902/400500 at Aeropuerto de Sevilla, 956/150010 at Aeropuerto Jerez de la Frontera airport* 🌐*www.iberia.es*). **Monarch** (✉*Aeropuerto Federico Garcí Lorca, Graanada* ☎*958/245245* 🌐*www.flymonarch.com*). **Ryanair** (☎*0818/303030 fromU.K.* 🌐*www.ryanair.com*). **Spanair** (✉*Aeropuerto de Sevilla, Seville* ☎*902/131415* 🌐*www.spanair.com*). **Vueling** (✉*Aeropuerto Federico Garcí Lorca, Granada* ☎*902/333933* 🌐*www.vueling.com*).

BY BOAT & FERRY

From Cádiz, Trasmediterránea operates ferry services to the Canary Islands with stops at Las Palmas de Gran Canaria (39 hours) and connecting ferries on to La Palma (8 hours) and Santa Cruz de Tenerife (6.5 hours). There are no direct ferries to Seville.

Contacts Trasmediterránea (✉*Estación Marítima* ☎*956/227421 or 902/454645* 🌐*www.trasmediterranea.es*).

BY BUS

Seville has two bus stations: Estación del Prado de San Sebastián, serving the west and northwest, and the Estación Plaza de Armas, which serves central and eastern Spain. Cádiz also has two bus stations: Comes, which serves most destinations in Andalusia, and Los Amarillos, which serves Jerez, Seville, Córdoba, Puerto de Santa María, Sanlúcar de Barrameda, and Chipiona. The bus station in Jerez, on Plaza Madre de Dios, is served by two companies: La Valenciana and Los Amarillos. Granada's bus station is at Carretera de Jaen, 3 km northwest of the center of town beyond the end of Avenida de Madrid. All services operate from here except for a few to nearby destinations such as Fuente Vaqueros, Viznar and Sierra Nevada. Luggage lockers (*la consigna*) cost €2. Alsina Graells buses run to Las Alpujarras, Córdoba 8 times daily Seville 10 times daily, Malaga 14 times daily and Jaen, Baeza, Ubeda, Cazorla, Almeria, Almuñecar and Nerja several times daily.

Seville's urban bus service is efficient and covers the greater city area. Buses C1, C2, C3, and C4 run circular routes linking the main transportation terminals with the city center. The C1 goes east in a clockwise direction, from the Santa Justa train station via Avenida de Carlos V, Avenida de María Luisa, Triana, the Isla de la Cartuja, and Calle de Resolana. The C2 follows the same route in reverse. The C3 runs from the Avenida Menéndez Pelayo to the Puerta de Jerez, Triana, Plaza de Armas, and Calle de Recaredo. The C4 does the same route counterclockwise. Buses do not run within the Barrio de Santa Cruz because the streets are too narrow, though convenient access points around the periphery of this popular tourist area are amply served.

Seville's city buses operate limited night service between midnight and 2 AM, with no service between 2 and 4 AM. Single rides cost €1, but it is more economical to buy a ticket for 10 rides, which costs €5.30 for use on any bus. A special tourist pass (Tarjeta Turística) valid for one or three days of unlimited bus travel cost (respectively) €3.11 and €7.25. Tickets are on sale at newspaper kiosks and at the main bus station, Prado de San Sebastián.

Granada and Córdoba have extensive public bus networks. The average waiting time usually does not exceed 15 minutes. Normally, buses in both cities start running around 6:30 to 7 AM and stop around 11 PM in Granada and midnight in Córdoba. However, schedules can be slightly reduced for some lines. In Granada, you can buy 6- and 21-trip discount passes on the buses and 10-trip passes at newsstands. In Córdoba, newsstands and the bus office at Plaza de Colón sell 10-trip discount tickets. The single-trip fares are €1 in Granada and Córdoba. Rober and Aucorsa manage the bus networks in Granada and Córdoba, respectively.

Bus Lines **Alsa** (☎ *902/422242* 🌐 *www.alsa.es*). **Alsina Gräells** (☎ *950/238197 in Almería, 957/278100 in Córdoba, 958/185480 in Granada, 953/255014 in Jaén, 95/2341738 in Málaga, 95/4418811 in Seville* 🌐 *www.alsinagraells.es*). **Aucorsa** (☎ *957/764676* 🌐 *www.aucorsa.net*). **Autocares Bonal** (☎ *958/273100*). **Comes** (✉ *Pl. Hispanidad, Cádiz* ☎ *956/224271*). **La Valenciana** (✉ *Bus station, Pl. Madre de Dios, Jerez de la Frontera* ☎ *956/341063*). **Los Amarillos** (✉ *Calle Diego Fernández Herreras 34, Cádiz* ☎ *956/285852, 956/329347 Jerez*). **Rober** (☎ *958/813750 or 900/710900* 🌐 *www.transportesrober.com*).

Bus Stations **Cádiz–Estación de Autobuses Comes** (✉ *Pl. de la Hispanidad 1* ☎ *956/342174*). **Córdoba** (✉ *Glorieta de las Tres Culturas, Córdoba* ☎ *957/404040*). **Huelva** (✉ *Av. Doctor Rubio s/n* ☎ *959/256900*). **Granada** (✉ *Ctra. Jaén, Granada* ☎ *958/185480*). **Jerez de la Frontera** (✉ *Calle de la Cartuja* ☎ *956/345207*). **Seville–Estación del Prado de San Sebastián** (✉ *Prado de San Sebastián s/n* ☎ *95/441–7111*). **Seville–Estación Plaza de Armas** (✉ *Calle Cristo de la Expiración* ☎ *95/490–7737*).

BY CAR

The main road from Madrid is the A4/E5 through Córdoba to Seville, a four-lane *autovía* (highway). From Granada or Málaga, head for Antequera; then take A92 *autovía* by way of Osuna to Seville. Road trips from Seville to Córdoba, Granada, and the Costa del Sol (by way of Ronda) are slow but scenic. Along the Costa del Sol, A7/E15 connects Almería with Algeciras in under three hours traveling at the standard Spanish 120–140 kph (72–84 mph) freeway cruising speed. The old coastal N340 highway is useful for slow and panoramic beach touring around Estepona and Motril but has otherwise been replaced by the A7/E15 freeway. Driving within Western Andalusia is easy—the terrain is mostly flat land or slightly hilly, and the roads are straight. From Seville to Jerez and Cádiz, the A4/E5 toll road gets you to Cádiz in under an hour. The only way to access Doñana National Park by road is to take the A49/E1 Seville–Huelva highway, exit for Almonte/Bollullos par del Condado, then follow the signs for El Rocío and Matalascañas. The A49/E1 west of Seville will also lead you to the freeway to Portugal and the Algarve.

With the exception of parts of La Alpujarra, most roads in this region are smooth; touring by car is one of the most enjoyable ways to see the countryside. Local tourist offices can advise about scenic drives. One good route heads northwest from Seville on the N433 passing through stunning scenery; turn northeast on the N435 to Santa Olalla de Cala to the village of Zufre, dramatically set at the edge of a gorge. Backtrack and continue on to Aracena. Return via the Minas de Riotinto (signposted from Aracena), which will bring you back to the N433 heading east to Seville.

Getting in and out of Seville is not difficult thanks to the SE30 ring road, but getting around the city by car is problematic. In Seville and Cádiz, avoid the lunchtime rush hour (around 2–3 PM) and the evening 7:15–8:30 PM rush hour. Bringing a car to Cádiz at Carnival time (pre-Lent) or to Seville during Holy Week or the April Fair can be difficult as processions close most of the streets to traffic. Check with your hotel about access to hotel parking during these ferias.

In the big cities, especially Granada and Córdoba, it's best to park in an underground lot or your hotel garage or parking area. Follow the large blue "P" signs, which will guide you to the city center and the nearest underground lot. You can expect to pay around €1.20 an hour. Blue lines on the street mean you must pay at the nearest meter to park during working hours, around €0.50 an hour. Yellow lines mean no parking. If your car is towed, you will be fined about €150.

Local car-rental agencies can be less expensive than the international chains. *See Spain Essentials in the back of the book for contact information for national rental agencies.*

Rental Agencies **Autopro** (*Carril de Montañez 49, Málaga* *952/176030* *www.autopro.es*). **Crown Car Hire** (*952/176486* *www.crowncarhire.com*). **Niza Cars** (*952/236179* *www.nizacars.com*).

BY SUBWAY

The first line of a three-line metro opened in Seville in late 2006. The Seville subway system covers a distance of 19 km (13 mi) and runs from Mairena de Aljarafe to Montequinto with 23 stations, including Puerta de Jerez and Plaza de Cuba. *www.metrodesevilla.net.*

BY TAXI

Taxis are plentiful throughout Andalusia and may be hailed on the street or from specified taxi stands marked TAXI. Restaurants are usually obliging and will also call you a taxi, if required. Fares are reasonable, and meters are strictly used; the minimum fare is about €4. Fares are based on the time of the day, and are higher at night and on public holidays. Taxis charge an additional amount (usually about €0.50) for picking up passengers at the train station, as well as for each piece of luggage. You are not required to tip taxi drivers, although rounding off the amount is appreciated.

In Seville and Granada there are taxi stations, or *paradas de taxis,* in almost every major area, or phone Tele Radio Taxi or Asociación de Radio Taxi. In Córdoba there are taxi stations at Avenida de América near the Hotel Gran Capitán, at the corner of El Corte Inglés, and near the hotel Meliá, among other locations; or call Call Radio Taxi. In Seville or Granada, expect to pay around €20 for cab fare from the airport to the city center.

Taxi Companies **Asociació de RadioTaxi** (✉ *Granada* ☎ *958/132323*). **Radio Taxi** (✉ *Córdoba* ☎ *957/764444*). **Radio Teléfono Giralda** (✉ *Seville* ☎ *95/467–5555*). **Tele Radio Taxi** (✉ *Granada* ☎ *958/280654*). **Tele Taxi** (✉ *Jerez de la Frontera* ☎ *956/344860*). **Tele Taxi** (✉ *Huelva* ☎ *959/250022*). **Unitaxi** (✉ *Cádiz* ☎ *956/212121*).

BY TRAIN

Seville, Córdoba, Jerez, and Cádiz all lie on the main rail line from Madrid to southern Spain. Trains leave from Madrid for Seville (via Córdoba) almost hourly, most of them high-speed ones that reach Seville in 2½ hours. Two of the non-AVE trains continue on to Jerez and Cádiz; travel time from Seville to Cádiz is 1½ to 2 hours. Trains also depart regularly for Barcelona (3 daily, 11 hours), Cáceres (1 daily, 6 hours), and Huelva (4 daily, 1½ hours). From Granada, Málaga, Ronda, and Algeciras, trains go to Seville by way of Bobadilla, where, more often than not, you have to change. A dozen or more local trains each day connect Cádiz with Seville, Puerto de Santa María, and Jerez. There are no trains to Doñana National Park, Sanlúcar de Barrameda, or Arcos de la Frontera, or between Cádiz and the Costa del Sol.

Train Information **RENFE** (☎ *902/240202* 🌐 *www.renfe.es*).

Train Stations **Cádiz** (✉ *Plaza de Sevilla s/n* ☎ *956/251010*). **Córdoba** (✉ *Glorieta de las Tres Culturas s/n* ☎ *957/403480*). **Granada** (✉ *Av. de los Andaluces s/n* ☎ *958/271272*). **Huelva** (✉ *Av. de Italia* ☎ *959/246666*). **Jerez de la Frontera** (✉ *Pl. de la Estación s/n, off Calle Diego Fernández Herrera* ☎ *956/342319*). **Seville–Estación Santa Justa** (✉ *Av. Kansas City* ☎ *95/454–0202*).

CONTACTS & RESOURCES

BANKS & EXCHANGING SERVICES

Banks are generally in town and city centers; the majority will have an ATM. Banks are open from 8:30 AM to 2 PM weekdays, plus on Saturday from October to April. Currency-exchange offices are also common—however, they generally charge a higher commission than the banks. You can also change money in your hotel, although this again will cost you more than the banks. One of the main banks in Spain is BBVA: www.bbva.es.

EMERGENCIES

In an emergency, call one of the Spain-wide emergency numbers, for police, ambulance, or fire services. The local Red Cross (Cruz Roja) can also dispatch an ambulance in case of an emergency. For nonemergencies, there are private medical clinics throughout the region; they often have staff members who can speak some English. Every town has at least one pharmacy open 24 hours; the address of the on-duty pharmacy is posted on the front door of all pharmacies. You can also dial Spain's general information number (11818) for the location of a doctor's office or pharmacy that's open nearest you.

Emergency Services **Fire, Police or Ambulance** (☎ *112*). **La Cruz Roja (Red Cross).** (✉ *Calle Amor de Dios 31, Seville* ☎ *954/376613*), (✉ *Cuesta Escoriaza 8, Granada* ☎ *958/221420*), (✉ *Paseo Victoria s/n, Córdoba* ☎ *957/420666*). **Guardia Civil** (☎ *062*). **Insalud** (*Public health service* ☎ *061*). **Policía Local** (*Local police* ☎ *092*). **Policía Nacional** (*National police* ☎ *091*). **Servicio Marítimo** (*Air-Sea Rescue* ☎ *902/202202*).

INTERNET, MAIL & SHIPPING

Internet cafés with competitive prices are plentiful in major cities. In Seville's provincial tourist office between Plaza Nueva and Calle Sierpes there are work stations with free Internet access for an hour; the office can also provide you with a list of local Internet cafés. The main post office in Seville is opposite the cathedral. It's open weekdays 8:30–8:30 and Saturday 9:30–2. Several international courier companies have branches at Seville airport, including DHL. National courier companies include Seur and MRW; both have branches and drop-off locations throughout the country. Granada's main post office is in the Plaza Real. The main office in Córdoba—the only one open in the afternoon—is north of the mosque near the Plaza de las Tendillas.

Internet Cafés **First Centre** (✉ *Av. de la Constitucíon 34, Centro, Seville* ☎ *95/421–5622*). **Hostal "El Pilar del Potro"** (✉ *Calle Lucano, 12, Córdoba* ☎ *957/492966*). **Internet Granada** (✉ *Calle del Pintor Zuloaga 29, Granada* ☎ *958/535025*). **Seville Internet Centre** (✉ *C. Almirantazgo 2, Centro, Seville* ☎ *95/450–0275*). **Turismo de la Provincia** (✉ *Pl. del Triunfo 1, Centro, Seville* ☎ *95/450–1001*).

Couriers **DHL** (✉ *Aeropuerto de Seville* ☎ *902/122–424*). **MRW** (✉ *Aeropuerto de Seville* ☎ *900/300–400*). **SEUR** (✉ *Aeropuerto de Seville* ☎ *902/101–010*)

SAFETY

Seville has long been notorious for petty crime. Tourists continue to be thieves' favored victims, so take common sense precautions. Drive with your doors locked, lock your luggage out of sight in the trunk, and keep a wary eye on scooter riders, who have snatched purses and even smashed windows of moving cars. When walking around, carry only a small amount of cash and one credit card. Leave your passport and other credit cards in the hotel safe.

VISITOR INFORMATION

Seville has both regional and provincial tourist offices and also has branches at the Seville Airport and Santa Justa railway station. Tourist offices are generally open 9–2 and 3–7. Seville's provincial tourist office publishes a monthly events guide, *El Giraldillo*; it is in Spanish but is easy to understand for novice readers. Also in Seville you can pick up the free *Sevilla Welcome and Olé!* The best Web site for the region is andalucia.org.

Regional Tourist Offices **Seville** (✉ *Av. de la Constitución 21* ☎ *95/422–1404, 95/421–8157, or 95/444–9128* 🌐 *www.andalucia.org*). **Cádiz** (✉ *Av. Ramón de Carranza s/n* ☎ *956/258646*).

Provincial Tourist Offices **Cádiz** (✉ *Pl. de San Antonio 3, 2nd fl.* ☎ *956/807061*). **Córdoba** (✉ *Palacio de Exposiciones, Calle Torrijos 10, opposite mosque, Judería* ☎ *957/471235*). **Granada** (✉ *Pl. Mariana Pineda, 10, Centro* ☎ *958/247146* 🌐 *www.turismodegranada.org*). **Huelva** (✉ *Av. Alemania 12* ☎ *959/257403*). **Seville** (✉ *Pl. de Triunfo 1–3, Santa Cruz* ☎ *95/421–0005* 🌐 *www.turismosevilla.org*).

Local Tourist Offices **Almonte** (✉ *Calle Alonso Pérez 1* ☎ *959/450419*). **Aracena** (✉ *Pl. de San Pedro s/n* ☎ *959/128825*). **Arcos de la Frontera** (✉ *Pl. del Cabildo s/n* ☎ *959/502121*). **Baeza** (✉ *Pl. del Pópulo* ☎ *953/740444*). **Cádiz** (✉ *Pl. San Juan de Dios 11* ☎ *956/241001* 🌐 *www.cadizturismo.com*). **Carmona** (✉ *Arco de la Puerta de Sevilla* ☎ *95/419–0955* 🌐 *www.turismo.carmona.org*). **Córdoba** (✉ *Pl. Juda Levi, Judería* ☎ *957/200522* 📠 *957/200277*). **Granada** (✉ *Pl. Mariana Pineda 10, Centro* ☎ *958/247128*). **El Rocío** (✉ *Calle La Canalieja s/n* ☎ *959/443908* 🌐 *www.parquenacionaldonana.com*). **Isla Cristina** (✉ *Calle Ayamonte s/n* ☎ *959/332694*). **Islantilla** (✉ *Av. de Riofrio s/n* ☎ *959/646013*). **Jaén** (✉ *C. Maestra, 13-Bajo* ☎ *953/242624*). **Jerez de la Frontera** (✉ *Calle Larga 39* ☎ *956/331150 or 956/331162* 🌐 *www.turismojerez.com*). **La Rábida** (✉ *Paraje de la Rábida s/n* ☎ *959/531137*). **Matalascañas** (✉ *Av. las Adelfas s/n* ☎ *959/430086*). **Mazagón** (✉ *Av. de los Conquistadores s/n* ☎ *959/376300*). **Moguer** (✉ *Calle del Castillo s/n* ☎ *959/371898* 🌐 *www.aytomoguer.es*). **Montilla** (✉ *Capitán Alonso de Vargas 3* ☎ *957/652462* 🌐 *www.turismomontilla.com*). **Puerto de Santa María** (✉ *Calle Luna 22* ☎ *956/542413* 🌐 *www.elpuertosm.es*). **Rota** (✉ *Castillo de Luna, Cuna 2* ☎ *956/846345*). **Seville** (✉ *Av. de la Constitucíon 21, Arenal* ☎ *95/422–1404* 🌐 *www.sevilla.org* ✉ *Costurero de la Reina, Paseo de las Delicias 9, Arenal* ☎ *95/423–4465*). **Úbeda** (✉ *Palacio Marqués del Contadero, C. Baja del Marqués 4* ☎ *953/750897*).

The Costa del Sol

12

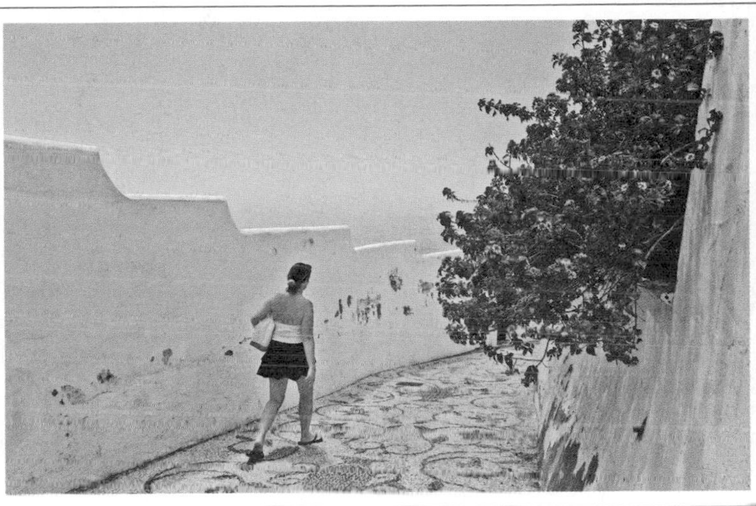

Nerja, Málaga province

WORD OF MOUTH

"Málaga is a terrific place to stay as a base for some great day trips as well as some wonderful sights within Málaga itself if you're interested in art and architecture."

—Artlover

www.fodors.com/forums

WELCOME TO THE COSTA DEL SOL

TOP REASONS TO GO

★ **Sun & Sand:** Relax at the plethora of packed (in summer) beaches; they're all free.

★ **Lovely Strolls:** Spend a morning in Marbella's old town, stopping for a drink at Plaza de los Naranjos (Oranges Square).

★ **Rich Environs:** Bask in the five-star splendor of Puerto Banús, where everything is exclusive, extravagant, and expensive.

★ **Sensational Seafood:** Tuck into a dish of delicious *fritura malagueño* (fried fish, anchovies, and squid) at a beach restaurant in Torremolinos.

★ **Natural Refuges:** Head to Cabo de Gato Nature Reserve, one of the wildest and most beautiful stretches of coast in Spain.

★ **Souvenir Shopping:** Check out the weekly market in one of the Costa resorts—the best place to pick up bargain-price souvenirs, such as ceramics or Spanish music CDs.

1 Almería. Just west of the Murcia Coast, this handsome, underrated city boasts a dynamic and gracious historic center.

2 Ronda. Intrinsically Andalusian, this town is enhanced by the stunning surrounding Serranía de Ronda countryside, which is dotted with *pueblos blancos.*

3 Málaga. This vibrant Spanish city has a fascinating historic center with narrow pedestrian streets flanked by sun-baked ocher buildings and tapas bars.

Horsemen in El Real de la Feria, Fuengirola, Málaga province,

Resort views in Torremolinos.

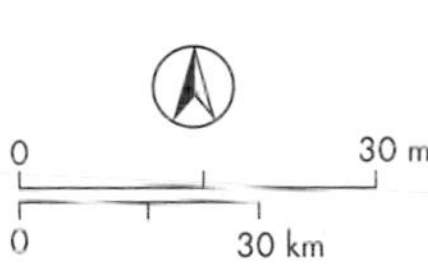

Winding *pueblo* roads in the Málaga province.

GETTING ORIENTED

The towns and resorts along the Costa del Sol vary considerably according to whether they lie to the east or to the west of Málaga. To the east lies the Costa del Almería and Costa Tropical, less developed stretches of coastline. Towns such as Nerja also act as a gateway to the dramatic mountainous region of La Axarquía. Heading west from Málaga along the Costa del Sol proper, the strip between Torremolinos and Marbella is the most densely populated. Seamless though it may appear, as one resort merges into the next, each town has a distinctive character, with its own sights, charm, and activities.

4 Beach resorts. The main ones are Torremolinos, appealing to young families; Fuengirola, with a large foreign resident population; and Marbella, which is more exclusive—and expensive.

5 The Axarquía. This is one of the most agriculturally lush regions in the south of Spain. The bleached dazzle of villages seems almost luminescent against the looming dark backdrop of the Sierra Tejeda mountains.

THE COSTA DEL SOL PLANNER

When to Go

Fall and spring are the best times to visit the coast. There's plenty of sunshine but fewer tourists, although golfers often prefer these cooler times. Winter can have bright sunny days, but you may feel chilled; many hotels in the lower price bracket have heating for only a few hours a day. You can also expect several days of rain. Avoid July and August; it's too hot and crowded. May, June, and the fall are better, with longer days and more space on the beach. Holy Week offers memorable celebrations.

Ferias & Fiestas

Málaga's **Semana Santa** (Holy Week; the week before Easter) processions are dramatic. Nerja and Estepona celebrate **San Isidro** (May 15) with typically Andalusian ferias with plenty of flamenco and *fino* (sherry). The feast of **San Juan** (June 23 and 24), is marked by midnight bonfires on beaches along the coast. Coastal communities honor the **Virgen del Carmen**, the patron saint of fishermen, on her feast day (July 16). The annual **ferias** (more general and usually lengthier celebrations than fiestas) in Málaga (early August) and Fuengirola (early October) are among the best for sheer exuberance.

Getting There & Around

Air Plus Comet operates a weekly direct flight from New York to Málaga, although at press time it had been temporarily suspended. All other flights from the United States connect in Madrid. Iberia and British Airways fly once daily from London to Málaga and numerous British budget airlines, such as easyJet and Monarch, link London with Málaga. There are direct flights to Málaga from most other major European cities on Iberia or other national airlines. Iberia has up to eight flights daily from Madrid (flying time is 1 hour), three flights a day from Barcelona (1½ hours), and regular flights from other Spanish cities.

By far the region's busiest point of entry, Málaga's Pablo Picasso airport is 10 km (6 mi) west of town. Trains from the airport into town run every half hour (7 AM–midnight, journey time 12 minutes, €1.20 single) and from the airport southwest to Fuengirola every half hour (5:45 AM–10:45 PM, journey time 25 minutes, €1.65 single), stopping at several resorts en route, including Torremolinos and Benalmádena. There's a bus service to Málaga every half hour from 6:30 AM to 11:30 PM at a fare of €1. Ten daily buses (more July–September) run between the airport and Marbella, with a journey time of one hour and fare of €4 single. Taxis fares to Málaga, Torremolinos, and other resorts are posted inside the terminal. The trip from the airport to Marbella costs about €45, to Torremolinos €12, to Fuengiorola €26. Many of the better hotels and all tour companies will arrange for pickup at the airport.

Buses are the best way to reach the Costa del Sol from Seville or Granada, and the best way to get around once you're here. Larger towns usually have a bus station where all out-of-town buses stop.

Málaga is the main rail terminus in the area, with eight trains a day from Madrid and one from Barcelona and Valencia.

By car you will have the freedom to explore some of Andalusia's mountain villages. Mountain driving can be a hair-raising adventure, but it's getting more manageable as highways are improved.

See The Costa del Sol Essentials at the end of this chapter for more transportation information.

Bird-Watching in Costa del Sol

Costa del Sol attracts ornithologists throughout the year; however, the variety of birds increases in spring.

Not surprisingly, the Strait of Gibraltar is a key point of passage for raptors, storks, and other birds migrating between Africa and Europe. Overall, northern migrations take place between mid-February and June, while those birds heading south will set off between late July and early November when there's a westerly wind. Gibraltar itself is generally good for bird-watchers, although when there is not much wind, the Tarifa region on the Atlantic coast can be better.

Soaring birds, such as raptors and storks, cross the Strait of Gibraltar because they rely on thermals and updrafts, which occur only over narrower expanses of water. One of the most impressive sights over the Strait is a crossing of flocks of storks, from August to October, which sometimes numbers up to 3,000.

The more hilly inland parts of the Costa del Sol are the best places to see resident raptor species circling high in the sky.

WHAT IT COSTS In Euros

	$$$$	$$$	$$	$	¢
RESTAURANTS	over €20	€15–€20	€10–€15	€6–€10	under €6
HOTELS	over €180	€100–€180	€60–€100	€40–€60	under €40

WHAT IT COSTS In Pounds in Gibraltar

RESTAURANTS	Over £25	£18–£25	£12–£18	£5–£12	under £5
HOTELS	over £165	£120–£165	£80–£120	£30–£80	under £30

Restaurant prices are per person for a main course at dinner. Hotel prices are for two people in a standard double room in high season, excluding tax.

Planning Your Time

Travelers with their own wheels who want a real taste of the area in just a few days should start by exploring the relatively unspoiled villages of the Costa Tropical. Wander around quaint **Salobreña** before hitting the larger coastal resort of **Nerja** and heading inland for a wander around pretty **Frigiliana.** Move on to **Málaga,** which has plenty on offer—including museums, excellent restaurants, and some of the best tapas bars in the province. Don't miss the stunning mountaintop town of **Ronda** (also on the bus route), which has plenty of atmosphere and memorable sights. Hit the coast at **Marbella,** the Costa del Sol's swankiest resort, followed by a leisurely stroll around **Puerto Banús.** Next head west to **Gibraltar** for a day of shopping and sightseeing before returning to the coast and **Torremolinos** for a night on the town. If you have more time, explore rural Andalusia: **Setenil de las Bodegas, Olvera,** and **Grazalema.**

By Mary McLean

THE STRETCH OF ANDALUSIAN SHORE known as the Costa del Sol runs west from the Costa Tropical, near Granada, to the tip of Tarifa, the southernmost tip of Europe, just beyond Gibraltar. For most of the Europeans who have flocked here over the past 40 years, though, the Sunshine Coast has been largely restricted to the 70-km (43-mi) sprawl of hotels, vacation villas, golf courses, marinas, and nightclubs between Torremolinos, just west of Málaga, and Estepona, down toward Gibraltar. Since the late 1950s this area has mushroomed from a group of impoverished fishing villages into an overdeveloped seaside playground and retirement haven.

Construction continued unabated along the coast until the early '90s, which saw a brief economic slump caused, in part, by a drop in international airfares. Travelers became more adventurous, and Spain's favorite coast was now competing with seemingly more sophisticated locations. Local municipalities poured money into elaborate landscaping, and better roads and infrastructure. It paid off. In 1997 the prestigious Ryder Cup was held in Sotogrande, seeming to mark the Costa del Sol's return to the world stage. The result was more golf courses, luxury marinas, villa developments, and upscale hotels. The Costa averages some 320 days of sunshine a year, and balmy days are not unknown even in January or February. Despite the hubbub, you *can* unwind here, basking or strolling on mile after mile of sandy beach.

Choose your base carefully. Málaga is a vibrant Spanish city, virtually untainted by tourism. Despite the tour bus trade, Ronda is also intrinsically Andalusian, with the added perk of a stunning inland setting. Back on the coast, Torremolinos is a budget destination catering almost exclusively to the mass market; it appeals to young families, the gay community, and to those who come purely for the sun-bronzing and the late-night scene. Fuengirola is quieter, with a large, and notably middle-aged, foreign resident population; farther west, the Marbella–San Pedro de Alcántara area is more exclusive and expensive.

EXPLORING THE COSTA DEL SOL

ABOUT THE BEACHES

Lobster-pink sun worshippers from northern Europe pack these beaches in summer so that there's little towel space on the sand. Beach chairs can be rented for around €4 a day. Beaches range from shingle and pebbles (Almuñecar, Nerja, Málaga) to fine, gritty sand (from Torremolinos westward). The best—and most crowded—beaches are El Bajondillo and La Carihuela, in Torremolinos; the stretch between Carvajal, Los Boliches, and Fuengirola; and those around Marbella. You may find a secluded beach west of Estepona. Shingle beaches are popular with European vacationers. For wide beaches of fine golden sand, head west past Gibraltar, to Tarifa and the Cádiz coast—though you'll probably find that the winds are quite strong, hence all the sails.

All beaches are free and packed July through August and on Sunday May through October. It's acceptable for women to go topless; if you want to take it *all* off, go to beaches designated *playa naturista*. The most popular nude beaches are in Maro (near Nerja) and near Tarifa.

SHORT- & LONG-TERM STAYS

There's no shortage of apartments and villas for both short- and long-term stays. Accommodations range from traditional Andalusian farmhouses to luxury villas. An excellent source for apartment and villa rentals is *www.andalucia.com*. You can also try **Gilmar** at (*Av. Ricardo Soriano 56, Marbella, 29600* *952/861341* *www.gilmarinmobiliaria.com*) or **Viajes Rural Andalus** (*Calle Montes de Oca 18, Málaga, 29007* *952/276229* *www.ruralandalus.es*).

ABOUT THE RESTAURANTS

Spain's southern coast is known for fresh seafood, breaded with fine flour and fried quickly in sizzling olive oil. Sardines barbecued on skewers at beachside restaurants are another popular and unforgettable treat. Gazpacho and *ajo blanco* (a cold soup based on almonds, grapes, and garlic) are typical cold soups that are refreshing in hot weather. Málaga is best for traditional Spanish cooking, with a wealth of bars and seafood restaurants serving *fritura malagueña,* the city's famous fried fish. Torremolinos' Carihuela district is also a locus for lovers of Spanish seafood. The resorts serve every conceivable foreign cuisine as well, from Thai to the Scandinavian smorgasbord. Expect to pay more at the internationally renowned restaurants in Marbella.

At the other end of the scale, and often even more enjoyable, are the *chiringuitos*. Strung out along the beaches, these rough-and-ready, summer-only restaurants serve seafood fresh off the boats. Because there are so many foreigners, meals on the coast are served earlier than elsewhere in Andalusia, with restaurants opening at 1 PM or 1:30 PM for lunch and 7 PM or 8 PM for dinner. Reservations are advisable for the pricier restaurants in Marbella and Málaga; elsewhere, they're rarely necessary. Expect beach restaurants to be packed after 3 PM on Sunday.

ABOUT THE HOTELS

Most hotels on the developed stretch, between Torremolinos and Fuengirola, offer large, functional rooms near the sea at competitive rates. The area's popularity as a budget destination means that most such hotels are booked in high season by package-tour operators. Finding a room at Easter, in July and August, or over holiday weekends can be difficult if you haven't reserved in advance. Málaga has several new lodging establishments, but it's still poorly endowed with high-quality hotels for a city of its size, aside from an excellent but small parador that can be hard to book. Marbella, conversely, has more than its fair share of grand hotels, including some of Spain's most expensive accommodations. Rooms in Gibraltar's handful of hotels tend to be more expensive than most comparable lodgings in Spain.

Numbers in the text correspond to numbers in the margin and on the Costa del Sol and Gibraltar maps.

THE COSTA DE ALMERÍA

West of Spain's Murcia Coast lie the shores of Andalusia, beginning with the Costa de Almería. Its highlights include the archaeological site of Los Millares, near the village of Santa Fé de Mondújar, and the otherworldly landscape of Tabernas, Europe's only desert, which can mesmerize you with its stark beauty. The mineral riches of the surrounding mountains gave rise to Iberia's first true civilization, whose capital can still be glimpsed in the 4,700-year-old ruins of Los Millares. The towns of Níjar and Sorbas maintain an ages-old tradition of pottery-making and other crafts, and the western coast of Almería has tapped unexpected wealth from a parched land, thanks to modern farming techniques. In contrast to that inhospitable landscape, the mountain-fringed Andarax Valley has a cool climate and gentle landscape, both conducive to making fine wines.

AGUA AMARGA

❶ *22 km (14 mi) north of San José and 55 km (30 mi) west of Almeria.*

Agua Amarga is perhaps the most pleasant village on the Cabo de Gata coast. Like other coastal hamlets, it started out in the 18th century as a tuna-fishing port. Today it attracts more visitors, but remains a fishing village at heart, less developed than San José. One of the coast's best beaches is just to the north: the dramatically named **Playa de los Muertos** (Beach of the Dead), a long stretch of fine sand bookended with volcanic outcrops.

SAN JOSÉ & THE CABO DE GATA NATURE RESERVE

❷ *40 km (25 mi) east of Almería, 86 km (53 mi) south of Mojácar.*

San José is the largest village in the southern part of the park and has a very nice bay, but these days it has rather outgrown itself and can get busy in the summer months. Those preferring smaller, quieter places should look a little farther north at places such as La Isleta and Agua Amarga and the often-deserted beaches between them. Just south of San José is the **Parque Natural Marítimo y Terrestre Cabo de Gata–Níjar** (⊠*Road from Almería to Cabo de Gata, Km 6* ☎📠*950/160435*). Birds are the main attraction at this nature reserve; it is home to several species native to Africa, including the *camachuelo trompetero* (large beaked bullfinch), which is not found anywhere else outside Africa. The **Centro Las Amuladeras visitor center,** at the park entrance, has an exhibit and information on the region. For beach time, follow signs south to the **Playa Los Genoveses** and **Playa Monsul.** A dirt track follows the coast around the spectacular cape, eventually linking up with the N332 to Almería.

WHERE TO STAY

$$$–$$$$ **Mikasa.** Specifically designed for rest and relaxation, this stylish hotel has some rooms with king-size beds and whirlpools as well as sea views; a gourmet breakfast is served on the terrace or in the delightful garden, and the restaurant, exclusively for guests, serves an intriguing mix of local and international cuisine. If you don't fancy the beach, relax at one of the two pools (one is heated) or luxuriate in the spa. ⊠*Ctra. de Carboneras s/n, Agua Amarga, 04149* ☎*950/138073* 🌐*www.mikasasuites.com* *20 rooms* *In-hotel: restaurant, bar, pools, spa* 💳*AE, DC, MC, V.*

ALMERÍA

❸ *219 km (136 mi) southwest of Murcia, 183 km (114 mi) east of Málaga.*

Warmed by the sunniest climate in Andalusia, Almería is a youthful Mediterranean city, basking in sweeping views of the sea from its coastal perch. Almería is also a capital of the grape industry, thanks to its wonderfully mild climate in spring and fall. Rimmed by tree-lined boulevards and some landscaped squares, the city's core is still a maze of narrow, winding alleys formed by flat-roof, distinctly Mudéjar houses. Though now surrounded by modern apartment blocks, these dazzling-white older homes give Almería an Andalusian flavor. Dominating the city is its **Alcazaba** *(Fortress)* built by Caliph Abd ar-Rahman I and given a bell tower by Carlos III. From here you have sweeping views of the port and city. Among the ruins of the fortress, damaged by earthquakes in 1522 and 1560, are landscaped gardens of rock flowers and cacti. ✉ *C. Almanzor* ☎ *950/271617* 🎫 *€1.50; free for EU citizens* ⏲ *Apr.–Oct., Tues.–Sun. 10–8; Nov.–Mar., Tues.–Sun. 9–6:30.* Below the Alcazaba stands the **cathedral**, whose buttressed towers make it look like a castle. It is Gothic in design, but with some classical touches around the doors. 🎫 *€3* ⏲ *Weekdays 10:30–4:30, Sat. 10–1.*

WHERE TO STAY & EAT

$$ ✕ **Veracruz.** In Almería's beach barrio, El Zapillo, this justly popular seafood restaurant has its own storage tank for oysters, clams, prawns, and lobsters. The specialty is *parillada de pescado*, a mixed grill of everything that swims in the Mediterranean. ✉ *Av. Cabo de Gata 119* ☎ *950/251220* 💳 *AE, MC, V.*

$–$$ ✕ **Valentin.** This popular, central spot serves fine regional specialties, such as *cazuela de rape* (monkfish baked in a sauce of almonds and pine nuts). The surroundings are Andalusian: white walls, wood, and glass. Come on the early side (around 9) to get a table. ✉ *Tenor Iribarne 7* ☎ *950/264475* 💳 *AE, MC, V* ⏲ *Closed Mon. No dinner Sun.*

$$ ✕🏨 **Torreluz III.** Value is the overriding attraction of this comfortable yet elegant modern hotel. Guest rooms are slick and bright, with the kind of installations for which you'd expect to pay more. Its restaurant, Torreluz Mediterráneo, is famous among locals for robust portions and brisk lunchtime service. It serves an excellent cross section of southeastern fare—try the *zarzuela de marisco a la marinera* (mixed seafood in a zesty red marinade). The cheaper Torreluz Hotel, with just 24 rooms ($) next door (with the same phone number) is also good value, as are the nearby apartments, which offer more space for the same price as the main hotel. ✉ *Plaza Flores 3, 04001* ☎ *950/234399* 📠 *950/281428* 🌐 *www.torreluz.com* *94 rooms* *In-hotel: 2 restaurants, bar* 💳 *AE, DC, MC, V.*

$$ 🏨 **NH Ciudad de Almería.** One of the newest hotels in Almería, this has the appealing mix of traditional and modern style—including avant-garde art pieces—often found in NH hotels, and offers larger rooms than is usually expected in the region. It also has a fine strategic location, just to the east of the town center and directly across from the train and bus station. ✉ *Jardín de Medina s/n, 04006* ☎ *950/182500* 📠 *950/273010* 🌐 *www.nh-hotels.com* *139 rooms* *In-hotel: restaurant, bar, laundry facilities, public Internet* 💳 *AE, DC, MC, V.*

$ 🏨 **Hostal Sevilla.** If you want inexpensive comfort, look no further. In the labyrinth of the old town, you'll find healthy doses of Andalusian style and charm. The rooms vary; those on the street side have small terraces, whereas those on the quiet interior look over the courtyards and rooftops of the old town. All have ceramic-tile floors. ✉ *Granada 25, 04001* ☎📠 *950/230009* *37 rooms* 💳 *MC, V.*

NIGHTLIFE

Nocturnal action centers on **Plaza Flores**, moving down to the beach in summer. In town, try the small **Cajón de Sastre** (✉ *Plaza Marques de Heredia 8*) for typical *copas* (libations) and a mainly Spanish crowd.

OFF THE BEATEN PATH

The Desierto de Tabernas, 25 km (15 mi) north of Almería, is billed as the only true desert in Europe, receiving an average of 8 inches of rainfall a year. The striking, almost lunar landscape of scrub and parched hills bears a similarity to the American desert—a fact not lost on filmmakers. More than 300 westerns were made in the area between 1950 and 1990, most of them of the "spaghetti western" genre. Several of the old film sets still stand, and two of them are open to the public, Mini Hollywood (***N340, Km 364 950/365236 €16 Tues.-Sun. 10-7***) **and** Western Leone (***A92, Km 378.9 950/165405 €6.50 Daily 10-dusk***).

THE COSTA TROPICAL

East of Málaga and west of Almería lies the Costa Tropical. It has escaped the worst excesses of the property developers, and its tourist onslaught has been mild. A flourishing farming center, this area earns its keep from tropical fruit, including avocados, mangoes, and papaws (also known as custard apples). Housing developments are generally inspired by Andalusian village architecture rather than bland high-rise design. You may find packed beaches and traffic-choked roads at the height of the season, but for most of the year the Costa Tropical is relatively free of tourists, if not also devoid of expatriates.

SALOBREÑA

4 *102 km (63 mi) east of Málaga.*

You can reach Salobreña by descending through the mountains from Granada or by continuing west from Almería on N340. A detour to the left from the highway brings you to this unspoiled village of near-perpendicular streets and old white houses, slapped onto a steep hill beneath a Moorish fortress. It's a true Andalusian *pueblo*, separated from the beachfront restaurants and bars in the newer part of town.

ALMUÑECAR

5 *85 km (53 mi) east of Málaga.*

Almuñecar has been a fishing village since Phoenician times, 3,000 years ago, when it was called Sexi. Later, the Moors built a castle here for the treasures of Granada's kings. Today Almuñecar is a small-time resort with a shingle beach, popular with Spanish and northern-European vacationers. The road west from Motril and Salobreña passes through the former empire of the sugar barons who brought prosperity to Málaga's province in the 19th century. The cane fields are now giving way to litchis, limes, mangoes, papaws, and olives; avocado groves line your route as you descend into Almuñecar. The village is actually two, separated by the dramatic rocky headland of Punta de la Mona. To the east is Almuñecar proper, and to the west is **La Herradura,** a quiet fishing community. Between the two is the Marina del Este yacht harbor, a popular diving center along with La Herradura.

Crowning Almuñecar is the **Castillo de San Miguel** *(St. Michael's Castle)*. A Roman fortress once stood here, later enlarged by the Moors, but the castle's present aspect owes more to 16th-century additions. The building was bombarded during the Peninsular War at the beginning of the 19th century, and what was left became initially a cemetery until the 1990s, when excavation and restoration began. You can wander the ramparts and peer into the dungeon; the skeleton at the bottom is a reproduction of human remains discovered on the spot. *€2, includes admission to Cueva de Siete Palacios ⏲July and Aug., Tues.–Sat. 10:30–1:30 and 6–9, Sun. 10–2; Sept.–June, Tues.–Sat. 10:30–1:30 and 4–6:30, Sun. 10:30–2.*

Beneath the Castillo de San Miguel is a large, vaulted stone cellar of Roman origin, the **Cueva de Siete Palacios** *(Cave of Seven Palaces)*, now Almuñecar's archaeological museum. The collection is small but interesting, with Phoenician, Roman, and Moorish artifacts. *€2, includes admission to Castillo de San Miguel ⏲July and Aug., Tues.–Sat. 10:30–1:30 and 6–9, Sun. 10–2; Sept.–June, Tues.–Sat. 10:30–1:30 and 4–6:30, Sun. 10:30–2.*

WHERE TO STAY & EAT

$$ ✕ **Jacquy-Cotobro.** One of the finest French restaurants on Spain's southern coast, Jacquy-Cotobro is cozy, with bare brick walls and green wicker chairs; a beachfront terrace is open in summer. Try the *menú de degustación*, with three courses plus dessert; it might include fresh pasta topped with oyster mushrooms and prawns, lobster salad with truffle oil, or duck in orange sauce. Finish with the calorific delight of strawberry mousse drizzled with Kirsch. ✉*Edificio Río, Playa Cotobro* ☎*958/631802* ▭*MC, V* ⏲*Closed Mon.*

$$$ **Sol Los Fenicios.** Near the beach in La Herradura, this modern, Andalusian-style hotel has views of the bay and the cliffs of Punta de Mona to the east and the rocky headland of Cerro Gordo to the west. The rooms have recently benefited from a major revamp. They are set around a traditional interior patio, complete with pond; ask for a room with a sea view. ✉*Paseo de Andrés Segovia s/n, La Herradura 18697* ☎*958/827900* 🖷*958/827910* 🌐*www.sollosfenicios.solmelia.com* *42 rooms* *In-room: Wi-Fi. In-hotel: restaurant, pool, parking (fee)* ▭*AE, DC, MC, V* 🍽*BP* ⏲*Closed late Nov.–early Mar.*

$–$$ **Casablanca.** There's something quaint about this family-run hotel with its neo-Moorish façade sitting next to the beach and near the botanical park. The rooms, which are all different, have modern fittings juxtaposed with antiques and the occasional four-poster bed. All have private balconies or large picture windows. The restaurant specializes in traditional cuisine, such as *migas* (breadcrumbs fried with sausage and spices) and paella. ✉*Pl. San Cristóbal 4, 18690* ☎*958/635575* 🌐*www.almunecar.info/casablanca/* *35 rooms* *In-hotel: restaurant, bar, public Internet, parking* ▭*D, MC, V.*

NERJA

6 ★ *52 km (32 mi) east of Málaga, 22 km (14 mi) west of Almuñecar.*

Nerja—the name comes from the Moorish word *narixa,* meaning "abundant springs"—has a large foreign resident community living mainly outside town in *urbanizaciones* ("village" developments). The old village is on a headland above small beaches and rocky coves, which offer reasonable swimming despite the gray, gritty sand. In high season, Nerja is packed with tourists, but the rest of the year it's a pleasure to wander the old town's narrow streets. Nerja's highlight is the **Balcón de Europa,** a tree-lined promenade with magnificent views, on a promontory just off the central square. The **Cuevas de Nerja** *(Nerja Caves)* lie between Almuñecar and Nerja on a road surrounded by giant cliffs and dramatic seascapes. Signs point to the cave entrance above the village of Maro, 4 km (2½ mi) east of Nerja. Its spires and turrets created by millennia of dripping water are now floodlighted for better views. One suspended pinnacle, 200 feet long, is in fact the world's largest known stalactite. The awesome subterranean chambers create an evocative setting for concerts and ballets during the Nerja Festival of Music and Dance, held annually during the second and third weeks of July. *952/529520 www.cuevanerja.com €6 Oct.–Apr., daily 10–2 and 4–6:30; May–Sept., daily 10–2 and 4–8.*

WHERE TO STAY & EAT

$$–$$$ **Udo Heimer.** Your eponymous host, a genial German, welcomes you warmly to this stylish art deco villa in a development east of Nerja. The visual flair extends to the food, which mixes German and Spanish flavors. Try the rack of lamb with rosemary and thyme, or prawns wrapped in bacon with cayenne rice and a sweet curry sauce. The excellent wine list has rarities from all over Spain. *Pueblo Andaluz 27 952/520032 MC, V Closed Wed. No lunch.*

$$ **Casa Luque.** One of Nerja's most authentic Spanish restaurants, Casa Luque is in an old Andalusian house in a lovely square just off the Balcón de Europa. The menu has dishes from northern Spain, often of Basque or Navarrese origin, with an emphasis on meat and game; tapas and seafood are also on offer. Ask to sit on the patio in summer. *Pl. Cavana 2 952/521004 AE, DC, MC, V Closed Wed. No dinner Sun.*

$$–$$$ ★ **Hotel Carabeo.** Tucked away down a side street near the center of town and the sea, this British-owned boutique hotel has bookshelves, antiques, and cozy overstuffed sofas in the downstairs sitting room. The walls throughout are hung with colorful oil paintings by local artist David Broadhead. In the main building there are seven rooms, five with sea views, and a private terrace overlooking the sea. In the newer annex there are six more rooms, plus a small gym and games room. *C. Hernando de Carabeo 34, 29780 952/525444 952/522677 www.hotelcarabeo.com 20 rooms In-hotel: restaurant, bar, pool, gym, public Internet MC, V Closed end-Oct.-mid–Mar. CP.*

NIGHTLIFE & THE ARTS

El Colono (✉ *Granada 6, Nerja* ☎ *952/521826*) is a flamenco club in the town center. Although the show is obviously geared toward tourists, the club has an authentic olé atmosphere. The food is good, and local specialties, including paella, are served. Dinner shows begin at 9 PM on Wednesday and Friday from February until the end of October.

FRIGILIANA

❼ *58 km (36 mi) east of Málaga.*

The village of Frigiliana, on a mountain ridge overlooking the sea, was the site of one of the last battles between the Christians and the Moors. The short drive off the highway rewards you with spectacular views and an old quarter of narrow, cobbled streets and dazzling white houses decorated with pots of geraniums. (If you don't have a car, take a bus here from Nerja.)

THE AXARQUÍA

❽ *Vélez-Málaga: 36 km (22 mi) east of Málaga.*

The Axarquía region is in the eastern third of Málaga's province, stretching from Nerja to Málaga. The area's charm lies in its mountainous interior, peppered with pueblos, vineyards, and tiny farms. Its coast consists of narrow, pebbly beaches and drab fishing villages on either side of the high-rise resort town of Torre del Mar. The four-lane E15 highway speeds across the region a few miles in from the coast; traffic on the old coastal road (N340) is slower. **Vélez-Málaga** is the capital of the Axarquía. A pleasant agricultural town of white houses, Vélez-Málaga is a center for strawberry fields and vineyards. Worth quick visits are the **Thursday market,** the ruins of a **Moorish castle,** and the church of **Santa María la Mayor,** built in Mudejar style on the site of a mosque that was destroyed when the town fell to the Christians in 1487.

If you have a car and an up-to-date road map, explore the Axarquía's inland villages. You can follow the **Ruta del Vino** *(Wine Route)* 22 km (14 mi) from the coast, stopping at villages that produce the sweet, earthy local wine, particularly Cómpeta. Alternatively you can take the **Ruta de la Pasa** *(Raisin Route)* through Moclinejo, El Borge, and Comares. Comares perches like an eagle's nest atop one of La Serrazuela's highest mountains and dates back to Moorish times. This area is especially spectacular during the late-summer grape-harvest season or in late autumn, when the leaves of the vines turn gold. A short detour to Macharaviaya (7 km [4 mi] north of Rincón de la Victoria) might lead you to ponder the past glory of this now sleepy village: in 1776 one of its sons, Bernardo de Gálvez, became Spanish governor of Louisiana and later fought in the American Revolution (Galveston, Texas, takes its name from the governor). Macharaviaya prospered under his heirs and for many years enjoyed a lucrative monopoly on the manufacture of playing cards for South America. Both the Ruta del Vino and the Ruta de la Pasa are signposted locally.

WHERE TO STAY & EAT

$$$ **Molino de Santillán.** This small country hotel and restaurant is typically Andalusian, with arches, terra-cotta floors, and dark oak furniture. There are superb countryside views from the rooms as well as from the timbered restaurant ($$–$$$), where the cooks use organic ingredients grown at the hotel (try the fresh quince salad with Burgos cheese). At the end of a signposted dirt road north of the main highway, the hotel is a short drive away from the Añoreta golf club and 5 km (2½ mi) from the nearest beach. Pottery and woodcarving workshops are regularly held here. ✉ *Ctra. de Macharaviaya, Km 3, Rincón de la Victoria, 29730* ☎ *952/400949* 🖷 *952/115782* 🌐 *www.molinodesantillan.es* *22 rooms* *In-hotel: restaurant, tennis, pool, public Wi-Fi, some pets allowed* 💳 *AE, DC, MC, V.*

¢–$ ★ **El Molino de los Abuelos.** Under a canopy of jasmine and bougainvillea, this former olive mill has a cobbled courtyard where you can enjoy a glass of *fino* (sherry) at sundown. The rooms are all different, varying from small and simple with shared bath to a sumptuous suite with hot tub. The restaurant has fabulous views; its menu has an emphasis on fish—despite the fact that Axarquía sits some 3,000 feet above sea level. ✉ *Plaza 2, Comares, 29195* ☎ *952/509309* 🖷 *952/214220* *6 rooms* *In-room: no TV (some). In-hotel: restaurant, no elevator* 💳 *AE, MC, V.*

MÁLAGA PROVINCE

The city of Málaga and the provincial towns of the upland hills and valleys to the north create the kind of contrast that makes travel in Spain so tantalizing. The region's Moorish legacy is a unifying visual theme, connecting the tiny streets honeycombing the steamy depths of Málaga, the rocky cliffs and gorges between Alora and Archidona, the layout of the farms, and the crops themselves, including olives, grapes, oranges, and lemons. Ronda and the whitewashed villages of the mountains behind the Costa del Sol form one of Spain's most scenic and emblematic driving routes.

> **GOLFING IN SUNSHINE**
>
> Nicknamed the Costa del Golf, the Sun Coast has some 40 golf courses within putting distance of the Mediterranean, making it a prime golfing destination. Most of the courses are between Rincón de la Victoria (east of Málaga) and Gibraltar. The best season is October to June; greens fees are lower in summer. Pick up *Sun Golf*, a free magazine, at hotels and golf clubs.

To the west of Málaga along the coast, the sprawling outskirts of Torremolinos signal that you're leaving the "real" Spain and entering, well, the "real" Costa del Sol, with its beaches, high-rise hotels, and serious tourist activity. On the far west, you can still see Estepona's fishing village and Moorish old quarter amid its booming coastal development. Just inland, Casares piles whitewashed houses over the bright-blue Mediterranean below.

MÁLAGA

175 km (109 mi) southeast of Córdoba.

With about 550,000 residents, the city of Málaga is technically the capital of the Costa del Sol, though most travelers head straight for the beaches west of the city. Approaching Málaga from the airport, you'll be greeted by huge 1970s high-rises that march determinedly toward Torremolinos. But don't despair: in its center and its eastern suburbs, Málaga is a pleasant port city, with ancient streets and lovely villas amid exotic foliage. Blessed with a subtropical climate, it's covered in lush vegetation and averages some 324 days of sunshine a year.

Málaga has been spruced up with tastefully restored historic buildings and the gradual emergence of more sophisticated shops, bars, and restaurants. The opening of the prestigious Picasso Museum has similarly boosted tourism to this Costa capital, although there are still far fewer visitors here than in the other grand-slam Andalusian cities of Seville, Córdoba, and Granada. Most hotels organize sightseeing tours, and there's an inexpensive open-top tourist bus that travels to the major sights. Tickets (€13) allow you to hop on and off as many times as you like in 24 hours. ⚠ *Note that more tourists usually means more pickpockets, so stay alert, particularly around the historic city center.*

Arriving from Nerja, you'll enter Málaga through the suburbs of El Palo and Pedregalejo, once traditional fishing villages in their own right. Here you can eat fresh fish in the numerous *chiringuitos* (beach-side bars) and stroll Pedregalejos' seafront promenade or the tree-lined streets of El Limonar. At sunset, walk along the **Paseo Marítimo** and watch the lighthouse start its nightly vigil. A few blocks inland from here is Málaga's bullring, **La Malagueta,** built in 1874. Continuing west you soon reach the city center and inviting **Plaza de la Marina;** with cafés and an illuminated fountain overlooking the port, it's a pleasant place for a drink. From here, stroll through the shady, palm-lined gardens of the **Paseo del Parque** or browse on **Calle Marqués de Larios,** the elegant pedestrian-only main shopping street.

WHAT TO SEE

The narrow streets and alleys on each side of Calle Marqués de Larios have charms of their own. Wander the warren of passageways around
9 **Pasaje Chinitas,** off Plaza de la Constitución, and peep into the dark, vaulted bodegas, where old men down glasses of *seco añejo* or *Málaga Virgen,* local wines made from Málaga's muscatel grapes. Silversmiths and vendors of religious books and statues ply their trades in shops that have changed little since the early 1900s. Backtrack across Larios, and, in the streets leading to Calle Nueva, you can see shoeshine boys, lottery-ticket vendors, Gypsy guitarists, and tapas bars with wine served from huge barrels.

10 From the Plaza Felix Saenz, at the southern end of Calle Nueva, turn onto Sagasta to reach the **Mercado de Atarazanas,** the most colorful market in all of Andalusia. Stalls sell fresh fish, spices, and vegetables. The typical 19th-century iron structure incorporates the original **Puerta de Atarazanas,** the exquisitely crafted 14th-century Moorish gate that once connected the city with the port.

NEED A BREAK?

The Antigua Casa de Guardia (✉ *Alameda 18* ☎ *952/214680*), around the corner from the Mercado de Atarazanas, is Málaga's oldest bar, founded in 1840. Andalusian wines flow straight from the barrel, and the floor is ankle-deep in discarded shrimp shells.

11 Málaga's **cathedral,** built between 1528 and 1782, is a triumph, although a generally unappreciated one, having been left unfinished when funds ran out. Because it lacks one of its two towers, the building is nicknamed *La Manquita* (The One-Armed Lady). The enclosed choir, which miraculously survived the burnings of the civil war, is the work of 17th-century artist Pedro de Mena, who carved the wood wafer-thin in some places to express the fold of a robe or shape of a finger. The choir also has a pair of massive 18th-century pipe organs, one of which is still used for the occasional concert. Adjoining the cathedral is a small museum of religious art and artifacts, and a walk around the cathedral on Calle Cister will take you to the magnificent Gothic Puerta del Sagrario. ✉ *C. de Molina Larios* ☎ *952/215917* *€3.50* ⊙ *Mon.–Sat. 10–6:45.*

Alcazaba 15
Cathedral 11
Fundación Picasso 14
Gibralfaro 16
La Concepción 18
Mercado de Atarazanas 10
Museo de Artes Populares 17
Museo Picasso . 13
Palacio Episcopal 12
Pasaje Chinitas ..9

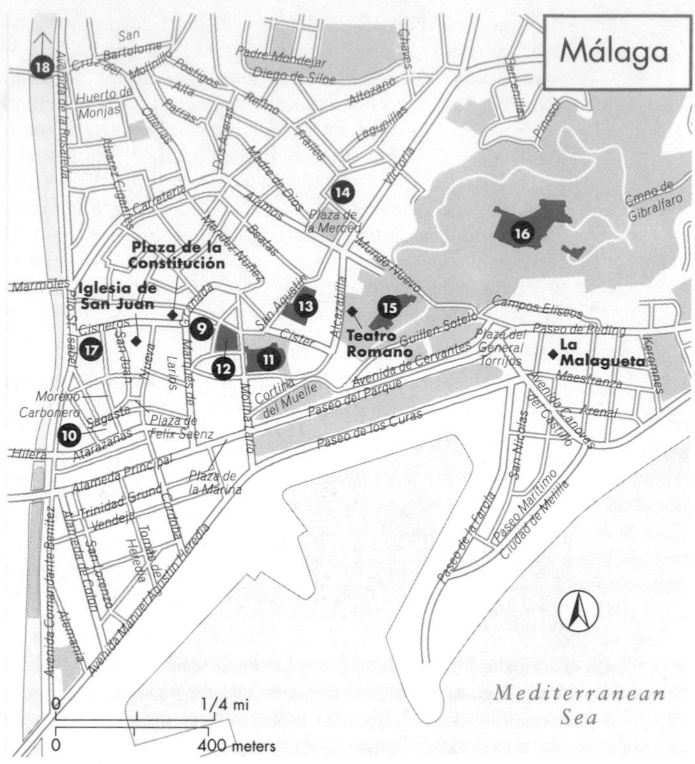

⓬ **Palacio Episcopa** *(Bishop's Palace)*, which faces the cathedral's main entrance, has one of the most stunning facades in the city. It's now a venue for temporary art exhibitions. ✉*Pl. Obispo 6* ☎*952/602722* *Free* ⏲*Tues.–Sun. 10–2 and 6–9.*

⓭ Fodor's Choice ★ The charm of the **Museo Picasso,** the city's most prestigious museum, is that it's such a family affair. These are the works that Pablo Picasso kept for himself or gave to his family and include the heartfelt *Paulo con gorro blanco* (Paulo with a white cap), a portrait of his firstborn son painted in the early 1920s. The holdings were largely donated by two family members—Christine and Bernard Ruiz-Picasso, the artist's daughter-in-law and grandson. The works are displayed in chronological order according to the periods that marked his development as an artist, from Blue and Rose to Cubism, and beyond. The museum is housed in a former palace where, during restoration work, Roman and Moorish remains were discovered. These are now on display, together with the permanent collection of Picassos and temporary exhibitions. ✉*C. de San Agustín* ☎*952/602731* *Permanent exhibition €6, combined permanent and temporary exhibition €8, last Sun. of every month free* ⏲*Tues.–Thurs. 10–8, Fri. and Sat. 10–9.*

14 On the Plaza de la Merced, No. 15 was the childhood home of Málaga's most famous native son, Pablo Picasso, born here in 1881. Now the **Fundación Picasso,** the building has been painted and furnished in the style of the era and houses a permanent exhibition of Picasso's early sketches and sculptures, as well as memorabilia, including the artist's christening robe and family photographs. ✉ *Pl. de la Merced 15* ☎ *952/600215* 🎟 *€1* ⏲ *Mon.–Sat. 10–8, Sun. 10–2.*

15 Just beyond the ruins of a Roman theater on Calle Alcazabilla, the Moorish **Alcazaba** is Málaga's greatest monument. This fortress was begun in the 8th century, when Málaga was the principal port of the Moorish kingdom, though most of the present structure dates from the 11th century. The inner palace was built between 1057 and 1063, when the Moorish emirs took up residence; and Ferdinand and Isabella lived here for a while after conquering Málaga in 1487. The ruins are dappled with orange trees and bougainvillea and include a small museum; from the highest point you can see over the park and port. ✉ *Entrance on Alcazabilla* 🎟 *€1.90, €3.15 combined entry with Gibralfaro* ⏲ *Nov.–Mar., Tues.–Sun. 8.30–7; Apr.–Oct., Tues.–Sun. 9:30–8.*

16 Magnificent vistas beckon at **Gibralfaro,** which is floodlighted at night. The fortifications were built for Yusuf I in the 14th century; the Moors called them Jebelfaro, from the Arab word for "mount" and the Greek word for "lighthouse," after a beacon that stood here to guide ships into the harbor and warn of pirates. The beacon has been succeeded by a small parador. You can drive here by way of Calle Victoria or take a minibus that leaves 10 times a day between 11 and 7, or roughly every hour, from the bus stop in the park near the Plaza de la Marina. ✉ *Gibralfaro Mountain* ☎ *952/220043* 🎟 *€1.90, €3.15 combined entry with Alcazaba* ⏲ *Nov.–Mar., daily 9–5:45; Apr.–Oct., daily 9–7:45.*

17 In the old Mesón de la Victoria, a 17th-century inn, is the **Museo de Artes Populares** *(Arts and Crafts Museum)*. On display are horse-drawn carriages and carts, old agricultural implements, folk costumes, a forge, a bakery, an ancient grape press, and Malagueño painted clay figures and ceramics. ✉ *Pasillo de Santa Isabel 10* ☎ *952/217137* 🎟 *€2* ⏲ *Oct.–May, weekdays 10–1:30 and 4–7, Sat. 10–1:30; June–Sept., weekdays 10–1:30 and 5–8, Sat., 10–1:30.*

18 A 150-year-old botanical garden, **La Concepción** was created by the daughter of the British consul, who married a Spanish shipping magnate—the captains of the Spaniard's fleet had standing orders to bring back seedlings and cuttings from every "exotic" port of call. The garden is just off the exit road to Granada—too far to walk, but well worth the cab fare from the city center. ✉ *Ctra. de las Pedrizas, Km 166* ☎ *952/252148* 🎟 *€3.15* ⏲ *Tues.–Sun. 10* AM*–dusk.*

WHERE TO STAY & EAT

$$–$$$ ✕ **El Chinitas.** Decorated with traditional mosaic tiles and original paintings by Malagueño artists, this place sits at one end of Pasaje Chinitas, Málaga's most *típico* (typical) street. The tapas bar is popular, especially for its cured ham. The second floor has three private dining rooms—groups of 12 to 20 can reserve the Sala Antequera, with a Camelot-style

round table—and a banquet hall. Try the *sopa castellana* (soup made with fresh garlic, bread, paprika, and egg), followed by *solomillo al vino de Málaga* (fillet steak in Málaga wine sauce). ✉*Moreno Monroy 4* ☎*952/210972* 🌐*www.chinitas.arrakis.es* ▭*AE, DC, MC, V.*

$$–$$$ ✕ **La Ménsula.** Head here if you want to sample traditional Andalusian cuisine in an elegant, yet cozy atmosphere. The setting is warm and woody, with arches, beams, and a barrel vault ceiling. Stone-cooked steak, warm fish salad, and king prawns with *setas* (oyster mushrooms) are included on the menu. The restaurant is between the port and the city center. ✉*C. Trinidad Grund 28* ☎*952/221314* ▭*DC, MC, V* ⊙*Closed Sun.*

$ ✕ **El Vegetariano de la Alcazabilla.** This restaurant is arguably the best of the handful of vegetarian restaurants on the carnivorous Costa. The location is pleasantly atmospheric, tucked up a side street just around the corner from the Roman amphitheater. Dishes include vegan options and more mainstream vegetarian choices, such as spinach cannelloni, Roquefort-and-celery turnovers, and plenty of salads. The daily set menu prices fluctuate from a reasonable €6.50 to €8.50, and refreshingly, this restaurant is not too pious to include a healthy wine list and some delicious calorie-laden desserts. ✉*Pozo del Rey 5* ☎*952/214858* ▭*MC, V* ⊙*Closed Sun.*

$ ✕ **Tintero.** Come to this sprawling and noisy restaurant for the entertainment rather than the food. There's no menu—the waiters circle the restaurant carrying various dishes, and you choose whatever looks good to you. The bill is totaled up according to the number and size of the plates on the table at the end of the meal. On the El Palo seafront, Tintero specializes in catch-of-the-day seafood, such as *boquerones* (fresh anchovies), *sepia* (cuttlefish), and the all-time familiar classic, *gambas* (prawns). ✉*Playa del Dedo, El Palo* ☎*952/204464* ▭*No credit cards* ⊙*No dinner.*

¢–$ Fodor'sChoice ★ ✕ **Logueno.** This traditional tapas bar has two dining spaces: the original well-loved bar shoehorned into a deceptively small space on a side street near Calle Larios and a more recent expansion across the street. Check out the original with its L-shape wooden bar crammed with a choice of more than 75 tantalizing tapas, including many Logueno originals, such as grilled oyster mushrooms with garlic, parsley, and goat cheese. There's an excellent selection of Rioja wines, and the service is fast and good, despite the lack of elbow room. ✉*Marin Garcia s/n* ☎*No phone* ▭*No credit cards* ⊙*Closed Sun.*

$$$ Fodor'sChoice ★ ✕🏨 **Parador de Málaga–Gibralfaro.** Surrounded by pine trees on top of Gibralfaro, 3 km (2 mi) above the city, this cozy, gray-stone parador has spectacular views of Málaga and the bay. Rooms are attractive—with blue curtains and bedspreads, and woven rugs on bare tile floors—and are some of the best in Málaga. Reserve well in advance. The restaurant ($–$$$) excels at such classic Mediterranean dishes as calamari and fried green peppers. ✉*Monte de Gibralfaro s/n, 29016* ☎*952/221902* 📠*952/221904* 🌐*www.parador.es* ⇜*38 rooms* 👍*In-room: Ethernet. In-hotel: restaurant, bar, pool, parking (no fee)* ▭*AE, DC, MC, V.*

$$$$ **Larios.** On the central Plaza de la Constitución, Larios is inside a 19th-century building that's been elegantly restored. Black-and-white tile floors lend subdued elegance to the second-floor lobby; the rooms are furnished in art deco style with photographs and jazzy bedspreads. The roof terrace has views of the cathedral, and the restaurant has a Japanese menu. There are special discount weekend rates. ✉*Marqués de Larios 2, 29005* ☎*952/222200* 🖷*952/222407* 🌐*www.hotel-larios.com* *34 rooms, 6 suites* *In-room: Wi-Fi. In-hotel: restaurant* ▭*AE, DC, MC, V* *BP.*

$$ **Don Curro.** Just around the corner from the cathedral, this family classic is going through continual renovations, but an old-fashioned air permeates the wood-panel common rooms and fireplace lounge. The revamped rooms have parquet floors, spot lighting, and classy cream and white fabrics. The ground floor bingo parlor is a quirky surprise. Prices drop considerably on weekends. ✉*Sancha de Lara 9, 29015* ☎*952/227200* 🖷*952/215946* 🌐*www.hoteldoncurro.com* *112 rooms, 6 suites* *In-room: dial-up. In-hotel: public Wi-Fi, restaurant, parking (fee)* ▭*AE, DC, MC, V.*

$$ Fodor's Choice ★ **Humaina.** In this small hotel 16 km (10 mi) north of the city, the rooms are painted a sunny yellow and are furnished with terra-cotta tiled floors. Balconies overlook a thickly forested park of olive, pine, and oak trees. Solar energy, an organic garden, and serious recycling are part of the ecofriendly package; horseback riding, bird-watching, and rambling excursions can be arranged. The restaurant dishes up healthful, tasty dishes, and vegetarians are happily accommodated—a rarity in these parts. ✉*Parque Natural Montes de Málaga, Carretera del Colmenar s/n, 29013* ☎*952/641025* 🖷*952/640115* 🌐*www.hotelhumaina.es* *10 rooms, 4 suites* *In-hotel: restaurant, pool, no elevator* ▭*MC, V* *BP.*

$ **Lis.** This older hotel is housed in an elegant building in between the center and the port. The public areas, with original marble floors, have a scuffed, lived-in feel, but a planned renovation (no definite dates given) could change this. The rooms are butter-colored and have dark wood trim. The bathrooms have tubs, as well as showers. ✉C. *Cordoba 7, 29001* ☎*952/227300* *51 rooms* *In-hotel: bar* ▭*MC, V* *EP.*

NIGHTLIFE & THE ARTS

The region's main theater is the **Teatro Cervantes** (✉*Ramos Marín* ☎*952/224109 or 952/220237* 🌐*www.teatrocervantes.com*), whose programs include Spanish-language plays, concerts, and flamenco. The **Málaga Symphony Orchestra** has a winter season of orchestral concerts and chamber music, with most performances held at the Teatro Cervantes. In summer, larger concerts are staged in the bullring or the **Palacio Municipal de Deportes** (☎*952/176392* 🌐*www.palaciodeportes-malaga.com*); past big-name billings have included Bryan Ferry and Bob Dylan. Málaga's main nightlife districts are Maestranza, between the bullring and the Paseo Marítimo, and the beachfront in the suburb of Pedregalejos. Central Málaga also has a lively bar scene.

ANTEQUERA

 *64 km (40 mi) northwest of Málaga and 108 km (67 mi) northeast of Ronda, via Pizarra.*

Antequera became a stronghold of the Moors after their defeat at Córdoba and Seville in the 13th century. Its fall to the Christians in 1410 paved the way for the reconquest of Granada—the Moors retreated, leaving a fortress on the town heights.

WHAT TO SEE

Next door to the town fortress is the former church of **Santa María la Mayor,** one of 27 churches, convents, and monasteries in Antequera. Built of sandstone in the 16th century, it has a fine ribbed vault and is now a concert hall. The church of **San Sebastián** has a brick baroque Mudejar tower topped by a winged figure called the Angelote ("big angel"), the symbol of Antequera. The church of **Nuestra Señora del Carmen** (Our Lady of Carmen) has an extraordinary baroque altarpiece that towers to the ceiling.

Antequera's pride and joy is *Efebo,* a beautiful bronze statue of a boy that dates back to Roman times. Standing almost 5 feet high, it's on display in the **Museo Municipal.** ⊠ *Pl. Coso Vieja* ☎ *952/704051* 🎫 *€3* ⊙ *Tues.–Fri. 10–1:30 and 4:30–6:30, Sat. 10–1:30, Sun. 11–1:30.*

The mysterious prehistoric **dolmens** are megalithic burial chambers, built some 4,000 years ago out of massive slabs of stone weighing more than 100 tons each. The best-preserved dolmen is La Menga. They're just outside Antequera. ⊠ *Signposted off Málaga exit Rd.* 🎫 *Free* ⊙ *Tues. 9–3:30, Wed.–Sat. 9–6, Sun. 9:30–2:30.*

Europe's major nesting area for the greater flamingo is **Fuente de Piedra,** a shallow saltwater lagoon. In February and March, these birds arrive from Africa by the thousands to breed, returning to Africa in August when the water dries up. The visitor center has information on wildlife. Don't forget your binoculars. ⊠ *10 km (6 mi) northwest of Antequera, off A92 to Seville* ☎ *952/111715* 🎫 *Free* ⊙ *May–Sept., Wed.–Sun. 10–2 and 4–6; Oct.–Apr., Wed.–Sun. 10–2 and 6–8.*

East of Antequera, along N342, is the dramatic silhouette of the **Peña de los Enamorados** *(Lovers' Rock),* an Andalusian landmark. Legend has it that a Moorish princess and a Christian shepherd boy eloped here one night and cast themselves to their deaths from the peak the next morning. The rock's outline is often likened to the profile of the Córdoban bullfighter Manolete.

About 8 km (5 mi) from Antequera's Lovers' Rock, the village of **Archidona** winds its way up a steep mountain slope beneath the ruins of a Moorish castle. This unspoiled village is worth a detour for its **Plaza Ochavada,** a magnificent 17th-century square resplendent with contrasting red and ocher stone. ⊠ *8 km (5 mi) beyond Peña de los Enamorados, along N342, Antequera.*

Well-marked walking trails guide you at the **Parque Natural del Torcal de Antequera** *(El Torcal Nature Park).* You can walk among eerie pillars of pink limestone sculpted by aeons of wind and rain. Keep to the well-marked paths. A guide can be arranged for longer hikes. The visitor center includes a small museum. ✉ *Centro de Visitantes, Ctra. C3310, 10 km (6 mi) south of Antequera* ☎ *649/472688* 🎫 *Free* ⊙ *Daily 10–5.*

WHERE TO STAY & EAT

$$ Fodor'sChoice ★ ✕ **El Angelote.** Across the square from the Museo Municipal, El Angelote's two wood-beam dining rooms are usually packed. Try the *porrilla de setas* (wild mushrooms in an almond-and-wine sauce) or *perdiz hortelana* (stewed partridge). Antequera's typical dessert is *bienmesabe* (literally, "tastes good to me"), a delicious concoction of almonds, chocolate, and apple custard. ✉ *Pl. Coso Viejo* ☎ *952/703465* ▭ *DC, MC, V* ⊙ *Closed Mon. No dinner Sun.*

$ ✕ **Caserío San Benito.** If it weren't for the cell-phone transmission tower looming next to this country restaurant 11 km (7 mi) north of Antequera, you might think you've stumbled into an 18th-century scene. Many of the items found during the renovation of this former farmhouse fronted by a cobbled courtyard are displayed in a small adjacent museum. Popular dishes include *porra antequerana* (a thick version of gazpacho) and *migas* (fried bread crumbs with sausage and spices). ✉ *Ctra. Málaga–Córdoba, Km 108* ☎ *952/111103* ▭ *AE, MC, V* ⊙ *Closed Mon. and 1st 2 wks in July. No dinner Tues.–Thurs.*

$$–$$$$ 🏨 **La Posada del Torcal.** Surrounded by the lunar landscape of El Torcal, this small hotel is just the place to chill out and relax after a long day on the trail. There are king-size beds (a rarity in Spain!) and a fireplace in each room. You can find skillful copies of Spanish paintings throughout. The Posada's restaurant uses organic, locally produced ingredients to cook up Spanish dishes with an innovative twist. ✉ *Partido de Jeva, Villanueva de la Concepción, 29230* ☎ *952/031177* 📠 *952/031006* 🌐 *www.laposadadeltorcal.com* *10 rooms* *In-hotel: restaurant, bar, tennis court, pool, gym, no elevator* ▭ *AE, MC, V* ⊙ *Closed Dec. and Jan.* 🍽 *BP.*

$ 🏨 **Castillo.** Despite its name, this hotel is modern, although housed in an elegant building in the historic center. The rooms are not fancy, but they are bright and comfortable; try for one with a balcony overlooking the bustling street. The downstairs restaurant serves good traditional food, including tapas, *raciones,* (large tapa) and grilled meats. ✉ C. *Don Fernando 40* ☎ *952/843090* 🌐 *www.castillahotel.com* *18* rooms *In hotel: restaurant* ▭ *MC, V* 🍽.

THE GUADALHORCE VALLEY

20 *Leave Antequera via the El Torcal exit and turn right onto A343.*

From the village of Alora, follow a small road north to the awe-inspiring **Garganta del Chorro** *(Gorge of the Stream),* a deep limestone chasm where the Guadalhorce River churns and snakes its way some 600 feet below the road. The railroad track that worms in and out of tunnels in the cleft is, amazingly, the main line heading north from Málaga for Bobadilla junction and, eventually, Madrid. Clinging to the cliff side is the **Caminito del Rey** *(King's Walk),* a suspended catwalk built for a visit by King Alfonso XIII at the beginning of the 19th century. At this writing, the catwalk is closed for major construction and renovations.

North of the gorge, the Guadalhorce has been dammed to form a series of scenic reservoirs surrounded by piney hills, which constitute the **Parque de Ardales** nature area. Informal, open-air restaurants overlook the lakes and a number of picnic spots. Driving along the southern shore of the lake, you reach Ardales and, turning onto A357, the old spa town of **Carratraca.** Once a favorite watering hole for both Spanish and foreign aristocracy, it has a Moorish-style *ayuntamiento* (town hall) and an unusual **polygonal bullring.** Carratraca's old hotel, the **Hostal del Príncipe,** once sheltered Empress Eugénie, wife of Napoléon III; Lord Byron also came seeking the cure. The splendid Roman-style marble-and-tile **bathhouse** has benefited from extensive restoration.

TORREMOLINOS

21 *11 km (7 mi) west of Málaga, 16 km (10 mi) northeast of Fuengirola, 43 km (27 mi) east of Marbella.*

Torremolinos is all about fun in the sun. It may be more subdued than it was in the action-packed '60s and '70s, but scantily attired northern Europeans of all ages still jam its streets in season, shopping for bargains on Calle San Miguel, downing sangría in the bars of La Nogalera, and congregating in the karaoke bars and English pubs. By day, the sunseekers flock to the beaches El Bajondillo and La Carihuela, where, in high summer, it's hard to find towel space on the sand.

Torremolinos has two sections. The first, **Central Torremolinos,** is built around the Plaza Costa del Sol; Calle San Miguel, the main shopping street; and the brash Nogalera Plaza, which is full of overpriced bars and restaurants. The Pueblo Blanco area, off Calle Casablanca, is more pleasant; and the Cuesta del Tajo, at the far end of Calle San Miguel, winds down a steep slope to Bajondillo Beach. Here, crumbling walls, bougainvillea-clad patios, and old cottages hint at the quiet fishing village of bygone years. The second, much nicer, section of Torremolinos is **La Carihuela.** (To find it, head west out of town on Avenida Carlota Alessandri and turn left following the signs.) Far more authentically Spanish, the Carihuela still has a few fishermen's cottages and excellent seafood restaurants. The traffic-free esplanade makes for a pleasurable stroll, especially on a summer evening or Sunday at lunchtime, when it's packed with Spanish families.

Just inland on the Churriana road, **Senda** bird park, botanical garden, and minizoo opened in 2005 in former historical gardens. Exhibits include an aquarium, reptile enclosure, and plenty of exotic birds, all viewed in a lush tropical setting. ✉ *Ctra. Coín, Km 88, Churriana* ☎ *952/623540* 🌐 *www.sendaelretiro.com* 🎫 *€20* ⏲ *May–Sept., daily 10–10; Oct.–Apr., daily 10–6.*

WHERE TO STAY & EAT

SAVE YOUR SWEET TOOTH

In seafood restaurants here, the desserts tend to be disappointing: frozen, commercially made, and overpriced. Skip dessert and enjoy an ice-cream cone on the beach instead.

$$$ ★ ✕ **Med.** Med is tucked away around the corner from the car-free San Miguel. An elevator whisks you up to an elegant restaurant with wooden beams, a blue-and-white nautical setting, seamless Mediterranean views, and impeccable service. The beautifully presented food is from a menu (written in Spanish) that changes every six months, with dishes such as *solomillo de ternero con setas, patata machacona y tempura de verduras* (braised veal with oyster mushrooms, creamed potatoes, and vegetable tempura) followed by *sorbete de limón o mandarina con cava* (lemon or orange sorbet with champagne). There's also an excellent wine selection. ✉*Las Mercedes 12* ☎*952/058830* *Reservations essential* *AE, DC, MC, V.*

$$ ✕ **Casa Juan.** This restaurant is an institution among malagueño families, who flock here on weekends to sample the legendary fresh seafood. Try for a table on the square overlooking the mermaid fountain. This is a good place to indulge in *fritura malagueña* (fried seafood) or *arroz marinera* (seafood with rice), another specialty. ✉*Plaza San Gines, La Carihuela* ☎*952/373512* *MC, V* *Closed Mon.*

$ ✕ **Matahambre.** Opened in mid-2005, this restaurant has a stylish yet rustic feel, with brick barrel-vault ceiling, terra-cotta tiles, and walls washed in dark ocher and sky blue. There are outside tables on the Plaza del Panorama—aptly named, as the views of the coast from here are stunning. The affordable restaurant takes its wines seriously, with more than 80 reds to choose from. To accompany your tipple choose from dishes such as *carpaccio de salmón y espinacas con vinagreta pesto* (carpaccio of salmon and spinach with pesto vinaigrette), or, for lightweights, goat-cheese salad with bacon and walnuts. ✉*Las Mercedes 14* ☎*952/381212* *MC, V* *Closed Mon.*

$$$ **Don Pedro.** Extremely comfortable and well maintained, this three-story hotel was built in traditional low-rise Andalusian-style with ocher-painted walls. The rooms are spacious and have balconies; sea views get snapped up fast. The bodega-style bar gets popular at happy hour; nightly entertainment there includes flamenco shows. The hearty breakfast buffet should set you up for the day. ✉*Av. del Lido, 29620* ☎*952/386844* *952/386935* *www.solmelia.com* *524 rooms* *In-hotel: restaurant, pools, beachfront* *AE, DC, MC, V* *BP.*

$$$ **Tropicana.** On the beach at the far end of the Carihuela, in one of the most pleasant parts of Torremolinos, you'll find this low-rise resort hotel, which has its own beach club. A tropical theme runs throughout, from the purple passion-flower climbers covering the brickwork to the common areas, with exotic plants, raffia floor mats, and bamboo furniture, to the rooms, with their warm color schemes complemented

by lashings of white linen. The hotel has a friendly, homey feel that keeps many guests returning year after year. ✉*Trópico 6, La Carihuela, 29620* ☎*952/386600* 🖷*952/380568* 🌐*www.hoteltropicana.es* *84 rooms* *In-room: refrigerator. In-hotel: restaurant, bar, pool, public Wi-Fi, beach* 💳*AE, DC, MC, V* 🍴*BP.*

$$ **Miami.** Something of a find, this small hotel dates from 1950, when it was designed by Manolo Blascos, Picasso's cousin, for the well-known flamenco Gypsy dancer Lola Medina. Rooms are individually furnished, if a little dated, and there's a sitting area with a TV, cozy fireplace, and small library. The inn is surrounded by a shady garden west of the Carihuela, making a stay here like visiting a private Spanish home. Reserve ahead. ✉*Aladino 14, at C. Miami, 29620* ☎*952/385255* 🌐*www.residencia-miami.com* *26 rooms* *In-room: no TV. In-hotel: bar, pool, some pets allowed* 💳*No credit cards* 🍴*CP.*

$ **Cabello.** The rooms at this small hotel have few frills, but most have impressive sea views—it's just a block from the beach, in La Carihuela. Near the ground-floor bar is a comfortable sitting area, with overstuffed chairs, a piano, and a pool table. The owners are friendly and helpful, though they speak only Spanish. ✉*Calle Chiriva 28, 29620* ☎*952/384505* *19 rooms* *In-hotel: bar, no elevator* 💳*No credit cards.*

NIGHTLIFE & THE ARTS

Most nocturnal action is in the center of town. Many of the better hotels stage flamenco shows, but you may also want to check out the **Taberna Flamenca Pepe López** (✉*Pl. de la Gamba Alegre* ☎*952/381284*). There are nightly shows at 10 PM from April to October. The rest of the year shows are on weekends only.

BENALMÁDENA

22 *9 km (5½ mi) west of Torremolinos, 9 km (5½ mi) east of Mijas.*

★ **Benalmádena-Pueblo,** the village proper, is on the mountainside 7 km (4 mi) from the coast. It is surprisingly unspoiled and offers a glimpse of the old Andalusia. **Benalmádena-Costa,** the beach resort, is practically an extension of Torremolinos; it is run almost exclusively by package-tour operators, however the marina does have shops, restaurants, and bars aimed at a sophisticated clientele that may appeal to the independent traveler.

In Benalmádena-Costa's marina, **Sea Life Benalmádena**is an above-average aquarium with fish from local waters, including rays, sharks, and sunfish. Adjacent is a pirate-theme miniature golf course. 🎟€6 ✉*Puerto Marina Benalmádena* ☎*952/560150* 🌐*www.sealife.es* 🎟*€10.95* ⏲*May–Sept., daily 10 AM–midnight; Oct.–Apr., daily 10–6.*

The Costa del Sol's leading amusement park is **Tivoli World,** with rides, Wild West shows, and 40-odd restaurants and snack bars. A 4,000-seat, open-air auditorium showcases international stars alongside cancan, flamenco, and Spanish ballet performances. Take a cable car to the top of Calamorro Mountain for hiking trails. ✉ *Av. Tivoli s/n, Arroyo de la Miel* ☎ *952/7577016* 🌐 *www.tivoli.es* 🎟 *€6, Sun. 11–2* ⏲ *May–Sept., daily 1 PM–1 AM; Oct.–Apr., weekends noon–8.*

WHERE TO STAY & EAT

$$$–$$$$ ✕ **Mar de Alborán.** Next to the yacht harbor, this restaurant has a touch more class than most of its peers, including a decent wine list. Fish dishes, such as the Basque-inspired *lomo de merluza con kokotxas y almejas* (hake stew with clams) or *bacalao al pil-pil* (salted cod in a spicy sauce) can be a welcome switch from standard Costa fare. ✉ *Av. de Alay 5* ☎ *952/446427* ▭ *AE, MC, V* ⏲ *Closed Mon. mid-Dec.–mid-Jan. No dinner Sun.*

$–$$ ✕ **Casa Fidel.** This Benalmádena-Pueblo restaurant is in a typical Andalusian house complete with arches, terra-cotta tiles, a large fireplace, and a small leafy patio. For a starter, try *crema fría de aguacate con salmón marinado* (cold avocado soup with marinated salmon) or *ensalada templada de setas y gambas* (warm salad with shrimp and wild mushrooms). Main courses include *langostinos con chalotas y puré de garbanzos* (king prawns with shallots and garbanzos) and T-bone steak for two. ✉ *Maestra Ayala 1* ☎ *952/449165* ▭ *AE, DC, MC, V* ⏲ *Closed Tues. and Aug. 1–15. No lunch Wed.*

$–$$ ★ ✕ **Ventorillo de la Perra.** If you've been scouring the coast for something typically Spanish, you may find it at this old inn, which dates from 1785. Outside, there's a leafy patio; inside is a cozy dining room and bar with hams hanging from the ceiling. Choose between local Malagueño cooking, including *gazpacuelo malagueño* (a warm gazpacho of potatoes, rice, and shrimp), and typical Spanish food, such as *conejo en salsa de almendras* (rabbit in almond sauce). The *ajo blanco* (a cold, garlicky almond-based soup) is particularly good. ✉ *Av. Constitución 115, Km 13, Arroyo de la Miel* ☎ *952/441966* ▭ *AE, DC, MC, V* ⏲ *Closed Mon. and Nov.*

$$ 🏨 **La Fonda.** You'll find a true taste of Andalusia at this small hotel on one of the prettiest streets in the pueblo. Rooms have white walls, marble floors, and bright floral fabrics. Some rooms have peerless views of the coast and the Mediterranean; others look onto the cool interior patio shaded by palms. In the same building, under different management, is an excellent restaurant run by Málaga's official hotel school; it's open for lunch on weekdays. ✉ *Santo Domingo 7, 29639* ☎ *952/568324* 📠 *952/568273* 🌐 *www.fondahotel.com* 🛏 *26 rooms* ♿ *In-hotel: bar, pool* ▭ *AE, DC, MC, V* 🍽 *BP.*

NIGHTLIFE

For discos, piano bars, and karaoke, head for the port. The **Fortuna Nightclub** in the **Casino Torrequebrada** (✉ *Av. del Sol s/n, Benalmádena-Costa* ☎ *952/446000* 🌐 *www.torrequebrada.com*) has flamenco and an international dance show with a live orchestra, starting at 10:30 PM. A passport, jacket, and tie are required in the casino, open daily 9 PM–4 AM.

FUENGIROLA

23 *16 km (10 mi) west of Torremolinos, 27 km (17 mi) east of Marbella.*

Fuengirola is less frenetic than Torremolinos. Many of its waterfront high-rises are vacation apartments that cater to budget-minded sun-seekers from northern Europe and, in summer, a large contingent from Córdoba and other parts of Spain. The town is also a haven for British retirees (with plenty of English and Irish pubs to serve them) and a shopping and business center for the rest of the Costa del Sol. Its Tuesday market is the largest on the coast, and a major tourist attraction.

The most prominent landmark in Fuengirola is **Castillo de Sohail.** The original structure dates from the 12th century, but the castle served as a military fortress until the early 19th century. Just west of town, the castle makes a dramatic performance venue for the annual summer season of music and dance. *€1.30 Tues.–Sun. 10–3.*

WHERE TO STAY & EAT

$$–$$$ Fodor'sChoice ★ **Guy Massey.** A celebrated chef from the United Kingdom, Guy Massey took over the helm of the acclaimed Patrick Bausier restaurant in fall 2006 and renamed it to reflect that change. The menu continues to be French inspired. Starters include crab salad and vegetable soup with crispy beetroot. Main dishes like roast pheasant, Barbary duck, and turbot follow. The salmon and goat's cheese salad garnished with pomegranate seeds comes particularly recommended. There's complimentary champagne and hors d'oeuvres. *Rotondade la Luna 1, Pueblo López 952/585120 Reservations essential AE, MC, V Closed Sun. No lunch.*

$–$$ **Bistro.** This restaurant is in the most charming part of Fuengirola, a neighborhood with low-rise buildings punctuated by the occasional fisherman's cottage. With a series of pine-clad rooms, the Bistro has a loyal following of foreign residents, who come for the reliably good food and reasonable prices. The cuisine caters to international palates with such dishes as chicken salad with Philadelphia cheese sauce, crepes stuffed with spinach, and fillet steak with a choice of sauces. The bow-tied waiters are charming and efficient. *Calle Palangreros 30 952/477701 MC, V Closed Sun.*

$–$$ **Mo Mo.** Tucked down a side street, this gem of a restaurant has a vegetarian menu that changes daily. Among the choices you might find are moussaka, tofu kebabs, and lentil and coriander patties. The soothing classical music combined with a pine interior and contemporary art for sale results in a mellow dining experience. There are additional tables outside on the attractive pedestrian street. *Calle Marbella 8 952/197321 MC, V Closed Sun. and Mon. dinner.*

$$ **Villa de Laredo.** At the quieter end of the promenade, just a Frisbee throw from the beach, this hotel has a mildy scuffed, old-fahioned feel, but it is excellently priced given the location and facilities. The rooms are washed in pale cream and have striped Regency-style fabrics. There are small terraces with sea views. Its restaurant ($–$$) offers an aquarium of catch-of-the-day options to choose from. *Paseo Marítimo 42, Rey de España, 29640 952/477689 952/477950 www.hotelvilladelaredo.com*

50 rooms In-room: dial-up. In-hotel: restaurant, pool AE, DC, MC, V.

$ **Hostal Italia.** Right off the main plaza and near the beach, this small, family-run hotel is deservedly popular. People come here year after year, particularly during the October *feria*. The rooms are small yet comfy, and nearly all have balconies. There's a larger sun terrace for catching the rays. *C. de la Cruz 1, 29640 952/474193 952/461909 www.hostal-italia.com 40 rooms MC, V.*

NIGHTLIFE & THE ARTS

Amateur local troupes regularly stage plays and musicals in English at the **Salón de Variétés Theater** (*Emancipación 30 952/474542*). For concerts—from classical to rock to jazz—check out the modern **Palacio de la Paz** (*Recinto Ferial, Av. Jesús Santo Rein 952/589349*) between Los Boliches and the town center.

MIJAS

24 ★ *8 km (5 mi) north of Fuengirola, 18 km (11 mi) west of Torremolinos.*

Mijas is in the foothills of the sierra just north of the coast. Buses leave Fuengirola every half hour for the 20-minute drive through hills peppered with villas. If you have a car and don't mind a mildly hair-raising drive, take the more dramatic approach from Benalmádena-Pueblo, a winding mountain road with splendid views. Mijas was discovered long ago by foreign retirees, and though the large, touristy square may look like an extension of the Costa, beyond this are hilly residential streets with time-worn homes. Try to arrive late in the afternoon, after the tour buses have left. Park in the underground parking garage signposted on the approach to the village. The **Museo Mijas** occupies the former town hall. Themed rooms, including an old-fashioned bakery and bodega, surround a patio. Regular art exhibitions are mounted in the upstairs gallery. *Plaza de la Libertad 952/590380 Free Daily 10–2 and 5–8.*

Bullfights take place year-round, usually on Sunday at 4:30 PM, at Mijas's tiny **bullring.** One of the few square bullrings in Spain, it's off the Plaza Constitución—Mijas's old village square—and up the slope beside the Mirlo Blanco restaurant. *Pl. Constitución 952/485248 Museum entrance fee, €3 June–Sept., daily 10–10; Oct.–Feb., daily 9:30–7; Mar., daily 10–7:30; Apr. and May, daily 10–8:30.*

Worth a visit is the delightful village church **Iglesia Parroquial de la Inmaculada Concepción** *(The Immaculate Conception)*. It's impeccably decorated, especially at Easter, and the terrace and spacious gardens have a splendid panoramic view. The church is up the hill from the Mijas bullring. *Pl. Constitución.*

NEED A BREAK?

The Bar Porras on Plaza de la Libertad (at the base of Calle San Sebastián—the most photographed street in the village) attracts a regular crowd of crusty locals with its good-value tasty tapas.

Mijas extends down to the coast, and the coastal strip between Fuengirola and Marbella is officially called **Mijas-Costa.** This area has several hotels, restaurants, and golf courses.

WHERE TO STAY & EAT

$$$–$$$$ ✕**El Padrastro.** Perched on a cliff above the Plaza Virgen de la Peña, "The Stepfather" is accessible by an elevator from the square or, if you're energetic, by stairs. A view over Fuengirola and the coast is the restaurant's main draw. Dishes might include *lubina cocida con ragout de alcachofa y mantequilla al limón* (sea bass cooked with ragout of artichokes and lemon butter). When the weather's right, you can dine alfresco on the large terrace. ✉*Paseo del Compás 22* ☎*952/485000* ▭*AE, DC, MC, V.*

$$$ ✕**Mirlo Blanco.** In an old house on the pleasant Plaza de la Constitución, with a terrace for outdoor dining, this place is run by a Basque family that has been in the Costa del Sol restaurant business for decades. Good choices here are such Basque specialties as *txangurro* (spider crab) and *kokotxas de bacalau* (cod cheeks). ✉*Pl. de la Constitución 2* ☎*952/485700* ▭*AE, MC, V* ⊙*Closed Jan.*

$$–$$$ ✕**Valparaíso.** Halfway up the road from Fuengirola to Mijas, this sprawling villa stands in its own garden, complete with swimming pool. There's live music nightly ranging from flamenco to opera and jazz. Valparaíso is a favorite among local (mainly British) expatriates, some of whom come in full evening dress to celebrate their birthdays. In winter, logs burn in a cozy fireplace. Try the *pato a la naranja* (duck in orange sauce). ✉*Ctra. de Mijas–Fuengirola, Km 4* ☎*952/485996* ▭*AE, DC, MC, V* ⊙*No dinner Sun. No lunch Oct.–June.*

$$$$ ★ ✕🏨**Gran Hotel Guadalpin Byblos.** On the edge of Mijas's golf course (closer to Fuengirola than to Mijas) and in a huge garden of palms, cypresses, and fountains, this is one of the most exclusive hotels on the Costa del Sol. It's primarily a spa known for its thalassotherapy, a skin treatment using seawater and seaweed, which is applied in a Roman-like temple of cool, white-and-blue marble tiles. Three outstanding restaurants ($$$–$$$$) serve savory regional and international dishes. The menu changes according to season but may include such gourmet delights as roast duck breast flambéed with Jerez brandy. Check the Web site for reduced-price package deals. ✉*Urbanización Mijas-Golf, Mijas-Costa, 29640* ☎*952/473050* 📠*952/476783* 🌐*www.byblos-andaluz.com* *109 rooms, 35 suites* *In-room: Ethernet. In-hotel: 3 restaurants, bars, golf courses, tennis courts, pools, gym, spa, public Internet, public Wi-Fi, some pets allowed* ▭*AE, DC, MC, V* 🍽*BP.*

$$$ Fodor'sChoice ★ 🏨**Beach House.** The epitomé of cool Mediterranean-inspired decor, the Beach House seems not so much like a hotel, but rather like a sumptuous villa owned by a hospitable (and wealthy) friend. From the pleasing viewpoint of the bougainvillea-draped bar, the pool merges seamlessly with the sea. The interior is all clean lines, sparkling marble, and minimalist good taste. The town and restaurants of Fuengirola are 10 minutes due east on N340. ✉*Urbanización El Chaparral, CN340, Km 203, 19648* ☎*952/494540* 🌐*www.beachhouse.nu* *10 rooms* *In-room: Ethernet. In-hotel: pool, no elevator* ▭*MC, V* 🍽*CP.*

$$ **TRH Mijas.** It's easy to unwind here, thanks to the poolside restaurant and bar, and the gardens with views of the hillsides stretching down to Fuengirola and the sea. The tasteful decor is marked by marble floors throughout, wrought-iron window grilles, and wooden shutters. The lobby is large and airy, and there's an attractive glass-roof terrace. All rooms are well furnished, with wood fittings and marble floors. TRH Mijas is at the entrance to Mijas village. *Urbanización Tamisa, 29650 952/485800 952/485825 www.trhhoteles.es 204 rooms, 2 suites In-room: dial-up. In-hotel: restaurant, tennis court, pool, gym AE, DC, MC, V.*

MARBELLA

25 *27 km (17 mi) west of Fuengirola, 28 km (17 mi) east of Estepona, 50 km (31 mi) southeast of Ronda.*

Playground of the rich and home of movie stars, rock musicians, and dispossessed royal families, Marbella has attained the top rung on Europe's social ladder. Dip into any Spanish gossip magazine and chances are the glittering parties that fill its pages are set in Marbella. Much of this action takes place on the fringes—grand hotels and luxury restaurants line the waterfront for 20 km (12 mi) on each side of the town center. In the town itself, you may well wonder how Marbella became so famous. The main thoroughfare, Avenida Ricardo Soriano, is distinctly charmless, and the Paseo Marítimo, though pleasant enough, with a mix of seafood restaurants and pizzerias overlooking an ordinary beach, is far from spectacular.

Marbella's appeal lies in the heart of the **old village**, which remains miraculously intact. Here, a block or two back from the main highway, narrow alleys of whitewashed houses cluster around the central **Plaza de los Naranjos** (Orange Square), where colorful, albeit pricey, restaurants vie for space under the orange trees. Climb onto what remains of the old fortifications and stroll along the Calle Virgen de los Dolores to the Plaza de Santo Cristo.

The **Museo del Grabado Español Contemporáneo,** in a restored 16th-century palace in the heart of the old town, has contemporary Spanish prints and temporary exhibitions. *Hospital Bazán 952/765741 www.museodelgrabado.com €2.50 Tues.–Sat. 10–2 and 5:30–8:30.*

In a modern building just east of Marbella's old quarter, the **Museo de Bonsai** has a collection of miniature trees, including a 300-year-old olive tree from China. *Parque Arroyo de la Repesa, Av. Dr. Maiz Viñal 952/862926 €3 June–Sept., daily 10:30–1:30 and 5–8:30; Oct.–May., daily 10:30–1:30 and 4–7.*

Marbella's wealth glitters most brightly along the Golden Mile, a tiara of star-studded clubs, restaurants, and hotels west of town stretching from Marbella to **Puerto Banús.** Here, a mosque, Arab banks, and the onetime residence of Saudi Arabia's King Fahd betray the influence of oil money in this wealthy enclave. About 7 km (4½ mi) west of central Marbella (between Km 175 and Km 174), a sign indicates the turnoff leading down to Puerto Banús. Though now hemmed in by a belt of high-rises, Marbella's plush marina, with 915 berths, is a gem of ostentatious wealth, a Spanish answer to St. Tropez. Huge and flashy yachts, beautiful people, and countless expensive stores and restaurants make up the glittering parade that marches long into the night. The backdrop is an Andalusian pueblo—built in the 1960s to resemble the fishing villages that once lined this coast.

WHERE TO STAY & EAT

$$$–$$$$ ✕ **La Hacienda.** In a large, pleasant villa 12 km (7 mi) east of Marbella, the Hacienda was founded in the early '70s by the late Belgian chef Paul Schiff, who helped transform the Costa del Sol culinary scene with his modern approach and judicious use of local ingredients. His legacy lives on here through his family. Schiff's signature dish, *pintada con pasas al vino de Málaga* (guinea fowl with raisins in Málaga wine sauce), is often available. ✉ *Urbanización Las Chapas, N340, Km 193* ☎ *952/831267* ✍ *Reservations essential* ▭ *AE, MC, V* ⊙ *Closed Mon. and Tues. mid-Nov.–mid-Dec. No lunch July and Aug.*

$$$–$$$$ ✕ **Santiago.** Facing the seafront promenade, this busy place has long been considered the best fish restaurant in Marbella. Try the *ensalada de langosta* (lobster salad), followed by *besugo al horno* (baked red bream). The menu also has roasts, such as *cochinillo* (pig) and *cordero* (lamb) of the owner's native Castile. Around the corner from the original restaurant (and sharing the same phone number) is Santiago's popular tapas bar. ✉ *Paseo Marítimo 5* ☎ *952/770078* ▭ *AE, DC, MC, V* ⊙ *Closed Nov.*

$$–$$$ ✕ **Aquavit.** Cream-and-yellow paintwork, titanium cutlery, and handcrafted tables provide a sunny, snazzy look. Asian-style starters include nori rolls, Thai fish cakes, and fresh arugula salad; the signature dish just has to be the potato-and-anchovy gratin with a shot of (what else?) chilled aquavit. More than 35 different vodkas are available, as well as some unusual wines and liqueurs. ✉ *Plaza del Puerto, Puerto Banús* ☎ *952/819127* ▭ *AE, MC, V* ⊙ *No lunch.*

$$–$$$ ✕ **La Comedia.** This Swedish-run restaurant is on one of the old town's most traditional Andalusian plazas and has one of the most imaginative menus among Marbella's 600-plus restaurants. Starters include such delights as blue mussel carpaccio topped with grilled scallops and truffles. Entrées include avocado-and-salmon spring rolls with mango and marie rose sauce (a thousand island–style dressing) and tandoori sweet curried chicken. For dessert there's an unusual deep-fried apple-cinnamon wonton with vanilla and white chocolate mousse. ✉ *Plaza de la Victoria* ☎ *952/776478* ✍ *Reservations essential* ▭ *AE, DC, MC, V* ⊙ *Closed Mon. No lunch.*

$$–$$$ Fodor's Choice ★ ✕ **Zozoi.** Tucked into the corner of one of the town's squares, upbeat, art deco Zozoi receives rave reviews from the local press. The fashionably Mediterranean menu makes little distinction between starters and main courses; all the portions are generous. Imaginative use of ingredients is shown in such dishes as grilled fillet of sea bass with saffron fettucini and green asparagus, and roasted duck breast with black cherries and pepper. For dessert, try the red forest fruits with *mille feuilles*

(puff pastry) or lemon sorbet spiked with vodka. ✉*Plaza Altamirano 1* ☎*952/858868* *Reservations essential* ▭*MC, V.*

$$$$ **Marbella Club.** The grande dame of Marbella hotels was a creation of the late Alfonso von Hohenlohe, a Mexican-Austrian aristocrat who turned Marbella into a playground for the rich and famous. The exquisite grounds have lofty palm trees, dazzling flower beds, and a beachside tropical pool area. The bungalow-style rooms vary in size; some have private pools. The main restaurant has a classy eclectic menu of modern Mediterranean cuisine. If you can't afford to stay, at least stop by for afternoon tea, served daily 4–6:30, with a selection of finger sandwiches, pastries, and strawberries and cream (in summer). ✉*Blvd. Principe Alfonso von Hohenlohe at Ctra. de Cádiz, Km 178, 3 km (2 mi) west of Marbella, 29600* ☎*952/822211* *952/829884* *www.marbellaclub.com* *84 rooms, 37 suites, 16 bungalows* *In-room: Ethernet, dial-up, Wi-Fi. In-hotel: 3 restaurants, pools, gym, public Internet, parking (no fee)* ▭*AE, DC, MC, V* *BP.*

Fodor'sChoice ★

$$$$ **Puente Romano.** West of Marbella, between the Marbella Club and Puerto Banús, is this palatial hotel designed like an Andalusian pueblo, complete with gardens and trickling fountains. As the name suggests, there's a genuine Roman bridge on the grounds running right down to the beach. There are four restaurants, including El Puente, and Roberto; the latter serves Italian food in the hotel's beach club, a popular summer nightlife venue. In summer there's a beachfront *chiringuito* (seafood restaurant), where you can sample fresh fish. ✉*Ctra. Cádiz, Km 177, 29600* ☎*952/820900* *952/775766* *www.puenteromano.com* *149 rooms, 77 suites* *In-room: Wi-Fi. In-hotel: 4 restaurants, tennis courts, pools* ▭*AE, DC, MC, V* *BP.*

★

$$$ **The Town House.** In a choice location in one of old town Marbella's prettiest squares, this former family house has been exquisitely transformed into a boutique hotel. A combination of antiques and modern fittings make for luxurious rooms, accentuated by earthy colors. The spacious bathrooms are decked out in shiny marble with plenty of complimentary suds to encourage pampering. There is an attractive bar and plenty of restaurants nearby. ✉*C. Alderete 7, Plaza Tetuan, 29600* ☎*952/901791* *www.townhouse.nu* *9 rooms* *In-hotel: bar, no elevator* ▭*MC, V.*

Fodor'sChoice ★

$$ **Lima.** Here's a good midrange option in downtown Marbella, two blocks from the beach. The tastefully decorated rooms have dark-wood furniture, bright floral bedspreads, and balconies; corner rooms are the largest. Underground parking is available for a fee. ✉*Av. Antonio Belón 2, 29600* ☎*952/770500* *952/863091* *www.hotellimamarbella.com* *64 rooms* *In-hotel: parking (fee)* ▭*AE, DC, MC, V.*

¢ **Juan.** On a quiet street, this no-frills cheapie with a small courtyard is a short stroll from the beach and Marbella's historic center. Because the rooms have refrigerators, this is a good place if you're economizing on eating out. ✉*Calle Luna 18, 29600* ☎*952/779475* *4 rooms* *In-room: no a/c, refrigerator, no elevator* ▭*No credit cards* *EP.*

NIGHTLIFE & THE ARTS

Art exhibits are held in private galleries and in several of Marbella's leading hotels, notably the Puente Romano. The **tourist office** (✉ *Glorieta de la Fontanilla* ☎ *952/822818* 🌐 *www.pgb.es/marbella*) can provide a map of town and monthly calendar of exhibits and events.

Much of the nighttime action revolves around the **Puerto Banús,** in such bars as Sinatra's and Joy's Bar. Marbella's most famous nightspot is the

Fodor's Choice ★ **Olivia Valére disco** (✉ *Ctra. de Istán, Km 0.8* ☎ *952/828861*), decorated to resemble a Moorish palace; head inland from the town's mosque (an easy-to-spot landmark).

The trendy **Dreamers** (✉ *CN 340 km, Puerto Banús* ☎ *952/812080*) attracts a young, streetwise crowd with its live bands, go-go girls, and a massive dance space. The **Casino Nueva Andalucía** (✉ *Bajos Hotel Andalucía Pl., N340* ☎ *952/814000*), open 8 PM to 6 AM May through October (until 5 AM November through April), is a chic gambling spot in the Hotel Andalucía Plaza, just west of Puerto Banús. Jacket and tie are required for men, and passports for all. In the center of Marbella, **Ana María** (✉ *Pl. de Santo Cristo 5* ☎ *952/775646*) is a popular flamenco venue but open only from May to September.

OJÉN

26 *10 km (6 mi) north of Marbella.*

For a contrast to the glamour of the coast, drive up to Ojén, in the hills above Marbella. Take note of the beautiful pottery and, if you're here the first week in August, don't miss the **Fiesta de Flamenco,** which attracts some of Spain's most respected flamenco names, including the Juan Peña El Lebrijano, Chiquetete, and El Cabrero. Four kilometers (2½ mi) from Ojén is the **Refugio del Juanar,** a former hunting lodge in the heart of the Sierra Blanca, at the southern edge of the Serranía de Ronda, a mountainous wilderness. Not far from the Refugio, you might spot the wild ibex that dwell among the rocky crags; the best times to watch are dawn and dusk, when they descend from their hiding places. A bumpy trail takes you a mile from the Refugio to the **Mirador** (lookout), with a sweeping view of the Costa del Sol and the coast of northern Africa.

WHERE TO STAY & EAT

$$$ ✕🏨 **Castillo de Monda.** Designed to resemble a castle, this hotel incorporates the ruins of Monda's Moorish fortress, some of which date back to the 8th century. The interior is decorated with ceramic tiles, elaborate arches, and extensive use of Moorish-style stucco bas-relief. The guest rooms are sumptuous and fun, with four-poster beds, marble heated bathroom floors, and colorful fabrics. The main restaurant ($$–$$$), which resembles a medieval banquet hall, has terrific views of the surrounding countryside. There are weeklong relaxation skills courses available. ✉ *Monda, 29110* ☎ *952/457142* 📠 *952/457336* 🌐 *www.mondacastle.com* *17 rooms, 6 suites* *In-room: dial-up. In-hotel: restaurant, bar, pool, public Wi-Fi* 💳 *AE, MC, V.*

$$–$$$ **Refugio del Juanar.** Once an aristocratic hunting lodge (King Alfonso XIII came here), this secluded hotel and restaurant was sold to its staff in 1984 for the symbolic sum of 1 peseta. The hunting theme prevails, both in the common areas—where a log fire roars in winter—and on the restaurant menu, where game is emphasized. The rooms are simply decorated in a rustic style, and six (including the three suites) have their own fireplace. *Sierra Blanca s/n, 29610 952/881000 www.juanar.com 23 rooms, 3 suites In-hotel: restaurant, tennis court, pool AE, DC, MC, V.*

RONDA

27 *61 km (38 mi) northwest of Marbella, 108 km (67 mi) southwest of Antequera (via Pizarra).*

Fodor'sChoice ★

Ronda, one of the oldest towns in Spain, is known for its spectacular position and views. Secure in its mountain fastness on a rock high over the River Guadalevín, the town was a stronghold for the legendary Andalusian bandits who held court here from the 18th to early 20th century. Ronda's most dramatic element is its ravine (360 feet deep and 210 feet across)—known as **El Tajo**—which divides La Ciudad, the old Moorish town, from El Mercadillo, the "new town," which sprang up after the Christian Reconquest of 1485. Tour buses roll in daily with sightseers from the coast 49 km (30 mi) away, and on weekends affluent Sevillanos flock to their second homes here. Stay overnight midweek to see this noble town's true colors.

The most attractive approach is from the south. The winding but well-maintained A376 from San Pedro de Alcántara travels north up through the mountains of the Serranía de Ronda. Take the first turnoff to Ronda from A376. Entering the lowest part of town, known as El Barrio, you can see parts of the old walls, including the 13th-century Puerta de Almocobar and the 16th-century Puerta de Carlos V gates. The road climbs past the Iglesia del Espíritu Santo (Church of the Holy Spirit) and up into the heart of town.

WHAT TO SEE

Begin in El Mercadillo, where the **tourist office** (*Paseo de Bas Infante s/n 952/187119 www.andalucia.org Weekdays 9:30–6:30, weekends 10–2*) in the Plaza de España can supply you with a map.

Immediately south of the Plaza de España is Ronda's most famous bridge, the **Puente Nuevo** *(New Bridge)*, an architectural marvel built between 1755 and 1793. The bridge's lantern-lighted parapet offers dizzying views of the awesome gorge. Just how many people have met their ends here nobody knows, but the architect of the Puente Nuevo fell to his death while inspecting work on the bridge. During the civil war, hundreds of victims were hurled from it.

Cross the Puente Nuevo into **La Ciudad**, the old Moorish town, and wander the twisting streets of white houses with birdcage balconies.

The so-called House of the Moorish King, **Casa del Rey Moro,** was actually built in 1709 on the site of an earlier Moorish residence. Despite the name and the *azulejo* (painted tile) plaque depicting a Moor on the facade, it's unlikely that Moorish rulers ever lived here. The garden has a great view of the gorge, and from here a stairway of some 365 steps, known as **La Mina,** descends to the river. However, the steps are steep and poorly lighted and should be tackled only by the agile. The house, across the Puente Nuevo on Calle Santo Domingo, is being converted into a luxury hotel due for completion in mid-2008, although you can visit the gardens and La Mina. ✉ *Calle Santo Domingo 17* ☎ *952/187200* 🎫 *€4* ⏲ *May–Sept., daily 10–8; Oct.–Apr., daily 10–7.*

PICASSO'S CUBES

It's been suggested that Picasso, who was born in Málaga, was inspired to create cubism by the pueblos *blancos* of his youth. The story may or may not be apocryphal, but it's nonetheless easy to imagine—there *is* something wondrous and inspiring about Andalusia's whitewashed villages, with their dwellings that seem to tumble down the mountain slopes like giant dice. Perhaps it's the contrast in color: the bright white against the pine green. Or perhaps the mountaintop isolation: at these altitudes, the morning light breaks silently over the slopes, the only movement a far-off shepherd guiding his flock.

The excavated remains of the **Baños Arabes** *(Arab Baths)* date from Ronda's tenure as capital of a Moorish *taifa* (kingdom). The star-shape vents in the roof are an inferior imitation of the ceiling of the beautiful bathhouse in Granada's Alhambra. The baths are beneath the Puente Arabe (Arab Bridge) in a ravine below the Palacio del Marqués de Salvatierra. 🎫 *€2* ⏲ *Weekdays 10–6, weekends 10–3.*

The collegiate church of **Santa María la Mayor,** which serves as Ronda's cathedral, has roots in Moorish times: originally the Great Mosque of Ronda, the tower and adjacent galleries, built for viewing festivities in the square, retain their Islamic design. After the mosque was destroyed (when the Moors were overthrown), it was rebuilt as a church and dedicated to the Virgen de la Encarnacion after the Reconquest. The naves are late Gothic, and the main altar is heavy with baroque gold leaf. The church is around the corner from the remains of a mosque, Minarete Árabe (Moorish Minaret) at the end of the Marqués de Salvatierra. ✉ *Pl. Duquesa de Parcent* 🎫 *€2* ⏲ *May–Sept., daily 10–8; Oct.–Apr., daily 10–6.*

A stone palace with twin Mudejar towers, the **Palacio de Mondragón** *(Palace of Mondragón)* was probably the residence of Ronda's Moorish kings. Ferdinand and Isabella appropriated it after their victory in 1485. Today you can wander through the patios, with their brick arches and delicate, Mudejar stucco tracery, and admire the mosaics and *artesonado* (coffered) ceiling. The second floor holds a small museum with archaeological items found near Ronda, plus the reproduction of a dolmen. ✉ *Plaza Mondragón* ☎ *952/878450* 🎫 *€2* ⏲ *Apr.–Oct.,* *weekdays 10–6, weekends 10–3; May–Sept., weekdays 10–8, weekends 10–3.*

The main sight in Ronda's commercial center, El Mercadillo, is the **Plaza de Toros.** Pedro Romero (1754–1839), the father of modern bullfighting and Ronda's most famous native son, is said to have killed 5,600 bulls here during his long career. In the museum beneath the plaza you can see posters for Ronda's very first fights, held here in 1785. The plaza was once owned by the late bullfighter Antonio Ordóñez, on whose nearby ranch Orson Welles's ashes were scattered (as directed in his will)—indeed, the ring has become a favorite of filmmakers. Every September, the bullring is the scene of Ronda's *corridas goyescas,* named after Francisco Goya, whose bullfight sketches (*tauromaquias*) were inspired by the skill and art of Pedro Romero. Both participants and the dignitaries in the audience don the costumes of Goya's time for the occasion. Seats for these fights cost a small fortune and are booked far in advance. Other than that, the plaza is rarely used for fights except during Ronda's May festival and sometimes in September. *952/874132 €5 Daily 10–6; May–Sept. 10–8*

WHERE TO STAY & EAT

$$$$ ★ **Tragabuches.** Málagueño chef Benito Goméz is famed for his daringly innovative menu. The *menú de degustación,* a taster's menu of five courses and two desserts, includes imaginative choices, such as a casserole of noodles with octopus sashimi and butter and white-garlic ice cream with pine nuts. Traditional and modern furnishings blend in the two dining rooms (one with a picture window). The restaurant is around the corner from Ronda's parador and the tourist office. You can purchase a cookbook at the restaurant that contains some of its best-loved dishes. *José Aparicio 1 952/190291 AE, DC, MC, V Closed Mon. No dinner Sun.*

$$ **Pedro Romero.** Named after the father of modern bullfighting, this restaurant opposite the bullring is packed with colorful bullfight paraphernalia. Mounted bull heads peer down at you as you tuck into the *sopa de la casa* (house soup, made with ham and eggs), *rabo de toro,* (oxtail) or *perdiz estofada con salsa de vino blanco y hierbas* (stewed partridge with white-wine-and-herb sauce), and, for dessert, *helado de higos con chocolate* (fig ice cream topped with house-made chocolate sauce). *Virgen de la Paz 18 952/871110 AE, DC, MC, V.*

$$$ **Ancinipo.** The artistic legacy of its former owners, Ronda artist Téllez Loriguillo and acclaimed Japanese watercolor painter Miki Haruta, is evidenced throughout this boutique hotel. The interior has exposed stone panels, steel and glass fittings, and mosaic-tile bathrooms—and many murals and paintings. There are dramatic mountain views from most of the rooms, and the Atrium restaurant ($$) dishes up such traditional favorites as *migas* (fried breadcrumbs with sausage and spices) and oxtail stew, followed by chestnuts with brandy and cream. *José Aparicio 7, 29400 952/161002 www.hotelacinipo.com 14 rooms In-room: Wi-Fi. In-hotel: restaurant, bar AE, DC, MC, V.*

$$$ **El Molino del Santo.** In the now-converted "Saint's Mill" next to a rushing stream near Benaoján, 10 km (7 mi) from Ronda, this British-run establishment was one of Andalusia's first country hotels. Guest rooms are arranged around a pleasant patio and come in different sizes, some with a terrace. This is a good base for walks in the mountains, and the hotel rents mountain bikes as well. There's also a small station nearby with trains to Ronda and other villages. The restaurant ($–$$) has an excellent reputation and offers vegetarian options. The hotel uses solar panels for hot water and the pool. ✉*Estación de Benaoján s/n, Benaoján, 29370* ☎*952/167151* *952/167327* *www.andalucia.com/molino* *18 rooms* *In-hotel: restaurant, pool, bicycles, no elevator* *AE, DC, MC, V* *Closed mid-Nov.–mid-Feb.* *BP.*

$$ **Alavera de los Baños.** This small, German-run hotel was used as a backdrop for the film classic *Carmen.* Fittingly, given its location next to the Moorish baths, there's an Arab-influenced theme throughout, with terra-cotta tiles, graceful arches, and pastel-color washes. The two rooms on the first floor have their own terraces, opening up onto the split-level garden. The restaurant is open for dinner and uses predominantly organic foods. ✉*Hoya San Miguel s/n, 29400* ☎*952/879143* *www.andalucia.com/alavera* *9 rooms* *In-room: no a/c. In-hotel: restaurant, bar, pool, no elevator* *MC, V* *BP.*

$$$ **Husa Reina Victoria.** Built in 1906 by the Gibraltar British as a weekend stop for passengers on the rail line between Algeciras and Bobadilla, this classic Spanish hotel rose to fame in 1912, when the ailing German poet Rainer Maria Rilke came here to convalesce. (His room has been preserved as a museum.) The Queen Victoria still exudes old-fashioned charm with large Edwardian-style windows, hunting prints, and gracious lounges. The views from the cliff-top gardens, hanging over a roughly 500-foot precipice, are particularly dramatic. ✉*Jerez 25, 29400* ☎*952/871240* *952/871075* *www.husa.es* *90 rooms* *In-hotel: restaurant, pool, parking (fee), some pets allowed* *AE, DC, MC, V.*

$$ **Finca la Guzmana.** This traditional Andalusian *corijo* (cottage) 4 km (2½ mi) east of Ronda has been lovingly restored with bright, fresh decor to complement the original beams, the wood-burning stoves, and a sublime setting surrounded by olive trees and grapevines. Walkers, bird-watchers, and painters are frequent guests. The owners also organize trips (guided or unguided) through the white villages in a classic sports car. The breakfast is more generous than most, with homemade bread, preserves, and local cheeses. ✉*Aptdo de Correos 408, 29400* ☎*600/006305* *www.laguzmana.com* *5 rooms* *In-hotel: pool, no elevator* *No credit cards* *CP.*

$$ ★ **San Gabriel.** In the oldest part of Ronda, this hotel is run by a family who converted their 18th-century home into an elegant, informal hotel (the family still lives in part of the building). The common areas, furnished with antiques, are warm and cozy, and include a DVD screening room with autographed photos of actors. (John Lithgow, Isabella Rossellini, and Bob Hoskins, in town to film the 2000 television movie version of *Don Quixote,* were among the first to stay at the hotel.)

12

CLOSE UP

Olive Oil, the Golden Nectar

Inland from the Costa de Sol's clamor and crowds, the landscape is stunning. Far in the distance, tiny villages cling precariously to the mountainside like a tumble of sugar cubes, while in the foreground, brilliant red poppies and a blaze of yellow mimosa are set against a rippling quilt of cool green olive trees and burnt ocher soil.

Up close, most of the trees have dark twisted branches and gnarled trunks, which denote a lifetime that can span more than a century. It is believed that many of the olive trees here are born from seeds of the original crop brought to the Mediterranean shores in the 7th century BC by Greek and Phoenician traders. Since that time, the oil produced has been used for innumerable purposes, ranging from monetary to medicinal.

These days, the benefits of olive oil are well-known. The locals don't need convincing. Olive oil has long been an integral part of the traditional cuisine and is used lavishly in every meal, including breakfast. This is when the country bars fill up with old men wearing flat caps who start their day with coffee, brandy, and black tobacco along with slabs of toasted white bread generously laden with lashings of olive oil, garlic, and salt.

Spain's most southerly province produces a copious 653 metric tons of olive oil each year, or 90% of the entire Spanish production. The area currently exports to more than 95 countries, with the main buyers of bulk oil being Italy, France, Germany, Portugal, and the United Kingdom. The type and grade of oil varies according to the destination. Some oils taste sweet and smooth; others have great body and character, and varying intensities of bitterness. North Americans like their oil to be light, with little distinctive taste, while Mexicans prefer olive oil that is dark and strong.

It has been about 30 years since a published medical study revealed that people living in the southern Mediterranean countries had the lowest case of heart disease in the Western world. This has resulted in increased use of olive oil throughout the West, not only for salad dressing but also as a healthy and tasty substitute for butter and vegetable oil in almost every aspect of cooking—except, that is, as a spread for toast; it may take several decades more before olive oil on toast becomes standard breakfast fare anywhere else but in rural Andalucia!

Some guest rooms have small sitting areas; all are stylishly furnished with antiques. ✉ *Marqués de Moctezuma 19, 29400* ☎ *952/190392* 📠 *952/190117* 🌐 *www.hotelsangabriel.com* *15 rooms, 1 suite* *In-hotel: restaurant, parking (no fee), no elevator* ▭ *AE, MC, V.*

AROUND RONDA: CAVES, ROMANS & PUEBLOS BLANCOS

This area of spectacular gorges, remote mountain villages, and ancient caves is fascinating to explore and a dramatic contrast with the clamor and crowds of the coast.

About 20 km (12 mi) west of Ronda toward Seville is the prehistoric **Cueva de la Pileta** *(Pileta Cave)*. Exit left for the village of Benaoján—

from here the caves are well signposted. A Spanish-speaking guide will hand you a paraffin lamp and lead you on a roughly 90-minute walk that reveals prehistoric wall paintings of bison, deer, and horses outlined in black, red, and ocher. One highlight is the Cámara del Pescado (Chamber of the Fish), whose drawing of a huge fish is thought to be 15,000 years old. ☎*952/167343* 🎫*€6* ⏲*Nov.–Apr., daily 10–1 and 4–6; May–Oct., daily 10–1 and 4–5.*

Ronda la Vieja (Old Ronda), 20 km (12 mi) north of Ronda, is the site of the old Roman settlement of **Acinipo.** A thriving town in the 1st century AD, Acinipo was abandoned for reasons that still baffle historians. Today it's a windswept hillside with piles of stones, the foundations of a few Roman houses, and what remains of a theater. Excavations are often under way at the site, in which case it will be closed to the public. Call the tourist office in Setenil (see number below) before visiting to get an update. ✉*Take A376 toward Algodonales; turnoff for ruins is 9 km (5 mi) from Ronda on MA449* ☎*956/134261* 🌐*www.setenil.com* 🎫*Free* ⏲*Weekdays 10–2:30 and 5–8, weekends noon–2 and 5–8.*

28 **Setenil de las Bodegas,** 8 km (5 mi) north of Acinipo, is in a cleft in the rock cut by the Guadalporcín River. The streets resemble long, narrow caves, and on many houses the roof is formed by a projecting ledge of heavy rock.

29 In **Olvera,** 13 km (8 mi) north of Setenil, two imposing silhouettes dominate the crest of its hill: the 11th-century castle Vallehermoso, a legacy of the Moors, and the neoclassical church of La Encarnación, reconstructed in the 19th century on the foundations of the old Moorish mosque.

30 A solitary watchtower dominates a crag above the village of **Zahara de la Sierra,** its outline visible for miles around. The tower is all that remains of a Moorish castle where King Alfonso X once fought the emir of Morocco; the building remained a Moorish stronghold until it fell to the Christians in 1470. Along the streets you can see door knockers fashioned like the hand of Fatima: the fingers represent the five laws of the Koran and serve to ward off evil. ✉*From Olvera, drive 21 km (13 mi) southwest to village of Algodonales then south on A376 to Zahara de la Sierra 5 km (3 mi).*

SIERRA DE GRAZALEMA

Village of Grazalema: 28 km (17 mi) northwest of Ronda, 23 km (14 mi) northeast of Ubrique.

The 323-square-km (125-square-mi) Sierra de Grazalema straddles the provinces of Málaga and Cádiz. These mountains trap the rain clouds that roll in from the Atlantic and thus have the distinction of being the wettest place in Spain, with an average annual rainfall of 88 inches. Thanks to the park's altitude and prevailing humidity, it's one of the last habitats for the rare fir tree *Abies pinsapo*; it's also home to ibex, vultures, and birds of prey. Parts of the park are restricted, accessible only on foot and accompanied by an official guide.

31 Standing dramatically at the entrance to the park, the village of **Grazalema** is the prettiest of the pueblos blancos. Its cobblestone streets of houses with pink-and-ocher roofs wind up the hillside, red geraniums splash white walls, and black wrought-iron lanterns and grilles cling to the house fronts.

From Grazalema, A374 takes you to **Ubrique,** on the slopes of the Saltadero Mountains, and known for its leather tanning and embossing industry. Look for the **Convento de los Capuchinos** (Capuchin Convent), the church of **San Pedro,** and 4 km (2½ mi) away the ruins of the Moorish castle **El Castillo de Fátima.**

Another excursion from Grazalema takes you through the heart of the nature park: follow the A344 west through dramatic mountain scenery, past Benamahoma, to **El Bosque,** home to a trout stream and information center.

WHERE TO STAY

$ **La Mejorana.** This is the place to find rural simplicity. A mere 20 years old, the house has been cleverly designed and built to resemble an old-fashioned village home, complete with beams, tiled floors, and thick whitewashed walls. The rooms have simple wrought-iron beds, but the mountain views are stunning. There is a tranquil flower-filled garden for sunny days, and when temperatures drop, the cozy alternative of a fireplace in the communal sitting room. ✉ *C. Santa Clara 6, 11610* ☎ *956/132327* 🌐 *www.lamejorana.net* *5 rooms* *In-room: no TV. In-hotel: pool, no elevator* *CP.*

ESTEPONA

32 *17 km (11 mi) west of San Pedro de Alcántara and 22 km (13 mi) west of Marbella.*

Estepona is a pleasant and relatively tranquil seaside resort, despite being surrounded by an ever-increasing number of urban developments. The beach, more than 1 km (½ mi) long, also has better-quality sand than the Costa norm, and the promenade is lined with well-kept, aromatic flower gardens. The gleaming white **Puerto Deportivo** is lively and packed with restaurants, serving everything from fresh fish to pizza and Chinese food. Back from the main Avenida de España, the old quarter of narrow streets and bars is surprisingly unspoiled.

WHERE TO STAY & EAT

$$–$$$ ✕ **Alcaría de Ramos.** José Ramos, a winner of Spain's National Gastronomy Prize, opened this restaurant in the El Paraíso complex, between Estepona and San Pedro de Alcántara, and has watched it garner a large and enthusiastic following. Try the *ensalada de lentejas con salmón ahumado* (with lentils and smoked salmon), followed by *zarzuela de pescados y mariscos* (seafood casserole), leaving room for Ramos's exemplary crêpes suzette with raspberry sauce. ✉ *Urbanización El Paraíso, Ctra. N340, Km 167* ☎ *952/886178* *MC, V* *Closed Sun. No lunch.*

$ ✕ **La Escollera.** This cheerful, family-friendly seafood restaurant is appropriately located at the fishing boat end of the port. Expect no-frills decor and paper tablecloths but excellent fresh fish and seafood. This place is a favorite with locals—always a good sign. The menu changes according to the catch of the day. ✉ *Puerto Pesquero de Estepona* ☎ *952/806354* ▭ *No credit cards* ⏲ *Closed Mon.*

$$$$ ★ ✕ **Las Dunas.** Rising like a multicolor apparition next to the beach, this spectacular hotel is halfway between Estepona and Marbella. Trickling fountains and copious exotic plants help create a sense of the palatial, and the large guest rooms are suitably sumptuous. Sea views command a premium. The El Lido Restaurant ($$$$) serves first-rate international cuisine; chef Juan Carlos Jiménez was awarded Best Chef 2005 by the Academia Gastronómica de Málaga. The health center offers several alternative therapies, and families will appreciate the well-organized children's club. ✉ *La Boladilla Baja, Ctra. de Cádiz, Km 163.5, 29689* ☎ *952/794345* 🖷 *952/794825* 🌐 *www.las-dunas.com* *33 rooms, 39 suites, 33 apartments* *In-room: Ethernet, Wi-Fi. In-hotel: 3 restaurants, pools, gym, spa, children's programs (ages 6–12), parking (no fee)* ▭ *AE, DC, MC, V* *BP.*

$$$$ **Kempinski.** From the outside, this luxury resort between the coastal highway and the beach looks like a cross between a Moroccan casbah and the Hanging Gardens of Babylon. Tropical gardens, with a succession of large swimming pools, meander down to the beach. The rooms are spacious, modern, and luxurious, with faux–North African furnishings and balconies overlooking the Mediterranean. The Sunday-afternoon jazz brunch, with a live band and lavish buffet, is something of a social occasion for locals. ✉ *Playa El Padrón, Ctra. N340, Km 159, 29680* ☎ *952/809500* 🖷 *952/809550* 🌐 *www.kempinski-spain.com* *133 rooms, 16 suites* *In-room: Ethernet, dial-up, Wi-Fi. In-hotel: 4 restaurants, pools, gym, children's programs (ages 5–12), some pets allowed* ▭ *AE, DC, MC, V* *BP.*

$$$ ★ **Albero Lodge.** Owner Myriam Perez Torres' love for travel infuses this boutique hotel, where each room is named after a city, with decor to match. Exotic Fez has rich fabrics and colors; European rooms, such as Florence and Berlin, are elegantly decorated with antiques. In playful contrast, the New York room is dramatically avant-garde with a black-and-white theme. There are private terraces, and a sandy path leads to the beach. Myriam can arrange hiking, horse riding, and boat trips, as well as therapeutic massages. ✉ *Urb. Finca La Cancelada, Calle Támesis 16, 29689* ☎ *952/880700* 🖷 *952/885238* 🌐 *www.alberolodge.com* *9 rooms* *In-hotel: pool, no elevator* ▭ *AE, DC, MC, V.*

CASARES

33 *20 km (12 mi) northwest of Estepona.*

The mountain village of Casares lies high above Estepona in the Sierra Bermeja. Streets of ancient white houses piled one on top of the other perch on the slopes beneath a ruined but impressive Moorish castle. The heights afford stunning views over orchards, olive groves, and cork woods to the Mediterranean, sparkling in the distance.

GIBRALTAR

The tiny British colony of Gibraltar—nicknamed Gib, or simply the Rock—whose impressive silhouette dominates the strait between Spain and Morocco, was one of the two Pillars of Hercules in ancient times, marking the western limits of the known world. Gibraltar today is a bizarre anomaly of Moorish, Spanish, and British influences in an ace position commanding the narrow pathway between the Mediterranean Sea and the Atlantic Ocean.

The Moors, headed by Tariq ibn Ziyad, seized the peninsula in 711 as a preliminary to the conquest of Spain. After the Moors had ruled for 750 years, the Spaniards recaptured Tariq's Rock in 1462. The English, heading an Anglo-Dutch fleet in the War of the Spanish Succession, gained control in 1704, and, after several years of local skirmishes, Gibraltar was finally ceded to Great Britain in 1713 by the Treaty of Utrecht. Spain has been trying to get it back ever since. In 1779 a combined French and Spanish force laid siege to the Rock for three years to no avail. During the Napoléonic Wars, Gibraltar served as Admiral Horatio Nelson's base for the decisive naval Battle of Trafalgar, and during the two World Wars, it served the Allies well as a naval and air base. In 1967 Franco closed the land border with Spain to strengthen his claims over the colony, and it remained closed until 1985.

The Rock is like Britain with a suntan. There are double-decker buses, policemen in helmets, and bright red mailboxes. Millions of dollars have been spent in developing the Rock's tourist potential, while a steady flow of expatriate Britons come here from Spain to shop at Morrisons supermarket and High Street shops. Gibraltar's economy is further boosted by its important status as an offshore financial center. Britain and Spain have been talking about joint Anglo-Spanish sovereignty, much to the ire of the majority of Gibraltarians, who remain fiercely patriotic to the crown. The relationship between the two traditional foes has relaxed a little with the introduction of flights from the Spanish mainland to Gibraltar in November 2006.

EXPLORING THE ROCK

20 km (12 mi) east of Algeciras, 77 km (48 mi) southwest of Marbella.

There are likely few places in the world that you enter by walking or driving across an airport runway, but that's what happens in Gibraltar. First, show your passport; then make your way out onto the narrow strip of land linking Spain's La Linea with Britain's Rock. Unless you have a good reason to take your car—such as loading up on cheap gas or duty-free goodies—you're best off leaving it in a guarded parking area in La Linea, the Spanish border town—and don't bother hanging around here; it's a seedy place. In Gibraltar you can hop on buses and taxis that expertly maneuver the narrow, congested streets. The Official Rock Tour—conducted either by minibus or, at a greater cost, taxi—takes about 90 minutes and includes all the major sights, allowing you to choose which places to come back to and linger at later. When you call Gibraltar from Spain, the area code is 9567; when you call from another country, the code is 350. Prices in this section are given in British pounds; Gibraltar permits the use of U.K. currency and its own sterling government notes and coins. Euros can also be used in most of the shops, but the exchange rate may be unfavorable.

WHAT TO SEE

34 **Catalan Bay,** a fishing village founded by Genoese settlers, is now a resort on the eastern shores. The massive water catchments once supplied the colony's drinking water. ✉ *From the Rock's eastern side, go left down Devil's Tower Rd. as you enter Gibraltar.*

35 From **Europa Point,** have a look across the straits to Morocco, 23 km (14 mi) away. You're now standing on one of the two ancient Pillars of Hercules. In front of you, the lighthouse has dominated the meeting place of the Atlantic and the Mediterranean since 1841; sailors can see its light from a distance of 27 km (17 mi). ✉ *Continue along coast road to the Rock's southern tip.*

36 To the north of the lighthouse is the **Shrine of Our Lady of Europe,** venerated by seafarers since 1462. Once a mosque, the small Catholic chapel has a little museum with a 1462 statue of the Virgin and some documents. ✉ *Just north of Europa Point and lighthouse, along Rock's southern tip* 🎫 *Free* ⏲ *Weekdays 10–7.*

37 For a fine view, drive high above **Rosia Bay,** to which Nelson's flagship, HMS *Victory,* was towed after the Battle of Trafalgar in 1805. On board were the dead, who were buried in Trafalgar Cemetery on the southern edge of town—except for Admiral Nelson, whose body was returned to England preserved in a barrel of rum. ✉ *From Europa Flats, follow Queensway back along the Rock's western slopes.*

38 The **Upper Rock Nature Preserve,** accessible from Jews' Gate, includes St. Michael's Cave, the Apes' Den, the Great Siege Tunnels, the Moorish Castle, and the Military Heritage Center, which chronicles the British regiments who have served on the Rock. ✉ *From Rosia Bay, drive along Queensway and Europa Rd. as far as Casino, above Alameda Gardens. Make a sharp right here up Engineer Rd. to Jews' Gate, a lookout over docks and Bay of Gibraltar toward Algeciras.* 🎫 *£8, includes all attractions, plus £1.50 per vehicle* ⏲ *Daily 9:30–6:30.*

39 **St. Michael's Cave** is the largest of Gibraltar's 150 caves. A series of underground chambers hung with stalactites and stalagmites, it's an ideal performing-arts venue. Sound-and-light shows are held here most days at 11 AM and 4 PM. The skull of a Neanderthal woman (now in the British Museum) was found at nearby Forbes Quarry eight years *before* the world-famous discovery in Germany's Neander Valley in 1856; nobody paid much attention to it at the time, which is why this prehistoric race is called Neanderthals rather than *Homo calpensis* (literally, "Gibraltar Man"—after the Romans' name for the Rock, *Calpe*). St. Michael's is on Queens Road.

CLOSE UP

The Full Monty on Gibraltar's Past

Plenty of places in Spain are culturally a country apart, but Gibraltar is—literally—a country apart. As a little piece of Britain tucked onto the underside of Spain, Gibraltar has an amusing mix of tea-and-biscuits culture paired with the baking sun of its Mediterranean surroundings. This strategic spot, a quick skip into Africa and a perfect point of departure around the base of Europe, has inspired a fair amount of turf wars, ultimately placing it in the hands of the British. Today that relationship is amicable, however in the beginning it was anything but.

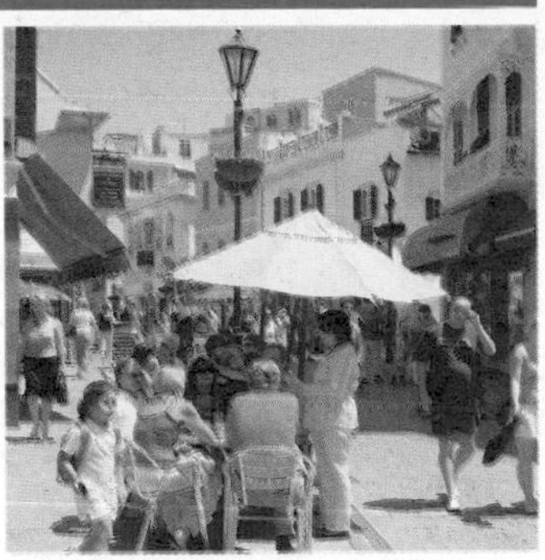

Although the Romans ruled the area from 500 BC to AD 475, it was left to the Moors to establish the first settlement here in 1160. The Duke of Medina Sidonia recaptured the Rock for Spain in 1462. In 1501 Isabel the Catholic declared Gibraltar a crown property and the following year it received the Royal Warrant that bestowed on it a coat-of-arms consisting of a castle and a key. In 1704 an Anglo-Dutch force eventually captured Gibraltar—and this developed into Spain's ceding of Gibraltar to Britain in 1713.

In 1779, combined Spanish and French forces totaling over 50,000 troops laid the final Great Siege against a mere 5,000 defenders. The attack highlighted all the unusual problems defending Gibraltar. The great north face of the Rock guarded the entrance to Gibraltar, but it seemed impossible to mount guns on it. Taking into account the characteristics of limestone, Sergeant Ince came up with an answer: tunnels. Of course the solution had one major problem: cannons are designed to fire upward, not down. They circumvented the problem by digging tunnels that sloped downward. Later, in World War II, tunnels were used again to defend Gibraltar. General Eisenhower conducted the Allied invasion of North Africa from one of the tunnels—and all of them remain under military control today.

From 1963 to 1964 Gibraltar's future was debated at the United Nations, but in a referendum on September 10, 1967, which has now become Gibraltar's National Day, 99.9% of Gibraltarians voted to remain a part of Britain. In 1969 this resulted in a new constitution granting self-government. These events severely provoked General Franco and he closed the costal border that same year. It stayed closed until February 5, 1985. Despite this, Spain occasionally decided to make the crossing more difficult. In 2002, finally, the governments of the U.K. and Spain reached an agreement in principle on joint sovereignty. Another referendum resulted in 99% voting against the idea. Nevertheless, this led to the creation of a tripartite forum, including the Gibraltar government and, in turn, direct flights from Madrid were started in December 2006.

★ You can reach St. Michael's Cave—or ride all the way to the top of Gibraltar—on a **cable car.** The car doesn't go high off the ground, but the views of Spain and Africa from the Rock's pinnacle are superb. It leaves from a station at the southern end of Main Street. *Cable car £8 round-trip* *Daily 9:30–5:45.*

40 The famous Barbary Apes are a breed of cinnamon-color, tailless monkeys native to Morocco's Atlas Mountains. Legend holds that as long as the apes remain in Gibraltar, the British will keep the Rock; Winston Churchill went so far as to issue an order for their preservation when the apes' numbers began to dwindle during World War II. They are publicly fed twice daily, at 8 and 4, at **Apes' Den,** a rocky area down Old Queens Road and near the Wall of Charles V (this is the famous wall built in 1552 after an attack by Turkish pirates). Among the apes' mischievous talents are grabbing food, purses, and cameras.

GIBRALTAR FACTS

- Gibraltar has been a self-governing Crown Colony of the United Kingdom since 1830.
- Currency on the rock is the pound sterling and although Gibraltar issues its own notes and coins, U.K. notes and coins are equally accepted, as are euros.
- The official language is English, but a mixed English–Spanish dialect, known as Llanito is commonly used.
- Century-old rituals such as the Changing of the Guard and the Ceremony of the Keys continue to draw the largest crowds of visitors.

41 The **Great Siege Tunnels,** formerly known as the Upper Galleries, were carved out during the Great Siege of 1779–82 at the northern end of Old Queen's Road. You can plainly see the openings from where the guns were pointed at the Spanish invaders. These tunnels form part of what is arguably the most impressive defense system anywhere in the world.

42 The **Moorish Castle** was built by the descendants of Tariq, who conquered the Rock in 711. The present Tower of Homage dates from 1333, and its besieged walls bear the scars of stones from medieval catapults (and, later, cannonballs). Admiral George Rooke hoisted the British flag from its summit when he captured the Rock in 1704, and it has flown here ever since. The castle is on Willis's Road but may be viewed from outside only.

43 **Casemates Square,** in the northern part of town, is Gibraltar's social hub. It has been pedestrianized, and there are plenty of places to sit out with a drink and watch the world go by. There's a **tourist office** (*9567/50762* *Weekdays 9–5:30, weekends 10–4* PM) branch here.

44 The colorful, congested **town of Gibraltar** is where the dignified Regency architecture of Great Britain blends well with the shutters, balconies, and patios of southern Spain. Shops, restaurants, and pubs beckon on busy Main Street; at the Governor's Residence, the ceremonial Changing of the Guard takes place six times a year and the Ceremony of the Keys takes place twice a year. Also make sure you see the Law

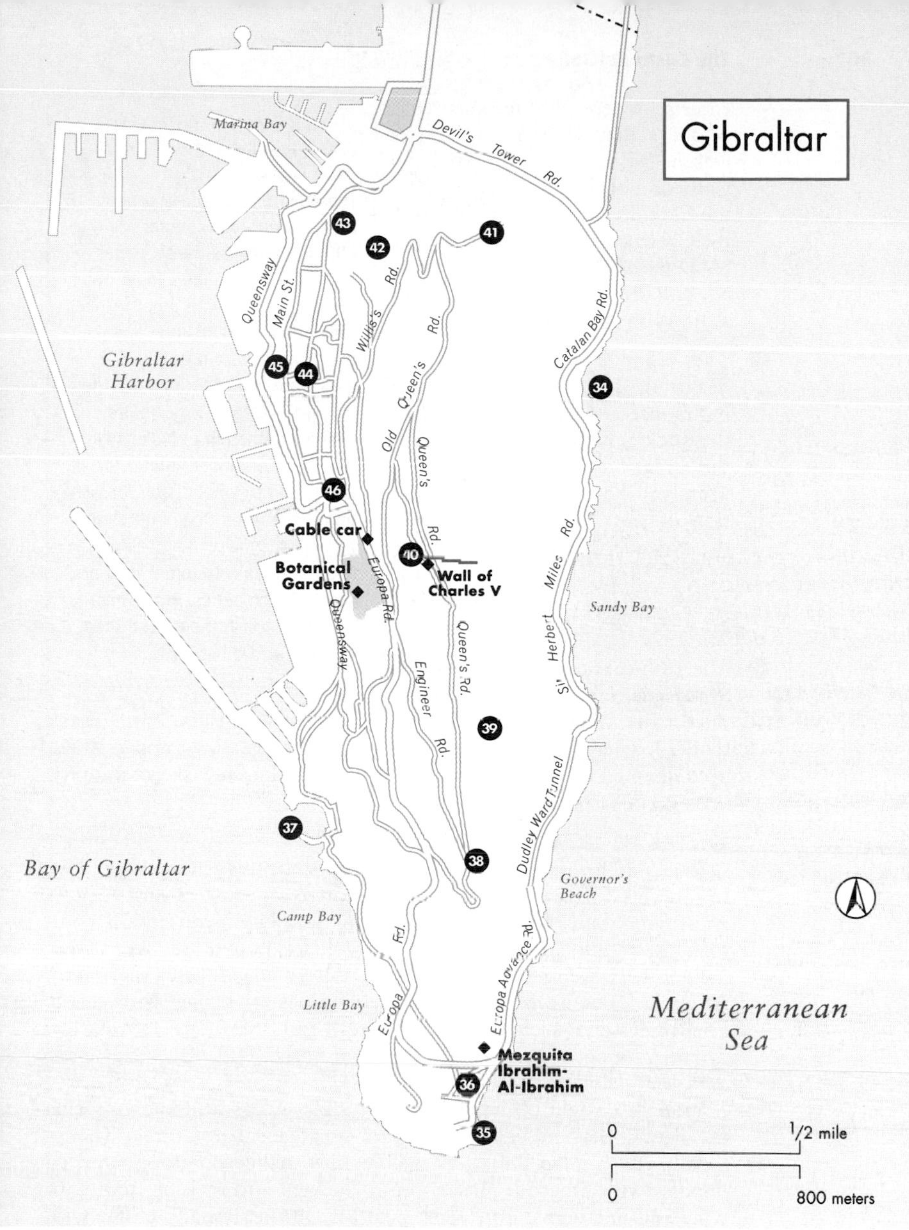

- Apes' Den **40**
- Casemates Square **43**
- Catalan Bay **34**
- Europa Point **35**
- Gibraltar Museum **45**
- Great Siege Tunnels **41**
- Moorish Castle **42**
- Nefusot Yehudada Synagogue **46**
- Rosia Bay **37**
- Shrine of Our Lady of Europe **36**
- St. Michael's Cave **39**
- Town of Gibraltar **44**
- Upper Rock Nature Reserve **38**

Courts, where the famous case of the sailing ship *Mary Celeste* was heard in 1872; the Anglican Cathedral of the Holy Trinity; and the Catholic Cathedral of St. Mary the Crowned. The **main tourist office** (✉ *Duke of Kent House, Cathedral Sq.* ☎ *9567/45000* ⏲ *Weekdays 9–5:30*) is on Cathedral Square.

45 The **Gibraltar Museum** houses a beautiful 14th-century Moorish bathhouse and an 1865 model of the Rock; it has displays that evoke the Great Siege and the Battle of Trafalgar. There's also a reproduction of the "Gibraltar Woman," the Neanderthal skull discovered here in 1848. ✉ *Bomb House La.* ☎ *9567/74289* *£2* ⏲ *Weekdays 10–6, Sat. 10–2.*

46 The 18th-century **Nefusot Yehudada Synagogue,** on Line Wall Road, is one of the oldest synagogues on the Iberian Peninsula, dating back to 1724. There are guided tours twice a day at 12:30 PM and 2:30 PM, accompanied by a short history of the Gibraltar Jewish community. ☎ *9567/78804.*

MONKEYING AROUND ON THE ROCK

The most privileged—and popular—residents of Gibraltar are the 200 or so tailless Barbary apes, the only wild primates in all of Europe. Treated with great respect, the apes receive health care at the local military hospital as if they were any other patient. They live in the Upper Rock Nature Reserve (although occasionally one is seen wandering into the town), and a popular stop for visitors is the Ape's Den. With their friendly, playful, and inquisitive nature, it's easy to forget they are semi-wild creatures. But remember: don't touch them, feed them, or go near the babies.

WHERE TO STAY & EAT

$$–$$$ ✕ **Terrace Restaurant.** Upstairs from the casino, this is one of the best restaurants for sea views. Tarifa's colorful kite-surfers and Africa's Atlas Mountains are visible on a clear day. The menu here is comfortably traditional and as good as the black bow-tie service. Dishes include beef Wellington, chicken Roquefort, and lobster thermidor. Afterward, choose from the diet-defying dessert trolley with classic English desserts, such as trifle, and fresh fruit tarts. ✉ *7 Europa Rd.* ☎ *9567/76666* *Reservations essential* *AE, DC, MC, V* ⏲ *Closed Sun. No lunch.*

$ ✕ **Sacarello's.** Right off Main Street, this place is as well known for its excellent coffee and cakes as it is for its adjacent restaurant. There's a daily lavish salad buffet, as well as filled baked potatoes; panfried noodles with broccoli, mussels, and chicken; and rack of lamb with wine and fine herbs. Top your meal off with a specialty coffee with cream and vanilla. The restaurant has several rooms warmly decorated in English-pub style, with cozy corners, dark-wood furnishings, and low ceilings. ✉ *57 Irish Town* ☎ *9567/70625* *MC, V* ⏲ *No dinner Sun.*

$$$$ **The Eliott.** If you want to stay at the most slick and modern of the Rock's hotels, try this place right in the center of the town, in what used to be the Gibraltar Holiday Inn. Rooms have been revamped over the past couple of years, so you can expect all the extras. Ask for

a room at the top of the hotel, with a view over the Bay of Gibraltar. ✉*2 Governor's Parade* ☎*9567/70500* 🖷*9567/70243* 🌐*www.ocallaghanhotels.com* *106 rooms, 8 suites* *In-room: dial-up, Wi-Fi. In-hotel: 2 restaurants, bars, pool, no-smoking rooms* ▭*AE, DC, MC, V* *BP.*

$$$$ **The Rock.** Overlooking Gibraltar, this hotel first opened in 1932. Furnishings in the rooms and restaurants are modern and colorful, yet they manage to preserve something of the English colonial style—bamboo, ceiling fans, and a fine terrace bar with a wisteria-covered terrace. There's a 20% discount if you book online. ✉*3 Europa Rd.* ☎*9567/73000* 🖷*9567/73513* 🌐*www.rockhotelgibraltar.com* *101 rooms, 2 suites* *In-room: dial-up, Wi-Fi. In-hotel: restaurant, bar, pool* ▭*AE, DC, MC, V* *BP.*

$ **Bristol.** This colonial-style hotel in the heart of town has splendid views of the bay and the cathedral. Rooms are spacious and comfortable, and the downstairs lounge exudes a faded elegance with sink-into sofas and chandeliers. The tropical garden is a haven. ✉*10 Cathedral Sq.* ☎*9567/76800* 🖷*9567/77613* 🌐*www.bristolhotel.gi* *60 rooms* *In-hotel: bar, pool, parking (no fee)* ▭*AE, DC, MC, V.*

NIGHTLIFE

At the **Ladbrokes Casino** (✉*7 Europa Rd.* ☎*9567/76666*) the gaming room is open 9 PM–4 AM, the cocktail bar 7:30 PM–4 AM. Dress is smart casual.

SPORTS & THE OUTDOORS

Bird- and dolphin-watching, diving, and fishing are popular activities on the Rock. For details on tours and outfitters, visit the Gibraltar government Web site's "On Holiday" page (🌐*www.gibraltar.gov.uk*) or call the local tourist office (☎9567/745000).

SIDE TRIPS FROM GIBRALTAR

SAN ROQUE

47 *92 km (57 mi) southwest of Ronda, 64 km (40 mi) west of Marbella, 40 km (25 mi) west of Estepona, 14 km (9 mi) east of Gibraltar, and 35 km (22 mi) east of Tarifa.*

The town of San Roque was founded within sight of Gibraltar by Spaniards who fled the Rock when the British captured it in 1704. Almost 300 years of British occupation have done little to diminish the ideals of San Roque's inhabitants, who still see themselves as the only genuine Gibraltarians. Fourteen kilometers (10 mi) east of San Roque is the luxury **Sotogrande** complex, a gated community with sprawling millionaires' villas, a yacht marina, and four golf courses, including the legendary Valderrama, which once hosted the Ryder Cup.

WHERE TO STAY & EAT

$$–$$$ ✕**Los Remos.** The dining room in this gracious colonial villa has peach-color walls with quasi-baroque adornments: gilt rococo mirrors, swirling cherubs, friezes of grapes, and crystal lamps. It overlooks a formal, leafy garden full of palms, cedars, and trailing ivy. Entrées include *potaje de sepia con garbanzos* (cuttlefish stew with chickpeas). All the seafood comes from the Bay of Algeciras area—the restaurant's name means "The Oars"—and the wine cellar contains some 20,000 bottles. ✉ *Villa Victoria, Campomento de San Roque* ☎ *956/698412* ▭ *AE, DC, MC, V* ⊙ *Closed Mon. No dinner Sun.*

$$$$ **San Roque Club.** In this Moorish-Andalusian-style pueblo, the main building houses the reception area, golf clubhouse, and two restaurants, one specializing in Japanese food. The rooms and suites are in white houses scattered around a garden with fountains and exotic plants; each room has a little garden patio, and each suite has an enclosed courtyard as well. The houses are connected by paved paths, on which the cleaning staff tool around on golf carts. The hotel is next to the San Roque golf course, halfway between the village and Sotogrande. ✉ *San Roque Club, N340, Km 127, 11360* ☎ *956/613030* 📠 *956/613360* 🌐 *www.sanroqueclub.com* *50 rooms, 50 suites* *In-room: dial-up. In-hotel: 2 restaurants, golf course, tennis courts, pool, some pets allowed* ▭ *AE, DC, MC, V* 🍽 *BP.*

$$$ **NH Almenara Golf Hotel & Spa.** This deluxe Sotogrande resort is a complex of semidetached Andalusian-style houses clustered around a main building on the edge of an 18-hole golf course, 6 km (4 mi) from the coast. Gardens surround each house, accessible via golf cart. Each house also has a private terrace or patio. Facilities at the marble-clad spa include a Finnish sauna, Turkish bath, and hydromassage pool. ✉ *Av. Almenara s/n, Sotogrande, 11310* ☎ *956/582000* 📠 *956/582001* 🌐 *www.sotogrande.com* *136 rooms, 12 suites* *In-room: dial-up, Wi-Fi. In-hotel: restaurant, bar, golf courses, pool, spa* ▭ *AE, DC, MC, V.*

NIGHTLIFE

The **Casino de San Roque** (✉ *N340, Km 124* ☎ *956/780100* ⊙ *Mar.–Sept., daily 8 PM–5 AM; Oct.–Feb., daily 9 PM–5 AM*) has a gaming room with roulette and blackjack tables and a less formal slot-machine area. Passports, and a jacket and tie for men, are required in the casino.

TARIFA

48 *35 km (21 mi) west of San Roque.*

Fodor's Choice ★

On the Straits of Gibraltar at the southernmost tip of mainland Europe—where the Mediterranean and the Atlantic meet—Tarifa was one of the earliest Moorish settlements in Spain. Strong winds kept Tarifa off the tourist maps for years, but they have ultimately proven a source of wealth; the vast wind farm on the surrounding hills creates electricity, and the wide, white-sand beaches stretching north of the town have become Europe's biggest wind- and kite-surfing center. As a result, the town has continued to grow and prosper. Downtown cafés, which a couple of years ago were filled with men in flat caps playing dominoes and drinking *anís,* now serve croissants with their *café con leche* and make fancier tapas for a more cosmopolitan crowd.

Tarifa's 10th-century **castle** is famous for its siege of 1292, when the defender Guzmán el Bueno refused to surrender even though the attacking Moors threatened to kill his captive son. In defiance, he flung his own dagger down to them, shouting, "Here, use this"—or something to that effect. (And they did indeed kill his son afterward.) The Spanish military turned the castle over to the town in the mid-1990s, and it now has a **museum** on Guzmán and the sacrifice of his son. *€1.50 Tues.–Sun. 10–2 and 4–6.*

Ten kilometers (6 mi) north of Tarifa on the Atlantic coast are the Roman ruins of **Baelo Claudia.** This settlement was a thriving production center of *garum,* a salty fish paste appreciated in Rome. *956/688530 Free July–mid-Sept., Tues.–Sat. 10–6, Sun. 10–2; mid-Sept.–June, Tues.–Sat. 10–5, Sun. 10–2.*

WHERE TO STAY & EAT

$$ **100% Fun.** This funky hotel across from Tarifa's sandy strip is popular with the wind- and kite-surfing crowd. There's an exotic Amazonian theme here, with thatched roofs, bubbling fountains, and thick, exuberant greenery. In bungalows surrounding the pool, rooms are washed in shades of ocher, nicely complimented by crisp white bedding and terracotta tiles. The restaurant ($) serves Tex Mex dishes, including sizzling prawn fajitas, chilli con carne, and several vegetarian options. The predominantly young, fun-loving crowd makes peace and quiet hard to find. *Ctra. Cádiz-Málaga, Km 76, 11380 956/680330 www.tarifa.net/100fun 22 rooms In-room: no a/c In-hotel: restaurant, bar, pool MC, V EP.*

$$ **Convento de San Francisco.** Rooms are comfortable and basic, but the main draw here is the setting: a restored 17th-century convent in the spectacular village of Vejer, just west of Tarifa, overlooking the coast. Breakfast is served in the former refectory. *La Plazuela, 11150 956/451001 956/451004 www.tugasa.com 25 rooms In-hotel: restaurant MC, V EP.*

THE COSTA DEL SOL ESSENTIALS

To research prices, get advice from other travelers, and book travel arrangements, visit www.fodors.com.

TRANSPORTATION

For more on travel to and in Costa del Sol, see the Costa del Sol Planner at the beginning of this chapter.

BY AIR

Airports Aeropuerto de Almería (*☎950/213700*). **Aeropuerto de Málaga (AGP)** (*Pablo Picasso Airport ✉Av. García Morato s/n ☎952/048804 🌐www.ccoo-agp.com*). **Gibraltar Airport (GIB)** (*✉Winston Churchill Ave. ☎9567/73026*).

Carriers Air Plus Comet (*☎212/983–1277 🌐www.airpluscomet.com*). **British Airways** (*☎800/247–9297 🌐www.ba.com*). **easyJet** (*🌐www.easyjet.com*). **Iberia** (*☎952/136166 at airport, 902/400500 inquiries 🌐www.iberia.com*). **Monarch** (*☎800/099260 🌐www.flymonarch.com*).

BY BIKE

The Costa del Sol is famous for its sun and sand, but many people supplement their beach time with mountain-bike forays into the hilly interior, particularly around Ojén, near Marbella, and also along the mountain roads around Ronda. A popular route, which affords sweeping vistas, is via the mountain road from Ojén west to Istán. The Costa del Sol's temperate climate is ideal for biking, though it's best not to exert yourself on the trails in July and August, when temperatures soar. There are numerous bike-rental shops around the Costa del Sol, particularly in Marbella, Ronda, and Ojén; many shops can also arrange bike excursions. The cost to rent a mountain bike for the day ranges between €15 and €20. Guided bike excursions, which include the bikes and support staff and cars, generally start at about €62 a day.

Bike Rentals Monte Aventura (*✉Pl. de Andalucía 1, Ojén ☎952/881519*). **Sierra Cycling** (*✉Urbanization Pueblo Castillo No. 7, Fuengirola ☎952/471720 🌐www.sierracycling.com*). **Spanish Cycling Federation** (*✉Ferraz 16, 28008 Madrid ☎91/542–0421*).

BY BOAT & FERRY

ARRIVING & DEPARTING There are no direct ferries to Andalusia; the only possible option is to go to the northern Spanish coast from the United Kingdom (on P&O Ferries) via the Portsmouth-to-Bilboa route or the Plymouth-to-Santander route and then catch a train south.

GETTING AROUND If you opt for the P&O ferry from the United Kingdom to northern Spain, you can take the RENFE train from Bilboa to Málaga (journey time 14 hours, one daily). Alternatively, it is quicker to catch a train to Madrid (journey time 7 hours, 30 minutes, three daily) and catch a further train south to Málaga (journey time 4 hours).

Information P&O Ferries (*☎944/234477 🌐www.poferries.com*). **RENFE Trains** (*☎942/360611 or 902/240202 🌐www.renfe.es*).

12

BY BUS

During holidays it is wise to reserve your bus seat in advance for long-distance bus travel. On the Costa del Sol, the bus service connects Málaga with Cádiz (4 daily), with Córdoba (5 daily), with Granada (18 daily), and with Seville (12 daily). In Fuengirola you can catch buses for Mijas, Marbella, Estepona, and Algeciras. The Portillo bus company serves most of the Costa del Sol. Alsina Gräells serves Granada, Córdoba, Seville, and Nerja. Los Amarillos serves Cádiz, Jerez, Ronda, and Seville. Málaga's tourist office has details on other bus lines.

Bus Lines Alsina Gräells (☎ *952/318295*). **Los Amarillos** (✉ *Málaga bus station* ☎ *902/210317*). **Portillo** (✉ *Málaga bus station* ☎ *952/360191*).

Bus Stations Algeciras (✉ *Av. Virgen del Carmen 15* ☎ *956/51055*). **Estepona** (✉ *Av. de España* ☎ *952/800249*). **Fuengirola** (✉ *Av. Alfonso X111* ☎ *952/475066*). **Málaga** (✉ *Paseo de los Tilos* ☎ *952/350061*). **Marbella** (✉ *Av. Trapiche* ☎ *952/764400*). **Torremolinos** (✉ *Calle Hoyo* ☎ *952/382419*).

BY CAR

Málaga is 580 km (360 mi) from Madrid, taking the N–IV to Córdoba, then N331 to Antequera and the N321; 182 km (114 mi) from Córdoba via Antequera; 214 km (134 mi) from Seville; and 129 km (81 mi) from Granada by the shortest route of N342 to Loja, then N321 to Málaga.

There are some beautiful scenic drives here about which the respective tourist offices can advise you. The A369 heading southwest from Ronda to Guacín passes through stunning whitewashed villages. Another camera-clicking route is the N334 from Churriana to Coín, via Alhaurín de la Torre and Alhaurín el Grande. From here, continue on to Coín, then take the N337 toward Marbella, which travels via the villages of Monda and Ojen, finally ending at the coast just north of Marbella.

On major roads and motorways the speed limit is 120 kph (75 mph); in urban areas it is 50 kph (31 mph), and on other roads it is either 90 kph (55 mph) or 100 kph (63 mph).

Parking in the smaller villages can be fraught with danger (such as getting your vehicle sideswiped on winding, narrow streets), so it is advisable to park on the edge of the center and walk. In larger towns head for the nearest parking garage. The major resorts have improved their parking, and you should have no problem. You can expect to pay around €1.20 an hour. Blue lines on the street mean you must pay at the nearest meter to park during working hours, around €0.50 an hour. Yellow lines mean no parking. If your car is towed, you will be fined approximately €65 to claim it.

To take a car into Gibraltar you need, in theory, an insurance certificate and a logbook (a certificate of vehicle ownership). In practice, all you need is your passport. Prepare for parking problems on the Rock, as space is scarce.

Local car-rental agencies can be less expensive than the large chains (*See Essentials at the back of the book for contact information for international chains*).

Car-Rental Agencies Autopro (✉ *Carril de Montañez 49, Málaga* ☎ *952/176030* 🌐 *www.autopro.es*). **Crown Car Hire** (✉ *At Málaga Airport* ☎ *952/176486* 🌐 *www.crowncarhire.com*). **Niza Cars** (✉ *At Málaga Airport* ☎ *952/236179* 🌐 *www.nizacars.com*).

BY TAXI

Taxis are plentiful throughout the Costa del Sol and may be hailed on the street or from specified taxi ranks marked TAXI. Restaurants are usually obliging and will call you a taxi, if requested. Fares are reasonable and meters are strictly used. There are extra charges for luggage. You are not required to tip taxi drivers, although rounding off the amount will be appreciated.

Taxi Companies Morales Rodriguez–Málaga (☎ *952/430077*). **Radio Taxi Torremolinos** (☎ *952/380600*) .**Radio Taxi Fuengirola** (☎ *952/471000*).

BY TRAIN

Most Madrid–Málaga trains leave Madrid from Atocha station (⇨Chapter 2), though some leave from Chamartín. Travel time varies between 4½ and 10 hours; the best and fastest train is the daytime *Talgo 200* from Atocha. All Madrid–Málaga trains stop at Córdoba. A new AVE high-speed service is under construction that will connect Málaga to Madrid in around 2½ hours. The current date for completion is set for late 2007. From both Seville (4 hours, five daily) and Granada (3–3½ hours, three daily) to Málaga, you have to change at Bobadilla, making buses a more efficient mode of travel from those cities. In fact, aside from the direct Madrid–Córdoba–Málaga line, trains in Andalusia can be slow because of the hilly terrain. Málaga's train station is a 15-minute walk from the city center, across the river. Check the RENFE Web site for schedules and fares. You can book tickets online for most services.

RENFE connects Málaga, Torremolinos, and Fuengirola, stopping at the airport and all resorts along the way. The train leaves Málaga every half hour between 6 AM and 10:30 PM and Fuengirola every half hour from 6:35 AM to 11:35 PM. For the city center get off at the last stop—Centro-Alameda—not the previous stop, which will land you at Málaga's RENFE station. A daily train connects Málaga and Ronda via the dramatic Chorro gorge, with a change at Bobadilla. Travel time is about three hours. Three trains a day make the direct two-hour trip between Ronda and Algeciras on a spectacular mountain track. All routes are operated by RENFE.

Information AVE (☎ *902/240202* 🌐 *www.renfe.es*).**Málaga train station** (✉ *Explanada de la Estación* ☎ *952/360202*). **RENFE** (☎ *902/240202* 🌐 *www.renfe.es*).

CONTACTS & RESOURCES

EMERGENCIES

In an emergency, call one of the Spain-wide emergency numbers for police, ambulance, or fire services. The local Red Cross (Cruz Roja) can also dispatch an ambulance in case of an emergency. Also, there are numerous private ambulance services, which are listed under *ambulancias* (ambulances) in the *Paginas Amarillas* (Yellow Pages). The Hospital Carlos Haya in Málaga has a 24-hour emergency department. For nonemergencies, there are private medical clinics throughout the Costa del Sol, which often have staff members who can speak some English. Every town has at least one pharmacy open 24 hours; the address of the on-duty pharmacy is posted on the front door of all pharmacies. You can also dial Spain's general information number for the location of a doctor's office or pharmacy that's open nearest you.

Emergency Services Directory Enquiries (☎ *11818*). **Emergencies** (☎ *112*). **Fire department** (☎ *080*). **Hospital Carlos Haya** (☎ *952/390400*). **Local police** (☎ *092*). **Medical service** (☎ *061*). **National police** (☎ *091*). **Red Cross** (☎ *952/443545*).

INTERNET, MAIL & SHIPPING

For shipping, most of the international couriers have representatives on the Costa del Sol, including MRW and Mail Boxes Etc.

Internet Cafés Cristanet (✉ *Cristamar Commercial Centre, Puerto Bánus, Marbella* ☎ *952/799591*). **Microfun** (✉ *Av. de Los Boliches, Fuengirola* ☎ *952/661424*). **Navegaweb** (✉ *Calle Molina Lario 11, Málaga* ☎ *952/352300*).

Courier Services Mail Boxes Etc. (✉ *C. Medellin 1, Málaga 29006* ☎ *952/311482*). **MRW** (✉ *C. Paris 45, Málaga 29006* ☎ *952/171760*).

TOUR OPTIONS

Many one- and two-day excursions from Costa del Sol resorts are run by the national company Pullmantur and by smaller firms. All local travel agents and most hotels can book you a tour; excursions leave from Málaga, Torremolinos, Fuengirola, Marbella, and Estepona, with prices varying by departure point. Most tours last half a day, and in most cases you can be picked up at your hotel. Popular tours include Málaga, Gibraltar, the Cuevas de Nerja, Mijas, Marbella, and Puerto Banús; a burro safari in Coín; and a countryside tour of Alhaurín de la Torre, Alhaurín el Grande, Coín, Ojén, and Ronda. Night tours include a barbecue evening, a bullfighting evening with dinner, and a night at the Casino Torrequebrada. The varied landscape here is also wonderful for hiking and walking, and several companies offer walking tours. All provide comprehensive information on their Web sites.

If you plan to visit Málaga independently, but are on a tight schedule, the colorful, open-topped Málaga Tour City Sightseeing Bus is a good way to view the city's attractions within a day. The bus stops at all the major sights in town, including the Gibralfaro and the cathedral.

Tour Operators Málaga Tour City Sightseeing Bus (✉ *Málaga* ☎ *952/363133* 🌐 *www.citysightseeing-spain.com*). **Pullmantur** (✉ *Av. Imperial, Torremolinos* ☎ *952/384400* 🌐 *www.pullmantur-spain.com*). **Walking Holidays** (☎ *0207/494--2699* from U.K. 🌐 *www.walksinspain.com*).

VISITOR INFORMATION

The official Web site of the Andalucian government is www.andalucia.org; it has further information on sightseeing and events as well as contact details for the following regional and local tourist offices. Tourist offices are generally open 10–2 and 5–8 Monday–Saturday.

Regional Tourist Office Málaga (✉ *Pasaje de Chinitas 4* ☎ *952/213445*).

Local Tourist Offices Almuñecar (✉ *Palacete de La Najarra, Av. Europa* ☎ *958/631125*). **Antequera** (✉ *Palacio de Najera, Coso Viejo* ☎ *952/702505*). **Benalmádena Costa** (✉ *Av. Antonio Machado 14* ☎ *952/442494*). **Estepona** (✉ *Av. San Lorenzo 1* ☎ *952/802002*). **Fuengirola** (✉ *Av. Jesús Santos Rein 6* ☎ *952/467625*). **Gibraltar** (✉ *6 Duke of Kent House, Cathedral Sq.* ☎ *9567/45000*). **Málaga** (✉ *Av. Cervantes 1, Paseo del Parque* ☎ *952/604410*). **Marbella** (✉ *Glorieta de la Fontanilla* ☎ *952/822818* 🌐 *www.pgb.es/marbella*). **Nerja** (✉ *Puerta del Mar 2* ☎ *952/521531*). **Ronda** (✉ *Pl. de España 1* ☎ *952/871272*). **Ronda** (✉ *Paseo de Bas Infante s/n* ☎ *952/187119*). **Torremolinos** (✉ *Pl. Blas Infante 1* ☎ *952/379512*).

Extremadura

13

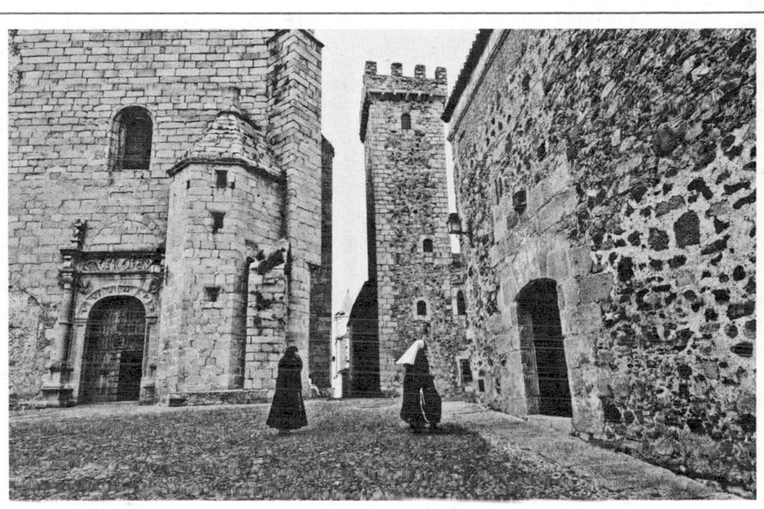

Square and Church of San Mateo and Torre de las Cigüeñas, Caceres

WORD OF MOUTH

"Mérida is known for the Roman ruins that are still within the city. I was expecting these to be somewhere outside the city, but no. You turn a corner, and BAM! There is the Templo Diana mixed in with the shops!"

—Chele60

www.fodors.com/forums

WELCOME TO EXTREMADURA

TOP REASONS TO GO

★ **Stuck-in-a-time-warp Cáceres:** The walled old city is wonderfully evocative, particularly at dusk when the skyline takes on an otherworldly air with its ancient spires, towers, and cupolas.

★ **In the pink:** Impress the folks back home with photographs of the beautiful cherry blossoms in the spectacular Jerte Valley.

★ **A medieval blockbuster:** Enjoy a coffee or *cerveza* in Trujillo's plaza while ogling the ancient buildings, with not a modern block in sight.

★ **Heady views:** Splurge on a night at the parador in Guadalupe; the views will have you waxing lyrical for weeks.

1 Three Valleys. In the far northeast of the province are three beautiful valleys: Valle de Jerte, La Vera, and the Valle del Ambroz. They stretch down to the grand old city of Plasencia and its environs. The region is superb for hiking.

2 Monumental Cities. Cáceres and Trujillo are the two cities that most tourists visit in Extremadura, and for good reason: they are headily historic and have plenty of appeal. They are in the center of the province and roads are good, so traveling between the two is easy either via your own wheels or an efficient bus system.

3 Natural Spaces. The vast natural park of Monfragüe covers some 178.5 square km (111 square mi) stretching across to Trujillo with Cáceres to the west. This area is renowned for its flora and fauna, such as Eurasian vultures, black stork carob, and the wild olive tree.

4 Southern Appeal. Mérida has Spain's most extensive Roman ruins, Olivenza has a Portuguese heritage, Badajoz is a capital city; and right at the southern tip, Zafra is a whitewashed delight of a town.

A Roman amphitheatre in Mérida.

Trujillo: Cradle of the Conquistadors.

GETTING ORIENTED

Extremadura covers an area of 41,602 square km (25,793 square mi) and consists of two provinces: Cáceres to the north and Badajoz to the south, divided by the Toledo Mountains. To the west, this region borders Portugal; to the south, Andalusia; and to the east, Castilla–La Mancha. The north is typified by stunning mountain scenery with green valleys and unspoiled villages and towns, while southern Extremadura contains verdant rich farmland between Badajoz and Mérida. South of here to Zafra, the area is mainly flat and a harsh landscape until you reach the lush Sierra Morena mountain range on the border of Andalusia.

Inhabitants of Las Hurdes in Cáceres dress for Carnaval.

EXTREMADURA PLANNER

When to Go

Summer in Extremadura can get brutally hot, particularly in the south. If you have to visit at this time of year, then head for the cooler mountains and natural parks in the north. **Spring is an ideal season,** especially for the countryside when the valleys and hills are covered with a dazzle of wild flowers. If you can time it right, the stunning spectacle of cherry-blossom season in the Jerte Valley and the Vera takes place around mid-March. Bird-watchers should try and time their visit in late February, after the migrating storks have arrived to nest and before the European cranes have returned to northern Europe. Fall is also a good time for Extremadura, when the weather cools down considerably and the summer crowds have left. You may have rain starting in late October.

Getting There & Around

If you're traveling to and around Extremadura via public transportation, buses are the way to go. There are trains to and within Extremadura; however, train stations tend to be some distance from town centers. Bus links between Extremadura and the other Spanish provinces are far more plentiful and reliable, as well as being the least expensive way of getting around the province. Buses, some of them express, frequently serve Extremadura's main cities from Madrid, Seville, Lisbon, Valladolid, Salamanca, and Barcelona. The first bus of the day on lesser routes tends to set off very early in the morning, so plan carefully to avoid getting stranded. Some examples of destinations from Madrid are: Badajoz (7 daily); Cáceras (8 daily), Guadalupe (2 daily); Trujillo (10 daily); and Mérida (8 daily). Bus routes within the vicinity are similarly well serviced; the following routes run frequently from Badajoz: Cáeres (7 daily); Caia, on the Portuguese border (4 daily); Mérida (8 daily); Olienza (12 daily); and Zafra (8 daily). In addition, buses serve virtually every village in Extremadura and you can generally pick up a detailed schedule from local tourist offices.

If you opt for a rental car, all the larger towns and cities have rental car agencies, including Badajoz, Cáceres, Mérida, Trujillo, and Plasencia. Note that it is invariably more economical to rent a car via a car-rental Web site than to book in person (*see* Spain Essentials in the back of the book for car rental contact information).

Traffic moves quickly on the four-lane A5, the main highway from Madrid to Extremadura. The A66, or Vía de la Plata, which crosses Extremadura from north to south, is also effective. The fastest route to Portugal is on the A6, which runs from Badajoz to Lisbon.

Taxis are available at train and bus stations, outside most tourist sights, and in city and town centers. They are particularly efficient and reasonable for short trips, while longer journeys will clock up the price.

There are no airports in Extremadura. The nearest international airports are in Madrid and Seville.

See Extremadura Essentials at the end of this chapter for train and bus line/station contact information.

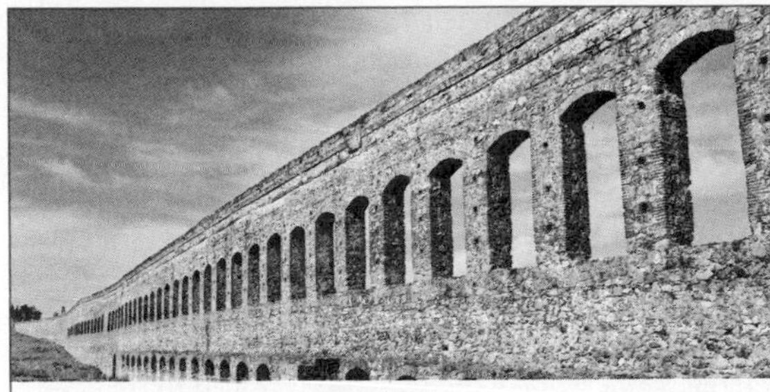

Extremadura By Bike

A great way to really get under the skin of this varied and dramatic province is by bike. You can cut down on the map reading by following the Ruta Vía de la Plata. It runs through Extremadura from north to south along A66, dividing it in two, and passes by such villages as Plasencia, Cáceres, Mérida, and Zafra. This route more or less follows the ancient Roman walkway Via de la Plata. Parts of the road are still preserved and rideable. Note that the region north of the province of Cáceres, including the Jerte Valley, the Vera, and the area surrounding Guadalupe, is mountainous and uneven. If you attempt it, be prepared for a bumpy and exhausting ride. The regional government has opened a Vía Verde, which goes from Logrosán (a couple of miles southwest of Guadalupe) to Villanueva de la Serena (east of Mérida and near Don Benito). This path is a roughly cleared walkway, more like a nature walkway, and not for vehicles.

Other options for bicyclists are the paved areas of the national parks of Monfragüe (near Cáceres). If you want to cycle with others, try one of the numerous tour companies that arrange cycling tours. Ask the local tourist offices about tours and where to rent bikes. Rural lodgings also sometimes provide bikes for their guests.

WHAT IT COSTS In Euros

	$$$$	$$$	$$	$	¢
RESTAU-RANTS	over €20	€15–€20	€10–€15	€6–€10	under €6
HOTELS	over €180	€100–€180	€60–€100	€40–€60	under €40

Prices are per person for a main course at dinner. Prices are for two people in a standard double room in high season, excluding tax.

Planning Your Time

You can get a lightning impression of Extremadura in a day's drive from Madrid. It's about 2½ hours from Madrid to **Jerte;** from there, you can take the A66 south to **Cáceres,** then head east to **Trujillo** on the N521. Split your time evenly between Cáceres and Trujillo.

If you have a weekend to explore Extremadura, divide your time with a day at the **Parque Natural de Monfragüe,** an evening and morning in **Trujillo,** and lunch and afternoon sightseeing in **Cáceres.** If time allows, spend a third day exploring the Roman monuments in **Mérida**. Those with time for a longer stay should from here travel west on A5 to the provincial capital of **Badajoz** and also make a side trip to **Olivenza,** 25 km (15 mi) southwest of Badajoz. Spend at least one night at the sumptuous parador in Jarandilla de la Vera. While there, you can visit the nearby Monasterio de Yuste.

Euro-Economizing

Most museums and galleries are free on Monday. You also can save money by traveling in spring and autumn, when hotel prices are often slashed by up to a third. Another way to penny pinch is by choosing the *menu del día* instead of à la carte at restaurants or cafés. These set meals, typically composed of three courses plus a drink, cost in the €6–€10 range.

13

By Mary McLean

THE VERY NAME EXTREMADURA—"THE FAR end of the Duero"—suggests the wild, remote, and isolated character of this haunting region. With its poor soil and minimal industry, Extremadura has not experienced the kind of economic gains typical of other parts of Spain. However, tourism to the region *is* steadily increasing. Also, in recent decades a series of dams has brightened Extremadura's agricultural outlook. All the same, it's hard to believe that, in the distant past, it was one of Spain's most important and wealthy regions. No other place in Spain has as many Roman monuments as Mérida, the capital of the vast Roman province of Lusitania (the Iberian Peninsula). Mérida guarded the Vía de la Plata, the major Roman highway that crossed Extremadura from north to south, connecting Gijón with Seville. The economy and the arts declined after the Romans left, but the region revived in the 16th century, when explorers and conquerors of the New World—from Francisco Pizarro and Hernán Cortés to Nuñez de Balboa and Francisco de Orellana, first navigator of the Amazon—returned to their birthplace. These men built the magnificent palaces that now glorify towns such as Cáceres and Trujillo, and they turned the remote monastery of Guadalupe into one of the great artistic repositories of Spain.

EXPLORING EXTREMADURA

The rugged Extremadura is a boon for those who like the outdoors. The lush Jerte Valley and the craggy peaks of the Sierra de Gredos mark Upper Extremadura's fertile landscape. South of the Jerte Valley is the historical town of Plasencia and the 15th-century Yuste Monastery. In Extremadura's central interior is the provincial capital of Cáceres and the Monfrague Nature Park. Lower Extremadura's main towns—Mérida, Badajoz, Olivenza, and Zafra—have long exuded a Portuguese flavor, bolstered by the sizeable Portuguese population.

ABOUT THE RESTAURANTS

Extremaduran food reflects the austerity of the landscape: true peasant fare, with a strong character. In addition to fresh produce, Extremadurans rely on pigs, of which every part is used, including the *criadillas* (testicles—don't confuse them with *criadillas de la tierra,* which are "earth testicles," also known as truffles). The dressed meats are outstanding, most notably the sweetish cured hams from Montánchez; chorizo (spiced sausage); and *morcilla* (blood pudding), which is often made here with potatoes. The *caldereta de cordero* (lamb stew) is particularly tasty, as is the beef from the *retinto,* a local breed of longhorn cattle. Game is also common, and *perdiz al modo de Alcántara,* partridge cooked with truffles, is a specialty. Local lake tench and river trout are also worth trying. Extremadurans make a gazpacho based on cucumbers, green peppers, and broth rather than tomatoes and water. A common accompaniment is *migas,* bread crumbs soaked in water and fried in olive oil with garlic, peppers, and sausage.

Local cheeses generally have a crumbly texture and strong flavors. If you have a chance, savor *tortas,* the round, semisoft cheeses of Cáceres; those from Casar and La Serena are especially prized. Favorite *extremeño* desserts include the *técula mécula* (an almond-flavor marzipan tart), which combines the flavors of Spain and Portugal. Marketed under the generic appellation "Ribera del Guadiana," Extremadura's little-known, light and fruity red wines are good values; try Lar de Lares. Typical digestifs include liqueurs made from cherries or acorns.

ABOUT THE HOTELS

Extremadura's paradores are remarkable, occupying buildings of great historic or architectural interest in all major tourist areas. Reserve well in advance for a weekend stay. The Extremaduran government runs a few *hospederías,* a sort of regional version of the parador chain; some have historic quarters in scenic areas. Most other high-end hotels, with a few exceptions, are modern boxes with little character. Throughout Extremadura's countryside are a number of charming bed-and-breakfast inns (*hoteles rurales*) and 135 guesthouses (*casa rurales*). Despite their number, space in popular guesthouses is limited, so reservations are a must. Your best base for a series of day trips might be Cáceres.

Numbers in the text correspond to numbers in the margin and on chapter maps.

UPPER EXTREMADURA

JERTE & EL VALLE DEL JERTE (JERTE VALLEY)

1 *220 km (137 mi) west of Madrid. For a scenic route, follow N110 southwest from Ávila to Plasencia.*

There's no more striking introduction to Extremadura than the **Puerto de Tornavacas** *(Tornavacas Pass)* —literally, the "point where the cows turn back." Part of the N110 road northeast of Plasencia, the pass marks the border between Extremadura and the stark plateau of Castile. At 4,183 feet above sea level, it has a breathtaking view of the valley formed by the fast-flowing Jerte River. The valley's lower slopes are covered with a dense mantle of ash, chestnut, and cherry trees, whose richness contrasts with the granite cliffs of Castile's Sierra de Gredos. Cherries are the principal crop. To catch their brilliant blossoms, visit in the spring. Camping is popular in this region, and even the most experienced hikers can find some challenging trails.

Cabezuela del Valle, full of half-timber stone houses, is one of the valley's best preserved villages. Follow N110 to Plasencia or, if you have a taste for mountain scenery, detour from the village of Jerte to Hervás, traveling a narrow road that winds 35 km (22 mi) through forests of low-growing oak trees and over the Honduras Pass.

WHERE TO STAY & EAT

$ ✕🏨 **Valle del Jerte.** Service is always cheerful in this family-run inn just off the N110 in the village of Jerte. Specialties at the restaurant include gazpacho, *cabrito* (kid), and local trout. The homemade, regional desserts are outstanding, with many featuring the Jerte Valley's famed cherries; try the *tarta de cerezas* (cherry tart) or the *queso fresco de*

IF YOU LIKE

FIESTAS

Extremadura is not a land of running bulls, except for the fiestas de **San Juan** in Coria, Cáceres, on the week of June 24, or the **Capeas,** in Segura de León, Badajoz, around September 14, when locals show off their bullfighting skills. Instead, the province of Cáceres has its share of festivals commemorating past saints and sinners. February 3 is the day to toast **San Blas** (St. Blaise), believed to heal sore throats, with hot cakes bearing his name, and multiple feasts.

Semana Santa (Holy Week) is celebrated with rituals in cities throughout the region. In early May Trujillo's **Feria del Queso** (Cheese Festival) is popular with foodies. For Cáceres's September **Celebración del Cerdo y Vino** (Pig and Wine Celebration), the area's innumerable pork products are prepared in public demonstrations. On December 7, Jarandilla de la Vera fills the city with bonfires to celebrate **Los Escobazos,** when locals play-fight with torches made out of brooms.

In Badajoz the year opens the 16th and 17th of January with **La Encamisá,** in Navalvillar de Pela. Horsemen re-create a medieval battle of the town's citizens against Arab invaders. During the **Carnival** celebration in Badajoz, parades of thousands wear extravagant costumes. Also colorful are the **Holy Week** celebrations at Oliva de la Frontera. Badajoz says *adios* to winter with the fiestas of **La Primavera** (Spring Festival) and **Los Mayos** (May Days), usually at the end of April and beginning of May. A significant date in Badajoz is May 3, **El Día de la Santa Cruz** (the Exaltation of the Holy Cross), celebrated in the villages of Corte de Peleas and Feria, where a local family is selected a month in advance to prepare a processional floral cross in its home. Some of these crosses become magnificent works of art and patience, tended to the point of depleting hard-earned savings.

REMOTE VILLAGES

North of Plasencia is Las Hurdes, a rocky barren landscape where visitors were so rare that as recently as the 1950s the inhabitants would hide when any outsider arrived. This isolation has resulted in some charmingly primitive villages where you can hire a donkey as transport. Interesting stops are Nuñomaral, La Huetre, and the dramatically situated El Gasco. Continue your explorations with the Sierra de Gata on the western border; elderly villagers here speak *maniego,* a combination of Castilian, Spanish, and Portuguese. Villages with a special atmosphere include Robledillo and Santibáñez el Alto, a hilltop village where the buildings are made out of stone, seemingly sculptured out of the rock face.

WILDLIFE

You can keep busy with trails in the Gredos and Tormantos ranges; forests of oak, poplar, and cherry; massive gorges; and the winding waterways of the Jerte Valley, where the blossoming of the cherry trees in March attracts tourists from all over the country. In Monfragüe Nature Park and in the smaller and less touristy Cornalvo Nature Park, bird-watchers might spot eagles, falcons, and vultures. Thousands of European cranes spend the winter in eastern Badajoz.

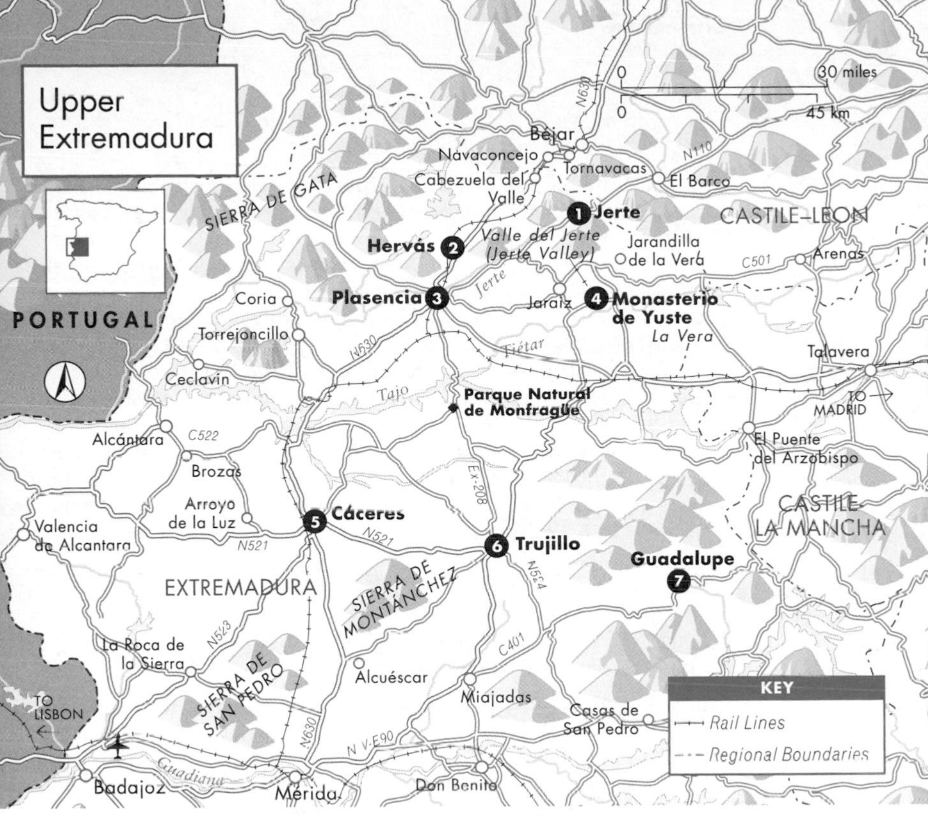

cabra con miel cerezo (goat cheese topped with cherry-flavored honey). Ask to see the wonderful old wine cellar. The charming La Sotorriza *casa rural* upstairs has five comfortable guest rooms with chestnut furniture, cotton bedspreads, and beam ceilings. ✉ *Gargantilla 16, Jerte, 10612* ☎ *927/470052* 📠 *927/470448* 🌐 *www.donbellota.com* 🛏 *5 rooms* 👍 *In-hotel: restaurant, no elevator* 💳 *MC, V* 🍽 *BP.*

$$ 🏨 **La Casería.** This rambling home is on a 120-acre working farm, once part of a 16th-century Franciscan convent. One of the first rural guesthouses established in Extremadura, it's run by a couple who also raise sheep. This place is strictly for animal lovers, as the household includes lots of dogs and cats. Aside from the six rooms in the main lodge, there are three cottages, each of which can sleep two to four. Activities such as horseback riding, mountain biking, and paragliding can be arranged. It's wise to reserve in advance, and to keep your eyes peeled as you approach: the sign is easy to miss. ✉ *N110, Km 378.6, Navaconcejo, 10613* ☎ *927/173141* 📠 *927/177384* 🌐 *www.lacaseria.net* 🛏 *6 rooms, 3 cottages* 👍 *In-room: no a/c, no TV. In-hotel: pool, no elevator* 💳 *MC, V.*

HERVÁS

2 *42 km (26 mi) northeast of Plasencia, 115 km (72 mi) northeast of Cáceres, 20 km (13 mi) northwest of Jerte.*

Surrounded by pine and chestnut groves, this charming, hilly village makes an interesting detour from either the Jerte Valley or Plasencia. Hervás, it's believed, grew into a predominantly Jewish settlement during the Middle Ages, populated by Jews escaping Christian and Muslim persecution in Spain's larger cities. In 1492, when the Jews were expelled from the country altogether during the Inquisition, their neighborhood was left intact but their possessions were ceded to the local nobility. Stripped of its wealth, the village lost its commercial reputation and was forgotten. Now fully restored, the **Judería** (Jewish Quarter) is among the best-preserved in Spain. It contains the 17th-century **Convento de los Trinitarios** (☎*927/474828*), part of which has been turned into a tastefully furnished *hospedería.*At the top of the quarter there's a 16th- to 17th-century Renaissance church called the **Santa Maria de Aguas Vivas.**

PLASENCIA

 *255 km (160 mi) west of Madrid, 79 km (49 mi) north of Cáceres, 42 km (26 mi) southwest of Hervás.*

Rising dramatically from the banks of the narrow Jerte River and backed by the peaks of the Sierra de Gredos, this community was founded by Alfonso VIII in 1180, just after he captured the entire area from the Moors. The town's motto, *placeat Deo et hominibus* ("It pleases both God and men"), might well have been a ploy on Alfonso's part to attract settlers to this wild, isolated place on the southern border of the former kingdom of León. Badly damaged during the Peninsular War of 1808, Plasencia retains far less of its medieval quarter than other Extremaduran towns, but it still has extensive remains of its early walls and a smattering of fine old buildings. In addition to being a site for visiting ruins, the city makes a good base for side trips to Hervás and the Jerte Valley, the Monasterio de Yuste and Monfragüe Nature Park, or, farther northwest, the wild Las Hurdes and Sierra de Gata.

Plasencia's **cathedral** was founded in 1189 and rebuilt after 1320 in an austere Gothic style that looks a bit incongruous looming over the town's red-tile roofs. In 1498 the great architect Enrique Egas designed a new structure, intending to complement or even overshadow the original, but despite the later efforts of other notable architects of the time, such as Juan de Alava and Francisco de Colonia, his plans were never fully realized. The entrance to this incomplete, curious, and not wholly satisfactory complex is through a door on the cathedral's ornate but somber north facade. The dark interior of the new cathedral is notable for the beauty of its pilasters, which sprout like trees into the ribs of the vaulting. You enter the old cathedral through the Gothic cloister, which has four enormous lemon trees. Off the cloister stands the building's oldest surviving section, a 13th-century chapter house (now the chapel of **San Pablo**)—a late-Romanesque structure with an idiosyncratic, Moorish-inspired dome. Inside are medieval hymnals and a 13th-century gilded wood sculpture of the Virgen del Perdón. The **museum** in the truncated nave of the old cathedral has ecclesiastical and archaeological objects. ☎*927/414852* *Old cathedral €3* *Oct.–Apr., Mon.–Sat. 9–12:30 and 4–5:30, Sun. 9–1; May–Sept., Mon.–Sat. 9–12:30 and 5–6:30, Sun. 9–1.*

The cloister of the elegant **Palacio Episcopal** (*Bishop's Palace* ✉*Pl. de la Catedral*) is open weekdays from 9 to 2.

Lined with orange trees, the narrow, carefully preserved **Plaza de San Vicente** is at the northwest end of the old medieval quarter. At one end is the 15th-century church of **San Vicente Ferrer,** with an adjoining convent that's now a parador. The north side of the square is dominated by the Renaissance **Palacio de Mirabel** (*Palace of the Marquis of Mirabel* ☎*927/410701*)—go through the central arch for a back view. The hours can be sporadic, but it's usually open daily 10 to 2 and 4 to 6; tip the caretaker.

East of the Plaza de San Vicente, at the other end of the Rúa Zapatería, is the cheerful, arcaded square **Plaza Mayor.** The mechanical figure clinging to the town-hall clock tower depicts the clock maker and is called the **Mayorga** in honor of his Castilian hometown.Also east of the Plaza de San Viccnte you can find a large section of the town's **medieval wall** on the other side of which is a heavily restored Roman aqueduct.Walk southeast from the Plaza de San Vicente to the **Parque de los Pinos,** home to wildlife that includes peacocks, cranes, swans, pheasants, and monkeys.

WHERE TO STAY & EAT

$$$ **Hotel Alfonso VIII.** Grand but slightly past its prime, with bland modern rooms and a predominance of beige, this curious Franco-era relic is still strangely agreeable. There is disabled access and some rooms have private terraces. The Alfonso's restaurant ($$–$$$) has long been regionally renowned for its food; the *ensalada de perdiz* (salad with partridge) makes for a tasty starter. ✉*Alfonso VIII 32, 10600* ☎*927/410250* *927/418042* *www.hotelalfonsoviii.com* *55 rooms, 2 suites* *In-room: dial-up. In-hotel: restaurant, public Wi-Fi, parking (fee)* *AE, DC, MC, V.*

$ **Rincón Extremeño.** Just off the Plaza Mayor in the heart of the old quarter, this property is basic and well maintained. The ground floor has a popular bar and restaurant, the latter serving regional dishes like *caracoles de tierra* (snails in a spicy sauce). You'll have pleasanter views, though more noise, in a guest room facing the street. ✉*Vidrieras 6, 10600* ☎*927/411150* *927/420627* *www.hotelrincon.com* *13 rooms, 7 with bath* *In-hotel: restaurant, bar* *MC, V.*

$$$ **Parador de Plasencia.** In a 15th-century Gothic convent, this parador cultivates a medieval environment. The common areas are majestic and somber, and the guest rooms are decorated with monastic motifs and heavy wood furniture. Rooms are spacious and comfortable with stylishly modern bathrooms; most have sitting rooms. The high-ceil-

ing, stone-and-wood-beam restaurant—called the Refectory—is almost intimidating in its architectural magnificence. Parking adds a hefty €12 nightly. ✉ *Pl. de San Vicente Ferrer, 10600* ☎ *927/425870* 📠 *927/425872* 🌐 *www.parador.es* 66 *rooms* *In-room: dial-up, Wi-Fi. In-hotel: restaurant, bar, pool, parking (fee)* 💳 *AE, D, MC, V.*

SHOPPING

If you happen to be in Plasencia on a Tuesday morning, head for the Plaza Mayor and do what the locals have been doing since the 12th century: scouting bargains in the weekly market. On the first Tuesday of August the market is much larger, with vendors from all over the region. For local art and crafts, try **Bámbara de Artesanía** (✉ *Sancho Polo 12* ☎ *927/411766*). Near the parador is **Artesanías Canillas** (✉ *C. San Vicente Ferrer s/n* ☎ *927/411668*), which has regional costumes, pottery, and handmade straw hats. At **Casa del Jamón** (✉ *C. Sol 18, east of Pl. Mayor* ☎ *927/419328* ✉ *C. Zapatería 17, between Pl. Mayor and parador* ☎ *927/419328*), stock up on sausages, *jamón ibérico* (Iberian ham), cheeses, Extremeño wines, and cherry liqueur.

LA VERA & MONASTERIO DE YUSTE

❹ *45 km (28 mi) from Plasencia. Turn left off C501 at Cuacos and follow signs for the monastery (1 km [½ mi]).*

In the heart of **La Vera,** a place of steep ravines (*gargantas*), rushing rivers, and villages, lies **Monasterio de Yuste** *(Yuste Monastery)*. It was founded by Hieronymite monks in the early 15th century. Badly damaged in the Peninsular War, it was left to decay after the suppression of Spain's monasteries in 1835, but it has since been restored and taken over once more by the Hieronymites. Carlos V (1500–58), founder of Spain's vast 16th-century empire, spent his last two years in the Royal Chambers, enabling the emperor to attend Mass within a short stumble of his bed. The required guided tour also covers the church, the crypt where Carlos V was buried before being moved to El Escorial (near Madrid), and a glimpse of the monastery's cloisters. ☎ *927/172130* 🌐 *www.yuste.org/monasterio* *€2.50* ⏲ *Mon.–Sat. 9:30–12:30 and 3–6, Sun. 9:30–11:15 and 3–6.*

EN ROUTE

Following the road that climbs from the monastery into the mountains for 6 km (4 mi), you come to the delightful village of Garganta La Olla. As you approach it, the road winds through cherry orchards and eventually dips into the village's narrow, twisting streets.

WHERE TO STAY & EAT

$$$ ✕🏨 **Parador de Jarandilla de la Vera.** Nestled in the town of Jarandilla, this parador (sometimes called Parador Carlos V) was built in the early 16th century as a fortified palace. Carlos V stayed here for three months while he waited for his quarters at Yuste to be completed. The halls have stylish medieval furnishings, and the regal dining room is the perfect place to indulge royal fantasies. In the restaurant ($$–$$$), start with a humble classic, *huevos fritos con migas* (fried eggs with bread crumbs); then savor one of the house specialties: *caldereta de cordero*

(lamb stew). ✉Av. García Prieto 1, 59 km (36 mi) east of Plasencia, 17 km (11 mi) west of Monasterio de Yuste, 10450 ☎927/560117 📠927/560088 🌐www.parador.es 53 rooms In-room: dial-up. In-hotel: restaurant, bar, tennis court, pool, public Wi-Fi ▭AE, DC, MC, V.

> **WORD OF MOUTH**
>
> "If you have ever dreamed of spending the night in a castle, look no further (than the Parador de Jarandilla de la Vera)."
>
> –ekscrunchy

$$ **Camino Real.** In a village in the highest valley of the Vera, this hotel is in a mansion. Rooms have exposed stone walls and wooden beam ceilings. There's a sitting room with fireplace, plus an outside hot tub. The rate includes a lavish buffet breakfast. The owners organize local excursions. *✉C. El Monje 27, Guijo de Santa Bárbara, 10459 ☎927/561119 📠927/561119 🌐www.casaruralcaminoreal.com 10 rooms In-hotel: restaurant, public Wi-Fi, no elevator ▭MC, V BP.*

$–$$ **Finca Valvellidos.** An exquisitely restored farmhouse, this *casa rural* offers a choice of double rooms or bungalows; the latter with kitchens and sitting rooms complete with fireplace. Rooms in the main house are spacious and rustic with terra-cotta tiles, exposed brick, and cotton rugs. Horse-riding lessons are available and there are bicycles to rent. *✉Torremenga 10413, Km 15, Jaraiz de la Vera, 10400 ☎927/194143 🌐www.valvellidos.com 5 rooms, 6 bungalows In-hotel: no elevator ▭MC, V BP.*

EN ROUTE

At the junction of the rivers Tiétar and Tajo, 20 km (12 mi) south of Plasencia on the EX208, is the Parque Natural de Monfragüe. This rocky-mountain wilderness is known for its plant and animal life, including lynx, boar, deer, fox, black storks, imperial eagles, and the world's largest colony of black vultures. Bring binoculars and find the lookout point called Salto del Gitano (Gypsy's Leap), on the C524 just south of the Tajo River—this is where the vultures can often be spotted wheeling in the dozens at close range. Nearby is the excellent Camping Monfragüe campground, with plenty of tenting sites, plus a pool and bike rental. The park's visitor center and main entrance is in the hamlet of Villareal de San Carlos. *☎927/199134 ⏲May–Sept., daily 9–2:30 and 4:30–7:30; Oct.–Apr., daily 9–2:30 and 4–6; audiovisual show every hr on ½ hr.*

CÁCERES

5 Fodor'sChoice ★ *307 km (190 mi) west of Madrid, 79 km (49 mi) south of Plasencia; 125 km (78 mi) southwest of Monasterio de Yuste; 90 km (55 mi) west of Monasterio de Guadalupe.*

Cáceres, the provincial capital, is a prosperous agricultural town whose vibrant nightlife draws villagers from the surrounding pueblos every weekend. It is one of Spain's oldest cities. The Roman colony called Norba Caesarina was founded in 35 BC, but when the Moors took over in the 8th century, they named the city Quazris, which eventually morphed into the Spanish Cáceres. It has been prosperous ever since noble families helped Alfonso IX expel the Moors in 1229, and the pristine condition of the city's medieval and Renaissance quarter is the result of the families' continued occupancy of the palaces first erected in the 15th century.

Cáceres Viejo (Old Cáceres), which begins just east of Plaza San Juan, is the best part of town to stay in and explore. On the long, inclined, arcaded **Plaza Mayor,** you can see several outdoor cafés, tourist offices, and, on breezy summer nights, nearly everyone in town. In the middle of the arcade opposite the old quarter is the entrance to the lively Calle General Ezponda, lined with tapas bars, student hangouts, and discos that keep the neighborhood awake and moving until dawn.

On high ground on the eastern side of the Plaza Mayor, a portal beckons through the town's intact wall, which in turn surrounds one of the best-preserved old quarters in Spain. Literally packed with treasures, Cáceres's **Ciudad Monumental** (old town; also called the *casco antiguo*) is a marvel: small, but without a single modern building to distract from its aura. Storks are common in this area of Cáceres, and virtually every tower and spire is topped by nests of storks. The old town is virtually deserted in winter.Once you pass through the gate leading to the old quarter, note the **Palacio de los Golfines de Arriba** (☒*C. Adarve de Santa Ana*), dominated by a soaring tower dating from 1515. The ground floor is a stylish restaurant. The **Casa de Sanchez de Paredes** (☒*C. Ancha*), a 16th-century palace that now serves as a parador.

On the Plaza San Mateo is the **San Mateo church** (☒*C. Ancha*). Built mainly in the 14th century, but with a 16th-century choir, it has an austere interior, the main decorative notes being the baroque high altar and some heraldic crests. The battlement tower of the **Palacio de Las Cigüeñas** (☒*Pl. San Mateo*) is also known as the Torre de las Cigüeñas (Tower of the Storks) for obvious reasons. It's now a military residence, but some rooms are occasionally opened up for exhibitions.

The **Casa de las Veletas** *(House of the Weather Vanes)* is a 12th-century Moorish mansion that is now the **Museo de Cáceres.** Filled with archaeological finds, it's an excellent way to acquaint yourself with the area's many inhabitants. One highlight is the eerie but superb Moorish cistern—the *aljibe*—with arches supported by moldy stone pillars. It's downhill from Plaza San Mateo. ☒*1 Pl. de las Veletas* ☎*927/010877* 🌐*www.museosextremadura.com/caceres* 🎟*€1.20, free Sun. and for EU citizens* ⏲*Oct.–Apr., Tues.–Sat. 9–2:30 and 4–7, Sun. 10–2:30; May–Sept., 9–2:30 and 5–8, Sun. 10–2:30.*

The stony severity of the **Palacio de los Golfines de Abajo** (☒*Cuesta de la Companía*) seems appropriate when you consider it was once the headquarters of General Franco. However, the exterior is somewhat relieved by elaborate Mudejar and Renaissance decorative motifs.

The Gothic church of **Santa María,** built mainly in the 16th century, is now the town cathedral. The elegantly carved high altar, dating from

1551, is barely visible in the gloom. A small museum displays religious objects. ✉ *Cuesta de la Compañía* ☎ *927/215313* *Cathedral free, museum €2* ⏲ *Mon.–Sat. 10–2 and 5–8, Sun. 9:30–2 and 5–7:30.*

> **STORKS DROPPING BY**
>
> Storks are common in Cáceres old quarter, and virtually every tower and spire is topped by nests of storks. The battlement tower Palacio del Capitán Diego is even known as the Palace of the Storks.

Near the cathedral of Santa María is the elegant **Palacio de Carvajal,** the only old palace you can tour besides the Casa de las Veletas. It has an imposing granite facade and an arched doorway, and the interior has been restored, with period furnishings and art, to look as it did when the Carvajal family lived here in the 16th century. ✉ *Pl. de Santa María* *Free* ⏲ *Weekdays 8* AM*–9* PM*, Sat. 9:30–2 and 5–8, Sun. 10–3.*

From Santa María cathedral, a 110 yard walk down Calle Tiendas takes you to Cáceres's northern wall. Don't miss the 16th-century **Palacio de los Moctezuma-Toledo** (now a public-records office), built by Juan Cano de Saavedra with the dowry provided by his wife, an Aztec princess who was the daughter of Montezuma (aka Moctezuma). ✉ *Pl. Conde de Canilleros 1* ☎ *927/249294* *Free* ⏲ *Weekdays 8:30–2:30.*

The chief building of interest outside the wall of the old town is the church of **Santiago de los Caballeros** (✉ *C. Villalobos*), rebuilt in the 16th century by Rodrigo Gil de Hontañón, Spain's last great Gothic architect. Reach the church by exiting the old town on its west side, through the Socorro gate.

Just up the hill behind Cáceres's Ciudad Monumental is the **Santuario de la Virgen de la Montaña** *(Sanctuary of the Virgin of the Mountain).* Inside is a golden baroque altar and a statue of the patroness virgin, which is paraded through town each May. On a clear day the view of old Cáceres from the front of the building is spectacular, well worth the 15-minute drive up the hill. ✉ *Follow C. Cervantes until it becomes Ctra. Miajadas; the sanctuary is just off the town tourist map, which you can pick up from the local tourist office.* ☎ *927/220049* *Donation accepted* ⏲ *Daily 8:30–2 and 4–8.*

WHERE TO STAY & EAT

$$$$ Fodor's Choice ★ ✕ **Atrio.** On a side street off the southern end of Cáceres's leafy main boulevard, this elegant restaurant is the best in Extremadura, and possibly better than any in Andalusia, too. It specializes in highly refined modern cooking. The menu changes often, but you won't be disappointed with any of the selections, especially if they're venison, partridge, wild mushrooms, or truffles. ✉ *Av. de España 30* ☎ *927/242928* ▭ *AE, DC, MC, V* ⏲ *Closed Sept. 1–15. No dinner Sun.*

$$$ ✕ **Chez Manou.** Enjoying a prime location in Cáceres's historic old town, this French restaurant features a traditional menu, and most of the classics are here. Start with a slice of quiche lorraine, followed by one of the duck specialties, such as *à l'orange,* and finish with the chocolate mousse *par excellence.* The dining area was formerly horse stables and the atmosphere is still suitably rustic, with beamed ceiling, antiques,

and an eclectic selection of old prints and photos adorning the walls. During the warmer months you can sit at tables outside. ✉*Plaza de las Veletas 4* ☎*927/227682* 💳*MC, V* ⏲*Closed Sun. dinner and Mon.*

$$$ ✕🏨 **Parador de Cáceres.** A 14th-century Renaissance palace provides a noble setting for this comfortable parador decorated in soft cream and ocher tones offset by exposed stone walls and wood beams. The rooms are cozy and comfortable, and the public spaces are ancient and elegant. The Torreorgaz restaurant ($$–$$$), with tables in the patio terrace in summer, prepares local game specialties, including *lomo de venado a la Torta del Casar* (venison with the creamy Torta del Casar sheep cheese) or *cabrito asado al romero* (young goat roasted with rosemary). From Friday to Sunday, you can sample wines in the parador's wine cellar, Enoteca Torreorgaz. ✉*Ancha 6, 10003* ☎*927/211759* 📠*927/211729* 🌐*www.parador.es* *32 rooms, 1 suite* *In-room: dial-up. In-hotel: restaurant, parking (fee)* 💳*AE, DC, MC, V.*

$$$ ★ 🏨 **Meliá Cáceres.** This 16th-century palace built by the Marqueses de Oquendo is just outside the walls of the old town on the Plaza San Juan. The boutique hotel gracefully blends exposed brick and designer touches with antique furniture. Rooms have ample bathrooms with ornate fittings. La Cava del Emperador, a street-level bar and restaurant with a vaulted brick ceiling, is a popular meeting place for the town's well heeled. ✉*Pl. San Juan 11–13, 10003* ☎*927/215800* 📠*927/214070* 🌐*www.solmelia.com* *84 rooms, 2 suites* *In-room: dial-up. In-hotel: restaurant, room service, bar, laundry service, parking (fee)* 💳*AE, DC, MC, V.*

$ ★ 🏨 **Hotel Iberia Plaza Mayor.** You don't have to shift your credit card into overdrive to stay in this 18th-century, antique-furnished palace. The tastefully refurbished guest rooms have breezy blue tiled bathrooms and attractive dark-wood furniture. The location on a pedestrian shopping street just off Plaza Mayor is excellent but likely to be noisy—pack your earplugs. ✉*C. Pintores 2, 10003* ☎*927/247634* 🌐*www.iberia-hotel.com* *37 rooms* *In-hotel: some pets allowed* 💳*V.*

NIGHTLIFE & THE ARTS

Bars in Cáceres are lively until the wee hours. Nightlife centers on the **Plaza Mayor,** which fills after dinner with families out for a *paseo* (stroll) as well as students swigging *calimocho,* a mix of red wine and Coca-Cola. In the adjacent old town, you can take in some live music at **El Corral de las Cigueñas** (✉*Cuesta de Aldana 6*), which from October to April is open only Thursday to Sunday evenings. For livelier nightlife, head to nearby **Calle de Pizarro.** This block, south of Plaza de San Juan, is lined with cafés and bars, including **Mistura Brasileira,** at number 8, a Brazilian bar where you can perfect your hip-swinging steps with a live band beginning at 10:30 PM on Friday. The annual **WOMAD** (World of Music, Arts and Dance, 🌐www.bme.es/womad) festival is held in Cáceres center every May, attracting some 75,000 spectators.

OFF THE BEATEN PATH

Garovillas and Monasterio del Palancar. Garovillas, 10 km (6 mi) off the main road between Cáceres and Plasencia (turn left [northwest] onto the C522, 25 km [15 mi] north of Cáceres), is a perfectly preserved, though partially deserted, village. Its must-see square from the late 15th century has an

impressive *hospedería*. East of Garovillas and near the Portuguese border, lies the Puente de Alcántara, a 2nd-century Roman bridge over the River Tajo that is one of Spain's prized architectural marvels. On the same road to Plasencia, past the Puerto de los Castañeos, is a detour to the Monasterio del Palancar (☎ *927/192023*). In this Franciscan convent, friar San Pedro de Alcantára spent most of his life in a cell so tiny he had to sleep sitting up. It's open Thursday through Tuesday 10 to 1 and 4:30 to 6:45.

TRUJILLO

★ *48 km (30 mi) east of Cáceres, 250 km (155 mi) southwest of Madrid.*

Trujillo rises up from the fertile fields around it like a great granite schooner under full sail. Up close, the rooftops and towers seem medieval; down below, Renaissance architecture flourishes in squares such as Plaza Mayor, with its elegant San Martín church. The storks' nests that top many of the towers in and around the center of the old town have become a symbol of Trujillo. The city dates back at least to Roman times. The city was captured from the Moors in 1232 and colonized by a number of leading military families.

DISCOUNTS & DEALS

Trujillo has two different types of multisight passes. The first, at €4.50, provides access to Casa Museo Pizarro, the castle, the church of Santiago, and a guidebook (also sold separately). The second, at €6.50, grants access to the above plus Museo del Traje, Aljibe del Altamirano, and a guided tour.

It is practical to see Trujillo only on foot, as the streets are mostly cobbled or crudely paved with stone. The two main roads into Trujillo leave you at the town's unattractive bottom. Things get progressively older the farther you climb, but even on the lower slopes—where most of the shops are concentrated—you need walk only a few yards to step into what seems like the Middle Ages.

Trujillo's large **Plaza Mayor,** one of the finest in Spain, is a superb Renaissance creation and the site of the local tourist office. At the foot of the stepped platform on the plaza's north side stands a large, bronze equestrian statue of conqueror Francisco Pizarro—the work, curiously, of a U.S. sculptor, Charles Rumsey. The church behind the Pizarro statue, **San Martín,** is a Gothic structure from the early 16th century, with Renaissance tombs and an old organ. Some of Spain's most prominent kings prayed there, including Carlos V, Felipe II, and Felipe V. If you visit at dusk, you may hear the men's choir rehearsing, adding an inspiring note to eventide. ✉ *Pl. Mayor* 🎫 *€1.30* 🕐 *Mon.–Sat. 9:30–2 and 4:30–7:30, Sun. 9:30–12:30.*

The **Palacio de los Duques de San Carlos** *(Palace of the Dukes of San Carlos)* is next to the church of San Martín. The palace's majestically decorated facade dates from around 1600. The building is now a convent of Hieronymite nuns, who can occasionally be glimpsed on the balconies in full habit, hanging laundry or watering their flowers. To visit, ring the bell by pulling the chain in the foyer. The convent also produces and sells typical pastries, including *perrunillas* (small lard cakes) and *tocinillos del cielo* (custardlike egg-yolk sweets). ✉ *Pl. Mayor* ☎ *927/320058* 🎫 *€1.20* ⏲ *Mon.–Sat. 10–1 and 4:30–6, Sun. 10–12:30.*

NEED A BREAK?

If the intense summer sun leaves you parched and tired, revivify yourself at the Bar Pillete Cafeteria (✉ *Pl. Mayor 28* ☎ *927/321449*). It sells fresh-squeezed juices, shakes, and other exotic fruit concoctions—a rarity in these remote parts.

The **Palacio del Marqués de la Conquista** (*Palace of the Marquis of the Conquest* ✉ *Pl. Mayor*) is the most dramatic building on the square. Built by Francisco Pizarro's half-brother Hernando, the stone palace is immediately recognizable by its rich covering of early Renaissance plateresque ornamentation. Flanking its corner balcony are imaginative busts of the Pizarro family.

Adjacent to the Palacio de la Conquista is the arcaded former town hall, now a court of law; the alley that runs through its central arch takes you to the **Palacio de Orellana-Pizarro,** which functions as a school and has the most elegant Renaissance courtyard in town. Cervantes, on his way to thank the Virgin of Guadalupe for his release from prison, spent some time writing here. 🎫 *Free* ⏲ *Weekdays 10–1 and 4–6, weekends 11–2 and 4:30–7.*

Trujillo's oldest section, known as **La Villa,** is entirely surrounded by its original, much restored, walls. Follow the wall along Calle Almenas, which runs west from the Palacio de Orellana-Pizarro, beneath the **Alcázar de Los Chaves,** a castle-fortress that was turned into a guest lodge in the 15th century and hosted visiting dignitaries, including Ferdinand and Isabella. The building has seen better days and is now a college. Passing the Alcázar, continue west along the wall to the **Puerta de San Andrés,** one of La Villa's four surviving gates (there were originally seven). Walk through and you're in a world inhabited by storks, who, in spring and early summer, hunker down in the many crumbling chimneys and towers of Trujillo's palaces and churches.

Attached to a Romanesque bell tower, the Gothic church of **Santa María Mayor** is occasionally used for masses, but its interior has been virtually untouched since the 16th century. The upper choir has an exquisitely carved balustrade; the coats of arms at each end indicate the seats Ferdinand and Isabella occupied when they attended mass here. Note the high altar, circa 1480, adorned with great 15th-century Spanish paintings; to see it properly illuminated, place a coin in the box next to the church entrance. Climb up the tower for stunning views of the town and surrounding vast plains stretching toward Cáceres and the Sierra de Gredos. ✉ *Pl. de Santa María* 🎫 *€1.30* ⏲ *Oct.–Apr., daily 10–2 and 4:30–7; May–Sept., daily 10–2 and 4–8.*

Near the Puerta de la Coria, housed in a former Franciscan convent, is the **Museo de la Coria.** Its exhibits on Spain and Latin America's connection are similar to those in the Casa Museo de Pizarro (formerly the

Pizarro family home), but they're more impressive, with an emphasis on the troops as well as other (non-Pizarro) conquistadors who led missions over the water. *927/321898 Free Weekends 11:30–2.*

For spectacular views of the town and its surroundings, climb to the top of the fortress of Trujillo's large **castle,** built by the Moors on Roman foundations. To the south are silos, warehouses, and residential neighborhoods; to the north are only green fields and flowers, partitioned by a maze of nearly leveled Roman stone walls. *€1.30 May–Sept., daily 10–2 and 5–8:30; Oct.–Apr., daily 10–2 and 4–7.*

DID YOU KNOW?

Known as the Cradle of the Conquistadors, Trujillo spawned some of the leading explorers and conquerors of the Western Hemisphere. The most famous was Francisco Pizarro, conqueror of Peru, born in Trujillo in 1475.

WHERE TO STAY & EAT

$–$$$ ★ **Pizarro.** Traditional Extremaduran home cooking is the draw of this friendly restaurant right on the main plaza in a small but quiet and elegant upstairs dining room. A house specialty is *gallina trufada,* an elaborately prepared chicken dish prepared with cognac, truffles, and nutmeg. This was once a common Christmas dish, but few people today know how to make it. *Pl. Mayor 13 927/320255 MC, V Closed Tues.*

$–$$ **Mesón La Troya.** An institution in these parts, this restaurant is fronted by a noisy tapas bar papered with photos of celebrity diners happily posing aside the restaurant's elderly owner, Concha. The atmospheric dining room has a barrel-vaulted brick ceiling. If you choose the €20 prix-fixe meal, you're served a starter of *tortilla de patatas* (potato omelet), *chorizo ibérico* (pork sausage), and a salad. One notable main dish is the *pruebas de cerdo* (pork casserole with garlic and spices). Go here hungry—the portions are enormous. *Pl. Mayor 10 927/321364 MC, V.*

$$–$$$ ★ **Parador de Trujillo.** Originally the 16th-century Convent of Santa Clara, Trujillo's homey parador centers on a harmonious Renaissance courtyard complete with bubbling fountain. A living-museum quality is reflected in the furniture, paintings, and engravings. The back wall of the vaulted dining room is lined with shelves of regional plates and copper-ware as well as an exquisite mural painting. Go for the tomato soup spiced with cumin seeds or any of the *revueltos* (scrambled eggs) with asparagus or mushrooms. Carnivores may prefer one of the game dishes, such as wild boar in an acorn-and-wine sauce. *C. Santa Beatriz de Silva 1, 10200 927/321350 927/321366 www.parador.es 45 rooms, 1 suite In-room: Ethernet. In-hotel: restaurant, bar, public Wi-Fi AE, DC, MC, V.*

$$$ ★ **Meliá Trujillo.** Once a 16th-century convent, this boutique hotel has a reddish–ocher color scheme on its facade, in its cloisters, and in its courtyard, where there's a swimming pool surrounded by wrought-iron furniture. The restaurant in the former refectory serves regional dishes such as wild boar. *Pl. del Campillo 1, 10200 927/458900 927/323046 www.solmelia.com 74 rooms, 3 suites In-hotel: restaurant, bar, pool AE, DC, MC, V BP.*

$$ **Posada Dos Orillas.** In the historic center of town, this 16th-century former inn has rooms individually decorated in traditional Spanish colonial style with lots of wrought iron and dark-wood furniture. Guests can enjoy breakfast in the delightful patio with columns and leafy plants, or at an elegant restaurant, which serves classic Extramadura dishes with an innovative twist. ✉*Calle de Cambrones 6, 10200* ☎*927/659079* 🌐*www.dosorillas.com* *13 rooms* *In-hotel: restaurant, no elevator* *MC, V* *BP.*

$$ **Viña Las Torres.** This family-run rural hotel is in the mountains 6 mi south of Trujillo. A former private house, the rooms are individually decorated with rustic tiles, rugs, and wrought-iron headboards. Outside there is a delightful colonnaded terrace overlooking the gardens, complete with tennis court and pool. This area is renowned for its birdlife, thus ideal for bird-watching enthusiasts, as demonstrated by the following quote from a contented guest: "If you want to be serenaded by owls and nightingales outside your bedroom window, wake up to hoopoe and blue rock thrush on the hotel tower, and view the red-rumped swallows nesting in the courtyard, then this is THE place." ✉*EX208, Km 87.6, 10200* ☎*927/319350* 🌐*www.vinalastorres.com* *8 rooms* *In-hotel: pool, tennis court, no elevator* *MC, V* *BP.*

SHOPPING

Trujillo sells more folk arts and crafts than almost any other place in Extremadura, among the most attractive of which are multicolor rugs, blankets, and embroideries. **Eduardo Pablos Mateos** (✉*Plazuela de San Judas 12* ☎*927/321066*) specializes in local wood carvings, basketwork, and furniture. For other stores selling pottery, glass, or iron crafts, ask at the tourist office.Several shops on the **Plaza Mayor** have enticing selections; the one just across from the tourist office displays a centuries-old loom along with the work of local craftswoman Maribel Vallar; store hours are erratic.

GUADALUPE

7 ★ *200 km (125 mi) southwest of Madrid, 96 km (60 mi) east of Trujillo.*

The **Real Monasterio de Santa María de Guadalupe** *(Royal Monastery of Our Lady of Guadalupe)* is one of the most inspiring sights in Extremadura. Whether you come from Madrid, Trujillo, or Cáceres, the last stage of the ride takes you through wild, astonishingly beautiful mountain scenery. The monastery itself clings to the slopes, forming a profile that echoes the gaunt wall of mountains behind it. Pilgrims have been coming here since the 14th century, but for the past 10 years they have been joined by a growing number of tourists. Even so, the monastery's isolation—it's a good two-hour drive from the nearest town—has saved it from commercial excess. The story of Guadalupe goes back to around 1300, when a local shepherd uncovered a statue of the virgin, supposedly carved by St. Luke. King Alfonso XI, who often hunted here, had a church built to house the statue and later vowed to found a monastery should he defeat the Moors at the battle of Salado in

1340. After his victory, he kept his promise. The greatest period in the monastery's history was between the 15th and 18th centuries, when, under the rule of the Hieronymites, it was turned into a pilgrimage center rivaling Santiago de Compostela in importance. Documents authorizing Columbus's first voyage to the Western Hemisphere were signed here. The Virgin of Guadalupe became the patroness of Latin America, honored by the dedication of thousands of churches and towns in the New World. The monastery's decline coincided with Spain's loss of overseas territories in the 19th century. Abandoned for 70 years and left to decay, it was restored after the civil war.

MONASTERY DAY TRIP

From Madrid, you can easily do a one-day trip to the monastery of **Guadalupe.** A good scenic route takes three hours. Take the A5/E90 southwest from Madrid for 105 km (65 mi) to Talavera, and then turn left/south on N502. After reaching La Nava de Ricomalillo, around 48 km (30 mi) away, fork right onto CM411, signposted for Guadalupe, and drive 58 km (37 mi). On the return, a faster way back is via EX118 north of Guadalupe to Navalmoral de la Mata, then the A5/E90 to Madrid.

In the middle of the tiny, irregularly shaped **Plaza Mayor** (also known as the Plaza de Santa María de Guadalupe, and transformed during festivals into a bullring) is a 15th-century **fountain,** where Columbus's two American Indian servants were baptized in 1496. Looming in the background is the late-Gothic south facade of the **monastery church,** flanked by battlement towers. The entrance to the monastery is to the left of the church. From the large Mudejar cloister, the required guided tour progresses to the **chapter house,** with hymnals, vestments, and paintings, including a series of small panels by Zurbarán. The ornate 17th century **sacristy** has a series of eight Zurbarán paintings of 1638–47. These powerfully austere representations of monks of the Hieronymite order and scenes from the life of St. Jerome are the artist's only significant paintings still in the setting for which they were intended. The tour concludes with the garish, late-baroque **Camarín,** the chapel where the famous Virgen Morena (Black Virgin) is housed. The dark, mysterious wooden figure hides under a heavy veil and mantle of red and gold; painted panels tell the virgin's life story. Each September 8, the virgin is brought down from its altarpiece and a procession walks it around the cloister, with pilgrims following on their knees. Outside, the monastery's gardens have been restored to their original, geometric Moorish style. ✉*Entrance on Pl. Mayor* ☎*927/367000* 🎫*€3* 🕐*Daily 9:30–1 and 3:30–6, guided tours every ½ hr.*

EN ROUTE

Four kilometers (2½ mi) outside of Guadalupe toward Navalmoral de la Mata, there is a 15th-century Gothic hermitage, Ermita del Humilladero. On the same road immediately before it is a lookout point providing dramatic views of the monastery, with the small town of Guadalupe in the background.

WHERE TO STAY & EAT

$–$$ ✕ **Extremadura.** For a hearty meal, particularly if you like mushrooms, try this restaurant just down the road from the monastery. The menu *de la casa* (of the house) includes *migas, sopa de ajo* (garlic soup), pork chops with green beans, and steak topped with mushrooms. ✉ *Gregorio López 18* ☎ *927/367351.*

$–$$ ✕ **Mesón el Cordero.** This relaxed and rustic dining room has fine regional dishes at good prices. Grab a table by the window for some stunning mountain views. Chef and owner Doña Antonia is especially proud of her *escabeches de perdiz* (stewed partridge in preserves). ✉ *Av. Alfonso el Onceno, 27* ☎ *927/367131* ⏲ *Closed Mon. and Feb.*

ON THE BORDER

Spain's border with Portugal has remained virtually unchanged for centuries. From the mid-1400s, black slaves were frequently transferred from Portugal to Andalusia and Africa through Extremadura, resulting in a considerable black population that existed until relatively recent times. These days, however, Extremadura does not reflect any dramatic influence from its western neighbor, though subtle influences exist in certain aspects of the culture, including the cuisine and architecture. The traditional gateway town to Portugal is Badajoz.

$$$ ★ ✕ **Parador de Guadalupe.** The first autopsy in Spain was performed in this building, a 15th-century hospital and then pilgrim's hostel. Despite this prior use, the parador has an unusually luxurious feel, thanks to its Mudejar architecture, Moorish-style rooms, and exotic vegetation. The best rooms look out onto the monastery. The restaurant ($$–$$$) serves simple local dishes, such as *bacalao monacal* (cod with spinach and potatoes), migas, and *frite de cordero* (lamb stew). ✉ *C. Marqués de la Romana 12, 10140* ☎ *927/367075* 📠 *927/367076* 🌐 *www.parador.es* *41 rooms* *In-room: dial-up, Wi-Fi (some). In-hotel: restaurant, bar, tennis court, pool* 💳 *AE, DC, MC, V.*

$ Fodor's Choice ★ ✕ **Hospedería del Real Monasterio.** An excellent and considerably cheaper alternative to the town parador, this inn was built around the 16th-century Gothic cloister of the monastery itself. The courtyard of the cloister is used as an outdoor café, open to all from May to September. The simple, traditional rooms with wood-beam ceilings are exceptionally quiet. Fine local dishes at the restaurant ($–$$) include *caldereta de cabrito* (baby goat stew), *revuelto de cardillos* (scrambled eggs with thistle), and *morcilla de berza* (blood sausage with cabbage). ✉ *Pl. Juan Carlos I s/n, 10140* ☎ *927/367000* 📠 *927/367177* 🌐 *www.monasterioguadalupe.com* *46 rooms, 1 suite* *In-hotel: restaurant, bar* 💳 *MC, V* ⏲ *Closed mid-Jan.–mid-Feb.*

$$ ★ **La Clara.** Right in the center of town, across from the monastery, this small *casa rural* is decorated throughout with antiques. Friendly owner Maribel will welcome you with a shot of her homemade *cafe con puesto* (coffee liquor) in the small downstairs bar. The rooms have a homey appeal with flower-filled balconies overlooking the chairs on the square. ✉ *Plaza Sta. Maria de Guadalupe 44, 10140* ☎ *927/154067* *4 rooms* *In-hotel: bar, no elevator* 💳 *MC, V.*

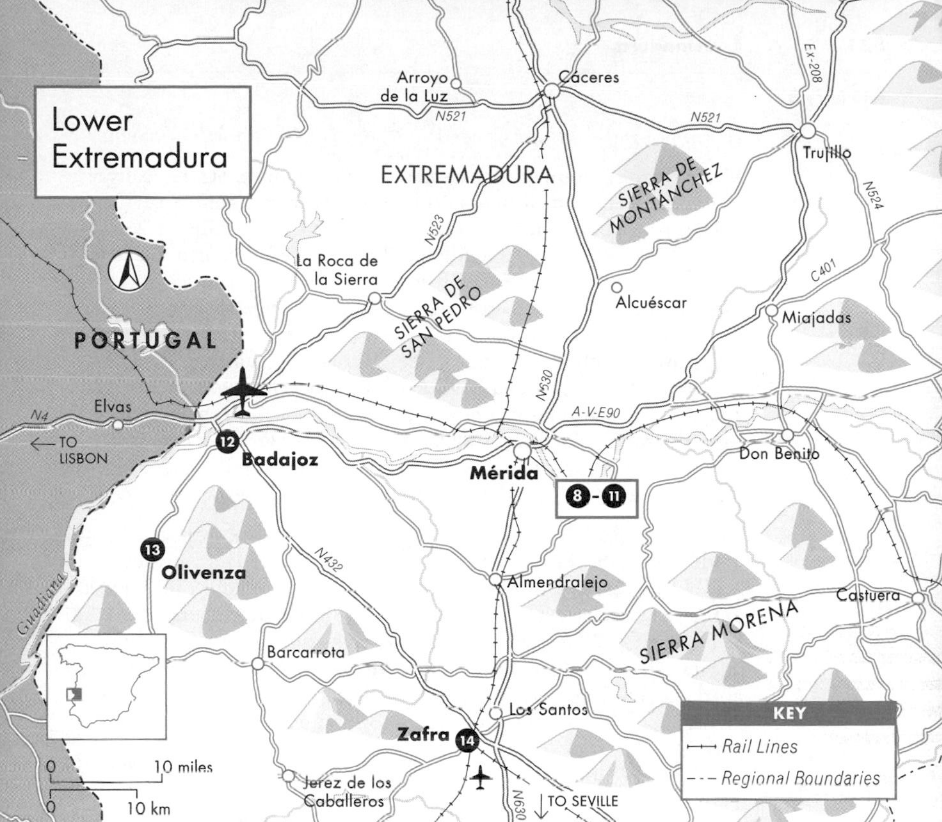

SHOPPING

On sale everywhere in Guadalupe is the copper-ware that has been crafted here since the 16th century.

LOWER EXTREMADURA

Extremadura's southern half sometimes seems more Andalusian or even Portuguese than classically Spanish. Long stretches of dusty farmland and whitewashed villages make it feel light-years away from Castile. Mérida was established in 25 BC as a settlement for Roman soldiers; it soon became the capital of the Roman province of Lusitania (the Iberian Peninsula), and its many ruins bear witness to its former splendor. Badajoz has also been a settlement since prehistoric times; Paleolithic remains have been found nearby. Minutes from the Portuguese border, it has long served as a gateway to Portugal and is home to many Portuguese as well as Portuguese descendants. Extremadura's links with Portugal come alive in Olivenza, whereas Zafra, near the southern end of the province, feels more like an Andalusian town.

MÉRIDA

70 km (43 mi) south of Cáceres, 250 km (155 mi) north of Seville.

Mérida is the administrative capital of Extremadura. Strategically situated at the junction of major Roman roads from León to Seville and Toledo to Lisbon, Mérida was founded by the Romans in 25 BC on the banks of the River Guadiana. Then named Augusta Emerita, it became the capital of the vast Roman province of Lusitania soon after its founding. A bishopric in Visigothic times, Mérida never regained the importance that it had under the Romans, and it's now a rather plain large town—with the exception of its Roman monuments; they pop up all over town, surrounded by thoroughly modern buildings. The glass-and-steel bus station is in a modern district on the other side of the river from the town center. It commands a good view of the exceptionally long **Roman bridge,** which spans two forks of this sluggish river. On the farther bank is the Alcazaba fortress.

Some other Roman sites require a drive. Across the train tracks in a modern neighborhood is the **circo** (circus), where chariot races were held. Little remains of the grandstands, which seated 30,000, but the outline of the circus is clearly visible and impressive for its size: 1,312 feet long and 377 feet wide. Of the existing aqueduct remains, the most impressive is the **Acueducto de los Milagros** (Aqueduct of Miracles), north of the train station. It carried water from the Roman dam of Proserpina, which still stands, 5 km (3 mi) away.

8 Fodor's Choice ★ If you're driving, reach Mérida's best-preserved **Roman monuments,** the **teatro** (theater) and **anfiteatro** (amphitheater), arranged in a verdant park, by following signs to the MUSEO DE ARTE ROMANO. The theater, the best-preserved in Spain, is used for a classical drama festival each July; it seats 6,000. The amphitheater, which holds 15,000 spectators, opened in 8 BC for gladiatorial contests. Parking is usually easy to find here. Next to the entrance to the Roman ruins is the **main tourist office,** where you can pick up maps and brochures. You can buy a ticket to see only the Roman ruins or, for a slightly higher fee, an *entrada conjunta* (joint admission), which also grants access to the Basílica de Santa Eulalia and the Alcazaba. ✉ *Calle Pedro Maria Plano s/n* ☎ *924/312530* 🎫 *Theater and amphitheater €6.50; combined admission to Roman sites, basilica, and Alcazaba €9* ⏲ *Oct.–Apr., daily 9:30–1:45 and 4–6:15; May–Sept., 9:30–1:45 and 5–7:15.*

9 ★ Across the street from the entrance to the Roman sites, and connected by an underground passageway, is Mérida's superb, modern **Museo Nacional de Arte Romano** *(National Museum of Roman Art)*, in a monumental building designed by the renowned Spanish architect Rafael Moneo. You walk through a series of passageways to the luminous, cathedral-like main exhibition hall, supported by arches the same proportion and size (50 feet) as the Roman arch in the center of Mérida, the Arco de Trajano (Trajan's Arch). The exhibits include mosaics, frescoes, jewelry, statues, pottery, household utensils, and other Roman works. Before leaving, be sure to visit the **crypt** beneath the museum—it houses the remains of several homes and a necropolis that were uncovered while

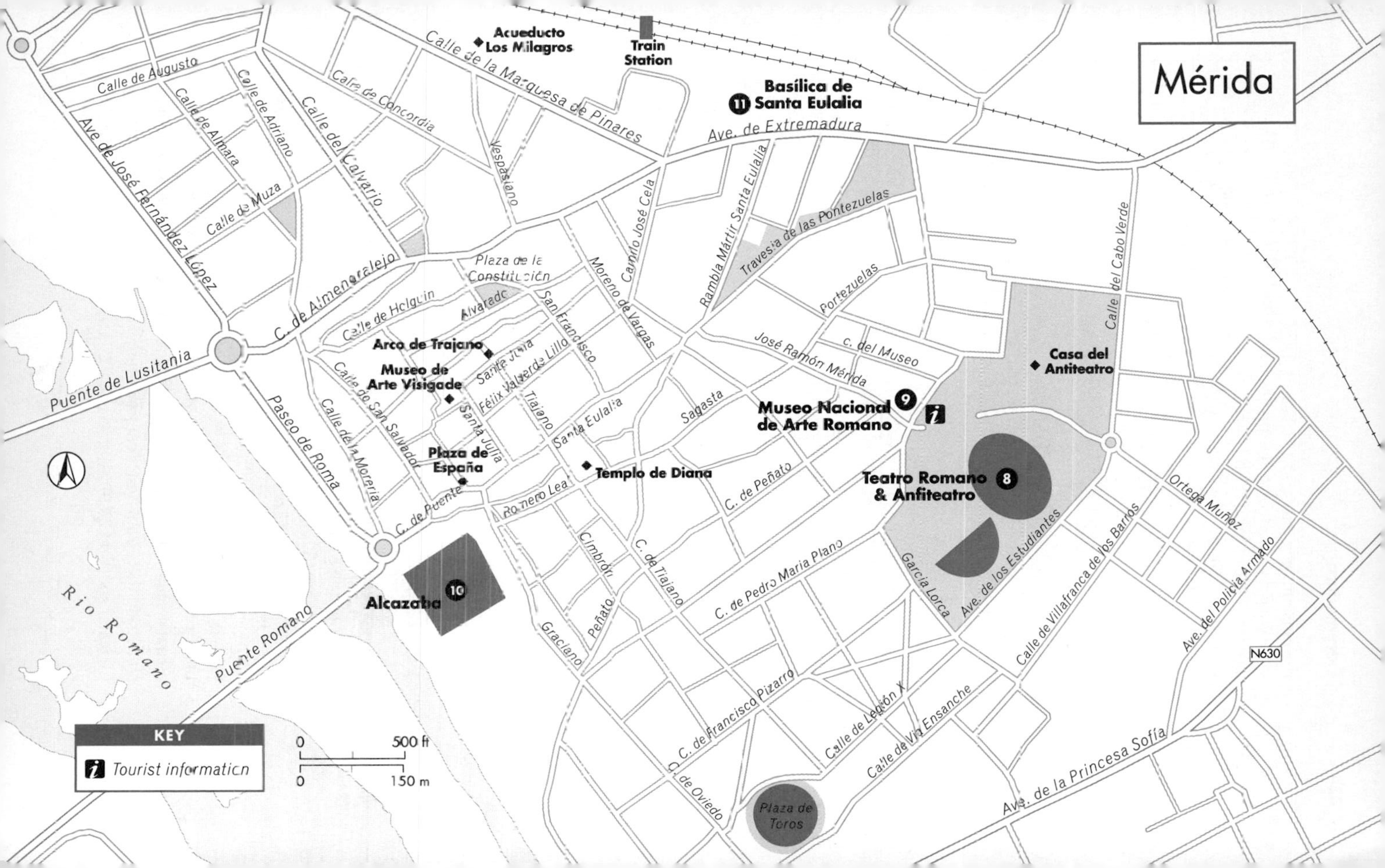

Mérida
Acueducto Los Milagros
Train Station
Basílica de Santa Eulalia
11
Casa del Antiteatro
Museo Nacional de Arte Romano
9
Teatro Romano & Anfiteatro
8
Templo de Diana
Arco de Trajano
Museo de Arte Visigade
Plaza de España
Alcazaba
10
Plaza de Toros
Plaza de la Constitución
Calle de la Marquesa de Pinares
Ave. de Extremadura
Calle de Augusto
Calle de Adriano
Calle de Almara
Calle de Muza
Ave de José Fernández López
Calle del Calvario
Calle de Concordia
Vespasiano
C. de Almendralejo
Calle de Holguin
Alvarado
Santa Julia
Félix Valverde Lillo
San Francisco
Tiajano
Santa Eulalia
Calle do San Salvador
Calle de la Moreria
Paseo de Roma
Puente de Lusitania
Puente Romano
Rio Romano
C. de Puente
Romero Leal
Camilo José Cela
Moreno de Vargas
Rambla Mártir Santa Eulalia
Travesía de las Pontezuelas
Portezuelas
José Ramón Mérida
c. del Museo
Sagasta
C. de Peñato
Cimbrón
Peñato
Graciano
C. de Tiajano
C. de Pedro Maria Plano
C. de Francisco Pizarro
C. de Oviedo
Calle de Legión X
Calle de Vía Ensanche
Ave. de la Princesa Sofía
Garcia Lorca
Ave. de los Estudiantes
Calle de Villafranca de los Barros
Ave. del Policía Armado
Ortega Muñoz
Calle del Cabo Verde
N630
KEY
Tourist information
0
500 ft
0
150 m

the museum was built, in 1981, and were incorporated into the project as part of the exhibits. The museum is wheelchair accessible. ✉ *José Ramón Mélida 2* ☎ *924/311690* 🌐 *www.mnar.es* 🎫 *€2.40, free Sat. afternoon and Sun.* ⏲ *Oct.–Apr., Tues.–Sat. 10–2 and 4–6, Sun. 10–2; May–Sept., Tues.–Sat. 10–2 and 5–7, Sun. 10–2.*

DISCOUNTS & DEALS

In Mérida, a multisight pass for €9 includes the Roman theater and amphitheater, Zona Arqueológica de Morerís, excavations of Basílica de Santa Eulalia, and Casa de Mitrea. If you just want to see the Roman theater and amphitheater, you can purchase a combined ticket for those attractions.

10 From the Museo Nacional de Arte Romano, make your way west down Suarez Somontes toward the river and the city center. Turn right at Calle Baños and you can see the towering columns of the **Templo de Diana,** the oldest of Mérida's Roman buildings. If you continue toward the river along Sagasta and Romera, you can come to the sturdy, square **Alcazaba** *(fortress)*, built by the Romans and later strengthened by the Visigoths and Moors. To go inside, follow the fortress walls around to the side farthest from the river. Climb up to the battlements for sweeping river views. ☎ *924/317309* 🎫 *€9, includes Roman theater and amphitheater* ⏲ *May–Sept., daily 9:30–1:45, 5–7:15; Oct.–Apr., daily 9:30–1:45 and 4–6.*

Mérida's main square, the **Plaza de España,** adjoins the northwestern corner of the fortress and is highly animated both day and night. The plaza's oldest building is a 16th-century palace, now a Meliá hotel. Behind the palace stretches Mérida's most charming area, with Andalusian-style white houses shaded by palms—in the midst of which stands the **Arco de Trajano,** part of a Roman city gate.

11 The **Basílica de Santa Eulalia,** originally a Visigothic structure, marks both the site of a Roman temple and supposedly where the child martyr Eulalia was roasted alive in AD 304 for spitting in the face of a Roman magistrate. In 1990, excavations surrounding the tomb of the famous saint revealed layer upon layer of Paleolithic, Visigothic, Byzantine, and Roman settlements. ✉ *Rambla Mártir Santa Eulalia* ☎ *924/303407* 🎫 *€3.50* ⏲ *Oct.–Apr., Mon.–Sat. 10–1:15 and 4–6:15; May–Sept., 10–1:15 and 5–7:15.*

OFF THE BEATEN PATH

Siberia Extremeña. For a taste of truly elemental Spain, drive to the "Extremaduran Siberia," between Mérida and the Castilian town of Ciudad Real (leave N430, which links the two towns, by following signs for Casas de Don Pedro, and continue south toward Talarrubias). This poor area of wild, rolling scrubland owes its nickname to the 12th duke of Osuna, a 19th-century Spanish ambassador to Russia who thought the terrain resembled the Siberian steppes. The oldest village is Puebla de Alcocer, which has an arcaded square. In nearby Peloche, to the north of Talarrubias, women still sit outside their front doors embroidering. Many people come to this region for water sports at its three reservoirs: Cíjara, García de Sola, and Orellana.

WHERE TO STAY & EAT

$$–$$$ ✕**Altair.** Under the same ownership as the renowned Atrio in Cáceres, Altair, on the bank of the river Guadiana, delivers high-quality regional food with a modern twist. The chef's specialties include *rollitos crujientes de prueba de ibérico* (crunchy pasta rolls stuffed with pork), *bacalo fresco con manitas de cerdo* (fresh cod with pig's trotters), and *patito asado con miel y higos* (roast duckling baked with honey and figs). Consider going for the six-course degustation menu if you can afford the €50 price tag. A translucent wall facing the river provides a silhouetted view of the Roman Bridge. ✉*Av. José Fernández López s/n* ☎*924/304512* ▭*AE, DC, MC, V* ⏲*Closed Sun.*

LINGUISTIC MÉLANGE

In general, Extremaduran (*extremeñu*) is the Spanish dialect spoken throughout the province. However, there are a few spots where the cultures, and subsequently, the languages, collide. In the Portuguese town of Barrancos, a dialect of Portuguese known as *barranquenho* is spoken; it is heavily influenced by Extremaduran. Similarly, in Olivenza, the elderly inhabitants can often be heard speaking Portuguese. And in the isolated region of Sierra de Gata, the elderly still speak *maniego*, a mixture of Castilian, Spanish, and Portuguese.

$$ ✕**Casa Benito.** Famous for its tasty tapas and local *pitarra* wine, this atmospheric bar-restaurant hidden on a square off Calle Santa Eulalia also has a small, rustic dining area in the back with a reasonably priced daily set menu as well as decent à la carte options. The walls at Benito's are covered with pictures and memorabilia of matadors and bullfights. ✉*C. San Francisco 3* ☎*924/330769* ▭*AE, MC, V* ⏲*Closed Sun.*

$$ ✕**Nicolás.** Mérida's best-known restaurant is in a distinctive house with yellow awnings, near the municipal market. There's a tavern serving tapas downstairs and a dining room upstairs. The regionally inspired food includes *perdiz en escabeche* (marinated partridge), lamb dishes, and frogs' legs. Desserts might include the traditional *tocino del cielo* made with honey and egg yolks, or creamy cheese from La Serena. The wine list is extensive, the service professional. ✉*Felix Valverde Lillo 13* ☎*924/319610* ▭*AE, DC, MC, V* ⏲*No dinner Sun.*

¢ ✕**Cervecería 100 Montaditos.** Don't be put off by the fact that this popular local eatery is part of a nationwide chain. This is an excellent informal restaurant specializing in *montaditos* (small filled rolls)—at least a hundred of them, with fillings varying from tortilla to *jamon iberico con aceite oliva virgin extra* (Iberian ham with extra-virgin olive oil). Washed down with draught beer, these light eats are tasty and excellent value, but don't expect dress-for-dinner surroundings. ✉*C. Félix Valverde Lillo 5* ☎*No phone* ▭*No credit cards.*

$$$ ★ ✕🏨**Parador de Mérida.** Built over the remains of what was first a Roman temple, then a baroque convent, then a prison, this spacious whitewashed building exudes an Andalusian cheerfulness, with hints at its Roman and Mudejar past. Also called Parador Via de la Plata, the hotel has bright guest rooms with traditional dark-wood furniture. The brilliant-white interior of the convent's former church has been turned into a restful lounge. Try the restaurant's ($$–$$$) *revuelto* (scrambled

eggs) prepared in myriad ways, including *con aroma de pimentón* (in paprika sauce) and with *cabrito al ajillo* (baby goat fried with garlic). ✉*Pl. Constitución 3, 06800* ☎*924/313800* 📠*924/319208* 🌐*www.parador.es* *80 rooms, 2 suites* *In-room: dial-up, Wi-Fi. In-hotel: restaurant, bar, pool, Wi-Fi, gym, parking (fee)* 💳*AE, DC, MC, V.*

NIGHTLIFE & THE ARTS

The highlight of the cultural calendar is the annual **Festival de Teatro Clásico,** held in the Roman theater from early July to mid-August. Contact the tourist office in advance for information and tickets. The many cafés, tapas bars, and restaurants surrounding the Plaza España and in the Plaza de la Constitución fill with boisterous crowds late into the evening. Calle John Lennon, off the northwest corner of the plaza, is your best bet for late-night dance action, especially in summer. As you walk south on Santa Eulalia, the bars get cheaper, the music louder. Locals pack **Rafael II** (✉*C. Santa Eulalia 13*) for ham, cheese, and sausages; there's also a small, cork-lined dining room in the back.

BADAJOZ

12 *66 km (40 mi) west of Mérida, 90 km (59 mi) southwest of Cáceres.*

A sprawling mass of concrete and glass amid desolate terrain, the border town of Badajoz looks like an urban oasis on approach and is indeed modern and well stocked, relative to the surrounding towns. Hardly an aesthetic haven, however, the city has little to offer the traveler; it tries (not quite successfully) to make up for its lack qualities with nighttime energy and the intellectual punch of its university.

The **Museo Extremeño e Iberoamericano de Arte Contemporáneo** is the main daytime incentive to spend a few hours here. Dedicated to contemporary Spanish and Latin American painting and sculpture, the museum is south of the city center in a striking circular building that was once the Badajoz prison. ✉*Nuestra Señora de Guadalupe s/n* ☎*924/013060* 🎟*Free* ⏲*Oct.–Apr., Tues.–Sat. 10:30–1:30 and 5–8, Sun. 10:30–1:30; May–Sept., Tues.–Sat. 10:30–1:30 and 6–9, Sun. 10:30–1:30.*

WHERE TO STAY & EAT

$$$–$$$$ ✕**Aldebarán.** Elegant touches, such as Bohemian glassware and embroidered tablecloths, set this restaurant with a spacious interior apart. A former head chef of the renowned Arzak in San Sebastián runs the kitchen. Specialties include *merluza al aroma de romero* (hake infused with rosemary), *manitas de cerdo con judías verdes* (pig's trotters) with green beans), and a supremely delicious cheese-and-walnut tart. ✉*Av. de Elvas s/n, Urb. Guadiana, Las Terrazas* ☎*924/274261* 💳*AE, DC, MC, V* ⏲*Closed Sun.*

$$ ✕🏨**Barceló Husa Zurbarán.** This modern building is near the River Guadiana and overlooks the Parque de Castelar. Although the exterior is bland, the rooms are large and decorated in warm, earthy tones of cream and soft browns. Service here is impeccable, and the elegant restaurant, Los Monjes, is one of the best in town, serving international cuisine, as well as *cordero asado* (roast lamb), Iberian hams

and sausages, local cheeses, and regional wines. ✉*Paseo Castelar s/n, 06001* ☎*924/001400* 📠*924/220142* 🌐*www.barcelo.com* *215 rooms* *In-room: Wi-Fi. In-hotel: restaurant, bar, pool, public Wi-Fi, parking (fee)* ▭*AE, DC, MC, V.*

NIGHTLIFE & THE ARTS

You'll find bars and tapas places around Plaza España, especially on Calles Zurbarán and Muñoz y Torrero.

OLIVENZA

13 *22 km (14 mi) south of Badajoz.*

Olivenza is worth seeing for its curious double personality. Looking at the airy, elongated main square, with its patterned cobblestones and facades in the Portuguese *estilo manuelino,* an architectural style popular in Portugal during the reign of Manuel I (1469–1521), you might think you've inadvertently crossed the border into Portugal. In fact, this originally Spanish town was occupied by Portugal in 1297, recaptured by the Spanish duke of San Germán in 1657, recovered by Portugal in 1668, and definitively reclaimed for Spain again in 1801.

Olivenza's Portuguese influence is most evident in the twisted *manuelina* columns and tiling in the **Iglesia de Santa María Magdalena** (*Church of Mary Magdalene* ✉*Pl. de la Constitución s/n*). As befits a long-disputed border town, Olivenza has numerous fortifications, the largest of which is the castle, with its 15th-century **Torre del Homenaje** (*Tower of Homage* ✉*Pl. de Santa María*).

Adjoining the Torre del Homenaje is the **Museo Etnográfico González Santana,** surprisingly ambitious for a town this size. One room is devoted to archaeological finds, but the main thrust is recent history: exhibits cover traditional trades and crafts along with collections of musical instruments, toys, and other paraphernalia of early 20th century daily rural life. ✉*Pl. de Santa María* ☎*924/490222* *€1* ⏲*Oct.–May, Tues.–Sun. 11–2 and 4–6; June–Sept., Tues.–Sun. 11–2 and 5–8.*

WHERE TO EAT

$$–$$$ ✕ **Alcañices.** Portuguese-accented cuisine makes this a good lunch or dinner choice. ✉*Colon 3* ☎*924/491570* ▭*MC, V* ⏲*No dinner Sun.*

ZAFRA

14 *62 km (38 mi) south of Mérida, 85 km (53 mi) southeast of Badajoz, 135 km (84 mi) north of Seville.*

Worth a stop on your way to or from Seville, Zafra is an attractive and lively town with a **Plaza Mayor** that's actually two contiguous squares: the 16th-century Plaza Chica, once a marketplace, and the 18th-century Plaza Grande, ringed by mansions flaunting their coats of arms. Connected by a graceful archway, both plazas make for enjoyable tapas crawls.There are several churches here, the finest being **Nuestra Señora de Candelaria** (✉*Conde de la Corte*) a block west off the Plaza Mayor and a short walk from the parador—its *retablo* (altarpiece) has nine extraordinary panels by Zurbarán. The main reason travelers stop in Zafra, however, is the parador itself, otherwise known as the 15th-century **Alcázar de los Duques de Feria** (✉*Pl. Corazón de María 7*).

During the first week of October, Zafra is the site of one of Spain's oldest and largest livestock fairs, the **Feria Internacional Ganadera**, which dates back to 1417. Breeders and traders come from all over the country, and hotel rates rise accordingly; reserve well in advance.

WHERE TO STAY & EAT

$$$ ★ **Parador Hernán Cortés.** This hotel is in the 15th-century castle where Cortés stayed before his voyage to Mexico. The military exterior conceals a refined elegant 16th-century courtyard attributed to Juan de Herrera. The suite and the chapel, which together now serve as a conference room, have an elaborate *artesonado* (coffered) ceiling. The rooms here are spacious and elegant, with high ceilings, antique furniture, and decorative ironwork. At the restaurant ($$), try *pierna de cordero asado* (roasted leg of lamb). Local desserts include delicious marzipan-and-acorn cakes. The menu is in English as well as Spanish. ✉*Pl. María Cristina 7, 06300* ☎*924/554540* 📠*924/551018* 🌐*www.parador.es* *44 rooms, 1 suite* *In-room: dial-up. In-hotel: restaurant, pool* 💳*AE, DC, MC, V.*

$$$ ★ **Rocamador.** Between Olivenza and Zafra, the hotel is a 16th-century monastery on top of a hill. You can stay in the former library, the kitchen, or the monks' cells, which have cavernous arches and wooden beam ceilings, brick-arch doorways, stone or clay tile floors, and rustic furniture. The monastery's chapel is a renowned restaurant with arches and columns run by two young, imaginative Basque chefs. The menu includes dishes like (*charlota de rabo con manzanas agridulces y salsa de puerros y anises* (oxtail with sweet-and-sour apples in a leek and aniseed sauce) and includes two fixed-price sampler menus. Reserve well in advance. ✉*Ctra. Nacional Badajoz–Huelva, Km 41.1, Almendral, 06160* ☎*924/489000* 📠*924/489001* 🌐*www.rocamador.com* *25 rooms, 5 suites* *In-hotel: restaurant, bar, pool, no elevator* 💳*AE, DC, MC, V.*

$$ **Huerta Honda.** Across a small square from the castle-parador, this gleaming-white Andalusian-style hotel has rooms painted in soothing pastel colors. Twelve luxurious Gran Clase rooms or suites have four-poster beds, sumptuous furnishings, and Jacuzzi baths; those on the ground floor, including one with wheelchair access, have patios. At Barbacana, savor gazpacho *a la extremeña* (Extremeño-style) or local beef. The Huerta's lively Mesón cafeteria serves more modest fare. There's also an English-style pub. ✉*Lopez Asme 30, 06300* ☎*924/554100* 📠*924/552504* 🌐*www.hotelhuertahonda.com* *45 rooms, 3 suites* *In-room: Wi-Fi. In-hotel: restaurant, bar, pool, public Wi-Fi* 💳*AE, DC, MC, V.*

EXTREMADURA ESSENTIALS

To research prices, get advice from other travelers, and book travel arrangements, visit www.fodors.com.

TRANSPORTATION

For more on travel to and in Extremadura, see the Extremadura Planner at the beginning of the chapter.

BY BUS

Bus travel is the most efficient and least costly mode of transport for getting around Extremadura. For schedules and prices, check the respective tourist office or contact the Auto Res bus line.

Bus Lines **Auto Res** (✉ *Pl. Conde de Casal 6, Madrid* ☎ *91/551–7200* 🌐 *www.auto-res.es* ✉ *Estación de Autobuses, Av. de la Libertad, Mérida* ☎ *924/371955*).

Bus Stations **Badajoz** (✉ *José Rebollo López s/n, Badajoz* ☎ *924/258661*). **Cáceres** (✉ *Ctra. Gijó–Sevilla, s/n, Cáceres* ☎ *927/232550*).

BY CAR

If you are heading here by car from Madrid, the main gateway, the four-lane NV, moves quickly. The N630, or Vía de la Plata, which crosses Extremadura from north to south, is also effective. The fastest approach from Portugal is the A6 from Lisbon to Badajoz. If you're in any kind of a hurry, driving is the most feasible way to get around Extremadura. The main roads are well surfaced and not too congested. Side roads—particularly those that cross the wilder mountainous districts, such as the Sierra de Guadalupe—can be poorly paved and badly marked, however, the Sierra de Guadalupe affords some of the most spectacular views in Extremadura. (For some of the best views, head north of Guadalupe on EX118, toward the village of Navalmoral.) The surrounding countryside is rugged and beautiful. For more scenic countryside, continue northwest from here on the EX102 at Cañamero and on to the main Navalmoral-Trujillo road near the Puerto de Miravete, where you can enjoy a fabulous lookout point with sweeping views of Trujillo in the distance.

On major roads and motorways the speed limit is 120 kmph (75 mph), in urban areas it is 50 kmph (31 mph), and on other roads it is either 90 kmph (55 mph) or 100 kmph (62.5 mph). Severe fines are enforced throughout Spain for driving under the influence of alcohol. Spot breath checks are often carried out, and if the level of alcohol in your bloodstream is found to be 0.05 percent or above, you could have your driver's license confiscated and be fined as much as €600.

See Spain Essentials in back of book for national car-rental agencies.

Local Agencies **Albarran Rent a Car** (✉ *Santa Ana 9, Badajoz* ☎ *924/250353* 🌐 *www.atesa.com*). **Automoviles Palma** (✉ *Poligrono Los Caños Badajoz* ☎ *607/151888*). **Lambea** (✉ *Ctra. Gijón–Sevilla s/n, Cáceres* ☎ *927/629091*). **Record Rent a Car** (✉ *Poligrono Las Capellaniás 223, Cáceres* ☎ *927/249097*).

Rent a Car Extremadura (✉ *Avenida Reina Sofía 11, Merida* ☎ *924/387562*). **Sales Rent a Car** (✉ *Ricardo Carapeto 97, Badajoz* ☎ *924/260896* 🌐 *www.carjet.com*).

BY TAXI

Taxis are readily available. You are not required to tip taxi drivers, though locals generally round off the amount.

Taxi Companies **Radio Taxi Badajoz** (☎ *924/243101*). **Radio Taxi Cáceres** (☎ *927/242424*). **Radio Taxi Mérida** (☎ *924/371111*). **Tele Taxi Mérida** (☎ *924/315756*).

BY TRAIN

Trains from Madrid stop at Monfragüe, Plasencia, Cáceres, Mérida, Zafra, and Badajoz. They run as often as six times daily. From Seville there are daily trains to Mérida, Cáceres, and Plasencia. The journey from Madrid to Cáceres takes about 5 hours; from Seville to Cáceres, 7½ hours. There is also a train from Lisbon to Badajoz, which takes 5 hours. Within the province there are services from Badajoz to Cáceres (2 daily, 1 hour 55 minutes) and to Mérida (7 daily, 1 hour); from Cáceres to Badajoz (3 daily, 2 hours), to Mérida (5 daily, 1 hour), to Plasencia (2 daily, 1 hour 20 minutes), and to Zafra (2 daily, 2 hours 10 minutes); from Plasencia to Badajoz (1 daily, 3 hours 30 minutes), to Cáceres (3 daily, 1 hour 20 minutes), and to Mérida (3 daily, 2 hours 20 minutes). Operators generally speak Spanish only, so check the RENFE Web site (www.renfe.es) for details in English. Note that train stations in Extremadura tend to be some distance from the town centers.

Train Information **RENFE** (☎ *902/240202* 🌐 *www.renfe.es*).

SPORTS & THE OUTDOORS

FISHING PERMITS

Trout fishing is popular in the Vera and Jerte districts, and tench, carp, royal carp, barbel, and pike abound in the Tajo and Guadiana rivers. Non-EU residents can apply for one of two possible licenses to fish in public waters. You'll need to pick up a *Modelo 50* form, available from most banks in Extremadura. The licenses are called *especial*; the special granting permission to fish for trout for a one-year period is €6.75; the annual nontrout license is €4.50. Note that the licenses are mailed to your home address, but the Modelo form serves as proof of license for up to two months.

Contacts **Dirección General del Medio Ambiente** (✉ *Av. de Portugal s/n, Mérida* ☎ *924/002211 or 924/002467*).

OUTDOOR ADVENTURE

Peña del Aguila organizes hiking, horseback riding, cycling, kayaking, and quad rallies throughout Extremadura but particularly in the Sierra de Montánchez region; English is spoken. Valle Aventura arranges similar activities in the Jerte Valley; if you want to hike here, ask the tourist office near Cabezuela for its helpful maps, which describe each hike and detail the route. To visit the Cornalvo Nature Park, the second-largest park in the region next to Monfragüe, contact (in advance) the nature park's department at the Dirección General del Medio Ambiente. Most of the park is private land, and it's a good idea to take a guide. The regional government has set up a Centro de Interpretación, an information and permit center, in Trujillanos.

Contacts **Centro de Interpretación** (✉ *Ctra. Trujillanos-Embalse de Cornalvo, Trujillanos* ☎ *924/002386*). **Dirección General del Medio Ambiente** (✉ *Av. de Portugal s/n, Mérida* ☎ *924/002520 or 924/002386* 🌐 *www.juntaex.es*). **Peña del Aguila** (✉ *10170 Montantánchez, Cáceres* ☎ *626/712724* 🌐 *www.pena-del-aguila.com/activities.htm*). **Valle Aventura** (✉ *Av. de Plasencia, Cabezuela del Valle* ☎ *927/472196* 🌐 *www.valleaventura.com*).

CONTACTS & RESOURCES

BANKS & EXCHANGING SERVICES

Banks are generally in town and city centers, and the majority will have an ATM, enabling you to withdraw euros with your credit or debit card, providing you have a valid PIN. Your card issuer is likely to charge you a fee for using an ATM abroad. Banks are open from 8:30 AM to 2 PM weekdays plus on Saturday mornings, October to April. Currency-exchange offices are also common; however, in general, they charge a higher commission than the banks.

DISABILITIES & ACCESSIBILITY

Extremadura abounds with ancient buildings that do not easily accommodate travelers with disabilities. In Cáceres, visitors with disabilities have access to the old part of the city and, with some help, the Concatedral de Santa María. Plasencia's only accessible site is the Museo Etnográfico-Textil. Trujillo's celebrated main square was renovated in 2002 to provide, among other things, easier access for people with disabilities. From there, tourists can move into the old area and visit, with the help of a ramp, the Iglesia of Santa María. In Mérida, the Roman ruins and the Basílica de Santa Eulalia are accessible with accompaniment, unlike the Alcazaba; the Museo Nacional de Arte Romano is accessible. In Badajoz, only the Museo Extremeño e Iberoamericano de Arte Contemporáneo provides access for travelers with disabilities.

EMERGENCIES

The Hospital Infanta Cristina is a large hospital in Badajoz with a 24-hour emergency department. For nonemergencies, there are private medical clinics throughout Extremadura, some with English-speaking staff members.

Every town has at least one pharmacy open 24 hours; the address of the on-duty pharmacy is posted on the front door of all pharmacies. You can also dial Spain's general information number—11818—for the location of a doctor's office or pharmacy that's open nearest you.

Emergency Services **Ambulance** (☎ *061*). **Guardia Civil** (☎ *062*). **Hospital Infanta Cristina** (*Hospital* ☎ *924/218199*). **Insalud** (*Public health service* ☎ *061*). **Policía Local** (*Local police* ☎ *092*). **Police Nacional** (*National police* ☎ *091*).

INTERNET, MAIL & SHIPPING

Courier Service **DHL** (✉ *Poligono Industrial, C. Villablino, Badajoz* ☎ *902/122424* 🌐 *www.dhl.es*). **MRW** (✉ *El Prado, Parcela 53, Mérida* ☎ *900/300400* 🌐 *www.mrw.es*).

Internet Cafés **Cibercity** (✉ *Plaza de Bruselas, Cáceres* ☎ *927/626093*). **Cibercafe Ciberalia** (✉ *C. Tienda 18, Trujillo* ☎ *927/659087*). **HDZ One** (✉ *Av. Antonio Montero Moreno 6, Badajoz* ☎ *924/248616*).

Information **Post Office** (✉ *Paseo Primo de Rivera 2, Cáceres*).

MEDIA

Extremadura's most popular local newspaper is *Diario Hoy*, which is published daily in Badajoz but also has sections on Cáceres, Mérida, and Plasencia. The local television station is Telefrontera, and several radio stations provide a mix of commentary and music, including Radio Extremadura (1.008 AM) and Radio Forum, which is broadcast in Merida (107.4 FM). El Corte Inglés stores in Mérida, Badajoz, Cáceres and Mérida have a limited selection of English language books, international newspapers and magazines. Tourist offices can also provide information on bookshops that stock English-language books—to avoid disappointment, bring your leisure-reading material with you.

VISITOR INFORMATION

Regional Tourist Offices **Badajoz** (✉ *Pl. de la Libertad 3* ☎ *924/013659*). **Cáceres** (✉ *Pl. Mayor 3* ☎ *927/010834*). **Mérida** (✉ *Av. José Álvarez Saez de Buruaga s/n, at entrance to Roman theater* ☎ *924/009730*). **Plasencia** (✉ *Plaza de Torre de Lucia s/n* ☎ *927/017840*). **Turismo Extremadura** (🌐 *www.turismoextremadura.com*).

Local Tourist Offices **Badajoz** (✉ *Pasaje de San Juan s/n* ☎ *924/224981*). **Guadalupe** (✉ *Pl. Mayor* ☎ *927/154128*). **Mérida** (✉ *C. Santa Eulalia* ☎ *924/330722*). **Olivenza** (✉ *Pl. de España s/n* ☎ *924/490151*). **Parque Nacional de Monfragüe** (✉ *Vilarreal de San Carlos* ☎ *927/199134*). **Plasencia** (✉ *El Rey 8* ☎ *927/423843*). **Trujillo** (✉ *Pl. Mayor s/n* ☎ *927/322677*). **Valle del Jerte (Jerte Valley)** (✉ *Paraje de Peñas Alba, just off N110 north of Cabezuela* ☎ *927/472122 or 927/472558*). **Zafra** (✉ *Pl. de España 30* ☎ *924/551036*).

Spain Essentials

PLANNING TOOLS, EXPERT INSIGHT, GREAT CONTACTS

There are planners and there are those who, excuse the pun, fly by the seat of their pants. We happily place ourselves among the planners. Our writers and editors try to anticipate all the issues you may face before and during any journey, and then they do their research. This section is the product of their efforts. Use it to get excited about your trip to Spain, to inform your travel planning, or to guide you on the road should the seat of your pants start to feel threadbare.

www.fodors.com

GETTING STARTED

We're really proud of our Web site: Fodors.com is a great place to begin any journey. Scan Travel Wire for suggested itineraries, travel deals, restaurant and hotel openings, and other up-to-the-minute info. Check out Booking to research prices and book plane tickets, hotel rooms, rental cars, and vacation packages. Head to Talk for on-the-ground pointers from travelers who frequent our message boards. You can also link to loads of other travel-related resources.

RESOURCES

ONLINE TRAVEL TOOLS

For more information on Spain, visit the Tourist Office of Spain at ⊕*www.okspain.org*. Also check out the sites ⊕*www.cyberspain.com* and ⊕*www.red2000.com/spain*. For a virtual brochure on Spain's paradores, go to ⊕*www.parador.es*. Go to ⊕*sispain.org/english* and then click on "Other Web Sites in or about Spain" for a wide selection of informational Web sites.

All About Spain

Currency Conversion Google (⊕www.google.com) does currency conversion. Just type in the amount you want to convert and an explanation of how you want it converted (e.g., "14 Swiss francs in dollars"), and then voilà. **Oanda.com** (⊕www.oanda.com) also allows you to print out a handy table with the current day's conversion rates. **XE.com** (⊕www.xe.com) is a good currency conversion Web site.

Safety Transportation Security Administration (TSA ⊕www.tsa.gov)

Time Zones Timeanddate.com (⊕www.timeanddate.com/worldclock) can help you figure out the correct time anywhere.

Weather Accuweather.com (⊕www.accuweather.com) is an independent weather-forecasting service. **Weather.com** (⊕www.weather.com) is the Web site for the Weather Channel.

WORD OF MOUTH

After your trip, be sure to rate the places you visited and share your experiences and travel tips with us and other Fodorites in Travel Ratings and Talk on www.fodors.com.

Other Resources CIA World Factbook (⊕www.odci.gov/cia/publications/factbook/index.html) has profiles of every country in the world. It's a good source if you need some quick facts and figures.

VISITOR INFORMATION

Before you go, consult the Tourist Office of Spain in your home country or on the World Wide Web. The site ⊕*www.okspain.org* provides a basic introduction; the Spain-based ⊕*www.spain.info* is more sophisticated.

Contacts Chicago (☎312/642–1992). **Los Angeles** (☎323/658–7188). **Miami** (☎305/358–1992). **New York** (☎212/265–8822).

THINGS TO CONSIDER

GOVERNMENT ADVISORIES

As different countries have different world views, look at travel advisories from a range of governments to get more of a sense of what's going on out there. And be sure to parse the language carefully. For example, a warning to "avoid all travel" carries more weight than one urging you to "avoid nonessential travel," and both are much stronger than a plea to "exercise caution." A U.S. government travel warning is more permanent (though not necessarily more serious) than a so-called public announcement, which carries an expiration date.

Consider registering online with the State Department (https://travelregistration.

state.gov/ibrs/), so the government will know to look for you should a crisis occur in the country you're visiting.

The U.S. Department of State's Web site has more than just travel warnings and advisories. The consular information sheets issued for every country have general safety tips, entry requirements (though be sure to verify these with the country's embassy), and other useful details.

General Information & Warnings **U.S. Department of State** (🌐www.travel.state.gov).

GEAR

Pack light. Although baggage carts are free and plentiful in most Spanish airports, they're rare in smaller train stations and most bus stations.Madrid, north and northeastern Spain, and Granada and the Sierra Nevada can be bitterly cold from late fall through early spring, while the Mediterranean and southern region are generally much more mild, if not warm. It makes sense to wear casual, comfortable clothing and shoes for sightseeing, but you'll want to dress up a bit in large cities, especially for fine restaurants and nightclubs. On the beach, anything goes; it's common to see females of all ages wearing only bikini bottoms, and many of the more remote beaches allow nude sunbathing.

PASSPORTS & VISAS

Visitors from the United States need a passport valid for a minimum of six months to enter Spain.

PASSPORTS

A passport verifies both your identity and nationality—a great reason to have one.

U.S. passports are valid for 10 years. You must apply in person if you're getting a passport for the first time; if your previous passport was lost, stolen, or damaged; or if your previous passport has expired and was issued more than 15 years ago or when you were under 16. All children under 18 must appear in person to apply for or renew a passport. Both parents must accompany any child under 14 (or send a notarized statement with their permission) and provide proof of their relationship to the child.

■TIP→ Before your trip, make two copies of your passport's data page (one for someone at home and another for you to carry separately). Or scan the page and e-mail it to someone at home and/or yourself.

There are 14 regional passport offices, as well as 7,000 passport acceptance facilities in post offices, public libraries, and other governmental offices. If you're renewing a passport, you can do so by mail. Forms are available at passport acceptance facilities and online.

The cost to apply for a new passport is $97 for adults, $82 for children under 16; renewals are $67. Allow six weeks for processing, both for first-time passports and renewals. For an expediting fee of $60 you can reduce this time to about two weeks. If your trip is less than two weeks away, you can get a passport even more rapidly by going to a passport office with the necessary documentation. Private expediters can get things done in as little as 48 hours, but charge hefty fees for their services.

VISAS

Visas are not necessary for those with a U.S. passport valid for a minimum of six months, and who plan to stay in Spain for tourist or business purposes for up to 90 days. Should you need a visa to stay longer than this, contact the nearest Spanish Consulate office to you in the U.S. to apply for the appropriate documents.

U.S. Passport Information **U.S. Department of State** (☎877/487–2778 🌐http://travel.state.qov/passport). For information regarding the whereabouts of Spanish Consular offices in the USA check this Web site 🌐www.mae.es

U.S. Passport & Visa Expediters **A. Briggs Passport & Visa Expeditors** (☎800/806–0581 or 202/338–0111 🌐www.abriggs.com). **American Passport Express**

(☎800/455-5166 or 800/841-6778 🌐www.americanpassport.com). **Passport Express** (☎800/362-8196 🌐www.passportexpress.com). **Travel Document Systems** (☎800/874-5100 or 202/638-3800 🌐www.traveldocs.com). **Travel the World Visas** (☎866/886-8472 or 301/495-7700 🌐www.world-visa.com).

TRIP INSURANCE

What kind of coverage do you honestly need? Do you even need trip insurance at all? Take a deep breath and read on.

We believe that comprehensive trip insurance is especially valuable, or indeed essential, for any trip and should be taken out at the date of booking, especially if that is six months or so in advance of the trip. But ultimately, whether or not you get insurance depends on how comfortable you are assuming all that risk yourself.

Comprehensive travel policies typically cover trip cancellation and interruption, and letting you cancel or cut your trip short because of a personal emergency, illness, or, in some cases, acts of terrorism in your destination. Such policies also cover evacuation and medical care. Some also cover you for trip delays because of bad weather or mechanical problems as well as for lost or delayed baggage (but be sure to check the small print as often only a small sum is allocated to electrical equipment like cameras, etc.). Another type of coverage to look for is financial default—that is, when your trip is disrupted because a tour operator, airline, or cruise line goes out of business. Generally you must buy this when you book your trip or shortly thereafter, and it's only available to you if your operator isn't on a list of excluded companies.

If you're going abroad, consider buying medical-only coverage at the very least. Neither Medicare nor some private insurers cover medical expenses anywhere outside of the United States (including time aboard a cruise ship, even if it leaves from a U.S. port). Medical-only policies typically reimburse you for medical care (excluding that related to preexisting conditions) and hospitalization abroad, and provide for evacuation. You still have to pay the bills and await reimbursement from the insurer, though.

Expect comprehensive travel insurance policies to cost about 4% to 8% of the total price of your trip (it's more like 8%–12% if you're over age 70). A medical-only policy may or may not be cheaper than a comprehensive policy. Always read the fine print of your policy to make sure that you are covered for the risks that are of most concern to you. Compare several policies to make sure you're getting the best price and range of coverage available.

Insurance Comparison Sites Insure My Trip.com (☎800/487-4722 🌐www.insuremytrip.com). Square Mouth.com (☎800/240-0369 or 727/490-5803 🌐www.squaremouth.com).

Comprehensive Travel Insurers Access America (☎800/729-6021 🌐www.accessamerica.com). CSA Travel Protection (☎800/873-9855 🌐www.csatravelprotection.com). HTH Worldwide (☎610/254-8700 or 888/243-2358 🌐www.hthworldwide.com). Travelex Insurance (☎800/228-9792 🌐www.travelex-insurance.com). Travel Guard International (☎715/345-0505 or 800/826-4919 🌐www.travelguard.com). Travel Insured International (☎800/243-3174 🌐www.travelinsured.com).

Medical-Only Insurers International Medical Group (☎800/628-4664 🌐www.imglobal.com). International SOS (🌐www.internationalsos.com). Wallach & Company (☎800/237-6615 or 540/687-3166 🌐www.wallach.com).

BOOKING YOUR TRIP

Unless your cousin is a travel agent, you're probably among the millions of people who make most of their travel arrangements online. But have you ever wondered just what the differences are between an online travel agent (a Web site through which you make reservations instead of going directly to the airline, hotel, or car-rental company), a discounter (a firm that does a high volume of business with a hotel chain or airline and accordingly gets good prices), a wholesaler (one that makes cheap reservations in bulk and then resells them to people like you), and an aggregator (one that compares all the offerings so you don't have to)? Is it truly better to book directly on an airline or hotel Web site? And when does a real live travel agent come in handy?

ONLINE

You really have to shop around. A travel wholesaler such as Hotels.com or HotelClub.net can be a source of good rates, as can discounters such as Hotwire or Priceline, particularly if you can bid for your hotel room or airfare. Indeed, such sites sometimes have deals that are unavailable elsewhere. They do, however, tend to work only with hotel chains (which makes them just plain useless for getting hotel reservations outside of major cities) or big airlines (so that often leaves out upstarts like jetBlue and some foreign carriers like Air India). Also, with discounters and wholesalers you must generally prepay, and everything is nonrefundable. And before you fork over the dough, be sure to check the terms and conditions, so you know what a given company will do for you if there's a problem and what you'll have to deal with on your own.

■TIP→To be absolutely sure everything was processed correctly, confirm reservations made through online travel agents, discounters, and wholesalers directly with your hotel or airline before leaving home.

Booking engines like Expedia, Travelocity, and Orbitz are actually travel agents, albeit high-volume, online ones. And airline travel packagers like American Airlines Vacations and Virgin Vacations—well, they're travel agents, too. But they may still not work with all the world's hotels.

An aggregator site will search many sites and pull the best prices for airfares, hotels, and rental cars from them. Most aggregators compare the major travel-booking sites such as Expedia, Travelocity, and Orbitz; some also look at airline Web sites, though rarely the sites of smaller budget airlines. Some aggregators also compare other travel products, including complex packages—a good thing, as you can sometimes get the best overall deal by booking an air-and-hotel package.

AGGREGATORS

Booking Engines **Cheap Tickets** (🌐www.cheaptickets.com) is a discounter. **Expedia** (🌐www.expedia.com) is a large online agency that charges a booking fee for airline tickets. **Hotwire** (🌐www.hotwire.com) is a discounter. **lastminute.com** (🌐www.lastminute.com) specializes in last-minute travel; the main site is for the U.K., but it has a link to a U.S. site. **Luxury Link** (🌐www.luxurylink.com) has auctions (surprisingly good deals) as well as offers on the high-end side of travel. **Onetravel.com** (🌐www.onetravel.com) is a discounter for hotels, car rentals, airfares, and packages. **Orbitz** (🌐www.orbitz.com) charges a booking fee for airline tickets, but gives a clear breakdown of fees and taxes before you book. **Priceline.com** (🌐www.priceline.com) is a discounter that also allows bidding. **Travel.com** (🌐www.travel.com) allows you to compare its rates with those of other booking engines. **Travelocity** (🌐www.travelocity.com) charges a booking fee for airline tickets, but promises good problem resolution.

Online Accommodations Hotelbook.com (🌐www.hotelbook.com) focuses on independent hotels worldwide. Hotel Club (🌐www.hotelclub.net) is good for major cities and some resort areas. Hotels.com (🌐www.hotels.com) is a big Expedia-owned wholesaler that offers rooms in hotels all over the world. Quikbook (🌐www.quikbook.com) offers "pay when you stay" reservations that allow you to settle your bill when you check out, not when you book; best for trips to U.S. and Canadian cities. Reservator (🌐www.reservator.com) is one of the best online sources focusing purely on hotels in Spain.

Other Resources Bidding For Travel (🌐www.biddingfortravel.com) is a good place to figure out what you can get and for how much before you start bidding on, say, Priceline.

WITH A TRAVEL AGENT

If you use an agent—brick-and-mortar or virtual—you'll pay a fee for the service. And know that the service you get from some online agents isn't comprehensive. For example Expedia and Travelocity don't search for prices on budget airlines like jetBlue, Southwest, or small foreign carriers. That said, some agents (online or not) *do* have access to fares that are difficult to find otherwise, and the savings can more than make up for any surcharge.

A knowledgeable brick-and-mortar travel agent can be a godsend if you're booking a cruise, a package trip that's not available to you directly, an air pass, or a complicated itinerary including several overseas flights. What's more, travel agents that specialize in a destination may have exclusive access to certain deals and insider information on things such as charter flights. Agents who specialize in types of travelers (senior citizens, gays and lesbians, naturists) or types of trips (cruises, luxury travel, safaris) can also be invaluable.

TIP→ Remember that Expedia, Travelocity, and Orbitz are travel agents, not just booking engines. To resolve any problems with a reservation made through these companies, contact them first.

Agent Resources American Society of Travel Agents (☎703/739–2782 🌐www.travelsense.org).

ACCOMMODATIONS

By law, hotel prices must be posted at the reception desk and should indicate whether or not the value-added tax (I.V.A.; 7%) is included. Note that high-season rates prevail not only in summer but also during Holy Week and local fiestas.

In much of Spain, breakfast is normally *not* included. However, in the resort destinations, such asthe Balearic Islands and the Costa del Sol, a buffet breakfast is often included.

TIP→ See each chapter's Planner section for accommodations price charts.

Most hotels and other lodgings require you to give your credit-card details before they will confirm your reservation. If you don't feel comfortable e-mailing this information, ask if you can fax it (some places even prefer faxes). However you book, get confirmation in writing and have a copy of it handy when you check in.

Be sure you understand the hotel's cancellation policy. Some places allow you to cancel without any kind of penalty—even if you prepaid to secure a discounted rate—if you cancel at least 24 hours in advance. Others require you to cancel a week in advance or penalize you the cost of one night. Small inns and B&Bs are most likely to require you to cancel far in advance. Most hotels allow children under a certain age to stay in their parents' room at no extra charge, but others charge for them as extra adults; find out the cutoff age for discounts.

TIP→ Assume that hotels operate on the European Plan (EP, no meals) unless we specify that they use the Breakfast Plan (BP, with full breakfast), Continental Plan (CP, continental breakfast), Full American Plan (FAP,

all meals), Modified American Plan (MAP, breakfast and dinner) or are all-inclusive (AI, all meals and most activities).

APARTMENT & HOUSE RENTALS

If you are interested in a single-destination vacation, or are staying in one place and using it as a base for exploring the local area, renting an apartment or a house can be a good idea. However, it is not always possible to ensure the quality beforehand, and you may be responsible for supplying your own bed linen, towels, etc.

Contacts Barclay International Group (☎516/364-0064 or 800/845-6636 🌐www.barclayweb.com). **Homes Away** (☎416/920-1873 or 800/374-6637 🌐www.homesaway.com). **Hometours International** (☎865/690-8484 🌐thor.he.net/~hometour). **Interhome** (☎954/791-8282 or 800/882-6864 🌐www.interhome.us). **Villanet** (☎206/417-3444 or 800/964-1891 🌐www.rentavilla.com). **Villas & Apartments Abroad** (☎212/213-6435 or 800/433-3020 🌐www.vaanyc.com). **Villas International** (☎415/499-9490 or 800/221-2260 🌐www.villasintl.com).

HOME EXCHANGES

With a direct home exchange you stay in someone else's home while they stay in yours. Some outfits also deal with vacation homes, so you're not actually staying in someone's full-time residence, just their vacant weekend place.

Exchange Clubs Home Exchange.com (☎800/877-8723 🌐www.homeexchange.com); $59.95 for a 1-year online listing. **HomeLink International** (☎800/638-3841 🌐www.homelink.org); $90 yearly for Web-only membership; $140 includes Web access and two catalogs. **Intervac U.S.** (☎800/756-4663 🌐www.intervacus.com); $78.88 for Web-only membership; $126 includes Web access and a catalog.

HOSTELS

Hostels offer bare-bones lodging at low, low prices—often in shared dorm rooms with shared baths—to people of all ages, though the primary market is young travelers, especially students. Most hos-

10 WAYS TO SAVE

1. Join "frequent guest" programs. You may get preferential treatment in room choice and/or upgrades in your favorite chains.

2. Call direct. You can sometimes get a better price if you call a hotel's local toll-free number rather than a central reservations number.

3. Check online. Check hotel Web sites, as not all chains are represented on all travel sites.

4. Look for specials. Always inquire about packages and corporate rates.

5. Look for price guarantees. For overseas trips, look for guaranteed rates. With your rate locked in you won't pay more, even if the price goes up in the local currency.

6. Look for weekend deals at business hotels. High-end chains catering to business travelers are busy only on weekdays; to fill rooms they often drop rates on weekends.

7. Ask about taxes. Verify whether local hotel taxes are included in quoted rates. In some places taxes can add 20% or more to your bill.

8. Read the fine print. Watch for add-ons, including resort fees, energy surcharges, and "convenience" fees for such things as unlimited local phone service you won't use or a free newspaper in a language you can't read.

9. Know when to go. Find out the destination's high season. Ask when rates go down, though: if your dates straddle peak and nonpeak seasons, a property may still charge peak-season rates for the entire stay.

10. Weigh your options. Weigh transportation times and costs against the savings of staying in a hotel that's cheaper because it's out of the way.

tels serve breakfast; dinner and/or shared cooking facilities may also be available. In some hostels you aren't allowed to be in your room during the day, and there may be a curfew at night. Nevertheless, hostels provide a sense of community, with public rooms where travelers often gather to share stories. Many hostels are affiliated with Hostelling International (HI), an umbrella group of hostel associations with some 4,500 member properties in more than 70 countries. Other hostels are completely independent and may be nothing more than a really cheap hotel.

Membership in any HI association, open to travelers of all ages, allows you to stay in HI-affiliated hostels at member rates. One-year membership is about $28 for adults; hostels charge about $10–$30 per night. Members have priority if the hostel is full; they're also eligible for discounts around the world, even on rail and bus travel in some countries.

Youth hostels (*albergue juvenil*) in Spain are usually large and impersonal (but clean) with dorm-style beds. Most are geared to students, though many have a few private rooms suitable for families and couples. These rooms fill up quickly, so book at least a month in advance. Other budget options are the university student dorms *(residencia estudiantil)*, some of which offer accommodation in the summer months, when students are away. Note that dorm availability changes from year to year, so inquire at the tourist office when you arrive. The rooms are often small, basic, and sparsely furnished, but the cost is low.

■ TIP→**Note that in Spain hostales are not the same as the dorm-style youth hostels common elsewhere in Europe—hostales are inexpensive hotels with individual rooms, not communal quarters.**

Information **Hostelling International—USA** (☎ 301/495–1240 ⊕ www.hiusa.org).

WORD OF MOUTH

Did the resort look as good in real life as it did in the photos? Did you sleep like a baby, or were the walls paper thin? Did you get your money's worth? Rate hotels and write your own reviews in Travel Ratings or start a discussion about your favorite places in Travel Talk on www.fodors.com. Your comments might even appear in our books. Yes, you, too, can be a correspondent!

HOTELS & BED-AND-BREAKFASTS

The Spanish government classifies hotels with one to five stars, with an additional rating of five-star GL (Gran Luxo) indicating the highest quality. Although quality is a factor, **the rating is technically only an indication of how many facilities the hotel offers.** For example, a three-star hotel may be just as comfortable as a four-star hotel but may lack a swimming pool. Similarly, Fodor's price categories (¢–$$$$) indicate room rates only, so you might find a well-kept $$$ inn more charming than the famous $$$$ property down the street.

All hotel entrances are marked with a blue plaque bearing the letter H and the number of stars. The letter R (standing for *residencia*) after the letter H indicates an establishment with no meal service, with the possible exception of breakfast. The designations *fonda* (F), *pensión* (P), *casa de huéspedes* (CH), and *hostal* (Hs) indicate budget accommodations. In most cases, especially in smaller villages, rooms in such buildings will be basic but clean; in large cities, these rooms can be downright dreary.

All hotels listed have private bath and air-conditioning (*aire acondicionado*) unless otherwise noted. When inquiring in Spanish about whether a hotel has a private bath, ask if it's an *habitación con baño*.

Although a single room (*habitación sencilla*) is usually available, singles are often on the small side. Solo travelers might prefer to pay a bit extra for single occupancy of a double room (*habitación doble uso individual.*) Make sure you request a double bed (*matrimonial*) if you want one—if you don't ask, you may end up with two singles placed together.

Spain's major private hotel groups include the Sol Meliá, Tryp, and Hotusa. The NH chain, which is concentrated in major cities, appeals to business travelers. Dozens of reasonably priced beachside high-rises along the various coasts cater to package tours.

There's a growing trend in Spain toward small country hotels and agrotourism. Estancias de España is an association of more than 40 independently owned hotels in restored palaces, monasteries, mills, and estates, generally in rural Spain; contact them for a free directory. Similar associations serve individual regions, and tourist offices also provide lists of establishments. In Galicia, *Pozos* are a beautiful old, often stately, homes converted into small luxury hotels and Pozos de Galicia is the main organization for them. In Cantabria *casonas* are small to large country houses, but as they don't have individual Web sites it is necessary to check the regional tourist office Web sites.

A number of *casas rurales* (country houses similar to bed-and-breakfasts) offer pastoral lodging either in guest rooms or in self-catering cottages. You may also come across the term *finca,* which is a country estate house. Many of the accommodations designated agroturismo are fincas that people have inherited and converted to upscale B&Bs. Comfort and conveniences vary widely; it's best to book these types of accommodation through one of the appropriate regional associations. Ask the local tourist office about casas rurales and fincas in the area.

INFORMATION

Small Hotels AHRA (Andalusian Association of Rural Hotels ☎957/540801 🌐www.ahra.es). **Estancias de España** (✉Calle Luxemburgo, 4, Pozuelo de Alarcón28224 ☎91/3454141 🌐www.estancias.com). **Hosterías y Hospederías Reales** (Hotels in Castile–La Mancha ✉CalleFrailes 1, Villanueva de los Infantes13320, Ciudad Real ☎902/202010 🌐www.hosteriasreales.com) .

Major Spanish Chains Hotusa (☎93/268-1010 🌐www.hotusa.es). **NH Hoteles** (☎902/115116 🌐www.nh-hoteles.es). **Sol Meliá** (☎902/144444 🌐www.solmelia.com).

PARADORES

The Spanish government runs 91 *paradores*—upmarket hotels in historic buildings or near significant sites. Some are in castles on a hill with sweeping views; others are in monasteries or convents filled with artistic treasures; still others are in modern buildings on choice beachfront, alpine, or pastoral property. Rates are reasonable, considering that most paradores have four- or five-star amenities; and the premises are invariably immaculate and tastefully furnished, often with antiques or reproductions. However, be advised that in most instances they do not offer many rooms with double beds (*matrimoniales*), so a special request is necessary. Each parador has a restaurant serving regional specialties, and you can stop in for a meal or a drink without spending the night. Breakfast, however, is an expensive buffet, so if you just want coffee and a roll, you'll do better to walk down the street to a local café.

Paradores are extremely popular with foreigners and Spaniards alike, so make reservations well in advance. If you plan to spend at least five nights in the paradors, the "five-night card" or *Tarjeta Cinco Noches* in Spanish offers excellent savings. You can purchase and use the card at any parador within the valid calendar period; in most paradors, discounted nights aren't offered during the high-season summer months of June, July, and August, and are offered only Sunday through Thursday in spring. Note that you can still use the card during these

10 WAYS TO SAVE

1. Nonrefundable is best. If saving money is more important than flexibility, then nonrefundable tickets work. Just remember that you'll pay dearly (as much as $200) if you change your plans.

2. **Comparison shop.** Web sites and travel agents can have different arrangements with the airlines and offer different prices for exactly the same flights.

3. Beware the listed prices. Many airline Web sites—and most ads—show prices *without* taxes and surcharges. Don't buy until you know the full price.

4. Stay loyal. Stick with one or two frequent-flier programs. You'll rack up free trips faster and you'll accumulate more quickly the perks that make trips easier. On some airlines these include a special reservations number, early boarding, access to upgrades, and more roomy economy-class seating.

5. Watch those ticketing fees. Surcharges are usually added when you buy your ticket anywhere but on an airline Web site.

6. Check often. Start looking for cheap fares from three months out to about one month. Keep looking till you find a price you like.

7. Don't work alone. Some Web sites have tracking features that will e-mail you immediately when good deals are posted.

8. Jump on the good deals. Waiting even a few minutes might mean paying more.

9. Be flexible. Look for departures on Tuesday, Wednesday, and Saturday, typically the cheapest days to travel.

10. Weigh your options. What you get can be as important as what you save. A cheaper flight might have a long layover, or it might land at a secondary airport, where your ground transportation costs might be higher.

periods, but you'll be paying the difference between the official and discounted rate. The card does not guarantee a room; you must make reservations in advance. The paradores offer 35% discounts to those 60 and over, usually in May and June, though the months may vary. Those 30 and under also qualify for special discounted deals "Young Person's Getaway" (with the buffet breakfast included in the price), that is valid throughout the year but with limited availability so check the website before you leave.

In Spain Paradores de España (✉Central de Reservas, Requena 3, Madrid 28013 ☎91/516-6666 🌐www.parador.es).

In the U.S. Marketing Ahead (✉381 Park Ave. S, Suite 718, New York, NY 10016 ☎212/686-9213 or 800/223-1356 🌐www.marketingahead.com).

In the U.K. Keytel International (✉402 Edgeware Rd., London W2 1ED ☎020/7616-0300 🌐www.keytel.co.uk).

AIRLINE TICKETS

Most domestic airline tickets are electronic; international tickets may be either electronic or paper. With an e-ticket the only thing you receive is an e-mailed receipt citing your itinerary and reservation and ticket numbers. The greatest advantage of an e-ticket is that if you lose your receipt, you can simply print out another copy or ask the airline to do it for you at check-in. You usually pay a surcharge (up to $50) to get a paper ticket, if you can get one at all. The sole advantage of a paper ticket is that it may be easier to endorse over to another airline if your flight is canceled and the airline with which you booked can't accommodate you on another flight.

TIP→ Discount air passes that let you travel economically in a country or region must often be purchased before you leave home. In some cases you can only get them through a travel agent.

The least expensive airfares to Spain are priced for round-trip travel and must usually be purchased in advance. Airlines generally allow you to change your return date for a fee; most low-fare tickets, however, are nonrefundable.

You can fly as a courier to Spain, though not within Spain.

If you buy a round-trip transatlantic ticket on Iberia, you might want to purchase a **Visit Spain** Airpass, good for three or more domestic flights during your trip. The pass must be purchased before you arrive in Spain, and all flights must be booked in advance; the cost starts at $248. The maximum number of coupons you may purchase is nine, and the pass is valid for one year. On certain days of the week, Iberia also offers *minitarifas* (minifares), which can save you up to 40% on domestic flights. Tickets must be purchased at least two days in advance, and you must stay over Saturday night. Another option is to join the Iberia Plus Internet club, which can offer exceptionally low fares.

Air Pass Info **FlightPass** (☎888/387-2479 EuropebyAir 🌐www.europebyair.com). **Iberia** (☎800/772-4642 🌐www.iberia.com).

RENTAL CARS

When you reserve a car, ask about cancellation penalties, taxes, drop-off charges (if you're planning to pick up the car in one city and leave it in another), and surcharges (for being under or over a certain age, for additional drivers, or for driving across state or country borders or beyond a specific distance from your point of rental). All these things can add substantially to your costs. Request car seats and extras such as GPS when you book.

Rates are sometimes—but not always—better if you book in advance or reserve through a rental agency's Web site. There are other reasons to book ahead, though: for popular destinations, during busy times of the year, or to ensure that you get certain types of cars (vans, SUVs, exotic sports cars).

TIP→ Make sure that a confirmed reservation guarantees you a car. Agencies sometimes overbook, particularly for busy weekends and holiday periods.

Alamo, Avis, Budget, Europcar, Hertz, and National (partnered in Spain with the Spanish agency Atesa) have branches at major Spanish airports and in large cities. Smaller, regional companies and wholesalers offer lower rates. All agencies have a range of models, but virtually all cars in Spain have a manual transmission—if you don't want a stick shift, reserve weeks in advance and specify automatic transmission, then call to reconfirm your automatic car before you leave for Spain. Rates in Madrid begin at the equivalents of U.S. $65 a day and $300 a week for an economy car with air-conditioning, manual transmission, and unlimited mileage. Add to this a 16% tax on car rentals. Although you should always rent the size car that makes you feel safest, a small car, aside from saving you money, is prudent for the tiny roads and parking spaces in many parts of Spain.

Anyone over 18 with a valid license can drive in Spain, but some rental agencies will not rent cars to drivers under 21.

Your driver's license may not be recognized outside your home country. You may not be able to rent a car without an International Driving Permit (IDP), which can be used only in conjunction with a valid driver's license and which translates your license into 10 languages. Check the AAA Web site for more info as well as for IDPs ($10) themselves.

Automobile Associations U.S.: **American Automobile Association** (AAA ☎315/797-5000 🌐www.aaa.com); most contact with the organization is through state and regional members. **National Automobile Club** (☎650/294-7000 🌐www.thenac.com); membership is open to California residents only.

LOCAL AGENCIES

Major Agencies **Alamo** (☎800/522-9696 🌐www.alamo.com). **Avis** (☎800/331-1084, 902/135531 in Spain 🌐www.avis.com). **Budget** (☎800/472-3325, 901/201212 in Spain 🌐www.budget.com). **Europcar** (☎902/105030 in Spain 🌐www.europcar.es). **Hertz** (☎800/654-3001, 902/402405 in Spain 🌐www.hertz.com). **National Car Rental/Atesa** /(☎800/227-7368, 902100101 in Spain 🌐www.nationalcar.com). **Pepe Car** (☎902/360535 in Spain 🌐www.pepecar.com)

Wholesalers **Mondialautos** (☎971/453000 🌐www.mondialautos.com). **Auto Europe** (☎888/223-5555 🌐www.autoeurope.com). **Europe by Car** (☎800/223-1516, 212/581-3040 in New York 🌐www.europebycar.com). **Eurovacations** (☎877/471-3876 🌐www.eurovacations.com). **Kemwel** (☎877/820-0668 🌐www.kemwel.com).

CAR-RENTAL INSURANCE

Everyone who rents a car wonders whether the insurance that the rental companies offer is worth the expense. No one—including us—has a simple answer. It all depends on how much regular insurance you have, how comfortable you are with risk, and whether money is an issue. More and more, companies are offering fully comprehensive insurance as an integral part of the price—and this is far and away the most preferred option.

If you own a car, your personal auto insurance may cover a rental to some degree, though not all policies protect you abroad; always read your policy's fine print. If you don't have auto insurance, then seriously consider buying the collision- or loss-damage waiver (CDW or LDW) from the car-rental company, which eliminates your liability for damage to the car. Some credit cards offer CDW coverage, but it's usually supplemental to your own insurance and rarely covers SUVs, minivans, luxury models, and the like. If your coverage is secondary, you may still be liable for loss-of-use costs from the car-rental company. But no credit-card insurance is valid unless you use that card for *all* transactions, from reserving to paying the final bill. All companies exclude car rental in some countries, so be sure to find out about the destination to which you are traveling.

■TIP➜ Diners Club offers primary CDW coverage on all rentals reserved and paid for with the card. This means that Diners Club's company—not your own car insurance—pays in case of an accident. It *doesn't* **mean your car-insurance company won't raise your rates once it discovers you had an accident.**

Some countries require you to purchase CDW coverage or require car-rental companies to include it in quoted rates. Ask your rental company about issues like these in your destination. In most cases it's cheaper to add a supplemental CDW plan to your comprehensive travel-insurance policy *(⇨Trip Insurance under Things to Consider in Getting Started, above)* than to purchase it from a rental company. That said, you don't want to pay for a supplement if you're required to buy insurance from the rental company.

■TIP➜ You can decline the insurance from the rental company and purchase it through a third-party provider such as Travel Guard (www.travelguard.com)—$9 per day for $35,000 of coverage. That's sometimes just under half the price of the CDW offered by some car-rental companies.

VACATION PACKAGES

Packages *are not* guided excursions. Packages combine airfare, accommodations, and perhaps a rental car or other extras (theater tickets, guided excursions, boat trips, reserved entry to popular museums, transit passes), but they let you do your own thing. During busy periods packages may be your only option, as flights and rooms may be sold out otherwise. Packages will definitely save you time. They can also save you money, particularly in peak seasons, but—and this is a really big "but"—you should price each part of the package separately to be sure. And be aware that prices advertised on Web sites and in newspapers rarely include service charges or taxes, which can up your costs by hundreds of dollars.

TIP→ Some packages and cruises are sold only through travel agents. Don't always assume that you can get the best deal by booking everything yourself.

Each year consumers are stranded or lose their money when packagers—even large ones with excellent reputations—go out of business. How can you protect yourself? First, always pay with a credit card; if you have a problem, your credit-card company may help you resolve it. Second, buy trip insurance that covers default. Third, choose a company that belongs to the United States Tour Operators Association, whose members must set aside funds to cover defaults. Finally, choose a company that also participates in the Tour Operator Program of the American Society of Travel Agents (ASTA), which will act as mediator in any disputes. You can also check on the tour operator's reputation among travelers by posting an inquiry on one of the Fodors.com forums.

Organizations American Society of Travel Agents (ASTA ☎703/739–2782 or 800/965–2782 🌐www.astanet.com). **United States Tour Operators Association** (USTOA ☎212/599–6599 🌐www.ustoa.com).

TIP→ Local tourism boards can provide information about lesser-known and small-niche operators that sell packages to only a few destinations.

GUIDED TOURS

Guided tours are a good option when you don't want to do it all yourself. You travel along with a group (sometimes large, sometimes small), stay in prebooked hotels, eat with your fellow travelers (the cost of meals sometimes included in the price of your tour, sometimes not), and follow a schedule. But not all guided tours are an if-it's-Tuesday-this-must-be-Belgium experience. A knowledgeable guide can take you places that you might never discover on your own, and you may be pushed to see more than you would have otherwise. Tours aren't for everyone, but they can be just the thing for trips to places where making travel arrangements is difficult or time-consuming (particularly when you don't speak the language). Whenever you book a guided tour, find out what's included and what isn't. A "land-only" tour includes all your travel (by bus, in most cases) in the destination, but not necessarily your flights to and from or even within it. Also, in most cases prices in tour brochures don't include fees and taxes. And remember that you'll be expected to tip your guide (in cash) at the end of the tour.

SPECIAL-INTEREST TOURS

ART

For art and culture tours try **Escorted Spain Tours** (☎800/942–3301 🌐www.escortedspaintours.com).

Another company in Spain that offers interesting art and historical tours to Spain is **Ole Spain Tours** (☎91/551–5294 🌐www.olespaintours.com).

Based in Switzerland **Art Tours** (☎41/41–410–50–60 🌐www.art-tours.com) offers a wide array of art tours to Spain.

BIRD-WATCHING

The Coto Doñana National Park in Andalucía offers, most probably, the widest array of bird-watching in Spain and **Discovering Doñana Ltd.** (☎959/442–466 🌐www.discoveringdonana.com) offers the best expeditions here.

CULINARY

Based in Madrid **Cellar Tours** (☎91/521–3939 🌐www.cellartours.com) offer a wide array of wine and cooking tours to Spain.

GOLF

The following two Spanish-based companies offer a fine selection of golf tours and information. **Golf Spain** (☎91/4263726 or 902/196877 🌐www.golfspain.com). **Golf in Spain** (☎952/474-848 🌐www.golfinspain.com).

HIKING

For a company that offers all kinds of adventure tours in Spain check out **Spain Adventures** (☎877/717-7246 🌐www.spainadventures.com).

LANGUAGE PROGRAMS

One of the best resources for language schools in Spain is **Go Abroad** (☎720/570-1702 🌐www.goabroad.com).

VOLUNTEER PROGRAMS

The best resource for volunteering in Spain is **Go Abroad** (☎720/570-1702 🌐www.goabroad.com).

WINE

Artisans of Leisure (☎800/214-8144 🌐www.artisansofleisure.com) offers personalized and tailor-made food and wine and cultural tours to Spain.

CRUISES

Barcelona is the busiest cruise port in Spain and Europe. Other popular ports of call in the country are Málaga, Alicante, and Palma de Mallorca. Nearby Gibraltar is also a popular stop. Although cruise lines such as Silversea and Costa traditionally offer cruises that take in parts of Spain and other Mediterranean countries such as Italy and Greece, it is becoming increasingly common to package tours wholly within Spain. Two popular routes consist of island-hopping in the Balaerics or around the Canary Islands. Among the many cruise lines that call on Spain are Royal Caribbean, Holland America Line, the Norwegian Cruise Line, and Princess Cruises.

Cruise Lines **Celebrity Cruises** (☎800/647-2251 🌐www.celebrity.com). **Costa Cruises** (☎800/445-8020 🌐www.costacruise.com). **Crystal Cruises** (☎800/804-1500 🌐www.crystalcruises.com). **Cunard Line** (☎800/728-6273 🌐www.cunard.com). **Holland America Line** (☎206/281-3535 or 877/932-4259 🌐www.hollandamerica.com). **Mediterranean Shipping Cruises** (☎212/764-4800 or 800/666-9333 🌐www.msccruises.com). **Norwegian Cruise Line** (☎866/625-1166 🌐www.ncl.com). **Oceania Cruises** (☎305/514-2300 or 800/531-5659 🌐www.oceaniacruises.com). **Princess Cruises** (☎661/753-0000 or 800/774-6237 🌐www.princess.com). **Regent Seven Seas Cruises** (☎877/505-5370 🌐www.rssc.com). **Royal Caribbean International** (☎305/539-6000 or 800/327-6700 🌐www.royalcaribbean.com). **Seabourn Cruise Line** (☎305/463-3000 or 800/929-9391 🌐www.seabourn.com). **SeaDream Yacht Club** (☎800/707-4911 🌐www.seadreamyachtclub.com). **Silversea Cruises** (☎954/522-4477 or 800/722-9955 🌐www.silversea.com). **Star Clippers** (☎305/442-0550 or 800/442-0551 🌐www.starclippers.com). **Windstar Cruises** (☎877/827-7245 🌐www.windstarcruises.com).

TRANSPORTATION

BY AIR

Flying time from New York to Madrid is about 7 hours; from London, just over 2.

Regular nonstop flights serve Spain from many major cities in the eastern United States; flying from other North American cities usually involves a stop. If you're coming from North America and would like to land in a city other than Madrid or Barcelona, consider flying a British or other European carrier, and know that you may have to stay overnight in London or another European city on your way home.

Since 2004, there's been a revolution in cheap flights from the United Kingdom to Spain, with the emergence of scores of new carriers such as Monarch and Flybmi providing competition to the market's main players—easyJet and Ryanair. All these carriers offer frequent flights, cover small cities as well as large ones, and have very competitive fares. Attitude Travel (*www.attitudetravel.com/lowcostairlines*) is the most comprehensive site on the Internet for low-cost airlies worldwide.

There are no nonstop flights to Spain from Australia or New Zealand.

Smoking policies vary from carrier to carrier. Many airlines prohibit smoking on all of their flights; others allow smoking only on certain routes or departures. There is no smoking on domestic flights in Spain.

Airline Security Issues Transportation Security Administration (www.tsa.gov) has answers for almost every question that might come up.

AIRPORTS

Most flights from the United States and Canada land in, or pass through, Madrid's Barajas (MAD). The other major gateway is Barcelona's El Prat de Llobregat (BCN). From England and elsewhere in Europe, regular flights also land in Málaga (AGP), Alicante (ALC), Palma de Mallorca (PMI), and many other smaller cities too. Many of the new budget airlines flying from the United Kingdom to Barcelona land at the increasingly busy Girona airport, some 90 minutes north of Barcelona. The bus company Sagalés runs a shuttle service between Girona's airport and Barcelona in conjunction with the departure and arrival times of Ryanair flights. Check the Web site (www.sagales.com) for timetables and fares.

AIRPORT INFORMATION

Madrid-Barajas (91/305-8343 www.aena.es). **Barcelona-El Prat de Llobregat** (93/298-3838 www.aena.es). **Girona-Girona** (972/186600). **Sagalés Buses** (93/231-2756 www.sagales.com).

GROUND TRANSPORTATION

In Madrid, the Metro service runs directly into town, although a little away from the center. In Barcelona the train or bus will take you right into the center of town. In other destinations it is necessary to take a bus connection.

FLIGHTS

From North America, Air Europa, Continental, Spanair, and USAirways fly to Madrid; American, Delta, and Iberia fly to Madrid and Barcelona—note that some of these airlines use shared facilities and do not operate their own flights. Within Spain, Iberia is the main domestic airline, but Air Europa and Spanair fly most domestic routes at lower prices. The budget airline Vueling heavily promotes its Internet bookings, which are often the country's cheapest domestic flight prices. The airline is servicing more and more major Spanish cities on and off the mainland and outside of Spain offers cheap flights to Amsterdam, Brussels, Berlin, Lisbon, Milan, Rome, and Paris.

The further from your travel date you purchase the ticket, the more bargains you're likely to find. Air Europa and Spanair also travel both within Spain and to the rest of Europe.

Iberia runs a shuttle, the *puente aereo,* between Madrid and Barcelona from around 7 AM to 11 PM; planes depart hourly and around every 15 to 20 minutes during the morning and afternoon commute hours. You don't need to reserve ahead; you can buy your tickets at the airport ticket counter upon arriving or book online at Iberia.com. Passengers can now also use the newly installed self-service check-in counters to avoid queues. Terminal C in the Barcelona airport is used exclusively by the shuttle; in Madrid, the shuttle departs from the newly opened Terminal 4.

Airline Contacts **Air Europa** (☎888/238-7672 and 902/401501 🌐www.air-europa.com). **American Airlines** (☎800/433-7300 🌐www.aa.com). **Continental Airlines** (☎800/523-3273 for U.S. and Mexico reservations, 800/231-0856 for international reservations 🌐www.continental.com). **Delta Airlines** (☎800/221-1212 for U.S. reservations, 800/241-4141 for international reservations 🌐www.delta.com). **Iberia** (☎800/772-4642 🌐www.iberia.com). **Northwest Airlines** (☎800/225-2525 🌐www.nwa.com). **Spanair** (☎888/545-5757 🌐www.spanair.com). **United Airlines** (☎800/864-8331 for U.S. reservations, 800/538-2929 for international reservations 🌐www.united.com). **USAirways** (☎800/428-4322 for U.S. and Canada reservations, 800/622-1015 for international reservations 🌐www.usairways.com).

Within Spain **Air Europa** (☎902/401501 🌐www.air-europa.com). **Iberia** (☎902/400500 🌐www.iberia.com). **Spanair** (☎902/131415 🌐www.spanair.com). **Vueling** (☎902/333933 🌐www.vueling.com).

BY BOAT

Regular car ferries connect the United Kingdom with northern Spain. Brittany Ferries sails from Plymouth to Santander, P&O European Ferries from Portsmouth to Bilbao. Trasmediterránea connects mainland Spain to the Balearic and Canary islands. If you want to drive from Spain to Morocco directly (using the ferry) there are only two options, with one being much faster than the other. Otherwise, it is necessary to travel to either Ceuta or Melilla, two Spanish enclaves on the North African coast, and then move on to Morocco. Trasmediterránea operates services from Algeciras either to Ceuta or directly to Tangier, and from Málaga and Almería to Melilla. Buquebus operates fast ferries from Algeciras to Ceuta. However, the fastest and most direct route to Africa proper is from Tarifa to Tangier and operated by FRS.

INFORMATION

U.K. to Spain **Brittany Ferries** (☎0239/289-2200 🌐www.brittany-ferries.com). **P&O European Ferries** (☎0239/230-1000 🌐www.poferries.com).

In Spain **Buquebus** (☎902/414242 🌐www.buquebus.es). **FRS** (☎956/681830 🌐www.frs.es). **Trasmediterránea** (☎902/454645 🌐www.trasmediterranea.com).

BY BUS

Within Spain, a mix of private companies provide bus services that range from knee-crunchingly basic to luxurious. Fares are lower than the corresponding train fares, and service is more extensive: if you want to reach a town not served by train, you can be sure a bus goes there. Smaller towns don't usually have a central bus depot, so ask the tourist office where to wait for the bus to your destination. Note that service is less frequent on weekends. Spain's major national long-haul bus line is Alsa-Enatcar. For a longer haul, you can travel to Spain by bus (Eurolines/National EXpress, for example) from London, Paris, Rome, Frankfurt, Prague, and other major European cities. It's a long journey, but the buses are modern. Although it may once have been the case that international bus travel was significantly cheaper than air travel, new budget airlines have changed the equation. For perhaps a little more money and a large savings of travel hours, flying is increasingly the better option.

Most of Spain's larger bus companies have buses with comfortable seats and adequate legroom; on longer journeys (two hours or longer), a movie is shown on board, and earphones are provided. Except for smaller, regional buses that travel only short hops, all buses have a bathroom on board. Nonetheless, most long-haul buses usually stop at least once every two to three hours for a snack and bathroom break. Smoking is prohibited on buses.

Road and traffic conditions can make or break the journey; Spain's highways, particularly along major routes, are well maintained. That may not be the case in the country's more rural areas, where you could be in for a bumpy ride—sometimes exacerbated by older buses with worn shock absorbers. Alsa-Enatcar has two luxury classes in addition to its regular seating. Supra Clase includes roomy leather seats and on board meals; also, you have the option of *asientos individuales,* individual seats (with no other seat on either side) that line one side of the bus. The next class is the Eurobus, with comfortable seats and plenty of legroom. The Supra Clase and Eurobus usually cost, respectively, up to one-third and one-fourth more than the regular seats.

If you plan to return to your initial destination, you can save by buying a round-trip ticket, instead of one-way. Also, some of Spain's smaller, regional bus lines offer multitrip bus passes, which are worthwhile if you plan to make multiple trips between two fixed destinations within the region. Generally, these tickets offer a savings of 20% per journey; you can buy these tickets only in the bus station (not on the bus). The general rule for children is that if they occupy a seat, they pay. Check the bus Web sites for deals (*ofertas*); you'll often find discounts for mid-week and/or round-trip tickets to specific destinations.

In Spain's larger cities, you can pick up schedule and fare information at the bus station; smaller towns may not have a bus station but just a bus stop. Schedules are sometimes listed at the bus stop; otherwise, call the bus company directly or ask at the tourist office, which can usually supply all schedule and fare information.

At bus station ticket counters, generally all major credit cards (except American Express) are accepted. If you buy your ticket on the bus, it's cash only. Traveler's checks are almost never accepted. Big lines such as Enatcar are now encouraging online purchasing. Once your ticket is booked, there's no need to go to the terminal sales desk—it's simply a matter of showing up at the bus with your ticket number and ID. The smaller regional services are increasingly providing online purchasing, too, but will often require that your ticket be picked up at the terminal sales desk.

During peak travel times (Easter, August, and Christmas), it's a good idea to make a reservation at least a week in advance.

From the U.K. Eurolines/National Express (☎01582/404511 or 0990/143219 🌐www.eurolines.com).

In Spain Alsa-Enatcar (✉Estación Sur de Autobuses, Calle Méndez Álvaro, Madrid ☎902/422242 🌐www.enatcar.com).

Bus Tours Marsans (✉Gran Vía 59, Madrid ☎902/306090). **Pullmantur** (✉Pl. de Oriente 8, Madrid ☎91/541–1805 🌐www.pullmantur-spain.com).

BY CAR

Your own driver's license is valid in Spain, but you may want to get an International Driver's Permit for extra assurance, as having one may save you a problem with local authorities. Permits are available from the American or Canadian Automobile Association (AAA or CAA), or, in the United Kingdom, from the Automobile Association or Royal Automobile Club (AA or RAC). These international permits, valid only in conjunction with your regular driver's license (so have both on hand), are universally recognized.

Driving is the best way to see Spain's rural areas. The main cities are connected by a network of excellent four-lane *s* (freeways) and *autopistas* (toll freeways; "toll" is *peaje*), which are designated with the letter A and have speed limits of up to 120 km/h (74 mph). The letter N indicates a *carretera nacional* (basic national route), which may have four or two lanes, but these days they have largely been replaced with an E prefix, denoting the European route number, and an A prefix, denoting the new national route number. Smaller towns and villages are connected by a network of secondary roads maintained by regional, provincial, and local governments. Spain's major routes bear heavy traffic, especially during holidays. Drive with care: Spain has a yearly road toll that is ghastly—most accidents are speed related. The roads are shared by a potentially perilous mixture of local drivers and non-Spanish vacationers, some of whom are accustomed to driving on the left side of the road. Be prepared, too, for heavy truck traffic on national routes, which, in the case of two-lane roads, can have you creeping along for hours.

GASOLINE

Gas stations are plentiful, and most on major routes and in big cities are open 24 hours. On less-traveled routes, gas stations are usually open 7 AM–11 PM. If a gas station is closed, it's required by law to post the address and directions to the nearest open station—but this is rarely adhered to, so plan your trip carefully. Most stations are self-service, though prices are the same as those at full-service stations. You punch in the amount of gas you want (in euros, not in liters), unhook the nozzle, pump the gas, and then pay. At night, however, you must pay before you fill up. Most pumps offer a choice of gas, including leaded, unleaded, and diesel, so be careful to pick the right one for your car. All newer cars in Spain use *gasolina sin plomo* (unleaded gas), which is available in two grades, 95 and 98 octane. *Super,* regular 97-octane leaded gas, is gradually being phased out. Prices vary little among stations and were at this writing €1 a liter for leaded, 97 octane; €1 a liter for unleaded, 95 octane; and €1.05 a liter for unleaded, 98 octane. Credit cards are widely accepted.

PARKING

Parking is, almost without exception, a nightmare in all Spanish cities and towns. Although parking meters are frequently used, finding an empty space to park in is another matter altogether. Parking lots are available, often underground, but spaces are at a premium. Another frequent problem is that many cities now have one-way systems, and it can be more than frustrating to drive around and around trying to find an empty space. The lesson is that if you don't need to go into a city or town center with your car then leave it at your hotel and take public transport or a taxi.

ROAD CONDITIONS

Spain's highway system includes some 6,000 km (3,600 mi) of beautifully maintained superhighways. Still, you'll find some stretches of major national highways that are only two lanes wide, where traffic often backs up behind slow, heavy trucks. *Autopista* tolls are steep, but as a result, these highways are often less crowded than the free ones. If you're driving down through Catalonia, be aware that there are more tolls here than anywhere else in Spain. This can result in a quicker journey, but at a sizeable cost. If you spring for the autopistas, you'll find that many of the rest stops are nicely landscaped and have cafeterias with reasonable but overpriced food. Rather than ordering a plate of food, a cheese or ham *bocadillo* (baguette-style sandwich) offers a much cheaper and often tastier alternative.

Most Spanish cities have notoriously long morning and evening rush hours. Traffic jams are especially bad in and around Barcelona and Madrid. If possible, avoid the morning rush, which can last until noon, and the evening rush, which lasts from 7 to 9. Also be aware that on the dates corresponding to the beginning, the middle, and the end of July and August, the country suffers its worst traffic jams (delays of six to eight hours are common) as millions of Spaniards embark on, or return from, their annual vacations.

ROADSIDE EMERGENCIES

The rental agencies Hertz and Avis have 24 hour breakdown service. If you belong to an auto club (AAA, CAA, or AA), you can get emergency assistance from the Spanish counterpart, RACE.

Emergency Services RACE (✉José Abascal 10, Madrid ☎900/200093).

RULES OF THE ROAD

Spaniards drive on the right; they pass on the left—so stay in the right-hand slow lane when not passing. Horns are banned in cities, but that doesn't keep people from blasting away. Children under 10 may not ride in the front seat, and seat belts are compulsory for both front and backseat riders. Speed limits are 50 km/h (31 mph) in cities, 100 km/h (62 mph) on N roads, 120 km/h (74 mph) on the *autopista* or *autovía,* and, unless otherwise signposted, 90 km/h (56 mph) on other roads.

Spanish highway police are increasingly vigilant about speeding and illegal passing. Fines start at €90, and police are empowered to demand payment from non-Spanish drivers on the spot. It is an unfortunate reality that rental-car drivers are disproportionately targeted by police for speeding and illegal passing, so play it safe.

Although local drivers, especially in cities such as Madrid, will park their cars just about anywhere, you should park only in legal spots. Parking fines are steep, and your car might well be towed, resulting in fines, hassles, and wasted time.

BY TRAIN

International overnight trains run from Madrid to Lisbon and from Barcelona and Madrid to Paris (both around 11½ hours). An overnight train also runs from Barcelona to Geneva (10 hours) and Zurich (13 hours).

Spain's wonderful high-speed train, the 290-km/h (180-mph) AVE, travels between Madrid and Seville (with a stop in Córdoba) in less than three hours at prices starting around €86 each way. The AVE also travels from Madrid to Lleida (with a stop in Zaragoza), and there are plans to extend it to Barcelona by 2007. The trip to Zaragoza is just under two hours, and starts at €63 each way; to Lleida, the trip is just under three hours and starts at €70 each way. The fast Talgo service is also efficient.

However, the rest of the state-run rail system—known as RENFE—remains below par by European standards. Local train travel within cities is efficient, but many long-distance trips are tediously slow. Although some overnight trains have comfortable sleeper cars, first-class fares that include a sleeping compartment are comparable to, or more expensive than, airfares.

For shorter routes with convenient schedules, trains are the most economical way to go. First- and second-class seats are reasonably priced, and you can get a bunk in a compartment with five other people for a supplement of about €32.

Commuter trains and most long-distance trains forbid smoking, though some long-distance trains have smoking cars.

If you're coming from the United States or Canada and are planning extensive train travel throughout Europe, check Rail Europe for Eurail passes. Whichever of the many available passes you choose, remember that you must buy your pass before you leave for Europe.

Spain is one of 17 European countries in which you can use the Eurail Global Pass, which buys you unlimited first-class rail travel in all participating countries for the duration of the pass. If you plan to rack up the miles, get a standard pass. These are available for 15 days ($651), 21 days ($846), one month ($1,050), two months ($1,482), and three months ($1,829). If your needs are more limited, look into a Eurail Global Pass Flexi, which costs less than a Global Pass and buys you either 10 days in 2 months at $770 or 15 days in 2 months for $1,012.

In addition to these Rail Europe sells the Eurail Global Pass Youth (you must be younger than 26), and a wide variety of other passes in different formats.

If Spain is your only destination, check into Rail Europe's Spain passes. Consider a Eurail Spain Pass that provies any 3 days of unlimited train travel in Spain in a 2 month period for $244 1st class and $190 2nd class, or the Eurail Spain Rail 'n Drive Pass that combines 3 days unlimited train travel and 2 days in a rental car. There are also combination passes for those visiting Spain and Portugal, Spain and France, and Spain and Italy.

You should also check for RENFE discounts in Spain. If you purchase a round-trip ticket on AVE or any of RENFE's Grandes Lineas, which are its faster, long-distance trains (including the Talgo) while in Spain, you'll get a 20% discount. You have up to 60 days to use the return portion of your ticket. Passengers with international airline tickets who are traveling on the AVE within 48 hours of their arrival receive a 25% discount on their AVE ticket. This discount also applies to passengers with national airline tickets for travel to or from the Canary and Balearic Islands and Melilla. On regional trains, you receive a 10% discount on round-trip tickets, and you have up to 15 days to use the return portion. Children and students also receive good discounts. Note that even if you just buy a one-way ticket to your destination, you can still receive the round-trip discount if you present your ticket stub at the train station when buying your return (provided your return is within the allotted time frame, either 15 or 60 days).

Most Spaniards buy train tickets in advance at the train station's *taquilla* (ticket office). The lines can be long, so give yourself plenty of time. For popular train routes, you will need to reserve tickets more than a few days in advance and pick them up at least a day before traveling; call RENFE to inquire. The ticket clerks at the stations rarely speak English, so if you need help or advice in planning a more complex train journey, you may be better off going to a travel agency that displays the blue-and-yellow RENFE sign. The price is the same. For shorter, regional train trips, you can often buy your tickets directly from machines in the main train stations. Note that if your itinerary is set in stone and has little room for error, you can buy RENFE tickets through Rail Europe before you leave home.

You can buy train tickets with a major credit card (except for American Express) at most city train stations. In the smaller towns and villages, it's cash only. Traveler's checks are no longer accepted.

Seat reservations are required on most long-distance and some other trains, particularly high-speed trains, and are wise on any train that might be crowded. You'll also need a reservation if you want a sleeping berth. Many travelers assume that rail passes guarantee them seats on the trains they wish to ride: not so. Reserve seats in advance even if you're using a rail pass.

The easiest way to make reservations is to use the TIKNET service on the RENFE Web site. TIKNET involves registering and providing your credit-card information. When you make the reservation, you'll be given a car and seat assignment and a *localizador* (translated as "localizer" on the English version of the site; it is similar to a confirmation number). Print out the reservations page or write down the car number, seat number, and localizer. When traveling, go to your assigned seat on the train. When the conductor comes around, give him the localizer, and he will issue the ticket on the spot. You'll need your passport and, in most cases, the credit card you used for the reservation (in Spain, credit cards are often used for an additional form of ID). The AVE trains check you in at the gate to the platform, where you provide the localizer. You can review your pending reservations online at any time.

Caveats: the first time you use TIKNET, you must pick up the tickets at a RENFE station (most major airports have a RENFE booth, so you can retrieve your tickets as soon as you get off your plane). A 15% cancellation fee is charged if you cancel more than two hours after making the reservation. You cannot buy tickets online for certain regional lines or for commuter lines (*cercanias*). Station agents cannot alter TIKNET reservations: you must do this yourself online. If a train is booked, the TIKNET process doesn't reveal this until the final stage of the reservation attempt—then it gives you a cryptic error message in a little box—but if you reserve a few days in advance, it's unlikely you'll encounter this problem except at Easter, Christmas, or during the first week of August.

There's no line per se at the train station for advance tickets (and often for information); you take a number and wait until it's called. Ticket clerks at stations rarely speak English, so if you need help or advice in planning a more complex train journey, you may be better off going to a travel agency that displays the blue-and-yellow RENFE sign. A small commission (American Express Viajes charges €3) should be expected.

Information **RENFE** (☎902/240202 ⊕www.renfe.es).

Rail Passes **Rail Europe** (☎877/456-7245 or 800/361-7245 ⊕www.raileurope.com). **RENFE** (☎902/157507 ⊕www.renfe.es).

FROM THE U.K.

Train services to Spain from the United Kingdom are not as frequent, fast, or affordable as flights, and you have to change trains—and stations—in Paris. Allow 2 hours for the changing process, then 13 hours for the trip from Paris to Madrid. It's worth paying extra for the Talgo or Puerta del Sol express trains to avoid changing trains again at the Spanish border. If you're under 26 years old, Eurotrain has excellent deals.

Information **Eurotrain** (✉52 Grosvenor Gardens, London SW1W 0AG, U.K. ☎0207/730-8832). **Transalpino** (✉71-75 Buckingham Palace Rd., London SW1W 0RE, U.K. ☎0207/834-9656).

ON THE GROUND

COMMUNICATIONS

INTERNET

The Internet boom came a bit late to Spain, with few or limited Internet cafés in the big cities at the turn of this century. But all that has changed, and the Internet is now in full swing. Huge increases in migration to the country's bigger cities means demand has skyrocketed for *locutorios* (cheap international phone centers), which double as places to get on the Internet. In addition to the locutorios, where Internet access is not always reliable, there are upmarket cafés and bars that provide Internet service, often at faster speeds. The most you're likely to pay for Internet access is about €3 an hour.

Internet cafés are most common in tourist and student precincts. If you can't find one easily, ask at either the tourist office or a hotel's front desk. There's no perfect guide to the many cybercafés in Spain, but Ocio Latino's Web site (🌐*www.ociolatino.com*) is probably the best. Click on "Guía Latina" and then "locutorios."

Internet access within Spanish hotels is not widespread and tends to be offered only in the more expensive hotels. And those that do offer Internet access have varying services: Internet kiosks or rooms, in-room data ports or DSL, and/or Wi-Fi (either free or with a fee; sometimes in-room, sometimes in common areas).

Contacts Cybercafes (🌐www.cybercafes.com) lists over 4,000 Internet cafés worldwide.

PHONES

The good news is that you can now make a direct-dial telephone call from virtually any point on earth. The bad news? You can't always do so cheaply. Calling from a hotel is almost always the most expensive option; hotels usually add huge surcharges to all calls, particularly international ones. In some countries you can phone from call centers or even the post office. Calling cards usually keep costs to a minimum, but only if you purchase them locally. And then there are mobile phones, which are sometimes more prevalent—particularly in the developing world—than land lines; as expensive as mobile phone calls can be, they are still usually a much cheaper option than calling from your hotel.

Spain's phone system is perfectly efficient but can be expensive. Direct dialing is the norm. Most travelers buy phone cards, which for €5 or €6 allows for about three hours of calls nationally and internationally. Phone cards can be used with any hotel, bar, or public telephone. Although some phone cards from Australia, the United Kingdom, and the United States can be used in Spain, those with the best value are found in Spain itself. There are many cards that work for only certain regions of the country, but the all-encompassing *Fantastic* card works for anywhere in the world. Phone cards can be bought at any tobacco shop or at most Internet cafés. Such cafés also often provide phone booths that allow you to call at cheaper rates. If you do use coins, be aware that the public phones in the street are cheaper than the green and blue phones found inside most bars and restaurants. Spain's main telephone company is Telefónica.

Note that only cell phones conforming to the European GSM standard will work in Spain. Buying a cell phone without a contract (i.e., paying for your calls by adding money to your phone either via a cell-phone card or at a cell-phone store) is popular in Spain. If you're going to be traveling in Spain for an extended period of time and plan on using a cell phone frequently to call within Spain, then buying a phone will often turn out to be a big money-saver. Using a Spanish cell phone means avoiding the hefty long-distance charges accrued when using your cell phone from home to call within Spain. Prices fluctuate, but offers start at about €40 for a phone with about €30 worth of calls.

The country code for Spain is 34. The country code is 1 for the United States and Canada.

CALLING WITHIN SPAIN

For general information in Spain, dial 1003. International operators, who generally speak English, are at 025.

All area codes begin with a 9. To call within Spain—even locally—dial the area code first. Numbers preceded by a 900 code are no longer toll-free and often have long wait times, which can be expensive. Phone numbers starting with a 6 are going to a cellular phone. Note that when calling a cell phone, you do not need to dial the area code first; also, calls to cell phones are significantly more expensive than calls to regular phones.

You'll find pay phones in individual booths, in special telephone offices (*locutorios*), and in many bars and restaurants. Most have a digital readout so you can see your money ticking away. If you're calling with coins, you need at least €0.15 to call locally and €0.45 to call another province. Simply insert the coins and wait for a dial tone. (With older models, you line coins up in a groove on top of the dial and they drop down as needed.) Note that rates are reduced on weekends and after 8 PM during the week.

CALLING OUTSIDE SPAIN

International calls are awkward from coin-operated pay phones because of the many coins needed; and they can be expensive from hotels, as the hotel often adds a hefty surcharge. Your best bet is to use a public phone that accepts phone cards or go to the local telephone office, the *locutorio:* every town has one, and major cities have several. The locutorios near the center of town are generally more expensive; farther from the center, the rates are sometimes as much as one-third less. You converse in a quiet, private booth, and you're charged according to the meter. If the call ends up costing around €4 or more, you can usually pay with Visa or MasterCard.

To make an international call yourself, dial 00, then the country code, then the area code and number.

The country code for the United States is 1.

Madrid's main telephone office is at Gran Vía 28. There's another at the main post office, and a third at Paseo Recoletos 43, just off Plaza Colón. In Barcelona you can phone overseas from the office at Carrer de Fontanella 4, off Plaça de Catalunya.

Before you leave home, find out your long-distance company's access code in Spain (⇨ *Access Codes, below*).

ACCESS CODES

AT&T Direct (☎900/990011). **MCI WorldPhone** (☎900/990014). **Sprint International Access** (☎900/990013).

General Information AT&T (☎800/222-0300). **MCI WorldCom** (☎800/444-4444). **Sprint** (☎800/793-1153).

CALLING CARDS

To use a newer pay phone you need a special phone card (*tarjeta telefónica*), which you can buy at any tobacco shop or newsstand, in various denominations. Some such phones also accept credit cards, but phone cards are more reliable.

MOBILE PHONES

If you have a multiband phone (some countries use different frequencies than what's used in the United States) and your service provider uses the world-standard GSM network (as do T-Mobile, Cingular, and Verizon), you can probably use your phone abroad. Roaming fees can be steep, however: 99¢ a minute is considered reasonable. And overseas you normally pay the toll charges for incoming

LOCAL DO'S & TABOOS

GREETINGS

When addressing Spaniards with whom you are not well acquainted or who are elderly, use the formal *usted* rather than the familiar *tu*.

DRESS

Some town councils are cracking down on people wearing swimsuits in public spaces. Use your common sense—it's unlikely you'd be allowed entry in a bar or restaurant wearing swimming attire back home, so don't do it when overseas. Be respectful when visiting churches: casual dress is fine if it's not gaudy or unkempt. Spaniards object to men going bare-chested anywhere other than the beach or poolside.

OUT ON THE TOWN

These days, the Spanish are generally very informal, and casual-smart dress is accepted in most places.

DOING BUSINESS

Spanish office hours can be confusing to the uninitiated. Some offices stay open more or less continuously from 9 to 3, with a very short lunch break. Others open in the morning, break up the day with a long lunch break of two to three hours, then reopen at 4 or 5 until 7 or 8. Spaniards enjoy a certain notoriety for their lack of punctuality, but this has changed dramatically in recent years, and you are expected to show up for meetings on time. Smart dress is the norm.

Spaniards in international fields tend to conduct business with foreigners in English. If you speak Spanish, address new colleagues with the formal *usted* and the corresponding verb conjugations, then follow their lead in switching to the familiar *tu* once a working relationship has been established.

LANGUAGE

One of the best ways to avoid being an Ugly American is to learn a little of the local language. You need not strive for fluency; even just mastering a few basic words and terms is bound to make chatting with the locals more rewarding.

Although Spaniards exported their language to all of Central and South America, Spanish is not the principal language in all of Spain. Outside their big cities, the Basques speak Euskera. In Catalonia, you'll hear Catalan throughout the region, just as you'll hear Gallego in Galicia and Valenciano in Valencia (the latter, as with Mallorquín in Majorca and Menorquín in Menorca, are considered Catalan dialects). Although almost everyone in these regions also speaks and understands Spanish, local radio and television stations may broadcast in their respective languages, and road signs may be printed (or spray-painted over) with the preferred regional language. Spanish is referred to as Castellano, or Castilian.

Fortunately, Spanish is fairly easy to pick up, and your efforts to speak it will be graciously received. Learn at least the following basic phrases: *buenos días* (hello—until 2 PM), *buenas tardes* (good afternoon—until 8 PM), *buenas noches* (hello—after dark), *por favor* (please), *gracias* (thank you), *adiós* (goodbye), *sí* (yes), *no* (no), *los servicios* (the toilets), *la cuenta* (bill/check), and *habla inglés?* (do you speak English?), *no comprendo* (I don't understand). If your Spanish breaks down, you should have no trouble finding people who speak English in major cities and coastal resorts, but you won't necessarily be able to count on the bus driver or the passerby on the street. It's much more likely that you'll find an English-language speaker if you approach people under age 30.

calls. It's almost always cheaper to send a text message than to make a call, since text messages have a very low set fee (often less than 5¢).

If you just want to make local calls, consider buying a new SIM card (note that your provider may have to unlock your phone for you to use a different SIM card) and a prepaid service plan in the destination. You'll then have a local number and can make local calls at local rates. If your trip is extensive, you could also simply buy a new cell phone in your destination, as the initial cost will be offset over time.

TIP→If you travel internationally frequently, save one of your old mobile phones or buy a cheap one on the Internet; ask your cell phone company to unlock it for you, and take it with you as a travel phone, buying a new SIM card with pay-as-you-go service in each destination.

Contacts **Cellular Abroad** (800/287-5072 www.cellularabroad.com) rents and sells GMS phones and sells SIM cards that work in many countries. **Mobal** (888/888-9162 www.mobalrental.com) rents mobiles and sells GSM phones (starting at $49) that will operate in 140 countries. Per-call rates vary throughout the world. **Planet Fone** (888/988-4777 www.planetfone.com) rents cell phones, but the per-minute rates are expensive.

CUSTOMS & DUTIES

You're always allowed to bring goods of a certain value back home without having to pay any duty or import tax. But there's a limit on the amount of tobacco and liquor you can bring back duty-free, and some countries have separate limits for perfumes; for exact figures, check with your customs department. The values of so-called "duty-free" goods are included in these amounts. When you shop abroad, save all your receipts, as customs inspectors may ask to see them as well as the items you purchased. If the total value of your goods is more than the duty-free limit, you'll have to pay a tax (most often a flat percentage) on the value of everything beyond that limit.

From countries that are not part of the European Union, visitors age 15 and over may *enter* Spain duty-free with up to 200 cigarettes or 50 cigars, up to 1 liter of alcohol over 22 proof, and up to 2 liters of wine.

U.S. Information U.S. Customs and Border Protection (www.cbp.gov).

EATING OUT

Sitting around a table eating and talking is a huge part of Spanish culture, defining much of people's daily routines. Sitting in the middle of a typical bustling restaurant here goes a long way toward showing how fundamental food can be to Spanish lives.

Although Spain has always had an extraordinary range of regional cuisine, in the past decade or so its restaurants have won it international recognition at the highest levels. A new generation of Spanish chefs—led by the revolutionary Ferran Adrià—has transformed classic dishes to suit contemporary tastes, drawing on some of the freshest ingredients in Europe.

One of the major drawbacks of drinking and eating in Spanish bars and restaurants has been the unbridled smoking in almost all of them. The new antismoking laws introduced by the national government at the beginning of 2006 is changing all that. Establishments within shopping malls, theaters, and cinemas are now strictly no-smoking. All establishments that measure 100 meters squared or more are obliged to provide a no-smoking section. Children may not eat outside this section. However, establishments smaller than this size retain the option for the time being to permit smoking across the board or to ban it altogether. With a few exceptions, the proprietors of these establishments have maintained the status quo, presumably because of the fact that one in three Spaniards smoke, and they are fearful of losing clients. This may change over time as locals become more accustomed to the new regulations forbidding smoking in public places, shops, and places of work. All eating and drinking establishments are obliged to inform clients by posting a sign at the entrance. *Se permite fumar* means you can smoke, *No se permite fumar* means you can't, and *Sala habilitada para no fumadores* means a nonsmoking section is available.

MEALS & MEALTIMES

Most restaurants in Spain do not serve breakfast (*desayuno*); for coffee and carbs, head to a bar or *cafetería*. Outside major hotels, which serve morning buffets, breakfast in Spain is usually limited to coffee and toast or a roll. Lunch (*comida* or *almuerzo*) traditionally consists of an appetizer, a main course, and dessert, followed by coffee and perhaps a liqueur. Between lunch and dinner the best way to snack is to sample some tapas (appetizers) at a bar; normally you can choose from quite a variety. Dinner (*cena*) is somewhat lighter, with perhaps only one course. In addition to an à la carte menu, most restaurants offer a daily fixed-price menu (*menú del día*), consisting of two courses, wine, and dessert at a very attractive price (usually between €6 and €12). Coffee usually costs extra. If your waiter does not suggest the menú del día when you're seated, ask for it—"*Hay menú del día, por favor?*" Restaurants in many of the larger tourist areas will have the menú del día posted outside. The menú del día is traditionally offered only at lunch, but increasingly it's also offered at dinner in popular tourist destinations.

Mealtimes in Spain are later than elsewhere in Europe, and later still in Madrid and the southern region of Andalusia. Lunch starts around 2 or 2:30 (closer to 3 in Madrid), and dinner after 9 (later in Madrid). Weekend eating times, especially dinner, can begin upward of about an hour later. In areas with heavy tourist traffic, some restaurants open a bit earlier.

WORD OF MOUTH

Was the service stellar or not up to snuff? Did the food give you shivers of delight or leave you cold? Did the prices and portions make you happy or sad? Rate restaurants and write your own reviews in Travel Ratings or start a discussion about your favorite places in Travel Talk on www.fodors.com. Your comments might even appear in our books. Yes, you, too, can be a correspondent!

Unless otherwise noted, the restaurants listed in this guide are open daily for lunch and dinner.

PAYING

Credit cards are widely accepted in Spanish restaurants, but beware that smaller establishments often do not take them. If you pay by credit card and you want to leave a small tip above and beyond the service charge, leave the tip in cash.

For guidelines see Tipping.

RESERVATIONS & DRESS

Regardless of where you are, it's a good idea to make a reservation if you can. In some places, it's expected. We only mention them specifically when reservations are essential (there's no other way you'll ever get a table) or when they are not accepted. For popular restaurants, book as far ahead as you can (often 30 days), and reconfirm as soon as you arrive. (Large parties should always call ahead to check the reservations policy.) We mention dress only when men are required to wear a jacket or a jacket and tie.

WINES, BEER & SPIRITS

Apart from its famous wines, Spain produces many brands of lager, the most popular of which are San Miguel, Cruzcampo, Aguila, Mahou, and Estrella.

Jerez de la Frontera is Europe's largest producer of brandy and is a major source of sherry. Catalonia produces most of the world's *cava* (sparkling wine). Spanish law prohibits the sale of alcohol to people under 18.

ELECTRICITY

Spain's electrical current is 220 volts, 50 cycles alternating current (AC); wall outlets take Continental-type plugs, with two round prongs.

Consider making a small investment in a universal adapter, which has several types of plugs in one lightweight, compact unit. Most laptops and mobile phone chargers are dual voltage (i.e., they operate equally well on 110 and 220 volts), so require only an adapter. These days the same is true of small appliances such as hair dryers. Always check labels and manufacturer instructions to be sure. Don't use 110 volt outlets marked FOR SHAVERS ONLY for high-wattage appliances such as hair-dryers.

Contacts Steve Kropla's Help for World Travelers (www.kropla.com) has information on electrical and telephone plugs around the world. **Walkabout Travel Gear** (www.walkabouttravelgear.com) has a good coverage of electricity under "adapters."

EMERGENCIES

The pan-European emergency phone number (112) is operative in some parts of Spain, but not all. If it doesn't work, dial the emergency numbers below for the national police, local police, fire department, or medical services. On the road, there are emergency phones marked SOS at regular intervals on *autovías* (freeways) and *autopistas* (toll highways). If your documents are stolen, contact both the local police and your embassy. If you lose a credit card, phone the issuer immediately.

Foreign Embassies Fuengirola (Av. Juan Goméz 8, Apt. 1c 952/474891). **Madrid** (C. Serrano 75, Salamanca 91/587-2200). **Seville** (Paseo de las Delicias 7, Arenal 95/423-1885).

General Emergency Contacts

National police (091). **Local police** (092). **Fire department** (080). **Medical service** (061).

HEALTH

The most common types of illnesses are caused by contaminated food and water. Make sure food has been thoroughly cooked and is served to you fresh and hot; avoid vegetables and fruits that you haven't washed (in bottled or purified water) or peeled yourself. If you have problems, mild cases of traveler's diarrhea may respond to Imodium (known generically as loperamide) or Pepto-Bismol. Be sure to drink plenty of fluids; if you can't keep fluids down, seek medical help immediately.

Infectious diseases can be airborne or passed via mosquitoes and ticks and through direct or indirect physical contact with animals or people. Some, including Norwalk-like viruses that affect your digestive tract, can be passed along through contaminated food. Condoms can help prevent most sexually transmitted diseases, but they aren't absolutely reliable and their quality varies from country to country. Speak with your physician and/or check the CDC or World Health Organization Web sites for health alerts, particularly if you're pregnant, traveling with children, or have a chronic illness.

TIP→ If you travel a lot internationally—particularly to developing nations—refer to the CDC's *Health Information for International Travel* **(aka Traveler's Health Yellow Book). Info from it is posted on the CDC Web site (www.cdc.gov/travel/yb), or you can buy a copy from your local bookstore for $24.95.**

SPECIFIC ISSUES IN SPAIN

Medical care is good in Spain, but nursing is perfunctory, as relatives are expected to stop by and look after patients' needs. In some popular destinations, such as the Costa del Sol, there are volunteer English interpreters on hand. In 2004, Spain was documented by the World Health Organization as having the highest number of cumulative AIDS cases in Europe, and like many European countries, it is once again experiencing increased rate of HIV infections. If you're applying for a work permit, you'll be asked for proof that you are HIV-negative.

In the summer, sunburn and sunstroke are real risks in Spain. On the hottest sunny days, even if you're not normally bothered by strong sun, you should cover yourself up, carry sunblock lotion (*protector solar*), drink plenty of fluids, and limit sun time for the first few days. If you require medical attention for any problem, ask your hotel's front desk for assistance or go to the nearest public **Centro de Salud** (day hospital); in serious cases, you'll be referred to the regional hospital.

OVER-THE-COUNTER REMEDIES

Over-the-counter remedies are available at any *farmacia* (pharmacy), recognizable by the large green crosses outside. Some will look familiar, such as *aspirina* (aspirin), and other medications are sold under various brand names. If you get traveler's diarrhea, ask for *un antidiarreico* (the general term for antidiarrheal medicine); Fortasec is a well-known brand. Mild cases may respond to Imodium (known generically as loperamide) or Pepto-Bismol. To keep from getting dehydrated, drink plenty of purified water or herbal tea. In severe cases, rehydrate yourself with a salt-sugar solution—½ teaspoon salt (*sal*) and 4 tablespoons sugar (*azúcar*) per quart of water.

If you regularly take a nonprescription medicine, take a sample box or bottle with you, and the Spanish pharmacist will provide you with its local equivalent.

HOURS OF OPERATION

The ritual of a long afternoon siesta is no longer as ubiquitous as it once was. However, the tradition does remain, and many people take a postlunch nap before returning to work or continuing on with their day. The two- to three-hour lunch makes it possible to eat and then snooze. Siestas generally begin at 1 or 2 and end between 4 and 5, depending on the city and the sort of business. The midafternoon siesta—often a half-hour power nap in front of the TV—fits naturally into the workday cycle, since Spaniards tend to work until 7 or 8 PM.

Traditionally, Spain's climate created the siesta as a time to preserve energy while afternoon temperatures spiked. After the sun began setting, Spaniards went back to working, shopping, and taking their leisurely *paseo,* or stroll. In the big cities—particularly with the advent of air-conditioning—the heat has less of an effect on the population; in the small towns in the south of Spain, however, many still use a siesta as a way to wait out the weather.

Until a decade or so ago, it was common for many businesses to close for a month in the July/August period. Europeanization, changing trading hours, and a booming consumerism are gradually altering that custom. These days many small businesses are more likely to close down for two weeks only, maybe three. When open, they often run on a summer schedule, which can mean a longer-than-usual siesta (sometimes up to four hours), a shorter working day (until 3 PM only), and no Saturday afternoon trading at all.

Banks are generally open weekdays from 8:30 or 9 until 2 or 2:30. From October to May the major banks open on Saturday from 8:30 or 9 until 2 or 2:30, and savings banks are also open Thursday 4:30 to 8. Currency exchanges at airports, train stations, and in the city center stay open later; you can also cash traveler's checks at El Corte Inglés department stores until 10 PM (some branches close at 9 PM or 9:30 PM). Most government offices are open weekdays 9 to 2.

Most museums are open from 9:30 to 2 and 4 to 7 six days a week, every day but Monday. Schedules are subject to change, particularly between the high and low seasons, so confirm opening hours before you make plans. A few large museums, such as Madrid's Prado and Reina Sofía and Barcelona's Picasso Museum, stay open all day, without a siesta.

Pharmacies keep normal business hours (9 to 1:30 and 5 to 8), but every midsize town (or city neighborhood) has a duty pharmacy that stays open 24 hours. The location of the duty pharmacy is usually posted on the front door of all pharmacies.

When planning a shopping trip, remember that almost all shops in Spain close between 1 and 2 PM for at least two hours. The only exceptions are large supermarkets and the department-store chain El Corte Inglés. Stores are generally open somewhere between 9 or 10 to 1:30 or 2 and from somewhere between 4 and 5 to 7:30 or 8. Most shops are closed on Sunday, and in Madrid and several other places they're also closed Saturday afternoon. Larger shops in tourist areas may stay open Sunday in summer and during the Christmas holiday.

HOLIDAYS

Spain's national holidays are January 1, January 6 (Epiphany), Good Friday, Easter, May 1 (May Day), August 15 (Assumption), October 12 (National Day), November 1 (All Saints' Day), December 6 (Constitution), December 8 (Immaculate Conception), and December 25.

In addition, each region, city, and town has its own holidays honoring political events and patron saints. Madrid holidays are May 2 (Madrid Day), May 15 (St. Isidro), and November 9 (Almudena). Barcelona celebrates April 23 (St. George), September 11 (Catalonia Day), and September 24 (Merce).

Many stores close during *Semana Santa* (Holy Week—also sometimes translated as Easter Week); it is the week that precedes Easter.

If a public holiday falls on a Tuesday or Thursday, remember that many businesses also close on the nearest Monday or Friday for a long weekend, called a *puente* (bridge). If a major holiday falls on a Sun day, businesses close on Monday.

MAIL

Spain's postal system, the *correos,* does work, but delivery times can vary widely. An airmail letter to the United States may take anywhere from four days to two weeks; delivery to other destinations is equally unpredictable. Sending your letters by priority mail (*urgente*) or the cheaper registered mail *certificado* ensures speedier and safer arrival.

Airmail letters to the United States and Canada cost €0.78 up to 20 grams. Letters to the United Kingdom and other EU countries cost €0.57 up to 20 grams. Letters within Spain are €0.29. Postcards carry the same rates as letters. You can buy stamps at post offices and at licensed tobacco shops.

Because mail delivery in Spain can often be slow and unreliable, it's best to have your mail held at a Spanish post office; have it addressed to LISTA DE CORREOS (the equivalent of poste restante) in a town you'll be visiting. Postal addresses should include the name of the province in parentheses, for example, Marbella (Málaga).

SHIPPING PACKAGES

When time is of the essence, or when you're sending valuable items or documents overseas, you can use a courier (*mensajero*). The major international agencies, such as Federal Express, UPS, and DHL, have representatives in Spain; the biggest Spanish courier service is Seur. MRW is another local courier that provides express delivery worldwide.

EXPRESS SERVICES

DHL (☎902/122424). **Federal Express** (☎900/100871). **MRW** (☎900/300400). **Seur** (☎902/101010). **UPS** (☎902/888820).

MONEY

Spain is no longer a budget destination, even less so in the expensive cities of Barcelona, San Sebastian, and Madrid. However, prices still compare slightly favorably with those elsewhere in Europe. Coffee (depending if it's a smaller espresso or a latte) in a bar generally costs anywhere from €0.80 to €2, again, depending on if you're standing or sitting at a bar, sitting at an inside table, or sitting at an outside terrace table. The latter is always the most expensive option—whether you're ordering coffee, a beer, or a packet of chips. Tap beer (regular size) in a bar: €1 standing or sitting at a bar, €1.50–€2 seated inside, and €1.50–€2.50 sitting outside. Small glass of wine in a bar: €1–€2.50. Soft drink: €1.20–€1.80 a bottle. Ham-and-cheese sandwich: €1.80–€2.70. Two-kilometer (1-mi) taxi ride: €2.40, but the meter keeps ticking in traffic jams. Local bus or subway ride: €0.90–€1.30. Movie ticket: €4–€6. Foreign newspaper: €2.

Prices throughout this guide are given for adults. Substantially reduced fees are almost always available for children, students, and senior citizens.

■TIP→ Banks never have every foreign currency on hand, and it may take as long as a week to order. If you're planning to exchange funds before leaving home, don't wait until the last minute.

ATMS & BANKS

Your own bank will probably charge a fee for using ATMs abroad; the foreign bank you use may also charge a fee. Nevertheless, you'll usually get a better rate of exchange at an ATM than you will at a currency-exchange office or even when changing money in a bank. And extracting funds as you need them is a safer option than carrying around a large amount of cash.

■TIP→ PIN numbers with more than four digits are not recognized at ATMs in many countries. If yours has five or more, remember to change it before you leave.

You'll find ATMs in every major city in Spain, as well as most smaller cities. ATMs will be part of the Cirrus and/or Plus networks, and will allow you to withdraw euros with your credit or debit card, provided you have a valid PIN (pronounced *peen*). Make sure your PIN code is four digits, which is required in Spain. Also, if you tend to rely on muscle memory to punch in your code, memorize the numerical equivalents before going to Spain; at some ATMs the keyboard is reverse from the American keyboard starting with a 9 in the top left.

The Spanish banking system has been hailed as Europe's most efficient on several occasions. Bank branches mushroom all over the country, especially in the cities. Banks are generally located in the town and city centers, and the majority will have an ATM. Major banks in Spain are Banco Popular (🌐*www.bancopopular.es*), Banesto (🌐*www.banesto.es*), BBVA (Banco Bilbao-Vizcaya Argentara 🌐*www.bbva.es*), and BSCH (Banco Santander Central Hispano 🌐*www.gruposantander.com*). *See Hours of Operation.*

CREDIT CARDS

Throughout this guide, the following abbreviations are used: **AE,** American Express; **DC,** Diners Club; **MC,** MasterCard; and **V,** Visa.

It's a good idea to inform your credit-card company before you travel, especially if you're going abroad and don't travel internationally very often. Otherwise, the credit-card company might put a hold on your card owing to unusual activity—not a good thing halfway through your trip. Record all your credit-card numbers—as well as the phone numbers to call if your cards are lost or stolen—in a safe place, so you're prepared should something go wrong. Both MasterCard and Visa have general numbers you can call (collect if you're abroad) if your card is lost, but you're better off calling the number of your issuing bank, since MasterCard and Visa usually just transfer you to your bank; your bank's number is usually printed on your card.

If you plan to use your credit card for cash advances, you'll need to apply for a PIN at least two weeks before your trip. Although it's usually cheaper (and safer) to use a credit card abroad for large purchases (so you can cancel payments or be reimbursed if there's a problem), note that some credit-card companies *and* the banks that issue them add substantial percentages to all foreign transactions, whether they're in a foreign currency or not. Check on these fees before leaving home, so there won't be any surprises when you get the bill.

■ **TIP→ Before you charge something, ask the merchant whether he or she plans to do a dynamic currency conversion (DCC). In such a transaction the credit-card *processor* (shop, restaurant, or hotel, not Visa or MasterCard) converts the currency and charges you in dollars. In most cases you'll pay the merchant a 3% fee for this service in addition to any credit-card company and issuing-bank foreign-transaction surcharges.**

Dynamic currency conversion programs are becoming increasingly widespread. Merchants who participate in them are supposed to ask whether you want to be charged in dollars or the local currency, but they don't always do so. And even if they do offer you a choice, they may well avoid mentioning the additional surcharges. The good news is that you *do* have a choice. And if this practice really gets your goat, you can avoid it entirely thanks to American Express; with its cards, DCC simply isn't an option.

Reporting Lost Cards American Express (☎800/528–4800 in the U.S., 336/393–1111 collect from abroad 🌐www.americanexpress.com). **Diners Club** (☎800/234–6377 in the U.S., 303/799–1504 collect from abroad 🌐www.dinersclub.com). **MasterCard** (☎800/627–8372 in the U.S., 636/722–7111 collect from abroad 🌐www.mastercard.com). **Visa** (☎800/847–2911 in the U.S. 🌐www.visa.com).

Use these toll free numbers in Spain. **American Express** (☎917/437000). **Diners Club** (☎901/101011). **MasterCard** (☎900/971231). **Visa** (☎900/991124).

CURRENCY & EXCHANGE

Since 2002, Spain has used the European monetary unit, the euro; other countries that also have adopted it are Austria, Belgium, Finland, France, Germany, Greece, Ireland, Italy, Luxembourg, the Netherlands, and Portugal. Euro notes come in denominations of 5, 10, 20, 50, 100, 200, and 500; coins are worth 1 cent of a euro, 2 cents, 5 cents, 10 cents, 20 cents, 50 cents, 1 euro, and 2 euros. Forgery is quite commonplace in parts of Spain, especially with 50-euro notes. You can generally tell a forgery by the feel of the paper: they tend to be smoother than the legal notes, and the metalic line down the middle is darker than those in real bills.

At this writing the euro is fairly strong against the U.S. dollar and other currencies: €0.84 to the U.S. dollar, €1.46 to the pound sterling, €0.72 to the Canadian dollar, €0.62 to the Australian dollar, €0.56 to the New Zealand dollar, and €0.14 to the South African rand.

■ TIP→ Even if a currency-exchange booth has a sign promising no commission, rest assured that there's some kind of huge, hidden fee. (Oh . . . that's right. The sign didn't say no *fee*.). And as for rates, you're almost always better off getting foreign currency at an ATM or exchanging money at a bank.

TRAVELER'S CHECKS & CARDS

Some consider this the currency of the cave man, and it's true that fewer establishments accept traveler's checks these days. Nevertheless, they're a cheap and secure way to carry extra money, particularly on trips to urban areas. Both Citibank (under the Visa brand) and American Express issue traveler's checks in the United States, but Amex is better known and more widely accepted; you can also avoid hefty surcharges by cashing Amex checks at Amex offices. Whatever you do, keep track of all the serial numbers in case the checks are lost or stolen.

American Express now offers a stored-value card called a Travelers Cheque Card, which you can use wherever American Express credit cards are accepted, including ATMs. The card can carry a minimum of $300 and a maximum of $2,750, and it's a very safe way to carry your funds. Although you can get replacement funds in 24 hours if your card is lost or stolen, it doesn't really strike us as a very good deal. In addition to a high initial cost ($14.95 to set up the card, plus $5 each time you "reload"), you still have to pay a 2% fee for each purchase in a foreign currency (similar to that of any credit card). Further, each time you use the card in an ATM you pay a transaction fee of $2.50 on top of the 2% transaction fee for the conversion—add it all up and it can be considerably more than you would pay when simply using your own ATM card. Regular traveler's checks are just as secure and cost less.

Contacts American Express (☎888/412-6945 in the U.S., 801/945-9450 collect outside of the U.S. to add value or speak to customer service 🌐www.americanexpress.com).

RESTROOMS

Spain has some public restrooms (*servicios*), including, in larger cities, small coin-operated booths, but they are few and far between. Your best option is to use the facilities in a bar or cafeteria, remembering that at the discretion of the establishment you may have to order something. Gas stations have restrooms (you usually have to request the key to use them), but they are more often than not in terrible condition.

Find a Loo The Bathroom Diaries (🌐www.thebathroomdiaries.com) is flush with unsanitized info on restrooms the world over—each one located, reviewed, and rated.

SAFETY

Petty crime is a huge problem in Spain's most popular tourist destinations. The most frequent offenses are pickpocketing (particularly in Madrid and Barcelona) and theft from cars (all over the country). Never leave anything valuable in a parked car, no matter how friendly the area feels, how quickly you'll return, or how invisible the item seems once you lock it in the trunk. Thieves can spot rental cars a mile away, and they work very efficiently. In airports, laptop computers are choice prey. Except when traveling between the airport or train station and your hotel, don't wear a money belt or a waist pack, both of which peg you as a tourist. (If you do use a money belt while traveling, opt for a concealed one and don't reach into it once you're in public.) Distribute your cash and any valuables (including your credit cards and passport) between a deep front pocket or an inside jacket or vest pocket. When walking the streets, particularly in large cities, carry as little cash as possible. Men should carry their wallets in the front pocket; women who need to carry purses should strap them across the front of their bodies. Another alternative is to carry money or important documents in both your front pockets. Leave the rest of your valuables in the safe at your hotel. On the beach, in cafés, and restaurants (particularly in the well-touristed areas), and in Internet centers, always keep your belongings on your lap or tied to your person in some way.

It's not advisable to sleep on beaches—no matter how well you store your possessions, you are an easy target for those who prey there in the early morning. Additionally, be cautious of any odd or unnecessary human contact, verbal or physical, whether it's a tap on the shoulder, someone asking you for a light for their cigarette, someone spilling their drink at your table, and so on. Thieves often work in twos, so while one is attracting your attention, the other could be swiping your wallet.

In the tourist areas of Madrid and Barcelona you'll sometimes see a raucous group standing around a makeshift cardboard table and cheering on a guy who appears to be playing the ancient game of hiding the seed under one of three walnut shells. He goads passersby to pick a shell, any shell, to see if they can guess where the seed is; someone takes the bait, and the con game has begun. You'll choose correctly and "win" at the beginning. The moment you start handing over betting money, it becomes noticeably more difficult—and all but impossible—to guess the right shell. This is a scam, through and through, and the people standing around cheering the guy on are his friends or paid accomplices. The whole thing is actually very entertaining to watch—but if you do so, stand at a distance, be aware of those around you, and continue on your way sooner rather than later. Also, be cautious when a group of people approaches you in sightseeing areas to sell flowers or otherwise barter for items on the street. While you're distracted, they could be picking your pocket—or that of the person you're with.

TAXES

Value-added tax, similar to sales tax, is called I.V.A. in Spain (pronounced "*ee*-vah," for *impuesto sobre el valor añadido*). It's levied on both products and services, such as hotel rooms and restaurant meals. When in doubt about whether tax is included, ask, "*Está incluido el I.V.A.*"?

The I.V.A. rate for hotels and restaurants is 7%, regardless of their number of stars. A special tax law for the Canary Islands allows hotels and restaurants there to charge 4% I.V.A. Menus will generally say at the bottom whether tax is included (*I.V.A. incluido*) or not (*más 7% I.V.A.*).

Although food, pharmaceuticals, and household items are taxed at the lowest rate, most consumer goods are taxed at 16%. A number of shops participate in Global Refund (formerly Europe Tax-Free Shopping), a V.A.T. refund service that makes getting your money back relatively hassle-free. You cannot get a refund on the V.A.T. for such items as meals or services such as hotel accommodation, or taxi fares. There are also some taxable goods for which the refund doesn't apply, such as consumable items such as perfume.

When making a purchase, ask for a V.A.T. refund form and find out whether the merchant gives refunds—not all stores do, nor are they required to. Have the form stamped like any customs form by customs officials when you leave the country or, if you're visiting several European Union countries, when you leave the EU. After you're through passport control, take the form to a refund-service counter for an on-the-spot refund (which is usually the quickest and easiest option), or mail it to the address on the form (or the envelope with it) after you arrive home. You receive the total refund stated on the form, but the processing time can be long, especially if you request a credit-card adjustment.

Global Refund is a Europe-wide service with 225,000 affiliated stores and more than 700 refund counters at major airports and border crossings. Its refund form, called a Tax Free Check, is the most common across the European continent. The service issues refunds in the form of cash, check, or credit-card adjustment.

V.A.T. Refunds Global Refund (☎800/566-9828 🌐www.globalrefund.com).

TIME

Spain is on central European time, one hour ahead of Greenwich mean time, and six hours ahead of eastern standard time. Like the rest of the European Union, Spain switches to daylight saving time on the last weekend in March and switches back on the last weekend in October.

TIPPING

Service staff expect to be tipped, and you can be sure that your contribution will be appreciated. On the other hand, if you experience bad or surly service, don't feel obligated to leave a tip.

Restaurant checks do not list a service charge on the bill, but consider the tip included. If you want to leave a small tip in addition to the bill, do not tip more than 10% of the bill, and leave less if you eat tapas or sandwiches at a bar—just enough to round out the bill to the nearest €1. Tip cocktail servers €0.30–€0.50 a drink, depending on the bar.

Tip taxi drivers about 10% of the total fare, plus a supplement to help with luggage. Note that rides from airports carry an official surcharge plus a small handling fee for each piece of luggage.

Tip hotel porters €0.50 a bag, and the bearer of room service €0.50. A doorman who calls a taxi for you gets €0.50. If you stay in a hotel for more than two nights, tip the maid about €0.50 per night. The concierge should receive a tip for any additional help he or she provides.

Tour guides should be tipped about €2, ushers in theaters or at bullfights €0.15–€0.20, barbers €0.50, and women's hairdressers at least €1 for a wash and style. Restroom attendants are tipped €0.15.

INDEX

H

I

J

T

PHOTO CREDITS

Cover Photo (The Corrida, San Fermin Festival, Pamplona): *Alan Copson/age fotostock*. 5, *Javier Larrea/age fotostock*. **Chapter 1: Experience Spain:** 9, *J.D. Dallet/age fotostock*. 10, *Kolvenbach/Alamy*. 11 (left), *J.D. Dallet/age fotostock*. 11 (right), *Javier Larrea/age fotostock*. 12, *Joe Viesti/viestiphoto.com*. 13 (left), *Corbis*. 13 (right), *Wojtek Buss/age fotostock*. 14, *Thomas Dressler/age fotostock*. 15 (left), *Javier Larrea/age fotostock*. 15 (right), *Joe Viesti/viestiphoto.com*. 16, *Gonzalo Azumendi/age fotostock*. 17, *Factoria Singular/age fotostock*. 18, *Doco Dalfiano/age fotostock*. 19 (left), *Juan José Pascual/age fotostock*. 19 (right), *Doug Scott/age fotostock*. 20, *Juan Manuel Silva/age fotostock*. 21 (left), *Alex Segre/Alamy*. 21 (right), *Nils-Johan Norenlind/age fotostock*. 22 (left), *Malcolm Case-Green/Alamy*. 22 (top center), *Javier Larrea/age fotostock*. 22 (bottom center), *Fougras G./age fotostock*. 22 (right), *Adriaan Thomas Snaaijer/Shutterstock*. 23 (top left), *Atlantide S.N.C./age fotostock*. 23 (bottom left), *Victor Kotler/age fotostock*. 23 (bottom center), *Paco Gómez García/age fotostock*. 23 (right), *José Fuste Raga/age fotostock*. 24, *Joe Viesti/viestiphoto.com*. 25 (left and right), *J.D. Dallet/age fotostock*. 26, *Felipe Rodriguez/*

Alamy. 27, *Alan Copson/age fotostock.* 28, *Atlantide S.N.C./age fotostock.* 29 (left), *Corbis.* 29 (right), *Francesc Guillamet.* 35, *Ezio Bocci/age fotostock.* 36, *Howard/age fotostock.* 37 (left), *Juan Manuel Silva/age fotostock.* 37 (right), *Ken Welsh/age fotostock.* 38, *Pedro Salaverría/age fotostock.* 39 (left), *J.D. Dallet/age fotostock.* 39 (right), *Alberto Paredes/age fotostock.* 42, *Carlos Nieto/age fotostock.* 43, *Javier Larrea/age fotostock.* 44 (top), *The Print Collector/Alamy.* 44 (bottom), *Pictorial Press Ltd./Alamy.* 45 (top), *Paradores de Turismo de España, S.A.* 45 (bottom), *Jean Dominique Dallet/Alamy.* 46 (all), *Paradores de Turismo de España, S.A.* 47 (top and center), *Tourist Office of Spain, NY.* 47 (bottom), *Alberto Paredes/age fotostock.* 48, *Fernando Fernández/age fotostock.* **Chapter 2: Madrid:** 49, *David Noton/age fotostock.* 50, *Sergio Pitamitz/age fotostock.* 51, *Scott Warren/Aurora Photos.* 53, *Factoria Singular/age fotostock.* 78, *Peter Barritt/Alamy.* 79, *David R. Frazier Photolibrary, Inc./Alamy.* 80 (top), *Factoria Singular/age fotostock.* 80 (bottom), *Susana Vera/Reuters/Newscom.* 82 (top), *Mary Evans Picture Library/Alamy.* 84 (bottom center), *A.H.C./age fotostock.* 84 (bottom), *Tramonto/age fotostock.* 91 and 108, *Sergio Pitamitz/age fotostock.* 92, *Kevin Foy/Alamy.* 122, *Berchery/age fotostock.* 123, *imagebroker/Alamy.* 124, *G. Haling/age fotostock.* 125 (top left), *sebastiancastella.net.* 125 (bottom left), *Marcelo del Pozo/Reuters.* 125 (center right), *Felipe Rodriguez/Alamy.* 125 (bottom right), *Heino Kalis/Reuters.* 126 (top), *Paco Ayala/age fotostock.* 126 (center), *Charles Sturge/Alamy.* 126 (bottom), *Jean Du Boisberranger/Hemis.fr/Aurora Photos.* 127, *Vinicius Tupinamba/Shutterstock.* 92, *Kevin Foy/Alamy.* 93, *Renaud Visage/age fotostock.* **Chapter 3: Castile-León & Castile-La Mancha:** 155, *José Fuste Raga/age fotostock.* 156, *Juan Carlos Muñoz/age fotostock.* 157 (top), *J.D. Dallet/age fotostock.* 157 (bottom), *Juan José Pascual/age fotostock.* 158, *J.D. Dallet/age fotostock.* 159, *Josep Curto/age fotostock.* 207 (top and bottom), *J.D. Dallet/age fotostock.* 208 (top), *Javier Larrea/age fotostock.* 208 (center), *Mary Evans Picture Library/Alamy.* 208 (bottom), *Robert Harding Picture Library Ltd./Alamy.* 210 (top), *Daniel P. Acevedo/age fotostock.* 210 (bottom) and 211, *Javier Larrea/age fotostock.* 212 (top), *Oso Media/Alamy.* 212 (second from top), *Wild Horse Winery (Forrest L. Doud).* 212 (third from top), *Napa Valley Conference Bureau.* 212 (fourth from top), *Panther Creek Cellars (Ron Kaplan).* 212 (fifth from top), *Napa Valley Conference Bureau.* 212 (sixth from top), *Clos du Val (Marvin Collins).* 212 (bottom), *Panther Creek Cellars (Ron Kaplan).* 213 (top left), *Mauro Winery.* 213 (second from top left), *Cephas Picture Library/Alamy.* 213 (third from top left), *Alvaro Palacios Winery.* 213 (top right), *Mas Martinet Winery.* 213 (bottom), *Mike Randolph.* **Chapter 4: Galicia & Asturia:** 233, *Aguililla & Marín/age fotostock.* 234, *Alberto Paredes/age fotostock.* 235 (top), *David Freire/age fotostock.* 235 (bottom left), *Juan José Pascual/age fotostock.* 235 (bottom right), *Alan Copson/age fotostock.* 236, *Aguililla & Marín/age fotostock.* 237 (top), *Alberto Paredes/age fotostock.* 237 (bottom), *Arco Images/Alamy.* 243, *imagebroker/Alamy.* 244, *Schütze Rodemann/age fotostock.* 245 (top), *John Warburton-Lee Photography/Alamy.* 245 (bottom), *Visual Arts Library (London)/Alamy.* 246 (top), *Javier Larrea/age fotostock.* 246 (bottom), *R. Matina/age fotostock.* 247, *J.D. Dallet/age fotostock.* 248 (top left), *Toño Labra/age fotostock.* 248 (bottom center), *Anthony Collins/Alamy.* 248 (top right), *Ian Dagnall/Alamy.* 249 (left), *Javier Larrea/age fotostock.* 249 (right), *Miguel Angel Munoz Pellicer/Alamy.* 257, *Kevin Foy/Alamy.* **Chapter 5: Bilbao & the Basque Country:** 283, *Tolo Balaguer/age fotostock.* 284 (top), *Javier Larrea/age fotostock.* 284 (bottom), *Juan Carlos Muñoz/age fotostock.* 285 (top and bottom), *Javier Larrea/age fotostock.* 286, *Gonzalo Azumendi/age fotostock.* 293, *Bernager E./age fotostock.* 294 (top left and top right), *Javier Larrea/age fotostock.* 294 (bottom), *Profimedia International s.r.o./Alamy.* 295 (top right), *Robert Fried/Alamy.* 295 (left center), *Le Naviose/age fotostock.* 295 (right center and bottom) and 296, *Mark Baynes/Alamy.* 304, *Javier Larrea/age fotostock.* 314-15, *Alan Copson City Pictures/Alamy.* 314 (bottom), *Jon Arnold Images/Alamy.* 316 (top), *Tom Till/Alamy.* 316 (second from top), *mediacolor's/Alamy.* 316 (third from top), *Ramon Grosso Dolarea/Shutterstock.* 316 (bottom), *Peter Cassidy/age fotostock.* 317 (left), *Kathleen Melis/Shutterstock.* 317 (top right), *Mark Baynes/Alamy.* 317 (second from top right), *Alex Segre/Alamy.* 317 (third from top right), *Peter Cassidy/age fotostock.* 317 (bottom right), *Frank Heuer/laif/Aurora Photos.* **Chapter 6: The Pyrenees:** 349, *Martin Siepmann/age fotostock.* 350 (top), *Gonzalo Azumendi/age fotostock.* 350 (bottom), *Guy Christian/age fotostock.* 351 (top), *Matz Sjöberg/age fotostock.* 351 (bottom), *Javier Larrea/age fotostock.* 352, *Tolo Balaguer/age fotostock.* **Chapter 7: Barcelona:** 399, *Rene Mattes/age fotostock.* 403, *Matz Sjöberg/age fotostock.* 410, *Lagui/Shutterstock.* 411, *Sandra Baker/Alamy.* 412 (second from top), *Zina Seletskaya/Shutterstock.* 412 (third from top), *Kevin Foy/Alamy.* 412 (bottom left), *Gonzalo Azumendi/age fotostock.* 412 (bottom right), *Luis M. Seco/Shutterstock.* 413, *Javier Larrea/age fotostock.* 413 (bottom left), *Matz Sjöberg/age fotostock.* 413 (bottom right), *Steven Newton/Shutterstock.* 414 (top), *SuperStock/age fotostock.* 414 (bottom), *Jan van der Hoeven/Shutterstock.* 414 (top left), *Vibrant Pictures/Alamy.* 414 (bottom left), *rubiphoto/Shutterstock.* 414 (top right), *Elena Solodovnikova/Shutterstock.* 452, *Ian Dagnall/Alamy.* 467, *Hotel Majestic.* 484, *Visual & Written SL/Alamy.* **Chapter 8: Catalonia & the Levante:** 501, *Hermes/age fotostock.* 502, *Bjorn Svensson/age fotostock.* 503 (left), *Barry Mason/Alamy.* 503 (right), *Rafael Campillo/age fotostock.* 504, *Oscar García*

Bayerri/age fotostock. 517, *Francesc Guillamet*. 518 (top row and center photo), *Francesc Guillamet*. 518 (bottom), *Patricia Esteve/age fotostock*. 519 (top left), *Peter Arnold, Inc./Alamy*. 519 (bottom left), *Francesc Guillamet*. 519 (top center), *Kari Marttila/Alamy*. 519 (bottom center), *Francesc Guillamet*. 519 (right), *Sol Melia Hotels & Resorts*. 520, *Vittorio Sciosia/age fotostock*. 521 (top and bottom), *Javier Espinosa*. **Chapter 9: The Balearic Islands:** 555, *Stuart Pearce/age fotostock*. 556 (top), *Casteran/age fotostock*. 556 (bottom), *Factoria Singular/age fotostock*. 557 (top), *Martin Siepmann/age fotostock*. 557 (bottom), *Salvador Álvaro Nebot/age fotostock*. 558, *Joan Mercadal/age fotostock*. **Chapter 10: The Southeast:** 605-06, *Alan Copson/age fotostock*. 607 (top), *Juan Carlos Muñoz/age fotostock*. 607 (bottom), *Hidalgo & Lopesino/age fotostock*. 608, *Luis Alberto Aldonza/age fotostock*. **Chapter 11: Andalusia:** 637, *Javier Larrea/age fotostock*. 638, *Sylvain Grandadam/age fotostock*. 639 (top), *Paco Ayala/age fotostock*. 639 (bottom), *Johnny Stockshooter/age fotostock*. 641 (top), *José Fuste Raga/age fotostock*. 641 (bottom), *J.D. Dallet/age fotostock*. 664, *Marina Spironetti/Alamy*. 665, *Kimball Hall/Alamy*. 666, *Profimedia International s.r.o./Alamy*. 667 (top), *Amjad El-Geoushi/Alamy*. 667 (center), *Redferns Music Picture Library/Alamy*. 667 (bottom), *Felipe Trueba/Alamy*. 668, *Christina Wilson/Alamy*. 669 (top left), *Marco Brindicci/Reuters/Corbis*. 669 (bottom left), *AFP/Getty Images*. 669 (top right), *Ted Pink/Alamy*. 669 (bottom right), *Christina Wilson/Alamy*. 723, *JLImages/Alamy*. 724, *Peter Horree/Alamy*. 725, *Jerónimo Alba/age fotostock*. 726 (top), *Werner Otto/age fotostock*. 726 (second from top), *Sylvain Grandadam/age fotostock*. 726 (third from top), *Tom Wright/earthscapes/Alamy*. 726 (fourth from top), *Ken Welsh/age fotostock*. 726 (bottom), *Victor Kotler/age fotostock*. 727, *Javier Larrea/age fotostock*. 728, *Hideo Kurihara/Alamy*. 729 (top and bottom), *Javier Larrea/age fotostock*. 730, *Jerónimo Alba/age fotostock*. **Chapter 12: The Costa del Sol:** 755, *Jordi Puig/age fotostock*. 756 (top), *Philippe Renault/age fotostock*. 756 (bottom) and 757 (top), *Jerónimo Alba/age fotostock*. 757 (bottom), *José Francisco Ruiz/age fotostock*. 759 (top), *Michael Reckling/age fotostock*. 759 (bottom), *Taka/age fotostock*. 799, *Ken Welsh/age fotostock*. **Chapter 13: Extremadura:** 811, *José Antonio Moreno/age fotostock*. 812, *José Fuste Raga/age fotostock*. 813 (top), *Carlos Nieto/age fotostock*. 813 (bottom), *Aguililla & Marín/age fotostock*. 814, *José Antonio Moreno/age fotostock*. 815, *Nacho Moro/age fotostock*. **Color Section:** *Step into 14th-century Spain at Majorca's Bellver Castle: Alvaro Leiva/age fotostock. Wine makers roll barrels of sherry in Cádiz: Jean-Dominique Dallet/age fotostock. Asturian house: Juan Carlos Muñoz/age fotostock. Gaudí's Casa Battlló: Jean-Dominique Dallet/age fotostock. Valencia's City of Arts & Sciences complex: José Fuste Raga/age fotostock. Alhambra, Granada: Javier Larrea/age fotostock. Viura grapes are harvested for white wine in the Rueda region: Cephas Picture Library/Alamy. Candles reflect pilgrims' devotion at Montserrat's monastery: John Ivern/age fotostock. Moroccan Barbary Ape sits atop a cannon in Gilbraltar: Ludke and Sparrow/Alamy. Guggenheim Museum, Bilbao: Ken Ross/viestiphoto.com. Galicia's Celtic roots pop up in its modern port city of A Coruña: Juan José Pascual/age fotostock. Tapas entice in Jerez de la Frontera: San Rostro/age fotostock. Parador, Olite: Joe Viesti/viestiphoto.com. Guernica at the Queen Sofía Art Center: Sergio Pitamitz/age fotostock. La Endiablada in Cuenca: Joe Viesti/viestiphoto.com. Horses carry festive pilgrims in El Rocío to the Virgin of the Dew site: travelstock44/Alamy. Yachts in Marina Bay transport vacationers around the Rock of Gibraltar: Ken Welsh/age fotostock.*

NOTES

ABOUT OUR WRITERS

Ben Curtis escaped to Madrid to pursue his passion for photography, languages, and travel. He has since written about living and traveling in Spain for guidebooks and travel Web sites, and is currently working with his Spanish wife on his Notes from Spain Web site and podcasts.

Born and raised in Madrid, economist **Ignacio Gómez** spent three years living and working in New York and rode the online journalism wave in Madrid, serving as a writer and editor for a Spanish technology and economy Web magazine. He now writes for both the online and print versions of *20 minutos* and is a frequent contributor for the weekly entertainment and culture magazine *OnMadrid.*

Journalist **Michael Kessler** writes almost exclusively on Spanish music, food, theater, film, travel, art, sports, and politics for the Australian press and a range of Spanish, American, and British magazines.

Jared Lubarsky is a university teacher and freelance journalist who has been writing for Fodor's since 1997, first on Japan, where he lived for 30 years, and more recently—having relocated to Barcelona—on Spain. He contributes to a range of in-flight and general-interest magazines, guides, and newspapers, and is happiest exploring the myriad ways that the arts impact social and economic affairs.

Journalist **Mary McLean** is from England and has worked in California, the Middle East, and—since 1990—Spain. Mary writes for many magazines and travel publications, including in-flight magazines and guidebooks. She has covered Portugal, Italy, and various regions of Spain and contributes to travel-related Web sites. In her spare time she likes nothing better than exploring the wilder regions of the Iberian Peninsula.

Norman Renouf was born in London and educated at Charlton Secondary School, Greenwich. He started writing travel guides, articles, and newspaper contributions in the early 1990s and has written about numerous European destinations, with particular emphasis on the Costa Tropical in Southern Spain, and on Portugal, Switzerland, and the Nordic countries.

Helio San Miguel is a wine and food writer and educator. He was born in Madrid and lives in New York, where he created and teaches the Wines of Spain Program at Instituto Cervantes. He is the New York correspondent of *Club de Gourmets,* Spain's leading wine and food magazine. He has a PhD in Philosophy and teaches at The New School.

Writer and journalist **George Semler** has lived in Spain for the last 30-odd years. During that time he has written on Spain, France, Morocco, Cuba, and the Mediterranean region for *Forbes, Sky, Saveur,* the *International Herald Tribune,* and the *Los Angeles Times* and has published walking guides to Madrid and Barcelona. When not sampling Catalonia's hottest restaurants, this James Beard Journalism Awards Finalist forges ahead on his magnum opus about the Pyrenees.

Will Shank writes frequently about art and culture. The head of conservation for many years at the San Francisco Museum of Modern Art, he was also the curator of the Guggenheim exhibition "A Hidden Picasso." His first book, *Celluloid San Francisco* with Jim van Buskirk, covers film locations of the Bay Area.

Stephen "Kip" Tobin is a freelance writer, journalist, music critic, English teacher, and DJ living in Madrid. He writes Spain-themed short stories, scripts, and blogs, and a slew of articles covering Spain-related travel, literature, music, film, and human interest. He currently is working on a script he's mulled over for years and a children's story for his nieces.